D0587729

COLLINS

POCKET SPANISH DICTIONARY

COLLINS

POCKET
SPANISH
DICTIONARY

SPANISH ▶ ENGLISH ENGLISH ▶ SPANISH

HarperCollins*Publishers*

second edition/segunda edición 1995

© **HarperCollins Publishers 1995**
© **William Collins Sons & Co. Ltd. 1990**

HarperCollins Publishers
P.O. Box, Glasgow G4 0NB, Great Britain
ISBN 0 00 470398 7

Grijalbo Mondadori S.A.
Aragó, 385 - 08013 Barcelona
ISBN 84 253 2821 7

Mike Gonzalez • Alicia de Benito de Harland
Soledad Pérez-López • José Ramón Parrondo

contributors to second edition/colaboradores en la segunda edición
Bob Grossmith • Teresa Álvarez García

editorial staff/redacción
Val McNulty • Sharon Hunter
Claire Evans

series editor/colección dirigida por
Lorna Sinclair Knight

Typeset by Morton Word Processing Ltd, Scarborough

Printed in Great Britain by
HarperCollins Manufacturing, Glasgow

INTRODUCTION

We are delighted that you have decided to buy the Collins Pocket Spanish Dictionary, and hope you will enjoy and benefit from using it at home, at school, on holiday or at work.

The innovative use of colour guides you quickly and efficiently to the word you want, and the comprehensive wordlist provides a wealth of modern and idiomatic phrases not normally found in a dictionary this size.

In addition, the supplement provides you with guidance on using the dictionary, along with entertaining ways of improving your dictionary skills.

We hope that you will enjoy using it and that it will significantly enhance your language studies.

Abbreviations	iv
Phonetic transcription	vi
Spanish verb forms	x
English verb forms	xii
Numbers	xiv
Time	xvi
SPANISH-ENGLISH	1-276
USING YOUR COLLINS POCKET DICTIONARY	1-48
ENGLISH-SPANISH	1-291

ABREVIATURAS		ABBREVIATIONS
adjetivo, locución adjetiva	adj	adjective, adjectival phrase
abreviatura	ab(b)r	abbreviation
adverbio, locución adverbial	adv	adverb, adverbial phrase
administración, lengua administrativa	ADMIN	administration
agricultura	AGR	agriculture
América Latina	AM	Latin America
anatomía	ANAT	anatomy
arquitectura	ARQ, ARCH	architecture
artículo	art	article
el automóvil	AUT(O)	the motor car and motoring
aviación, viajes aéreos	AVIAT	flying, air travel
biología	BIO(L)	biology
botánica, flores	BOT	botany
inglés británico	BRIT	British English
química	CHEM	chemistry
comercio, finanzas, banca	COM(M)	commerce, finance, banking
comparativo	compar	comparative
informática	COMPUT	computers
conjunción	conj	conjunction
construcción	CONSTR	building
compuesto	cpd	compound element
cocina	CULIN	cookery
definido	def	definite
demostrativo	demos	demonstrative
economía	ECON	economics
electricidad, electrónica	ELEC	electricity, electronics
enseñanza, sistema escolar y universitario	ESCOL	schooling, schools and universities
España	ESP	Spain
especialmente	esp	especially
exclamación, interjección	excl	exclamation, interjection
femenino	f	feminine
lengua familiar (! vulgar)	fam(!)	informal usage (! particularly offensive)
ferrocarril	FERRO	railways
uso figurado	fig	figurative use
fotografía	FOTO	photography
(verbo inglés) del cual la partícula es inseparable	fus	(phrasal verb) where the particle is inseparable
generalmente	gen	generally
geografía, geología	GEO	geography, geology
geometría	GEOM	geometry
indefinido	indef	indefinite
lengua familiar (! vulgar)	inf(!)	informal usage
infinitivo	infin	infinitive
informática	INFORM	computers
interrogativo	interr	interrogative
invariable	inv	invariable
irregular	irreg	irregular
lo jurídico	JUR	law

iv

ABREVIATURAS

ABBREVIATIONS

América Latina	LAM	Latin America
gramática, lingüística	LING	grammar, linguistics
masculino	m	masculine
matemáticas	MAT(H)	mathematics
medicina	MED	medical term, medicine
masculino/femenino	m/f	masculine/feminine
lo militar, ejército	MIL	military matters
música	MUS	music
sustantivo, nombre	n	noun
navegación, náutica	NAUT	sailing, navigation
sustantivo numérico	num	numeral noun
complemento	obj	(grammatical) object
	o.s.	oneself
peyorativo	pey, pej	derogatory, pejorative
fotografía	PHOT	photography
fisiología	PHYSIOL	physiology
plural	pl	plural
política	POL	politics
participio de pasado	pp	past participle
preposición	prep	preposition
pronombre	pron	pronoun
psicología, psiquiatría	PSICO, PSYCH	psychology, psychiatry
tiempo pasado	pt	past tense
química	QUIM	chemistry
ferrocarril	RAIL	railways
religión, lo eclesiástico	REL	religion, church service
	sb	somebody
enseñanza, sistema escolar y universitario	SCH	schooling, schools and universities
singular	sg	singular
España	SP	Spain
	sth	something
sujeto	su(b)j	(grammatical) subject
subjuntivo	subjun	subjunctive
superlativo	superl	superlative
tauromaquia	TAUR	bullfighting
también	tb	also
técnica, tecnología	TEC(H)	technical term, technology
telecomunicaciones	TELEC, TEL	telecommunications
televisión	TV	television
imprenta, tipografía	TIP, TYP	typography, printing
inglés norteamericano	US	American English
verbo	vb	verb
verbo intransitivo	vi	intransitive verb
verbo pronominal	vr	reflexive verb
verbo transitivo	vt	transitive verb
zoología, animales	ZOOL	zoology
marca registrada	®	registered trademark
indica un equivalente cultural	≈	introduces a cultural equivalent

SPANISH PRONUNCIATION

Consonants

b	[b, ß]	**b**oda **b**om**b**a la**b**or	see notes on **v** below
c	[k]	**c**aja	**c** before **a**, **o** or **u** is pronounced as in **c**at
ce, ci	[θe, θi]	**c**ero **c**ielo	**c** before **e** or **i** is pronounced as in **th**in
ch	[tʃ]	**ch**iste	**ch** is pronounced as **ch** in **ch**air
d	[d, ð]	**d**anés ciu**d**ad	at the beginning of a phrase or after **l** or **n**, **d** is pronounced as in English. In any other position it is pronounced like **th** in **th**e
g	[g, ɣ]	**g**afas pa**g**a	**g** before **a**, **o** or **u** is pronounced as in **g**ap, if at the beginning of a phrase or after **n**. In other positions the sound is softened
ge, gi	[xe, xi]	**g**ente **g**irar	**g** before **e** or **i** is pronounced similar to **ch** in Scottish lo**ch**
h		**h**aber	**h** is always silent in Spanish
j	[x]	**j**ugar	**j** is pronounced similar to **ch** in Scottish lo**ch**
ll	[ʎ]	ta**ll**e	**ll** is pronounced like the **lli** in mi**lli**on
ñ	[ɲ]	ni**ñ**o	**ñ** is pronounced like the **ni** in o**ni**on
q	[k]	**q**ue	**q** is pronounced as **k** in **k**ing
r, rr	[r, rr]	quita**r** ga**rr**a	**r** is always pronounced in Spanish, unlike the silent **r** in dance**r**. **rr** is trilled, like a Scottish **r**
s	[s]	quizá**s** i**s**la	**s** is usually pronounced as in pa**ss**, but before **b**, **d**, **g**, **l**, **m** or **n** it is pronounced as in ro**s**e
v	[b, ß]	**v**ía di**v**idir	**v** is pronounced something like **b**. At the beginning of a phrase or after **m** or **n** it is pronounced as **b** in **b**oy. In any other position the sound is softened
z	[θ]	tena**z**	**z** is pronounced as **th** in **th**in

f, **k**, **l**, **m**, **n**, **p**, **t** and **x** are pronounced as in English.

Vowels

a	[a]	p**a**t**a**	not as long as *a* in f**a**r. When followed by a consonant in the same syllable (i.e. in a closed syllable), as in am**a**nte, the *a* is short, as in b**a**t
e	[e]	m**e**	like *e* in th**e**y. In a closed syllable, as in g**e**nte, the *e* is short as in p**e**t
i	[i]	p**i**no	as in m**ea**n or mach**i**ne
o	[o]	l**o**	as in l**o**cal. In a closed syllable, as in c**o**ntrol, the *o* is short as in c**o**t
u	[u]	l**u**nes	as in r**u**le. It is silent after *q*, and in **gue, gui**, unless marked **güe, güi** e.g. antig**ü**edad, when it is pronounced like *w* in **w**olf

Semivowels

i, y	[j]	b**i**en h**i**elo **y**unta	pronounced like *y* in **y**es
u	[w]	h**u**evo f**u**ento antig**ü**edad	unstressed *u* between consonant and vowel is pronounced like *w* in **w**ell. See also notes on *u* above

Diphthongs

ai, ay	[ai]	b**ai**le	as *i* in r**i**de
au	[au]	**au**to	as *ou* in sh**ou**t
ei, ey	[ei]	b**uey**	as *ey* in gr**ey**
eu	[eu]	d**eu**da	both elements pronounced independently [e] + [u]
oi, oy	[oi]	h**oy**	as *oy* in t**oy**

Stress

The rules of stress in Spanish are as follows:

(a) when a word ends in a vowel or in *n* or *s*, the second last syllable is stressed: pa**ta**ta, pa**ta**tas, **co**me, **co**men

(b) when a word ends in a consonant other than *n* or *s*, the stress falls on the last syllable: pa**red**, ha**blar**

(c) when the rules set out in (a) and (b) are not applied, an acute accent appears over the stressed vowel: co**mún**, geogra**fía**, in**glés**

In the phonetic transcription, the symbol ['] precedes the syllable on which the stress falls.

PRONUNCIACIÓN INGLESA

Vocales y diptongos

	Ejemplo inglés	*Ejemplo español/explicación*
ɑ:	father	Entre *a* de p*a*dre y *o* de n*o*che
ʌ	but, come	*a* muy breve
æ	man, cat	Con los labios en la posición de *e* en p*e*na se pronuncia el sonido *a* parecido a la *a* de c*a*rro
ə	father, ago	Vocal neutra parecida a una *e* u *o* casi mudas
ə:	bird, heard	Entre *e* abierta, y *o* cerrada, sonido alargado
ɛ	get, bed	Como en p*e*rro
ɪ	it, big	Más breve que en s*i*
i:	tea, see	Como en f*i*no
ɔ	hot, wash	Como en t*o*rre
ɔ:	saw, all	Como en p*o*r
u	put, book	Sonido breve, más cerrado que b*u*rro
u:	too, you	Sonido largo, como en *u*no
aɪ	fly, high	Como en fr*ai*le
au	how, house	Como en p*au*sa
ɛə	there, bear	Casi como en v*ea*, pero el segundo elemento es la vocal neutra [ə]
eɪ	day, obey	*e* cerrada seguida por una *i* débil
ɪə	here, hear	Como en man*ía*, mezclándose el sonido *a* con la vocal neutra [ə]
əu	go, note	[ə] seguido por una breve *u*
ɔɪ	boy, oil	Como en v*oy*
uə	poor, sure	*u* bastante larga más la vocal neutra [ə]

Consonantes

	Ejemplo inglés	*Ejemplo español/explicación*
b	**b**ig, lo**bb**y	Como en tum**b**a
d	men**d**e**d**	Como en con**d**e, an**d**ar
g	**g**o, **g**et, bi**g**	Como en **g**rande, **g**ol
dʒ	**g**in, **j**udge	Como en la **ll** andaluza y en **G**eneralitat (catalán)
ŋ	si**ng**	Como en ví**n**culo
h	**h**ouse, **h**e	Como la jota hispanoamericana
j	**y**oung, **y**es	Como en **y**a
k	**c**ome, mo**ck**	Como en **c**aña, Es**c**ocia
r	**r**ed, t**r**ead	Se pronuncia con la punta de la lengua hacia atrás y sin hacerla vibrar
s	**s**and, ye**s**	Como en ca**s**a, **s**esión
z	ro**s**e, **z**ebra	Como en de**s**de, mi**s**mo
ʃ	**sh**e, ma**ch**ine	Como en **ch**ambre (francés), ro**x**o (portugués)
tʃ	**ch**in, ri**ch**	Como en **ch**ocolate
v	**v**alley	Como en f, pero se retiran los dientes superiores vibrándolos contra el labio inferior
w	**w**ater, **wh**ich	Como en la **u** de h**u**evo, p**u**ede
ʒ	vi**s**ion	Como en **j**ournal (francés)
θ	**th**ink, my**th**	Como en re**c**eta, **z**apato
ð	**th**is, **th**e	Como en la **d** de habla**d**o, verda**d**

p, f, m, n, l, t iguales que en español
El signo * indica que la r final escrita apenas se pronuncia en inglés británico cuando la palabra siguiente empieza con vocal. El signo ['] indica la sílaba acentuada.

SPANISH VERB TABLES

1 Gerund *2* Imperative *3* Present *4* Preterite *5* Future *6* Present subjunctive *7* Imperfect subjunctive *8* Past participle *9* Imperfect. *Etc* indicates that the irregular root is used for all persons of the tense, e.g. **oír**: *6* oiga *etc* = oigas, oigamos, oigáis, oigan. Forms which consist of the unmodified verb root + verb ending are not shown, e.g. acertamos, acertáis.

acertar *2* acierta *3* acierto, aciertas, acierta, aciertan *6* acierte, aciertes, acierte, acierten

acordar *2* acuerda *3* acuerdo, acuerdas, acuerda, acuerdan *6* acuerde, acuerdes, acuerde, acuerden

advertir *1* advirtiendo *2* advierte *3* advierto, adviertes, advierte, advierten *4* advirtió, advirtieron *6* advierta, adviertas, advierta, advirtamos, advirtáis, adviertan *7* advirtiera *etc*

agradecer *3* agradezco *6* agradezca *etc*

aparecer *3* aparezco *6* aparezca *etc*

aprobar *2* aprueba *3* apruebo, apruebas, aprueba, aprueban *6* apruebe, apruebes, apruebe, aprueben

atravesar *2* atraviesa *3* atravieso, atraviesas, atraviesa, atraviesan *6* atraviese, atravieses, atraviese, atraviesen

caber *3* quepo *4* cupe, cupiste, cupo, cupimos, cupisteis, cupieron *5* cabré *etc* *6* quepa *etc* *7* cupiera *etc*

caer *1* cayendo *3* caigo *4* cayó, cayeron *6* caiga *etc* *7* cayera *etc*

calentar *2* calienta *3* caliento, calientas, calienta, calientan *6* caliente, calientes, caliente, calienten

cerrar *2* cierra *3* cierro, cierras, cierra, cierran *6* cierre, cierres, cierre, cierren

COMER *1* comiendo *2* come, comed *3* como, comes, come, comemos, coméis, comen *4* comí, comiste, comió, comimos, comisteis, comieron *5* comeré, comerás, comerá, comeremos, comeréis, comerán *6* coma, comas, coma, comamos, comáis, coman *7* comiera, comieras, comiera, comiéramos, comierais, comieran *8* comido *9* comía, comías, comía, comíamos, comíais, comían

conocer *3* conozco *6* conozca *etc*

contar *2* cuenta *3* cuento, cuentas, cuenta, cuentan *6* cuente, cuentes, cuente, cuenten

costar *2* cuesta *3* cuesto, cuestas, cuesta, cuestan *6* cueste, cuestes, cueste, cuesten

dar *2* doy *4* di, diste, dio, dimos, disteis, dieron *7* diera *etc*

decir *2* di *3* digo *4* dije, dijiste, dijo, dijimos, dijisteis, dijeron *5* diré *etc* *6* diga *etc* *7* dijera

despertar *2* despierta *3* despierto, despiertas, despierta, despiertan *6* despierte, despiertes, despierte

divertir *1* divirtiendo *2* divierte *3* divierto, diviertes, divierte, divierten *4* divirtió, divirtieron *6* divierta, diviertas, divierta, divirtamos, divirtáis, diviertan *7* divirtiera *etc*

dormir *1* durmiendo *2* duerme *3* duermo, duermes, duerme, duermen *4* durmió, durmieron *6* duerma, duermas, duerma, durmamos, durmáis, duerman *7* durmiera *etc*

empezar *2* empieza *3* empiezo, empiezas, empieza, empiezan *4* empecé *6* empiece, empieces, empiece, empecemos, empecéis, empiecen

entender *2* entiende *3* entiendo, entiendes, entiende, entienden *6* entienda, entiendas, entienda, entiendan

ESTAR *2* está *3* estoy, estás, está, están *4* estuve, estuviste, estuvo, estuvimos, estuvisteis, estuvieron *6* esté, estés, esté, estén *7* estuviera *etc*

HABER *3* he, has, ha, hemos, han *4* hube, hubiste, hubo, hubimos, hubisteis, hubieron *5* habré *etc* *6* haya *etc* *7* hubiera *etc*

HABLAR *1* hablando *2* habla, hablad *3* hablo, hablas, habla, hablamos, habláis, hablan *4* hablé, hablaste, habló, hablamos, hablasteis, hablaron *5* hablaré, hablarás, hablará, hablaremos, hablaréis, hablarán *6* hable, hables, hable, hablemos, habléis, hablen *7* hablara, hablaras, hablara, habláramos, hablarais, hablaran *8* hablado *9* hablaba, hablabas, hablaba, hablábamos, hablabais, hablaban

hacer *2* haz *3* hago *4* hice, hiciste, hizo, hicimos, hicisteis, hicieron *5* haré *etc* *6* haga *etc* *7* hiciera *etc* *8* hecho

instruir *1* instruyendo *2* instruye *3* instruyo, instruyes, instruye, instruyen *4* instruyó, instruyeron *6* instruya *etc* *7* instruyera *etc*

ir *1* yendo *2* ve *3* voy, vas, va, vamos, van *4* fui, fuiste, fue, fuimos, fuisteis, fueron *6* vaya, vayas, vaya, vayamos, vayáis, vayan

7 fuera etc **9** iba, ibas, iba, íbamos, ibais, iban

jugar 2 juega 3 juego, juegas, juega, juegan 4 jugué 6 juegue etc

leer 1 leyendo 4 leyó, leyeron 7 leyera etc

morir 1 muriendo 2 muere 3 muero, mueres, muere, mueren 4 murió, murieron 6 muera, mueras, muera, muramos, muráis, mueran 7 muriera etc 8 muerto

mostrar 2 muestra 3 muestro, muestras, muestra, muestran 6 muestre, muestres, muestre, muestren

mover 2 mueve 3 muevo, mueves, mueve, mueven 6 mueva, muevas, mueva, muevan

negar 2 niega 3 niego, niegas, niega, niegan 4 negué 6 niegue, niegues, niegue, neguemos, neguéis, nieguen

ofrecer 3 ofrezco 6 ofrezca etc

oír 1 oyendo 2 oye 3 oigo, oyes, oye, oyen 4 oyó, oyeron 6 oiga etc 7 oyera etc

oler 2 huele 3 huelo, hueles, huele, huelen 6 huela, huelas, huela, huelan

parecer 3 parezco 6 parezca etc

pedir 1 pidiendo 2 pide 3 pido, pides, pide, piden 4 pidió, pidieron 6 pida etc 7 pidiera etc

pensar 2 piensa 3 pienso, piensas, piensa, piensan 6 piense, pienses, piense, piensen

perder 2 pierde 3 pierdo, pierdes, pierde, pierden 6 pierda, pierdas, pierda, pierdan

poder 1 pudiendo 2 puede 3 puedo, puedes, puede, pueden 4 pudiste, pudo, pudimos, pudisteis, pudieron 5 podré etc 6 pueda, puedas, pueda, puedan 7 pudiera etc

poner 1 pon 3 pongo 4 puse, pusiste, puso, pusimos, pusisteis, pusieron 5 pondré etc 6 ponga etc 7 pusiera etc 8 puesto

preferir 1 prefiriendo 2 prefiere 3 prefiero, prefieres, prefiere, prefieren 4 prefirió, prefirieron 6 prefiera, prefieras, prefiera, prefiramos, prefiráis, prefieran 7 prefiriera etc

querer 2 quiere 3 quiero, quieres, quiere, quieren 4 quise, quisiste, quiso, quisimos, quisisteis, quisieron 5 querré etc 6 quiera, quieras, quiera, quieran 7 quisiera etc

reír 2 ríe 3 río, ríes, ríe, ríen 4 rio, rieron 6 ría, rías, ría, riamos, riáis, rían 7 riera etc

repetir 1 repitiendo 2 repite 3 repito, repites, repite, repiten 4 repitió, repitieron 6 repita etc 7 repitiera etc

rogar 2 ruega 3 ruego, ruegas, ruega, ruegan 4 rogué 6 ruegue, ruegues, ruegue, roguemos, roguéis, rueguen

saber 3 sé 4 supe, supiste, supo, supimos, supisteis, supieron 5 sabré etc 6 sepa etc 7 supiera etc

salir 2 sal 3 salgo 5 saldré etc 6 salga etc

seguir 1 siguiendo 2 sigue 3 sigo, sigues, sigue, siguen 4 siguió, siguieron 6 siga etc 7 siguiera etc

sentar 2 sienta 3 siento, sientas, sienta, sientan 6 siente, sientes, siente, sienten

sentir 1 sintiendo 2 siente 3 siento, sientes, siente, sienten 4 sintió, sintieron 6 sienta, sientas, sienta, sintamos, sintáis, sientan 7 sintiera etc

SER 2 sé 3 soy, eres, es, somos, sois, son 4 fui, fuiste, fue, fuimos, fuisteis, fueron 6 sea etc 7 fuera etc 9 era, eras, era, éramos, erais, eran

servir 1 sirviendo 2 sirve 3 sirvo, sirves, sirve, sirven 4 sirvió, sirvieron 6 sirva etc 7 sirviera etc

soñar 2 sueña 3 sueño, sueñas, sueña, sueñan 6 sueñe, sueñes, sueñe, sueñen

tener 2 ten 3 tengo, tienes, tiene, tienen 4 tuve, tuviste, tuvo, tuvimos, tuvisteis, tuvieron 5 tendré etc 6 tenga etc 7 tuviera etc

traer 1 trayendo 3 traigo 4 traje, trajiste, trajo, trajimos, trajisteis, trajeron 6 traiga etc 7 trajera etc

valer 2 val 3 valgo 5 valdré etc 6 valga etc

venir 2 ven 3 vengo, vienes, viene, vienen 4 vine, viniste, vino, vinimos, vinisteis, vinieron 5 vendré etc 6 venga etc 7 viniera etc

ver 3 veo 6 vea etc 8 visto 9 veía etc

vestir 1 vistiendo 2 viste 3 visto, vistes, viste, visten 4 vistió, vistieron 6 vista etc 7 vistiera etc

VIVIR 1 viviendo 2 vive 3 vivid 3 vivo, vives, vive, vivimos, vivís, viven 4 viví, viviste, vivió, vivimos, vivisteis, vivieron 5 viviré, vivirás, vivirá, viviremos, viviréis, vivirán 6 viva, vivas, viva, vivamos, viváis, vivan 7 viviera, vivieras, viviera, viviéramos, vivierais, vivieran 8 vivido 9 vivía, vivías, vivía, vivíamos, vivíais, vivían

volver 2 vuelve 3 vuelvo, vuelves, vuelve, vuelven 6 vuelva, vuelvas, vuelva, vuelvan 8 vuelto

VERBOS IRREGULARES EN INGLÉS

present	pt	pp	present	pt	pp
arise	arose	arisen	feed	fed	fed
awake	awoke	awoken	feel	felt	felt
be (am, is, are; being)	was, were	been	fight	fought	fought
			find	found	found
bear	bore	born(e)	flee	fled	fled
beat	beat	beaten	fling	flung	flung
become	became	become	fly (flies)	flew	flown
begin	began	begun	forbid	forbade	forbidden
behold	beheld	beheld	forecast	forecast	forecast
bend	bent	bent	forego	forewent	foregone
beseech	besought	besought	foresee	foresaw	foreseen
beset	beset	beset	foretell	foretold	foretold
bet	bet, betted	bet, betted	forget	forgot	forgotten
bid	bid, bade	bid, bidden	forgive	forgave	forgiven
bind	bound	bound	forsake	forsook	forsaken
bite	bit	bitten	freeze	froze	frozen
bleed	bled	bled	get	got	got, (US) gotten
blow	blew	blown			
break	broke	broken	give	gave	given
breed	bred	bred	go (goes)	went	gone
bring	brought	brought	grind	ground	ground
build	built	built	grow	grew	grown
burn	burnt, burned	burnt, burned	hang	hung, hanged	hung, hanged
burst	burst	burst	have (has; having)	had	had
buy	bought	bought			
can	could	(been able)	hear	heard	heard
cast	cast	cast	hide	hid	hidden
catch	caught	caught	hit	hit	hit
choose	chose	chosen	hold	held	held
cling	clung	clung	hurt	hurt	hurt
come	came	come	keep	kept	kept
cost	cost	cost	kneel	knelt, kneeled	knelt, kneeled
creep	crept	crept			
cut	cut	cut	know	knew	known
deal	dealt	dealt	lay	laid	laid
dig	dug	dug	lead	led	led
do (3rd person: he/she/it does)	did	done	lean	leant, leaned	leant, leaned
			leap	leapt, leaped	leapt, leaped
draw	drew	drawn	learn	learnt, learned	learnt, learned
dream	dreamed, dreamt	dreamed, dreamt			
drink	drank	drunk	leave	left	left
drive	drove	driven	lend	lent	lent
dwell	dwelt	dwelt	let	let	let
eat	ate	eaten	lie (lying)	lay	lain
fall	fell	fallen	light	lit, lighted	lit, lighted

present	pt	pp	present	pt	pp
lose	lost	lost	spell	spelt, spelled	spelt, spelled
make	made	made			
may	might	—	spend	spent	spent
mean	meant	meant	spill	spilt, spilled	spilt, spilled
meet	met	met			
mistake	mistook	mistaken	spin	spun	spun
mow	mowed	mown, mowed	spit	spat	spat
must	(had to)	(had to)	split	split	split
pay	paid	paid	spoil	spoiled, spoilt	spoiled, spoilt
put	put	put			
quit	quit, quitted	quit, quitted	spread	spread	spread
			spring	sprang	sprung
read	read	read	stand	stood	stood
rid	rid	rid	steal	stole	stolen
ride	rode	ridden	stick	stuck	stuck
ring	rang	rung	sting	stung	stung
rise	rose	risen	stink	stank	stunk
run	ran	run	stride	strode	stridden
saw	sawed	sawn	strike	struck	struck, stricken
say	said	said			
see	saw	seen	strive	strove	striven
seek	sought	sought	swear	swore	sworn
sell	sold	sold	sweep	swept	swept
send	sent	sent	swell	swelled	swollen, swelled
set	set	set			
shake	shook	shaken	swim	swam	swum
shall	should	—	swing	swung	swung
shear	sheared	shorn, sheared	take	took	taken
shed	shed	shed	teach	taught	taught
shine	shone	shone	tear	tore	torn
shoot	shot	shot	tell	told	told
show	showed	shown	think	thought	thought
shrink	shrank	shrunk	throw	threw	thrown
shut	shut	shut	thrust	thrust	thrust
sing	sang	sung	tread	trod	trodden
sink	sank	sunk	wake	woke	woken
sit	sat	sat	waylay	waylaid	waylaid
slay	slew	slain	wear	wore	worn
sleep	slept	slept	weave	wove, weaved	woven, weaved
slide	slid	slid			
sling	slung	slung	wed	wedded, wed	wedded, wed
slit	slit	slit			
smell	smelt, smelled	smelt, smelled	weep	wept	wept
			win	won	won
sow	sowed	sown, sowed	wind	wound	wound
speak	spoke	spoken	wring	wrung	wrung
speed	sped, speeded	sped, speeded	write	wrote	written

LOS NÚMEROS   # NUMBERS

un, uno(a)	1	one
dos	2	two
tres	3	three
cuatro	4	four
cinco	5	five
seis	6	six
siete	7	seven
ocho	8	eight
nueve	9	nine
diez	10	ten
once	11	eleven
doce	12	twelve
trece	13	thirteen
catorce	14	fourteen
quince	15	fifteen
dieciséis	16	sixteen
diecisiete	17	seventeen
dieciocho	18	eighteen
diecinueve	19	nineteen
veinte	20	twenty
veintiuno	21	twenty-one
veintidós	22	twenty-two
treinta	30	thirty
treinta y uno(a)	31	thirty-one
treinta y dos	32	thirty-two
cuarenta	40	forty
cuarenta y uno(a)	41	forty-one
cincuenta	50	fifty
sesenta	60	sixty
setenta	70	seventy
ochenta	80	eighty
noventa	90	ninety
cien, ciento	100	a hundred, one hundred
ciento uno(a)	101	a hundred and one
doscientos(as)	200	two hundred
doscientos(as) uno(a)	201	two hundred and one
trescientos(as)	300	three hundred
trescientos(as) uno(a)	301	three hundred and one
cuatrocientos(as)	400	four hundred
quiniento(as)	500	five hundred
seiscientos(as)	600	six hundred
setecientos(as)	700	seven hundred
ochocientos(as)	800	eight hundred
novecientos(as)	900	nine hundred
mil	1000	a thousand
mil dos	1002	a thousand and two
cinco mil	5000	five thousand
un millón	1000000	a million

LOS NÚMEROS

NUMBERS

primer, primero(a), 1º, 1er (1ª, 1era)	first, 1st
segundo(a), 2º (2ª)	second, 2nd
tercer, tercero(a), 3º (3ª)	third, 3rd
cuarto(a), 4º (4ª)	fourth, 4th
quinto(a), 5º (5ª)	fifth, 5th
sexto(a), 6º (6ª)	sixth, 6th
séptimo(a)	seventh
octavo(a)	eighth
noveno(a)	ninth
décimo(a)	tenth
undécimo(a)	eleventh
duodécimo(a)	twelfth
decimotercio(a)	thirteenth
decimocuarto(a)	fourteenth
decimoquinto(a)	fifteenth
decimosexto(a)	sixteenth
decimoséptimo(a)	seventeenth
decimoctavo(a)	eighteenth
decimonoveno(a)	nineteenth
vigésimo(a)	twentieth
vigésimo(a) primero(a)	twenty-first
vigésimo(a) segundo(a)	twenty-second
trigésimo(a)	thirtieth
centésimo(a)	hundredth
centésimo(a) primero(a)	hundred-and-first
milésimo(a)	thousandth

Números Quebrados etc

Fractions etc

un medio	a half
un tercio	a third
dos tercios	two thirds
un cuarto	a quarter
un quinto	a fifth
cero coma cinco, 0,5	(nought) point five, 0.5
tres coma cuatro, 3,4	three point four, 3.4
diez por cien(to)	ten per cent
cien por cien	a hundred per cent

Ejemplos

Examples

va a llegar el 7 (de mayo)	he's arriving on the 7th (of May)
vive en el número 7	he lives at number 7
el capítulo/la página 7	chapter/page 7
llegó séptimo	he came in 7th

N.B. In Spanish the ordinal numbers from 1 to 10 are commonly used; from 11 to 20 rather less; above 21 they are rarely written and almost never heard in speech. The custom is to replace the forms for 21 and above by the cardinal number.

LA HORA

THE TIME

¿qué hora es?

what time is it?

es/son

it's o it is

medianoche, las doce (de la noche)	midnight, twelve p.m.
la una (de la madrugada)	one o'clock (in the morning), one (a.m.)
la una y cinco	five past one
la una y diez	ten past one
la una y cuarto *or* quince	a quarter past one, one fifteen
la una y veinticinco	twenty-five past one, one twenty-five
la una y media *or* treinta	half-past one, one thirty
las dos menos veinticinco, la una treinta y cinco	twenty-five to two, one thirty-five
las dos menos veinte, la una cuarenta	twenty to two, one forty
las dos menos cuarto, la una cuarenta y cinco	a quarter to two, one forty-five
las dos menos diez, la una cincuenta	ten to two, one fifty
mediodía, las doce (de la tarde)	twelve o'clock, midday, noon
la una (de la tarde)	one o'clock (in the afternoon), one (p.m.)
las siete (de la tarde)	seven o'clock (in the evening), seven (p.m.)

¿a qué hora?

(at) what time?

a medianoche	at midnight
a las siete	at seven o'clock
en veinte minutos	in twenty minutes
hace quince minutos	fifteen minutes ago

ESPAÑOL - INGLÉS
SPANISH - ENGLISH

A a

a [a] (*a*+ *el* = *al*) *prep* **1** (*dirección*) to;
fueron ~ Madrid/Grecia they went to
Madrid/Greece; **me voy ~ casa** I'm
going home
2 (*distancia*): **está ~ 15 km de aquí** it's
15 kms from here
3 (*posición*): **estar ~ la mesa** to be at
table; **al lado de** next to, beside; *ver tb*
puerta
4 (*tiempo*): **~ las 10/~ medianoche** at
10/midnight; **~ la mañana siguiente** the
following morning; **~ los pocos días**
after a few days; **estamos ~ 9 de julio**
it's the ninth of July; **~ los 24 años** at
the age of 24; **al año/~ la semana** (*AM*) a
year/week later
5 (*manera*): **~ la francesa** the French
way; **~ caballo** on horseback; **~ oscuras**
in the dark
6 (*medio, instrumento*): **~ lápiz** in pencil;
~ mano by hand; **cocina ~ gas** gas
stove
7 (*razón*): **~ 30 ptas el kilo** at 30 pesetas
a kilo; **~ más de 50 km/h** at more than
50 kms per hour
8 (*dativo*): **se lo di ~ él** I gave it to him;
vi al policía I saw the policeman; **se lo
compré ~ él** I bought it from him
9 (*tras ciertos verbos*): **voy ~ verle** I'm
going to see him; **empezó ~ trabajar** he
started working *o* to work
10 (+ *infin*): **al verle, le reconocí
inmediatamente** when I saw him I recognized him at once; **el camino ~
recorrer** the distance we (*etc*) have to
travel; **¡~ callar!** keep quiet!; **¡~ comer!**
let's eat!

abad, esa [aˈβað, ˈðesa] *nm/f* abbot/

abbess; **~ía** *nf* abbey
abajo [aˈβaxo] *adv* (*situación*) (down)
below, underneath; (*en edificio*)
downstairs; (*dirección*) down,
downwards; **el piso de ~** the downstairs
flat; **la parte de ~** the lower part; **¡~ el
gobierno!** down with the government!;
cuesta/río ~ downhill/downstream; **de
arriba ~** from top to bottom; **el ~
firmante** the undersigned; **más ~** lower
o further down
abalanzarse [aβalanˈθarse] *vr*: **~ sobre** *o*
contra to throw o.s. at
abalorios [aβaˈlorjos] *nmpl* (*chucherías*)
trinkets
abanderado [aβandeˈraðo] *nm* standard
bearer
abandonado, a [aβandoˈnaðo, a] *adj*
derelict; (*desatendido*) abandoned;
(*desierto*) deserted; (*descuidado*) neglected
abandonar [aβandoˈnar] *vt* to leave;
(*persona*) to abandon, desert; (*cosa*) to
abandon, leave behind; (*descuidar*) to
neglect; (*renunciar a*) to give up; (*INFORM*)
to quit; **~se** *vr*: **~se a** to abandon o.s. to;
abandono *nm* (*acto*) desertion,
abandonment; (*estado*) abandon, neglect;
(*renuncia*) withdrawal, retirement;
ganar por abandono to win by default
abanicar [aβaniˈkar] *vt* to fan; **abanico**
nm fan; (*NAUT*) derrick
abaratar [aβaraˈtar] *vt* to lower the price
of ♦ *vi* to go *o* come down in price; **~se**
vr to go *o* come down in price
abarcar [aβarˈkar] *vt* to include, embrace;
(*AM*) to monopolize
abarrotado, a [aβarroˈtaðo, a] *adj* packed
abarrotar [aβarroˈtar] *vt* (*local, estadio,
teatro*) to fill, pack
abarrotero, a [aβarroˈtero, a] (*AM*) *nm/f*
grocer; **abarrotes** *nmpl* (*AM*) groceries,

provisions

abastecer [aβaste'θer] *vt*: ~ **(de)** to supply (with); **abastecimiento** *nm* supply

abasto [a'βasto] *nm* supply; (*abundancia*) abundance; **no dar ~ a** to be unable to cope with

abatido, a [aβa'tiðo, a] *adj* dejected, downcast

abatimiento [aβati'mjento] *nm* (*depresión*) dejection, depression

abatir [aβa'tir] *vt* (*muro*) to demolish; (*pájaro*) to shoot o bring down; (*fig*) to depress; ~**se** *vr* to get depressed; ~**se sobre** to swoop o pounce on

abdicación [aβðika'θjon] *nf* abdication

abdicar [aβði'kar] *vi* to abdicate

abdomen [aß'ðomen] *nm* abdomen; **abdominales** *nmpl* (*tb: ejercicios abdominales*) sit-ups

abecedario [aβeθe'ðarjo] *nm* alphabet

abedul [aße'ðul] *nm* birch

abeja [a'βexa] *nf* bee

abejorro [aβe'xorro] *nm* bumblebee

aberración [aβerra'θjon] *nf* aberration

abertura [aßer'tura] *nf* = **apertura**

abeto [a'βeto] *nm* fir

abierto, a [a'βjerto, a] *pp de* **abrir** ♦ *adj* open; (*fig*) vast, enormous

abigarrado, a [aβiɣa'rraðo, a] *adj* multi-coloured

abismal [aßis'mal] *adj* (*fig*) vast, enormous

abismar [aßis'mar] *vt* to humble, cast down; ~**se** *vr* to sink; ~**se en** (*fig*) to be plunged into

abismo [a'βismo] *nm* abyss

abjurar [aßxu'rar] *vi*: ~ **de** to abjure, forswear

ablandar [aßlan'dar] *vt* to soften ♦ *vi* to get softer; ~**se** *vr* to get softer

abnegación [aßneɣa'θjon] *nf* self-denial

abnegado, a [aßne'ɣaðo, a] *adj* self-sacrificing

abocado, a [aßo'kaðo, a] *adj*: **verse ~ al desastre** to be heading for disaster

abochornar [aßotʃor'nar] *vt* to embarrass

abofetear [aßofete'ar] *vt* to slap (in the face)

abogado, a [aßo'ɣaðo, a] *nm/f* lawyer; (*notario*) solicitor; (*en tribunal*) barrister (*BRIT*), attorney (*US*); ~ **defensor** defence lawyer o attorney (*US*)

abogar [aßo'ɣar] *vi*: ~ **por** to plead for; (*fig*) to advocate

abolengo [aßo'lengo] *nm* ancestry, lineage

abolición [aßoli'θjon] *nf* abolition

abolir [aßo'lir] *vt* to abolish; (*cancelar*) to cancel

abolladura [aßoʎa'ðura] *nf* dent

abollar [aßo'ʎar] *vt* to dent

abominable [aßomi'naßle] *adj* abominable

abonado, a [aßo'naðo, a] *adj* (*deuda*) paid(-up) ♦ *nm/f* subscriber

abonar [aßo'nar] *vt* (*deuda*) to settle; (*terreno*) to fertilize; (*idea*) to endorse; ~**se** *vr* to subscribe; **abono** *nm* payment; fertilizer; subscription

abordar [aßor'ðar] *vt* (*barco*) to board; (*asunto*) to broach

aborigen [aßo'rixen] *nm/f* aborigine

aborrecer [aßorre'θer] *vt* to hate, loathe

abortar [aßor'tar] *vi* (*malparir*) to have a miscarriage; (*deliberadamente*) to have an abortion; **aborto** *nm* miscarriage; abortion

abotonar [aßoto'nar] *vt* to button (up), do up

abovedado, a [aßoße'ðaðo, a] *adj* vaulted, domed

abrasar [aßra'sar] *vt* to burn (up); (*AGR*) to dry up, parch

abrazadera [aßraθa'ðera] *nf* bracket

abrazar [aßra'θar] *vt* to embrace, hug

abrazo [a'βraθo] *nm* embrace, hug; **un ~** (*en carta*) with best wishes

abrebotellas [aßreßo'teʎas] *nm inv* bottle opener

abrecartas [aßre'kartas] *nm inv* letter opener

abrelatas [aßre'latas] *nm inv* tin (*BRIT*) o can opener

abreviar [aßre'βjar] *vt* to abbreviate; (*texto*) to abridge; (*plazo*) to reduce; **abreviatura** *nf* abbreviation

abridor [aßri'ðor] *nm* bottle opener; (*de latas*) tin (*BRIT*) o can opener

abrigar [aβri'ɣar] *vt* (*proteger*) to shelter; (*suj: ropa*) to keep warm; (*fig*) to cherish

abrigo [a'βriɣo] *nm* (*prenda*) coat, overcoat; (*lugar protegido*) shelter

abril [a'βril] *nm* April

abrillantar [aβriʎan'tar] *vt* to polish

abrir [a'βrir] *vt* to open (up) ♦ *vi* to open; ~**se** *vr* to open (up); (*extenderse*) to open out; (*cielo*) to clear; ~**se paso** to find *o* force a way through

abrochar [aβro'tʃar] *vt* (*con botones*) to button (up); (*zapato, con broche*) to do up

abrumar [aβru'mar] *vt* to overwhelm; (*sobrecargar*) to weigh down

abrupto, a [a'βrupto, a] *adj* abrupt; (*empinado*) steep

absceso [aβs'θeso] *nm* abscess

absentismo [aβsen'tismo] *nm* absenteeism

absolución [aβsolu'θjon] *nf* (*REL*) absolution; (*JUR*) acquittal

absoluto, a [aβso'luto, a] *adj* absolute; **en ~** *adv* not at all

absolver [aβsol'βer] *vt* to absolve; (*JUR*) to pardon; (: *acusado*) to acquit

absorbente [aβsor'βente] *adj* absorbent; (*interesante*) absorbing

absorber [aβsor'βer] *vt* to absorb; (*embeber*) to soak up

absorción [aβsor'θjon] *nf* absorption; (*COM*) takeover

absorto, a [aβ'sorto, a] *pp de* **absorber** ♦ *adj* absorbed, engrossed

abstemio, a [aβs'temjo, a] *adj* teetotal

abstención [aβsten'θjon] *nf* abstention

abstenerse [aβste'nerse] *vr*: ~ (**de**) to abstain *o* refrain (from)

abstinencia [aβsti'nenθja] *nf* abstinence; (*ayuno*) fasting

abstracción [aβstrak'θjon] *nf* abstraction

abstracto, a [aβ'strakto, a] *adj* abstract

abstraer [aβstra'er] *vt* to abstract; ~**se** *vr* to be *o* become absorbed

abstraído, a [aβstra'iðo, a] *adj* absent-minded

absuelto [aβ'swelto] *pp de* **absolver**

absurdo, a [aβ'surðo, a] *adj* absurd

abuchear [aβutʃe'ar] *vt* (*a actor, orador*) to boo

abuelo, a [a'βwelo, a] *nm/f* grandfather/mother; ~**s** *nmpl* grandparents

abulia [a'βulja] *nf* apathy

abultado, a [aβul'taðo, a] *adj* bulky

abultar [aβul'tar] *vt* to enlarge; (*aumentar*) to increase; (*fig*) to exaggerate ♦ *vi* to be bulky

abundancia [aβun'danθja] *nf*: **una ~ de** plenty of; **abundante** *adj* abundant, plentiful

abundar [aβun'dar] *vi* to abound, be plentiful

aburguesarse [aβurɣe'sarse] *vr* to become middle-class

aburrido, a [aβu'rriðo, a] *adj* (*hastiado*) bored; (*que aburre*) boring; **aburrimiento** *nm* boredom, tedium

aburrir [aβu'rrir] *vt* to bore; ~**se** *vr* to be bored, get bored

abusar [aβu'sar] *vi* to go too far; ~ **de** to abuse

abusivo, a [aβu'siβo, a] *adj* (*precio*) exorbitant

abuso [a'βuso] *nm* abuse

abyecto, a [aβ'jekto, a] *adj* wretched, abject

acá [a'ka] *adv* (*lugar*) here; ¿**de cuándo ~**? since when?

acabado, a [aka'βaðo, a] *adj* finished, complete; (*perfecto*) perfect; (*agotado*) worn out; (*fig*) masterly ♦ *nm* finish

acabar [aka'βar] *vt* (*llevar a su fin*) to finish, complete; (*consumir*) to use up; (*rematar*) to finish off ♦ *vi* to finish, end; ~**se** *vr* to finish, stop; (*terminarse*) to be over; (*agotarse*) to run out; ~ **con** to put an end to; ~ **de llegar** to have just arrived; ~ **por hacer** to end (up) by doing; ¡**se acabó**! it's all over!; (*¡basta!*) that's enough!

acabóse [aka'βose] *nm*: **esto es el ~** this is the last straw

academia [aka'ðemja] *nf* academy; **académico, a** *adj* academic

acaecer [akae'θer] *vi* to happen, occur

acallar [aka'ʎar] *vt* (*persona*) to silence; (*protestas, rumores*) to suppress

acalorado, a [akalo'raðo, a] *adj* (*discusión*) heated

acalorarse [akaloˈrarse] *vr* (*fig*) to get heated

acampar [akamˈpar] *vi* to camp

acantilado [akantiˈlaðo] *nm* cliff

acaparar [akapaˈrar] *vt* to monopolize; (*acumular*) to hoard

acariciar [akariˈθjar] *vt* to caress; (*esperanza*) to cherish

acarrear [akarreˈar] *vt* to transport; (*fig*) to cause, result in

acaso [aˈkaso] *adv* perhaps, maybe ♦ *nm* chance; (**por**) **si ~** (just) in case

acatamiento [akataˈmjento] *nm* respect; (*ley*) observance

acatar [akaˈtar] *vt* to respect; (*ley*) obey

acatarrarse [akataˈrrarse] *vr* to catch a cold

acaudalado, a [akauðaˈlaðo, a] *adj* well-off

acaudillar [akauðiˈʎar] *vt* to lead, command

acceder [akθeˈðer] *vi*: **~ a** (*petición etc*) to agree to; (*tener acceso a*) to have access to; (*INFORM*) to access

accesible [akθeˈsiβle] *adj* accessible

acceso [akˈθeso] *nm* access, entry; (*camino*) access, approach; (*MED*) attack, fit

accesorio, a [akθeˈsorjo, a] *adj, nm* accessory

accidentado, a [akθiðenˈtaðo, a] *adj* uneven; (*montañoso*) hilly; (*azaroso*) eventful ♦ *nm/f* accident victim

accidental [akθiðenˈtal] *adj* accidental; **accidentarse** *vr* to have an accident

accidente [akθiˈðente] *nm* accident; **~s** *nmpl* (*de terreno*) unevenness *sg*

acción [akˈθjon] *nf* action; (*acto*) action, act; (*COM*) share; (*JUR*) action, lawsuit; **~ ordinaria/preferente** ordinary/preference share; **accionar** *vt* to work, operate; (*INFORM*) to drive

accionista [akθjoˈnista] *nm/f* shareholder, stockholder

acebo [aˈθeβo] *nm* holly; (*árbol*) holly tree

acechar [aθeˈtʃar] *vt* to spy on; (*aguardar*) to lie in wait for; **acecho** *nm*: **estar al acecho (de)** to lie in wait (for)

aceitar [aθeiˈtar] *vt* to oil, lubricate

aceite [aˈθeite] *nm* oil; (*de oliva*) olive oil; **~ra** *nf* oilcan; **aceitoso, a** *adj* oily

aceituna [aθeiˈtuna] *nf* olive

acelerador [aθelera'ðor] *nm* accelerator

acelerar [aθeleˈrar] *vt* to accelerate

acelga [aˈθelɣa] *nf* chard, beet

acento [aˈθento] *nm* accent; (*acentuación*) stress

acentuar [aθenˈtwar] *vt* to accent; to stress; (*fig*) to accentuate

acepción [aθepˈθjon] *nf* meaning

aceptable [aθepˈtaβle] *adj* acceptable

aceptación [aθeptaˈθjon] *nf* acceptance; (*aprobación*) approval

aceptar [aθepˈtar] *vt* to accept; (*aprobar*) to approve

acequia [aˈθekja] *nf* irrigation ditch

acera [aˈθera] *nf* pavement (*BRIT*), sidewalk (*US*)

acerca [aˈθerka]: **~ de** *prep* about, concerning

acercar [aθerˈkar] *vt* to bring *o* move nearer; **~se** *vr* to approach, come near

acerico [aθeˈriko] *nm* pincushion

acero [aˈθero] *nm* steel

acérrimo, a [aˈθerrimo, a] *adj* (*partidario*) staunch; (*enemigo*) bitter

acertado, a [aθerˈtaðo, a] *adj* correct; (*apropiado*) apt; (*sensato*) sensible

acertar [aθerˈtar] *vt* (*blanco*) to hit; (*solución*) to get right; (*adivinar*) to guess ♦ *vi* to get it right, be right; **~ a** to manage to; **~ con** to happen *o* hit on

acertijo [aθerˈtixo] *nm* riddle, puzzle

achacar [atʃaˈkar] *vt* to attribute

achacoso, a [atʃaˈkoso, a] *adj* sickly

achantar [atʃanˈtar] (*fam*) *vt* to scare, frighten; **~se** *vr* to back down

achaque *etc* [aˈtʃake] *vb ver* **achacar** ♦ *nm* ailment

achicar [atʃiˈkar] *vt* to reduce; (*humillar*) to humiliate; (*NAUT*) to bale out

achicharrar [atʃitʃaˈrrar] *vt* to scorch, burn

achicoria [atʃiˈkorja] *nf* chicory

aciago, a [aˈθjaɣo, a] *adj* ill-fated, fateful

acicalar [aθikaˈlar] *vt* to polish; (*persona*) to dress up; **~se** *vr* to get dressed up

acicate [aθi'kate] *nm* spur

acidez [aθi'ðeθ] *nf* acidity

acido, a ['aθiðo, a] *adj* sour, acid ♦ *nm* acid

acierto *etc* [a'θjerto] *vb ver* acertar ♦ *nm* success; (*buen paso*) wise move; (*solución*) solution; (*habilidad*) skill, ability

aclamación [aklama'θjon] *nf* acclamation; (*aplausos*) applause

aclamar [akla'mar] *vt* to acclaim; (*aplaudir*) to applaud

aclaración [aklara'θjon] *nf* clarification, explanation

aclarar [akla'rar] *vt* to clarify, explain; (*ropa*) to rinse ♦ *vi* to clear up; ~**se** *vr* (*explicarse*) to understand; ~**se la garganta** to clear one's throat

aclaratorio, a [aklara'torjo, a] *adj* explanatory

aclimatación [aklimata'θjon] *nf* acclimatization

aclimatar [aklima'tar] *vt* to acclimatize; ~**se** *vr* to become acclimatized

acné [ak'ne] *nm* acne

acobardar [akoβar'ðar] *vt* to intimidate

acodarse [ako'ðarse] *vr*: ~ **en** to lean on

acogedor, a [akoxe'ðor, a] *adj* welcoming; (*hospitalario*) hospitable

acoger [ako'xer] *vt* to welcome; (*abrigar*) to shelter; ~**se** *vr* to take refuge

acogida [ako'xiða] *nf* reception; refuge

acolchar [akol'tʃar] *vt* to pad; (*fig*) to cushion

acometer [akome'ter] *vt* to attack; (*emprender*) to undertake; **acometida** *nf* attack, assault

acomodado, a [akomo'ðaðo, a] *adj* (*persona*) well-to-do

acomodador, a [akomoða'ðor, a] *nm/f* usher(ette)

acomodar [akomo'ðar] *vt* to adjust; (*alojar*) to accommodate; ~**se** *vr* to conform; (*instalarse*) to install o.s.; (*adaptarse*): ~**se (a)** to adapt (to)

acomodaticio, a [akomoða'tiθjo, a] *adj* (*pey*) accommodating, obliging; (*manejable*) pliable

acompañar [akompa'ɲar] *vt* to accompany; (*documentos*) to enclose

acondicionar [akondiθjo'nar] *vt* to arrange, prepare; (*pelo*) to condition

acongojar [akoŋgo'xar] *vt* to distress, grieve

aconsejar [akonse'xar] *vt* to advise, counsel; ~**se** *vr*: ~**se con** to consult

acontecer [akonte'θer] *vi* to happen, occur; **acontecimiento** *nm* event

acopio [a'kopjo] *nm* store, stock

acoplamiento [akopla'mjento] *nm* coupling, joint; **acoplar** *vt* to fit; (*ELEC*) to connect; (*vagones*) to couple

acorazado, a [akora'θaðo, a] *adj* armourplated, armoured ♦ *nm* battleship

acordar [akor'ðar] *vt* (*resolver*) to agree, resolve; (*recordar*) to remind; ~**se** *vr* to agree; ~**se (de algo)** to remember (sth); **acorde** *adj* (*MUS*) harmonious; **acorde con** (*medidas etc*) in keeping with ♦ *nm* chord

acordeón [akorðe'on] *nm* accordion

acordonado, a [akorðo'naðo, a] *adj* (*calle*) cordoned-off

acorralar [akorra'lar] *vt* to round up, corral

acortar [akor'tar] *vt* to shorten; (*duración*) to cut short; (*cantidad*) to reduce; ~**se** *vr* to become shorter

acosar [ako'sar] *vt* to pursue relentlessly; (*fig*) to hound, pester

acostar [akos'tar] *vt* (*en cama*) to put to bed; (*en suelo*) to lay down; (*barco*) to bring alongside; ~**se** *vr* to go to bed; to lie down; ~**se con uno** to sleep with sb

acostumbrado, a [akostum'braðo, a] *adj* usual; ~ **a** used to

acostumbrar [akostum'brar] *vt*: ~ **a uno a algo** to get sb used to sth ♦ *vi*: ~ **(a) hacer** to be in the habit of doing; ~**se** *vr*: ~**se a** to get used to

acotación [akota'θjon] *nf* marginal note; (*GEO*) elevation mark; (*de límite*) boundary mark; (*TEATRO*) stage direction

ácrata ['akrata] *adj*, *nm/f* anarchist

acre ['akre] *adj* (*sabor*) sharp, bitter; (*olor*) acrid; (*fig*) biting ♦ *nm* acre

acrecentar [akreθen'tar] *vt* to increase, augment

acreditar [akreði'tar] *vt* (*garantizar*) to vouch for, guarantee; (*autorizar*) to authorize; (*dar prueba de*) to prove; (*COM: abonar*) to credit; (*embajador*) to accredit; **~se** *vr* to become famous

acreedor, a [akree'ðor, a] *adj*: ~ **de** worthy of ♦ *nm/f* creditor

acribillar [akriβi'ʎar] *vt*: ~ **a balazos** to riddle with bullets

acrimonia [akri'monja] *nf* acrimony

acritud [akri'tuð] *nf* = **acrimonia**

acróbata [a'kroβata] *nm/f* acrobat

acta ['akta] *nf* certificate; (*de comisión*) minutes *pl*, record; ~ **de nacimiento/de matrimonio** birth/marriage certificate; ~ **notarial** affidavit

actitud [akti'tuð] *nf* attitude; (*postura*) posture

activar [akti'βar] *vt* to activate; (*acelerar*) to speed up

actividad [aktiβi'ðað] *nf* activity

activo, a [ak'tiβo, a] *adj* active; (*vivo*) lively ♦ *nm* (*COM*) assets *pl*

acto ['akto] *nm* act, action; (*ceremonia*) ceremony; (*TEATRO*) act; **en el ~** immediately

actor [ak'tor] *nm* actor; (*JUR*) plaintiff ♦ *adj*: **parte ~a** prosecution

actriz [ak'triθ] *nf* actress

actuación [aktwa'θjon] *nf* action; (*comportamiento*) conduct, behaviour; (*JUR*) proceedings *pl*; (*desempeño*) performance

actual [ak'twal] *adj* present(-day), current; **~idad** *nf* present; **~idades** *nfpl* (*noticias*) news *sg*; **en la ~idad** at present; (*hoy día*) nowadays

actualizar [aktwali'θar] *vt* to update, modernize

actualmente [aktwal'mente] *adv* at present; (*hoy día*) nowadays

actuar [ak'twar] *vi* (*obrar*) to work, operate; (*actor*) to act, perform ♦ *vt* to work, operate; ~ **de** to act as

acuarela [akwa'rela] *nf* watercolour

acuario [a'kwarjo] *nm* aquarium; (*ASTROLOGÍA*): **A~** Aquarius

acuartelar [akwarte'lar] *vt* (*MIL: disciplinar*) to confine to barracks

acuático, a [a'kwatiko, a] *adj* aquatic

acuchillar [akutʃi'ʎar] *vt* (*TEC*) to plane (down), smooth

acuciante [aku'θjante] *adj* urgent

acuciar [aku'θjar] *vt* to urge on

acudir [aku'ðir] *vi* (*asistir*) to attend; (*ir*) to go; ~ **a** (*fig*) to turn to; ~ **en ayuda de** to go to the aid of

acuerdo *etc* [a'kwerðo] *vb ver* **acordar** ♦ *nm* agreement; **¡de ~!** agreed!; **de ~ con** (*persona*) in agreement with; (*acción, documento*) in accordance with; **estar de ~** to be agreed, agree

acumular [akumu'lar] *vt* to accumulate, collect

acuñar [aku'ɲar] *vt* (*moneda*) to mint; (*frase*) to coin

acupuntura [akupun'tura] *nf* acupuncture

acurrucarse [akurru'karse] *vr* to crouch; (*ovillarse*) to curl up

acusación [akusa'θjon] *nf* accusation

acusar [aku'sar] *vt* to accuse; (*revelar*) to reveal; (*denunciar*) to denounce

acuse [a'kuse] *nm*: ~ **de recibo** acknowledgement of receipt

acústica [a'kustika] *nf* acoustics *pl*

acústico, a [a'kustiko, a] *adj* acoustic

adaptación [aðapta'θjon] *nf* adaptation

adaptador [aðapta'ðor] *nm* (*ELEC*) adapter

adaptar [aðap'tar] *vt* to adapt; (*acomodar*) to fit

adecuado, a [aðe'kwaðo, a] *adj* (*apto*) suitable; (*oportuno*) appropriate

adecuar [aðe'kwar] *vt* to adapt; to make suitable

a. de J.C. *abr* (= *antes de Jesucristo*) B.C.

adelantado, a [aðelan'taðo, a] *adj* advanced; (*reloj*) fast; **pagar por ~** to pay in advance

adelantamiento [aðelanta'mjento] *nm* advance, advancement; (*AUTO*) overtaking

adelantar [aðelan'tar] *vt* to move forward; (*avanzar*) to advance; (*acelerar*) to speed up; (*AUTO*) to overtake ♦ *vi* to go forward, advance; **~se** *vr* to go forward, advance

adelante [aðe'lante] *adv* forward(s), ahead ♦ *excl* come in!; **de hoy en ~** from now on; **más ~** later on; (*más allá*)

urther on
delanto [aðe'lanto] *nm* advance;
(*mejora*) improvement; (*progreso*)
progress
delgazar [aðelɣa'θar] *vt* to thin (down)
♦ *vi* to get thin; (*con régimen*) to slim
down, lose weight
demán [aðe'man] *nm* gesture; ade-
manes *nmpl* manners; en ~ de as if to
demás [aðe'mas] *adv* besides; (*por otra
parte*) moreover; (*también*) also; ~ de
besides, in addition to
dentrarse [aðen'trarse] *vr*: ~ en to go
into, get inside; (*penetrar*) to penetrate
(into)
dentro [a'ðentro] *adv* inside, in; mar ~
out at sea; tierra ~ inland
depto, a [a'ðepto, a] *nm/f* supporter
derezar [aðere'θar] *vt* (*ensalada*) to
dress; (*comida*) to season; aderezo *nm*
dressing; seasoning
deudar [aðeu'ðar] *vt* to owe; ~se *vr* to
run into debt
dherirse [aðe'rirse] *vr*: ~ a to adhere to;
(*partido*) to join
dhesión [aðe'sjon] *nf* adhesion; (*fig*)
adherence
dicción [aðik'θjon] *nf* addiction
dición [aði'θjon] *nf* addition
dicto, a [a'ðikto, a] *adj*: ~ a addicted to;
dedicado) devoted to ♦ *nm/f* supporter,
follower; (*toxicómano etc*) addict
diestrar [aðjes'trar] *vt* to train, teach;
(*guiar*) to guide, lead; ~se *vr* to
practise; (*enseñarse*) to train o.s.
dinerado, a [aðine'raðo, a] *adj* wealthy
diós [a'ðjos] *excl* (*para despedirse*)
goodbye!, cheerio!; (*al pasar*) hello!
ditivo [aði'tiβo] *nm* additive
divinanza [aðiβi'nanθa] *nf* riddle
divinar [aðiβi'nar] *vt* to prophesy;
(*conjeturar*) to guess; adivino, a *nm/f*
fortune-teller
dj *abr* (= adjunto) encl.
djetivo [aðxe'tiβo] *nm* adjective
djudicación [aðxuðika'θjon] *nf* award;
adjudication
djudicar [aðxuði'kar] *vt* to award; ~se
vr: ~se algo to appropriate sth

adjuntar [aðxun'tar] *vt* to attach, enclose;
adjunto, a *adj* attached, enclosed ♦ *nm/f*
assistant
administración [aðministra'θjon] *nf*
administration; (*dirección*) management;
administrador, a *nm/f* administrator;
manager(ess)
administrar [aðminis'trar] *vt* to
administer; administrativo, a *adj*
administrative
admirable [aðmi'raβle] *adj* admirable
admiración [aðmira'θjon] *nf* admiration;
(*asombro*) wonder; (*LING*) exclamation
mark
admirar [aðmi'rar] *vt* to admire;
(*extrañar*) to surprise; ~se *vr* to be
surprised
admisible [aðmi'siβle] *adj* admissible
admisión [aðmi'sjon] *nf* admission;
(*reconocimiento*) acceptance
admitir [aðmi'tir] *vt* to admit; (*aceptar*) to
accept
admonición [aðmoni'θjon] *nf* warning
adobar [aðo'βar] *vt* (*CULIN*) to season
adobe [a'ðoβe] *nm* adobe, sun-dried brick
adoctrinar [aðoktri'nar] *vt*: ~ en to
indoctrinate with
adolecer [aðole'θer] *vi*: ~ de to suffer
from
adolescente [aðoles'θente] *nm/f*
adolescent, teenager
adonde [a'ðonðe] *conj* (to) where
adónde [a'ðonde] *adv* = dónde
adopción [aðop'θjon] *nf* adoption
adoptar [aðop'tar] *vt* to adopt
adoptivo, a [aðop'tiβo, a] *adj* (*padres*)
adoptive; (*hijo*) adopted
adoquín [aðo'kin] *nm* paving stone
adorar [aðo'rar] *vt* to adore
adormecer [aðorme'θer] *vt* to put to
sleep; ~se *vr* to become sleepy;
(*dormirse*) to fall asleep
adornar [aðor'nar] *vt* to adorn
adorno [a'ðorno] *nm* adornment;
(*decoración*) decoration
adosado, a [aðo'saðo, a] *adj*: casa ado-
sada semi-detached house
adquiero *etc vb ver* adquirir
adquirir [aðki'rir] *vt* to acquire, obtain

adquisición [aðkisi'θjon] *nf* acquisition

adrede [a'ðreðe] *adv* on purpose

adscribir [aðskri'βir] *vt* to appoint

adscrito *pp de* **adscribir**

aduana [a'ðwana] *nf* customs *pl*

aduanero, a [aðwa'nero, a] *adj* customs *cpd* ♦ *nm/f* customs officer

aducir [aðu'θir] *vt* to adduce; (*dar como prueba*) to offer as proof

adueñarse [aðwe'ɲarse] *vr*: ~ **de** to take possession of

adulación [aðula'θjon] *nf* flattery

adular [aðu'lar] *vt* to flatter

adulterar [aðulte'rar] *vt* to adulterate ♦ *vi* to commit adultery

adulterio [aðul'terjo] *nm* adultery

adúltero, a [a'ðultero, a] *adj* adulterous ♦ *nm/f* adulterer/adulteress

adulto, a [a'ðulto, a] *adj, nm/f* adult

adusto, a [a'ðusto, a] *adj* stern; (*austero*) austere

advenedizo, a [aðβene'ðiθo, a] *nm/f* upstart

advenimiento [aðβeni'mjento] *nm* arrival; (*al trono*) accession

adverbio [að'βerβjo] *nm* adverb

adversario, a [aðβer'sarjo, a] *nm/f* adversary

adversidad [aðβersi'ðað] *nf* adversity; (*contratiempo*) setback

adverso, a [að'βerso, a] *adj* adverse

advertencia [aðβer'tenθja] *nf* warning; (*prefacio*) preface, foreword

advertir [aðβer'tir] *vt* to notice; (*avisar*): ~ **a uno de** to warn sb about *o* of

Adviento [að'βjento] *nm* Advent

advierto *etc vb ver* **advertir**

adyacente [aðja'θente] *adj* adjacent

aéreo, a [a'ereo, a] *adj* aerial

aerobic [ae'roβik] *nm* aerobics *sg*

aerodeslizador [aeroðesliθa'ðor] *nm* hovercraft

aeromozo, a [aero'moθo, a] *nm/f* (*AM*) air steward(ess)

aeronáutica [aero'nautika] *nf* aeronautics *sg*

aeronave [aero'naβe] *nm* spaceship

aeroplano [aero'plano] *nm* aeroplane

aeropuerto [aero'pwerto] *nm* airport

aerosol [aero'sol] *nm* aerosol

afabilidad [afaβili'ðað] *nf* friendliness; **afable** *adj* affable

afamado, a [afa'maðo, a] *adj* famous

afán [a'fan] *nm* hard work; (*deseo*) desire

afanar [afa'nar] *vt* to harass; (*fam*) to pinch; ~**se** *vr*: ~**se por hacer** to strive to do; **afanoso, a** *adj* (*trabajo*) hard; (*trabajador*) industrious

afear [afe'ar] *vt* to disfigure

afección [afek'θjon] *nf* (*MED*) disease

afectación [afekta'θjon] *nf* affectation; **afectado, a** *adj* affected

afectar [afek'tar] *vt* to affect

afectísimo, a [afek'tisimo, a] *adj* affectionate; ~ **suyo** yours truly

afectivo, a [afek'tiβo, a] *adj* (*problema etc*) emotional

afecto [a'fekto] *nm* affection; **tenerle ~ a uno** to be fond of sb

afectuoso, a [afek'twoso, a] *adj* affectionate

afeitar [afei'tar] *vt* to shave; ~**se** *vr* to shave

afeminado, a [afemi'naðo, a] *adj* effeminate

aferrar [afe'rrar] *vt* to grasp; (*barco*) to moor ♦ *vi* to moor

Afganistán [afɣanis'tan] *nm* Afghanistan

afianzamiento [afjanθa'mjento] *nm* strengthening; security

afianzar [afjan'θar] *vt* to strengthen; to secure; ~**se** *vr* to become established

afiche [a'fitʃe] (*AM*) *nm* poster

afición [afi'θjon] *nf* fondness, liking; **la ~** the fans *pl*; **pinto por ~** I paint as a hobby; **aficionado, a** *adj* keen, enthusiastic; (*no profesional*) amateur ♦ *nm/f* enthusiast, fan; amateur; **ser aficionado a algo** to be very keen on *o* fond of sth

aficionar [afiθjo'nar] *vt*: ~ **a uno a algo** to make sb like sth; ~**se** *vr*: ~**se a algo** to grow fond of sth

afilado, a [afi'laðo, a] *adj* sharp

afilar [afi'lar] *vt* to sharpen

afiliarse [afi'ljarse] *vr* to affiliate

afín [a'fin] *adj* (*parecido*) similar; (*conexo*) related

afinar [afiˈnar] *vt* (*TEC*) to refine; (*MUS*) to tune ♦ *vi* (*tocar*) to play in tune; (*cantar*) to sing in tune

afincarse [afinˈkarse] *vr* to settle

afinidad [afiniˈðað] *nf* affinity; (*parentesco*) relationship; **por ~** by marriage

afirmación [afirmaˈθjon] *nf* affirmation

afirmar [afirˈmar] *vt* to affirm, state; (*reforzar*) to strengthen; **afirmativo, a** *adj* affirmative

aflicción [aflikˈθjon] *nf* affliction; (*dolor*) grief

afligir [afliˈxir] *vt* to afflict; (*apenar*) to distress; **~se** *vr* to grieve

aflojar [afloˈxar] *vt* to slacken; (*desatar*) to loosen, undo; (*relajar*) to relax ♦ *vi* to drop; (*bajar*) to go down; **~se** *vr* to relax

aflorar [afloˈrar] *vi* to come to the surface, emerge

afluente [afluˈente] *adj* flowing ♦ *nm* tributary

afluir [afluˈir] *vi* to flow

afmo, a *abr* (= *afectísimo(a) suyo(a)*) Yours

afónico, a [aˈfoniko, a] *adj*: **estar ~** to have a sore throat; to have lost one's voice

aforo [aˈforo] *nm* (*de teatro etc*) capacity

afortunado, a [afortuˈnaðo, a] *adj* ~~fortunate, lucky~~

afrancesado, a [afranθeˈsaðo, a] *adj* francophile; (*pey*) Frenchified

afrenta [aˈfrenta] *nf* affront, insult; (*deshonra*) dishonour, shame

África [ˈafrika] *nf* Africa; **~ del Sur** South Africa; **~ del Norte** North Africa; **africano, a** *adj, nm/f* African

afrontar [afronˈtar] *vt* to confront; (*poner cara a cara*) to bring face to face

afuera [aˈfwera] *adv* out, outside; **~s** *nfpl* outskirts

agachar [aɣaˈtʃar] *vt* to bend, bow; **~se** *vr* to stoop, bend

agalla [aˈɣaʎa] *nf* (*ZOOL*) gill; **tener ~s** (*fam*) to have guts

agarradera [aɣarraˈðera] (*esp AM*) *nf* handle

agarrado, a [aɣaˈrraðo, a] *adj* mean, stingy

agarrar [aɣaˈrrar] *vt* to grasp, grab; (*AM*) to take, catch; (*recoger*) to pick up ♦ *vi* (*planta*) to take root; **~se** *vr* to hold on (tightly)

agarrotar [aɣarroˈtar] *vt* (*persona*) to squeeze tightly; (*reo*) to garrotte; **~se** *vr* (*motor*) to seize up; (*MED*) to stiffen

agasajar [aɣasaˈxar] *vt* to treat well, fête

agazaparse [aɣaθaˈparse] *vr* to crouch down

agencia [aˈxenθja] *nf* agency; **~ inmobiliaria** estate (*BRIT*) o real estate (*US*) agent's (office); **~ de viajes** travel agency

agenciarse [axenˈθjarse] *vr* to obtain, procure

agenda [aˈxenda] *nf* diary

agente [aˈxente] *nm/f* agent; (*de policía*) policeman/policewoman; **~ inmobiliario** estate agent (*BRIT*), realtor (*US*); **~ de seguros** insurance agent

ágil [ˈaxil] *adj* agile, nimble; **agilidad** *nf* agility, nimbleness

agilizar [axiliˈθar] *vt* (*trámites*) to speed up

agitación [axitaˈθjon] *nf* (*de mano etc*) shaking, waving; (*de líquido etc*) stirring; (*fig*) agitation

agitado, a [axiˈtaðo, a] *adj* hectic; (*viaje*) ~~bumpy~~

agitar [axiˈtar] *vt* to wave, shake; (*líquido*) to stir; (*fig*) to stir up, excite; **~se** *vr* to get excited; (*inquietarse*) to get worried o upset

aglomeración [aɣlomeraˈθjon] *nf*: **~ de tráfico/gente** traffic jam/mass of people

aglomerar [aɣlomeˈrar] *vt* to crowd together; **~se** *vr* to crowd together

agnóstico, a [aɣˈnostiko, a] *adj, nm/f* agnostic

agobiar [aɣoˈβjar] *vt* to weigh down; (*oprimir*) to oppress; (*cargar*) to burden

agolparse [aɣolˈparse] *vr* to crowd together

agonía [aɣoˈnia] *nf* death throes *pl*; (*fig*) agony, anguish

agonizante [aɣoniˈθante] *adj* dying

agonizar [aɣoniˈθar] *vi* (*tb*: **estar agonizando**) to be dying

agosto [a'ɣosto] *nm* August

agotado, a [aɣo'taðo, a] *adj* (*persona*) exhausted; (*libros*) out of print; (*acabado*) finished; (*COM*) sold out

agotador, a [aɣota'ðor, a] *adj* exhausting

agotamiento [aɣota'mjento] *nm* exhaustion

agotar [aɣo'tar] *vt* to exhaust; (*consumir*) to drain; (*recursos*) to use up, deplete; **~se** *vr* to be exhausted; (*acabarse*) to run out; (*libro*) to go out of print

agraciado, a [aɣra'θjaðo, a] *adj* (*atractivo*) attractive; (*en sorteo etc*) lucky

agradable [aɣra'ðaβle] *adj* pleasant, nice

agradar [aɣra'ðar] *vt*: **él me agrada** I like him

agradecer [aɣraðe'θer] *vt* to thank; (*favor etc*) to be grateful for; **agradecido, a** *adj* grateful; **¡muy agradecido!** thanks a lot!; **agradecimiento** *nm* thanks *pl*; gratitude

agradezco *etc vb ver* **agradecer**

agrado [a'ɣraðo] *nm*: **ser de tu** *etc* **~** to be to your *etc* liking

agrandar [aɣran'dar] *vt* to enlarge; (*fig*) to exaggerate; **~se** *vr* to get bigger

agrario, a [a'ɣrarjo, a] *adj* agrarian, land *cpd*; (*política*) agricultural, farming

agravante [aɣra'βante] *adj* aggravating ♦ *nf*: **con la ~ de que ...** with the further difficulty that ....

agravar [aɣra'βar] *vt* (*pesar sobre*) to make heavier; (*irritar*) to aggravate; **~se** *vr* to worsen, get worse

agraviar [aɣra'βjar] *vt* to offend; (*ser injusto con*) to wrong; **~se** *vr* to take offence; **agravio** *nm* offence; wrong; (*JUR*) grievance

agredir [aɣre'ðir] *vt* to attack

agregado, a [aɣre'ɣaðo, a] *nm/f*: **A~** ≈ teacher (*who is not head of department*) ♦ *nm* aggregate; (*persona*) attaché

agregar [aɣre'ɣar] *vt* to gather; (*añadir*) to add; (*persona*) to appoint

agresión [aɣre'sjon] *nf* aggression

agresivo, a [aɣre'siβo, a] *adj* aggressive

agriar [a'ɣrjar] *vt* to (turn) sour; **~se** *vr* to turn sour

agrícola [a'ɣrikola] *adj* farming *cpd*, agricultural

agricultor, a [aɣrikul'tor, a] *nm/f* farmer

agricultura [aɣrikul'tura] *nf* agriculture, farming

agridulce [aɣri'ðulθe] *adj* bittersweet; (*CULIN*) sweet and sour

agrietarse [aɣrje'tarse] *vr* to crack; (*piel*) to chap

agrimensor, a [aɣrimen'sor, a] *nm/f* surveyor

agrio, a ['aɣrjo, a] *adj* bitter

agronomía [aɣrono'mia] *nf* agronomy, agriculture

agropecuario, a [aɣrope'kwarjo, a] *adj* farming *cpd*, agricultural

agrupación [aɣrupa'θjon] *nf* group; (*acto*) grouping

agrupar [aɣru'par] *vt* to group

agua ['aɣwa] *nf* water; (*NAUT*) wake; (*ARQ*) slope of a roof; **~s** *nfpl* (*de piedra*) water *sg*, sparkle *sg*; (*MED*) water *sg*, urine *sg*; (*NAUT*) waters; **~s abajo/arriba** downstream/upstream; **~ bendita/destilada/ potable** holy/distilled/drinking water; **~ caliente** hot water; **~ corriente** running water; **~ de colonia** eau de cologne; **~ mineral (con/sin gas)** (carbonated/ uncarbonated) mineral water; **~ oxigenada** hydrogen peroxide; **~s jurisdiccionales** territorial waters

aguacate [aɣwa'kate] *nm* avocado (pear)

aguacero [aɣwa'θero] *nm* (heavy) shower, downpour

aguado, a [a'ɣwaðo, a] *adj* watery, watered down

aguafiestas [aɣwa'fjestas] *nm/f inv* spoilsport, killjoy

aguanieve [aɣwa'njeβe] *nf* sleet

aguantar [aɣwan'tar] *vt* to bear, put up with; (*sostener*) to hold up ♦ *vi* to last; **~se** *vr* to restrain o.s.; **aguante** *nm* (*paciencia*) patience; (*resistencia*) endurance

aguar [a'ɣwar] *vt* to water down

aguardar [aɣwar'ðar] *vt* to wait for

aguardiente [aɣwar'ðjente] *nm* brandy, liquor

aguarrás [aɣwa'rras] *nm* turpentine

agudeza [aɣu'ðeθa] *nf* sharpness;

(*ingenio*) wit

agudizar [aɣuði'θar] *vt* (*crisis*) to make worse; **~se** *vr* to get worse

agudo, a [a'ɣuðo, a] *adj* sharp; (*voz*) high-pitched, piercing; (*dolor, enfermedad*) acute

agüero [a'ɣwero] *nm*: **buen/mal ~** good/bad omen

aguijón [aɣi'xon] *nm* sting; (*fig*) spur

águila ['aɣila] *nf* eagle; (*fig*) genius

aguileño, a [aɣi'leɲo, a] *adj* (*nariz*) aquiline; (*rostro*) sharp-featured

aguinaldo [aɣi'naldo] *nm* Christmas box

aguja [a'ɣuxa] *nf* needle; (*de reloj*) hand; (*ARQ*) spire; (*de reloj*) firing-pin; **~s** *nfpl* (*ZOOL*) ribs; (*FERRO*) points

agujerear [aɣuxere'ar] *vt* to make holes in

agujero [aɣu'xero] *nm* hole

agujetas [aɣu'xetas] *nfpl* stitch *sg*; (*rigidez*) stiffness *sg*

aguzar [aɣu'θar] *vt* to sharpen; (*fig*) to incite

ahí [a'i] *adv* there; **de ~ que** so that, with the result that; **~ llega** here he comes; **por ~** that way; (*allá*) over there; **200 o por ~** 200 or so

ahijado, a [ai'xaðo, a] *nm/f* godson/daughter

ahínco [a'inko] *nm* earnestness

ahíto, a [a'ito, a] *adj*: **estoy ~** I'm full up

ahogar [ao'ɣar] *vt* to drown; (*asfixiar*) to suffocate, smother; (*fuego*) to put out; **~se** *vr* (*en el agua*) to drown; (*por asfixia*) to suffocate

ahogo [a'oɣo] *nm* breathlessness; (*fig*) financial difficulty

ahondar [aon'dar] *vt* to deepen, make deeper; (*fig*) to study thoroughly ♦ *vi*: **~ en** to study thoroughly

ahora [a'ora] *adv* now; (*hace poco*) a moment ago, just now; (*dentro de poco*) in a moment; **~ voy** I'm coming; **~ mismo** right now; **~ bien** now then; **por ~** for the present

ahorcar [aor'kar] *vt* to hang; **~se** *vr* to hang o.s.

ahorita [ao'rita] (*fam: esp AM*) *adv* right now

ahorrar [ao'rrar] *vt* (*dinero*) to save; (*esfuerzos*) to save, avoid; **ahorro** *nm* (*acto*) saving; (*frugalidad*) thrift; **ahorros** *nmpl* (*dinero*) savings

ahuecar [awe'kar] *vt* to hollow (out); (*voz*) to deepen; **~se** *vr* to give o.s. airs

ahumar [au'mar] *vt* to smoke, cure; (*llenar de humo*) to fill with smoke ♦ *vi* to smoke; **~se** *vr* to fill with smoke

ahuyentar [aujen'tar] *vt* to drive off, frighten off; (*fig*) to dispel

airado, a [ai'raðo, a] *adj* angry

airar [ai'rar] *vt* to anger; **~se** *vr* to get angry

aire ['aire] *nm* air; (*viento*) wind; (*corriente*) draught; (*MUS*) tune; **~s** *nmpl*: **darse ~s** to give o.s. airs; **al ~ libre** in the open air; **~ acondicionado** air conditioning; **airearse** *vr* (*persona*) to go out for a breath of fresh air; **airoso, a** *adj* windy; draughty; (*fig*) graceful

aislado, a [ais'laðo, a] *adj* isolated; (*incomunicado*) cut-off; (*ELEC*) insulated

aislar [ais'lar] *vt* to isolate; (*ELEC*) to insulate

ajardinado, a [axarði'naðo, a] *adj* landscaped

ajedrez [axe'ðreθ] *nm* chess

ajeno, a [a'xeno, a] *adj* (*que pertenece a otro*) somebody else's; **~ a** foreign to; **~ de** free from, devoid of

ajetreado, a [axetre'aðo, a] *adj* busy

ajetreo [axe'treo] *nm* bustle

ají [a'xi] (*AM*) *nm* chil(l)i, red pepper; (*salsa*) chil(l)i sauce

ajo ['axo] *nm* garlic

ajuar [a'xwar] *nm* household furnishings *pl*; (*de novia*) trousseau; (*de niño*) layette

ajustado, a [axus'taðo, a] *adj* (*tornillo*) tight; (*cálculo*) right; (*ropa*) tight(-fitting); (*DEPORTE: resultado*) close

ajustar [axus'tar] *vt* (*adaptar*) to adjust; (*encajar*) to fit; (*TEC*) to engage; (*IMPRENTA*) to make up; (*apretar*) to tighten; (*concertar*) to agree (on); (*reconciliar*) to reconcile; (*cuentas, deudas*) to settle ♦ *vi* to fit; **~se** *vr*: **~se a** (*precio etc*) to be in keeping with, fit in with; **~ las cuentas a uno** to get even with sb

ajuste [a'xuste] *nm* adjustment; (*COSTURA*) fitting; (*acuerdo*) compromise; (*de cuenta*) settlement

al [al] (= **a** + **el**) *ver* **a**

ala ['ala] *nf* wing; (*de sombrero*) brim; (*futbolista*) winger

alabanza [ala'ßanθa] *nf* praise

alabar [ala'ßar] *vt* to praise

alacena [ala'θena] *nf* kitchen cupboard (*BRIT*), kitchen closet (*US*)

alacrán [ala'kran] *nm* scorpion

alado, a [a'laðo, a] *adj* winged

alambique [alam'bike] *nm* still

alambrada [alam'braða] *nf* wire fence; (*red*) wire netting

alambrado [alam'braðo] *nm* = **alambrada**

alambre [a'lambre] *nm* wire; ~ **de púas** barbed wire

alameda [ala'meða] *nf* (*plantío*) poplar grove; (*lugar de paseo*) avenue, boulevard

álamo ['alamo] *nm* poplar; ~ **temblón** aspen

alarde [a'larðe] *nm* show, display; **hacer** ~ **de** to boast of

alargador [alarɣa'ðor] *nm* (*ELEC*) extension lead

alargar [alar'ɣar] *vt* to lengthen, extend; (*paso*) to hasten; (*brazo*) to stretch out; (*cuerda*) to pay out; (*conversación*) to spin out; ~**se** *vr* to get longer

alarido [ala'riðo] *nm* shriek

alarma [a'larma] *nf* alarm

alarmar *vt* to alarm; ~**se** to get alarmed; **alarmante** [alar'mante] *adj* alarming

alba ['alßa] *nf* dawn

albacea [alßa'θea] *nm/f* executor/executrix

albahaca [alß'aka] *nf* basil

Albania [al'ßanja] *nf* Albania

albañal [alßa'ɲal] *nm* drain, sewer

albañil [alßa'ɲil] *nm* bricklayer; (*cantero*) mason

albarán [alßa'ran] *nm* (*COM*) delivery note, invoice

albaricoque [alßari'koke] *nm* apricot

albedrío [alße'ðrio] *nm*: **libre** ~ free will

alberca [al'ßerka] *nf* reservoir; (*AM*) swimming pool

albergar [alßer'ɣar] *vt* to shelter

albergue *etc* [al'ßerɣe] *vb ver* **albergar**
♦ *nm* shelter, refuge; ~ **juvenil** youth hostel

albóndiga [al'ßondiɣa] *nf* meatball

albornoz [alßor'noθ] *nm* (*de los árabes*) burnous; (*para el baño*) bathrobe

alborotar [alßoro'tar] *vi* to make a row
♦ *vt* to agitate, stir up; ~**se** *vr* to get excited; (*mar*) to get rough; **alboroto** *nm* row, uproar

alborozar [alßoro'θar] *vt* to gladden; ~**se** *vr* to rejoice

alborozo [alßo'roθo] *nm* joy

álbum ['alßum] (*pl* ~**s**, ~**es**) *nm* album; ~ **de recortes** scrapbook

alcachofa [alka'tʃofa] *nf* artichoke

alcalde, esa [al'kalde, esa] *nm/f* mayor(ess)

alcaldía [alkal'dia] *nf* mayoralty; (*lugar*) mayor's office

alcance *etc* [al'kanθe] *vb ver* **alcanzar**
♦ *nm* reach; (*COM*) adverse balance

alcantarilla [alkanta'riʎa] *nf* (*de aguas cloacales*) sewer; (*en la calle*) gutter

alcanzar [alkan'θar] *vt* (*algo: con la mano, el pie*) to reach; (*alguien: en el camino etc*) to catch up (with); (*autobús*) to catch; (*suj: bala*) to hit, strike ♦ *vi* (*ser suficiente*) to be enough; ~ **a hacer** to manage to do

alcaparra [alka'parra] *nf* caper

alcayata [alka'jata] *nf* hook

alcázar [al'kaθar] *nm* fortress; (*NAUT*) quarter-deck

alcoba [al'koßa] *nf* bedroom

alcohol [al'kol] *nm* alcohol; ~ **metílico** methylated spirits *pl* (*BRIT*), wood alcohol (*US*); **alcohólico, a** *adj, nm/f* alcoholic

alcoholímetro [alko'limetro] *nm* Breathalyser ® (*BRIT*), drunkometer (*US*)

alcoholismo [alko'lismo] *nm* alcoholism

alcornoque [alkor'noke] *nm* cork tree; (*fam*) idiot

alcurnia [al'kurnja] *nf* lineage

aldaba [al'daßa] *nf* (*door*) knocker

aldea [al'dea] *nf* village; ~**no, a** *adj* village *cpd* ♦ *nm/f* villager

aleación [alea'θjon] *nf* alloy

aleatorio, a [alea'torjo, a] *adj* random

aleccionar [alekθjo'nar] *vt* to instruct; (*adiestrar*) to train

alegación [aleva'θjon] *nf* allegation

alegar [ale'var] *vt* to allege; (*JUR*) to plead ♦ *vi* (*AM*) to argue

alegato [ale'vato] *nm* (*JUR*) allegation; (*AM*) argument

alegoría [alevo'ria] *nf* allegory

alegrar [ale'vrar] *vt* (*causar alegría*) to cheer (up); (*fuego*) to poke; (*fiesta*) to liven up; **~se** *vr* (*fam*) to get merry *o* tight; **~se de** to be glad about

alegre [a'levre] *adj* happy, cheerful; (*fam*) merry, tight; (*chiste*) risqué, blue; **alegría** *nf* happiness; merriment

alejamiento [alexa'mjento] *nm* removal; (*distancia*) remoteness

alejar [ale'xar] *vt* to remove; (*fig*) to estrange; **~se** *vr* to move away

alemán, ana [ale'man, ana] *adj, nm/f* German ♦ *nm* (*LING*) German

Alemania [ale'manja] *nf*: **~ Occidental/Oriental** West/East Germany

alentador, a [alenta'ðor, a] *adj* encouraging

alentar [alen'tar] *vt* to encourage

alergia [a'lerxja] *nf* allergy

alero [a'lero] *nm* (*de tejado*) eaves *pl*; (*de carruaje*) mudguard

alerta [a'lerta] *adj, nm* alert

aleta [a'leta] *nf* (*de pez*) fin; (*de ave*) wing; (*de foca, DEPORTE*) flipper; (*AUTO*) mudguard

aletargar [aletar'var] *vt* to make drowsy; (*entumecer*) to make numb; **~se** *vr* to grow drowsy; to become numb

aletear [alete'ar] *vi* to flutter

alevín [ale'ßin] *nm* fry, young fish

alevino [ale'ßino] *nm* = **alevín**

alevosía [aleßo'sia] *nf* treachery

alfabeto [alfa'ßeto] *nm* alphabet

alfalfa [al'falfa] *nf* alfalfa, lucerne

alfarería [alfare'ria] *nf* pottery; (*tienda*) pottery shop; **alfarero, a** *nm/f* potter

alféizar [al'feiθar] *nm* window-sill

alférez [al'fereθ] *nm* (*MIL*) second lieutenant; (*NAUT*) ensign

alfil [al'fil] *nm* (*AJEDREZ*) bishop

alfiler [alfi'ler] *nm* pin; (*broche*) clip; (*pinza*) clothes peg

alfiletero [alfile'tero] *nm* needlecase

alfombra [al'fombra] *nf* carpet; (*más pequeña*) rug; **alfombrar** *vt* to carpet; **alfombrilla** *nf* rug, mat

alforja [al'forxa] *nf* saddlebag

algarabía [alvara'ßia] (*fam*) *nf* gibberish; (*griterío*) hullabaloo

algas ['alvas] *nfpl* seaweed

álgebra ['alxeßra] *nf* algebra

álgido, a ['alxiðo] *adj* icy, chilly; (*momento etc*) crucial, decisive

algo ['alvo] *pron* something; anything ♦ *adv* somewhat, rather; **¿~ más?** anything else?; (*en tienda*) is that all?; **por ~ será** there must be some reason for it

algodón [alvo'ðon] *nm* cotton; (*planta*) cotton plant; **~ de azúcar** candy floss (*BRIT*), cotton candy (*US*); **~ hidrófilo** cotton wool (*BRIT*), absorbent cotton (*US*)

algodonero, a [alvoðo'nero, a] *adj* cotton *cpd* ♦ *nm/f* cotton grower ♦ *nm* cotton plant

alguacil [alvwa'θil] *nm* bailiff; (*TAUR*) mounted official

alguien ['alvjen] *pron* someone, somebody; (*en frases interrogativas*) anyone, anybody

alguno, a [al'vuno, a] *adj* (*delante de nm*: **algún**) some; (*después de n*): **no tiene talento ~** he has no talent, he doesn't have any talent ♦ *pron* (*alguien*) someone, somebody; **algún que otro libro** some book or other; **algún día iré** I'll go one *o* some day; **sin interés ~** without the slightest interest; **~ que otro** an occasional one; **~s piensan** some (people) think

alhaja [a'laxa] *nf* jewel; (*tesoro*) precious object, treasure

alhelí [ale'li] *nm* wallflower, stock

aliado, a [a'ljaðo, a] *adj* allied

alianza [a'ljanθa] *nf* alliance; (*anillo*) wedding ring

aliar [a'ljar] *vt* to ally; **~se** *vr* to form an alliance

alias ['aljas] *adv* alias

alicates [ali'kates] *nmpl* pliers; ~ **de uñas** nail clippers

aliciente [ali'θjente] *nm* incentive; (*atracción*) attraction

alienación [aljena'θjon] *nf* alienation

aliento [a'ljento] *nm* breath; (*respiración*) breathing; **sin ~** breathless

aligerar [alixe'rar] *vt* to lighten; (*reducir*) to shorten; (*aliviar*) to alleviate; (*mitigar*) to ease; (*paso*) to quicken

alijo [a'lixo] *nm* consignment

alimaña [ali'maɲa] *nf* pest

alimentación [alimenta'θjon] *nf* (*comida*) food; (*acción*) feeding; (*tienda*) grocer's (shop); **alimentador** *nm*: **alimentador de papel** sheet-feeder

alimentar [alimen'tar] *vt* to feed; (*nutrir*) to nourish; **~se** *vr* to feed

alimenticio, a [alimen'tiθjo, a] *adj* food *cpd*; (*nutritivo*) nourishing, nutritious

alimento [ali'mento] *nm* food; (*nutrición*) nourishment; **~s** *nmpl* (*JUR*) alimony *sg*

alineación [alinea'θjon] *nf* alignment; (*DEPORTE*) line-up

alinear [aline'ar] *vt* to align; **~se** *vr* (*DEPORTE*) to line up; **~se en** to fall in with

aliñar [ali'ɲar] *vt* (*CULIN*) to season; **aliño** *nm* (*CULIN*) dressing

alioli [ali'oli] *nm* garlic mayonnaise

alisar [ali'sar] *vt* to smooth

aliso [a'liso] *nm* alder

alistarse [alis'tarse] *vr* to enlist; (*inscribirse*) to enrol

aliviar [ali'βjar] *vt* (*carga*) to lighten; (*persona*) to relieve; (*dolor*) to relieve, alleviate

alivio [a'liβjo] *nm* alleviation, relief

aljibe [al'xiβe] *nm* cistern

allá [a'ʎa] *adv* (*lugar*) there; (*por ahí*) over there; (*tiempo*) then; ~ **abajo** down there; **más ~** further on; **más ~ de** beyond; **¡~ tú!** that's your problem!

allanamiento [aʎana'mjento] *nm*: ~ **de morada** burglary

allanar [aʎa'nar] *vt* to flatten, level (out); (*igualar*) to smooth (out); (*fig*) to subdue; (*JUR*) to burgle, break into; **~se** *vr* to fall down; **~se a** to submit to, accept

allegado, a [aʎe'ɣaðo, a] *adj* near, close ♦ *nm/f* relation

allí [a'ʎi] *adv* there; ~ **mismo** right there; **por ~** over there; (*por ese camino*) that way

alma ['alma] *nf* soul; (*persona*) person; (*TEC*) core

almacén [alma'θen] *nm* (*depósito*) warehouse, store; (*MIL*) magazine; (*AM*) shop; **(grandes) almacenes** *nmpl* department store *sg*; **almacenaje** *nm* storage

almacenar [almaθe'nar] *vt* to store, put in storage; (*proveerse*) to stock up with; **almacenero** *nm* (*AM*) shopkeeper

almanaque [alma'nake] *nm* almanac

almeja [al'mexa] *nf* clam

almendra [al'mendra] *nf* almond; **almendro** *nm* almond tree

almíbar [al'miβar] *nm* syrup

almidón [almi'ðon] *nm* starch; **almidonar** *vt* to starch

almirante [almi'rante] *nm* admiral

almirez [almi'reθ] *nm* mortar

almizcle [al'miθkle] *nm* musk

almohada [almo'aða] *nf* pillow; (*funda*) pillowcase; **almohadilla** *nf* cushion; (*TEC*) pad; (*AM*) pincushion

almohadón [almoa'ðon] *nm* large pillow; bolster

almorranas [almo'rranas] *nfpl* piles, haemorrhoids

almorzar [almor'θar] *vt*: ~ **una tortilla** to have an omelette for lunch ♦ *vi* to (have) lunch

almuerzo *etc* [al'mwerθo] *vb ver* **almorzar** ♦ *nm* lunch

alocado, a [alo'kaðo, a] *adj* crazy

alojamiento [aloxa'mjento] *nm* lodging(s) (*pl*); (*viviendas*) housing

alojar [alo'xar] *vt* to lodge; **~se** *vr* to lodge, stay

alondra [a'londra] *nf* lark, skylark

alpargata [alpar'ɣata] *nf* rope-soled sandal, espadrille

Alpes ['alpes] *nmpl*: **los ~** the Alps

alpinismo [alpi'nismo] *nm* mountaineering, climbing; **alpinista** *nm/f* mountaineer, climber

alpiste [al'piste] *nm* birdseed

alquilar [alki'lar] *vt* (*suj: propietario*: *inmuebles*) to let, rent (out); (: *coche*) to hire out; (: *TV*) to rent (out); (*suj*: *alquilador*: *inmuebles, TV*) to rent (: *coche*) to hire; **"se alquila casa"** "house to let (*BRIT*) o for rent (*US*)"

alquiler [alki'ler] *nm* renting; letting; hiring; (*arriendo*) rent; hire charge; ~ **de automóviles** car hire; **de** ~ for hire

alquimia [al'kimja] *nf* alchemy

alquitrán [alki'tran] *nm* tar

alrededor [alreðe'ðor] *adv* around, about; ~ **de** around, about; **mirar a su** ~ to look (round) about one; ~**es** *nmpl* surroundings

alta ['alta] *nf* (certificate of) discharge; **dar de** ~ to discharge

altanería [altane'ria] *nf* haughtiness, arrogance; **altanero, a** *adj* arrogant, haughty

altar [al'tar] *nm* altar

altavoz [alta'βoθ] *nm* loudspeaker; (*amplificador*) amplifier

alteración [altera'θjon] *nf* alteration; (*alboroto*) disturbance

alterar [alte'rar] *vt* to alter; to disturb; ~**se** *vr* (*persona*) to get upset

altercado [alter'kaðo] *nm* argument

alternar [alter'nar] *vt* to alternate ♦ *vi* to alternate; (*turnar*) to take turns; ~**se** *vr* to alternate; to take turns; ~ **con** to mix with; **alternativa** *nf* alternative; (*elección*) choice; **alternativo, a** *adj* alternative; (*alterno*) alternating; **alterno, a** *adj* alternate; (*ELEC*) alternating

Alteza [al'teθa] *nf* (*tratamiento*) Highness

altibajos [alti'βaxos] *nmpl* ups and downs

altiplanicie [altiplа'niθje] *nf* high plateau

altiplano [alti'plano] *nm* = **altiplanicie**

altisonante [altiso'nante] *adj* high-flown, high-sounding

altitud [alti'tuð] *nf* height; (*AVIAT, GEO*) altitude

altivez [alti'βeθ] *nf* haughtiness, arrogance; **altivo, a** *adj* haughty, arrogant

alto, a ['alto, a] *adj* high; (*persona*) tall; (*sonido*) high, sharp; (*noble*) high, lofty ♦ *nm* halt; (*MUS*) alto; (*GEO*) hill; (*AM*) pile ♦ *adv* (*de sitio*) high; (*de sonido*) loud, loudly ♦ *excl* halt!; **la pared tiene 2 metros de** ~ the wall is 2 metres high; **en alta mar** on the high seas; **en voz alta** in a loud voice; **las altas horas de la noche** the small o wee hours; **en lo de** at the top of; **pasar por** ~ to overlook

altoparlante [altopar'lante] (*AM*) *nm* loudspeaker

altruismo [altru'ismo] *nm* altruism

altura [al'tura] *nf* height; (*NAUT*) depth; (*GEO*) latitude; **la pared tiene 1.80 de** ~ the wall is 1 metre 80cm high; **a estas** ~**s** at this stage; **a estas** ~**s del año** at this time of the year

alubia [a'luβja] *nf* French bean, kidney bean

alucinación [aluθina'θjon] *nf* halluci-nation

alucinar [aluθi'nar] *vi* to hallucinate ♦ *vt* to deceive; (*fascinar*) to fascinate

alud [a'luð] *nm* avalanche; (*fig*) flood

aludir [alu'ðir] *vi*: ~ **a** to allude to; **darse por aludido** to take the hint

alumbrado [alum'braðo] *nm* lighting; **alumbramiento** *nm* lighting; (*MED*) childbirth, delivery

alumbrar [alum'brar] *vt* to light (up) ♦ *vi* (*MED*) to give birth

aluminio [alu'minjo] *nm* aluminium (*BRIT*), aluminum (*US*)

alumno, a [a'lumno, a] *nm/f* pupil, student

alunizar [aluni'θar] *vi* to land on the moon

alusión [alu'sjon] *nf* allusion

alusivo, a [alu'siβo, a] *adj* allusive

aluvión [alu'βjon] *nm* alluvium; (*fig*) flood

alverja [al'βerxa] (*AM*) *nf* pea

alza ['alθa] *nf* rise; (*MIL*) sight

alzada [al'θaða] *nf* (*de caballos*) height; (*JUR*) appeal

alzamiento [alθa'mjento] *nm* (*aumento*) rise, increase; (*acción*) lifting, raising; (*mejor postura*) higher bid; (*rebelión*) rising; (*COM*) fraudulent bankruptcy

alzar [al'θar] *vt* to lift (up); (*precio, muro*)

to raise; (*cuello de abrigo*) to turn up; (*AGR*) to gather in; (*IMPRENTA*) to gather; ~**se** *vr* to get up, rise; (*rebelarse*) to revolt; (*COM*) to go fraudulently bankrupt; (*JUR*) to appeal

ama ['ama] *nf* lady of the house; (*dueña*) owner; (*institutriz*) governess; (*madre adoptiva*) foster mother; ~ **de casa** housewife; ~ **de llaves** housekeeper

amabilidad [amaβili'ðað] *nf* kindness; (*simpatía*) niceness; **amable** *adj* kind; nice; **es usted muy amable** that's very kind of you

amaestrado, a [amaes'traðo, a] *adj* (*animal: en circo etc*) performing

amaestrar [amaes'trar] *vt* to train

amago [a'maɣo] *nm* threat; (*gesto*) threatening gesture; (*MED*) symptom

amainar [amai'nar] *vi* (*viento*) to die down

amalgama [amal'ɣama] *nf* amalgam; **amalgamar** *vt* to amalgamate; (*combinar*) to combine, mix

amamantar [amaman'tar] *vt* to suckle, nurse

amanecer [amane'θer] *vi* to dawn ♦ *nm* dawn; ~ **afiebrado** to wake up with a fever

amanerado, a [amane'raðo, a] *adj* affected

amansar [aman'sar] *vt* to tame; (*persona*) to subdue; ~**se** *vr* (*persona*) to calm down

amante [a'mante] *adj*: ~ **de** fond of ♦ *nm/f* lover

amapola [ama'pola] *nf* poppy

amar [a'mar] *vt* to love

amargado, a [amar'ɣaðo, a] *adj* bitter

amargar [amar'ɣar] *vt* to make bitter; (*fig*) to embitter; ~**se** *vr* to become embittered

amargo, a [a'marɣo, a] *adj* bitter; **amargura** *nf* bitterness

amarillento, a [amari'ʎento, a] *adj* yellowish; (*tez*) sallow; **amarillo, a** *adj*, *nm* yellow

amarrar [ama'rrar] *vt* to moor; (*sujetar*) to tie up

amarras [a'marras] *nfpl*: **soltar** ~ to set sail

amartillar [amarti'ʎar] *vt* (*fusil*) to cock

amasar [ama'sar] *vt* (*masa*) to knead; (*mezclar*) to mix, prepare; (*confeccionar*) to concoct; **amasijo** *nm* kneading; mixing; (*fig*) hotchpotch

amateur ['amatur] *nm/f* amateur

amatista [ama'tista] *nf* amethyst

amazona [ama'θona] *nf* horsewoman; **A~s** *nm*: **el A~s** the Amazon

ambages [am'baxes] *nmpl*: **sin** ~ in plain language

ámbar ['ambar] *nm* amber

ambición [ambi'θjon] *nf* ambition; **ambicionar** *vt* to aspire to; **ambicioso, a** *adj* ambitious

ambidextro, a [ambi'ðekstro, a] *adj* ambidextrous

ambientación [ambjenta'θjon] *nf* (*CINE, TEATRO etc*) setting; (*RADIO*) sound effects

ambiente [am'bjente] *nm* (*tb fig*) atmosphere; (*medio*) environment

ambigüedad [ambiɣwe'ðað] *nf* ambiguity; **ambiguo, a** *adj* ambiguous

ámbito ['ambito] *nm* (*campo*) field; (*fig*) scope

ambos, as ['ambos, as] *adj pl, pron pl* both

ambulancia [ambu'lanθja] *nf* ambulance

ambulante [ambu'lante] *adj* travelling *cpd*, itinerant

ambulatorio [ambula'torio] *nm* state health-service clinic

amedrentar [ameðren'tar] *vt* to scare

amén [a'men] *excl* amen; ~ **de** besides

amenaza [ame'naθa] *nf* threat

amenazar [amena'θar] *vt* to threaten ♦ *vi*: ~ **con hacer** to threaten to do

amenidad [ameni'ðað] *nf* pleasantness

ameno, a [a'meno, a] *adj* pleasant

América [a'merika] *nf* America; ~ **del Norte/del Sur** North/South America; ~ **Central/Latina** Central/Latin America; **americana** *nf* coat, jacket; *ver tb* **americano**; **americano, a** *adj*, *nm/f* American

amerizar [ameri'θar] *vi* (*avión*) to land (on the sea)

ametralladora [ametraʎa'ðora] *nf* machine gun

amianto [a'mjanto] *nm* asbestos
amigable [ami'ɣaβle] *adj* friendly
amígdala [a'miɣðala] *nf* tonsil;
  amigdalitis *nf* tonsillitis
amigo, a [a'miɣo, a] *adj* friendly ♦ *nm/f*
  friend; (*amante*) lover; **ser ~ de algo** to
  be fond of sth; **ser muy ~s** to be close
  friends
amilanar [amila'nar] *vt* to scare; **~se** *vr* to
  get scared
aminorar [amino'rar] *vt* to diminish;
  (*reducir*) to reduce; **~ la marcha** to slow
  down
amistad [amis'tað] *nf* friendship; **~es** *nfpl*
  (*amigos*) friends; **amistoso, a** *adj*
  friendly
amnesia [am'nesja] *nf* amnesia
amnistía [amnis'tia] *nf* amnesty
amo ['amo] *nm* owner; (*jefe*) boss
amodorrarse [amoðo'rrarse] *vr* to get
  sleepy
amoldar [amol'dar] *vt* to mould; (*adaptar*)
  to adapt
amonestación [amonesta'θjon] *nf*
  warning; **amonestaciones** *nfpl* (*REL*)
  marriage banns
amonestar [amones'tar] *vt* to warn; (*REL*)
  to publish the banns of
amontonar [amonto'nar] *vt* to collect, pile
  up; **~se** *vr* to crowd together; (*acumularse*) to pile up
amor [a'mor] *nm* love; (*amante*) lover;
  hacer el ~ to make love; **~ propio** self-
  respect
amoratado, a [amora'taðo, a] *adj* purple
amordazar [amorða'θar] *vt* to muzzle;
  (*fig*) to gag
amorfo, a [a'morfo, a] *adj* amorphous,
  shapeless
amoroso, a [amo'roso, a] *adj*
  affectionate, loving
amortajar [amorta'xar] *vt* to shroud
amortiguador [amortiɣwa'ðor] *nm* shock
  absorber; (*parachoques*) bumper; **~es**
  nmpl (*AUTO*) suspension *sg*
amortiguar [amorti'ɣwar] *vt* to deaden;
  (*ruido*) to muffle; (*color*) to soften
amortización [amortiθa'θjon] *nf* (*de
  deuda*) repayment; (*de bono*) redemption

amotinar [amoti'nar] *vt* to stir up, incite
  (to riot); **~se** *vr* to mutiny
amparar [ampa'rar] *vt* to protect; **~se** *vr*
  to seek protection; (*de la lluvia etc*) to
  shelter; **amparo** *nm* help, protection; **al
  amparo de** under the protection of
amperio [am'perjo] *nm* ampère, amp
ampliación [amplja'θjon] *nf* enlargement;
  (*extensión*) extension
ampliar [am'pljar] *vt* to enlarge; to extend
amplificación [amplifika'θjon] *nf*
  enlargement; **amplificador** *nm* amplifier
amplificar [amplifi'kar] *vt* to amplify
amplio, a ['ampljo, a] *adj* spacious; (*de
  falda etc*) full; (*extenso*) extensive;
  (*ancho*) wide; **amplitud** *nf* spaciousness;
  extent; (*fig*) amplitude
ampolla [am'poʎa] *nf* blister; (*MED*)
  ampoule
ampuloso, a [ampu'loso, a] *adj*
  bombastic, pompous
amputar [ampu'tar] *vt* to cut off,
  amputate
amueblar [amwe'βlar] *vt* to furnish
amurallar [amura'ʎar] *vt* to wall up *o* in
anacronismo [anakro'nismo] *nm* anach-
  ronism
anales [a'nales] *nmpl* annals
analfabetismo [analfaβe'tismo] *nm*
  illiteracy; **analfabeto, a** *adj, nm/f*
  illiterate
analgésico [anal'xesiko] *nm* painkiller,
  analgesic
análisis [a'nalisis] *nm inv* analysis
analista [ana'lista] *nm/f* (*gen*) analyst
analizar [anali'θar] *vt* to analyse
analogía [analo'xia] *nf* analogy
analógico, a [ana'loxiko, a] *adj* (*INFORM*)
  analog; (*reloj*) analogue (*BRIT*), analog (*US*)
análogo, a [a'naloɣo, a] *adj* analogous,
  similar
ananá(s) [ana'na(s)] (*AM*) *nm* pineapple
anaquel [ana'kel] *nm* shelf
anarquía [anar'kia] *nf* anarchy;
  anarquismo *nm* anarchism; **anarquista**
  nm/f anarchist
anatomía [anato'mia] *nf* anatomy
anca ['anka] *nf* rump, haunch; **~s** *nfpl*
  (*fam*) behind *sg*

ancho, a ['antʃo, a] *adj* wide; (*falda*) full; (*fig*) liberal ♦ *nm* width; (*FERRO*) gauge; **ponerse ~** to get conceited; **estar a sus anchas** to be at one's ease

anchoa [an'tʃoa] *nf* anchovy

anchura [an'tʃura] *nf* width; (*extensión*) wideness

anciano, a [an'θjano, a] *adj* old, aged ♦ *nm/f* old man/woman; elder

ancla ['ankla] *nf* anchor; **~dero** *nm* anchorage; **anclar** *vi* to (drop) anchor

andadura [anda'ðura] *nf* gait; (*de caballo*) pace

Andalucía [andalu'θia] *nf* Andalusia; **andaluz, a** *adj, nm/f* Andalusian

andamiaje [anda'mjaxe] *nm* = **andamio**

andamio [an'damjo] *nm* scaffold(ing)

andar [an'dar] *vt* to go, cover, travel ♦ *vi* to go, walk, travel; (*funcionar*) to go, work; (*estar*) to be ♦ *nm* walk, gait, pace; **~se** *vr* to go away; **~ a pie/a caballo/en bicicleta** to go on foot/on horseback/by bicycle; **~ haciendo algo** to be doing sth; **¡anda!** (*sorpresa*) go on!; **anda por** *o* **en los 40** he's about 40

andariego, a [anda'rjeɣo, a] *adj* (*itinerante*) wandering

andén [an'den] *nm* (*FERRO*) platform; (*NAUT*) quayside; (*AM: de la calle*) pavement (*BRIT*), sidewalk (*US*)

Andes ['andes] *nmpl*: **los ~** the Andes

Andorra [an'dorra] *nf* Andorra

andrajo [an'draxo] *nm* rag; **~so, a** *adj* ragged

anduve *etc* [an'duße] *vb ver* **andar**

anécdota [a'nekðota] *nf* anecdote, story

anegar [ane'ɣar] *vt* to flood; (*ahogar*) to drown; **~se** *vr* to drown; (*hundirse*) to sink

anejo, a [a'nexo, a] *adj, nm* = **anexo**

anemia [a'nemja] *nf* anaemia

anestesia [anes'tesja] *nf* anaesthesia

anestésico [anes'tesiko] *nm* anaesthetic

anexar [anek'sar] *vt* to annex; (*documento*) to attach; **anexión** *nf* annexation; **anexionamiento** *nm* annexation; **anexo, a** *adj* attached ♦ *nm* annexe

anfibio, a [an'fißjo, a] *adj* amphibious ♦ *nm* amphibian

anfiteatro [anfite'atro] *nm* amphitheatre; (*TEATRO*) dress circle

anfitrión, ona [anfi'trjon, ona] *nm/f* host(ess)

ángel ['anxel] *nm* angel; **~ de la guarda** guardian angel; **tener ~** to be charming; **angelical** *adj*, **angélico, a** *adj* angelic(al)

angina [an'xina] *nf* (*MED*) inflammation of the throat; **~ de pecho** angina; **tener ~s** to have tonsillitis

anglicano, a [angli'kano, a] *adj, nm/f* Anglican

anglosajón, ona [anglosa'xon, ona] *adj* Anglo-Saxon

angosto, a [an'gosto, a] *adj* narrow

anguila [an'gila] *nf* eel; **~s** *nfpl* (*NAUT*) slipway *sg*

angula [an'gula] *nf* elver, baby eel

ángulo ['angulo] *nm* angle; (*esquina*) corner; (*curva*) bend

angustia [an'gustja] *nf* anguish; **angustiar** *vt* to distress, grieve

anhelar [ane'lar] *vt* to be eager for; (*desear*) to long for, desire ♦ *vi* to pant, gasp; **anhelo** *nm* eagerness; desire

anidar [ani'ðar] *vi* to nest

anillo [a'niʎo] *nm* ring; **~ de boda** wedding ring

animación [anima'θjon] *nf* liveliness; (*vitalidad*) life; (*actividad*) activity; bustle

animado, a [ani'maðo, a] *adj* lively; (*vivaz*) animated; **animador, a** *nm/f* (*TV*) host(ess), compère; (*DEPORTE*) cheerleader

animadversión [animaðßer'sjon] *nf* ill-will, antagonism

animal [ani'mal] *adj* animal; (*fig*) stupid ♦ *nm* animal; (*fig*) fool; (*bestia*) brute

animar [ani'mar] *vt* (*BIO*) to animate, give life to; (*fig*) to liven up, brighten up, cheer up; (*estimular*) to stimulate; **~se** *vr* to cheer up; to feel encouraged; (*decidirse*) to make up one's mind

ánimo ['animo] *nm* (*alma*) soul; (*mente*) mind; (*valentía*) courage ♦ *excl* cheer up!

animoso, a [ani'moso, a] *adj* brave; (*vivo*) lively

aniquilar [aniki'lar] *vt* to annihilate, destroy

anís [a'nis] *nm* aniseed; (*licor*) anisette

aniversario [aniβer'sarjo] *nm* anniversary

anoche [a'notʃe] *adv* last night; **antes de ~** the night before last

anochecer [anotʃe'θer] *vi* to get dark ♦ *nm* nightfall, dark; **al ~** at nightfall

anodino, a [ano'ðino, a] *adj* dull, anodyne

anomalía [anoma'lia] *nf* anomaly

anonadado, a [anona'ðaðo, a] *adj*: **estar/quedar/sentirse ~** to be overwhelmed o amazed

anonimato [anoni'mato] *nm* anonymity

anónimo, a [a'nonimo, a] *adj* anonymous; (*COM*) limited ♦ *nm* (*carta*) anonymous letter; (: *maliciosa*) poison-pen letter

anormal [anor'mal] *adj* abnormal

anotación [anota'θjon] *nf* note; annotation

anotar [ano'tar] *vt* to note down; (*comentar*) to annotate

anquilosamiento [ankilosa'mjento] *nm* (*fig*) paralysis; stagnation

anquilosarse [ankilo'sarse] *vr* (*fig: persona*) to get out of touch; (*método, costumbres*) to go out of date

ansia ['ansja] *nf* anxiety; (*añoranza*) yearning; **ansiar** *vt* to long for

ansiedad [ansje'ðað] *nf* anxiety

ansioso, a [an'sjoso, a] *adj* anxious; (*anhelante*) eager; **~ de** o **por algo** greedy for sth

antagónico, a [anta'ɣoniko, a] *adj* antagonistic; (*opuesto*) contrasting; **antagonista** *nm/f* antagonist

antaño [an'taɲo] *adv* long ago, formerly

Antártico [an'tartiko] *nm*: **el ~** the Antarctic

ante ['ante] *prep* before, in the presence of; (*problema etc*) faced with ♦ *nm* (*piel*) suede; **~ todo** above all

anteanoche [antea'notʃe] *adv* the night before last

anteayer [antea'jer] *adv* the day before yesterday

antebrazo [ante'βraθo] *nm* forearm

antecedente [anteθe'ðente] *adj* previous ♦ *nm* antecedent; **~s** *nmpl* (*JUR*): **~s** penales criminal record; (*procedencia*) background

anteceder [anteθe'ðer] *vt* to precede, go before

antecesor, a [anteθe'sor, a] *nm/f* predecessor

antedicho, a [ante'ðitʃo, a] *adj* aforementioned

antelación [antela'θjon] *nf*: **con ~** in advance

antemano [ante'mano]: **de ~** *adv* beforehand, in advance

antena [an'tena] *nf* antenna; (*de televisión etc*) aerial; **~ parabólica** satellite dish

anteojo [ante'oxo] *nm* eyeglass; **~s** *nmpl* (*AM*) glasses, spectacles

antepasados [antepa'saðos] *nmpl* ancestors

antepecho [ante'petʃo] *nm* guardrail, parapet; (*repisa*) ledge, sill

anteponer [antepo'ner] *vt* to place in front; (*fig*) to prefer

anteproyecto [antepro'jekto] *nm* preliminary sketch; (*fig*) blueprint

anterior [ante'rjor] *adj* preceding, previous; **~idad** *nf*: **con ~idad a** prior to, before

antes ['antes] *adv* (*con prioridad*) before ♦ *prep*: **~ de** before ♦ *conj*: **~ de ir/de que te vayas** before going/before you go; **~ bien** (but) rather; **dos días ~** two days before o previously; **no quiso venir ~** she didn't want to come any earlier; **tomo el avión ~ que el barco** I take the plane rather than the boat; **~ que yo** before me; **lo ~ posible** as soon as possible; **cuanto ~ mejor** the sooner the better

antiaéreo, a [antia'ereo, a] *adj* anti-aircraft

antibalas [anti'βalas] *adj inv*: **chaleco ~** bullet-proof jacket

antibiótico [anti'βjotiko] *nm* antibiotic

anticiclón [antiθi'klon] *nm* anticyclone

anticipación [antiθipa'θjon] *nf* anticipation; **con 10 minutos de ~** 10 minutes early

anticipado, a [antiθi'paðo, a] *adj* (*pago*) advance; **por ~** in advance

anticipar [antiθi'par] *vt* to anticipate; (*adelantar*) to bring forward; (*COM*) to advance; **~se** *vr*: **~se a su época** to be ahead of one's time

anticipo [anti'θipo] *nm* (*COM*) advance

anticonceptivo, a [antikonθep'tiβo, a] *adj, nm* contraceptive

anticongelante [antikonxe'lante] *nm* antifreeze

anticuado, a [anti'kwaðo, a] *adj* out-of-date, old-fashioned; (*desusado*) obsolete

anticuario [anti'kwarjo] *nm* antique dealer

anticuerpo [anti'kwerpo] *nm* (*MED*) antibody

antídoto [an'tiðoto] *nm* antidote

antiestético, a [anties'tetiko, a] *adj* unsightly

antifaz [anti'faθ] *nm* mask; (*velo*) veil

antigualla [anti'ɣwaʎa] *nf* antique; (*reliquia*) relic

antiguamente [antiɣwa'mente] *adv* formerly; (*hace mucho tiempo*) long ago

antigüedad [antiɣwe'ðað] *nf* antiquity; (*artículo*) antique; (*rango*) seniority

antiguo, a [an'tiɣwo, a] *adj* old, ancient; (*que fue*) former

Antillas [an'tiʎas] *nfpl*: **las ~** the West Indies

antílope [an'tilope] *nm* antelope

antinatural [antinatu'ral] *adj* unnatural

antipatía [antipa'tia] *nf* antipathy, dislike; **antipático, a** *adj* disagreeable, unpleasant

antirrobo [anti'rroβo] *adj inv* (*alarma etc*) anti-theft

antisemita [antise'mita] *adj* anti-Semitic ♦ *nm/f* anti-Semite

antiséptico, a [anti'septiko, a] *adj* antiseptic ♦ *nm* antiseptic

antítesis [an'titesis] *nf inv* antithesis

antojadizo, a [antoxa'ðiθo, a] *adj* capricious

antojarse [anto'xarse] *vr* (*desear*): **se me antoja comprarlo** I have a mind to buy it; (*pensar*): **se me antoja que** ¶ I have a feeling that

antojo [an'toxo] *nm* caprice, whim; (*rosa*) birthmark; (*lunar*) mole

antología [antolo'xia] *nf* anthology

antorcha [an'tortʃa] *nf* torch

antro ['antro] *nm* cavern

antropófago, a [antro'pofaɣo, a] *adj, nm/f* cannibal

antropología [antropolo'xia] *nf* anthropology

anual [a'nwal] *adj* annual; **~idad** *nf* annuity

anuario [a'nwarjo] *nm* yearbook

anudar [anu'ðar] *vt* to knot, tie; (*unir*) to join; **~se** *vr* to get tied up

anulación [anula'θjon] *nf* annulment; (*cancelación*) cancellation

anular [anu'lar] *vt* (*contrato*) to annul, cancel; (*ley*) to revoke, repeal; (*suscripción*) to cancel ♦ *nm* ring finger

anunciación [anunθja'θjon] *nf* announcement; (*REL*): **A~** Annunciation

anunciante [anun'θjante] *nm/f* (*COM*) advertiser

anunciar [anun'θjar] *vt* to announce; (*proclamar*) to proclaim; (*COM*) to advertise

anuncio [a'nunθjo] *nm* announcement; (*señal*) sign; (*COM*) advertisement; (*cartel*) poster

anzuelo [an'θwelo] *nm* hook; (*para pescar*) fish hook

añadidura [aɲaði'ðura] *nf* addition, extra; **por ~** besides, in addition

añadir [aɲa'ðir] *vt* to add

añejo, a [a'ɲexo, a] *adj* old; (*vino*) mellow

añicos [a'ɲikos] *nmpl*: **hacer ~** to smash, shatter

añil [a'ɲil] *nm* (*BOT, color*) indigo

año ['aɲo] *nm* year; **¡Feliz A~ Nuevo!** Happy New Year!; **tener 15 ~s** to be 15 (years old); **los ~ 90** the nineties; **~ bisiesto/escolar** leap/school year; **el ~ que viene** next year

añoranza [aɲo'ranθa] *nf* nostalgia; (*anhelo*) longing

apabullar [apaβu'ʎar] *vt* (*tb fig*) to crush, squash

apacentar [apaθen'tar] *vt* to pasture, graze

apacible [apa'θiβle] *adj* gentle, mild

apaciguar [apaθi'ɣwar] *vt* to pacify, calm (down)

apadrinar [apaðri'nar] *vt* to sponsor, support; (*REL*) to be godfather to

apagado, a [apa'ɣaðo, a] *adj* (*volcán*) extinct; (*color*) dull; (*voz*) quiet; (*sonido*) muted, muffled; (*persona: apático*) listless; **estar ~** (*fuego, luz*) to be out; (*RADIO, TV etc*) to be off

apagar [apa'ɣar] *vt* to put out; (*ELEC, RADIO, TV*) to turn off; (*sonido*) to silence, muffle; (*sed*) to quench

apagón [apa'ɣon] *nm* blackout; power cut

apalabrar [apala'βrar] *vt* to agree to; (*contratar*) to engage

apalear [apale'ar] *vt* to beat, thrash; (*AGR*) to winnow

apañar [apa'ɲar] *vt* to pick up; (*asir*) to take hold of, grasp; (*reparar*) to mend, patch up; **~se** *vr* to manage, get along

aparador [apara'ðor] *nm* sideboard; (*escaparate*) shop window

aparato [apa'rato] *nm* apparatus; (*máquina*) machine; (*doméstico*) appliance; (*boato*) ostentation; **~ de facsímil** facsimile (machine), fax; **~ digestivo** (*ANAT*) digestive system; **~so, a** *adj* showy, ostentatious

aparcamiento [aparka'mjento] *nm* car park (*BRIT*), parking lot (*US*)

aparcar [apar'kar] *vt, vi* to park

aparear [apare'ar] *vt* (*objetos*) to pair, match; (*animales*) to mate; **~se** *vr* to make a pair; to mate

aparecer [apare'θer] *vi* to appear; **~se** *vr* to appear

aparejado, a [apare'xaðo, a] *adj* fit, suitable; **llevar** *o* **traer ~** to involve; **aparejador, a** *nm/f* (*ARQ*) master builder

aparejo [apa'rexo] *nm* preparation; harness; rigging; (*de poleas*) block and tackle

aparentar [aparen'tar] *vt* (*edad*) to look; (*fingir*) **~ tristeza** to pretend to be sad

aparente [apa'rente] *adj* apparent; (*adecuado*) suitable

aparezco *etc vb ver* **aparecer**

aparición [apari'θjon] *nf* appearance; (*de libro*) publication; (*espectro*) apparition

apariencia [apa'rjenθja] *nf* (outward) appearance; **en ~** outwardly, seemingly

apartado, a [apar'taðo, a] *adj* separate; (*lejano*) remote ♦ *nm* (*tipográfico*) paragraph; **~ (de correos)** post office box

apartamento [aparta'mento] *nm* apartment, flat (*BRIT*)

apartamiento [aparta'mjento] *nm* separation; (*aislamiento*) remoteness, isolation; (*AM*) apartment, flat (*BRIT*)

apartar [apar'tar] *vt* to separate; (*quitar*) to remove; (*MINERALOGÍA*) to extract; **~se** *vr* to separate, part; (*irse*) to move away; to keep away

aparte [a'parte] *adv* (*separadamente*) separately; (*además*) besides ♦ *nm* aside; (*tipográfico*) new paragraph

apasionado, a [apasjo'naðo, a] *adj* passionate; biassed, prejudiced

apasionar [apasjo'nar] *vt* to excite; **le apasiona el fútbol** she's crazy about football; **~se** *vr* to get excited

apatía [apa'tia] *nf* apathy

apático, a [a'patiko, a] *adj* apathetic

apátrida [a'patrida] *adj* stateless

Apdo *abr* (= *Apartado (de Correos)*) PO Box

apeadero [apea'ðero] *nm* halt, stop, stopping place

apearse [ape'arse] *vr* (*jinete*) to dismount; (*bajarse*) to get down *o* out; (*AUTO, FERRO*) to get off *o* out

apechugar [apetʃu'ɣar] *vr*: **~ con algo** to face up to sth

apedrear [apeðre'ar] *vt* to stone

apegarse [ape'ɣarse] *vr*: **~ a** to become attached to; **apego** *nm* attachment, devotion

apelación [apela'θjon] *nf* appeal

apelar [ape'lar] *vi* to appeal; **~ a** (*fig*) to resort to

apellidar [apeʎi'ðar] *vt* to call, name; **~se** *vr*: **se apellida Pérez** her (sur)name's Pérez

apellido [ape'ʎiðo] *nm* surname

apelmazarse [apelma'θarse] *vr* (*masa, arroz*) to go hard; (*prenda de tana*) to shrink

apenar [ape'nar] *vt* to grieve, trouble; (*AM: avergonzar*) to embarrass; **~se** *vr* to grieve; (*AM*) to be embarrassed

apenas [a'penas] *adv* scarcely, hardly ♦ *conj* as soon as, no sooner

apéndice [a'pendiθe] *nm* appendix; **apendicitis** *nf* appendicitis

aperitivo [aperi'tiβo] *nm* (*bebida*) aperitif; (*comida*) appetizer

apero [a'pero] *nm* (*AGR*) implement; **~s** *nmpl* farm equipment *sg*

apertura [aper'tura] *nf* opening; (*POL*) liberalization

apesadumbrar [apesaðum'brar] *vt* to grieve, sadden; **~se** *vr* to distress o.s.

apestar [apes'tar] *vt* to infect ♦ *vi*: **~ (a)** to stink (of)

apetecer [apete'θer] *vt*: *¿te apetece un café?* do you fancy a (cup of) coffee?; **apetecible** *adj* desirable; (*comida*) appetizing

apetito [ape'tito] *nm* appetite; **~so, a** *adj* appetizing; (*fig*) tempting

apiadarse [apja'ðarse] *vr*: **~ de** to take pity on

ápice ['apiθe] *nm* apex; (*fig*) whit, iota

apilar [api'lar] *vt* to pile o heap up; **~se** *vr* to pile up

apiñarse [api'narse] *vr* to crowd o press together

apio ['apjo] *nm* celery

apisonadora [apisona'ðora] *nf* (*máquina*) steamroller

aplacar [apla'kar] *vt* to placate; **~se** *vr* to calm down

aplanar [apla'nar] *vt* to smooth, level; (*allanar*) to roll flat, flatten

aplastante [aplas'tante] *adj* overwhelming; (*lógica*) compelling

aplastar [aplas'tar] *vt* to squash (flat); (*fig*) to crush

aplatanarse [aplata'narse] *vr* to get lethargic

aplaudir [aplau'ðir] *vt* to applaud

aplauso [a'plauso] *nm* applause; (*fig*) approval, acclaim

aplazamiento [aplaθa'mjento] *nm* postponement

aplazar [apla'θar] *vt* to postpone, defer

aplicación [aplika'θjon] *nf* application; (*esfuerzo*) effort

aplicado, a [apli'kaðo, a] *adj* diligent, hard-working

aplicar [apli'kar] *vt* (*ejecutar*) to apply; **~se** *vr* to apply o.s.

aplique *etc* [a'plike] *vb ver* **aplicar** ♦ *nm* wall light

aplomo [a'plomo] *nm* aplomb, self-assurance

apocado, a [apo'kaðo, a] *adj* timid

apocarse [apo'karse] *vr* to feel small o humiliated

apodar [apo'ðar] *vt* to nickname

apoderado [apoðe'raðo] *nm* agent, representative

apoderar [apoðe'rar] *vt* to authorize, empower; (*JUR*) to grant (a) power of attorney to; **~se** *vr*: **~se de** to take possession of

apodo [a'poðo] *nm* nickname

apogeo [apo'xeo] *nm* peak, summit

apolillarse [apoli'ʎarse] *vr* to get moth-eaten

apología [apolo'xia] *nf* eulogy; (*defensa*) defence

apoltronarse [apoltro'narse] *vr* to get lazy

apoplejía [apople'xia] *nf* apoplexy, stroke

apoquinar [apoki'nar] (*fam*) *vt* to fork out, cough up

aporrear [aporre'ar] *vt* to beat (up)

aportar [apor'tar] *vt* to contribute ♦ *vi* to reach port; **~se** *vr* (*AM: llegar*) to arrive, come

aposento [apo'sento] *nm* lodging; (*habitación*) room

aposta [a'posta] *adv* deliberately, on purpose

apostar [apos'tar] *vt* to bet, stake; (*tropas etc*) to station, post ♦ *vi* to bet

apóstol [a'postol] *nm* apostle

apóstrofo [a'postrofo] *nm* apostrophe

apoyar [apo'jar] *vt* to lean, rest; (*fig*) to support, back; **~se** *vr*: **~se en** to lean on; **apoyo** *nm* (*gen*) support; backing, help

apreciable [apre'θjaβle] *adj* considerable; (*fig*) esteemed

apreciar [apre'θjar] *vt* to evaluate, assess; (*COM*) to appreciate, value; (*persona*) to respect; (*tamaño*) to gauge, assess; (*detalles*) to notice

aprecio [a'preθjo] *nm* valuation, estimate; (*fig*) appreciation

aprehender [apreen'der] *vt* to apprehend, detain; **aprehensión** *nf* detention, capture

apremiante [apre'mjante] *adj* urgent, pressing

apremiar [apre'mjar] *vt* to compel, force ♦ *vi* to be urgent, press; **apremio** *nm* urgency

aprender [apren'der] *vt*, *vi* to learn

aprendiz, a [apren'diθ, a] *nm/f* apprentice; (*principiante*) learner; ~ **de conductor** learner driver; ~**aje** *nm* apprenticeship

aprensión [apren'sjon] *nm* apprehension, fear; **aprensivo, a** *adj* apprehensive

apresar [apre'sar] *vt* to seize; (*capturar*) to capture

aprestar [apres'tar] *vt* to prepare, get ready; (*TEC*) to prime, size; ~**se** *vr* to get ready

apresurado, a [apresu'raðo, a] *adj* hurried, hasty; **apresuramiento** *nm* hurry, haste

apresurar [apresu'rar] *vt* to hurry, accelerate; ~**se** *vr* to hurry, make haste

apretado, a [apre'taðo, a] *adj* tight; (*escritura*) cramped

apretar [apre'tar] *vt* to squeeze; (*TEC*) to tighten; (*presionar*) to press together, pack ♦ *vi* to be too tight

apretón [apre'ton] *nm* squeeze; ~ **de manos** handshake

aprieto [a'prjeto] *nm* squeeze; (*dificultad*) difficulty; **estar en un** ~ to be in a fix

aprisa [a'prisa] *adv* quickly, hurriedly

aprisionar [aprisjo'nar] *vt* to imprison

aprobación [aproβa'θjon] *nf* approval

aprobar [apro'βar] *vt* to approve (of); (*examen, materia*) to pass ♦ *vi* to pass

apropiación [apropja'θjon] *nf* appropriation

apropiado, a [apro'pjaðo, a] *adj* appropriate

apropiarse [apro'pjarse] *vr*: ~ **de** to appropriate

aprovechado, a [aproβe'tʃaðo, a] *adj* industrious, hard-working; (*económico*) thrifty; (*pey*) unscrupulous; **aprovechamiento** *nm* use; exploitation

aprovechar [aproβe'tʃar] *vt* to use; (*explotar*) to exploit; (*experiencia*) to profit from; (*oferta, oportunidad*) to take advantage of ♦ *vi* to progress, improve; ~**se** *vr*: ~**se de** to make use of; to take advantage of; ¡**que aproveche**! enjoy your meal!

aproximación [aproksima'θjon] *nf* approximation; (*de lotería*) consolation prize; **aproximado, a** *adj* approximate

aproximar [aproksi'mar] *vt* to bring nearer; ~**se** *vr* to come near, approach

apruebo *etc vb ver* **aprobar**

aptitud [apti'tuð] *nf* aptitude

apto, a ['apto, a] *adj* suitable

apuesta [a'pwesta] *nf* bet, wager

apuesto, a [a'pwesto, a] *adj* neat, elegant

apuntador [apunta'ðor] *nm* prompter

apuntalar [apunta'lar] *vt* to prop up

apuntar [apun'tar] *vt* (*con arma*) to aim at; (*con dedo*) to point at *o* to; (*anotar*) to note (down); (*TEATRO*) to prompt; ~**se** *vr* (*DEPORTE: tanto, victoria*) to score; (*ESCOL*) to enrol

apunte [a'punte] *nm* note

apuñalar [apuɲa'lar] *vt* to stab

apurado, a [apu'raðo, a] *adj* needy; (*difícil*) difficult; (*peligroso*) dangerous; (*AM*) hurried, rushed

apurar [apu'rar] *vt* (*agotar*) to drain; (*recursos*) to use up; (*molestar*) to annoy; ~**se** *vr* (*preocuparse*) to worry; (*darse prisa*) to hurry

apuro [a'puro] *nm* (*aprieto*) fix, jam; (*escasez*) want, hardship; (*vergüenza*) embarrassment; (*AM*) haste, urgency

aquejado, a [ake'xaðo, a] *adj*: ~ **de** (*MED*) afflicted by

aquél, aquélla [a'kel, a'keʎa] (*pl* **aquéllos, as**) *pron* that (one); (*pl*) those (ones)

aquel, aquella [a'kel, a'keʎa] (*pl* **aquellos, as**) *adj* that; (*pl*) those

aquello [a'keʎo] *pron* that, that business

aquí [a'ki] *adv* (*lugar*) here; (*tiempo*) now;

~ **arriba** up here; ~ **mismo** right here; ~ **yace** here lies; **de** ~ **a siete días** a week from now

aquietar [akje'tar] *vt* to quieten (down), calm (down)

ara ['ara] *nf*: **en ~s de** for the sake of

árabe ['araβe] *adj, nm/f* Arab ♦ *nm* (*LING*) Arabic

Arabia [a'raβja] *nf*: ~ **Saudí** *o* **Saudita** Saudi Arabia

arado [a'raðo] *nm* plough

Aragón [ara'ɣon] *nm* Aragon; **aragonés, esa** *adj, nm/f* Aragonese

arancel [aran'θel] *nm* tariff, duty; ~ **de aduanas** customs (duty)

arandela [aran'dela] *nf* (*TEC*) washer

araña [a'raɲa] *nf* (*ZOOL*) spider; (*lámpara*) chandelier

arañar [ara'ɲar] *vt* to scratch

arañazo [ara'ɲaθo] *nm* scratch

arar [a'rar] *vt* to plough, till

arbitraje [arβi'traxe] *nm* arbitration

arbitrar [arβi'trar] *vt* to arbitrate in; (*DEPORTE*) to referee ♦ *vi* to arbitrate

arbitrariedad [arβitrarje'ðað] *nf* arbitrariness; (*acto*) arbitrary act; **arbitrario, a** *adj* arbitrary

arbitrio [ar'βitrjo] *nm* free will; (*JUR*) adjudication, decision

árbitro ['arβitro] *nm* arbitrator; (*DEPORTE*) referee; (*TENIS*) umpire

árbol ['arβol] *nm* (*BOT*) tree; (*NAUT*) mast; (*TEC*) axle, shaft; **arbolado, a** *adj* wooded; (*camino etc*) tree-lined ♦ *nm* woodland

arboleda [arβo'leða] *nf* grove, plantation

arbusto [ar'βusto] *nm* bush, shrub

arca ['arka] *nf* chest, box

arcada [ar'kaða] *nf* arcade; (*de puente*) arch, span; ~s *nfpl* (*náuseas*) retching *sg*

arcaico, a [ar'kaiko, a] *adj* archaic

arce ['arθe] *nm* maple tree

arcén [ar'θen] *nm* (*de autopista*) hard shoulder; (*de carretera*) verge

archipiélago [artʃi'pjelaɣo] *nm* archipelago

archivador [artʃiβa'ðor] *nm* filing cabinet

archivar [artʃi'βar] *vt* to file (away); **archivo** *nm* file, archive(s) (*pl*)

arcilla [ar'θiʎa] *nf* clay

arco ['arko] *nm* arch; (*MAT*) arc; (*MIL, MUS*) bow; ~ **iris** rainbow

arder [ar'ðer] *vi* to burn; **estar que arde** (*persona*) to fume

ardid [ar'ðið] *nm* ploy, trick

ardiente [ar'ðjente] *adj* burning, ardent

ardilla [ar'ðiʎa] *nf* squirrel

ardor [ar'ðor] *nm* (*calor*) heat; (*fig*) ardour; ~ **de estómago** heartburn

arduo, a ['arðwo, a] *adj* arduous

área ['area] *nf* area; (*DEPORTE*) penalty area

arena [a'rena] *nf* sand; (*de una lucha*) arena; ~ **movedizas** quicksand *sg*

arenal [are'nal] *nm* (*arena movediza*) quicksand

arengar [aren'gar] *vt* to harangue

arenisca [are'niska] *nf* sandstone; (*cascajo*) grit

arenoso, a [are'noso, a] *adj* sandy

arenque [a'renke] *nm* herring

arete [a'rete] *nm* earring

argamasa [arɣa'masa] *nf* mortar, plaster

Argel [ar'xel] *n* Algiers; **Argelia** *nf* Algeria; **argelino, a** *adj, nm/f* Algerian

Argentina [arxen'tina] *nf*: **(la) ~** Argentina

argentino, a [arxen'tino, a] *adj* Argentinian; (*de plata*) silvery ♦ *nm/f* Argentinian

argolla [ar'ɣoʎa] *nf* (large) ring

argot [ar'ɣo] (*pl* ~s) *nm* slang

argucia [ar'ɣuθja] *nf* subtlety, sophistry

argüir [ar'ɣwir] *vt* to deduce; (*discutir*) to argue; (*indicar*) to indicate, imply; (*censurar*) to reproach ♦ *vi* to argue

argumentación [arɣumenta'θjon] *nf* (line of) argument

argumentar [arɣumen'tar] *vt, vi* to argue

argumento [arɣu'mento] *nm* argument; (*razonamiento*) reasoning; (*de novela etc*) plot; (*CINE, TV*) storyline

aria ['arja] *nf* aria

aridez [ari'ðeθ] *nf* aridity, dryness

árido, a ['ariðo, a] *adj* arid, dry; ~s *nmpl* (*COM*) dry goods

Aries ['arjes] *nm* Aries

ario, a ['arjo, a] *adj* Aryan

arisco, a [aˈrisko, a] *adj* surly; (*insociable*) unsociable

aristócrata [arisˈtokrata] *nm/f* aristocrat

aritmética [aritˈmetika] *nf* arithmetic

arma [ˈarma] *nf* arm; **~s** *nfpl* arms; ~ **blanca** blade, knife; (*espada*) sword; ~ **de fuego** firearm; **~s cortas** small arms

armada [arˈmaða] *nf* armada; (*flota*) fleet

armadillo [armaˈðiʎo] *nm* armadillo

armado, a [arˈmaðo, a] *adj* armed; (*TEC*) reinforced

armador [armaˈðor] *nm* (*NAUT*) shipowner

armadura [armaˈðura] *nf* (*MIL*) armour; (*TEC*) framework; (*ZOOL*) skeleton; (*FÍSICA*) armature

armamento [armaˈmento] *nm* armament; (*NAUT*) fitting-out

armar [arˈmar] *vt* (*soldado*) to arm; (*máquina*) to assemble; (*navío*) to fit out; **~la**, ~ **un lío** to start a row, kick up a fuss

armario [arˈmarjo] *nm* wardrobe; (*de cocina, baño*) cupboard

armatoste [armaˈtoste] *nm* (*mueble*) monstrosity; (*máquina*) contraption

armazón [armaˈθon] *nf o m* body, chassis; (*de mueble etc*) frame; (*ARQ*) skeleton

armería [armeˈria] *nf* (*museo*) military museum; (*tienda*) gunsmith's

armiño [arˈmiɲo] *nm* stoat; (*piel*) ermine

armisticio [armisˈtiθjo] *nm* armistice

armonía [armoˈnia] *nf* harmony

armónica [arˈmonika] *nf* harmonica

armonioso, a [armoˈnjoso, a] *adj* harmonious

armonizar [armoniˈθar] *vt* to harmonize; (*diferencias*) to reconcile ♦ *vi*: ~ **con** (*fig*) to be in keeping with; (*colores*) to tone in with, blend

arnés [arˈnes] *nm* armour; **arneses** *nmpl* (*de caballo etc*) harness *sg*

aro [ˈaro] *nm* ring; (*tejo*) quoit; (*AM: pendiente*) earring

aroma [aˈroma] *nm* aroma, scent

aromático, a [aroˈmatiko, a] *adj* aromatic

arpa [ˈarpa] *nf* harp

arpía [arˈpia] *nf* shrew

arpillera [arpiˈʎera] *nf* sacking, sackcloth

arpón [arˈpon] *nm* harpoon

arquear [arkeˈar] *vt* to arch, bend; **~se** *vr* to arch, bend

arqueología [arkeoloˈxia] *nf* archaeology; **arqueólogo, a** *nm/f* archaeologist

arquero [arˈkero] *nm* archer, bowman

arquetipo [arkeˈtipo] *nm* archetype

arquitecto [arkiˈtekto] *nm* architect; **arquitectura** *nf* architecture

arrabal [arraˈβal] *nm* suburb; (*AM*) slum; **~es** *nmpl* (*afueras*) outskirts

arraigado, a [arraiˈɣaðo, a] *adj* deep-rooted; (*fig*) established

arraigar [arraiˈɣar] *vt* to establish ♦ *vi* to take root; **~se** *vr* to take root; (*persona*) to settle

arrancar [arranˈkar] *vt* (*sacar*) to extract, pull out; (*arrebatar*) to snatch (away); (*INFORM*) to boot; (*fig*) to extract ♦ *vi* (*AUTO, máquina*) to start; (*ponerse en marcha*) to get going; ~ **de** to stem from

arranque *etc* [aˈrranke] *vb ver* **arrancar** ♦ *nm* sudden start; (*AUTO*) start; (*fig*) fit, outburst

arrasar [arraˈsar] *vt* (*aplanar*) to level, flatten; (*destruir*) to demolish

arrastrado, a [arrasˈtraðo, a] *adj* poor, wretched; (*AM*) servile

arrastrar [arrasˈtrar] *vt* to drag (along); (*fig*) to drag down, degrade; (*suj: agua, viento*) to carry away ♦ *vi* to drag, trail on the ground; **~se** *vr* to crawl; (*fig*) to grovel; **llevar algo arrastrado** to drag sth along

arrastre [aˈrrastre] *nm* drag, dragging

arre [ˈarre] *excl* gee up!

arrear [arreˈar] *vt* to drive on, urge on ♦ *vi* to hurry along

arrebatado, a [arreβaˈtaðo, a] *adj* rash, impetuous; (*repentino*) sudden, hasty

arrebatar [arreβaˈtar] *vt* to snatch (away), seize; (*fig*) to captivate; **~se** *vr* to get carried away, get excited

arrebato [arreˈβato] *nm* fit of rage, fury; (*éxtasis*) rapture

arrecife [arreˈθife] *nm* (*tb:* ~ **de coral**) reef

arredrarse [arreˈðrarse] *vr*: ~ (**ante algo**) to be intimidated (by sth)

arreglado, a [arreˈɣlaðo, a] *adj* (*ordenado*) neat, orderly; (*moderado*) moderate, reasonable

arreglar [arre'ɣlar] *vt* (*poner orden*) to tidy up; (*algo roto*) to fix, repair; (*problema*) to solve; **~se** *vr* to reach an understanding; **arreglárselas** (*fam*) to get by, manage

arreglo [a'rreɣlo] *nm* settlement; (*orden*) order; (*acuerdo*) agreement; (*MUS*) arrangement, setting

arrellanarse [arreʎa'narse] *vr*: **~ en** to sit back in/on

arremangar [arreman'ɡar] *vt* to roll up, turn up; **~se** *vr* to roll up one's sleeves

arremeter [arreme'ter] *vi*: **~ contra** to attack, rush at

arrendamiento [arrenda'mjento] *nm* letting; (*alquilar*) hiring; (*contrato*) lease; (*alquiler*) rent; **arrendar** *vt* to let, lease; to rent; **arrendatario, a** *nm/f* tenant

arreo [a'rreo] *nm* adornment; **~s** *nmpl* (*de caballo*) harness *sg*, trappings

arrepentimiento [arrepenti'mjento] *nm* regret, repentance

arrepentirse [arrepen'tirse] *vr* to repent; **~ de** to regret

arrestar [arres'tar] *vt* to arrest; (*encarcelar*) to imprison; **arresto** *nm* arrest; (*MIL*) detention; (*audacia*) boldness, daring; **arresto domiciliario** house arrest

arriar [a'rrjar] *vt* (*velas*) to haul down; (*bandera*) to lower, strike; (*cable*) to pay out

---

PALABRA CLAVE

---

arriba [a'rriβa] *adv* **1** (*posición*) above; **desde ~** from above; **~ de todo** at the very top, right on top; **Juan está ~** Juan is upstairs; **lo ~ mencionado** the aforementioned

2 (*dirección*): **calle ~** up the street

3: **de ~ abajo** from top to bottom; **mirar a uno de ~ abajo** to look sb up and down

4: **para ~**: **de 5000 pesetas para ~** from 5000 pesetas up(wards)

♦ *adj*: **de ~**: **el piso de ~** the upstairs flat (*BRIT*) *o* apartment; **la parte de ~** the top *o* upper part

♦ *prep*: **~ de** (*AM*) above; **~ de 200 dólares** more than 200 dollars

♦ *excl*: **¡~!** up!; **¡manos ~!** hands up!; **¡~ España!** long live Spain!

---

arribar [arri'βar] *vi* to put into port; (*llegar*) to arrive

arribista [arri'βista] *nm/f* parvenu(e), upstart

arriendo *etc* [a'rrjendo] *vb ver* **arrendar**

♦ *nm* = **arrendamiento**

arriero [a'rrjero] *nm* muleteer

arriesgado, a [arrjes'ɣaðo, a] *adj* (*peligroso*) risky; (*audaz*) bold, daring

arriesgar [arrjes'ɣar] *vt* to risk; (*poner en peligro*) to endanger; **~se** *vr* to take a risk

arrimar [arri'mar] *vt* (*acercar*) to bring close; (*poner de lado*) to set aside; **~se** *vr* to come close *o* closer; **~se a** to lean on

arrinconar [arrinko'nar] *vt* (*colocar*) to put in a corner; (*enemigo*) to corner; (*fig*) to put on one side; (*abandonar*) to push aside

arrodillarse [arroði'ʎarse] *vr* to kneel (down)

arrogancia [arro'ɣanθja] *nf* arrogance; **arrogante** *adj* arrogant

arrojar [arro'xar] *vt* to throw, hurl; (*humo*) to emit, give out; (*COM*) to yield, produce; **~se** *vr* to throw *o* hurl o.s

arrojo [a'rroxo] *nm* daring

arrollador, a [arroʎa'ðor, a] *adj* overwhelming

arrollar [arro'ʎar] *vt* (*AUTO etc*) to run over, knock down; (*DEPORTE*) to crush

arropar [arro'par] *vt* to cover, wrap up; **~se** *vr* to wrap o.s. up

arrostrar [arros'trar] *vt* to face (up to); **~se** *vr*: **~se con uno** to face up to sb

arroyo [a'rrojo] *nm* stream; (*de la calle*) gutter

arroz [a'rroθ] *nm* rice; **~ con leche** rice pudding

arruga [a'rruɣa] *nf* fold; (*de cara*) wrinkle; (*de vestido*) crease

arrugar [arru'ɣar] *vt* to fold; to wrinkle; to crease; **~se** *vr* to get creased

arruinar [arrwi'nar] *vt* to ruin, wreck; **~se**

vr to be ruined, go bankrupt
arrullar [arru'ʎar] *vi* to coo ♦ *vt* to lull to sleep
arsenal [arse'nal] *nm* naval dockyard; (*MIL*) arsenal
arsénico [ar'seniko] *nm* arsenic
arte ['arte] (*gen m en sg y siempre f en pl*) *nm* art; (*maña*) skill, guile; **~s** *nfpl* (*bellas ~s*) arts
artefacto [arte'fakto] *nm* appliance; (*ARQUEOLOGÍA*) artefact
arteria [ar'terja] *nf* artery
artesanía [artesa'nia] *nf* craftsmanship; (*artículos*) handicrafts *pl*; **artesano, a** *nm/f* artisan, craftsman/woman
ártico, a ['artiko, a] *adj* Arctic ♦ *nm*: **el Á~** the Arctic
articulación [artikula'θjon] *nf* articulation; (*MED, TEC*) joint; **articulado, a** *adj* articulated; jointed
articular [artiku'lar] *vt* to articulate; to join together
artículo [ar'tikulo] *nm* article; (*cosa*) thing, article; **~s** *nmpl* (*COM*) goods
artífice [ar'tifiθe] *nm/f* artist, craftsman/woman; (*fig*) architect
artificial [artifi'θjal] *adj* artificial
artificio [arti'fiθjo] *nm* art, skill; (*artesanía*) craftsmanship; (*astucia*) cunning
artillería [artiʎe'ria] *nf* artillery
artillero [arti'ʎero] *nm* artilleryman, gunner
artilugio [arti'luxjo] *nm* gadget
artimaña [arti'maɲa] *nf* trap, snare; (*astucia*) cunning
artista [ar'tista] *nm/f* (*pintor*) artist, painter; (*TEATRO*) artist, artiste; **~ de cine** film actor/actress; **artístico, a** *adj* artistic
artritis [ar'tritis] *nf* arthritis
arveja [ar'βexa] (*AM*) *nf* pea
arzobispo [arθo'βispo] *nm* archbishop
as [as] *nm* ace
asa ['asa] *nf* handle; (*fig*) lever
asado [a'saðo] *nm* roast (meat); (*AM*: *barbacoa*) barbecue
asador [asa'ðor] *nm* spit
asadura [asa'ðura] *nf* entrails *pl*, offal

asalariado, a [asala'rjaðo, a] *adj* paid, salaried ♦ *nm/f* wage earner
asaltador, a [asalta'ðor, a] *nm/f* assailant
asaltante [asal'tante] *nm/f* = **asaltador, a**
asaltar [asal'tar] *vt* to attack, assault; (*fig*) to assail; **asalto** *nm* attack, assault; (*DEPORTE*) round
asamblea [asam'blea] *nf* assembly; (*reunión*) meeting
asar [a'sar] *vt* to roast
asbesto [as'βesto] *nm* asbestos
ascendencia [asθen'denθja] *nf* ancestry; (*AM*) ascendancy; **de ~ francesa** of French origin
ascender [asθen'der] *vi* (*subir*) to ascend, rise; (*ser promovido*) to gain promotion ♦ *vt* to promote; **~ a** to amount to; **ascendiente** *nm* influence ♦ *nm/f* ancestor
ascensión [asθen'sjon] *nf* ascent; (*REL*): **la A~** the Ascension
ascenso [as'θenso] *nm* ascent; (*promoción*) promotion
ascensor [asθen'sor] *nm* lift (*BRIT*), elevator (*US*)
ascético, a [as'θetiko, a] *adj* ascetic
asco ['asko] *nm*: **¡qué ~!** how revolting *o* disgusting; **el ajo me da ~** I hate *o* loathe garlic; **estar hecho un ~** to be filthy
ascua ['askwa] *nf* ember; **estar en ~s** to be on tenterhooks
aseado, a [ase'aðo, a] *adj* clean; (*arreglado*) tidy; (*pulcro*) smart
asear [ase'ar] *vt* to clean, wash; to tidy (up)
asediar [ase'ðjar] *vt* (*MIL*) to besiege, lay siege to; (*fig*) to chase, pester; **asedio** *nm* siege; (*COM*) run
asegurado, a [aseɣu'raðo, a] *adj* insured; **asegurador, a** *nm/f* insurer
asegurar [aseɣu'rar] *vt* (*consolidar*) to secure, fasten; (*dar garantía de*) to guarantee; (*preservar*) to safeguard; (*afirmar, dar por cierto*) to assure, affirm; (*tranquilizar*) to reassure; (*tomar un seguro*) to insure; **~se** *vr* to assure o.s., make sure

asemejarse [aseme'xarse] *vr* to be alike; ~ **a** to be like, resemble

asentado, a [asen'taðo, a] *adj* established, settled

asentar [asen'tar] *vt* (*sentar*) to seat, sit down; (*poner*) to place, establish; (*alisar*) to level, smooth down *o* out; (*anotar*) to note down ♦ *vi* to be suitable, suit

asentir [asen'tir] *vi* to assent, agree; ~ **con la cabeza** to nod (one's head)

aseo [a'seo] *nm* cleanliness; ~**s** *nmpl* (*servicios*) toilet *sg* (*BRIT*), cloakroom *sg* (*BRIT*), restroom *sg* (*US*)

aséptico, a [a'septiko, a] *adj* germ-free, free from infection

asequible [ase'kiβle] *adj* (*precio*) reasonable; (*meta*) attainable; (*persona*) approachable

aserradero [aserra'ðero] *nm* sawmill; **aserrar** *vt* to saw

asesinar [asesi'nar] *vt* to murder; (*POL*) to assassinate; **asesinato** *nm* murder; assassination

asesino, a [ase'sino, a] *nm/f* murderer, killer; (*POL*) assassin

asesor, a [ase'sor, a] *nm/f* adviser, consultant

asesorar [aseso'rar] *vt* (*JUR*) to advise, give legal advice to; (*COM*) to act as consultant to; ~**se** *vr*: ~**se con** *o* **de** to take advice from, consult; **asesoría** *nf* (*cargo*) consultancy; (*oficina*) consultant's office

asestar [ases'tar] *vt* (*golpe*) to deal, strike; (*arma*) to aim; (*tiro*) to fire

asfalto [as'falto] *nm* asphalt

asfixia [as'fiksja] *nf* asphyxia, suffocation

asfixiar [asfik'sjar] *vt* to asphyxiate, suffocate; ~**se** *vr* to be asphyxiated, suffocate

asgo *etc vb ver* **asir**

así [a'si] *adv* (*de esta manera*) in this way, like this, thus; (*aunque*) although; (*tan pronto como*) as soon as; ~ **que** so; ~ **como** as well as; ~ **y todo** even so; ¿**no es** ~? isn't it?, didn't you? *etc*; ~ **de grande** this big

Asia ['asja] *nf* Asia; **asiático, a** *adj*, *nm/f* Asian, Asiatic

asidero [asi'ðero] *nm* handle

asiduidad [asiðwi'ðað] *nf* assiduousness; **asiduo, a** *adj* assiduous; (*frecuente*) frequent ♦ *nm/f* regular (customer)

asiento [a'sjento] *nm* (*mueble*) seat, chair; (*de coche, en tribunal etc*) seat; (*localidad*) seat, place; (*fundamento*) site; ~ **delantero/trasero** front/back seat

asignación [asixna'θjon] *nf* (*atribución*) assignment; (*reparto*) allocation; (*sueldo*) salary; ~ (**semanal**) pocket money

asignar [asix'nar] *vt* to assign, allocate

asignatura [asixna'tura] *nf* subject; course

asilado, a [asi'laðo, a] *nm/f* inmate; (*POL*) refugee

asilo [a'silo] *nm* (*refugio*) asylum, refuge; (*establecimiento*) home, institution; ~ **político** political asylum

asimilación [asimila'θjon] *nf* assimilation

asimilar [asimi'lar] *vt* to assimilate

asimismo [asi'mismo] *adv* in the same way, likewise

asir [a'sir] *vt* to seize, grasp

asistencia [asis'tenθja] *nf* audience; (*MED*) attendance; (*ayuda*) assistance; **asistente** *nm/f* assistant; **los asistentes** those present; **asistente social** social worker

asistido, a [asis'tiðo, a] *adj*: ~ **por ordenador** computer-assisted

asistir [asis'tir] *vt* to assist, help ♦ *vi*: ~ **a** to attend, be present at

asma ['asma] *nf* asthma

asno ['asno] *nm* donkey; (*fig*) ass

asociación [asoθja'θjon] *nf* association; (*COM*) partnership; **asociado, a** *adj* associate ♦ *nm/f* associate; (*COM*) partner

asociar [aso'θjar] *vt* to associate

asolar [aso'lar] *vt* to destroy

asolearse [asole'arse] *vr* to sunbathe

asomar [aso'mar] *vt* to show, stick out ♦ *vi* to appear; ~**se** *vr* to appear, show up; ~ **la cabeza por la ventana** to put one's head out of the window

asombrar [asom'brar] *vt* to amaze, astonish; ~**se** *vr* (*sorprenderse*) to be amazed; (*asustarse*) to get a fright; **asombro** *nm* amazement, astonishment; (*susto*) fright; **asombroso, a** *adj* astonishing, amazing

asomo [a'somo] *nm* hint, sign

aspa ['aspa] *nf* (*cruz*) cross; (*de molino*) sail; **en ~** X-shaped

aspaviento [aspa'ßjento] *nm* exaggerated display of feeling; (*fam*) fuss

aspecto [as'pekto] *nm* (*apariencia*) look, appearance; (*fig*) aspect

aspereza [aspe'reθa] *nf* roughness; (*agrura*) sourness; (*de carácter*) surliness; **áspero, a** *adj* rough; bitter, sour; harsh

aspersión [asper'sjon] *nf* sprinkling

aspiración [aspira'θjon] *nf* breath, inhalation; (*MUS*) short pause; **aspiraciones** *nfpl* (*ambiciones*) aspirations

aspirador [aspira'ðor] *nm* = **aspiradora**

aspiradora [aspira'ðora] *nf* vacuum cleaner, Hoover ®

aspirante [aspi'rante] *nm/f* (*candidato*) candidate; (*DEPORTE*) contender

aspirar [aspi'rar] *vt* to breathe in ♦ *vi*: **~ a** to aspire to

aspirina [aspi'rina] *nf* aspirin

asquear [aske'ar] *vt* to sicken ♦ *vi* to be sickening; **~se** *vr* to feel disgusted; **asqueroso, a** *adj* disgusting, sickening

asta ['asta] *nf* lance; (*arpón*) spear; (*mango*) shaft, handle; (*ZOOL*) horn; **a media ~** at half mast

astado, a [as'taðo, a] *adj* horned ♦ *nm* bull

asterisco [aste'risko] *nm* asterisk

astilla [as'tiʎa] *nf* splinter; (*pedacito*) chip; **~s** *nfpl* (*leña*) firewood *sg*

astillero [asti'ʎero] *nm* shipyard

astringente [astrin'xente] *adj, nm* astringent

astro ['astro] *nm* star

astrología [astrolo'xia] *nf* astrology; **astrólogo, a** *nm/f* astrologer

astronauta [astro'nauta] *nm/f* astronaut

astronave [astro'naße] *nm* spaceship

astronomía [astrono'mia] *nf* astronomy; **astrónomo, a** *nm/f* astronomer

astucia [as'tuθja] *nf* astuteness; (*ardid*) clever trick; **astuto, a** *adj* astute; (*taimado*) cunning

asueto [a'sweto] *nm* holiday; (*tiempo libre*) time off *no pl*

asumir [asu'mir] *vt* to assume

asunción [asun'θjon] *nf* assumption; (*REL*): **A~** Assumption

asunto [a'sunto] *nm* (*tema*) matter, subject; (*negocio*) business

asustar [asus'tar] *vt* to frighten; **~se** *vr* to be (*o* become) frightened

atacar [ata'kar] *vt* to attack

atadura [ata'ðura] *nf* bond, tie

atajar [ata'xar] *vt* (*enfermedad, mal*) to stop ♦ *vi* (*persona*) to take a short cut

atajo [a'taxo] *nm* short cut; (*DEPORTE*) tackle

atañer [ata'ɲer] *vi*: **~ a** to concern

ataque *etc* [a'take] *vb ver* **atacar** ♦ *nm* attack; **~ cardíaco** heart attack

atar [a'tar] *vt* to tie, tie up

atardecer [atarðe'θer] *vi* to get dark ♦ *nm* evening; (*crepúsculo*) dusk

atareado, a [atare'aðo, a] *adj* busy

atascar [atas'kar] *vt* to clog up; (*obstruir*) to jam; (*fig*) to hinder; **~se** *vr* to stall; (*cañería*) to get blocked up; **atasco** *nm* obstruction; (*AUTO*) traffic jam

ataúd [ata'uð] *nm* coffin

ataviar [ata'ßjar] *vt* to deck, array; **~se** *vr* to dress up

atavío [ata'ßio] *nm* attire, dress; **~s** *nmpl* finery *sg*

atemorizar [atemori'θar] *vt* to frighten, scare; **~se** *vr* to get scared

Atenas [a'tenas] *n* Athens

atención [aten'θjon] *nf* attention; (*bondad*) kindness ♦ *excl* (be) careful!, look out!

atender [aten'der] *vt* to attend to, look after ♦ *vi* to pay attention

atenerse [ate'nerse] *vr*: **~ a** to abide by, adhere to

atentado [aten'taðo] *nm* crime, illegal act; (*asalto*) assault; **~ contra la vida de uno** attempt on sb's life

atentamente [atenta'mente] *adv*: **Le saluda ~** Yours faithfully

atentar [aten'tar] *vi*: **~ a** *o* **contra** to commit an outrage against

atento, a [a'tento, a] *adj* attentive, observant; (*cortés*) polite, thoughtful

atenuante [ate'nwante] *adj* extenuating

atenuar [ate'nwar] *vt* (*disminuir*) to lessen, minimize

ateo, a [a'teo, a] *adj* atheistic ♦ *nm/f* atheist

aterciopelado, a [aterθjope'laðo, a] *adj* velvety

aterido, a [ate'riðo, a] *adj*: ~ **de frío** frozen stiff

aterrador, a [aterra'ðor, a] *adj* frightening

aterrar [ate'rrar] *vt* to frighten; to terrify; ~**se** *vr* to be frightened; to be terrified

aterrizaje [aterri'θaxe] *nm* (*AVIAT*) landing

aterrizar [aterri'θar] *vi* to land

aterrorizar [aterrori'θar] *vt* to terrify

atesorar [ateso'rar] *vt* to hoard, store up

atestado, a [ates'taðo, a] *adj* packed ♦ *nm* (*JUR*) affidavit

atestar [ates'tar] *vt* to pack, stuff; (*JUR*) to attest, testify to

atestiguar [atesti'ɣwar] *vt* to testify to, bear witness to

atiborrar [atiβo'rrar] *vt* to fill, stuff; ~**se** *vr* to stuff o.s

ático ['atiko] *nm* attic; ~ **de lujo** penthouse (flat (*BRIT*) o apartment)

atildar [atil'dar] *vt* to criticize; ~**se** *vr* to spruce o.s. up

atinado, a [ati'naðo, a] *adj* (*sensato*) wise; (*correcto*) right, correct

atinar [ati'nar] *vi* (*al disparar*): ~ **al blanco** to hit the target; (*fig*) to be right

atisbar [atis'βar] *vt* to spy on; (*echar una ojeada*) to peep at

atizar [ati'θar] *vt* to poke; (*horno etc*) to stoke; (*fig*) to stir up, rouse

atlántico, a [at'lantiko, a] *adj* Atlantic ♦ *nm*: **el (océano) A~** the Atlantic (Ocean)

atlas ['atlas] *nm* atlas

atleta [at'leta] *nm* athlete; **atlético, a** *adj* athletic; **atletismo** *nm* athletics *sg*

atmósfera [at'mosfera] *nf* atmosphere

atolladero [atoʎa'ðero] *nm* (*fig*) jam, fix

atolondramiento [atolondra'mjento] *nm* bewilderment; (*insensatez*) silliness

atómico, a [a'tomiko, a] *adj* atomic

atomizador [atomiθa'ðor] *nm* atomizer; (*de perfume*) spray

átomo ['atomo] *nm* atom

atónito, a [a'tonito, a] *adj* astonished, amazed

atontado, a [aton'taðo, a] *adj* stunned; (*bobo*) silly, daft

atontar [aton'tar] *vt* to stun; ~**se** *vr* to become confused

atormentar [atormen'tar] *vt* to torture; (*molestar*) to torment; (*acosar*) to plague, harass

atornillar [atorni'ʎar] *vt* to screw on o down

atosigar [atosi'ðar] *vt* (*fig*) to harass, pester

atracador, a [atraka'ðor, a] *nm/f* robber

atracar [atra'kar] *vt* (*NAUT*) to moor; (*robar*) to hold up, rob ♦ *vi* to moor; ~**se** *vr*: ~**se (de)** to stuff o.s. (with)

atracción [atrak'θjon] *nf* attraction

atraco [a'trako] *nm* holdup, robbery

atracón [atra'kon] *nm*: **darse** o **pegarse un ~ (de)** (*fam*) to stuff o.s. (with)

atractivo, a [atrak'tiβo, a] *adj* attractive ♦ *nm* appeal

atraer [atra'er] *vt* to attract

atragantarse [atraɣan'tarse] *vr*: ~ **(con)** to choke (on); **se me ha atragantado el chico** I can't stand the boy

atrancar [atran'kar] *vt* (*puerta*) to bar, bolt

atrapar [atra'par] *vt* to trap; (*resfriado etc*) to catch

atrás [a'tras] *adv* (*movimiento*) back (-wards); (*lugar*) behind; (*tiempo*) previously; **ir hacia** ~ to go back(wards); to go to the rear; **estar** ~ to be behind o at the back

atrasado, a [atra'saðo, a] *adj* slow; (*pago*) overdue, late; (*país*) backward

atrasar [atra'sar] *vi* to be slow; ~**se** *vr* to remain behind; (*tren*) to be o run late; **atraso** *nm* slowness; lateness, delay; (*de país*) backwardness; **atrasos** *nmpl* (*COM*) arrears

atravesar [atraβe'sar] *vt* (*cruzar*) to cross (over); (*traspasar*) to pierce; to go through; (*poner al través*) to lay o put across; ~**se** *vr* to come in between; (*intervenir*) to interfere

atravieso *etc vb ver* **atravesar**

atrayente [atra'jente] *adj* attractive

atreverse [atre'βerse] *vr* to dare; (*insolentarse*) to be insolent; **atrevido, a** *adj* daring; insolent; **atrevimiento** *nm* daring; insolence

atribución [atriβu'θjon] *nf*: **atribuciones** (*POL*) powers; (*ADMIN*) responsibilities

atribuir [atriβu'ir] *vt* to attribute; (*funciones*) to confer

atribular [atriβu'lar] *vt* to afflict, distress

atributo [atri'βuto] *nm* attribute

atril [a'tril] *nm* (*para libro*) lectern; (*MUS*) music stand

atrocidad [atroθi'ðað] *nf* atrocity, outrage

atropellar [atrope'ʎar] *vt* (*derribar*) to knock over *o* down; (*empujar*) to push (aside); (*agraviar*) to run over, run down; (*agraviar*) to insult; **~se** *vr* to act hastily; **atropello** *nm* (*AUTO*) accident; (*empujón*) push; (*agravio*) wrong; (*atrocidad*) outrage

atroz [a'troθ] *adj* atrocious, awful

atto, a *abr* = **atento**

atuendo [a'twendo] *nm* attire

atún [a'tun] *nm* tuna

aturdir [atur'ðir] *vt* to stun; (*de ruido*) to deafen; (*fig*) to dumbfound, bewilder

atusar [atu'sar] *vt* to smooth (down)

audacia [au'ðaθja] *nf* boldness, audacity; **audaz** *adj* bold, audacious

audible [au'ðiβle] *adj* audible

audición [auði'θjon] *nf* hearing; (*TEATRO*) audition

audiencia [au'ðjenθja] *nf* audience; **A~** (*JUR*) High Court

audífono [au'ðifono] *nm* (*para sordos*) hearing aid

auditor [auði'tor] *nm* (*JUR*) judge advocate; (*COM*) auditor

auditorio [auði'torjo] *nm* audience; (*sala*) auditorium

auge ['auxe] *nm* boom; (*clímax*) climax

augurar [auɣu'rar] *vt* to predict; (*presagiar*) to portend

augurio [au'ɣurjo] *nm* omen

aula ['aula] *nf* classroom; (*en universidad etc*) lecture room

aullar [au'ʎar] *vi* to howl, yell

aullido [au'ʎiðo] *nm* howl, yell

aumentar [aumen'tar] *vt* to increase; (*precios*) to put up; (*producción*) to step up; (*con microscopio, anteojos*) to magnify ♦ *vi* to increase, be on the increase; **~se** *vr* to increase, be on the increase; **aumento** *nm* increase; rise

aun [a'un] *adv* even; **~ así** even so; **~ más** even *o* yet more

aún [a'un] *adv*: **~ está aquí** he's still here; **~ no lo sabemos** we don't know yet; **¿no ha venido ~?** hasn't she come yet?

aunque [a'unke] *conj* though, although, even though

aúpa [a'upa] *excl* come on!

aureola [aure'ola] *nf* halo

auricular [auriku'lar] *nm* (*TEL*) earpiece, receiver; **~es** *nmpl* (*para escuchar música etc*) headphones

aurora [au'rora] *nf* dawn

auscultar [auskul'tar] *vt* (*MED*: *pecho*) to listen to, sound

ausencia [au'senθja] *nf* absence

ausentarse [ausen'tarse] *vr* to go away; (*por poco tiempo*) to go out

ausente [au'sente] *adj* absent

auspicios [aus'piθjos] *nmpl* auspices; (*protección*) protection *sg*

austeridad [austeri'ðað] *nf* austerity; **austero, a** *adj* austere

austral [aus'tral] *adj* southern ♦ *nm* monetary unit of Argentina

Australia [aus'tralja] *nf* Australia; **australiano, a** *adj, nm/f* Australian

Austria ['austrja] *nf* Austria; **austríaco, a** *adj, nm/f* Austrian

auténtico, a [au'tentiko, a] *adj* authentic

auto ['auto] *nm* (*JUR*) edict, decree; (: *orden*) writ; (*AUTO*) car; **~s** *nmpl* (*JUR*) proceedings; (: *acta*) court record *sg*

autoadhesivo [autoaðe'siβo] *adj* self-adhesive; (*sobre*) self-sealing

autobiografía [autoβjoɣra'fia] *nf* autobiography

autobús [auto'βus] *nm* bus

autocar [auto'kar] *nm* coach (*BRIT*), (passenger) bus (*US*)

autóctono, a [au'toktono, a] *adj* native,

indigenous

autodefensa [autoðe'fensa] *nf* self-defence

autodeterminación [autoðetermina'θjon] *nf* self-determination

autodidacto, a [autoði'ðakto, a] *adj* self-taught

autoescuela [autoes'kwela] *nf* driving school

autógrafo [au'toɣrafo] *nm* autograph

automación [automa'θjon] *nf* = **automatización**

autómata [au'tomata] *nm* automaton

automático, a [auto'matiko, a] *adj* automatic ♦ *nm* press stud

automatización [automatiθa'θjon] *nf* automation

automotor, triz [automo'tor, 'triθ] *adj* self-propelled ♦ *nm* diesel train

automóvil [auto'moβil] *nm* (motor) car (*BRIT*), automobile (*US*); **automovilismo** *nm* (*actividad*) motoring; (*DEPORTE*) motor racing; **automovilista** *nm/f* motorist, driver; **automovilístico, a** *adj* (*industria*) motor *cpd*

autonomía [autono'mia] *nf* autonomy; **autónomo, a** (*ESP*), **autonómico, a** (*ESP*) *adj* (*POL*) autonomous

autopista [auto'pista] *nf* motorway (*BRIT*), freeway (*US*); ~ **de peaje** toll road (*BRIT*), turnpike road (*US*)

autopsia [au'topsja] *nf* autopsy, postmortem

autor, a [au'tor, a] *nm/f* author

autoridad [autori'ðað] *nf* authority; **autoritario, a** *adj* authoritarian

autorización [autoriθa'θjon] *nf* authorization; **autorizado, a** *adj* authorized; (*aprobado*) approved

autorizar [autori'θar] *vt* to authorize; (*aprobar*) to approve

autorretrato [autorre'trato] *nm* self-portrait

autoservicio [autoser'βiθjo] *nm* (*tienda*) self-service shop (*BRIT*) o store (*US*); (*restaurante*) self-service restaurant

autostop [auto'stop] *nm* hitch-hiking; **hacer** ~ to hitch-hike; **~ista** *nm/f* hitch-hiker

autosuficiencia [autosufi'θjenθja] *nf* self-sufficiency

autovía [auto'βia] *nf* ≈ A-road (*BRIT*), dual carriageway (*BRIT*), ≈ state highway (*US*)

auxiliar [auksi'ljar] *vt* to help ♦ *nm/f* assistant; **auxilio** *nm* assistance, help; **primeros auxilios** first aid *sg*

Av *abr* (= *Avenida*) Av(e).

aval [a'βal] *nm* guarantee; (*persona*) guarantor

avalancha [aβa'lantʃa] *nf* avalanche

avance [a'βanθe] *nm* advance; (*pago*) advance payment; (*CINE*) trailer

avanzar [aβan'θar] *vt, vi* to advance

avaricia [aβa'riθja] *nf* avarice, greed; **avaricioso, a** *adj* avaricious, greedy

avaro, a [a'βaro, a] *adj* miserly, mean ♦ *nm/f* miser

avasallar [aβasa'ʎar] *vt* to subdue, subjugate

Avda *abr* (= *Avenida*) Av(e).

AVE ['aβe] *nm abr* (= *Alta Velocidad Española*) ≈ bullet train

ave ['aβe] *nf* bird; ~ **de rapiña** bird of prey

avecinarse [aβeθi'narse] *vr* (*tormenta, fig*) to be on the way

avellana [aβe'ʎana] *nf* hazelnut; **avellano** *nm* hazel tree

avemaría [aβema'ria] *nm* Hail Mary, Ave Maria

avena [a'βena] *nf* oats *pl*

avenida [aβe'niða] *nf* (*calle*) avenue

avenir [aβe'nir] *vt* to reconcile; **~se** *vr* to come to an agreement, reach a compromise

aventajado, a [aβenta'xaðo, a] *adj* outstanding

aventajar [aβenta'xar] *vt* (*sobrepasar*) to surpass, outstrip

aventar [aβen'tar] *vt* to fan, blow; (*grano*) to winnow

aventura [aβen'tura] *nf* adventure; **aventurado, a** *adj* risky; **aventurero, a** *adj* adventurous

avergonzar [aβerɣon'θar] *vt* to shame; (*desconcertar*) to embarrass; **~se** *vr* to be ashamed; to be embarrassed

avería [aβe'ria] *nf* (*TEC*) breakdown, fault

averiado, a [aβe'rjaðo, a] *adj* broken

down; "**~**" "out of order"

averiguación [aβeɾiɣwa'θjon] *nf* investigation; (*descubrimiento*) ascertainment

averiguar [aβeɾi'ɣwar] *vt* to investigate; (*descubrir*) to find out, ascertain

aversión [aβer'sjon] *nf* aversion, dislike

avestruz [aβes'truθ] *nm* ostrich

aviación [aβja'θjon] *nf* aviation; (*fuerzas aéreas*) air force

aviador, a [aβja'ðor, a] *nm/f* aviator, airman/woman

avicultura [aβikul'tura] *nf* poultry farming

avidez [aβi'ðeθ] *nf* avidity, eagerness; **ávido, a** *adj* avid, eager

avinagrado, a [aβina'ɣraðo, a] *adj* sour, acid

avío [a'βio] *nm* preparation; **~s** *nmpl* (*equipamiento*) gear *sg*, kit *sg*

avión [a'βjon] *nm* aeroplane; (*ave*) martin; **~ de reacción** jet (plane)

avioneta [aβjo'neta] *nf* light aircraft

avisar [aβi'sar] *vt* (*advertir*) to warn, notify; (*informar*) to tell; (*aconsejar*) to advise, counsel; **aviso** *nm* warning; (*noticia*) notice

avispa [a'βispa] *nf* wasp

avispado, a [aβis'paðo, a] *adj* sharp, clever

avispero [aβis'pero] *nm* wasp's nest

avispón [aβis'pon] *nm* hornet

avistar [aβis'tar] *vt* to sight, spot

avituallar [aβitwa'ʎar] *vt* to supply with food

avivar [aβi'βar] *vt* to strengthen, intensify; **~se** *vr* to revive, acquire new life

axila [ak'sila] *nf* armpit

axioma [ak'sjoma] *nm* axiom

ay [ai] *excl* (*dolor*) ow!, ouch!; (*aflicción*) oh!, oh dear!; **¡~ de mi!** poor me!

aya ['aja] *nf* governess; (*niñera*) nanny

ayer [a'jer] *adv, nm* yesterday; **antes de ~** the day before yesterday

ayote [a'jote] (*AM*) *nm* pumpkin

ayuda [a'juða] *nf* help, assistance ♦ *nm* page; **ayudante, a** *nm/f* assistant, helper; (*ESCOL*) assistant; (*MIL*) adjutant

ayudar [aju'ðar] *vt* to help, assist

ayunar [aju'nar] *vi* to fast; **ayunas** *nfpl*: **estar en ayunas** (*no haber comido*) to be fasting; (*ignorar*) to be in the dark; **ayuno** *nm* fast; fasting

ayuntamiento [ajunta'mjento] *nm* (*consejo*) town (*o* city) council; (*edificio*) town (*o* city) hall

azabache [aθa'βatʃe] *nm* jet

azada [a'θaða] *nf* hoe

azafata [aθa'fata] *nf* air stewardess

azafrán [aθa'fran] *nm* saffron

azahar [aθa'ar] *nm* orange/lemon blossom

azar [a'θar] *nm* (*casualidad*) chance, fate; (*desgracia*) misfortune, accident; **por ~** by chance; **al ~** at random

azoramiento [aθora'mjento] *nm* alarm; (*confusión*) confusion

azorar [aθo'rar] *vt* to alarm; **~se** *vr* to get alarmed

Azores [a'θores] *nfpl*: **las ~** the Azores

azotar [aθo'tar] *vt* to whip, beat; (*pegar*) to spank; **azote** *nm* (*látigo*) whip; (*latigazo*) lash, stroke; (*en las nalgas*) spank; (*calamidad*) calamity

azotea [aθo'tea] *nf* (flat) roof

azteca [aθ'teka] *adj, nm/f* Aztec

azúcar [a'θukar] *nm* sugar; **azucarado, a** *adj* sugary, sweet

azucarero, a [aθuka'rero, a] *adj* sugar *cpd* ♦ *nm* sugar bowl

azucena [aθu'θena] *nf* white lily

azufre [a'θufre] *nm* sulphur

azul [a'θul] *adj, nm* blue; **~ marino** navy blue

azulejo [aθu'lexo] *nm* tile

azuzar [aθu'θar] *vt* to incite, egg on

B b

B.A. *abr* (= *Buenos Aires*) B.A.

baba ['baβa] *nf* spittle, saliva; **babear** *vi* to drool, slaver

babero [ba'βero] *nm* bib

babor [ba'βor] *nm* port (side)

baboso, a [ba'βoso, a] (*AM: fam*) *adj* silly

baca ['baka] *nf* (*AUTO*) luggage *o* roof rack

bacalao [baka'lao] *nm* cod(fish)

bache ['batʃe] nm pothole, rut; (fig) bad patch

bacteria [bak'terja] nf bacterium, germ

báculo ['bakulo] nm stick, staff

bagaje [ba'yaxe] nm baggage, luggage

Bahama [ba'ama]: **las (Islas)** ~ nfpl the Bahamas

bahía [ba'ia] nf bay

bailar [bai'lar] vt, vi to dance; ~**ín**, **ina** nm/f (ballet) dancer; **baile** nm dance; (formal) ball

baja ['baxa] nf drop, fall; (MIL) casualty; **dar de** ~ (soldado) to discharge; (empleado) to dismiss

bajada [ba'xaða] nf descent; (camino) slope; (de aguas) ebb

bajar [ba'xar] vi to go down, come down; (temperatura, precios) to drop, fall ♦ vt (cabeza) to bow; (escalera) to go down, come down; (precio, voz) to lower; (llevar abajo) to take down; ~**se** vr (de coche) to get out; (de autobús, tren) to get off; ~ **de** (coche) to get out of; (autobús, tren) to get off

bajeza [ba'xeθa] nf baseness no pl; (una ~) vile deed

bajío [ba'xio] nm shoal, sandbank; (AM) lowlands pl

bajo, a ['baxo, a] adj (mueble, número, precio) low; (piso) ground; (de estatura) small, short; (color) pale; (sonido) faint, soft, low; (voz: en tono) deep; (metal) base; (humilde) low, humble ♦ adv (hablar) softly, quietly; (volar) low ♦ prep under, below, underneath ♦ nm (MUS) bass; ~ **la lluvia** in the rain

bajón [ba'xon] nm fall, drop

bala ['bala] nf bullet

balance [ba'lanθe] nm (COM) balance; (: libro) balance sheet; (: cuenta general) stocktaking

balancear [balanθe'ar] vt to balance ♦ vi to swing (to and fro); (vacilar) to hesitate; ~**se** vr to swing (to and fro); to hesitate; **balanceo** nm swinging

balanza [ba'lanθa] nf scales pl, balance; (ASTROLOGÍA): **B**~ Libra; ~ **comercial** balance of trade; ~ **de pagos** balance of payments

balar [ba'lar] vi to bleat

balaustrada [balaus'traða] nf balustrade; (pasamanos) banisters pl

balazo [ba'laθo] nm (golpe) shot; (herida) bullet wound

balbucear [balβuθe'ar] vi, vt to stammer, stutter; **balbuceo** nm stammering, stuttering

balbucir [balβu'θir] vi, vt to stammer, stutter

balcón [bal'kon] nm balcony

balde ['balde] nm bucket, pail; **de** ~ (for) free, for nothing; **en** ~ in vain

baldío, a [bal'dio, a] adj uncultivated; (terreno) waste ♦ nm waste land

baldosa [bal'dosa] nf (azulejo) floor tile; (grande) flagstone; **baldosin** nm (small) tile

Baleares [bale'ares] nfpl: **las (Islas)** ~ the Balearic Islands

balido [ba'liðo] nm bleat, bleating

balín [ba'lin] nm pellet; **balines** nmpl buckshot sg

baliza [ba'liθa] nf (AVIAT) beacon; (NAUT) buoy

ballena [ba'ʎena] nf whale

ballesta [ba'ʎesta] nf crossbow; (AUTO) spring

ballet [ba'le] (pl ~s) nm ballet

balneario, a [balne'arjo, a] adj: **estación balnearia** (bathing) resort ♦ nm spa, health resort

balón [ba'lon] nm ball

baloncesto [balon'θesto] nm basketball

balonmano [balon'mano] nm handball

balonvolea [balombo'lea] nm volleyball

balsa ['balsa] nf raft; (BOT) balsa wood

bálsamo ['balsamo] nm balsam, balm

baluarte [ba'lwarte] nm bastion, bulwark

bambolear [bambole'ar] vi to swing, sway; (silla) to wobble; ~**se** vr to swing, sway; to wobble; **bamboleo** nm swinging, swaying; wobbling

bambú [bam'bu] nm bamboo

banana [ba'nana] (AM) nf banana; **banano** (AM) nm banana tree

banca ['banka] nf (asiento) bench; (COM) banking

bancario, a [ban'karjo, a] adj banking

cpd, bank *cpd*

bancarrota [banka'rrota] *nf* bankruptcy; **hacer** ~ to go bankrupt

banco ['banko] *nm* bench; (*ESCOL*) desk; (*COM*) bank; (*GEO*) stratum; ~ **de crédito/de ahorros** credit/savings bank; ~ **de arena** sandbank; ~ **de datos** databank; ~ **de hielo** iceberg

banda ['banda] *nf* band; (*pandilla*) gang; (*NAUT*) side, edge; **la B~ Oriental** Uruguay; ~ **sonora** soundtrack

bandada [ban'daða] *nf* (*de pájaros*) flock; (*de peces*) shoal

bandazo [ban'daθo] *nm*: **dar ~s** to sway from side to side

bandeja [ban'dexa] *nf* tray

bandera [ban'dera] *nf* (*de tela*) flag; (*estandarte*) banner

banderilla [bande'riʎa] *nf* banderilla

banderín [bande'rin] *nm* pennant, small flag

bandido [ban'diðo] *nm* bandit

bando ['bando] *nm* (*edicto*) edict, proclamation; (*facción*) faction; **los ~s** (*REL*) the banns

bandolera [bando'lera] *nf*: **llevar en ~** to wear across one's chest

bandolero [bando'lero] *nm* bandit, brigand

Bangladesh [baeŋglo'deʃ] *nm* Bangladesh

banquero [ban'kero] *nm* banker

banqueta [ban'keta] *nf* stool; (*AM*: *en la calle*) pavement (*BRIT*), sidewalk (*US*)

banquete [ban'kete] *nm* banquet; (*para convidados*) formal dinner

banquillo [ban'kiʎo] *nm* (*JUR*) dock, prisoner's bench; (*banco*) bench; (*para los pies*) footstool

bañador [baɲa'ðor] *nm* swimming costume (*BRIT*), bathing suit (*US*)

bañar [ba'ɲar] *vt* to bath, bathe; (*objeto*) to dip; (*de barniz*) to coat; ~**se** *vr* (*en el mar*) to bathe, swim; (*en la bañera*) to have a bath

bañera [ba'ɲera] *nf* bath(tub)

bañero, a [ba'ɲero, a] (*AM*) *nm/f* lifeguard

bañista [ba'ɲista] *nm/f* bather

baño ['baɲo] *nm* (*en bañera*) bath; (*en río*) dip, swim; (*cuarto*) bathroom;

(*bañera*) bath(tub); (*capa*) coating

baqueta [ba'keta] *nf* (*MUS*) drumstick

bar [bar] *nm* bar

barahúnda [bara'unda] *nf* uproar, hubbub

baraja [ba'raxa] *nf* pack (of cards); **barajar** *vt* (*naipes*) to shuffle; (*fig*) to jumble up

baranda [ba'randa] *nf* = **barandilla**

barandilla [baran'diʎa] *nf* rail, railing

baratija [bara'tixa] *nf* trinket

baratillo [bara'tiʎo] *nm* (*tienda*) junkshop; (*subasta*) bargain sale; (*conjunto de cosas*) secondhand goods *pl*

barato, a [ba'rato, a] *adj* cheap ♦ *adv* cheap, cheaply

baraúnda [bara'unda] *nf* = **barahúnda**

barba ['barβa] *nf* (*mentón*) chin; (*pelo*) beard

barbacoa [barβa'koa] *nf* (*parrilla*) barbecue; (*carne*) barbecued meat

barbaridad [barβari'ðað] *nf* barbarity; (*acto*) barbarism; (*atrocidad*) outrage; **una ~** (*fam*) loads; **¡qué ~!** (*fam*) how awful!

barbarie [bar'βarje] *nf* barbarism, savagery; (*crueldad*) barbarity

barbarismo [barβa'rismo] *nm* = **barbarie**

bárbaro, a ['barβaro, a] *adj* barbarous, cruel; (*grosero*) rough, uncouth ♦ *nm/f* barbarian ♦ *adv*: **lo pasamos ~** (*fam*) we had a great time; **¡qué ~!** (*fam*) how marvellous!; **un éxito ~** (*fam*) a terrific success; **es un tipo ~** (*fam*) he's a great bloke

barbecho [bar'βetʃo] *nm* fallow land

barbero [bar'βero] *nm* barber, hairdresser

barbilampiño [barβilam'piɲo] *adj* clean-shaven, smooth-faced; (*fig*) inexperienced

barbilla [bar'βiʎa] *nf* chin, tip of the chin

barbo ['barβo] *nm*: ~ **de mar** red mullet

barbotear [barβote'ar] *vt*, *vi* to mutter, mumble

barbudo, a [bar'βuðo, a] *adj* bearded

barca ['barka] *nf* (small) boat; ~ **pesquera** fishing boat; ~ **de pasaje** ferry; ~**za** *nf* barge; ~**za de desembarco** landing craft

Barcelona [barθe'lona] *n* Barcelona

barcelonés, esa [barθelo'nes, esa] *adj* of
o from Barcelona
barco ['barko] *nm* boat; (*buque*) ship; ~
de carga cargo boat; ~ **de vela** sailing
ship
baremo [ba'remo] *nm* (*MAT, fig*) scale
barítono [ba'ritono] *nm* baritone
barman ['barman] *nm* barman
Barna. *abr* = **Barcelona**
barniz [bar'niθ] *nm* varnish; (*en la loza*)
glaze; (*fig*) veneer; ~**ar** *vt* to varnish;
(*loza*) to glaze
barómetro [ba'rometro] *nm* barometer
barquero [bar'kero] *nm* boatman
barquillo [bar'kiʎo] *nm* cone, cornet
barra ['barra] *nf* bar, rod; (*de un bar,
café*) bar; (*de pan*) French stick;
(*palanca*) lever; ~ **de carmín** *o* **de
labios** lipstick; ~ **libre** free bar
barraca [ba'rraka] *nf* hut, cabin
barranco [ba'rranko] *nm* ravine; (*fig*)
difficulty
barrena [ba'rrena] *nf* drill; **barrenar** *vt* to
drill (through), bore; **barreno** *nm* large
drill
barrer [ba'rrer] *vt* to sweep; (*quitar*) to
sweep away
barrera [ba'rrera] *nf* barrier
barriada [ba'rrjaða] *nf* quarter, district
barricada [barri'kaða] *nf* barricade
barrida [ba'rriða] *nf* sweep, sweeping
barrido [ba'rriðo] *nm* = **barrida**
barriga [ba'rriɣa] *nf* belly; (*panza*)
paunch; **barrigón, ona** *adj* potbellied;
barrigudo, a *adj* potbellied
barril [ba'rril] *nm* barrel, cask
barrio ['barrjo] *nm* (*vecindad*) area,
neighborhood (*US*); (*en las afueras*)
suburb; ~ **chino** red-light district
barro ['barro] *nm* (*lodo*) mud; (*objetos*)
earthenware; (*MED*) pimple
barroco, a [ba'rroko, a] *adj, nm* baroque
barrote [ba'rrote] *nm* (*de ventana*) bar
barruntar [barrun'tar] *vt* (*conjeturar*) to
guess; (*presentir*) to suspect; **barrunto**
nm guess; suspicion
bartola [bar'tola]: **a la** ~ *adv*: **tirarse a la**
~ to take it easy, be lazy
bártulos ['bartulos] *nmpl* things,

belongings
barullo [ba'ruʎo] *nm* row, uproar
basar [ba'sar] *vt* to base; ~**se** *vr*: ~**se en**
to be based on
basca ['baska] *nf* nausea
báscula ['baskula] *nf* (platform) scales
base ['base] *nf* base; **a** ~ **de** on the basis
of; (*mediante*) by means of; ~ **de datos**
(*INFORM*) database
básico, a ['basiko, a] *adj* basic
basílica [ba'silika] *nf* basilica

| PALABRA CLAVE |

bastante [bas'tante] *adj* **1** (*suficiente*)
enough; ~ **dinero** enough *o* sufficient
money; ~**s libros** enough books
2 (*valor intensivo*): ~ **gente** quite a lot of
people; **tener** ~ **calor** to be rather hot
♦ *adv*: ~ **bueno/malo** quite good/rather
bad; ~ **rico** pretty rich; **(lo)** ~
inteligente (como) para hacer algo
clever enough *o* sufficiently clever to do
sth

---

bastar [bas'tar] *vi* to be enough *o*
sufficient; ~**se** *vr* to be self-sufficient; ~
para to be enough to; **¡basta!** (that's)
enough!
bastardilla [bastar'ðiʎa] *nf* italics
bastardo, a [bas'tarðo, a] *adj, nm/f*
bastard
bastidor [basti'ðor] *nm* frame; (*de coche*)
chassis; (*TEATRO*) wing; **entre** ~**es** (*fig*)
behind the scenes
basto, a ['basto, a] *adj* coarse, rough; ~**s**
nmpl (*NAIPES*) ≈ clubs
bastón [bas'ton] *nm* stick, staff; (*para
pasear*) walking stick
bastoncillo [baston'θiʎo] *nm* cotton bud
bastos ['bastos] *nmpl* (*NAIPES*) clubs
basura [ba'sura] *nf* rubbish (*BRIT*), garbage
(*US*)
basurero [basu'rero] *nm* (*hombre*)
dustman (*BRIT*), garbage man (*US*); (*lugar*)
dump; (*cubo*) (rubbish) bin (*BRIT*), trash
can (*US*)
bata ['bata] *nf* (*gen*) dressing gown;
(*cubretodo*) smock, overall; (*MED, TEC etc*)
lab(oratory) coat

batalla [ba'taʎa] *nf* battle; **de ~** (*fig*) for everyday use

batallar [bata'ʎar] *vi* to fight

batallón [bata'ʎon] *nm* battalion

batata [ba'tata] (*AM*) *nf* sweet potato

batería [bate'ria] *nf* battery; (*MUS*) drums; **~ de cocina** kitchen utensils

batido, a [ba'tiðo, a] *adj* (*camino*) beaten, well-trodden ♦ *nm* (*CULIN*): **~ (de leche)** milk shake

batidora [bati'ðora] *nf* beater, mixer; **~ eléctrica** food mixer, blender

batir [ba'tir] *vt* to beat, strike; (*vencer*) to beat, defeat; (*revolver*) to beat, mix; **~se** *vr* to fight; **~ palmas** to clap, applaud

batuta [ba'tuta] *nf* baton; **llevar la ~** (*fig*) to be the boss, be in charge

baúl [ba'ul] *nm* trunk; (*AUTO*) boot (*BRIT*), trunk (*US*)

bautismo [bau'tismo] *nm* baptism, christening

bautizar [bauti'θar] *vt* to baptize, christen; (*fam: diluir*) to water down; **bautizo** *nm* baptism, christening

baya ['baja] *nf* berry

bayeta [ba'jeta] *nf* floorcloth

bayo, a ['bajo, a] *adj* bay

bayoneta [bajo'neta] *nf* bayonet

baza ['baθa] *nf* trick; **meter ~** to butt in

bazar [ba'θar] *nm* bazaar

bazofia [ba'θofja] *nf* pigswill (*BRIT*), hogwash (*US*); (*libro etc*) trash

beato, a [be'ato, a] *adj* blessed; (*piadoso*) pious

bebé [be'βe] (*pl* **~s**) *nm* baby

bebedero [beβe'ðero] *nm* (*para animales*) drinking trough

bebedor, a [beβe'ðor, a] *adj* hard-drinking

beber [be'βer] *vt, vi* to drink

bebida [be'βiða] *nf* drink; **bebido, a** *adj* drunk

beca ['beka] *nf* grant, scholarship

becario, a [be'karjo, a] *nm/f* scholarship holder, grant holder

bedel [be'ðel] *nm* (*ESCOL*) janitor; (*UNIV*) porter

béisbol ['beisβol] *nm* (*DEPORTE*) baseball

belén [be'len] *nm* (*de navidad*) nativity scene, crib; **B~** Bethlehem

belga ['belɣa] *adj, nm/f* Belgian

Bélgica ['belxika] *nf* Belgium

bélico, a ['beliko, a] *adj* (*actitud*) warlike; **belicoso, a** *adj* (*guerrero*) warlike; (*agresivo*) aggressive, bellicose

beligerante [belixe'rante] *adj* belligerent

belleza [be'ʎeθa] *nf* beauty

bello, a ['beʎo, a] *adj* beautiful, lovely; **Bellas Artes** Fine Art

bellota [be'ʎota] *nf* acorn

bemol [be'mol] *nm* (*MUS*) flat; **esto tiene ~es** (*fam*) this is a tough one

bencina [ben'θina] (*AM*) *nf* (*gasolina*) petrol (*BRIT*), gasoline (*US*)

bendecir [bende'θir] *vt* to bless

bendición [bendi'θjon] *nf* blessing

bendito, a [ben'dito, a] *pp de* **bendecir** ♦ *adj* holy; (*afortunado*) lucky; (*feliz*) happy; (*sencillo*) simple ♦ *nm/f* simple soul

beneficencia [benefi'θenθja] *nf* charity

beneficiar [benefi'θjar] *vt* to benefit, be of benefit to; **~se** *vr* to benefit, profit; **~io, a** *nm/f* beneficiary

beneficio [bene'fiθjo] *nm* (*bien*) benefit, advantage; (*ganancia*) profit, gain; **~so, a** *adj* beneficial

benéfico, a [be'nefiko, a] *adj* charitable

beneplácito [bene'plaθito] *nm* approval, consent

benevolencia [beneβo'lenθja] *nf* benevolence, kindness; **benévolo, a** *adj* benevolent, kind

benigno, a [be'niɣno, a] *adj* kind; (*suave*) mild; (*MED: tumor*) benign, non-malignant

berberecho [berβe'retʃo] *nm* (*ZOOL, CULIN*) cockle

berenjena [beren'xena] *nf* aubergine (*BRIT*), eggplant (*US*)

Berlín [ber'lin] *n* Berlin; **berlinés, esa** *adj* of *o* from Berlin ♦ *nm/f* Berliner

bermudas [ber'muðas] *nfpl* Bermuda shorts

berrear [berre'ar] *vi* to bellow, low

berrido [be'rriðo] *nm* bellow(ing)

berrinche [be'rrintʃe] (*fam*) *nm* temper, tantrum

berro ['berro] *nm* watercress

berza ['berθa] *nf* cabbage

besamel [besa'mel] *nf* (*CULIN*) white sauce, bechamel sauce

besar [be'sar] *vt* to kiss; (*fig: tocar*) to graze; **~se** *vr* to kiss (one another); **beso** *nm* kiss

bestia ['bestja] *nf* beast, animal; (*fig*) idiot; ~ **de carga** beast of burden

bestial [bes'tjal] *adj* bestial; (*fam*) terrific; **~idad** *nf* bestiality; (*fam*) stupidity

besugo [be'suɣo] *nm* sea bream; (*fam*) idiot

besuquear [besuke'ar] *vt* to cover with kisses; **~se** *vr* to kiss and cuddle

betún [be'tun] *nm* shoe polish; (*QUÍMICA*) bitumen

biberón [biβe'ron] *nm* feeding bottle

Biblia ['biβlja] *nf* Bible

bibliografía [biβljoɣra'fia] *nf* bibliography

biblioteca [biβljo'teka] *nf* library; (*mueble*) bookshelves; ~ **de consulta** reference library; **~rio, a** *nm/f* librarian

BIC [bik] *nf abr* (*ESP*: = *Brigada de Investigación Criminal*) ≈ CID (*BRIT*), FBI (*US*)

bicarbonato [bikarβo'nato] *nm* bicarbonate

bicho ['bitʃo] *nm* (*animal*) small animal; (*sabandija*) bug, insect; (*TAUR*) bull

bici ['biθi] (*fam*) *nf* bike

bicicleta [biθi'kleta] *nf* bicycle, cycle; **ir en** ~ to cycle

bidé [bi'ðe] (*pl* **~s**) *nm* bidet

bidón [bi'ðon] *nm* (*de aceite*) drum; (*de gasolina*) can

PALABRA CLAVE

---

bien [bjen] *nm* **1** (*bienestar*) good; **te lo digo por tu** ~ I'm telling you for your own good; **el** ~ **y el mal** good and evil
2 (*posesión*): **~es** goods; **~es de consumo** consumer goods; **~es inmuebles** *o* **raíces/~es muebles** real estate *sg/* personal property *sg*
♦ *adv* **1** (*de manera satisfactoria, correcta etc*) well; **trabaja/come** ~ she works/ eats well; **contestó** ~ he answered correctly; **me siento** ~ I feel fine; **no me siento** ~ I don't feel very well; **se está** ~

aquí it's nice here
2 (*frases*): **hiciste** ~ **en llamarme** you were right to call me
3 (*valor intensivo*) very; **un cuarto** ~ **caliente** a nice warm room; ~ **se ve que** ... it's quite clear that ...
4: **estar** ~: **estoy muy** ~ **aquí** I feel very happy here; **está** ~ **que vengan** it's all right for them to come; **¡está ~!** lo haré oh all right, I'll do it
5 (*de buena gana*): **yo** ~ **que iría pero** ... I'd gladly go but ...
♦ *excl*: **¡~!** (*aprobación*) O.K!; **¡muy ~!** well done!
♦ *adj inv* (*matiz despectivo*): **niño** ~ rich kid; **gente** ~ posh people
♦ *conj* **1**: ~ ... ~: ~ **en coche** ~ **en tren** either by car or by train
2: **no** ~ (*esp AM*): **no** ~ **llegue te llamaré** as soon as I arrive I'll call you
3: **si** ~ even though; *ver tb* **más**

---

bienal [bje'nal] *adj* biennial

bienaventurado, a [bjenaβentu'raðo, a] *adj* (*feliz*) happy, fortunate

bienestar [bjenes'tar] *nm* well-being, welfare

bienhechor, a [bjene'tʃor, a] *adj* beneficent ♦ *nm/f* benefactor/benefactress

bienvenida [bjembe'niða] *nf* welcome; **dar la** ~ **a uno** to welcome sb

bienvenido [bjembe'niðo] *excl* welcome!

bife ['bife] (*AM*) *nm* steak

bifurcación [bifurka'θjon] *nf* fork

bifurcarse [bifur'karse] *vr* (*camino, carretera, río*) to fork

bigamia [bi'ɣamja] *nf* bigamy; **bígamo, a** *adj* bigamous ♦ *nm/f* bigamist

bigote [bi'ɣote] *nm* moustache; **bigotudo, a** *adj* with a big moustache

bikini [bi'kini] *nm* bikini; (*CULIN*) toasted ham and cheese sandwich

bilbaíno, a [bilβa'ino, a] *adj* from *o* of Bilbao

bilingüe [bi'lingwe] *adj* bilingual

billar [bi'ʎar] *nm* billiards *sg*; (*lugar*) billiard hall; (*mini-casino*) amusement arcade; ~ **americano** pool

billete [bi'ʎete] *nm* ticket; (*de banco*)

(bank)note (BRIT), bill (US); (carta) note; ~ **sencillo, ~ de ida solamente** single (BRIT) o one-way (US) ticket; ~ **de ida y vuelta** return (BRIT) o round-trip (US) ticket; ~ **de 20 libras** £20 note

billetera [biʎe'tera] nf wallet

billetero [biʎe'tero] nm = **billetera**

billón [bi'ʎon] nm billion

bimensual [bimen'swal] adj twice monthly

bimotor [bimo'tor] adj twin-engined ♦ nm twin-engined plane

bingo ['biŋgo] nm bingo

biodegradable [bioðeɣra'ðaßle] adj biodegradable

biografía [bjoɣra'fia] nf biography; **biógrafo, a** nm/f biographer

biología [bjolo'xia] nf biology; **biológico, a** adj biological; **biólogo, a** nm/f biologist

biombo ['bjombo] nm (folding) screen

biopsia [bi'opsja] nf biopsy

biquini [bi'kini] nm bikini

birlar [bir'lar] (fam) vt to pinch

Birmania [bir'manja] nf Burma

birria ['birrja] nf: **ser una** ~ (película, libro) to be rubbish

bis [bis] excl encore! ♦ adv: **viven en el 27** ~ they live at 27a

bisabuelo, a [bisa'ßwelo, a] nm/f great-grandfather/mother

bisagra [bi'saɣra] nf hinge

bisbisar [bisßi'sar] vt to mutter, mumble

bisbisear [bisßise'ar] vt = **bisbisar**

bisiesto [bi'sjesto] adj: **año** ~ leap year

bisnieto, a [bis'njeto, a] nm/f great-grandson/daughter

bisonte [bi'sonte] nm bison

bisté [bis'te] nm = **bistec**

bistec [bis'tek] nm steak

bisturí [bistu'ri] nm scalpel

bisutería [bisute'ria] nf imitation o costume jewellery

bit [bit] nm (INFORM) bit

bizco, a ['biθko, a] adj cross-eyed

bizcocho [biθ'kotʃo] nm (CULIN) sponge cake

bizquear [biθke'ar] vi to squint

blanca ['blaŋka] nf (MUS) minim; **estar** sin ~ to be broke; ver tb **blanco**

blanco, a ['blaŋko, a] adj white ♦ nm/f white man/woman, white ♦ nm (color) white; (en texto) blank; (MIL, fig) target; **en** ~ blank; **noche en** ~ sleepless night

blancura [blaŋ'kura] nf whiteness

blandir [blan'dir] vt to brandish

blando, a ['blando, a] adj soft; (tierno) tender, gentle; (carácter) mild; (fam) cowardly; **blandura** nf softness; tenderness; mildness

blanquear [blaŋke'ar] vt to whiten; (fachada) to whitewash; (paño) to bleach ♦ vi to turn white; **blanquecino, a** adj whitish

blasfemar [blasfe'mar] vi to blaspheme, curse; **blasfemia** nf blasphemy

blasón [bla'son] nm coat of arms; (fig) honour; **blasonar** vt to emblazon ♦ vi to boast, brag

bledo ['bleðo] nm: **me importa un** ~ I couldn't care less

blindado, a [blin'daðo, a] adj (MIL) armour-plated; (antibala) bullet-proof; **coche** (ESP) o **carro** (AM) ~ armoured car

blindaje [blin'daxe] nm armour, armour-plating

bloc [blok] (pl ~s) nm writing pad

bloque ['bloke] nm block; (POL) bloc; ~ **de cilindros** cylinder block

bloquear [bloke'ar] vt to blockade; **bloqueo** nm blockade; (COM) freezing, blocking

blusa ['blusa] nf blouse

boato [bo'ato] nm show, ostentation

bobada [bo'ßaða] nf foolish action; foolish statement; **decir** ~s to talk nonsense

bobería [boße'ria] nf = **bobada**

bobina [bo'ßina] nf (TEC) bobbin; (FOTO) spool; (ELEC) coil

bobo, a ['boßo, a] adj (tonto) daft, silly; (cándido) naïve ♦ nm/f fool, idiot ♦ nm (TEATRO) clown, funny man

boca ['boka] nf mouth; (de crustáceo) pincer; (de cañón) muzzle; (entrada) mouth, entrance; ~s nfpl (de río) mouth sg; ~ **abajo/arriba** face down/up; **se me hace agua la** ~ my mouth is watering

bocacalle [boka'kaʎe] *nf* (entrance to a) street; **la primera** ~ the first turning *o* street

bocadillo [boka'ðiʎo] *nm* sandwich

bocado [bo'kaðo] *nm* mouthful, bite; (*de caballo*) bridle; ~ **de Adán** Adam's apple

bocajarro [boka'xarro]: **a** ~ *adv* (*disparar, preguntar*) point-blank

bocanada [boka'naða] *nf* (*de vino*) mouthful, swallow; (*de aire*) gust, puff

bocata [bo'kata] (*fam*) *nm* sandwich

bocazas [bo'kaθas] (*fam*) *nm inv* bigmouth

boceto [bo'θeto] *nm* sketch, outline

bochorno [bo'tʃorno] *nm* (*vergüenza*) embarrassment; (*calor*): **hace** ~ it's very muggy; **~so, a** *adj* muggy; embarrassing

bocina [bo'θina] *nf* (*MUS*) trumpet; (*AUTO*) horn; (*para hablar*) megaphone

boda ['boða] *nf* (*tb*: ~**s**) wedding, marriage; (*fiesta*) wedding reception; ~**s de plata/de oro** silver/golden wedding

bodega [bo'ðeɣa] *nf* (*de vino*) (wine) cellar; (*depósito*) storeroom; (*de barco*) hold

bodegón [boðe'ɣon] *nm* (*ARTE*) still life

bofe ['bofe] *nm* (*tb*: ~**s**: *de res*) lights

bofetada [bofe'taða] *nf* slap (in the face)

bofetón [bofe'ton] *nm* = **bofetada**

boga ['boɣa] *nf*: **en** ~ (*fig*) in vogue

bogar [bo'ɣar] *vi* (*remar*) to row; (*navegar*) to sail

Bogotá [boɣo'ta] *n* Bogota

bohemio, a [bo'emjo, a] *adj, nm/f* Bohemian

boicot [boi'kot] (*pl* ~**s**) *nm* boycott; **~ear** *vt* to boycott; **~eo** *nm* boycott

boina ['boina] *nf* beret

bola ['bola] *nf* ball; (*canica*) marble; (*NAIPES*) (grand) slam; (*betún*) shoe polish; (*mentira*) tale, story; ~**s** (*AM*) *nfpl* bolas *sg*; ~ **de billar** billiard ball; ~ **de nieve** snowball

bolchevique [boltʃe'ßike] *adj, nm/f* Bolshevik

boleadoras [bolea'ðoras] (*AM*) *nfpl* bolas *sg*

bolera [bo'lera] *nf* skittle *o* bowling alley

boleta [bo'leta] (*AM*) *nf* (*billete*) ticket; (*permiso*) pass, permit

boletería [bolete'ria] (*AM*) *nf* ticket office

boletín [bole'tin] *nm* bulletin; (*periódico*) journal, review; ~ **de noticias** news bulletin

boleto [bo'leto] *nm* ticket

boli ['boli] (*fam*) *nm* Biro ®, pen

boliche [bo'litʃe] *nm* (*bola*) jack; (*juego*) bowls *sg*; (*lugar*) bowling alley

bolígrafo [bo'liɣrafo] *nm* ball-point pen, Biro ®

bolívar [bo'lißar] *nm* monetary unit of Venezuela

Bolivia [bo'lißja] *nf* Bolivia; **boliviano, a** *adj, nm/f* Bolivian

bollo ['boʎo] *nm* (*pan*) roll; (*bulto*) bump, lump; (*abolladura*) dent

bolo ['bolo] *nm* skittle; (*píldora*) (large) pill; (**juego de**) ~**s** *nmpl* skittles *sg*

bolsa ['bolsa] *nf* (*cartera*) purse; (*saco*) bag; (*AM*) pocket; (*ANAT*) cavity, sac; (*COM*) stock exchange; (*MINERÍA*) pocket; **de** ~ *cpd*; ~ **de agua caliente** hot water bottle; ~ **de aire** air pocket; ~ **de papel** paper bag; ~ **de plástico** plastic bag

bolsillo [bol'siʎo] *nm* pocket; (*cartera*) purse; **de** ~ pocket(-size)

bolsista [bol'sista] *nm/f* stockbroker

bolso ['bolso] *nm* (*bolsa*) bag; (*de mujer*) handbag

bomba ['bomba] *nf* (*MIL*) bomb; (*TEC*) pump ♦ (*fam*) *adj*: **noticia** ~ bombshell ♦ (*fam*) *adv*: **pasarlo** ~ to have a great time; ~ **atómica/de humo/de retardo** atomic/smoke/time bomb; ~ **de gasolina** petrol pump

bombardear [bombarðe'ar] *vt* to bombard; (*MIL*) to bomb; **bombardeo** *nm* bombardment; bombing

bombardero [bombar'ðero] *nm* bomber

bombear [bombe'ar] *vt* (*agua*) to pump (out *o* up); (*MIL*) to bomb; **~se** *vr* to warp

bombero [bom'bero] *nm* fireman

bombilla [bom'biʎa] (*ESP*) *nf* (light) bulb

bombín [bom'bin] *nm* bowler hat

bombo ['bombo] *nm* (*MUS*) bass drum; (*TEC*) drum

bombón [bom'bon] *nm* chocolate

bombona [bom'bona] *nf (de butano, oxígeno)* cylinder

bonachón, ona [bona'tʃon, ona] *adj* good-natured, easy-going

bonanza [bo'nanθa] *nf (NAUT)* fair weather; *(fig)* bonanza; *(MINERÍA)* rich pocket *o* vein

bondad [bon'dað] *nf* goodness, kindness; **tenga la ~ de** (please) be good enough to; **~oso, a** *adj* good, kind

bonificación [bonifika'θjon] *nf* bonus

bonito, a [bo'nito, a] *adj* pretty; *(agradable)* nice ♦ *nm (atún)* tuna (fish)

bono ['bono] *nm* voucher; *(FINANZAS)* bond

bonobús [bono'βus] *(ESP) nm* bus pass

boquerón [boke'ron] *nm (pez)* (kind of) anchovy; *(agujero)* large hole

boquete [bo'kete] *nm* gap, hole

boquiabierto, a [bokia'βjerto, a] *adj*: **quedar ~** to be amazed *o* flabbergasted

boquilla [bo'kiʎa] *nf (para riego)* nozzle; *(para cigarro)* cigarette holder; *(MUS)* mouthpiece

borbotón [borβo'ton] *nm*: **salir a borbotones** to gush out

borda ['borða] *nf (NAUT)* (ship's) rail; **tirar algo/caerse por la ~** to throw sth/fall overboard

bordado [bor'ðaðo] *nm* embroidery

bordar [bor'ðar] *vt* to embroider

borde ['borðe] *nm* edge, border; *(de camino etc)* side; *(en la costura)* hem; **al ~ de** *(fig)* on the verge *o* brink of; **ser ~** *(ESP: fam)* to be a pain (in the neck); **~ar** *vt* to border

bordillo [bor'ðiʎo] *nm* kerb *(BRIT)*, curb *(US)*

bordo ['borðo] *nm (NAUT)* side; **a ~** on board

borinqueño, a [borin'kenjo, a] *adj, nm/f* Puerto Rican

borla ['borla] *nf (adorno)* tassel

borra ['borra] *nf (pelusa)* fluff; *(sedimento)* sediment

borrachera [borra'tʃera] *nf (ebriedad)* drunkenness; *(orgía)* spree, binge

borracho, a [bo'rratʃo, a] *adj* drunk ♦ *nm/f (que bebe mucho)* drunkard, drunk; *(temporalmente)* drunk, drunk

man/woman

borrador [borra'ðor] *nm (escritura)* first draft, rough sketch; *(cuaderno)* scribbling pad; *(goma)* rubber *(BRIT)*, eraser

borrar [bo'rrar] *vt* to erase, rub out

borrasca [bo'rraska] *nf* storm

borrico, a [bo'rriko, a] *nm/f* donkey/she-donkey; *(fig)* stupid man/woman

borrón [bo'rron] *nm (mancha)* stain

borroso, a [bo'rroso, a] *adj* vague, unclear; *(escritura)* illegible

bosque ['boske] *nm* wood; *(grande)* forest

bosquejar [boske'xar] *vt* to sketch; **bosquejo** *nm* sketch

bostezar [boste'θar] *vi* to yawn; **bostezo** *nm* yawn

bota ['bota] *nf (calzado)* boot; *(saco)* leather wine bottle; **~s de agua, ~ de goma** Wellingtons

botánica [bo'tanika] *nf (ciencia)* botany; *ver tb* **botánico**

botánico, a [bo'taniko, a] *adj* botanical ♦ *nm/f* botanist

botar [bo'tar] *vt* to throw, hurl; *(NAUT)* to launch; *(fam)* to throw out ♦ *vi* to bounce

bote ['bote] *nm (salto)* bounce; *(golpe)* thrust; *(vasija)* tin, can; *(embarcación)* boat; **de ~ en ~** packed, jammed full; **~ de la basura** *(AM)* dustbin *(BRIT)*, trashcan *(US)*; **~ salvavidas** lifeboat

botella [bo'teʎa] *nf* bottle; **botellín** *nm* small bottle

botica [bo'tika] *nf* chemist's (shop) *(BRIT)*, pharmacy; **~rio, a** *nm/f* chemist *(BRIT)*, pharmacist

botijo [bo'tixo] *nm (earthenware)* jug

botín [bo'tin] *nm (calzado)* half boot; *(polaina)* spat; *(MIL)* booty

botiquín [boti'kin] *nm (armario)* medicine cabinet; *(portátil)* first-aid kit

botón [bo'ton] *nm* button; *(BOT)* bud; *(de florete)* tip; **~ de oro** buttercup

botones [bo'tones] *nm inv* bellboy *(BRIT)*, bellhop *(US)*

bóveda ['boβeða] *nf (ARQ)* vault

boxeador [boksea'ðor] *nm* boxer

boxear [bokse'ar] *vi* to box

boxeo [bok'seo] *nm* boxing

boya ['boja] *nf* (*NAUT*) buoy; (*flotador*) float

boyante [bo'jante] *adj* prosperous

bozal [bo'θal] *nm* (*de caballo*) halter; (*de perro*) muzzle

bracear [braθe'ar] *vi* (*agitar los brazos*) to wave one's arms

bracero [bra'θero] *nm* labourer; (*en el campo*) farmhand

braga ['braɣa] *nf* (*cuerda*) sling, rope; (*de bebé*) nappy (*BRIT*), diaper (*US*); ~**s** *nfpl* (*de mujer*) panties, knickers (*BRIT*)

bragueta [bra'ɣeta] *nf* fly, flies *pl*

braille [breil] *nm* braille

bramar [bra'mar] *vi* to bellow, roar; **bramido** *nm* bellow, roar

brasa ['brasa] *nf* live o hot coal

brasero [bra'sero] *nm* brazier

Brasil [bra'sil] *nm*: (**el**) ~ Brazil; **brasileño, a** *adj*, *nm/f* Brazilian

bravata [bra'βata] *nf* boast

braveza [bra'βeθa] *nf* (*valor*) bravery; (*ferocidad*) ferocity

bravío, a [bra'βio, a] *adj* wild; (*feroz*) fierce

bravo, a ['braβo, a] *adj* (*valiente*) brave; (*bueno*) fine, splendid; (*feroz*) ferocious; (*salvaje*) wild; (*mar etc*) rough, stormy ♦ *excl* bravo!; **bravura** *nf* bravery; ferocity; (*pey*) boast

braza ['braθa] *nf* fathom; **nadar a la** ~ to swim (the) breast-stroke

brazada [bra'θaða] *nf* stroke

brazado [bra'θaðo] *nm* armful

brazalete [braθa'lete] *nm* (*pulsera*) bracelet; (*banda*) armband

brazo ['braθo] *nm* arm; (*ZOOL*) foreleg; (*BOT*) limb, branch; **luchar a** ~ **partido** to fight hand-to-hand; **ir cogidos del** ~ to walk arm in arm

brea ['brea] *nf* pitch, tar

brebaje [bre'βaxe] *nm* potion

brecha ['bretʃa] *nf* (*hoyo, vacío*) gap, opening; (*MIL*, *fig*) breach

brega ['breɣa] *nf* (*lucha*) struggle; (*trabajo*) hard work

breve ['breβe] *adj* short, brief ♦ *nf* (*MUS*) breve; ~**dad** *nf* brevity, shortness

brezo ['breθo] *nm* heather

bribón, ona [bri'βon, ona] *adj* idle, lazy ♦ *nm/f* (*vagabundo*) vagabond; (*pícaro*) rascal, rogue

bricolaje [briko'laxe] *nm* do-it-yourself, DIY

brida ['briða] *nf* bridle, rein; (*TEC*) clamp; **a toda** ~ at top speed

bridge [britʃ] *nm* bridge

brigada [bri'ɣaða] *nf* (*unidad*) brigade; (*trabajadores*) squad, gang ♦ *nm* ≈ staff-sergeant, sergeant-major

brillante [bri'ʎante] *adj* brilliant ♦ *nm* diamond

brillar [bri'ʎar] *vi* (*tb fig*) to shine; (*joyas*) to sparkle

brillo ['briʎo] *nm* shine; (*brillantez*) brilliance; (*fig*) splendour; **sacar** ~ **a** to polish

brincar [brin'kar] *vi* to skip about, hop about, jump about; **está que brinca** he's hopping mad

brinco ['brinko] *nm* jump, leap

brindar [brin'dar] *vi*: ~ **a** o **por** to drink (a toast) to ♦ *vt* to offer, present

brindis ['brindis] *nm inv* toast; (*TAUR*) (ceremony of) dedication

brío ['brio] *nm* spirit, dash; **brioso, a** *adj* spirited, dashing

brisa ['brisa] *nf* breeze

británico, a [bri'taniko, a] *adj* British ♦ *nm/f* Briton, British person

brizna ['briθna] *nf* (*de hierba, paja*) blade; (*de tabaco*) leaf

broca ['broka] *nf* (*TEC*) drill, bit

brocal [bro'kal] *nm* rim

brocha ['brotʃa] *nf* (*large*) paintbrush; ~ **de afeitar** shaving brush

broche ['brotʃe] *nm* brooch

broma ['broma] *nf* joke; **en** ~ in fun, as a joke; ~ **pesada** practical joke; **bromear** *vi* to joke

bromista [bro'mista] *adj* fond of joking ♦ *nm/f* joker, wag

bronca ['bronka] *nf* row; **echar una** ~ **a uno** to tick sb off

bronce ['bronθe] *nm* bronze; ~**ado, a** *adj* bronze; (*por el sol*) tanned ♦ *nm* (sun)tan; (*TEC*) bronzing

bronceador [bronθea'ðor] *nm* suntan lotion

broncearse [bronθe'arse] *vr* to get a suntan

bronco, a ['bronko, a] *adj (manera)* rude, surly; *(voz)* harsh

bronquio ['bronkjo] *nm (ANAT)* bronchial tube

bronquitis [bron'kitis] *nf inv* bronchitis

brotar [bro'tar] *vi (BOT)* to sprout; *(aguas)* to gush (forth); *(MED)* to break out

brote ['brote] *nm (BOT)* shoot; *(MED, fig)* outbreak

bruces ['bruθes]: **de ~** *adv*: **caer** *o* **dar de ~** to fall headlong, fall flat

bruja ['bruxa] *nf* witch; **brujería** *nf* witchcraft

brujo ['bruxo] *nm* wizard, magician

brújula ['bruxula] *nf* compass

bruma ['bruma] *nf* mist; **brumoso, a** *adj* misty

bruñir [bru'ɲir] *vt* to polish

brusco, a ['brusko, a] *adj (súbito)* sudden; *(áspero)* brusque

Bruselas [bru'selas] *n* Brussels

brutal [bru'tal] *adj* brutal

brutalidad [brutali'ðað] *nf* brutality

bruto, a ['bruto, a] *adj (idiota)* stupid; *(bestial)* brutish; *(peso)* gross; **en ~** raw, unworked

Bs.As. *abr (= Buenos Aires)* B.A.

bucal [bu'kal] *adj* oral; **por vía ~** orally

bucear [buθe'ar] *vi* to dive ♦ *vt* to explore; **buceo** *nm* diving; *(fig)* investigation

bucle ['bukle] *nm* curl

budismo [bu'ðismo] *nm* Buddhism

buen [bwen] *adj m ver* **bueno**

buenamente [bwena'mente] *adv (fácilmente)* easily; *(voluntariamente)* willingly

buenaventura [bwenaßen'tura] *nf (suerte)* good luck; *(adivinación)* fortune

PALABRA CLAVE

bueno, a ['bweno, a] *adj (antes de nmsg:* **buen**) **1** *(excelente etc)* good; **es un libro ~, es un buen libro** it's a good book; **hace ~, hace buen tiempo** the weather

is fine, it is fine; **el ~ de Paco** good old Paco; **fue muy ~ conmigo** he was very nice *o* kind to me

2 *(apropiado)*: **ser ~ para** to be good for; **creo que vamos por buen camino** I think we're on the right track

3 *(irónico)*: **le di un buen rapapolvo** I gave him a good *o* real ticking off; **¡buen conductor estás hecho!** some *o* a fine driver you are!; **¡estaría ~ que ...!** a fine thing it would be if ...!

4 *(atractivo, sabroso)*: **está ~ este bizcocho** this sponge is delicious; **Carmen está muy buena** Carmen is looking good

5 *(saludos)*: **¡buen día!, ¡~s días!** (good) morning!; **¡buenas (tardes)!** (good) afternoon!; *(más tarde)* (good) evening!; **¡buenas noches!** good night!

6 *(otras locuciones)*: **estar de buenas** to be in a good mood; **por las buenas o por las malas** by hook or by crook; **de buenas a primeras** all of a sudden

♦ *excl*: **¡~!** all right!; **~, ¿y qué?** well, so what?

Buenos Aires *nm* Buenos Aires

buey [bwei] *nm* ox

búfalo ['bufalo] *nm* buffalo

bufanda [bu'fanda] *nf* scarf

bufar [bu'far] *vi* to snort

bufete [bu'fete] *nm (despacho de abogado)* lawyer's office

buffer ['bufer] *nm (INFORM)* buffer

bufón [bu'fon] *nm* clown

buhardilla [buar'ðiʎa] *nf (desván)* attic

búho ['buo] *nm* owl; *(fig)* hermit, recluse

buhonero [buo'nero] *nm* pedlar

buitre ['bwitre] *nm* vulture

bujía [bu'xia] *nf (vela)* candle; *(ELEC)* candle (power); *(AUTO)* spark plug

bula ['bula] *nf (papal)* bull

bulbo ['bulßo] *nm* bulb

bulevar [bule'ßar] *nm* boulevard

Bulgaria [bul'ɣarja] *nf* Bulgaria; **búlgaro, a** *adj, nm/f* Bulgarian

bulla ['buʎa] *nf (ruido)* uproar; *(de gente)* crowd

bullicio [bu'ʎiθjo] *nm (ruido)* uproar;

(*movimiento*) bustle

bullir [buˈʎir] *vi* (*hervir*) to boil; (*burbujear*) to bubble; (*mover*) to move, stir

bulto [ˈbulto] *nm* (*paquete*) package; (*fardo*) bundle; (*tamaño*) size, bulkiness; (MED) swelling, lump; (*silueta*) vague shape; (*estatua*) bust, statue

buñuelo [buˈɲwelo] *nm* ≈ doughnut (BRIT), ≈ donut (US); (*fruta de sartén*) fritter

BUP [bup] *nm abr* (ESP: = *Bachillerato Unificado Polivalente*) *secondary education and leaving certificate for 14–17 age group*

buque [ˈbuke] *nm* ship, vessel

burbuja [burˈβuxa] *nf* bubble; **burbujear** *vi* to bubble

burdel [burˈðel] *nm* brothel

burdo, a [ˈburðo, a] *adj* coarse, rough

burgués, esa [burˈɣes, esa] *adj* middle-class, bourgeois; **burguesía** *nf* middle class, bourgeoisie

burla [ˈburla] *nf* (*mofa*) gibe; (*broma*) joke; (*engaño*) trick

burladero [burlaˈðero] *nm* (bullfighter's) refuge

burlar [burˈlar] *vt* (*engañar*) to deceive; (*seducir*) to seduce ♦ *vi* to joke; **~se** *vr* to joke; **~se de** to make fun of

burlesco, a [burˈlesko, a] *adj* burlesque

burlón, ona [burˈlon, ona] *adj* mocking

burocracia [buroˈkraθja] *nf* civil service; (*pey*) bureaucracy

burócrata [buˈrokrata] *nm/f* civil servant; (*pey*) bureaucrat

burrada [buˈrraða] *nf*: **decir/soltar ~s** to talk nonsense; **hacer ~s** to act stupid; **una ~ a** (a hell of a) lot

burro, a [ˈburro] *nm/f* donkey/she-donkey; (*fig*) ass, idiot

bursátil [burˈsatil] *adj* stock-exchange *cpd*

bus [bus] *nm* bus

busca [ˈbuska] *nf* search, hunt ♦ *nm* (TEL) bleeper; **en ~ de** in search of

buscar [busˈkar] *vt* to look for, search for, seek ♦ *vi* to look, search, seek; **se busca secretaria** secretary wanted

busque *etc vb ver* **buscar**

búsqueda [ˈbuskeða] *nf* = **busca** *nf*

busto [ˈbusto] *nm* (ANAT, ARTE) bust

butaca [buˈtaka] *nf* armchair; (*de cine, teatro*) stall, seat

butano [buˈtano] *nm* butane (gas)

buzo [ˈbuθo] *nm* diver

buzón [buˈθon] *nm* (*en puerta*) letter box; (*en la calle*) pillar box

C c

C. *abr* (= *centígrado*) C; (= *compañía*) Co.

c. *abr* (= *capítulo*) ch.

C/ *abr* (= *calle*) St

c.a. *abr* (= *corriente alterna*) AC

cabal [kaˈβal] *adj* (*exacto*) exact; (*correcto*) right, proper; (*acabado*) finished, complete; **~es** *nmpl*: **estar en sus ~es** to be in one's right mind

cábalas [ˈkaβalas] *nfpl*: **hacer ~** to guess

cabalgar [kaβalˈɣar] *vt, vi* to ride

cabalgata [kaβalˈɣata] *nf* procession

caballa [kaˈβaʎa] *nf* mackerel

caballeresco, a [kaβaʎeˈresko, a] *adj* noble, chivalrous

caballería [kaβaʎeˈria] *nf* mount; (MIL) cavalry

caballeriza [kaβaʎeˈriθa] *nf* stable; **caballerizo** *nm* groom, stableman

caballero [kaβaˈʎero] *nm* (*hombre galante*) gentleman; (*de la orden de caballería*) knight; (*trato directo*) sir

caballerosidad [kaβaʎerosiˈðað] *nf* chivalry

caballete [kaβaˈʎete] *nm* (ARTE) easel; (TEC) trestle

caballito [kaβaˈʎito] *nm* (*caballo pequeño*) small horse, pony; **~s** *nmpl* (*en verbena*) roundabout, merry-go-round

caballo [kaˈβaʎo] *nm* horse; (AJEDREZ) knight; (NAIPES) queen; **ir en ~** to ride; **~ de vapor o de fuerza** horsepower; **~ de carreras** racehorse

cabaña [kaˈβaɲa] *nf* (*casita*) hut, cabin

cabaré [kaβaˈre] (*pl* **~s**) *nm* cabaret

cabaret [kaβaˈre] (*pl* **~s**) *nm* cabaret

cabecear [kaβeθeˈar] *vt, vi* to nod

cabecera [kaβe'θera] *nf* head; *(de distrito)* chief town; *(IMPRENTA)* headline

cabecilla [kaβe'θiʎa] *nm* ringleader

cabellera [kaβe'ʎera] *nf* (head of) hair; *(de cometa)* tail

cabello [ka'βeʎo] *nm* (*tb:* ~s) hair

caber [ka'βer] *vi* *(entrar)* to fit, go; **caben 3 más** there's room for 3 more

cabestrillo [kaβes'triʎo] *nm* sling

cabestro [ka'βestro] *nm* halter

cabeza [ka'βeθa] *nf* head; *(POL)* chief, leader; ~ **rapada** skinhead; ~**da** *nf* *(golpe)* butt; **dar** ~**das** to nod off; **cabezón, ona** *adj* *(vino)* heady; *(fam: persona)* pig-headed

cabida [ka'βiða] *nf* space

cabildo [ka'βildo] *nm* *(de iglesia)* chapter; *(POL)* town council

cabina [ka'βina] *nf* cabin; *(de camión)* cab; ~ **telefónica** telephone box *(BRIT)* o booth

cabizbajo, a [kaβiθ'βaxo, a] *adj* crestfallen, dejected

cable ['kaβle] *nm* cable

cabo ['kaβo] *nm* *(de objeto)* end, extremity; *(MIL)* corporal; *(NAUT)* rope, cable; *(GEO)* cape; **al ~ de 3 días** after 3 days

cabra ['kaβra] *nf* goat

cabré *etc vb ver* **caber**

cabrear [kaβre'ar] *(fam)* *vt* to bug; ~**se** *vr* *(enfadarse)* to fly off the handle

cabrío, a [ka'βrio, a] *adj* goatish; **macho** ~ (he-)goat, billy goat

cabriola [ka'βrjola] *nf* caper

cabritilla [kaβri'tiʎa] *nf* kid, kidskin

cabrito [ka'βrito] *nm* kid

cabrón [ka'βron] *nm* cuckold; *(fam!)* bastard *(!)*

caca ['kaka] *(fam)* *nf* shit *(!)*; *(usado para/por niños)* pooh

cacahuete [kaka'wete] *(ESP)* *nm* peanut

cacao [ka'kao] *nm* cocoa; *(BOT)* cacao

cacarear [kakare'ar] *vi* *(persona)* to boast; *(gallina)* to crow

cacería [kaθe'ria] *nf* hunt

cacerola [kaθe'rola] *nf* pan, saucepan

cachalote [katʃa'lote] *nm* *(ZOOL)* sperm whale

cacharro [ka'tʃarro] *nm* earthenware pot; ~**s** *nmpl* pots and pans

cachear [katʃe'ar] *vt* to search, frisk

cachemir [katʃe'mir] *nm* cashmere

cacheo [ka'tʃeo] *nm* searching, frisking

cachete [ka'tʃete] *nm* *(ANAT)* cheek; *(bofetada)* slap (in the face)

cachiporra [katʃi'porra] *nf* truncheon

cachivache [katʃi'βatʃe] *nm* *(trasto)* piece of junk; ~**s** *nmpl* junk *sg*

cacho ['katʃo] *nm* (small) bit; *(AM: cuerno)* horn

cachondeo [katʃon'deo] *(fam)* *nm* farce, joke

cachondo, a [ka'tʃondo, a] *adj* *(ZOOL)* on heat; *(fam)* sexy; *(gracioso)* funny

cachorro, a [ka'tʃorro, a] *nm/f* *(perro)* pup, puppy; *(león)* cub

cacique [ka'θike] *nm* chief, local ruler; *(POL)* local party boss; **caciquismo** *nm* system of control by the local boss

caco ['kako] *nm* pickpocket

cacto ['kakto] *nm* cactus

cactus ['kaktus] *nm inv* cactus

cada ['kaða] *adj inv* each; *(antes de número)* every; ~ **día** each day, every day; ~ **dos días** every other day; ~ **uno/a** each one, every one; ~ **vez más/menos** more and more/less and less; ~ **uno de ~ diez** one out of every ten

cadalso [ka'ðalso] *nm* scaffold

cadáver [ka'ðaβer] *nm* (dead) body, corpse

cadena [ka'ðena] *nf* chain; *(TV)* channel; **trabajo en** ~ assembly line work; ~ **perpetua** *(JUR)* life imprisonment

cadencia [ka'ðenθja] *nf* rhythm

cadera [ka'ðera] *nf* hip

cadete [ka'ðete] *nm* cadet

caducar [kaðu'kar] *vi* to expire; **caduco, a** *adj* expired; *(persona)* very old

C.A.E. *abr* (= *cóbrese al entregar*) C.O.D.

caer [ka'er] *vi* to fall (down); ~**se** *vr* to fall (down); **me cae bien/mal** I get on well with him/I can't stand him; ~ **en la cuenta** to catch on; **su cumpleaños cae en viernes** her birthday falls on a Friday

café [ka'fe] *(pl* ~**s***)* *nm* *(bebida, planta)*

coffee; (*lugar*) café ♦ *adj* (*color*) brown; ~ **con leche** white coffee; ~ **solo** black coffee

cafetera [kafe'tera] *nf* coffee pot

cafetería [kafete'ria] *nf* (*gen*) café

cafetero, a [kafe'tero, a] *adj* coffee *cpd*; **ser muy** ~ to be a coffee addict

cagar [ka'ɣar] (*fam!*) *vt* to shit (*!*); to bungle, mess up ♦ *vi* to have a shit (*!*)

caída [ka'iða] *nf* fall; (*declive*) slope; (*disminución*) fall, drop

caído, a [ka'iðo, a] *adj* drooping

caiga *etc vb ver* **caer**

caimán [kai'man] *nm* alligator

caja ['kaxa] *nf* box; (*para reloj*) case; (*de ascensor*) shaft; (*COM*) cashbox; (*donde se hacen los pagos*) checkdesk; (: *en supermercado*) checkout, till; ~ **de ahorros** savings bank; ~ **de cambios** gearbox; ~ **fuerte**, ~ **de caudales** safe, strongbox

cajero, a [ka'xero, a] *nm/f* cashier; ~ **automático** cash dispenser

cajetilla [kaxe'tiʎa] *nf* (*de cigarrillos*) packet

cajón [ka'xon] *nm* big box; (*de mueble*) drawer

cal [kal] *nf* lime

cala ['kala] *nf* (*GEO*) cove, inlet; (*de barco*) hold

calabacín [kalaβa'θin] *nm* (*BOT*) baby marrow; (: *más pequeño*) courgette (*BRIT*), zucchini (*US*)

calabaza [kala'βaθa] *nf* (*BOT*) pumpkin

calabozo [kala'βoθo] *nm* (*cárcel*) prison; (*celda*) cell

calada [ka'laða] *nf* (*de cigarrillo*) puff

calado, a [ka'laðo, a] *adj* (*prenda*) lace *cpd* ♦ *nm* (*NAUT*) draught

calamar [kala'mar] *nm* squid *no pl*

calambre [ka'lambre] *nm* (*tb*: ~**s**) cramp

calamidad [kalami'ðað] *nf* calamity, disaster

calar [ka'lar] *vt* to soak, drench; (*penetrar*) to pierce, penetrate; (*comprender*) to see through; (*vela*) to lower; ~**se** *vr* (*AUTO*) to stall; ~**se las gafas** to stick one's glasses on

calavera [kala'βera] *nf* skull

calcañal [kalka'ɲal] *nm* = **calcañar**

calcañar [kalka'ɲar] *nm* heel

calcaño [kal'kaɲo] *nm* = **calcañar**

calcar [kal'kar] *vt* (*reproducir*) to trace; (*imitar*) to copy

calcetín [kalθe'tin] *nm* sock

calcinar [kalθi'nar] *vt* to burn, blacken

calcio ['kalθjo] *nm* calcium

calco ['kalko] *nm* tracing

calcomanía [kalkoma'nia] *nf* transfer

calculador, a [kalkula'ðor, a] *adj* (*persona*) calculating

calculadora [kalkula'ðora] *nf* calculator

calcular [kalku'lar] *vt* (*MAT*) to calculate, compute; ~ **que ...** to reckon that ...;

cálculo *nm* calculation

caldear [kalde'ar] *vt* to warm (up), heat (up)

caldera [kal'dera] *nf* boiler

calderilla [kalde'riʎa] *nf* (*moneda*) small change

caldero [kal'dero] *nm* small boiler

caldo ['kaldo] *nm* stock; (*consomé*) consommé

calefacción [kalefak'θjon] *nf* heating; ~ **central** central heating

calendario [kalen'darjo] *nm* calendar

calentador [kalenta'ðor] *nm* heater

calentamiento [kalenta'mjento] *nm* (*DEPORTE*) warm-up

calentar [kalen'tar] *vt* to heat (up); ~**se** *vr* to heat up, warm up; (*fig: discusión etc*) to get heated

calentura [kalen'tura] *nf* (*MED*) fever, (high) temperature

calibrar [kali'βrar] *vt* to gauge, measure;

calibre *nm* (*de cañón*) calibre, bore; (*diámetro*) diameter; (*fig*) calibre

calidad [kali'ðað] *nf* quality; **de** ~ quality *cpd*; **en** ~ **de** in the capacity of, as

cálido, a ['kaliðo, a] *adj* hot; (*fig*) warm

caliente *etc* [ka'ljente] *vb ver* **calentar** ♦ *adj* hot; (*fig*) fiery; (*disputa*) heated; (*fam: cachondo*) randy

calificación [kalifika'θjon] *nf* qualification; (*de alumno*) grade, mark

calificar [kalifi'kar] *vt* to qualify; (*alumno*) to grade, mark; ~ **de** to describe as

calima [ka'lima] *nf* (*cerca del mar*) mist

cáliz ['kaliθ] nm chalice
caliza [ka'liθa] nf limestone
calizo, a [ka'liθo, a] adj lime cpd
callado, a [ka'ʎaðo, a] adj quiet
callar [ka'ʎar] vt (asunto delicado) to keep
quiet about, say nothing about; (persona,
opinión) to silence ♦ vi to keep quiet, be
silent; ~se vr to keep quiet, be silent;
¡cállate! be quiet!, shut up!
calle ['kaʎe] nf street; (DEPORTE) lane; ~
arriba/abajo up/down the street; ~ de
un solo sentido one-way street
calleja [ka'ʎexa] nf alley, narrow street;
callejear vi to wander (about) the
streets; callejero, a adj street cpd ♦ nm
street map; callejón nm alley, passage;
callejón sin salida cul-de-sac; callejuela
nf side-street, alley
callista [ka'ʎista] nm/f chiropodist
callo ['kaʎo] nm callus; (en el pie) corn;
~s nmpl (CULIN) tripe sg; ~so, a adj
callused
calma ['kalma] nf calm; (pachorra)
slowness
calmante [kal'mante] nm sedative,
tranquillizer
calmar [kal'mar] vt to calm, calm down
♦ vi (tempestad) to abate; (mente etc) to
become calm
calmoso, a [kal'moso, a] adj calm, quiet
calor [ka'lor] nm heat; (agradable)
warmth; hace ~ it's hot; tener ~ to be
hot
caloría [kalo'ria] nf calorie
calumnia [ka'lumnja] nf calumny,
slander; calumnioso, a adj slanderous
caluroso, a [kalu'roso, a] adj hot; (sin
exceso) warm; (fig) enthusiastic
calva ['kalβa] nf bald patch; (en bosque)
clearing
calvario [kal'βarjo] nm stations pl of the
cross
calvicie [kal'βiθje] nf baldness
calvo, a ['kalβo, a] adj bald; (terreno)
bare, barren; (tejido) threadbare
calza ['kalθa] nf wedge, chock
calzada [kal'θaða] nf roadway, highway
calzado, a [kal'θaðo, a] adj shod ♦ nm
footwear

calzador [kalθa'ðor] nm shoehorn
calzar [kal'θar] vt (zapatos etc) to wear;
(un mueble) to put a wedge under; ~se
vr: ~se los zapatos to put on one's
shoes; ¿qué (número) calza? what size
do you take?
calzón [kal'θon] nm (tb: calzones nmpl)
shorts; (AM: de hombre) (under)pants;
(: de mujer) panties
calzoncillos [kalθon'θiʎos] nmpl
underpants
cama ['kama] nf bed; (GEO) stratum; ~
individual/de matrimonio single/
double bed
camada [ka'maða] nf litter; (de personas)
gang, band
camafeo [kama'feo] nm cameo
camaleón [kamale'on] nm (ZOOL)
chameleon
cámara ['kamara] nf chamber;
(habitación) room; (sala) hall; (CINE) cine
camera; (fotográfica) camera; ~ de aire
inner tube; ~ de comercio chamber of
commerce; ~ frigorífica cold-storage
room
camarada [kama'raða] nm comrade,
companion
camarera [kama'rera] nf (en restaurante)
waitress; (en casa, hotel) maid
camarero [kama'rero] nm waiter
camarilla [kama'riʎa] nf (clan) clique;
(POL) lobby
camarón [kama'ron] nm shrimp
camarote [kama'rote] nm cabin
cambiable [kam'bjaβle] adj (variable)
changeable, variable; (intercambiable)
interchangeable
cambiante [kam'bjante] adj variable
cambiar [kam'bjar] vt to change; (dinero)
to exchange ♦ vi to change; ~se vr
(mudarse) to move; (de ropa) to change;
~ de idea to change one's mind; ~ de
ropa to change (one's clothes)
cambiazo [kam'bjaθo] nm: dar el ~ a
uno to swindle sb
cambio ['kambjo] nm change; (trueque)
exchange; (COM) rate of exchange;
(oficina) bureau de change; (dinero
menudo) small change; en ~ on the other

hand; (*en lugar de*) instead; ~ **de divisas** foreign exchange; ~ **de velocidades** gear lever; ~ **de vía** points *pl*

camelar [kame'lar] *vt* (*con mujer*) to flirt with; (*persuadir*) to cajole

camello [ka'meʎo] *nm* camel; (*fam: traficante*) pusher

camerino [kame'rino] *nm* (*TEATRO*) dressing room

camilla [ka'miʎa] *nf* (*MED*) stretcher

caminante [kami'nante] *nm/f* traveller

caminar [kami'nar] *vi* (*marchar*) to walk, go; (*viajar*) to travel, journey ♦ *vt* (*recorrer*) to cover, travel

caminata [kami'nata] *nf* long walk; (*por el campo*) hike

camino [ka'mino] *nm* way, road; (*sendero*) track; **a medio** ~ halfway (there); **en el** ~ on the way, en route; ~ **de** on the way to; ~ **particular** private road

camión [ka'mjon] *nm* lorry (*BRIT*), truck (*US*); ~ **cisterna** tanker; **camionero, a** *nm/f* lorry o truck driver

camioneta [kamjo'neta] *nf* van, light truck

camisa [ka'misa] *nf* shirt; (*BOT*) skin; ~ **de fuerza** straitjacket; **camisería** *nf* outfitter's (shop)

camiseta [kami'seta] *nf* (*prenda*) tee-shirt; (: *ropa interior*) vest; (*de deportista*) top

camisón [kami'son] *nm* nightdress, nightgown

camorra [ka'morra] *nf*: **armar** o **buscar** ~ to look for trouble, kick up a fuss

campamento [kampa'mento] *nm* camp

campana [kam'pana] *nf* bell; ~ **de cristal** bell jar; ~**da** *nf* peal; ~**rio** *nm* belfry

campanilla [kampa'niʎa] *nf* small bell

campaña [kam'paɲa] *nf* (*MIL*, *POL*) campaign

campechano, a [kampe'tʃano, a] *adj* (*franco*) open

campeón, ona [kampe'on, ona] *nm/f* champion; **campeonato** *nm* championship

campesino, a [kampe'sino, a] *adj* country *cpd*, rural; (*gente*) peasant *cpd* ♦ *nm/f* countryman/woman; (*agricultor*) farmer

campestre [kam'pestre] *adj* country *cpd*, rural

camping ['kampin] (*pl* ~**s**) *nm* camping; (*lugar*) campsite; **ir de** o **hacer** ~ to go camping

campo ['kampo] *nm* (*fuera de la ciudad*) country, countryside; (*AGR*, *ELEC*) field; (*de fútbol*) pitch; (*de golf*) course; (*MIL*) camp; ~ **de batalla** battlefield; ~ **de deportes** sports ground, playing field

camposanto [kampo'santo] *nm* cemetery

camuflaje [kamu'flaxe] *nm* camouflage

cana ['kana] *nf* white o grey hair; **tener** ~**s** to be going grey

Canadá [kana'ða] *nm* Canada; **canadiense** *adj*, *nm/f* Canadian ♦ *nf* fur-lined jacket

canal [ka'nal] *nm* canal; (*GEO*) channel, strait; (*de televisión*) channel; (*de tejado*) gutter; ~ **de Panamá** Panama Canal; ~**izar** *vt* to channel

canalla [ka'naʎa] *nf* rabble, mob ♦ *nm* swine

canalón [kana'lon] *nm* (*conducto vertical*) drainpipe; (*del tejado*) gutter

canapé [kana'pe] (*pl* ~**s**) *nm* sofa, settee; (*CULIN*) canapé

Canarias [ka'narjas] *nfpl*: (**las Islas**) ~ the Canary Islands, the Canaries

canario, a [ka'narjo, a] *adj*, *nm/f* (native) of the Canary Isles ♦ *nm* (*ZOOL*) canary

canasta [ka'nasta] *nf* (round) basket; **canastilla** *nf* small basket; (*de niño*) layette

canasto [ka'nasto] *nm* large basket

cancela [kan'θela] *nf* gate

cancelación [kanθela'θjon] *nf* cancellation

cancelar [kanθe'lar] *vt* to cancel; (*una deuda*) to write off

cáncer ['kanθer] *nm* (*MED*) cancer; (*ASTROLOGÍA*): **C**~ Cancer

cancha ['kantʃa] *nf* (*de baloncesto, tenis etc*) court; (*AM: de fútbol*) pitch

canciller [kanθi'ʎer] *nm* chancellor

canción [kan'θjon] *nf* song; ~ **de cuna** lullaby; **cancionero** *nm* song book

candado [kan'daðo] *nm* padlock

candente [kan'dente] *adj* red-hot; (*fig: tema*) burning

candidato, a [kandi'ðato, a] *nm/f*

candidate
candidez [kandi'ðeθ] *nf* (*sencillez*) simplicity; (*simpleza*) naiveté; **cándido, a** *adj* simple; naive
candil [kan'dil] *nm* oil lamp; **~ejas** *nfpl* (TEATRO) footlights
candor [kan'dor] *nm* (*sinceridad*) frankness; (*inocencia*) innocence
canela [ka'nela] *nf* cinnamon
cangrejo [kan'grexo] *nm* crab
canguro [kan'guro] *nm* kangaroo; **hacer de ~** to babysit
caníbal [ka'niβal] *adj, nm/f* cannibal
canica [ka'nika] *nf* marble
canijo, a [ka'nixo, a] *adj* frail, sickly
canino, a [ka'nino, a] *adj* canine ♦ *nm* canine (tooth)
canjear [kanxe'ar] *vt* to exchange
cano, a ['kano, a] *adj* grey-haired, white-haired
canoa [ka'noa] *nf* canoe
canon ['kanon] *nm* canon; (*pensión*) rent; (COM) tax
canónigo [ka'noniγo] *nm* canon
canonizar [kanoni'θar] *vt* to canonize
canoso, a [ka'noso, a] *adj* grey-haired
cansado, a [kan'saðo, a] *adj* tired, weary; (*tedioso*) tedious, boring
cansancio [kan'sanθjo] *nm* tiredness, fatigue
cansar [kan'sar] *vt* (*fatigar*) to tire, tire out; (*aburrir*) to bore; (*fastidiar*) to bother; **~se** *vr* to tire, get tired; (*aburrirse*) to get bored
cantábrico, a [kan'taβriko, a] *adj* Cantabrian; **mar C~** Bay of Biscay
cantante [kan'tante] *adj* singing ♦ *nm/f* singer
cantar [kan'tar] *vt* to sing ♦ *vi* to sing; (*insecto*) to chirp; (*rechinar*) to squeak ♦ *nm* (*acción*) singing; (*canción*) song; (*poema*) poem
cántara ['kantara] *nf* large pitcher
cántaro ['kantaro] *nm* pitcher, jug; **llover a ~s** to rain cats and dogs
cante ['kante] *nm*: **~ jondo** flamenco singing
cantera [kan'tera] *nf* quarry
cantidad [kanti'ðað] *nf* quantity, amount

cantilena [kanti'lena] *nf* = **cantinela**
cantimplora [kantim'plora] *nf* (*frasco*) water bottle, canteen
cantina [kan'tina] *nf* canteen; (*de estación*) buffet
cantinela [kanti'nela] *nf* ballad, song
canto ['kanto] *nm* singing; (*canción*) song; (*borde*) edge, rim; (*de un cuchillo*) back; **~ rodado** boulder
cantor, a [kan'tor, a] *nm/f* singer
canturrear [kanturre'ar] *vi* to sing softly
canuto [ka'nuto] *nm* (*tubo*) small tube; (*fam: droga*) joint
caña ['kaɲa] *nf* (BOT: *tallo*) stem, stalk; (*carrizo*) reed; (*vaso*) tumbler; (*de cerveza*) glass of beer; (ANAT) shinbone; **~ de azúcar** sugar cane; **~ de pescar** fishing rod
cañada [ka'ɲaða] *nf* (*entre dos montañas*) gully, ravine; (*camino*) cattle track
cáñamo ['kaɲamo] *nm* hemp
cañería [kaɲe'ria] *nf* (*tubo*) pipe
caño ['kaɲo] *nm* (*tubo*) tube, pipe; (*de albañil*) sewer; (MUS) pipe; (*de fuente*) jet
cañón [ka'ɲon] *nm* (MIL) cannon; (*de fusil*) barrel; (GEO) canyon, gorge
caoba [ka'oβa] *nf* mahogany
caos ['kaos] *nm* chaos
cap. *abr* (= *capítulo*) ch
capa ['kapa] *nf* cloak, cape; (GEO) layer, stratum; **so ~ de** under the pretext of; **~ de ozono** ozone layer
capacidad [kapaθi'ðað] *nf* (*medida*) capacity; (*aptitud*) capacity, ability
capacitar [kapaθi'tar] *vt*: **~ a algn para (hacer)** to enable sb to (do)
capar [ka'par] *vt* to castrate, geld
caparazón [kapara'θon] *nm* shell
capataz [kapa'taθ] *nm* foreman
capaz [ka'paθ] *adj* able, capable; (*amplio*) capacious, roomy
capcioso, a [kap'θjoso, a] *adj* wily, deceitful
capellán [kape'ʎan] *nm* chaplain; (*sacerdote*) priest
caperuza [kape'ruθa] *nf* hood
capicúa [kapi'kua] *adj inv* (*número, fecha*) reversible
capilla [ka'piʎa] *nf* chapel

capital [kapi'tal] *adj* capital ♦ *nm* (COM) capital ♦ *nf* (*ciudad*) capital; ~ **social** share *o* authorized capital

capitalismo [kapita'lismo] *nm* capitalism; **capitalista** *adj*, *nm/f* capitalist

capitán [kapi'tan] *nm* captain

capitanear [kapitane'ar] *vt* to captain

capitulación [kapitula'θjon] *nf* (*rendición*) capitulation, surrender; (*acuerdo*) agreement, pact; **capitulaciones (matrimoniales)** *nfpl* marriage contract *sg*

capitular [kapitu'lar] *vi* to come to terms, make an agreement

capítulo [ka'pitulo] *nm* chapter

capó [ka'po] *nm* (AUTO) bonnet

capón [ka'pon] *nm* (*gallo*) capon

capota [ka'pota] *nf* (*de mujer*) bonnet; (AUTO) hood (BRIT), top (US)

capote [ka'pote] *nm* (*abrigo: de militar*) greatcoat; (: *de torero*) cloak

capricho [ka'pritʃo] *nm* whim, caprice; ~**so, a** *adj* capricious

Capricornio [kapri'kornjo] *nm* Capricorn

cápsula ['kapsula] *nf* capsule

captar [kap'tar] *vt* (*comprender*) to understand; (RADIO) to pick up; (*atención, apoyo*) to attract

captura [kap'tura] *nf* capture; (JUR) arrest; **capturar** *vt* to capture; to arrest

capucha [ka'putʃa] *nf* hood, cowl

capullo [ka'puʎo] *nm* (BOT) bud; (ZOOL) cocoon; (*fam*) idiot

caqui ['kaki] *nm* khaki

cara ['kara] *nf* (ANAT, *de moneda*) face; (*aspecto*) appearance; (*de disco*) side; (*fig*) boldness; ~ **a** facing; **de** ~ opposite, facing; **dar la** ~ to face the consequences; ¿~ **o cruz?** heads or tails?; **¡qué ~ (más dura)!** what a nerve!

carabina [kara'βina] *nf* carbine, rifle; (*persona*) chaperone

Caracas [ka'rakas] *n* Caracas

caracol [kara'kol] *nm* (ZOOL) snail; (*concha*) (sea) shell

carácter [ka'rakter] (*pl* **caracteres**) *nm* character; **tener buen/mal** ~ to be good natured/bad tempered

característica [karakte'ristika] *nf* characteristic

característico, a [karakte'ristiko, a] *adj* characteristic

caracterizar [karakteri'θar] *vt* (*distinguir*) to characterize, typify; (*honrar*) to confer (a) distinction on

caradura [kara'ðura] *nm/f*: **es un** ~ he's got a nerve

carajillo [kara'xiʎo] *nm* coffee with a dash of brandy

carajo [ka'raxo] (*fam!*) *nm*: ¡~! shit! (*!*)

caramba [ka'ramba] *excl* good gracious!

carámbano [ka'rambano] *nm* icicle

caramelo [kara'melo] *nm* (*dulce*) sweet; (*azúcar fundida*) caramel

caravana [kara'βana] *nf* caravan; (*fig*) group; (AUTO) tailback

carbón [kar'βon] *nm* coal; **papel** ~ carbon paper; **carboncillo** *nm* (ARTE) charcoal; **carbonero, a** *nm/f* coal merchant; **carbonilla** [-'niʎa] *nf* coal dust

carbonizar [karβoni'θar] *vt* to carbonize; (*quemar*) to char

carbono [kar'βono] *nm* carbon

carburador [karβura'ðor] *nm* carburettor

carburante [karβu'rante] *nm* (*para motor*) fuel

carcajada [karka'xaða] *nf* (loud) laugh, guffaw

cárcel ['karθel] *nf* prison, jail; (TEC) clamp; **carcelero, a** *adj* prison *cpd* ♦ *nm/f* warder

carcoma [kar'koma] *nf* woodworm

carcomer [karko'mer] *vt* to bore into, eat into; (*fig*) to undermine; ~**se** *vr* to become worm-eaten; (*fig*) to decay

cardar [kar'ðar] *vt* (*pelo*) to backcomb

cardenal [karðe'nal] *nm* (REL) cardinal; (MED) bruise

cardíaco, a [kar'ðiako, a] *adj* cardiac, heart *cpd*

cardinal [karði'nal] *adj* cardinal

cardo ['karðo] *nm* thistle

carearse [kare'arse] *vr* to come face to face, meet

carecer [kare'θer] *vi*: ~ **de** to lack, be in need of

carencia [ka'renθja] *nf* lack; (*escasez*) shortage; (MED) deficiency

carente [ka'rente] *adj*: ~ **de** lacking in, devoid of

carestía [kares'tia] *nf* (*escasez*) scarcity, shortage; (*COM*) high cost

careta [ka'reta] *nf* mask

carga ['karɣa] *nf* (*peso, ELEC*) load; (*de barco*) cargo, freight; (*MIL*) charge; (*obligación, responsabilidad*) duty, obligation

cargado, a [kar'ɣaðo, a] *adj* loaded; (*ELEC*) live; (*café, té*) strong; (*cielo*) overcast

cargamento [karɣa'mento] *nm* (*acción*) loading; (*mercancías*) load, cargo

cargar [kar'ɣar] *vt* (*barco, arma*) to load; (*ELEC*) to charge; (*COM: algo en cuenta*) to charge; (*INFORM*) to load ♦ *vi* (*MIL: enemigo*) to charge; (*AUTO*) to load (up); (*inclinarse*) to lean; ~ **con** to pick up, carry away; (*peso, fig*) to shoulder, bear; ~**se** (*fam*) *vr* (*estropear*) to break; (*matar*) to bump off

cargo ['karɣo] *nm* (*puesto*) post, office; (*responsabilidad*) duty, obligation; (*fig*) weight, burden; (*JUR*) charge; **hacerse ~ de** to take charge of *o* responsibility for

carguero [kar'ɣero] *nm* freighter, cargo boat; (*avión*) freight plane

Caribe [ka'riße] *nm*: **el ~** the Caribbean; **del ~** Caribbean

caribeño, a [kari'ßeɲo, a] *adj* Caribbean

caricatura [karika'tura] *nf* caricature

caricia [ka'riθja] *nf* caress

caridad [kari'ðað] *nf* charity

caries ['karjes] *nf inv* (*MED*) tooth decay

cariño [ka'riɲo] *nm* affection, love; (*caricia*) caress; (*en carta*) love ...; **tener ~ a** to be fond of; **~so, a** *adj* affectionate

carisma [ka'risma] *nm* charisma

caritativo, a [karita'tißo, a] *adj* charitable

cariz [ka'riθ] *nm*: **tener** *o* **tomar buen/mal ~** to look good/bad

carmesí [karme'si] *adj, nm* crimson

carmín [kar'min] *nm* lipstick

carnal [kar'nal] *adj* carnal; **primo ~** first cousin

carnaval [karna'ßal] *nm* carnival

carne ['karne] *nf* flesh; (*CULIN*) meat; ~ **de cerdo/cordero/ternera/vaca** pork/lamb/veal/beef; ~ **de gallina** (*fig*): **se me pone la ~ de gallina sólo verlo** I get the creeps just seeing it

carné [kar'ne] (*pl* ~**s**) *nm*: ~ **de conducir** driving licence (*BRIT*), driver's license (*US*); ~ **de identidad** identity card

carnero [kar'nero] *nm* sheep, ram; (*carne*) mutton

carnet [kar'ne] (*pl* ~**s**) *nm* = **carné**

carnicería [karniθe'ria] *nf* butcher's (shop); (*fig: matanza*) carnage, slaughter

carnicero, a [karni'θero, a] *adj* carnivorous ♦ *nm/f* (*tb fig*) butcher; (*carnívoro*) carnivore

carnívoro, a [kar'nißoro, a] *adj* carnivorous

carnoso, a [kar'noso, a] *adj* beefy, fat

caro, a ['karo, a] *adj* dear; (*COM*) dear, expensive ♦ *adv* dear, dearly

carpa ['karpa] *nf* (*pez*) carp; (*de circo*) big top; (*AM: de camping*) tent

carpeta [kar'peta] *nf* folder, file

carpintería [karpinte'ria] *nf* carpentry, joinery; **carpintero** *nm* carpenter

carraspear [karraspe'ar] *vi* to clear one's throat

carraspera [karras'pera] *nf* hoarseness

carrera [ka'rrera] *nf* (*acción*) run(ning); (*espacio recorrido*) run; (*certamen*) race; (*trayecto*) course; (*profesión*) career; (*ESCOL*) course

carreta [ka'rreta] *nf* wagon, cart

carrete [ka'rrete] *nm* reel, spool; (*TEC*) coil

carretera [karre'tera] *nf* (*main*) road, highway; ~ **de circunvalación** ring road; ~ **nacional** ≈ A road (*BRIT*), ≈ state highway (*US*)

carretilla [karre'tiʎa] *nf* trolley; (*AGR*) (wheel)barrow

carril [ka'rril] *nm* furrow; (*de autopista*) lane; (*FERRO*) rail

carrillo [ka'rriʎo] *nm* (*ANAT*) cheek; (*TEC*) pulley

carro ['karro] *nm* cart, wagon; (*MIL*) tank; (*AM: coche*) car

carrocería [karroθe'ria] *nf* bodywork, coachwork

carroña [ka'rroɲa] *nf* carrion *no pl*

carroza [ka'rroθa] *nf* (*carruaje*) coach

carrusel [karru'sel] *nm* merry-go-round, roundabout

carta ['karta] *nf* letter; (*CULIN*) menu; (*naipe*) card; (*mapa*) map; (*JUR*) document; ~ **de ajuste** (*TV*) test card; ~ **de crédito** credit card; ~ **certificada** registered letter; ~ **marítima** chart; ~ **verde** (*AUTO*) green card

cartabón [karta'βon] *nm* set square

cartel [kar'tel] *nm* (*anuncio*) poster, placard; (*ESCOL*) wall chart; (*COM*) cartel; ~**era** *nf* hoarding, billboard; (*en periódico etc*) entertainments guide; **"en ~era"** "showing"

cartera [kar'tera] *nf* (*de bolsillo*) wallet; (*de colegial, cobrador*) satchel; (*de señora*) handbag; (*para documentos*) briefcase; (*COM*) portfolio; **ocupa la ~ de Agricultura** she is Minister of Agriculture

carterista [karte'rista] *nm/f* pickpocket

cartero [kar'tero] *nm* postman

cartilla [kar'tiʎa] *nf* primer, first reading book; ~ **de ahorros** savings book

cartón [kar'ton] *nm* cardboard; ~ **piedra** papier-mâché

cartucho [kar'tutʃo] *nm* (*MIL*) cartridge

cartulina [kartu'lina] *nf* card

casa ['kasa] *nf* house; (*hogar*) home; (*edificio*) building; (*COM*) firm, company; **en** ~ at home; ~ **consistorial** town hall; ~ **de huéspedes** boarding house; ~ **de socorro** first aid post

casado, a [ka'saðo, a] *adj* married ♦ *nm/f* married man/woman

casamiento [kasa'mjento] *nm* marriage, wedding

casar [ka'sar] *vt* to marry; (*JUR*) to quash, annul; ~**se** *vr* to marry, get married

cascabel [kaska'βel] *nm* (small) bell

cascada [kas'kaða] *nf* waterfall

cascanueces [kaska'nweθes] *nm inv* nutcrackers *pl*

cascar [kas'kar] *vt* to crack, split, break (open); ~**se** *vr* to crack, split, break (open)

cáscara ['kaskara] *nf* (*de huevo, fruta seca*) shell; (*de fruta*) skin; (*de limón*) peel

casco ['kasko] *nm* (*de bombero, soldado*) helmet; (*NAUT: de barco*) hull; (*ZOOL: de caballo*) hoof; (*botella*) empty bottle; (*de ciudad*): **el ~ antiguo** the old part; **el ~ urbano** the town centre; **los ~s azules** the UN peace-keeping force, the blue berets

cascote [kas'kote] *nm* rubble

caserío [kase'rio] *nm* hamlet; (*casa*) country house

casero, a [ka'sero, a] *adj* (*pan etc*) home-made ♦ *nm/f* (*propietario*) landlord/lady; (*COM*) house agent; **ser muy** ~ to be home-loving; **"comida casera"** "home cooking"

caseta [ka'seta] *nf* hut; (*para bañista*) cubicle; (*de feria*) stall

casete [ka'sete] *nm o f* cassette

casi ['kasi] *adv* almost, nearly; ~ **nada** hardly anything; ~ **nunca** hardly ever, almost never; ~ **te caes** you almost fell

casilla [ka'siʎa] *nf* (*casita*) hut, cabin; (*TEATRO*) box office; (*AJEDREZ*) square; (*para cartas*) pigeonhole; **casillero** *nm* (*para cartas*) pigeonholes *pl*

casino [ka'sino] *nm* club; (*de juego*) casino

caso ['kaso] *nm* case; **en ~ de ...** in case of ...; **en ~ de que ...** in case ...; **el ~ es que** the fact is that; **en ese ~** in that case; **hacer** ~ **a** to pay attention to; **hacer** *o* **venir al** ~ to be relevant

caspa ['kaspa] *nf* dandruff

cassette [ka'sete] *nm o f* = **casete**

casta ['kasta] *nf* caste; (*raza*) breed; (*linaje*) lineage

castaña [kas'taɲa] *nf* chestnut

castañetear [kastaɲete'ar] *vi* (*dientes*) to chatter

castaño, a [kas'taɲo, a] *adj* chestnut (-coloured), brown ♦ *nm* chestnut tree

castañuelas [kasta'ɲwelas] *nfpl* castanets

castellano, a [kaste'ʎano, a] *adj, nm/f* Castilian ♦ *nm* (*LING*) Castilian, Spanish

castidad [kasti'ðað] *nf* chastity, purity

castigar [kasti'ɣar] *vt* to punish; (*DEPORTE*) to penalize; (*afligir*) to afflict; **castigo** *nm* punishment; (*DEPORTE*) penalty

Castilla [kas'tiʎa] *nf* Castille

castillo [kas'tiʎo] *nm* castle

castizo, a [kas'tiθo, a] *adj* (*LING*) pure; (*de buena casta*) purebred, pedigree

casto, a ['kasto, a] *adj* chaste, pure

castor [kas'tor] *nm* beaver

castrar [kas'trar] *vt* to castrate

castrense [kas'trense] *adj* (*disciplina, vida*) military

casual [ka'swal] *adj* chance, accidental; ~**idad** *nf* chance, accident; (*combinación de circunstancias*) coincidence; **¡qué ~idad!** what a coincidence!

cataclismo [kata'klismo] *nm* cataclysm

catador, a [kata'ðor, a] *nm/f* wine taster

catalán, ana [kata'lan, ana] *adj, nm/f* Catalan ♦ *nm* (*LING*) Catalan

catalizador [kataliθa'ðor] *nm* catalyst; (*AUT*) catalytic convertor

catalogar [katalo'ɣar] *vt* to catalogue; ~ **a algn (de)** (*fig*) to categorize sb (as)

catálogo [ka'taloɣo] *nm* catalogue

Cataluña [kata'luɲa] *nf* Catalonia

catar [ka'tar] *vt* to taste, sample

catarata [kata'rata] *nf* (*GEO*) waterfall; (*MED*) cataract

catarro [ka'tarro] *nm* catarrh; (*constipado*) cold

catástrofe [ka'tastrofe] *nf* catastrophe

catear [kate'ar] (*fam*) *vt* (*examen, alumno*) to fail

cátedra ['kateðra] *nf* (*UNIV*) chair, professorship

catedral [kate'ðral] *nf* cathedral

catedrático, a [kate'ðratiko, a] *nm/f* professor

categoría [kateɣo'ria] *nf* category; (*rango*) rank, standing; (*calidad*) quality; **de ~** (*hotel*) top-class

categórico, a [kate'ɣoriko, a] *adj* categorical

cateto, a ['kateto, a] (*pey*) *nm/f* peasant

catolicismo [katoli'θismo] *nm* Catholicism

católico, a [ka'toliko, a] *adj, nm/f* Catholic

catorce [ka'torθe] *num* fourteen

cauce ['kauθe] *nm* (*de río*) riverbed; (*fig*) channel

caucho ['kautʃo] *nm* rubber; (*AM: llanta*) tyre

caución [kau'θjon] *nf* bail; **caucionar** *vt* (*JUR*) to bail, go bail for

caudal [kau'ðal] *nm* (*de río*) volume, flow; (*fortuna*) wealth; (*abundancia*) abundance; ~**oso, a** *adj* (*río*) large; (*persona*) wealthy, rich

caudillo [kau'ðiʎo] *nm* leader, chief

causa ['kausa] *nf* cause; (*razón*) reason; (*JUR*) lawsuit, case; **a ~ de** because of

causar [kau'sar] *vt* to cause

cautela [kau'tela] *nf* caution, cautiousness; **cauteloso, a** *adj* cautious, wary

cautivar [kauti'ßar] *vt* to capture; (*fig*) to captivate

cautiverio [kauti'ßerjo] *nm* captivity

cautividad [kautißi'ðað] *nf* = **cautiverio**

cautivo, a [kau'tißo, a] *adj, nm/f* captive

cauto, a ['kauto, a] *adj* cautious, careful

cava ['kaßa] *nm* champagne-type wine

cavar [ka'ßar] *vt* to dig

caverna [ka'ßerna] *nf* cave, cavern

cavidad [kaßi'ðað] *nf* cavity

cavilar [kaßi'lar] *vt* to ponder

cayado [ka'jaðo] *nm* (*de pastor*) crook; (*de obispo*) crozier

cayendo *etc vb ver* **caer**

caza ['kaθa] *nf* (*acción: gen*) hunting; (*: con fusil*) shooting; (*una ~*) hunt, chase; (*animales*) game ♦ *nm* (*AVIAT*) fighter

cazador, a [kaθa'ðor, a] *nm/f* hunter; **cazadora** *nf* jacket

cazar [ka'θar] *vt* to hunt; (*perseguir*) to chase; (*prender*) to catch

cazo ['kaθo] *nm* saucepan

cazuela [ka'θwela] *nf* (*vasija*) pan; (*guisado*) casserole

CD *abbr* (= *compact disc*) CD

CD-ROM *abbr m* CD-ROM

CE *nf abr* (= *Comunidad Europea*) EC

cebada [θe'ßaða] *nf* barley

cebar [θe'ßar] *vt* (*animal*) to fatten (up); (*anzuelo*) to bait; (*MIL, TEC*) to prime

cebo ['θeßo] *nm* (*para animales*) feed, food; (*para peces, fig*) bait; (*de arma*) charge

cebolla [θe'ßoʎa] *nf* onion; **cebollín** *nm*

spring onion

cebra [ˈθeβra] *nf* zebra

cecear [θeθeˈar] *vi* to lisp; **ceceo** *nm* lisp

ceder [θeˈðer] *vt* to hand over, give up, part with ♦ *vi* (*renunciar*) to give in, yield; (*disminuir*) to diminish, decline; (*romperse*) to give way

cedro [ˈθeðro] *nm* cedar

cédula [ˈθeðula] *nf* certificate, document

cegar [θeˈɣar] *vt* to blind; (*tubería etc*) to block up, stop up ♦ *vi* to go blind; **~se** *vr*: **~se (de)** to be blinded (by)

ceguera [θeˈɣera] *nf* blindness

CEI *abbr* (= *Confederación de Estados Independientes*) CIS

ceja [ˈθexa] *nf* eyebrow

cejar [θeˈxar] *vi* (*fig*) to back down

celada [θeˈlaða] *nf* ambush, trap

celador, a [θelaˈðor, a] *nm/f* (*de edificio*) watchman; (*de museo etc*) attendant

celda [ˈθelda] *nf* cell

celebración [θeleβraˈθjon] *nf* celebration

celebrar [θeleˈβrar] *vt* to celebrate; (*alabar*) to praise ♦ *vi* to be glad; **~se** *vr* to occur, take place

célebre [ˈθelebre] *adj* famous

celebridad [θeleβriˈðað] *nf* fame; (*persona*) celebrity

celeste [θeˈleste] *adj* sky-blue; celestial, heavenly

celestial [θelesˈtjal] *adj* celestial, heavenly

celibato [θeliˈβato] *nm* celibacy

célibe [ˈθeliβe] *adj*, *nm/f* celibate

celo¹ [ˈθelo] *nm* zeal; (*REL*) fervour; (*ZOOL*): **en ~** on heat; **~s** *nmpl* (*envidia*) jealousy *sg*; **tener ~s** to be jealous

celo² [ˈθelo] ® *nm* Sellotape ®

celofán [θeloˈfan] *nm* cellophane

celoso, a [θeˈloso, a] *adj* (*envidioso*) jealous; (*trabajador*) zealous; (*desconfiado*) suspicious

celta [ˈθelta] *adj* Celtic ♦ *nm/f* Celt

célula [ˈθelula] *nf* cell; **~ solar** solar cell

celulitis [θeluˈlitis] *nf* cellulite

celuloide [θeluˈloiðe] *nm* celluloid

cementerio [θemenˈterjo] *nm* cemetery, graveyard

cemento [θeˈmento] *nm* cement;

(*hormigón*) concrete; (*AM*: *cola*) glue

cena [ˈθena] *nf* evening meal, dinner

cenagal [θenaˈɣal] *nm* bog, quagmire

cenar [θeˈnar] *vt* to have for dinner ♦ *vi* to have dinner

cenicero [θeniˈθero] *nm* ashtray

cenit [θeˈnit] *nm* zenith

ceniza [θeˈniθa] *nf* ash, ashes *pl*

censo [ˈθenso] *nm* census; **~ electoral** electoral roll

censura [θenˈsura] *nf* (*POL*) censorship; (*moral*) censure, criticism

censurar [θensuˈrar] *vt* (*idea*) to censure; (*cortar*: *película*) to censor

centella [θenˈteʎa] *nf* spark

centellear [θenteʎeˈar] *vi* (*metal*) to gleam; (*estrella*) to twinkle; (*fig*) to sparkle

centenar [θenteˈnar] *nm* hundred

centenario, a [θenteˈnarjo, a] *adj* centenary; hundred-year-old ♦ *nm* centenary

centeno [θenˈteno] *nm* (*BOT*) rye

centésimo, a [θenˈtesimo, a] *adj* hundredth

centígrado [θenˈtiɣraðo] *adj* centigrade

centímetro [θenˈtimetro] *nm* centimetre (*BRIT*), centimeter (*US*)

céntimo [ˈθentimo] *nm* cent

centinela [θentiˈnela] *nm* sentry, guard

centollo [θenˈtoʎo] *nm* spider crab

central [θenˈtral] *adj* central ♦ *nf* head office; (*TEC*) plant; (*TEL*) exchange; **~ eléctrica** power station; **~ nuclear** nuclear power station

centralizar [θentraliˈθar] *vt* to centralize

centrar [θenˈtrar] *vt* to centre

céntrico, a [ˈθentriko, a] *adj* central

centrifugar [θentrifuˈɣar] *vt* to spin-dry

centrista [θenˈtrista] *adj* centre *cpd*

centro [ˈθentro] *nm* centre; **~ comercial** shopping centre; **~ juvenil** youth club

centroamericano, a [θentroameriˈkano, a] *adj*, *nm/f* Central American

ceñido, a [θeˈɲiðo, a] *adj* (*chaqueta*, *pantalón*) tight(-fitting)

ceñir [θeˈɲir] *vt* (*rodear*) to encircle, surround; (*ajustar*) to fit (tightly); (*apretar*) to tighten

ceño ['θeɲo] nm frown, scowl; **fruncir el ~** to frown, knit one's brow

CEOE nf abr (ESP: = Confederación Española de Organizaciones Empresariales) ≈ CBI (BRIT), employers' organization

cepillar [θepi'ʎar] vt to brush; (madera) to plane (down)

cepillo [θe'piʎo] nm brush; (para madera) plane; **~ de dientes** toothbrush

cera ['θera] nf wax

cerámica [θe'ramika] nf pottery; (arte) ceramics

cerca ['θerka] nf fence ♦ adv near, nearby, close ♦ nm: **~s** foreground sg; **~ de** near, close to

cercanía [θerka'nia] nf nearness, closeness; **~s** nfpl (afueras) outskirts, suburbs

cercano, a [θer'kano, a] adj close, near

cercar [θer'kar] vt to fence in; (rodear) to surround

cerciorar [θerθjo'rar] vt (asegurar) to assure; **~se** vr (descubrir) to find out; (asegurarse) to make sure

cerco ['θerko] nm (AGR) enclosure; (AM) fence; (MIL) siege

cerdo, a ['θerðo, a] nm/f pig/sow

cereal [θere'al] nm cereal; **~es** nmpl cereals, grain sg

cerebro [θe'reβro] nm brain; (fig) brains pl

ceremonia [θere'monja] nf ceremony; **ceremonial** adj, nm ceremonial; **ceremonioso, a** adj ceremonious; (cumplido) formal

cereza [θe'reθa] nf cherry

cerilla [θe'riʎa] nf (fósforo) match

cernerse [θer'nerse] vr to hover

cero ['θero] nm nothing, zero

cerrado, a [θe'rraðo, a] adj closed, shut; (con llave) locked; (tiempo) cloudy, overcast; (curva) sharp; (acento) thick, broad

cerradura [θerra'ðura] nf (acción) closing; (mecanismo) lock

cerrajero [θerra'xero] nm locksmith

cerrar [θe'rrar] vt to close, shut; (paso, carretera) to close; (grifo) to turn off; (cuenta, negocio) to close ♦ vi to close, shut; (la noche) to come down; **~se** vr to close, shut; **~ con llave** to lock; **~ un trato** to strike a bargain

cerro ['θerro] nm hill

cerrojo [θe'rroxo] nm (herramienta) bolt; (de puerta) latch

certamen [θer'tamen] nm competition, contest

certero, a [θer'tero, a] adj (gen) accurate

certeza [θer'teθa] nf certainty

certidumbre [θerti'ðumbre] nf = **certeza**

certificado [θertifi'kaðo] nm certificate

certificar [θertifi'kar] vt (asegurar, atestar) to certify

cervatillo [θerβa'tiʎo] nm fawn

cervecería [θerβeθe'ria] nf (fábrica) brewery; (bar) public house, pub

cerveza [θer'βeθa] nf beer

cesante [θe'sante] adj redundant

cesantía [θesan'tia] nf unemployment

cesar [θe'sar] vi to cease, stop ♦ vt (funcionario) to remove from office

cesárea [θe'sarea] nf (MED) Caesarean operation o section

cese ['θese] nm (de trabajo) dismissal; (de pago) suspension

césped ['θespeð] nm grass, lawn

cesta ['θesta] nf basket

cesto ['θesto] nm (large) basket, hamper

cetro ['θetro] nm sceptre

cfr abr (= confróntese) cf.

chabacano, a [tʃaβa'kano, a] adj vulgar, coarse

chabola [tʃa'βola] nf shack; **~s** nfpl shanty town sg

chacal [tʃa'kal] nm jackal

chacha ['tʃatʃa] (fam) nf maid

cháchara ['tʃatʃara] nf chatter; **estar de ~** to chatter away

chacra ['tʃakra] (AM) nf smallholding

chafar [tʃa'far] vt (aplastar) to crush; (arruinar) to ruin

chal [tʃal] nm shawl

chalado, a [tʃa'laðo, a] (fam) adj crazy

chalé [tʃa'le] (pl **~s**) nm villa; ≈ detached house

chaleco [tʃa'leko] nm waistcoat, vest (US); **~ salvavidas** life jacket

chalet [tʃa'le] (pl ~s) nm = **chalé**

champán [tʃam'pan] nm champagne

champaña [tʃam'paɲa] nm = **champán**

champiñón [tʃampi'ɲon] nm mushroom

champú [tʃam'pu] (pl **champúes**, **champús**) nm shampoo

chamuscar [tʃamus'kar] vt to scorch, sear, singe

chance [tʃanθe] (AM) nm chance

chancho, a [tʃantʃo, a] (AM) nm/f pig

chanchullo [tʃan'tʃuʎo] (fam) nm fiddle

chandal [tʃan'dal] nm tracksuit

chantaje [tʃan'taxe] nm blackmail

chapa ['tʃapa] nf (de metal) plate, sheet; (de madera) board, panel; (AM: AUTO) number (BRIT) o license (US) plate

chaparrón [tʃapa'rron] nm downpour, cloudburst

chapotear [tʃapote'ar] vi to splash about

chapucero, a [tʃapu'θero, a] adj rough, crude ♦ nm/f bungler

chapurrear [tʃapurre'ar] vt (idioma) to speak badly

chapuza [tʃa'puθa] nf botched job

chapuzón [tʃapu'θon] nm: **darse un ~** to go for a dip

chaqueta [tʃa'keta] nf jacket

chaquetón [tʃake'ton] nm long jacket

charca ['tʃarka] nf pond, pool

charco ['tʃarko] nm pool, puddle

charcutería [tʃarkute'ria] nf (tienda) shop selling chiefly pork meat products; (productos) cooked pork meats pl

charla ['tʃarla] nf talk, chat; (conferencia) lecture

charlar [tʃar'lar] vi to talk, chat

charlatán, ana [tʃarla'tan, ana] nm/f chatterbox; (estafador) trickster

charol [tʃa'rol] nm varnish; (cuero) patent leather

chascarrillo [tʃaska'rriʎo] (fam) nm funny story

chasco ['tʃasko] nm (broma) trick, joke; (desengaño) disappointment

chasis ['tʃasis] nm inv chassis

chasquear [tʃaske'ar] vt (látigo) to crack; (lengua) to click; **chasquido** nm crack; click

chatarra [tʃa'tarra] nf scrap (metal)

chato, a ['tʃato, a] adj flat; (nariz) snub

chaval, a [tʃa'βal, a] nm/f kid, lad/lass

checo, a ['tʃeko, a] adj, nm/f Czech ♦ nm (LING) Czech

checo(e)slovaco, a [tʃeko(e)slo'βako, a] adj, nm/f Czech, Czechoslovak

Checo(e)slovaquia [tʃeko(e)slo'βakja] nf Czechoslovakia

cheque ['tʃeke] nm cheque (BRIT), check (US); **~ de viajero** traveller's cheque (BRIT), traveler's check (US)

chequeo [tʃe'keo] nm (MED) check-up; (AUTO) service

chequera [tʃe'kera] (AM) nf chequebook (BRIT), checkbook (US)

chicano, a [tʃi'kano, a] adj, nm/f chicano

chícharo ['tʃitʃaro] (AM) nm pea

chichón [tʃi'tʃon] nm bump, lump

chicle ['tʃikle] nm chewing gum

chico, a ['tʃiko, a] adj small, little ♦ nm/f (niño) child; (muchacho) boy/girl

chiflado, a [tʃi'flaðo, a] adj crazy

chiflar [tʃi'flar] vt to hiss, boo

Chile ['tʃile] nm Chile; **chileno, a** adj, nm/f Chilean

chile ['tʃile] nm chilli pepper

chillar [tʃi'ʎar] vi (persona) to yell, scream; (animal salvaje) to howl; (cerdo) to squeal; (puerta) to creak

chillido [tʃi'ʎiðo] nm (de persona) yell, scream; (de animal) howl; (de frenos) screech(ing)

chillón, ona [tʃi'ʎon, ona] adj (niño) noisy; (color) loud, gaudy

chimenea [tʃime'nea] nf chimney; (hogar) fireplace

China ['tʃina] nf: **(la) ~** China

chinche ['tʃintʃe] nf (insecto) (bed)bug; (TEC) drawing pin (BRIT), thumbtack (US) ♦ nm/f nuisance, pest

chincheta [tʃin'tʃeta] nf drawing pin (BRIT), thumbtack (US)

chino, a ['tʃino, a] adj, nm/f Chinese ♦ nm (LING) Chinese

chipirón [tʃipi'ron] nm (ZOOL, CULIN) squid

Chipre ['tʃipre] nf Cyprus; **chipriota** adj, nm/f Cypriot

chiquillo, a [tʃi'kiʎo, a] nm/f (fam) kid

chiringuito [tʃirin'vito] nm small open-air

bar

chiripa [tʃi'ripa] *nf* fluke

chirriar [tʃi'rrjar] *vi (goznes etc)* to creak, squeak; *(pájaros)* to chirp, sing

chirrido [tʃi'rriðo] *nm* creak(ing), squeak(ing); *(de pájaro)* chirp(ing)

chis [tʃis] *excl* sh!

chisme ['tʃisme] *nm (habladurías)* piece of gossip; *(fam: objeto)* thingummyjig

chismoso, a [tʃis'moso, a] *adj* gossiping ♦ *nm/f* gossip

chispa ['tʃispa] *nf* spark; *(fig)* sparkle; *(ingenio)* wit; *(fam)* drunkenness

chispear [tʃispe'ar] *vi* to spark; *(lloviznar)* to drizzle

chisporrotear [tʃisporrote'ar] *vi (fuego)* to throw out sparks; *(leña)* to crackle; *(aceite)* to hiss, splutter

chiste ['tʃiste] *nm* joke, funny story

chistoso, a [tʃis'toso, a] *adj (gracioso)* funny, amusing; *(bromista)* witty

chivo, a ['tʃiβo, a] *nm/f* (billy-/nanny-) goat; ~ **expiatorio** scapegoat

chocante [tʃo'kante] *adj* startling; *(extraño)* odd; *(ofensivo)* shocking

chocar [tʃo'kar] *vi (coches etc)* to collide, crash; *(MIL, fig)* to clash ♦ *vt* to shock; *(sorprender)* to startle; ~ **con** to collide with; *(fig)* to run into, run up against; ¡**chócala!** *(fam)* put it there!

chochear [tʃotʃe'ar] *vi* to dodder, be senile

chocho, a ['tʃotʃo, a] *adj* doddering, senile; *(fig)* soft, doting

chocolate [tʃoko'late] *adj, nm* chocolate; **chocolatina** *nf* chocolate

chofer [tʃo'fer] *nm* = **chófer**

chófer ['tʃofer] *nm* driver

chollo ['tʃoʎo] *(fam) nm* bargain, snip

choque *etc* ['tʃoke] *vb ver* **chocar** ♦ *nm (impacto)* impact; *(golpe)* jolt; *(AUTO)* crash; *(fig)* conflict; ~ **frontal** head-on collision

chorizo [tʃo'riθo] *nm* hard pork sausage, *(type of)* salami

chorrada [tʃo'rraða] *(fam) nf:* ¡**es una ~!** that's crap! *(!)*; **decir ~s** to talk crap *(!)*

chorrear [tʃorre'ar] *vi* to gush (out), spout (out); *(gotear)* to drip, trickle

chorro ['tʃorro] *nm* jet; *(fig)* stream

choza ['tʃoθa] *nf* hut, shack

chubasco [tʃu'βasko] *nm* squall

chubasquero [tʃuβas'kero] *nm* lightweight raincoat

chuchería [tʃutʃe'ria] *nf* trinket

chuleta [tʃu'leta] *nf* chop, cutlet

chulo ['tʃulo] *nm (pícaro)* rascal; *(rufián)* pimp

chupar [tʃu'par] *vt* to suck; *(absorber)* to absorb; **~se** *vr* to grow thin

chupete [tʃu'pete] *nm* dummy *(BRIT)*, pacifier *(US)*

churro, a ['tʃurro, a] *adj* coarse ♦ *nm* (type of) fritter

chusma ['tʃusma] *nf* rabble, mob

chutar [tʃu'tar] *vi (DEPORTE)* to shoot (at goal)

Cía *abr* (= *compañía*). Co.

cianuro [θja'nuro] *nm* cyanide

cicatriz [θika'triθ] *nf* scar; **~arse** *vr* to heal (up), form a scar

ciclismo [θi'klismo] *nm* cycling

ciclista [θi'lista] *adj* cycle *cpd* ♦ *nm/f* cyclist

ciclo ['θiklo] *nm* cycle

ciclón [θi'klon] *nm* cyclone

ciego, a ['θjeɣo, a] *adj* blind ♦ *nm/f* blind man/woman

cielo ['θjelo] *nm* sky; *(REL)* heaven; ¡**~s!** good heavens!

ciempiés [θjem'pjes] *nm inv* centipede

cien [θjen] *num ver* **ciento**

ciénaga ['θjenaɣa] *nf* marsh, swamp

ciencia ['θjenθja] *nf* science; **~s** *nfpl* *(ESCOL)* science *sg*; **~-ficción** *nf* science fiction

cieno ['θjeno] *nm* mud, mire

científico, a [θjen'tifiko, a] *adj* scientific ♦ *nm/f* scientist

ciento ['θjento] *(tb:* **cien***) num* hundred; **pagar al 10 por ~** to pay at 10 per cent

cierne *etc* ['θjerne] *nm:* **en ~** in blossom

cierre *etc* ['θjerre] *vb ver* **cerrar** ♦ *nm* closing, shutting; *(con llave)* locking; ~ **de cremallera** zip (fastener)

cierro *etc vb ver* **cerrar**

cierto, a ['θjerto, a] *adj* sure, certain; *(un tal)* a certain; *(correcto)* right, correct; ~

hombre a certain man; **ciertas personas** certain *o* some people; **sí, es ~** yes, that's correct

ciervo ['θjerßo] *nm* (ZOOL) deer; (: *macho*) stag

cierzo ['θjerθo] *nm* north wind

cifra ['θifra] *nf* number, numeral; (*cantidad*) number, quantity; (*secreta*) code

cifrar [θi'frar] *vt* to code, write in code; (*resumir*) to abridge

cigala [θi'γala] *nf* Norway lobster

cigarra [θi'γarra] *nf* cicada

cigarrera [θiγa'rrera] *nf* cigar case

cigarrillo [θiγa'rriλo] *nm* cigarette

cigarro [θi'γarro] *nm* cigarette; (*puro*) cigar

cigüeña [θi'γweŋa] *nf* stork

cilíndrico, a [θi'lindriko, a] *adj* cylindrical

cilindro [θi'lindro] *nm* cylinder

cima ['θima] *nf* (*de montaña*) top, peak; (*de árbol*) top; (*fig*) height

cimbrearse [θimbre'arse] *vr* to sway

cimentar [θimen'tar] *vt* to lay the foundations of; (*fig: fundar*) to found

cimiento [θi'mjento] *nm* foundation

cinc [θink] *nm* zinc

cincel [θin'θel] *nm* chisel; **~ar** *vt* to chisel

cinco ['θinko] *num* five

cincuenta [θin'kwenta] *num* fifty

cine ['θine] *nm* cinema

cineasta [θine'asta] *nm/f* (*director de cine*) film director

cinematográfico, a [θinemato'γrafiko, a] *adj* cine-, film *cpd*

cínico, a ['θiniko, a] *adj* cynical ♦ *nm/f* cynic

cinismo [θi'nismo] *nm* cynicism

cinta ['θinta] *nf* band, strip; (*de tela*) ribbon; (*película*) reel; (*de máquina de escribir*) ribbon; **~ adhesiva** sticky tape; **~ de vídeo** videotape; **~ magnetofónica** tape; **~ métrica** tape measure

cinto ['θinto] *nm* belt

cintura [θin'tura] *nf* waist

cinturón [θintu'ron] *nm* belt; **~ de seguridad** safety belt

ciprés [θi'pres] *nm* cypress (tree)

circo ['θirko] *nm* circus

circuito [θir'kwito] *nm* circuit

circulación [θirkula'θjon] *nf* circulation; (AUTO) traffic

circular [θirku'lar] *adj, nf* circular ♦ *vi, vt* to circulate ♦ *vi* (AUTO) to drive; **"circule por la derecha"** "keep (to the) right"

círculo ['θirkulo] *nm* circle; **~ vicioso** vicious circle

circuncidar [θirkunθi'dar] *vt* to circumcise

circundar [θirkun'dar] *vt* to surround

circunferencia [θirkunfe'renθja] *nf* circumference

circunscribir [θirkunskri'ßir] *vt* to circumscribe; **~se** *vr* to be limited

circunscripción [θirkunskrip'θjon] *nf* division; (POL) constituency

circunspecto, a [θirkuns'pekto, a] *adj* circumspect, cautious

circunstancia [θirkuns'tanθja] *nf* circumstance

cirio ['θirjo] *nm* (wax) candle

ciruela [θi'rwela] *nf* plum; **~ pasa** prune

cirugía [θiru'xia] *nf* surgery; **~ estética** *o* **plástica** plastic surgery

cirujano [θiru'xano] *nm* surgeon

cisne ['θisne] *nm* swan

cisterna [θis'terna] *nf* cistern, tank

cita ['θita] *nf* appointment, meeting; (*de novios*) date; (*referencia*) quotation

citación [θita'θjon] *nf* (JUR) summons *sg*

citar [θi'tar] *vt* (*gen*) to make an appointment with; (JUR) to summons; (*un autor, texto*) to quote; **~se** *vr*: **se citaron en el cine** they arranged to meet at the cinema

cítricos ['θitrikos] *nmpl* citrus fruit(s)

ciudad [θju'ðað] *nf* town; (*más grande*) city; **~anía** *nf* citizenship; **~ano, a** *nm/f* citizen

cívico, a ['θißiko, a] *adj* civic

civil [θi'ßil] *adj* civil ♦ *nm* (*guardia*) policeman

civilización [θißiliθa'θjon] *nf* civilization

civilizar [θißili'θar] *vt* to civilize

civismo [θi'ßismo] *nm* public spirit

cizaña [θi'θaŋa] *nf* (*fig*) discord

cl. *abr* (= *centilitro*) cl.

clamar [kla'mar] *vt* to clamour for, cry

out for ♦ *vi* to cry out, clamour
clamor [kla'mor] *nm* (*grito*) cry, shout; (*fig*) clamour, protest
clandestino, a [klandes'tino, a] *adj* clandestine; (*POL*) underground
clara ['klara] *nf* (*de huevo*) egg white
claraboya [klara'βoja] *nf* skylight
clarear [klare'ar] *vi* (*el día*) to dawn; (*el cielo*) to clear up, brighten up; ~**se** *vr* to be transparent
clarete [kla'rete] *nm* rosé (wine)
claridad [klari'ðað] *nf* (*del día*) brightness; (*de estilo*) clarity
clarificar [klarifi'kar] *vt* to clarify
clarín [kla'rin] *nm* bugle
clarinete [klari'nete] *nm* clarinet
clarividencia [klariβi'ðenθja] *nf* clairvoyance; (*fig*) far-sightedness
claro, a ['klaro, a] *adj* clear; (*luminoso*) bright; (*color*) light; (*evidente*) clear, evident; (*poco espeso*) thin ♦ *nm* (*en bosque*) clearing ♦ *adv* clearly ♦ *excl* (*tb*: ~ *que sí*) of course!
clase ['klase] *nf* class; ~ **alta/media/obrera** upper/middle/working class; ~**s particulares** private lessons, private tuition *sg*
clásico, a ['klasiko, a] *adj* classical; (*fig*) classic
clasificación [klasifika'θjon] *nf* classification; (*DEPORTE*) league (table)
clasificar [klasifi'kar] *vt* to classify
claudicar [klauði'kar] *vi* (*fig*) to back down
claustro ['klaustro] *nm* cloister
cláusula ['klausula] *nf* clause
clausura [klau'sura] *nf* closing, closure; **clausurar** *vt* (*congreso etc*) to bring to a close
clavar [kla'βar] *vt* (*clavo*) to hammer in; (*cuchillo*) to stick, thrust; (*tablas etc*) to nail (together)
clave ['klaβe] *nf* key; (*MUS*) clef
clavel [kla'βel] *nm* carnation
clavícula [kla'βikula] *nf* collar bone
clavija [kla'βixa] *nf* peg, dowel, pin; (*ELEC*) plug
clavo ['klaβo] *nm* (*de metal*) nail; (*BOT*) clove

claxon ['klakson] (*pl* ~**s**) *nm* horn
clemencia [kle'menθja] *nf* mercy, clemency
cleptómano, a [klep'tomano, a] *nm/f* kleptomaniac
clerical [kleri'kal] *adj* clerical
clérigo ['klerivo] *nm* priest
clero ['klero] *nm* clergy
cliché [kli'tʃe] *nm* cliché; (*FOTO*) negative
cliente, a ['kljente, a] *nm/f* client, customer
clientela [kljen'tela] *nf* clientele, customers *pl*
clima ['klima] *nm* climate
climatizado, a [klimati'θaðo, a] *adj* air-conditioned
clímax ['klimaks] *nm inv* climax
clínica ['klinika] *nf* clinic; (*particular*) private hospital
clip [klip] (*pl* ~**s**) *nm* paper clip
clítoris ['klitoris] *nm inv* (*ANAT*) clitoris
cloaca [klo'aka] *nf* sewer
cloro ['kloro] *nm* chlorine
club [klub] (*pl* ~**s** *o* ~**es**) *nm* club; ~ **de jóvenes** youth club
cm *abr* (= *centímetro, centímetros*) cm
C.N.T. (*ESP*) *abr* = Confederación Nacional de Trabajo
coacción [koak'θjon] *nf* coercion, compulsion; **coaccionar** *vt* to compel
coagular [koavu'lar] *vt* (*leche, sangre*) to clot; ~**se** *vr* to clot; **coágulo** *nm* clot
coalición [koali'θjon] *nf* coalition
coartada [koar'taða] *nf* alibi
coartar [koar'tar] *vt* to limit, restrict
coba ['koβa] *nf*: **dar** ~ **a uno** to soft-soap sb
cobarde [ko'βarðe] *adj* cowardly ♦ *nm* coward; **cobardía** *nf* cowardice
cobaya [ko'βaja] *nf* guinea pig
cobertizo [koβer'tiθo] *nm* shelter
cobertura [koβer'tura] *nf* cover
cobija [ko'βixa] (*AM*) *nf* blanket
cobijar [koβi'xar] *vt* (*cubrir*) to cover; (*abrigar*) to shelter; **cobijo** *nm* shelter
cobra ['koβra] *nf* cobra
cobrador, a [koβra'ðor, a] *nm/f* (*de autobús*) conductor/conductress; (*de impuestos, gas*) collector

cobrar [ko'ßrar] *vt* (*cheque*) to cash; (*sueldo*) to collect, draw; (*objeto*) to recover; (*precio*) to charge; (*deuda*) to collect ♦ *vi* to draw one's pay; **~se** *vr* to recover, get well; **cóbrese al entregar** cash on delivery

cobre ['koßre] *nm* copper; **~s** *nmpl* (*MUS*) brass instruments

cobro ['koßro] *nm* (*de cheque*) cashing; (*pago*) payment; **presentar al ~** to cash

Coca-Cola ['koka'kola] ® *nf* Coca-Cola ®

cocaína [koka'ina] *nf* cocaine

cocción [kok'θjon] *nf* (*CULIN*) cooking; (: *el hervir*) boiling

cocear [koθe'ar] *vi* to kick

cocer [ko'θer] *vt*, *vi* to cook; (*en agua*) to boil; (*en horno*) to bake

coche ['kotʃe] *nm* (*AUTO*) car (*BRIT*), automobile (*US*); (*de tren, de caballos*) coach, carriage; (*para niños*) pram (*BRIT*), baby carriage (*US*); **ir en ~** to drive; **~ celular** Black Maria, prison van; **~ de bomberos** fire engine; **~ fúnebre** hearse; **coche-cama** (*pl* **coches-cama**) *nm* (*FERRO*) sleeping car, sleeper

cochera [ko'tʃera] *nf* garage; (*de autobuses, trenes*) depot

coche restaurante (*pl* **coches restaurante**) *nm* (*FERRO*) dining car, diner

cochino, a [ko'tʃino, a] *adj* filthy, dirty ♦ *nm/f* pig

cocido [ko'θiðo] *nm* stew

cocina [ko'θina] *nf* kitchen; (*aparato*) cooker, stove; (*acto*) cookery; **~ eléctrica/de gas** electric/gas cooker; **~ francesa** French cuisine; **cocinar** *vt*, *vi* to cook

cocinero, a [koθi'nero, a] *nm/f* cook

coco ['koko] *nm* coconut

cocodrilo [koko'ðrilo] *nm* crocodile

cocotero [koko'tero] *nm* coconut palm

cóctel ['koktel] *nm* cocktail

codazo [ko'ðaθo] *nm*: **dar un ~ a uno** to nudge sb

codicia [ko'ðiθja] *nf* greed; (*fig*) lust; **codiciar** *vt* to covet; **codicioso, a** *adj* covetous

código ['koðiɣo] *nm* code; **~ de barras** bar code; **~ civil** common law; **~ de (la)**

circulación highway code; **~ postale** postcode

codillo [ko'ðiʎo] *nm* (*ZOOL*) knee; (*TEC*) elbow (joint)

codo ['koðo] *nm* (*ANAT, de tubo*) elbow; (*ZOOL*) knee

codorniz [koðor'niθ] *nf* quail

coerción [koer'θjon] *nf* coercion

coetáneo, a [koe'taneo, a] *adj, nm/f* contemporary

coexistir [koe(k)sis'tir] *vi* to coexist

cofradía [kofra'ðia] *nf* brotherhood, fraternity

cofre ['kofre] *nm* (*de joyas*) case; (*de dinero*) chest

coger [ko'xer] (*ESP*) *vt* to take (hold of); (*objeto caído*) to pick up; (*frutas*) to pick, harvest; (*resfriado, ladrón, pelota*) to catch ♦ *vi*: **~ por el buen camino** to take the right road; **~se** *vr* (*el dedo*) to catch; **~se a algo** to get hold of sth

cogollo [ko'ɣoʎo] *nm* (*de lechuga*) heart

cogote [ko'ɣote] *nm* back o nape of the neck

cohabitar [koaßi'tar] *vi* to live together, cohabit

cohecho [ko'etʃo] *nm* (*acción*) bribery; (*soborno*) bribe

coherente [koe'rente] *adj* coherent

cohesión [koe'sjon] *nm* cohesion

cohete [ko'ete] *nm* rocket

cohibido, a [koi'ßiðo, a] *adj* (*PSICO*) inhibited; (*tímido*) shy

cohibir [koi'ßir] *vt* to restrain, restrict

coincidencia [koinθi'ðenθja] *nf* coincidence

coincidir [koinθi'ðir] *vi* (*en idea*) to coincide, agree; (*en lugar*) to coincide

coito ['koito] *nm* intercourse, coitus

coja *etc vb ver* **coger**

cojear [koxe'ar] *vi* (*persona*) to limp, hobble; (*mueble*) to wobble, rock

cojera [ko'xera] *nf* lameness; (*andar cojo*) limp

cojín [ko'xin] *nm* cushion; **cojinete** *nm* small cushion, pad; (*TEC*) ball bearing

cojo, a *etc* [ko'xo, a] *vb ver* **coger** ♦ *adj* (*que no puede andar*) lame, crippled; (*mueble*) wobbly ♦ *nm/f* lame person, cripple

cojón [ko'xon] (*fam*) *nm*: ¡**cojones!** shit! (*!*); **cojonudo, a** (*fam*) *adj* great, fantastic

col [kol] *nf* cabbage; **~es de Bruselas** Brussels sprouts

cola ['kola] *nf* tail; (*de gente*) queue; (*lugar*) end, last place; (*para pegar*) glue, gum; **hacer ~** to queue (up)

colaborador, a [kolaβora'ðor, a] *nm/f* collaborator

colaborar [kolaβo'rar] *vi* to collaborate

colada [ko'laða] *nf*: **hacer la ~** to do the washing

colador [kola'ðor] *nm* (*de té*) strainer; (*para verduras etc*) colander

colapso [ko'lapso] *nm* collapse; **~ nervioso** nervous breakdown

colar [ko'lar] *vt* (*líquido*) to strain off; (*metal*) to cast ♦ *vi* to ooze, seep (through); **~se en** to get into the queue; **~se en** to get into without paying; (*fiesta*) to gatecrash

colateral [kolate'ral] *nm* collateral

colcha ['koltʃa] *nf* bedspread

colchón [kol'tʃon] *nm* mattress; **~ inflable** *o* **neumático** air bed, air mattress

colchoneta [koltʃo'neta] *nf* (*en gimnasio*) mattress

colear [kole'ar] *vi* (*perro*) to wag its tail

colección [kolek'θjon] *nf* collection; **coleccionar** *vt* to collect; **coleccionista** *nm/f* collector

colecta [ko'lekta] *nf* collection

colectivo, a [kolek'tiβo, a] *adj* collective, joint ♦ *nm* (*AM*) (small) bus

colector [kolek'tor] *nm* collector; (*sumidero*) sewer

colega [ko'leɣa] *nm/f* colleague

colegial, a [kole'xjal, a] *nm/f* schoolboy/girl

colegio [ko'lexjo] *nm* college; (*escuela*) school; (*de abogados etc*) association; **~ electoral** polling station; **~ mayor** hall of residence

colegir [kole'xir] *vt* (*juntar*) to collect, gather; (*deducir*) to infer, conclude

cólera ['kolera] *nf* (*ira*) anger; (*MED*)

cholera; **colérico, a** [ko'leriko, a] *adj* irascible, bad-tempered

colesterol [koleste'rol] *nm* cholesterol

coleta [ko'leta] *nf* pigtail

colgante [kol'ɣante] *adj* hanging ♦ *nm* (*joya*) pendant

colgar [kol'ɣar] *vt* to hang (up); (*ropa*) to hang out ♦ *vi* to hang; (*teléfono*) to hang up

cólico ['koliko] *nm* colic

coliflor [koli'flor] *nf* cauliflower

colilla [ko'liʎa] *nf* cigarette end, butt

colina [ko'lina] *nf* hill

colindante [kolin'dante] *adj* adjacent, neighbouring

colisión [koli'sjon] *nf* collision; **~ de frente** head-on crash

collar [ko'ʎar] *nm* necklace; (*de perro*) collar

colmado, a [kol'maðo, a] *adj* full

colmar [kol'mar] *vt* to fill to the brim; (*fig*) to fulfil, realize

colmena [kol'mena] *nf* beehive

colmillo [kol'miʎo] *nm* (*diente*) eye tooth; (*de elefante*) tusk; (*de perro*) fang

colmo ['kolmo] *nm* height, summit; ¡**es el ~!** it's the limit!

colocación [koloka'θjon] *nf* (*acto*) placing; (*empleo*) job, position; (*situación*) place, position

colocar [kolo'kar] *vt* to place, put, position; (*dinero*) to invest; (*poner en empleo*) to find a job for; **~se** *vr* to get a job

Colombia [ko'lombja] *nf* Colombia; **colombiano, a** *adj, nm/f* Colombian

colonia [ko'lonja] *nf* colony; (*de casas*) housing estate; (*agua de ~*) cologne

colonización [koloniθa'θjon] *nf* colonization; **colonizador, a** [koloniθa'ðor, a] *adj* colonizing ♦ *nm/f* colonist, settler

colonizar [koloni'θar] *vt* to colonize

coloquio [ko'lokjo] *nm* conversation; (*congreso*) conference

color [ko'lor] *nm* colour

colorado, a [kolo'raðo, a] *adj* (*rojo*) red; (*LAM: chiste*) rude

colorante [kolo'rante] *nm* colouring

colorear [kolore'ar] *vt* to colour

colorete [kolo'rete] *nm* blusher

colorido [kolo'riðo] *nm* colouring

columna [ko'lumna] *nf* column; (*pilar*) pillar; (*apoyo*) support

columpiar [kolum'pjar] *vt* to swing; **~se** *vr* to swing; **columpio** *nm* swing

coma ['koma] *nf* comma ♦ *nm* (*MED*) coma

comadre [ko'maðre] *nf* (*madrina*) godmother; (*vecina*) neighbour; (*chismosa*) gossip; **comadrona** *nf* midwife

comandancia [koman'danθja] *nf* command

comandante [koman'dante] *nm* commandant

comarca [ko'marka] *nf* region

comba ['komba] *nf* (*curva*) curve; (*cuerda*) skipping rope; **saltar a la ~** to skip

combar [kom'bar] *vt* to bend, curve

combate [kom'bate] *nm* fight; (*fig*) battle; **combatiente** *nm* combatant

combatir [komba'tir] *vt* to fight, combat

combinación [kombina'θjon] *nf* combination; (*QUÍMICA*) compound; (*bebida*) cocktail; (*plan*) scheme, setup; (*prenda*) slip

combinar [kombi'nar] *vt* to combine

combustible [kombus'tiβle] *nm* fuel

combustión [kombus'tjon] *nf* combustion

comedia [ko'meðja] *nf* comedy; (*TEATRO*) play, drama

comediante [kome'ðjante] *nm/f* (comic) actor/actress

comedido, a [kome'ðiðo, a] *adj* moderate

comedor, a [kome'ðor, a] *nm/f* (*persona*) glutton ♦ *nm* (*habitación*) dining room; (*restaurante*) restaurant; (*cantina*) canteen

comensal [komen'sal] *nm/f* fellow guest (*o* diner)

comentar [komen'tar] *vt* to comment on; (*fam*) to discuss

comentario [komen'tarjo] *nm* comment, remark; (*literario*) commentary; **~s** *nmpl* (*chismes*) gossip *sg*

comentarista [komenta'rista] *nm/f* commentator

comenzar [komen'θar] *vt, vi* to begin, start, commence; **~ a hacer algo** to begin *o* start doing sth

comer [ko'mer] *vt* to eat; (*DAMAS, AJEDREZ*) to take, capture ♦ *vi* to eat; (*almorzar*) to have lunch; **~se** *vr* to eat up

comercial [komer'θjal] *adj* commercial; (*relativo al negocio*) business *cpd*;

comercializar *vt* (*producto*) to market; (*pey*) to commercialize

comerciante [komer'θjante] *nm/f* trader, merchant

comerciar [komer'θjar] *vi* to trade, do business

comercio [ko'merθjo] *nm* commerce, trade; (*negocio*) business; (*fig*) dealings *pl*

comestible [komes'tiβle] *adj* eatable, edible; **~s** *nmpl* food *sg*, foodstuffs

cometa [ko'meta] *nm* comet ♦ *nf* kite

cometer [kome'ter] *vt* to commit

cometido [kome'tiðo] *nm* (*misión*) task, assignment; (*deber*) commitment

comezón [kome'θon] *nf* itch, itching

cómic ['komik] *nm* (*historieta*) comic

comicios [ko'miθjos] *nmpl* elections

cómico, a [ko'miko, a] *adj* comic(al) ♦ *nm/f* comedian; (*de teatro*) (comic) actor/actress

comida [ko'miða] *nf* (*alimento*) food; (*almuerzo, cena*) meal; (*de mediodía*) lunch

comidilla [komi'ðiʎa] *nf*: **ser la ~ de la ciudad** to be the talk of the town

comienzo *etc* [ko'mjenθo] *vb ver* **comenzar** ♦ *nm* beginning, start

comillas [ko'miʎas] *nfpl* quotation marks

comilona [komi'lona] (*fam*) *nf* blow-out

comino [ko'mino] *nm*: **(no) me importa un ~** I don't give a damn

comisaría [komisa'ria] *nf* (*de policía*) police station; (*MIL*) commissariat

comisario [komi'sarjo] *nm* (*MIL etc*) commissary; (*POL*) commissar

comisión [komi'sjon] *nf* commission

comité [komi'te] (*pl* **~s**) *nm* committee

comitiva [komi'tiβa] *nf* retinue

como ['komo] *adv* as; (*tal ~*) like; (*aproximadamente*) about, approximately ♦ *conj* (*ya que, puesto que*) as, since; (*en cuanto*) as soon as; **¡~ no!** of course!; **~ no lo haga hoy** unless he does it today;

~ si as if; **es tan alto ~ ancho** it is as high as it is wide

cómo ['komo] *adv* how?, why? ♦ *excl* what?, I beg your pardon? ♦ *nm*: **el ~ y el porqué** the whys and wherefores

cómoda ['komoða] *nf* chest of drawers

comodidad [komoði'ðað] *nf* comfort; **venga a su ~** come at your convenience

comodín [komo'ðin] *nm* joker

cómodo, a ['komoðo, a] *adj* comfortable; *(práctico, de fácil uso)* convenient

compact disc *nm* compact disk player

compacto, a [kom'pakto, a] *adj* compact

compadecer [kompaðe'θer] *vt* to pity, be sorry for; **~se** *vr*: **~se de** to pity, be *o* feel sorry for

compadre [kom'paðre] *nm* (*padrino*) godfather; (*amigo*) friend, pal

compañero, a [kompa'nero, a] *nm/f* companion; (*novio*) boy/girlfriend; **~ de clase** classmate

compañía [kompa'nia] *nf* company

comparación [kompara'θjon] *nf* comparison; **en ~ con** in comparison with

comparar [kompa'rar] *vt* to compare

comparativo, a [kompara'tiβo, a] *adj* comparative

comparecer [kompare'θer] *vi* to appear (in court)

comparsa [kom'parsa] *nm/f* (*TEATRO*) extra

compartimiento [komparti'mjento] *nm* (*FERRO*) compartment

compartir [kompar'tir] *vt* to share; (*dinero, comida etc*) to divide (up), share (out)

compás [kom'pas] *nm* (*MUS*) beat, rhythm; (*MAT*) compasses *pl*; (*NAUT etc*) compass

compasión [kompa'sjon] *nf* compassion, pity

compasivo, a [kompa'siβo, a] *adj* compassionate

compatibilidad [kompatiβili'ðað] *nf* compatibility

compatible [kompa'tiβle] *adj* compatible

compatriota [kompa'trjota] *nm/f* compatriot, fellow countryman/woman

compendiar [kompen'djar] *vt* to summarize; (*libro*) to abridge;

compendio *nm* summary; abridgement

compenetrarse [kompene'trarse] *vr* (*persona*) to see eye to eye

compensación [kompensa'θjon] *nf* compensation

compensar [kompen'sar] *vt* to compensate

competencia [kompe'tenθja] *nf* (*incumbencia*) domain, field; (*JUR, habilidad*) competence; (*rivalidad*) competition

competente [kompe'tente] *adj* (*JUR, persona*) competent; (*conveniente*) suitable

competición [kompeti'θjon] *nf* competition

competir [kompe'tir] *vi* to compete

compilar [kompi'lar] *vt* to compile

complacencia [kompla'θenθja] *nf* (*placer*) pleasure; (*tolerancia excesiva*) complacency

complacer [kompla'θer] *vt* to please; **~se** *vr* to be pleased

complaciente [kompla'θjente] *adj* kind, obliging, helpful

complejo, a [kom'plexo, a] *adj, nm* complex

complementario, a [komplemen'tarjo, a] *adj* complementary

completar [komple'tar] *vt* to complete

completo, a [kom'pleto, a] *adj* complete; (*perfecto*) perfect; (*lleno*) full ♦ *nm* full complement

complicado, a [kompli'kaðo, a] *adj* complicated; **estar ~ en** to be mixed up in

complicar [kompli'kar] *vt* to complicate

cómplice ['kompliθe] *nm/f* accomplice

complot [kom'plo(t)] (*pl* **~s**) *nm* plot; (*conspiración*) conspiracy

componer [kompo'ner] *vt* to make up, put together; (*MUS, LITERATURA, IMPRENTA*) to compose; (*algo roto*) to mend, repair; (*arreglar*) to arrange; **~se** *vr*: **~se de** to consist of; **componérselas para hacer algo** to manage to do sth

comportamiento [komporta'mjento] *nm* behaviour, conduct

comportarse [kompor'tarse] *vr* to behave

composición [komposi'θjon] *nf*
composition

compositor, a [komposi'tor, a] *nm/f*
composer

compostura [kompos'tura] *nf*
(*composición*) composition; (*reparación*)
mending, repair; (*acuerdo*) agreement;
(*actitud*) composure

compra ['kompra] *nf* purchase; ~s *nfpl*
purchases, shopping *sg*; **ir de** ~s to go
shopping; **comprador, a** *nm/f* buyer,
purchaser

comprar [kom'prar] *vt* to buy, purchase

comprender [kompren'der] *vt* to
understand; (*incluir*) to comprise,
include

comprensión [kompren'sjon] *nf*
understanding; (*totalidad*) comprehen-
siveness; **comprensivo, a** *adj* comprehensive; (*actitud*) understanding

compresa [kom'presa] *nf*: ~ **higiénica**
sanitary towel (*BRIT*) o napkin (*US*)

comprimido, a [kompri'miðo, a] *adj*
compressed ♦ *nm* (*MED*) pill, tablet

comprimir [kompri'mir] *vt* to compress;
(*fig*) to control

comprobante [kompro'ßante] *nm* proof;
(*COM*) voucher; ~ **de recibo** receipt

comprobar [kompro'ßar] *vt* to check;
(*probar*) to prove; (*TEC*) to check, test

comprometer [komprome'ter] *vt* to
compromise; (*exponer*) to endanger; ~**se**
vr to compromise o.s.; (*involucrarse*) to
get involved

compromiso [kompro'miso] *nm*
(*obligación*) obligation; (*cometido*)
commitment; (*convenio*) agreement; (*dificultad*) awkward situation

compuesto, a [kom'pwesto, a] *adj*: ~ **de**
composed of, made up of ♦ *nm*
compound

computador [komputa'ðor] *nm* computer;
~ **central** mainframe computer; ~
personal personal computer

computadora [komputa'ðora] *nf* =
computador

cómputo ['komputo] *nm* calculation

comulgar [komul'var] *vi* to receive
communion

común [ko'mun] *adj* common ♦ *nm*: **el** ~
the community

comunicación [komunika'θjon] *nf*
communication; (*informe*) report

comunicado [komuni'kado] *nm*
announcement; ~ **de prensa** press
release

comunicar [komuni'kar] *vt, vi* to
communicate; ~**se** *vr* to communicate;
está comunicando (*TEL*) the line's
engaged (*BRIT*) o busy (*US*); **comunicativo,
a** *adj* communicative

comunidad [komuni'ðað] *nf* community;
~ **autónoma** (*POL*) autonomous region;
C~ Económica Europea European
Economic Community

comunión [komu'njon] *nf* communion

comunismo [komu'nismo] *nm*
communism; **comunista** *adj, nm/f*
communist

PALABRA CLAVE

---

con [kon] *prep* **1** (*medio, compañía*) with;
comer ~ **cuchara** to eat with a spoon;
pasear ~ **uno** to go for a walk with sb

2 (*a pesar de*): ~ **todo, merece nuestros
respetos** all the same, he deserves our
respect

3 (*para* ~): **es muy bueno para** ~ **los
niños** he's very good with (the) children

4 (+ *infin*): ~ **llegar tan tarde se quedó
sin comer** by arriving so late he missed
out on eating

♦ *conj*: ~ **que: será suficiente** ~ **que le
escribas** it will be sufficient if you write
to her

---

conato [ko'nato] *nm* attempt; ~ **de robo**
attempted robbery

concebir [konθe'ßir] *vt, vi* to conceive

conceder [konθe'ðer] *vt* to concede

concejal, a [konθe'xal, a] *nm/f* town
councillor

concentración [konθentra'θjon] *nf*
concentration

concentrar [konθen'trar] *vt* to
concentrate; ~**se** *vr* to concentrate

concepción [konθep'θjon] *nf* conception

concepto [kon'θepto] *nm* concept

concernir [konθer'nir] *vi* to concern; **en lo que concierne a ...** (*cosa*) as far as ... is concerned; **en lo que a mí concierne** as far as I'm concerned

concertar [konθer'tar] *vt* (*MUS*) to harmonize; (*acordar: precio*) to agree; (: *tratado*) to conclude; (*trato*) to arrange, fix up; (*combinar: esfuerzos*) to coordinate; (*reconciliar: personas*) to reconcile ♦ *vi* to harmonize, be in tune

concesión [konθe'sjon] *nf* concession

concesionario [konθesjo'narjo] *nm* (licensed) dealer, agent

concha ['kontʃa] *nf* shell

conciencia [kon'θjenθja] *nf* conscience; **tener/tomar ~ de** to be/become aware of; **tener la ~ limpia/tranquila** to have a clear conscience

concienciar [konθjen'θjar] *vt* to make aware; **~se** *vr* to become aware

concienzudo, a [konθjen'θuðo, a] *adj* conscientious

concierto *etc* [kon'θjerto] *vb ver* **concertar** ♦ *nm* concert; (*obra*) concerto

conciliar [konθi'ljar] *vt* to reconcile

concilio [kon'θiljo] *nm* council

conciso, a [kon'θiso, a] *adj* concise

conciudadano, a [konθjuða'ðano, a] *nm/f* fellow citizen

concluir [konklu'ir] *vt, vi* to conclude; **~se** *vr* to conclude

conclusión [konklu'sjon] *nf* conclusion

concluyente [konklu'jente] *adj* (*prueba, información*) conclusive

concordar [konkor'ðar] *vt* to reconcile ♦ *vi* to agree, tally

concordia [kon'korðja] *nf* harmony

concretar [konkre'tar] *vt* to make concrete, make more specific; **~se** *vr* to become more definite

concreto, a [kon'kreto, a] *adj, nm* (*AM*) concrete; **en ~** (*en resumen*) to sum up; (*especificamente*) specifically; **no hay nada en ~** there's nothing definite

concurrencia [konku'rrenθja] *nf* turnout

concurrido, a [konku'rriðo, a] *adj* (*calle*) busy; (*local, reunión*) crowded

concurrir [konku'rrir] *vi* (*juntarse: ríos*) to meet, come together; (: *personas*) to

gather, meet

concursante [konkur'sante] *nm/f* competitor

concurso [kon'kurso] *nm* (*de público*) crowd; (*ESCOL, DEPORTE, competencia*) competition; (*ayuda*) help, cooperation

condal [kon'dal] *adj*: **la Ciudad C~** Barcelona

conde ['konde] *nm* count

condecoración [kondekora'θjon] *nf* (*MIL*) medal

condecorar [kondeko'rar] *vt* (*MIL*) to decorate

condena [kon'dena] *nf* sentence

condenación [kondena'θjon] *nf* condemnation; (*REL*) damnation

condenar [konde'nar] *vt* to condemn; (*JUR*) to convict; **~se** *vr* (*JUR*) to confess (one's guilt); (*REL*) to be damned

condensar [konden'sar] *vt* to condense

condesa [kon'desa] *nf* countess

condescender [kondesθen'der] *vi* to acquiesce, comply

condición [kondi'θjon] *nf* condition; **condicional** *adj* conditional

condicionar [kondiθjo'nar] *vt* (*acondicionar*) to condition; **~ algo a** to make sth conditional on

condimento [kondi'mento] *nm* seasoning

condolerse [kondo'lerse] *vr* to sympathize

condón [kon'don] *nm* condom

conducir [kondu'θir] *vt* to take, convey; (*AUTO*) to drive ♦ *vi* to drive; (*fig*) to lead; **~se** *vr* to behave

conducta [kon'dukta] *nf* conduct, behaviour

conducto [kon'dukto] *nm* pipe, tube; (*fig*) channel

conductor, a [konduk'tor, a] *adj* leading, guiding ♦ *nm* (*FÍSICA*) conductor; (*de vehículo*) driver

conduje *etc vb ver* **conducir**

conduzco *etc vb ver* **conducir**

conectado, a [konek'taðo, a] *adj* (*INFORM*) on-line

conectar [konek'tar] *vt* to connect (up); (*enchufar*) plug in

conejillo [kone'xiʎo] *nm*: **~ de Indias**

(ZOOL) guinea pig

conejo [ko'nexo] *nm* rabbit

conexión [konek'sjon] *nf* connection

confección [confe(k)'θjon] *nf* preparation; (*industria*) clothing industry

confeccionar [konfekθjo'nar] *vt* to make (up)

confederación [konfeðera'θjon] *nf* confederation

conferencia [konfe'renθja] *nf* conference; (*lección*) lecture; (*TEL*) call

conferir [konfe'rir] *vt* to award

confesar [konfe'sar] *vt* to confess, admit

confesión [konfe'sjon] *nf* confession

confesionario [konfesjo'narjo] *nm* confessional

confeti [kon'feti] *nm* confetti

confiado, a [kon'fjaðo, a] *adj* (*crédulo*) trusting; (*seguro*) confident; (*presumido*) conceited, vain

confianza [kon'fjanθa] *nf* trust; (*aliento*, *confidencia*) confidence; (*familiaridad*) intimacy, familiarity; (*pey*) vanity, conceit

confiar [kon'fjar] *vt* to entrust ♦ *vi* to trust

confidencia [konfi'ðenθja] *nf* confidence

confidencial [konfiðen'θjal] *adj* confidential

confidente [konfi'ðente] *nm/f* confidant/e; (*policial*) informer

configurar [konfiɣu'rar] *vt* to shape, form

confín [kon'fin] *nm* limit; **confines** *nmpl* confines, limits

confinar [konfi'nar] *vi* to confine; (*desterrar*) to banish

confirmar [konfir'mar] *vt* to confirm

confiscar [konfis'kar] *vt* to confiscate

confite [kon'fite] *nm* sweet (*BRIT*), candy (*US*)

confitería [konfite'ria] *nf* confectionery; (*tienda*) confectioner's (shop)

confitura [konfi'tura] *nf* jam

conflictivo, a [konflik'tiβo, a] *adj* (*asunto*, *propuesta*) controversial; (*país*, *situación*) troubled

conflicto [kon'flikto] *nm* conflict; (*fig*) clash

confluir [kon'flwir] *vi* (*ríos*) to meet;

(*gente*) to gather

conformar [konfor'mar] *vt* to shape, fashion ♦ *vi* to agree; ~**se** *vr* to conform; (*resignarse*) to resign o.s

conforme [kon'forme] *adj* (*correspondiente*): ~ **con** in line with; (*de acuerdo*): **estar ~s (con algo)** to be in agreement (with sth) ♦ *adv* as ♦ *excl* agreed! ♦ *prep*: ~ **a** in accordance with; **quedarse ~ (con algo)** to be satisfied (with sth)

conformidad [konformi'ðað] *nf* (*semejanza*) similarity; (*acuerdo*) agreement; (*resignación*) resignation; **conformista** *adj*, *nm/f* conformist

confortable [konfor'taβle] *adj* comfortable

confortar [konfor'tar] *vt* to comfort

confrontar [konfron'tar] *vt* to confront; (*dos personas*) to bring face to face; (*cotejar*) to compare ♦ *vi* to border

confundir [konfun'dir] *vt* (*borrar*) to blur; (*equivocar*) to mistake, confuse; (*mezclar*) to mix; (*turbar*) to confuse; ~**se** *vr* (*hacerse borroso*) to become blurred; (*turbarse*) to get confused; (*equivocarse*) to make a mistake; (*mezclarse*) to mix

confusión [konfu'sjon] *nf* confusion

confuso, a [kon'fuso, a] *adj* confused

congelado, a [konxe'laðo, a] *adj* frozen; ~**s** *nmpl* frozen food(s); **congelador** *nm* (*aparato*) freezer, deep freeze; **congeladora** *nf* freezer, deep freeze

congelar [konxe'lar] *vt* to freeze; ~**se** *vr* (*sangre*, *grasa*) to congeal

congeniar [konxe'njar] *vi* to get on (*BRIT*) o along (*US*) well

congestión [konxes'tjon] *nf* congestion

congestionar [konxestjo'nar] *vt* to congest; ~**se** *vr*: **se le congestionó la cara** his face became flushed

congoja [kon'goxa] *nf* distress, grief

congraciarse [kongra'θjarse] *vr* to ingratiate o.s.

congratular [kongratu'lar] *vt* to congratulate

congregación [kongreɣa'θjon] *nf* congregation

congregar [kongre'ɣar] *vt* to gather together; ~**se** *vr* to gather together

congresista [kongre'sista] *nm/f* delegate,

congressman/woman
congreso [kon'greso] *nm* congress
conjetura [konxe'tura] *nf* guess;
  conjeturar *vt* to guess
conjugar [konxu'ɣar] *vt* to combine, fit
  together; (*LING*) to conjugate
conjunción [konxun'θjon] *nf* conjunction
conjunto, a [kon'xunto, a] *adj* joint,
  united ♦ *nm* whole; (*MUS*) band; **en** ~ as
  a whole
conjurar [konxu'rar] *vt* (*REL*) to exorcise;
  (*fig*) to ward off ♦ *vi* to plot
conmemoración [konmemora'θjon] *nf*
  commemoration
conmemorar [konmemo'rar] *vt* to
  commemorate
conmigo [kon'miɣo] *pron* with me
conminar [konmi'nar] *vt* to threaten
conmoción [konmo'θjon] *nf* shock; (*fig*)
  upheaval; ~ **cerebral** (*MED*) concussion
conmovedor, a [konmoße'ðor, a] *adj*
  touching, moving; (*emocionante*) exciting
conmover [konmo'ßer] *vt* to shake,
  disturb; (*fig*) to move
conmutador [konmuta'ðor] *nm* switch;
  (*AM*: *TEL*: *centralita*) switchboard;
  (: *central*) telephone exchange
cono ['kono] *nm* cone
conocedor, a [konoθe'ðor, a] *adj* expert,
  knowledgeable ♦ *nm/f* expert
conocer [kono'θer] *vt* to know; (*por
  primera vez*) to meet, get to know;
  (*entender*) to know about; (*reconocer*) to
  recognize; ~**se** *vr* (*una persona*) to know
  o.s.; (*dos personas*) to (get to) know each
  other
conocido, a [kono'θiðo, a] *adj* (well-)
  known ♦ *nm/f* acquaintance
conocimiento [konoθi'mjento] *nm* knowledge; (*MED*) consciousness; ~**s** *nmpl*
  (*personas*) acquaintances; (*saber*)
  knowledge *sg*
conozco *etc vb ver* **conocer**
conque ['konke] *conj* and so, so then
conquista [kon'kista] *nf* conquest;
  conquistador, a *adj* conquering ♦ *nm*
  conqueror
conquistar [konkis'tar] *vt* to conquer
consagrar [konsa'ɣrar] *vt* (*REL*) to

consecrate; (*fig*) to devote
consciente [kons'θjente] *adj* conscious
consecución [konseku'θjon] *nf*
  acquisition; (*de fin*) attainment
consecuencia [konse'kwenθja] *nf*
  consequence, outcome; (*firmeza*)
  consistency
consecuente [konse'kwente] *adj*
  consistent
consecutivo, a [konseku'tißo, a] *adj*
  consecutive
conseguir [konse'ɣir] *vt* to get, obtain;
  (*sus fines*) to attain
consejero, a [konse'xero, a] *nm/f* adviser,
  consultant; (*POL*) councillor
consejo [kon'sexo] *nm* advice; (*POL*)
  council; ~ **de administración** (*COM*)
  board of directors; ~ **de guerra** court
  martial; ~ **de ministros** cabinet meeting
consenso [kon'senso] *nm* consensus
consentimiento [konsenti'mjento] *nm*
  consent
consentir [konsen'tir] *vt* (*permitir, tolerar*)
  to consent to; (*mimar*) to pamper, spoil;
  (*aguantar*) to put up with ♦ *vi* to agree,
  consent; ~ **que uno haga algo** to allow
  sb to do sth
conserje [kon'serxe] *nm* caretaker;
  (*portero*) porter
conservación [konserßa'θjon] *nf*
  conservation; (*de alimentos, vida*) preservation
conservador, a [konserßa'ðor, a] *adj*
  (*POL*) conservative ♦ *nm/f* conservative
conservante [konser'ßante] *nm*
  preservative
conservar [konser'ßar] *vt* to conserve,
  keep; (*alimentos, vida*) to preserve; ~**se**
  vr to survive
conservas [kon'serßas] *nfpl* canned
  food(s) (*pl*)
conservatorio [konserßa'torjo] *nm* (*MUS*)
  conservatoire, conservatory
considerable [konsiðe'raßle] *adj*
  considerable
consideración [konsiðera'θjon] *nf*
  consideration; (*estimación*) respect
considerado, a [konsiðe'raðo, a] *adj*
  (*atento*) considerate; (*respetado*)

respected

considerar [konsiðe'rar] *vt* to consider

consigna [kon'siɣna] *nf* (*orden*) order, instruction; (*para equipajes*) left-luggage office

consigo *etc* [kon'siɣo] *vb ver* **conseguir**
 ♦ *pron* (*m*) with him; (*f*) with her; (*Vd*) with you; (*reflexivo*) with o.s.

consiguiendo *etc vb ver* **conseguir**

consiguiente [konsi'ɣjente] *adj* consequent; **por ~** and so, therefore, consequently

consistente [konsis'tente] *adj* consistent; (*sólido*) solid, firm; (*válido*) sound

consistir [konsis'tir] *vi*: **~ en** (*componerse de*) to consist of; (*ser resultado de*) to be due to

consolación [konsola'θjon] *nf* consolation

consolar [konso'lar] *vt* to console

consolidar [konsoli'ðar] *vt* to consolidate

consomé [konso'me] (*pl* **~s**) *nm* consommé, clear soup

consonante [konso'nante] *adj* consonant, harmonious ♦ *nf* consonant

consorcio [kon'sorθjo] *nm* consortium

conspiración [konspira'θjon] *nf* conspiracy

conspirador, a [konspira'ðor, a] *nm/f* conspirator

conspirar [konspi'rar] *vi* to conspire

constancia [kons'tanθja] *nf* constancy; **dejar ~ de** to put on record

constante [kons'tante] *adj, nf* constant

constar [kons'tar] *vi* (*evidenciarse*) to be clear *o* evident; **~ de** to consist of

constatar [konsta'tar] *vt* (*controlar*) to check; (*observar*) to note

consternación [konsterna'θjon] *nf* consternation

constipado, a [konsti'paðo, a] *adj*: **estar ~** to have a cold ♦ *nm* cold

constitución [konstitu'θjon] *nf* constitution; **constitucional** *adj* constitutional

constituir [konstitu'ir] *vt* (*formar, componer*) to constitute, make up; (*fundar, erigir, ordenar*) to constitute, establish

constituyente [konstitu'jente] *adj* constituent

constreñir [konstre'ɲir] *vt* (*restringir*) to restrict

construcción [konstruk'θjon] *nf* construction, building

constructor, a [konstruk'tor, a] *nm/f* builder

construir [konstru'ir] *vt* to build, construct

construyendo *etc vb ver* **construir**

consuelo [kon'swelo] *nm* consolation, solace

cónsul ['konsul] *nm* consul; **consulado** *nm* consulate

consulta [kon'sulta] *nf* consultation; (*MED*): **horas de ~** surgery hours

consultar [konsul'tar] *vt* to consult

consultorio [konsul'torjo] *nm* (*MED*) surgery

consumar [konsu'mar] *vt* to complete, carry out; (*crimen*) to commit; (*sentencia*) to carry out

consumición [konsumi'θjon] *nf* consumption; (*bebida*) drink; (*comida*) food; **~ mínima** cover charge

consumidor, a [konsumi'ðor, a] *nm/f* consumer

consumir [konsu'mir] *vt* to consume; **~se** *vr* to be consumed; (*persona*) to waste away

consumismo [konsu'mismo] *nm* consumerism

consumo [kon'sumo] *nm* consumption

contabilidad [kontaßili'ðað] *nf* accounting, book-keeping; (*profesión*) accountancy; **contable** *nm/f* accountant

contacto [kon'takto] *nm* contact; (*AUTO*) ignition

contado, a [kon'taðo, a] *adj*: **~s** (*escasos*) numbered, scarce, few ♦ *nm*: **pagar al ~** to pay (in) cash

contador [konta'ðor] *nm* (*aparato*) meter; (*AM: contante*) accountant

contagiar [konta'xjar] *vt* (*enfermedad*) to pass on, transmit; (*persona*) to infect; **~se** *vr* to become infected

contagio [kon'taxjo] *nm* infection; **contagioso, a** *adj* infectious; (*fig*) catching

contaminación [kontamina'θjon] *nf* contamination; (*polución*) pollution

contaminar [kontami'nar] *vt* to contaminate; (*aire, agua*) to pollute

contante [kon'tante] *adj*: **dinero ~ (y sonante)** cash

contar [kon'tar] *vt* (*páginas, dinero*) to count; (*anécdota, chiste etc*) to tell ♦ *vi* to count; **~ con** to rely on, count on

contemplación [kontempla'θjon] *nf* contemplation

contemplar [kontem'plar] *vt* to contemplate; (*mirar*) to look at

contemporáneo, a [kontempo'raneo, a] *adj, nm/f* contemporary

contendiente [konten'djente] *nm/f* contestant

contenedor [kontene'ðor] *nm* container

contener [konte'ner] *vt* to contain, hold; (*retener*) to hold back, contain; **~se** *vr* to control o restrain o.s.

contenido, a [konte'niðo, a] *adj* (*moderado*) restrained; (*risa etc*) suppressed ♦ *nm* contents *pl*, content

contentar [konten'tar] *vt* (*satisfacer*) to satisfy; (*complacer*) to please; **~se** *vr* to be satisfied

contento, a [kon'tento, a] *adj* contented, content; (*alegre*) pleased; (*feliz*) happy

contestación [kontesta'θjon] *nf* answer, reply

contestador [kontesta'ðor] *nm*: **~ automático** answering machine

contestar [kontes'tar] *vt* to answer, reply; (*JUR*) to corroborate, confirm

contexto [kon'te(k)sto] *nm* context

contienda [kon'tjenda] *nf* contest

contigo [kon'tiɣo] *pron* with you

contiguo, a [kon'tiɣwo, a] *adj* (*de al lado*) next; (*vecino*) adjacent, adjoining

continente [konti'nente] *adj, nm* continent

contingencia [kontin'xenθja] *nf* contingency; (*riesgo*) risk; **contingente** *adj, nm* contingent

continuación [kontinwa'θjon] *nf* continuation; **a ~** then, next

continuar [konti'nwar] *vt* to continue, go on with ♦ *vi* to continue, go on; **~ hablando** to continue talking o to talk

continuidad [kontinwi'ðað] *nf* continuity

continuo, a [kon'tinwo, a] *adj* (*sin interrupción*) continuous; (*acción perseverante*) continual

contorno [kon'torno] *nm* outline; (*GEO*) contour; **~s** *nmpl* neighbourhood *sg*, surrounding area *sg*

contorsión [kontor'sjon] *nf* contortion

contra ['kontra] *prep, ad* against ♦ *nm inv* **con** ♦ *nf*: **la C~** (*de Nicaragua*) the Contras *pl*

contraataque [kontraa'take] *nm* counter-attack

contrabajo [kontra'βaxo] *nm* double bass

contrabandista [kontraβan'dista] *nm/f* smuggler

contrabando [kontra'βando] *nm* (*acción*) smuggling; (*mercancías*) contraband

contracción [kontrak'θjon] *nf* contraction

contrachapado [kontratʃa'paðo] *nm* plywood

contracorriente [kontrako'rrjente] **(a) ~** *adv* against the current

contradecir [kontraðe'θir] *vt* to contradict

contradicción [kontraðik'θjon] *nf* contradiction

contradictorio, a [kontraðik'torjo, a] *adj* contradictory

contraer [kontra'er] *vt* to contract; (*limitar*) to restrict; **~se** *vr* to contract; (*limitarse*) to limit o.s.

contraluz [kontra'luθ] *nf*: **a ~** against the light

contramaestre [kontrama'estre] *nm* foreman

contrapartida [kontrapar'tiða] *nf*: **como ~ (de)** in return (for)

contrapelo [kontra'pelo]: **a ~** *adv* the wrong way

contrapesar [kontrape'sar] *vt* to counterbalance; (*fig*) to offset; **contrapeso** *nm* counterweight

contraportada [kontrapor'taða] *nf* (*de revista*) back cover

contraproducente [kontraproðu'θente] *adj* counterproductive

contrariar [kontra'rjar] *vt* (*oponerse*) to oppose; (*poner obstáculo*) to impede;

(*enfadar*) to vex

contrariedad [kontrarje'ðað] *nf* (*oposición*) opposition; (*obstáculo*) obstacle, setback; (*disgusto*) vexation, annoyance

contrario, a [kon'trarjo, a] *adj* contrary; (*persona*) opposed; (*sentido, lado*) opposite ♦ *nm/f* enemy, adversary; (*DEPORTE*) opponent; **al/por el ~** on the contrary; **de lo ~** otherwise

contrarreloj [kontrarre'lo] *nf* (*tb: prueba ~*) time trial

contrarrestar [kontrarres'tar] *vt* to counteract

contrasentido [kontrasen'tiðo] *nm:* **es un ~ que él ...** it doesn't make sense for him to ...

contraseña [kontra'seɲa] *nf* (*INFORM*) password

contrastar [kontras'tar] *vt* to resist ♦ *vi* to contrast

contraste [kon'traste] *nm* contrast

contratar [kontra'tar] *vt* (*firmar un acuerdo para*) to contract for; (*empleados, obreros*) to hire, engage; **~se** *vr* to sign on

contratiempo [kontra'tjempo] *nm* setback

contratista [kontra'tista] *nm/f* contractor

contrato [kon'trato] *nm* contract

contravenir [kontraße'nir] *vi:* **~ a** to contravene, violate

contraventana [kontraßen'tana] *nf* shutter

contribución [kontrißu'θjon] *nf* (*municipal etc*) tax; (*ayuda*) contribution

contribuir [kontrißu'ir] *vt, vi* to contribute; (*COM*) to pay (in taxes)

contribuyente [kontrißu'jente] *nm/f* (*COM*) taxpayer; (*que ayuda*) contributor

contrincante [kontrin'kante] *nm* opponent

control [kon'trol] *nm* control; (*inspección*) inspection, check; **~ador, a** *nm/f* controller; **~ador aéreo** air-traffic controller

controlar [kontro'lar] *vt* to control; (*inspeccionar*) to inspect, check

controversia [kontro'ßersja] *nf* controversy

contundente [kontun'dente] *adj* (*instrumento*) blunt; (*argumento, derrota*) overwhelming

contusión [kontu'sjon] *nf* bruise

convalecencia [kombale'θenθja] *nf* convalescence

convalecer [kombale'θer] *vi* to convalesce, get better

convaleciente [kombale'θjente] *adj, nm/f* convalescent

convalidar [kombali'ðar] *vt* (*título*) to recognize

convencer [komben'θer] *vt* to convince; (*persuadir*) to persuade

convencimiento [kombenθi'mjento] *nm* (*acción*) convincing; (*persuasión*) persuasion; (*certidumbre*) conviction

convención [komben'θjon] *nf* convention

conveniencia [kombe'njenθja] *nf* suitability; (*conformidad*) agreement; (*utilidad, provecho*) usefulness; **~s** *nfpl* (*convenciones*) conventions; (*COM*) property *sg*

conveniente [kombe'njente] *adj* suitable; (*útil*) useful

convenio [kom'benjo] *nm* agreement, treaty

convenir [kombe'nir] *vi* (*estar de acuerdo*) to agree; (*ser conveniente*) to suit, be suitable

convento [kom'bento] *nm* convent

convenza *etc vb ver* **convencer**

converger [komber'xer] *vi* to converge

convergir [komber'xir] *vi* = **converger**

conversación [kombersa'θjon] *nf* conversation

conversar [komber'sar] *vi* to talk, converse

conversión [komber'sjon] *nf* conversion

convertir [komber'tir] *vt* to convert

convicción [kombik'θjon] *nf* conviction

convicto, a [kom'bikto, a] *adj* convicted, found guilty; (*condenado*) condemned

convidado, a [kombi'ðaðo, a] *nm/f* guest

convidar [kombi'ðar] *vt* to invite

convincente [kombin'θente] *adj* convincing

convite [kom'bite] *nm* invitation; (*banquete*) banquet

convivencia [kombi'ßenθja] *nf* coexistence, living together convivir [kombi'ßir] vi to live together

convocar [kombo'kar] vt to summon, call (together)

convocatoria [komboka'torja] nf (de oposiciones, elecciones) notice; (de huelga) call

convulsión [kombul'sjon] nf convulsion

conyugal [konju'val] adj conjugal; cónyuge ['konjuxe] nm/f spouse

coñac [ko'ɲa(k)] (pl ~s) nm cognac, brandy

coño ['koɲo] (fam!) excl (enfado) shit! (!); (sorpresa) bloody hell! (!)

cooperación [koopera'θjon] nf cooperation

cooperar [koope'rar] vi to cooperate

cooperativa [koopera'tißa] nf cooperative

coordinadora [koordina'ðora] nf (comité) coordinating committee

coordinar [koordi'nar] vt to coordinate

copa ['kopa] nf cup; (vaso) glass; (tomar una) ~ to (have a) drink; (de árbol) top; (de sombrero) crown; ~s nfpl (NAIPES) ≈ hearts

copia ['kopja] nf copy; ~ de respaldo o seguridad (INFORM) back-up copy; copiar vt to copy

copioso, a [ko'pjoso, a] adj copious, plentiful

copla ['kopla] nf verse; (canción) (popular) song

copo ['kopo] nm: ~ de nieve snowflake; ~s de maíz cornflakes

copropietarios [kopropje'tarjos] nmpl joint owners

coqueta [ko'keta] adj flirtatious, coquettish; coquetear vi to flirt

coraje [ko'raxe] nm courage; (ánimo) spirit; (ira) anger

coral [ko'ral] adj choral ♦ nf (MUS) choir ♦ nm (ZOOL) coral

coraza [ko'raθa] nf (armadura) armour; (blindaje) armour-plating

corazón [kora'θon] nm heart

corazonada [koraθo'naða] nf impulse; (presentimiento) hunch

corbata [kor'ßata] nf tie

corchete [kor'tʃete] nm catch, clasp

corcho ['kortʃo] nm cork; (PESCA) float

cordel [kor'ðel] nm cord, line

cordero [kor'ðero] nm lamb

cordial [kor'ðjal] adj cordial; ~idad nf warmth, cordiality

cordillera [korði'ʎera] nf range (of mountains)

Córdoba ['korðoßa] n Cordova

cordón [kor'ðon] nm (cuerda) cord, string; (de zapatos) lace; (MIL etc) cordon

cordura [kor'ðura] nf: con ~ (obrar, hablar) sensibly

corneta [kor'neta] nf bugle

cornisa [kor'nisa] nf (ARQ) cornice

coro ['koro] nm chorus; (conjunto de cantores) choir

corona [ko'rona] nf crown; (de flores) garland; coronación nf coronation; coronar vt to crown

coronel [koro'nel] nm colonel

coronilla [koro'niʎa] nf (ANAT) crown (of the head)

corporación [korpora'θjon] nf corporation

corporal [korpo'ral] adj corporal, bodily

corpulento, a [korpu'lento a] adj (persona) heavily-built

corral [ko'rral] nm farmyard

correa [ko'rrea] nf strap; (cinturón) belt; (de perro) lead, leash

corrección [korrek'θjon] nf correction; (reprensión) rebuke; correccional nm reformatory

correcto, a [ko'rrekto, a] adj correct; (persona) well-mannered

corredizo, a [korre'ðiθo, a] adj (puerta etc) sliding

corredor, a [korre'ðor, a] adj running ♦ nm (pasillo) corridor; (balcón corrido) gallery; (COM) agent, broker ♦ nm/f (DEPORTE) runner

corregir [korre'xir] vt (error) to correct; (amonestar, reprender) to rebuke, reprimand; ~se vr to reform

correo [ko'rreo] nm post, mail; (persona) courier; C~s nmpl Post Office sg; ~ aéreo airmail

correr [ko'rrer] vt to run; (viajar) to cover, travel; (cortinas) to draw; (cerrojo) to shoot ♦ vi to run; (líquido) to run, flow; ~se vr to slide, move; (colores) to run

correspondencia [korrespon'denθja] *nf*
correspondence; (*FERRO*) connection

corresponder [korrespon'der] *vi* to
correspond; (*convenir*) to be suitable;
(*pertenecer*) to belong; (*tocar*) to concern;
~se *vr* (*por escrito*) to correspond;
(*amarse*) to love one another

correspondiente [korrespon'djente] *adj*
corresponding

corresponsal [korrespon'sal] *nm/f*
correspondent

corrida [ko'rriða] *nf* (*de toros*) bullfight

corrido, a [ko'rriðo, a] *adj* (*avergonzado*)
abashed; **3 noches corridas** 3 nights
running; **un kilo ~** a good kilo

corriente [ko'rrjente] *adj* (*agua*) running;
(*fig*) flowing; (*dinero etc*) current;
(*común*) ordinary, normal ♦ *nf* current
♦ *nm* current month; **~ eléctrica** electric
current

corrija *etc vb ver* **corregir**

corrillo [ko'rriʎo] *nm* ring, circle (of
people); (*fig*) clique

corro ['korro] *nm* ring, circle (of people)

corroborar [korroβo'rar] *vt* to corroborate

corroer [korro'er] *vt* to corrode; (*GEO*) to
erode

corromper [korrom'per] *vt* (*madera*) to
rot; (*fig*) to corrupt

corrosivo, a [korro'siβo, a] *adj* corrosive

corrupción [korrup'θjon] *nf* rot, decay;
(*fig*) corruption

corsé [kor'se] *nm* corset

cortacésped [korta'θespeð] *nm* lawn
mower

cortado, a [kor'taðo, a] *adj* (*gen*) cut;
(*leche*) sour; (*confuso*) confused; (*desconcertado*) embarrassed ♦ *nm* coffee (with a
little milk)

cortar [kor'tar] *vt* to cut; (*suministro*) to
cut off; (*un pasaje*) to cut out ♦ *vi* to cut;
~se *vr* (*turbarse*) to become embarrassed; (*leche*) to turn, curdle; **~se el
pelo** to have one's hair cut

cortauñas [korta'uɲas] *nm inv* nail
clippers *pl*

corte ['korte] *nm* cut, cutting; (*de tela*)
piece, length ♦ *nf*: **las C~s** the Spanish

Parliament; **~ y confección** dress-
making; **~ de luz** power cut

cortejar [korte'xar] *vt* to court

cortejo [kor'texo] *nm* entourage; **~
fúnebre** funeral procession

cortés [kor'tes] *adj* courteous, polite

cortesía [korte'sia] *nf* courtesy

corteza [kor'teθa] *nf* (*de árbol*) bark; (*de
pan*) crust

cortina [kor'tina] *nf* curtain

corto, a ['korto, a] *adj* (*breve*) short;
(*tímido*) bashful; **~ de luces** not very
bright; **~ de vista** short-sighted; **estar ~
de fondos** to be short of funds; **~circuito**
nm short circuit; **~metraje** *nm* (*CINE*)
short

cosa ['kosa] *nf* thing; (*asunto*) affair; **~ de**
about; **eso es ~ mía** that's my business

coscorrón [kosko'rron] *nm* bump on the
head

cosecha [ko'setʃa] *nf* (*AGR*) harvest; (*de
vino*) vintage

cosechar [kose'tʃar] *vt* to harvest, gather
(in)

coser [ko'ser] *vt* to sew

cosmético, a [kos'metiko, a] *adj, nm*
cosmetic

cosquillas [kos'kiʎas] *nfpl*: **hacer ~** to
tickle; **tener ~** to be ticklish

costa ['kosta] *nf* (*GEO*) coast; **C~ Brava**
Costa Brava; **C~ Cantábrica** Cantabrian
Coast; **C~ del Sol** Costa del Sol; **a toda
~** at any price

costado [kos'taðo] *nm* side

costar [kos'tar] *vt* (*valer*) to cost;
(*necesitar*) to require, need; **me cuesta
hablarle** I find it hard to talk to him

Costa Rica *nf* Costa Rica;
costarricense *adj, nm/f* Costa Rican;
costarriqueño, a *adj, nm/f* Costa Rican

coste ['koste] *nm* = **costo**

costear [koste'ar] *vt* to pay for

costero, a [kos'tero, a] *adj* (*pueblecito,
camino*) coastal

costilla [kos'tiʎa] *nf* rib; (*CULIN*) cutlet

costo ['kosto] *nm* cost, price; **~ de la
vida** cost of living; **~so, a** *adj* costly,
expensive

costra ['kostra] *nf* (*corteza*) crust; (*MED*)

scab
costumbre [kos'tumbre] *nf* custom, habit
costura [kos'tura] *nf* sewing, needlework; (*zurcido*) seam
costurera [kostu'rera] *nf* dressmaker
costurero [kostu'rero] *nm* sewing box *o* case
cotejar [kote'xar] *vt* to compare
cotidiano, a [koti'ðjano, a] *adj* daily, day to day
cotilla [ko'tiʎa] *nm/f* (*fam*) gossip; **cotillear** *vi* to gossip; **cotilleo** *nm* gossip(ing)
cotización [kotiθa'θjon] *nf* (*COM*) quotation, price; (*de club*) dues *pl*
cotizar [koti'θar] *vt* (*COM*) to quote, price; **~se** *vr*: **~se a** to sell at, fetch; (*BOLSA*) to stand at, be quoted at
coto ['koto] *nm* (*terreno cercado*) enclosure; (*de caza*) reserve
cotorra [ko'torra] *nf* parrot
COU [kou] (*ESP*) *nm abr* (= *Curso de Orientación Universitaria*) *1 year course leading to final school-leaving certificate and university entrance examinations*
coyote [ko'jote] *nm* coyote, prairie wolf
coyuntura [kojun'tura] *nf* (*ANAT*) joint; (*fig*) juncture, occasion
coz [koθ] *nf* kick
crack (*m droga*) crack
cráneo ['kraneo] *nm* skull, cranium
cráter ['krater] *nm* crater
creación [krea'θjon] *nf* creation
creador, a [krea'ðor, a] *adj* creative ♦ *nm/f* creator
crear [kre'ar] *vt* to create, make
crecer [kre'θer] *vi* to grow; (*precio*) to rise
creces ['kreθes]: **con ~** *adv* amply, fully
crecido, a [kre'θiðo, a] *adj* (*persona, planta*) full-grown; (*cantidad*) large
creciente [kre'θjente] *adj* growing; (*cantidad*) increasing; (*luna*) crescent ♦ *nm* crescent
crecimiento [kreθi'mjento] *nm* growth; (*aumento*) increase
credenciales [kreðen'θjales] *nfpl* credentials
crédito ['kreðito] *nm* credit
credo ['kreðo] *nm* creed

crédulo, a ['kreðulo, a] *adj* credulous
creencia [kre'enθja] *nf* belief
creer [kre'er] *vt, vi* to think, believe; **~se** *vr* to believe o.s. (to be); **~ en** to believe in; **¡ya lo creo!** I should think so!
creíble [kre'iβle] *adj* credible, believable
creído, a [kre'iðo, a] *adj* (*engreído*) conceited
crema ['krema] *nf* cream; (*natillas*) custard; **~ pastelera** (confectioner's) custard
cremallera [krema'ʎera] *nf* zip (fastener)
crematorio [krema'torjo] *nm* (*tb: horno ~*) crematorium
crepitar [krepi'tar] *vi* to crackle
crepúsculo [kre'puskulo] *nm* twilight, dusk
crespo, a ['krespo, a] *adj* (*pelo*) curly
cresta ['kresta] *nf* (*GEO, ZOOL*) crest
creyendo *vb ver* **creer**
creyente [kre'jente] *nm/f* believer
creyó *etc vb ver* **creer**
crezco *etc vb ver* **crecer**
cría *etc* ['kria] *vb ver* **criar** ♦ *nf* (*de animales*) rearing, breeding; (*animal*) young; *ver tb* **crío**
criadero [kria'ðero] *nm* nursery; (*ZOOL*) breeding place
criado, a [kri'aðo, a] *nm* servant ♦ *nf* servant, maid
criador [kria'ðor] *nm* breeder
crianza [kri'anθa] *nf* rearing, breeding; (*fig*) breeding
criar [kri'ar] *vt* (*amamantar*) to suckle, feed; (*educar*) to bring up; (*producir*) to grow, produce; (*animales*) to breed
criatura [kria'tura] *nf* creature; (*niño*) baby, (small) child
criba ['kriβa] *nf* sieve; **cribar** *vt* to sieve
crimen ['krimen] *nm* crime
criminal [krimi'nal] *adj, nm/f* criminal
crin [krin] *nf* (*tb: ~es nfpl*) mane
crío, a ['krio, a] (*fam*) *nm/f* (*niño*) kid
crisis ['krisis] *nf inv* crisis; **~ nerviosa** nervous breakdown
crispar [kris'par] *vt* (*músculo*) to tense (up); (*nervios*) to set on edge
cristal [kris'tal] *nm* crystal; (*de ventana*) glass, pane; (*lente*) lens; **~ino, a** *adj*

crystalline; (*fig*) clear ♦ *nm* lens (of the eye); ~izar *vt, vi* to crystallize

cristiandad [kristjan'daθ] *nf* Christendom

cristianismo [kristja'nismo] *nm* Christianity

cristiano, a [kris'tjano, a] *adj, nm/f* Christian

Cristo ['kristo] *nm* Christ; (*crucifijo*) crucifix

criterio [kri'terjo] *nm* criterion; (*juicio*) judgement

crítica ['kritika] *nf* criticism; *ver tb* **crítico**

criticar [kriti'kar] *vt* to criticize

crítico, a ['kritiko, a] *adj* critical ♦ *nm/f* critic

Croacia *nf* Croatia

croar [kro'ar] *vi* to croak

cromo ['kromo] *nm* chrome

crónica ['kronika] *nf* chronicle, account

crónico, a ['kroniko, a] *adj* chronic

cronómetro [kro'nometro] *nm* (*DEPORTE*) stopwatch

croqueta [kro'keta] *nf* (*CULIN*) croquette

cruce *etc* ['kruθe] *vb ver* **cruzar** ♦ *nm* crossing; (*de carreteras*) crossroads

crucificar [kruθifi'kar] *vt* to crucify

crucifijo [kruθi'fixo] *nm* crucifix

crucigrama [kruθi'vrama] *nm* crossword (puzzle)

crudo, a ['kruðo, a] *adj* raw; (*no maduro*) unripe; (*petróleo*) crude; (*rudo, cruel*) cruel ♦ *nm* crude (oil)

cruel [krwel] *adj* cruel; ~dad *nf* cruelty

crujido [kru'xiðo] *nm* (*de madera etc*) creak

crujiente [kru'xjente] *adj* (*galleta etc*) crunchy

crujir [kru'xir] *vi* (*madera etc*) to creak; (*dedos*) to crack; (*dientes*) to grind; (*nieve, arena*) to crunch

cruz [kruθ] *nf* cross; (*de moneda*) tails *sg*; ~ **gamada** swastika

cruzada [kru'θaða] *nf* crusade

cruzado, a [kru'θaðo, a] *adj* crossed ♦ *nm* crusader

cruzar [kru'θar] *vt* to cross; ~se *vr* (*líneas etc*) to cross; (*personas*) to pass each other

Cruz Roja *nf* Red Cross

cuaderno [kwa'ðerno] *nm* notebook; (*de escuela*) exercise book; (*NAUT*) logbook

cuadra ['kwaðra] *nf* (*caballeriza*) stable; (*AM*) block

cuadrado, a [kwa'ðraðo, a] *adj* square ♦ *nm* (*MAT*) square

cuadrar [kwa'ðrar] *vt* to square ♦ *vi*: ~ **con** to square with, tally with; ~se *vr* (*soldado*) to stand to attention

cuadrilátero [kwaðri'latero] *nm* (*DEPORTE*) boxing ring; (*GEOM*) quadrilateral

cuadrilla [kwa'ðriʎa] *nf* party, group

cuadro ['kwaðro] *nm* square; (*ARTE*) painting; (*TEATRO*) scene; (*diagrama*) chart; (*DEPORTE, MED*) team; (*POL*) executive; **tela a ~s** checked (*BRIT*) o chequered (*US*) material

cuádruple ['kwaðruple] *adj* quadruple

cuádruplo, a ['kwaðruplo, a] *adj* quadruple

cuajar [kwa'xar] *vt* to thicken; (*leche*) to curdle; (*sangre*) to congeal; (*adornar*) to adorn; (*CULIN*) to set; ~se *vr* to curdle; to congeal; to set; (*llenarse*) to fill up

cuajo ['kwaxo] *nm*: **de ~** (*arrancar*) by the roots; (*cortar*) completely

cual [kwal] *adv* like, as ♦ *pron*: **el ~** *etc* which; (*persona: sujeto*) who; (: *objeto*) whom ♦ *adj* such as; **cada ~** each one; **tal ~** just as it is

cuál [kwal] *pron interr* which (one)

cualesquier(a) [kwales'kjer(a)] *pl de* **cualquier(a)**

cualidad [kwali'ðaθ] *nf* quality

cualquier [kwal'kjer] *adj ver* **cualquiera**

cualquiera [kwal'kjera] (*pl* **cualesquiera**) *adj* (*delante de nm y f*: **cualquier**) any ♦ *pron* anybody; **un coche ~ servirá** any car will do; **no es un hombre ~** he isn't just anybody; **cualquier día/libro** any day/book; **eso ~ lo sabe hacer** anybody can do that; **es un ~** he's a nobody

cuando ['kwando] *adv* when; (*aún si*) if, even if ♦ *conj* (*puesto que*) since ♦ *prep*: **yo, ~ niño ...** when I was a child ...; ~ **no sea así** even if it is not so; ~ **más** at (the) most; ~ **menos** at least; ~ **no** if not, otherwise; **de ~ en ~** from time to time

cuándo ['kwando] *adv* when; **¿desde ~?**, **¿de ~ acá?** since when?

cuantía [kwan'tia] *nf* (*importe: de pérdidas, deuda, daños*) extent

cuantioso, a [kwan'tjoso, a] *adj* substantial

PALABRA CLAVE

---

cuanto, a ['kwanto, a] *adj* **1** (*todo*): **tiene todo ~ desea** he's got everything he wants; **le daremos ~s ejemplares necesite** we'll give him as many copies as *o* all the copies he needs; **~s hombres la ven** all the men who see her

2: **unos ~s**: **había unos ~s periodistas** there were (quite) a few journalists

3 (*+ más*): **~ más vino bebes peor te sentirás** the more wine you drink the worse you'll feel

♦ *pron*: **tiene ~ desea** he has everything he wants; **tome ~/~s quiera** take as much/many as you want

♦ *adv*: **en ~: ~ profesor** as a teacher; **en ~ a mí** as for me; *ver tb* **antes**

♦ *conj* **1**: **~ más gana menos gasta** the more he earns the less he spends; **~ más joven se es más se es confiado** the younger you are the more trusting you are

2: **en ~**: **en ~ llegue/llegué** as soon as I arrive/arrived

---

cuánto, a ['kwanto, a] *adj* (*exclamación*) what a lot of; (*interr: sg*) how much?; (: *pl*) how many? ♦ *pron, adv* how; (*interr: sg*) how much?; (: *pl*) how many?; **¡cuánta gente!** what a lot of people!; **¿~ cuesta?** how much does it cost?; **¿a ~s estamos?** what's the date?; **Señor no sé ~s** Mr. So-and-So

cuarenta [kwa'renta] *num* forty

cuarentena [kwaren'tena] *nf* quarantine

cuaresma [kwa'resma] *nf* Lent

cuarta ['kwarta] *nf* (*MAT*) quarter, fourth; (*palmo*) span

cuartear [kwarte'ar] *vt* to quarter; (*dividir*) to divide up; **~se** *vr* to crack, split

cuartel [kwar'tel] *nm* (*de ciudad*) quarter, district; (*MIL*) barracks *pl*; **~ general** headquarters *pl*

cuarteto [kwar'teto] *nm* quartet

cuarto, a ['kwarto, a] *adj* fourth ♦ *nm* (*MAT*) quarter, fourth; (*habitación*) room; **~ de baño** bathroom; **~ de estar** living room; **~ de hora** quarter (of an) hour; **~ de kilo** quarter kilo

cuatro ['kwatro] *num* four

Cuba ['kuβa] *nf* Cuba; **cubano, a** *adj, nm/f* Cuban

cuba ['kuβa] *nf* cask, barrel

cúbico, a ['kuβiko, a] *adj* cubic

cubierta [ku'βjerta] *nf* cover, covering; (*neumático*) tyre; (*NAUT*) deck

cubierto, a [ku'βjerto, a] *pp de* **cubrir** ♦ *adj* covered ♦ *nm* cover; (*en la mesa*) place; **~s** *nmpl* cutlery *sg*; **a ~ de** covered with *o* in

cubil [ku'βil] *nm* den; **~ete** *nm* (*en juegos*) cup

cubito [ku'βito] *nm*: **~ de hielo** ice-cube

cubo ['kuβo] *nm* cube; (*balde*) bucket, tub; (*TEC*) drum

cubrecama [kuβre'kama] *nm* bedspread

cubrir [ku'βrir] *vt* to cover; **~se** *vr* (*cielo*) to become overcast

cucaracha [kuka'ratʃa] *nf* cockroach

cuchara [ku'tʃara] *nf* spoon; (*TEC*) scoop; **~da** *nf* spoonful; **~dita** *nf* teaspoonful

cucharilla [kutʃa'riʎa] *nf* teaspoon

cucharón [kutʃa'ron] *nm* ladle

cuchichear [kutʃitʃe'ar] *vi* to whisper

cuchilla [ku'tʃiʎa] *nf* (large) knife; (*de arma blanca*) blade; **~ de afeitar** razor blade

cuchillo [ku'tʃiʎo] *nm* knife

cuchitril [kutʃi'tril] *nm* hovel; (*habitación etc*) pigsty

cuclillas [ku'kliʎas] *nfpl*: **en ~** squatting

cuco, a ['kuko, a] *adj* pretty; (*astuto*) sharp ♦ *nm* cuckoo

cucurucho [kuku'rutʃo] *nm* cornet

cuello ['kweʎo] *nm* (*ANAT*) neck; (*de vestido, camisa*) collar

cuenca ['kwenka] *nf* (*ANAT*) eye socket; (*GEO*) bowl, deep valley

cuenco ['kwenko] *nm* bowl

cuenta *etc* ['kwenta] *vb ver* **contar** ♦ *nf* (*cálculo*) count, counting; (*en café, restaurante*) bill (*BRIT*), check (*US*); (*COM*) account; (*de collar*) bead; (*fig*) account; **a fin de ~s** in the end; **caer en la ~** to catch on; **darse ~ de** to realize; **tener en ~** to bear in mind; **echar ~s** to take stock; **~ corriente/de ahorros** current/savings account; **~ atrás** countdown; **~kilómetros** *nm inv* ≈ milometer; (*de velocidad*) speedometer

cuento *etc* ['kwento] *vb ver* **contar** ♦ *nm* story

cuerda ['kwerða] *nf* rope; (*hilo*) string; (*de reloj*) spring; **dar ~ a un reloj** to wind up a clock; **~ floja** tightrope

cuerdo, a ['kwerðo, a] *adj* sane; (*prudente*) wise, sensible

cuerno ['kwerno] *nm* horn

cuero ['kwero] *nm* (*ZOOL*) skin, hide; (*TEC*) leather; **en ~s** stark naked; **~ cabelludo** scalp

cuerpo ['kwerpo] *nm* body

cuervo ['kwerßo] *nm* crow

cuesta *etc* ['kwesta] *vb ver* **costar** ♦ *nf* slope; (*en camino etc*) hill; **~ arriba/abajo** uphill/downhill; **a ~s** on one's back

cueste *etc vb ver* **costar**

cuestión [kwes'tjon] *nf* matter, question, issue; (*riña*) quarrel, dispute

cueva ['kweßa] *nf* cave

cuidado [kwi'ðaðo] *nm* care, carefulness; (*preocupación*) care, worry ♦ *excl* careful!, look out!

cuidadoso, a [kwiða'ðoso, a] *adj* careful; (*preocupado*) anxious

cuidar [kwi'ðar] *vt* (*MED*) to care for; (*ocuparse de*) to take care of, look after ♦ *vi*: **~ de** to take care of, look after; **~se** *vr* to look after o.s.; **~se de hacer algo** to take care to do sth

culata [ku'lata] *nf* (*de fusil*) butt

culebra [ku'leßra] *nf* snake

culebrón [kule'ßron] (*fam*) *nm* (*TV*) soap (-opera)

culinario, a [kuli'narjo, a] *adj* culinary, cooking *cpd*

culminación [kulmina'θjon] *nf* culmination

culo ['kulo] *nm* bottom, backside; (*de vaso, botella*) bottom

culpa ['kulpa] *nf* fault; (*JUR*) guilt; **por ~ de** because of, through; **tener la (de)** to be to blame (for); **~bilidad** *nf* guilt; **~ble** *adj* guilty ♦ *nm/f* culprit

culpar [kul'par] *vt* to blame; (*acusar*) to accuse

cultivar [kulti'ßar] *vt* to cultivate

cultivo [kul'tißo] *nm* (*acto*) cultivation; (*plantas*) crop

culto, a ['kulto, a] *adj* (*cultivado*) cultivated; (*que tiene cultura*) cultured, educated ♦ *nm* (*homenaje*) worship; (*religión*) cult

cultura [kul'tura] *nf* culture

culturismo [kultu'rismo] *nm* body-building

cumbre ['kumbre] *nf* summit, top

cumpleaños [kumple'aɲos] *nm inv* birthday

cumplido, a [kum'pliðo, a] *adj* complete, perfect; (*abundante*) plentiful; (*cortés*) courteous ♦ *nm* compliment; **visita de ~** courtesy call

cumplidor, a [kumpli'ðor, a] *adj* reliable

cumplimentar [kumplimen'tar] *vt* to congratulate

cumplimiento [kumpli'mjento] *nm* (*de un deber*) fulfilment; (*acabamiento*) completion

cumplir [kum'plir] *vt* (*orden*) to carry out, obey; (*promesa*) to carry out, fulfil; (*condena*) to serve; (*años*) to reach, attain ♦ *vi*: **~ con** (*deberes*) to carry out, fulfil; **~se** *vr* (*plazo*) to expire; **hoy cumple dieciocho años** he is eighteen today

cúmulo ['kumulo] *nm* heap

cuna ['kuna] *nf* cradle, cot

cundir [kun'dir] *vi* (*noticia, rumor, pánico*) to spread; (*rendir*) to go a long way

cuneta [ku'neta] *nf* ditch

cuña ['kuɲa] *nf* wedge

cuñado, a [ku'ɲaðo, a] *nm/f* brother-/sister-in-law

cuota ['kwota] *nf* (*parte proporcional*) share; (*cotización*) fee, dues *pl*

cupe *etc vb ver* **caber**
cupiera *etc vb ver* **caber**
cupo ['kupo] *vb ver* **caber** ♦ *nm* quota
cupón [ku'pon] *nm* coupon
cúpula ['kupula] *nf* dome
cura ['kura] *nf* (*curación*) cure; (*método curativo*) treatment ♦ *nm* priest
curación [kura'θjon] *nf* cure; (*acción*) curing
curandero, a [kuran'dero, a] *nm/f* quack
curar [ku'rar] *vt* (MED: *herida*) to treat, dress; (: *enfermo*) to cure; (CULIN) to cure, salt; (*cuero*) to tan ♦ *vi* to get well, recover; **~se** *vr* to get well, recover
curiosear [kurjose'ar] *vt* to glance at, look over ♦ *vi* to look round, wander round; (*explorar*) to poke about
curiosidad [kurjosi'ðað] *nf* curiosity
curioso, a [ku'rjoso, a] *adj* curious ♦ *nm/f* bystander, onlooker
currante [ku'rrante] (*fam*) *nm/f* worker
currar [ku'rrar] (*fam*) *vi* to work
currelar [kurre'lar] (*fam*) *vi* to work
currículo [ku'rrikulo] = **curriculum**
curriculum [ku'rrikulum] *nm* curriculum vitae
curro ['kurro] (*fam*) *nm* work, job
cursi ['kursi] (*fam*) *adj* pretentious; (*amanerado*) affected
cursillo [kur'siʎo] *nm* short course
cursiva [kur'siβa] *nf* italics *pl*
curso ['kurso] *nm* course; **en ~** (*año*) current; (*proceso*) going on, under way
cursor [kur'sor] *nm* (INFORM) cursor
curtido, a [kur'tiðo, a] *adj* (*cara etc*) weather-beaten; (*fig: persona*) experienced
curtir [kur'tir] *vt* (*cuero etc*) to tan
curva ['kurβa] *nf* curve, bend
curvo, a ['kurβo, a] *adj* (*gen*) curved; (*torcido*) bent
cúspide ['kuspiðe] *nf* (GEO) peak; (*fig*) top
custodia [kus'toðja] *nf* safekeeping; custody; (*custodiar vt* (*conservar*) to take care of; (*vigilar*) to guard
cutícula [ku'tikula] *nf* cuticle
cutis ['kutis] *nm inv* skin, complexion
cutre ['kutre] (*fam*) *adj* (*lugar*) grotty; (*persona*) naff

cuyo, a ['kujo, a] *pron* (*de quien*) whose; (*de que*) whose, of which; **en ~ caso** in which case
C.V. *abr* (= *caballos de vapor*) H.P.

D d

D. *abr* (= *Don*) Esq.
Da. *abr* = **Doña**
dádiva ['daðiβa] *nf* (*donación*) donation; (*regalo*) gift; **dadivoso, a** *adj* generous
dado, a ['daðo, a] *pp de* **dar** ♦ *nm* die; **~s** *nmpl* dice; **~ que** given that
daltónico, a [dal'toniko, a] *adj* colour-blind
dama ['dama] *nf* (*gen*) lady; (*AJEDREZ*) queen; **~s** *nfpl* (*juego*) draughts *sg*
damnificar [damnifi'kar] *vt* to harm; (*persona*) to injure
danés, esa [da'nes, esa] *adj* Danish ♦ *nm/f* Dane
danzar [dan'θar] *vt, vi* to dance
dañar [da'ɲar] *vt* (*objeto*) to damage; (*persona*) to hurt; **~se** *vr* (*objeto*) to get damaged
dañino, a [da'ɲino, a] *adj* harmful
daño ['daɲo] *nm* (*a un objeto*) damage; (*a una persona*) harm, injury; **~s y perjuicios** (*JUR*) damages; **hacer ~ a** to damage; (*persona*) to hurt, injure; **hacerse ~** to hurt o.s.

PALABRA CLAVE
---

dar [dar] *vt* **1** (*gen*) to give; (*obra de teatro*) to put on; (*film*) to show; (*fiesta*) to hold; **~ algo a uno** to give sb sth *o* sth to sb; **~ de beber a uno** to give sb a drink
2 (*producir: intereses*) to yield; (*fruta*) to produce
3 (*locuciones* + *n*): **da gusto escucharle** it's a pleasure to listen to him; *ver tb* **paseo** *y otros sustantivos*
4 (+ *n*: = *perífrasis de verbo*): **me da pena/asco** it frightens/sickens me
5 (*considerar*): **~ algo por descontado/entendido** to take sth for granted/as read; **~ algo por concluido** to consider

sth finished
6 (*hora*): **el reloj dio las 6** the clock
struck 6 (o'clock)
7: **me da lo mismo** it's all the same to
me; *ver tb* **igual**, **más**
♦ *vi* 1: **~ con: dimos con él dos horas
más tarde** we came across him two
hours later; **al final di con la solución**
I eventually came up with the answer
2: **~ en: ~ en** (*blanco, suelo*) to hit; **el
sol me da en la cara** the sun is shining
(right) on my face
3: **~ de sí** (*zapatos etc*) to stretch, give
♦ **~se** *vr* 1: **~se por vencido** to give up
2 (*ocurrir*): **se han dado muchos casos**
there have been a lot of cases
3: **~se a: se ha dado a la bebida** he's
taken to drinking
4: **se me dan bien/mal las ciencias** I'm
good/bad at science
5: **dárselas de: se las da de experto** he
fancies himself *o* poses as an expert

dardo ['darðo] *nm* dart
dársena ['darsena] *nf* dock
datar [da'tar] *vi*: **~ de** to date from
dátil ['datil] *nm* date
dato ['dato] *nm* fact, piece of information
DC *abbr m* (= *disco compacto*) CD
dcha. *abr* (= *derecha*) r.h.
d. de J.C. *abr* (= *después de Jesucristo*)
A.D.

PALABRA CLAVE

de [de] *prep* (*de+el* = *del*) 1 (*posesión*) of;
la casa ~ Isabel/mis padres Isabel's/
my parents' house; **es ~ ellos** it's theirs
2 (*origen, distancia, con números*) from;
soy ~ Gijón I'm from Gijón; **~ 8 a 20**
from 8 to 20; **salir del cine** to go out of
o leave the cinema; **~ ... en ...** from ... to
...; **~ 2 en 2** 2 by 2, 2 at a time
3 (*valor descriptivo*): **una copa ~ vino** a
glass of wine; **la mesa ~ la cocina** the
kitchen table; **un billete ~ 1000 pesetas**
a 1000 peseta note; **un niño ~ tres años**
a three-year-old (child); **una máquina ~
coser** a sewing machine; **ir vestido ~
gris** to be dressed in grey; **la niña del**

vestido azul the girl in the blue dress;
trabaja ~ profesora she works as a
teacher; **~ lado** sideways; **~ atrás/
delante** rear/front
4 (*hora, tiempo*): **a las 8 ~ la mañana** at
8 o'clock in the morning; **~ día/noche**
by day/night; **~ hoy en ocho días** a
week from now; **~ niño era gordo** as a
child he was fat
5 (*comparaciones*): **más/menos ~ cien
personas** more/less than a hundred
people; **el más caro ~ la tienda** the
most expensive in the shop; **menos/más
~ lo pensado** less/more than expected
6 (*causa*): **del calor** from the heat; **~
puro tonto** out of sheer stupidity
7 (*tema*): about; **clases ~ inglés** English
classes; **¿sabes algo ~ él?** do you know
anything about him?; **un libro ~ física**
a physics book
8 (*adj + de + infin*): **fácil ~ entender**
easy to understand
9 (*oraciones pasivas*): **fue respetado ~
todos** he was loved by all
10 (*condicional + infin*) if; **~ ser posible**
if possible; **~ no terminarlo hoy** if I *etc*
don't finish it today

dé *vb ver* **dar**
deambular [deambu'lar] *vi* to stroll,
wander
debajo [de'βaxo] *adv* underneath; **~ de**
below, under; **por ~ de** beneath
debate [de'βate] *nm* debate; **debatir** *vt* to
debate
deber [de'βer] *nm* duty ♦ *vt* to owe ♦ *vi*:
debe (de) it must, it should; **~es** *nmpl*
(*ESCOL*) homework; **debo hacerlo** I must
do it; **debe de ir** he should go; **~se** *vr*:
~se a to be owing *o* due to
debido, a [de'βiðo, a] *adj* proper, just; **~
a** due to, because of
débil ['deβil] *adj* (*persona, carácter*) weak;
(*luz*) dim; **debilidad** *nf* weakness;
dimness
debilitar [deβili'tar] *vt* to weaken; **~se** *vr*
to grow weak
debutar [deβu'tar] *vi* to make one's debut
década ['dekaða] *nf* decade

decadencia [deka'ðenθja] *nf* (*estado*) decadence; (*proceso*) decline, decay

decaer [deka'er] *vi* (*declinar*) to decline; (*debilitarse*) to weaken

decaído, a [deka'iðo, a] *adj*: **estar ~** (*abatido*) to be down

decaimiento [dekai'mjento] *nm* (*declinación*) decline; (*desaliento*) discouragement; (*MED*: *estado débil*) weakness

decano, a [de'kano, a] *nm/f* (*de universidad etc*) dean

decapitar [dekapi'tar] *vt* to behead

decena [de'θena] *nf*: **una ~** ten (or so)

decencia [de'θenθja] *nf* (*modestia*) modesty; (*honestidad*) respectability

decente [de'θente] *adj* (*correcto*) seemly, proper; (*honesto*) respectable

decepción [deθep'θjon] *nf* disappointment

decepcionar [deθepθjo'nar] *vt* to disappoint

decidir [deθi'ðir] *vt* (*persuadir*) to convince, persuade; (*resolver*) to decide ♦ *vi* to decide; **~se** *vr*: **~se a** to make up one's mind to

décimo, a ['deθimo, a] *adj* tenth ♦ *nm* tenth

decir [de'θir] *vt* (*expresar*) to say; (*contar*) to tell; (*hablar*) to speak ♦ *nm* saying; **~se** *vr*: **se dice que** it is said that; **~ para o entre sí** to say to o.s.; **querer ~** to mean; **¡dígame!** (*TEL*) hello!; (*en tienda*) can I help you?

decisión [deθi'sjon] *nf* (*resolución*) decision; (*firmeza*) decisiveness

decisivo, a [deθi'siβo, a] *adj* decisive

declamar [dekla'mar] *vt, vi* to declaim

declaración [deklara'θjon] *nf* (*manifestación*) statement; (*explicación*) explanation; **~ de ingresos o de la renta o fiscal** income-tax return

declarar [dekla'rar] *vt* to declare ♦ *vi* to declare; (*JUR*) to testify; **~se** *vr* to propose

declinar [dekli'nar] *vt* (*gen*) to decline; (*JUR*) to reject ♦ *vi* (*el día*) to draw to a close

declive [de'kliβe] *nm* (*cuesta*) slope; (*fig*) decline

decodificador [dekoðifika'ðor] *nm* decoder

decolorarse [dekolo'rarse] *vr* to become discoloured

decoración [dekora'θjon] *nf* decoration

decorado [deko'raðo] *nm* (*CINE, TEATRO*) scenery, set

decorar [deko'rar] *vt* to decorate; **decorativo, a** *adj* ornamental, decorative

decoro [de'koro] *nm* (*respeto*) respect; (*dignidad*) decency; (*recato*) propriety; **~so, a** *adj* (*decente*) decent; (*modesto*) modest; (*digno*) proper

decrecer [dekre'θer] *vi* to decrease, diminish

decrépito, a [de'krepito, a] *adj* decrepit

decretar [dekre'tar] *vt* to decree; **decreto** *nm* decree

dedal [de'ðal] *nm* thimble

dedicación [deðika'θjon] *nf* dedication

dedicar [deði'kar] *vt* (*libro*) to dedicate; (*tiempo, dinero*) to devote; (*palabras: decir, consagrar*) to dedicate, devote; **dedicatoria** *nf* (*de libro*) dedication

dedo ['deðo] *nm* finger; **~ (del pie)** toe; **~ pulgar** thumb; **~ índice** index finger; **~ mayor o cordial** middle finger; **~ anular** ring finger; **~ meñique** little finger; **hacer ~** (*fam*) to hitch (a lift)

deducción [deðuk'θjon] *nf* deduction

deducir [deðu'θir] *vt* (*concluir*) to deduce, infer; (*COM*) to deduct

defecto [de'fekto] *nm* defect, flaw; **defectuoso, a** *adj* defective, faulty

defender [defen'der] *vt* to defend

defensa [de'fensa] *nf* defence ♦ *nm* (*DEPORTE*) defender, back; **defensivo, a** *adj* defensive; **a la defensiva** on the defensive

defensor, a [defen'sor, a] *adj* defending ♦ *nm/f* (*abogado ~*) defending counsel; (*protector*) protector

deficiencia [defi'θjenθja] *nf* deficiency

deficiente [defi'θjente] *adj* (*defectuoso*) defective; **~ en** lacking o deficient in; **ser un ~ mental** to be mentally handicapped

déficit ['defiθit] (*pl* **~s**) *nm* deficit

definición [defini'θjon] *nf* definition

definir [defi'nir] *vt* (*determinar*) to determine, establish; (*decidir*) to define; (*aclarar*) to clarify; **definitivo, a** *adj* definitive; **en definitiva** definitively; (*en resumen*) in short

deformación [deforma'θjon] *nf* (*alteración*) deformation; (*RADIO etc*) distortion

deformar [defor'mar] *vt* (*gen*) to deform; **~se** *vr* to become deformed; **deforme** *adj* (*informe*) deformed; (*feo*) ugly; (*malhecho*) misshapen

defraudar [defrau'ðar] *vt* (*decepcionar*) to disappoint; (*estafar*) to cheat; to defraud

defunción [defun'θjon] *nf* death, demise

degeneración [dexenera'θjon] *nf* (*de las células*) degeneration; (*moral*) degeneracy

degenerar [dexene'rar] *vi* to degenerate

degollar [deɣo'ʎar] *vt* to behead; (*fig*) to slaughter

degradar [deɣra'ðar] *vt* to debase, degrade; **~se** *vr* to demean o.s

degustación [deɣusta'θjon] *nf* sampling, tasting

deificar [deifi'kar] *vt* (*persona*) to deify

dejadez [dexa'ðeθ] *nf* (*negligencia*) neglect; (*descuido*) untidiness, carelessness

dejar [de'xar] *vt* to leave; (*permitir*) to allow, let; (*abandonar*) to abandon, forsake; (*beneficios*) to produce, yield
♦ *vi*: **~ de** (*parar*) to stop; (*no hacer*) to fail to; **no dejes de comprar un billete** make sure you buy a ticket; **~ a un lado** to leave *o* set aside

dejo ['dexo] *nm* (*LING*) accent

del [del] (= **de**+ **el**) *ver* **de**

delantal [delan'tal] *nm* apron

delante [de'lante] *adv* in front, (*enfrente*) opposite; (*adelante*) ahead; **~ de** in front of, before

delantera [delan'tera] *nf* (*de vestido, casa etc*) front part; (*DEPORTE*) forward line; **llevar la ~ (a uno)** to be ahead (of sb)

delantero, a [delan'tero, a] *adj* front
♦ *nm* (*DEPORTE*) forward, striker

delatar [dela'tar] *vt* to inform on *o* against, betray; **delator, a** *nm/f* informer

delegación [deleɣa'θjon] *nf* (*acción, delegados*) delegation; (*COM: oficina*) office, branch; **~ de policía** police station

delegado, a [dele'ɣaðo, a] *nm/f* delegate; (*COM*) agent

delegar [dele'ɣar] *vt* to delegate

deletrear [deletre'ar] *vt* to spell (out)

deleznable [deleθ'naβle] *adj* brittle; (*excusa, idea*) feeble

delfín [del'fin] *nm* dolphin

delgadez [delɣa'ðeθ] *nf* thinness, slimness

delgado, a [del'ɣaðo, a] *adj* thin; (*persona*) slim, thin; (*tierra*) poor; (*tela etc*) light, delicate

deliberación [deliβera'θjon] *nf* deliberation

deliberar [deliβe'rar] *vt* to debate, discuss

delicadeza [delika'ðeθa] *nf* (*gen*) delicacy; (*refinamiento, sutileza*) refinement

delicado, a [deli'kaðo, a] *adj* (*gen*) delicate; (*sensible*) sensitive; (*quisquilloso*) touchy

delicia [de'liθja] *nf* delight

delicioso, a [deli'θjoso, a] *adj* (*gracioso*) delightful; (*exquisito*) delicious

delimitar [delimi'tar] *vt* (*funciones, responsabilidades*) to define

delincuencia [delin'kwenθja] *nf* delinquency; **delincuente** *nm/f* delinquent; (*criminal*) criminal

delineante [deline'ante] *nm/f* draughtsman/woman

delinear [deline'ar] *vt* (*dibujo*) to draw; (*fig, contornos*) to outline

delinquir [delin'kir] *vi* to commit an offence

delirante [deli'rante] *adj* delirious

delirar [deli'rar] *vi* to be delirious, rave

delirio [de'lirjo] *nm* (*MED*) delirium; (*palabras insensatas*) ravings *pl*

delito [de'lito] *nm* (*gen*) crime; (*infracción*) offence

delta ['delta] *nm* delta

demacrado, a [dema'kraðo, a] *adj*: **estar ~** to look pale and drawn, be wasted away

demagogo, a [dema'ɣoɣo, a] *nm/f*

demagogue

demanda [de'manda] *nf* (*pedido*, COM)
demand; (*petición*) request; (*JUR*) action,
lawsuit

demandante [deman'dante] *nm/f*
claimant

demandar [deman'dar] *vt* (*gen*) to
demand; (*JUR*) to sue, file a lawsuit
against

demarcación [demarka'θjon] *nf* (*de
terreno*) demarcation

demás [de'mas] *adj*: **los ~ niños** the
other children, the remaining children
♦ *pron*: **los/las ~** the others, the rest (of
them); **lo ~** the rest (of it)

demasía [dema'sia] *nf* (*exceso*) excess,
surplus; **comer en ~** to eat to excess

demasiado, a [dema'sjaðo, a] *adj*: **~ vino**
too much wine ♦ *adv* (*antes de adj, adv*)
too; **~s libros** too many books; **¡esto es
~!** that's the limit!; **hace ~ calor** it's too
hot; **~ despacio** too slowly; **~s** too many

demencia [de'menθja] *nf* (*locura*)
madness; **demente** *nm/f* lunatic ♦ *adj*
mad, insane

democracia [demo'kraθja] *nf* democracy

demócrata [de'mokrata] *nm/f* democrat;
democrático, a *adj* democratic

demoler [demo'ler] *vt* to demolish;
demolición *nf* demolition

demonio [de'monjo] *nm* devil, demon;
¡~s! hell!, damn!; **¿cómo ~s?** how the
hell?

demora [de'mora] *nf* delay; **demorar** *vt*
(*retardar*) to delay, hold back; (*detener*)
to hold up ♦ *vi* to linger, stay on; **~se** *vr*
to be delayed

demos *vb ver* **dar**

demostración [demostra'θjon] *nf* (*MAT*)
proof; (*de afecto*) show, display

demostrar [demos'trar] *vt* (*probar*) to
prove; (*mostrar*) to show; (*manifestar*) to
demonstrate

demudado, a [demu'ðaðo, a] *adj* (*rostro*)
pale

den *vb ver* **dar**

denegar [dene'var] *vt* (*rechazar*) to
refuse; (*JUR*) to reject

denigrar [deni'vrar] *vt* (*desacreditar,*
infamar) to denigrate; (*injuriar*) to insult

denominación [denomina'θjon] *nf* (*clase*)
denomination

denotar [deno'tar] *vt* (*indicar*) to indicate;
(*significar*) to denote

densidad [densi'ðað] *nf* (*FÍSICA*) density;
(*fig*) thickness

denso, a ['denso, a] *adj* (*apretado*) solid;
(*espeso, pastoso*) thick; (*fig*) heavy

dentadura [denta'ðura] *nf* (set of) teeth
pl; **~ postiza** false teeth *pl*

dentera [den'tera] *nf* (*sensación
desagradable*) the shivers *pl*

dentífrico, a [den'tifriko, a] *adj* dental
♦ *nm* toothpaste

dentista [den'tista] *nm/f* dentist

dentro ['dentro] *adv* inside ♦ *prep*: **~ de**
in, inside, within; **por ~** (on the) inside;
mirar por ~ to look inside; **~ de tres
meses** within three months

denuncia [de'nunθja] *nf* (*delación*)
denunciation; (*acusación*) accusation; (*de
accidente*) report; **denunciar** *vt* to report;
(*delatar*) to inform on *o* against

departamento [departa'mento] *nm*
(*sección administrativa*) department,
section; (*AM: apartamento*) flat (*BRIT*),
apartment

dependencia [depen'denθja] *nf* depend-
ence; (*POL*) dependency; (*COM*) office,
section

depender [depen'der] *vi*: **~ de** to depend
on

dependienta [depen'djenta] *nf*
saleswoman, shop assistant

dependiente [depen'djente] *adj*
dependent ♦ *nm* salesman, shop
assistant

depilar [depi'lar] *vt* (*con cera*) to wax;
(*cejas*) to pluck; **depilatorio** *nm* hair
remover

deplorable [deplo'raßle] *adj* deplorable

deplorar [deplo'rar] *vt* to deplore

deponer [depo'ner] *vt* to lay down ♦ *vi*
(*JUR*) to give evidence; (*declarar*) to make
a statement

deportar [depor'tar] *vt* to deport

deporte [de'porte] *nm* sport; **hacer ~** to
play sports; **deportista** *adj* sports *cpd*

♦ *nm/f* sportsman/woman; **deportivo, a** *adj* (*club, periódico*) sports *cpd* ♦ *nm* sports car

depositante [deposiˈtante] *nm/f* depositor

depositar [depoˈsitar] *vt* (*dinero*) to deposit; (*mercancías*) to put away, store; (*persona*) to confide; **~se** *vr* to settle; **~io, a** *nm/f* trustee

depósito [deˈposito] *nm* (*gen*) deposit; (*almacén*) warehouse, store; (*de agua, gasolina etc*) tank; **~ de cadáveres** mortuary

depreciar [depreˈθjar] *vt* to depreciate, reduce the value of; **~se** *vr* to depreciate, lose value

depredador, a [depreðaˈðor, a] *adj* predatory ♦ *nm* predator

depresión [depreˈsjon] *nf* depression

deprimido, a [depriˈmiðo, a] *adj* depressed

deprimir [depriˈmir] *vt* to depress; **~se** *vr* (*persona*) to become depressed

deprisa [deˈprisa] *adv* quickly, hurriedly

depuración [depuraˈθjon] *nf* purification; (*POL*) purge

depurar [depuˈrar] *vt* to purify; (*purgar*) to purge

derecha [deˈretʃa] *nf* right(-hand) side; (*POL*) right; **a la ~** (*estar*) on the right; (*torcer etc*) (to the) right

derecho, a [deˈretʃo, a] *adj* right, right-hand ♦ *nm* (*privilegio*) right; (*lado*) right(-hand) side; (*leyes*) law ♦ *adv* straight, directly; **~s** *nmpl* (*de aduana*) duty *sg*; (*de autor*) royalties; **tener ~ a** to have a right to

deriva [deˈriβa] *nf*: **ir o estar a la ~** to drift, be adrift

derivado [deriˈβaðo] *nm* (*COM*) by-product

derivar [deriˈβar] *vt* to derive; (*desviar*) to direct ♦ *vi* to derive, be derived; (*NAUT*) to drift; **~se** *vr* to derive, be derived; to drift

derramamiento [derramaˈmjento] *nm* (*dispersión*) spilling; **~ de sangre** bloodshed

derramar [derraˈmar] *vt* to spill; (*verter*) to pour out; (*esparcir*) to scatter; **~se** *vr* to pour out; **~ lágrimas** to weep

derrame [deˈrrame] *nm* (*de líquido*) spilling; (*de sangre*) shedding; (*de tubo etc*) overflow; (*pérdida*) leakage; (*MED*) discharge; (*declive*) slope

derredor [derreˈðor] *adv*: **al o en ~ de** around, about

derretido, a [derreˈtiðo, a] *adj* melted; (*metal*) molten

derretir [derreˈtir] *vt* (*gen*) to melt; (*nieve*) to thaw; (*fig*) to squander; **~se** *vr* to melt

derribar [derriˈβar] *vt* to knock down; (*construcción*) to demolish; (*persona, gobierno, político*) to bring down

derrocar [derroˈkar] *vt* (*gobierno*) to bring down, overthrow

derrochar [derroˈtʃar] *vt* to squander; **derroche** *nm* (*despilfarro*) waste, squandering

derrota [deˈrrota] *nf* (*NAUT*) course; (*MIL, DEPORTE etc*) defeat, rout; **derrotar** *vt* (*gen*) to defeat; **derrotero** *nm* (*rumbo*) course

derruir [derruˈir] *vt* (*edificio*) to demolish

derrumbar [derrumˈbar] *vt* (*edificio*) to knock down; **~se** *vr* to collapse

derruyendo *etc vb ver* **derruir**

des *vb ver* **dar**

desabotonar [desaβotoˈnar] *vt* to unbutton, undo ♦ *vi* (*flores*) to bloom; **~se** *vr* to come undone

desabrido, a [desaˈβriðo, a] *adj* (*comida*) insipid, tasteless; (*persona*) rude, surly; (*respuesta*) sharp; (*tiempo*) unpleasant

desabrochar [desaβroˈtʃar] *vt* (*botones, broches*) to undo, unfasten; **~se** *vr* (*ropa etc*) to come undone

desacato [desaˈkato] *nm* (*falta de respeto*) disrespect; (*JUR*) contempt

desacertado, a [desaθerˈtaðo, a] *adj* (*equivocado*) mistaken; (*inoportuno*) unwise

desacierto [desaˈθjerto] *nm* mistake, error

desaconsejado, a [desakonseˈxaðo, a] *adj* ill-advised

desaconsejar [desakonseˈxar] *vt* to advise against

desacreditar [desakreðiˈtar] *vt* (*desprestigiar*) to discredit, bring into disrepute; (*denigrar*) to run down

desacuerdo [desa'kwerðo] *nm* (*conflicto*) disagreement, discord; (*error*) error, blunder

desafiar [desa'fjar] *vt* (*retar*) to challenge; (*enfrentarse a*) to defy

desafilado, a [desafi'laðo, a] *adj* blunt

desafinado, a [desafi'naðo, a] *adj*: **estar ~** to be out of tune

desafinar [desafi'nar] *vi* (*al cantar*) to be *o* sing out of tune

desafío *etc* [desa'fio] *vb ver* **desafiar** ♦ *nm* (*reto*) challenge; (*combate*) duel; (*resistencia*) defiance

desaforado, a [desafo'raðo, a] *adj* (*grito*) ear-splitting; (*comportamiento*) outrageous

desafortunadamente [desafortunaða-'mente] *adv* unfortunately

desafortunado, a [desafortu'naðo, a] *adj* (*desgraciado*) unfortunate, unlucky

desagradable [desaɣra'ðaßle] *adj* (*fastidioso, enojoso*) unpleasant; (*irritante*) disagreeable

desagradar [desaɣra'ðar] *vi* (*disgustar*) to displease; (*molestar*) to bother

desagradecido, a [desaɣraðe'θiðo, a] *adj* ungrateful

desagrado [desa'ɣraðo] *nm* (*disgusto*) displeasure; (*contrariedad*) dissatisfaction

desagraviar [desaɣra'ßjar] *vt* to make amends to

desagüe [des'aɣwe] *nm* (*de un líquido*) drainage; (*cañería*) drainpipe; (*salida*) outlet, drain

desaguisado, a [desaɣi'saðo, a] *adj* illegal ♦ *nm* outrage

desahogado, a [desao'ɣaðo, a] *adj* (*holgado*) comfortable; (*espacioso*) roomy, large

desahogar [desao'ɣar] *vt* (*aliviar*) to ease, relieve; (*ira*) to vent; **~se** *vr* (*relajarse*) to relax; (*desfogarse*) to let off steam

desahogo [desa'oɣo] *nm* (*alivio*) relief; (*comodidad*) comfort, ease

desahuciar [desau'θjar] *vt* (*enfermo*) to give up hope for; (*inquilino*) to evict;

desahucio *nm* eviction

desairar [desai'rar] *vt* (*menospreciar*) to slight, snub; (*cosa*) to disregard

desaire [des'aire] *nm* (*menosprecio*) slight; (*falta de garbo*) unattractiveness

desajustar [desaxus'tar] *vt* (*desarreglar*) to disarrange; (*desconcertar*) to throw off balance; **~se** *vr* to get out of order; (*aflojarse*) to loosen

desajuste [desa'xuste] *nm* (*de máquina*) disorder; (*situación*) imbalance

desalentador, a [desalenta'ðor, a] *adj* discouraging

desalentar [desalen'tar] *vt* (*desanimar*) to discourage

desaliento *etc* [desa'ljento] *vb ver* **desalentar** ♦ *nm* discouragement

desaliño [desa'liɲo] *nm* (*negligencia*) slovenliness

desalmado, a [desal'maðo, a] *adj* (*cruel*) cruel, heartless

desalojar [desalo'xar] *vt* (*expulsar, echar*) to eject; (*abandonar*) to move out of ♦ *vi* to move out

desamor [desa'mor] *nm* (*frialdad*) indifference; (*odio*) dislike

desamparado, a [desampa'raðo, a] *adj* (*persona*) helpless; (*lugar: expuesto*) exposed; (*desierto*) deserted

desamparar [desampa'rar] *vt* (*abandonar*) to desert, abandon; (*JUR*) to leave defenceless; (*barco*) to abandon

desandar [desan'dar] *vt*: **~ lo andado** *o* **el camino** to retrace one's steps

desangrar [desan'grar] *vt* to bleed; (*fig: persona*) to bleed dry; **~se** *vr* to lose a lot of blood

desanimado, a [desani'maðo, a] *adj* (*persona*) downhearted; (*espectáculo, fiesta*) dull

desanimar [desani'mar] *vt* (*desalentar*) to discourage; (*deprimir*) to depress; **~se** *vr* to lose heart

desapacible [desapa'θißle] *adj* (*gen*) unpleasant

desaparecer [desapare'θer] *vi* (*gen*) to disappear; (*el sol, la luz*) to vanish; **desaparecido, a** *adj* missing; **desaparecidos** *nmpl* (*en accidente*) people missing; **desaparición** *nf* disappearance

desapasionado, a [desapasjo'naðo, a] *adj* dispassionate, impartial

desapego [desa'peɣo] *nm* (*frialdad*) coolness; (*distancia*) detachment

desapercibido, a [desaperθi'βiðo, a] *adj* (*desprevenido*) unprepared; **pasar** ~ to go unnoticed

desaprensivo, a [desapren'siβo, a] *adj* unscrupulous

desaprobar [desapro'βar] *vt* (*reprobar*) to disapprove of; (*condenar*) to condemn; (*no consentir*) to reject

desaprovechado, a [desaproβe'tʃaðo, a] *adj* (*oportunidad, tiempo*) wasted; (*estudiante*) slack

desaprovechar [desaproβe'tʃar] *vt* to waste

desarmar [desar'mar] *vt* (*MIL, fig*) to disarm; (*TEC*) to take apart, dismantle; **desarme** *nm* disarmament

desarraigar [desarrai'ɣar] *vt* to uproot; **desarraigo** *nm* uprooting

desarreglar [desarre'ɣlar] *vt* (*desordenar*) to disarrange; (*trastocar*) to upset, disturb

desarreglo [desa'rreɣlo] *nm* (*de casa, persona*) disorder; (*desorden*) disorder

desarrollar [desarro'ʎar] *vt* (*gen*) to develop; (*extender*) to unfold; ~**se** *vr* to develop; (*extenderse*) to open (out); (*FOTO*) to develop; **desarrollo** *nm* development

desarticular [desartiku'lar] *vt* (*hueso*) to dislocate; (*objeto*) to take apart; (*fig*) to break up

desasir [desa'sir] *vt* to loosen; ~**se** *vr* to extricate o.s.; ~**se de** to let go, give up

desasosegar [desasose'ɣar] *vt* (*inquietar*) to disturb, make uneasy; ~**se** *vr* to become uneasy

desasosiego *etc* [desaso'sjeɣo] *vb ver* **desasosegar** ♦ *nm* (*intranquilidad*) uneasiness, restlessness; (*ansiedad*) anxiety

desastrado, a [desas'traðo, a] *adj* (*desaliñado*) shabby; (*sucio*) dirty

desastre [de'sastre] *nm* disaster; **desastroso, a** *adj* disastrous

desatado, a [desa'taðo, a] *adj* (*desligado*)

untied; (*violento*) violent, wild

desatar [desa'tar] *vt* (*nudo*) to untie; (*paquete*) to undo; (*separar*) to detach; ~**se** *vr* (*zapatos*) to come untied; (*tormenta*) to break

desatascar [desatas'kar] *vt* (*cañería*) to unblock, clear

desatender [desaten'der] *vt* (*no prestar atención a*) to disregard; (*abandonar*) to neglect

desatento, a [desa'tento, a] *adj* (*distraído*) inattentive; (*descortés*) discourteous

desatinado, a [desati'naðo, a] *adj* foolish, silly; **desatino** *nm* (*idiotez*) foolishness, folly; (*error*) blunder

desatornillar [desatorni'ʎar] *vt* to unscrew

desatrancar [desatran'kar] *vt* (*puerta*) to unbolt; (*cañería*) to clear, unblock

desautorizado, a [desautori'θaðo, a] *adj* unauthorized

desautorizar [desautori'θar] *vt* (*oficial*) to deprive of authority; (*informe*) to deny

desavenencia [desaβe'nenθja] *nf* (*desacuerdo*) disagreement; (*discrepancia*) quarrel

desayunar [desaju'nar] *vi* to have breakfast ♦ *vt* to have for breakfast; **desayuno** *nm* breakfast

desazón [desa'θon] *nf* (*angustia*) anxiety; (*fig*) annoyance

desazonar [desaθo'nar] *vt* (*fig*) to annoy, upset; ~**se** *vr* (*enojarse*) to be annoyed; (*preocuparse*) to worry, be anxious

desbandarse [desβan'darse] *vr* (*MIL*) to disband; (*fig*) to flee in disorder

desbarajuste [desβara'xuste] *nm* confusion, disorder

desbaratar [desβara'tar] *vt* (*deshacer, destruir*) to ruin

desbloquear [desβloke'ar] *vt* (*negociaciones, tráfico*) to get going again; (*COM: cuenta*) to unfreeze

desbocado, a [desβo'kaðo, a] *adj* (*caballo*) runaway

desbordar [desβor'ðar] *vt* (*sobrepasar*) to go beyond; (*exceder*) to exceed ♦ *vi* (*río*) to overflow; (*entusiasmo*) to erupt; ~**se** *vr* to overflow; to erupt

descabalgar [deskaβal'ɣar] *vi* to dismount

descabellado, a [deskaβe'ʎaðo, a] *adj* (*disparatado*) wild, crazy

descafeinado, a [deskafei'naðo, a] *adj* decaffeinated ♦ *nm* decaffeinated coffee

descalabro [deska'laβro] *nm* blow; (*desgracia*) misfortune

descalificar [deskalifi'kar] *vt* to disqualify; (*desacreditar*) to discredit

descalzar [deskal'θar] *vt* (*zapato*) to take off; **descalzo, a** *adj* barefoot(ed); (*fig*) destitute

descambiar [deskam'bjar] *vt* to exchange

descaminado, a [deskami'naðo, a] *adj* (*equivocado*) on the wrong road; (*fig*) misguided

descampado [deskam'paðo] *nm* open space

descansado, a [deskan'saðo, a] *adj* (*gen*) rested; (*que tranquiliza*) restful

descansar [deskan'sar] *vt* (*gen*) to rest ♦ *vi* to rest, have a rest; (*echarse*) to lie down

descansillo [deskan'siʎo] *nm* (*de escalera*) landing

descanso [des'kanso] *nm* (*reposo*) rest; (*alivio*) relief; (*pausa*) break; (*DEPORTE*) interval, half time

descapotable [deskapo'taβle] *nm* (*tb: coche ~*) convertible

descarado, a [deska'raðo, a] *adj* shameless; (*insolente*) cheeky

descarga [des'karɣa] *nf* (*ARQ , ELEC , MIL*) discharge; (*NAUT*) unloading

descargar [deskar'ɣar] *vt* to unload; (*golpe*) to let fly; **~se** *vr* to unburden o.s.; **descargo** *nm* (*COM*) receipt; (*JUR*) evidence

descarnado, a [deskar'naðo, a] *adj* scrawny; (*fig*) bare

descaro [des'karo] *nm* nerve

descarriar [deska'rrjar] *vt* (*descaminar*) to misdirect; (*fig*) to lead astray; **~se** *vr* (*perderse*) to lose one's way; (*separarse*) to stray; (*pervertirse*) to err, go astray

descarrilamiento [deskarrila'mjento] *nm* (*de tren*) derailment

descarrilar [deskarri'lar] *vi* to be derailed

descartar [deskar'tar] *vt* (*rechazar*) to reject; (*eliminar*) to rule out; **~se** *vr* (*NAIPES*) to discard; **~se de** to shirk

descascarillado, a [deskaskari'ʎaðo, a] *adj* (*paredes*) peeling

descendencia [desθen'denθja] *nf* (*origen*) origin, descent; (*hijos*) offspring

descender [desθen'der] *vt* (*bajar: escalera*) to go down ♦ *vi* to descend; (*temperatura, nivel*) to fall, drop; **~ de** to be descended from

descendiente [desθen'djente] *nm/f* descendant

descenso [des'θenso] *nm* descent; (*de temperatura*) drop

descifrar [desθi'frar] *vt* to decipher; (*mensaje*) to decode

descolgar [deskol'ɣar] *vt* (*bajar*) to take down; (*teléfono*) to pick up; **~se** *vr* to let o.s. down

descolorido, a [deskolo'riðo, a] *adj* faded; (*pálido*) pale

descompasado, a [deskompa'saðo, a] *adj* (*sin proporción*) out of all proportion; (*excesivo*) excessive

descomponer [deskompo'ner] *vt* (*desordenar*) to disarrange, disturb; (*TEC*) to put out of order; (*dividir*) to break down (into parts); (*fig*) to provoke; **~se** *vr* (*corromperse*) to rot, decompose; (*el tiempo*) to change (for the worse); (*TEC*) to break down

descomposición [deskomposi'θjon] *nf* (*gen*) breakdown; (*de fruta etc*) decomposition; **~ de vientre** stomach upset, diarrhoea

descompostura [deskompos'tura] *nf* (*TEC*) breakdown; (*desorganización*) disorganization; (*desorden*) untidiness

descompuesto, a [deskom'pwesto, a] *adj* (*corrompido*) decomposed; (*roto*) broken

descomunal [deskomu'nal] *adj* (*enorme*) huge

desconcertado, a [deskonθer'taðo, a] *adj* disconcerted, bewildered

desconcertar [deskonθer'tar] *vt* (*confundir*) to baffle; (*incomodar*) to upset, put out; **~se** *vr* (*turbarse*) to be upset

desconchado, a [deskon'tʃaðo, a] *adj*
(*pintura*) peeling

desconcierto *etc* [deskon'θjerto] *vb ver*
desconcertar ♦ *nm* (*gen*) disorder;
(*desorientación*) uncertainty; (*inquietud*)
uneasiness

desconectar [deskonek'tar] *vt* to
disconnect

desconfianza [deskon'fjanθa] *nf* distrust

desconfiar [deskon'fjar] *vi* to be
distrustful; ~ **de** to distrust, suspect

descongelar [deskonxe'lar] *vt* to defrost;
(*COM, POL*) to unfreeze

descongestionar [deskonxestjo'nar] *vt*
(*cabeza, tráfico*) to clear

desconocer [deskono'θer] *vt* (*ignorar*) not
to know, be ignorant of; (*no aceptar*) to
deny; (*repudiar*) to disown

desconocido, a [deskono'θiðo, a] *adj*
unknown ♦ *nm/f* stranger

desconocimiento [deskonoθi'mjento] *nm*
(*falta de conocimientos*) ignorance;
(*repudio*) disregard

desconsiderado, a [deskonsiðe'raðo, a]
adj inconsiderate; (*insensible*) thoughtless

desconsolar [deskonso'lar] *vt* to distress;
~**se** *vr* to despair

desconsuelo *etc* [deskon'swelo] *vb ver*
desconsolar ♦ *nm* (*tristeza*) distress;
(*desesperación*) despair

descontado, a [deskon'taðo, a] *adj*: **dar
por** ~ **(que)** to take (it) for granted
(that)

descontar [deskon'tar] *vt* (*deducir*) to take
away, deduct; (*rebajar*) to discount

descontento, a [deskon'tento, a] *adj*
dissatisfied ♦ *nm* dissatisfaction,
discontent

descorazonar [deskoraθo'nar] *vt* to
discourage, dishearten

descorchar [deskor'tʃar] *vt* to uncork

descorrer [desko'rrer] *vt* (*cortinas,
cerrojo*) to draw back

descortés [deskor'tes] *adj* (*mal educado*)
discourteous; (*grosero*) rude

descoser [desko'ser] *vt* to unstitch; ~**se**
vr to come apart (at the seams)

descosido, a [desko'siðo, a] *adj* (*COSTURA*)
unstitched; (*desordenado*) disjointed

descrédito [des'kreðito] *nm* discredit

descreído, a [deskre'iðo, a] *adj*
(*incrédulo*) incredulous; (*falto de fe*)
unbelieving

descremado, a [deskre'maðo, a] *adj*
skimmed

describir [deskri'βir] *vt* to describe;
descripción [deskrip'θjon] *nf* description

descrito [des'krito] *pp de* **describir**

descuartizar [deskwarti'θar] *vt* (*animal*)
to cut up

descubierto, a [desku'βjerto, a] *pp de*
descubrir ♦ *adj* uncovered, bare;
(*persona*) bareheaded ♦ *nm* (*bancario*)
overdraft; **al** ~ in the open

descubrimiento [deskuβri'mjento] *nm*
(*hallazgo*) discovery; (*revelación*) revelation

descubrir [desku'βrir] *vt* to discover, find;
(*inaugurar*) to unveil; (*vislumbrar*) to
detect; (*revelar*) to reveal, show;
(*destapar*) to uncover; ~**se** *vr* to reveal
o.s.; (*quitarse sombrero*) to take off one's
hat; (*confesar*) to confess

descuento *etc* [des'kwento] *vb ver*
descontar ♦ *nm* discount

descuidado, a [deskwi'ðaðo, a] *adj* (*sin
cuidado*) careless; (*desordenado*) untidy;
(*olvidadizo*) forgetful; (*dejado*) neglected;
(*desprevenido*) unprepared

descuidar [deskwi'ðar] *vt* (*dejar*) to
neglect; (*olvidar*) to overlook ♦ *vi*
(*distraerse*) to be careless; (*estar
desaliñado*) to let o.s. go; (*desprevenirse*)
to drop one's guard; ~**se** *vr* to be
careless; to let o.s. go; to drop one's
guard; **¡descuida!** don't worry!;
descuido *nm* (*dejadez*) carelessness;
(*olvido*) negligence

PALABRA CLAVE
---

desde ['desðe] *prep* **1** (*lugar*) from; ~
Burgos hasta mi casa hay 30 km it's
30 kms from Burgos to my house
2 (*posición*): **hablaba** ~ **el balcón** she
was speaking from the balcony
3 (*tiempo*: + *ad, n*): ~ **ahora** from now
on; ~ **la boda** since the wedding; ~ **niño**

since I *etc* was a child; ~ **3 años atrás** since 3 years ago

4 (*tiempo:* +*vb*) since; for; **nos conocemos ~ 1978/ ~ hace 20 años** we've known each other since 1978/for 20 years; **no le veo ~ 1983/~ hace 5 años** I haven't seen him since 1983/for 5 years

5 (*gama*): ~ **los más lujosos hasta los más económicos** from the most luxurious to the most reasonably priced

6: ~ **luego (que no)** of course (not)

♦ *conj*: ~ **que**: ~ **que recuerdo** for as long as I can remember; ~ **que llegó no ha salido** he hasn't been out since he arrived

desdecirse [desðe'θirse] *vr* to retract; ~ **de** to go back on

desdén [des'ðen] *nm* scorn

desdeñar [desðe'ɲar] *vt* (*despreciar*) to scorn

desdicha [des'ðitʃa] *nf* (*desgracia*) misfortune; (*infelicidad*) unhappiness; **desdichado, a** *adj* (*sin suerte*) unlucky; (*infeliz*) unhappy

desdoblar [desðo'βlar] *vt* (*extender*) to spread out; (*desplegar*) to unfold

desear [dese'ar] *vt* to want, desire, wish for

desecar [dese'kar] *vt* to dry up; ~**se** *vr* to dry up

desechar [dese'tʃar] *vt* (*basura*) to throw out *o* away; (*ideas*) to reject, discard; **desechos** *nmpl* rubbish *sg*, waste *sg*

desembalar [desemba'lar] *vt* to unpack

desembarazado, a [desembara'θaðo, a] *adj* (*libre*) clear, free; (*desenvuelto*) free and easy

desembarazar [desembara'θar] *vt* (*desocupar*) to clear; (*desenredar*) to free; ~**se** *vr*: ~**se de** to free o.s. of, get rid of

desembarcar [desembar'kar] *vt* (*mercancías etc*) to unload ♦ *vi* to disembark; ~**se** *vr* to disembark

desembocadura [desemboka'ðura] *nf* (*de río*) mouth; (*de calle*) opening

desembocar [desembo'kar] *vi* to flow into; (*fig*) to result in

desembolso [desem'bolso] *nm* payment

desembragar [desembra'ɣar] *vi* to declutch

desembrollar [desembro'ʎar] *vt* (*madeja*) to unravel; (*asunto, malentendido*) to sort out

desemejanza [deseme'xanθa] *nf* dissimilarity

desempaquetar [desempake'tar] *vt* (*regalo*) to unwrap; (*mercancía*) to unpack

desempatar [desempa'tar] *vi* to replay, hold a play-off; **desempate** *nm* (*FÚTBOL*) replay, play-off; (*TENIS*) tie-break(er)

desempeñar [desempe'ɲar] *vt* (*cargo*) to hold; (*papel*) to perform; (*lo empeñado*) to redeem; ~**se** *vr* to get out of debt; ~ **un papel** (*fig*) to play (a role)

desempeño [desem'peɲo] *nm* redeeming; (*de cargo*) occupation

desempleado, a [desemple'aðo, a] *nm/f* unemployed person; **desempleo** *nm* unemployment

desempolvar [desempol'βar] *vt* (*muebles etc*) to dust; (*lo olvidado*) to revive

desencadenar [desenkaðe'nar] *vt* to unchain; (*ira*) to unleash; ~**se** *vr* to break loose; (*tormenta*) to burst; (*guerra*) to break out

desencajar [desenka'xar] *vt* (*hueso*) to dislocate; (*mecanismo, pieza*) to disconnect, disengage

desencanto [desen'kanto] *nm* disillusionment

desenchufar [desentʃu'far] *vt* to unplug

desenfadado, a [desenfa'ðaðo, a] *adj* (*desenvuelto*) uninhibited; (*descarado*) forward; **desenfado** *nm* (*libertad*) freedom; (*comportamiento*) free and easy manner; (*descaro*) forwardness

desenfocado, a [desenfo'kaðo, a] *adj* (*FOTO*) out of focus

desenfrenado, a [desenfre'naðo, a] *adj* (*descontrolado*) uncontrolled; (*inmoderado*) unbridled; **desenfreno** *nm* (*vicio*) wildness; (*de las pasiones*) lack of self-control

desenganchar [desengan'tʃar] *vt* (*gen*) to unhook; (*FERRO*) to uncouple

desengañar [desenga'ɲar] *vt* to disillusion; **~se** *vr* to become disillusioned; **desengaño** *nm* disillusionment; (*decepción*) disappointment

desenlace [desen'laθe] *nm* outcome

desenmarañar [desenmara'ɲar] *vt* (*fig*) to unravel

desenmascarar [desenmaska'rar] *vt* to unmask

desenredar [desenre'ðar] *vt* (*pelo*) to untangle; (*problema*) to sort out

desenroscar [desenros'kar] *vt* to unscrew

desentenderse [desenten'derse] *vr*: ~ **de** to pretend not to know about; (*apartarse*) to have nothing to do with

desenterrar [desente'rrar] *vt* to exhume; (*tesoro*, *fig*) to unearth, dig up

desentonar [desento'nar] *vi* (*MUS*) to sing (*o* play) out of tune; (*color*) to clash

desentrañar [desentra'ɲar] *vt* (*misterio*) to unravel

desentumecer [desentume'θer] *vt* (*pierna etc*) to stretch; (*DEPORTE*) to loosen up

desenvoltura [desenβol'tura] *nf* (*libertad*, *gracia*) ease; (*descaro*) free and easy manner

desenvolver [desenβol'βer] *vt* (*paquete*) to unwrap; (*fig*) to develop; **~se** *vr* (*desarrollarse*) to unfold, develop; (*arreglárselas*) to cope

deseo [de'seo] *nm* desire, wish; **~so, a** *adj*: **estar ~so de** to be anxious to

desequilibrado, a [desekili'βraðo, a] *adj* unbalanced

desertar [deser'tar] *vi* to desert

desértico, a [de'sertiko, a] *adj* desert *cpd*

desesperación [desespera'θjon] *nf* (*impaciencia*) desperation, despair; (*irritación*) fury

desesperar [desespe'rar] *vt* to drive to despair; (*exasperar*) to drive to distraction ♦ *vi*: ~ **de** to despair of; **~se** *vr* to despair, lose hope

desestabilizar [desestaβili'θar] *vt* to destabilize

desestimar [desesti'mar] *vt* (*menospreciar*) to have a low opinion of; (*rechazar*) to reject

desfachatez [desfatʃa'teθ] *nf* (*insolencia*) impudence; (*descaro*) rudeness

desfalco [des'falko] *nm* embezzlement

desfallecer [desfaʎe'θer] *vi* (*perder las fuerzas*) to become weak; (*desvanecerse*) to faint

desfasado, a [desfa'saðo, a] *adj* (*anticuado*) old-fashioned; **desfase** *nm* (*diferencia*) gap

desfavorable [desfaβo'raβle] *adj* unfavourable

desfigurar [desfiɣu'rar] *vt* (*cara*) to disfigure; (*cuerpo*) to deform

desfiladero [desfila'ðero] *nm* gorge

desfilar [desfi'lar] *vi* to parade; **desfile** *nm* procession

desfogarse [desfo'ɣarse] *vr* (*fig*) to let off steam

desgajar [desɣa'xar] *vt* (*arrancar*) to tear off; (*romper*) to break off; **~se** *vr* to come off

desgana [des'ɣana] *nf* (*falta de apetito*) loss of appetite; (*renuencia*) unwillingness; **~do, a** *adj*: **estar ~do** (*sin apetito*) to have no appetite; (*sin entusiasmo*) to have lost interest

desgarrador, a [desɣarra'ðor, a] *adj* (*fig*) heartrending

desgarrar [desɣa'rrar] *vt* to tear (up); (*fig*) to shatter; **desgarro** *nm* (*en tela*) tear; (*aflicción*) grief; (*descaro*) impudence

desgastar [desɣas'tar] *vt* (*deteriorar*) to wear away *o* down; (*estropear*) to spoil; **~se** *vr* to get worn out; **desgaste** *nm* wear (and tear)

desglosar [desɣlo'sar] *vt* (*factura*) to break down

desgracia [des'ɣraθja] *nf* misfortune; (*accidente*) accident; (*vergüenza*) disgrace; (*contratiempo*) setback; **por ~** unfortunately

desgraciado, a [desɣra'θjaðo, a] *adj* (*sin suerte*) unlucky, unfortunate; (*miserable*) wretched; (*infeliz*) miserable

desgravación [desɣraβa'θjon] *nf* (*COM*): ~ **fiscal** tax relief

desgravar [desɣra'βar] *vt* (*impuestos*) to reduce the tax *o* duty on

desgreñado, a [desɣre'ɲaðo, a] *adj* dishevelled

deshabitado, a [desaßi'taðo, a] *adj* uninhabited

deshacer [desa'θer] *vt* (*casa*) to break up; (*TEC*) to take apart; (*enemigo*) to defeat; (*diluir*) to melt; (*contrato*) to break; (*intriga*) to solve; **~se** *vr* (*disolverse*) to melt; (*despedazarse*) to come apart *o* undone; **~se de** to get rid of; **~se en lágrimas** to burst into tears

desharrapado, a [desarra'paðo, a] *adj* (*persona*) shabby

deshecho, a [des'etʃo, a] *adj* undone; (*roto*) smashed; (*persona*): **estar ~** to be shattered

desheredar [desere'ðar] *vt* to disinherit

deshidratar [desiðra'tar] *vt* to dehydrate

deshielo [des'jelo] *nm* thaw

deshonesto, a [deso'nesto, a] *adj* indecent

deshonra [des'onra] *nf* (*deshonor*) dishonour; (*vergüenza*) shame

deshora [des'ora]: **a ~** *adv* at the wrong time

deshuesar [deswe'sar] *vt* (*carne*) to bone; (*fruta*) to stone

desierto, a [de'sjerto, a] *adj* (*casa, calle, negocio*) deserted ♦ *nm* desert

designar [desiɣ'nar] *vt* (*nombrar*) to designate; (*indicar*) to fix

designio [de'siɣnjo] *nm* plan

desigual [desi'ɣwal] *adj* (*terreno*) uneven; (*lucha etc*) unequal

desilusión [desilu'sjon] *nf* disillusionment; (*decepción*) disappointment; **desilusionar** *vt* to disillusion; to disappoint; **desilusionarse** *vr* to become disillusioned

desinfectar [desinfek'tar] *vt* to disinfect

desinflar [desin'flar] *vt* to deflate

desintegración [desinteɣra'θjon] *nf* disintegration

desinterés [desinte'res] *nm* (*objetividad*) disinterestedness; (*altruismo*) unselfishness

desintoxicarse [desintoksi'karse] *vr* (*drogadicto*) to undergo detoxification

desistir [desis'tir] *vi* (*renunciar*) to stop, desist

desleal [desle'al] *adj* (*infiel*) disloyal; (*COM: competencia*) unfair; **~tad** *nf* disloyalty

desleír [desle'ir] *vt* (*líquido*) to dilute; (*sólido*) to dissolve

deslenguado, a [deslen'gwaðo, a] *adj* (*grosero*) foul-mouthed

desligar [desli'ɣar] *vt* (*desatar*) to untie, undo; (*separar*) to separate; **~se** *vr* (*de un compromiso*) to extricate o.s.

desliz [des'liθ] *nm* (*fig*) lapse; **~ar** *vt* to slip, slide

deslucido, a [deslu'θiðo, a] *adj* dull; (*torpe*) awkward, graceless; (*deslustrado*) tarnished

deslumbrar [deslum'brar] *vt* to dazzle

desmadrarse [desma'ðrarse] (*fam*) *vr* (*descontrolarse*) to run wild; (*divertirse*) to let one's hair down; **desmadre** (*fam*) *nm* (*desorganización*) chaos; (*jaleo*) commotion

desmán [des'man] *nm* (*exceso*) outrage; (*abuso de poder*) abuse

desmandarse [desman'darse] *vr* (*portarse mal*) to behave badly; (*excederse*) to get out of hand; (*caballo*) to bolt

desmantelar [desmante'lar] *vt* (*deshacer*) to dismantle; (*casa*) to strip

desmaquillador [desmakiʎa'ðor] *nm* make-up remover

desmayado, a [desma'jaðo, a] *adj* (*sin sentido*) unconscious; (*carácter*) dull; (*débil*) faint, weak

desmayar [desma'jar] *vi* to lose heart; **~se** *vr* (*MED*) to faint; **desmayo** *nm* (*MED: acto*) faint; (: *estado*) unconsciousness; (*depresión*) dejection

desmedido, a [desme'ðiðo, a] *adj* excessive

desmejorar [desmexo'rar] *vt* (*dañar*) to impair, spoil; (*MED*) to weaken

desmembrar [desmem'brar] *vt* (*MED*) to dismember; (*fig*) to separate

desmemoriado, a [desmemo'rjaðo, a] *adj* forgetful

desmentir [desmen'tir] *vt* (*contradecir*) to contradict; (*refutar*) to deny ♦ *vi*: **~ de** to refute; **~se** *vr* to contradict o.s.

desmenuzar [desmenu'θar] *vt* (*deshacer*) to crumble; (*carne*) to chop; (*examinar*) to examine closely

desmerecer [desmere'θer] *vt* to be unworthy of ♦ *vi* (*deteriorarse*) to deteriorate

desmesurado, a [desmesu'raðo, a] *adj* disproportionate

desmontable [desmon'taβle] *adj* (*que se quita*: *pieza*) detachable; (*que sa pueda plegar etc*) collapsible, folding

desmontar [desmon'tar] *vt* (*deshacer*) to dismantle; (*tierra*) to level ♦ *vi* to dismount

desmoralizar [desmorali'θar] *vt* to demoralize

desmoronar [desmoro'nar] *vt* to wear away, erode; ~**se** *vr* (*edificio, dique*) to fall into disrepair; (*economía*) to decline

desnatado, a [desna'taðo, a] *adj* skimmed

desnivel [desni'βel] *nm* (*de terreno*) unevenness

desnudar [desnu'ðar] *vt* (*desvestir*) to undress; (*despojar*) to strip; ~**se** *vr* (*desvestirse*) to get undressed; desnudo, a *adj* naked ♦ *nm/f* nude; **desnudo de** devoid *o* bereft of

desnutrición [desnutri'θjon] *nf* malnutrition; **desnutrido, a** *adj* undernourished

desobedecer [desoβeðe'θer] *vt, vi* to disobey; **desobediencia** *nf* disobedience

desocupado, a [desoku'paðo, a] *adj* at leisure; (*desempleado*) unemployed; (*deshabitado*) empty, vacant

desocupar [desoku'par] *vt* to vacate

desodorante [desoðo'rante] *nm* deodorant

desolación [desola'θjon] *nf* (*lugar*) desolation; (*fig*) grief

desolar [deso'lar] *vt* to ruin, lay waste

desorbitado, a [desorβi'taðo, a] *adj* (*excesivo*: *ambición*) boundless; (*deseos*) excessive; (: *precio*) exorbitant

desorden [des'orðen] *nm* confusion; (*político*) disorder, unrest

desorganizar [desorvani'θar] *vt* (*desordenar*) to disorganize; **desorganización** *nf* (*de persona*) disorganization; (*en empresa, oficina*) disorder, chaos

desorientar [desorjen'tar] *vt* (*extraviar*) to mislead; (*confundir, desconcertar*) to confuse; ~**se** *vr* (*perderse*) to lose one's way

despabilado, a [despaβi'laðo, a] *adj* (*despierto*) wide-awake; (*fig*) alert, sharp

despabilar [despaβi'lar] *vt* (*el ingenio*) to sharpen ♦ *vi* to wake up; (*fig*) to get a move on; ~**se** *vr* to wake up; to get a move on

despachar [despa'tʃar] *vt* (*negocio*) to do, complete; (*enviar*) to send, dispatch; (*vender*) to sell, deal in; (*billete*) to issue; (*mandar ir*) to send away

despacho [des'patʃo] *nm* (*oficina*) office; (*de paquetes*) dispatch; (*venta*) sale; (*comunicación*) message

despacio [des'paθjo] *adv* slowly

desparpajo [despar'paxo] *nm* self-confidence; (*pey*) nerve

desparramar [desparra'mar] *vt* (*esparcir*) to scatter; (*líquido*) to spill

despavorido, a [despaβo'riðo, a] *adj* terrified

despecho [des'petʃo] *nm* spite; **a ~ de** in spite of

despectivo, a [despek'tiβo, a] *adj* (*despreciativo*) derogatory; (*LING*) pejorative

despedazar [despeða'θar] *vt* to tear to pieces

despedida [despe'ðiða] *nf* (*adiós*) farewell; (*de obrero*) sacking

despedir [despe'ðir] *vt* (*visita*) to see off, show out; (*empleado*) to dismiss; (*inquilino*) to evict; (*objeto*) to hurl; (*olor etc*) to give out *o* off; ~**se** *vr*: ~**se de** to say goodbye to

despegar [despe'var] *vt* to unstick ♦ *vi* (*avión*) to take off; ~**se** *vr* to come loose, come unstuck; **despego** *nm* detachment

despegue *etc* [des'peve] *vb ver* **despegar** ♦ *nm* takeoff

despeinado, a [despei'naðo, a] *adj* dishevelled, unkempt

despejado, a [despe'xaðo, a] *adj* (*lugar*) clear, free; (*cielo*) clear; (*persona*) wide-awake, bright

despejar [despe'xar] *vt* (*gen*) to clear; (*misterio*) to clear up ♦ *vi* (*el tiempo*) to clear; ~**se** *vr* (*tiempo, cielo*) to clear (up); (*misterio*) to become clearer; (*cabeza*) to clear

despellejar [despeʎeˈxar] *vt* (*animal*) to skin

despensa [desˈpensa] *nf* larder

despeñadero [despeɲaˈðero] *nm* (GEO) cliff, precipice

despeñarse [despeˈɲarse] *vr* to hurl o.s. down; (*coche*) to tumble over

desperdicio [desperˈðiθjo] *nm* (*despilfarro*) squandering; ~**s** *nmpl* (*basura*) rubbish *sg* (BRIT), garbage *sg* (US); (*residuos*) waste *sg*

desperdigarse [desperðiˈɣarse] *vr* (*rebaño, familia*) to scatter, spread out; (*granos de arroz, semillas*) to scatter

desperezarse [despereˈθarse] *vr* to stretch

desperfecto [desperˈfekto] *nm* (*deterioro*) slight damage; (*defecto*) flaw, imperfection

despertador [despertaˈðor] *nm* alarm clock

despertar [desperˈtar] *nm* awakening ♦ *vt* (*persona*) to wake up; (*recuerdos*) to revive; (*sentimiento*) to arouse ♦ *vi* to awaken, wake up; ~**se** *vr* to awaken, wake up

despiadado, a [despjaˈðaðo, a] *adj* (*ataque*) merciless; (*persona*) heartless

despido *etc* [desˈpiðo] *vb ver* **despedir** ♦ *nm* dismissal, sacking

despierto, a *etc* [desˈpjerto, a] *vb ver* **despertar** ♦ *adj* awake; (*fig*) sharp, alert

despilfarro [despilˈfarro] *nm* (*derroche*) squandering; (*lujo desmedido*) extravagance

despistar [despisˈtar] *vt* to throw off the track *o* scent; (*fig*) to mislead, confuse; ~**se** *vr* to take the wrong road; (*fig*) to become confused

despiste [desˈpiste] *nm* absentmindedness; **un** ~ a mistake, slip

desplazamiento [desplaθaˈmjento] *nm* displacement

desplazar [desplaˈθar] *vt* to move; (NAUT) to displace; (INFORM) to scroll; (*fig*) to oust; ~**se** *vr* (*persona*) to travel

desplegar [despleˈɣar] *vt* (*tela, papel*) to unfold, open out; (*bandera*) to unfurl; **despliegue** *etc* [desˈplexe] *vb ver* **desplegar** ♦ *nm* display

desplomarse [desploˈmarse] *vr* (*edificio, gobierno, persona*) to collapse

desplumar [despluˈmar] *vt* (*ave*) to pluck; (*fam: estafar*) to fleece

despoblado, a [despoˈβlaðo, a] *adj* (*sin habitantes*) uninhabited

despojar [despoˈxar] *vt* (*alguien: de sus bienes*) to divest of, deprive of; (*casa*) to strip, leave bare; (*alguien: de su cargo*) to strip of

despojo [desˈpoxo] *nm* (*acto*) plundering; (*objetos*) plunder, loot; ~**s** *nmpl* (*de ave, res*) offal

desposado, a [despoˈsaðo, a] *adj, nm/f* newly-wed

desposar [despoˈsar] *vt* to marry; ~**se** *vr* to get married

desposeer [despoˈseer] *vt*: ~ **a uno de** (*puesto, autoridad*) to strip sb of

déspota [ˈdespota] *nm/f* despot

despreciar [despreˈθjar] *vt* (*desdeñar*) to despise, scorn; (*afrentar*) to slight; **desprecio** *nm* scorn, contempt; slight

desprender [desprenˈder] *vt* (*broche*) to unfasten; (*olor*) to give off; ~**se** *vr* (*botón: caerse*) to fall off; (*broche*) to come unfastened; (*olor, perfume*) to be given off; ~**se de algo que** ... to draw from sth that ...

desprendimiento [desprendiˈmjento] *nm* (*gen*) loosening; (*generosidad*) disinterestedness; (*indiferencia*) detachment; (*de gas*) leak; (*de tierra, rocas*) landslide

despreocupado, a [despreokuˈpaðo, a] *adj* (*sin preocupación*) unworried, nonchalant; (*negligente*) careless

despreocuparse [despreokuˈparse] *vr* not to worry; ~ **de** to have no interest in

desprestigiar [desprestiˈxjar] *vt* (*criticar*) to run down; (*desacreditar*) to discredit

desprevenido, a [despreβeˈniðo, a] *adj* (*no preparado*) unprepared, unready

desproporcionado, a [desproporθjoˈnaðo, a] *adj* disproportionate, out of proportion

desprovisto, a [desproˈβisto, a] *adj*: ~ **de** devoid of

después [des'pwes] *adv* afterwards, later; (*próximo paso*) next; ~ **de comer** after lunch; **un año** ~ a year later; ~ **se debatió el tema** next the matter was discussed; ~ **de corregido el texto** after the text had been corrected; ~ **de todo** after all

desquiciado, a [deski'θjaðo, a] *adj* deranged

desquite [des'kite] *nm* (*satisfacción*) satisfaction; (*venganza*) revenge

destacar [desta'kar] *vt* to emphasize, point up; (*MIL*) to detach, detail ♦ *vi* (*resaltarse*) to stand out; (*persona*) to be outstanding *o* exceptional; ~**se** *vr* to stand out; to be outstanding *o* exceptional

destajo [des'taxo] *nm*: **trabajar a** ~ to do piecework

destapar [desta'par] *vt* (*botella*) to open; (*cacerola*) to take the lid off; (*descubrir*) to uncover; ~**se** *vr* (*revelarse*) to reveal one's true character

destartalado, a [destarta'laðo, a] *adj* (*desordenado*) untidy; (*ruinoso*) tumble-down

destello [des'teʎo] *nm* (*de estrella*) twinkle; (*de faro*) signal light

destemplado, a [destem'plaðo, a] *adj* (*MUS*) out of tune; (*voz*) harsh; (*MED*) out of sorts; (*tiempo*) unpleasant, nasty

desteñir [deste'ɲir] *vt* to fade ♦ *vi* to fade; ~**se** *vr* to fade; **esta tela no destiñe** this fabric will not run

desternillarse [desterni'ʎarse] *vr*: ~ **de risa** to split one's sides laughing

desterrar [deste'rrar] *vt* (*exilar*) to exile; (*fig*) to banish, dismiss

destiempo [des'tjempo]: **a** ~ *adv* out of turn

destierro *etc* [des'tjerro] *vb ver* **desterrar** ♦ *nm* exile

destilar [desti'lar] *vt* to distil; **destilería** *nf* distillery

destinar [desti'nar] *vt* (*funcionario*) to appoint, assign; (*fondos*) ~ **(a)** to set aside (for)

destinatario, a [destina'tarjo, a] *nm/f* addressee

destino [des'tino] *nm* (*suerte*) destiny; (*de avión, viajero*) destination

destituir [destitu'ir] *vt* to dismiss

destornillador [destorniʎa'ðor] *nm* screwdriver

destornillar [destorni'ʎar] *vt* (*tornillo*) to unscrew; ~**se** *vr* to unscrew

destreza [des'treθa] *nf* (*habilidad*) skill; (*maña*) dexterity

destrozar [destro'θar] *vt* (*romper*) to smash, break (up); (*estropear*) to ruin; (*nervios*) to shatter

destrozo [des'troθo] *nm* (*acción*) destruction; (*desastre*) smashing; ~**s** *nmpl* (*pedazos*) pieces; (*daños*) havoc *sg*

destrucción [destruk'θjon] *nf* destruction

destruir [destru'ir] *vt* to destroy

desuso [des'uso] *nm* disuse; **caer en** ~ to become obsolete

desvalido, a [desβa'liðo, a] *adj* (*desprotegido*) destitute; (*sin fuerzas*) helpless

desvalijar [desβali'xar] *vt* (*persona*) to rob; (*casa, tienda*) to burgle; (*coche*) to break into

desván [des'βan] *nm* attic

desvanecer [desβane'θer] *vt* (*disipar*) to dispel; (*borrar*) to blur; ~**se** *vr* (*humo etc*) to vanish, disappear; (*color*) to fade; (*recuerdo, sonido*) to fade away; (*MED*) to pass out; (*duda*) to be dispelled

desvanecimiento [desβaneθi'mjento] *nm* (*desaparición*) disappearance; (*de colores*) fading; (*evaporación*) evaporation; (*MED*) fainting fit

desvariar [desβa'rjar] *vi* (*enfermo*) to be delirious; **desvarío** *nm* delirium

desvelar [desβe'lar] *vt* to keep awake; ~**se** *vr* (*no poder dormir*) to stay awake; (*vigilar*) to be vigilant *o* watchful

desvelos [des'βelos] *nmpl* worrying *sg*

desvencijado, a [desβenθi'xaðo, a] *adj* (*silla*) rickety; (*máquina*) broken-down

desventaja [desβen'taxa] *nf* disadvantage

desventura [desβen'tura] *nf* misfortune

desvergonzado, a [desβervon'θaðo, a] *adj* shameless

desvergüenza [desβer'ɣwenθa] *nf* (*descaro*) shamelessness; (*insolencia*) impudence; (*mala conducta*) effrontery

desvestir [desβes'tir] *vt* to undress; **~se**
vr to undress
desviación [desβja'θjon] *nf* deviation;
(*AUTO*) diversion, detour
desviar [des'βjar] *vt* to turn aside; (*río*) to
alter the course of; (*navío*) to divert, re-
route; (*conversación*) to sidetrack; **~se** *vr*
(*apartarse del camino*) to turn aside;
(: *barco*) to go off course
desvío *etc* [des'βio] *vb ver* **desviar** ♦ *nm*
(*desviación*) detour, diversion; (*fig*)
indifference
desvirtuar [desβir'twar] *vt* to spoil; **~se** *vr*
to spoil
desvivirse [desβi'βirse] *vr*: **~ por**
(*anhelar*) to long for, crave for; (*hacer lo
posible por*) to do one's utmost for
detallar [deta'ʎar] *vt* to detail
detalle [de'taʎe] *nm* detail; (*fig*) gesture,
token; **al ~** in detail; (*COM*) retail
detallista [deta'ʎista] *nm/f* retailer
detective [detek'tiβe] *nm/f* detective
detener [dete'ner] *vt* (*gen*) to stop; (*JUR*) to
arrest; (*objeto*) to keep; **~se** *vr* to stop;
(*demorarse*): **~se en** to delay over, linger
over
detenidamente [deteniða'mente] *adv*
(*minuciosamente*) carefully; (*extensa-
mente*) at great length
detenido, a [dete'niðo, a] *adj* (*arrestado*)
under arrest; (*minucioso*) detailed ♦ *nm/f*
person under arrest, prisoner
detenimiento [deteni'mjento] *nm*: **con ~**
thoroughly; (*observar, considerar*)
carefully
detergente [deter'xente] *nm* detergent
deteriorar [deterjo'rar] *vt* to spoil,
damage; **~se** *vr* to deteriorate; **deterioro**
nm deterioration
determinación [determina'θjon] *nf*
(*empeño*) determination; (*decisión*)
decision; **determinado, a** *adj* specific
determinar [determi'nar] *vt* (*plazo*) to fix;
(*precio*) to settle; **~se** *vr* to decide
detestar [detes'tar] *vt* to detest
detractor, a [detrak'tor, a] *nm/f*
slanderer, libeller
detrás [de'tras] *adv* behind; (*atrás*) at the
back; **~ de** behind

detrimento [detri'mento] *nm*: **en ~ de** to
the detriment of
deuda ['deuða] *nf* (*condición*)
indebtedness, debt; (*cantidad*) debt
devaluación [deβalwa'θjon] *nf*
devaluation
devastar [deβas'tar] *vt* (*destruir*) to
devastate
devoción [deβo'θjon] *nf* devotion
devolución [deβolu'θjon] *nf* (*reenvío*)
return, sending back; (*reembolso*)
repayment; (*JUR*) devolution
devolver [deβol'βer] *vt* to return; (*lo
extraviado, lo prestado*) to give back;
(*carta al correo*) to send back; (*COM*) to
repay, refund; (*lo prestado*) to give back
♦ *vi* (*vomitar*) to be sick
devorar [deβo'rar] *vt* to devour
devoto, a [de'βoto, a] *adj* devout ♦ *nm/f*
admirer
devuelto *pp de* **devolver**
devuelva *etc vb ver* **devolver**
di *vb ver* **dar; decir**
día ['dia] *nm* day; **¿qué ~ es?** what's the
date?; **estar/poner al ~** to be/keep up to
date; **el ~ de hoy/de mañana** today/
tomorrow; **al ~ siguiente** (on) the
following day; **vivir al ~** to live from
hand to mouth; **de ~** by day, in daylight;
en pleno ~ in full daylight; **D~ de
Reyes** Epiphany; **~ festivo** (*ESP*) o
feriado (*AM*) holiday; **~ libre** day off
diabetes [dja'βetes] *nf* diabetes
diablo ['djaβlo] *nm* devil; **diablura** *nf*
prank
diadema [dja'ðema] *nf* tiara
diafragma [dja'fraɣma] *nm* diaphragm
diagnosis [djaɣ'nosis] *nf inv* diagnosis
diagnóstico [djaɣ'nostiko] *nm* = **diagnosis**
diagonal [djaɣo'nal] *adj* diagonal
diagrama [dja'ɣrama] *nm* diagram; **~ de
flujo** flowchart
dial ['djal] *nm* dial
dialecto [dja'lekto] *nm* dialect
dialogar [djalo'ɣar] *vi*: **~ con** (*POL*) to hold
talks with
diálogo ['djaloɣo] *nm* dialogue
diamante [dja'mante] *nm* diamond

diana ['djana] *nf* (*MIL*) reveille; (*de blanco*) centre, bull's-eye

diapositiva [djaposi'tiβa] *nf* (*FOTO*) slide, transparency

diario, a ['djarjo, a] *adj* daily ♦ *nm* newspaper; **a ~** daily; **de ~** everyday

diarrea [dja'rrea] *nf* diarrhoea

dibujar [diβu'xar] *vt* to draw, sketch; **dibujo** *nm* drawing; **dibujos animados** cartoons

diccionario [dikθjo'narjo] *nm* dictionary

dice *etc vb ver* **decir**

dicho, a ['ditʃo, a] *pp de* **decir** ♦ *adj*: **en ~s países** in the aforementioned countries ♦ *nm* saying

dichoso, a [di'tʃoso, a] *adj* happy

diciembre [di'θjembre] *nm* December

dictado [dik'taðo] *nm* dictation

dictador [dikta'ðor] *nm* dictator; **dictadura** *nf* dictatorship

dictamen [dik'tamen] *nm* (*opinión*) opinion; (*juicio*) judgment; (*informe*) report

dictar [dik'tar] *vt* (*carta*) to dictate; (*JUR*: *sentencia*) to pronounce; (*decreto*) to issue; (*AM*: *clase*) to give

didáctico, a [di'ðaktiko, a] *adj* educational

diecinueve [djeθi'nweβe] *num* nineteen

dieciocho [djeθi'otʃo] *num* eighteen

dieciséis [djeθi'seis] *num* sixteen

diecisiete [djeθi'sjete] *num* seventeen

diente ['djente] *nm* (*ANAT, TEC*) tooth; (*ZOOL*) fang; (: *de elefante*) tusk; (*de ajo*) clove; **hablar entre ~s** to mutter, mumble

diera *etc vb ver* **dar**

diesel ['disel] *adj*: **motor ~** diesel engine

diestro, a ['djestro, a] *adj* (*derecho*) right; (*hábil*) skilful

dieta ['djeta] *nf* diet; **diétetico, a** *adj* diet (*atr*), dietary

diez [djeθ] *num* ten

diezmar [djeθ'mar] *vt* (*población*) to decimate

difamar [difa'mar] *vt* (*JUR*: *hablando*) to slander; (: *por escrito*) to libel

diferencia [dife'renθja] *nf* difference; **diferenciar** *vt* to differentiate between

♦ *vi* to differ; **diferenciarse** *vr* to differ, be different; (*distinguirse*) to distinguish o.s.

diferente [dife'rente] *adj* different

diferido [dife'riðo] *nm*: **en ~** (*TV etc*) recorded

difícil [di'fiθil] *adj* difficult

dificultad [difikul'taθ] *nf* difficulty; (*problema*) trouble; (*objeción*) objection

dificultar [difikul'tar] *vt* (*complicar*) to complicate, make difficult; (*estorbar*) to obstruct

difteria [dif'terja] *nf* diphtheria

difundir [difun'dir] *vt* (*calor, luz*) to diffuse; (*RADIO, TV*) to broadcast; **~ una noticia** to spread a piece of news; **~se** *vr* to spread (out)

difunto, a [di'funto, a] *adj* dead, deceased ♦ *nm/f* deceased (person)

difusión [difu'sjon] *nf* (*RADIO, TV*) broadcasting

diga *etc vb ver* **decir**

digerir [dixe'rir] *vt* to digest; (*fig*) to absorb; **digestión** *nf* digestion; **digestivo, a** *adj* digestive

digital [dixi'tal] *adj* (*INFORM*) digital

dignarse [diɣ'narse] *vr* to deign to

dignatario, a [diɣna'tarjo, a] *nm/f* dignitary

dignidad [diɣni'ðaθ] *nf* dignity

digno, a ['diɣno, a] *adj* worthy

digo *etc vb ver* **decir**

dije *etc vb ver* **decir**

dilapidar [dilapi'ðar] *vt* (*dinero, herencia*) to squander, waste

dilatar [dila'tar] *vt* (*cuerpo*) to dilate; (*prolongar*) to prolong; (*aplazar*) to delay

dilema [di'lema] *nm* dilemma

diligencia [dili'xenθja] *nf* diligence; (*ocupación*) errand, job; **~s** *nfpl* (*JUR*) formalities; **diligente** *adj* diligent

diluir [dilu'ir] *vt* to dilute

diluvio [di'luβjo] *nm* deluge, flood

dimensión [dimen'sjon] *nf* dimension

diminuto, a [dimi'nuto, a] *adj* tiny, diminutive

dimitir [dimi'tir] *vi* to resign

dimos *vb ver* **dar**

Dinamarca [dina'marka] *nf* Denmark

dinámico, a [di'namiko, a] *adj* dynamic

dinamita [dina'mita] *nf* dynamite

dínamo ['dinamo] *nf* dynamo

dineral [dine'ral] *nm* large sum of money, fortune

dinero [di'nero] *nm* money; ~ **contante**, ~ **efectivo** (ready) cash; ~ **suelto** (loose) change

dio *vb ver* **dar**

dios [djos] *nm* god; **¡D~ mío!** (oh,) my God!

diosa ['djosa] *nf* goddess

diploma [di'ploma] *nm* diploma

diplomacia [diplo'maθja] *nf* diplomacy; (*fig*) tact

diplomado, a [diplo'maðo, a] *adj* qualified

diplomático, a [diplo'matiko, a] *adj* diplomatic ♦ *nm/f* diplomat

diputación [diputa'θjon] *nf* (*tb:* ~ **provincial**) ≈ county council

diputado, a [dipu'taðo, a] *nm/f* delegate; (*POL*) ≈ member of parliament (*BRIT*), ≈ representative (*US*)

dique ['dike] *nm* dyke

diré *etc vb ver* **decir**

dirección [direk'θjon] *nf* direction; (*señas*) address; (*AUTO*) steering; (*gerencia*) management; (*POL*) leadership; ~ **única/prohibida** one-way street/no entry

directa [di'rekta] *nf* (*AUT*) top gear

directiva [direk'tißa] *nf* (*DEP, tb: junta ~*) board of directors

directo, a [di'rekto, a] *adj* direct; (*RADIO, TV*) live; **transmitir en** ~ to broadcast live

director, a [direk'tor, a] *adj* leading ♦ *nm/f* director; (*ESCOL*) head(teacher) (*BRIT*), principal (*US*); (*gerente*) manager(ess); (*PRENSA*) editor; ~ **de cine** film director; ~ **general** managing director

dirigente [diri'xente] *nm/f* (*POL*) leader

dirigir [diri'xir] *vt* to direct; (*carta*) to address; (*obra de teatro, film*) to direct; (*MUS*) to conduct; (*comercio*) to manage; **~se** *vr*: **~se a** to go towards, make one's way towards; (*hablar con*) to speak to

dirija *etc vb ver* **dirigir**

discernir [disθer'nir] *vt* (*distinguir,*

discriminar) to discern

disciplina [disθi'plina] *nf* discipline

discípulo, a [dis'θipulo, a] *nm/f* disciple

disco ['disko] *nm* disc; (*DEPORTE*) discus; (*TEL*) dial; (*AUTO: semáforo*) light; (*MUS*) record; (*INFORM*): ~ **flexible/rígido** floppy/hard disk; ~ **compacto/de larga duración** compact disc/long-playing record; ~ **de freno** brake disc

disconforme [diskon'forme] *adj* differing; **estar ~ (con)** to be in disagreement (with)

discordia [dis'korðja] *nf* discord

discoteca [disko'teka] *nf* disco(theque)

discreción [diskre'θjon] *nf* discretion; (*reserva*) prudence; **comer a ~** to eat as much as one wishes; **discrecional** *adj* (*facultativo*) discretionary

discrepancia [diskre'panθja] *nf* (*diferencia*) discrepancy; (*desacuerdo*) disagreement

discreto, a [dis'kreto, a] *adj* (*diplomático*) discreet; (*sensato*) sensible; (*reservado*) quiet; (*sobrio*) sober

discriminación [diskrimina'θjon] *nf* discrimination

disculpa [dis'kulpa] *nf* excuse; (*pedir perdón*) apology; **pedir ~s a/por** to apologize to/for; **disculpar** *vt* to excuse, pardon; **disculparse** *vr* to excuse o.s.; to apologize

discurrir [disku'rrir] *vi* (*pensar, reflexionar*) to think, meditate; (*recorrer*) to roam, wander; (*el tiempo*) to pass, go by

discurso [dis'kurso] *nm* speech

discusión [disku'sjon] *nf* (*diálogo*) discussion; (*riña*) argument

discutir [disku'tir] *vt* (*debatir*) to discuss; (*pelear*) to argue about; (*contradecir*) to argue against ♦ *vi* to discuss; (*disputar*) to argue

disecar [dise'kar] *vt* (*conservar: animal*) to stuff; (: *planta*) to dry

diseminar [disemi'nar] *vt* to disseminate, spread

diseño [di'seɲo] *nm* design; (*ARTE*) drawing

disfraz [dis'fraθ] *nm* (*máscara*) disguise; (*excusa*) pretext; **~ar** *vt* to disguise;

~arse *vr*: **~arse de** to disguise o.s. as

disfrutar [disfru'tar] *vt* to enjoy ♦ *vi* to enjoy o.s.; **~ de** to enjoy, possess

disgregarse [disɣre'ɣarse] *vr* (*muchedumbre*) to disperse

disgustar [disɣus'tar] *vt* (*no gustar*) to displease; (*contrariar, enojar*) to annoy, upset; **~se** *vr* to be annoyed; (*dos personas*) to fall out

disgusto [dis'ɣusto] *nm* (*repugnancia*) disgust; (*contrariedad*) annoyance; (*tristeza*) grief; (*riña*) quarrel; (*avería*) misfortune

disidente [disi'ðente] *nm* dissident

disimular [disimu'lar] *vt* (*ocultar*) to hide, conceal ♦ *vi* to dissemble

disipar [disi'par] *vt* to dispel; (*fortuna*) to squander; **~se** *vr* (*nubes*) to vanish; (*indisciplinarse*) to dissipate

dislocarse [dislo'karse] *vr* (*articulación*) to sprain, dislocate

disminución [disminu'θjon] *nf* decrease, reduction

disminuido, a [disminu'iðo, a] *nm/f*: **~ mental/físico** mentally/physically handicapped person

disminuir [disminu'ir] *vt* to decrease, diminish

disociarse [diso'θjarse] *vr*: **~ (de)** to dissociate o.s. (from)

disolver [disol'βer] *vt* (*gen*) to dissolve; **~se** *vr* to dissolve; (*COM*) to go into liquidation

dispar [dis'par] *adj* different

disparar [dispa'rar] *vt, vi* to shoot, fire

disparate [dispa'rate] *nm* (*tontería*) foolish remark; (*error*) blunder; **decir ~s** to talk nonsense

disparo [dis'paro] *nm* shot

dispensar [dispen'sar] *vt* to dispense; (*disculpar*) to excuse

dispersar [disper'sar] *vt* to disperse; **~se** *vr* to scatter

disponer [dispo'ner] *vt* (*arreglar*) to arrange; (*ordenar*) to put in order; (*preparar*) to prepare, get ready ♦ *vi*: **~ de** to have, own; **~se** *vr*: **~se a** *o* **para hacer** to prepare to do

disponible [dispo'niβle] *adj* available

disposición [disposi'θjon] *nf* arrangement, disposition; (*aptitud*) aptitude; (*INFORM*) layout; **a la ~ de** at the disposal of; **~ de ánimo** state of mind

dispositivo [disposi'tiβo] *nm* device, mechanism

dispuesto, a [dis'pwesto, a] *pp de* **disponer** ♦ *adj* (*arreglado*) arranged; (*preparado*) disposed

disputar [dispu'tar] *vt* (*discutir*) to dispute, question; (*contender*) to contend for ♦ *vi* to argue

disquete [dis'kete] *nm* floppy disk, diskette

distancia [dis'tanθja] *nf* distance

distanciar [distan'θjar] *vt* to space out; **~se** *vr* to become estranged

distante [dis'tante] *adj* distant

distar [dis'tar] *vi*: **dista 5km de aquí** it is 5km from here

diste *vb ver* **dar**

disteis ['disteis] *vb ver* **dar**

distension [disten'sjon] *nf* (*en las relaciones*) relaxation; (*POL*) détente; (*muscular*) strain

distinción [distin'θjon] *nf* distinction; (*elegancia*) elegance; (*honor*) honour

distinguido, a [distin'ɡiðo, a] *adj* distinguished

distinguir [distin'ɡir] *vt* to distinguish; (*escoger*) to single out; **~se** *vr* to be distinguished

distintivo [distin'tiβo] *nm* badge; (*fig*) characteristic

distinto, a [dis'tinto, a] *adj* different; (*claro*) clear

distracción [distrak'θjon] *nf* distraction; (*pasatiempo*) hobby, pastime; (*olvido*) absent-mindedness, distraction

distraer [distra'er] *vt* (*atención*) to distract; (*divertir*) to amuse; (*fondos*) to embezzle; **~se** *vr* (*entretenerse*) to amuse o.s.; (*perder la concentración*) to allow one's attention to wander

distraído, a [distra'iðo, a] *adj* (*gen*) absent-minded; (*entretenido*) amusing

distribuidor, a [distriβui'ðor, a] *nm/f* distributor; (*AUT*) distributor;

distribuidora nf (COM) dealer, agent; (CINE) distributor

distribuir [distriβu'ir] vt to distribute

distrito [dis'trito] nm (sector, territorio) region; (barrio) district

disturbio [dis'turβjo] nm disturbance; (desorden) riot

disuadir [diswa'ðir] vt to dissuade

disuelto [di'swelto] pp de **disolver**

disyuntiva [disjun'tiβa] nf dilemma

DIU nm abr (= dispositivo intrauterino) IUD

diurno, a ['djurno, a] adj day cpd

divagar [diβa'ɣar] vi (desviarse) to digress

diván [di'βan] nm divan

divergencia [diβer'xenθja] nf divergence

diversidad [diβersi'ðað] nf diversity, variety

diversificar [diβersifi'kar] vt to diversify

diversión [diβer'sjon] nf (gen) entertainment; (actividad) hobby, pastime

diverso, a [di'βerso, a] adj diverse; ~s **libros** several books; ~s nmpl sundries

divertido, a [diβer'tiðo, a] adj (chiste) amusing; (fiesta etc) enjoyable

divertir [diβer'tir] vt (entretener, recrear) to amuse; ~se vr (pasarlo bien) to have a good time; (distraerse) to amuse o.s

dividendos [diβi'ðendos] nmpl (COM) dividends

dividir [diβi'ðir] vt (gen) to divide; (separar) to separate; (distribuir) to distribute, share out

divierta etc vb ver **divertir**

divino, a [di'βino, a] adj divine

divirtiendo etc vb ver **divertir**

divisa [di'βisa] nf (emblema, moneda) emblem, badge; ~s nfpl foreign exchange sg

divisar [diβi'sar] vt to make out, distinguish

división [diβi'sjon] nf (gen) division; (de partido) split; (de país) partition

divorciar [diβor'θjar] vt to divorce; ~se vr to get divorced; **divorcio** nm divorce

divulgar [diβul'βar] vt (desparramar) to spread; (hacer circular) to divulge, circulate; ~se vr to leak out

DNI (ESP) nm abr (= Documento Nacional de Identidad) national identity card

Dña. abr (= doña) Mrs

do [do] nm (MUS) do, C

dobladillo [doβla'ðiʎo] nm (de vestido) hem; (de pantalón: vuelta) turn-up (BRIT), cuff (US)

doblar [do'βlar] vt to double; (papel) to fold; (caño) to bend; (la esquina) to turn, go round; (film) to dub ♦ vi to turn; (campana) to toll; ~se vr (plegarse) to fold (up), crease; (encorvarse) to bend

doble ['doβle] adj double; (de dos aspectos) dual; (fig) two-faced ♦ nm double ♦ nm/f (TEATRO) double, stand-in; ~s nmpl (DEPORTE) doubles sg; **con sentido** ~ with a double meaning

doblegar [doβle'βar] vt to fold, crease; ~se vr to yield

doblez [do'βleθ] nm fold, hem ♦ nf insincerity, duplicity

doce ['doθe] num twelve; ~na nf dozen

docente [do'θente] adj: **centro/personal** ~ teaching establishment/staff

dócil ['doθil] adj (pasivo) docile; (obediente) obedient

docto, a ['dokto, a] adj: ~ **en** instructed in

doctor, a [dok'tor, a] nm/f doctor

doctorado [dokto'raðo] nm doctorate

doctrina [dok'trina] nf doctrine, teaching

documentación [dokumenta'θjon] nf documentation, papers pl

documental [dokumen'tal] adj, nm documentary

documento [doku'mento] nm (certificado) document; ~ **national de identidad** identity card

dólar ['dolar] nm dollar

doler [do'ler] vt, vi to hurt; (fig) to grieve; ~se vr (de su situación) to grieve, feel sorry; (de las desgracias ajenas) to sympathize; **me duele el brazo** my arm hurts

dolor [do'lor] nm pain; (fig) grief, sorrow; ~ **de cabeza** headache; ~ **de estómago** stomachache

domar [do'mar] vt to tame

domesticar [domesti'kar] vt = **domar**

doméstico, a [do'mestiko, a] *adj* (*vida, servicio*) home; (*tareas*) household; (*animal*) tame, pet

domiciliación [domiθilia'θjon] *nf*: ~ **de pagos** (*COM*) standing order

domicilio [domi'θiljo] *nm* home; ~ **particular** private residence; ~ **social** (*COM*) head office; **sin ~ fijo** of no fixed abode

dominante [domi'nante] *adj* dominant; (*persona*) domineering

dominar [domi'nar] *vt* (*gen*) to dominate; (*idiomas*) to be fluent in ♦ *vi* to dominate, prevail; ~**se** *vr* to control o.s.

domingo [do'miŋgo] *nm* Sunday

dominio [do'minjo] *nm* (*tierras*) domain; (*autoridad*) power, authority; (*de las pasiones*) grip, hold; (*de idiomas*) command

don [don] *nm* (*talento*) gift; ~ **Juan Gómez** Mr Juan Gómez, Juan Gómez Esq (*BRIT*)

donaire [do'naire] *nm* charm

donar [do'nar] *vt* to donate

donativo [dona'tiβo] *nm* donation

doncella [don'θeʎa] *nf* (*criada*) maid

donde ['donde] *adv* where ♦ *prep*: **el coche está allí ~ el farol** the car is over there by the lamppost *o* where the lamppost is; **por ~** through which; **en ~** where, in which

dónde ['donde] *adv interrogativo* where?; **¿a ~ vas?** where are you going (to)?; **¿de ~ vienes?** where have you come from?; **¿por ~?** where?, whereabouts?

dondequiera [donde'kjera] *adv* anywhere; **por ~** everywhere, all over the place ♦ *conj*: ~ **que** wherever

doña ['doɲa] *nf*: ~ **Alicia** Alicia; ~ **Victoria Benito** Mrs Victoria Benito

dorado, a [do'raðo, a] *adj* (*color*) golden; (*TEC*) gilt

dormir [dor'mir] *vt*: ~ **la siesta por la tarde** to have an afternoon nap ♦ *vi* to sleep; ~**se** *vr* to fall asleep

dormitar [dormi'tar] *vi* to doze

dormitorio [dormi'torjo] *nm* bedroom; ~ **común** dormitory

dorsal [dor'sal] *nm* (*DEPORTE*) number

dorso ['dorso] *nm* (*de mano*) back; (*de hoja*) other side

dos [dos] *num* two

dosis ['dosis] *nf inv* dose, dosage

dotado, a [do'taðo, a] *adj* gifted; ~ **de** endowed with

dotar [do'tar] *vt* to endow; **dote** *nf* dowry; **dotes** *nfpl* (*talentos*) gifts

doy *vb ver* **dar**

dragaminas [draɣa'minas] *nm* minesweeper

dragar [dra'ɣar] *vt* (*río*) to dredge; (*minas*) to sweep

drama ['drama] *nm* drama

dramaturgo [drama'turɣo] *nm* dramatist, playwright

drástico, a ['drastiko, a] *adj* drastic

drenaje [dre'naxe] *nm* drainage

droga ['droɣa] *nf* drug

drogadicto, a [droɣa'ðikto, a] *nm/f* drug addict

droguería [droɣe'ria] *nf* hardware shop (*BRIT*) *o* store (*US*)

ducha ['dutʃa] *nf* (*baño*) shower; (*MED*) douche; **ducharse** *vr* to take a shower

duda ['duða] *nf* doubt; **dudar** *vt, vi* to doubt; **dudoso, a** [du'ðoso, a] *adj* (*incierto*) hesitant; (*sospechoso*) doubtful

duela *etc vb ver* **doler**

duelo ['dwelo] *vb ver* **doler** ♦ *nm* (*combate*) duel; (*luto*) mourning

duende ['dwende] *nm* imp, goblin

dueño, a ['dweɲo, a] *nm/f* (*propietario*) owner; (*de pensión, taberna*) landlord/lady; (*empresario*) employer

duermo *etc vb ver* **dormir**

dulce ['dulθe] *adj* sweet ♦ *adv* gently, softly ♦ *nm* sweet

dulzura [dul'θura] *nf* sweetness; (*ternura*) gentleness

duna ['duna] *nf* (*GEO*) dune

dúo ['duo] *nm* duet

duplicar [dupli'kar] *vt* (*hacer el doble de*) to duplicate; ~**se** *vr* to double

duque ['duke] *nm* duke; ~**sa** *nf* duchess

duración [dura'θjon] *nf* (*de película, disco etc*) length; (*de pila etc*) life; (*curso: de acontecimientos etc*) duration

duradero, a [dura'ðero, a] *adj* (*tela etc*)

hard-wearing; (*fe, paz*) lasting
durante [du'rante] *prep* during
durar [du'rar] *vi* (*permanecer*) to last;
(*recuerdo*) to remain
durazno [du'raθno] (*AM*) *nm* (*fruta*) peach;
(*árbol*) peach tree
durex ['dureks] (*AM*) *nm* (*tira adhesiva*)
Sellotape ® (*BRIT*), Scotch tape ® (*US*)
dureza [du'reθa] *nf* (*calidad*) hardness
duro, a ['duro, a] *adj* hard; (*carácter*)
tough ♦ *adv* hard ♦ *nm* (*moneda*) five
peseta coin *o* piece

E e

E *abr* (= *este*) E
e [e] *conj* and
ebanista [eβa'nista] *nm/f* cabinetmaker
ébano ['eβano] *nm* ebony
ebrio, a ['eβrjo, a] *adj* drunk
ebullición [eβuʎi'θjon] *nf* boiling
eccema [ek'θema] *nf* (*MED*) eczema
echar [e'tʃar] *vt* to throw; (*agua, vino*) to
pour (out); (*empleado: despedir*) to fire,
sack; (*hojas*) to sprout; (*cartas*) to post;
(*humo*) to emit, give out ♦ *vi*: ~ a
correr/llorar to run off/burst into
tears; ~**se** *vr* to lie down; ~ **llave a** to
lock (up); ~ **abajo** (*gobierno*) to
overthrow; (*edificio*) to demolish; ~
mano a to lay hands on; ~ **una mano a**
uno (*ayuda*) to give sb a hand; ~ **de**
menos to miss
eclesiástico, a [ekle'sjastiko, a] *adj*
ecclesiastical
eclipse [e'klipse] *nm* eclipse
eco ['eko] *nm* echo; **tener ~** to catch on
ecología [ekolo'via] *nf* ecology;
ecológico, a *adj* (*producto, método*)
environmentally-friendly; (*agricultura*)
organic; **ecologista** *adj* ecological,
environmental ♦ *nm/f* environmentalist
economato [ekono'mato] *nm* cooperative
store
economía [ekono'mia] *nf* (*sistema*)
economy; (*cualidad*) thrift
económico, a [eko'nomiko, a] *adj* (*barato*) cheap, economical; (*persona*)

thrifty; (*COM: año etc*) financial;
(: *situación*) economic
economista [ekono'mista] *nm/f* econo-
mist
ECU [eku] *nm* ECU
ecuador [ekwa'ðor] *nm* equator; **(el) E~**
Ecuador
ecuánime [e'kwanime] *adj* (*carácter*)
level-headed; (*estado*) calm
ecuatoriano, a [ekwato'rjano, a] *adj, nm/
f* Ecuadorian
ecuestre [e'kwestre] *adj* equestrian
eczema [ek'θema] *nm* = **eccema**
edad [e'ðað] *nf* age; **¿qué ~ tienes?** how
old are you?; **tiene ocho años de ~** 'he
is eight (years old); **de ~ mediana/**
avanzada middle-aged/advanced in
years; **la E~ Media** the Middle Ages
edición [eði'θjon] *nf* (*acto*) publication;
(*ejemplar*) edition
edicto [e'ðikto] *nm* edict, proclamation
edificio [eði'fiθjo] *nm* building; (*fig*)
edifice, structure
Edimburgo [eðim'burvo] *nm* Edinburgh
editar [eði'tar] *vt* (*publicar*) to publish;
(*preparar textos*) to edit
editor, a [eði'tor, a] *nm/f* (*que publica*)
publisher; (*redactor*) editor ♦ *adj*: **casa**
~**a** publishing house, publisher; ~**ial** *adj*
editorial ♦ *nm* leading article, editorial;
casa ~ial publishing house, publisher
edredon [eðre'ðon] *nm* duvet
educación [eðuka'θjon] *nf* education;
(*crianza*) upbringing; (*modales*) (good)
manners *pl*
educar [eðu'kar] *vt* to educate; (*criar*) to
bring up; (*voz*) to train
EE. UU. *nmpl abr* (= *Estados Unidos*)
US(A)
efectista [efek'tista] *adj* sensationalist
efectivamente [efektiβa'mente] *adv* (*como
respuesta*) exactly, precisely;
(*verdaderamente*) really; (*de hecho*) in
fact
efectivo, a [efek'tiβo, a] *adj* effective;
(*real*) actual, real ♦ *nm*: **pagar en ~** to
pay (in) cash; **hacer ~ un cheque** to
cash a cheque
efecto [e'fekto] *nm* effect, result; ~**s** *nmpl*

(*~s personales*) effects; (*bienes*) goods; (*COM*) assets; **en ~** in fact; (*respuesta*) exactly, indeed; **~ invernadero** greenhouse effect

efectuar [efek'twar] *vt* to carry out; (*viaje*) to make

eficacia [efi'kaθja] *nf* (*de persona*) efficiency; (*de medicamento etc*) effectiveness

eficaz [efi'kaθ] *adj* (*persona*) efficient; (*acción*) effective

eficiente [efi'θjente] *adj* efficient

efusivo, a [efu'siβo, a] *adj* effusive; **mis más efusivas gracias** my warmest thanks

EGB (*ESP*) *nf abr* (*ESCOL*) = *Educación General Básica*

egipcio, a [e'xipθjo, a] *adj, nm/f* Egyptian

Egipto [e'xipto] *nm* Egypt

egoísmo [exo'ismo] *nm* egoism

egoísta [exo'ista] *adj* egoistical, selfish
♦ *nm/f* egoist

egregio, a [e'xrexjo, a] *adj* eminent, distinguished

Eire ['eire] *nm* Eire

ej. *abr* (= *ejemplo*) eg

eje ['exe] *nm* (*GEO, MAT*) axis; (*de rueda*) axle; (*de máquina*) shaft, spindle

ejecución [exeku'θjon] *nf* execution; (*cumplimiento*) fulfilment; (*actuación*) performance; (*JUR: embargo de deudor*) attachment

ejecutar [exeku'tar] *vt* to execute, carry out; (*matar*) to execute; (*cumplir*) to fulfil; (*MUS*) to perform; (*JUR: embargar*) to attach, distrain (on)

ejecutivo, a [exeku'tiβo, a] *adj* executive; **el (poder) ~** the executive (power)

ejemplar [exem'plar] *adj* exemplary ♦ *nm* example; (*ZOOL*) specimen; (*de libro*) copy; (*de periódico*) number, issue

ejemplo [e'xemplo] *nm* example; **por ~** for example

ejercer [exer'θer] *vt* to exercise; (*influencia*) to exert; (*un oficio*) to practise ♦ *vi* (*practicar*): **~ (de)** to practise (as); (*tener oficio*) to hold office

ejercicio [exer'θiθjo] *nm* exercise;

(*período*) tenure; **~ comercial** financial year

ejército [e'xerθito] *nm* army; **entrar en el ~** to join the army, join up

ejote [e'xote] (*AM*) *nm* green bean

┌─────────────────┐
│ **PALABRA CLAVE** │
└─────────────────┘

el [el] (*f* **la**, *pl* **los**, **las**, *neutro* **lo**) *art def*
1 the; **el libro/la mesa/los estudiantes** the book/table/students
2 (*con n abstracto: no se traduce*): **el amor/la juventud** love/youth
3 (*posesión: se traduce a menudo por adj posesivo*): **romperse el brazo** to break one's arm; **levantó la mano** he put his hand up; **se puso el sombrero** she put her hat on
4 (*valor descriptivo*): **tener la boca grande/los ojos azules** to have a big mouth/blue eyes
5 (*con días*) on; **me iré el viernes** I'll leave on Friday; **los domingos suelo ir a nadar** on Sundays I generally go swimming
6 (*lo + adj*): **lo difícil/caro** what is difficult/expensive; (= *cuán*): **no se da cuenta de lo pesado que es** he doesn't realise how boring he is
♦ *pron demos* **1**: **mi libro y el de usted** my book and yours; **las de Pepe son mejores** Pepe's are better; **no la(s) blanca(s) sino la(s) gris(es)** not the white one(s) but the grey one(s)
2: **lo de: lo de ayer** what happened yesterday; **lo de las facturas** that business about the invoices
♦ *pron relativo*: **el que** *etc* **1** (*indef*): **el (los) que** **quiera(n) que se vaya(n)** anyone who wants to can leave; **llévese el que más le guste** take the one you like best
2 (*def*): **el que compré ayer** the one I bought yesterday; **los que se van** those who leave
3: **lo que: lo que pienso yo/más me gusta** what I think/like most
♦ *conj*: **el que: el que lo diga** the fact that he says so; **el que sea tan vago me molesta** his being so lazy bothers me

♦ *excl*: ¡el susto que me diste! what a fright you gave me!
♦ *pron personal* **1** (*persona: m*) him; (: *f*) her; (: *pl*) them; **lo/las veo** I can see him/them
2 (*animal, cosa: sg*) it; (: *pl*) them; **lo** (*o* **la**) **veo** I can see it; **los** (*o* **las**) **veo** I can see them
3: lo (*como sustituto de frase*): **no lo sabía** I didn't know; **ya lo entiendo** I understand now

él [el] *pron* (*persona*) he; (*cosa*) it; (*después de prep: persona*) him; (: *cosa*) it; **de ~** his
elaborar [elaβo'rar] *vt* (*producto*) to make, manufacture; (*preparar*) to prepare; (*madera, metal etc*) to work; (*proyecto etc*) to work on *o* out
elasticidad [elastiθi'ðað] *nf* elasticity
elástico, a [e'lastiko, a] *adj* elastic; (*flexible*) flexible ♦ *nm* elastic; (*un ~*) elastic band
elección [elek'θjon] *nf* election; (*selección*) choice, selection
electorado [elekto'raðo] *nm* electorate, voters *pl*
electricidad [elektriθi'ðað] *nf* electricity
electricista [elektri'θista] *nm/f* electrician
eléctrico, a [e'lektriko, a] *adj* electric
electro... [elektro] *prefijo* electro...;
~cardiograma *nm* electrocardiogram;
~cutar *vt* to electrocute; **~do** *nm* electrode; **~domésticos** *nmpl* (electrical) household appliances; **~magnético, a** *adj* electromagnetic
electrónica [elek'tronika] *nf* electronics *sg*
electrónico, a [elek'troniko, a] *adj* electronic
electrotecnia [elektro'teknja] *nf* electrical engineering; **electrotécnico, a** *nm/f* electrical engineer
elefante [ele'fante] *nm* elephant
elegancia [ele'γanθja] *nf* elegance, grace; (*estilo*) stylishness
elegante [ele'γante] *adj* elegant, graceful; (*estiloso*) stylish, fashionable
elegía [ele'xia] *nf* elegy
elegir [ele'xir] *vt* (*escoger*) to choose, select; (*optar*) to opt for; (*presidente*) to elect
elemental [elemen'tal] *adj* (*claro, obvio*) elementary; (*fundamental*) elemental, fundamental
elemento [ele'mento] *nm* element; (*fig*) ingredient; **~s** *nmpl* elements, rudiments
elenco [e'lenko] *nm* (TEATRO, CINE) cast
elepé [ele'pe] (*pl*: **elepés**) *nm* L.P.
elevación [eleβa'θjon] *nf* elevation; (*acto*) raising, lifting; (*de precios*) rise; (GEO *etc*) height, altitude; (*de persona*) nobleness
elevar [ele'βar] *vt* to raise, lift (up); (*precio*) to put up; **~se** *vr* (*edificio*) to rise; (*precios*) to go up; (*transportarse, enajenarse*) to get carried away
eligiendo *etc vb ver* **elegir**
elija *etc vb ver* **elegir**
eliminar [elimi'nar] *vt* to eliminate, remove
eliminatoria [elimina'torja] *nf* heat, preliminary (round)
elite [e'lite] *nf* elite
ella ['eʎa] *pron* (*persona*) she; (*cosa*) it; (*después de prep: persona*) her; (: *cosa*) it; **de ~** hers
ellas ['eʎas] *pron* (*personas y cosas*) they; (*después de prep*) them; **de ~** theirs
ello ['eʎo] *pron* it
ellos ['eʎos] *pron* they; (*después de prep*) them; **de ~** theirs
elocuencia [elo'kwenθja] *nf* eloquence
elogiar [elo'xjar] *vt* to praise, eulogize; **elogio** *nm* praise
elote [e'lote] (AM) *nm* corn on the cob
eludir [elu'ðir] *vt* (*evitar*) to avoid, evade; (*escapar*) to escape, elude
emanar [ema'nar] *vi*: **~ de** to emanate from, come from; (*derivar de*) to originate in
emancipar [emanθi'par] *vt* to emancipate; **~se** *vr* to become emancipated, free o.s.
embadurnar [embaður'nar] *vt* to smear
embajada [emba'xaða] *nf* embassy
embajador, a [embaxa'ðor, a] *nm/f* ambassador/ambassadress
embalaje [emba'laxe] *nm* packing
embalar [emba'lar] *vt* (*envolver*) to parcel, wrap (up); (*envasar*) to package; **~se** *vr*

to go fast

embalsamar [embalsaˈmar] *vt* to embalm

embalse [emˈbalse] *nm* (*presa*) dam;
(*lago*) reservoir

embarazada [embaraˈθaða] *adj* pregnant
♦ *nf* pregnant woman

embarazar [embaraˈθar] *vt* to obstruct,
hamper; **~se** *vr* (*aturdirse*) to become
embarrassed; (*confundirse*) to get into a
mess

embarazo [embaˈraθo] *nm* (*de mujer*)
pregnancy; (*impedimento*) obstacle,
obstruction; (*timidez*) embarrassment;
embarazoso, a *adj* awkward,
embarrassing

embarcación [embarkaˈθjon] *nf* (*barco*)
boat, craft; (*acto*) embarkation, boarding

embarcadero [embarkaˈðero] *nm* pier,
landing stage

embarcar [embarˈkar] *vt* (*cargamento*) to
ship, stow; (*persona*) to embark, put on
board; **~se** *vr*: to embark, go on board

embargar [embarˈɣar] *vt* (*JUR*) to seize,
impound

embargo [emˈbarɣo] *nm* (*JUR*) seizure;
(*COM, POL*) embargo

embargue [emˈbarɣe] *etc vb ver*
embargar

embarque *etc* [emˈbarke] *vb ver*
embarcar ♦ *nm* shipment, loading

embaucar [embauˈkar] *vt* to trick, fool

embeber [embeˈβer] *vt* (*absorber*) to
absorb, soak up; (*empapar*) to saturate
♦ *vi* to shrink; **~se** *vr*: **~se en un libro**
to be engrossed *o* absorbed in a book

embellecer [embeʎeˈθer] *vt* to embellish,
beautify

embestida [embesˈtiða] *nf* attack,
onslaught; (*carga*) charge

embestir [embesˈtir] *vt* to attack, assault;
to charge, attack ♦ *vi* to attack

emblema [emˈblema] *nm* emblem

embobado, a [emboˈβaðo, a] *adj*
(*atontado*) stunned, bewildered

embolia [emˈbolja] *nf* (*MED*) clot

émbolo [ˈembolo] *nm* (*AUTO*) piston

embolsar [embolˈsar] *vt* to pocket, put in
one's pocket

emborrachar [emborraˈtʃar] *vt* to make

drunk, intoxicate; **~se** *vr* to get drunk

emboscada [embosˈkaða] *nf* (*celada*)
ambush

embotar [emboˈtar] *vt* to blunt, dull; **~se**
vr (*adormecerse*) to go numb

embotellamiento [emboteʎaˈmjento] *nm*
(*AUTO*) traffic jam

embotellar [emboteˈʎar] *vt* to bottle; **~se**
vr (*circulación*) to get into a jam

embozo [emˈboθo] *nm* (*de sábana*)
turndown

embrague [emˈbraɣe] *nm* (*tb: pedal de* ~)
clutch

embriagar [embrjaˈɣar] *vt* (*emborrachar*)
to make drunk; (*alegrar*) to delight; **~se**
vr (*emborracharse*) to get drunk

embriaguez [embrjaˈɣeθ] *nf* (*borrachera*)
drunkenness

embrión [emˈbrjon] *nm* embryo

embrollar [embroˈʎar] *vt* (*el asunto*) to
confuse, complicate; (*persona*) to involve,
embroil; **~se** *vr* (*confundirse*) to get into
a muddle *o* mess

embrollo [emˈbroʎo] *nm* (*enredo*) muddle,
confusion; (*aprieto*) fix, jam

embrujado, a [embruˈxado, a] *adj*
bewitched; **casa embrujada** haunted
house

embrutecer [embruteˈθer] *vt* (*atontar*) to
stupefy; **~se** *vr* to be stupefied

embudo [emˈbuðo] *nm* funnel

embuste [emˈbuste] *nm* trick; (*mentira*)
lie; (*hum*) fib; **~ro, a** *adj* lying, deceitful
♦ *nm/f* (*tramposo*) cheat; (*mentiroso*) liar;
(*humorístico*) fibber

embutido [embuˈtiðo] *nm* (*CULIN*) sausage;
(*TEC*) inlay

embutir [embuˈtir] *vt* (*TEC*) to inlay;
(*llenar*) to pack tight, cram

emergencia [emerˈxenθja] *nf* emergency;
(*surgimiento*) emergence

emerger [emerˈxer] *vi* to emerge, appear

emigración [emiɣraˈθjon] *nf* emigration;
(*de pájaros*) migration

emigrar [emiˈɣrar] *vi* (*personas*) to
emigrate; (*pájaros*) to migrate

eminencia [emiˈnenθja] *nf* eminence;
eminente *adj* eminent, distinguished;
(*elevado*) high

emisario [emi'sarjo] *nm* emissary

emisión [emi'sjon] *nf (acto)* emission; *(COM etc)* issue; *(RADIO, TV: acto)* broadcasting; *(: programa)* broadcast, programme *(BRIT)*, program *(US)*

emisora [emi'sora] *nf* radio *o* broadcasting station

emitir [emi'tir] *vt (olor etc)* to emit, give off; *(moneda etc)* to issue; *(opinión)* to express; *(RADIO)* to broadcast

emoción [emo'θjon] *nf* emotion; *(excitación)* excitement; *(sentimiento)* feeling

emocionante [emoθjo'nante] *adj (excitante)* exciting, thrilling

emocionar [emoθjo'nar] *vt (excitar)* to excite, thrill; *(conmover)* to move, touch; *(impresionar)* to impress

emotivo, a [emo'tiβo, a] *adj* emotional

empacar [empa'kar] *vt (gen)* to pack; *(en caja)* to bale, crate

empacho [em'patʃo] *nm (MED)* indigestion; *(fig)* embarrassment

empadronarse [empaðro'narse] *vr (POL: como elector)* to register

empalagoso, a [empala'ɣoso, a] *adj* cloying; *(fig)* tiresome

empalizada [empali'θaða] *nf (valla)* fence

empalmar [empal'mar] *vt* to join, connect ♦ *vi (dos caminos)* to meet, join; **empalme** *nm* joint, connection; junction; *(de trenes)* connection

empanada [empa'naða] *nf* pie, pasty

empantanarse [empanta'narse] *vr* to get swamped; *(fig)* to get bogged down

empañarse [empa'ɲarse] *vr (cristales etc)* to steam up

empapar [empa'par] *vt (mojar)* to soak, saturate; *(absorber)* to soak up, absorb; ~**se** *vr*: ~**se de** to soak up

empapelar [empape'lar] *vt (paredes)* to paper

empaquetar [empake'tar] *vt* to pack, parcel up

emparedado [empare'ðaðo] *nm* sandwich

empastar [empas'tar] *vt (embadurnar)* to paste; *(diente)* to fill

empaste [em'paste] *nm (de diente)* filling

empatar [empa'tar] *vi* to draw, tie;

empate *nm* draw, tie

empecé *etc vb ver* **empezar**

empedernido, a [empeðer'niðo, a] *adj* hard, heartless; *(fijado)* hardened, inveterate

empedrado, a [empe'ðraðo, a] *adj* paved ♦ *nm* paving

empeine [em'peine] *nm (de pie, zapato)* instep

empellón [empe'ʎon] *nm* push, shove

empeñado, a [empe'ɲaðo, a] *adj (persona)* determined; *(objeto)* pawned

empeñar [empe'ɲar] *vt (objeto)* to pawn, pledge; *(persona)* to compel; ~**se** *vr (obligarse)* to bind o.s., pledge o.s.; *(endeudarse)* to get into debt; ~**se en** to be set on, be determined to

empeño [em'peɲo] *nm (determinación, insistencia)* determination, insistence; *(cosa prendada)* pledge; **casa de** ~**s** pawnshop

empeorar [empeo'rar] *vt* to make worse, worsen ♦ *vi* to get worse, deteriorate

empequeñecer [empekeɲe'θer] *vt* to dwarf; *(fig)* to belittle

emperador [empera'ðor] *nm* emperor; **emperatriz** *nf* empress

empezar [empe'θar] *vt, vi* to begin, start

empiece *etc vb ver* **empezar**

empiezo *etc vb ver* **empezar**

empinar [empi'nar] *vt* to raise; ~**se** *vr (persona)* to stand on tiptoe; *(animal)* to rear up; *(camino)* to climb steeply

empírico, a [em'piriko, a] *adj* empirical

emplasto [em'plasto] *nm (MED)* plaster

emplazamiento [emplaθa'mjento] *nm* site, location; *(JUR)* summons *sg*

emplazar [empla'θar] *vt (ubicar)* to site, place, locate; *(JUR)* to summons; *(convocar)* to summon

empleado, a [emple'aðo, a] *nm/f (gen)* employee; *(de banco etc)* clerk

emplear [emple'ar] *vt (usar)* to use, employ; *(dar trabajo a)* to employ; ~**se** *vr (conseguir trabajo)* to be employed; *(ocuparse)* to occupy o.s.

empleo [em'pleo] *nm (puesto)* job; *(puestos: colectivamente)* employment; *(uso)* use, employment

empobrecer [empoβre'θer] *vt* to impoverish; **~se** *vr* to become poor *o* impoverished

empollar [empo'ʎar] *(fam) vt, vi* to swot (up); **empollón, ona** *(fam) nm/f* swot

empolvarse [empol'βarse] *vr* to powder one's face

emporio [em'porjo] *nm* emporium, trading centre; *(AM:* gran almacén) department store

empotrado, a [empo'traðo, a] *adj (armario etc)* built-in

emprender [empren'der] *vt (empezar)* to begin, embark on; *(acometer)* to tackle, take on

empresa [em'presa] *nf (de espíritu etc)* enterprise; *(COM)* company, firm; **~rio, a** *nm/f (COM)* manager

empréstito [em'prestito] *nm* (public) loan

empujar [empu'xar] *vt* to push, shove; **empuje** *nm* thrust; *(presión)* pressure; *(fig)* vigour, drive

empujón [empu'xon] *nm* push, shove

empuñar [empu'ɲar] *vt (asir)* to grasp, take (firm) hold of

emular [emu'lar] *vt* to emulate; *(rivalizar)* to rival

PALABRA CLAVE

en [en] *prep* **1** *(posición)* in; *(: sobre)* on; **está ~ el cajón** it's in the drawer; **~ Argentina/La Paz** in Argentina/La Paz; **~ la oficina/el colegio** at the office/school; **está ~ el suelo/quinto piso** it's on the floor/the fifth floor

2 *(dirección)* into; **entró ~ el aula** she went into the classroom; **meter algo ~ el bolso** to put sth into one's bag

3 *(tiempo)* in; on; **~ 1605/3 semanas/invierno** in 1605/3 weeks/winter; **~ (el mes de) enero** in (the month of) January; **~ aquella ocasión/época** on that occasion/at that time

4 *(precio)* for; **lo vendió ~ 20 dólares** he sold it for 20 dollars

5 *(diferencia)* by; **reducir/aumentar ~ una tercera parte/un 20 por ciento** to reduce/increase by a third/20 per cent

6 *(manera)*: **~ avión/autobús** by plane/

bus; **escrito ~ inglés** written in English

7 *(después de vb que indica gastar etc)* on; **han cobrado demasiado ~ dietas** they've charged too much to expenses; **se le va la mitad del sueldo ~ comida** he spends half his salary on food

8 *(tema, ocupación)*: **experto ~ la materia** expert on the subject; **trabaja ~ la construcción** he works in the building industry

9 *(adj + ~ + infin)*: **lento ~ reaccionar** slow to react

---

enaguas [e'naɣwas] *nfpl* petticoat *sg*, underskirt *sg*

enajenación [enaxena'θjon] *nf (fig: distracción)* absent-mindedness; *(: embelesamiento)* rapture, trance

enajenamiento [enaxena'mjento] *nm* = **enajenación**

enajenar [enaxe'nar] *vt* to alienate; *(fig)* to carry away

enamorado, a [enamo'raðo, a] *adj* in love ♦ *nm/f* lover

enamorar [enamo'rar] *vt* to win the love of; **~se** *vr*: **~se de alguien** to fall in love with sb

enano, a [e'nano, a] *adj* tiny ♦ *nm/f* dwarf

enardecer [enarðe'θer] *vt (pasiones)* to fire, inflame; *(persona)* to fill with enthusiasm; **~se** *vr*: **~se por** to get excited about; *(entusiasmarse)* to get enthusiastic about

encabezamiento [enkaβeθa'mjento] *nm (de carta)* heading; *(de periódico)* headline; *(preámbulo)* foreword, preface

encabezar [enkaβe'θar] *vt (movimiento, revolución)* to lead, head; *(lista)* to head, be at the top of; *(carta)* to put a heading to; *(libro)* to entitle

encadenar [enkaðe'nar] *vt* to chain (together); *(poner grilletes a)* to shackle

encajar [enka'xar] *vt (ajustar)*: **~ (en)** to fit (into); *(fam: golpe)* to give, deal; *(entrometer)* to insert ♦ *vi* to fit (well); *(fig: corresponder a)* to match; **~se** *vr*: **~se en un sillón** to squeeze into a chair

encaje [en'kaxe] *nm (labor)* lace

encalar [enka'lar] *vt* (*pared*) to whitewash

encallar [enka'ʎar] *vi* (*NAUT*) to run aground

encaminar [enkami'nar] *vt* to direct, send; **~se** *vr*: **~se a** to set out for

encandilar [enkandi'lar] *vt* to dazzle

encantado, a [enkan'taðo, a] *adj* (*hechizado*) bewitched; (*muy contento*) delighted; ¡**~!** how do you do, pleased to meet you

encantador, a [enkanta'ðor, a] *adj* charming, lovely ♦ *nm/f* magician, enchanter/enchantress

encantar [enkan'tar] *vt* to charm, delight; (*hechizar*) to bewitch, cast a spell on; **encanto** *nm* (*magia*) spell, charm; (*fig*) charm, delight

encarcelar [enkarθe'lar] *vt* to imprison, jail

encarecer [enkare'θer] *vt* to put up the price of ♦ *vi* to get dearer; **~se** *vr* to get dearer

encarecimiento [enkareθi'mjento] *nm* price increase

encargado, a [enkar'ɣaðo, a] *adj* in charge ♦ *nm/f* agent, representative; (*responsable*) person in charge

encargar [enkar'ɣar] *vt* to entrust; (*recomendar*) to urge, recommend; **~se** *vr*: **~se de** to look after, take charge of

encargo [en'karɣo] *nm* (*pedido*) assignment, job; (*responsabilidad*) responsibility; (*recomendación*) recommendation; (*COM*) order

encariñarse [enkari'narse] *vr*: **~ con** to grow fond of, get attached to

encarnación [enkarna'θjon] *nf* incarnation, embodiment

encarnizado, a [enkarni'θaðo, a] *adj* (*lucha*) bloody, fierce

encarrilar [enkarri'lar] *vt* (*tren*) to put back on the rails; (*fig*) to correct, put on the right track

encasillar [enkasi'ʎar] *vt* (*tb fig*) to pigeonhole; (*actor*) to typecast

encasquetar [enkaske'tar] *vt* (*gorro, sombrero*) to pull on, stick on; **~se** *vr* to pull on, stick on

encauzar [enkau'θar] *vt* to channel

encendedor [enθende'ðor] *nm* lighter

encender [enθen'der] *vt* (*con fuego*) to light; (*incendiar*) to set fire to; (*luz, radio*) to put on, switch on; (*avivar: pasiones*) to inflame; **~se** *vr* to catch fire; (*excitarse*) to get excited; (*de cólera*) to flare up; (*el rostro*) to blush

encendido [enθen'diðo] *nm* (*AUTO*) ignition

encerado [enθe'raðo] *nm* (*ESCOL*) blackboard

encerar [enθe'rar] *vt* (*suelo*) to wax, polish

encerrar [enθe'rrar] *vt* (*confinar*) to shut in, shut up; (*comprender, incluir*) to include, contain

encharcado, a [entʃar'kaðo, a] *adj* (*terreno*) flooded

encharcarse [entʃar'karse] *vr* to get flooded

enchufado, a [entʃu'faðo, a] (*fam*) *nm/f* well-connected person

enchufar [entʃu'far] *vt* (*ELEC*) to plug in; (*TEC*) to connect, fit together; **enchufe** *nm* (*ELEC: clavija*) plug; (: *toma*) socket; (*de dos tubos*) joint, connection; (*fam: influencia*) contact, connection; (: *puesto*) cushy job

encía [en'θia] *nf* gum

encienda *etc vb ver* **encender**

encierro *etc* [en'θjerro] *vb ver* **encerrar** ♦ *nm* shutting in, shutting up; (*calabozo*) prison

encima [en'θima] *adv* (*sobre*) above, over; (*además*) besides; **~ de** (*en*) on, on top of; (*sobre*) above, over; (*además de*) besides, on top of; **por ~ de** over; ¿**llevas dinero ~?** have you (got) any money on you?; **se me vino ~** it took me by surprise

encinta [en'θinta] *adj* pregnant

enclenque [en'klenke] *adj* weak, sickly

encoger [enko'xer] *vt* to shrink, contract; (*fig: asustar*) to scare; **~se** *vr* to shrink, contract; (*fig*) to cringe; **~se de hombros** to shrug one's shoulders

encolar [enko'lar] *vt* (*engomar*) to glue, paste; (*pegar*) to stick down

encolerizar [enkoleri'θar] *vt* to anger, provoke; **~se** *vr* to get angry

encomendar [enkomen'dar] *vt* to entrust,

commend; **~se** *vr*: **~se a** to put one's trust in

encomiar [enko'mjar] *vt* to praise, pay tribute to

encomienda *etc* [enko'mjenda] *vb ver* **encomendar ♦** *nf* (*encargo*) charge, commission; (*elogio*) tribute; **~ postal** (*AM*) parcel post

encontrado, a [enkon'traðo, a] *adj* (*contrario*) contrary, conflicting; (*hostil*) hostile

encontrar [enkon'trar] *vt* (*hallar*) to find; (*inesperadamente*) to meet, run into; **~se** *vr* to meet (each other); (*situarse*) to be (situated); (*entrar en conflicto*) to crash, collide; **~se con** to meet; **~se bien (de salud)** to feel well

encorvar [enkor'βar] *vt* to curve; (*inclinar*) to bend (down); **~se** *vr* to bend down, bend over

encrespar [enkres'par] *vt* (*cabellos*) to curl; (*fig*) to anger, irritate; **~se** *vr* (*el mar*) to get rough; (*fig*) to get cross, get irritated

encrucijada [enkruθi'xaða] *nf* crossroads *sg*; (*empalme*) junction

encuadernación [enkwaðerna'θjon] *nf* binding

encuadernador, a [enkwaðerna'ðor, a] *nm/f* bookbinder

encuadrar [enkwa'ðrar] *vt* (*retrato*) to frame; (*ajustar*) to fit, insert; (*encerrar*) to contain

encubrir [enku'βrir] *vt* (*ocultar*) to hide, conceal; (*criminal*) to harbour, shelter

encuentro *etc* [en'kwentro] *vb ver* **encontrar ♦** *nm* (*de personas*) meeting; (*AUTO etc*) collision, crash; (*DEPORTE*) match, game; (*MIL*) encounter

encuesta [en'kwesta] *nf* inquiry, investigation; (*sondeo*) (public) opinion poll; **~ judicial** post mortem

encumbrar [enkum'brar] *vt* (*persona*) to exalt; **~se** *vr* (*fig*) to become conceited

endeble [en'deβle] *adj* (*argumento, excusa, persona*) weak

endémico, a [en'demiko, a] *adj* (*MED*) endemic; (*fig*) rife, chronic

endemoniado, a [endemo'njaðo, a] *adj*

possessed (of the devil); (*travieso*) devilish

enderezar [endere'θar] *vt* (*poner derecho*) to straighten (out); (*: verticalmente*) to set upright; (*fig*) to straighten o sort out; (*dirigir*) to direct; **~se** *vr* (*persona sentada*) to straighten up

endeudarse [endeu'ðarse] *vr* to get into debt

endiablado, a [endja'βlaðo, a] *adj* devilish, diabolical; (*travieso*) mischievous

endilgar [endil'yar] (*fam*) *vt*: **~le algo a uno** to lumber sb with sth; **~le un sermón a uno** to lecture sb

endiñar [endi'ɲar] (*fam*) *vt* (*bofetón*) to land, belt

endosar [endo'sar] *vt* (*cheque etc*) to endorse

endulzar [endul'θar] *vt* to sweeten; (*suavizar*) to soften

endurecer [endure'θer] *vt* to harden; **~se** *vr* to harden, grow hard

enema [e'nema] *nm* (*MED*) enema

enemigo, a [ene'miyo, a] *adj* enemy, hostile ♦ *nm/f* enemy

enemistad [enemis'tað] *nf* enmity

enemistar [enemis'tar] *vt* to make enemies of, cause a rift between; **~se** *vr* to become enemies; (*amigos*) to fall out

energía [ener'xia] *nf* (*vigor*) energy, drive; (*empuje*) push; (*TEC, ELEC*) energy, power; **~ eólica** wind power; **~ solar** solar energy/power

enérgico, a [e'nerxiko, a] *adj* (*gen*) energetic; (*voz, modales*) forceful

energúmeno, a [ener'xumeno, a] (*fam*) *nm/f* (*fig*) madman/woman

enero [e'nero] *nm* January

enfadado, a [enfa'ðaðo, a] *adj* angry, annoyed

enfadar [enfa'ðar] *vt* to anger, annoy; **~se** *vr* to get angry o annoyed

enfado [en'faðo] *nm* (*enojo*) anger, annoyance; (*disgusto*) trouble, bother

énfasis ['enfasis] *nm* emphasis, stress

enfático, a [en'fatiko, a] *adj* emphatic

enfermar [enfer'mar] *vt* to make ill ♦ *vi* to fall ill, be taken ill

enfermedad [enfermeˈðað] *nf* illness; ~ **venérea** venereal disease

enfermera [enferˈmera] *nf* nurse

enfermería [enfermeˈria] *nf* infirmary; (*de colegio etc*) sick bay

enfermero [enferˈmero] *nm* (male) nurse

enfermizo, a [enferˈmiθo, a] *adj* (*persona*) sickly, unhealthy; (*fig*) unhealthy

enfermo, a [enˈfermo, a] *adj* ill, sick ♦ *nm/f* invalid, sick person; (*en hospital*) patient

enflaquecer [enflakeˈθer] *vt* (*adelgazar*) to make thin; (*debilitar*) to weaken

enfocar [enfoˈkar] *vt* (*foto etc*) to focus; (*problema etc*) to consider, look at

enfoque *etc* [enˈfoke] *vb ver* **enfocar** ♦ *nm* focus.

enfrascarse [enfrasˈkarse] *vr*: ~ **en algo** to bury o.s. in sth

enfrentar [enfrenˈtar] *vt* (*peligro*) to face (up to), confront; (*oponer*) to bring face to face; ~**se** *vr* (*dos personas*) to face o confront each other; (*DEPORTE: dos equipos*) to meet; ~**se a** *o* **con** to face up to, confront

enfrente [enˈfrente] *adv* opposite; **la casa de** ~ the house opposite, the house across the street; ~ **de** opposite, facing

enfriamiento [enfriaˈmjento] *nm* chilling, refrigeration; (*MED*) cold, chill

enfriar [enfriˈar] *vt* (*alimentos*) to cool, chill; (*algo caliente*) to cool down; (*habitación*) to air, freshen; ~**se** *vr* to cool down; (*MED*) to catch a chill; (*amistad*) to cool

enfurecer [enfureˈθer] *vt* to enrage, madden; ~**se** *vr* to become furious, fly into a rage; (*mar*) to get rough

engalanar [engalaˈnar] *vt* (*adornar*) to adorn; (*ciudad*) to decorate; ~**se** *vr* to get dressed up

enganchar [enganˈtʃar] *vt* to hook; (*ropa*) to hang up; (*dos vagones*) to hitch up; (*TEC*) to couple, connect; (*MIL*) to recruit; (*fam: persona*) to rope in; ~**se** *vr* (*MIL*) to enlist, join up

enganche [enˈgantʃe] *nm* hook; (*TEC*) coupling, connection; (*acto*) hooking (up); (*MIL*) recruitment, enlistment; (*AM:*

depósito) deposit

engañar [engaˈɲar] *vt* to deceive; (*estafar*) to cheat, swindle; ~**se** *vr* (*equivocarse*) to be wrong; (*disimular la verdad*) to deceive o.s.

engaño [enˈgaɲo] *nm* deceit; (*estafa*) trick, swindle; (*error*) mistake, misunderstanding; (*ilusión*) delusion; ~**so, a** *adj* (*tramposo*) crooked; (*mentiroso*) dishonest, deceitful; (*aspecto*) deceptive; (*consejo*) misleading

engarzar [engarˈθar] *vt* (*joya*) to set, mount; (*fig*) to link, connect

engatusar [engatuˈsar] (*fam*) *vt* to coax

engendrar [enxenˈdrar] *vt* to breed; (*procrear*) to beget; (*fig*) to cause, produce; **engendro** *nm* (*BIO*) foetus; (*fig*) monstrosity; (*idea*) brainchild

englobar [engloˈβar] *vt* (*incluir*) to include, comprise

engordar [engorˈðar] *vt* to fatten ♦ *vi* to get fat, put on weight

engorroso, a [engoˈrroso, a] *adj* bothersome, trying

engranaje [engraˈnaxe] *nm* (*AUTO*) gear

engrandecer [engrandeˈθer] *vt* to enlarge, magnify; (*alabar*) to praise, speak highly of; (*exagerar*) to exaggerate

engrasar [engraˈsar] *vt* (*TEC: poner grasa*) to grease; (: *lubricar*) to lubricate, oil; (*manchar*) to make greasy

engreído, a [engreˈiðo, a] *adj* vain, conceited

engrosar [engroˈsar] *vt* (*ensanchar*) to enlarge; (*aumentar*) to increase; (*hinchar*) to swell

enhebrar [eneˈβrar] *vt* to thread

enhorabuena [enoraˈβwena] *excl*: ¡~! congratulations! ♦ *nf*: **dar la** ~ **a** to congratulate

enigma [eˈniɣma] *nm* enigma; (*problema*) puzzle; (*misterio*) mystery

enjabonar [enxaβoˈnar] *vt* to soap; (*fam: adular*) to soft-soap; (: *regañar*) to tick off

enjambre [enˈxambre] *nm* swarm

enjaular [enxauˈlar] *vt* to (put in a) cage; (*fam*) to jail, lock up

enjuagar [enxwaˈɣar] *vt* (*ropa*) to rinse

(out)

enjuague *etc* [en'xwaɣe] *vb ver* **enjuagar**
♦ *nm* (*MED*) mouthwash; (*de ropa*) rinse, rinsing

enjugar [enxu'ɣar] *vt* to wipe (off); (*lágrimas*) to dry; (*déficit*) to wipe out

enjuiciar [enxwi'θjar] *vt* (*JUR*: *procesar*) to prosecute, try; (*fig*) to judge

enjuto, a [en'xuto, a] *adj* dry, dried up; (*fig*) lean, skinny

enlace [en'laθe] *nm* link, connection; (*relación*) relationship; (*tb*: ~ *matrimonial*) marriage; (*de carretera, trenes*) connection; ~ **sindical** shop steward

enlatado, a [enla'taðo, a] *adj* (*comida, productos*) tinned, canned

enlazar [enla'θar] *vt* (*unir con lazos*) to bind together; (*atar*) to tie; (*conectar*) to link, connect; (*AM*) to lasso

enlodar [enlo'ðar] *vt* to cover in mud; (*fig: manchar*) to stain; (: *rebajar*) to debase

enloquecer [enloke'θer] *vt* to drive mad ♦ *vi* to go mad; ~**se** *vr* to go mad

enlutado, a [enlu'taðo, a] *adj* (*persona*) in mourning

enmarañar [enmara'ɲar] *vt* (*enredar*) to tangle (up), entangle; (*complicar*) to complicate; (*confundir*) to confuse; ~**se** *vr* (*enredarse*) to become entangled; (*confundirse*) to get confused

enmarcar [enmar'kar] *vt* (*cuadro*) to frame

enmascarar [enmaska'rar] *vt* to mask; ~**se** *vr* to put on a mask

enmendar [enmen'dar] *vt* to emend, correct; (*constitución etc*) to amend; (*comportamiento*) to reform; ~**se** *vr* to reform, mend one's ways; **enmienda** *nf* correction; amendment; reform

enmohecerse [enmoe'θerse] *vr* (*metal*) to rust, go rusty; (*muro, plantas*) to get mouldy

enmudecer [enmuðe'θer] *vi* (*perder el habla*) to fall silent; (*guardar silencio*) to remain silent; ~**se** *vr* to fall silent; to remain silent

ennegrecer [ennexre'θer] *vt* (*poner negro*) to blacken; (*oscurecer*) to darken; ~**se** *vr*

to turn black; (*oscurecerse*) to get dark, darken

ennoblecer [ennoβle'θer] *vt* to ennoble

enojar [eno'xar] *vt* (*encolerizar*) to anger; (*disgustar*) to annoy, upset; ~**se** *vr* to get angry; to get annoyed

enojo [e'noxo] *nm* (*cólera*) anger; (*irritación*) annoyance; ~**so, a** *adj* annoying

enorgullecerse [enorɣuʎe'θerse] *vr* to be proud; ~ **de** to pride o.s. on, be proud of

enorme [e'norme] *adj* enormous, huge; (*fig*) monstrous; **enormidad** *nf* hugeness, immensity

enrarecido, a [enrare'θiðo, a] *adj* (*atmósfera, aire*) rarefied

enredadera [enreða'ðera] *nf* (*BOT*) creeper, climbing plant

enredar [enre'ðar] *vt* (*cables, hilos etc*) to tangle (up), entangle; (*situación*) to complicate, confuse; (*meter cizaña*) to sow discord among o between; (*implicar*) to embroil, implicate; ~**se** *vr* to get entangled, get tangled (up); (*situación*) to get complicated; (*persona*) to get embroiled; (*AM: fam*) to meddle

enredo [en'reðo] *nm* (*maraña*) tangle; (*confusión*) mix-up, confusion; (*intriga*) intrigue

enrejado [enre'xaðo] *nm* fence, railings *pl*

enrevesado, a [enreβe'saðo, a] *adj* (*asunto*) complicated, involved

enriquecer [enrike'θer] *vt* to make rich, enrich; ~**se** *vr* to get rich

enrojecer [enroxe'θer] *vt* to redden ♦ *vi* (*persona*) to blush; ~**se** *vr* to blush

enrolar [enro'lar] *vt* (*MIL*) to enlist; (*reclutar*) to recruit; ~**se** *vr* (*MIL*) to join up; (*afiliarse*) to enrol

enrollar [enro'ʎar] *vt* to roll (up), wind (up)

enroscar [enros'kar] *vt* (*torcer, doblar*) to coil (round), wind; (*tornillo, rosca*) to screw in; ~**se** *vr* to coil, wind

ensalada [ensa'laða] *nf* salad; **ensaladilla** (**rusa**) *nf* Russian salad

ensalzar [ensal'θar] *vt* (*alabar*) to praise, extol; (*exaltar*) to exalt

ensambladura [ensambla'ðura] *nf*

assembly; (*TEC*) joint

ensamblaje [ensam'blaxe] *nm* = **ensambladura**

ensanchar [ensan'tʃar] *vt* (*hacer más ancho*) to widen; (*agrandar*) to enlarge, expand; (*COSTURA*) to let out; **~se** *vr* to get wider, expand; (*pey*) to give o.s. airs; **ensanche** *nm* (*de calle*) widening; (*de negocio*) expansion

ensangrentar [ensangren'tar] *vt* to stain with blood

ensañar [ensa'ɲar] *vt* to enrage; **~se con** to treat brutally

ensartar [ensar'tar] *vt* (*cuentas, perlas etc*) to string (together)

ensayar [ensa'jar] *vt* to test, try (out); (*TEATRO*) to rehearse

ensayista [ensa'jista] *nm/f* essayist

ensayo [en'sajo] *nm* test, trial; (*QUÍMICA*) experiment; (*TEATRO*) rehearsal; (*DEPORTE*) try; (*ESCOL, LITERATURA*) essay

enseguida [ense'ɣiða] *adv* at once, right away

ensenada [ense'naða] *nf* inlet, cove

enseñanza [ense'ɲanθa] *nf* (*educación*) education; (*acción*) teaching; (*doctrina*) teaching, doctrine

enseñar [ense'ɲar] *vt* (*educar*) to teach; (*instruir*) to teach, instruct; (*mostrar, señalar*) to show

enseres [en'seres] *nmpl* belongings

ensillar [ensi'ʎar] *vt* to saddle (up)

ensimismarse [ensimis'marse] *vr* (*abstraerse*) to become lost in thought; (*estar absorto*) to be lost in thought; (*AM*) to become conceited

ensombrecer [ensombre'θer] *vt* to darken, cast a shadow over; (*fig*) to overshadow, put in the shade

ensordecer [ensorðe'θer] *vt* to deafen ♦ *vi* to go deaf

ensortijado, a [ensorti'xaðo, a] *adj* (*pelo*) curly

ensuciar [ensu'θjar] *vt* (*manchar*) to dirty, soil; (*fig*) to defile; **~se** *vr* to get dirty; (*niño*) to wet o.s.

ensueño [en'sweɲo] *nm* (*sueño*) dream, fantasy; (*ilusión*) illusion; (*soñando despierto*) daydream

entablar [enta'βlar] *vt* (*recubrir*) to board (up); (*AJEDREZ, DAMAS*) to set up; (*conversación*) to strike up; (*JUR*) to file ♦ *vi* to draw

entablillar [entaβli'ʎar] *vt* (*MED*) to (put in a) splint

entallar [enta'ʎar] *vt* (*traje*) to tailor ♦ *vi*: **el traje entalla bien** the suit fits well

ente ['ente] *nm* (*organización*) body, organization; (*fam: persona*) odd character

entender [enten'der] *vt* (*comprender*) to understand; (*darse cuenta*) to realize; (*querer decir*) to mean ♦ *vi* to understand; (*creer*) to think, believe; **~se** *vr* (*comprenderse*) to be understood; (*2 personas*) to get on together; (*ponerse de acuerdo*) to agree, reach an agreement; **~ de** to know all about; **~ algo de** to know a little about; **~ en** to deal with, have to do with; **~se mal** (*2 personas*) to get on badly

entendido, a [enten'diðo, a] *adj* (*comprendido*) understood; (*hábil*) skilled; (*inteligente*) knowledgeable ♦ *nm/f* (*experto*) expert ♦ *excl* agreed!; **entendimiento** *nm* (*comprensión*) understanding; (*inteligencia*) mind, intellect; (*juicio*) judgement

enterado, a [ente'raðo, a] *adj* well-informed; **estar ~ de** to know about, be aware of

enteramente [entera'mente] *adv* entirely, completely

enterar [ente'rar] *vt* (*informar*) to inform, tell; **~se** *vr* to find out, get to know

entereza [ente'reθa] *nf* (*totalidad*) entirety; (*fig: carácter*) strength of mind; (: *honradez*) integrity

enternecer [enterne'θer] *vt* (*ablandar*) to soften; (*apiadar*) to touch, move; **~se** *vr* to be touched, be moved

entero, a [en'tero, a] *adj* (*total*) whole, entire; (*fig: recto*) honest; (: *firme*) firm, resolute ♦ *nm* (*COM: punto*) point; (*AM: pago*) payment

enterrador [enterra'ðor] *nm* gravedigger

enterrar [ente'rrar] *vt* to bury

entibiar [enti'βjar] *vt* (*enfriar*) to cool;

(*calentar*) to warm; **~se** *vr* (*fig*) to cool

entidad [enti'ðað] *nf* (*empresa*) firm, company; (*organismo*) body; (*sociedad*) society; (*FILOSOFÍA*) entity

entiendo *etc vb ver* **entender**

entierro [en'tjerro] *nm* (*acción*) burial; (*funeral*) funeral

entomología [entomolo'xia] *nf* entomology

entonación [entona'θjon] *nf* (*LING*) intonation; (*fig*) conceit

entonar [ento'nar] *vt* (*canción*) to intone; (*colores*) to tone; (*MED*) to tone up ♦ *vi* to be in tune; **~se** *vr* (*engreírse*) to give o.s. airs

entonces [en'tonθes] *adv* then, at that time; **desde ~** since then; **en aquel ~** at that time; (**pues**) **~** and so

entornar [entor'nar] *vt* (*puerta, ventana*) to half close, leave ajar; (*los ojos*) to screw up

entorpecer [entorpe'θer] *vt* (*entendimiento*) to dull; (*impedir*) to obstruct, hinder; (: *tránsito*) to slow down, delay

entrada [en'traða] *nf* (*acción*) entry, access; (*sitio*) entrance, way in; (*INFORM*) input; (*COM*) receipts *pl*, takings *pl*; (*CULIN*) starter; (*DEPORTE*) innings *sg*; (*TEATRO*) house, audience; (*para el cine etc*) ticket; (*COM*): **~s y salidas** income and expenditure; (*TEC*): **~ de aire** air intake *o* inlet; **de ~** from the outset

entrado, a [en'traðo, a] *adj*: **~ en años** elderly; **una vez ~ el verano** in the summer(time), when summer comes

entramparse [entram'parse] *vr* to get into debt

entrante [en'trante] *adj* next, coming; **mes/año ~** next month/year

entraña [en'traɲa] *nf* (*fig: centro*) heart, core; (*raíz*) root; **~s** *nfpl* (*ANAT*) entrails; (*fig*) heart *sg*; **sin ~s** (*fig*) heartless; **entrañable** *adj* close, intimate; **entrañar** *vt* to entail

entrar [en'trar] *vt* (*introducir*) to bring in; (*INFORM*) to input ♦ *vi* (*meterse*) to go in, come in, enter; (*comenzar*): **~ diciendo** to begin by saying; **hacer ~** to show in;

no me entra I can't get the hang of it

entre ['entre] *prep* (*dos*) between; (*más de dos*) among(st)

entreabrir [entrea'ßrir] *vt* to half-open, open halfway

entrecejo [entre'θexo] *nm*: **fruncir el ~** to frown

entrecortado, a [entrekor'taðo, a] *adj* (*respiración*) difficult; (*habla*) faltering

entredicho [entre'ðitʃo] *nm* (*JUR*) injunction; **poner en ~** to cast doubt on; **estar en ~** to be banned

entrega [en'treɣa] *nf* (*de mercancías*) delivery; (*de novela etc*) instalment

entregar [entre'ɣar] *vt* (*dar*) to hand (over), deliver; **~se** *vr* (*rendirse*) to surrender, give in, submit; (*dedicarse*) to devote o.s.

entrelazar [entrela'θar] *vt* to entwine

entremeses [entre'meses] *nmpl* hors d'œuvres

entremeter [entreme'ter] *vt* to insert, put in; **~se** *vr* to meddle, interfere; **entremetido, a** *adj* meddling, interfering

entremezclar [entremeθ'klar] *vt* to intermingle; **~se** *vr* to intermingle

entrenador, a [entrena'ðor, a] *nm/f* trainer, coach

entrenarse [entre'narse] *vr* to train

entrepierna [entre'pjerna] *nf* crotch

entresacar [entresa'kar] *vt* to pick out, select

entresuelo [entre'swelo] *nm* mezzanine

entretanto [entre'tanto] *adv* meanwhile, meantime

entretejer [entrete'xer] *vt* to interweave

entretener [entrete'ner] *vt* (*divertir*) to entertain, amuse; (*detener*) to hold up, delay; (*mantener*) to maintain; **~se** *vr* (*divertirse*) to amuse o.s.; (*retrasarse*) to delay, linger; **entretenido, a** *adj* entertaining, amusing; **entretenimiento** *nm* entertainment, amusement; (*mantenimiento*) upkeep, maintenance

entrever [entre'ßer] *vt* to glimpse, catch a glimpse of

entrevista [entre'ßista] *nf* interview; **entrevistar** *vt* to interview;

entrevistarse *vr* to have an interview

entristecer [entriste'θer] *vt* to sadden, grieve; **~se** *vr* to grow sad

entrometerse [entrome'terse] *vr*: **~ (en)** to interfere (in *o* with)

entroncar [entron'kar] *vi* to be connected *o* related

entumecer [entume'θer] *vt* to numb, benumb; **~se** *vr* (*por el frío*) to go *o* become numb; **entumecido, a** *adj* numb, stiff

enturbiar [entur'βjar] *vt* (*el agua*) to make cloudy; (*fig*) to confuse; **~se** *vr* (*oscurecerse*) to become cloudy; (*fig*) to get confused, become obscure

entusiasmar [entusjas'mar] *vt* to excite, fill with enthusiasm; (*gustar mucho*) to delight; **~se** *vr*: **~se con** *o* **por** to get enthusiastic *o* excited about

entusiasmo [entu'sjasmo] *nm* enthusiasm; (*excitación*) excitement

entusiasta [entu'sjasta] *adj* enthusiastic ♦ *nm/f* enthusiast

enumerar [enume'rar] *vt* to enumerate

enunciación [enunθja'θjon] *nf* enunciation

enunciado [enun'θjaðo] *nm* enunciation; (*declaración*) declaration, statement

envainar [embai'nar] *vt* to sheathe

envalentonar [embalento'nar] *vt* to give courage to; **~se** *vr* (*pey: jactarse*) to boast, brag

envanecer [embane'θer] *vt* to make conceited; **~se** *vr* to grow conceited

envasar [emba'sar] *vt* (*empaquetar*) to pack, wrap; (*enfrascar*) to bottle; (*enlatar*) to can; (*embolsar*) to pocket

envase [em'base] *nm* (*en paquete*) packing, wrapping; (*en botella*) bottling; (*en lata*) canning; (*recipiente*) container; (*paquete*) package; (*botella*) bottle; (*lata*) tin (*BRIT*), can

envejecer [embexe'θer] *vt* to make old, age ♦ *vi* (*volverse viejo*) to grow old; (*parecer viejo*) to age; **~se** *vr* to grow old; to age

envenenar [embene'nar] *vt* to poison; (*fig*) to embitter

envergadura [emberɣa'ðura] *nf* (*fig*) scope, compass

envés [em'bes] *nm* (*de tela*) back, wrong side

enviar [em'bjar] *vt* to send

enviciarse [embi'θjarse] *vr*: **~ (con)** to get addicted (to)

envidia [em'biðja] *nf* envy; **tener ~ a** to envy, be jealous of; **envidiar** *vt* (*desear*) to envy; (*tener celos de*) to be jealous of

envío [em'bio] *nm* (*acción*) sending; (*de mercancías*) consignment; (*de dinero*) remittance

enviudar [embju'ðar] *vi* to be widowed

envoltura [embol'tura] *nf* (*cobertura*) cover; (*embalaje*) wrapper, wrapping; **envoltorio** *nm* package

envolver [embol'βer] *vt* to wrap (up); (*cubrir*) to cover; (*enemigo*) to surround; (*implicar*) to involve, implicate

envuelto [em'bwelto] *pp de* **envolver**

enyesar [enje'sar] *vt* (*pared*) to plaster; (*MED*) to put in plaster

enzarzarse [enθar'θarse] *vr*: **~ en** (*en pelea*) to get mixed up in; (*en disputa*) to get involved in

épica ['epika] *nf* epic

épico, a ['epiko, a] *adj* epic

epidemia [epi'ðemja] *nf* epidemic

epilepsia [epi'lepsja] *nf* epilepsy

epílogo [e'pilovo] *nm* epilogue

episodio [epi'soðjo] *nm* episode

epístola [e'pistola] *nf* epistle

época ['epoka] *nf* period, time; (*HISTORIA*) age, epoch; **hacer ~** to be epoch-making

equidad [eki'ðað] *nf* equity

equilibrar [ekili'βrar] *vt* to balance; **equilibrio** *nm* balance, equilibrium; **equilibrista** *nm/f* (*funámbulo*) tightrope walker; (*acróbata*) acrobat

equipaje [eki'paxe] *nm* luggage; (*avíos*) equipment, kit; **~ de mano** hand luggage

equipar [eki'par] *vt* (*proveer*) to equip

equipararse [ekipa'rarse] *vr*: **~ con** to be on a level with

equipo [e'kipo] *nm* (*conjunto de cosas*) equipment; (*DEPORTE*) team; (*de obreros*) shift

equis ['ekis] *nf inv* (the letter) X

equitación [ekita'θjon] *nf* (*acto*) riding;

(*arte*) horsemanship

equitativo, a [ekita'tiβo, a] *adj* equitable, fair

equivalente [ekiβa'lente] *adj, nm* equivalent

equivaler [ekiβa'ler] *vi* to be equivalent *o* equal

equivocación [ekiβoka'θjon] *nf* mistake, error

equivocado, a [ekiβo'kaðo, a] *adj* wrong, mistaken

equivocarse [ekiβo'karse] *vr* to be wrong, make a mistake; ~ **de camino** to take the wrong road

equívoco, a [e'kiβoko, a] *adj* (*dudoso*) suspect; (*ambiguo*) ambiguous ♦ *nm* ambiguity; (*malentendido*) misunderstanding

era ['era] *vb ver* **ser** ♦ *nf* era, age

erais *vb ver* **ser**

éramos *vb ver* **ser**

eran *vb ver* **ser**

erario [e'rarjo] *nm* exchequer (*BRIT*), treasury

eras *vb ver* **ser**

erección [erek'θjon] *nf* erection

eres *vb ver* **ser**

erguir [er'ɣir] *vt* to raise, lift; (*poner derecho*) to straighten; ~**se** *vr* to straighten up

erigir [eri'xir] *vt* to erect, build; ~**se** *vr*: ~**se en** to set o.s. up as

erizarse [eri'θarse] *vr* (*pelo: de perro*) to bristle; (*: de persona*) to stand on end

erizo [e'riθo] *nm* (*ZOOL*) hedgehog; ~ **de mar** sea-urchin

ermita [er'mita] *nf* hermitage

ermitaño, a [ermi'taɲo, a] *nm/f* hermit

erosion [ero'sjon] *nf* erosion

erosionar [erosjo'nar] *vt* to erode

erótico, a [e'rotiko, a] *adj* erotic; **erotismo** *nm* eroticism

erradicar [erraði'kar] *vt* to eradicate

errante [e'rrante] *adj* wandering, errant

errar [e'rrar] *vi* (*vagar*) to wander, roam; (*equivocarse*) to be mistaken ♦ *vt*: ~ **el camino** to take the wrong road; ~ **el tiro** to miss

erróneo, a [e'rroneo, a] *adj* (*equivocado*)

wrong, mistaken; (*falso*) false, untrue

error [e'rror] *nm* error, mistake; (*INFORM*) bug; ~ **de imprenta** misprint

eructar [eruk'tar] *vt* to belch, burp

erudito, a [eru'ðito, a] *adj* erudite, learned

erupción [erup'θjon] *nf* eruption; (*MED*) rash

es *vb ver* **ser**

esa ['esa] (*pl* **esas**) *adj demos ver* **ese**

ésa ['esa] (*pl* **ésas**) *pron ver* **ése**

esbelto, a [es'βelto, a] *adj* slim, slender

esbozo [es'βoθo] *nm* sketch, outline

escabeche [eska'βetʃe] *nm* brine; (*de aceitunas etc*) pickle; **en** ~ pickled

escabroso, a [eska'βroso, a] *adj* (*accidentado*) rough, uneven; (*fig*) tough, difficult; (: *atrevido*) risqué

escabullirse [eskaβu'ʎirse] *vr* to slip away, to clear out

escafandra [eska'fandra] *nf* (*buzo*) diving suit; (~ *espacial*) space suit

escala [es'kala] *nf* (*proporción, MUS*) scale; (*de mano*) ladder; (*AVIAT*) stopover; **hacer** ~ **en** to stop *o* call in at

escalafón [eskala'fon] *nm* (*escala de salarios*) salary scale, wage scale

escalar [eska'lar] *vt* to climb, scale

escalera [eska'lera] *nf* stairs *pl*, staircase; (*escala*) ladder; (*NAIPES*) run; ~ **mecánica** escalator; ~ **de caracol** spiral staircase

escalfar [eskal'far] *vt* (*huevos*) to poach

escalinata [eskali'nata] *nf* staircase

escalofriante [eskalo'frjante] *adj* chilling

escalofrío [eskalo'frio] *nm* (*MED*) chill; ~**s** *nmpl* (*fig*) shivers

escalón [eska'lon] *nm* step, stair; (*de escalera*) rung

escalope [eska'lope] *nm* (*CULIN*) escalope

escama [es'kama] *nf* (*de pez, serpiente*) scale; (*de jabón*) flake; (*fig*) resentment

escamar [eska'mar] *vt* (*fig*) to make wary *o* suspicious

escamotear [eskamote'ar] *vt* (*robar*) to lift, swipe; (*hacer desaparecer*) to make disappear

escampar [eskam'par] *vb impers* to stop raining

escandalizar [eskandali'θar] *vt* to

scandalize, shock; ~se *vr* to be shocked;
(*ofenderse*) to be offended

escándalo [es'kandalo] *nm* scandal;
(*alboroto, tumulto*) row, uproar;
escandaloso, a *adj* scandalous, shocking

escandinavo, a [eskandi'naβo, a] *adj,
nm/f* Scandinavian

escaño [es'kaɲo] *nm* bench; (POL) seat

escapar [eska'par] *vi* (*gen*) to escape, run
away; (DEPORTE) to break away; ~se *vr* to
escape, get away; (*agua, gas*) to leak
(out)

escaparate [eskapa'rate] *nm* shop window

escape [es'kape] *nm* (*de agua, gas*) leak;
(*de motor*) exhaust; (*de persona*) escape

escarabajo [eskara'βaxo] *nm* beetle

escaramuza [eskara'muθa] *nf* skirmish;
(*fig*) brush

escarbar [eskar'βar] *vt* (*gallina*) to
scratch; (*fig*) to inquire into, investigate

escarceos [eskar'θeos] *nmpl* (*fig*): **en mis
~ con la política ...** in my dealings with
politics ...; **~ amorosos** love affairs

escarcha [es'kartʃa] *nf* frost

escarchado, a [eskar'tʃaðo, a] *adj* (CULIN:
fruta) crystallized

escarlata [eskar'lata] *adj inv* scarlet;
escarlatina *nf* scarlet fever

escarmentar [eskarmen'tar] *vt* to punish
severely ♦ *vi* to learn one's lesson

escarmiento *etc* [eskar'mjento] *vb ver*
escarmentar ♦ *nm* (*ejemplo*) lesson;
(*castigo*) punishment

escarnio [es'karnjo] *nm* mockery;
(*injuria*) insult

escarola [eska'rola] *nf* endive

escarpado, a [eskar'paðo, a] *adj*
(*pendiente*) sheer, steep; (*rocas*) craggy

escasear [eskase'ar] *vi* to be scarce

escasez [eska'seθ] *nf* (*falta*) shortage,
scarcity; (*pobreza*) poverty

escaso, a [es'kaso, a] *adj* (*poco*) scarce;
(*raro*) rare; (*ralo*) thin, sparse; (*limitado*)
limited

escatimar [eskati'mar] *vt* (*limitar*) to
skimp (on), be sparing with

escayola [eska'jola] *nf* plaster

escena [es'θena] *nf* scene

escenario [esθe'narjo] *nm* (TEATRO) stage;

(CINE) set; (*fig*) scene; **escenografía** *nf* set
design

escepticismo [esθepti'θismo] *nm*
scepticism; **escéptico, a** *adj* sceptical
♦ *nm/f* sceptic

escisión [esθi'sjon] *nf* (*de partido, secta*)
split

esclarecer [esklare'θer] *vt* (*iluminar*) to
light up, illuminate; (*misterio, problema*)
to shed light on

esclavitud [esklaβi'tuð] *nf* slavery

esclavizar [esklaβi'θar] *vt* to enslave

esclavo, a [es'klaβo, a] *nm/f* slave

esclusa [es'klusa] *nf* (*de canal*) lock;
(*compuerta*) floodgate

escoba [es'koβa] *nf* broom

escocer [esko'θer] *vi* to burn, sting; ~se
vr to chafe, get chafed

escocés, esa [esko'θes, esa] *adj* Scottish
♦ *nm/f* Scotsman/woman, Scot

Escocia [es'koθja] *nf* Scotland

escoger [esko'xer] *vt* to choose, pick,
select; **escogido, a** *adj* chosen, selected;
(*calidad*) choice, select

escolar [esko'lar] *adj* school *cpd* ♦ *nm/f*
schoolboy/girl, pupil

escollo [es'koʎo] *nm* reef

escolta [es'kolta] *nf* escort; **escoltar** *vt* to
escort

escombros [es'kombros] *nmpl* (*basura*)
rubbish *sg*; (*restos*) debris *sg*

esconder [eskon'der] *vt* to hide, conceal;
~se *vr* to hide; **escondidas** (AM) *nfpl*: **a
escondidas** secretly; **escondite** *nm*
hiding place; (*juego*) hide-and-seek;
escondrijo *nm* hiding place, hideout

escopeta [esko'peta] *nf* shotgun

escoria [es'korja] *nf* (*de alto horno*) slag;
(*fig*) scum, dregs *pl*

Escorpio [es'korpjo] *nm* Scorpio

escorpión [eskor'pjon] *nm* scorpion

escotado, a [esko'taðo, a] *adj* low-cut

escote [es'kote] *nm* (*de vestido*) low neck;
pagar a ~ to share the expenses

escotilla [esko'tiʎa] *nf* (NAUT) hatch(way)

escozor [esko'θor] *nm* (*dolor*) sting(ing)

escribir [eskri'βir] *vt, vi* to write; **~ a
máquina** to type; **¿cómo se escribe?**
how do you spell it?

escrito, a [es'krito, a] *pp de* **escribir**
♦ *nm* (*documento*) document; (*manuscrito*) text, manuscript; **por ~** in writing

escritor, a [eskri'tor, a] *nm/f* writer

escritorio [eskri'torjo] *nm* desk; (*oficina*) office

escritura [eskri'tura] *nf* (*acción*) writing; (*caligrafía*) (hand)writing; (*JUR: documento*) deed

escrúpulo [es'krupulo] *nm* scruple; (*minuciosidad*) scrupulousness; **escrupuloso, a** *adj* scrupulous

escrutar [eskru'tar] *vt* to scrutinize, examine; (*votos*) to count

escrutinio [eskru'tinjo] *nm* (*examen atento*) scrutiny; (*POL: recuento de votos*) count(ing)

escuadra [es'kwaðra] *nf* (*MIL etc*) squad; (*NAUT*) squadron; (*de coches etc*) fleet; **escuadrilla** *nf* (*de aviones*) squadron; (*AM: de obreros*) gang

escuadrón [eskwa'ðron] *nm* squadron

escuálido, a [es'kwaliðo, a] *adj* skinny, scraggy; (*sucio*) squalid

escuchar [esku'tʃar] *vt* to listen to ♦ *vi* to listen

escudilla [esku'ðiʎa] *nf* bowl, basin

escudo [es'kuðo] *nm* shield

escudriñar [eskuðri'ɲar] *vt* (*examinar*) to investigate, scrutinize; (*mirar de lejos*) to scan

escuela [es'kwela] *nf* school; **~ de artes y oficios** (*ESP*) ≈ technical college; **~ normal** teacher training college

escueto, a [es'kweto, a] *adj* plain; (*estilo*) simple

escuincle [es'kwinkle] (*AM: fam*) *nm/f* kid

esculpir [eskul'pir] *vt* to sculpt; (*grabar*) to engrave; (*tallar*) to carve; **escultor, a** *nm/f* sculptor/tress; **escultura** *nf* sculpture

escupidera [eskupi'ðera] *nf* spittoon

escupir [esku'pir] *vt, vi* to spit (out)

escurreplatos [eskurre'platos] *nm inv* plate rack

escurridizo, a [eskurri'ðiθo, a] *adj* slippery

escurridor [eskurri'ðor] *nm* colander

escurrir [esku'rrir] *vt* (*ropa*) to wring out; (*verduras, platos*) to drain ♦ *vi* (*líquidos*) to drip; **~se** *vr* (*secarse*) to drain; (*resbalarse*) to slip, slide; (*escaparse*) to slip away

ese ['ese] (*f* **esa**, *pl* **esos, esas**) *adj demos* (*sg*) that; (*pl*) those

ése ['ese] (*f* **ésa**, *pl* **ésos, ésas**) *pron* (*sg*) that (one); (*pl*) those (ones); **~ ... éste ...** the former ... the latter ...; **no me vengas con ésas** don't give me any more of that nonsense

esencia [e'senθja] *nf* essence; **esencial** *adj* essential

esfera [es'fera] *nf* sphere; (*de reloj*) face; **esférico, a** *adj* spherical

esforzarse [esfor'θarse] *vr* to exert o.s., make an effort

esfuerzo *etc* [es'fwerθo] *vb ver* **esforzar** ♦ *nm* effort

esfumarse [esfu'marse] *vr* (*apoyo, esperanzas*) to fade away

esgrima [es'yrima] *nf* fencing

esgrimir [esyri'mir] *vt* (*arma*) to brandish; (*argumento*) to use

esguince [es'yinθe] *nm* (*MED*) sprain

eslabón [esla'ßon] *nm* link

eslovaco, a [eslo'ßako, a] *adj, nm/f* Slovak, Slovakian ♦ *nm* (*LING*) Slovak, Slovakian

Eslovaquia [eslo'ßakja] *nf* Slovakia

esmaltar [esmal'tar] *vt* to enamel; **esmalte** *nm* enamel; **esmalte de uñas** nail varnish *o* polish

esmerado, a [esme'raðo, a] *adj* careful, neat

esmeralda [esme'ralda] *nf* emerald

esmerarse [esme'rarse] *vr* (*aplicarse*) to take great pains, exercise great care; (*afanarse*) to work hard

esmero [es'mero] *nm* (great) care

esnob [es'nob] (*pl* **~s**) *adj* (*persona*) snobbish; (*coche etc*) posh ♦ *nm/f* snob; **~ismo** *nm* snobbery

eso ['eso] *pron* that, that thing *o* matter; **~ de su coche** that business about his car; **~ de ir al cine** all that going to the cinema; **a ~ de las cinco** at about five o'clock; **en ~** thereupon, at that point; ~ es that's it; ¡~ sí que es vida! now that is really living!; por ~ te lo dije that's why I told you; y ~ que llovía in spite of the fact it was raining

esófago [e'sofaɣo] nm (ANAT) oesophagus

esos ['esos] adj demos ver ese

ésos ['esos] pron ver ése

espabilar etc [espaβi'lar] = despabilar etc

espacial [espa'θjal] adj (del espacio) space cpd

espaciar [espa'θjar] vt to space (out)

espacio [es'paθjo] nm space; (MUS) interval; (RADIO, TV) programme (BRIT), program (US); el ~ space; ~so, a adj spacious, roomy

espada [es'paða] nf sword; ~s nfpl (NAIPES) spades

espaguetis [espa'ɣetis] nmpl spaghetti sg

espalda [es'palda] nf (gen) back; ~s nfpl (hombros) shoulders; a ~s de uno behind sb's back; tenderse de ~s to lie (down) on one's back; volver la ~ a alguien to cold-shoulder sb

espantadizo, a [espanta'ðiθo, a] adj timid, easily frightened

espantajo [espan'taxo] nm = espantapájaros

espantapájaros [espanta'paxaros] nm inv scarecrow

espantar [espan'tar] vt (asustar) to frighten, scare; (ahuyentar) to frighten off; (asombrar) to horrify, appal; ~se vr to get frightened o scared; to be appalled

espanto [es'panto] nm (susto) fright; (terror) terror; (asombro) astonishment; ~so, a adj frightening; terrifying; astonishing

España [es'paɲa] nf Spain; español, a adj Spanish ♦ nm/f Spaniard ♦ nm (LING) Spanish

esparadrapo [espara'ðrapo] nm (sticking) plaster (BRIT), adhesive tape (US)

esparcimiento [esparθi'mjento] nm (dispersión) spreading; (derramamiento) scattering; (fig) cheerfulness

esparcir [espar'θir] vt to spread; (derramar) to scatter; ~se vr to spread (out); to scatter; (divertirse) to enjoy o.s.

espárrago [es'parraɣo] nm asparagus

esparto [es'parto] nm esparto (grass)

espasmo [es'pasmo] nm spasm

espátula [es'patula] nf spatula

especia [es'peθja] nf spice

especial [espe'θjal] adj special; ~idad nf speciality (BRIT), specialty (US)

especie [es'peθje] nf (BIO) species; (clase) kind, sort; en ~ in kind

especificar [espeθifi'kar] vt to specify; específico, a adj specific

espécimen [es'peθimen] (pl especímenes) nm specimen

espectáculo [espek'takulo] nm (gen) spectacle; (TEATRO etc) show

espectador, a [espekta'ðor, a] nm/f spectator

espectro [es'pektro] nm ghost; (fig) spectre

especular [espeku'lar] vt, vi to speculate

espejismo [espe'xismo] nm mirage

espejo [es'pexo] nm mirror; (fig) model; ~ retrovisor rear-view mirror

espeluznante [espeluθ'nante] adj horrifying, hair-raising

espera [es'pera] nf (pausa, intervalo) wait; (JUR: plazo) respite; en ~ de waiting for; (con expectativa) expecting

esperanza [espe'ranθa] nf (confianza) hope; (expectativa) expectation; hay pocas ~s de que venga there is little prospect of his coming

esperar [espe'rar] vt (aguardar) to wait for; (tener expectativa de) to expect; (desear) to hope for ♦ vi to wait; to expect; to hope

esperma [es'perma] nf sperm

espesar [espe'sar] vt to thicken; ~se vr to thicken, get thicker

espeso, a [es'peso, a] adj thick; espesor nm thickness

espía [es'pia] nm/f spy; espiar vt (observar) to spy on ♦ vi: ~ para to spy for

espiga [es'piɣa] nf (BOT: de trigo etc) ear

espigón [espi'ɣon] nm (BOT) ear; (NAUT) breakwater

espina [es'pina] nf thorn; (de pez) bone; ~ dorsal (ANAT) spine

espinaca [espi'naka] nf spinach

espinazo [espi'naθo] nm spine, backbone

espinilla [espi'niʎa] *nf (ANAT: tibia)* shin(bone); *(grano)* blackhead

espino [es'pino] *nm* hawthorn

espinoso, a [espi'noso, a] *adj (planta)* thorny, prickly; *(fig)* difficult

espionaje [espjo'naxe] *nm* spying, espionage

espiral [espi'ral] *adj, nf* spiral

espirar [espi'rar] *vt* to breathe out, exhale

espiritista [espiri'tista] *adj; nm/f* spiritualist

espíritu [es'piritu] *nm* spirit; **espiritual** *adj* spiritual

espita [es'pita] *nf* tap

espléndido, a [es'plendiðo, a] *adj (magnífico)* magnificent, splendid; *(generoso)* generous

esplendor [esplen'dor] *nm* splendour

espolear [espole'ar] *vt* to spur on

espoleta [espo'leta] *nf (de bomba)* fuse

espolón [espo'lon] *nm* sea wall

espolvorear [espolßore'ar] *vt* to dust, sprinkle

esponja [es'ponxa] *nf* sponge; *(fig)* sponger; **esponjoso, a** *adj* spongy

espontaneidad [espontanei'ðað] *nf* spontaneity; **espontáneo, a** *adj* spontaneous

esposa [es'posa] *nf* wife; **~s** *nfpl* handcuffs; **esposar** *vt* to handcuff

esposo [es'poso] *nm* husband

espuela [es'pwela] *nf* spur

espuma [es'puma] *nf* foam; *(de cerveza)* froth, head; *(de jabón)* lather; **espumadera** *nf (utensilio)* skimmer; **espumoso, a** *adj* frothy, foamy; *(vino)* sparkling

esqueje [es'kexe] *nm (de planta)* cutting

esqueleto [eske'leto] *nm* skeleton

esquema [es'kema] *nm (diagrama)* diagram; *(dibujo)* plan; *(plan)* scheme; *(FILOSOFÍA)* schema

esquí [es'ki] *(pl ~s) nm (objeto)* ski; *(DEPORTE)* skiing; **~ acuático** waterskiing; **esquiar** *vi* to ski

esquilar [eski'lar] *vt* to shear

esquimal [eski'mal] *adj, nm/f* Eskimo

esquina [es'kina] *nf* corner

esquinazo [eski'naθo] *nm:* **dar ~ a algn** to give sb the slip

esquirol [eski'rol] *nm* blackleg

esquivar [eski'ßar] *vt* to avoid; *(evadir)* to dodge, elude

esquivo, a [es'kißo, a] *adj* evasive; *(tímido)* reserved; *(huraño)* unsociable

esta ['esta] *adj demos ver* **este²**

está *vb ver* **estar**

ésta ['esta] *pron ver* **éste**

estabilidad [estaßili'ðað] *nf* stability; **estable** *adj* stable

establecer [estaßle'θer] *vt* to establish; **~se** *vr* to establish o.s.; *(echar raíces)* to settle (down); **establecimiento** *nm* establishment

establo [es'taßlo] *nm (AGR)* stable

estaca [es'taka] *nf* stake, post; *(de tienda de campaña)* peg

estacada [esta'kaða] *nf (cerca)* fence, fencing; *(palenque)* stockade

estación [esta'θjon] *nf* station; *(del año)* season; **~ de autobuses** bus station; **~ balnearia** seaside resort; **~ de servicio** service station

estacionamiento [estaθjona'mjento] *nm (AUTO)* parking; *(MIL)* stationing

estacionar [estaθjo'nar] *vt (AUTO)* to park; *(MIL)* to station; **~io, a** *adj* stationary; *(COM: mercado)* slack

estadio [es'taðjo] *nm (fase)* stage, phase; *(DEPORTE)* stadium

estadista [esta'ðista] *nm (POL)* statesman; *(ESTADÍSTICA)* statistician

estadística [esta'ðistika] *nf* figure, statistic; *(ciencia)* statistics *sg*

estado [es'taðo] *nm (POL: condición)* state; **~ de animo** state of mind; **~ de cuenta** bank statement; **~ de sitio** state of siege; **~ civil** marital status; **~ mayor** staff; **estar en ~** to be pregnant; **(los) E~s Unidos** *nmpl* the United States (of America) *sg*

estadounidense [estaðouni'ðense] *adj* United States *cpd*, American ♦ *nm/f* American

estafa [es'tafa] *nf* swindle, trick; **estafar** *vt* to swindle, defraud

estafeta [esta'feta] *nf (oficina de correos)* post office; **~ diplomática** diplomatic bag

estáis *vb ver* **estar**

estallar [esta'ʎar] *vi* to burst; (*bomba*) to explode, go off; (*epidemia, guerra, rebelión*) to break out; ~ **en llanto** to burst into tears; **estallido** *nm* explosion; (*fig*) outbreak

estampa [es'tampa] *nf* (*impresión, imprenta*) print, engraving; (*imagen, figura: de persona*) appearance

estampado, a [estam'paðo, a] *adj* printed ♦ *nm* (*impresión: acción*) printing; (: *efecto*) print; (*marca*) stamping

estampar [estam'par] *vt* (*imprimir*) to print; (*marcar*) to stamp; (*metal*) to engrave; (*poner sello en*) to stamp; (*fig*) to stamp, imprint

estampida [estam'piða] *nf* stampede

estampido [estam'piðo] *nm* bang, report

estampilla [estam'piʎa] *nf* stamp

están *vb ver* **estar**

estancado, a [estan'kaðo, a] *adj* stagnant

estancar [estan'kar] *vt* (*aguas*) to hold up, hold back; (*COM*) to monopolize; (*fig*) to block, hold up; ~**se** *vr* to stagnate

estancia [es'tanθja] *nf* (*permanencia*) stay; (*sala*) room; (*AM*) farm, ranch; **estanciero** (*AM*) *nm* farmer, rancher

estanco, a [es'tanko, a] *adj* watertight ♦ *nm* tobacconist's (shop), cigar store (*US*)

estándar [es'tandar] *adj, nm* standard; **estandarizar** *vt* to standardize

estandarte [estan'darte] *nm* banner, standard

estanque [es'tanke] *nm* (*lago*) pool, pond; (*AGR*) reservoir

estanquero, a [estan'kero, a] *nm/f* tobacconist

estante [es'tante] *nm* (*armario*) rack, stand; (*biblioteca*) bookcase; (*anaquel*) shelf; (*AM*) prop; **estantería** *nf* shelving, shelves *pl*

estaño [es'taɲo] *nm* tin

PALABRA CLAVE

estar [es'tar] *vi* **1** (*posición*) to be; **está en la plaza** it's in the square; **¿está Juan?** is Juan in?; **estamos a 30 km de Junín**

we're 30 kms from Junín

2 (+ *adj: estado*) to be; ~ **enfermo** to be ill; **está muy elegante** he's looking very smart; **¿cómo estás?** how are you keeping?

3 (+ *gerundio*) to be; **estoy leyendo** I'm reading

4 (*uso pasivo*): **está condenado a muerte** he's been condemned to death; **está envasado en ...** it's packed in ...

5 (*con fechas*): **¿a cuántos estamos?** what's the date today?; **estamos a 5 de mayo** it's the 5th of May

6 (*locuciones*): **¿estamos?** (*¿de acuerdo?*) okay?; (*¿listo?*) ready?; **¡ya está bien!** that's enough!

7: ~ **de**: ~ **de vacaciones/viaje** to be on holiday/away *o* on a trip; **está de camarero** he's working as a waiter

8: ~ **para**: **está para salir** he's about to leave; **no estoy para bromas** I'm not in the mood for jokes

9: ~ **por** (*propuesta etc*) to be in favour of; (*persona etc*) to support, side with; **está por limpiar** it still has to be cleaned

10: ~ **sin**: ~ **sin dinero** to have no money; **está sin terminar** it isn't finished yet

♦ ~**se** *vr*: **se estuvo en la cama toda la tarde** he stayed in bed all afternoon

---

estas ['estas] *adj demos ver* **este**[2]

éstas ['estas] *pron ver* **éste**

estatal [esta'tal] *adj* state *cpd*

estático, a [es'tatiko, a] *adj* static

estatua [es'tatwa] *nf* statue

estatura [esta'tura] *nf* stature, height

estatuto [esta'tuto] *nm* (*JUR*) statute; (*de ciudad*) bye-law; (*de comité*) rule

este[1] ['este] *nm* east

este[2] ['este] (*f* **esta**, *pl* **estos, estas**) *adj demos* (*sg*) this; (*pl*) these

esté *etc vb ver* **estar**

éste ['este] (*f* **ésta**, *pl* **éstos, éstas**) *pron* (*sg*) this (one); (*pl*) these (ones); **ése ... ~ ...** the former ... the latter ...

estela [es'tela] *nf* wash; (*fig*) trail

estelar [este'lar] *adj* (*ASTRO*) stellar;

(*actuación, reparto*) star (*atr*)

estén *etc vb ver* **estar**

estenografía [estenoɣra'fia] *nf* shorthand (*BRIT*), stenography (*US*)

estepa [es'tepa] *nf* (*GEO*) steppe

estera [es'tera] *nf* mat(ting)

estéreo [es'tereo] *adj inv, nm* stereo; **estereotipo** *nm* stereotype

estéril [es'teril] *adj* sterile, barren; (*fig*) vain, futile; **esterilizar** *vt* to sterilize

esterlina [ester'lina] *adj*: **libra ~** pound sterling

estés *etc vb ver* **estar**

estética [es'tetika] *nf* aesthetics *sg*

estético, a [es'tetiko, a] *adj* aesthetic

estibador [estiβa'ðor] *nm* stevedore, docker

estiércol [es'tjerkol] *nm* dung, manure

estigma [es'tiɣma] *nm* stigma

estilarse [esti'larse] *vr* to be in fashion

estilo [es'tilo] *nm* style; (*TEC*) stylus; (*NATACIÓN*) stroke; **algo por el ~** something along those lines

estima [es'tima] *nf* esteem, respect

estimación [estima'θjon] *nf* (*evaluación*) estimation; (*aprecio, afecto*) esteem, regard

estimar [esti'mar] *vt* (*evaluar*) to estimate; (*valorar*) to value; (*apreciar*) to esteem, respect; (*pensar, considerar*) to think, reckon

estimulante [estimu'lante] *adj* stimulating ♦ *nm* stimulant

estimular [estimu'lar] *vt* to stimulate; (*excitar*) to excite

estímulo [es'timulo] *nm* stimulus; (*ánimo*) encouragement

estío [es'tio] *nm* summer

estipulación [estipula'θjon] *nf* stipulation, condition

estipular [estipu'lar] *vt* to stipulate

estirado, a [esti'raðo, a] *adj* (*tenso*) (stretched *o* drawn) tight; (*fig: persona*) stiff, pompous

estirar [esti'rar] *vt* to stretch; (*dinero, suma etc*) to stretch out; **~se** *vr* to stretch

estirón [esti'ron] *nm* pull, tug; (*crecimiento*) spurt, sudden growth; **dar**

un ~ (*niño*) to shoot up

estirpe [es'tirpe] *nf* stock, lineage

estival [esti'βal] *adj* summer *cpd*

esto ['esto] *pron* this, this thing *o* matter; **~ de la boda** this business about the wedding

Estocolmo [esto'kolmo] *nm* Stockholm

estofado [esto'faðo] *nm* (*CULIN*) stew

estofar [esto'far] *vt* (*CULIN*) to stew

estómago [es'tomaɣo] *nm* stomach; **tener ~** to be thick-skinned

estorbar [estor'βar] *vt* to hinder, obstruct; (*fig*) to bother, disturb ♦ *vi* to be in the way; **estorbo** *nm* (*molestia*) bother, nuisance; (*obstáculo*) hindrance, obstacle

estornudar [estornu'ðar] *vi* to sneeze

estos ['estos] *adj demos ver* **este²**

éstos ['estos] *pron ver* **éste**

estoy *vb ver* **estar**

estrado [es'traðo] *nm* platform

estrafalario, a [estrafa'larjo, a] *adj* odd, eccentric; (*desarreglado*) slovenly, sloppy

estrago [es'traɣo] *nm* ruin, destruction; **hacer ~s en** to wreak havoc among

estragón [estra'ɣon] *nm* tarragon

estrambótico, a [estram'botiko, a] *adj* (*persona*) eccentric; (*peinado, ropa*) outlandish

estrangulador, a [estrangula'ðor, a] *nm/f* strangler ♦ *nm* (*TEC*) throttle; (*AUTO*) choke

estrangular [estrangu'lar] *vt* (*persona*) to strangle; (*MED*) to strangulate

estraperlo [estra'perlo] *nm* black market

estratagema [estrata'xema] *nf* (*MIL*) stratagem; (*astucia*) cunning

estrategia [estra'texja] *nf* strategy; **estratégico, a** *adj* strategic

estrato [es'trato] *nm* stratum, layer

estrechamente [es'tretʃamente] *adv* (*íntimamente*) closely, intimately; (*pobremente: vivir*) poorly

estrechar [estre'tʃar] *vt* (*reducir*) to narrow, take in; (*COSTURA*) to take in; (*persona*) to hug, embrace; **~se** *vr* (*reducirse*) to narrow, grow narrow; (*2 personas*) to embrace; **~ la mano** to shake hands

estrechez [estre'tʃeθ] *nf* narrowness; (*de ropa*) tightness; (*intimidad*) intimacy;

(COM) want o shortage of money;
estrecheces *nfpl* (*dificultades económicas*) financial difficulties

estrecho, a [es'tretʃo, a] *adj* narrow; (*apretado*) tight; (*íntimo*) close, intimate; (*miserable*) mean ♦ *nm* strait; ~ **de miras** narrow-minded

estrella [es'treʎa] *nf* star; ~ **de mar** (ZOOL) starfish; ~ **fugaz** shooting star; **estrellado, a** *adj* (*forma*) star-shaped; (*cielo*) starry

estrellar [estre'ʎar] *vt* (*hacer añicos*) to smash (to pieces); (*huevos*) to fry; ~**se** *vr* to smash; (*chocarse*) to crash; (*fracasar*) to fail

estremecer [estreme'θer] *vt* to shake; ~**se** *vr* to shake, tremble; **estremecimiento** *nm* (*temblor*) trembling, shaking

estrenar [estre'nar] *vt* (*vestido*) to wear for the first time; (*casa*) to move into; (*película, obra de teatro*) to première; ~**se** *vr* (*persona*) to make one's début; **estreno** *nm* (*primer uso*) first use; (CINE etc) première

estreñido, a [estre'ɲiðo, a] *adj* constipated

estreñimiento [estreɲi'mjento] *nm* constipation

estrépito [es'trepito] *nm* noise, racket; (*fig*) fuss; **estrepitoso, a** *adj* noisy; (*fiesta*) rowdy

estría [es'tria] *nf* groove

estribación [estriβa'θjon] *nf* (GEO) spur, foothill

estribar [estri'βar] *vi*: ~ **en** to rest on, be supported by

estribillo [estri'βiʎo] *nm* (LITERATURA) refrain; (MUS) chorus

estribo [es'triβo] *nm* (*de jinete*) stirrup; (*de coche, tren*) step; (*de puente*) support; (GEO) spur; **perder los ~s** to fly off the handle

estribor [estri'βor] *nm* (NAUT) starboard

estricto, a [es'trikto, a] *adj* (*riguroso*) strict; (*severo*) severe

estridente [estri'ðente] *adj* (*color*) loud; (*voz*) raucous

estropajo [estro'paxo] *nm* scourer

estropear [estrope'ar] *vt* (*arruinar*) to

spoil; (*dañar*) to damage; ~**se** *vr* (*objeto*) to get damaged; (*persona: la piel etc*) to be ruined

estructura [estruk'tura] *nf* structure

estruendo [es'trwendo] *nm* (*ruido*) racket, din; (*fig: alboroto*) uproar, turmoil

estrujar [estru'xar] *vt* (*apretar*) to squeeze; (*aplastar*) to crush; (*fig*) to drain, bleed

estuario [es'twarjo] *nm* estuary

estuche [es'tutʃe] *nm* box, case

estudiante [estu'ðjante] *nm/f* student; **estudiantil** *adj* student *cpd*

estudiar [estu'ðjar] *vt* to study

estudio [es'tuðjo] *nm* study; (CINE, ARTE, RADIO) studio; ~**s** *nmpl* studies; (*erudición*) learning *sg*; ~**so, a** *adj* studious

estufa [es'tufa] *nf* heater, fire

estupefaciente [estupefa'θjente] *nm* drug, narcotic

estupefacto, a [estupe'fakto, a] *adj* speechless, thunderstruck

estupendo, a [estu'pendo, a] *adj* wonderful, terrific; (*fam*) great; ¡~! that's great!, fantastic!

estupidez [estupi'ðeθ] *nf* (*torpeza*) stupidity; (*acto*) stupid thing (to do)

estúpido, a [es'tupiðo, a] *adj* stupid, silly

estupor [estu'por] *nm* stupor; (*fig*) astonishment, amazement

estupro [es'tupro] *nm* rape

estuve *etc vb ver* **estar**

esvástica [es'βastika] *nf* swastika

ETA ['eta] (ESP) *nf abr* (= *Euskadi ta Askatasuna*) ETA

etapa [e'tapa] *nf* (*de viaje*) stage; (DEPORTE) leg; (*parada*) stopping place; (*fig*) stage, phase

etarra [e'tarra] *nm/f* member of ETA

etc. *abr* (= *etcétera*) etc

etcétera [et'θetera] *adv* etcetera

eternidad [eterni'ðað] *nf* eternity; **eterno, a** *adj* eternal, everlasting

ética ['etika] *nf* ethics *pl*

ético, a ['etiko, a] *adj* ethical

etiqueta [eti'keta] *nf* (*modales*) etiquette; (*rótulo*) label, tag

Eucaristía [eukaris'tia] *nf* Eucharist

eufemismo [eufe'mismo] *nm* euphemism

euforia [eu'forja] *nf* euphoria

eunuco [eu'nuko] *nm* eunuch

eurodiputado, a [eurodipu'taðo, a] *nm/f* Euro MP, MEP

Europa [eu'ropa] *nf* Europe; **europeo, a** *adj, nm/f* European

Euskadi [eus'kaði] *nm* the Basque Country *o* Provinces *pl*

euskera [eus'kera] *nm* (LING) Basque

evacuación [eβakwa'θjon] *nf* evacuation

evacuar [eβa'kwar] *vt* to evacuate

evadir [eβa'ðir] *vt* to evade, avoid; **~se** *vr* to escape

evaluar [eβa'lwar] *vt* to evaluate

evangelio [eβan'xeljo] *nm* gospel

evaporar [eβapo'rar] *vt* to evaporate; **~se** *vr* to vanish

evasión [eβa'sjon] *nf* escape, flight; (*fig*) evasion; **~ de capitales** flight of capital

evasiva [eβa'siβa] *nf* (*pretexto*) excuse

evasivo, a [eβa'siβo, a] *adj* evasive, non-committal

evento [e'βento] *nm* event

eventual [eβen'twal] *adj* possible, conditional (upon circumstances); (*trabajador*) casual, temporary

evidencia [eβi'ðenθja] *nf* evidence, proof; **evidenciar** *vt* (*hacer patente*) to make evident; (*probar*) to prove, show; **evidenciarse** *vr* to be evident

evidente [eβi'ðente] *adj* obvious, clear, evident

evitar [eβi'tar] *vt* (*evadir*) to avoid; (*impedir*) to prevent

evocar [eβo'kar] *vt* to evoke, call forth

evolución [eβolu'θjon] *nf* (*desarrollo*) evolution, development; (*cambio*) change; (MIL) manoeuvre; **evolucionar** *vi* to evolve; to manoeuvre

ex [eks] *adj* ex-; **el ~ ministro** the former minister, the ex-minister

exacerbar [eksaθer'βar] *vt* to irritate, annoy

exactamente [eksakta'mente] *adv* exactly

exactitud [eksakti'tuð] *nf* exactness; (*precisión*) accuracy; (*puntualidad*) punctuality; **exacto, a** *adj* exact; accurate; punctual; **¡exacto!** exactly!

exageración [eksaxera'θjon] *nf* exaggeration

exagerar [eksaxe'rar] *vt, vi* to exaggerate

exaltado, a [eksal'taðo, a] *adj* (*apasionado*) over-excited, worked-up; (*exagerado*) extreme

exaltar [eksal'tar] *vt* to exalt, glorify; **~se** *vr* (*excitarse*) to get excited *o* worked-up

examen [ek'samen] *nm* examination

examinar [eksami'nar] *vt* to examine; **~se** *vr* to be examined, take an examination

exasperar [eksaspe'rar] *vt* to exasperate; **~se** *vr* to get exasperated, lose patience

Exca. *abr* = **Excelencia**

excavadora [ekskaβa'ðora] *nf* excavator

excavar [ekska'βar] *vt* to excavate

excedencia [eksθe'ðenθja] *nf*: **estar en ~** to be on leave; **pedir** *o* **solicitar la ~** to ask for leave

excedente [eksθe'ðente] *adj, nm* excess, surplus

exceder [eksθe'ðer] *vt* to exceed, surpass; **~se** *vr* (*extralimitarse*) to go too far; (*sobrepasarse*) to excel o.s.

excelencia [eksθe'lenθja] *nf* excellence; **E~** Excellency; **excelente** *adj* excellent

excentricidad [eksθentri'θi'ðað] *nf* eccentricity; **excéntrico, a** *adj, nm/f* eccentric

excepción [eksθep'θjon] *nf* exception; **excepcional** *adj* exceptional

excepto [eks'θepto] *adv* excepting, except (for)

exceptuar [eksθep'twar] *vt* to except, exclude

excesivo, a [eksθe'siβo, a] *adj* excessive

exceso [eks'θeso] *nm* (*gen*) excess; (*COM*) surplus; **~ de equipaje/peso** excess luggage/weight

excitación [eksθita'θjon] *nf* (*sensación*) excitement; (*acción*) excitation

excitado, a [eksθi'taðo, a] *adj* excited; (*emociones*) aroused

excitar [eksθi'tar] *vt* to excite; (*incitar*) to urge; **~se** *vr* to get excited

exclamación [eksklama'θjon] *nf* exclamation

exclamar [ekskla'mar] *vi* to exclaim

excluir [eksklu'ir] *vt* to exclude; (*dejar fuera*) to shut out; (*descartar*) to reject;

exclusión *nf* exclusion

exclusiva [eksklu'sißa] *nf* (*PRENSA*) exclusive, scoop; (*COM*) sole right

exclusivo, a [eksklu'sißo, a] *adj* exclusive; **derecho ~** sole *o* exclusive right

Excmo. *abr* = **excelentísmo**

excomulgar [ekskomul'ɣar] *vt* (*REL*) to excommunicate

excomunión [ekskomu'njon] *nf* excommunication

excursión [ekskur'sjon] *nf* excursion, outing; **excursionista** *nm/f* (*turista*) sightseer

excusa [eks'kusa] *nf* excuse; (*disculpa*) apology

excusar [eksku'sar] *vt* to excuse; (*evitar*) to avoid, prevent; **~se** *vr* (*disculparse*) to apologize

exento, a [ek'sento, a] *adj* exempt

exequias [ek'sekjas] *nfpl* funeral rites

exhalar [eksa'lar] *vt* to exhale, breathe out; (*olor etc*) to give off; (*suspiro*) to breathe, heave

exhaustivo, a [eksaus'tißo, a] *adj* (*análisis*) thorough; (*estudio*) exhaustive

exhausto, a [ek'sausto, a] *adj* exhausted

exhibición [eksißi'θjon] *nf* exhibition, display, show

exhibir [eksi'ßir] *vt* to exhibit, display, show

exhortar [eksor'tar] *vt*: **~ a** to exhort to

exigencia [eksi'xenθja] *nf* demand, requirement; **exigente** *adj* demanding

exigir [eksi'xir] *vt* (*gen*) to demand, require; **~ el pago** to demand payment

exiliado, a [eksi'ljaðo, a] *adj* exiled ♦ *nm/f* exile

exilio [ek'siljo] *nm* exile

eximir [eksi'mir] *vt* to exempt

existencia [eksis'tenθja] *nf* existence; **~s** *nfpl* stock(s) (*pl*)

existir [eksis'tir] *vi* to exist, be

éxito ['eksito] *nm* (*resultado*) result, outcome; (*triunfo*) success; (*MUS etc*) hit; **tener ~** to be successful

exonerar [eksone'rar] *vt* to exonerate; **~ de una obligación** to free from an obligation

exorbitante [eksorßi'tante] *adj* (*precio*) exorbitant; (*cantidad*) excessive

exorcizar [eksorθi'θar] *vt* to exorcize

exótico, a [ek'sotiko, a] *adj* exotic

expandir [ekspan'dir] *vt* to expand

expansión [ekspan'sjon] *nf* expansion

expansivo, a [ekspan'sißo, a] *adj*: **onda ~a** shock wave

expatriarse [ekspa'trjarse] *vr* to emigrate; (*POL*) to go into exile

expectativa [ekspekta'tißa] *nf* (*espera*) expectation; (*perspectiva*) prospect

expedición [ekspeði'θjon] *nf* (*excursión*) expedition

expediente [ekspe'ðjente] *nm* expedient; (*JUR: procedimento*) action, proceedings *pl*; (: *papeles*) dossier, file, record

expedir [ekspe'ðir] *vt* (*despachar*) to send, forward; (*pasaporte*) to issue

expendedor, a [ekspende'ðor, a] *nm/f* (*vendedor*) dealer

expensas [eks'pensas] *nfpl*: **a ~ de** at the expense of

experiencia [ekspe'rjenθja] *nf* experience

experimentado, a [eksperimen'taðo, a] *adj* experienced

experimentar [eksperimen'tar] *vt* (*en laboratorio*) to experiment with; (*probar*) to test, try out; (*notar, observar*) to experience; (*deterioro, pérdida*) to suffer; **experimento** *nm* experiment

experto, a [eks'perto, a] *adj* expert, skilled ♦ *nm/f* expert

expiar [ekspi'ar] *vt* to atone for

expirar [ekspi'rar] *vi* to expire

explanada [eskpla'naða] *nf* (*llano*) plain

explayarse [ekspla'jarse] *vr* (*en discurso*) to speak at length; **~ con uno** to confide in sb

explicación [eksplika'θjon] *nf* explanation

explicar [ekspli'kar] *vt* to explain; **~se** *vr* to explain (o.s.)

explícito, a [eks'pliθito, a] *adj* explicit

explique *etc vb ver* **explicar**

explorador, a [eksplora'ðor, a] *nm/f* (*pionero*) explorer; (*MIL*) scout ♦ *nm* (*MED*) probe; (*TEC*) (radar) scanner

explorar [eksplo'rar] *vt* to explore; (*MED*) to probe; (*radar*) to scan

explosión [eksplo'sjon] *nf* explosion;
explosivo, a *adj* explosive
explotación [eksplota'θjon] *nf*
exploitation; (*de planta etc*) running
explotar [eksplo'tar] *vt* to exploit; to run,
operate ♦ *vi* to explode
exponer [ekspo'ner] *vt* to expose; (*cuadro*)
to display; (*vida*) to risk; (*idea*) to
explain; **~se** *vr*: **~se a (hacer) algo** to
run the risk of (doing) sth
exportación [eksporta'θjon] *nf* (*acción*)
export; (*mercancías*) exports *pl*
exportar [ekspor'tar] *vt* to export
exposición [eksposi'θjon] *nf* (*gen*)
exposure; (*de arte*) show, exhibition;
(*explicación*) explanation; (*narración*)
account, statement
expresamente [ekspresa'mente] *adv*
(*decir*) clearly; (*a propósito*) expressly
expresar [ekspre'sar] *vt* to express;
expresión *nf* expression
expresivo, a [ekspre'sißo, a] *adj* (*persona,
gesto, palabras*) expressive; (*cariñoso*)
affectionate
expreso, a [eks'preso, a] *pp de* **expresar**
♦ *adj* (*explícito*) express; (*claro*) specific,
clear; (*tren*) fast ♦ *adv*: **mandar ~** to
send by express (delivery)
express [eks'pres] (*AM*) *adv*: **enviar algo
~** to send sth special delivery
exprimidor [eksprimi'ðor] *nm* squeezer
exprimir [ekspri'mir] *vt* (*fruta*) to squeeze;
(*zumo*) to squeeze out
expropiar [ekspro'pjar] *vt* to expropriate
expuesto, a [eks'pwesto, a] *pp de*
exponer ♦ *adj* exposed; (*cuadro etc*) on
show, on display
expulsar [ekspul'sar] *vt* (*echar*) to eject,
throw out; (*alumno*) to expel; (*despedir*)
to sack, fire; (*DEPORTE*) to send off;
expulsión *nf* expulsion; sending-off
exquisito, a [ekski'sito, a] *adj* exquisite;
(*comida*) delicious
éxtasis ['ekstasis] *nm* ecstasy
extender [eksten'der] *vt* to extend; (*los
brazos*) to stretch out, hold out; (*mapa,
tela*) to spread (out), open (out);
(*mantequilla*) to spread; (*certificado*) to
issue; (*cheque, recibo*) to make out;

(*documento*) to draw up; **~se** *vr* (*gen*) to
extend; (*persona: en el suelo*) to stretch
out; (*epidemia*) to spread; **extendido, a**
adj (*abierto*) spread out, open; (*brazos*)
outstretched; (*costumbre*) widespread;
(*pey*) rife
extensión [eksten'sjon] *nf* (*de terreno,
mar*) expanse, stretch; (*de tiempo*) length,
duration; (*TEL*) extension; **en toda la ~
de la palabra** in every sense of the
word
extenso, a [eks'tenso, a] *adj* extensive
extenuar [ekste'nwar] *vt* (*debilitar*) to
weaken
exterior [ekste'rjor] *adj* (*de fuera*)
external; (*afuera*) outside, exterior;
(*apariencia*) outward; (*deuda, relaciones*)
foreign ♦ *nm* (*gen*) exterior, outside;
(*aspecto*) outward appearance; (*DEPORTE*)
wing(er); (*países extranjeros*) abroad; **en
el ~** abroad; **al ~** outwardly, on the
surface
exterminar [ekstermi'nar] *vt* to
exterminate; **exterminio** *nm*
extermination
externo, a [eks'terno, a] *adj* (*exterior*)
external, outside; (*superficial*) outward
♦ *nm/f* day pupil
extinguir [ekstin'gir] *vt* (*fuego*) to
extinguish, put out; (*raza, población*) to
wipe out; **~se** *vr* (*fuego*) to go out; (*BIO*)
to die out, become extinct
extinto, a [eks'tinto, a] *adj* extinct
extintor [ekstin'tor] *nm* (*fire*) extinguisher
extirpar [ekstir'par] *vt* (*MED*) to remove
(surgically)
extorsión [ekstor'sjon] *nf* (*FIN, JUR*)
blackmail; (*molestia*) inconvenience
extra ['ekstra] *adj inv* (*tiempo*) extra;
(*chocolate, vino*) good-quality ♦ *nm/f*
extra ♦ *nm* extra; (*bono*) bonus
extracción [ekstrak'θjon] *nf* extraction;
(*en lotería*) draw
extracto [eks'trakto] *nm* extract
extradición [ekstraði'θjon] *nf* extradition
extraer [ekstra'er] *vt* to extract, take out
extraescolar [ekstraesko'lar] *adj*:
actividad ~ extracurricular activity
extralimitarse [ekstralimi'tarse] *vr* to go

too far

extranjero, a [ekstran'xero, a] *adj* foreign
♦ *nm/f* foreigner ♦ *nm* foreign countries
pl; **en el ~** abroad

extrañar [ekstra'ɲar] *vt* (*sorprender*) to
find strange *o* odd; (*echar de menos*) to
miss; **~se** *vr* (*sorprenderse*) to be amazed,
be surprised; (*distanciarse*) to become
estranged, grow apart

extrañeza [ekstra'ɲeθa] *nf* (*rareza*)
strangeness, oddness; (*asombro*)
amazement, surprise

extraño, a [eks'traɲo, a] *adj* (*extranjero*)
foreign; (*raro, sorprendente*) strange, odd

extraordinario, a [ekstraorði'narjo, a] *adj*
extraordinary; (*edición, número*) special
♦ *nm* (*de periódico*) special edition;
horas extraordinarias overtime *sg*

extrarradio [ekstra'rraðjo] *nm poor
suburban area*

extravagancia [ekstraβa'γanθja] *nf*
oddness; outlandishness; **extravagante**
adj (*excéntrico*) eccentric; (*estrafalario*)
outlandish

extraviado, a [ekstra'βjaðo, a] *adj* lost,
missing

extraviar [ekstra'βjar] *vt* (*persona:
desorientar*) to mislead, misdirect;
(*perder*) to lose, misplace; **~se** *vr* to lose
one's way, get lost; **extravío** *nm* loss;
(*fig*) deviation

extremar [ekstre'mar] *vt* to carry to
extremes; **~se** *vr* to do one's utmost,
make every effort

extremaunción [ekstremaun'θjon] *nf*
extreme unction

extremidad [ekstremi'ðað] *nf* (*punta*)
extremity; (*fila*) edge; **~es** *nfpl* (ANAT)
extremities

extremo, a [eks'tremo, a] *adj* extreme;
(*último*) last ♦ *nm* end; (*límite, grado
sumo*) extreme; **en último ~** as a last
resort

extrovertido, a [ekstroβer'tiðo, a] *adj,
nm/f* extrovert

exuberancia [eksuβe'ranθja] *nf*
exuberance; **exuberante** *adj* exuberant;
(*fig*) luxuriant, lush

eyacular [ejaku'lar] *vt, vi* to ejaculate

F f

f.a.b. *abr* (= *franco a bordo*) f.o.b.

fábrica ['faβrika] *nf* factory; **marca de ~**
trademark; **precio de ~** factory price

fabricación [faβrika'θjon] *nf* (*manufactura*) manufacture; (*producción*)
production; **de ~ casera** home-made; **~
en serie** mass production

fabricante [faβri'kante] *nm/f*
manufacturer

fabricar [faβri'kar] *vt* (*manufacturar*) to
manufacture, make; (*construir*) to build;
(*cuento*) to fabricate, devise

fábula ['faβula] *nf* (*cuento*) fable; (*chisme*)
rumour; (*mentira*) fib

fabuloso, a [faβu'loso, a] *adj*
(*oportunidad, tiempo*) fabulous, great

facción [fak'θjon] *nf* (POL) faction;
facciones *nfpl* (*del rostro*) features

faceta [fa'θeta] *nf* facet

facha ['fatʃa] *nf* (*fam*) (*aspecto*) look;
(*cara*) face

fachada [fa'tʃaða] *nf* (ARQ) façade, front

fácil ['faθil] *adj* (*simple*) easy; (*probable*)
likely

facilidad [faθili'ðað] *nf* (*capacidad*) ease;
(*sencillez*) simplicity; (*de palabra*)
fluency; **~es** *nfpl* facilities

facilitar [faθili'tar] *vt* (*hacer fácil*) to make
easy; (*proporcionar*) to provide

fácilmente ['faθilmente] *adv* easily

facsímil [fak'simil] *nm* facsimile, fax

factible [fak'tiβle] *adj* feasible

factor [fak'tor] *nm* factor

factura [fak'tura] *nf* (*cuenta*) bill;
(*hechura*) manufacture; **facturar** *vt* (COM)
to invoice, charge for; (*equipaje*) to
register (BRIT), check (US)

facultad [fakul'tað] *nf* (*aptitud, ESCOL etc*)
faculty; (*poder*) power

faena [fa'ena] *nf* (*trabajo*) work;
(*quehacer*) task, job

faisán [fai'san] *nm* pheasant

faja ['faxa] *nf* (*para la cintura*) sash; (*de
mujer*) corset; (*de tierra*) strip

fajo ['faxo] *nm* (*de papeles*) bundle; (*de*

billetes) wad
falacia [fa'laθja] *nf* fallacy
falda ['falda] *nf* (*prenda de vestir*) skirt
falla ['faʎa] *nf* (*defecto*) fault, flaw
fallar [fa'ʎar] *vt* (*JUR*) to pronounce
sentence on ♦ *vi* (*memoria*) to fail;
(*motor*) to miss
fallecer [faʎe'θer] *vi* to pass away, die;
fallecimiento *nm* decease, demise
fallido, a [fa'ʎiðo, a] *adj* (*gen*) frustrated,
unsuccessful
fallo ['faʎo] *nm* (*JUR*) verdict, ruling;
(*fracaso*) failure; ~ **cardíaco** heart
failure
falo ['falo] *nm* phallus
falsedad [false'ðað] *nf* falseness;
(*hipocresía*) hypocrisy; (*mentira*)
falsehood
falsificar [falsifi'kar] *vt* (*firma etc*) to
forge; (*voto etc*) to rig; (*moneda*) to
counterfeit
falso, a ['falso, a] *adj* false; (*erróneo*)
mistaken; (*documento, moneda etc*) fake;
en ~ falsely
falta ['falta] *nf* (*defecto*) fault, flaw;
(*privación*) lack, want; (*ausencia*)
absence; (*carencia*) shortage; (*equivocación*) mistake; (*DEPORTE*) foul; **echar en** ~
to miss; **hacer** ~ **hacer algo** to be
necessary to do sth; **me hace** ~ **una
pluma** I need a pen; ~ **de educación**
bad manners *pl*
faltar [fal'tar] *vi* (*escasear*) to be lacking,
be wanting; (*ausentarse*) to be absent, be
missing; **faltan 2 horas para llegar**
there are 2 hours to go till arrival; ~ **al
respeto a uno** to be disrespectful to sb;
¡**no faltaba más!** that's the last straw!
falto, a ['falto, a] *adj* (*desposeído*)
deficient, lacking; (*necesitado*) poor,
wretched
fama ['fama] *nf* (*renombre*) fame;
(*reputación*) reputation
famélico, a [fa'meliko, a] *adj* starving
familia [fa'milja] *nf* family; ~ **política** in-
laws *pl*
familiar [fami'ljar] *adj* (*relativo a la
familia*) family *cpd*; (*conocido, informal*)
familiar ♦ *nm* relative, relation; ~**idad** *nf*

(*gen*) familiarity; (*informalidad*)
homeliness; ~**izarse** *vr*: ~**izarse con** to
familiarize o.s. with
famoso, a [fa'moso, a] *adj* (*renombrado*)
famous
fanático, a [fa'natiko, a] *adj* fanatical
♦ *nm/f* fanatic; (*CINE, DEPORTE*) fan;
fanatismo *nm* fanaticism
fanfarrón, ona [fanfa'rron, ona] *adj*
boastful; (*pey*) showy
fango ['fango] *nm* mud; ~**so, a** *adj*
muddy
fantasía [fanta'sia] *nf* fantasy,
imagination; **joyas de** ~ imitation
jewellery *sg*
fantasma [fan'tasma] *nm* (*espectro*) ghost,
apparition; (*presumido*) show-off
fantástico, a [fan'tastiko, a] *adj* fantastic
farmacéutico, a [farma'θeutiko, a] *adj*
pharmaceutical ♦ *nm/f* chemist (*BRIT*),
pharmacist
farmacia [far'maθja] *nf* chemist's (shop)
(*BRIT*), pharmacy; ~ **de turno** duty
chemist; ~ **de guardia** all-night chemist
fármaco ['farmako] *nm* drug
faro ['faro] *nm* (*NAUT: torre*) lighthouse;
(*AUTO*) headlamp; (*foco*) floodlight; ~**s
antiniebla** fog lamps; ~**s delanteros/
traseros** headlights/rear lights
farol [fa'rol] *nm* lantern, lamp
farola [fa'rola] *nf* street lamp (*BRIT*) *o* light
(*US*)
farsa ['farsa] *nf* (*gen*) farce
farsante [far'sante] *nm/f* fraud, fake
fascículo [fas'θikulo] *nm* (*de revista*) part,
instalment
fascinar [fasθi'nar] *vt* (*gen*) to fascinate
fascismo [fas'θismo] *nm* fascism; **fascista**
adj, nm/f fascist
fase ['fase] *nf* phase
fastidiar [fasti'ðjar] *vt* (*disgustar*) to
annoy, bother; (*estropear*) to spoil; ~**se**
vr (*disgustarse*) to get annoyed *o* cross;
¡**que se fastidie!** (*fam*) he'll just have to
put up with it!
fastidio [fas'tiðjo] *nm* (*disgusto*)
annoyance; ~**so, a** *adj* (*molesto*)
annoying
fastuoso, a [fas'twoso, a] *adj* (*banquete,*

boda) lavish; (*acto*) pompous

fatal [fa'tal] *adj* (*gen*) fatal; (*desgraciado*) ill-fated; (*fam: malo, pésimo*) awful; **~idad** *nf* (*destino*) fate; (*mala suerte*) misfortune

fatiga [fa'tiɣa] *nf* (*cansancio*) fatigue, weariness

fatigar [fati'ɣar] *vt* to tire, weary; **~se** *vr* to get tired

fatigoso, a [fati'ɣoso, a] *adj* (*cansador*) tiring

fatuo, a ['fatwo, a] *adj* (*vano*) fatuous; (*presuntuoso*) conceited

fauces ['fauθes] *nfpl* jaws, mouth *sg*

favor [fa'βor] *nm* favour; **estar a ~ de** to be in favour of; **haga el ~ de...** would you be so good as to..., kindly...; **por ~** please; **~able** *adj* favourable

favorecer [faβore'θer] *vt* to favour; (*vestido etc*) to become, flatter; **este peinado le favorece** this hairstyle suits him

favorito, a [faβo'rito, a] *adj, nm/f* favourite

faz [faθ] *nf* face; **la ~ de la tierra** the face of the earth

fe [fe] *nf* (*REL*) faith; (*confianza*) belief; (*documento*) certificate; **prestar ~ a** to believe, credit; **actuar con buena/mala ~** to act in good/bad faith; **dar ~ de** to bear witness to

fealdad [feal'dað] *nf* ugliness

febrero [fe'βrero] *nm* February

febril [fe'βril] *adj* (*fig: actividad*) hectic; (*mente, mirada*) feverish

fecha ['fetʃa] *nf* date; **~ de caducidad** (*de producto alimenticio*) sell-by date; (*de contrato etc*) expiry date; **con ~ adelantada** postdated; **en ~ próxima** soon; **hasta la ~** to date, so far; **poner ~ to** date; **fechar** *vt* to date

fecundar [fekun'dar] *vt* (*generar*) to fertilize, make fertile; **fecundo, a** *adj* (*fértil*) fertile; (*fig*) prolific; (*productivo*) productive

federación [feðera'θjon] *nf* federation

federal [feðe'ral] *adj* federal

felicidad [feliθi'ðað] *nf* (*satisfacción, contento*) happiness; **~es** *nfpl* (*felicita-*

ciones) best wishes, congratulations

felicitación [feliθita'θjon] *nf*: **¡felicitaciones!** congratulations!

felicitar [feliθi'tar] *vt* to congratulate

feligrés, esa [feli'ɣres, esa] *nm/f* parishioner

feliz [fe'liθ] *adj* (*contento*) happy; (*afortunado*) lucky

felpudo [fel'puðo] *nm* doormat

femenino, a [feme'nino, a] *adj, nm* feminine

feminista [femi'nista] *adj, nm/f* feminist

fenómeno [fe'nomeno] *nm* phenomenon; (*fig*) freak, accident ♦ *adj* great! ♦ *excl* great!, marvellous!; **fenomenal** *adj* = **fenómeno**

feo, a ['feo, a] *adj* (*gen*) ugly; (*desagradable*) bad, nasty

féretro ['feretro] *nm* (*ataúd*) coffin; (*sarcófago*) bier

feria ['ferja] *nf* (*gen*) fair; (*descanso*) holiday, rest day; (*AM: mercado*) village market; (: *cambio*) loose o small change

fermentar [fermen'tar] *vi* to ferment

ferocidad [feroθi'ðað] *nf* fierceness, ferocity

feroz [fe'roθ] *adj* (*cruel*) cruel; (*salvaje*) fierce

férreo, a ['ferreo, a] *adj* iron

ferretería [ferrete'ria] *nf* (*tienda*) ironmonger's (shop) (*BRIT*), hardware store

ferrocarril [ferroka'rril] *nm* railway

ferroviario, a [ferro'βjarjo, a] *adj* rail *cpd*

fértil ['fertil] *adj* (*productivo*) fertile; (*rico*) rich; **fertilidad** *nf* (*gen*) fertility; (*productividad*) fruitfulness

ferviente [fer'βjente] *adj* fervent

fervor [fer'βor] *nm* fervour; **~oso, a** *adj* fervent

festejar [feste'xar] *vt* (*celebrar*) to celebrate

festejo [fes'texo] *nm* celebration; **festejos** *nmpl* (*fiestas*) festivals

festín [fes'tin] *nm* feast, banquet

festival [festi'βal] *nm* festival

festividad [festiβi'ðað] *nf* festivity

festivo, a [fes'tiβo, a] *adj* (*de fiesta*) festive; (*fig*) witty; (*CINE, LITERATURA*) humorous; **día ~** holiday

fétido, a ['fetiðo, a] *adj* (*hediondo*) foul-smelling

feto ['feto] *nm* foetus

fiable ['fjaßle] *adj* (*persona*) trustworthy; (*máquina*) reliable

fiador, a [fia'ðor, a] *nm/f* (*JUR*) surety, guarantor; (*COM*) backer; **salir ~ por uno** to stand bail for sb

fiambre ['fjambre] *nm* cold meat

fianza ['fjanθa] *nf* surety; (*JUR*): **libertad bajo ~** release on bail

fiar [fi'ar] *vt* (*salir garante de*) to guarantee; (*vender a crédito*) to sell on credit; (*secreto*): **~ a** to confide (to) ♦ *vi* to trust; **~se** *vr* to trust (in), rely on; **~se de uno** to rely on sb

fibra ['fißra] *nf* fibre; **~ óptica** optical fibre

ficción [fik'θjon] *nf* fiction

ficha ['fitʃa] *nf* (*TEL*) token; (*en juegos*) counter, marker; (*tarjeta*) (index) card; **fichar** *vt* (*archivar*) to file, index; (*DEPORTE*) to sign; **estar fichado** to have a record; **fichero** *nm* box file; (*INFORM*) file

ficticio, a [fik'tiθjo, a] *adj* (*imaginario*) fictitious; (*falso*) fabricated

fidelidad [fiðeli'ðað] *nf* (*lealtad*) fidelity, loyalty; **alta ~** high fidelity, hi-fi

fideos [fi'ðeos] *nmpl* noodles

fiebre ['fjeßre] *nf* (*MED*) fever; (*fig*) fever, excitement; **~ amarilla/del heno** yellow/hay fever; **~ palúdica** malaria; **tener ~** to have a temperature

fiel [fjel] *adj* (*leal*) faithful, loyal; (*fiable*) reliable; (*exacto*) accurate, faithful ♦ *nm*: **los ~es** the faithful

fieltro ['fjeltro] *nm* felt

fiera ['fjera] *nf* (*animal feroz*) wild animal *o* beast; (*fig*) dragon; *ver tb* **fiero**

fiero, a ['fjero, a] *adj* (*cruel*) cruel; (*feroz*) fierce; (*duro*) harsh ♦ *nm/f* (*fig*) fiend

fiesta ['fjesta] *nf* party; (*de pueblo*) festival; (*vacaciones, tb*: **~s**) holiday *sg*; (*REL*): **~ de guardar** day of obligation

figura [fi'ɣura] *nf* (*gen*) figure; (*forma, imagen*) shape, form; (*NAIPES*) face card

figurar [fiɣu'rar] *vt* (*representar*) to represent; (*fingir*) to figure ♦ *vi* to figure; **~se** *vr* (*imaginarse*) to imagine; (*suponer*) to suppose

fijador [fixa'ðor] *nm* (*FOTO etc*) fixative; (*de pelo*) gel

fijar [fi'xar] *vt* (*gen*) to fix; (*estampilla*) to affix, stick (on); (*fig*) to settle (on), decide; **~se** *vr*: **~se en** to notice

fijo, a ['fixo, a] *adj* (*gen*) fixed; (*firme*) firm; (*permanente*) permanent ♦ *adv*: **mirar ~** to stare

fila ['fila] *nf* row; (*MIL*) rank; (*cadena*) line; **ponerse en ~** to line up, get into line

filántropo, a [fi'lantropo, a] *nm/f* philanthropist

filatelia [fila'telja] *nf* philately, stamp collecting

filete [fi'lete] *nm* (*carne*) fillet steak; (*pescado*) fillet

filiación [filja'θjon] *nf* (*POL*) affiliation

filial [fi'ljal] *adj* filial ♦ *nf* subsidiary

Filipinas [fili'pinas] *nfpl*: **las ~** the Philippines; **filipino, a** *adj, nm/f* Philippine

filmar [fil'mar] *vt* to film, shoot

filo ['filo] *nm* (*gen*) edge; **sacar ~ a** to sharpen; **al ~ del mediodía** at about midday; **de doble ~** double-edged

filón [fi'lon] *nm* (*MINERÍA*) vein, lode; (*fig*) goldmine

filosofía [filoso'fia] *nf* philosophy; **filósofo, a** *nm/f* philosopher

filtrar [fil'trar] *vt, vi* to filter, strain; **~se** *vr* to filter; (*fig: dinero*) to dwindle; **filtro** *nm* (*TEC, utensilio*) filter

fin [fin] *nm* end; (*objetivo*) aim, purpose; **al ~ y al cabo** when all's said and done; **a ~ de** in order to; **por ~** finally; **en ~** in short; **~ de semana** weekend

final [fi'nal] *adj* final ♦ *nm* end, conclusion ♦ *nf* final; **~idad** *nf* (*propósito*) purpose, intention; **~ista** *nm/f* finalist; **~izar** *vt* to end, finish; (*INFORM*) to log out *o* off ♦ *vi* to end, come to an end

financiar [finan'θjar] *vt* to finance; **financiero, a** *adj* financial ♦ *nm/f* financier

finca ['finka] *nf* (*bien inmueble*) property, land; (*casa de campo*) country house;

(AM) farm

fingir [fin'xir] vt (simular) to simulate, feign; (pretextar) to sham, fake ♦ vi (aparentar) to pretend; **~se** vr to pretend to be

finlandés, esa [finlan'des, esa] adj Finnish ♦ nm/f Finn ♦ nm (LING) Finnish

Finlandia [fin'landja] nf Finland

fino, a ['fino, a] adj fine; (delgado) slender; (de buenas maneras) polite, refined; (jerez) fino, dry

firma ['firma] nf signature; (COM) firm, company

firmamento [firma'mento] nm firmament

firmar [fir'mar] vt to sign

firme ['firme] adj firm; (estable) stable; (sólido) solid; (constante) steady; (decidido) resolute ♦ nm road (surface); **~mente** adv firmly; **~za** nf firmness; (constancia) steadiness; (solidez) solidity

fiscal [fis'kal] adj fiscal ♦ nm/f public prosecutor; **año ~** tax o fiscal year

fisco ['fisko] nm (hacienda) treasury, exchequer (BRIT)

fisgar [fis'var] vt to pry into

fisgonear [fisvone'ar] vt to poke one's nose into ♦ vi to pry, spy

física ['fisika] nf physics sg; ver tb físico

físico, a ['fisiko, a] adj physical ♦ nm physique ♦ nm/f physicist

fisura [fi'sura] nf crack; (MED) (hairline) fracture

flac(c)ido, a ['fla(k)θiðo, a] adj flabby

flaco, a ['flako, a] adj (muy delgado) skinny, thin; (débil) weak, feeble

flagrante [fla'vrante] adj flagrant

flamante [fla'mante] (fam) adj brilliant; (nuevo) brand-new

flamenco, a [fla'menko, a] adj (de Flandes) Flemish; (baile, música) flamenco ♦ nm (baile, música) flamenco

flan [flan] nm creme caramel

flaqueza [fla'keθa] nf (delgadez) thinness, leanness; (fig) weakness

flash [flaʃ] (pl ~s o ~es) nm (FOTO) flash

flauta ['flauta] nf (MUS) flute

flecha ['fletʃa] nf arrow

flechazo [fle'tʃaθo] nm love at first sight

fleco ['fleko] nm fringe

flema ['flema] nm phlegm

flequillo [fle'kiʎo] nm (pelo) fringe

flete ['flete] nm (carga) freight; (alquiler) charter; (precio) freightage

flexible [flek'siβle] adj flexible

flexo ['flekso] nm adjustable table-lamp

flojera [flo'xera] (AM: fam) nf: **me da ~** I can't be bothered

flojo, a ['floxo, a] adj (gen) loose; (sin fuerzas) limp; (débil) weak

flor [flor] nf flower; (piropo) compliment; **a ~ de** on the surface of; **~ecer** vi (BOT) to flower, bloom; (fig) to flourish; **~eciente** adj (BOT) in flower, flowering; (fig) thriving; **~ero** nm vase; **~istería** nf florist's (shop)

flota ['flota] nf fleet

flotador [flota'ðor] nm (gen) float; (para nadar) rubber ring

flotar [flo'tar] vi (gen) to float; **flote** nm: **a flote** afloat; **salir a flote** (fig) to get back on one's feet

fluctuar [fluk'twar] vi (oscilar) to fluctuate

fluidez [flui'ðeθ] nf fluidity; (fig) fluency

flúido, a ['fluiðo, a] adj, nm fluid

fluir [flu'ir] vi to flow

flujo ['fluxo] nm flow; **~ y reflujo** ebb and flow; **~ de sangre** (MED) loss of blood

fluvial [fluβi'al] adj (navegación, cuenca) fluvial, river cpd

foca ['foka] nf seal

foco ['foko] nm focus; (ELEC) floodlight; (AM) (light) bulb

fofo, a ['fofo, a] adj soft, spongy; (carnes) flabby

fogata [fo'vata] nf bonfire

fogón [fo'von] nm (de cocina) ring, burner

fogoso, a [fo'voso, a] adj spirited

folio ['foljo] nm folio, page

follaje [fo'ʎaxe] nm foliage

folletín [foʎe'tin] nm newspaper serial

folleto [fo'ʎeto] nm (POL) pamphlet

follón [fo'ʎon] (fam) nm (lío) mess; (conmoción) fuss; **armar un ~** to kick up a row

fomentar [fomen'tar] vt (MED) to foment; **fomento** nm (promoción) promotion

fonda ['fonda] *nf* inn

fondear [fonde'ar] *vt* to search

fondo ['fondo] *nm* (*de mar*) bottom; (*de coche, sala*) back; (*ARTE etc*) background; (*reserva*) fund; **~s** *nmpl* (*COM*) funds, resources; **una investigación a ~** a thorough investigation; **en el ~** at bottom, deep down

fontanería [fontane'ria] *nf* plumbing; **fontanero, a** *nm/f* plumber

footing ['futin] *nm* jogging; **hacer ~** to jog, go jogging

foráneo, a [fo'raneo, a] *adj* foreign

forastero, a [foras'tero, a] *nm/f* stranger

forcejear [forθexe'ar] *vi* (*luchar*) to struggle

forense [fo'rense] *nm/f* pathologist

forjar [for'xar] *vt* to forge

forma ['forma] *nf* (*figura*) form, shape; (*molde*) mould, pattern; (*MED*) fitness; (*método*) way, means; **las ~s** the conventions; **estar en ~** to be fit

formación [forma'θjon] *nf* (*gen*) formation; (*educación*) education; **~ profesional** vocational training

formal [for'mal] *adj* (*gen*) formal; (*fig: persona*) serious; (: *de fiar*) reliable; **~idad** *nf* formality; seriousness; **~izar** *vt* (*JUR*) to formalize; (*situación*) to put in order, regularize; **~izarse** *vr* (*situación*) to be put in order, be regularized

formar [for'mar] *vt* (*componer*) to form, shape; (*constituir*) to make up, constitute; (*ESCOL*) to train, educate; **~se** (*ESCOL*) to be trained, educated; (*cobrar forma*) to form, take form; (*desarrollarse*) to develop

formatear [formate'ar] *vt* to format

formativo, a [forma'tiβo, a] *adj* (*lecturas, años*) formative

formato [for'mato] *nm* format

formidable [formi'ðaβle] *adj* (*temible*) formidable; (*asombroso*) tremendous

fórmula ['formula] *nf* formula

formular [formu'lar] *vt* (*queja*) to make, lodge; (*petición*) to draw up; (*pregunta*) to pose

formulario [formu'larjo] *nm* form

fornido, a [for'niðo, a] *adj* well-built

forrar [fo'rrar] *vt* (*abrigo*) to line; (*libro*) to cover; **forro** *nm* (*de cuaderno*) cover; (*COSTURA*) lining; (*de sillón*) upholstery

fortalecer [fortale'θer] *vt* to strengthen

fortaleza [forta'leθa] *nf* (*MIL*) fortress, stronghold; (*fuerza*) strength; (*determinación*) resolution

fortuito, a [for'twito, a] *adj* accidental

fortuna [for'tuna] *nf* (*suerte*) fortune, (good) luck; (*riqueza*) fortune, wealth

forzar [for'θar] *vt* (*puerta*) to force (open); (*compeler*) to compel

forzoso, a [for'θoso, a] *adj* necessary

fosa ['fosa] *nf* (*sepultura*) grave; (*en tierra*) pit; (*MED*) cavity; **~s nasales** nostrils

fósforo ['fosforo] *nm* (*QUÍMICA*) phosphorus; (*AM*) match

foso ['foso] *nm* ditch; (*TEATRO*) pit; (*AUTO*): **~ de reconocimiento** inspection pit

foto ['foto] *nf* photo, snap(shot); **sacar una ~** to take a photo o picture

fotocopia [foto'kopja] *nf* photocopy; **fotocopiadora** *nf* photocopier; **fotocopiar** *vt* to photocopy

fotografía [fotoɣra'fia] *nf* (*ARTE*) photography; (*una ~*) photograph; **fotografiar** *vt* to photograph

fotógrafo, a [fo'toɣrafo, a] *nm/f* photographer

fracasar [fraka'sar] *vi* (*gen*) to fail

fracaso [fra'kaso] *nm* (*desgracia, revés*) failure

fracción [frak'θjon] *nf* fraction; (*POL*) faction; **fraccionamiento** (*AM*) *nm* housing estate

fractura [frak'tura] *nf* fracture, break

fragancia [fra'ɣanθja] *nf* (*olor*) fragrance, perfume

frágil ['fraxil] *adj* (*débil*) fragile; (*COM*) breakable

fragmento [fraɣ'mento] *nm* (*pedazo*) fragment

fragua ['fraɣwa] *nf* forge; **fraguar** *vt* to forge; (*fig*) to concoct ♦ *vi* to harden

fraile ['fraile] *nm* (*REL*) friar; (: *monje*) monk

frambuesa [fram'bwesa] *nf* raspberry

francamente [franka'mente] *adv* (*hablar, decir*)

frankly; (*realmente*) really

francés, esa [fran'θes, esa] *adj* French
♦ *nm/f* Frenchman/woman ♦ *nm* (*LING*)
French

Francia ['franθja] *nf* France

franco, a ['franko, a] *adj* (*cándido*) frank,
open; (*COM: exento*) free ♦ *nm* (*moneda*)
franc

francotirador, a [frankotira'ðor, a] *nm/f*
sniper

franela [fra'nela] *nf* flannel

franja ['franxa] *nf* fringe

franquear [franke'ar] *vt* (*camino*) to clear;
(*carta, paquete postal*) to frank, stamp;
(*obstáculo*) to overcome

franqueo [fran'keo] *nm* postage

franqueza [fran'keθa] *nf* (*candor*)
frankness

frasco ['frasko] *nm* bottle, flask; ~ **al
vacío** (vacuum) flask

frase ['frase] *nf* sentence; ~ **hecha** set
phrase; (*pey*) stock phrase

fraterno, a [fra'terno, a] *adj* brotherly,
fraternal

fraude ['frauðe] *nm* (*cualidad*) dishonesty;
(*acto*) fraud; **fraudulento, a** *adj*
fraudulent

frazada [fra'saða] (*AM*) *nf* blanket

frecuencia [fre'kwenθja] *nf* frequency;
con ~ frequently, often

frecuentar [frekwen'tar] *vt* to frequent

fregadero [freɣa'ðero] *nm* (kitchen) sink

fregar [fre'ɣar] *vt* (*frotar*) to scrub;
(*platos*) to wash (up); (*AM*) to annoy

fregona [fre'ɣona] *nf* (*utensilio*) mop;
(*pey: sirvienta*) skivvy

freír [fre'ir] *vt* to fry

frenar [fre'nar] *vt* to brake; (*fig*) to check

frenazo [fre'naθo] *nm*: **dar un** ~ to brake
sharply

frenesí [frene'si] *nm* frenzy; **frenético, a**
adj frantic

freno ['freno] *nm* (*TEC, AUTO*) brake; (*de
cabalgadura*) bit; (*fig*) check

frente ['frente] *nm* (*ARQ, POL*) front; (*de
objeto*) front part ♦ *nf* forehead, brow; ~
a in front of; (*en situación opuesta de*)
opposite; **al** ~ **de** (*fig*) at the head of;
chocar de ~ to crash head-on; **hacer** ~ **a**

to face up to

fresa ['fresa] (*ESP*) *nf* strawberry

fresco, a ['fresko, a] *adj* (*nuevo*) fresh;
(*frío*) cool; (*descarado*) cheeky ♦ *nm*
(*aire*) fresh air; (*ARTE*) fresco; (*AM: jugo*)
fruit drink ♦ *nm/f* (*fam*): **ser un** ~ to
have a nerve; **tomar el** ~ to get some
fresh air; **frescura** *nf* freshness; (*descaro*)
cheek, nerve; (*calma*) calmness

frialdad [frial'dað] *nf* (*gen*) coldness;
(*indiferencia*) indifference

fricción [frik'θjon] *nf* (*gen*) friction; (*acto*)
rub(bing); (*MED*) massage

frigidez [frixi'ðeθ] *nf* frigidity

frigorífico [friɣo'rifiko] *nm* refrigerator

frijol [fri'xol] *nm* kidney bean

frío, a *etc* ['frio, a] *vb ver* **freír** ♦ *adj* cold;
(*indiferente*) indifferent ♦ *nm* cold; indifference; **hace** ~ it's cold; **tener** ~ to be
cold

frito, a ['frito, a] *adj* fried; **me trae** ~ **ese
hombre** I'm sick and tired of that man;
fritos *nmpl* fried food

frívolo, a ['friβolo, a] *adj* frivolous

frontal [fron'tal] *adj* frontal; **choque** ~
head-on collision

frontera [fron'tera] *nf* frontier; **fronterizo,
a** *adj* frontier *cpd*; (*contiguo*) bordering

frontón [fron'ton] *nm* (*DEPORTE: cancha*)
pelota court; (: *juego*) pelota

frotar [fro'tar] *vt* to rub; ~**se** *vr*: ~**se las
manos** to rub one's hands

fructífero, a [fruk'tifero, a] *adj* fruitful

frugal [fru'ɣal] *adj* frugal

fruncir [frun'θir] *vt* to pucker; (*COSTURA*) to
pleat; ~ **el ceño** to knit one's brow

frustrar [frus'trar] *vt* to frustrate

fruta ['fruta] *nf* fruit; **frutería** *nf* fruit
shop; **frutero, a** *adj* fruit *cpd* ♦ *nm/f*
fruiterer ♦ *nm* fruit bowl

frutilla [fru'tiʎa] (*AM*) *nf* strawberry

fruto ['fruto] *nm* fruit; (*fig: resultado*)
result; (: *utilidad*) benefit; ~**s secos** nuts;
(*pasas etc*) dried fruit *sg*

fue *vb ver* **ser**; **ir**

fuego ['fweɣo] *nm* (*gen*) fire; **a** ~ **lento**
on a low heat; **¿tienes** ~? have you (got)
a light?; ~**s artificiales** *o* **de artificio**
fireworks

fuente ['fwente] *nf* fountain; (*manantial*, *fig*) spring; (*origen*) source; (*plato*) large dish

fuera *etc* ['fwera] *vb ver* **ser, ir** ♦ *adv* out(side); (*en otra parte*) away; (*excepto*, *salvo*) except, save ♦ *prep*: ~ **de** outside; (*fig*) besides; ~ **de sí** beside o.s.; **por** ~ (on the) outside

fuerte ['fwerte] *adj* strong; (*golpe*) hard; (*ruido*) loud; (*comida*) rich; (*lluvia*) heavy; (*dolor*) intense ♦ *adv* strongly; hard; loud(ly)

fuerza *etc* ['fwerθa] *vb ver* **forzar** ♦ *nf* (*fortaleza*) strength; (*TEC, ELEC*) power; (*coacción*) force; (*MIL: tb*: ~s) forces *pl*; **a** ~ **de** by dint of; **cobrar** ~s to recover one's strength; **tener** ~s **para** to have the strength to; **a la** ~ forcibly, by force; **por** ~ of necessity; ~ **de voluntad** willpower

fuga ['fuɣa] *nf* (*huida*) flight, escape; (*de gas etc*) leak

fugarse [fu'ɣarse] *vr* to flee, escape

fugaz [fu'ɣaθ] *adj* fleeting

fugitivo, a [fuxi'tiβo, a] *adj, nm/f* fugitive

fui *vb ver* **ser; ir**

fulano, a [fu'lano, a] *nm/f* so-and-so, what's-his-name/what's-her-name

fulminante [fulmi'nante] *adj* (*fig: mirada*) fierce; (*MED: enfermedad, ataque*) sudden; (*fam: éxito, golpe*) sudden

fumador, a [fuma'ðor, a] *nm/f* smoker

fumar [fu'mar] *vt, vi* to smoke; ~**se** *vr* (*disipar*) to squander; ~ **en pipa** to smoke a pipe

función [fun'θjon] *nf* function; (*de puesto*) duties *pl*; (*espectáculo*) show; **entrar en funciones** to take up one's duties

funcionar [funθjo'nar] *vi* (*gen*) to function; (*máquina*) to work; **"no funciona"** "out of order"

funcionario, a [funθjo'narjo, a] *nm/f* official; (*público*) civil servant

funda ['funda] *nf* (*gen*) cover; (*de almohada*) pillowcase

fundación [funda'θjon] *nf* foundation

fundamental [fundamen'tal] *adj* fundamental, basic

fundamentar [fundamen'tar] *vt* (*poner*

base) to lay the foundations of; (*establecer*) to found; (*fig*) to base; **fundamento** *nm* (*base*) foundation

fundar [fun'dar] *vt* to found; ~**se** *vr*: ~**se en** to be founded on

fundición [fundi'θjon] *nf* fusing; (*fábrica*) foundry

fundir [fun'dir] *vt* (*gen*) to fuse; (*metal*) to smelt, melt down; (*nieve etc*) to melt; (*COM*) to merge; (*estatua*) to cast; ~**se** *vr* (*colores etc*) to merge, blend; (*unirse*) to fuse together; (*ELEC: fusible, lámpara etc*) to fuse, blow; (*nieve etc*) to melt

fúnebre ['funeβre] *adj* funeral *cpd*, funereal

funeral [fune'ral] *nm* funeral; **funeraria** *nf* undertaker's

funesto, a [fu'nesto, a] *adj* (*día*) ill-fated; (*decisión*) fatal

furgón [fur'ɣon] *nm* wagon; **furgoneta** *nf* (*AUTO, COM*) (transit) van (*BRIT*), pick-up (truck) (*US*)

furia ['furja] *nf* (*ira*) fury; (*violencia*) violence; **furibundo, a** *adj* furious; **furioso, a** *adj* (*iracundo*) furious; (*violento*) violent; **furor** *nm* (*cólera*) rage

furtivo, a [fur'tiβo, a] *adj* furtive ♦ *nm* poacher

fusible [fu'siβle] *nm* fuse

fusil [fu'sil] *nm* rifle; ~**ar** *vt* to shoot

fusión [fu'sjon] *nf* (*gen*) melting; (*unión*) fusion; (*COM*) merger

fusta ['fusta] *nf* (*látigo*) riding crop

fútbol ['futβol] *nm* football; **futbolista** *nm* footballer

fútil ['futil] *adj* trifling

futuro, a [fu'turo, a] *adj, nm* future

G g

gabardina [gaβar'ðina] *nf* raincoat, gabardine

gabinete [gaβi'nete] *nm* (*POL*) cabinet; (*estudio*) study; (*de abogados etc*) office

gaceta [ga'θeta] *nf* gazette

gachas ['gatʃas] *nfpl* porridge *sg*

gafas ['gafas] *nfpl* glasses; ~ **de sol** sunglasses

gafe ['gafe] *nm* jinx
gaita ['gaita] *nf* bagpipes *pl*
gajes ['gaxes] *nmpl*: **los ~ del oficio** occupational hazards
gajo ['gaxo] *nm* (*de naranja*) segment
gala ['gala] *nf* (*traje de etiqueta*) full dress; (*fig: lo mejor*) cream, flower; **~s** *nfpl* (*ropa*) finery *sg*; **estar de ~** to be in one's best clothes; **hacer ~ de** to display, show off
galante [ga'lante] *adj* gallant; **galantear** *vt* (*hacer la corte a*) to court, woo;
galantería *nf* (*caballerosidad*) gallantry; (*cumplido*) politeness; (*comentario*) compliment
galápago [ga'lapaxo] *nm* (*ZOOL*) turtle
galardón [galar'ðon] *nm* award, prize
galaxia [ga'laksja] *nf* galaxy
galera [ga'lera] *nf* (*nave*) galley; (*carro*) wagon; (*IMPRENTA*) galley
galería [gale'ria] *nf* (*gen*) gallery; (*balcón*) veranda(h); (*pasillo*) corridor
Gales ['gales] *nm* (*tb: País de ~*) Wales; **galés, esa** *adj* Welsh ♦ *nm/f* Welshman/woman ♦ *nm* (*LING*) Welsh
galgo, a ['galxo, a] *nm/f* greyhound
galimatías [galima'tias] *nmpl* (*lenguaje*) gibberish *sg*, nonsense *sg*
gallardía [gaʎar'ðia] *nf* (*galantería*) dash; (*valor*) bravery; (*elegancia*) elegance
gallego, a [ga'ʎexo, a] *adj, nm/f* Galician
galleta [ga'ʎeta] *nf* biscuit (*BRIT*), cookie (*US*)
gallina [ga'ʎina] *nf* hen ♦ *nm/f* (*fam: cobarde*) chicken; **gallinero** *nm* henhouse; (*TEATRO*) top gallery
gallo ['gaʎo] *nm* cock, rooster
galón [ga'lon] *nm* (*MIL*) stripe; (*COSTURA*) braid; (*medida*) gallon
galopar [galo'par] *vi* to gallop
gama ['gama] *nf* (*fig*) range
gamba ['gamba] *nf* prawn (*BRIT*), shrimp (*US*)
gamberro, a [gam'berro, a] *nm/f* hooligan, lout
gamuza [ga'muθa] *nf* chamois
gana ['gana] *nf* (*deseo*) desire, wish; (*apetito*) appetite; (*voluntad*) will; (*añoranza*) longing; **de buena ~**

willingly; **de mala ~** reluctantly; **me da ~s de** I feel like, I want to; **no me da la ~** I don't feel like it; **tener ~s de** to feel like
ganadería [ganaðe'ria] *nf* (*ganado*) livestock; (*ganado vacuno*) cattle *pl*; (*cría, comercio*) cattle raising
ganado [ga'naðo] *nm* livestock; **~ lanar** sheep *pl*; **~ mayor** cattle *pl*; **~ porcino** pigs *pl*
ganador, a [gana'ðor, a] *adj* winning ♦ *nm/f* winner
ganancia [ga'nanθja] *nf* (*lo ganado*) gain; (*aumento*) increase; (*beneficio*) profit; **~s** *nfpl* (*ingresos*) earnings; (*beneficios*) profit *sg*, winnings
ganar [ga'nar] *vt* (*obtener*) to get, obtain; (*sacar ventaja*) to gain; (*salario etc*) to earn; (*DEPORTE, premio*) to win; (*derrotar a*) to beat; (*alcanzar*) to reach ♦ *vi* (*DEPORTE*) to win; **~se** *vr*: **~se la vida** to earn one's living
ganchillo [gan'tʃiʎo] *nm* crochet
gancho ['gantʃo] *nm* (*gen*) hook; (*colgador*) hanger
gandul, a [gan'dul, a] *adj, nm/f* good-for-nothing, layabout
ganga ['ganga] *nf* (*cosa buena y barata*) bargain; (*buena situación*) cushy job
gangrena [gan'grena] *nf* gangrene
gansada [gan'saða] (*fam*) *nf* stupid thing to do
ganso, a ['ganso, a] *nm/f* (*ZOOL*) goose; (*fam*) idiot
ganzúa [gan'θua] *nf* skeleton key
garabatear [garaβate'ar] *vi, vt* (*al escribir*) to scribble, scrawl
garabato [gara'βato] *nm* (*escritura*) scrawl, scribble
garaje [ga'raxe] *nm* garage
garante [ga'rante] *adj* responsible ♦ *nm/f* guarantor
garantía [garan'tia] *nf* guarantee
garantizar [garanti'θar] *vt* (*hacerse responsable de*) to vouch for; (*asegurar*) to guarantee
garbanzo [gar'βanθo] *nm* chickpea (*BRIT*), garbanzo (*US*)
garbo ['garβo] *nm* grace, elegance

garfio ['garfjo] *nm* grappling iron

garganta [gar'yanta] *nf* (*ANAT*) throat; (*de botella*) neck; **gargantilla** *nf* necklace

gárgaras ['garyaras] *nfpl*: **hacer ~** to gargle

garita [ga'rita] *nf* cabin, hut; (*MIL*) sentry box

garra ['garra] *nf* (*de gato*, *TEC*) claw; (*de ave*) talon; (*fam*) hand, paw

garrafa [ga'rrafa] *nf* carafe, decanter

garrapata [garra'pata] *nf* tick

garrote [ga'rrote] *nm* (*palo*) stick; (*porra*) cudgel; (*suplicio*) garrotte

garza ['garθa] *nf* heron

gas [gas] *nm* gas

gasa ['gasa] *nf* gauze

gaseosa [gase'osa] *nf* lemonade

gaseoso, a [gase'oso, a] *adj* gassy, fizzy

gasoil [ga'soil] *nm* diesel (oil)

gasóleo [ga'soleo] *nm* = **gasoil**

gasolina [gaso'lina] *nf* petrol, gas(oline) (*US*); **gasolinera** *nf* petrol (*BRIT*) o gas (*US*) station

gastado, a [gas'taðo, a] *adj* (*rendido*) spent; (*raído*) worn out; (*usado*: *frase etc*) trite

gastar [gas'tar] *vt* (*dinero, tiempo*) to spend; (*fuerzas*) to use up; (*desperdiciar*) to waste; (*llevar*) to wear; **~se** *vr* to wear out; (*estropearse*) to waste; **~ en** to spend on; **~ bromas** to crack jokes; **¿qué número gastas?** what size (shoe) do you take?

gasto ['gasto] *nm* (*desembolso*) expenditure, spending; (*consumo, uso*) use; **~s** *nmpl* (*desembolsos*) expenses; (*cargos*) charges, costs

gastronomía [gastrono'mia] *nf* gastronomy

gatear [gate'ar] *vi* (*andar a gatas*) to go on all fours

gatillo [ga'tiʎo] *nm* (*de arma de fuego*) trigger; (*de dentista*) forceps

gato, a ['gato, a] *nm/f* cat ♦ *nm* (*TEC*) jack; **andar a gatas** to go on all fours

gaviota [ga'βjota] *nf* seagull

gay [ge] *adj inv, nm* gay, homosexual

gazpacho [gaθ'patʃo] *nm* gazpacho

gel [xel] *nm* (*tb*: **~ de baño/ducha**) gel

gelatina [xela'tina] *nf* jelly; (*polvos etc*) gelatine

gema ['xema] *nf* gem

gemelo, a [xe'melo, a] *adj, nm/f* twin; **~s** *nmpl* (*de camisa*) cufflinks; **~s de campo** field glasses, binoculars

gemido [xe'miðo] *nm* (*quejido*) moan, groan; (*aullido*) howl

Géminis ['xeminis] *nm* Gemini

gemir [xe'mir] *vi* (*quejarse*) to moan, groan; (*aullar*) to howl

generación [xenera'θjon] *nf* generation

general [xene'ral] *adj* general ♦ *nm* general; **por lo** o **en ~** in general; **G~itat** *nf* Catalan parliament; **~izar** *vt* to generalize; **~izarse** *vr* to become generalized, spread; **~mente** *adv* generally

generar [xene'rar] *vt* to generate

género ['xenero] *nm* (*clase*) kind, sort; (*tipo*) type; (*BIO*) genus; (*LING*) gender; (*COM*) material; **~ humano** human race

generosidad [xenerosi'ðað] *nf* generosity; **generoso, a** *adj* generous

genial [xe'njal] *adj* inspired; (*idea*) brilliant; (*afable*) genial

genio ['xenjo] *nm* (*carácter*) nature, disposition; (*humor*) temper; (*facultad creadora*) genius; **de mal ~** bad-tempered

genital [xeni'tal] *adj* genital; **genitales** *nmpl* genitals

gente ['xente] *nf* (*personas*) people *pl*; (*raza*) race; (*nación*) nation; (*parientes*) relatives *pl*

gentil [xen'til] *adj* (*elegante*) graceful; (*encantador*) charming; **~eza** *nf* grace; charm; (*cortesía*) courtesy

gentío [xen'tio] *nm* crowd, throng

genuino, a [xe'nwino, a] *adj* genuine

geografía [xeoyra'fia] *nf* geography

geología [xeolo'xia] *nf* geology

geometría [xeome'tria] *nf* geometry

gerencia [xe'renθja] *nf* management; **gerente** *nm/f* (*supervisor*) manager; (*jefe*) director

geriatría [xeria'tria] *nf* (*MED*) geriatrics *sg*

germen ['xermen] *nm* germ

germinar [xermi'nar] *vi* to germinate

gesticular [xestiku'lar] *vi* to gesticulate;

(*hacer muecas*) to grimace; gesticulación *nf* gesticulation; (*mueca*) grimace

gestión [xes'tjon] *nf* management; (*diligencia, acción*) negotiation; gestionar *vt* (*lograr*) to try to arrange; (*llevar*) to manage

gesto ['xesto] *nm* (*mueca*) grimace; (*ademán*) gesture

Gibraltar [xiβral'tar] *nm* Gibraltar; gibraltareño, a *adj, nm/f* Gibraltarian

gigante [xi'ɣante] *adj, nm/f* giant; gigantesco, a *adj* gigantic

gilipollas [xili'poʎas] (*fam*) *adj inv* daft ♦ *nm/f inv* wally

gimnasia [xim'nasja] *nf* gymnastics *pl*; gimnasio *nm* gymnasium; gimnasta *nm/f* gymnast

gimotear [ximote'ar] *vi* to whine, whimper

ginebra [xi'neβra] *nf* gin

ginecólogo, a [xine'koloɣo, a] *nm/f* gynaecologist

gira ['xira] *nf* tour, trip

girar [xi'rar] *vt* (*dar la vuelta*) to turn (around); (: *rápidamente*) to spin; (*COM: giro postal*) to draw; (*comerciar: letra de cambio*) to issue ♦ *vi* to turn (round); (*rápido*) to spin; (*COM*) to draw

girasol [xira'sol] *nm* sunflower

giratorio, a [xira'torjo, a] *adj* (*gen*) revolving; (*puente*) swing

giro ['xiro] *nm* (*movimiento*) turn, revolution; (*LING*) expression; (*COM*) draft; ~ bancario/postal bank giro/postal order

gis [xis] (*AM*) *nm* chalk

gitano, a [xi'tano, a] *adj, nm/f* gypsy

glacial [gla'θjal] *adj* icy, freezing

glaciar [gla'θjar] *nm* glacier

glándula ['glandula] *nf* gland

global [glo'βal] *adj* global

globo ['gloβo] *nm* (*esfera*) globe, sphere; (*aerostato, juguete*) balloon

glóbulo ['gloβulo] *nm* globule; (*ANAT*) corpuscle

gloria ['glorja] *nf* glory

glorieta [glo'rjeta] *nf* (*de jardín*) bower, arbour; (*plazoleta*) roundabout (*BRIT*), traffic circle (*US*)

glorificar [glorifi'kar] *vt* (*enaltecer*) to glorify, praise

glorioso, a [glo'rjoso, a] *adj* glorious

glosa ['glosa] *nf* comment

glosario [glo'sarjo] *nm* glossary

glotón, ona [glo'ton, ona] *adj* gluttonous, greedy ♦ *nm/f* glutton

glucosa [glu'kosa] *nf* glucose

gobernador, a [goβerna'ðor, a] *adj* governing ♦ *nm/f* governor; gobernante *adj* governing

gobernar [goβer'nar] *vt* (*dirigir*) to guide, direct; (*POL*) to rule, govern ♦ *vi* to govern; (*NAUT*) to steer

gobierno *etc* [go'βjerno] *vb ver* gobernar ♦ *nm* (*POL*) government; (*dirección*) guidance, direction; (*NAUT*) steering

goce *etc* ['goθe] *vb ver* gozar ♦ *nm* enjoyment

gol [gol] *nm* goal

golf [golf] *nm* golf

golfa ['golfa] (*fam*) *nf* (*mujer*) slut, whore

golfo, a ['golfo, a] *nm* (*GEO*) gulf ♦ *nm/f* (*fam: niño*) urchin; (*gamberro*) lout

golondrina [golon'drina] *nf* swallow

golosina [golo'sina] *nf* titbit; (*dulce*) sweet; goloso, a *adj* sweet-toothed

golpe ['golpe] *nm* blow; (*de puño*) punch; (*de mano*) smack; (*de remo*) stroke; (*fig: choque*) clash; **no dar** ~ to be bone idle; **de un** ~ with one blow; **de** ~ suddenly; ~ **(de estado)** coup (d'état); golpear *vt*, *vi* to strike, knock; (*asestar*) to beat; (*de puño*) to punch; (*golpetear*) to tap

goma ['goma] *nf* (*caucho*) rubber; (*elástico*) elastic; (*una* ~) elastic band; ~ **espuma** foam rubber; ~ **de pegar** gum, glue

gordo, a ['gorðo, a] *adj* (*gen*) fat; (*persona*) plump; (*fam*) enormous; **el (premio)** ~ (*en lotería*) first prize; gordura *nf* fat; (*corpulencia*) fatness, stoutness

gorila [go'rila] *nm* gorilla

gorjear [gorxe'ar] *vi* to twitter, chirp

gorra ['gorra] *nf* cap; (*de niño*) bonnet; (*militar*) bearskin; **entrar de** ~ (*fam*) to gatecrash; **ir de** ~ to sponge

gorrión [go'rrjon] *nm* sparrow

gorro ['gorro] *nm* (*gen*) cap; (*de niño*,

mujer) bonnet
gorrón, ona [go'rron, ona] *nm/f*
scrounger; **gorronear** (*fam*) *vi* to
scrounge
gota ['gota] *nf* (*gen*) drop; (*de sudor*)
bead; (*MED*) gout; **gotear** *vi* to drip;
(*lloviznar*) to drizzle; **gotera** *nf* leak
gozar [go'θar] *vi* to enjoy o.s.; ~ **de**
(*disfrutar*) to enjoy; (*poseer*) to possess
gozne ['goθne] *nm* hinge
gozo ['goθo] *nm* (*alegría*) joy; (*placer*)
pleasure
gr. *abr* (= *gramo, gramos*) g
grabación [graβa'θjon] *nf* recording
grabado [gra'βaðo] *nm* print, engraving
grabadora [graβa'ðora] *nf* tape-recorder
grabar [gra'βar] *vt* to engrave; (*discos,
cintas*) to record
gracia ['graθja] *nf* (*encanto*) grace, grace-
fulness; (*humor*) humour, wit; **¡(muchas)
~s!** thanks (very much)!; **~s a** thanks to;
tener ~ (*chiste etc*) to be funny; **no me
hace ~** I am not keen; **gracioso, a** *adj*
(*divertido*) funny, amusing; (*cómico*)
comical ♦ *nm/f* (*TEATRO*) comic character
grada ['graða] *nf* (*de escalera*) step; (*de
anfiteatro*) tier, row; **~s** *nfpl* (*DEPORTE: de
estadio*) terraces
gradación [graða'θjon] *nf* gradation
gradería [graðe'ria] *nf* (*gradas*) (flight of)
steps *pl*; (*de anfiteatro*) tiers *pl*, rows *pl*;
(*DEPORTE: de estadio*) terraces *pl*; **~
cubierta** covered stand
grado ['graðo] *nm* degree; (*de aceite, vino*)
grade; (*grada*) step; (*MIL*) rank; **de buen
~** willingly
graduación [graðwa'θjon] *nf* (*del alcohol*)
proof, strength; (*ESCOL*) graduation; (*MIL*)
rank
gradual [gra'ðwal] *adj* gradual
graduar [gra'ðwar] *vt* (*gen*) to graduate;
(*MIL*) to commission; **~se** *vr* to graduate;
~se la vista to have one's eyes tested
gráfica ['grafika] *nf* graph
gráfico, a ['grafiko, a] *adj* graphic ♦ *nm*
diagram; **~s** *nmpl* (*INFORM*) graphics
grajo ['graxo] *nm* rook
Gral *abr* (= *General*) Gen.
gramática [gra'matika] *nf* grammar

gramo ['gramo] *nm* gramme (*BRIT*), gram
(*US*)
gran [gran] *adj ver* **grande**
grana ['grana] *nf* (*BOT*) seedling; (*color,
tela*) scarlet
granada [gra'naða] *nf* pomegranate; (*MIL*)
grenade
granate [gra'nate] *adj* (*color*) deep red
Gran Bretaña [-bre'taɲa] *nf* Great
Britain
grande ['grande] (*antes de nmsg*: **gran**)
adj (*de tamaño*) big, large; (*alto*) tall;
(*distinguido*) great; (*impresionante*) grand
♦ *nm* grandee; **grandeza** *nf* greatness
grandioso, a [gran'djoso, a] *adj*
magnificent, grand
granel [gra'nel]: **a ~** *adv* (*COM*) in bulk
granero [gra'nero] *nm* granary, barn
granito [gra'nito] *nm* (*AGR*) small grain;
(*roca*) granite
granizado [grani'θaðo] *nm* iced drink
granizar [grani'θar] *vi* to hail; **granizo** *nm*
hail
granja ['granxa] *nf* (*gen*) farm; **granjear**
vt to win, gain; **granjearse** *vr* to win,
gain; **granjero, a** *nm/f* farmer
grano ['grano] *nm* grain; (*semilla*) seed;
(*baya*) berry; (*MED*) pimple, spot; **~s** *nmpl*
(*cereales*) cereals
granuja [gra'nuxa] *nm/f* rogue; (*golfillo*)
urchin
grapa ['grapa] *nf* staple; (*TEC*) clamp;
grapadora *nf* stapler
grasa ['grasa] *nf* (*gen*) grease; (*de cocina*)
fat, lard; (*sebo*) suet; (*mugre*) filth;
grasiento, a *adj* greasy; (*de aceite*) oily;
graso, a *adj* (*leche, queso, carne*) fatty;
(*pelo, piel*) greasy
gratificación [gratifika'θjon] *nf* (*propina*)
tip; (*bono*) bonus; (*recompensa*) reward
gratificar [gratifi'kar] *vt* to tip; to reward
gratinar [grati'nar] *vt* to cook au gratin
gratis ['gratis] *adv* free
gratitud [grati'tuð] *nf* gratitude
grato, a ['grato, a] *adj* (*agradable*)
pleasant, agreeable; (*bienvenido*)
welcome
gratuito, a [gra'twito, a] *adj* (*gratis*) free;
(*sin razón*) gratuitous

gravamen [graˈβamen] nm (*carga*) burden; (*impuesto*) tax

gravar [graˈβar] vt to burden; (*COM*) to tax

grave [ˈgraβe] adj heavy; (*serio*) grave, serious; ~**dad** nf gravity

gravilla [graˈβiʎa] nf gravel

gravitar [graβiˈtar] vi to gravitate; ~ **sobre** to rest on

graznar [graθˈnar] vi (*cuervo*) to squawk; (*pato*) to quack; (*hablar ronco*) to croak

Grecia [ˈgreθja] nf Greece

gremio [ˈgremjo] nm (*asociación*) trade, industry

greña [ˈgreɲa] nf (*cabellos*) shock of hair; (*maraña*) tangle

gresca [ˈgreska] nf uproar

griego, a [ˈgrjeβo, a] adj, nm/f Greek

grieta [ˈgrjeta] nf crack

grifo [ˈgrifo] nm tap; (*AM: AUTO*) petrol (*BRIT*) o gas (*US*) station

grilletes [griˈʎetes] nmpl fetters

grillo [ˈgriʎo] nm (*ZOOL*) cricket; (*BOT*) shoot

gripe [ˈgripe] nf flu, influenza

gris [gris] adj (*color*) grey

gritar [griˈtar] vt, vi to shout, yell; **grito** nm shout, yell; (*de horror*) scream

grosella [groˈseʎa] nf (red)currant; ~ **negra** blackcurrant

grosería [groseˈria] nf (*actitud*) rudeness; (*comentario*) vulgar comment; **grosero, a** adj (*poco cortés*) rude, bad-mannered; (*ordinario*) vulgar, crude

grosor [groˈsor] nm thickness

grotesco, a [groˈtesko, a] adj grotesque

grúa [ˈgrua] nf (*TEC*) crane; (*de petróleo*) derrick

grueso, a [ˈgrweso, a] adj thick; (*persona*) stout ♦ nm bulk; **el ~ de** the bulk of

grulla [ˈgruʎa] nf crane

grumo [ˈgrumo] nm clot, lump

gruñido [gruˈɲiðo] nm grunt; (*fig*) grumble

gruñir [gruˈɲir] vi (*animal*) to growl; (*fam*) to grumble

grupa [ˈgrupa] nf (*ZOOL*) rump

grupo [ˈgrupo] nm group; (*TEC*) unit, set

gruta [ˈgruta] nf grotto

guadaña [gwaˈðaɲa] nf scythe

guagua [ˈgwaɣwa] (*AM*) nf (*niño*) baby; (*bus*) bus

guante [ˈgwante] nm glove

guapo, a [ˈgwapo, a] adj good-looking, attractive; (*elegante*) smart

guarda [ˈgwarða] nm/f (*persona*) guard, keeper ♦ nf (*acto*) guarding; (*custodia*) custody; ~**bosques** nm inv gamekeeper; ~**costas** nm inv coastguard vessel ♦ nm/f guardian, protector; ~**espaldas** nm/f inv bodyguard; ~**meta** nm/f goalkeeper; **guardar** vt (*gen*) to keep; (*vigilar*) to guard, watch over; (*dinero: ahorrar*) to save; **guardarse** vr (*preservarse*) to preserve o.s.; (*evitar*) to avoid; **guardar cama** to stay in bed; ~**rropa** nm (*armario*) wardrobe; (*en establecimiento público*) cloakroom

guardería [gwarðeˈria] nf nursery

guardia [ˈgwarðja] nf (*MIL*) guard; (*cuidado*) care, custody ♦ nm/f guard; (*policía*) policeman/woman; **estar de ~** to be on guard; **montar ~** to mount guard; **G~ Civil** Civil Guard; **G~ Nacional** National Guard

guardián, ana [gwarˈðjan, ana] nm/f (*gen*) guardian, keeper

guarecer [gwareˈθer] vt (*proteger*) to protect; (*abrigar*) to shelter; ~**se** vr to take refuge

guarida [gwaˈriða] nf (*de animal*) den, lair; (*refugio*) refuge

guarnecer [gwarneˈθer] vt (*equipar*) to provide; (*adornar*) to adorn; (*TEC*) to reinforce; **guarnición** nf (*de vestimenta*) trimming; (*de piedra*) mount; (*CULIN*) garnish; (*arneses*) harness; (*MIL*) garrison

guarro, a [ˈgwarro, a] nm/f pig

guasa [ˈgwasa] nf joke; **guasón, ona** adj witty; (*bromista*) joking ♦ nm/f wit; joker

Guatemala [gwateˈmala] nf Guatemala

guay [gwai] (*fam*) adj super, great

gubernativo, a [guβernaˈtiβo, a] adj governmental

guerra [ˈgerra] nf war; (*pelea*) struggle; ~ **civil** civil war; ~ **fría** cold war; **dar ~** to annoy; **guerrear** vi to wage war; **guerrero, a** adj fighting; (*carácter*)

warlike ♦ *nm/f* warrior
guerrilla [geˈrriʎa] *nf* guerrilla warfare;
(tropas) guerrilla band *o* group
guía *etc* [ˈgia] *vb ver* **guiar** ♦ *nm/f*
(persona) guide ♦ *nf* *(libro)* guidebook;
G~ Girl Guide; **~ de ferrocarriles**
railway timetable; **~ telefónica**
telephone directory
guiar [giˈar] *vt* to guide, direct; *(AUTO)* to
steer; **~se** *vr*: **~se por** to be guided by
guijarro [giˈxarro] *nm* pebble
guillotina [giʎoˈtina] *nf* guillotine
guinda [ˈginda] *nf* morello cherry
guindilla [ginˈdiʎa] *nf* chilli pepper
guiñapo [giˈɲapo] *nm* *(harapo)* rag;
(persona) reprobate, rogue
guiñar [giˈɲar] *vt* to wink
guión [giˈon] *nm* *(LING)* hyphen, dash;
(CINE) script; **guionista** *nm/f* scriptwriter
guiri [ˈgiri] *(fam: pey)* *nm/f* foreigner
guirnalda [girˈnalda] *nf* garland
guisado [giˈsaðo] *nm* stew
guisante [giˈsante] *nm* pea
guisar [giˈsar] *vt, vi* to cook; **guiso** *nm*
cooked dish
guitarra [giˈtarra] *nf* guitar
gula [ˈgula] *nf* gluttony, greed
gusano [guˈsano] *nm* maggot; *(lombriz)*
earthworm
gustar [gusˈtar] *vt* to taste, sample ♦ *vi* to
please, be pleasing; **~ de algo** to like *o*
enjoy sth; **me gustan las uvas** I like
grapes; **le gusta nadar** she likes *o*
enjoys swimming
gusto [ˈgusto] *nm* *(sentido, sabor)* taste;
(placer) pleasure; **tiene ~ a menta** it
tastes of mint; **tener buen ~** to have
good taste; **sentirse a ~** to feel at ease;
mucho ~ (en conocerle) pleased to
meet you; **el ~ es mío** the pleasure is
mine; **con ~** willingly, gladly; **~so, a** *adj*
(sabroso) tasty; *(agradable)* pleasant

H h

ha *vb ver* **haber**
haba [ˈaßa] *nf* bean
Habana [aˈßana] *nf*: **la ~** Havana

habano [aˈßano] *nm* Havana cigar
habéis *vb ver* **haber**

PALABRA CLAVE
---

haber [aˈßer] *vb aux* **1** *(tiempos
compuestos)* to have; **había comido** I
have/had eaten; **antes/después de ~lo
visto** before seeing/after seeing *o* having
seen it
2: **¡~lo dicho antes!** you should have
said so before!
3: **~ de**: **he de hacerlo** I have to do it;
ha de llegar mañana it should arrive
tomorrow
♦ *vb impers* **1** *(existencia: sg)* there is;
(: pl) there are; **hay un hermano/dos
hermanos** there is one brother/there
are two brothers; **¿cuánto hay de aquí
a Sucre?** how far is it from here to
Sucre?
2 *(obligación)*: **hay que hacer algo**
something must be done; **hay que
apuntarlo para acordarse** you have to
write it down to remember
3: **¡hay que ver!** well I never!
4: **¡no hay de *o* por (AM) qué!** don't
mention it!, not at all!
5: **¿qué hay?** *(¿qué pasa?)* what's up?,
what's the matter?; *(¿qué tal?)* how's it
going?
♦ **~se** *vr*: **habérselas con uno** to have it
out with sb
♦ *vt*: **he aquí unas sugerencias** here
are some suggestions; **no hay cintas
blancas pero sí las hay rojas** there
aren't any white ribbons but there are
some red ones
♦ *nm* *(en cuenta)* credit side; **~es** *nmpl*
assets; **¿cuánto tengo en el ~?** how
much do I have in my account?; **tiene
varias novelas en su ~** he has several
novels to his credit

---

habichuela [aßiˈtʃwela] *nf* kidney bean
hábil [ˈaßil] *adj* *(listo)* clever, smart;
(capaz) fit, capable; *(experto)* expert; **día
~** working day; **habilidad** *nf* *(gen)* skill,
ability; *(inteligencia)* cleverness
habilitar [aßiliˈtar] *vt* *(capacitar)* to

enable; (*dar instrumentos*) to equip; (*financiar*) to finance

hábilmente [aβil'mente] *adv* skilfully, expertly

habitación [aβita'θjon] *nf* (*cuarto*) room; (*casa*) dwelling, abode; (*BIO: morada*) habitat; ~ **sencilla** *o* **individual** single room; ~ **doble** *o* **de matrimonio** double room

habitante [aβi'tante] *nm/f* inhabitant

habitar [aβi'tar] *vt* (*residir en*) to inhabit; (*ocupar*) to occupy ♦ *vi* to live

hábito ['aβito] *nm* habit

habitual [aβi'twal] *adj* usual

habituar [aβi'twar] *vt* to accustom; ~**se** *vr*: ~**se a** to get used to

habla ['aβla] *nf* (*capacidad de hablar*) speech; (*idioma*) language; (*dialecto*) dialect; **perder el** ~ to become speechless; **de** ~ **francesa** French-speaking; **estar al** ~ to be in contact; (*TEL*) to be on the line; **¡González al** ~! (*TEL*) González speaking!

hablador, a [aβla'ðor, a] *adj* talkative ♦ *nm/f* chatterbox

habladuría [aβlaðu'ria] *nf* rumour; ~**s** *nfpl* gossip *sg*

hablante [a'βlante] *adj* speaking ♦ *nm/f* speaker

hablar [a'βlar] *vt* to speak, talk ♦ *vi* to speak; ~**se** *vr* to speak to each other; ~ **con** to speak to; ~ **de** to speak of *o* about; **"se habla inglés"** "English spoken here"; **¡ni** ~! it's out of the question!

habré *etc vb ver* **haber**

hacendado [asen'daðo] (*AM*) *nm* large landowner

hacendoso, a [aθen'doso, a] *adj* industrious

PALABRA CLAVE

hacer [a'θer] *vt* **1** (*fabricar, producir*) to make; (*construir*) to build; ~ **una película/un ruido** to make a film/noise; **el guisado lo hice yo** I made *o* cooked the stew

2 (*ejecutar: trabajo etc*) to do; ~ **la colada** to do the washing; ~ **la comida** to do the cooking; **¿qué haces?** what are you doing?; ~ **el malo** *o* **el papel del malo** (*TEATRO*) to play the villain

3 (*estudios, algunos deportes*) to do; ~ **español/económicas** to do *o* study Spanish/economics; ~ **yoga/gimnasia** to do yoga/go to gym

4 (*transformar, incidir en*): **esto lo hará más difícil** this will make it more difficult; **salir te hará sentir mejor** going out will make you feel better

5 (*cálculo*): **2 y 2 hacen 4** 2 and 2 make 4; **éste hace 100** this one makes 100

6 (+ *sub*): **esto hará que ganemos** this will make us win; **harás que no quiera venir** you'll stop him wanting to come

7 (*como sustituto de vb*) to do; **él bebió y yo hice lo mismo** he drank and I did likewise

8: **no hace más que criticar** all he does is criticize

♦ *vb semi-aux*: **hacer** + *infin* **1** (*directo*): **les hice venir** I made *o* had them come; ~ **trabajar a los demás** to get others to work

2 (*por intermedio de otros*): ~ **reparar algo** to get sth repaired

♦ *vi* **1**: **haz como que no lo sabes** act as if you don't know

2 (*ser apropiado*): **si os hace** if it's alright with you

3: ~ **de**: ~ **de madre para uno** to be like a mother to sb; (*TEATRO*): ~ **de Otelo** to play Othello

♦ *vb impers* **1**: **hace calor/frío** it's hot/cold; *ver tb* **bueno**; **seco**; **tiempo**

2 (*tiempo*): **hace 3 años** 3 years ago; **hace un mes que voy/no voy** I've been going/I haven't been for a month

3: **¿cómo has hecho para llegar tan rápido?** how did you manage to get here so quickly?

♦ ~**se** *vr* **1** (*volverse*) to become; **se hicieron amigos** they became friends

2 (*acostumbrarse*): ~**se a** to get used to

3: **se hace con huevos y leche** it's made out of eggs and milk; **eso no se hace** that's not done

4 (*obtener*): ~**se de** *o* **con algo** to get

hold of sth

5 (*fingirse*): **~se el sueco** to turn a deaf ear

hacha ['atʃa] *nf* axe; (*antorcha*) torch
hachís [a'tʃis] *nm* hashish
hacia ['aθja] *prep* (*en dirección de*) towards; (*cerca de*) near; (*actitud*) towards; **~ arriba/abajo** up(wards)/down(wards); **~ mediodía** about noon
hacienda [a'θjenda] *nf* (*propiedad*) property; (*finca*) farm; (*AM*) ranch; **~ pública** public finance; **(Ministerio de) H~** Exchequer (*BRIT*), Treasury Department (*US*)
hada ['aða] *nf* fairy
hago *etc vb ver* **hacer**
Haití [ai'ti] *nm* Haiti
halagar [ala'ɣar] *vt* (*lisonjear*) to flatter
halago [a'laɣo] *nm* (*adulación*) flattery; **halagüeño, a** *adj* flattering
halcón [al'kon] *nm* falcon, hawk
hallar [a'ʎar] *vt* (*gen*) to find; (*descubrir*) to discover; (*toparse con*) to run into; **~se** *vr* to be (situated); **hallazgo** *nm* discovery; (*cosa*) find
halterofilia [altero'filja] *nf* weightlifting
hamaca [a'maka] *nf* hammock
hambre ['ambre] *nf* hunger; (*carencia*) famine; (*fig*) longing; **tener ~** to be hungry; **hambriento, a** *adj* hungry, starving
hamburguesa [ambur'ɣesa] *nf* hamburger
han *vb ver* **haber**
haragán, ana [ara'ɣan, ana] *adj, nm/f* good-for-nothing
harapiento, a [ara'pjento, a] *adj* tattered, in rags
harapos [a'rapos] *nmpl* rags
haré *etc vb ver* **hacer**
harina [a'rina] *nf* flour
hartar [ar'tar] *vt* to satiate, glut; (*fig*) to tire, sicken; **~se** *vr* (*de comida*) to fill o.s., gorge o.s.; (*cansarse*) to get fed up (*de* with); **hartazgo** *nm* surfeit, glut; **harto, a** *adj* (*lleno*) full; (*cansado*) fed up ♦ *adv* (*bastante*) enough; (*muy*) very; **estar harto de** to be fed up with

has *vb ver* **haber**
hasta ['asta] *adv* even ♦ *prep* (*alcanzando a*) as far as; up to; down to; (*de tiempo: a tal hora*) till, until; (*antes de*) before ♦ *conj*: **~ que** until; **~ luego/el sábado** see you soon/on Saturday
hastiar [as'tjar] *vt* (*gen*) to weary; (*aburrir*) to bore; **~se** *vr*: **~se de** to get fed up with; **hastío** *nm* weariness; boredom
hatillo [a'tiʎo] *nm* belongings *pl*, kit; (*montón*) bundle, heap
hay *vb ver* **haber**
Haya ['aja] *nf*: **la ~** The Hague
haya *etc* ['aja] *vb ver* **haber** ♦ *nf* beech tree
haz [aθ] *vb ver* **hacer** ♦ *nm* bundle, bunch; (*rayo: de luz*) beam
hazaña [a'θaɲa] *nf* feat, exploit
hazmerreír [aθmerre'ir] *nm inv* laughing stock
he *vb ver* **haber**
hebilla [e'βiʎa] *nf* buckle, clasp
hebra ['eβra] *nf* thread; (*BOT: fibra*) fibre, grain
hebreo, a [e'βreo, a] *adj, nm/f* Hebrew ♦ *nm* (*LING*) Hebrew
hechizar [etʃi'θar] *vt* to cast a spell on, bewitch
hechizo [e'tʃiθo] *nm* witchcraft, magic; (*acto de magía*) spell, charm
hecho, a ['etʃo, a] *pp de* **hacer** ♦ *adj* complete; (*maduro*) mature; (*COSTURA*) ready-to-wear ♦ *nm* deed, act; (*dato*) fact; (*cuestión*) matter; (*suceso*) event ♦ *excl* agreed!, done!; **¡bien ~!** well done!; **de ~** in fact, as a matter of fact
hechura [e'tʃura] *nf* making, creation; (*producto*) product; (*forma*) form, shape; (*de persona*) build; (*TEC*) craftsmanship
hectárea [ek'tarea] *nf* hectare
heder [e'ðer] *vi* to stink, smell; (*fig*) to be unbearable
hediondo, a [e'ðjondo, a] *adj* stinking
hedor [e'ðor] *nm* stench
helada [e'laða] *nf* frost
heladera [ela'ðera] (*AM*) *nf* (*refrigerador*) refrigerator
helado, a [e'laðo, a] *adj* frozen; (*glacial*)

icy; (*fig*) chilly, cold ♦ *nm* ice cream
helar [e'lar] *vt* to freeze, ice (up); (*dejar atónito*) to amaze; (*desalentar*) to discourage ♦ *vi* to freeze; **~se** *vr* to freeze
helecho [e'letʃo] *nm* fern
hélice ['eliθe] *nf* spiral; (*TEC*) propeller
helicóptero [eli'koptero] *nm* helicopter
hembra ['embra] *nf* (*BOT, ZOOL*) female; (*mujer*) woman; (*TEC*) nut
hemorragia [emo'rraxja] *nf* haemorrhage
hemorroides [emo'rroiðes] *nfpl* haemorrhoids, piles
hemos *vb ver* **haber**
hendidura [endi'ðura] *nf* crack, split; (*GEO*) fissure
heno ['eno] *nm* hay
herbicida [erßi'θiða] *nm* weedkiller
heredad [ere'ðað] *nf* landed property; (*granja*) farm
heredar [ere'ðar] *vt* to inherit; **heredero, a** *nm/f* heir(ess)
hereje [e'rexe] *nm/f* heretic
herencia [e'renθja] *nf* inheritance
herida [e'riða] *nf* wound, injury; *ver tb* **herido**
herido, a [e'riðo, a] *adj* injured, wounded ♦ *nm/f* casualty
herir [e'rir] *vt* to wound, injure; (*fig*) to offend
hermanastro, a [erma'nastro, a] *nm/f* stepbrother/sister
hermandad [erman'dað] *nf* brotherhood
hermano, a [er'mano, a] *nm/f* brother/sister; **~ gemelo** twin brother; **hermana gemela** twin sister; **~ político** brother-in-law; **hermana política** sister-in-law
hermético, a [er'metiko, a] *adj* hermetic; (*fig*) watertight
hermoso, a [er'moso, a] *adj* beautiful, lovely; (*estupendo*) splendid; (*guapo*) handsome; **hermosura** *nf* beauty
hernia ['ernja] *nf* hernia
héroe ['eroe] *nm* hero
heroína [ero'ina] *nf* (*mujer*) heroine; (*droga*) heroin
heroísmo [ero'ismo] *nm* heroism
herradura [erra'ðura] *nf* horseshoe
herramienta [erra'mjenta] *nf* tool

herrero [e'rrero] *nm* blacksmith
herrumbre [e'rrumbre] *nf* rust
hervidero [erßi'ðero] *nm* (*fig*) swarm; (*POL etc*) hotbed
hervir [er'ßir] *vi* to boil; (*burbujear*) to bubble; (*fig*): **~ de** to teem with; **~ a fuego lento** to simmer; **hervor** *nm* boiling; (*fig*) ardour, fervour
heterosexual [eterosek'swal] *adj* heterosexual
hice *etc vb ver* **hacer**
hidratante [iðra'tante] *adj*: **crema ~** moisturizing cream, moisturizer; **hidratar** *vt* (*piel*) to moisturize; **hidrato** *nm*: **hidratos de carbono** carbohydrates
hidráulica [i'ðraulika] *nf* hydraulics *sg*
hidráulico, a [i'ðrauliko, a] *adj* hydraulic
hidro... [iðro] *prefijo* hydro..., water-...; **~eléctrico, a** *adj* hydroelectric; **~fobia** *nf* hydrophobia, rabies; **hidrógeno** *nm* hydrogen
hiedra ['jeðra] *nf* ivy
hiel [jel] *nf* gall, bile; (*fig*) bitterness
hiela *etc vb ver* **helar**
hielo ['jelo] *nm* (*gen*) ice; (*escarcha*) frost; (*fig*) coldness, reserve
hiena ['jena] *nf* hyena
hierba ['jerßa] *nf* (*pasto*) grass; (*CULIN, MED: planta*) herb; **mala ~** weed; (*fig*) evil influence; **~buena** *nf* mint
hierro ['jerro] *nm* (*metal*) iron; (*objeto*) iron object
hígado ['ixaðo] *nm* liver
higiene [i'xjene] *nf* hygiene; **higiénico, a** *adj* hygienic
higo ['ixo] *nm* fig; **higuera** *nf* fig tree
hijastro, a [i'xastro, a] *nm/f* stepson/daughter
hijo, a ['ixo, a] *nm/f* son/daughter, child; **~s** *nmpl* children, sons and daughters; **~ de papá/mamá** daddy's/mummy's boy; **~ de puta** (*fam!*) bastard (*!*), son of a bitch (*!*)
hilar [i'lar] *vt* to spin; **~ fino** to split hairs
hilera [i'lera] *nf* row, file
hilo ['ilo] *nm* thread; (*BOT*) fibre; (*metal*) wire; (*de agua*) trickle, thin stream; (*de luz*) beam, ray

hilvanar [ilβa'nar] *vt* (*COSTURA*) to tack (*BRIT*), baste (*US*); (*fig*) to do hurriedly

himno ['imno] *nm* hymn; ~ **nacional** national anthem

hincapié [inka'pje] *nm*: **hacer** ~ **en** to emphasize

hincar [in'kar] *vt* to drive (in), thrust (in); ~**se** *vr*: ~**se de rodillas** to kneel down

hincha ['intʃa] (*fam*) *nm/f* fan

hinchado, a [in'tʃaðo, a] *adj* (*gen*) swollen; (*persona*) pompous

hinchar [in'tʃar] *vt* (*gen*) to swell; (*inflar*) to blow up, inflate; (*fig*) to exaggerate; ~**se** *vr* (*inflarse*) to swell up; (*fam*: *llenarse*) to stuff o.s.; **hinchazón** *nf* (*MED*) swelling; (*altivez*) arrogance

hinojo [i'noxo] *nm* fennel

hipermercado [ipermer'kaðo] *nm* hypermarket, superstore

hípico, a ['ipiko, a] *adj* horse *cpd*

hipnotismo [ipno'tismo] *nm* hypnotism; **hipnotizar** *vt* to hypnotize

hipo ['ipo] *nm* hiccups *pl*

hipocresía [ipokre'sia] *nf* hypocrisy; **hipócrita** *adj* hypocritical ♦ *nm/f* hypocrite

hipódromo [i'poðromo] *nm* racetrack

hipopótamo [ipo'potamo] *nm* hippopotamus

hipoteca [ipo'teka] *nf* mortgage

hipótesis [i'potesis] *nf inv* hypothesis

hiriente [i'rjente] *adj* offensive, wounding

hispánico, a [is'paniko, a] *adj* Hispanic

hispano, a [is'pano, a] *adj* Hispanic, Spanish, Hispano- ♦ *nm/f* Spaniard; **H~américa** *nf* Latin America; ~**americano, a** *adj*, *nm/f* Latin American

histeria [is'terja] *nf* hysteria

historia [is'torja] *nf* history; (*cuento*) story, tale; ~**s** *nfpl* (*chismes*) gossip *sg*; **dejarse de** ~**s** to come to the point; **pasar a la** ~ to go down in history; ~**dor, a** *nm/f* historian; **historial** *nm* (*profesional*) curriculum vitae, C.V.; (*MED*) case history; **histórico, a** *adj* historical; (*fig*) historic

historieta [isto'rjeta] *nf* tale, anecdote; (*dibujos*) comic strip

hito ['ito] *nm* (*fig*) landmark; (*objetivo*) goal, target

hizo *vb ver* **hacer**

Hnos *abr* (= *Hermanos*) Bros.

hocico [o'θiko] *nm* snout; (*fig*) grimace

hockey ['xoki] *nm* hockey; ~ **sobre hielo** ice hockey

hogar [o'ɣar] *nm* fireplace, hearth; (*casa*) home; (*vida familiar*) home life; ~**eño, a** *adj* home *cpd*; (*persona*) home-loving

hoguera [o'ɣera] *nf* (*gen*) bonfire

hoja ['oxa] *nf* (*gen*) leaf; (*de flor*) petal; (*de papel*) sheet; (*página*) page; ~ **de afeitar** razor blade

hojalata [oxa'lata] *nf* tin(plate)

hojaldre [o'xaldre] *nm* (*CULIN*) puff pastry

hojear [oxe'ar] *vt* to leaf through, turn the pages of

hola ['ola] *excl* hello!

Holanda [o'landa] *nf* Holland; **holandés, esa** *adj* Dutch ♦ *nm/f* Dutchman/woman ♦ *nm* (*LING*) Dutch

holgado, a [ol'ɣaðo, a] *adj* loose, baggy; (*rico*) well-to-do

holgar [ol'ɣar] *vi* (*descansar*) to rest; (*sobrar*) to be superfluous; **huelga decir que** it goes without saying that

holgazán, ana [olɣa'θan, ana] *adj* idle, lazy ♦ *nm/f* loafer

holgura [ol'ɣura] *nf* looseness, bagginess; (*TEC*) play, free movement; (*vida*) comfortable living, luxury

hollín [o'ʎin] *nm* soot

hombre ['ombre] *nm* (*gen*) man; (*raza humana*): **el** ~ man(kind); (*uno*) man ♦ *excl*: ¡**sí** ~! (*claro*) of course!; (*para énfasis*) man, old boy; ~ **de negocios** businessman; ~ **de pro** honest man; ~**rana** frogman

hombrera [om'brera] *nf* shoulder strap

hombro ['ombro] *nm* shoulder

hombruno, a [om'bruno, a] *adj* mannish

homenaje [ome'naxe] *nm* (*gen*) homage; (*tributo*) tribute

homicida [omi'θiða] *adj* homicidal ♦ *nm/f* murderer; **homicidio** *nm* murder, homicide

homologar [omolo'ðar] *vt* (*COM*: *productos, tamaños*) to standardize; **homólogo,**

a *nm/f*: **su** *etc* **homólogo** his *etc*
counterpart *o* opposite number
homosexual [omosek'swal] *adj*, *nm/f*
homosexual
hondo, a ['ondo, a] *adj* deep; **lo ~** the
depth(s) (*pl*), the bottom; **~nada** *nf*
hollow, depression; (*cañón*) ravine; (*GEO*)
lowland
Honduras [on'duras] *nf* Honduras
hondureño, a [ondu'reɲo, a] *adj*, *nm/f*
Honduran
honestidad [onesti'ðað] *nf* purity,
chastity; (*decencia*) decency; **honesto, a**
adj chaste; decent, honest; (*justo*) just
hongo ['ongo] *nm* (*BOT*: *gen*) fungus;
(: *comestible*) mushroom; (: *venenoso*)
toadstool
honor [o'nor] *nm* (*gen*) honour; (*gloria*)
glory; **en ~ a la verdad** to be fair; **~able**
adj honourable
honorario, a [ono'rarjo, a] *adj* honorary;
~s *nmpl* fees
honra ['onra] *nf* (*gen*) honour; (*renombre*)
good name; **~dez** *nf* honesty; (*de
persona*) integrity; **~do, a** *adj* honest,
upright
honrar [on'rar] *vt* to honour; **~se** *vr*: **~se
con algo/de hacer algo** to be honoured
by sth/to do sth
honroso, a [on'roso, a] *adj* (*honrado*)
honourable; (*respetado*) respectable
hora ['ora] *nf* (*una* ~) hour; (*tiempo*) time;
¿qué ~ es? what time is it?; **¿a qué ~?**
at what time?; **media ~** half an hour; **a
la ~ de recreo** at playtime; **a primera ~**
first thing (in the morning); **a última ~**
at the last moment; **a altas ~s** in the
small hours; **¡a buena ~!** about time,
too!; **dar la ~** to strike the hour; **~s de
oficina/de trabajo** office/working
hours; **~s de visita** visiting times; **~s
extras** *o* **extraordinarias** overtime *sg*;
~s punta rush hours
horadar [ora'ðar] *vt* to drill, bore
horario, a [o'rarjo, a] *adj* hourly, hour
cpd ♦ *nm* timetable; **~ comercial**
business hours *pl*
horca ['orka] *nf* gallows *sg*
horcajadas [orka'xaðas]: **a ~** *adv* astride

horchata [or'tʃata] *nf* cold drink made
from tiger nuts and water, tiger nut milk
horizontal [oriθon'tal] *adj* horizontal
horizonte [ori'θonte] *nm* horizon
horma ['orma] *nf* mould
hormiga [or'miɣa] *nf* ant; **~s** *nfpl* (*MED*)
pins and needles
hormigón [ormi'ɣon] *nm* concrete; **~
armado/pretensado** reinforced/pre-
stressed concrete
hormigueo [ormi'ɣeo] *nm* (*comezón*) itch;
(*fig*) uneasiness
hormona [or'mona] *nf* hormone
hornada [or'naða] *nf* batch (of loaves *etc*)
hornillo [or'niʎo] *nm* (*cocina*) portable
stove
horno ['orno] *nm* (*CULIN*) oven; (*TEC*)
furnace; **alto ~** blast furnace
horóscopo [o'roskopo] *nm* horoscope
horquilla [or'kiʎa] *nf* hairpin; (*AGR*)
pitchfork
horrendo, a [o'rrendo, a] *adj* horrendous,
frightful
horrible [o'rriβle] *adj* horrible, dreadful
horripilante [orripi'lante] *adj* hair-raising,
horrifying
horror [o'rror] *nm* horror, dread;
(*atrocidad*) atrocity; **¡qué ~!** (*fam*) how
awful!; **~izar** *vt* to horrify, frighten;
~izarse *vr* to be horrified; **~oso, a** *adj*
horrifying, ghastly
hortaliza [orta'liθa] *nf* vegetable
hortelano, a [orte'lano, a] *nm/f* (market)
gardener
hortera [or'tera] (*fam*) *adj* tacky
hosco, a ['osko, a] *adj* dark; (*persona*)
sullen, gloomy
hospedar [ospe'ðar] *vt* to put up; **~se** *vr*
to stay, lodge
hospital [ospi'tal] *nm* hospital
hospitalario, a [ospita'larjo, a] *adj*
(*acogedor*) hospitable; **hospitalidad** *nf*
hospitality
hostal [os'tal] *nm* small hotel
hostelería [ostele'ria] *nf* hotel business *o*
trade
hostia ['ostja] *nf* (*REL*) host, consecrated
wafer; (*fam*: *golpe*) whack, punch ♦ *excl*
(*fam!*): **¡~(s)!** damn!

hostigar [osti'ɣar] *vt* to whip; (*fig*) to harass, pester

hostil [os'til] *adj* hostile; **~idad** *nf* hostility

hotel [o'tel] *nm* hotel; **~ero, a** *adj* hotel *cpd* ♦ *nm/f* hotelier

hoy [oi] *adv* (*este día*) today; (*la actualidad*) now(adays) ♦ *nm* present time; **~ (en) día** now(adays)

hoyo ['ojo] *nm* hole, pit; **hoyuelo** *nm* dimple

hoz [oθ] *nf* sickle

hube *etc vb ver* **haber**

hucha ['utʃa] *nf* money box

hueco, a ['weko, a] *adj* (*vacío*) hollow, empty; (*resonante*) booming ♦ *nm* hollow, cavity

huelga *etc* ['welɣa] *vb ver* **holgar** ♦ *nf* strike; **declararse en ~** to go on strike, come out on strike; **~ de hambre** hunger strike

huelguista [wel'ɣista] *nm/f* striker

huella ['weʎa] *nf* (*acto de pisar, pisada*) tread(ing); (*marca del paso*) footprint, footstep; (: *de animal, máquina*) track; **~ digital** fingerprint

huelo *etc vb ver* **oler**

huérfano, a ['werfano, a] *adj* orphan(ed) ♦ *nm/f* orphan

huerta ['werta] *nf* market garden; (*en Murcia y Valencia*) irrigated region

huerto ['werto] *nm* kitchen garden; (*de árboles frutales*) orchard

hueso ['weso] *nm* (*ANAT*) bone; (*de fruta*) stone

huésped, a ['wespeð, a] *nm/f* (*invitado*) guest; (*habitante*) resident; (*anfitrión*) host(ess)

huesudo, a [we'suðo, a] *adj* bony, big-boned

huevera [we'ßera] *nf* eggcup

huevo ['weßo] *nm* egg; **~ duro/escalfado/frito** (*ESP*) o **estrellado** (*AM*)/**pasado por agua** hard-boiled/poached/fried/soft-boiled egg; **~s revueltos** scrambled eggs

huida [u'iða] *nf* escape, flight

huidizo, a [ui'ðiθo, a] *adj* (*tímido*) shy; (*pasajero*) fleeting

huir [u'ir] *vi* (*escapar*) to flee, escape; (*evadir*) to avoid; **~se** *vr* (*escaparse*) to escape

hule ['ule] *nm* (*encerado*) oilskin

humanidad [umani'ðað] *nf* (*género humano*) man(kind); (*cualidad*) humanity

humanitario, a [umani'tarjo, a] *adj* humanitarian

humano, a [u'mano, a] *adj* (*gen*) human; (*humanitario*) humane ♦ *nm* human; **ser ~** human being

humareda [uma'reða] *nf* cloud of smoke

humedad [ume'ðað] *nf* (*del clima*) humidity; (*de pared etc*) dampness; **a prueba de ~** damp-proof; **humedecer** *vt* to moisten, wet; **humedecerse** *vr* to get wet

húmedo, a ['umeðo, a] *adj* (*mojado*) damp, wet; (*tiempo etc*) humid

humildad [umil'dað] *nf* humility, humbleness; **humilde** *adj* humble, modest

humillación [umiʎa'θjon] *nf* humiliation; **humillante** *adj* humiliating

humillar [umi'ʎar] *vt* to humiliate; **~se** *vr* to humble o.s., grovel

humo ['umo] *nm* (*de fuego*) smoke; (*gas nocivo*) fumes *pl*; (*vapor*) steam, vapour; **~s** *nmpl* (*fig*) conceit *sg*

humor [u'mor] *nm* (*disposición*) mood, temper; (*lo que divierte*) humour; **de buen/mal ~** in a good/bad mood; **~ista** *nm/f* comic; **~ístico, a** *adj* funny, humorous

hundimiento [undi'mjento] *nm* (*gen*) sinking; (*colapso*) collapse

hundir [un'dir] *vt* to sink; (*edificio, plan*) to ruin, destroy; **~se** *vr* to sink, collapse

húngaro, a ['ungaro, a] *adj, nm/f* Hungarian

Hungría [un'gria] *nf* Hungary

huracán [ura'kan] *nm* hurricane

huraño, a [u'raɲo, a] *adj* shy; (*antisocial*) unsociable

hurgar [ur'ɣar] *vt* to poke, jab; (*remover*) to stir (up); **~se** *vr*: **~se (las narices)** to pick one's nose

hurón, ona [u'ron, ona] *nm* (*ZOOL*) ferret

hurtadillas [urta'ðiʎas]: **a ~** *adv*

stealthily, on the sly

hurtar [ur'tar] *vt* to steal; **hurto** *nm* theft, stealing

husmear [usme'ar] *vt* (*oler*) to sniff out, scent; (*fam*) to pry into ♦ *vi* to smell bad

huyo *etc vb ver* **huir**

I i

iba *etc vb ver* **ir**

ibérico, a [i'βeriko, a] *adj* Iberian

iberoamericano, a [iβeroameri'kano, a] *adj, nm/f* Latin American

Ibiza [i'βiθa] *nf* Ibiza

iceberg [iθe'βer] *nm* iceberg

ícono ['ikono] *nm* ikon, icon

iconoclasta [ikono'klasta] *adj* iconoclastic ♦ *nm/f* iconoclast

ictericia [ikte'riθja] *nf* jaundice

ida ['iða] *nf* going, departure; ~ **y vuelta** round trip, return

idea [i'ðea] *nf* idea; **no tengo la menor ~** I haven't a clue

ideal [iðe'al] *adj, nm* ideal; **~ista** *nm/f* idealist; **~izar** *vt* to idealize

idear [iðe'ar] *vt* to think up; (*aparato*) to invent; (*viaje*) to plan

ídem ['iðem] *pron* ditto

idéntico, a [i'ðentiko, a] *adj* identical

identidad [iðenti'ðað] *nf* identity

identificación [iðentifika'θjon] *nf* identification

identificar [iðentifi'kar] *vt* to identify; **~se** *vr*: **~se con** to identify with

ideología [iðeolo'xia] *nf* ideology

idilio [i'ðiljo] *nm* love-affair

idioma [i'ðjoma] *nm* (*gen*) language

idiota [i'ðjota] *adj* idiotic ♦ *nm/f* idiot; **idiotez** *nf* idiocy

ídolo ['iðolo] *nm* (*tb: fig*) idol

idóneo, a [i'ðoneo, a] *adj* suitable

iglesia [i'ɣlesja] *nf* church

ignominia [iɣno'minja] *nf* ignominy

ignorancia [iɣno'ranθja] *nf* ignorance; **ignorante** *adj* ignorant, uninformed ♦ *nm/f* ignoramus

ignorar [iɣno'rar] *vt* not to know, be ignorant of; (*no hacer caso a*) to ignore

igual [i'ɣwal] *adj* (*gen*) equal; (*similar*) like, similar; (*mismo*) (the) same; (*constante*) constant; (*temperatura*) even ♦ *nm/f* equal; ~ **que** like, the same as; **me da** *o* **es** ~ I don't care; **son ~es** they're the same; **al ~ que** *prep, conj* like, just like

igualada [iɣwa'laða] *nf* equaliser

igualar [iɣwa'lar] *vt* (*gen*) to equalize, make equal; (*allanar, nivelar*) to level (off), even (out); **~se** *vr* (*platos de balanza*) to balance out

igualdad [iɣwal'dað] *nf* equality; (*similaridad*) sameness; (*uniformidad*) uniformity

igualmente [iɣwal'mente] *adv* equally; (*también*) also, likewise ♦ *excl* the same to you!

ikurriña [iku'rriɲa] *nf* Basque flag

ilegal [ile'ɣal] *adj* illegal

ilegítimo, a [ile'xitimo, a] *adj* illegitimate

ileso, a [i'leso, a] *adj* unhurt

ilícito, a [i'liθito, a] *adj* illicit

ilimitado, a [ilimi'taðo, a] *adj* unlimited

ilógico, a [i'loxiko, a] *adj* illogical

iluminación [ilumina'θjon] *nf* illumination; (*alumbrado*) lighting

iluminar [ilumi'nar] *vt* to illuminate, light (up); (*fig*) to enlighten

ilusión [ilu'sjon] *nf* illusion; (*quimera*) delusion; (*esperanza*) hope; **hacerse ilusiones** to build up one's hopes; **ilusionado, a** *adj* excited; **ilusionar** *vi*: **le ilusiona ir de vacaciones** he's looking forward to going on holiday; **ilusionarse** *vr*: **ilusionarse (con)** to get excited (about)

ilusionista [ilusjo'nista] *nm/f* conjurer

iluso, a [i'luso, a] *adj* easily deceived ♦ *nm/f* dreamer

ilusorio, a [ilu'sorjo, a] *adj* (*de ilusión*) illusory, deceptive; (*esperanza*) vain

ilustración [ilustra'θjon] *nf* illustration; (*saber*) learning, erudition; **la I~** the Enlightenment; **ilustrado, a** *adj* illustrated; learned

ilustrar [ilus'trar] *vt* to illustrate; (*instruir*) to instruct; (*explicar*) to explain, make clear; **~se** *vr* to acquire knowledge

ilustre [i'lustre] *adj* famous, illustrious

imagen [i'maxen] *nf* (*gen*) image; (*dibujo*) picture

imaginación [imaxina'θjon] *nf* imagination

imaginar [imaxi'nar] *vt* (*gen*) to imagine; (*idear*) to think up; (*suponer*) to suppose; ~**se** *vr* to imagine; ~**io**, **a** *adj* imaginary; **imaginativo**, **a** *adj* imaginative

imán [i'man] *nm* magnet

imbécil [im'beθil] *nm/f* imbecile, idiot

imitación [imita'θjon] *nf* imitation

imitar [imi'tar] *vt* to imitate; (*parodiar*, *remedar*) to mimic, ape

impaciencia [impa'θjenθja] *nf* impatience; **impaciente** *adj* impatient; (*nervioso*) anxious

impacto [im'pakto] *nm* impact

impar [im'par] *adj* odd

imparcial [impar'θjal] *adj* impartial, fair

impartir [impar'tir] *vt* to impart, give

impasible [impa'siβle] *adj* impassive

impávido, a [im'paβiðo, a] *adj* fearless, intrepid

impecable [impe'kaβle] *adj* impeccable

impedimento [impeði'mento] *nm* impediment, obstacle

impedir [impe'ðir] *vt* (*obstruir*) to impede, obstruct; (*estorbar*) to prevent

impenetrable [impene'traβle] *adj* impenetrable; (*fig*) incomprehensible

imperar [impe'rar] *vi* (*reinar*) to rule, reign; (*fig*) to prevail, reign; (*precio*) to be current

imperativo, a [impera'tiβo, a] *adj* (*persona*) imperious; (*urgente*, LING) imperative

imperceptible [imperθep'tiβle] *adj* imperceptible

imperdible [imper'ðiβle] *nm* safety pin

imperdonable [imperðo'naβle] *adj* unforgivable, inexcusable

imperfección [imperfek'θjon] *nf* imperfection

imperfecto, a [imper'fekto, a] *adj* imperfect

imperial [impe'rjal] *adj* imperial; ~**ismo** *nm* imperialism

imperio [im'perjo] *nm* empire; (*autoridad*) rule, authority; (*fig*) pride, haughtiness; ~**so, a** *adj* imperious; (*urgente*) urgent; (*imperativo*) imperative

impermeable [imperme'aβle] *adj* (*a prueba de agua*) waterproof ♦ *nm* raincoat, mac (BRIT)

impersonal [imperso'nal] *adj* impersonal

impertinencia [imperti'nenθja] *nf* impertinence; **impertinente** *adj* impertinent

imperturbable [impertur'βaβle] *adj* imperturbable

ímpetu ['impetu] *nm* (*impulso*) impetus, impulse; (*impetuosidad*) impetuosity; (*violencia*) violence

impetuoso, a [impe'twoso, a] *adj* impetuous; (*río*) rushing; (*acto*) hasty

impío, a [im'pio, a] *adj* impious, ungodly

implacable [impla'kaβle] *adj* implacable

implantar [implan'tar] *vt* to introduce

implicar [impli'kar] *vt* to involve; (*entrañar*) to imply

implícito, a [im'pliθito, a] *adj* (*tácito*) implicit; (*sobreentendido*) implied

implorar [implo'rar] *vt* to beg, implore

imponente [impo'nente] *adj* (*impresionante*) impressive, imposing; (*solemne*) grand

imponer [impo'ner] *vt* (*gen*) to impose; (*exigir*) to exact; ~**se** *vr* to assert o.s.; (*prevalecer*) to prevail; **imponible** *adj* (COM) taxable

impopular [impopu'lar] *adj* unpopular

importación [importa'θjon] *nf* (*acto*) importing; (*mercancías*) imports *pl*

importancia [impor'tanθja] *nf* importance; (*valor*) value, significance; (*extensión*) size, magnitude; **importante** *adj* important; valuable, significant

importar [impor'tar] *vt* (*del extranjero*) to import; (*costar*) to amount to ♦ *vi* to be important, matter; **me importa un rábano** I couldn't care less; **no importa** it doesn't matter; **¿le importa que fume?** do you mind if I smoke?

importe [im'porte] *nm* (*total*) amount; (*valor*) value

importunar [importu'nar] *vt* to bother, pester

imposibilidad [imposiβili'ðað] *nf* impossibility; **imposibilitar** *vt* to make impossible, prevent

imposible [impo'siβle] *adj* (*gen*) impossible; (*insoportable*) unbearable, intolerable

imposición [imposi'θjon] *nf* imposition; (*COM: impuesto*) tax; (: *inversión*) deposit

impostor, a [impos'tor, a] *nm/f* impostor

impotencia [impo'tenθja] *nf* impotence; **impotente** *adj* impotent

impracticable [imprakti'kaβle] *adj* (*irrealizable*) impracticable; (*intransitable*) impassable

impreciso, a [impre'θiso, a] *adj* imprecise, vague

impregnar [impreɣ'nar] *vt* to impregnate; **~se** *vr* to become impregnated

imprenta [im'prenta] *nf* (*acto*) printing; (*aparato*) press; (*casa*) printer's; (*letra*) print

imprescindible [impresθin'diβle] *adj* essential, vital

impresión [impre'sjon] *nf* (*gen*) impression; (*IMPRENTA*) printing; (*edición*) edition; (*FOTO*) print; (*marca*) imprint; **~ digital** fingerprint

impresionable [impresjo'naβle] *adj* (*sensible*) impressionable

impresionante [impresjo'nante] *adj* impressive; (*tremendo*) tremendous; (*maravilloso*) great, marvellous

impresionar [impresjo'nar] *vt* (*conmover*) to move; (*afectar*) to impress, strike; (*película fotográfica*) to expose; **~se** *vr* to be impressed; (*conmoverse*) to be moved

impreso, a [im'preso, a] *pp de* **imprimir** ♦ *adj* printed; **~s** *nmpl* printed matter; **impresora** *nf* printer

imprevisto, a [impre'βisto, a] *adj* (*gen*) unforeseen; (*inesperado*) unexpected

imprimir [impri'mir] *vt* to imprint, impress, stamp; (*textos*) to print; (*INFORM*) to output, print out

improbable [impro'βaβle] *adj* improbable; (*inverosímil*) unlikely

improcedente [improθe'ðente] *adj* inappropriate

improductivo, a [improðuk'tiβo, a] *adj* unproductive

improperio [impro'perjo] *nm* insult

impropio, a [im'propjo, a] *adj* improper

improvisado, a [improβi'saðo, a] *adj* improvised

improvisar [improβi'sar] *vt* to improvise

improviso, a [impro'βiso, a] *adj*: **de ~** unexpectedly, suddenly

imprudencia [impru'ðenθja] *nf* imprudence; (*indiscreción*) indiscretion; (*descuido*) carelessness; **imprudente** *adj* unwise, imprudent; (*indiscreto*) indiscreet

impúdico, a [im'puðiko, a] *adj* shameless; (*lujurioso*) lecherous

impudor [impu'ðor] *nm* shamelessness; (*lujuria*) lechery

impuesto, a [im'pwesto, a] *adj* imposed ♦ *nm* tax; **~ sobre el valor añadido** value added tax

impugnar [impuɣ'nar] *vt* to oppose, contest; (*refutar*) to refute, impugn

impulsar [impul'sar] *vt* = **impeler**

impulsivo, a [impul'siβo, a] *adj* impulsive; **impulso** *nm* impulse; (*fuerza, empuje*) thrust, drive; (*fig: sentimiento*) urge, impulse

impune [im'pune] *adj* unpunished

impureza [impu'reθa] *nf* impurity; (*fig*) lewdness; **impuro, a** *adj* impure; lewd

imputar [impu'tar] *vt*: **~ a** to attribute to

inacabable [inaka'βaβle] *adj* (*infinito*) endless; (*interminable*) interminable

inaccesible [inakθe'siβle] *adj* inaccessible

inacción [inak'θjon] *nf* inactivity

inaceptable [inaθep'taβle] *adj* unacceptable

inactividad [inaktiβi'ðað] *nf* inactivity; (*COM*) dullness; **inactivo, a** *adj* inactive

inadecuado, a [inaðe'kwaðo, a] *adj* (*insuficiente*) inadequate; (*inapto*) unsuitable

inadmisible [inaðmi'siβle] *adj* inadmissible

inadvertido, a [inaðβer'tiðo, a] *adj* (*no visto*) unnoticed

inagotable [inaɣo'taβle] *adj* inexhaustible

inaguantable [inaɣwan'taβle] *adj* unbearable

inalterable [inalte'raβle] *adj* immutable, unchangeable
inanición [inani'θjon] *nf* starvation
inanimado, a [inani'maðo, a] *adj* inanimate
inapreciable [inapre'θjaβle] *adj* (*cantidad, diferencia*) imperceptible; (*ayuda, servicio*) invaluable
inaudito, a [inau'ðito, a] *adj* unheard-of
inauguración [inauɣura'θjon] *nf* inauguration; opening
inaugurar [inauɣu'rar] *vt* to inaugurate; (*exposición*) to open
I.N.B. (*ESP*) *abr* (= *Instituto Nacional de Bachillerato*) ≈ comprehensive school (*BRIT*), ≈ high school (*US*)
inca ['inka] *nm/f* Inca
incalculable [inkalku'laβle] *adj* incalculable
incandescente [inkandes'θente] *adj* incandescent
incansable [inkan'saβle] *adj* tireless, untiring
incapacidad [inkapaθi'ðað] *nf* incapacity; (*incompetencia*) incompetence; ~ **física/mental** physical/mental disability
incapacitar [inkapaθi'tar] *vt* (*inhabilitar*) to incapacitate, render unfit; (*descalificar*) to disqualify
incapaz [inka'paθ] *adj* incapable
incautación [inkauta'θjon] *nf* confiscation
incautarse [inkau'tarse] *vr*: ~ **de** to seize, confiscate
incauto, a [in'kauto, a] *adj* (*imprudente*) incautious, unwary
incendiar [inθen'djar] *vt* to set fire to; (*fig*) to inflame; ~**se** *vr* to catch fire; ~**io, a** *adj* incendiary
incendio [in'θendjo] *nm* fire
incentivo [inθen'tiβo] *nm* incentive
incertidumbre [inθerti'ðumbre] *nf* (*inseguridad*) uncertainty; (*duda*) doubt
incesante [inθe'sante] *adj* incessant
incesto [in'θesto] *nm* incest
incidencia [inθi'ðenθja] *nf* (*MAT*) incidence
incidente [inθi'ðente] *nm* incident
incidir [inθi'ðir] *vi* (*influir*) to influence; (*afectar*) to affect; ~ **en un error** to fall into error

incienso [in'θjenso] *nm* incense
incierto, a [in'θjerto, a] *adj* uncertain
incineración [inθinera'θjon] *nf* incineration; (*de cadáveres*) cremation
incinerar [inθine'rar] *vt* to burn; (*cadáveres*) to cremate
incipiente [inθi'pjente] *adj* incipient
incisión [inθi'sjon] *nf* incision
incisivo, a [inθi'siβo, a] *adj* sharp, cutting; (*fig*) incisive
incitar [inθi'tar] *vt* to incite, rouse
inclemencia [inkle'menθja] *nf* (*severidad*) harshness, severity; (*del tiempo*) inclemency
inclinación [inklina'θjon] *nf* (*gen*) inclination; (*de tierras*) slope, incline; (*de cabeza*) nod, bow; (*fig*) leaning, bent
inclinar [inkli'nar] *vt* to incline; (*cabeza*) to nod, bow ♦ *vi* to lean, slope; ~**se** *vr* to bow; (*encorvarse*) to stoop; ~**se a** (*parecerse a*) to take after, resemble; ~**se ante** to bow down to; **me inclino a pensar que** I'm inclined to think that
incluir [inklu'ir] *vt* to include; (*incorporar*) to incorporate; (*meter*) to enclose
inclusive [inklu'siβe] *adv* inclusive ♦ *prep* including
incluso, a [in'kluso, a] *adj* included ♦ *adv* inclusively; (*hasta*) even
incógnita [in'koɣnita] *nf* (*MAT*) unknown quantity
incógnito [in'koɣnito] *nm*: **de** ~ incognito
incoherente [inkoe'rente] *adj* incoherent
incoloro, a [inko'loro, a] *adj* colourless
incólume [in'kolume] *adj* (*gen*) safe; (*indemne*) unhurt, unharmed
incomodar [inkomo'ðar] *vt* to inconvenience; (*molestar*) to bother, trouble; (*fastidiar*) to annoy; ~**se** *vr* to put o.s. out; (*fastidiarse*) to get annoyed
incomodidad [inkomoði'ðað] *nf* inconvenience; (*fastidio, enojo*) annoyance; (*de vivienda*) discomfort
incómodo, a [in'komoðo, a] *adj* (*inconfortable*) uncomfortable; (*molesto*) annoying; (*inconveniente*) inconvenient
incomparable [inkompa'raβle] *adj* incomparable
incompatible [inkompa'tiβle] *adj*

incompatible

incompetencia [inkompe'tenθja] *nf* incompetence; **incompetente** *adj* incompetent

incompleto, a [inkom'pleto, a] *adj* incomplete, unfinished

incomprensible [inkompren'sißle] *adj* incomprehensible

incomunicado, a [inkomuni'kaðo, a] *adj* (*aislado*) cut off, isolated; (*confinado*) in solitary confinement

inconcebible [inkonθe'ßißle] *adj* inconceivable

incondicional [inkondiθjo'nal] *adj* unconditional; (*apoyo*) wholehearted; (*partidario*) staunch

inconexo, a [inko'nekso, a] *adj* (*gen*) unconnected; (*desunido*) disconnected

inconfundible [inkonfun'dißle] *adj* unmistakable

incongruente [inkon'grwente] *adj* incongruous

inconsciencia [inkons'θjenθja] *nf* unconsciousness; (*fig*) thoughtlessness; **inconsciente** *adj* unconscious; thoughtless

inconsecuente [inkonse'kwente] *adj* inconsistent

inconsiderado, a [inkonsiðe'raðo, a] *adj* inconsiderate

inconsistente [inkonsis'tente] *adj* weak; (*tela*) flimsy

inconstancia [inkon'stanθja] *nf* inconstancy; (*inestabilidad*) unsteadiness; **inconstante** *adj* inconstant

incontable [inkon'taßle] *adj* countless, innumerable

incontestable [inkontes'taßle] *adj* unanswerable; (*innegable*) undeniable

incontinencia [inkonti'nenθja] *nf* incontinence

inconveniencia [inkombe'njenθja] *nf* unsuitability, inappropriateness; (*descortesía*) impoliteness; **inconveniente** *adj* unsuitable; impolite ♦ *nm* obstacle; (*desventaja*) disadvantage; **el inconveniente es que ...** the trouble is that ...

incordiar [inkor'ðjar] (*fam*) *vt* to bug,

annoy

incorporación [inkorpora'θjon] *nf* incorporation

incorporar [inkorpo'rar] *vt* to incorporate; **~se** *vr* to sit up

incorrección [inkorrek'θjon] *nf* (*gen*) incorrectness, inaccuracy; (*descortesía*) bad-mannered behaviour; **incorrecto, a** *adj* (*gen*) incorrect, wrong; (*comportamiento*) bad-mannered

incorregible [inkorre'xißle] *adj* incorrigible

incredulidad [inkreðuli'ðað] *nf* incredulity; (*escepticismo*) scepticism; **incrédulo, a** *adj* incredulous, unbelieving; sceptical

increíble [inkre'ißle] *adj* incredible

incremento [inkre'mento] *nm* increment; (*aumento*) rise, increase

increpar [inkre'par] *vt* to reprimand

incruento, a [in'krwento, a] *adj* bloodless

incrustar [inkrus'tar] *vt* to incrust; (*piedras: en joya*) to inlay

incubar [inku'ßar] *vt* to incubate; (*fig*) to hatch

inculcar [inkul'kar] *vt* to inculcate

inculpar [inkul'par] *vt* (*acusar*) to accuse; (*achacar, atribuir*) to charge, blame

inculto, a [in'kulto, a] *adj* (*persona*) uneducated; (*grosero*) uncouth ♦ *nm/f* ignoramus

incumplimiento [inkumpli'mjento] *nm* non-fulfilment; **~ de contrato** breach of contract

incurrir [inku'rrir] *vi*: **~ en** to incur; (*crimen*) to commit; **~ en un error** to make a mistake

indagación [indaγa'θjon] *nf* investigation; (*búsqueda*) search; (*JUR*) inquest

indagar [inda'γar] *vt* to investigate; to search; (*averiguar*) to ascertain

indecente [inde'θente] *adj* indecent, improper; (*lascivo*) obscene

indecible [inde'θißle] *adj* unspeakable; (*indescriptible*) indescribable

indeciso, a [inde'θiso, a] *adj* (*por decidir*) undecided; (*vacilante*) hesitant

indefenso, a [inde'fenso, a] *adj* defenceless

indefinido, a [indefi'niðo, a] *adj* indefinite; (*vago*) vague, undefined

indeleble [inde'leßle] *adj* indelible

indemne [in'demne] *adj* (*objeto*) undamaged; (*persona*) unharmed, unhurt

indemnizar [indemni'θar] *vt* to indemnify; (*compensar*) to compensate

independencia [indepen'denθja] *nf* independence

independiente [indepen'djente] *adj* (*libre*) independent; (*autónomo*) self-sufficient

indeterminado, a [indetermi'naðo, a] *adj* indefinite; (*desconocido*) indeterminate

India ['indja] *nf*: **la ~** India

indicación [indika'θjon] *nf* indication; (*señal*) sign; (*sugerencia*) suggestion, hint

indicado, a [indi'kaðo, a] *adj* (*momento, método*) right; (*tratamiento*) appropriate; (*solución*) likely

indicador [indika'ðor] *nm* indicator; (*TEC*) gauge, meter

indicar [indi'kar] *vt* (*mostrar*) to indicate, show; (*termómetro etc*) to read, register; (*señalar*) to point to

índice ['indiθe] *nm* index; (*catálogo*) catalogue; (*ANAT*) index finger, forefinger

indicio [in'diθjo] *nm* indication, sign; (*en pesquisa etc*) clue

indiferencia [indife'renθja] *nf* indifference; (*apatía*) apathy; **indiferente** *adj* indifferent

indígena [in'dixena] *adj* indigenous, native ♦ *nm/f* native

indigencia [indi'xenθja] *nf* poverty, need

indigestión [indixes'tjon] *nf* indigestion

indigesto, a [indi'xesto, a] *adj* undigested; (*indigestible*) indigestible; (*fig*) turgid

indignación [indixna'θjon] *nf* indignation

indignar [indix'nar] *vt* to anger, make indignant; **~se** *vr*: **~se por** to get indignant about

indigno, a [in'dixno, a] *adj* (*despreciable*) low, contemptible; (*inmerecido*) unworthy

indio, a ['indjo, a] *adj, nm/f* Indian

indirecta [indi'rekta] *nf* insinuation, innuendo; (*sugerencia*) hint

indirecto, a [indi'rekto, a] *adj* indirect

indiscreción [indiskre'θjon] *nf* (*impruden-*cia*) indiscretion; (*irreflexión*) tactlessness; (*acto*) gaffe, faux pas

indiscreto, a [indis'kreto, a] *adj* indiscreet

indiscriminado, a [indiskrimi'naðo, a] *adj* indiscriminate

indiscutible [indisku'tißle] *adj* indisputable, unquestionable

indispensable [indispen'saßle] *adj* indispensable, essential

indisponer [indispo'ner] *vt* to spoil, upset; (*salud*) to make ill; **~se** *vr* to fall ill; **~se con uno** to fall out with sb

indisposición [indisposi'θjon] *nf* indisposition

indispuesto, a [indis'pwesto, a] *adj* (*enfermo*) unwell, indisposed

indistinto, a [indis'tinto, a] *adj* indistinct; (*vago*) vague

individual [indißi'ðwal] *adj* individual; (*habitación*) single ♦ *nm* (*DEPORTE*) singles *sg*

individuo, a [indi'ßiðwo, a] *adj, nm* individual

índole ['indole] *nf* (*naturaleza*) nature; (*clase*) sort, kind

indolencia [indo'lenθja] *nf* indolence, laziness

indómito, a [in'domito, a] *adj* indomitable

inducir [indu'θir] *vt* to induce; (*inferir*) to infer; (*persuadir*) to persuade

indudable [indu'ðaßle] *adj* undoubted; (*incuestionable*) unquestionable

indulgencia [indul'xenθja] *nf* indulgence

indultar [indul'tar] *vt* (*perdonar*) to pardon, reprieve; (*librar de pago*) to exempt; **indulto** *nm* pardon; exemption

industria [in'dustrja] *nf* industry; (*habilidad*) skill; **industrial** *adj* industrial ♦ *nm* industrialist

inédito, a [in'eðito, a] *adj* (*texto*) unpublished; (*nuevo*) new

inefable [ine'faßle] *adj* ineffable, indescribable

ineficaz [inefi'kaθ] *adj* (*inútil*) ineffective; (*ineficiente*) inefficient

ineludible [inelu'ðißle] *adj* inescapable, unavoidable

ineptitud [inepti'tuð] *nf* ineptitude, incompetence; **inepto, a** *adj* inept, incompetent

inequívoco, a [ine'kiβoko, a] *adj* unequivocal; *(inconfundible)* unmistakable

inercia [in'erθja] *nf* inertia; *(pasividad)* passivity

inerme [in'erme] *adj (sin armas)* unarmed; *(indefenso)* defenceless

inerte [in'erte] *adj* inert; *(inmóvil)* motionless

inesperado, a [inespe'raðo, a] *adj* unexpected, unforeseen

inestable [ines'taβle] *adj* unstable

inevitable [ineβi'taβle] *adj* inevitable

inexactitud [ineksakti'tuð] *nf* inaccuracy; **inexacto, a** *adj* inaccurate; *(falso)* untrue

inexperto, a [inek'sperto, a] *adj (novato)* inexperienced

infalible [infa'liβle] *adj* infallible; *(plan)* foolproof

infame [in'fame] *adj* infamous; *(horrible)* dreadful; **infamia** *nf* infamy; *(deshonra)* disgrace

infancia [in'fanθja] *nf* infancy, childhood

infantería [infante'ria] *nf* infantry

infantil [infan'til] *adj (pueril, aniñado)* infantile; *(cándido)* childlike; *(literatura, ropa etc)* children's

infarto [in'farto] *nm (tb: ~ de miocardio)* heart attack

infatigable [infati'γaβle] *adj* tireless, untiring

infección [infek'θjon] *nf* infection; **infeccioso, a** *adj* infectious

infectar [infek'tar] *vt* to infect; ~**se** *vr* to become infected

infeliz [infe'liθ] *adj* unhappy, wretched ♦ *nm/f* wretch

inferior [infe'rjor] *adj* inferior; *(situación)* lower ♦ *nm/f* inferior, subordinate

inferir [infe'rir] *vt (deducir)* to infer, deduce; *(causar)* to cause

infestar [infes'tar] *vt* to infest

infidelidad [infiðeli'ðað] *nf (gen)* infidelity, unfaithfulness

infiel [in'fjel] *adj* unfaithful, disloyal; *(erróneo)* inaccurate ♦ *nm/f* infidel, unbeliever

infierno [in'fjerno] *nm* hell

infiltrarse [infil'trarse] *vr*: ~ **en** to infiltrate in(to); *(persona)* to work one's way in(to)

ínfimo, a ['infimo, a] *adj (más bajo)* lowest; *(despreciable)* vile, mean

infinidad [infini'ðað] *nf* infinity; *(abundancia)* great quantity

infinito, a [infi'nito, a] *adj, nm* infinite

inflación [infla'θjon] *nf (hinchazón)* swelling; *(monetaria)* inflation; *(fig)* conceit; **inflacionario, a** *adj* inflationary

inflamar [infla'mar] *vt (MED, fig)* to inflame; ~**se** *vr* to catch fire; to become inflamed

inflar [in'flar] *vt (hinchar)* to inflate, blow up; *(fig)* to exaggerate; ~**se** *vr* to swell (up); *(fig)* to get conceited

inflexible [inflek'siβle] *adj* inflexible; *(fig)* unbending

infligir [infli'xir] *vt* to inflict

influencia [influ'enθja] *nf* influence; **influenciar** *vt* to influence

influir [influ'ir] *vt* to influence

influjo [in'fluxo] *nm* influence

influya *etc vb ver* **influir**

influyente [influ'jente] *adj* influential

información [informa'θjon] *nf* information; *(noticias)* news *sg*; *(JUR)* inquiry; **I~** *(oficina)* Information Office; *(mostrador)* Information Desk; *(TEL)* Directory Enquiries

informal [infor'mal] *adj (gen)* informal

informar [infor'mar] *vt (gen)* to inform; *(revelar)* to reveal, make known ♦ *vi (JUR)* to plead; *(denunciar)* to inform; *(dar cuenta de)* to report on; ~**se** *vr* to find out; ~**se de** to inquire into

informática [infor'matika] *nf* computer science, information technology

informe [in'forme] *adj* shapeless ♦ *nm* report

infortunio [infor'tunjo] *nm* misfortune

infracción [infrak'θjon] *nf* infraction, infringement

infranqueable [infranke'aβle] *adj* impassable; *(fig)* insurmountable

infravalorar [infrabalo'rar] *vt* to undervalue, underestimate

infringir [infrin'xir] *vt* to infringe, contravene

infructuoso, a [infruk'twoso, a] *adj* fruitless, unsuccessful

infundado, a [infun'daðo, a] *adj* groundless, unfounded

infundir [infun'dir] *vt* to infuse, instil

infusión [infu'sjon] *nf* infusion; ~ **de manzanilla** camomile tea

ingeniar [inxe'njar] *vt* to think up, devise; ~**se** *vr*: ~**se para** to manage to

ingeniería [inxenje'ria] *nf* engineering; ~ **genética** genetic engineering; **ingeniero, a** *nm/f* engineer; **ingeniero de caminos/de sonido** civil engineer/ sound engineer

ingenio [in'xenjo] *nm* (*talento*) talent; (*agudeza*) wit; (*habilidad*) ingenuity, inventiveness; (*TEC*): ~ **azucarero** sugar refinery

ingenioso, a [inxe'njoso, a] *adj* ingenious, clever; (*divertido*) witty

ingenuidad [inxenwi'ðað] *nf* ingenuousness; (*sencillez*) simplicity; **ingenuo, a** *adj* ingenuous

ingerir [inxe'rir] *vt* to ingest; (*tragar*) to swallow; (*consumir*) to consume

Inglaterra [ingla'terra] *nf* England

ingle ['ingle] *nf* groin

inglés, esa [in'gles, esa] *adj* English ♦ *nm/f* Englishman/woman ♦ *nm* (*LING*) English

ingratitud [ingrati'tuð] *nf* ingratitude; **ingrato, a** *adj* (*gen*) ungrateful

ingrediente [ingre'ðjente] *nm* ingredient

ingresar [ingre'sar] *vt* (*dinero*) to deposit ♦ *vi* to come in; ~ **en un club** to join a club; ~ **en el hospital** to go into hospital

ingreso [in'greso] *nm* (*entrada*) entry; (: *en hospital etc*) admission; ~**s** *nmpl* (*dinero*) income *sg*; (: *COM*) takings *pl*

inhabitable [inaßi'taßle] *adj* uninhabitable

inhalar [ina'lar] *vt* to inhale

inherente [ine'rente] *adj* inherent

inhibir [ini'ßir] *vt* to inhibit; (*REL*) to restrain

inhóspito, a [i'nospito, a] *adj* (*región, paisaje*) inhospitable

inhumano, a [inu'mano, a] *adj* inhuman

INI ['ini] (*ESP*) *nm abr* (= *Instituto Nacional de Industria*) ≈ NEB (*BRIT*)

inicial [ini'θjal] *adj, nf* initial

iniciar [ini'θjar] *vt* (*persona*) to initiate; (*empezar*) to begin, commence; (*conversación*) to start up

iniciativa [iniθja'tißa] *nf* initiative; **la ~ privada** private enterprise

ininterrumpido, a [ininterrum'piðo, a] *adj* uninterrupted

injerencia [inxe'renθja] *nf* interference

injertar [inxer'tar] *vt* to graft; **injerto** *nm* graft

injuria [in'xurja] *nf* (*agravio, ofensa*) offence; (*insulto*) insult; **injuriar** *vt* to insult; **injurioso, a** *adj* offensive; insulting

injusticia [inxus'tiθja] *nf* injustice

injusto, a [in'xusto, a] *adj* unjust, unfair

inmadurez [inmaðu'reθ] *nf* immaturity

inmediaciones [inmeðja'θjones] *nfpl* neighbourhood *sg*, environs

inmediato, a [inme'ðjato, a] *adj* immediate; (*contiguo*) adjoining; (*rápido*) prompt; (*próximo*) neighbouring, next; **de ~** immediately

inmejorable [inmexo'raßle] *adj* unsurpassable; (*precio*) unbeatable

inmenso, a [in'menso, a] *adj* immense, huge

inmerecido, a [inmere'θiðo, a] *adj* undeserved

inmigración [inmiɣra'θjon] *nf* immigration

inmiscuirse [inmisku'irse] *vr* to interfere, meddle

inmobiliaria [inmoßi'ljarja] *nf* estate agency

inmobiliario, a [inmoßi'ljarjo, a] *adj* real-estate *cpd*, property *cpd*

inmolar [inmo'lar] *vt* to immolate, sacrifice

inmoral [inmo'ral] *adj* immoral

inmortal [inmor'tal] *adj* immortal; ~**izar** *vt* to immortalize

inmóvil [in'moßil] *adj* immobile
inmueble [in'mweßle] *adj*: **bienes ~s** real estate, landed property ♦ *nm* property
inmundicia [inmun'diθja] *nf* filth; **inmundo, a** *adj* filthy
inmune [in'mune] *adj*: **~ (a)** (MED) immune (to)
inmunidad [inmuni'ðað] *nf* immunity
inmutarse [inmu'tarse] *vr* to turn pale; **no se inmutó** he didn't turn a hair
innato, a [in'nato, a] *adj* innate
innecesario, a [inneθe'sarjo, a] *adj* unnecessary
innoble [in'noßle] *adj* ignoble
innovación [innoßa'θjon] *nf* innovation
innovar [inno'ßar] *vt* to introduce
inocencia [ino'θenθja] *nf* innocence
inocentada [inoθen'taða] *nf* practical joke
inocente [ino'θente] *adj* (*ingenuo*) naive, innocent; (*inculpable*) innocent; (*sin malicia*) harmless ♦ *nm/f* simpleton
inodoro [ino'ðoro] *nm* toilet, lavatory (BRIT)
inofensivo, a [inofen'sißo, a] *adj* inoffensive, harmless
inolvidable [inolßi'ðaßle] *adj* unforgettable
inopinado, a [inopi'naðo, a] *adj* unexpected
inoportuno, a [inopor'tuno, a] *adj* untimely; (*molesto*) inconvenient
inoxidable [inoksi'ðaßle] *adj*: **acero ~** stainless steel
inquebrantable [inkeßran'taßle] *adj* unbreakable
inquietar [inkje'tar] *vt* to worry, trouble; **~se** *vr* to worry, get upset; **inquieto, a** *adj* anxious, worried; **inquietud** *nf* anxiety, worry
inquilino, a [inki'lino, a] *nm/f* tenant
inquirir [inki'rir] *vt* to enquire into, investigate
insaciable [insa'θjaßle] *adj* insatiable
insalubre [insa'lußre] *adj* unhealthy
inscribir [inskri'ßir] *vt* to inscribe; **~ a uno en** (*lista*) to put sb on; (*censo*) to register sb on
inscripción [inskrip'θjon] *nf* inscription; (ESCOL *etc*) enrolment; (*censo*) registration

insecticida [insekti'θiða] *nm* insecticide
insecto [in'sekto] *nm* insect
inseguridad [inseɣuri'ðað] *nf* insecurity
inseguro, a [inse'ɣuro, a] *adj* insecure; (*inconstante*) unsteady; (*incierto*) uncertain
insensato, a [insen'sato, a] *adj* foolish, stupid
insensibilidad [insensißili'ðað] *nf* (*gen*) insensitivity; (*dureza de corazón*) callousness
insensible [insen'sißle] *adj* (*gen*) insensitive; (*movimiento*) imperceptible; (*sin sentido*) numb
insertar [inser'tar] *vt* to insert
inservible [inser'ßißle] *adj* useless
insidioso, a [insi'ðjoso, a] *adj* insidious
insignia [in'siɣnja] *nf* (*señal distintiva*) badge; (*estandarte*) flag
insignificante [insiɣnifi'kante] *adj* insignificant
insinuar [insi'nwar] *vt* to insinuate, imply; **~se** *vr*: **~se con uno** to ingratiate o.s. with sb
insípido, a [in'sipiðo, a] *adj* insipid
insistencia [insis'tenθja] *nf* insistence
insistir [insis'tir] *vi* to insist; **~ en algo** to insist on sth; (*enfatizar*) to stress sth
insolación [insola'θjon] *nf* (MED) sunstroke
insolencia [inso'lenθja] *nf* insolence; **insolente** *adj* insolent
insólito, a [in'solito, a] *adj* unusual
insoluble [inso'lußle] *adj* insoluble
insolvencia [insol'ßenθja] *nf* insolvency
insomnio [in'somnjo] *nm* insomnia
insondable [inson'daßle] *adj* bottomless; (*fig*) impenetrable
insonorizado, a [insonori'θaðo, a] *adj* (*cuarto etc*) soundproof
insoportable [insopor'taßle] *adj* unbearable
insospechado, a [insospe'tʃaðo, a] *adj* (*inesperado*) unexpected
inspección [inspek'θjon] *nf* inspection, check; **inspeccionar** *vt* (*examinar*) to inspect, examine; (*controlar*) to check
inspector, a [inspek'tor, a] *nm/f* inspector

inspiración [inspira'θjon] *nf* inspiration

inspirar [inspi'rar] *vt* to inspire; (*MED*) to inhale; **~se** *vr*: **~se en** to be inspired by

instalación [instala'θjon] *nf* (*equipo*) fittings *pl*, equipment; **~ eléctrica** wiring

instalar [insta'lar] *vt* (*establecer*) to instal; (*erguir*) to set up, erect; **~se** *vr* to establish o.s.; (*en una vivienda*) to move into

instancia [ins'tanθja] *nf* (*JUR*) petition; (*ruego*) request; **en última ~** as a last resort

instantánea [instan'tanea] *nf* snap(shot)

instantáneo, a [instan'taneo, a] *adj* instantaneous; **café ~** instant coffee

instante [ins'tante] *nm* instant, moment

instar [ins'tar] *vt* to press, urge

instaurar [instau'rar] *vt* (*costumbre*) to establish; (*normas, sistema*) to bring in, introduce; (*gobierno*) to instal

instigar [insti'ɣar] *vt* to instigate

instinto [ins'tinto] *nm* instinct; **por ~** instinctively

institución [institu'θjon] *nf* institution, establishment

instituir [institu'ir] *vt* to establish; (*fundar*) to found; **instituto** *nm* (*gen*) institute; **Instituto Nacional de Enseñanza** (*ESP*) ≈ comprehensive (*BRIT*) *o* high (*US*) school

institutriz [institu'triθ] *nf* governess

instrucción [instruk'θjon] *nf* instruction

instructivo, a [instruk'tiβo, a] *adj* instructive

instruir [instru'ir] *vt* (*gen*) to instruct; (*enseñar*) to teach, educate

instrumento [instru'mento] *nm* (*gen*) instrument; (*herramienta*) tool, implement

insubordinarse [insuβorði'narse] *vr* to rebel

insuficiencia [insufi'θjenθja] *nf* (*carencia*) lack; (*inadecuación*) inadequacy; **insuficiente** *adj* (*gen*) insufficient; (*ESCOL: calificación*) unsatisfactory

insufrible [insu'friβle] *adj* insufferable

insular [insu'lar] *adj* insular

insultar [insul'tar] *vt* to insult; **insulto** *nm* insult

insumiso, a [insu'miso, a] *nm/f* (*POL*) person who refuses to do military service or its substitute, community service

insuperable [insupe'raβle] *adj* (*excelente*) unsurpassable; (*problema etc*) insurmountable

insurgente [insur'xente] *adj, nm/f* insurgent

insurrección [insurrek'θjon] *nf* insurrection, rebellion

intachable [inta'tʃaβle] *adj* irreproachable

intacto, a [in'takto, a] *adj* intact

integral [inte'ɣral] *adj* integral; (*completo*) complete; **pan ~** wholemeal (*BRIT*) *o* wholewheat (*US*) bread

integrar [inte'ɣrar] *vt* to make up, compose; (*MAT*) to integrate

integridad [inteɣri'ðað] *nf* wholeness; (*carácter*) integrity; **íntegro, a** *adj* whole, entire; (*honrado*) honest

intelectual [intelek'twal] *adj, nm/f* intellectual

inteligencia [inteli'xenθja] *nf* intelligence; (*ingenio*) ability; **inteligente** *adj* intelligent

inteligible [inteli'xiβle] *adj* intelligible

intemperie [intem'perje] *nf*: **a la ~** out in the open, exposed to the elements

intempestivo, a [intempes'tiβo, a] *adj* untimely

intención [inten'θjon] *nf* (*gen*) intention, purpose; **con segundas intenciones** maliciously; **con ~** deliberately

intencionado, a [intenθjo'naðo, a] *adj* deliberate; **bien ~** well-meaning; **mal ~** ill-disposed, hostile

intensidad [intensi'ðað] *nf* (*gen*) intensity; (*ELEC, TEC*) strength; **llover con ~** to rain hard

intenso, a [in'tenso, a] *adj* intense; (*sentimiento*) profound, deep

intentar [inten'tar] *vt* (*tratar*) to try, attempt; **intento** *nm* (*intención*) intention, purpose; (*tentativa*) attempt

interactivo, a [interak'tiβo, a] *adj* (*INFORM*) interactive

intercalar [interka'lar] *vt* to insert

intercambio [inter'kambjo] *nm* exchange, swap

interceder [interθe'ðer] *vi* to intercede

interceptar [interθep'tar] *vt* to intercept

intercesión [interθe'sjon] *nf* intercession

interés [inte'res] *nm* (*gen*) interest; (*parte*) share, part; (*pey*) self-interest; **intereses creados** vested interests

interesado, a [intere'saðo, a] *adj* interested; (*prejuiciado*) prejudiced; (*pey*) mercenary, self-seeking

interesante [intere'sante] *adj* interesting

interesar [intere'sar] *vt, vi* to interest, be of interest to; ~**se** *vr*: ~**se en** *o* **por** to take an interest in

interface [inter'faθe] *nm* (*INFORM*) interface

interfase [inter'fase] *nm* = **interface**

interferir [interfe'rir] *vt* to interfere with; (*TEL*) to jam ♦ *vi* to interfere

interfono [inter'fono] *nm* intercom

interino, a [inte'rino, a] *adj* temporary ♦ *nm/f* temporary holder of a post; (*MED*) locum; (*ESCOL*) supply teacher

interior [inte'rjor] *adj* inner, inside; (*COM*) domestic, internal ♦ *nm* interior, inside; (*fig*) soul, mind; **Ministerio del I~** ≈ Home Office (*BRIT*), ≈ Department of the Interior (*US*)

interjección [interxek'θjon] *nf* interjection

interlocutor, a [interloku'tor, a] *nm/f* speaker

intermediario, a [interme'ðjarjo, a] *nm/f* intermediary

intermedio, a [inter'meðjo, a] *adj* intermediate ♦ *nm* interval

interminable [intermi'naβle] *adj* endless

intermitente [intermi'tente] *adj* intermittent ♦ *nm* (*AUTO*) indicator

internacional [internaθjo'nal] *adj* international

internado [inter'naðo] *nm* boarding school

internar [inter'nar] *vt* to intern; (*en un manicomio*) to commit; ~**se** *vr* (*penetrar*) to penetrate

interno, a [in'terno, a] *adj* internal, interior; (*POL etc*) domestic ♦ *nm/f* (*alumno*) boarder

interponer [interpo'ner] *vt* to interpose, put in; ~**se** *vr* to intervene

interpretación [interpreta'θjon] *nf* interpretation

interpretar [interpre'tar] *vt* to interpret; (*TEATRO, MUS*) to perform, play; **intérprete** *nm/f* (*LING*) interpreter, translator; (*MUS, TEATRO*) performer, artist(e)

interrogación [interroɣa'θjon] *nf* interrogation; (*LING: tb: signo de* ~) question mark

interrogar [interro'ɣar] *vt* to interrogate, question

interrumpir [interrum'pir] *vt* to interrupt

interrupción [interrup'θjon] *nf* interruption

interruptor [interrup'tor] *nm* (*ELEC*) switch

intersección [intersek'θjon] *nf* intersection

interurbano, a [interur'βano, a] *adj*: **llamada interurbana** long-distance call

intervalo [inter'βalo] *nm* interval; (*descanso*) break; **a ~s** at intervals, every now and then

intervenir [interβe'nir] *vt* (*controlar*) to control, supervise; (*MED*) to operate on ♦ *vi* (*participar*) to take part, participate; (*mediar*) to intervene

interventor, a [interβen'tor, a] *nm/f* inspector; (*COM*) auditor

interviú [inter'βju] *nf* interview

intestino [intes'tino] *nm* intestine

intimar [inti'mar] *vi* to become friendly

intimidad [intimi'ðað] *nf* intimacy; (*familiaridad*) familiarity; (*vida privada*) private life; (*JUR*) privacy

íntimo, a ['intimo, a] *adj* intimate

intolerable [intole'raβle] *adj* intolerable, unbearable

intoxicación [intoksika'θjon] *nf* poisoning

intranquilizarse [intrankili'θarse] *vr* to get worried *o* anxious; **intranquilo, a** *adj* worried

intransigente [intransi'xente] *adj* intransigent

intransitable [intransi'taβle] *adj* impassable

intrépido, a [in'trepiðo, a] *adj* intrepid

intriga [in'triɣa] *nf* intrigue; (*plan*) plot;

intrigar [*vt, vi*] to intrigue
intrincado, a [intrin'kaðo, a] *adj* intricate
intrínseco, a [in'trinseko, a] *adj* intrinsic
introducción [introðuk'θjon] *nf* introduction
introducir [introðu'θir] *vt* (*gen*) to introduce; (*moneda etc*) to insert; (*INFORM*) to input, enter
intromisión [intromi'sjon] *nf* interference, meddling
introvertido, a [introßer'tiðo, a] *adj, nm/f* introvert
intruso, a [in'truso, a] *adj* intrusive
♦ *nm/f* intruder
intuición [intwi'θjon] *nf* intuition
inundación [inunda'θjon] *nf* flood(ing); **inundar** *vt* to flood; (*fig*) to swamp, inundate
inusitado, a [inusi'taðo, a] *adj* unusual, rare
inútil [in'util] *adj* useless; (*esfuerzo*) vain, fruitless; **inutilidad** *nf* uselessness
inutilizar [inutili'θar] *vt* to make o render useless; **~se** *vr* to become useless
invadir [imba'ðir] *vt* to invade
inválido, a [im'baliðo, a] *adj* invalid
♦ *nm/f* invalid
invariable [imba'rjaßle] *adj* invariable
invasión [imba'sjon] *nf* invasion
invasor, a [imba'sor, a] *adj* invading
♦ *nm/f* invader
invención [imben'θjon] *nf* invention
inventar [imben'tar] *vt* to invent
inventario [imben'tarjo] *nm* inventory
inventiva [imben'tißa] *nf* inventiveness
invento [im'bento] *nm* invention
inventor, a [imben'tor, a] *nm/f* inventor
invernadero [imberna'ðero] *nm* greenhouse
inverosímil [imbero'simil] *adj* implausible
inversión [imber'sjon] *nf* (*COM*) investment
inverso, a [im'berso, a] *adj* inverse, opposite; **en el orden ~** in reverse order; **a la inversa** inversely, the other way round
inversor, a [imber'sor, a] *nm/f* (*COM*) investor
invertir [imber'tir] *vt* (*COM*) to invest;

(*volcar*) to turn upside down; (*tiempo etc*) to spend
investigación [imbestiɣa'θjon] *nf* investigation; (*ESCOL*) research; **~ de mercado** market research
investigar [imbesti'ɣar] *vt* to investigate; (*ESCOL*) to do research into
invierno [im'bjerno] *nm* winter
invisible [imbi'sißle] *adj* invisible
invitado, a [imbi'taðo, a] *nm/f* guest
invitar [imbi'tar] *vt* to invite; (*incitar*) to entice; (*pagar*) to buy, pay for
invocar [imbo'kar] *vt* to invoke, call on
involucrar [imbolu'krar] *vt*: **~ en** to involve in; **~se** *vr* (*persona*): **~ en** to get mixed up in
involuntario, a [imbolun'tarjo, a] *adj* (*movimiento, gesto*) involuntary; (*error*) unintentional
inyección [injek'θjon] *nf* injection
inyectar [injek'tar] *vt* to inject

| PALABRA CLAVE |

ir [ir] *vi* **1** to go; (*a pie*) to walk; (*viajar*) to travel; **~ caminando** to walk; **fui en tren** I went o travelled by train; **¡(ahora) voy!** (I'm just) coming!
2: **~ (a) por**: **~ (a) por el médico** to fetch the doctor
3 (*progresar: persona, cosa*) to go; **el trabajo va muy bien** work is going very well; **¿cómo te va?** how are things going?; **me va muy bien** I'm getting on very well; **le fue fatal** it went awfully badly for him
4 (*funcionar*): **el coche no va muy bien** the car isn't running very well
5: **te va estupendamente ese color** that colour suits you fantastically well
6 (*locuciones*): **¿vino? – ¡que va!** did he come? – of course not!; **vamos, no llores** come on, don't cry; **¡vaya coche!** what a car!, that's some car!
7: **no vaya a ser**: **tienes que correr, no vaya a ser que pierdas el tren** you'll have to run so as not to miss the train
8 (+ *pp*): **iba vestido muy bien** he was very well dressed
9: **no me** *etc* **va ni me viene** I *etc* don't

care
♦ *vb aux* **1**: ~ **a**: **voy/iba a hacerlo hoy**
I am/was going to do it today
2 (+ *gerundio*): **iba anocheciendo** it was
getting dark; **todo se me iba aclarando**
everything was gradually becoming
clearer to me
3 (+ *pp* = *pasivo*): **van vendidos 300
ejemplares** 300 copies have been sold so
far
♦ ~**se** *vr* **1**: **¿por dónde se va al
zoológico?** which is the way to the zoo?
2 (*marcharse*) to leave; **ya se habrán
ido** they must already have left *o* gone

ira ['ira] *nf* anger, rage
iracundo, a [ira'kundo, a] *adj* irascible
Irak [i'rak] *nm* = **Iraq**
Irán [i'ran] *nm* Iran; **iraní** *adj, nm/f*
Iranian
Iraq [i'rak] *nm* Iraq; **iraquí** *adj, nm/f*
Iraqui
iris ['iris] *nm inv* (*tb*: **arco ~**) rainbow;
(*ANAT*) iris
Irlanda [ir'landa] *nf* Ireland; **irlandés, esa**
adj ♦ *nm/f* Irishman/woman; **los
irlandeses** the Irish
ironía [iro'nia] *nf* irony; **irónico, a** *adj*
ironic(al)
irreal [irre'al] *adj* unreal
irrecuperable [irrekupe'raßle] *adj*
irrecoverable, irretrievable
irreflexión [irreflek'sjon] *nf* thoughtlessness
irregular [irreɣu'lar] *adj* (*gen*) irregular;
(*situación*) abnormal
irremediable [irreme'ðjaßle] *adj*
irremediable; (*vicio*) incurable
irreparable [irrepa'raßle] *adj* (*daños*)
irreparable; (*pérdida*) irrecoverable
irresoluto, a [irreso'luto, a] *adj*
irresolute, hesitant
irrespetuoso, a [irrespe'twoso, a] *adj*
disrespectful
irresponsable [irrespon'saßle] *adj*
irresponsible
irreversible [irreßer'sible] *adj* irreversible
irrigar [irri'ɣar] *vt* to irrigate
irrisorio, a [irri'sorjo, a] *adj* derisory,

ridiculous
irritar [irri'tar] *vt* to irritate, annoy
irrupción [irrup'θjon] *nf* irruption;
(*invasión*) invasion
isla ['isla] *nf* island
islandés, esa [islan'des, esa] *adj*
Icelandic ♦ *nm/f* Icelander
Islandia [is'landja] *nf* Iceland
isleño, a [is'leɲo, a] *adj* island *cpd*
♦ *nm/f* islander
Israel [isra'el] *nm* Israel; **israelí** *adj, nm/f*
Israeli
istmo ['istmo] *nm* isthmus
Italia [i'talja] *nf* Italy; **italiano, a** *adj,
nm/f* Italian
itinerario [itine'rarjo] *nm* itinerary, route
IVA ['ißa] *nm abr* (= *impuesto sobre el
valor añadido*) VAT
I y D *abr* (= *Investigación y Desarrollo*)
R & D
izar [i'θar] *vt* to hoist
izdo, a *abr* (= *izquierdo, a*) l.
izquierda [iθ'kjerda] *nf* left; (*POL*) left
(wing); **a la ~** (*estar*) on the left; (*torcer
etc*) (to the) left
izquierdista [iθkjer'ðista] *nm/f* left-
winger, leftist
izquierdo, a [iθ'kjerðo, a] *adj* left

J j

jabalí [xaßa'li] *nm* wild boar
jabalina [xaßa'lina] *nf* javelin
jabón [xa'ßon] *nm* soap; **jabonar** *vt* to
soap
jaca ['xaka] *nf* pony
jacinto [xa'θinto] *nm* hyacinth
jactarse [xak'tarse] *vr* to boast, brag
jadear [xaðe'ar] *vi* to pant, gasp for
breath; **jadeo** *nm* panting, gasping
jaguar [xa'ɣwar] *nm* jaguar
jalea [xa'lea] *nf* jelly
jaleo [xa'leo] *nm* racket, uproar; **armar
un ~** to kick up a racket
jalón [xa'lon] (*AM*) *nm* tug
Jamaica [xa'maika] *nf* Jamaica
jamás [xa'mas] *adv* never; (*interrogación*)
ever

jamón [xa'mon] *nm* ham; **~ dulce**, **~ de York** cooked ham; **~ serrano** cured ham

Japón [xa'pon] *nm*: **el ~** Japan; **japonés, esa** *adj, nm/f* Japanese ♦ *nm* (*LING*) Japanese

jaque ['xake] *nm*: **~ mate** checkmate

jaqueca [xa'keka] *nf* (very bad) headache, migraine

jarabe [xa'raße] *nm* syrup

jarcia ['xarθja] *nf* (*NAUT*) ropes *pl*, rigging

jardín [xar'ðin] *nm* garden; **~ de (la) infancia** (*ESP*) *o* **de niños** (*AM*) nursery (school); **jardinería** *nf* gardening; **jardinero, a** *nm/f* gardener

jarra ['xarra] *nf* jar; (*jarro*) jug

jarro ['xarro] *nm* jug

jaula ['xaula] *nf* cage

jauría [xau'ria] *nf* pack of hounds

J. C. *abr* (= *Jesucristo*) J.C.

jefa ['xefa] *nf ver* **jefe**

jefatura [xefa'tura] *nf*: **~ de policía** police headquarters *sg*

jefe, a ['xefe, a] *nm/f* (*gen*) chief, head; (*patrón*) boss; **~ de cocina** chef; **~ de estación** stationmaster; **~ de estado** head of state

jengibre [xen'xißre] *nm* ginger

jeque ['xeke] *nm* sheik

jerarquía [xerar'kia] *nf* (*orden*) hierarchy; (*rango*) rank; **jerárquico, a** *adj* hierarchic(al)

jerez [xe'reθ] *nm* sherry

jerga ['xerya] *nf* (*tela*) coarse cloth; (*lenguaje*) jargon

jeringa [xe'ringa] *nf* syringe; (*AM*) annoyance, bother; **~ de engrase** grease gun; **jeringar** (*AM*) *vt* to annoy, bother

jeroglífico [xero'ylifiko] *nm* hieroglyphic

jersey [xer'sei] (*pl* **~s**) *nm* jersey, pullover, jumper

Jerusalén [xerusa'len] *n* Jerusalem

Jesucristo [xesu'kristo] *nm* Jesus Christ

jesuita [xe'swita] *adj, nm* Jesuit

Jesús [xe'sus] *nm* Jesus; **¡~!** good heavens!; (*al estornudar*) bless you!

jinete, a [xi'nete, a] *nm/f* horseman/woman, rider

jipijapa [xipi'xapa] (*AM*) *nm* straw hat

jirafa [xi'rafa] *nf* giraffe

jirón [xi'ron] *nm* rag, shred

jocoso, a [xo'koso, a] *adj* humorous, jocular

jofaina [xo'faina] *nf* washbasin

jornada [xor'naða] *nf* (*viaje de un día*) day's journey; (*camino o viaje entero*) journey; (*día de trabajo*) working day

jornal [xor'nal] *nm* (day's) wage; **~ero** *nm* (day) labourer

joroba [xo'roßa] *nf* hump, hunched back; **~do, a** *adj* hunchbacked ♦ *nm/f* hunchback

jota ['xota] *nf* (the letter) J; (*danza*) Aragonese dance; (*fam*) jot, iota; **no saber ni ~** to have no idea

joven ['xoßen] (*pl* **jóvenes**) *adj* young ♦ *nm* young man, youth ♦ *nf* young woman, girl

jovial [xo'ßjal] *adj* cheerful, jolly

joya ['xoja] *nf* jewel, gem; (*fig: persona*) gem; **joyería** *nf* (*joyas*) jewellery; (*tienda*) jeweller's (shop); **joyero** *nm* (*persona*) jeweller; (*caja*) jewel case

juanete [xwa'nete] *nm* (*del pie*) bunion

jubilación [xußila'θjon] *nf* (*retiro*) retirement

jubilado, a [xußi'laðo, a] *adj* retired ♦ *nm/f* pensioner (*BRIT*), senior citizen

jubilar [xußi'lar] *vt* to pension off, retire; (*fam*) to discard; **~se** *vr* to retire

júbilo ['xußilo] *nm* joy, rejoicing; **jubiloso, a** *adj* jubilant

judía [xu'ðia] *nf* (*CULIN*) bean; **~ verde** French bean; *ver tb* **judío**

judicial [xuði'θjal] *adj* judicial

judío, a [xu'ðio, a] *adj* Jewish ♦ *nm/f* Jew(ess)

judo ['juðo] *nm* judo

juego *etc* ['xweyo] *vb ver* **jugar** ♦ *nm* (*gen*) play; (*pasatiempo, partido*) game; (*en casino*) gambling; (*conjunto*) set; **fuera de ~** (*DEPORTE: persona*) offside; (*: pelota*) out of play; **J~s Olímpicos** Olympic Games

juerga ['xwerya] *nf* binge; (*fiesta*) party; **ir de ~** to go out on a binge

jueves ['xweßes] *nm inv* Thursday

juez [xweθ] *nm/f* judge; **~ de línea** linesman; **~ de salida** starter

jugada [xu'ɣaða] *nf* play; **buena ~** good move/shot/stroke *etc*

jugador, a [xuɣa'ðor, a] *nm/f* player; (*en casino*) gambler

jugar [xu'ɣar] *vt, vi* to play; (*en casino*) to gamble; (*apostar*) to bet; **~ al fútbol** to play football

juglar [xu'ɣlar] *nm* minstrel

jugo ['xuɣo] *nm* (*BOT*) juice; (*fig*) essence, substance; **~ de fruta** (*AM*) fruit juice; **~so, a** *adj* juicy; (*fig*) substantial, important

juguete [xu'ɣete] *nm* toy; **~ar** *vi* to play; **~ría** *nf* toyshop

juguetón, ona [xuɣe'ton, ona] *adj* playful

juicio ['xwiθjo] *nm* judgement; (*razón*) sanity, reason; (*opinión*) opinion; **estar fuera de ~** to be out of one's mind; **~so, a** *adj* wise, sensible

julio ['xuljo] *nm* July

junco ['xunko] *nm* rush, reed

jungla ['xungla] *nf* jungle

junio ['xunjo] *nm* June

junta ['xunta] *nf* (*asamblea*) meeting, assembly; (*comité, consejo*) board, council, committee; (*articulación*) joint

juntar [xun'tar] *vt* to join, unite; (*maquinaria*) to assemble, put together; (*dinero*) to collect; **~se** *vr* to join, meet; (*reunirse: personas*) to meet, assemble; (*arrimarse*) to approach, draw closer; **~se con uno** to join sb

junto, a ['xunto, a] *adj* joined; (*unido*) united; (*anexo*) near, close; (*contiguo, próximo*) next, adjacent ♦ *adv*: **todo ~** all at once; **~s** together; **~ a** near (to), next to

jurado [xu'raðo] *nm* (*JUR: individuo*) juror; (: *grupo*) jury; (*de concurso: grupo*) panel (of judges); (: *individuo*) member of a panel

juramento [xura'mento] *nm* oath; (*maldición*) oath, curse; **prestar ~** to take the oath; **tomar ~ a** to swear in, administer the oath to

jurar [xu'rar] *vt, vi* to swear; **~ en falso** to commit perjury; **jurárselas a uno** to have it in for sb

jurídico, a [xu'riðiko, a] *adj* legal

jurisdicción [xurisðik'θjon] *nf* (*poder, autoridad*) jurisdiction; (*territorio*) district

jurisprudencia [xurispru'ðenθja] *nf* jurisprudence

jurista [xu'rista] *nm/f* jurist

justamente [xusta'mente] *adv* justly, fairly; (*precisamente*) just, exactly

justicia [xus'tiθja] *nf* justice; (*equidad*) fairness, justice; **justiciero, a** *adj* just, righteous

justificación [xustifika'θjon] *nf* justification; **justificar** *vt* to justify

justo, a ['xusto, a] *adj* (*equitativo*) just, fair, right; (*preciso*) exact, correct; (*ajustado*) tight ♦ *adv* (*precisamente*) exactly, precisely; (*AM: apenas a tiempo*) just in time

juvenil [xuße'nil] *adj* youthful

juventud [xußen'tuð] *nf* (*adolescencia*) youth; (*jóvenes*) young people *pl*

juzgado [xuθ'ɣaðo] *nm* tribunal; (*JUR*) court

juzgar [xuθ'ɣar] *vt* to judge; **a ~ por ...** to judge by ..., judging by ...

K k

kg *abr* (= *kilogramo*) kg

kilo ['kilo] *nm* kilo ♦ *pref*: **~gramo** *nm* kilogramme; **~metraje** *nm* distance in kilometres, ≈ mileage; **kilómetro** *nm* kilometre; **~vatio** *nm* kilowatt

kiosco ['kjosko] *nm* = **quiosco**

km *abr* (= *kilómetro*) km

kv *abr* (= *kilovatio*) kw

L l

l *abr* (= *litro*) l

la [la] *art def* the ♦ *pron* her; (*Ud.*) you; (*cosa*) it ♦ *nm* (*MUS*) la; **~ del sombrero rojo** the girl in the red hat; *tb ver* **el**

laberinto [laße'rinto] *nm* labyrinth

labia ['laßja] *nf* fluency; (*pey*) glib tongue

labio ['laßjo] *nm* lip

labor [la'ßor] *nf* labour; (*AGR*) farm work;

(*tarea*) job, task; (*COSTURA*) needlework; **~able** *adj* (*AGR*) workable; **día ~able** working day; **~al** *adj* (*accidente*) at work; (*jornada*) working

laboratorio [laβora'torjo] *nm* laboratory

laborioso, a [laβo'rjoso, a] *adj* (*persona*) hard-working; (*trabajo*) tough

laborista [laβo'rista] *adj*: **Partido L~** Labour Party

labrado, a [la'βraðo, a] *adj* worked; (*madera*) carved; (*metal*) wrought ♦ *nm* (*AGR*) cultivated field

labrador, a [laβra'ðor, a] *adj* farming *cpd* ♦ *nm/f* farmer

labranza [la'βranθa] *nf* (*AGR*) cultivation

labrar [la'βrar] *vt* (*gen*) to work; (*madera etc*) to carve; (*fig*) to cause, bring about

labriego, a [la'βrjeɣo, a] *nm/f* peasant

laca ['laka] *nf* lacquer

lacayo [la'kajo] *nm* lackey

lacio, a [la'θjo, a] *adj* (*pelo*) lank, straight

lacónico, a [la'koniko, a] *adj* laconic

lacra ['lakra] *nf* (*fig*) blot; **lacrar** *vt* (*cerrar*) to seal (with sealing wax); **lacre** *nm* sealing wax

lactancia [lak'tanθja] *nf* lactation

lactar [lak'tar] *vt*, *vi* to suckle

lácteo, a ['lakteo, a] *adj*: **productos ~s** dairy products

ladear [laðe'ar] *vt* to tip, tilt ♦ *vi* to tilt; **~se** *vr* to lean

ladera [la'ðera] *nf* slope

lado ['laðo] *nm* (*gen*) side; (*fig*) protection; (*MIL*) flank; **al ~ de** beside; **poner de ~** to put on its side; **poner a un ~** to put aside; **por todos ~s** on all sides, all round (*BRIT*)

ladrar [la'ðrar] *vi* to bark; **ladrido** *nm* bark, barking

ladrillo [la'ðriʎo] *nm* (*gen*) brick; (*azulejo*) tile

ladrón, ona [la'ðron, ona] *nm/f* thief

lagartija [laɣar'tixa] *nf* (*ZOOL*) (small) lizard

lagarto [la'ɣarto] *nm* (*ZOOL*) lizard

lago ['laɣo] *nm* lake

lágrima ['laɣrima] *nf* tear

laguna [la'ɣuna] *nf* (*lago*) lagoon; (*hueco*) gap

laico, a ['laiko, a] *adj* lay

lamentable [lamen'taβle] *adj* lamentable, regrettable; (*miserable*) pitiful

lamentar [lamen'tar] *vt* (*sentir*) to regret; (*deplorar*) to lament; **lo lamento mucho** I'm very sorry; **~se** *vr* to lament; **lamento** *nm* lament

lamer [la'mer] *vt* to lick

lámina ['lamina] *nf* (*plancha delgada*) sheet; (*para estampar, estampa*) plate

lámpara ['lampara] *nf* lamp; **~ de alcohol/gas** spirit/gas lamp; **~ de pie** standard lamp

lamparón [lampa'ron] *nm* grease spot

lampiño [lam'piɲo] *adj* clean-shaven

lana ['lana] *nf* wool

lance *etc* ['lanθe] *vb ver* **lanzar** ♦ *nm* (*golpe*) stroke; (*suceso*) event, incident

lancha ['lantʃa] *nf* launch; **~ de pesca** fishing boat; **~ salvavidas/torpedera** lifeboat/torpedo boat

langosta [lan'gosta] *nf* (*crustáceo*) lobster; (: *de río*) crayfish; **langostino** *nm* Dublin Bay prawn; (: *de río*) crayfish

languidecer [langiðe'θer] *vi* to languish; **languidez** *nf* languor; **lánguido, a** *adj* (*gen*) languid; (*sin energía*) listless

lanilla [la'niʎa] *nf* nap

lanza ['lanθa] *nf* (*arma*) lance, spear

lanzamiento [lanθa'mjento] *nm* (*gen*) throwing; (*NAUT, COM*) launch, launching; **~ de peso** putting the shot

lanzar [lan'θar] *vt* (*gen*) to throw; (*DEPORTE*: *pelota*) to bowl; (*NAUT, COM*) to launch; (*JUR*) to evict; **~se** *vr* to throw o.s.

lapa ['lapa] *nf* limpet

lapicero [lapi'θero] *nm* propelling (*BRIT*) o mechanical (*US*) pencil; (*AM*: *bolígrafo*) Biro ®

lápida ['lapiða] *nf* stone; **~ mortuoria** headstone; **~ conmemorativa** memorial stone; **lapidario** *a adj*, *nm* lapidary

lápiz ['lapiθ] *nm* pencil; **~ de color** coloured pencil; **~ de labios** lipstick

lapón, ona [la'pon, ona] *nm/f* Laplander, Lapp

lapso ['lapso] *nm* (*de tiempo*) interval; (*error*) error

lapsus ['lapsus] *nm inv* error, mistake
largar [lar'ɣar] *vt* (*soltar*) to release; (*aflojar*) to loosen; (*lanzar*) to launch; (*fam*) to let fly; (*velas*) to unfurl; (*AM*) to throw; ~**se** *vr* (*fam*) to beat it; ~**se a** (*AM*) to start to
largo, a ['larɣo, a] *adj* (*longitud*) long; (*tiempo*) lengthy; (*fig*) generous ♦ *nm* length; (*MUS*) largo; **dos años** ~**s** two long years; **tiene 9 metros de** ~ it is 9 metres long; **a lo** ~ **de** along; (*tiempo*) all through, throughout; ~**metraje** *nm* feature film
laringe [la'rinxe] *nf* larynx; **laringitis** *nf* laryngitis
larva ['larβa] *nf* larva
las [las] *art def* the ♦ *pron* them; ~ **que cantan** the ones/women/girls who sing; *tb ver* **el**
lascivo, a [las'θiβo, a] *adj* lewd
láser ['laser] *nm* laser
lástima ['lastima] *nf* (*pena*) pity; **dar** ~ to be pitiful; **es una** ~ **que** it's a pity that; **¡qué** ~! what a pity!; **ella está hecha una** ~ she looks pitiful
lastimar [lasti'mar] *vt* (*herir*) to wound; (*ofender*) to offend; ~**se** *vr* to hurt o.s.; **lastimero, a** *adj* pitiful, pathetic
lastre ['lastre] *nm* (*TEC, NAUT*) ballast; (*fig*) dead weight
lata ['lata] *nf* (*metal*) tin; (*caja*) tin (*BRIT*), can; (*fam*) nuisance; **en** ~ tinned (*BRIT*), canned; **dar (la)** ~ to be a nuisance
latente [la'tente] *adj* latent
lateral [late'ral] *adj* side *cpd*, lateral ♦ *nm* (*TEATRO*) wings
latido [la'tiðo] *nm* (*del corazón*) beat
latifundio [lati'fundjo] *nm* large estate; **latifundista** *nm/f* owner of a large estate
latigazo [lati'ɣaθo] *nm* (*golpe*) lash; (*sonido*) crack
látigo ['latiɣo] *nm* whip
latín [la'tin] *nm* Latin
latino, a [la'tino, a] *adj* Latin; ~**americano, a** *adj, nm/f* Latin-American
latir [la'tir] *vi* (*corazón, pulso*) to beat
latitud [lati'tuð] *nf* (*GEO*) latitude
latón [la'ton] *nm* brass

latoso, a [la'toso, a] *adj* (*molesto*) annoying; (*aburrido*) boring
laúd [la'uð] *nm* lute
laurel [lau'rel] *nm* (*BOT*) laurel; (*CULIN*) bay
lava ['laβa] *nf* lava
lavabo [la'βaβo] *nm* (*jofaina*) washbasin; (*tb:* ~**s**) toilet
lavado [la'βaðo] *nm* washing; (*de ropa*) laundry; (*ARTE*) wash; ~ **de cerebro** brainwashing; ~ **en seco** dry-cleaning
lavadora [laβa'ðora] *nf* washing machine
lavanda [la'βanda] *nf* lavender
lavandería [laβande'ria] *nf* laundry; ~ **automática** launderette
lavaplatos [laβa'platos] *nm inv* dishwasher
lavar [la'βar] *vt* to wash; (*borrar*) to wipe away; ~**se** *vr* to wash o.s.; ~**se las manos** to wash one's hands; ~ **y marcar** (*pelo*) to shampoo and set; ~ **en seco** to dry-clean
lavavajillas [laβaβa'xiʎas] *nm inv* dishwasher
laxante [lak'sante] *nm* laxative
lazada [la'θaða] *nf* bow
lazarillo [laθa'riʎo] *nm*: **perro** ~ guide dog
lazo ['laθo] *nm* knot; (*lazada*) bow; (*para animales*) lasso; (*trampa*) snare; (*vínculo*) tie
le [le] *pron* (*directo*) him (*o* her); (: *usted*) you; (*indirecto*) to him (*o* her *o* it); (: *usted*) to you
leal [le'al] *adj* loyal; ~**tad** *nf* loyalty
lección [lek'θjon] *nf* lesson
leche ['letʃe] *nf* milk; **tiene mala** ~ (*fam!*) he's a swine (*!*); ~ **condensada/ en polvo** condensed/powdered milk; ~ **desnatada** skimmed milk; ~**ra** *nf* (*vendedora*) milkmaid; (*recipiente*) (milk) churn; (*AM*) cow; ~**ro, a** *adj* dairy
lecho ['letʃo] *nm* (*cama, de río*) bed; (*GEO*) layer
lechón [le'tʃon] *nm* sucking (*BRIT*) *o* suckling (*US*) pig
lechoso, a [le'tʃoso, a] *adj* milky
lechuga [le'tʃuɣa] *nf* lettuce
lechuza [le'tʃuθa] *nf* owl
lector, a [lek'tor, a] *nm/f* reader

lectura [lek'tura] *nf* reading

leer [le'er] *vt* to read

legado [le'ɣaðo] *nm* (*don*) bequest; (*herencia*) legacy; (*enviado*) legate

legajo [le'ɣaxo] *nm* file

legal [le'ɣal] *adj* (*gen*) legal; (*persona*) trustworthy; **~idad** *nf* legality; **~izar** *vt* to legalize; (*documento*) to authenticate

legaña [le'ɣaɲa] *nf* sleep (*in eyes*)

legar [le'ɣar] *vt* to bequeath, leave

legendario, a [lexen'darjo, a] *adj* legendary

legión [le'xjon] *nf* legion; **legionario, a** *adj* legionary ♦ *nm* legionnaire

legislación [lexisla'θjon] *nf* legislation

legislar [lexis'lar] *vi* to legislate

legislatura [lexisla'tura] *nf* (*POL*) period of office

legitimar [lexiti'mar] *vt* to legitimize; **legítimo, a** *adj* (*genuino*) authentic; (*legal*) legitimate

lego, a ['leɣo, a] *adj* (*REL*) secular; (*ignorante*) ignorant ♦ *nm* layman

legua ['leɣwa] *nf* league

legumbres [le'ɣumbres] *nfpl* pulses

leído, a [le'iðo, a] *adj* well-read

lejanía [lexa'nia] *nf* distance; **lejano, a** *adj* far-off; (*en el tiempo*) distant; (*fig*) remote

lejía [le'xia] *nf* bleach

lejos ['lexos] *adv* far, far away; **a lo ~** in the distance; **de** *o* **desde ~** from afar; **~ de** far from

lelo, a ['lelo, a] *adj* silly ♦ *nm/f* idiot

lema ['lema] *nm* motto; (*POL*) slogan

lencería [lenθe'ria] *nf* linen, drapery

lengua ['lengwa] *nf* tongue; (*LING*) language; **morderse la ~** to hold one's tongue

lenguado [len'gwaðo] *nm* sole

lenguaje [len'gwaxe] *nm* language

lengüeta [len'gweta] *nf* (*ANAT*) epiglottis; (*zapatos*) tongue, (*MUS*) reed

lente ['lente] *nf* lens; (*lupa*) magnifying glass; **~s** *nfpl* (*gafas*) glasses; **~s de contacto** contact lenses

lenteja [len'texa] *nf* lentil; **lentejuela** *nf* sequin

lentilla [len'tiʎa] *nf* contact lens

lentitud [lenti'tuð] *nf* slowness; **con ~** slowly

lento, a ['lento, a] *adj* slow

leña ['leɲa] *nf* firewood; **~dor, a** *nm/f* woodcutter

leño ['leɲo] *nm* (*trozo de árbol*) log; (*madera*) timber; (*fig*) blockhead

Leo ['leo] *nm* Leo

león [le'on] *nm* lion; **~ marino** sea lion

leopardo [leo'parðo] *nm* leopard

leotardos [leo'tarðos] *nmpl* tights

lepra ['lepra] *nf* leprosy; **leproso, a** *nm/f* leper

lerdo, a ['lerðo, a] *adj* (*lento*) slow; (*patoso*) clumsy

les [les] *pron* (*directo*) them; (*: ustedes*) you; (*indirecto*) to them; (*: ustedes*) to you

lesbiana [les'βjana] *adj, nf* lesbian

lesión [le'sjon] *nf* wound, lesion; (*DEPORTE*) injury; **lesionado, a** *adj* injured ♦ *nm/f* injured person

letal [le'tal] *adj* lethal

letanía [leta'nia] *nf* litany

letargo [le'tarɣo] *nm* lethargy

letra ['letra] *nf* letter; (*escritura*) handwriting; (*MUS*) lyrics *pl*; **~ de cambio** bill of exchange; **~ de imprenta** print; **~do, a** *adj* learned; (*fam*) pedantic ♦ *nm* lawyer; **letrero** *nm* (*cartel*) sign; (*etiqueta*) label

letrina [le'trina] *nf* latrine

leucemia [leu'θemja] *nf* leukaemia

levadizo [leβa'ðiθo] *adj*: **puente ~** drawbridge

levadura [leβa'ðura] *nf* (*para el pan*) yeast; (*de la cerveza*) brewer's yeast

levantamiento [leβanta'mjento] *nm* raising, lifting; (*rebelión*) revolt, rising; **~ de pesos** weight-lifting

levantar [leβan'tar] *vt* (*gen*) to raise; (*del suelo*) to pick up; (*hacia arriba*) to lift (up); (*plan*) to make, draw up; (*mesa*) to clear; (*campamento*) to strike; (*fig*) to cheer up, hearten; **~se** *vr* to get up; (*enderezarse*) to straighten up; (*rebelarse*) to rebel; **~ el ánimo** to cheer up

levante [le'βante] *nm* east coast; **el L~** *region of Spain extending from Castellón* to Murcia

levar [le'ßar] *vt* to weigh anchor

leve ['leße] *adj* light; (*fig*) trivial; **~dad** *nf* lightness

levita [le'ßita] *nf* frock coat

léxico ['leksiko] *nm* (*vocabulario*) vocabulary

ley [lei] *nf* (*gen*) law; (*metal*) standard

leyenda [le'jenda] *nf* legend

leyó *etc vb ver* **leer**

liar [li'ar] *vt* to tie (up); (*unir*) to bind; (*envolver*) to wrap (up); (*enredar*) to confuse; (*cigarrillo*) to roll; **~se** *vr* (*fam*) to get involved; **~se a palos** to get involved in a fight

Líbano ['lißano] *nm*: **el ~** (the) Lebanon

libelo [li'ßelo] *nm* satire, lampoon; (*JUR*) petition

libélula [li'ßelula] *nf* dragonfly

liberación [lißera'θjon] *nf* liberation; (*de la cárcel*) release

liberal [liße'ral] *adj, nm/f* liberal; **~idad** *nf* liberality, generosity

liberar [liße'rar] *vt* to liberate

libertad [lißer'tað] *nf* liberty, freedom; **~ de culto/de prensa/de comercio** freedom of worship/of the press/of trade; **~ condicional** probation; **~ bajo palabra** parole; **~ bajo fianza** bail

libertar [lißer'tar] *vt* (*preso*) to set free; (*de una obligación*) to release; (*eximir*) to exempt

libertino, a [lißer'tino, a] *adj* permissive ♦ *nm/f* permissive person

libra ['lißra] *nf* pound; (*ASTROLOGÍA*): **L~** Libra; **~ esterlina** pound sterling

libramiento [lißra'mjento] *nm* rescue; (*COM*) delivery

libranza [li'ßranθa] *nf* (*COM*) draft; (*letra de cambio*) bill of exchange

librar [li'ßrar] *vt* (*de peligro*) to save; (*batalla*) to wage, fight; (*de impuestos*) to exempt; (*cheque*) to make out; (*JUR*) to exempt; **~se** *vr*: **~se de** to escape from, free o.s. from

libre ['lißre] *adj* free; (*lugar*) unoccupied; (*asiento*) vacant; (*de deudas*) free of debts; **~ de impuestos** free of tax; **tiro ~** free kick; **los 100 metros ~** the 100

metres free-style (race); **al aire ~** in the open air

librería [liße'rria] *nf* (*tienda*) bookshop; **librero, a** *nm/f* bookseller

libreta [li'ßreta] *nf* notebook; **~ de ahorros** savings book

libro ['lißro] *nm* book; **~ de bolsillo** paperback; **~ de caja** cashbook; **~ de cheques** chequebook (*BRIT*), checkbook (*US*); **~ de texto** textbook

Lic. *abr* = **licenciado, a**

licencia [li'θenθja] *nf* (*gen*) licence; (*permiso*) permission; **~ por enfermedad/con goce de sueldo** sick leave/paid leave; **~ de caza** game licence; **~do, a** *adj* licensed ♦ *nm/f* graduate; **licenciar** *vt* (*empleado*) to dismiss; (*permitir*) to permit, allow; (*soldado*) to discharge; (*estudiante*) to confer a degree upon; **licenciarse** *vr*: **licenciarse en letras** to graduate in arts

licencioso, a [liθen'θjoso, a] *adj* licentious

licitar [liθi'tar] *vt* to bid for; (*AM*) to sell by auction

lícito, a ['liθito, a] *adj* (*legal*) lawful; (*justo*) fair, just; (*permisible*) permissible

licor [li'kor] *nm* spirits *pl* (*BRIT*), liquor (*US*); (*de frutas etc*) liqueur

licuadora [likwa'ðora] *nf* blender

licuar [li'kwar] *vt* to liquidize

lid [lið] *nf* combat; (*fig*) controversy

líder ['liðer] *nm/f* leader; **liderato** *nm* leadership; **liderazgo** *nm* leadership

lidia ['liðja] *nf* bullfighting; (*una ~*) bullfight; **toros de ~** fighting bulls; **lidiar** *vt, vi* to fight

liebre ['ljeßre] *nf* hare

lienzo ['ljenθo] *nm* linen; (*ARTE*) canvas; (*ARQ*) wall

liga ['liɣa] *nf* (*de medias*) garter, suspender; (*AM: gomita*) rubber band; (*confederación*) league

ligadura [liɣa'ðura] *nf* bond, tie; (*MED, MUS*) ligature

ligamento [liɣa'mento] *nm* (*ANAT*) ligament; (*atadura*) tie; (*unión*) bond

ligar [li'ɣar] *vt* (*atar*) to tie; (*unir*) to join;

(*MED*) to bind up; (*MUS*) to slur ♦ *vi* to mix, blend; (*fam*): **(él) liga mucho** he pulls a lot of women; **~se** *vr* to commit o.s.

ligereza [lixe'reθa] *nf* lightness; (*rapidez*) swiftness; (*agilidad*) agility; (*superficialidad*) flippancy

ligero, a [li'xero, a] *adj* (*de peso*) light; (*tela*) thin; (*rápido*) swift, quick; (*ágil*) agile, nimble; (*de importancia*) slight; (*de carácter*) flippant, superficial ♦ *adv*: **a la ligera** superficially

liguero [li'γero] *nm* suspender (*BRIT*) o garter (*US*) belt

lija ['lixa] *nf* (*ZOOL*) dogfish; (*tb: papel de ~*) sandpaper

lila ['lila] *nf* lilac

lima ['lima] *nf* file; (*BOT*) lime; **~ de uñas** nailfile; **limar** *vt* to file

limitación [limita'θjon] *nf* limitation, limit; **~ de velocidad** speed limit

limitar [limi'tar] *vt* to limit; (*reducir*) to reduce, cut down ♦ *vi*: **~ con** to border on; **~se** *vr*: **~se a** to limit o.s. to

límite ['limite] *nm* (*gen*) limit; (*fin*) end; (*frontera*) border; **~ de velocidad** speed limit

limítrofe [li'mitrofe] *adj* bordering, neighbouring

limón [li'mon] *nm* lemon ♦ *adj*: **amarillo ~** lemon-yellow; **limonada** *nf* lemonade

limosna [li'mosna] *nf* alms *pl*; **vivir de ~** to live on charity

limpiaparabrisas [limpjapara'βrisas] *nm inv* windscreen (*BRIT*) o windshield (*US*) wiper

limpiar [lim'pjar] *vt* to clean; (*con trapo*) to wipe away; (*quitar*) to wipe away; (*zapatos*) to shine, polish; (*fig*) to clean up

limpieza [lim'pjeθa] *nf* (*estado*) cleanliness; (*acto*) cleaning; (: *de las calles*) cleansing; (: *de zapatos*) polishing; (*habilidad*) skill; (*fig: POLICÍA*) clean-up; (*pureza*) purity; (*MIL*): **operación de ~** mopping-up operation; **~ en seco** dry cleaning

limpio, a ['limpjo, a] *adj* clean; (*moralmente*) pure; (*COM*) clear, net; (*fam*) honest ♦ *adv*: **jugar ~** to play fair; **pasar**

a (*ESP*) o **en** (*AM*) **~** to make a clean copy

linaje [li'naxe] *nm* lineage, family

lince ['linθe] *nm* lynx

linchar [lin'tʃar] *vt* to lynch

lindar [lin'dar] *vi* to adjoin; **~ con** to border on; **linde** *nm* o *f* boundary; **lindero, a** *adj* adjoining ♦ *nm* boundary

lindo, a ['lindo, a] *adj* pretty, lovely ♦ *adv*: **nos divertimos de lo ~** we had a marvellous time; **canta muy ~** (*AM*) he sings beautifully

línea ['linea] *nf* (*gen*) line; **en ~** (*INFORM*) on line; **~ aérea** airline; **~ de meta** goal line; (*de carrera*) finishing line; **~ recta** straight line

lingote [lin'gote] *nm* ingot

lingüista [lin'gwista] *nm/f* linguist; **lingüística** *nf* linguistics *sg*

linimento [lini'mento] *nm* liniment

lino ['lino] *nm* linen; (*BOT*) flax

linóleo [li'noleo] *nm* lino, linoleum

linterna [lin'terna] *nf* lantern, lamp; **~ eléctrica** o **a pilas** torch (*BRIT*), flashlight (*US*)

lío ['lio] *nm* bundle; (*fam*) fuss; (*desorden*) muddle, mess; **armar un ~** to make a fuss

liquen ['liken] *nm* lichen

liquidación [likiða'θjon] *nf* liquidation; **venta de ~** clearance sale

liquidar [liki'ðar] *vt* (*mercancías*) to liquidate; (*deudas*) to pay off; (*empresa*) to wind up

líquido, a ['likiðo, a] *adj* liquid; (*ganancia*) net ♦ *nm* liquid; **~ imponible** net taxable income

lira ['lira] *nf* (*MUS*) lyre; (*moneda*) lira

lírico, a ['liriko, a] *adj* lyrical

lirio ['lirjo] *nm* (*BOT*) iris

lirón [li'ron] *nm* (*ZOOL*) dormouse; (*fig*) sleepyhead

Lisboa [lis'βoa] *n* Lisbon

lisiado, a [li'sjaðo, a] *adj* injured ♦ *nm/f* cripple

lisiar [li'sjar] *vt* to maim; **~se** *vr* to injure o.s

liso, a ['liso, a] *adj* (*terreno*) flat; (*cabello*) straight; (*superficie*) even; (*tela*) plain

lisonja [li'sonxa] *nf* flattery; **lisonjear** *vt*

to flatter; (*fig*) to please

lista ['lista] *nf* list; (*de alumnos*) school register; (*de libros*) catalogue; (*de platos*) menu; (*de precios*) price list; **pasar** ~ to call the roll; ~ **de correos** poste restante; ~ **de espera** waiting list; **tela a** ~**s** striped material

listo, a ['listo, a] *adj* (*perspicaz*) smart, clever; (*preparado*) ready

listón [lis'ton] *nm* (*tela*) ribbon; (*de madera, metal*) strip

litera [li'tera] *nf* (*en barco, tren*) berth; (*en dormitorio*) bunk, bunk bed

literal [lite'ral] *adj* literal

literario, a [lite'rarjo, a] *adj* literary

literato, a [lite'rato, a] *adj* literary ♦ *nm/f* writer

literatura [litera'tura] *nf* literature

litigar [liti'γar] *vi* to fight ♦ *vi* (*JUR*) to go to law; (*fig*) to dispute, argue

litigio [li'tixjo] *nm* (*JUR*) lawsuit; (*fig*): **en** ~ **con** in dispute with

litografía [litoγra'fia] *nf* lithography; (*una* ~) lithograph

litoral [lito'ral] *adj* coastal ♦ *nm* coast, seaboard

litro ['litro] *nm* litre

liviano, a [li'βjano, a] *adj* (*persona*) fickle; (*cosa, objeto*) trivial

lívido, a ['liβiðo, a] *adj* livid

llaga ['ʎaγa] *nf* wound

llama ['ʎama] *nf* flame; (*ZOOL*) llama

llamada [ʎa'maða] *nf* call; ~ **al orden** call to order; ~ **a pie de página** reference note

llamamiento [ʎama'mjento] *nm* call

llamar [ʎa'mar] *vt* to call; (*atención*) to attract ♦ *vi* (*por teléfono*) to telephone; (*a la puerta*) to knock (*o* ring); (*por señas*) to beckon; (*MIL*) to call up; ~**se** *vr* to be called, be named; ¿**cómo se llama usted?** what's your name?

llamarada [ʎama'raða] *nf* (*llamas*) blaze; (*rubor*) flush; (*fig*) flare-up

llamativo, a [ʎama'tiβo, a] *adj* showy; (*color*) loud

llano, a ['ʎano, a] *adj* (*superficie*) flat; (*persona*) straightforward; (*estilo*) clear

♦ *nm* plain, flat ground

llanta ['ʎanta] *nf* (*wheel*) rim; (*AM*): ~ **(de goma)** tyre; (: *cámara*) inner (tube)

llanto ['ʎanto] *nm* weeping

llanura [ʎa'nura] *nf* plain

llave ['ʎaβe] *nf* key; (*del agua*) tap; (*MECÁNICA*) spanner; (*de la luz*) switch; (*MUS*) key; ~ **inglesa** monkey wrench; ~ **maestra** master key; ~ **de contacto** (*AUTO*) ignition key; ~ **de paso** stopcock; **echar** ~ **a** to lock up; ~**ro** *nm* keyring

llegada [ʎe'γaða] *nf* arrival

llegar [ʎe'γar] *vi* to arrive; (*alcanzar*) to reach; (*bastar*) to be enough; ~**se** *vr*: ~**se a** to approach; ~ **a** to manage to, succeed in; ~ **a saber** to find out; ~ **a ser** to become; ~ **a las manos de** to come into the hands of

llenar [ʎe'nar] *vt* to fill; (*espacio*) to cover; (*formulario*) to fill in *o* up; (*fig*) to heap

lleno, a ['ʎeno, a] *adj* full, filled; (*repleto*) full up ♦ *nm* (*abundancia*) abundance; (*TEATRO*) full house; **dar de** ~ **contra un muro** to hit a wall head-on

llevadero, a [ʎeβa'ðero, a] *adj* bearable, tolerable

llevar [ʎe'βar] *vt* to take; (*ropa*) to wear; (*cargar*) to carry; (*quitar*) to take away; (*en coche*) to drive; (*transportar*) to transport; (*traer: dinero*) to carry; (*conducir*) to lead; (*MAT*) to carry ♦ *vi* (*suj: camino etc*): ~ **a** to lead to; ~**se** *vr* to carry off, take away; **llevamos dos días aquí** we have been here for two days; **él me lleva 2 años** he's 2 years older than me; (*COM*): ~ **los libros** to keep the books; ~**se bien** to get on well (together)

llorar [ʎo'rar] *vt, vi* to cry, weep; ~ **de risa** to cry with laughter

lloriquear [ʎorike'ar] *vi* to snivel, whimper

lloro ['ʎoro] *nm* crying, weeping; **llorón, ona** *adj* tearful ♦ *nm/f* cry-baby; ~**so, a** *adj* (*gen*) weeping, tearful; (*triste*) sad, sorrowful

llover [ʎo'βer] *vi* to rain

llovizna [ʎo'βiθna] *nf* drizzle; **lloviznar** *vi* to drizzle

llueve *etc vb ver* **llover**

lluvia ['ʎuβja] *nf* rain; ~ **radioactiva** (radioactive) fallout; **lluvioso, a** *adj* rainy

lo [lo] *art def*: ~ **bello** the beautiful, what is beautiful, that which is beautiful
♦ *pron (persona)* him; *(cosa)* it; *tb ver* **el**

loable [lo'aβle] *adj* praiseworthy; **loar** *vt* to praise

lobato [lo'βato] *nm (ZOOL)* wolf cub; **L~** Cub Scout

lobo ['loβo] *nm* wolf; ~ **de mar** *(fig)* sea dog; ~ **marino** seal

lóbrego, a ['loβreɣo, a] *adj* dark; *(fig)* gloomy

lóbulo ['loβulo] *nm* lobe

local [lo'kal] *adj* local ♦ *nm* place, site; *(oficinas)* premises *pl*; **~idad** *nf (barrio)* locality; *(lugar)* location; *(TEATRO)* seat, ticket; **~izar** *vt (ubicar)* to locate, find; *(restringir)* to localize; *(situar)* to place

loción [lo'θjon] *nf* lotion

loco, a ['loko, a] *adj* mad ♦ *nm/f* lunatic, mad person

locomoción [lokomo'θjon] *nf* locomotion

locomotora [lokomo'tora] *nf* engine, locomotive

locuaz [lo'kwaθ] *adj* loquacious

locución [loku'θjon] *nf* expression

locura [lo'kura] *nf* madness; *(acto)* crazy act

locutor, a [loku'tor, a] *nm/f (RADIO)* announcer; *(comentarista)* commentator; *(TV)* newsreader

locutorio [loku'torjo] *nm (en telefónica)* telephone booth

lodo ['loðo] *nm* mud

lógica ['loxika] *nf* logic

lógico, a ['loxiko, a] *adj* logical

logística [lo'xistika] *nf* logistics *sg*

logotipo [loðo'tipo] *nm* logo

logrado, a [lo'ðraðo, a] *adj (interpretación, reproducción)* polished, excellent

lograr [lo'ɣrar] *vt* to achieve; *(obtener)* to get, obtain; ~ **hacer** to manage to do; ~ **que uno venga** to manage to get sb to come

logro ['loɣro] *nm* achievement, success

loma ['loma] *nf* hillock *(BRIT)*, small hill

lombriz [lom'briθ] *nf* worm

lomo ['lomo] *nm (de animal)* back; *(CULIN: de cerdo)* pork loin; *(: de vaca)* rib steak; *(de libro)* spine

lona ['lona] *nf* canvas

loncha ['lontʃa] *nf* = **lonja**

lonche ['lontʃe] *(AM) nm* lunch; **~ría** *(AM) nf* snack bar, diner *(US)*

Londres ['londres] *n* London

longaniza [longa'niθa] *nf* pork sausage

longitud [lonxi'tuð] *nf* length; *(GEO)* longitude; **tener 3 metros de** ~ to be 3 metres long; ~ **de onda** wavelength

lonja ['lonxa] *nf* slice; *(de tocino)* rasher; ~ **de pescado** fish market

loro ['loro] *nm* parrot

los [los] *art def* the ♦ *pron* them; *(ustedes)* you; **mis libros y** ~ **de Ud** my books and yours; *tb ver* **el**

losa ['losa] *nf* stone; ~ **sepulcral** gravestone

lote ['lote] *nm* portion; *(COM)* lot

lotería [lote'ria] *nf* lottery; *(juego)* lotto

loza ['loθa] *nf* crockery

lozanía [loθa'nia] *nf (lujo)* luxuriance; **lozano, a** *adj* luxuriant; *(animado)* lively

lubricante [luβri'kante] *nm* lubricant

lubricar [luβri'kar] *vt* to lubricate

lucha ['lutʃa] *nf* fight, struggle; ~ **de clases** class struggle; ~ **libre** wrestling; **luchar** *vi* to fight

lucidez [luθi'ðeθ] *nf* lucidity

lúcido, a ['luθiðo, a] *adj (persona)* lucid; *(mente)* logical; *(idea)* crystal-clear

luciérnaga [lu'θjernaɣa] *nf* glow-worm

lucir [lu'θir] *vt* to illuminate, light (up); *(ostentar)* to show off ♦ *vi (brillar)* to shine; **~se** *vr (irónico)* to make a fool of o.s.

lucro ['lukro] *nm* profit, gain

lúdico, a ['luðiko, a] *adj (aspecto, actividad)* play *atr*

luego ['lweɣo] *adv (después)* next; *(más tarde)* later, afterwards

lugar [lu'ɣar] *nm* place; *(sitio)* spot; **en** ~ **de** instead of; **hacer** ~ to make room; **fuera de** ~ out of place; **tener** ~ to take place; ~ **común** commonplace

lugareño, a [luɣa'reɲo, a] *adj* village *cpd* ♦ *nm/f* villager

lugarteniente [luɣarte'njente] *nm* deputy
lúgubre ['luɣuβre] *adj* mournful
lujo ['luxo] *nm* luxury; (*fig*) profusion, abundance; **~so, a** *adj* luxurious
lujuria [lu'xurja] *nf* lust
lumbre ['lumbre] *nf* (*gen*) light
lumbrera [lum'brera] *nf* luminary
luminoso, a [lumi'noso, a] *adj* luminous, shining
luna ['luna] *nf* moon; (*de un espejo*) glass; (*de gafas*) lens; (*fig*) crescent; **~ llena/nueva** full/new moon; **estar en la ~** to have one's head in the clouds; **~ de miel** honeymoon
lunar [lu'nar] *adj* lunar ♦ *nm* (*ANAT*) mole; **tela a ~es** spotted material
lunes ['lunes] *nm inv* Monday
lupa ['lupa] *nf* magnifying glass
lustrar [lus'trar] *vt* (*mueble*) to polish; (*zapatos*) to shine; **lustre** *nm* polish; (*fig*) lustre; **dar lustre a** to polish; **lustroso, a** *adj* shining
luto ['luto] *nm* mourning; (*congoja*) grief, sorrow; **llevar el** *o* **vestirse de ~** to be in mourning
Luxemburgo [luksem'burɣo] *nm* Luxembourg
luz [luθ] (*pl* **luces**) *nf* light; **dar a ~ un niño** to give birth to a child; **sacar a la ~** to bring to light; **dar** *o* **encender** (*ESP*) *o* **prender** (*AM*)/**apagar la ~** to switch the light on/off; **a todas luces** by any reckoning; **hacer la ~ sobre** to shed light on; **tener pocas luces** to be dim *o* stupid; **~ roja/verde** red/green light; **~ de freno** brake light; **luces de tráfico** traffic lights; **traje de luces** bullfighter's costume

M m

m *abr* (= *metro*) m; (= *minuto*) m
macarrones [maka'rrones] *nmpl* macaroni *sg*
macedonia [maθe'ðonja] *nf*: **~ de frutas** fruit salad
macerar [maθe'rar] *vt* to macerate
maceta [ma'θeta] *nf* (*de flores*) pot of flowers; (*para plantas*) flowerpot
machacar [matʃa'kar] *vt* to crush, pound ♦ *vi* (*insistir*) to go on, keep on
machete [ma'tʃete] (*AM*) *nm* machete, (large) knife
machismo [ma'tʃismo] *nm* male chauvinism; **machista** *adj, nm* sexist
macho ['matʃo] *adj* male; (*fig*) virile ♦ *nm* male; (*fig*) he-man
macizo, a [ma'θiθo, a] *adj* (*grande*) massive; (*fuerte, sólido*) solid ♦ *nm* mass, chunk
madeja [ma'ðexa] *nf* (*de lana*) skein, hank; (*de pelo*) mass, mop
madera [ma'ðera] *nf* wood; (*fig*) nature, character; **una ~** a piece of wood
madero [ma'ðero] *nm* beam; (*fig*) ship
madrastra [ma'ðrastra] *nf* stepmother
madre ['maðre] *adj* mother *cpd*; (*AM*) tremendous ♦ *nf* mother; (*de vino etc*) dregs *pl*; **~ política/soltera** mother-in-law/unmarried mother
Madrid [ma'ðrið] *n* Madrid
madriguera [maðri'ɣera] *nf* burrow
madrileño, a [maðri'leɲo, a] *adj* of *o* from Madrid ♦ *nm/f* native of Madrid
madrina [ma'ðrina] *nf* godmother; (*ARQ*) prop, shore; (*TEC*) brace; **~ de boda** bridesmaid
madrugada [maðru'ɣaða] *nf* early morning; (*alba*) dawn, daybreak
madrugador, a [maðruɣa'ðor, a] *adj* early-rising
madrugar [maðru'ɣar] *vi* to get up early; (*fig*) to get ahead
madurar [maðu'rar] *vt, vi* (*fruta*) to ripen; (*fig*) to mature; **madurez** *nf* ripeness; maturity; **maduro, a** *adj* ripe; mature
maestra [ma'estra] *nf ver* **maestro**
maestría [maes'tria] *nf* mastery; (*habilidad*) skill, expertise
maestro, a [ma'estro, a] *adj* masterly; (*perito*) skilled, expert; (*principal*) main; (*educado*) trained ♦ *nm/f* master/mistress; (*profesor*) teacher ♦ *nm* (*autoridad*) authority; (*MUS*) maestro; (*AM*) skilled workman; **~ albañil** master mason
magia ['maxja] *nf* magic; **mágico, a** *adj*

magic(al) ♦ *nm/f* magician
magisterio [maxis'terjo] *nm* (*enseñanza*) teaching; (*profesión*) teaching profession; (*maestros*) teachers *pl*
magistrado [maxis'traðo] *nm* magistrate
magistral [maxis'tral] *adj* magisterial; (*fig*) masterly
magnánimo, a [may'nanimo, a] *adj* magnanimous
magnate [may'nate] *nm* magnate, tycoon
magnético, a [may'netiko, a] *adj* magnetic; **magnetizar** *vt* to magnetize
magnetófon [mayneto'fon] *nm* tape recorder; **magnetofónico, a** *adj*: **cinta magnetofónica** recording tape
magnetófono [mayne'tofono] *nm* = **magnetófon**
magnífico, a [may'nifiko, a] *adj* splendid, magnificent
magnitud [mayni'tuð] *nf* magnitude
mago, a ['mayo, a] *nm/f* magician; **los Reyes M~s** the Magi, the Three Wise Men
magro, a ['mayro, a] *adj* (*persona*) thin, lean; (*carne*) lean
maguey [ma'yei] *nm* agave
magullar [mayu'ʎar] *vt* (*amoratar*) to bruise; (*dañar*) to damage; (*fam: golpear*) to bash, beat
mahometano, a [maome'tano, a] *adj* Mohammedan
mahonesa [mao'nesa] *nf* = **mayonesa**
maíz [ma'iθ] *nm* maize (*BRIT*), corn (*US*); sweet corn
majadero, a [maxa'ðero, a] *adj* silly, stupid
majestad [maxes'tað] *nf* majesty; **majestuoso, a** *adj* majestic
majo, a ['maxo, a] *adj* nice; (*guapo*) attractive, good-looking; (*elegante*) smart
mal [mal] *adv* badly; (*equivocadamente*) wrongly; (*con dificultad*) with difficulty ♦ *adj* = **malo** ♦ *nm* evil; (*desgracia*) misfortune; (*daño*) harm, damage; (*MED*) illness; ~ **que bien** rightly or wrongly; **ir de** ~ **en peor** to get worse and worse
mala ['mala] *nf* spell of bad luck; **estar de** ~**s** to be in a bad mood; *ver tb* **malo**
malabarismo [malaβa'rismo] *nm* juggling;

malabarista *nm/f* juggler
malaria [ma'larja] *nf* malaria
malcriado, a [mal'krjaðo, a] *adj* (*consentido*) spoiled
maldad [mal'dað] *nf* evil, wickedness
maldecir [malde'θir] *vt* to curse ♦ *vi*: ~ **de** to speak ill of
maldición [maldi'θjon] *nf* curse
maldito, a [mal'dito, a] *adj* (*condenado*) damned; (*perverso*) wicked; ¡~ **sea!** damn it!
maleante [male'ante] *adj* wicked ♦ *nm/f* criminal, crook
maledicencia [maleði'θenθja] *nf* slander, scandal
maleducado, a [maleðu'kaðo, a] *adj* bad-mannered, rude
malentendido [malenten'diðo] *nm* misunderstanding
malestar [males'tar] *nm* (*gen*) discomfort; (*fig: inquietud*) uneasiness; (*POL*) unrest
maleta [ma'leta] *nf* case, suitcase; (*AUTO*) boot (*BRIT*), trunk (*US*); **hacer las** ~**s** to pack; **maletera** (*AM*) *nf* = **maletero**; **maletero** *nm* (*AUTO*) boot (*BRIT*), trunk (*US*); **maletín** *nm* small case, bag
malévolo, a [ma'leβolo, a] *adj* malicious, spiteful
maleza [ma'leθa] *nf* (*hierbas malas*) weeds *pl*; (*arbustos*) thicket
malgastar [malyas'tar] *vt* (*tiempo, dinero*) to waste; (*salud*) to ruin
malhechor, a [male'tʃor, a] *nm/f* delinquent
malhumorado, a [malumo'raðo, a] *adj* bad-tempered
malicia [ma'liθja] *nf* (*maldad*) wickedness; (*astucia*) slyness, guile; (*mala intención*) malice, spite; (*carácter travieso*) mischievousness; **malicioso, a** *adj* wicked, evil; sly, crafty; malicious, spiteful; mischievous
maligno, a [ma'liɣno, a] *adj* evil; (*malévolo*) malicious; (*MED*) malignant
malla ['maʎa] *nf* mesh; (*de baño*) swimsuit; (*de ballet, gimnasia*) leotard; ~**s** *nfpl* tights; ~ **de alambre** wire mesh
Mallorca [ma'ʎorka] *nf* Majorca
malo, a ['malo, a] *adj* bad; (*falso*) false

♦ *nm/f* villain; **estar** ~ to be ill

malograr [malo'ɣrar] *vt* to spoil; (*plan*) to upset; (*ocasión*) to waste; ~**se** *vr* (*plan etc*) to fail, come to grief; (*persona*) to die before one's time

malparado, a [malpa'raðo, a] *adj*: **salir** ~ to come off badly

malpensado, a [malpen'saðo, a] *adj* (*persona*) nasty

malsano, a [mal'sano, a] *adj* unhealthy

Malta ['malta] *nf* Malta

malteada [malte'aða] (*AM*) *nf* milk shake

maltratar [maltra'tar] *vt* to ill-treat, mistreat

maltrecho, a [mal'tretʃo, a] *adj* battered, damaged

malvado, a [mal'βaðo, a] *adj* evil, villainous

malversar [malβer'sar] *vt* to embezzle, misappropriate

Malvinas [mal'βinas]: **Islas** ~ *nfpl* Falkland Islands

malvivir [malβi'βir] *vi* to live poorly

mama ['mama] *nf* (*de animal*) teat; (*de mujer*) breast

mamá [ma'ma] (*pl* ~**s**) (*fam*) *nf* mum, mummy

mamar [ma'mar] *vt* (*pecho*) to suck; (*fig*) to absorb, assimilate ♦ *vi* to suck

mamarracho [mama'rratʃo] *nm* sight, mess

mamífero [ma'mifero] *nm* mammal

mampara [mam'para] *nf* (*entre habitaciones*) partition; (*biombo*) screen

mampostería [mamposte'ria] *nf* masonry

manada [ma'naða] *nf* (*ZOOL*) herd; (: *de leones*) pride; (: *de lobos*) pack

Managua [ma'naɣwa] *n* Managua

manantial [manan'tjal] *nm* spring; (*fuente*) fountain; (*fig*) source

manar [ma'nar] *vt* to run with, flow with ♦ *vi* to run, flow; (*abundar*) to abound

mancha ['mantʃa] *nf* stain, mark; (*ZOOL*) patch; (*boceto*) sketch, outline; **manchar** *vt* (*gen*) to stain, mark; (*ensuciar*) to soil, dirty

manchego, a [man'tʃeɣo, a] *adj* of o from La Mancha

manco, a ['manko, a] *adj* (*de un brazo*) one-armed; (*de una mano*) one-handed; (*fig*) defective, faulty

mancomunar [mankomu'nar] *vt* to unite, bring together; (*recursos*) to pool; (*JUR*) to make jointly responsible; **mancomunidad** *nf* union, association; (*comunidad*) community; (*JUR*) joint responsibility

mandamiento [manda'mjento] *nm* (*orden*) order, command; (*REL*) commandment; ~ **judicial** warrant

mandar [man'dar] *vt* (*ordenar*) to order; (*dirigir*) to lead, command; (*enviar*) to send; (*pedir*) to order, ask for ♦ *vi* to be in charge; (*pey*) to be bossy; **¿mande?** pardon?, excuse me?; ~ **hacer un traje** to have a suit made

mandarina [manda'rina] *nf* (*fruta*) tangerine, mandarin (orange)

mandatario, a [manda'tarjo, a] *nm/f* (*representante*) agent; **primer** ~ head of state

mandato [man'dato] *nm* (*orden*) order; (*INFORM*) command; (*POL: período*) term of office; (: *territorio*) mandate; ~ **judicial** (search) warrant

mandíbula [man'diβula] *nf* jaw

mandil [man'dil] *nm* (*delantal*) apron

mando ['mando] *nm* (*MIL*) command; (*de país*) rule; (*el primer lugar*) lead; (*POL*) term of office; (*TEC*) control; ~ **a la izquierda** left-hand drive

mandón, ona [man'don, ona] *adj* bossy, domineering

manejable [mane'xaβle] *adj* manageable

manejar [mane'xar] *vt* to manage; (*máquina*) to work, operate; (*caballo etc*) to handle; (*casa*) to run, manage; (*AM: AUTO*) to drive; ~**se** *vr* (*comportarse*) to act, behave; (*arreglárselas*) to manage; **manejo** *nm* management; handling; running; driving; (*facilidad de trato*) ease, confidence; **manejos** *nmpl* (*intrigas*) intrigues

manera [ma'nera] *nf* way, manner, fashion; ~**s** *nfpl* (*modales*) manners; **su** ~ **de ser** the way he is; (*aire*) his manner; **de ninguna** ~ no way, by no means; **de otra** ~ otherwise; **de todas** ~**s** at any rate; **no hay** ~ **de persuadirle** there's no way of convincing him

manga ['manga] *nf* (*de camisa*) sleeve; (*de riego*) hose

mangar [man'gar] (*fam*) *vt* to pinch, nick

mango ['mango] *nm* handle; (*BOT*) mango

mangonear [mangone'ar] *vi* (*meterse*) to meddle, interfere; (*ser mandón*) to boss people about

manguera [man'gera] *nf* (*de riego*) hose; (*tubo*) pipe

manía [ma'nia] *nf* (*MED*) mania; (*fig: moda*) rage, craze; (*disgusto*) dislike; (*malicia*) spite; **maníaco, a** *adj* maniac(al) ♦ *nm/f* maniac

maniatar [manja'tar] *vt* to tie the hands of

maniático, a [ma'njatiko, a] *adj* maniac(al) ♦ *nm/f* maniac

manicomio [mani'komjo] *nm* mental hospital (*BRIT*), insane asylum (*US*)

manifestación [manifesta'θjon] *nf* (*declaración*) statement, declaration; (*de emoción*) show, display; (*POL: desfile*) demonstration; (*: concentración*) mass meeting

manifestar [manifes'tar] *vt* to show, manifest; (*declarar*) to state, declare; **manifiesto, a** *adj* clear, manifest ♦ *nm* manifesto

manija [ma'nixa] *nf* handle

manillar [mani'ʎar] *nm* (*de bicicleta*) handlebars *pl*

maniobra [ma'njoβra] *nf* manœuvring; (*manejo*) handling; (*fig*) manœuvre; (*estratagema*) stratagem; **~s** *nfpl* (*MIL*) manœuvres; **maniobrar** *vt* to manœuvre; (*manejar*) to handle

manipulación [manipula'θjon] *nf* manipulation

manipular [manipu'lar] *vt* to manipulate; (*manejar*) to handle

maniquí [mani'ki] *nm* dummy ♦ *nm/f* model

manirroto, a [mani'rroto, a] *adj* lavish, extravagant ♦ *nm/f* spendthrift

manivela [mani'βela] *nf* crank

manjar [man'xar] *nm* (*tasty*) dish

mano ['mano] *nf* hand; (*ZOOL*) foot, paw; (*de pintura*) coat; (*serie*) lot, series; **a ~**

by hand; **a ~ derecha/izquierda** on the right(-hand side)/left(-hand side); **de primera ~** (at) first hand; **de segunda ~** (at) second hand; **robo a ~ armada** armed robbery; **~ de obra** labour, manpower; **estrechar la ~ a uno** to shake sb's hand

manojo [ma'noxo] *nm* handful, bunch; **~ de llaves** bunch of keys

manopla [ma'nopla] *nf* (*guante*) glove; (*paño*) face cloth

manoseado, a [manose'aðo, a] *adj* well-worn

manosear [manose'ar] *vt* (*tocar*) to handle, touch; (*desordenar*) to mess up, rumple; (*insistir en*) to overwork; (*AM*) to caress, fondle

manotazo [mano'taθo] *nm* slap, smack

mansalva [man'salβa]: **a ~** *adv* indiscriminately

mansedumbre [manse'ðumbre] *nf* gentleness, meekness

mansión [man'sjon] *nf* mansion

manso, a ['manso, a] *adj* gentle, mild; (*animal*) tame

manta ['manta] *nf* blanket; (*AM: poncho*) poncho

manteca [man'teka] *nf* fat; (*AM*) butter; **~ de cacahuete/cacao** peanut/cocoa butter; **~ de cerdo** lard

mantecado [mante'kaðo] (*AM*) *nm* ice cream

mantel [man'tel] *nm* tablecloth

mantendré *etc vb ver* **mantener**

mantener [mante'ner] *vt* to support, maintain; (*alimentar*) to sustain; (*conservar*) to keep; (*TEC*) to maintain, service; **~se** *vr* (*seguir de pie*) to be still standing; (*no ceder*) to hold one's ground; (*subsistir*) to sustain o.s., keep going; **mantenimiento** *nm* maintenance; (*sustento*) support

mantequilla [mante'kiʎa] *nf* butter

mantilla [man'tiʎa] *nf* mantilla; **~s** *nfpl* (*de bebé*) baby clothes

manto ['manto] *nm* (*capa*) cloak; (*de ceremonia*) robe, gown

mantuve *etc vb ver* **mantener**

manual [ma'nwal] *adj* manual ♦ *nm*

manual, handbook

manufactura [manufak'tura] *nf* manufacture; (*fábrica*) factory; **manufacturado, a** *adj* (*producto*) manufactured

manuscrito, a [manus'krito, a] *adj* handwritten ♦ *nm* manuscript

manutención [manuten'θjon] *nf* maintenance; (*sustento*) support

maña ['maɲa] *nf* (*gen*) skill, dexterity; (*pey*) guile; (*costumbre*) habit; (*destreza*) trick, knack

manzana [man'θana] *nf* apple; (*ARQ*) block (of houses)

mañana [ma'ɲana] *adv* tomorrow ♦ *nm* future ♦ *nf* morning; **de** *o* **por la ~** in the morning; **¡hasta ~!** see you tomorrow!; **~ por la ~** tomorrow morning

manzanilla [manθa'niʎa] *nf* (*planta*) camomile; (*infusión*) camomile tea

manzano [man'θano] *nm* apple tree

mañoso, a [ma'ɲoso, a] *adj* (*hábil*) skilful; (*astuto*) smart, clever

mapa ['mapa] *nm* map

maqueta [ma'keta] *nf* (scale) model

maquillaje [maki'ʎaxe] *nm* make-up; (*acto*) making up

maquillar [maki'ʎar] *vt* to make up; **~se** *vr* to put on (some) make-up

máquina ['makina] *nf* machine; (*de tren*) locomotive, engine; (*FOTO*) camera; (*AM: coche*) car; (*fig*) machinery; (: *proyecto*) plan, project; **escrito a ~** typewritten; **~ de escribir** typewriter; **~ de coser/ lavar** sewing/washing machine

maquinación [makina'θjon] *nf* machination, plot

maquinal [maki'nal] *adj* (*fig*) mechanical, automatic

maquinaria [maki'narja] *nf* (*máquinas*) machinery; (*mecanismo*) mechanism, works *pl*

maquinilla [maki'niʎa] *nf*: **~ de afeitar** razor

maquinista [maki'nista] *nm/f* (*de tren*) engine driver; (*TEC*) operator; (*NAUT*) engineer

mar [mar] *nm o f* sea; **~ adentro** *o*

afuera out at sea; **en alta ~** on the high seas; **la ~ de** (*fam*) lots of; **el M~ Negro/Báltico** the Black/Baltic Sea

maraña [ma'raɲa] *nf* (*maleza*) thicket; (*confusión*) tangle

maravilla [mara'βiʎa] *nf* marvel, wonder; (*BOT*) marigold; **maravillar** *vt* to astonish, amaze; **maravillarse** *vr* to be astonished, be amazed; **maravilloso, a** *adj* wonderful, marvellous

marca ['marka] *nf* (*gen*) mark; (*sello*) stamp; (*COM*) make, brand; **de ~** excellent, outstanding; **~ de fábrica** trademark; **~ registrada** registered trademark

marcado, a [mar'kaðo, a] *adj* marked, strong

marcador [marka'ðor] *nm* (*DEPORTE*) scoreboard; (: *persona*) scorer

marcar [mar'kar] *vt* (*gen*) to mark; (*número de teléfono*) to dial; (*gol*) to score; (*números*) to record, keep a tally of; (*pelo*) to set ♦ *vi* (*DEPORTE*) to score; (*TEL*) to dial

marcha ['martʃa] *nf* march; (*TEC*) running, working; (*AUTO*) gear; (*velocidad*) speed; (*fig*) progress; (*dirección*) course; **poner en ~** to put into gear; (*fig*) to set in motion, get going; **dar ~ atrás** to reverse, put into reverse; **estar en ~** to be under way, be in motion

marchar [mar'tʃar] *vi* (*ir*) to go; (*funcionar*) to work, go; **~se** *vr* to go (away), leave

marchitar [martʃi'tar] *vt* to wither, dry up; **~se** *vr* (*BOT*) to wither; (*fig*) to fade away; **marchito, a** *adj* withered, faded; (*fig*) in decline

marcial [mar'θjal] *adj* martial, military

marciano, a [mar'θjano, a] *adj*, *nm/f* Martian

marco ['marko] *nm* frame; (*DEPORTE*) goal posts *pl*; (*moneda*) mark; (*fig*) framework; **~ de chimenea** mantelpiece

marea [ma'rea] *nf* tide; (*llovizna*) drizzle

marear [mare'ar] *vt* (*fig*) to annoy, upset; (*MED*): **~ a uno** to make sb feel sick; **~se** *vr* (*tener náuseas*) to feel sick; (*desvane-*

cerse) to feel faint; (*aturdirse*) to feel dizzy; (*fam: emborracharse*) to get tipsy

maremoto [mare'moto] *nm* tidal wave

mareo [ma'reo] *nm* (*náusea*) sick feeling; (*en viaje*) travel sickness; (*aturdimiento*) dizziness; (*fam: lata*) nuisance

marfil [mar'fil] *nm* ivory

margarina [marɣa'rina] *nf* margarine

margarita [marɣa'rita] *nf* (*BOT*) daisy; (**rueda**) ~ daisywheel

margen ['marxen] *nm* (*borde*) edge, border; (*fig*) margin, space ♦ *nf* (*de río etc*) bank; **dar ~ para** to give an opportunity for; **mantenerse al ~** to keep out (of things)

marginar [marxi'nar] *vt* (*grupo, individuo: socialmente*) to marginalize, ostracize

marica [ma'rika] (*fam*) *nm* sissy

maricón [mari'kon] (*fam*) *nm* queer

marido [ma'riðo] *nm* husband

mariguana [mari'ɣwana], **marihuana** [mari'wana] *nf* marijuana, cannabis

marina [ma'rina] *nf* navy; ~ **mercante** merchant navy

marinero, a [mari'nero, a] *adj* sea *cpd*; (*barco*) seaworthy ♦ *nm* sailor, seaman

marino, a [ma'rino, a] *adj* sea *cpd*, marine ♦ *nm* sailor

marioneta [marjo'neta] *nf* puppet

mariposa [mari'posa] *nf* butterfly

mariquita [mari'kita] *nf* ladybird (*BRIT*), ladybug (*US*)

mariscos [ma'riskos] *nmpl* shellfish *inv*, seafood(s)

marítimo, a [ma'ritimo, a] *adj* sea *cpd*, maritime

mármol ['marmol] *nm* marble

marqués, esa [mar'kes, esa] *nm/f* marquis/marchioness

marrón [ma'rron] *adj* brown

marroquí [marro'ki] *adj, nm/f* Moroccan ♦ *nm* Morocco (leather)

Marruecos [ma'rrwekos] *nm* Morocco

martes ['martes] *nm inv* Tuesday

martillo [mar'tiʎo] *nm* hammer; ~ **neumático** pneumatic drill (*BRIT*), jackhammer

mártir ['martir] *nm/f* martyr; **martirio** *nm* martyrdom; (*fig*) torture, torment

Marxismo [mark'sismo] *nm* Marxism; **marxista** *adj, nm/f* Marxist

marzo ['marθo] *nm* March

┌─────────────────────┐
│ **PALABRA CLAVE** │
└─────────────────────┘

más [mas] *adj, adv* **1**: ~ **(que, de)** (*compar*) more (than), ...+ er (than); ~ **grande/inteligente** bigger/more intelligent; **trabaja ~ (que yo)** he works more (than me); *ver tb* **cada**

2 (*superl*): **el ~** the most, ...+ est; **el ~ grande/inteligente (de)** the biggest/most intelligent (in)

3 (*negativo*): **no tengo ~ dinero** I haven't got any more money; **no viene ~ por aquí** he doesn't come round here any more

4 (*adicional*): **no le veo ~ solución que ...** I see no other solution than to ...; **¿quién ~?** anybody else?

5 (+ *adj: valor intensivo*): **¡qué perro ~ sucio!** what a filthy dog!; **¡es ~ tonto!** he's so stupid!

6 (*locuciones*): ~ **o menos** more or less; **los ~** most people; **es ~** furthermore; ~ **bien** rather; **¡qué ~ da!** what does it matter!; *ver tb* **no**

7: **por ~**: **por ~ que te esfuerces** no matter how hard you try; **por ~ que quisiera ...** much as I should like to ...

8: **de ~**: **veo que aquí estoy de ~** I can see I'm not needed here; **tenemos uno de ~** we've got one extra

♦ *prep*: **2 ~ 2 son 4** 2 and *o* plus 2 are 4

♦ *nm inv*: **este trabajo tiene sus ~ y sus menos** this job's got its good points and its bad points

mas [mas] *conj* but

masa ['masa] *nf* (*mezcla*) dough; (*volumen*) volume, mass; (*FÍSICA*) mass; **en ~** en masse; **las ~s** (*POL*) the masses

masacre [ma'sakre] *nf* massacre

masaje [ma'saxe] *nm* massage

máscara ['maskara] *nf* (*gen*) mask ♦ *nm/f* masked person; **mascarilla** *nf* (*de belleza, MED*) mask

masculino, a [masku'lino, a] *adj* masculine; (*BIO*) male

masificación [masifika'θjon] *nf* overcrowding

masivo, a [ma'siβo, a] *adj (en masa)* mass

masón [ma'son] *nm* (free)mason

masoquista [maso'kista] *nm/f* masochist

masticar [masti'kar] *vt* to chew; *(fig)* to ponder

mástil ['mastil] *nm (de navío)* mast; *(de guitarra)* neck

mastín [mas'tin] *nm* mastiff

masturbación [masturβa'θjon] *nf* masturbation

masturbarse [mastur'βarse] *vr* to masturbate

mata ['mata] *nf (arbusto)* bush, shrub; *(de hierba)* tuft

matadero [mata'ðero] *nm* slaughter-house, abattoir

matador, a [mata'ðor, a] *adj* killing ♦ *nm/f* killer ♦ *nm (TAUR)* matador, bullfighter

matamoscas [mata'moskas] *nm inv (palo)* fly swat

matanza [ma'tanθa] *nf* slaughter

matar [ma'tar] *vt*, *vi* to kill; **~se** *vr (suicidarse)* to kill o.s., commit suicide; *(morir)* to be o get killed; **~ el hambre** to stave off hunger

matasellos [mata'seʎos] *nm inv* postmark

mate ['mate] *adj (sin brillo: color)* dull, matt ♦ *nm (en ajedrez)* (check)mate; *(AM: hierba)* maté; *(: vasija)* gourd

matemáticas [mate'matikas] *nfpl* mathematics; **matemático, a** *adj* mathematical ♦ *nm/f* mathematician

materia [ma'terja] *nf (gen)* matter; *(TEC)* material; *(ESCOL)* subject; **en ~ de** on the subject of; **~ prima** raw material; **material** *adj* material; *(dolor)* physical ♦ *nm* material; *(TEC)* equipment; **materialismo** *nm* materialism; **materialista** *adj* materialist(ic); **materialmente** *adv* materially; *(fig)* absolutely

maternal [mater'nal] *adj* motherly, maternal

maternidad [materni'ðað] *nf* motherhood, maternity; **materno, a** *adj* maternal; *(lengua)* mother *cpd*

matinal [mati'nal] *adj* morning *cpd*

matiz [ma'tiθ] *nm* shade; **~ar** *vt (variar)* to vary; *(ARTE)* to blend; **~ar de** to tinge with

matón [ma'ton] *nm* bully

matorral [mato'rral] *nm* thicket

matraca [ma'traka] *nf* rattle

matrícula [ma'trikula] *nf (registro)* register; *(AUTO)* registration number; *(: placa)* number plate; **matricular** *vt* to register, enrol

matrimonial [matrimo'njal] *adj* matrimonial

matrimonio [matri'monjo] *nm (pareja)* (married) couple; *(unión)* marriage

matriz [ma'triθ] *nf (ANAT)* womb; *(TEC)* mould; **casa ~** *(COM)* head office

matrona [ma'trona] *nf (persona de edad)* matron

maullar [mau'ʎar] *vi* to mew, miaow

maxilar [maksi'lar] *nm* jaw(bone)

máxima ['maksima] *nf* maxim

máxime ['maksime] *adv* especially

máximo, a ['maksimo, a] *adj* maximum; *(más alto)* highest; *(más grande)* greatest ♦ *nm* maximum

mayo ['majo] *nm* May

mayonesa [majo'nesa] *nf* mayonnaise

mayor [ma'jor] *adj* main, chief; *(adulto)* adult; *(de edad avanzada)* elderly; *(MUS)* major; *(compar: de tamaño)* bigger; *(: de edad)* older; *(superl: de tamaño)* biggest; *(: de edad)* oldest ♦ *nm* chief, boss; *(adulto)* adult; **al por ~** wholesale; **~ de edad** adult; **~es** *nmpl (antepasados)* ancestors

mayoral [majo'ral] *nm* foreman

mayordomo [major'ðomo] *nm* butler

mayoría [majo'ria] *nf* majority, greater part

mayorista [majo'rista] *nm/f* wholesaler

mayoritario, a [majori'tarjo, a] *adj* majority *cpd*

mayúscula [ma'juskula] *nf* capital letter

mayúsculo, a [ma'juskulo, a] *adj (fig)* big, tremendous

mazapán [maθa'pan] *nm* marzipan

mazo ['maθo] *nm (martillo)* mallet; *(de flores)* bunch; *(DEPORTE)* bat

me [me] *pron (directo)* me; *(indirecto)* (to)

me; *(reflexivo)* (to) myself; **¡dámelo!** give it to me!

mear [me'ar] *(fam)* *vi* to pee, piss *(!)*

mecánica [me'kanika] *nf (ESCOL)* mechanics *sg; (mecanismo)* mechanism; *ver tb* **mecánico**

mecánico, a [me'kaniko, a] *adj* mechanical ♦ *nm/f* mechanic

mecanismo [meka'nismo] *nm* mechanism; *(marcha)* gear

mecanografía [mekanoɣra'fia] *nf* typewriting; **mecanógrafo, a** *nm/f* typist

mecate [me'kate] *(AM) nm* rope

mecedora [meθe'ðora] *nf* rocking chair

mecer [me'θer] *vt (cuna)* to rock; **~se** *vr* to rock; *(ramo)* to sway

mecha ['metʃa] *nf (de vela)* wick; *(de bomba)* fuse

mechero [me'tʃero] *nm* (cigarette) lighter

mechón [me'tʃon] *nm (gen)* tuft; *(manojo)* bundle; *(de pelo)* lock

medalla [me'ðaʎa] *nf* medal

media [me'ðja] *nf (ESP)* stocking; *(AM)* sock; *(promedio)* average

mediado, a [me'ðjaðo, a] *adj* half-full; *(trabajo)* half-completed; **a ~s de** in the middle of, halfway through

mediano, a [me'ðjano, a] *adj (regular)* medium, average; *(mediocre)* mediocre

medianoche [meðja'notʃe] *nf* midnight

mediante [me'ðjante] *adv* by (means of), through

mediar [me'ðjar] *vi (interceder)* to mediate, intervene

medicación [meðika'θjon] *nf* medication, treatment

medicamento [meðika'mento] *nm* medicine, drug

medicina [meði'θina] *nf* medicine

medición [meði'θjon] *nf* measurement

médico, a ['meðiko, a] *adj* medical ♦ *nm/f* doctor

medida [me'ðiða] *nf* measure; *(medición)* measurement; *(prudencia)* moderation, prudence; **en cierta/gran ~** up to a point/to a great extent; **un traje a la ~** made-to-measure suit; **~ de cuello** collar size; **a ~ de** in proportion to; *(de acuerdo con)* in keeping with; **a ~ que** *(conforme)*

as

medio, a ['meðjo, a] *adj* half (a); *(punto)* mid, middle; *(promedio)* average ♦ *adv* half ♦ *nm (centro)* middle, centre; *(promedio)* average; *(método)* means, way; *(ambiente)* environment; **~s** *nmpl* means, resources; **~ litro** half a litre; **las tres y media** half past three; **medio ambiente** environment; **M~ Oriente** Middle East; **a ~ terminar** half finished; **pagar a medias** to share the cost; **~ambiental** *adj (política, efectos)* environmental

mediocre [me'ðjokre] *adj* middling, average; *(pey)* mediocre

mediodía [meðjo'ðia] *nm* midday, noon

medir [me'ðir] *vt, vi (gen)* to measure

meditar [meði'tar] *vt* to ponder, think over, meditate on; *(planear)* to think out

mediterráneo, a [meðite'rraneo, a] *adj* Mediterranean ♦ *nm:* **el M~** the Mediterranean (Sea)

médula ['meðula] *nf (ANAT)* marrow; **~ espinal** spinal cord

medusa [me'ðusa] *(ESP) nf* jellyfish

megafonía [meɣafo'nia] *nf* public address system, PA system; **megáfono** *nm* megaphone

megalómano, a [meɣa'lomano, a] *nm/f* megalomaniac

mejicano, a [mexi'kano, a] *adj, nm/f* Mexican

Méjico ['mexiko] *nm* Mexico

mejilla [me'xiʎa] *nf* cheek

mejillón [mexi'ʎon] *nm* mussel

mejor [me'xor] *adj, adv (compar)* better; *(superl)* best; **a lo ~** probably; *(quizá)* maybe; **~ dicho** rather; **tanto ~** so much the better

mejora [me'xora] *nf* improvement; **mejorar** *vt* to improve, make better ♦ *vi* to improve, get better; **mejorarse** *vr* to improve, get better

melancólico, a [melan'koliko, a] *adj (triste)* sad, melancholy; *(soñador)* dreamy

melena [me'lena] *nf (de persona)* long hair; *(ZOOL)* mane

mellizo, a [me'ʎiθo, a] *adj, nm/f* twin; **~s**

nmpl (*AM*) cufflinks

melocotón [meloko'ton] (*ESP*) *nm* peach

melodía [melo'ðia] *nf* melody, tune

melodrama [melo'ðrama] *nm* melodrama; **melodramático, a** *adj* melodramatic

melón [me'lon] *nm* melon

membrete [mem'brete] *nm* letterhead

membrillo [mem'briʎo] *nm* quince; **carne de ~** quince jelly

memorable [memo'raßle] *adj* memorable

memorándum [memo'randum] (*pl* ~**s**) *nm* (*libro*) notebook; (*comunicación*) memorandum

memoria [me'morja] *nf* (*gen*) memory; ~**s** *nfpl* (*de autor*) memoirs; ~ **intermedia** (*INFORM*) buffer; **memorizar** *vt* to memorize

menaje [me'naxe] *nm*: ~ **de cocina** kitchenware

mencionar [menθjo'nar] *vt* to mention

mendigar [mendi'var] *vt* to beg (for)

mendigo, a [men'diɣo, a] *nm/f* beggar

mendrugo [men'druɣo] *nm* crust

menear [mene'ar] *vt* to move; (*fig*) to handle; ~**se** *vr* to shake; (*balancearse*) to sway; (*moverse*) to move; (*fig*) to get a move on

menester [menes'ter] *nm* (*necesidad*) necessity; ~**es** *nmpl* (*deberes*) duties; **es ~** it is necessary

menestra [me'nestra] *nf*: ~ **de verduras** vegetable stew

menguante [men'gwante] *adj* decreasing, diminishing

menguar [men'gwar] *vt* to lessen, diminish; (*fig*) to discredit ♦ *vi* to diminish, decrease; (*fig*) to decline

menopausia [meno'pausja] *nf* menopause

menor [me'nor] *adj* (*más pequeño*: *compar*) smaller; (: *superl*) smallest; (*más joven*: *compar*) younger; (: *superl*) youngest; (*MUS*) minor ♦ *nm/f* (*joven*) young person, juvenile; **no tengo la ~ idea** I haven't the faintest idea; **al por ~** retail; ~ **de edad** person under age

Menorca [me'norka] *nf* Minorca

PALABRA CLAVE

menos [menos] *adj* 1: ~ **(que, de)**

(*compar*: *cantidad*) less (than); (: *número*) fewer (than); **con ~ entusiasmo** with less enthusiasm; ~ **gente** fewer people; *ver tb* **cada**

2 (*superl*): **es el que ~ culpa tiene** he is the least to blame

♦ *adv* 1 (*compar*): ~ **(que, de)** less (than); **me gusta ~ que el otro** I like it less than the other one

2 (*superl*): **es el ~ listo (de su clase)** he's the least bright in his class; **de todas ellas es la que ~ me agrada** out of all of them she's the one I like least; **(por) lo ~** at (the very) least

3 (*locuciones*): **no quiero verle y ~ visitarle** I don't want to see him let alone visit him; **tenemos 7 de ~** we're seven short

♦ *prep* except; (*cifras*) minus; **todos ~ él** everyone except (for) him; **5 ~ 2** 5 minus 2

♦ *conj*: **a ~ que: a ~ que venga mañana** unless he comes tomorrow

---

menospreciar [menospre'θjar] *vt* to underrate, undervalue; (*despreciar*) to scorn, despise

mensaje [men'saxe] *nm* message; ~**ro, a** *nm/f* messenger

menstruación [menstrua'θjon] *nf* menstruation

menstruar [mens'trwar] *vi* to menstruate

mensual [men'swal] *adj* monthly; **1000 ptas ~es** 1000 ptas a month; ~**idad** *nf* (*salario*) monthly salary; (*COM*) monthly payment, monthly instalment

menta ['menta] *nf* mint

mental [men'tal] *adj* mental; ~**idad** *nf* mentality; ~**izar** *vt* (*sensibilizar*) to make aware; (*convencer*) to convince; (*padres*) to prepare (mentally); ~**izarse** *vr* (*concienciarse*) to become aware; ~**izarse (de)** to get used to the idea (of); ~**izarse de que ...** (*convencerse*) to get it into one's head that ...

mentar [men'tar] *vt* to mention, name

mente ['mente] *nf* mind

mentir [men'tir] *vi* to lie

mentira [men'tira] *nf* (*una ~*) lie; (*acto*)

lying; (*invención*) fiction; **parece ~ que ...** it seems incredible that ..., I can't believe that ...

mentiroso, a [menti'roso, a] *adj* lying ♦ *nm/f* liar

menú [me'nu] (*pl* ~**s**) *nm* menu; (*AM*) set meal

menudo, a [me'nuðo, a] *adj* (*pequeño*) small, tiny; (*sin importancia*) petty, insignificant; **¡~ negocio!** (*fam*) some deal!; **a ~** often, frequently

meñique [me'ɲike] *nm* little finger

meollo [me'oʎo] *nm* (*fig*) core

mercaderías [merkaðe'rias] *nfpl* goods, merchandise *sg*

mercado [mer'kaðo] *nm* market; **M~ Común** Common Market

mercancía [merkan'θia] *nf* commodity; ~**s** *nfpl* goods, merchandise *sg*

mercantil [merkan'til] *adj* mercantile, commercial

mercenario, a [merθe'narjo, a] *adj, nm* mercenary

mercería [merθe'ria] *nf* haberdashery (*BRIT*), notions (*US*); (*tienda*) haberdasher's (*BRIT*), notions store (*US*); (*AM*) drapery

mercurio [mer'kurjo] *nm* mercury

merecer [mere'θer] *vt* to deserve, merit ♦ *vi* to be deserving, be worthy; **merece la pena** it's worthwhile; **merecido, a** *adj* (well) deserved; **llevar su merecido** to get one's deserts

merendar [meren'dar] *vt* to have for tea ♦ *vi* to have tea; (*en el campo*) to have a picnic

merengue [me'renge] *nm* meringue

meridiano [meri'ðjano] *nm* (*GEO*) meridian

merienda [me'rjenda] *nf* (light) tea, afternoon snack; (*de campo*) picnic

mérito ['merito] *nm* merit; (*valor*) worth, value

merluza [mer'luθa] *nf* hake

merma ['merma] *nf* decrease; (*pérdida*) wastage; **mermar** *vt* to reduce, lessen ♦ *vi* to decrease, dwindle

mermelada [merme'laða] *nf* jam

mero, a ['mero, a] *adj* mere; (*AM: fam*) very

merodear [meroðe'ar] *vi*: **~ por** to prowl about

mes [mes] *nm* month; (*salario*) month's pay

mesa ['mesa] *nf* table; (*de trabajo*) desk; (*GEO*) plateau; (*ARQ*) landing; **~ directiva** board; **~ redonda** (*reunión*) round table; **poner/quitar la ~** to lay/clear the table; **mesero, a** (*AM*) *nm/f* waiter/waitress

meseta [me'seta] *nf* (*GEO*) meseta, tableland; (*ARQ*) landing

mesilla [me'siʎa] *nf*: **~ (de noche)** bedside table

mesón [me'son] *nm* inn

mestizo, a [mes'tiθo, a] *adj* half-caste, of mixed race; (*ZOOL*) crossbred ♦ *nm/f* half-caste

mesura [me'sura] *nf* (*moderación*) moderation, restraint; (*cortesía*) courtesy

meta ['meta] *nf* goal; (*de carrera*) finish

metabolismo [metaβo'lismo] *nm* (*BIO*) metabolism

metáfora [me'tafora] *nf* metaphor

metal [me'tal] *nm* (*materia*) metal; (*MUS*) brass; **metálico, a** *adj* metallic; (*de metal*) metal ♦ *nm* (*dinero contante*) cash

metalurgia [meta'lurxja] *nf* metallurgy

meteoro [mete'oro] *nm* meteor; ~**logía** *nf* meteorology

meter [me'ter] *vt* (*colocar*) to put, place; (*introducir*) to put in, insert; (*involucrar*) to involve; (*causar*) to make, cause; ~**se** *vr*: ~**se en** to go into, enter; (*fig*) to interfere in, meddle in; ~**se a** to start; ~**se a escritor** to become a writer; ~**se con uno** to provoke sb, pick a quarrel with sb

meticuloso, a [metiku'loso, a] *adj* meticulous, thorough

metódico, a [me'toðiko, a] *adj* methodical

método ['metoðo] *nm* method

metralleta [metra'ʎeta] *nf* sub-machine-gun

métrico, a ['metriko, a] *adj* metric

metro ['metro] *nm* metre; (*tren*) underground (*BRIT*), subway (*US*)

México ['mexiko] *nm* Mexico; **Ciudad de ~** Mexico City

mezcla ['meθkla] *nf* mixture; **mezclar** *vt* to mix (up); **mezclarse** *vr* to mix, mingle; **mezclarse en** to get mixed up in, get involved in

mezquino, a [meθ'kino, a] *adj (cicatero)* mean

mezquita [meθ'kita] *nf* mosque

mg. *abr* (= *miligramo*) mg

mi [mi] *adj pos* my ♦ *nm* (MUS) E

mí [mi] *pron* me; myself

mía ['mia] *pron ver* **mío**

miaja ['mjaxa] *nf* crumb

michelín [mitʃe'lin] *(fam) nm (de grasa)* spare tyre

micro ['mikro] (AM) *nm* minibus

microbio [mi'kroβjo] *nm* microbe

micrófono [mi'krofono] *nm* microphone

microondas [mikro'ondas] *nm inv (tb: horno ~)* microwave (oven)

microordenador [mikro(o)rðena'ðor] *nm* microcomputer

microscopio [mikro'skopjo] *nm* microscope

miedo ['mjeðo] *nm* fear; *(nerviosismo)* apprehension, nervousness; **tener ~** to be afraid; **de ~** wonderful, marvellous; **hace un frío de ~** *(fam)* it's terribly cold; **~so, a** *adj* fearful, timid

miel [mjel] *nf* honey

miembro ['mjembro] *nm* limb; *(socio)* member; **~ viril** penis

mientras ['mjentras] *conj* while; *(duración)* as long as ♦ *adv* meanwhile; **~ tanto** meanwhile; **~ más tiene, más quiere** the more he has, the more he wants

miércoles ['mjerkoles] *nm inv* Wednesday

mierda ['mjerða] *(fam!) nf* shit (!)

miga ['miɣa] *nf* crumb; *(fig: meollo)* essence; **hacer buenas ~s** *(fam)* to get on well

migración [miɣra'θjon] *nf* migration

mil [mil] *num* thousand; **dos ~ libras** two thousand pounds

milagro [mi'laɣro] *nm* miracle; **~so, a** *adj* miraculous

milésima [mi'lesima] *nf (de segundo)* thousandth

mili ['mili] *(fam) nf*: **hacer la ~** to do

one's military service

milicia [mi'liθja] *nf* militia; *(servicio militar)* military service

milímetro [mi'limetro] *nm* millimetre

militante [mili'tante] *adj* militant

militar [mili'tar] *adj* military ♦ *nm/f* soldier ♦ *vi* to serve in the army; *(fig)* to be a member of a party

milla ['miʎa] *nf* mile

millar [mi'ʎar] *nm* thousand

millón [mi'ʎon] *num* million; **millonario, a** *nm/f* millionaire

mimar [mi'mar] *vt (gen)* to spoil, pamper

mimbre ['mimbre] *nm* wicker

mímica ['mimika] *nf (para comunicarse)* sign language; *(imitación)* mimicry

mimo ['mimo] *nm (caricia)* caress; *(de niño)* spoiling; *(TEATRO)* mime; *(: actor)* mime artist

mina ['mina] *nf* mine; **minar** *vt* to mine; *(fig)* to undermine

mineral [mine'ral] *adj* mineral ♦ *nm* (GEO) mineral; *(mena)* ore

minero, a [mi'nero, a] *adj* mining *cpd* ♦ *nm/f* miner

miniatura [minja'tura] *adj inv, nf* miniature

minifalda [mini'falda] *nf* miniskirt

mínimo, a ['minimo, a] *adj, nm* minimum

minino, a [mi'nino, a] *(fam) nm/f* puss, pussy

ministerio [minis'terjo] *nm* Ministry; **M~ de Hacienda/del Exterior** Treasury (BRIT), Treasury Department (US)/Foreign Office (BRIT), State Department (US)

ministro, a [mi'nistro, a] *nm/f* minister

minoría [mino'ria] *nf* minority

minucioso, a [minu'θjoso, a] *adj* thorough, meticulous; *(prolijo)* very detailed

minúscula [mi'nuskula] *nf* small letter

minúsculo, a [mi'nuskulo, a] *adj* tiny, minute

minusválido, a [minus'βaliðo, a] *adj* (physically) handicapped ♦ *nm/f* (physically) handicapped person

minuta [mi'nuta] *nf (de comida)* menu

minutero [minu'tero] *nm* minute hand

minuto [mi'nuto] *nm* minute

mío, a ['mio, a] *pron*: **el ~/la mía** mine; **un amigo ~** a friend of mine; **lo ~** what is mine

miope [mi'ope] *adj* short-sighted

mira ['mira] *nf* (*de arma*) sight(s) (*pl*); (*fig*) aim, intention

mirada [mi'raða] *nf* look, glance; (*expresión*) look, expression; **clavar la ~ en** to stare at; **echar una ~ a** to glance at

mirado, a [mi'raðo, a] *adj* (*sensato*) sensible; (*considerado*) considerate; **bien/mal ~** well/not well thought of; **bien ~** all things considered

mirador [mira'ðor] *nm* viewpoint, vantage point

mirar [mi'rar] *vt* to look at; (*observar*) to watch; (*considerar*) to consider, think over; (*vigilar, cuidar*) to watch, look after ♦ *vi* to look; (*ARQ*) to face; **~se** *vr* (*dos personas*) to look at each other; **~ bien/mal** to think highly of/have a poor opinion of; **~se al espejo** to look at o.s. in the mirror

mirilla [mi'riʎa] *nf* (*agujero*) spyhole, peephole

mirlo ['mirlo] *nm* blackbird

misa ['misa] *nf* (*REL*) mass

miserable [mise'raßle] *adj* (*avaro*) mean, stingy; (*nimio*) miserable, paltry; (*lugar*) squalid; (*fam*) vile, despicable ♦ *nm/f* (*malvado*) rogue

miseria [mi'serja] *nf* misery; (*pobreza*) poverty; (*tacañería*) meanness, stinginess; (*condiciones*) squalor; **una ~** a pittance

misericordia [miseri'korðja] *nf* (*compasión*) compassion, pity; (*piedad*) mercy

misil [mi'sil] *nm* missile

misión [mi'sjon] *nf* mission; **misionero, a** *nm/f* missionary

mismo, a ['mismo, a] *adj* (*semejante*) same; (*después de pron*) -self; (*para énfasis*) very ♦ *adv*: **aquí/hoy ~** right here/this very day; **ahora ~** right now ♦ *conj*: **lo ~ que** just like, just as; **el ~ traje** the same suit; **en ese ~ momento** at that very moment; **vino el ~ Ministro** the minister himself came; **yo ~ lo vi** I saw it myself; **lo ~ ~** the same (thing); **da lo ~** it's all the same; **quedamos en las mismas** we're no further forward; **por lo ~** for the same reason

misterio [mis'terjo] *nm* (*gen*) mystery; (*lo secreto*) secrecy; **~so, a** *adj* mysterious

mitad [mi'tað] *nf* (*medio*) half; (*centro*) middle; **a ~ de precio** (at) half-price; **en o a ~ del camino** halfway along the road; **cortar por la ~** to cut through the middle

mitigar [miti'ɣar] *vt* to mitigate; (*dolor*) to ease; (*sed*) to quench

mitin ['mitin] (*pl* **mítines**) *nm* meeting

mito ['mito] *nm* myth

mixto, a ['miksto, a] *adj* mixed

ml. *abr* (= *mililitro*) ml

mm. *abr* (= *milímetro*) mm

mobiliario [moßi'ljarjo] *nm* furniture

mochila [mo'tʃila] *nf* rucksack (*BRIT*), back-pack

moción [mo'θjon] *nf* motion

moco ['moko] *nm* mucus; **~s** *nmpl* (*fam*) snot; **quitarse los ~s de la nariz** (*fam*) to wipe one's nose

moda ['moða] *nf* fashion; (*estilo*) style; **a la o de ~** in fashion, fashionable; **pasado de ~** out of fashion

modales [mo'ðales] *nmpl* manners

modalidad [moðali'ðað] *nf* kind, variety

modelar [moðe'lar] *vt* to model

modelo [mo'ðelo] *adj inv, nm/f* model

módem ['moðem] *nm* (*INFORM*) modem

moderado, a [moðe'raðo, a] *adj* moderate

moderar [moðe'rar] *vt* to moderate; (*violencia*) to restrain, control; (*velocidad*) to reduce; **~se** *vr* to restrain o.s., control o.s.

modernizar [moðerni'θar] *vt* to modernize

moderno, a [mo'ðerno, a] *adj* modern; (*actual*) present-day

modestia [mo'ðestja] *nf* modesty; **modesto, a** *adj* modest

módico, a ['moðiko, a] *adj* moderate, reasonable

modificar [moðifi'kar] *vt* to modify

modisto, a [mo'ðisto, a] *nm/f* dressmaker

modo ['moðo] *nm* (*manera, forma*) way, manner; (*MUS*) mode; **~s** *nmpl* manners; **de ningún ~** in no way; **de todos ~s** at any rate; **~ de empleo** directions *pl* (for use)

modorra [mo'ðorra] *nf* drowsiness

mofa ['mofa] *nf*: **hacer ~ de** to mock; **mofarse** *vr*: **mofarse de** to mock, scoff at

mogollón [moɣo'ʎon] (*fam*) *adv* (*gustar, beber*) a hell of a lot

moho ['moo] *nm* (*BOT*) mould, mildew; (*en metal*) rust; **~so, a** *adj* mouldy; rusty

mojar [mo'xar] *vt* to wet; (*humedecer*) to damp(en), moisten; (*calar*) to soak; **~se** *vr* to get wet

mojón [mo'xon] *nm* boundary stone

molde ['molde] *nm* mould; (*COSTURA*) pattern; (*fig*) model; **~ar** *vt* to mould

mole ['mole] *nf* mass, bulk; (*edificio*) pile

moler [mo'ler] *vt* to grind, crush; (*cansar*) to tire out, exhaust

molestar [moles'tar] *vt* to bother; (*fastidiar*) to annoy; (*incomodar*) to inconvenience, put out ♦ *vi* to be a nuisance; **~se** *vr* to bother; (*incomodarse*) to go to trouble; (*ofenderse*) to take offence

molestia [mo'lestja] *nf* bother, trouble; (*incomodidad*) inconvenience; (*MED*) discomfort; **es una ~** it's a nuisance; **molesto, a** *adj* (*que fastidia*) annoying; (*incómodo*) inconvenient; (*inquieto*) uncomfortable, ill at ease; (*enfadado*) annoyed

molido, a [mo'liðo, a] *adj*: **estar ~** (*fig*) to be exhausted *o* dead beat

molinillo [moli'niʎo] *nm*: **~ de carne/café** mincer/coffee grinder

molino [mo'lino] *nm* (*edificio*) mill; (*máquina*) grinder

momentáneo, a [momen'taneo, a] *adj* momentary

momento [mo'mento] *nm* (*gen*) moment; (*TEC*) momentum; **de ~** at the moment, for the moment

momia ['momja] *nf* mummy

monarca [mo'narka] *nm/f* monarch, ruler; **monarquía** *nf* monarchy; **monárquico, a** *nm/f* royalist, monarchist

monasterio [monas'terjo] *nm* monastery

mondar [mon'dar] *vt* (*limpiar*) to clean; (*pelar*) to peel; **~se** *vr*: **~se de risa** (*fam*) to split one's sides laughing

moneda [mo'neða] *nf* (*tipo de dinero*) currency, money; (*pieza*) coin; **una ~ de 5 pesetas** a 5 peseta piece; **monedero** *nm* purse; **monetario, a** *adj* monetary, financial

monitor, a [moni'tor, a] *nm/f* instructor, coach ♦ *nm* (*TV*) set; (*INFORM*) monitor

monja ['monxa] *nf* nun

monje ['monxe] *nm* monk

mono, a ['mono, a] *adj* (*bonito*) lovely, pretty; (*gracioso*) nice, charming ♦ *nm/f* monkey, ape ♦ *nm* dungarees *pl*; (*overoles*) overalls *pl*

monopatín [monopa'tin] *nm* skateboard

monopolio [mono'poljo] *nm* monopoly; **monopolizar** *vt* to monopolize

monotonía [monoto'nia] *nf* (*sonido*) monotone; (*fig*) monotony

monótono, a [mo'notono, a] *adj* monotonous

monstruo ['monstrwo] *nm* monster ♦ *adj inv* fantastic; **~so, a** *adj* monstrous

montaje [mon'taxe] *nm* assembly; (*TEATRO*) décor; (*CINE*) montage

montaña [mon'taɲa] *nf* (*monte*) mountain; (*sierra*) mountains *pl*, mountainous area; (*AM: selva*) forest; **~ rusa** roller coaster; **montañero, a** *nm/f* mountaineer; **montañés, esa** *nm/f* highlander; **montañismo** *nm* mountaineering

montar [mon'tar] *vt* (*subir a*) to mount, get on; (*TEC*) to assemble, put together; (*negocio*) to set up; (*arma*) to cock; (*colocar*) to lift on to; (*CULIN*) to beat ♦ *vi* to mount, get on; (*sobresalir*) to overlap; **~ en cólera** to get angry; **~ a caballo** to ride, go horseriding

monte ['monte] *nm* (*montaña*) mountain; (*bosque*) woodland; (*área sin cultivar*) wild area, wild country; **M~ de Piedad** pawnshop

monto ['monto] *nm* total, amount

montón [mon'ton] *nm* heap, pile; (*fig*): **un ~ de** heaps of, lots of

monumento [monu'mento] *nm* monument

moño ['moɲo] *nm* bun

monzón [mon'θon] *nm* monsoon

moqueta [mo'keta] *nf* fitted carpet

mora ['mora] *nf* blackberry; *ver tb* **moro**

morada [mo'raða] *nf* (*casa*) dwelling, abode

morado, a [mo'raðo, a] *adj* purple, violet ♦ *nm* bruise

moral [mo'ral] *adj* moral ♦ *nf* (*ética*) ethics *pl*; (*moralidad*) morals *pl*, morality; (*ánimo*) morale

moraleja [mora'lexa] *nf* moral

moralidad [morali'ðað] *nf* morals *pl*, morality

morboso, a [mor'βoso, a] *adj* morbid

morcilla [mor'θiʎa] *nf* blood sausage, ≈ black pudding (*BRIT*)

mordaz [mor'ðaθ] *adj* (*crítica*) biting, scathing

mordaza [mor'ðaθa] *nf* (*para la boca*) gag; (*TEC*) clamp

morder [mor'ðer] *vt* to bite; (*mordisquear*) to nibble; (*fig: consumir*) to eat away, eat into; **mordisco** *nm* bite

moreno, a [mo'reno, a] *adj* (*color*) (dark) brown; (*de tez*) dark; (*de pelo ~*) dark-haired; (*negro*) black

morfina [mor'fina] *nf* morphine

moribundo, a [mori'βundo, a] *adj* dying

morir [mo'rir] *vi* to die; (*fuego*) to die down; (*luz*) to go out; **~se** *vr* to die; (*fig*) to be dying; **fue muerto en un accidente** he was killed in an accident; **~se por algo** to be dying for sth

moro, a ['moro, a] *adj* Moorish ♦ *nm/f* Moor

moroso, a [mo'roso, a] *nm/f* (*COM*) bad debtor, defaulter

morral [mo'rral] *nm* haversack

morro ['morro] *nm* (*ZOOL*) snout, nose; (*AUTO, AVIAT*) nose

morsa ['morsa] *nf* walrus

mortaja [mor'taxa] *nf* shroud

mortal [mor'tal] *adj* mortal; (*golpe*) deadly; **~idad** *nf* mortality

mortero [mor'tero] *nm* mortar

mortífero, a [mor'tifero, a] *adj* deadly, lethal

mortificar [mortifi'kar] *vt* to mortify

mosca ['moska] *nf* fly

Moscú [mos'ku] *n* Moscow

mosquearse [moske'arse] (*fam*) *vr* (*enojarse*) to get cross; (*ofenderse*) to take offence

mosquitero [moski'tero] *nm* mosquito net

mosquito [mos'kito] *nm* mosquito

mostaza [mos'taθa] *nf* mustard

mostrador [mostra'ðor] *nm* (*de tienda*) counter; (*de café*) bar

mostrar [mos'trar] *vt* to show; (*exhibir*) to display, exhibit; (*explicar*) to explain; **~se** *vr*: **~se amable** to be kind; to prove to be kind; **no se muestra muy inteligente** he doesn't seem (to be) very intelligent

mota ['mota] *nf* speck, tiny piece; (*en diseño*) dot

mote ['mote] *nm* (*apodo*) nickname

motín [mo'tin] *nm* (*del pueblo*) revolt, rising; (*del ejército*) mutiny

motivar [moti'βar] *vt* (*causar*) to cause, motivate; (*explicar*) to explain, justify; **motivo** *nm* motive, reason

moto ['moto] (*fam*) *nf* = **motocicleta**

motocicleta [motoθi'kleta] *nf* motorbike (*BRIT*), motorcycle

motor [mo'tor] *nm* motor, engine; **~ a chorro** *o* **de reacción/de explosión** jet engine/internal combustion engine

motora [mo'tora] *nf* motorboat

movedizo, a [moβe'ðiθo, a] *adj* (*inseguro*) unsteady; (*fig*) unsettled, changeable; (*persona*) fickle

mover [mo'βer] *vt* to move; (*cabeza*) to shake; (*accionar*) to drive; (*fig*) to cause, provoke; **~se** *vr* to move; (*fig*) to get a move on

móvil ['moβil] *adj* mobile; (*pieza de máquina*) moving; (*mueble*) movable ♦ *nm* motive; **movilidad** *nf* mobility;

movilizar *vt* to mobilize

movimiento [moßi'mjento] *nm* movement; (*TEC*) motion; (*actividad*) activity

mozo, a ['moθo, a] *adj* (*joven*) young ♦ *nm/f* (*joven*) youth, young man/girl; (*camarero*) waiter; (*camarera*) waitress

muchacho, a [mu'tʃatʃo, a] *nm/f* (*niño*) boy/girl; (*criado*) servant; (*criada*) maid

muchedumbre [mutʃe'ðumbre] *nf* crowd

PALABRA CLAVE
---

mucho, a ['mutʃo, a] *adj* 1 (*cantidad*) a lot of, much; (*número*) lots of, a lot of, many; ~ **dinero** a lot of money; **hace** ~ **calor** it's very hot; **muchas amigas** lots *o* a lot of friends

2 (*sg: grande*): **ésta es mucha casa para él** this house is much too big for him ♦ *pron*: **tengo** ~ **que hacer** I've got a lot to do; ~**s dicen que ...** a lot of people say that ...; *ver tb* **tener**

♦ *adv* 1: **me gusta** ~ I like it a lot; **lo siento** ~ I'm very sorry; **come** ~ he eats a lot; **¿te vas a quedar** ~? are you going to be staying long?

2 (*respuesta*) very; **¿estás cansado? – ¡**~! are you tired? – very!

3 (*locuciones*): **como** ~ at (the) most; **con** ~: **el mejor con** ~ by far the best; **ni** ~ **menos: no es rico ni** ~ **menos** he's far from being rich

4: **por** ~ **que: por** ~ **que le creas** no matter how *o* however much you believe her

---

muda ['muða] *nf* change of clothes

mudanza [mu'ðanθa] *nf* (*cambio*) change; (*de casa*) move

mudar [mu'ðar] *vt* to change; (*ZOOL*) to shed ♦ *vi* to change; ~**se** *vr* (*la ropa*) to change; ~**se de casa** to move house

mudo, a ['muðo, a] *adj* dumb; (*callado, CINE*) silent

mueble ['mweßle] *nm* piece of furniture; ~**s** *nmpl* furniture *sg*

mueca ['mweka] *nf* face, grimace; **hacer** ~**s a** to make faces at

muela ['mwela] *nf* (*diente*) tooth; (: *de atrás*) molar

muelle ['mweʎe] *nm* spring; (*NAUT*) wharf; (*malecón*) pier

muero *etc vb ver* **morir**

muerte ['mwerte] *nf* death; (*homicidio*) murder; **dar** ~ **a** to kill

muerto, a ['mwerto, a] *pp de* **morir** ♦ *adj* dead; (*color*) dull ♦ *nm/f* dead man/ woman; (*difunto*) deceased; (*cadáver*) corpse; **estar** ~ **de cansancio** to be dead tired

muestra ['mwestra] *nf* (*señal*) indication, sign; (*demostración*) demonstration; (*prueba*) proof; (*estadística*) sample; (*modelo*) model, pattern; (*testimonio*) token

muestreo [mwes'treo] *nm* sample, sampling

muestro *etc vb ver* **mostrar**

muevo *etc vb ver* **mover**

mugir [mu'xir] *vi* (*vaca*) to moo

mugre ['muɣre] *nf* dirt, filth; **mugriento, a** *adj* dirty, filthy

mujer [mu'xer] *nf* woman; (*esposa*) wife; ~**iego** *nm* womanizer

mula ['mula] *nf* mule

mulato, a [mu'lato, a] *adj*, *nm/f* mulatto

muleta [mu'leta] *nf* (*para andar*) crutch; (*TAUROMAQUIA*) stick with red cape attached

mullido, a [mu'ʎiðo, a] *adj* (*cama*) soft; (*hierba*) soft, springy

multa ['multa] *nf* fine; **poner una** ~ **a** to fine; **multar** *vt* to fine

multicopista [multiko'pista] *nm* duplicator

multinacional [multinaθjo'nal] *nf* (*COM*) multinational

múltiple ['multiple] *adj* multiple; (*pl*) many, numerous

multiplicar [multipli'kar] *vt* (*MAT*) to multiply; (*fig*) to increase; ~**se** *vr* (*BIO*) to multiply; (*fig*) to be everywhere at once

multitud [multi'tuð] *nf* (*muchedumbre*) crowd; ~ **de** lots of

mundano, a [mun'dano, a] *adj* worldly; (*de moda*) fashionable

mundial [mun'djal] *adj* world-wide, universal; (*guerra, récord*) world *cpd*

mundo ['mundo] *nm* world; **todo el ~** everybody; **tener ~** to be experienced, know one's way around

munición [muni'θjon] *nf (MIL: provisiones)* stores *pl*, supplies *pl*; (: *balas)* ammunition

municipal [muniθi'pal] *adj* municipal, local

municipio [muni'θipjo] *nm (ayuntamiento)* town council, corporation; (*territorio administrativo)* town, municipality

muñeca [mu'ɲeka] *nf (ANAT)* wrist; (*juguete)* doll

muñeco [mu'ɲeko] *nm (figura)* figure; (*marioneta)* puppet; (*fig)* puppet, pawn

mural [mu'ral] *adj* mural, wall *cpd* ♦ *nm* mural

muralla [mu'raʎa] *nf* (city) wall(s) (*pl)*

murciélago [mur'θjelaɣo] *nm* bat

murmullo [mur'muʎo] *nm* murmur(ing); (*cuchicheo)* whispering; (*de arroyo)* murmur, rippling

murmuración [murmura'θjon] *nf* gossip; **murmurar** *vi* to murmur, whisper; (*criticar)* to criticize; (*cotillear)* to gossip

muro ['muro] *nm* wall

muscular [musku'lar] *adj* muscular

músculo ['muskulo] *nm* muscle

museo [mu'seo] *nm* museum

musgo ['musyo] *nm* moss

música ['musika] *nf* music; *ver tb* **músico**

músico, a ['musiko, a] *adj* musical ♦ *nm/f* musician

musitar [musi'tar] *vt, vi* to mutter, mumble

muslo ['muslo] *nm* thigh

mustio, a ['mustjo, a] *adj (persona)* depressed, gloomy; (*planta)* faded, withered

musulmán, ana [musul'man, ana] *nm/f* Moslem

mutación [muta'θjon] *nf (BIO)* mutation; (*cambio)* (sudden) change

mutilar [muti'lar] *vt* to mutilate; (*a una persona)* to maim

mutismo [mu'tismo] *nm (de persona)* uncommunicativeness; (*de autoridades)* silence

mutuamente [mutwa'mente] *adv* mutual-ly

mutuo, a ['mutwo, a] *adj* mutual

muy [mwi] *adv* very; (*demasiado)* too; **M~ Señor mío** Dear Sir; **~ de noche** very late at night; **eso es ~ de él** that's just like him

N n

N *abr* (= *norte)* N

nabo ['naβo] *nm* turnip

nácar ['nakar] *nm* mother-of-pearl

nacer [na'θer] *vi* to be born; (*de huevo)* to hatch; (*vegetal)* to sprout; (*río)* to rise; **nací en Barcelona** I was born in Barcelona; **nació una sospecha en su mente** a suspicion formed in her mind; **nacido, a** *adj* born; **recién nacido** newborn; **naciente** *adj* new, emerging; (*sol)* rising; **nacimiento** *nm* birth; (*fig)* birth, origin; (*de Navidad)* Nativity; (*linaje)* descent, family; (*de río)* source

nación [na'θjon] *nf* nation; **nacional** *adj* national; **nacionalismo** *nm* nationalism; **nacionalista** *nm/f* nationalist; **nacionalizar** *vt* to nationalize; **nacionalizarse** *vr* (*persona)* to become naturalized

nada ['naða] *pron* nothing ♦ *adv* not at all, in no way; **no decir ~** to say nothing, not to say anything; **~ más** nothing else; **de ~** don't mention it

nadador, a [naða'ðor, a] *nm/f* swimmer

nadar [na'ðar] *vi* to swim

nadie ['naðje] *pron* nobody, no-one; **~ habló** nobody spoke; **no había ~** there was nobody there, there wasn't anybody there

nado ['naðo]: **a ~** *adv*: **pasar a ~** to swim across

nafta ['nafta] (*AM)* *nf* petrol (*BRIT)*, gas (*US)*

naipe ['naipe] *nm* (playing) card; **~s** *nmpl* cards

nalgas ['nalɣas] *nfpl* buttocks

nana ['nana] *nf* lullaby

naranja [na'ranxa] *adj inv, nf* orange; **media ~** (*fam)* better half; **naranjada** *nf* orangeade; **naranjo** *nm* orange tree

narciso [nar'θiso] *nm* narcissus

narcótico, a [nar'kotiko, a] *adj, nm*
narcotic; **narcotizar** *vt* to drug;
narcotráfico *nm* drug trafficking *o*
running
nardo ['narðo] *nm* lily
narigón, ona, [nari'ɣon, ona] *adj* big-
nosed
narigudo, a [nari'ɣuðo, a] *adj* = **narigón**
nariz [na'riθ] *nf* nose; **narices** *nfpl*
nostrils; **delante de las narices de uno**
under one's (very) nose
narración [narra'θjon] *nf* narration;
narrador, a *nm/f* narrator
narrar [na'rrar] *vt* to narrate, recount;
narrativa *nf* narrative, story
nata ['nata] *nf* cream
natación [nata'θjon] *nf* swimming
natal [na'tal] *adj*: **ciudad** ~ home town;
~**idad** *nf* birth rate
natillas [na'tiʎas] *nfpl* custard *sg*
nativo, a [na'tiβo, a] *adj, nm/f* native
nato, a ['nato, a] *adj* born; **un músico** ~
a born musician
natural [natu'ral] *adj* natural; *(fruta etc)*
fresh ♦ *nm/f* native ♦ *nm (disposición)*
nature
naturaleza [natura'leθa] *nf* nature; *(género)* nature, kind; ~ **muerta** still life
naturalidad [naturali'ðað] *nf* naturalness
naturalmente [natural'mente] *adv (de
modo natural)* in a natural way; ¡~! of
course!
naufragar [naufra'ɣar] *vi* to sink;
naufragio *nm* shipwreck; **náufrago, a**
nm/f castaway, shipwrecked person
nauseabundo, a [nausea'βundo, a] *adj*
nauseating, sickening
náuseas ['nauseas] *nfpl* nausea *sg*; **me da**
~ it makes me feel sick
náutico, a ['nautiko, a] *adj* nautical
navaja [na'βaxa] *nf (cortaplumas)* clasp
knife *(BRIT)*, penknife; *(de barbero,
peluquero)* razor
naval [na'βal] *adj (MIL: combate, escuela)*
naval
Navarra [na'βarra] *n* Navarre
nave ['naβe] *nf (barco)* ship, vessel; *(ARQ)*
nave; ~ **espacial** spaceship
navegación [naβeɣa'θjon] *nf* navigation;

(viaje) sea journey; ~ **aérea** air traffic; ~
costera coastal shipping; **navegante**
nm/f navigator; **navegar** *vi (barco)* to
sail; *(avión)* to fly ♦ *vt* to sail; to fly;
(dirigir el rumbo) to navigate
navidad [naβi'ðað] *nf* Christmas; ~**es** *nfpl*
Christmas time; **navideño, a** *adj*
Christmas *cpd*
navío [na'βio] *nm* ship
nazca *etc vb ver* **nacer**
nazi ['naθi] *adj, nm/f* Nazi
NE *abr (= nor(d)este)* NE
neblina [ne'βlina] *nf* mist
nebuloso, a [neβu'loso, a] *adj* foggy;
(calinoso) misty; *(indefinido)* nebulous,
vague ♦ *nf* nebula
necedad [neθe'ðað] *nf* foolishness; *(una
~)* foolish act
necesario, a [neθe'sarjo, a] *adj* necessary
neceser [neθe'ser] *nm* toilet bag; *(bolsa
grande)* holdall
necesidad [neθesi'ðað] *nf* need; *(lo
inevitable)* necessity; *(miseria)* poverty,
need; **en caso de** ~ in case of need *o*
emergency; **hacer sus** ~**es** to relieve o.s
necesitado, a [neθesi'taðo, a] *adj* needy,
poor; ~ **de** in need of
necesitar [neθesi'tar] *vt* to need, require
♦ *vi*: ~ **de** to have need of
necio, a ['neθjo, a] *adj* foolish
necrópolis [ne'kropolis] *nf inv* cemetery
nectarina [nekta'rina] *nf* nectarine
nefasto, a [ne'fasto, a] *adj* ill-fated,
unlucky
negación [neɣa'θjon] *nf* negation;
(rechazo) refusal, denial
negar [ne'ɣar] *vt (renegar, rechazar)* to
refuse; *(prohibir)* to refuse, deny;
(desmentir) to deny; ~**se** *vr*: ~**se a** to
refuse to
negativa [neɣa'tiβa] *nf* negative; *(rechazo)*
refusal, denial
negativo, a [neɣa'tiβo, a] *adj, nm*
negative
negligencia [neɣli'xenθja] *nf* negligence;
negligente *adj* negligent
negociable [neɣo'θjaβle] *adj (COM)*
negotiable
negociado [neɣo'θjaðo] *nm* department,

section

negociante [neɣo'θjante] *nm/f* businessman/woman

negociar [neɣo'θjar] *vt, vi* to negotiate; ~ **en** to deal in, trade in

negocio [ne'ɣoθjo] *nm* (*COM*) business; (*asunto*) affair, business; (*operación comercial*) deal, transaction; (*AM*) firm; (*lugar*) place of business; **los ~s** business *sg*; **hacer ~** to do business

negra ['neɣra] *nf* (*MUS*) crotchet; *ver tb* **negro**

negro, a ['neɣro, a] *adj* black; (*suerte*) awful ♦ *nm* black ♦ *nm/f* Negro/Negress, Black

nene, a ['nene, a] *nm/f* baby, small child

nenúfar [ne'nufar] *nm* water lily

neologismo [neolo'xismo] *nm* neologism

neón [ne'on] *nm*: **luces/lámpara de** ~ neon lights/lamp

neoyorquino, a [neojor'kino, a] *adj* (of) New York

nepotismo [nepo'tismo] *nm* nepotism

nervio ['nerβjo] *nm* (*ANAT*) nerve; (: *tendón*) tendon; (*fig*) vigour; **nerviosismo** *nm* nervousness, nerves *pl*; ~**so, a** *adj* nervous

neto, a ['neto, a] *adj* clear; (*limpio*) clean; (*COM*) net

neumático, a [neu'matiko, a] *adj* pneumatic ♦ *nm* (*ESP*) tyre (*BRIT*), tire (*US*); ~ **de recambio** spare tyre

neurasténico, a [neuras'teniko, a] *adj* (*fig*) hysterical

neurólogo, a [neu'roloɣo, a] *nm/f* neurologist

neurona [neu'rona] *nf* (*ANAT*) nerve cell

neutral [neu'tral] *adj* neutral; ~**izar** *vt* to neutralize; (*contrarrestar*) to counteract

neutro, a ['neutro, a] *adj* (*BIO, LING*) neuter

neutrón [neu'tron] *nm* neutron

nevada [ne'βaða] *nf* snowstorm; (*caída de nieve*) snowfall

nevar [ne'βar] *vi* to snow

nevera [ne'βera] (*ESP*) *nf* refrigerator (*BRIT*), icebox (*US*)

nevería [neβe'ria] (*AM*) *nf* ice-cream parlour

nexo ['nekso] *nm* link, connection

ni [ni] *conj* nor, neither; (*tb*: ~ **siquiera**) not ... even; ~ **que** not even if; ~ **blanco** ~ **negro** neither white nor black

Nicaragua [nika'raɣwa] *nf* Nicaragua; **nicaragüense** *adj, nm/f* Nicaraguan

nicho ['nitʃo] *nm* niche

nicotina [niko'tina] *nf* nicotine

nido ['niðo] *nm* nest; (*fig*) hiding place

niebla ['njeβla] *nf* fog; (*neblina*) mist

niego *etc vb ver* **negar**

nieto, a ['njeto, a] *nm/f* grandson/ daughter; ~**s** *nmpl* grandchildren

nieve *etc* ['njeβe] *vb ver* **nevar** ♦ *nf* snow; (*AM*) icecream

N.I.F *nm abr* (= *Número de Identificación Fiscal*) *personal identification number used for financial and tax purposes*

nimiedad [nimje'ðað] *nf* small-mindedness; (*trivialidad*) triviality

nimio, a ['nimjo, a] *adj* trivial, insignificant

ninfa ['ninfa] *nf* nymph

ninfómana [nin'fomana] *nf* nymphomaniac

ningún [nin'gun] *adj ver* **ninguno**

ninguno, a [nin'guno, a] (*delante de nm*: **ningún**) *adj* no ♦ *pron* (*nadie*) nobody; (*ni uno*) none, not one; (*ni uno ni otro*) neither; **de ninguna manera** by no means, not at all

niña ['niɲa] *nf* (*ANAT*) pupil; *ver tb* **niño**

niñera [ni'ɲera] *nf* nursemaid, nanny; **niñería** *nf* childish act

niñez [ni'ɲeθ] *nf* childhood; (*infancia*) infancy

niño, a ['niɲo, a] *adj* (*joven*) young; (*inmaduro*) immature ♦ *nm/f* child, boy/girl

nipón, ona [ni'pon, ona] *adj, nm/f* Japanese

níquel ['nikel] *nm* nickel; **niquelar** *vt* (*TEC*) to nickel-plate

níspero ['nispero] *nm* medlar

nitidez [niti'ðeθ] *nf* (*claridad*) clarity; (: *de atmósfera*) brightness; (: *de imagen*) sharpness; **nítido, a** *adj* clear; sharp

nitrato [ni'trato] *nm* nitrate

nitrógeno [ni'troxeno] *nm* nitrogen

nitroglicerina [nitroɣliθe'rina] *nf* nitroglycerine

nivel [ni'βel] *nm* (GEO) level; (*norma*) level, standard; (*altura*) height; ~ **de aceite** oil level; ~ **de aire** spirit level; ~ **de vida** standard of living; ~**ar** *vt* to level out; (*fig*) to even up; (COM) to balance

NN. UU. *nfpl abr* (= *Naciones Unidas*) UN *sg*

no [no] *adv* no; not; (*con verbo*) not ♦ *excl* no!; ~ **tengo nada** I don't have anything, I have nothing; ~ **es el mío** it's not mine; **ahora** ~ not now; ¿~ **lo sabes?** don't you know?; ~ **mucho** not much; ~ **bien termine, lo entregaré** as soon as I finish I'll hand it over; ~ **más: ayer** ~ **más** just yesterday; ¡**pase** ~ **más!** come in!; ¡**a que** ~ **lo sabes!** I bet you don't know!; ¡**cómo** ~! of course!; **los países** ~ **alineados** the non-aligned countries; **la** ~ **intervención** non-intervention

noble ['noβle] *adj, nm/f* noble; ~**za** *nf* nobility

noche ['notʃe] *nf* night, night-time; (*la tarde*) evening; (*fig*) darkness; **de** ~, **por la** ~ at night

nochebuena [notʃe'βwena] *nf* Christmas Eve

nochevieja [notʃe'βjexa] *nf* New Year's Eve

noción [no'θjon] *nf* notion

nocivo, a [no'θiβo, a] *adj* harmful

noctámbulo, a [nok'tambulo, a] *nm/f* sleepwalker

nocturno, a [nok'turno, a] *adj* (*de la noche*) nocturnal, night *cpd*; (*de la tarde*) evening *cpd* ♦ *nm* nocturne

nodriza [no'ðriθa] *nf* wet nurse; **buque** *o* **nave** ~ supply ship

nogal [no'ɣal] *nm* walnut tree

nómada ['nomaða] *adj* nomadic ♦ *nm/f* nomad

nombramiento [nombra'mjento] *nm* naming; (*a un empleo*) appointment

nombrar [nom'brar] *vt* (*designar*) to name; (*mencionar*) to mention; (*dar puesto a*) to appoint

nombre ['nombre] *nm* name; (*sustantivo*) noun; (*fama*) renown; ~ **y apellidos** name in full; ~ **común/propio** common/proper noun; ~ **de pila/de soltera** Christian/maiden name; **poner** ~ **a** to call, name

nomenclatura [nomenkla'tura] *nf* nomenclature

nomeolvides [nomeol'βiðes] *nm inv* forget-me-not

nómina ['nomina] *nf* (*lista*) list; (COM) payroll

nominal [nomi'nal] *adj* nominal

nominar [nomi'nar] *vt* to nominate

nominativo, a [nomina'tiβo, a] *adj* (COM): **cheque** ~ **a X** cheque made out to X

nono, a ['nono, a] *adj* ninth

nordeste [nor'ðeste] *adj* north-east, north-eastern, north-easterly ♦ *nm* north-east

nórdico, a ['norðiko, a] *adj* (*del norte*) northern, northerly; (*escandinavo*) Nordic

noreste [no'reste] *adj, nm* = **nordeste**

noria ['norja] *nf* (AGR) waterwheel; (*de carnaval*) big (BRIT) *o* Ferris (US) wheel

norma ['norma] *nf* rule (of thumb)

normal [nor'mal] *adj* (*corriente*) normal; (*habitual*) usual, natural; (**gasolina**) ~ two-star petrol; ~**idad** *nf* normality; **restablecer la** ~**idad** to restore order; ~**izar** *vt* (*reglamentar*) to normalize; (TEC) to standardize; ~**izarse** *vr* to return to normal

normando, a [nor'mando, a] *adj, nm/f* Norman

normativa [norma'tiβa] *nf* (set of) rules *pl*, regulations *pl*

noroeste [noro'este] *adj* north-west, north-western, north-westerly ♦ *nm* north-west

norte ['norte] *adj* north, northern, northerly ♦ *nm* north; (*fig*) guide

norteamericano, a [norteameri'kano, a] *adj, nm/f* (North) American

Noruega [no'rweɣa] *nf* Norway

noruego, a [no'rweɣo, a] *adj, nm/f* Norwegian

nos [nos] *pron* (*directo*) us; (*indirecto*) us; to us; for us; from us; (*reflexivo*) (to) ourselves; (*recíproco*) (to) each other; ~ **levantamos a las 7** we get up at 7

nosotros, as [no'sotros, as] *pron* (*sujeto*) we; (*después de prep*) us

nostalgia [nos'talxja] *nf* nostalgia

nota ['nota] *nf* note; (*ESCOL*) mark

notable [no'taßle] *adj* notable; (*ESCOL*) outstanding ♦ *nm/f* notable

notar [no'tar] *vt* to notice, note; **~se** *vr* to be obvious; **se nota que ...** one observes that ...

notarial [nota'rjal] *adj*: **acta ~** affidavit

notario [no'tarjo] *nm* notary

noticia [no'tiθja] *nf* (*información*) piece of news; **las ~s** the news *sg*; **tener ~s de alguien** to hear from sb

noticiero [noti'θjero] (*AM*) *nm* news bulletin

notificación [notifika'θjon] *nf* notification; **notificar** *vt* to notify, inform

notoriedad [notorje'ðað] *nf* fame, renown; **notorio, a** *adj* (*público*) well-known; (*evidente*) obvious

novato, a [no'ßato, a] *adj* inexperienced ♦ *nm/f* beginner, novice

novecientos, as [noße'θjentos, as] *num* nine hundred

novedad [noße'ðað] *nf* (*calidad de nuevo*) newness; (*noticia*) piece of news; (*cambio*) change, (new) development

novel [no'ßel] *adj* new; (*inexperto*) inexperienced ♦ *nm/f* beginner

novela [no'ßela] *nf* novel

novelero, a [noße'lero, a] *adj* highly imaginative

noveno, a [no'ßeno, a] *adj* ninth

noventa [no'ßenta] *num* ninety

novia ['noßja] *nf ver* **novio**

noviazgo [no'ßjaθɣo] *nm* engagement

novicio, a [no'ßiθjo, a] *nm/f* novice

noviembre [no'ßjembre] *nm* November

novillada [noßi'ʎaða] *nf* (*TAUROMAQUIA*) bullfight with young bulls; **novillero** *nm* novice bullfighter; **novillo** *nm* young bull, bullock; **hacer novillos** (*fam*) to play truant

novio, a ['noßjo, a] *nm/f* boyfriend/ girlfriend; (*prometido*) fiancé/fiancée; (*recién casado*) bridegroom/bride; **los ~s** the newly-weds

nubarrón [nußa'rron] *nm* storm cloud

nube ['nuße] *nf* cloud

nublado, a [nu'ßlaðo, a] *adj* cloudy ♦ *nm* storm cloud; **nublar** *vt* (*oscurecer*) to darken; (*confundir*) to cloud; **nublarse** *vr* to grow dark

nubosidad [nußosi'ðað] *nf* cloudiness; **había mucha ~** it was very cloudy

nuca ['nuka] *nf* nape of the neck

nuclear [nukle'ar] *adj* nuclear

núcleo ['nukleo] *nm* (*centro*) core; (*FÍSICA*) nucleus

nudillo [nu'ðiʎo] *nm* knuckle

nudista [nu'ðista] *adj* (*playa*) nudist

nudo ['nuðo] *nm* knot; (*unión*) bond; (*de problema*) crux; **~so, a** *adj* knotty

nuera ['nwera] *nf* daughter-in-law

nuestro, a ['nwestro, a] *adj pos* our ♦ *pron* ours; **~ padre** our father; **un amigo ~** a friend of ours; **es el ~** it's ours

nueva ['nweßa] *nf* piece of news

nuevamente [nweßa'mente] *adv* (*otra vez*) again; (*de nuevo*) anew

Nueva York [-jork] *n* New York

Nueva Zelandia [-θe'landja] *nf* New Zealand

nueve ['nweße] *num* nine

nuevo, a ['nweßo, a] *adj* (*gen*) new; **de ~** again

nuez [nweθ] *nf* (*fruto*) nut; (*del nogal*) walnut; **~ de Adán** Adam's apple; **~ moscada** nutmeg

nulidad [nuli'ðað] *nf* (*incapacidad*) incompetence; (*abolición*) nullity

nulo, a ['nulo, a] *adj* (*inepto, torpe*) useless; (*inválido*) (null and) void; (*DEPORTE*) drawn, tied

núm. *abr* (= *número*) no

numeración [numera'θjon] *nf* (*cifras*) numbers *pl*; (*arábiga, romana etc*) numerals *pl*

numeral [nume'ral] *nm* numeral

numerar [nume'rar] *vt* to number

número ['numero] *nm* (*gen*) number; (*tamaño: de zapato*) size; (*ejemplar: de diario*) number, issue; **sin ~** numberless, unnumbered; **~ de matrícula/de**

teléfono registration/telephone number; ~ **atrasado** back number
numeroso, a [nume'roso, a] *adj* numerous
nunca ['nunka] *adv* (*jamás*) never; ~ **lo pensé** I never thought it; **no viene** ~ he never comes; ~ **más** never again; **más que** ~ more than ever
nuncio ['nunθjo] *nm* (*REL*) nuncio
nupcias ['nupθjas] *nfpl* wedding *sg*, nuptials
nutria ['nutrja] *nf* otter
nutrición [nutri'θjon] *nf* nutrition
nutrido, a [nu'triðo, a] *adj* (*alimentado*) nourished; (*fig: grande*) large; (*abundante*) abundant
nutrir [nu'trir] *vt* (*alimentar*) to nourish; (*dar de comer*) to feed; (*fig*) to strengthen; **nutritivo, a** *adj* nourishing, nutritious
nylon [ni'lon] *nm* nylon

Ñ ñ

ñato, a ['ɲato, a] (*AM*) *adj* snub-nosed
ñoñería [ɲoɲe'ria] *nf* insipidness
ñoño, a ['ɲoɲo, a] *adj* (*AM: tonto*) silly, stupid; (*soso*) insipid; (*persona*) spineless

O o

O *abr* (= *oeste*) W
o [o] *conj* or
o/ *abr* (= *orden*) o.
oasis [o'asis] *nm inv* oasis
obcecar [oßθe'kar] *vt* to blind
obcecarse [oßθe'karse] *vr* to get o become stubborn
obedecer [oßeðe'θer] *vt* to obey; **obediencia** *nf* obedience; **obediente** *adj* obedient
obertura [oßer'tura] *nf* overture
obesidad [oßesi'ðað] *nf* obesity; **obeso, a** *adj* obese
obispo [o'ßispo] *nm* bishop

objeción [oßxe'θjon] *nf* objection; **poner objeciones** to raise objections
objetar [oßxe'tar] *vt, vi* to object
objetivo, a [oßxe'tißo, a] *adj, nm* objective
objeto [oß'xeto] *nm* (*cosa*) object; (*fin*) aim
objetor, a [oßxe'tor, a] *nm/f* objector
oblicuo, a [o'ßlikwo, a] *adj* oblique; (*mirada*) sidelong
obligación [oßliɣa'θjon] *nf* obligation; (*COM*) bond
obligar [oßli'ɣar] *vt* to force; ~**se** *vr* to bind o.s.; **obligatorio, a** *adj* compulsory, obligatory
oboe [o'ßoe] *nm* oboe
obra ['oßra] *nf* work; (*hechura*) piece of work; (*ARQ*) construction, building; (*TEATRO*) play; ~ **maestra** masterpiece; ~**s públicas** public works; **por** ~ **de** thanks to (the efforts of); **obrar** *vt* to work; (*tener efecto*) to have an effect on ♦ *vi* to act, behave; (*tener efecto*) to have an effect; **la carta obra en su poder** the letter is in his/her possession
obrero, a [o'ßrero, a] *adj* (*clase*) working; (*movimiento*) labour *cpd*; **clase obrera** working class ♦ *nm/f* (*gen*) worker; (*sin oficio*) labourer
obscenidad [oßsθeni'ðað] *nf* obscenity; **obsceno, a** *adj* obscene
obscu... = oscu...
obsequiar [oßse'kjar] *vt* (*ofrecer*) to present with; (*agasajar*) to make a fuss of, lavish attention on; **obsequio** *nm* (*regalo*) gift; (*cortesía*) courtesy, attention
observación [oßserßa'θjon] *nf* observation; (*reflexión*) remark
observador, a [oßserßa'ðor, a] *nm/f* observer
observar [oßser'ßar] *vt* to observe; (*anotar*) to notice; ~**se** *vr* to keep to, observe
obsesión [oßse'sjon] *nf* obsession; **obsesivo, a** *adj* obsessive
obsoleto, a [oßso'leto, a] *adj* (*máquina, técnica*) obsolete
obstaculizar [oßstakuli'θar] *vt* (*dificultar*) to hinder, hamper

(*impedimento*) hindrance, drawback
obstante [oβs'tante]: **no** ~ *adv*
nevertheless ♦ *prep* in spite of
obstinado, a [oβsti'naðo, a] *adj* (*gen*)
obstinate, stubborn
obstinarse [oβsti'narse] *vr* to be
obstinate; ~ **en** to persist in
obstrucción [oβstruk'θjon] *nf* obstruction;
obstruir *vt* to obstruct
obtener [oβte'ner] *vt* (*conseguir*) to
obtain; (*ganar*) to gain
obturador [oβtura'ðor] *nm* (*FOTO*) shutter
obtuso, a [oβ'tuso, a] *adj* (*filo*) blunt;
(*MAT, fig*) obtuse
obvio, a ['oββjo, a] *adj* obvious
ocasión [oka'sjon] *nf* (*oportunidad*)
opportunity, chance; (*momento*) occasion,
time; (*causa*) cause; **de** ~ secondhand;
ocasionar *vt* to cause
ocaso [o'kaso] *nm* (*fig*) decline
occidente [okθi'ðente] *nm* west
OCDE *nf abr* (= *Organización de*
Cooperación y Desarrollo Económico)
OECD
océano [o'θeano] *nm* ocean; **el** ~ **Índico**
the Indian Ocean
ochenta [o'tʃenta] *num* eighty
ocho ['otʃo] *num* eight; ~ **días** a week
ocio ['oθjo] *nm* (*tiempo*) leisure; (*pey*)
idleness; ~**so, a** *adj* (*inactivo*) idle;
(*inútil*) useless
octanaje [okta'naxe] *nm*: **de alto** ~ high
octane; **octano** *nm* octane
octavilla [okta'viʎa] *nf* leaflet, pamphlet
octavo, a [ok'taβo, a] *adj* eighth
octogenario, a [oktoxe'narjo, a] *adj*
octogenarian
octubre [ok'tuβre] *nm* October
ocular [oku'lar] *adj* ocular, eye *cpd*;
testigo ~ eyewitness
oculista [oku'lista] *nm/f* oculist
ocultar [okul'tar] *vt* (*esconder*) to hide;
(*callar*) to conceal; **oculto, a** *adj* hidden;
(*fig*) secret
ocupación [okupa'θjon] *nf* occupation
ocupado, a [oku'paðo, a] *adj* (*persona*)
busy; (*plaza*) occupied, taken; (*teléfono*)
engaged; **ocupar** *vt* (*gen*) to occupy;
ocuparse *vr*: **ocuparse de** *o* **en** (*gen*) to

concern o.s. with; (*cuidar*) to look after
ocurrencia [oku'rrenθja] *nf* (*suceso*)
incident, event; (*idea*) bright idea
ocurrir [oku'rrir] *vi* to happen; ~**se** *vr*: **se**
me ocurrió que ... it occurred to me
that ...
odiar [o'ðjar] *vt* to hate; **odio** *nm* (*gen*)
hate, hatred; (*disgusto*) dislike; **odioso, a**
adj (*gen*) hateful; (*malo*) nasty
odontólogo, a [oðon'toloɣo, a] *nm/f*
dentist, dental surgeon
OEA *nf abr* (= *Organización de Estados*
Americanos) OAS
oeste [o'este] *nm* west; **una película del**
~ a western
ofender [ofen'der] *vt* (*agraviar*) to offend;
(*insultar*) to insult; ~**se** *vr* to take
offence; **ofensa** *nf* offence; **ofensiva** *nf*
offensive; **ofensivo, a** *adj* (*insultante*)
insulting; (*MIL*) offensive
oferta [o'ferta] *nf* offer; (*propuesta*)
proposal; **la** ~ **y la demanda** supply and
demand; **artículos en** ~ goods on offer
oficial [ofi'θjal] *adj* official ♦ *nm* official;
(*MIL*) officer
oficina [ofi'θina] *nf* office; ~ **de correos**
post office; ~ **de turismo** tourist office;
oficinista *nm/f* clerk
oficio [o'fiθjo] *nm* (*profesión*) profession;
(*puesto*) post; (*REL*) service; **ser del** ~ to
be an old hand; **tener mucho** ~ to have
a lot of experience; ~ **de difuntos**
funeral service; **de** ~ officially
oficioso, a [ofi'θjoso, a] *adj* (*pey*)
officious; (*no oficial*) unofficial, informal
ofimática [ofi'matika] *nf* office
automation
ofrecer [ofre'θer] *vt* (*dar*) to offer;
(*proponer*) to propose; ~**se** *vr* (*persona*)
to offer o.s., volunteer; (*situación*) to
present itself; **¿qué se le ofrece?, ¿se le**
ofrece algo? what can I do for you?, can
I get you anything?
ofrecimiento [ofreθi'mjento] *nm* offer,
offering
ofrendar [ofren'dar] *vt* to offer, contribute
oftalmólogo, a [oftal'moloɣo, a] *nm/f*
ophthalmologist
ofuscación [ofuska'θjon] *nf* (*fig*)

bewilderment

ofuscar [ofusˈkar] *vt (confundir)* to bewilder; *(enceguecer)* to dazzle, blind

oída [oˈiða] *nf:* **de ~s** by hearsay

oído [oˈiðo] *nm (ANAT)* ear; *(sentido)* hearing

oigo *etc vb ver* **oír**

oír [oˈir] *vt (gen)* to hear; *(atender a)* to listen to; **¡oiga!** listen!; ~ **misa** to attend mass

OIT *nf abr* (= *Organización Internacional del Trabajo*) ILO

ojal [oˈxal] *nm* buttonhole

ojalá [oxaˈla] *excl* if only (it were so)!, some hope! ♦ *conj* if only ...!, would that ...!; ~ **que venga hoy** I hope he comes today

ojeada [oxeˈaða] *nf* glance

ojera [oˈxera] *nf:* **tener ~s** to have bags under one's eyes

ojeriza [oxeˈriθa] *nf* ill-will

ojeroso, a [oxeˈroso, a] *adj* haggard

ojo [ˈoxo] *nm* eye; *(de puente)* span; *(de cerradura)* keyhole ♦ *excl* careful!; **tener ~ para** to have an eye for; ~ **de buey** porthole

okupa [oˈkupa] *(fam) nm/f* squatter

ola [ˈola] *nf* wave

olé [oˈle] *excl* bravo!, olé!

oleada [oleˈaða] *nf* big wave, swell; *(fig)* wave

oleaje [oleˈaxe] *nm* swell

óleo [ˈoleo] *nm* oil; **oleoducto** *nm* (oil) pipeline

oler [oˈler] *vt (gen)* to smell; *(inquirir)* to pry into; *(fig: sospechar)* to sniff out ♦ *vi* to smell; ~ **a** to smell of

olfatear [olfateˈar] *vt* to smell; *(fig: sospechar)* to sniff out; *(inquirir)* to pry into; **olfato** *nm* sense of smell

oligarquía [oliɣarˈkia] *nf* oligarchy

olimpíada [olimˈpiaða] *nf:* **las O~s** the Olympics

oliva [oˈliβa] *nf (aceituna)* olive; **aceite de** ~ olive oil; **olivo** *nm* olive tree

olla [ˈoʎa] *nf* pan; *(comida)* stew; ~ **a presión** *o* **exprés** pressure cooker; ~ **podrida** type of Spanish stew

olmo [ˈolmo] *nm* elm (tree)

olor [oˈlor] *nm* smell; **~oso, a** *adj* scented

olvidadizo, a [olβiðaˈðiθo, a] *adj (desmemoriado)* forgetful; *(distraído)* absent-minded

olvidar [olβiˈðar] *vt* to forget; *(omitir)* to omit; **~se** *vr (fig)* to forget o.s.; **se me olvidó** I forgot

olvido [olˈβiðo] *nm* oblivion; *(despiste)* forgetfulness

ombligo [omˈbliɣo] *nm* navel

omisión [omiˈsjon] *nf (abstención)* omission; *(descuido)* neglect

omiso, a [oˈmiso, a] *adj:* **hacer caso ~ de** to ignore, pass over

omitir [omiˈtir] *vt* to omit

omnipotente [omnipoˈtente] *adj* omnipotent

omnívoro, a [omˈniβoro, a] *adj* omnivorous

omóplato [oˈmoplato] *nm* shoulder blade

OMS *nf abr* (= *Organización Mundial de la Salud*) WHO

once [ˈonθe] *num* eleven; **~s** *(AM) nfpl* tea break

onda [ˈonda] *nf* wave; ~ **corta/larga/media** short/long/medium wave; **ondear** *vt, vi* to wave; *(tener ondas)* to be wavy; *(agua)* to ripple; **ondearse** *vr* to swing, sway

ondulación [ondulaˈθjon] *nf* undulation; **ondulado, a** *adj* wavy ♦ *nm* wave

ondular [onduˈlar] *vt (el pelo)* to wave ♦ *vi* to undulate; **~se** *vr* to undulate

ONG *nf abr* (= *organización no gubernamental*) NGO

ONU [ˈonu] *nf abr* (= *Organización de las Naciones Unidas*) UNO

opaco, a [oˈpako, a] *adj* opaque; *(fig)* dull

opción [opˈθjon] *nf (gen)* option; *(derecho)* right, option

OPEP [ˈopep] *nf abr* (= *Organización de Países Exportadores de Petróleo*) OPEC

ópera [ˈopera] *nf* opera; ~ **bufa** *o* **cómica** comic opera

operación [operaˈθjon] *nf (gen)* operation; *(COM)* transaction, deal

operador, a [operaˈðor, a] *nm/f* operator; *(CINE: proyección)* projectionist; *(: rodaje)* cameraman

operar [ope'rar] *vt* (*producir*) to produce, bring about; (*MED*) to operate on ♦ *vi* (*COM*) to operate, deal; **~se** *vr* to occur; (*MED*) to have an operation

opereta [ope'reta] *nf* operetta

opinar [opi'nar] *vt* (*estimar*) to think ♦ *vi* (*enjuiciar*) to give one's opinion; **opinión** *nf* (*creencia*) belief; (*criterio*) opinion

opio ['opjo] *nm* opium

oponente [opo'nente] *nm/f* opponent

oponer [opo'ner] *vt* (*resistencia*) to put up, offer; (*negativa*) to raise; **~se** *vr* (*objetar*) to object; (*estar frente a frente*) to be opposed; (*dos personas*) to oppose each other; **~ A a B** to set A against B; **me opongo a pensar que ...** I refuse to believe *o* think that ...

oportunidad [oportuni'ðað] *nf* (*ocasión*) opportunity; (*posibilidad*) chance

oportunismo [oportu'nismo] *nm* opportunism; **oportunista** *nm/f* opportunist

oportuno, a [opor'tuno, a] *adj* (*en su tiempo*) opportune, timely; (*respuesta*) suitable; **en el momento ~** at the right moment

oposición [oposi'θjon] *nf* opposition; **oposiciones** *nfpl* (*ESCOL*) public examinations

opositor, a [oposi'tor, a] *nm/f* (*adversario*) opponent; (*candidato*): **~ (a)** candidate (for)

opresión [opre'sjon] *nf* oppression; **opresivo, a** *adj* oppressive; **opresor, a** *nm/f* oppressor

oprimir [opri'mir] *vt* to squeeze; (*fig*) to oppress

optar [op'tar] *vi* (*elegir*) to choose; **~ a** *o* **por** to opt for; **optativo, a** *adj* optional

óptico, a ['optiko, a] *adj* optic(al) ♦ *nm/f* optician; **óptica** *nf* optician's (shop); **desde esta óptica** from this point of view

optimismo [opti'mismo] *nm* optimism; **optimista** *nm/f* optimist

óptimo, a ['optimo, a] *adj* (*el mejor*) very best

opuesto, a [o'pwesto, a] *adj* (*contrario*) opposite; (*antagónico*) opposing

opulencia [opu'lenθja] *nf* opulence;

opulento, a *adj* opulent

oración [ora'θjon] *nf* (*discurso*) speech; (*REL*) prayer; (*LING*) sentence

orador, a [ora'ðor, a] *nm/f* (*conferenciante*) speaker, orator

oral [o'ral] *adj* oral

orangután [orangu'tan] *nm* orang-utan

orar [o'rar] *vi* (*REL*) to pray

oratoria [ora'torja] *nf* oratory

órbita ['orβita] *nf* orbit

orden ['orðen] *nm* (*gen*) order ♦ *nf* (*gen*) order; (*INFORM*) command; **~ del día** agenda; **de primer ~** first-rate; **en ~ de prioridad** in order of priority

ordenado, a [orðe'naðo, a] *adj* (*metódico*) methodical; (*arreglado*) orderly

ordenador [orðena'ðor] *nm* computer; **~ central** mainframe computer

ordenanza [orðe'nanθa] *nf* ordinance

ordenar [orðe'nar] *vt* (*mandar*) to order; (*poner orden*) to put in order, arrange; **~se** *vr* (*REL*) to be ordained

ordeñar [orðe'ɲar] *vt* to milk

ordinario, a [orði'narjo, a] *adj* (*común*) ordinary, usual; (*vulgar*) vulgar, common

orégano [o'reßano] *nm* oregano

oreja [o'rexa] *nf* ear; (*MECÁNICA*) lug, flange

orfanato [orfa'nato] *nm* orphanage

orfandad [orfan'dað] *nf* orphanhood

orfebrería [orfeßre'ria] *nf* gold/silver work

orgánico, a [or'ßaniko, a] *adj* organic

organigrama [orßani'ßrama] *nm* flow chart

organismo [orßa'nismo] *nm* (*BIO*) organism; (*POL*) organization

organización [orßaniθa'θjon] *nf* organization; **organizar** *vt* to organize

órgano ['orßano] *nm* organ

orgasmo [or'ßasmo] *nm* orgasm

orgía [or'xia] *nf* orgy

orgullo [or'ßuʎo] *nm* (*altanería*) pride; (*autorespeto*) self-respect; **orgulloso, a** *adj* (*gen*) proud; (*altanero*) haughty

orientación [orjenta'θjon] *nf* (*posición*) position; (*dirección*) direction

orientar [orjen'tar] *vt* (*situar*) to orientate;

(*señalar*) to point; (*dirigir*) to direct;
(*guiar*) to guide; ~**se** *vr* to get one's
bearings; (*decidirse*) to decide on a
course of action

oriente [o'rjente] *nm* east; **Cercano/
Medio/Lejano O~** Near/Middle/Far
East

origen [o'rixen] *nm* origin; (*nacimiento*)
lineage, birth

original [orixi'nal] *adj* (*nuevo*) original;
(*extraño*) odd, strange; ~**idad** *nf*
originality

originar [orixi'nar] *vt* to start, cause; ~**se**
vr to originate; ~**io, a** *adj* (*nativo*)
native; (*primordial*) original

orilla [o'riʎa] *nf* (*borde*) border; (*de río*)
bank; (*de bosque, tela*) edge; (*de mar*)
shore

orina [o'rina] *nf* urine; **orinal** *nm*
(chamber) pot; **orinar** *vi* to urinate;
orinarse *vr* to wet o.s.; **orines** *nmpl*
urine

oriundo, a [o'rjundo, a] *adj*: ~ **de** native
of

ornitología [ornitolo'xia] *nf* ornithology,
bird-watching

oro ['oro] *nm* gold; ~**s** *nmpl* (*NAIPES*)
hearts

oropel [oro'pel] *nm* tinsel

orquesta [or'kesta] *nf* orchestra; ~ **de
cámara/sinfónica** chamber/symphony
orchestra

orquídea [or'kiðea] *nf* orchid

ortiga [or'tiɣa] *nf* nettle

ortodoxo, a [orto'ðokso, a] *adj* orthodox

ortografía [ortoɣra'fia] *nf* spelling

ortopedia [orto'peðja] *nf* orthopaedics *sg*;
ortopédico, a *adj* orthopaedic

oruga [o'ruɣa] *nf* caterpillar

orzuelo [or'θwelo] *nm* (*MED*) stye

os [os] *pron* (*gen*) you; (*a vosotros*) to you

osa ['osa] *nf* (she-)bear; **O~ Mayor/
Menor** Great/Little Bear

osadía [osa'ðia] *nf* daring

osar [o'sar] *vi* to dare

oscilación [osθila'θjon] *nf* (*movimiento*)
oscillation; (*fluctuación*) fluctuation;
(*vacilación*) hesitation; (*columpio*) swinging, movement to and fro

oscilar [osθi'lar] *vi* to oscillate; to
fluctuate; to hesitate

oscurecer [oskure'θer] *vt* to darken ♦ *vi*
to grow dark; ~**se** *vr* to grow o get dark

oscuridad [oskuri'ðað] *nf* obscurity;
(*tinieblas*) darkness

oscuro, a [os'kuro, a] *adj* dark; (*fig*)
obscure; **a oscuras** in the dark

óseo, a ['oseo, a] *adj* bony

oso ['oso] *nm* bear; ~ **de peluche** teddy
bear; ~ **hormiguero** anteater

ostensible [osten'sißle] *adj* obvious

ostentación [ostenta'θjon] *nf* (*gen*)
ostentation; (*acto*) display

ostentar [osten'tar] *vt* (*gen*) to show; (*pey*)
to flaunt, show off; (*poseer*) to have,
possess

ostra ['ostra] *nf* oyster

OTAN ['otan] *nf abr* (= *Organización del
Tratado del Atlántico Norte*) NATO

otear [ote'ar] *vt* to observe; (*fig*) to look
into

otitis [o'titis] *nf* earache

otoñal [oto'ɲal] *adj* autumnal

otoño [o'toɲo] *nm* autumn

otorgar [otor'ɣar] *vt* (*conceder*) to
concede; (*dar*) to grant

otorrino, a [oto'rrino, a], **otorrinolarin-
gólogo, a** [otorrinolarin'goloɣo, a] *nm/f* ear,
nose and throat specialist

PALABRA CLAVE

---

otro, a ['otro, a] *adj* **1** (*distinto: sg*)
another; (: *pl*) other; **con ~s amigos**
with other o different friends
2 (*adicional*): **tráigame ~ café** (**más**),
por favor can I have another coffee
please; ~**s 10 días más** another ten days
♦ *pron* **1**: **el ~** the other one; (**los**) ~**s**
(the) others; **de ~** somebody else's; **que
lo haga** let somebody else do it
2 (*recíproco*): **se odian** (**la**) **una a** (**la**)
otra they hate one another o each other
3: ~ **tanto**: **comer ~ tanto** to eat the
same o as much again; **recibió una
decena de telegramas y otras tantas
llamadas** he got about ten telegrams
and as many calls

ovación [oβa'θjon] *nf* ovation
oval [o'βal] *adj* oval; ~ado, a *adj* oval; óvalo *nm* oval
ovario [o'βario] *nm* (*ANAT*) ovary
oveja [o'βexa] *nf* sheep
overol [oβe'rol] (*AM*) *nm* overalls *pl*
ovillo [o'βiʎo] *nm* (*de lana*) ball of wool; hacerse un ~ to curl up
OVNI ['oβni] *nm abr* (= *objeto volante no identificado*) UFO
ovulación [oβula'θjon] *nf* ovulation; óvulo *nm* ovum
oxidación [oksiða'θjon] *nf* rusting
oxidar [oksi'ðar] *vt* to rust; ~se *vr* to go rusty
óxido ['oksiðo] *nm* oxide
oxigenado, a [oksixe'naðo, a] *adj* (*QUÍMICA*) oxygenated; (*pelo*) bleached
oxígeno [ok'sixeno] *nm* oxygen
oyente [o'jente] *nm/f* listener, hearer
oyes *etc vb ver* oír
ozono [o'θono] *nm* ozone

P p

P *abr* (= *padre*) Fr.
pabellón [paβe'ʎon] *nm* bell tent; (*ARQ*) pavilion; (*de hospital etc*) block, section; (*bandera*) flag
pacer [pa'θer] *vi* to graze
paciencia [pa'θjenθja] *nf* patience
paciente [pa'θjente] *adj, nm/f* patient
pacificación [paθifika'θjon] *nf* pacification
pacificar [paθifi'kar] *vt* to pacify; (*tranquilizar*) to calm
pacífico, a [pa'θifiko, a] *adj* (*persona*) peaceable; (*existencia*) peaceful; el (océano) P~ the Pacific (Ocean)
pacifismo [paθi'fismo] *nm* pacifism; pacifista *nm/f* pacifist
pacotilla [pako'tiʎa] *nf*: de ~ (*actor, escritor*) third-rate; (*mueble etc*) cheap
pactar [pak'tar] *vt* to agree to *o* on ♦ *vi* to come to an agreement
pacto ['pakto] *nm* (*tratado*) pact; (*acuerdo*) agreement
padecer [paðe'θer] *vt* (*sufrir*) to suffer;

(*soportar*) to endure, put up with; (*engaño, error*) to be a victim of; padecimiento *nm* suffering
padrastro [pa'ðrastro] *nm* stepfather
padre ['paðre] *nm* father ♦ *adj* (*fam*): un éxito ~ a tremendous success; ~s *nmpl* parents
padrino [pa'ðrino] *nm* (*REL*) godfather; (*tb*: ~ de boda) best man; (*fig*) sponsor, patron; ~s *nmpl* godparents
padrón [pa'ðron] *nm* (*censo*) census, roll; (*de socios*) register
paella [pa'eʎa] *nf* paella, *dish of rice with meat, shellfish etc*
paga ['paɣa] *nf* (*pago*) payment; (*sueldo*) pay, wages *pl*
pagadero, a [paɣa'ðero, a] *adj* payable; ~ a plazos payable in instalments
pagano, a [pa'ɣano, a] *adj, nm/f* pagan, heathen
pagar [pa'ɣar] *vt* to pay; (*las compras, crimen*) to pay for; (*fig: favor*) to repay ♦ *vi* to pay; ~ al contado/a plazos to pay (in) cash/in instalments
pagaré [paɣa're] *nm* I.O.U.
página ['paxina] *nf* page
pago ['paɣo] *nm* (*dinero*) payment; (*fig*) return; estar ~ to be even *o* quits; ~ anticipado/a cuenta/contra reembolso/en especie advance payment/payment on account/cash on delivery/payment in kind
pág(s). *abr* (= *página(s)*) p(p).
pague *etc vb ver* pagar
país [pa'is] *nm* (*gen*) country; (*región*) land; los P~es Bajos the Low Countries; el P~ Vasco the Basque Country
paisaje [pai'saxe] *nm* countryside, scenery
paisano, a [pai'sano, a] *adj* of the same country ♦ *nm/f* (*compatriota*) fellow countryman/woman; vestir de ~ (*soldado*) to be in civvies; (*guardia*) to be in plain clothes
paja ['paxa] *nf* straw; (*fig*) rubbish (*BRIT*), trash (*US*)
pajarita [paxa'rita] *nf* (*corbata*) bow tie
pájaro ['paxaro] *nm* bird; ~ carpintero woodpecker

pajita [pa'xita] *nf* (drinking) straw

pala ['pala] *nf* spade, shovel; (*raqueta etc*) bat; (: *de tenis*) racquet; (*CULIN*) slice; ~ **matamoscas** fly swat

palabra [pa'laβra] *nf* word; (*facultad*) (power of) speech; (*derecho de hablar*) right to speak; **tomar la ~** (*en mitin*) to take the floor

palabrota [pala'brota] *nf* swearword

palacio [pa'laθjo] *nm* palace; (*mansión*) mansion, large house; ~ **de justicia** courthouse; ~ **municipal** town/city hall

paladar [pala'ðar] *nm* palate; **paladear** *vt* to taste

palanca [pa'lanka] *nf* lever; (*fig*) pull, influence

palangana [palan'gana] *nf* washbasin

palco ['palko] *nm* box

Palestina [pales'tina] *nf* Palestine; **palestino, a** *nm/f* Palestinian

paleta [pa'leta] *nf* (*de pintor*) palette; (*de albañil*) trowel; (*de ping-pong*) bat; (*AM*) ice lolly

paleto, a [pa'leto, a] (*fam, pey*) *nm/f* yokel

paliar [pa'ljar] *vt* (*mitigar*) to mitigate, alleviate; **paliativo** *nm* palliative

palidecer [paliðe'θer] *vi* to turn pale; **palidez** *nf* paleness; **pálido, a** *adj* pale

palillo [pa'liʎo] *nm* small stick; (*mondadientes*) toothpick; (*para comer*) chopstick

paliza [pa'liθa] *nf* beating, thrashing

palma ['palma] *nf* (*ANAT*) palm; (*árbol*) palm tree; **batir** *o* **dar ~s** to clap, applaud; **~da** *nf* slap; **~das** *nfpl* clapping *sg*, applause *sg*

palmar [pal'mar] (*fam*) *vi* (*tb*: ~*la*) to die, kick the bucket

palmear [palme'ar] *vi* to clap

palmera [pal'mera] *nf* (*BOT*) palm tree

palmo ['palmo] *nm* (*medida*) span; (*fig*) small amount; ~ **a** ~ inch by inch

palmotear [palmote'ar] *vi* to clap, applaud

palo ['palo] *nm* stick; (*poste*) post; (*de tienda de campaña*) pole; (*mango*) handle, shaft; (*golpe*) blow, hit; (*de golf*) club; (*de béisbol*) bat; (*NAUT*) mast; (*NAIPES*) suit

paloma [pa'loma] *nf* dove, pigeon

palomilla [palo'miʎa] *nf* moth; (*TEC: tuerca*) wing nut; (: *hierro*) angle iron

palomitas [palo'mitas] *nfpl* popcorn *sg*

palpar [pal'par] *vt* to touch, feel

palpitación [palpita'θjon] *nf* palpitation

palpitante [palpi'tante] *adj* palpitating; (*fig*) burning

palpitar [palpi'tar] *vi* to palpitate; (*latir*) to beat

palta ['palta] (*AM*) *nf* avocado (pear)

paludismo [palu'ðismo] *nm* malaria

pamela [pa'mela] *nf* picture hat, sun hat

pampa ['pampa] (*AM*) *nf* pampas, prairie

pan [pan] *nm* bread; (*una barra*) loaf; ~ **integral** wholemeal (*BRIT*) *o* wholewheat (*US*) bread; ~ **rallado** breadcrumbs *pl*

pana ['pana] *nf* corduroy

panadería [panaðe'ria] *nf* baker's (shop); **panadero, a** *nm/f* baker

Panamá [pana'ma] *nm* Panama; **panameño, a** *adj* Panamanian

pancarta [pan'karta] *nf* placard, banner

panda ['panda] *nm* (*ZOOL*) panda

pandereta [pande'reta] *nf* tambourine

pandilla [pan'diʎa] *nf* set, group; (*de criminales*) gang; (*pey: camarilla*) clique

panecillo [pane'θiʎo] *nm* (bread) roll

panel [pa'nel] *nm* panel; ~ **solar** solar panel

panfleto [pan'fleto] *nm* pamphlet

pánico ['paniko] *nm* panic

panorama [pano'rama] *nm* panorama; (*vista*) view

pantalla [pan'taʎa] *nf* (*de cine*) screen; (*de lámpara*) lampshade

pantalón [panta'lon] *nm* trousers; **pantalones** *nmpl* trousers

pantano [pan'tano] *nm* (*ciénaga*) marsh, swamp; (*depósito: de agua*) reservoir; (*fig*) jam, difficulty

panteón [pante'on] *nm*: ~ **familiar** family tomb

pantera [pan'tera] *nf* panther

panti(e)s ['pantis] *nmpl* tights

pantomima [panto'mima] *nf* pantomime

pantorrilla [panto'rriʎa] *nf* calf (of the leg)

pantufla [pan'tufla] *nf* slipper

panty(s) ['panti(s)] *nm(pl)* tights

panza ['panθa] *nf* belly, paunch

pañal [pa'ɲal] *nm* nappy (*BRIT*), diaper (*US*); **~es** *nmpl* (*fig*) early stages, infancy *sg*

paño ['paɲo] *nm* (*tela*) cloth; (*pedazo de tela*) (piece of) cloth; (*trapo*) duster, rag; **~ higiénico** sanitary towel; **~s menores** underclothes

pañuelo [pa'ɲwelo] *nm* handkerchief, hanky (*fam*); (*para la cabeza*) (head)scarf

papa ['papa] *nm*: **el P~** the Pope ♦ *nf* (*AM*) potato

papá [pa'pa] (*pl* **~s**) (*fam*) *nm* dad(dy), pa (*US*)

papada [pa'paða] *nf* (*ANAT*) double chin

papagayo [papa'ɣajo] *nm* parrot

papanatas [papa'natas] (*fam*) *nm inv* simpleton

paparrucha [papa'rrutʃa] *nf* piece of nonsense

papaya [pa'paja] *nf* papaya

papear [pape'ar] (*fam*) *vt, vi* to scoff

papel [pa'pel] *nm* paper; (*hoja de ~*) sheet of paper; (*TEATRO*, *fig*) role; **~ de calco/carbón/de cartas** tracing paper/carbon paper/stationery; **~ de envolver/pintado** wrapping paper/wallpaper; **~ de aluminio/higiénico** aluminium (*BRIT*) o aluminum (*US*)/toilet paper; **~ de estaño** o **plata** tinfoil; **~ de lija** sandpaper; **~ moneda** paper money; **~ secante** blotting paper

papeleo [pape'leo] *nm* red tape

papelera [pape'lera] *nf* wastepaper basket; (*escritorio*) desk

papelería [papele'ria] *nf* stationer's (shop)

papeleta [pape'leta] *nf* (*pedazo de papel*) slip of paper; (*POL*) ballot paper; (*ESCOL*) report

paperas [pa'peras] *nfpl* mumps *sg*

papilla [pa'piʎa] *nf* (*para niños*) baby food

paquete [pa'kete] *nm* (*de cigarrillos etc*) packet; (*CORREOS etc*) parcel; (*AM*) package tour; (: *fam*) nuisance, bore

par [par] *adj* (*igual*) like, equal; (*MAT*) even ♦ *nm* equal; (*de guantes*) pair; (*de veces*) couple; (*POL*) peer; (*GOLF*, *COM*) par;

abrir de ~ en ~ to open wide

para ['para] *prep* for; **no es ~ comer** it's not for eating; **decir ~ sí** to say to o.s.; **¿~ qué lo quieres?** what do you want it for?; **se casaron ~ separarse otra vez** they married only to separate again; **lo tendré ~ mañana** I'll have it (for) tomorrow; **ir ~ casa** to go home, head for home; **~ profesor es muy estúpido** he's very stupid for a teacher; **¿quién es usted ~ gritar así?** who are you to shout like that?; **tengo bastante ~ vivir** I have enough to live on; *ver tb* **con**

parabién [para'βjen] *nm* congratulations *pl*

parábola [pa'raβola] *nf* parable; (*MAT*) parabola; **parabólica** *nf* (*tb: antena ~*) satellite dish

parabrisas [para'βrisas] *nm inv* windscreen (*BRIT*), windshield (*US*)

paracaídas [paraka'iðas] *nm inv* parachute; **paracaidista** *nm/f* parachutist; (*MIL*) paratrooper

parachoques [para'tʃokes] *nm inv* (*AUTO*) bumper; (*MECÁNICA etc*) shock absorber

parada [pa'raða] *nf* stop; (*acto*) stopping; (*de industria*) shutdown, stoppage; (*lugar*) stopping place; **~ de autobús** bus stop

paradero [para'ðero] *nm* stopping-place; (*situación*) whereabouts

parado, a [pa'raðo, a] *adj* (*persona*) motionless, standing still; (*fábrica*) closed, at a standstill; (*coche*) stopped; (*AM*) standing (up); (*sin empleo*) unemployed, idle

paradoja [para'ðoxa] *nf* paradox

parador [para'ðor] *nm* parador, state-run hotel

paráfrasis [pa'rafrasis] *nf inv* paraphrase

paraguas [pa'raɣwas] *nm inv* umbrella

Paraguay [para'ɣwai] *nm*: **el ~** Paraguay; **paraguayo, a** *adj, nm/f* Paraguayan

paraíso [para'iso] *nm* paradise, heaven

paraje [pa'raxe] *nm* place, spot

paralelo, a [para'lelo, a] *adj* parallel

parálisis [pa'ralisis] *nf inv* paralysis; **paralítico, a** *adj, nm/f* paralytic

paralizar [parali'θar] *vt* to paralyse; **~se**

vr to become paralysed; (*fig*) to come to a standstill

paramilitar [paramili'tar] *adj* paramilitary

páramo ['paramo] *nm* bleak plateau

parangón [paran'gon] *nm*: **sin ~** incomparable

paranoico, a [para'noiko, a] *nm/f* paranoiac

parapléjico, a [para'plexiko, a] *adj, nm/f* paraplegic

parar [pa'rar] *vt* to stop; (*golpe*) to ward off ♦ *vi* to stop; **~se** *vr* to stop; (*AM*) to stand up; **ha parado de llover** it has stopped raining; **van a ~ en la comisaria** they're going to end up in the police station; **~se en** to pay attention to

pararrayos [para'rrajos] *nm inv* lightning conductor

parásito, a [pa'rasito, a] *nm/f* parasite

parcela [par'θela] *nf* plot, piece of ground

parche ['partʃe] *nm* (*gen*) patch

parchís [par'tʃis] *nm* ludo

parcial [par'θjal] *adj* (*pago*) part-; (*eclipse*) partial; (*JUR*) prejudiced, biased; (*POL*) partisan; **~idad** *nf* (*prejuicio*) prejudice, bias

parco, a ['parko, a] *adj* (*moderado*) moderate

pardillo, a [par'ðiʎo, a] (*pey*) *adj* yokel

parecer [pare'θer] *nm* (*opinión*) opinion, view; (*aspecto*) looks *pl* ♦ *vi* (*tener apariencia*) to seem, look; (*asemejarse*) to look o seem like; (*aparecer, llegar*) to appear; **~se** *vr* to look alike, resemble each other; **~se a** to look like, resemble; **según** *o* **a lo que parece** evidently, apparently; **me parece que** I think (that), it seems to me that

parecido, a [pare'θiðo, a] *adj* similar ♦ *nm* similarity, likeness, resemblance; **bien ~** good-looking, nice-looking

pared [pa'reð] *nf* wall

pareja [pa'rexa] *nf* (*par*) pair; (*dos personas*) couple; (*otro: de un par*) other one (of a pair); (*persona*) partner

parentela [paren'tela] *nf* relations *pl*

parentesco [paren'tesko] *nm* relationship

paréntesis [pa'rentesis] *nm inv* parenthesis; (*digresión*) digression; (*en escrito*)

bracket

parezco *etc vb ver* **parecer**

pariente, a [pa'rjente, a] *nm/f* relative, relation

parir [pa'rir] *vt* to give birth to ♦ *vi* (*mujer*) to give birth, have a baby

París [pa'ris] *n* Paris

parking ['parkin] *nm* car park (*BRIT*), parking lot (*US*)

parlamentar [parlamen'tar] *vi* (*negociar*) to parley

parlamentario, a [parlamen'tarjo, a] *adj* parliamentary ♦ *nm/f* member of parliament

parlamento [parla'mento] *nm* (*POL*) parliament

parlanchín, ina [parlan'tʃin, ina] *adj* indiscreet ♦ *nm/f* chatterbox

parlar [par'lar] *vi* to chatter (away)

paro ['paro] *nm* (*huelga*) stoppage (of work), strike; (*desempleo*) unemployment; **subsidio de ~** unemployment benefit; **hay ~ en la industria** work in the industry is at a standstill

parodia [pa'roðja] *nf* parody; **parodiar** *vt* to parody

parpadear [parpaðe'ar] *vi* (*ojos*) to blink; (*luz*) to flicker

párpado ['parpaðo] *nm* eyelid

parque ['parke] *nm* (*lugar verde*) park; **~ de atracciones/infantil/zoológico** fairground/playground/zoo

parquímetro [par'kimetro] *nm* parking meter

parra ['parra] *nf* (*grape*)vine

párrafo ['parrafo] *nm* paragraph; **echar un ~** (*fam*) to have a chat

parranda [pa'rranda] (*fam*) *nf* spree, binge

parrilla [pa'rriʎa] *nf* (*CULIN*) grill; (*de coche*) **(carne a la) ~** barbecue; **~da** *nf* barbecue

párroco ['parroko] *nm* parish priest

parroquia [pa'rrokja] *nf* parish; (*iglesia*) parish church; (*COM*) clientele, customers *pl*; **~no, a** *nm/f* parishioner; client, customer

parsimonia [parsi'monja] *nf* calmness, level-headedness

parte ['parte] *nm* message; (*informe*)

report ♦ *nf* part; (*lado, cara*) side; (*de reparto*) share; (*JUR*) party; **en alguna ~ de Europa** somewhere in Europe; **en/ por todas ~s** everywhere; **en gran ~** to a large extent; **la mayor ~ de los españoles** most Spaniards; **de un tiempo a esta ~** for some time past; **de ~ de alguien** on sb's behalf; **¿de ~ de quién?** (*TEL*) who is speaking?; **por ~ de** on the part of; **yo por mi ~** I for my part; **por otra ~** on the other hand; **dar ~** to inform; **tomar ~** to take part

partición [partiˈθjon] *nf* division, sharing-out; (*POL*) partition

participación [partiθipaˈθjon] *nf* (*acto*) participation, taking part; (*parte, COM*) share; (*de lotería*) shared prize; (*aviso*) notice, notification

participante [partiθiˈpante] *nm/f* participant

participar [partiθiˈpar] *vt* to notify, inform ♦ *vi* to take part, participate

partícipe [parˈtiθipe] *nm/f* participant

particular [partikuˈlar] *adj* (*especial*) particular, special; (*individual, personal*) private, personal ♦ *nm* (*punto, asunto*) particular, point; (*individuo*) individual; **tiene coche ~** he has a car of his own; **~izar** *vt* to distinguish; (*especificar*) to specify; (*detallar*) to give details about

partida [parˈtiða] *nf* (*salida*) departure; (*COM*) entry, item; (*juego*) game; (*grupo de personas*) band, group; **mala ~** dirty trick; **~ de nacimiento / matrimonio / defunción** birth/marriage/death certificate

partidario, a [partiˈðarjo, a] *adj* partisan ♦ *nm/f* supporter, follower

partido [parˈtiðo] *nm* (*POL*) party; (*DEPORTE: encuentro*) game, match; (: *equipo*) team; (*apoyo*) support; **sacar ~ de** to profit o benefit from; **tomar ~** to take sides

partir [parˈtir] *vt* (*dividir*) to split, divide; (*compartir, distribuir*) to share (out), distribute; (*romper*) to break open, split open; (*rebanada*) to cut (off) ♦ *vi* (*ponerse en camino*) to set off o out; (*comenzar*) to start (off o out); **~se** *vr* to crack o split o

break (in two *etc*); **a ~ de** (starting) from

partitura [partiˈtura] *nf* (*MUS*) score

parto [ˈparto] *nm* birth; (*fig*) product, creation; **estar de ~** to be in labour

parvulario [parβuˈlarjo] *nm* nursery school, kindergarten

pasa [ˈpasa] *nf* raisin; **~ de Corinto/de Esmirna** currant/sultana

pasada [paˈsaða] *nf* passing, passage; **de ~** in passing, incidentally; **una mala ~** a dirty trick

pasadizo [pasaˈðiθo] *nm* (*pasillo*) passage, corridor; (*callejuela*) alley

pasado, a [paˈsaðo, a] *adj* past; (*malo: comida, fruta*) bad; (*muy cocido*) over-done; (*anticuado*) out of date ♦ *nm* past; **~ mañana** the day after tomorrow; **el mes ~** last month

pasador [pasaˈðor] *nm* (*gen*) bolt; (*de pelo*) hair slide; (*horquilla*) grip

pasaje [paˈsaxe] *nm* passage; (*pago de viaje*) fare; (*los pasajeros*) passengers *pl*; (*pasillo*) passageway

pasajero, a [pasaˈxero, a] *adj* passing; (*situación, estado*) temporary; (*amor, enfermedad*) brief ♦ *nm/f* passenger

pasamanos [pasaˈmanos] *nm inv* (hand)rail; (*de escalera*) banisters *pl*

pasamontañas [pasamonˈtaɲas] *nm inv* balaclava helmet

pasaporte [pasaˈporte] *nm* passport

pasar [paˈsar] *vt* to pass; (*tiempo*) to spend; (*desgracias*) to suffer, endure; (*noticia*) to give, pass on; (*río*) to cross; (*barrera*) to pass through; (*falta*) to overlook, tolerate; (*contrincante*) to sur-pass, do better than; (*coche*) to overtake; (*CINE*) to show; (*enfermedad*) to give, infect with ♦ *vi* (*gen*) to pass; (*terminarse*) to be over; (*ocurrir*) to happen; **~se** *vr* (*flores*) to fade; (*comida*) to go bad o off; (*fig*) to overdo it, go too far; **~ de** to go beyond, exceed; **~ por** (*AM*) to fetch; **~lo bien/mal** to have a good/bad time; **¡pase!** come in!; **hacer ~** to show in; **~se al enemigo** to go over to the enemy; **se me pasó** I forgot; **no se le pasa nada** he misses nothing; **pase lo que pase** come what may

pasarela [pasa'rela] *nf* footbridge; (*en barco*) gangway

pasatiempo [pasa'tjempo] *nm* pastime, hobby

Pascua ['paskwa] *nf*: ~ **(de Resurrección)** Easter; ~ **de Navidad** Christmas; ~s *nfpl* Christmas (time); ¡**felices** ~s! Merry Christmas!

pase ['pase] *nm* pass; (*CINE*) performance, showing

pasear [pase'ar] *vt* to take for a walk; (*exhibir*) to parade, show off ♦ *vi* to walk, go for a walk; ~**se** *vr* to walk, go for a walk; ~ **en coche** *vr* to go for a drive; **paseo** *nm* (*avenida*) avenue; (*distancia corta*) walk, stroll; **dar un** *o* **ir de paseo** to go for a walk

pasillo [pa'siʎo] *nm* passage, corridor

pasión [pa'sjon] *nf* passion

pasivo, a [pa'siβo, a] *adj* passive; (*inactivo*) inactive ♦ *nm* (*COM*) liabilities *pl*, debts *pl*; (*LING*) passive

pasmar [pas'mar] *vt* (*asombrar*) to amaze, astonish; **pasmo** *nm* amazement, astonishment; (*resfriado*) chill; (*fig*) wonder, marvel; **pasmoso, a** *adj* amazing, astonishing

paso, a ['paso, a] *adj* dried ♦ *nm* step; (*modo de andar*) walk; (*huella*) footprint; (*rapidez*) speed, pace, rate; (*camino accesible*) way through, passage; (*cruce*) crossing; (*pasaje*) passing, passage; (*GEO*) pass; (*estrecho*) strait; ~ **a nivel** (*FERRO*) level-crossing; ~ **de peatones** pedestrian crossing; **a ese** ~ (*fig*) at that rate; **salir al** ~ **de** *o* **a** to waylay; **estar de** ~ to be passing through; ~ **elevado** flyover; **prohibido el** ~ no entry; **ceda el** ~ give way

pasota [pa'sota] (*fam*) *adj*, *nm/f* ≈ dropout; **ser un (tipo)** ~ to be a bit of a dropout; (*ser indiferente*) not to care about anything

pasta ['pasta] *nf* paste; (*CULIN: masa*) dough; (: *de bizcochos etc*) pastry; (*fam*) dough; ~**s** *nfpl* (*bizcochos*) pastries, small cakes; (*fideos, espaguetis etc*) pasta; ~ **de dientes** *o* **dentífrica** toothpaste

pastar [pas'tar] *vt*, *vi* to graze

pastel [pas'tel] *nm* (*dulce*) cake; ~ **de carne** meat pie; (*ARTE*) pastel; ~**ería** *nf* cake shop

pasteurizado, a [pasteuri'θaðo, a] *adj* pasteurized

pastilla [pas'tiʎa] *nf* (*de jabón, chocolate*) bar; (*píldora*) tablet, pill

pasto ['pasto] *nm* (*hierba*) grass; (*lugar*) pasture, field

pastor, a [pas'tor, a] *nm/f* shepherd/ess ♦ *nm* (*REL*) clergyman, pastor; ~ **alemán** Alsatian

pata ['pata] *nf* (*pierna*) leg; (*pie*) foot; (*de muebles*) leg; ~**s arriba** upside down; **metedura de** ~ (*fam*) gaffe; **meter la** ~ (*fam*) to put one's foot in it; (*TEC*): ~ **de cabra** crowbar; **tener buena/mala** ~ to be lucky/unlucky; ~**da** *nf* kick; (*en el suelo*) stamp

patalear [patale'ar] *vi* (*en el suelo*) to stamp one's feet

patata [pa'tata] *nf* potato; ~**s fritas** *o* **a la española** chips, French fries; ~**s fritas** (*de bolsa*) crisps

paté [pa'te] *nm* pâté

patear [pate'ar] *vt* (*pisar*) to stamp on, trample (on); (*pegar con el pie*) to kick ♦ *vi* to stamp (with rage), stamp one's feet

patentar [paten'tar] *vt* to patent

patente [pa'tente] *adj* obvious, evident; (*COM*) patent ♦ *nf* patent

paternal [pater'nal] *adj* fatherly, paternal; **paterno, a** *adj* paternal

patético, a [pa'tetiko, a] *adj* pathetic, moving

patilla [pa'tiʎa] *nf* (*de gafas*) side(piece)

patillas [pa'tiʎas] *nfpl* sideburns

patín [pa'tin] *nm* skate; (*de trineo*) runner; **patinaje** *nm* skating; **patinar** *vi* to skate; (*resbalarse*) to skid, slip; (*fam*) to slip up, blunder

patio ['patjo] *nm* (*de casa*) patio, courtyard; ~ **de recreo** playground

pato ['pato] *nm* duck; **pagar el** ~ (*fam*) to take the blame, carry the can

patológico, a [pato'loxiko, a] *adj* pathological

patoso, a [pa'toso, a] (*fam*) *adj* clumsy

patraña [pa'traɲa] *nf* story, fib

patria ['patrja] *nf* native land, mother country

patrimonio [patri'monjo] *nm* inheritance; (*fig*) heritage

patriota [pa'trjota] *nm/f* patriot; **patriotismo** *nm* patriotism

patrocinar [patroθi'nar] *vt* to sponsor; (*apoyar*) to back, support; **patrocinio** *nm* sponsorship; backing, support

patronal [patro'nal] *adj*: **la clase ~** management

patronato [patro'nato] *nm* sponsorship; (*acto*) patronage; (*fundación benéfica*) trust, foundation

patrón, ona [pa'tron, ona] *nm/f* (*jefe*) boss, chief, master/mistress; (*propietario*) landlord/lady; (*REL*) patron saint ♦ *nm* (*TEC, COSTURA*) pattern

patrulla [pa'truʎa] *nf* patrol

pausa ['pausa] *nf* pause, break

pausado, a [pau'saðo, a] *adj* slow, deliberate

pauta ['pauta] *nf* line, guide line

pavimento [paβi'mento] *nm* (*con losas*) pavement, paving

pavo ['paβo] *nm* turkey; **~ real** peacock

pavor [pa'βor] *nm* dread, terror

payaso, a [pa'jaso, a] *nm/f* clown

payo, a ['pajo] *nm/f* (*para gitanos*) non-gipsy

paz [paθ] *nf* peace; (*tranquilidad*) peacefulness, tranquillity; **hacer las paces** to make peace; (*fig*) to make up

P.D. *abr* (= *posdata*) P.S., p.s.

peaje [pe'axe] *nm* toll

peatón [pea'ton] *nm* pedestrian

peca ['peka] *nf* freckle

pecado [pe'kaðo] *nm* sin; **pecador, a** *adj* sinful ♦ *nm/f* sinner

pecaminoso, a [pekami'noso, a] *adj* sinful

pecar [pe'kar] *vi* (*REL*) to sin; (*fig*): **peca de generoso** he is generous to a fault

pecho ['petʃo] *nm* (*ANAT*) chest; (*de mujer*) breast(s) (*pl*), bosom; (*fig: corazón*) heart, breast; (: *valor*) courage, spirit; **dar el ~ a** to breast-feed; **tomar algo a ~** to take sth to heart

pechuga [pe'tʃuɣa] *nf* breast

peculiar [peku'ljar] *adj* special, peculiar; (*característico*) typical, characteristic; **~idad** *nf* peculiarity; special feature, characteristic

pedal [pe'ðal] *nm* pedal; **~ear** *vi* to pedal

pedante [pe'ðante] *adj* pedantic ♦ *nm/f* pedant; **~ría** *nf* pedantry

pedazo [pe'ðaθo] *nm* piece, bit; **hacerse ~s** (*romperse*) to smash, shatter

pedernal [peðer'nal] *nm* flint

pediatra [pe'ðjatra] *nm/f* paediatrician

pedido [pe'ðiðo] *nm* (*COM: mandado*) order; (*petición*) request

pedir [pe'ðir] *vt* to ask for, request; (*comida, COM: mandar*) to order; (*exigir: precio*) to ask; (*necesitar*) to need, demand, require ♦ *vi* to ask; **me pidió que cerrara la puerta** he asked me to shut the door; **¿cuánto piden por el coche?** how much are they asking for the car?

pedo ['peðo] (*fam!*) *nm* fart

pega ['peɣa] *nf* snag; **poner ~s (a)** to complain (about)

pegadizo, a [peɣa'ðiθo, a] *adj* (*MUS*) catchy

pegajoso, a [peɣa'xoso, a] *adj* sticky, adhesive

pegamento [peɣa'mento] *nm* gum, glue

pegar [pe'ɣar] *vt* (*papel, sellos*) to stick (on); (*cartel*) to stick up; (*coser*) to sew (on); (*unir: partes*) to join, fix together; (*MED*) to give, infect with; (*dar: golpe*) to give, deal ♦ *vi* (*adherirse*) to stick, adhere; (*ir juntos: colores*) to match, go together; (*golpear*) to hit; (*quemar: el sol*) to strike hot, burn (*fig*); **~se** *vr* (*gen*) to stick; (*dos personas*) to hit each other, fight; (*fam*): **~ un grito** to let out a yell; **~ un salto** to jump (with fright); **~ en** to touch; **~se un tiro** to shoot o.s.

pegatina [peɣa'tina] *nf* sticker

pegote [pe'ɣote] *nm* (*fig*) mess; (*fam, pey*) eyesore, sight

peinado [pei'naðo] *nm* (*en peluquería*) hairdo; (*estilo*) hair style

peinar [pei'nar] *vt* to comb; (*hacer estilo*) to style; **~se** *vr* to comb one's hair

peine ['peine] *nm* comb; ~ta *nf* ornamental comb

p.ej. *abr* (= *por ejemplo*) e.g.

Pekín [pe'kin] *n* Pekin(g)

pelado, a [pe'laðo, a] *adj* (*fruta, patata etc*) peeled; (*cabeza*) shorn; (*campo, fig*) bare; (*fam: sin dinero*) broke

pelaje [pe'laxe] *nm* (*ZOOL*) fur, coat; (*fig*) appearance

pelar [pe'lar] *vt* (*fruta, patatas etc*) to peel; (*cortar el pelo a*) to cut the hair of; (*quitar la piel: animal*) to skin; ~**se** *vr* (*la piel*) to peel off; **voy a** ~**me** I'm going to get my hair cut

peldaño [pel'daɲo] *nm* step

pelea [pe'lea] *nf* (*lucha*) fight; (*discusión*) quarrel, row

peleado, a [pele'aðo, a] *adj*: **estar** ~ (**con uno**) to have fallen out (with sb)

pelear [pele'ar] *vi* to fight; ~**se** *vr* to fight; (*reñirse*) to fall out, quarrel

peletería [pelete'ria] *nf* furrier's, fur shop

pelícano [pe'likano] *nm* pelican

película [pe'likula] *nf* film; (*cobertura ligera*) thin covering; (*FOTO: rollo*) roll o reel of film

peligro [pe'liɣro] *nm* danger; (*riesgo*) risk; **correr** ~ **de** to run the risk of; ~**so, a** *adj* dangerous; risky

pelirrojo, a [peli'rroxo, a] *adj* red-haired, red-headed ♦ *nm/f* redhead

pellejo [pe'ʎexo] *nm* (*de animal*) skin, hide

pellizcar [peʎiθ'kar] *vt* to pinch, nip

pelma ['pelma] (*fam*) *nm/f* pain (in the neck)

pelmazo [pel'maθo] (*fam*) *nm* = **pelma**

pelo ['pelo] *nm* (*cabellos*) hair; (*de barba, bigote*) whisker; (*de animal: pellejo*) hair, fur, coat; **al** ~ just right; **venir al** ~ to be exactly what one needs; **un hombre de** ~ **en pecho** a brave man; **por los** ~**s** by the skin of one's teeth; **no tener** ~**s en la lengua** to be outspoken, not mince words; **tomar el** ~ **a uno** to pull sb's leg

pelota [pe'lota] *nf* ball; (*fam: cabeza*) nut; **en** ~ stark naked; **hacer la** ~ (**a uno**) (*fam*) to creep (to sb); ~ **vasca** pelota

pelotari [pelo'tari] *nm* pelota player

pelotón [pelo'ton] *nm* (*MIL*) squad, detachment

peluca [pe'luka] *nf* wig

peluche [pe'lutʃe] *nm*: **oso/muñeco de** ~ teddy bear/soft toy

peludo, a [pe'luðo, a] *adj* hairy, shaggy

peluquería [peluke'ria] *nf* hairdresser's; (*para hombres*) barber's (shop); **peluquero, a** *nm/f* hairdresser; barber

pelusa [pe'lusa] *nf* (*BOT*) down; (*COSTURA*) fluff

pena ['pena] *nf* (*congoja*) grief, sadness; (*remordimiento*) regret; (*dificultad*) trouble; (*dolor*) pain; (*JUR*) sentence; **merecer** o **valer la** ~ to be worthwhile; **a duras** ~**s** with great difficulty; ~ **de muerte** death penalty; ~ **pecuniaria** fine; **¡qué** ~! what a shame!

penal [pe'nal] *adj* penal ♦ *nm* (*cárcel*) prison

penalidad [penali'ðað] *nf* (*problema, dificultad*) trouble, hardship; (*JUR*) penalty, punishment; ~**es** *nfpl* trouble, hardship

penalti [pe'nalti] (*pl* ~**s** o ~**es**) *nm* penalty (kick)

penalty [pe'nalti] (*pl* ~**s** o ~**es**) *nm* = **penalti**

penar [pe'nar] *vt* to penalize; (*castigar*) to punish ♦ *vi* to suffer

pendiente [pen'djente] *adj* pending, unsettled ♦ *nm* earring ♦ *nf* hill, slope

pene ['pene] *nm* penis

penetración [penetra'θjon] *nf* (*acto*) penetration; (*agudeza*) sharpness, insight

penetrante [pene'trante] *adj* (*herida*) deep; (*persona, arma*) sharp; (*sonido*) penetrating, piercing; (*mirada*) searching; (*viento, ironía*) biting

penetrar [pene'trar] *vt* to penetrate, pierce; (*entender*) to grasp ♦ *vi* to penetrate, go in; (*entrar*) to enter, go in; (*líquido*) to soak in; (*fig*) to pierce

penicilina [peniθi'lina] *nf* penicillin

península [pe'ninsula] *nf* peninsula; **peninsular** *adj* peninsular

penique [pe'nike] *nm* penny

penitencia [peni'tenθja] *nf* (*remordimiento*) penitence; (*castigo*) penance

penoso, a [pe'noso, a] *adj* (*difícil*) arduous, difficult

pensador, a [pensa'ðor, a] *nm/f* thinker

pensamiento [pensa'mjento] *nm* thought; (*mente*) mind; (*idea*) idea

pensar [pen'sar] *vt* to think; (*considerar*) to think over, think out; (*proponerse*) to intend, plan; (*imaginarse*) to think up, invent ♦ *vi* to think; ~ **en** to aim at, aspire to; **pensativo, a** *adj* thoughtful, pensive

pensión [pen'sjon] *nf* (*casa*) boarding o guest house; (*dinero*) pension; (*cama y comida*) board and lodging; ~ **completa** full board; **pensionista** *nm/f* (*jubilado*) (old-age) pensioner; (*huésped*) lodger

penúltimo, a [pe'nultimo, a] *adj* penultimate, last but one

penumbra [pe'numbra] *nf* half-light

penuria [pe'nurja] *nf* shortage, want

peña ['peɲa] *nf* (*roca*) rock; (*cuesta*) cliff, crag; (*grupo*) group, circle; (*AM: club*) folk club

peñasco [pe'ɲasko] *nm* large rock, boulder

peñón [pe'ɲon] *nm* wall of rock; **el P~** the Rock (of Gibraltar)

peón [pe'on] *nm* labourer; (*AM*) farm labourer, farmhand; (*AJEDREZ*) pawn

peonza [pe'onθa] *nf* spinning top

peor [pe'or] *adj* (*comparativo*) worse; (*superlativo*) worst ♦ *adv* worse; worst; **de mal en** ~ from bad to worse

pepinillo [pepi'niʎo] *nm* gherkin

pepino [pe'pino] *nm* cucumber; **(no) me importa un** ~ I don't care one bit

pepita [pe'pita] *nf* (*BOT*) pip; (*MINERÍA*) nugget

pequeñez [peke'ɲeθ] *nf* smallness, littleness; (*trivialidad*) trifle, triviality

pequeño, a [pe'keɲo, a] *adj* small, little

pera ['pera] *nf* pear; **peral** *nm* pear tree

percance [per'kanθe] *nm* setback, misfortune

percatarse [perka'tarse] *vr*: ~ **de** to notice, take note of

percepción [perθep'θjon] *nf* (*vista*) perception; (*idea*) notion, idea

perceptible [perθep'tiβle] *adj* perceptible,

noticeable; (*COM*) payable, receivable

percha ['pertʃa] *nf* (*ganchos*) coat hooks *pl*; (*colgador*) coat hanger; (*de ave*) perch

percibir [perθi'βir] *vt* to perceive, notice; (*COM*) to earn, get

percusión [perku'sjon] *nf* percussion

perdedor, a [perðe'ðor, a] *adj* losing ♦ *nm/f* loser

perder [per'ðer] *vt* to lose; (*tiempo, palabras*) to waste; (*oportunidad*) to lose, miss; (*tren*) to miss ♦ *vi* to lose; ~**se** *vr* (*extraviarse*) to get lost; (*desaparecer*) to disappear, be lost to view; (*arruinarse*) to be ruined; **echar a** ~ (*comida*) to spoil, ruin; (*oportunidad*) to waste

perdición [perði'θjon] *nf* perdition, ruin

pérdida ['perðiða] *nf* loss; (*de tiempo*) waste; ~**s** *nfpl* (*COM*) losses

perdido, a [per'ðiðo, a] *adj* lost

perdiz [per'ðiθ] *nf* partridge

perdón [per'ðon] *nm* (*disculpa*) pardon, forgiveness; (*clemencia*) mercy; ¡~! sorry!, I beg your pardon!; **perdonar** *vt* to pardon, forgive; (*la vida*) to spare; (*excusar*) to exempt, excuse; ¡**perdone (usted)!** sorry!, I beg your pardon!

perdurable [perðu'raβle] *adj* lasting; (*eterno*) everlasting

perdurar [perðu'rar] *vi* (*resistir*) to last, endure; (*seguir existiendo*) to stand, still exist

perecedero, a [pereθe'ðero, a] *adj* (*COM etc*) perishable

perecer [pere'θer] *vi* (*morir*) to perish, die; (*objeto*) to shatter

peregrinación [pereɣrina'θjon] *nf* (*REL*) pilgrimage

peregrino, a [pere'ðrino, a] *adj* (*idea*) strange, absurd ♦ *nm/f* pilgrim

perejil [pere'xil] *nm* parsley

perenne [pe'renne] *adj* everlasting, perennial

perentorio, a [peren'torjo, a] *adj* (*urgente*) urgent, peremptory; (*fijo*) set, fixed

pereza [pe'reθa] *nf* laziness, idleness; **perezoso, a** *adj* lazy, idle

perfección [perfek'θjon] *nf* perfection; **perfeccionar** *vt* to perfect; (*mejorar*) to improve; (*acabar*) to complete, finish

perfectamente [perfekta'mente] *adv* perfectly

perfecto, a [per'fekto, a] *adj* perfect; (*terminado*) complete, finished

perfidia [per'fiðja] *nf* perfidy, treachery

perfil [per'fil] *nm* profile; (*contorno*) silhouette, outline; (*ARQ*) (cross) section; **~es** *nmpl* features; (*fig*) social graces; **~ar** *vt* (*trazar*) to outline; (*fig*) to shape, give character to

perforación [perfora'θjon] *nf* perforation; (*con taladro*) drilling; **perforadora** *nf* punch

perforar [perfo'rar] *vt* to perforate; (*agujero*) to drill, bore; (*papel*) to punch a hole in ♦ *vi* to drill, bore

perfume [per'fume] *nm* perfume, scent

pericia [pe'riθja] *nf* skill, expertise

periferia [peri'ferja] *nf* periphery; (*de ciudad*) outskirts *pl*

periférico [peri'feriko] (*AM*) *nm* ring road (*BRIT*), beltway (*US*)

perímetro [pe'rimetro] *nm* perimeter

periódico, a [pe'rjoðiko, a] *adj* periodic(al) ♦ *nm* newspaper

periodismo [perjo'ðismo] *nm* journalism; **periodista** *nm/f* journalist

periodo [pe'rjoðo] *nm* period

período [pe'rioðo] *nm* = **periodo**

periquito [peri'kito] *nm* budgerigar, budgie

perito, a [pe'rito, a] *adj* (*experto*) expert; (*diestro*) skilled, skilful ♦ *nm/f* expert; skilled worker; (*técnico*) technician

perjudicar [perxuði'kar] *vt* (*gen*) to damage, harm; **perjudicial** *adj* damaging, harmful; (*en detrimento*) detrimental; **perjuicio** *nm* damage, harm

perjurar [perxu'rar] *vi* to commit perjury

perla ['perla] *nf* pearl; **me viene de ~** it suits me fine

permanecer [permane'θer] *vi* (*quedarse*) to stay, remain; (*seguir*) to continue to be

permanencia [perma'nenθja] *nf* permanence; (*estancia*) stay

permanente [perma'nente] *adj* permanent, constant ♦ *nf* perm

permisible [permi'siβle] *adj* permissible, allowable

permisivo, a [permi'siβo, a] *adj* permissive

permiso [per'miso] *nm* permission; (*licencia*) permit, licence; **con ~** excuse me; **estar de ~** (*MIL*) to be on leave; **~ de conducir** driving licence (*BRIT*), driver's license (*US*)

permitir [permi'tir] *vt* to permit, allow

pernera [per'nera] *nf* trouser leg

pernicioso, a [perni'θjoso, a] *adj* (*maligno, MED*) pernicious; (*persona*) wicked

pero ['pero] *conj* but; (*aún*) yet ♦ *nm* (*defecto*) flaw, defect; (*reparo*) objection

perpendicular [perpendiku'lar] *adj* perpendicular

perpetrar [perpe'trar] *vt* to perpetrate

perpetuar [perpe'twar] *vt* to perpetuate; **perpetuo, a** *adj* perpetual

perplejo, a [per'plexo, a] *adj* perplexed, bewildered

perra ['perra] *nf* (*ZOOL*) bitch; (*fam: dinero*) money; **estar sin una ~** to be flat broke

perrera ['pe'rrera] *nf* kennel

perro ['perro] *nm* dog

persa ['persa] *adj, nm/f* Persian

persecución [perseku'θjon] *nf* pursuit, chase; (*REL, POL*) persecution

perseguir [perse'xir] *vt* to pursue, hunt; (*cortejar*) to chase after; (*molestar*) to pester, annoy; (*REL, POL*) to persecute

perseverante [perseβe'rante] *adj* persevering, persistent

perseverar [perseβe'rar] *vi* to persevere, persist; **~ en** to persevere in, persist with

persiana [per'sjana] *nf* (Venetian) blind

persignarse [persix'narse] *vr* to cross o.s.

persistente [persis'tente] *adj* persistent

persistir [persis'tir] *vi* to persist

persona [per'sona] *nf* person; **~ mayor** elderly person; **10 ~s** 10 people

personaje [perso'naxe] *nm* important person, celebrity; (*TEATRO etc*) character

personal [perso'nal] *adj* (*particular*) personal; (*para una persona*) single, for one person ♦ *nm* personnel, staff; ~idad *nf* personality

personarse [perso'narse] *vr* to appear in person

personificar [personifi'kar] *vt* to personify

perspectiva [perspek'tiβa] *nf perspective; (vista, panorama)* view, panorama; *(posibilidad futura)* outlook, prospect

perspicacia [perspi'kaθja] *nf (fig)* discernment, perspicacity

perspicaz [perspi'kaθ] *adj* shrewd

persuadir [perswa'ðir] *vt (gen)* to persuade; *(convencer)* to convince; ~se *vr* to become convinced; **persuasión** *nf* persuasion; **persuasivo, a** *adj* persuasive; convincing

pertenecer [pertene'θer] *vi* to belong; *(fig)* to concern; **perteneciente** *adj*: **perteneciente a** belonging to; **pertenencia** *nf* ownership; **pertenencias** *nfpl (bienes)* possessions, property *sg*

pertenezca *etc vb ver* **pertenecer**

pértiga ['pertiɣa] *nf*: **salto de** ~ pole vault

pertinaz [perti'naθ] *adj (persistente)* persistent; *(terco)* obstinate

pertinente [perti'nente] *adj* relevant, pertinent; *(apropiado)* appropriate; ~ **a** concerning, relevant to

perturbación [perturβa'θjon] *nf (POL)* disturbance; *(MED)* upset, disturbance

perturbado, a [pertur'βaðo, a] *adj* mentally unbalanced

perturbador, a [perturβa'ðor, a] *adj* perturbing, disturbing; *(subversivo)* subversive

perturbar [pertur'βar] *vt (el orden)* to disturb; *(MED)* to upset, disturb; *(mentalmente)* to perturb

Perú [pe'ru] *nm*: **el** ~ Peru; **peruano, a** *adj, nm/f* Peruvian

perversión [perßer'sjon] *nf* perversion; **perverso, a** *adj* perverse; *(depravado)* depraved

pervertido, a [perßer'tiðo, a] *adj* perverted ♦ *nm/f* pervert

pervertir [perßer'tir] *vt* to pervert, corrupt

pesa ['pesa] *nf* weight; *(DEPORTE)* shot

pesadez [pesa'ðeθ] *nf (peso)* heaviness; *(lentitud)* slowness; *(aburrimiento)* tediousness

pesadilla [pesa'ðiʎa] *nf* nightmare, bad dream

pesado, a [pe'saðo, a] *adj* heavy; *(lento)* slow; *(difícil, duro)* tough, hard; *(aburrido)* boring, tedious; *(tiempo)* sultry

pesadumbre [pesa'ðumbre] *nf* grief, sorrow

pésame ['pesame] *nm* expression of condolence, message of sympathy; **dar el** ~ to express one's condolences

pesar [pe'sar] *vt* to weigh ♦ *vi* to weigh; *(ser pesado)* to weigh a lot, be heavy; *(fig: opinión)* to carry weight; **no pesa mucho** it doesn't weigh much ♦ *nm (arrepentimiento)* regret; *(pena)* grief, sorrow; **a** ~ **de** *o* **pese a (que)** in spite of, despite

pesca ['peska] *nf (acto)* fishing; *(lo pescado)* catch; **ir de** ~ to go fishing

pescadería [peskaðe'ria] *nf* fish shop, fishmonger's *(BRIT)*

pescadilla [peska'ðiʎa] *nf (pez)* whiting

pescado [pes'kaðo] *nm* fish

pescador, a [peska'ðor, a] *nm/f* fisherman/woman

pescar [pes'kar] *vt (tomar)* to catch; *(intentar tomar)* to fish for; *(conseguir: trabajo)* to manage to get ♦ *vi* to fish, go fishing

pescuezo [pes'kweθo] *nm (ZOOL)* neck

pesebre [pe'seβre] *nm* manger

peseta [pe'seta] *nf* peseta

pesimista [pesi'mista] *adj* pessimistic ♦ *nm/f* pessimist

pésimo, a ['pesimo, a] *adj* awful, dreadful

peso ['peso] *nm* weight; *(balanza)* scales *pl*; *(moneda)* peso; ~ **bruto/neto** gross/net weight; **vender a** ~ to sell by weight

pesquero, a [pes'kero, a] *adj* fishing *cpd*

pesquisa [pes'kisa] *nf* inquiry, investigation

pestaña [pes'taɲa] *nf (ANAT)* eyelash; *(borde)* rim; **pestañear** *vi* to blink

peste ['peste] *nf* plague; *(mal olor)* stink, stench

pesticida [pesti'θiða] *nm* pesticide
pestilencia [pesti'lenθja] *nf* (*mal olor*) stink, stench
pestillo [pes'tiʎo] *nm* (*cerrojo*) bolt; (*picaporte*) doorhandle
petaca [pe'taka] *nf* (*de cigarros*) cigarette case; (*de pipa*) tobacco pouch; (*AM: maleta*) suitcase
pétalo ['petalo] *nm* petal
petardo [pe'tarðo] *nm* firework, firecracker
petición [peti'θjon] *nf* (*pedido*) request, plea; (*memorial*) petition; (*JUR*) plea
petrificar [petrifi'kar] *vt* to petrify
petróleo [pe'troleo] *nm* oil, petroleum; **petrolero, a** *adj* petroleum *cpd* ♦ *nm* (*COM: persona*) oil man; (*buque*) (oil) tanker
peyorativo, a [pejora'tiβo, a] *adj* pejorative
pez [peθ] *nm* fish
pezón [pe'θon] *nm* teat, nipple
pezuña [pe'θuɲa] *nf* hoof
piadoso, a [pja'ðoso, a] *adj* (*devoto*) pious, devout; (*misericordioso*) kind, merciful
pianista [pja'nista] *nm/f* pianist
piano ['pjano] *nm* piano
piar [pjar] *vi* to cheep
pibe, a ['piβe, a] (*AM*) *nm/f* boy/girl
picadero [pika'ðero] *nm* riding school
picadillo [pika'ðiʎo] *nm* mince, minced meat
picado, a [pi'kaðo, a] *adj* pricked, punctured; (*CULIN*) minced, chopped; (*mar*) choppy; (*diente*) bad; (*tabaco*) cut; (*enfadado*) cross
picador [pika'ðor] *nm* (*TAUR*) picador; (*minero*) faceworker
picadura [pika'ðura] *nf* (*pinchazo*) puncture; (*de abeja*) sting; (*de mosquito*) bite; (*tabaco picado*) cut tobacco
picante [pi'kante] *adj* hot; (*comentario*) racy, spicy
picaporte [pika'porte] *nm* (*manija*) doorhandle; (*pestillo*) latch
picar [pi'kar] *vt* (*agujerear, perforar*) to prick, puncture; (*abeja*) to sting; (*mosquito, serpiente*) to bite; (*CULIN*) to

mince, chop; (*incitar*) to incite, goad; (*dañar, irritar*) to annoy, bother; (*quemar: lengua*) to burn, sting ♦ *vi* (*pez*) to bite, take the bait; (*sol*) to burn, scorch; (*abeja, MED*) to sting; (*mosquito*) to bite; **~se** *vr* (*agriarse*) to turn sour, go off; (*ofenderse*) to take offence
picardía [pikar'ðia] *nf* villainy; (*astucia*) slyness, craftiness; (*una ~*) dirty trick; (*palabra*) rude/bad word *o* expression
pícaro, a ['pikaro, a] *adj* (*malicioso*) villainous; (*travieso*) mischievous ♦ *nm* (*astuto*) crafty sort; (*sinvergüenza*) rascal, scoundrel
pichón [pi'tʃon] *nm* young pigeon
pico ['piko] *nm* (*de ave*) beak; (*punta*) sharp point; (*TEC*) pick, pickaxe; (*GEO*) peak, summit; **y ~** and a bit
picotear [pikote'ar] *vt* to peck ♦ *vi* to nibble, pick
picudo, a [pi'kuðo, a] *adj* pointed, with a point
pidió *etc vb ver* **pedir**
pido *etc vb ver* **pedir**
pie [pje] (*pl* **~s**) *nm* foot; (*fig: motivo*) motive, basis; (: *fundamento*) foothold; **ir a ~** to go on foot, walk; **estar de ~** to be standing (up); **ponerse de ~** to stand up; **de ~s a cabeza** from top to bottom; **al ~ de la letra** (*citar*) literally, verbatim; (*copiar*) exactly, word for word; **en ~ de guerra** on a war footing; **dar ~ a** to give cause for; **hacer ~** (*en el agua*) to touch (the) bottom
piedad [pje'ðað] *nf* (*lástima*) pity, compassion; (*clemencia*) mercy; (*devoción*) piety, devotion
piedra ['pjeðra] *nf* stone; (*roca*) rock; (*de mechero*) flint; (*METEOROLOGÍA*) hailstone
piel [pjel] *nf* (*ANAT*) skin; (*ZOOL*) skin, hide, fur; (*cuero*) leather; (*BOT*) skin, peel
pienso *etc vb ver* **pensar**
pierdo *etc vb ver* **perder**
pierna ['pjerna] *nf* leg
pieza ['pjeθa] *nf* piece; (*habitación*) room; **~ de recambio** *o* **repuesto** spare (part)
pigmeo, a [piɣ'meo, a] *adj, nm/f* pigmy
pijama [pi'xama] *nm* pyjamas *pl*
pila ['pila] *nf* (*ELEC*) battery; (*montón*)

heap, pile; (*lavabo*) sink

píldora ['pildora] *nf* pill; **la ~ (anticonceptiva)** the (contraceptive) pill

pileta [pi'leta] *nf* basin, bowl; (*AM*) swimming pool

pillaje [pi'ʎaxe] *nm* pillage, plunder

pillar [pi'ʎar] *vt* (*saquear*) to pillage, plunder; (*fam: coger*) to catch; (: *agarrar*) to grasp, seize; (: *entender*) to grasp, catch on to; ~**se** *vr*: ~**se un dedo con la puerta** to catch one's finger in the door

pillo, a ['piʎo, a] *adj* villainous; (*astuto*) sly, crafty ♦ *nm/f* rascal, rogue, scoundrel

piloto [pi'loto] *nm* pilot; (*de aparato*) (pilot) light; (*AUTO: luz*) tail *o* rear light; (: *conductor*) driver

pimentón [pimen'ton] *nm* paprika

pimienta [pi'mjenta] *nf* pepper

pimiento [pi'mjento] *nm* pepper, pimiento

pin [pin] (*pl* **pins**) *nm* badge

pinacoteca [pinako'teka] *nf* art gallery

pinar [pi'nar] *nm* pine forest (*BRIT*), pine grove (*US*)

pincel [pin'θel] *nm* paintbrush

pinchadiscos [pintʃa'ðiskos] *nm/f inv* disc-jockey, DJ

pinchar [pin'tʃar] *vt* (*perforar*) to prick, pierce; (*neumático*) to puncture; (*fig*) to prod

pinchazo [pin'tʃaθo] *nm* (*perforación*) prick; (*de neumático*) puncture; (*fig*) prod

pincho ['pintʃo] *nm* savoury (snack); ~ **moruno** shish kebab; ~ **de tortilla** small slice of omelette

ping-pong ['pin'pon] *nm* table tennis

pingüino [pin'gwino] *nm* penguin

pino ['pino] *nm* pine (tree)

pinta ['pinta] *nf* spot; (*de líquidos*) spot, drop; (*aspecto*) appearance, look(s) (*pl*); ~**do, a** *adj* spotted; (*de muchos colores*) colourful; ~**das** *nfpl* graffiti *sg*

pintar [pin'tar] *vt* to paint ♦ *vi* to paint; (*fam*) to count, be important; ~**se** *vr* to put on make-up

pintor, a [pin'tor, a] *nm/f* painter

pintoresco, a [pinto'resko, a] *adj* picturesque

pintura [pin'tura] *nf* painting; ~ **a la**

acuarela watercolour; ~ **al óleo** oil painting

pinza ['pinθa] *nf* (*ZOOL*) claw; (*para colgar ropa*) clothes peg; (*TEC*) pincers *pl*; ~**s** *nfpl* (*para depilar etc*) tweezers *pl*

piña ['piɲa] *nf* (*fruto del pino*) pine cone; (*fruta*) pineapple; (*fig*) group

piñon [pi'ɲon] *nm* (*fruto*) pine nut; (*TEC*) pinion

pío, a ['pio, a] *adj* (*devoto*) pious, devout; (*misericordioso*) merciful

piojo ['pjoxo] *nm* louse

pionero, a [pjo'nero, a] *adj* pioneering ♦ *nm/f* pioneer

pipa ['pipa] *nf* pipe; ~**s** *nfpl* (*BOT*) (edible) sunflower seeds

pipí [pi'pi] (*fam*) *nm*: **hacer ~** to have a wee(-wee) (*BRIT*), have to go (wee-wee) (*US*)

pique ['pike] *nm* (*resentimiento*) pique, resentment; (*rivalidad*) rivalry, competition; **irse a ~** to sink; (*esperanza, familia*) to be ruined

piqueta [pi'keta] *nf* pick(axe)

piquete [pi'kete] *nm* (*agujerito*) small hole; (*MIL*) squad, party; (*de obreros*) picket

pirado, a [pi'raðo, a] (*fam*) *adj* round the bend ♦ *nm/f* nutter

piragua [pi'raxwa] *nf* canoe; **piragüismo** *nm* canoeing

pirámide [pi'ramiðe] *nf* pyramid

pirata [pi'rata] *adj, nm* pirate ♦ *nm/f*: ~ **informático/a** hacker

Pirineo(s) [piri'neo(s)] *nm(pl)* Pyrenees *pl*

pirómano, a [pi'romano, a] *nm/f* (*MED, JUR*) arsonist

piropo [pi'ropo] *nm* compliment, (piece of) flattery

pirueta [pi'rweta] *nf* pirouette

pis [pis] (*fam*) *nm* pee, piss; **hacer ~** to have a pee; (*para niños*) to wee-wee

pisada [pi'saða] *nf* (*paso*) footstep; (*huella*) footprint

pisar [pi'sar] *vt* (*caminar sobre*) to walk on, tread on; (*apretar con el pie*) to press; (*fig*) to trample on, walk all over ♦ *vi* to tread, step, walk

piscina [pis'θina] *nf* swimming pool

Piscis ['pisθis] *nm* Pisces
piso ['piso] *nm* (*suelo, planta*) floor; (*apartamento*) flat (*BRIT*), apartment; **primer ~** (*ESP*) first floor; (*AM*) ground floor
pisotear [pisote'ar] *vt* to trample (on *o* underfoot)
pista ['pista] *nf* track, trail; (*indicio*) clue; **~ de aterrizaje** runway; **~ de baile** dance floor; **~ de hielo** ice rink; **~ de tenis** tennis court
pistola [pis'tola] *nf* pistol; (*TEC*) spray-gun; **pistolero, a** *nm/f* gunman/woman, gangster
pistón [pis'ton] *nm* (*TEC*) piston; (*MUS*) key
pitar [pi'tar] *vt* (*silbato*) to blow; (*rechiflar*) to whistle at, boo ♦ *vi* to whistle; (*AUTO*) to sound *o* toot one's horn; (*AM*) to smoke
pitillo [pi'tiʎo] *nm* cigarette
pito ['pito] *nm* whistle; (*de coche*) horn
pitón [pi'ton] *nm* (*ZOOL*) python
pitonisa [pito'nisa] *nf* fortune-teller
pitorreo [pito'rreo] *nm* joke; **estar de ~** to be joking
pizarra [pi'θarra] *nf* (*piedra*) slate; (*encerado*) blackboard
pizca ['piθka] *nf* pinch, spot; (*fig*) spot, speck; **ni ~** not a bit
placa ['plaka] *nf* plate; (*distintivo*) badge, insignia; **~ de matrícula** number plate
placentero, a [plaθen'tero, a] *adj* pleasant, agreeable
placer [pla'θer] *nm* pleasure ♦ *vt* to please
plácido, a ['plaθiðo, a] *adj* placid
plaga ['plaɣa] *nf* pest; (*MED*) plague; (*abundancia*) abundance; **plagar** *vt* to infest, plague; (*llenar*) to fill
plagio ['plaxjo] *nm* plagiarism
plan [plan] *nm* (*esquema, proyecto*) plan; (*idea, intento*) idea, intention; **tener ~** (*fam*) to have a date; **tener un ~** (*fam*) to have an affair; **en ~ económico** (*fam*) on the cheap; **vamos en ~ de turismo** we're going as tourists; **si te pones en ese ~ ...** if that's your attitude ...
plana ['plana] *nf* sheet (of paper), page; (*TEC*) trowel; **en primera ~** on the front

page; **~ mayor** staff
plancha ['plantʃa] *nf* (*para planchar*) iron; (*rótulo*) plate, sheet; (*NAUT*) gangway; **a la ~** (*CULIN*) grilled; **~do** *nm* ironing; **planchar** *vt* to iron ♦ *vi* to do the ironing
planeador [planea'ðor] *nm* glider
planear [plane'ar] *vt* to plan ♦ *vi* to glide
planeta [pla'neta] *nm* planet
planicie [pla'niθje] *nf* plain
planificación [planifika'θjon] *nf* planning; **~ familiar** family planning
plano, a ['plano, a] *adj* flat, level, even ♦ *nm* (*MAT, TEC, AVIAT*) plane; (*FOTO*) shot; (*ARQ*) plan; (*GEO*) map; (*de ciudad*) map, street plan; **primer ~** close-up; **caer de ~** to fall flat
planta ['planta] *nf* (*BOT, TEC*) plant; (*ANAT*) sole of the foot, foot; (*piso*) floor; (*AM: personal*) staff; **~ baja** ground floor
plantación [planta'θjon] *nf* (*AGR*) plantation; (*acto*) planting
plantar [plan'tar] *vt* (*BOT*) to plant; (*levantar*) to erect, set up; **~se** *vr* to stand firm; **~ a uno en la calle** to throw sb out; **dejar plantado a uno** (*fam*) to stand sb up
plantear [plante'ar] *vt* (*problema*) to pose; (*dificultad*) to raise
plantilla [plan'tiʎa] *nf* (*de zapato*) insole; (*personal*) personnel; **ser de ~** to be on the staff
plantón [plan'ton] *nm* (*MIL*) guard, sentry; (*fam*) long wait; **dar (un) ~ a uno** to stand sb up
plasmar [plas'mar] *vt* (*dar forma*) to mould, shape; (*representar*) to represent ♦ *vi*: **~ en** to take the form of
plasta ['plasta] (*fam*) *adj inv* boring ♦ *nm/f* bore
Plasticina [plasti'θina] ® *nf* Plasticine ®
plástico, a ['plastiko, a] *adj* plastic ♦ *nm* plastic
Plastilina [plasti'lina] ® *nf* Plasticine ®
plata ['plata] *nf* (*metal*) silver; (*cosas hechas de ~*) silverware; (*AM*) cash, dough; **hablar en ~** to speak bluntly *o* frankly
plataforma [plata'forma] *nf* platform; **~**

de lanzamiento/perforación launch(ing) pad/drilling rig

plátano ['platano] *nm* (*fruta*) banana; (*árbol*) plane tree; banana tree

platea [pla'tea] *nf* (*TEATRO*) pit

plateado, a [plate'aðo, a] *adj* silver; (*TEC*) silver-plated

plática ['platika] *nf* talk, chat; **platicar** *vi* to talk, chat

platillo [pla'tiʎo] *nm* saucer; ~**s** *nmpl* (*MUS*) cymbals; ~ **volador** *o* **volante** flying saucer

platino [pla'tino] *nm* platinum; ~**s** *nmpl* (*AUTO*) contact points

plato ['plato] *nm* plate, dish; (*parte de comida*) course; (*comida*) dish; ~ **combinado** set main course (*served on one plate*); ~ **fuerte** main course; **primer** ~ first course

playa ['plaja] *nf* beach; (*costa*) seaside; ~ **de estacionamiento** (*AM*) car park

playera [pla'jera] *nf* (*AM: camiseta*) T-shirt; ~**s** *nfpl* (*zapatos*) (slip-on) canvas shoes

plaza ['plaθa] *nf* square; (*mercado*) market(place); (*sitio*) room, space; (*en vehículo*) seat, place; (*colocación*) post, job; ~ **de toros** bullring

plazo ['plaθo] *nm* (*lapso de tiempo*) time, period; (*fecha de vencimiento*) expiry date; (*pago parcial*) instalment; **a corto/ largo** ~ short-/long-term; **comprar algo a** ~**s** to buy sth on hire purchase (*BRIT*) *o* on time (*US*)

plazoleta [plaθo'leta] *nf* small square

pleamar [plea'mar] *nf* high tide

plebe ['pleβe] *nf*: **la** ~ the common people *pl*, the masses *pl*; (*pey*) the plebs *pl*; ~**yo, a** *adj* plebeian; (*pey*) coarse, common

plebiscito [pleβis'θito] *nm* plebiscite

plegable [ple'γaβle] *adj* pliable; (*silla*) folding

plegar [ple'γar] *vt* (*doblar*) to fold, bend; (*COSTURA*) to pleat; ~**se** *vr* to yield, submit

pleito ['pleito] *nm* (*JUR*) lawsuit, case; (*fig*) dispute, feud

plenilunio [pleni'lunjo] *nm* full moon

plenitud [pleni'tuð] *nf* plenitude, fullness; (*abundancia*) abundance

pleno, a ['pleno, a] *adj* full; (*completo*) complete ♦ *nm* plenum; **en** ~ **día** in broad daylight; **en** ~ **verano** at the height of summer; **en plena cara** full in the face

pleuresía [pleure'sia] *nf* pleurisy

pliego *etc* ['pljeγo] *vb ver* **plegar** ♦ *nm* (*hoja*) sheet (of paper); (*carta*) sealed letter/document; ~ **de condiciones** details *pl*, specifications *pl*

pliegue *etc* ['pljeγe] *vb ver* **plegar** ♦ *nm* fold, crease; (*de vestido*) pleat

plomero [plo'mero] *nm* (*AM*) plumber

plomo ['plomo] *nm* (*metal*) lead; (*ELEC*) fuse; **sin** ~ unleaded

pluma ['pluma] *nf* feather; (*para escribir*): ~ **(estilográfica)** ink pen; ~ **fuente** (*AM*) fountain pen

plumero [plu'mero] *nm* (*quitapolvos*) feather duster

plumón [plu'mon] *nm* (*AM: fino*) felt-tip pen; (: *ancho*) marker

plural [plu'ral] *adj* plural; ~**idad** *nf* plurality; **una** ~**idad de votos** a majority of votes

pluriempleo [pluriem'pleo] *nm* having more than one job

plus [plus] *nm* bonus; ~**valía** *nf* (*COM*) appreciation

población [poβla'θjon] *nf* population; (*pueblo, ciudad*) town, city

poblado, a [po'βlaðo, a] *adj* inhabited ♦ *nm* (*aldea*) village; (*pueblo*) (small) town; **densamente** ~ densely populated

poblador, a [poβla'ðor, a] *nm/f* settler, colonist

poblar [po'βlar] *vt* (*colonizar*) to colonize; (*fundar*) to found; (*habitar*) to inhabit

pobre ['poβre] *adj* poor ♦ *nm/f* poor person; ~**za** *nf* poverty

pocilga [po'θilγa] *nf* pigsty

pócima ['poθima] *nf* = **poción**

PALABRA CLAVE

poco, a ['poko, a] *adj* **1** (*sg*) little, not much; ~ **tiempo** little *o* not much time; **de** ~ **interés** of little interest, not very interesting; **poca cosa** not much
2 (*pl*) few, not many; **unos** ~**s** a few,

some; **~s niños comen lo que les conviene** few children eat what they should
♦ *adv* **1** little, not much; **cuesta ~** it doesn't cost much
2 (+ *adj*: = *negativo, antónimo*): **~ amable/inteligente** not very nice/intelligent
3: por ~ me caigo I almost fell
4: a ~: a ~ de haberse casado shortly after getting married
5: ~ a ~ little by little
♦ *nm* a little, a bit; **un ~ triste/de dinero** a little sad/money

podar [po'ðar] *vt* to prune

| PALABRA CLAVE |
----

poder [po'ðer] *vi* **1** (*capacidad*) can, be able to; **no puedo hacerlo** I can't do it, I'm unable to do it
2 (*permiso*) can, may, be allowed to; **¿se puede?** may I (*o* we)?; **puedes irte ahora** you may go now; **no se puede fumar en este hospital** smoking is not allowed in this hospital
3 (*posibilidad*) may, might, could; **puede llegar mañana** he may *o* might arrive tomorrow; **pudiste haberte hecho daño** you might *o* could have hurt yourself; **¡podías habérmelo dicho antes!** you might have told me before!
4: puede ser: puede ser perhaps; **puede ser que lo sepa Tomás** Tomás may *o* might know
5: ¡no puedo más! I've had enough!; **no pude menos que dejarlo** I couldn't help but leave it; **es tonto a más no ~** he's as stupid as they come
6: ~ con: no puedo con este crío this kid's too much for me
♦ *nm* power; **~ adquisitivo** purchasing power; **detentar** *o* **ocupar** *o* **estar en el ~** to be in power

poderoso, a [poðe'roso, a] *adj* (*político, país*) powerful
podio ['poðjo] *nm* (*DEPORTE*) podium
podium ['poðjum] = **podio**

podrido, a [po'ðriðo, a] *adj* rotten, bad; (*fig*) rotten, corrupt
podrir [po'ðrir] = **pudrir**
poema [po'ema] *nm* poem
poesía [poe'sia] *nf* poetry
poeta [po'eta] *nm/f* poet; **poético, a** *adj* poetic(al)
poetisa [poe'tisa] *nf* (woman) poet
póker ['poker] *nm* poker
polaco, a [po'lako, a] *adj* Polish ♦ *nm/f* Pole
polar [po'lar] *adj* polar; **~idad** *nf* polarity; **~izarse** *vr* to polarize
polea [po'lea] *nf* pulley
polémica [po'lemika] *nf* polemics *sg*; (*una ~*) controversy, polemic
polen ['polen] *nm* pollen
policía [poli'θia] *nm/f* policeman/woman ♦ *nf* police; **~co, a** *adj* police *cpd*; **novela policíaca** detective story; **policial** *adj* police *cpd*
polideportivo [poliðepor'tiβo] *nm* sports centre *o* complex
polietileno [polieti'leno] *nm* polythene (*BRIT*), polyethylene (*US*)
poligamia [poli'ɣamja] *nf* polygamy
polilla [po'liʎa] *nf* moth
polio ['poljo] *nf* polio
política [po'litika] *nf* politics *sg*; (*económica, agraria etc*) policy; *ver tb* **político**
político, a [po'litiko, a] *adj* political; (*discreto*) tactful; (*de familia*) -in-law ♦ *nm/f* politician; **padre ~** father-in-law
póliza ['poliθa] *nf* certificate, voucher; (*impuesto*) tax stamp; **~ de seguros** insurance policy
polizón [poli'θon] *nm* (*en barco etc*) stowaway
pollera [po'ʎera] (*AM*) *nf* skirt
pollería [poʎe'ria] *nf* poulterer's (shop)
pollo ['poʎo] *nm* chicken
polo ['polo] *nm* (*GEO, ELEC*) pole; (*helado*) ice lolly; (*DEPORTE*) polo; (*suéter*) polo-neck; **~ Norte/Sur** North/South Pole
Polonia [po'lonja] *nf* Poland
poltrona [pol'trona] *nf* easy chair
polución [polu'θjon] *nf* pollution
polvera [pol'βera] *nf* powder compact

polvo ['polβo] *nm* dust; (*QUÍMICA, CULIN, MED*) powder; **~s** *nmpl* (*maquillaje*) powder *sg*; **~ de talco** talcum powder; **estar hecho ~** (*fam*) to be worn out *o* exhausted

pólvora ['polβora] *nf* gunpowder; (*fuegos artificiales*) fireworks *pl*

polvoriento, a [polβo'rjento, a] *adj* (*superficie*) dusty; (*sustancia*) powdery

pomada [po'maða] *nf* (*MED*) cream, ointment

pomelo [po'melo] *nm* grapefruit

pómez ['pomeθ] *nf*: **piedra ~** pumice stone

pomo ['pomo] *nm* doorknob

pompa ['pompa] *nf* (*burbuja*) bubble; (*bomba*) pump; (*esplendor*) pomp, splendour; **pomposo, a** *adj* splendid, magnificent; (*pey*) pompous

pómulo ['pomulo] *nm* cheekbone

pon [pon] *vb ver* **poner**

ponche ['pontʃe] *nm* punch

poncho ['pontʃo] (*AM*) *nm* poncho

ponderar [ponde'rar] *vt* (*considerar*) to weigh up, consider; (*elogiar*) to praise highly, speak in praise of

pondré *etc vb ver* **poner**

PALABRA CLAVE

---

poner [po'ner] *vt* **1** (*colocar*) to put; (*telegrama*) to send; (*obra de teatro*) to put on; (*película*) to show; **ponlo más fuerte** turn it up; **¿qué ponen en el Excelsior?** what's on at the Excelsior?

2 (*tienda*) to open; (*instalar: gas etc*) to put in; (*radio, TV*) to switch *o* turn on

3 (*suponer*): **pongamos que ...** let's suppose that ...

4 (*contribuir*): **el gobierno ha puesto otro millón** the government has contributed another million

5 (*TELEC*): **póngame con el Sr. López** can you put me through to Mr. López?

6: **~ de**: **le han puesto de director general** they've appointed him general manager

7 (+ *adj*) to make; **me estás poniendo nerviosa** you're making me nervous

8 (*dar nombre*): **al hijo le pusieron Diego** they called their son Diego

♦ *vi* (*gallina*) to lay

♦ **~se** *vr* **1** (*colocarse*): **se puso a mi lado** he came and stood beside me; **tú pónte en esa silla** you go and sit on that chair

2 (*vestido, cosméticos*) to put on; **¿por qué no te pones el vestido nuevo?** why don't you put on *o* wear your new dress?

3 (+ *adj*) to turn; to get; become; **se puso muy serio** he got very serious; **después de lavarla la tela se puso azul** after washing it the material turned blue

4: **~se a**: **se puso a llorar** he started to cry; **tienes que ~te a estudiar** you must get down to studying

5: **~se a bien con uno** to make it up with sb; **~se a mal con uno** to get on the wrong side of sb

---

pongo *etc vb ver* **poner**

poniente [po'njente] *nm* (*occidente*) west; (*viento*) west wind

pontífice [pon'tifiθe] *nm* pope, pontiff

popa ['popa] *nf* stern

popular [popu'lar] *adj* popular; (*cultura*) of the people, folk *cpd*; **~idad** *nf* popularity; **~izarse** *vr* to become popular

---

PALABRA CLAVE

---

por [por] *prep* **1** (*objetivo*) for; **luchar ~ la patria** to fight for one's country

2 (+ *infin*): **~ no llegar tarde** so as not to arrive late; **~ citar unos ejemplos** to give a few examples

3 (*causa*) out of, because of; **~ escasez de fondos** through *o* for lack of funds

4 (*tiempo*): **~ la mañana/noche** in the morning/at night; **se queda ~ una semana** she's staying (for) a week

5 (*lugar*): **pasar ~ Madrid** to pass through Madrid; **ir a Guayaquil ~ Quito** to go to Guayaquil via Quito; **caminar ~ la calle** to walk along the street; *ver tb* **todo**

6 (*cambio, precio*): **te doy uno nuevo ~ el que tienes** I'll give you a new one (in return) for the one you've got

7 (*valor distributivo*): **550 pesetas ~ hora/cabeza** 550 pesetas an *o* per hour/ a *o* per head

8 (*modo, medio*) by; **~ correo/avión** by post/air; **día ~ día** day by day; **entrar ~ la entrada principal** to go in through the main entrance

9: **10 ~ 10 son 100** 10 times 10 is 100

10 (*en lugar de*): **vino él ~ su jefe** he came instead of his boss

11: **~ mí que revienten** as far as I'm concerned they can drop dead

12: **¿~ qué?** why?; **¿~ qué no?** why not?

---

porcelana [porθe'lana] *nf* porcelain; (*china*) china

porcentaje [porθen'taxe] *nm* percentage

porción [por'θjon] *nf* (*parte*) portion, share; (*cantidad*) quantity, amount

pordiosero, a [porðjo'sero, a] *nm/f* beggar

porfiar [por'fjar] *vi* to persist, insist; (*disputar*) to argue stubbornly

pormenor [porme'nor] *nm* detail, particular

pornografía [pornoɤra'fia] *nf* pornography

poro ['poro] *nm* pore; **~so, a** *adj* porous

porque ['porke] *conj* (*a causa de*) because; (*ya que*) since; (*con el fin de*) so that, in order that

porqué [por'ke] *nm* reason, cause

porquería [porke'ria] *nf* (*suciedad*) filth, dirt; (*acción*) dirty trick; (*objeto*) small thing, trifle; (*fig*) rubbish

porra ['porra] *nf* (*arma*) stick, club

porrazo [po'rraθo] *nm* blow, bump

porro ['porro] *nm* (*droga*) joint (*fam*)

porrón [po'rron] *nm* glass wine jar with a *long spout*

portaaviones [porta'(a)βjones] *nm inv* aircraft carrier

portada [por'taða] *nf* (*de revista*) cover

portador, a [porta'ðor, a] *nm/f* carrier, bearer; (*COM*) bearer, payee

portaequipajes [portaeki'paxes] *nm inv* (*AUTO: maletero*) boot; (*: baca*) luggage rack

portal [por'tal] *nm* (*entrada*) vestibule,

hall; (*portada*) porch, doorway; (*puerta de entrada*) main door; (*DEPORTE*) goal

portamaletas [portama'letas] *nm inv* (*AUTO: maletero*) boot; (*: baca*) roof rack

portarse [por'tarse] *vr* to behave, conduct o.s.

portátil [por'tatil] *adj* portable

portavoz [porta'βoθ] *nm/f* (*persona*) spokesman/woman

portazo [por'taθo] *nm*: **dar un ~** to slam the door

porte ['porte] *nm* (*COM*) transport; (*precio*) transport charges *pl*

portento [por'tento] *nm* marvel, wonder; **~so, a** *adj* marvellous, extraordinary

porteño, a [por'teɲo, a] *adj* of *o* from Buenos Aires

portería [porte'ria] *nf* (*oficina*) porter's office; (*gol*) goal

portero, a [por'tero, a] *nm/f* porter; (*conserje*) caretaker; (*ujier*) doorman; (*DEPORTE*) goalkeeper; **~ automático** intercom

pórtico ['portiko] *nm* (*patio*) portico, porch; (*fig*) gateway; (*arcada*) arcade

portorriqueño, a [portorri'keɲo, a] *adj* Puerto Rican

Portugal [portu'ɣal] *nm* Portugal; **portugués, esa** *adj, nm/f* Portuguese ♦ *nm* (*LING*) Portuguese

porvenir [porβe'nir] *nm* future

pos [pos] *prep*: **en ~ de** after, in pursuit of

posada [po'saða] *nf* (*refugio*) shelter, lodging; (*mesón*) guest house; **dar ~ a** to give shelter to, take in

posaderas [posa'ðeras] *nfpl* backside *sg*, buttocks

posar [po'sar] *vt* (*en el suelo*) to lay down, put down; (*la mano*) to place, put gently ♦ *vi* to sit, pose; **~se** *vr* to settle; (*pájaro*) to perch; (*avión*) to land, come down

posdata [pos'ðata] *nf* postscript

pose ['pose] *nf* pose

poseedor, a [posee'ðor, a] *nm/f* owner, possessor; (*de récord, puesto*) holder

poseer [pose'er] *vt* to possess, own; (*ventaja*) to enjoy; (*récord, puesto*) to hold

posesión [pose'sjon] *nf* possession; **posesionarse** *vr*: **posesionarse de** to take possession of, take over

posesivo, a [pose'siβo, a] *adj* possessive

posgrado [pos'graðo] *nm*: **curso de ~** postgraduate course

posibilidad [posiβili'ðað] *nf* possibility; (*oportunidad*) chance; **posibilitar** *vt* to make possible; (*hacer realizable*) to make feasible

posible [po'siβle] *adj* possible; (*realizable*) feasible; **de ser ~** if possible; **en lo ~** as far as possible

posición [posi'θjon] *nf* position; (*rango social*) status

positivo, a [posi'tiβo, a] *adj* positive

poso ['poso] *nm* sediment; (*heces*) dregs *pl*

posponer [pospo'ner] *vt* to put behind/below; (*aplazar*) to postpone

posta ['posta] *nf*: **a ~** deliberately, on purpose

postal [pos'tal] *adj* postal ♦ *nf* postcard

poste ['poste] *nm* (*de telégrafos etc*) post, pole; (*columna*) pillar

póster ['poster] (*pl* **pósteres, pósters**) *nm* poster

postergar [poster'ɣar] *vt* to postpone, delay

posteridad [posteri'ðað] *nf* posterity

posterior [poste'rjor] *adj* back, rear; (*siguiente*) following, subsequent; (*más tarde*) later; **~idad** *nf*: **con ~idad** later, subsequently

postgrado [post'graðo] *nm* = **posgrado**

postizo, a [pos'tiθo, a] *adj* false, artificial ♦ *nm* hairpiece

postor, a [pos'tor, a] *nm/f* bidder

postre ['postre] *nm* sweet, dessert

postrero, a [pos'trero, a] (*delante de nmsg*: **postrer**) *adj* (*último*) last; (*que viene detrás*) rear

postulado [postu'laðo] *nm* postulate

póstumo, a ['postumo, a] *adj* posthumous

postura [pos'tura] *nf* (*del cuerpo*) posture, position; (*fig*) attitude, position

potable [po'taβle] *adj* drinkable; **agua ~** drinking water

potaje [po'taxe] *nm* thick vegetable soup

pote ['pote] *nm* pot, jar

potencia [po'tenθja] *nf* power

potencial [poten'θjal] *adj, nm* potential

potenciar [poten'θjar] *vt* to boost

potente [po'tente] *adj* powerful

potro, a ['potro, a] *nm/f* (*ZOOL*) colt/filly ♦ *nm* (*de gimnasia*) vaulting horse

pozo ['poθo] *nm* well; (*de río*) deep pool; (*de mina*) shaft

P.P. *abr* (= *porte pagado*) CP

práctica ['praktika] *nf* practice; (*método*) method; (*arte, capacidad*) skill; **en la ~** in practice

practicable [prakti'kaβle] *adj* practicable; (*camino*) passable

practicante [prakti'kante] *nm/f* (*MED*: *ayudante de doctor*) medical assistant; (: *enfermero*) male nurse; (*quien practica algo*) practitioner ♦ *adj* practising

practicar [prakti'kar] *vt* to practise; (*DEPORTE*) to go in for (*BRIT*) *o* out for (*US*), play; (*realizar*) to carry out, perform

práctico, a ['praktiko, a] *adj* practical; (*instruído*: *persona*) skilled, expert

practique *etc vb ver* **practicar**

pradera [pra'ðera] *nf* meadow; (*US etc*) prairie

prado ['praðo] *nm* (*campo*) meadow, field; (*pastizal*) pasture

Praga ['praɣa] *n* Prague

pragmático, a [praɣ'matiko, a] *adj* pragmatic

preámbulo [pre'ambulo] *nm* preamble, introduction

precario, a [pre'karjo, a] *adj* precarious

precaución [prekau'θjon] *nf* (*medida preventiva*) preventive measure, precaution; (*prudencia*) caution, wariness

precaver [preka'βer] *vt* to guard against; (*impedir*) to forestall; **~se** *vr*: **~se de** *o* **contra algo** to (be on one's) guard against sth; **precavido, a** *adj* cautious, wary

precedente [preθe'ðente] *adj* preceding; (*anterior*) former ♦ *nm* precedent

preceder [preθe'ðer] *vt, vi* to precede, go before, come before

precepto [pre'θepto] *nm* precept

preciado, a [pre'θjaðo, a] *adj (estimado)* esteemed, valuable

preciarse [pre'θjarse] *vr* to boast; **~se de** to pride o.s. on, boast of being

precinto [pre'θinto] *nm (tb: ~ de garantía)* seal

precio ['preθjo] *nm* price; *(costo)* cost; *(valor)* value, worth; *(de viaje)* fare; **~ al contado/de coste/de oportunidad** cash/cost/bargain price; **~ al detalle** *o* **al por menor** retail price; **~ tope** top price

preciosidad [preθjosi'ðað] *nf (valor)* (high) value, worth; *(encanto)* charm; *(cosa bonita)* beautiful thing; **es una ~** it's lovely, it's really beautiful

precioso, a [pre'θjoso, a] *adj* precious; *(de mucho valor)* valuable; *(fam)* lovely, beautiful

precipicio [preθi'piθjo] *nm* cliff, precipice; *(fig)* abyss

precipitación [preθipita'θjon] *nf* haste; *(lluvia)* rainfall

precipitado, a [preθipi'taðo, a] *adj (conducta)* hasty, rash; *(salida)* hasty, sudden

precipitar [preθipi'tar] *vt (arrojar)* to hurl down, throw; *(apresurar)* to hasten; *(acelerar)* to speed up, accelerate; **~se** *vr* to throw o.s.; *(apresurarse)* to rush; *(actuar sin pensar)* to act rashly

precisamente [preθisa'mente] *adv* precisely; *(exactamente)* precisely, exactly

precisar [preθi'sar] *vt (necesitar)* to need, require; *(fijar)* to determine exactly, fix; *(especificar)* to specify

precisión [preθi'sjon] *nf (exactitud)* precision

preciso, a [pre'θiso, a] *adj (exacto)* precise; *(necesario)* necessary, essential

preconcebido, a [prekonθe'βiðo, a] *adj* preconceived

precoz [pre'koθ] *adj (persona)* precocious; *(calvicie etc)* premature

precursor, a [prekur'sor, a] *nm/f* predecessor, forerunner

predecir [preðe'θir] *vt* to predict, forecast

predestinado, a [preðesti'naðo, a] *adj* predestined

predicar [preði'kar] *vt, vi* to preach

predicción [preðik'θjon] *nf* prediction

predilecto, a [preði'lekto, a] *adj* favourite

predisponer [preðispo'ner] *vt* to predispose; *(pey)* to prejudice; **predisposición** *nf* inclination; prejudice, bias

predominante [preðomi'nante] *adj* predominant

predominar [preðomi'nar] *vt* to dominate ♦ *vi* to predominate; *(prevalecer)* to prevail; **predominio** *nm* predominance; prevalence

preescolar [pre(e)sko'lar] *adj* preschool

prefabricado, a [prefaβri'kaðo, a] *adj* prefabricated

prefacio [pre'faθjo] *nm* preface

preferencia [prefe'renθja] *nf* preference; **de ~** preferably, for preference

preferible [prefe'riβle] *adj* preferable

preferir [prefe'rir] *vt* to prefer

prefiero *etc vb ver* **preferir**

pregonar [preɣo'nar] *vt* to proclaim, announce

pregunta [pre'ɣunta] *nf* question; **hacer una ~** to ask *o* put (forth (*US*)) a question

preguntar [preɣun'tar] *vt* to ask; *(cuestionar)* to question ♦ *vi* to ask; **~se** *vr* to wonder; **~ por alguien** to ask for sb

preguntón, ona [preɣun'ton, ona] *adj* inquisitive

prehistórico, a [preis'toriko, a] *adj* prehistoric

prejuicio [pre'xwiθjo] *nm (acto)* prejudgement; *(idea preconcebida)* preconception; *(parcialidad)* prejudice, bias

preliminar [prelimi'nar] *adj* preliminary

preludio [pre'luðjo] *nm* prelude

prematuro, a [prema'turo, a] *adj* premature

premeditación [premeðita'θjon] *nf* premeditation

premeditar [premeði'tar] *vt* to premeditate

premiar [preˈmjar] *vt* to reward; (*en un concurso*) to give a prize to

premio [ˈpremjo] *nm* reward; prize; (*COM*) premium

premonición [premoniˈθjon] *nf* premonition

prenatal [prenaˈtal] *adj* antenatal, prenatal

prenda [ˈprenda] *nf* (*ropa*) garment, article of clothing; (*garantía*) pledge; ~**s** *nfpl* (*talentos*) talents, gifts

prendedor, a [prendeˈðor] *nm* brooch

prender [prenˈder] *vt* (*captar*) to catch, capture; (*detener*) to arrest; (*COSTURA*) to pin, attach; (*sujetar*) to fasten ♦ *vi* to catch; (*arraigar*) to take root; ~**se** *vr* (*encenderse*) to catch fire

prendido, a [prenˈðiðo, a] (*AM*) *adj* (*luz etc*) on

prensa [ˈprensa] *nf* press; **la P~** the press; **prensar** *vt* to press

preñado, a [preˈɲaðo, a] *adj* (*ZOOL*) pregnant; ~ **de** pregnant with, full of

preocupación [preokupaˈθjon] *nf* worry, concern; (*ansiedad*) anxiety

preocupado, a [preokuˈpaðo, a] *adj* worried, concerned; (*ansioso*) anxious

preocupar [preokuˈpar] *vt* to worry; ~**se** *vr* to worry; ~**se de algo** (*hacerse cargo*) to take care of sth

preparación [preparaˈθjon] *nf* (*acto*) preparation; (*estado*) readiness; (*entrenamiento*) training

preparado, a [prepaˈraðo, a] *adj* (*dispuesto*) prepared; (*CULIN*) ready (to serve) ♦ *nm* preparation

preparar [prepaˈrar] *vt* (*disponer*) to prepare, get ready; (*TEC: tratar*) to prepare, process; (*entrenar*) to teach, train; ~**se** *vr*: ~**se a** *o* **para** to prepare to *o* for, get ready to *o* for; **preparativo, a** *adj* preparatory, preliminary; **preparativos** *nmpl* preparations; **preparatoria** (*AM*) *nf* sixth-form college (*BRIT*), senior high school (*US*)

prerrogativa [prerroɣaˈtiβa] *nf* prerogative, privilege

presa [ˈpresa] *nf* (*cosa apresada*) catch; (*víctima*) victim; (*de animal*) prey; (*de agua*) dam

presagiar [presaˈxjar] *vt* to presage, forebode; **presagio** *nm* omen

prescindir [presθinˈdir] *vi*: ~ **de** (*privarse de*) to do without, go without; (*descartar*) to dispense with

prescribir [preskriˈβir] *vt* to prescribe; **prescripción** *nf* prescription

presencia [preˈsenθja] *nf* presence; **presencial** *adj*: **testigo presencial** eyewitness; **presenciar** *vt* to be present at; (*asistir a*) to attend; (*ver*) to see, witness

presentación [presentaˈθjon] *nf* presentation; (*introducción*) introduction

presentador, a [presentaˈðor, a] *nm/f* presenter, compère

presentar [presenˈtar] *vt* to present; (*ofrecer*) to offer; (*mostrar*) to show, display; (*a una persona*) to introduce; ~**se** *vr* (*llegar inesperadamente*) to appear, turn up; (*ofrecerse como candidato*) to run, stand; (*aparecer*) to show, appear; (*solicitar empleo*) to apply

presente [preˈsente] *adj* present ♦ *nm* present; **hacer** ~ to state, declare; **tener** ~ to remember, bear in mind

presentimiento [presentiˈmjento] *nm* premonition, presentiment

presentir [presenˈtir] *vt* to have a premonition of

preservación [preserβaˈθjon] *nf* protection, preservation

preservar [preserˈβar] *vt* to protect, preserve; **preservativo** *nm* sheath, condom

presidencia [presiˈðenθja] *nf* presidency; (*de comité*) chairmanship

presidente [presiˈðente] *nm/f* president; (*de comité*) chairman/woman

presidiario [presiˈðjarjo] *nm* convict

presidio [preˈsiðjo] *nm* prison, penitentiary

presidir [presiˈðir] *vt* (*dirigir*) to preside at, preside over; (: *comité*) to take the chair at; (*dominar*) to dominate, rule ♦ *vi* to preside; to take the chair

presión [preˈsjon] *nf* pressure; **presionar** *vt* to press; (*fig*) to press, put pressure

on ♦ *vi*: **presionar para** to press for
preso, a ['preso, a] *nm/f* prisoner; **tomar**
o **llevar ~ a uno** to arrest sb, take sb
prisoner
prestación [presta'θjon] *nf* service;
(*subsidio*) benefit; **prestaciones** *nfpl* (TEC,
AUT) performance features
prestado, a [pres'taðo, a] *adj* on loan;
pedir ~ to borrow
prestamista [presta'mista] *nm/f*
moneylender
préstamo ['prestamo] *nm* loan; **~**
hipotecario mortgage
prestar [pres'tar] *vt* to lend, loan;
(*atención*) to pay; (*ayuda*) to give
presteza [pres'teθa] *nf* speed, promptness
prestigio [pres'tixjo] *nm* prestige; **~so, a**
adj (*honorable*) prestigious; (*famoso,
renombrado*) renowned, famous
presumido, a [presu'miðo, a] *adj*
(*persona*) vain
presumir [presu'mir] *vt* to presume ♦ *vi*
(*tener aires*) to be conceited; **según cabe**
~ as may be presumed, presumably;
presunción *nf* presumption; **presunto, a**
adj (*supuesto*) supposed, presumed; (*así
llamado*) so-called; **presuntuoso, a** *adj*
conceited, presumptuous
presuponer [presupo'ner] *vt* to
presuppose
presupuesto [presu'pwesto] *pp de*
presuponer ♦ *nm* (FINANZAS) budget;
(*estimación*: *de costo*) estimate
pretencioso, a [preten'θjoso, a] *adj*
pretentious
pretender [preten'der] *vt* (*intentar*) to try
to, seek to; (*reivindicar*) to claim;
(*buscar*) to seek, try for; (*cortejar*) to
woo, court; **~ que** to expect that;
pretendiente *nm/f* (*candidato*)
candidate, applicant; (*amante*) suitor;
pretensión *nf* (*aspiración*) aspiration;
(*reivindicación*) claim; (*orgullo*)
pretension
pretexto [pre'teksto] *nm* pretext; (*excusa*)
excuse
prevalecer [preβale'θer] *vi* to prevail
prevención [preβen'θjon] *nf* (*preparación*)
preparation; (*estado*) preparedness,

readiness; (*el evitar*) prevention;
(*previsión*) foresight, forethought;
(*precaución*) precaution
prevenido, a [preβe'niðo, a] *adj*
prepared, ready; (*cauteloso*) cautious
prevenir [preβe'nir] *vt* (*impedir*) to
prevent; (*prever*) to foresee, anticipate;
(*predisponer*) to prejudice, bias; (*avisar*)
to warn; (*preparar*) to prepare, get
ready; **~se** *vr* to get ready, prepare; **~se**
contra to take precautions against;
preventivo, a *adj* preventive,
precautionary
prever [pre'βer] *vt* to foresee
previo, a ['preβjo, a] *adj* (*anterior*)
previous; (*preliminar*) preliminary
♦ *prep*: **~ acuerdo de los otros** subject
to the agreement of the others
previsión [preβi'sjon] *nf* (*perspicacia*)
foresight; (*predicción*) forecast; **previsto,**
a *adj* anticipated, forecast
prima ['prima] *nf* (COM) bonus; **~ de**
seguro insurance premium; *ver tb*
primo
primacía [prima'θia] *nf* primacy
primario, a [pri'marjo, a] *adj* primary
primavera [prima'βera] *nf* spring(-time)
primera [pri'mera] *nf* (AUTO) first gear;
(FERRO: *tb*: **~ clase**) first class; **de ~** (*fam*)
first-class, first-rate
primero, a [pri'mero, a] (*delante de nmsg*:
primer) *adj* first; (*principal*) prime
♦ *adv* first; (*más bien*) sooner, rather;
primera plana front page
primicia [pri'miθja] *nf* (PRENSA) (*tb*: **~**
informativa) scoop
primitivo, a [primi'tiβo, a] *adj* primitive;
(*original*) original
primo, a ['primo, a] *adj* prime ♦ *nm/f*
cousin; (*fam*) fool, idiot; **~ hermano** first
cousin; **materias primas** raw materials
primogénito, a [primo'xenito, a] *adj*
first-born
primordial [primor'ðjal] *adj* basic,
fundamental
primoroso, a [primo'roso, a] *adj*
exquisite, delicate
princesa [prin'θesa] *nf* princess
principal [prinθi'pal] *adj* principal, main

♦ *nm* (*jefe*) chief, principal

príncipe ['prinθipe] *nm* prince

principiante [prinθi'pjante] *nm/f* beginner

principio [prin'θipjo] *nm* (*comienzo*) beginning, start; (*origen*) origin; (*primera etapa*) rudiment, basic idea; (*moral*) principle; **a ~s de** at the beginning of

pringoso, a [prin'ɣoso, a] *adj* (*grasiento*) greasy; (*pegajoso*) sticky

pringue ['pringe] *nm* (*grasa*) grease, fat, dripping

prioridad [priori'ðað] *nf* priority

prisa ['prisa] *nf* (*apresuramiento*) hurry, haste; (*rapidez*) speed; (*urgencia*) (sense of) urgency; **a** *o* **de ~** quickly; **correr ~** to be urgent; **darse ~** to hurry up; **estar de** *o* **tener ~** to be in a hurry

prisión [pri'sjon] *nf* (*cárcel*) prison; (*período de cárcel*) imprisonment; **prisionero, a** *nm/f* prisoner

prismáticos [pris'matikos] *nmpl* binoculars

privación [priβa'θjon] *nf* deprivation; (*falta*) want, privation

privado, a [pri'βaðo, a] *adj* private

privar [pri'βar] *vt* to deprive; **privativo, a** *adj* exclusive

privilegiado, a [priβile'xjaðo, a] *adj* privileged; (*memoria*) very good

privilegiar [priβile'xjar] *vt* to grant a privilege to; (*favorecer*) to favour

privilegio [priβi'lexjo] *nm* privilege; (*concesión*) concession

pro [pro] *nm* *o* *f* profit, advantage ♦ *prep*: **asociación ~ ciegos** association for the blind ♦ *prefijo*: **~ soviético/americano** pro-Soviet/American; **en ~ de** on behalf of, for; **los ~s y los contras** the pros and cons

proa ['proa] *nf* bow, prow; **de ~** bow *cpd*, fore

probabilidad [proβaβili'ðað] *nf* probability, likelihood; (*oportunidad*, *posibilidad*) chance, prospect; **probable** *adj* probable, likely

probador [proβa'ðor] *nm* (*en tienda*) fitting room

probar [pro'βar] *vt* (*demostrar*) to prove;

(*someter a prueba*) to test, try out; (*ropa*) to try on; (*comida*) to taste ♦ *vi* to try; **~se un traje** to try on a suit

probeta [pro'βeta] *nf* test tube

problema [pro'βlema] *nm* problem

procedente [proθe'ðente] *adj* (*razonable*) reasonable; (*conforme a derecho*) proper, fitting; **~ de** coming from, originating in

proceder [proθe'ðer] *vi* (*avanzar*) to proceed; (*actuar*) to act; (*ser correcto*) to be right (and proper), be fitting ♦ *nm* (*comportamiento*) behaviour, conduct; **~ de** to come from, originate in; **procedimiento** *nm* procedure; (*proceso*) process; (*método*) means *pl*, method

procesado, a [proθe'saðo, a] *nm/f* accused

procesador [proθesa'ðor] *nm*: **~ de textos** word processor

procesar [proθe'sar] *vt* to try, put on trial

procesión [proθe'sjon] *nf* procession

proceso [pro'θeso] *nm* process; (*JUR*) trial; (*lapso*) course (of time)

proclamar [prokla'mar] *vt* to proclaim

procreación [prokrea'θjon] *nf* procreation

procrear [prokre'ar] *vt*, *vi* to procreate

procurador, a [prokura'ðor, a] *nm/f* attorney

procurar [proku'rar] *vt* (*intentar*) to try, endeavour; (*conseguir*) to get, obtain; (*asegurar*) to secure; (*producir*) to produce

prodigio [pro'ðixjo] *nm* prodigy; (*milagro*) wonder, marvel; **~so, a** *adj* prodigious, marvellous

pródigo, a ['proðiɣo, a] *adj*: **hijo ~** prodigal son

producción [proðuk'θjon] *nf* (*gen*) production; (*producto*) product; **~ en serie** mass production

producir [proðu'θir] *vt* to produce; (*causar*) to cause, bring about; **~se** *vr* (*cambio*) to come about; (*accidente*) to take place; (*problema etc*) to arise; (*hacerse*) to be produced, be made; (*estallar*) to break out

productividad [proðuktiβi'ðað] *nf* productivity; **productivo, a** *adj* productive; (*provechoso*) profitable

producto [pro'ðukto] *nm* product; (*producción*) production

productor, a [proðuk'tor, a] *adj* productive, producing ♦ *nm/f* producer

proeza [pro'eθa] *nf* exploit, feat

profanar [profa'nar] *vt* to desecrate, profane; **profano, a** *adj* profane ♦ *nm/f* layman/woman

profecía [profe'θia] *nf* prophecy

proferir [profe'rir] *vt* (*palabra, sonido*) to utter; (*injuria*) to hurl, let fly

profesar [profe'sar] *vt* (*practicar*) to practise

profesión [profe'sjon] *nf* profession; **profesional** *adj* professional

profesor, a [profe'sor, a] *nm/f* teacher; **~ado** *nm* teaching profession

profeta [pro'feta] *nm/f* prophet; **profetizar** *vt, vi* to prophesy

prófugo, a ['profuɣo, a] *nm/f* fugitive; (MIL: *desertor*) deserter

profundidad [profundi'ðað] *nf* depth; **profundizar** *vt* (*fig*): **profundizar en** to go deeply into; **profundo, a** *adj* deep; (*misterio, pensador*) profound

profusión [profu'sjon] *nf* (*abundancia*) profusion; (*prodigalidad*) extravagance

progenitor [proxeni'tor] *nm* ancestor; **~es** *nmpl* (*padres*) parents

programa [pro'ɣrama] *nm* programme (BRIT), program (US); **~ción** *nf* programming; **~dor, a** *nm/f* programmer; **programar** *vt* to program

progresar [proɣre'sar] *vi* to progress, make progress; **progresista** *adj, nm/f* progressive; **progresivo, a** *adj* progressive; (*gradual*) gradual; (*continuo*) continuous; **progreso** *nm* progress

prohibición [proiβi'θjon] *nf* prohibition, ban

prohibir [proi'βir] *vt* to prohibit, ban, forbid; **se prohibe fumar, prohibido fumar** no smoking

prójimo, a ['proximo, a] *nm/f* fellow man; (*vecino*) neighbour

proletariado [proleta'rjaðo] *nm* proletariat

proletario, a [prole'tarjo, a] *adj, nm/f* proletarian

proliferación [prolifera'θjon] *nf* proliferation

proliferar [prolife'rar] *vi* to proliferate; **prolífico, a** *adj* prolific

prólogo ['proloɣo] *nm* prologue

prolongación [prolonga'θjon] *nf* extension; **prolongado, a** *adj* (*largo*) long; (*alargado*) lengthy

prolongar [prolon'ɣar] *vt* to extend; (*reunión etc*) to prolong; (*calle, tubo*) to extend

promedio [pro'meðjo] *nm* average; (*de distancia*) middle, mid-point

promesa [pro'mesa] *nf* promise

prometer [prome'ter] *vt* to promise ♦ *vi* to show promise; **~se** *vr* (*novios*) to get engaged; **prometido, a** *adj* promised; engaged ♦ *nm/f* fiancé/fiancée

prominente [promi'nente] *adj* prominent

promiscuo, a [pro'miskwo, a] *adj* promiscuous

promoción [promo'θjon] *nf* promotion

promotor [promo'tor] *nm* promoter; (*instigador*) instigator

promover [promo'βer] *vt* to promote; (*causar*) to cause; (*instigar*) to instigate, stir up

promulgar [promul'ɣar] *vt* to promulgate; (*fig*) to proclaim

pronombre [pro'nombre] *nm* pronoun

pronosticar [pronosti'kar] *vt* to predict, foretell, forecast; **pronóstico** *nm* prediction, forecast; **pronóstico del tiempo** weather forecast

pronto, a ['pronto, a] *adj* (*rápido*) prompt, quick; (*preparado*) ready ♦ *adv* quickly, promptly; (*en seguida*) at once, right away; (*dentro de poco*) soon; (*temprano*) early ♦ *nm*: **tener ~s de enojo** to be quick-tempered; **al ~** at first; **de ~** suddenly; **por lo ~** meanwhile, for the present

pronunciación [pronunθja'θjon] *nf* pronunciation

pronunciar [pronun'θjar] *vt* to pronounce; (*discurso*) to make, deliver; **~se** *vr* to revolt, rebel; (*declararse*) to declare o.s.

propagación [propaɣa'θjon] *nf* propagation

propaganda [propa'ɣanda] *nf* (*política*)
propaganda; (*comercial*) advertising

propagar [propa'ɣar] *vt* to propagate

propensión [propen'sjon] *nf* inclination,
propensity; **propenso, a** *adj* inclined to;
ser propenso a to be inclined to, have a
tendency to

propicio, a [pro'piθjo, a] *adj* favourable,
propitious

propiedad [propje'ðað] *nf* property;
(*posesión*) possession, ownership; ~
particular private property

propietario, a [propje'tarjo, a] *nm/f*
owner, proprietor

propina [pro'pina] *nf* tip

propio, a ['propjo, a] *adj* own, of one's
own; (*característico*) characteristic,
typical; (*debido*) proper; (*mismo*)
selfsame, very; **el ~ ministro** the
minister himself; **¿tienes casa propia?**
have you a house of your own?

proponer [propo'ner] *vt* to propose, put
forward; (*problema*) to pose; ~**se** *vr* to
propose, intend

proporción [propor'θjon] *nf* proportion;
(*MAT*) ratio; **proporciones** *nfpl*
(*dimensiones*) dimensions; (*fig*) size *sg*;
proporcionado, a *adj* proportionate;
(*regular*) medium, middling; (*justo*) just
right; **proporcionar** *vt* (*dar*) to give,
supply, provide

proposición [proposi'θjon] *nf* proposition;
(*propuesta*) proposal

propósito [pro'posito] *nm* purpose;
(*intento*) aim, intention ♦ *adv*: **a ~** by the
way, incidentally; (*a posta*) on purpose,
deliberately; **a ~ de** about, with regard
to

propuesta [pro'pwesta] *vb ver* **proponer**
♦ *nf* proposal

propulsar [propul'sar] *vt* to drive, propel;
(*fig*) to promote, encourage; **propulsión**
nf propulsion; **propulsión a chorro** *o*
por reacción jet propulsion

prórroga ['prorroɣa] *nf* extension; (*JUR*)
stay; (*COM*) deferment; (*DEPORTE*) extra
time; **prorrogar** *vt* (*período*) to extend;
(*decisión*) to defer, postpone

prorrumpir [prorrum'pir] *vi* to burst forth,

break out

prosa ['prosa] *nf* prose

proscrito, a [pro'skrito, a] *adj* (*prohibido,
desterrado*) banned

proseguir [prose'ɣir] *vt* to continue,
carry on ♦ *vi* to continue, go on

prospección [prospek'θjon] *nf*
exploration; (*del oro*) prospecting

prospecto [pros'pekto] *nm* prospectus

prosperar [prospe'rar] *vi* to prosper,
thrive, flourish; **prosperidad** *nf*
prosperity; (*éxito*) success; **próspero, a**
adj prosperous, flourishing; (*que tiene
éxito*) successful

prostíbulo [pros'tiβulo] *nm* brothel (*BRIT*),
house of prostitution (*US*)

prostitución [prostitu'θjon] *nf*
prostitution

prostituir [prosti'twir] *vt* to prostitute;
~**se** *vr* to prostitute o.s., become a
prostitute

prostituta [prosti'tuta] *nf* prostitute

protagonista [protaɣo'nista] *nm/f*
protagonist

protagonizar [protaɣoni'θar] *vt* to take
the chief rôle in

protección [protek'θjon] *nf* protection

protector, a [protek'tor, a] *adj* protective,
protecting ♦ *nm/f* protector

proteger [prote'xer] *vt* to protect;
protegido, a *nm/f* protégé/protégée

proteína [prote'ina] *nf* protein

protesta [pro'testa] *nf* protest;
(*declaración*) protestation

protestante [protes'tante] *adj* Protestant

protestar [protes'tar] *vt* to protest,
declare; (*fe*) to protest ♦ *vi* to protest

protocolo [proto'kolo] *nm* protocol

prototipo [proto'tipo] *nm* prototype

prov. *abr* (= *provincia*) prov

provecho [pro'βetʃo] *nm* advantage,
benefit; (*FINANZAS*) profit; **¡buen ~!** bon
appétit!; **en ~ de** to the benefit of; **sacar
~ de** to benefit from, profit by

proveer [proβe'er] *vt* to provide, supply
♦ *vi*: ~ **a** to provide for

provenir [proβe'nir] *vi*: ~ **de** to come
from, stem from

proverbio [pro'βerβjo] *nm* proverb

providencia [proβiˈðenθja] *nf* providence; (*previsión*) foresight

provincia [proˈβinθja] *nf* province; **~no, a** *adj* provincial; (*del campo*) country *cpd*

provisión [proβiˈsjon] *nf* provision; (*abastecimiento*) provision, supply; (*medida*) measure, step

provisional [proβisjoˈnal] *adj* provisional

provocación [proβokaˈθjon] *nf* provocation

provocar [proβoˈkar] *vt* to provoke; (*alentar*) to tempt, invite; (*causar*) to bring about, lead to; (*promover*) to promote; (*estimular*) to rouse, stimulate; **¿te provoca un café?** (*AM*) would you like a coffee?; **provocativo, a** *adj* provocative

próximamente [proksimaˈmente] *adv* shortly, soon

proximidad [proksimiˈðað] *nf* closeness, proximity; **próximo, a** *adj* near, close; (*vecino*) neighbouring; (*siguiente*) next

proyectar [projekˈtar] *vt* (*objeto*) to hurl, throw; (*luz*) to cast, shed; (*CINE*) to screen, show; (*planear*) to plan

proyectil [projekˈtil] *nm* projectile, missile

proyecto [proˈjekto] *nm* plan; (*estimación de costo*) detailed estimate

proyector [projekˈtor] *nm* (*CINE*) projector

prudencia [pruˈðenθja] *nf* (*sabiduría*) wisdom; (*cuidado*) care; **prudente** *adj* sensible, wise; (*conductor*) careful

prueba *etc* [ˈprweβa] *vb ver* **probar** ♦ *nf* proof; (*ensayo*) test, trial; (*degustación*) tasting, sampling; (*de ropa*) fitting; **a ~ on trial**; **a ~ de** proof against; **a ~ de agua/fuego** waterproof/fireproof; **someter a ~** to put to the test

prurito [pruˈrito] *nm* itch; (*de bebé*) nappy (*BRIT*) o diaper (*US*) rash

psico... [siko] *prefijo* psycho...; **~análisis** *nm inv* psychoanalysis; **~logía** *nf* psychology; **~lógico, a** *adj* psychological; **psicólogo, a** *nm/f* psychologist; **psicópata** *nm/f* psychopath; **~sis** *nf inv* psychosis

psiquiatra [siˈkjatra] *nm/f* psychiatrist; **psiquiátrico, a** *adj* psychiatric

psíquico, a [ˈsikiko, a] *adj* psychic(al)

PSOE [peˈsoe] *nm abr* = **Partido Socialista Obrero Español**

pta(s) *abr* = **peseta(s)**

pts *abr* = **pesetas**

púa [ˈpua] *nf* sharp point; (*BOT, ZOOL*) prickle, spine; (*para guitarra*) plectrum (*BRIT*), pick (*US*); **alambre de ~** barbed wire

pubertad [puβerˈtað] *nf* puberty

publicación [puβlikaˈθjon] *nf* publication

publicar [puβliˈkar] *vt* (*editar*) to publish; (*hacer público*) to publicize; (*divulgar*) to make public, divulge

publicidad [puβliθiˈðað] *nf* publicity; (*COM: propaganda*) advertising; **publicitario, a** *adj* publicity *cpd*; advertising *cpd*

público, a [ˈpuβliko, a] *adj* public ♦ *nm* public; (*TEATRO etc*) audience

puchero [puˈtʃero] *nm* (*CULIN: guiso*) stew; (: *olla*) cooking pot; **hacer ~s** to pout

pude *etc vb ver* **poder**

púdico, a [ˈpuðiko, a] *adj* modest

pudiente [puˈðjente] *adj* (*rico*) wealthy, well-to-do

pudiera *etc vb ver* **poder**

pudor [puˈðor] *nm* modesty

pudrir [puˈðrir] *vt* to rot; (*fam*) to upset, annoy; **~se** *vr* to rot, decay

pueblo [ˈpweβlo] *nm* people; (*nación*) nation; (*aldea*) village

puedo *etc vb ver* **poder**

puente [ˈpwente] *nm* bridge; **hacer ~** (*inf*) *to take extra days off work between 2 public holidays*; to take a long weekend; **~ aéreo** shuttle service; **~ colgante** suspension bridge

puerco, a [ˈpwerko, a] *nm/f* pig/sow ♦ *adj* (*sucio*) dirty, filthy; (*obsceno*) disgusting; **~ de mar** porpoise; **~ marino** dolphin

pueril [pweˈril] *adj* childish

puerro [ˈpwerro] *nm* leek

puerta [ˈpwerta] *nf* door; (*de jardín*) gate; (*portal*) doorway; (*fig*) gateway; (*portería*) goal; **a la ~** at the door; **a ~ cerrada** behind closed doors; **~ giratoria** revolving door

puerto ['pwerto] *nm* port; (*paso*) pass; (*fig*) haven, refuge

Puerto Rico [pwerto'riko] *nm* Puerto Rico; **puertorriqueño, a** *adj*, *nm/f* Puerto Rican

pues [pwes] *adv* (*entonces*) then; (*bueno*) well, well then; (*así que*) so ♦ *conj* (*ya que*) since; ¡~! (*sí*) yes!, certainly!

puesta ['pwesta] *nf* (*apuesta*) bet, stake; ~ **en marcha** starting; ~ **del sol** sunset

puesto, a ['pwesto, a] *pp de* **poner** ♦ *adj*: **tener algo** ~ to have sth on, be wearing sth ♦ *nm* (*lugar, posición*) place; (*trabajo*) post, job; (*COM*) stall ♦ *conj*: ~ **que** since, as

púgil ['puxil] *nm* boxer

pugna ['puɣna] *nf* battle, conflict; **pugnar** *vi* (*luchar*) to struggle, fight; (*pelear*) to fight

pujar [pu'xar] *vi* (*en subasta*) to bid; (*esforzarse*) to struggle, strain

pulcro, a ['pulkro, a] *adj* neat, tidy; (*bello*) exquisite

pulga ['pulɣa] *nf* flea

pulgada [pul'ɣaða] *nf* inch

pulgar [pul'ɣar] *nm* thumb

pulir [pu'lir] *vt* to polish; (*alisar*) to smooth; (*fig*) to polish up, touch up

pulla ['puʎa] *nf* cutting remark; (*expresión grosera*) obscene remark

pulmón [pul'mon] *nm* lung; **pulmonía** *nf* pneumonia

pulpa ['pulpa] *nf* pulp; (*de fruta*) flesh, soft part

pulpería [pulpe'ria] (*AM*) *nf* (*tienda*) small grocery store

púlpito ['pulpito] *nm* pulpit

pulpo ['pulpo] *nm* octopus

pulsación [pulsa'θjon] *nf* beat, pulsation; (*ANAT*) throb(bing)

pulsar [pul'sar] *vt* (*tecla*) to touch, tap; (*MUS*) to play; (*botón*) to press, push ♦ *vi* to pulsate; (*latir*) to beat, throb; (*MED*): ~ **a uno** to take sb's pulse

pulsera [pul'sera] *nf* bracelet

pulso ['pulso] *nm* (*ANAT*) pulse; (: *muñeca*) wrist; (*fuerza*) strength; (*firmeza*) steadiness, steady hand; (*tacto*) tact, good sense

pulverizador [pulßeriθa'ðor] *nm* spray, spray gun

pulverizar [pulßeri'θar] *vt* to pulverize; (*líquido*) to spray

puna ['puna] (*AM*) *nf* mountain sickness

punitivo, a [puni'tißo, a] *adj* punitive

punta ['punta] *nf* point, tip; (*extremidad*) end; (*fig*) touch, trace; **horas ~s** peak hours, rush hours; **sacar** ~ **a** to sharpen; **estar de** ~ to be edgy

puntada [pun'taða] *nf* (*COSTURA*) stitch

puntal [pun'tal] *nm* prop, support

puntapié [punta'pje] *nm* kick

puntear [punte'ar] *vt* to tick, mark

puntería [punte'ria] *nf* (*de arma*) aim, aiming; (*destreza*) marksmanship

puntero, a [pun'tero, a] *adj* leading ♦ *nm* (*palo*) pointer

puntiagudo, a [puntja'ɣuðo, a] *adj* sharp, pointed

puntilla [pun'tiʎa] *nf* (*encaje*) lace edging *o* trim; (**andar**) **de ~s** (to walk) on tiptoe

punto ['punto] *nm* (*gen*) point; (*señal diminuta*) spot, dot; (*COSTURA, MED*) stitch; (*lugar*) spot, place; (*momento*) point, moment; **a** ~ ready; **estar a** ~ **de** to be on the point of *o* about to; **en** ~ on the dot; ~ **muerto** dead centre; (*AUTO*) neutral (gear); ~ **final** full stop (*BRIT*), period (*US*); ~ **y coma** semicolon; ~ **de interrogación** question mark; ~ **de vista** point of view, viewpoint; **hacer** ~ (*tejer*) to knit

puntuación [puntwa'θjon] *nf* punctuation; (*puntos: en examen*) mark(s) (*pl*); (: *DEPORTE*) score

puntual [pun'twal] *adj* (*a tiempo*) punctual; (*exacto*) exact, accurate; (*seguro*) reliable; **~idad** *nf* punctuality; exactness, accuracy; reliability; **~izar** *vt* to fix, specify

puntuar [pun'twar] *vi* (*DEPORTE*) to score, count

punzada [pun'θaða] *nf* (*de dolor*) twinge

puñado [pu'ɲaðo] *nm* handful

puñal [pu'ɲal] *nm* dagger; **~ada** *nf* stab

punzante [pun'θante] *adj* (*dolor*) shooting, sharp; (*herramienta*) sharp; **punzar** *vt* to prick, pierce ♦ *vi* to shoot,

stab
puñetazo [puɲe'taθo] *nm* punch
puño ['puɲo] *nm* (*ANAT*) fist; (*cantidad*)
fistful, handful; (*COSTURA*) cuff; (*de herra-mienta*) handle
pupila [pu'pila] *nf* pupil
pupitre [pu'pitre] *nm* desk
puré [pu're] *nm* puree; (*sopa*) (thick)
soup; ~ **de patatas** mashed potatoes
pureza [pu'reθa] *nf* purity
purga ['purxa] *nf* purge; **purgante** *adj*,
nm purgative; **purgar** *vt* to purge
purgatorio [purxa'torjo] *nm* purgatory
purificar [purifi'kar] *vt* to purify; (*refinar*)
to refine
puritano, a [puri'tano, a] *adj* (*actitud*)
puritanical; (*iglesia, tradición*) puritan
♦ *nm/f* puritan
puro, a ['puro, a] *adj* pure; (*cielo*) clear;
(*verdad*) simple, plain ♦ *adv*: **de ~
cansado** out of sheer tiredness ♦ *nm*
cigar
púrpura ['purpura] *nf* purple; **purpúreo, a**
adj purple
pus [pus] *nm* pus
puse *etc vb ver* **poner**
pusiera *etc vb ver* **poner**
pústula ['pustula] *nf* pimple, sore
puta ['puta] *nf* whore, prostitute
putrefacción [putrefak'θjon] *nf* rotting,
putrefaction
pútrido, a ['putriðo, a] *adj* rotten
PVP *abr* (*ESP*: = *precio venta al público*)
RRP
pyme, PYME ['pime] *nf abr* (= *Pequeña
y Mediana Empresa*) SME

Q q

PALABRA CLAVE

que [ke] *conj* **1** (*con oración subordinada*:
muchas veces no se traduce) that; **dijo ~
vendría** he said (that) he would come;
espero ~ lo encuentres I hope (that)
you find it; *ver tb* **el**
2 (*en oración independiente*): ¡**~ entre!**
send him in; ¡**~ se mejore tu padre!** I

hope your father gets better
3 (*enfático*): ¿**me quieres?** – ¡**~ sí!** do
you love me? – of course!
4 (*consecutivo*: *muchas veces no se
traduce*) that; **es tan grande ~ no lo
puedo levantar** it's so big (that) I can't
lift it
5 (*comparaciones*) than; **yo ~ tú/él** if I
were you/him; *ver tb* **más; menos;
mismo**
6 (*valor disyuntivo*): **~ le guste o no**
whether he likes it or not; **~ venga o ~
no venga** whether he comes or not
7 (*porque*): **no puedo, ~ tengo ~
quedarme en casa** I can't, I've got to
stay in
♦ *pron* **1** (*cosa*) that, which; (+ *prep*)
which; **el sombrero ~ te compraste** the
hat (that *o* which) you bought; **la cama
en ~ dormí** the bed (that *o* which) I
slept in
2 (*persona: suj*) that, who; (: *objeto*) that,
whom; **el amigo ~ me acompañó al
museo** the friend that *o* who went to the
museum with me; **la chica ~ invité** the
girl (that *o* whom) I invited

qué [ke] *adj* what?, which? ♦ *pron* what?;
¡**~ divertido!** how funny!; ¿**~ edad
tienes?** how old are you?; ¿**de ~ me
hablas?** what are you saying to me?; ¿**~
tal?** how are you?, how are things?; ¿**~
hay (de nuevo)?** what's new?
quebrada [ke'βraða] *nf* ravine; *ver tb
quebrado*
quebradizo, a [keβra'ðiθo, a] *adj* fragile;
(*persona*) frail
quebrado, a [ke'βraðo, a] *adj* (*roto*)
broken ♦ *nm/f* bankrupt ♦ *nm* (*MAT*)
fraction
quebrantar [keβran'tar] *vt* (*infringir*) to
violate, transgress; **~se** *vr* (*persona*) to
fail in health
quebranto [ke'βranto] *nm* damage, harm;
(*decaimiento*) exhaustion; (*dolor*) grief,
pain
quebrar [ke'βrar] *vt* to break, smash ♦ *vi*
to go bankrupt; **~se** *vr* to break, get
broken; (*MED*) to be ruptured

quedar [ke'ðar] *vi* to stay, remain; (*encontrarse: sitio*) to be; (*restar*) to remain, be left; ~**se** *vr* to remain, stay (behind); ~**se (con) algo** to keep sth; ~ **en** (*acordar*) to agree on/to; ~ **en nada** to come to nothing; ~ **por hacer** to be still to be done; ~ **ciego/mudo** to be left blind/dumb; **no te queda bien ese vestido** that dress doesn't suit you; **eso queda muy lejos** that's a long way (away); **quedamos a las seis** we agreed to meet at six

quedo, a ['keðo, a] *adj* still ♦ *adv* softly, gently

quehacer [kea'θer] *nm* task, job; ~**es** (*domésticos*) *nmpl* household chores

queja ['kexa] *nf* complaint; **quejarse** *vr* (*enfermo*) to moan, groan; (*protestar*) to complain; **quejarse de que** to complain (about the fact) that; **quejido** *nm* moan

quemado, a [ke'maðo, a] *adj* burnt

quemadura [kema'ðura] *nf* burn, scald

quemar [ke'mar] *vt* to burn; (*fig: malgastar*) to burn up, squander ♦ *vi* to be burning hot; ~**se** *vr* (*consumirse*) to burn (up); (*del sol*) to get sunburnt

quemarropa [kema'rropa]: **a** ~ *adv* pointblank

quemazón [kema'θon] *nf* burn; (*calor*) intense heat; (*sensación*) itch

quepo *etc vb ver* **caber**

querella [ke'reʎa] *nf* (*JUR*) charge; (*disputa*) dispute; ~**se** *vr* (*JUR*) to file a complaint

PALABRA CLAVE

querer [ke'rer] *vt* **1** (*desear*) to want; **quiero más dinero** I want more money; **quisiera** *o* **querría un té** I'd like a tea; **sin** ~ unintentionally; **quiero ayudar/que vayas** I want to help/you to go
2 (*preguntas: para pedir algo*): **¿quiere abrir la ventana?** could you open the window?; **¿quieres echarme una mano?** can you give me a hand?
3 (*amar*) to love; (*tener cariño a*) to be fond of; **quiere mucho a sus hijos** he's very fond of his children
4 (*requerir*): **esta planta quiere más**

luz this plant needs more light
5: le pedí que me dejara ir pero no quiso I asked him to let me go but he refused

querido, a [ke'riðo, a] *adj* dear ♦ *nm/f* darling; (*amante*) lover

queso ['keso] *nm* cheese; ~ **crema** cream cheese

quicio ['kiθjo] *nm* hinge; **sacar a uno de** ~ to get on sb's nerves

quiebra ['kjeβra] *nf* break, split; (*COM*) bankruptcy; (*ECON*) slump

quiebro ['kjeβro] *nm* (*del cuerpo*) swerve

quien [kjen] *pron* who; **hay** ~ **piensa que** there are those who think that; **no hay** ~ **lo haga** no-one will do it

quién [kjen] *pron* who, whom; **¿**~ **es?** who's there?

quienquiera [kjen'kjera] (*pl* **quienesquiera**) *pron* whoever

quiero *etc vb ver* **querer**

quieto, a ['kjeto, a] *adj* still; (*carácter*) placid; **quietud** *nf* stillness

quilate [ki'late] *nm* carat

quilla ['kiʎa] *nf* keel

quimera [ki'mera] *nf* chimera; **quimérico, a** *adj* fantastic

químico, a ['kimiko, a] *adj* chemical ♦ *nm/f* chemist ♦ *nf* chemistry

quincalla [kin'kaʎa] *nf* hardware, ironmongery (*BRIT*)

quince ['kinθe] *num* fifteen; ~ **días** a fortnight; ~**añero, a** *nm/f* teenager; ~**na** *nf* fortnight; (*pago*) fortnightly pay; ~**nal** *adj* fortnightly

quiniela [ki'njela] *nf* football pools *pl*; ~**s** *nfpl* (*impreso*) pools coupon *sg*

quinientos, as [ki'njentos, as] *adj, num* five hundred

quinina [ki'nina] *nf* quinine

quinqui ['kinki] *nm* delinquent

quinto, a ['kinto, a] *adj* fifth ♦ *nf* country house; (*MIL*) call-up, draft

quiosco ['kjosko] *nm* (*de música*) bandstand; (*de periódicos*) news stand

quirófano [ki'rofano] *nm* operating theatre

quirúrgico, a [ki'rurxiko, a] *adj* surgical

quise *etc vb ver* **querer**

quisiera *etc vb ver* **querer**

quisquilloso, a [kiski'ʎoso, a] *adj* (*susceptible*) touchy; (*meticuloso*) pernickety

quiste ['kiste] *nm* cyst

quitaesmalte [kitaes'malte] *nm* nail-polish remover

quitamanchas [kita'mantʃas] *nm inv* stain remover

quitanieves [kita'njeβes] *nm inv* snowplough (*BRIT*), snowplow (*US*)

quitar [ki'tar] *vt* to remove, take away; (*ropa*) to take off; (*dolor*) to relieve; ¡**quita de ahí**! get away!; ~**se** *vr* to withdraw; (*ropa*) to take off; **se quitó el sombrero** he took off his hat

quitasol [kita'sol] *nm* sunshade (*BRIT*), parasol

quite ['kite] *nm* (*esgrima*) parry; (*evasión*) dodge

Quito ['kito] *n* Quito

quizá(s) [ki'θa(s)] *adv* perhaps, maybe

R r

rábano ['raβano] *nm* radish; **me importa un** ~ I don't give a damn

rabia ['raβja] *nf* (*MED*) rabies *sg*; (*fig: ira*) fury, rage; **rabiar** *vi* to have rabies; to rage, be furious; **rabiar por algo** to long for sth

rabieta [ra'βjeta] *nf* tantrum, fit of temper

rabino [ra'βino] *nm* rabbi

rabioso, a [ra'βjoso, a] *adj* rabid; (*fig*) furious

rabo ['raβo] *nm* tail

racha ['ratʃa] *nf* gust of wind: **buena/ mala** ~ (*fig*) spell of good/bad luck

racial [ra'θjal] *adj* racial, race *cpd*

racimo [ra'θimo] *nm* bunch

raciocinio [raθjo'θinjo] *nm* reason

ración [ra'θjon] *nf* portion; **raciones** *nfpl* rations

racional [raθjo'nal] *adj* (*razonable*) reasonable; (*lógico*) rational; ~**izar** *vt* to rationalize

racionar [raθjo'nar] *vt* to ration (out)

racismo [ra'θismo] *nm* racialism, racism;

racista *adj*, *nm/f* racist

radar [ra'ðar] *nm* radar

radiactivo, a [raðiak'tiβo, a] *adj* = **radioactivo**

radiador [raðja'ðor] *nm* radiator

radiante [ra'ðjante] *adj* radiant

radical [raði'kal] *adj*, *nm/f* radical

radicar [raði'kar] *vi* to take root; ~ **en** (*dificultad, problema*) to lie in; (*solución*) to consist in; ~**se** *vr* to establish o.s., put down (one's) roots

radio ['raðjo] *nf* radio; (*aparato*) radio (set) ♦ *nm* (*MAT*) radius; (*QUÍMICA*) radium; ~**actividad** *nf* radioactivity; ~**activo, a** *adj* radioactive; ~**difusión** *nf* broadcasting; ~**emisora** *nf* transmitter, radio station; ~**escucha** *nm/f* listener; ~**grafía** *nf* X-ray; ~**grafiar** *vt* to X-ray; ~**terapia** *nf* radiotherapy; ~**yente** *nm/f* listener

ráfaga ['rafaɣa] *nf* gust; (*de luz*) flash; (*de tiros*) burst

raído, a [ra'iðo, a] *adj* (*ropa*) threadbare

raigambre [rai'ɣambre] *nf* (*BOT*) roots *pl*; (*fig*) tradition

raíz [ra'iθ] *nf* root; ~ **cuadrada** square root; **a** ~ **de** as a result of

raja ['raxa] *nf* (*de melón etc*) slice; (*grieta*) crack; **rajar** *vt* to split; (*fam*) to slash; **rajarse** *vr* to split, crack; **rajarse de** to back out of

rajatabla [raxa'taβla]: **a** ~ *adv* (*estrictamente*) strictly, to the letter

rallador [raʎa'ðor] *nm* grater

rallar [ra'ʎar] *vt* to grate

RAM [ram] *nf abr* (= *memoria de acceso aleatorio*) RAM

rama ['rama] *nf* branch; ~**je** *nm* branches *pl*, foliage; **ramal** *nm* (*de cuerda*) strand; (*FERRO*) branch line (*BRIT*); (*AUTO*) branch (road) (*BRIT*)

rambla ['rambla] *nf* (*avenida*) avenue

ramera [ra'mera] *nf* whore

ramificación [ramifika'θjon] *nf* ramification

ramificarse [ramifi'karse] *vr* to branch out

ramillete [rami'ʎete] *nm* bouquet

ramo ['ramo] *nm* branch; (*sección*) department, section

rampa ['rampa] *nf* ramp

ramplón, ona [ram'plon, ona] *adj* uncouth, coarse

rana ['rana] *nf* frog; **salto de ~** leapfrog

ranchero [ran'tʃero] *nm* (AM) rancher; smallholder

rancho ['rantʃo] *nm* grub (*fam*); (AM: *grande*) ranch; (: *pequeño*) small farm

rancio, a ['ranθjo, a] *adj* (*comestibles*) rancid; (*vino*) aged, mellow; (*fig*) ancient

rango ['rango] *nm* rank, standing

ranura [ra'nura] *nf* groove; (*de teléfono etc*) slot

rapar [ra'par] *vt* to shave; (*los cabellos*) to crop

rapaz [ra'paθ] (*nf*: **rapaza**) *nm/f* young boy/girl ♦ *adj* (ZOOL) predatory

rape ['rape] *nm* quick shave; (*pez*) angler fish; **al ~** cropped

rapé [ra'pe] *nm* snuff

rapidez [rapi'ðeθ] *nf* speed, rapidity; **rápido, a** *adj* fast, quick ♦ *adv* quickly ♦ *nm* (FERRO) express; **rápidos** *nmpl* rapids

rapiña [ra'piɲa] *nm* robbery; **ave de ~** bird of prey

raptar [rap'tar] *vt* to kidnap; **rapto** *nm* kidnapping; (*impulso*) sudden impulse; (*éxtasis*) ecstasy, rapture

raqueta [ra'keta] *nf* racquet

raquítico, a [ra'kitiko, a] *adj* stunted; (*fig*) poor, inadequate; **raquitismo** *nm* rickets *sg*

rareza [ra'reθa] *nf* rarity; (*fig*) eccentricity

raro, a ['raro, a] *adj* (*poco común*) rare; (*extraño*) odd, strange; (*excepcional*) remarkable

ras [ras] *nm*: **a ~ de** level with; **a ~ de tierra** at ground level

rasar [ra'sar] *vt* (*igualar*) to level

rascacielos [raska'θjelos] *nm inv* skyscraper

rascar [ras'kar] *vt* (*con las uñas etc*) to scratch; (*raspar*) to scrape; **~se** *vr* to scratch (o.s.)

rasgar [ras'ɣar] *vt* to tear, rip (up)

rasgo ['rasɣo] *nm* (*con pluma*) stroke; **~s** *nmpl* (*facciones*) features, characteristics;

a grandes ~s in outline, broadly

rasguñar [rasɣu'ɲar] *vt* to scratch; **rasguño** *nm* scratch

raso, a ['raso, a] *adj* (*liso*) flat, level; (*a baja altura*) very low ♦ *nm* satin; **cielo ~** clear sky

raspadura [raspa'ðura] *nf* (*acto*) scrape, scraping; (*marca*) scratch; **~s** *nfpl* (*de papel etc*) scrapings

raspar [ras'par] *vt* to scrape; (*arañar*) to scratch; (*limar*) to file

rastra ['rastra] *nf* (AGR) rake; **a ~s** by dragging; (*fig*) unwillingly

rastreador [rastrea'ðor] *nm* tracker; **~ de minas** minesweeper

rastrear [rastre'ar] *vt* (*seguir*) to track

rastrero, a [ras'trero, a] *adj* (BOT, ZOOL) creeping; (*fig*) despicable, mean

rastrillo [ras'triʎo] *nm* rake

rastro ['rastro] *nm* (AGR) rake; (*pista*) track, trail; (*vestigio*) trace; **el R~** the Madrid fleamarket

rastrojo [ras'troxo] *nm* stubble

rasurador [rasura'ðor] (AM) *nm* electric shaver

rasuradora [rasura'ðora] (AM) *nf* = **rasurador**

rasurarse [rasu'rarse] *vr* to shave

rata ['rata] *nf* rat

ratear [rate'ar] *vt* (*robar*) to steal

ratero, a [ra'tero, a] *adj* light-fingered ♦ *nm/f* (*carterista*) pickpocket; (AM: *de casas*) burglar

ratificar [ratifi'kar] *vt* to ratify

rato ['rato] *nm* while, short time; **a ~s** from time to time; **hay para ~** there's still a long way to go; **al poco ~** soon afterwards; **pasar el ~** to kill time; **pasar un buen/mal ~** to have a good/rough time

ratón [ra'ton] *nm* mouse; **ratonera** *nf* mousetrap

raudal [rau'ðal] *nm* torrent; **a ~es** in abundance

raya ['raja] *nf* line; (*marca*) scratch; (*en tela*) stripe; (*de pelo*) parting; (*límite*) boundary; (*pez*) ray; (*puntuación*) dash; **a ~s** striped; **pasarse de la ~** to go too far: **tener a ~** to keep in check; **rayar** *vt* to

line; to scratch; (*subrayar*) to underline
♦ *vi*: **rayar en** *o* **con** to border on
rayo ['rajo] *nm* (*del sol*) ray, beam; (*de luz*) shaft; (*en una tormenta*) (flash of) lightning; **~s X** X-rays
raza ['raθa] *nf* race; **~ humana** human race
razón [ra'θon] *nf* reason; (*justicia*) right, justice; (*razonamiento*) reasoning; (*motivo*) reason, motive; (*MAT*) ratio; **a ~ de 10 cada día** at the rate of 10 a day; **"~: ..."** "inquiries to ..."; **en ~ de** with regard to; **dar ~ a uno** to agree that sb is right; **tener ~** to be right; **~ directa/inversa** direct/inverse proportion; **~ de ser** raison d'être; **razonable** *adj* reasonable; (*justo, moderado*) fair; **razonamiento** *nm* (*juicio*) judg(e)ment; (*argumento*) reasoning; **razonar** *vt, vi* to reason, argue
reacción [reak'θjon] *nf* reaction; **avión a ~** jet plane; **~ en cadena** chain reaction; **reaccionar** *vi* to react; **reaccionario, a** *adj* reactionary
reacio, a [re'aθjo, a] *adj* stubborn
reactivar [reakti'ßar] *vt* to revitalize
reactor [reak'tor] *nm* reactor
readaptación [reaðapta'θjon] *nf*: **~ profesional** industrial retraining
reajuste [rea'xuste] *nm* readjustment
real [re'al] *adj* real; (*del rey, fig*) royal
realce [re'alθe] *nm* (*TEC*) embossing; (*lustre, fig*) splendour; (*ARTE*) highlight; **poner de ~** to emphasize
realidad [reali'ðað] *nf* reality, fact; (*verdad*) truth
realista [rea'lista] *nm/f* realist
realización [realiθa'θjon] *nf* fulfilment; (*COM*) selling up (*BRIT*), conversion into money (*US*)
realizador, a [realiθa'ðor, a] *nm/f* (*TV etc*) producer
realizar [reali'θar] *vt* (*objetivo*) to achieve; (*plan*) to carry out; (*viaje*) to make, undertake; (*COM*) to sell up (*BRIT*), convert into money (*US*); **~se** *vr* to come about, come true
realmente [real'mente] *adv* really, actually

realquilar [realki'lar] *vt* (*subarrendar*) to sublet
realzar [real'θar] *vt* (*TEC*) to raise; (*embellecer*) to enhance; (*acentuar*) to highlight
reanimar [reani'mar] *vt* to revive; (*alentar*) to encourage; **~se** *vr* to revive
reanudar [reanu'ðar] *vt* (*renovar*) to renew; (*historia, viaje*) to resume
reaparición [reapari'θjon] *nf* reappearance
rearme [re'arme] *nm* rearmament
rebaja [re'ßaxa] *nf* (*COM*) reduction; (: *descuento*) discount; **~s** *nfpl* (*COM*) sale; **rebajar** *vt* (*bajar*) to lower; (*reducir*) to reduce; (*disminuir*) to lessen; (*humillar*) to humble
rebanada [reßa'naða] *nf* slice
rebañar [reßa'ɲar] *vt* (*comida*) to scrape up; (*plato*) to scrape clean
rebaño [re'ßaɲo] *nm* herd; (*de ovejas*) flock
rebasar [reßa'sar] *vt* (*tb*: **~ de**) to exceed
rebatir [reßa'tir] *vt* to refute
rebeca [re'ßeka] *nf* cardigan
rebelarse [reße'larse] *vr* to rebel, revolt
rebelde [re'ßelde] *adj* rebellious; (*niño*) unruly ♦ *nm/f* rebel; **rebeldía** *nf* rebelliousness; (*desobediencia*) disobedience
rebelión [reße'ljon] *nf* rebellion
reblandecer [reßlande'θer] *vt* to soften
rebobinar [reßoßi'nar] *vt* (*cinta, película de video*) to rewind
rebosante [reßo'sante] *adj* overflowing
rebosar [reßo'sar] *vi* (*líquido, recipiente*) to overflow; (*abundar*) to abound, be plentiful
rebotar [reßo'tar] *vt* to bounce; (*rechazar*) to repel ♦ *vi* (*pelota*) to bounce; (*bala*) to ricochet; **rebote** *nm* rebound; **de rebote** on the rebound
rebozado, a [reßo'θaðo, a] *adj* fried in batter *o* breadcrumbs
rebozar [reßo'θar] *vt* to wrap up; (*CULIN*) to fry in batter *o* breadcrumbs
rebuscado, a [reßus'kaðo, a] *adj* (*amanerado*) affected; (*palabra*) recherché; (*idea*) far-fetched
rebuscar [reßus'kar] *vi*: **~ (en/por)** to

search carefully (in/for)

rebuznar [reβuθ'nar] *vi* to bray

recabar [reka'βar] *vt* (*obtener*) to manage to get

recado [re'kaðo] *nm* message; **tomar un ~** (*TEL*) to take a message

recaer [reka'er] *vi* to relapse; **~ en** to fall to *o* on; (*criminal etc*) to fall back into, relapse into; **recaída** *nf* relapse

recalcar [rekal'kar] *vt* (*fig*) to stress, emphasize

recalcitrante [rekalθi'trante] *adj* recalcitrant

recalentar [rekalen'tar] *vt* (*volver a calentar*) to reheat; (*calentar demasiado*) to overheat

recámara [re'kamara] (*AM*) *nf* bedroom

recambio [re'kambjo] *nm* spare; (*de pluma*) refill

recapacitar [rekapaθi'tar] *vi* to reflect

recargado, a [rekar'γaðo, a] *adj* overloaded

recargar [rekar'γar] *vt* to overload; (*batería*) to recharge; **recargo** *nm* surcharge; (*aumento*) increase

recatado, a [reka'taðo, a] *adj* (*modesto*) modest, demure; (*prudente*) cautious

recato [re'kato] *nm* (*modestia*) modesty, demureness; (*cautela*) caution

recaudación [rekauða'θjon] *nf* (*acción*) collection; (*cantidad*) takings *pl*; (*en deporte*) gate; **recaudador, a** *nm/f* tax collector

recelar [reθe'lar] *vt*: **~ que** (*sospechar*) to suspect that; (*temer*) to fear that ♦ *vi*: **~ de** to distrust; **recelo** *nm* distrust, suspicion; **receloso, a** *adj* distrustful, suspicious

recepción [reθep'θjon] *nf* reception; **recepcionista** *nm/f* receptionist

receptáculo [reθep'takulo] *nm* receptacle

receptivo, a [reθep'tiβo, a] *adj* receptive

receptor, a [reθep'tor, a] *nm/f* recipient ♦ *nm* (*TEL*) receiver

recesión [reθe'sjon] *nf* (*COM*) recession

receta [re'θeta] *nf* (*CULIN*) recipe; (*MED*) prescription

rechazar [retʃa'θar] *vt* to repel, drive back; (*idea*) to reject; (*oferta*) to turn

down

rechazo [re'tʃaθo] *nm* (*de fusil*) recoil; (*rebote*) rebound; (*negación*) rebuff

rechifla [re'tʃifla] *nf* hissing, booing; (*fig*) derision

rechinar [retʃi'nar] *vi* to creak; (*dientes*) to grind

rechistar [retʃis'tar] *vi*: **sin ~** without a murmur

rechoncho, a [re'tʃontʃo, a] (*fam*) *adj* thickset (*BRIT*), heavy-set (*US*)

rechupete [retʃu'pete] (*LAM*): **de ~** (*comida*) delicious, scrumptious

recibidor, a [reθiβi'ðor, a] *nm* entrance hall

recibimiento [reθiβi'mjento] *nm* reception, welcome

recibir [reθi'βir] *vt* to receive; (*dar la bienvenida*) to welcome ♦ *vi* to entertain; **~se** *vr*: **~se de** to qualify as; **recibo** *nm* receipt

reciclar [reθi'klar] *vt* to recycle

recién [re'θjen] *adv* recently, newly; **los ~ casados** the newly-weds; **el ~ llegado** the newcomer; **el ~ nacido** the newborn child

reciente [re'θjente] *adj* recent; (*fresco*) fresh; **~mente** *adv* recently

recinto [re'θinto] *nm* enclosure; (*área*) area, place

recio, a ['reθjo, a] *adj* strong, tough; (*voz*) loud ♦ *adv* hard; loud(ly)

recipiente [reθi'pjente] *nm* receptacle

reciprocidad [reθiproθi'ðað] *nf* reciprocity; **recíproco, a** *adj* reciprocal

recital [reθi'tal] *nm* (*MUS*) recital; (*LITERATURA*) reading

recitar [reθi'tar] *vt* to recite

reclamación [reklama'θjon] *nf* claim, demand; (*queja*) complaint

reclamar [rekla'mar] *vt* to claim, demand ♦ *vi*: **~ contra** to complain about; **~ a uno en justicia** to take sb to court; **reclamo** *nm* (*anuncio*) advertisement; (*tentación*) attraction

reclinar [rekli'nar] *vt* to recline, lean; **~se** *vr* to lean back

recluir [reklu'ir] *vt* to intern, confine

reclusión [reklu'sjon] *nf* (*prisión*) prison;

(*refugio*) seclusion; ~ **perpetua** life imprisonment

recluta [reˈkluta] *nm/f* recruit ♦ *nf* recruitment; **reclutar** *vt* (*datos*) to collect; (*diñero*) to collect up

reclutamiento [reklutaˈmjento] *nm* recruitment

recobrar [rekoˈβrar] *vt* (*salud*) to recover; (*rescatar*) to get back; ~**se** *vr* to recover

recodo [reˈkoðo] *nm* (*de río, camino*) bend

recoger [rekoˈxer] *vt* (*país*) to collect; (*AGR*) to harvest; (*levantar*) to pick up; (*juntar*) to gather; (*pasar a buscar*) to come for, get; (*dar asilo*) to give shelter to; (*faldas*) to gather up; (*pelo*) to put up; ~**se** *vr* (*retirarse*) to retire; **recogido, a** *adj* (*lugar*) quiet, secluded; (*pequeño*) small ♦ *nf* (*CORREOS*) collection; (*AGR*) harvest

recolección [rekolekˈθjon] *nf* (*AGR*) harvesting; (*colecta*) collection

recomendación [rekomendaˈθjon] *nf* (*sugerencia*) suggestion, recommendation; (*referencia*) reference

recomendar [rekomenˈdar] *vt* to suggest, recommend; (*confiar*) to entrust

recompensa [rekomˈpensa] *nf* reward, recompense; **recompensar** *vt* to reward, recompense

recomponer [rekompoˈner] *vt* to mend

reconciliación [rekonθiljaˈθjon] *nf* reconciliation

reconciliar [rekonθiˈljar] *vt* to reconcile; ~**se** *vr* to become reconciled

recóndito, a [reˈkondito, a] *adj* (*lugar*) hidden, secret

reconfortar [rekonforˈtar] *vt* to comfort

reconocer [rekonoˈθer] *vt* to recognize; (*registrar*) to search; (*MED*) to examine; **reconocido, a** *adj* recognized; (*agradecido*) grateful; **reconocimiento** *nm* recognition; search; examination; gratitude; (*confesión*) admission

reconquista [rekonˈkista] *nf* reconquest; **la R~** the Reconquest (of Spain)

reconstituyente [rekonstituˈjente] *nm* tonic

reconstruir [rekonstruˈir] *vt* to reconstruct

reconversión [rekonβerˈsjon] *nf*: ~

industrial industrial rationalization

recopilación [rekopilaˈθjon] *nf* (*resumen*) summary; (*compilación*) compilation; **recopilar** *vt* to compile

récord [ˈrekorð] (*pl* ~**s**) *adj inv, nm* record

recordar [rekorˈðar] *vt* (*acordarse de*) to remember; (*acordar a otro*) to remind ♦ *vi* to remember

recorrer [rekoˈrrer] *vt* (*país*) to cross, travel through; (*distancia*) to cover; (*registrar*) to search; (*repasar*) to look over; **recorrido** *nm* run, journey; **tren de largo recorrido** main-line train

recortado, a [rekorˈtaðo, a] *adj* uneven, irregular

recortar [rekorˈtar] *vt* to cut out; **recorte** *nm* (*acción, de prensa*) cutting; (*de telas, chapas*) trimming; **recorte presupuestario** budget cut

recostado, a [rekosˈtaðo, a] *adj* leaning; **estar ~** to be lying down

recostar [rekosˈtar] *vt* to lean; ~**se** *vr* to lie down

recoveco [rekoˈβeko] *nm* (*de camino, río etc*) bend; (*en casa*) cubby hole

recreación [rekreaˈθjon] *nf* recreation

recrear [rekreˈar] *vt* (*entretener*) to entertain; (*volver a crear*) to recreate; **recreativo, a** *adj* recreational; **recreo** *nm* recreation; (*ESCOL*) break, playtime

recriminar [rekrimiˈnar] *vt* to reproach ♦ *vi* to recriminate; ~**se** *vr* to reproach each other

recrudecer [rekruðeˈθer] *vt, vi* to worsen; ~**se** *vr* to worsen

recrudecimiento [rekruðeθiˈmjento] *nm* upsurge

recta [ˈrekta] *nf* straight line

rectángulo, a [rekˈtangulo, a] *adj* rectangular ♦ *nm* rectangle

rectificar [rektifiˈkar] *vt* to rectify; (*volverse recto*) to straighten ♦ *vi* to correct o.s.

rectitud [rektiˈtuð] *nf* straightness; (*fig*) rectitude

recto, a [ˈrekto, a] *adj* straight; (*persona*) honest, upright ♦ *nm* rectum

rector, a [rekˈtor, a] *adj* governing

recuadro [re'kwaðro] *nm* box; (*TIPOGRAFÍA*) inset

recubrir [reku'ßrir] *vt*: ~ **(con)** (*pintura, crema,*) to cover (with)

recuento [re'kwento] *nm* inventory; **hacer el** ~ **de** to count o reckon up

recuerdo [re'kwerðo] *nm* souvenir; ~s *nmpl* (*memorias*) memories; ¡~s **a tu madre!** give my regards to your mother!

recular [reku'lar] *vi* to back down

recuperable [rekupe'raßle] *adj* recoverable

recuperación [rekupera'θjon] *nf* recovery

recuperar [rekupe'rar] *vt* to recover; (*tiempo*) to make up; ~**se** *vr* to recuperate

recurrir [reku'rrir] *vi* (*JUR*) to appeal; ~ **a** to resort to; (*persona*) to turn to; **recurso** *nm* resort; (*medios*) means *pl*, resources *pl*; (*JUR*) appeal

recusar [reku'sar] *vt* to reject, refuse

red [reð] *nf* net, mesh; (*FERRO etc*) network; (*trampa*) trap

redacción [reðak'θjon] *nf* (*acción*) editing; (*personal*) editorial staff; (*ESCOL*) essay, composition

redactar [reðak'tar] *vt* to draw up, draft; (*periódico*) to edit

redactor, a [reðak'tor, a] *nm/f* editor

redada [re'ðaða] *nf*: ~ **policial** police raid, round-up

rededor [reðe'ðor] *nm*: **al** o **en** ~ around, round about

redención [reðen'θjon] *nf* redemption

redicho, a [re'ðitʃo, a] *adj* affected

redil [re'ðil] *nm* sheepfold

redimir [reði'mir] *vt* to redeem

rédito ['reðito] *nm* interest, yield

redoblar [reðo'ßlar] *vt* to redouble ♦ *vi* (*tambor*) to play a roll on the drums

redomado, a [reðo'maðo, a] *adj* (*astuto*) sly, crafty; (*perfecto*) utter

redonda [re'ðonda] *nf*: **a la** ~ around, round about

redondear [reðonde'ar] *vt* to round, round off

redondel [reðon'del] *nm* (*círculo*) circle; (*TAUR*) bullring, arena; (*AUTO*) roundabout

redondo, a [re'ðondo, a] *adj* (*circular*) round; (*completo*) complete

reducción [reðuk'θjon] *nf* reduction

reducido, a [reðu'θiðo, a] *adj* reduced; (*limitado*) limited; (*pequeño*) small

reducir [reðu'θir] *vt* to reduce; to limit; ~**se** *vr* to diminish

redundancia [reðun'danθja] *nf* redundancy

reembolsar [re(e)mbol'sar] *vt* (*persona*) to reimburse; (*dinero*) to repay, pay back; (*depósito*) to refund; **reembolso** *nm* reimbursement; refund

reemplazar [re(e)mpla'θar] *vt* to replace; **reemplazo** *nm* replacement; **de reemplazo** (*MIL*) reserve

reencuentro [re(e)n'kwentro] *nm* reunion

referencia [refe'renθja] *nf* reference; **con** ~ **a** with reference to

referéndum [refe'rendum] (*pl* ~**s**) *nm* referendum

referente [refe'rente] *adj*: ~ **a** concerning, relating to

referir [refe'rir] *vt* (*contar*) to tell, recount; (*relacionar*) to refer, relate; ~**se** *vr*: ~**se a** to refer to

refilón [refi'lon]: **de** ~ *adv* obliquely

refinado, a [refi'naðo, a] *adj* refined

refinamiento [refina'mjento] *nm* refinement

refinar [refi'nar] *vt* to refine; **refinería** *nf* refinery

reflejar [refle'xar] *vt* to reflect; **reflejo, a** *adj* reflected; (*movimiento*) reflex ♦ *nm* reflection; (*ANAT*) reflex

reflexión [reflek'sjon] *nf* reflection; **reflexionar** *vt* to reflect on ♦ *vi* to reflect; (*detenerse*) to pause (to think)

reflexivo, a [reflek'sißo, a] *adj* thoughtful; (*LING*) reflexive

reflujo [re'fluxo] *nm* ebb

reforma [re'forma] *nf* reform; (*ARQ etc*) repair; ~ **agraria** agrarian reform

reformar [refor'mar] *vt* to reform; (*modificar*) to change, alter; (*ARQ*) to repair; ~**se** *vr* to mend one's ways

reformatorio [reforma'torjo] *nm* reformatory

reforzar [refor'θar] *vt* to strengthen; (*ARQ*) to reinforce; (*fig*) to encourage

refractario, a [refrak'tarjo, a] adj (TEC) heat-resistant

refrán [re'fran] nm proverb, saying

refregar [refre'ɣar] vt to scrub

refrenar [refre'nar] vt to check, restrain

refrendar [refren'dar] vt (firma) to endorse, countersign; (ley) to approve

refrescante [refres'kante] adj refreshing, cooling

refrescar [refres'kar] vt to refresh ♦ vi to cool down; ~**se** vr to get cooler; (tomar aire fresco) to go out for a breath of fresh air; (beber) to have a drink

refresco [re'fresko] nm soft drink, cool drink; "~**s**" "refreshments"

refriega [re'frjeɣa] nf scuffle, brawl

refrigeración [refrixera'θjon] nf refrigeration; (de sala) air-conditioning

refrigerador [refrixera'ðor] nm refrigerator (BRIT), icebox (US)

refrigeradora [refrixera'ðora] nf = **refrigerador**

refrigerar [refrixe'rar] vt to refrigerate; (sala) to air-condition

refuerzo [re'fwerθo] nm reinforcement; (TEC) support

refugiado, a [refu'xjaðo, a] nm/f refugee

refugiarse [refu'xjarse] vr to take refuge, shelter

refugio [re'fuxjo] nm refuge; (protección) shelter

refulgir [reful'xir] vi to shine, be dazzling

refunfuñar [refunfu'ɲar] vi to grunt, growl; (quejarse) to grumble

refutar [refu'tar] vt to refute

regadera [reɣa'ðera] nf watering can

regadío [reɣa'ðio] nm irrigated land

regalado, a [reɣa'laðo, a] adj comfortable, luxurious; (gratis) free, for nothing

regalar [reɣa'lar] vt (dar) to give (as a present); (entregar) to give away; (mimar) to pamper, make a fuss of

regalía [reɣa'lia] nf privilege, prerogative; (COM) bonus; (de autor) royalty

regaliz [reɣa'liθ] nm liquorice

regalo [re'ɣalo] nm (obsequio) gift, present; (gusto) pleasure; (comodidad) comfort

regañadientes [reɣaɲa'ðjentes]: **a** ~ adv reluctantly

regañar [reɣa'ɲar] vt to scold ♦ vi to grumble; **regañón, ona** adj nagging

regar [re'ɣar] vt to water, irrigate; (fig) to scatter, sprinkle

regatear [reɣate'ar] vt (COM) to bargain over; (escatimar) to be mean with ♦ vi to bargain, haggle; (DEPORTE) to dribble; **regateo** nm bargaining; dribbling; (del cuerpo) swerve, dodge

regazo [re'ɣaθo] nm lap

regeneración [rexenera'θjon] nf regeneration

regenerar [rexene'rar] vt to regenerate

regentar [rexen'tar] vt to direct, manage; **regente** nm (COM) manager; (POL) regent

régimen ['reximen] (pl **regímenes**) nm regime; (MED) diet

regimiento [rexi'mjento] nm regiment

regio, a ['rexjo, a] adj royal, regal; (fig: suntuoso) splendid; (AM: fam) great, terrific

región [re'xjon] nf region; **regionalista** nm/f regionalist

regir [re'xir] vt to govern, rule; (dirigir) to manage, run ♦ vi to apply, be in force

registrador [rexistra'ðor] nm registrar, recorder

registrar [rexis'trar] vt (buscar) to search; (: en cajón) to look through; (inspeccionar) to inspect; (anotar) to register, record; (INFORM) to log; ~**se** vr to register; (ocurrir) to happen

registro [re'xistro] nm (acto) registration; (MUS, libro) register; (inspección) inspection, search; ~ **civil** registry office

regla ['reɣla] nf (ley) rule, regulation; (de medir) ruler, rule; (MED: período) period

reglamentación [reɣlamenta'θjon] nf (acto) regulation; (lista) rules pl

reglamentar [reɣlamen'tar] vt to regulate; **reglamentario, a** adj statutory; **reglamento** nm rules pl, regulations pl

regocijarse [reɣoθi'xarse] vr: ~ **de** to rejoice at, be happy about; **regocijo** nm joy, happiness

regodearse [reɣoðe'arse] vr to be glad, be delighted; **regodeo** nm delight

regresar [reɣre'sar] *vi* to come back, go back, return; **regresivo,** *a adj* backward; (*fig*) regressive; **regreso** *nm* return

reguero [re'ɣero] *nm* (*de sangre etc*) trickle; (*de humo*) trail

regulador [reɣula'ðor] *nm* regulator; (*de radio etc*) knob, control

regular [reɣu'lar] *adj* regular; (*normal*) normal, usual; (*común*) ordinary; (*organizado*) regular, orderly; (*mediano*) average; (*fam*) not bad, so-so ♦ *adv* so-so, alright ♦ *vt* (*controlar*) to control, regulate; (*TEC*) to adjust; **por lo ~** as a rule; **~idad** *nf* regularity; **~izar** *vt* to regularize

regusto [re'ɣusto] *nm* aftertaste

rehabilitación [reaßilita'θjon] *nf* rehabilitation; (*ARQ*) restoration

rehabilitar [reaßili'tar] *vt* to rehabilitate; (*ARQ*) to restore; (*reintegrar*) to reinstate

rehacer [rea'θer] *vt* (*reparar*) to mend, repair; (*volver a hacer*) to redo, repeat; **~se** *vr* (*MED*) to recover

rehén [re'en] *nm* hostage

rehuir [reu'ir] *vt* to avoid, shun

rehusar [reu'sar] *vt, vi* to refuse

reina ['reina] *nf* queen; **~do** *nm* reign

reinante [rei'nante] *adj* (*fig*) prevailing

reinar [rei'nar] *vi* to reign

reincidir [reinθi'ðir] *vi* to relapse

reincorporarse [reinkorpo'rarse] *vr*: **~ a** to rejoin

reino ['reino] *nm* kingdom; **el R~ Unido** the United Kingdom

reintegrar [reinte'ɣrar] *vt* (*reconstituir*) to reconstruct; (*persona*) to reinstate; (*dinero*) to refund, pay back; **~se** *vr*: **~se a** to return to

reír [re'ir] *vi* to laugh; **~se** *vr* to laugh; **~se de** to laugh at

reiterar [reite'rar] *vt* to reiterate

reivindicación [reißindika'θjon] *nf* (*demanda*) claim, demand; (*justificación*) vindication

reivindicar [reißindi'kar] *vt* to claim

reja ['rexa] *nf* (*de ventana*) grille, bars *pl*; (*en la calle*) grating

rejilla [re'xiʎa] *nf* grating, grille; (*muebles*) wickerwork; (*de ventilación*) vent; (*de coche etc*) luggage rack

rejoneador [rexonea'ðor] *nm* mounted bullfighter

rejuvenecer [rexuβene'θer] *vt, vi* to rejuvenate

relación [rela'θjon] *nf* relation, relationship; (*MAT*) ratio; (*narración*) report; **relaciones públicas** public relations; **con ~ a, en ~ con** in relation to; **relacionar** *vt* to relate, connect; **relacionarse** *vr* to be connected, be linked

relajación [relaxa'θjon] *nf* relaxation

relajado, *a* [rela'xaðo, a] *adj* (*disoluto*) loose; (*cómodo*) relaxed; (*MED*) ruptured

relajar [rela'xar] *vt* to relax; **~se** *vr* to relax

relamerse [rela'merse] *vr* to lick one's lips

relamido, *a* [rela'miðo, a] *adj* (*pulcro*) overdressed; (*afectado*) affected

relámpago [re'lampaɣo] *nm* flash of lightning; **visita/huelga ~** lightning visit/strike; **relampaguear** *vi* to flash

relatar [rela'tar] *vt* to tell, relate

relativo, *a* [rela'tiβo, a] *adj* relative; **en lo ~ a** concerning

relato [re'lato] *nm* (*narración*) story, tale

relegar [rele'ɣar] *vt* to relegate

relevante [rele'βante] *adj* eminent, outstanding

relevar [rele'βar] *vt* (*sustituir*) to relieve; **~se** *vr* to relay; **~ a uno de un cargo** to relieve sb of his post

relevo [re'leβo] *nm* relief; **carrera de ~s** relay race

relieve [re'ljeβe] *nm* (*ARTE, TEC*) relief; (*fig*) prominence, importance; **bajo ~** bas-relief

religión [reli'xjon] *nf* religion; **religioso,** *a adj* religious ♦ *nm/f* monk/nun

relinchar [relin'tʃar] *vi* to neigh; **relincho** *nm* neigh; (*acto*) neighing

reliquia [re'likja] *nf* relic; **~ de familia** heirloom

rellano [re'ʎano] *nm* (*ARQ*) landing

rellenar [reʎe'nar] *vt* (*llenar*) to fill up; (*CULIN*) to stuff; (*COSTURA*) to pad; **relleno,** *a adj* full up; stuffed ♦ *nm* stuffing; (*de* *tapicería*) padding

reloj [re'lo(x)] *nm* clock; ~ **(de pulsera)** wristwatch; ~ **despertador** alarm (clock); **poner el** ~ to set one's watch (*o* the clock); ~**ero, a** *nm/f* clockmaker; watchmaker

reluciente [relu'θjente] *adj* brilliant, shining

relucir [relu'θir] *vi* to shine; (*fig*) to excel

relumbrar [relum'brar] *vi* to dazzle, shine brilliantly

remachar [rema'tʃar] *vt* to rivet; (*fig*) to hammer home, drive home; **remache** *nm* rivet

remanente [rema'nente] *nm* remainder; (*COM*) balance; (*de producto*) surplus

remangar [reman'gar] *vt* to roll up

remanso [re'manso] *nm* pool

remar [re'mar] *vi* to row

rematado, a [rema'taðo, a] *adj* complete, utter

rematar [rema'tar] *vt* to finish off; (*COM*) to sell off cheap ♦ *vi* to end, finish off; (*DEPORTE*) to shoot

remate [re'mate] *nm* end, finish; (*punta*) tip; (*DEPORTE*) shot; (*ARQ*) top; (*COM*) auction sale; **de** *o* **para** ~ to crown it all (*BRIT*), to top it off

remedar [reme'ðar] *vt* to imitate

remediar [reme'ðjar] *vt* to remedy; (*subsanar*) to make good, repair; (*evitar*) to avoid

remedio [re'meðjo] *nm* remedy; (*alivio*) relief, help; (*JUR*) recourse, remedy; **poner** ~ **a** to correct, stop; **no tener más** ~ to have no alternative; **¡qué** ~**!** there's no choice!; **sin** ~ hopeless

remedo [re'meðo] *nm* imitation; (*pey*) parody

remendar [remen'dar] *vt* to repair; (*con parche*) to patch

remesa [re'mesa] *nf* remittance; (*COM*) shipment

remiendo [re'mjendo] *nm* mend; (*con parche*) patch; (*cosido*) darn

remilgado, a [remil'gaðo, a] *adj* prim; (*afectado*) affected

remilgo [re'milɣo] *nm* primness; (*afectación*) affectation

reminiscencia [reminis'θenθja] *nf* reminiscence

remiso, a [re'miso, a] *adj* slack, slow

remite [re'mite] *nm* (*en sobre*) name and address of sender

remitir [remi'tir] *vt* to remit, send ♦ *vi* to slacken; (*en carta*): **remite: X** sender: X; **remitente** *nm/f* sender

remo ['remo] *nm* (*de barco*) oar; (*DEPORTE*) rowing

remojar [remo'xar] *vt* to steep, soak; (*galleta etc*) to dip, dunk

remojo [re'moxo] *nm*: **dejar la ropa en** ~ to leave clothes to soak

remolacha [remo'latʃa] *nf* beet, beetroot

remolcador [remolka'ðor] *nm* (*NAUT*) tug; (*AUTO*) breakdown lorry

remolcar [remol'kar] *vt* to tow

remolino [remo'lino] *nm* eddy; (*de agua*) whirlpool; (*de viento*) whirlwind; (*de gente*) crowd

remolque [re'molke] *nm* tow, towing; (*cuerda*) towrope; **llevar a** ~ to tow

remontar [remon'tar] *vt* to mend; ~**se** *vr* to soar; ~**se a** (*COM*) to amount to; ~ **el vuelo** to soar

remorder [remor'ðer] *vt* to distress, disturb; ~**le la conciencia a uno** to have a guilty conscience; **remordimiento** *nm* remorse

remoto, a [re'moto, a] *adj* remote

remover [remo'βer] *vt* to stir; (*tierra*) to turn over; (*objetos*) to move round

remozar [remo'θar] *vt* (*ARQ*) to refurbish

remuneración [remunera'θjon] *nf* remuneration

remunerar [remune'rar] *vt* to remunerate; (*premiar*) to reward

renacer [rena'θer] *vi* to be reborn; (*fig*) to revive; **renacimiento** *nm* rebirth; **el Renacimiento** the Renaissance

renacuajo [rena'kwaxo] *nm* (*ZOOL*) tadpole

renal [re'nal] *adj* renal, kidney *cpd*

rencilla [ren'θiʎa] *nf* quarrel

rencor [ren'kor] *nm* rancour, bitterness; ~**oso, a** *adj* spiteful

rendición [rendi'θjon] *nf* surrender

rendido, a [ren'diðo, a] *adj* (*sumiso*) submissive; (*cansado*) worn-out, exhausted

rendija [ren'dixa] *nf* (*hendedura*) crack, cleft

rendimiento [rendi'mjento] *nm* (*producción*) output; (*TEC, COM*) efficiency

rendir [ren'dir] *vt* (*vencer*) to defeat; (*producir*) to produce; (*dar beneficio*) to yield; (*agotar*) to exhaust ♦ *vi* to pay; **~se** *vr* (*someterse*) to surrender; (*cansarse*) to wear o.s. out; **~ homenaje** *o* **culto a** to pay homage to

renegar [rene'var] *vi* (*renunciar*) to renounce; (*blasfemar*) to blaspheme; (*quejarse*) to complain

RENFE ['renfe] *nf abr* (= *Red Nacional de los Ferrocarriles Españoles*) ≈ BR (*BRIT*)

renglón [ren'glon] *nm* (*línea*) line; (*COM*) item, article; **a ~ seguido** immediately after

renombrado, a [renom'braðo, a] *adj* renowned

renombre [re'nombre] *nm* renown

renovación [renoβa'θjon] *nf* (*de contrato*) renewal; (*ARQ*) renovation

renovar [reno'βar] *vt* to renew; (*ARQ*) to renovate

renta ['renta] *nf* (*ingresos*) income; (*beneficio*) profit; (*alquiler*) rent; **~ vitalicia** annuity; **rentable** *adj* profitable; **rentar** *vt* to produce, yield

renuncia [re'nunθja] *nf* resignation

renunciar [renun'θjar] *vt* to renounce; (*tabaco, alcohol etc*): **~ a** to give up; (*oferta, oportunidad*) to turn down; (*puesto*) to resign ♦ *vi* to resign

reñido, a [re'niðo, a] *adj* (*batalla*) bitter, hard-fought; **estar ~ con uno** to be on bad terms with sb

reñir [re'nir] *vt* (*regañar*) to scold ♦ *vi* (*estar peleado*) to quarrel, fall out; (*combatir*) to fight

reo ['reo] *nm/f* culprit, offender; **~ de muerte** prisoner condemned to death

reojo [re'oxo]: **de ~** *adv* out of the corner of one's eye

reparación [repara'θjon] *nf* (*acto*) mending, repairing; (*TEC*) repair; (*fig*) amends, reparation

reparar [repa'rar] *vt* to repair; (*fig*) to make amends for; (*observar*) to observe ♦ *vi*: **~ en** (*darse cuenta de*) to notice; (*prestar atención a*) to pay attention to

reparo [re'paro] *nm* (*advertencia*) observation; (*duda*) doubt; (*dificultad*) difficulty; **poner ~s (a)** to raise objections (to)

repartición [reparti'θjon] *nf* distribution; (*división*) division; **repartidor, a** *nm/f* distributor

repartir [repar'tir] *vt* to distribute, share out; (*CORREOS*) to deliver; **reparto** *nm* distribution; delivery; (*TEATRO, CINE*) cast; (*AM: urbanización*) housing estate (*BRIT*), real estate development (*US*)

repasar [repa'sar] *vt* (*ESCOL*) to revise; (*MECÁNICA*) to check, overhaul; (*COSTURA*) to mend; **repaso** *nm* revision; overhaul, checkup; mending

repatriar [repa'trjar] *vt* to repatriate

repecho [re'petʃo] *nm* steep incline

repelente [repe'lente] *adj* repellent, repulsive

repeler [repe'ler] *vt* to repel

repensar [repen'sar] *vt* to reconsider

repente [re'pente] *nm*: **de ~** suddenly; **~ de ira** fit of anger

repentino, a [repen'tino, a] *adj* sudden

repercusión [reperku'sjon] *nf* repercussion

repercutir [reperku'tir] *vi* (*objeto*) to rebound; (*sonido*) to echo; **~ en** (*fig*) to have repercussions on

repertorio [reper'torjo] *nm* list; (*TEATRO*) repertoire

repetición [repeti'θjon] *nf* repetition

repetir [repe'tir] *vt* to repeat; (*plato*) to have a second helping of ♦ *vi* to repeat; (*sabor*) to come back; **~se** *vr* (*volver sobre un tema*) to repeat o.s.

repetitivo, a [repeti'tiβo, a] *adj* repetitive, repetitious

repicar [repi'kar] *vt* (*campanas*) to ring

repique [re'pike] *nm* pealing, ringing; **~so** *nm* pealing; (*de tambor*) drumming

repisa [re'pisa] *nf* ledge, shelf; (*de ventana*) windowsill; **~ de chimenea** mantelpiece

repito *etc vb ver* **repetir**

replantearse [replante'arse] *vr*: ~ **un problema** to reconsider a problem

replegarse [reple'ɣarse] *vr* to fall back, retreat

repleto, a [re'pleto, a] *adj* replete, full up

réplica ['replika] *nf* answer; (*ARTE*) replica

replicar [repli'kar] *vi* to answer; (*objetar*) to argue, answer back

repliegue [re'pljeɣe] *nm* (*MIL*) withdrawal

repoblación [repoβla'θjon] *nf* repopulation; (*de río*) restocking; ~ **forestal** reafforestation

repoblar [repo'βlar] *vt* to repopulate; (*con árboles*) to reafforest

repollo [re'poʎo] *nm* cabbage

reponer [repo'ner] *vt* to replace, put back; (*TEATRO*) to revive; ~**se** *vr* to recover; ~ **que** to reply that

reportaje [repor'taxe] *nm* report, article

reportero, a [repor'tero, a] *nm/f* reporter

reposacabezas [reposaka'βeθas] *nm inv* headrest

reposado, a [repo'saðo, a] *adj* (*descansado*) restful; (*tranquilo*) calm

reposar [repo'sar] *vi* to rest, repose

reposición [reposi'θjon] *nf* replacement; (*CINE*) remake

reposo [re'poso] *nm* rest

repostar [repos'tar] *vt* to replenish; (*AUTO*) to fill up (with petrol (*BRIT*) o gasoline (*US*))

repostería [reposte'ria] *nf* confectioner's (shop); **repostero, a** *nm/f* confectioner

reprender [repren'der] *vt* to reprimand

represa [re'presa] *nf* dam; (*lago artificial*) lake, pool

represalia [repre'salja] *nf* reprisal

representación [representa'θjon] *nf* representation; (*TEATRO*) performance; **representante** *nm/f* representative; performer

representar [represen'tar] *vt* to represent; (*TEATRO*) to perform; (*edad*) to look; ~**se** *vr* to imagine; **representativo, a** *adj* representative

represión [repre'sjon] *nf* repression

reprimenda [repri'menda] *nf* reprimand, rebuke

reprimir [repri'mir] *vt* to repress

reprobar [repro'βar] *vt* to censure, reprove

reprochar [repro'tʃar] *vt* to reproach; **reproche** *nm* reproach

reproducción [reproðuk'θjon] *nf* reproduction

reproducir [reproðu'θir] *vt* to reproduce; ~**se** *vr* to breed; (*situación*) to recur

reproductor, a [reproðuc'tor, a] *adj* reproductive

reptil [rep'til] *nm* reptile

república [re'puβlika] *nf* republic; **republicano, a** *adj, nm/f* republican

repudiar [repu'ðjar] *vt* to repudiate; (*fe*) to renounce

repuesto [re'pwesto] *nm* (*pieza de recambio*) spare (part); (*abastecimiento*) supply; **rueda de** ~ spare wheel

repugnancia [repuɣ'nanθja] *nf* repugnance; **repugnante** *adj* repugnant, repulsive

repugnar [repuɣ'nar] *vt* to disgust

repulsa [re'pulsa] *nf* rebuff

repulsión [repul'sjon] *nf* repulsion, aversion; **repulsivo, a** *adj* repulsive

reputación [reputa'θjon] *nf* reputation

reputar [repu'tar] *vt* to consider, deem

requemado, a [reke'maðo, a] *adj* (*quemado*) scorched; (*bronceado*) tanned

requerimiento [rekeri'mjento] *nm* request; (*JUR*) summons

requerir [reke'rir] *vt* (*pedir*) to ask, request; (*exigir*) to require; (*llamar*) to send for, summon

requesón [reke'son] *nm* cottage cheese

requete... [re'kete] *prefijo* extremely

réquiem ['rekjem] (*pl* ~**s**) *nm* requiem

requisito [reki'sito] *nm* requirement, requisite

res [res] *nf* beast, animal

resaca [re'saka] *nf* (*en el mar*) undertow, undercurrent; (*fig*) backlash; (*fam*) hangover

resaltar [resal'tar] *vi* to project, stick out; (*fig*) to stand out

resarcir [resar'θir] *vt* to compensate; ~**se** *vr* to make up for

resbaladizo, a [resβala'ðiθo, a] *adj* slippery

resbalar [resβa'lar] *vi* to slip, slide; *(fig)* to slip (up); **~se** *vr* to slip, slide; to slip (up); **resbalón** *nm (acción)* slip

rescatar [reska'tar] *vt (salvar)* to save, rescue; *(objeto)* to get back, recover; *(cautivos)* to ransom

rescate [res'kate] *nm* rescue; *(de objeto)* recovery; **pagar un ~** to pay a ransom

rescindir [resθin'dir] *vt* to rescind

rescisión [resθi'sjon] *nf* cancellation

rescoldo [res'koldo] *nm* embers *pl*

resecar [rese'kar] *vt* to dry thoroughly; *(MED)* to cut out, remove; **~se** *vr* to dry up

reseco, a [re'seko, a] *adj* very dry; *(fig)* skinny

resentido, a [resen'tiðo, a] *adj* resentful

resentimiento [resenti'mjento] *nm* resentment, bitterness

resentirse [resen'tirse] *vr (debilitarse: persona)* to suffer; **~ de** *(consecuencias)* to feel the effects of; **~ de** *(o por) algo* to resent sth, be bitter about sth

reseña [re'seɲa] *nf (cuenta)* account; *(informe)* report; *(LITERATURA)* review

reseñar [rese'ɲar] *vt* to describe; *(LITERATURA)* to review

reserva [re'serβa] *nf* reserve; *(reservación)* reservation; **a ~ de que ...** unless ...; **con toda ~** in strictest confidence

reservado, a [reser'βaðo, a] *adj* reserved; *(retraído)* cold, distant ♦ *nm* private room

reservar [reser'βar] *vt (guardar)* to keep; *(habitación, entrada)* to reserve; **~se** *vr* to save o.s.; *(callar)* to keep to o.s.

resfriado [resfri'aðo] *nm* cold; **resfriarse** *vr* to cool; *(MED)* to catch (a) cold

resguardar [resɣwar'ðar] *vt* to protect, shield; **~se** *vr*: **~se de** to guard against; **resguardo** *nm* defence; *(vale)* voucher; *(recibo)* receipt, slip

residencia [resi'ðenθja] *nf* residence; **~l** *nf (urbanización)* housing estate

residente [resi'ðente] *adj*, *nm/f* resident

residir [resi'ðir] *vi* to reside, live; **~ en** to reside in, lie in

residuo [re'siðwo] *nm* residue

resignación [resiɣna'θjon] *nf* resignation;

resignarse *vr*: **resignarse a** *o* **con** to resign o.s. to, be resigned to

resina [re'sina] *nf* resin

resistencia [resis'tenθja] *nf (dureza)* endurance, strength; *(oposición, ELEC)* resistance; **resistente** *adj* strong, hardy; resistant

resistir [resis'tir] *vt (soportar)* to bear; *(oponerse a)* to resist, oppose; *(aguantar)* to put up with ♦ *vi* to resist; *(aguantar)* to last, endure; **~se** *vr*: **~se a** to refuse to, resist

resollar [reso'ʎar] *vi* to breathe noisily, wheeze

resolución [resolu'θjon] *nf* resolution; *(decisión)* decision; **resoluto, a** *adj* resolute

resolver [resol'βer] *vt* to resolve; *(solucionar)* to solve, resolve; *(decidir)* to decide, settle; **~se** *vr* to make up one's mind

resonancia [reso'nanθja] *nf (del sonido)* resonance; *(repercusión)* repercussion

resonar [reso'nar] *vi* to ring, echo

resoplar [reso'plar] *vi* to snort; **resoplido** *nm* heavy breathing

resorte [re'sorte] *nm* spring; *(fig)* lever

respaldar [respal'dar] *vt* to back (up), support; **~se** *vr* to lean back; **~se con** *o* **en** *(fig)* to take one's stand on; **respaldo** *nm (de sillón)* back; *(fig)* support, backing

respectivo, a [respek'tiβo, a] *adj* respective; **en lo ~ a** with regard to

respecto [res'pekto] *nm*: **al ~** on this matter; **con ~ a**, **~ de** with regard to, in relation to

respetable [respe'taβle] *adj* respectable

respetar [respe'tar] *vt* to respect; **respeto** *nm* respect; *(acatamiento)* deference; **respetos** *nmpl* respects; **respetuoso, a** *adj* respectful

respingo [res'pingo] *nm* start, jump

respiración [respira'θjon] *nf* breathing; *(MED)* respiration; *(ventilación)* ventilation

respirar [respi'rar] *vi* to breathe; **respiratorio, a** *adj* respiratory; **respiro** *nm* breathing; *(fig: descanso)* respite

resplandecer [resplande'θer] *vi* to shine; **resplandeciente** *adj* resplendent, shining; **resplandor** *nm* brilliance, brightness; (*de luz, fuego*) blaze

responder [respon'der] *vt* to answer ♦ *vi* to answer; (*fig*) to respond; (*pey*) to answer back; **~ de** *o* **por** to answer for; **respondón, ona** *adj* cheeky

responsabilidad [responsaβili'ðað] *nf* responsibility

responsabilizarse [responsaβili'θarse] *vr* to make o.s. responsible, take charge

responsable [respon'saβle] *adj* responsible

respuesta [res'pwesta] *nf* answer, reply

resquebrajar [reskeβra'xar] *vt* to crack, split; **~se** *vr* to crack, split

resquemor [reske'mor] *nm* resentment

resquicio [res'kiθjo] *nm* chink; (*hendedura*) crack

resta ['resta] *nf* (*MAT*) remainder

restablecer [restaβle'θer] *vt* to re-establish, restore; **~se** *vr* to recover

restallar [resta'ʎar] *vi* to crack

restante [res'tante] *adj* remaining; **lo ~** the remainder

restar [res'tar] *vt* (*MAT*) to subtract; (*fig*) to take away ♦ *vi* to remain, be left

restauración [restaura'θjon] *nf* restoration

restaurante [restau'rante] *nm* restaurant

restaurar [restau'rar] *vt* to restore

restitución [restitu'θjon] *nf* return, restitution

restituir [restitu'ir] *vt* (*devolver*) to return, give back; (*rehabilitar*) to restore

resto ['resto] *nm* (*residuo*) rest, remainder; (*apuesta*) stake; **~s** *nmpl* remains

restregar [restre'ɣar] *vt* to scrub, rub

restricción [restrik'θjon] *nf* restriction

restrictivo, a [restrik'tiβo, a] *adj* restrictive

restringir [restrin'xir] *vt* to restrict, limit

resucitar [resuθi'tar] *vt, vi* to resuscitate, revive

resuello [re'sweʎo] *nm* (*aliento*) breath; **estar sin ~** to be breathless

resuelto, a [re'swelto, a] *pp de* **resolver** ♦ *adj* resolute, determined

resultado [resul'taðo] *nm* result; (*conclusión*) outcome; **resultante** *adj* resulting, resultant

resultar [resul'tar] *vi* (*ser*) to be; (*llegar a ser*) to turn out to be; (*salir bien*) to turn out well; (*COM*) to amount to; **~ de** to stem from; **me resulta difícil hacerlo** it's difficult for me to do it

resumen [re'sumen] (*pl* **resúmenes**) *nm* summary, résumé; **en ~** in short

resumir [resu'mir] *vt* to sum up; (*cortar*) to abridge, cut down; (*condensar*) to summarize

resurgir [resur'xir] *vi* (*reaparecer*) to reappear

resurrección [resurre(k)'θjon] *nf* resurrection

retablo [re'taβlo] *nm* altarpiece

retaguardia [reta'ɣwarðja] *nf* rearguard

retahíla [reta'ila] *nf* series, string

retal [re'tal] *nm* remnant

retar [re'tar] *vt* to challenge; (*desafiar*) to defy, dare

retardar [retar'ðar] *vt* (*demorar*) to delay; (*hacer más lento*) to slow down; (*retener*) to hold back

retazo [re'taθo] *nm* snippet (*BRIT*), fragment

retener [rete'ner] *vt* (*intereses*) to withhold

reticente [reti'θente] *adj* (*tono*) insinuating; (*postura*) reluctant; **ser ~ a hacer algo** to be reluctant *o* unwilling to do sth

retina [re'tina] *nf* retina

retintín [retin'tin] *nm* jangle, jingle

retirada [reti'raða] *nf* (*MIL, refugio*) retreat; (*de dinero*) withdrawal; (*de embajador*) recall; **retirado, a** *adj* (*lugar*) remote; (*vida*) quiet; (*jubilado*) retired

retirar [reti'rar] *vt* to withdraw; (*quitar*) to remove; (*jubilar*) to retire, pension off; **~se** *vr* to retreat, withdraw; to retire; (*acostarse*) to retire, go to bed; **retiro** *nm* retreat; retirement; (*pago*) pension

reto ['reto] *nm* dare, challenge

retocar [reto'kar] *vt* (*fotografía*) to touch up, retouch

retoño [re'toɲo] *nm* sprout, shoot; (*fig*)

offspring, child

retoque [re'toke] *nm* retouching

retorcer [retor'θer] *vt* to twist; (*manos, lavado*) to wring; **~se** *vr* to become twisted; (*mover el cuerpo*) to writhe

retorcido, a [retor'θiðo, a] *adj* (*persona*) devious

retórica [re'torika] *nf* rhetoric; (*pey*) affectedness; **retórico, a** *adj* rhetorical

retornar [retor'nar] *vt* to return, give back ♦ *vi* to return, go/come back; **retorno** *nm* return

retortijón [retorti'xon] *nm* twist, twisting

retozar [reto'θar] *vi* (*juguetear*) to frolic, romp; (*saltar*) to gambol; **retozón, ona** *adj* playful

retracción [retrak'θjon] *nf* retraction

retractarse [retrak'tarse] *vr* to retract; **me retracto** I take that back

retraerse [retra'erse] *vr* to retreat, withdraw; **retraído, a** *adj* shy, retiring; **retraimiento** *nm* retirement; (*timidez*) shyness

retransmisión [retransmi'sjon] *nf* repeat (broadcast)

retransmitir [retransmi'tir] *vt* (*mensaje*) to relay; (*TV etc*) to repeat, retransmit; (: *en vivo*) to broadcast live

retrasado, a [retra'saðo, a] *adj* late; (*MED*) mentally retarded; (*país etc*) backward, underdeveloped

retrasar [retra'sar] *vt* (*demorar*) to postpone, put off; (*retardar*) to slow down ♦ *vi* (*atrasarse*) to be late; (*reloj*) to be slow; (*producción*) to fall (off); (*quedarse atrás*) to lag behind; **~se** *vr* to be late; to be slow; to fall (off); to lag behind

retraso [re'traso] *nm* (*demora*) delay; (*lentitud*) slowness; (*tardanza*) lateness; (*atraso*) backwardness; **~s** (*FINANZAS*) *nmpl* arrears; **llegar con ~** to arrive late; **~ mental** mental deficiency

retratar [retra'tar] *vt* (*ARTE*) to paint the portrait of; (*fotografiar*) to photograph; (*fig*) to depict, describe; **~se** *vr* to have one's portrait painted; to have one's photograph taken; **retrato** *nm* portrait; (*fig*) likeness; **retrato-robot** *nm* Identikit

® picture

retreta [re'treta] *nf* retreat

retrete [re'trete] *nm* toilet

retribución [retriβu'θjon] *nf* (*recompensa*) reward; (*pago*) pay, payment

retribuir [retri'βwir] *vt* (*recompensar*) to reward; (*pagar*) to pay

retro... ['retro] *prefijo* retro...

retroactivo, a [retroak'tiβo, a] *adj* retroactive, retrospective

retroceder [retroθe'ðer] *vi* (*echarse atrás*) to move back(wards); (*fig*) to back down

retroceso [retro'θeso] *nm* backward movement; (*MED*) relapse; (*fig*) backing down

retrógrado, a [re'troɣraðo, a] *adj* retrograde, retrogressive; (*POL*) reactionary

retropropulsión [retropropul'sjon] *nf* jet propulsion

retrospectivo, a [retrospek'tiβo, a] *adj* retrospective

retrovisor [retroβi'sor] *nm* (*tb: espejo ~*) rear-view mirror

retumbar [retum'bar] *vi* to echo, resound

reuma ['reuma] *nm* rheumatism

reumatismo [reuma'tismo] *nm* = **reuma**

reunificar [reunifi'kar] *vt* to reunify

reunión [reu'njon] *nf* (*asamblea*) meeting; (*fiesta*) party

reunir [reu'nir] *vt* (*juntar*) to reunite, join (together); (*recoger*) to gather (together); (*personas*) to get together; (*cualidades*) to combine; **~se** *vr* (*personas: en asamblea*) to meet, gather

revalidar [reβali'ðar] *vt* (*ratificar*) to confirm, ratify

revalorizar [reβalori'θar] *vt* to revalue, reassess

revancha [re'βantʃa] *nf* revenge

revelación [reβela'θjon] *nf* revelation

revelado [reβe'laðo] *nm* developing

revelar [reβe'lar] *vt* to reveal; (*FOTO*) to develop

reventa [re'βenta] *nf* (*de entradas: para concierto*) touting

reventar [reβen'tar] *vt* to burst, explode

reventón [reβen'ton] *nm* (*AUTO*) blow-out (*BRIT*), flat (*US*)

reverberación [reßerßera'θjon] *nf*
reverberation

reverberar [reßerße'rar] *vi* to reverberate

reverencia [reße'renθja] *nf* reverence;
reverenciar *vt* to revere

reverendo, a [reße'rendo, a] *adj* reverend

reverente [reße'rente] *adj* reverent

reversible [reßer'sißle] *adj* (*prenda*)
reversible

reverso [re'ßerso] *nm* back, other side;
(*de moneda*) reverse

revertir [reßer'tir] *vi* to revert

revés [re'ßes] *nm* back, wrong side; (*fig*)
reverse, setback; (*DEPORTE*) backhand; **al
~** the wrong way round; (*de arriba
abajo*) upside down; (*ropa*) inside out;
volver algo al ~ to turn sth round;
(*ropa*) to turn sth inside out

revestir [reßes'tir] *vt* (*poner*) to put on;
(*cubrir*) to cover, coat; **~ con o de** to
invest with

revisar [reßi'sar] *vt* (*examinar*) to check;
(*texto etc*) to revise; **revisión** *nf* revision

revisor, a [reßi'sor, a] *nm/f* inspector;
(*FERRO*) ticket collector

revista [re'ßista] *nf* magazine, review;
(*TEATRO*) revue; (*inspección*) inspection;
pasar ~ a to review, inspect

revivir [reßi'ßir] *vi* to revive

revocación [reßoka'θjon] *nf* repeal

revocar [reßo'kar] *vt* to revoke

revolcarse [reßol'karse] *vr* to roll about

revolotear [reßolote'ar] *vi* to flutter

revoltijo [reßol'tixo] *nm* mess, jumble

revoltoso, a [reßol'toso, a] *adj* (*travieso*)
naughty, unruly

revolución [reßolu'θjon] *nf* revolution;
revolucionar *vt* to revolutionize;
revolucionario, a *adj, nm/f*
revolutionary

revolver [reßol'ßer] *vt* (*desordenar*) to
disturb, mess up; (*mover*) to move about;
(*POL*) to stir up ♦ *vi*: **~ en** to go through,
rummage (about) in; **~se** *vr* (*volver
contra*) to turn on o against

revólver [re'ßolßer] *nm* revolver

revuelo [re'ßwelo] *nm* fluttering; (*fig*)
commotion

revuelta [re'ßwelta] *nf* (*motín*) revolt;

(*agitación*) commotion

revuelto, a [re'ßwelto, a] *pp de* **revolver**
♦ *adj* (*mezclado*) mixed-up, in disorder

revulsivo [reßul'sißo] *nm* enema

rey [rei] *nm* king; **Día de R~es** Twelfth
Night

reyerta [re'jerta] *nf* quarrel, brawl

rezagado, a [reθa'ɣaðo, a] *nm/f* straggler

rezagar [reθa'sar] *vt* (*dejar atrás*) to leave
behind; (*retrasar*) to delay, postpone

rezar [re'θar] *vi* to pray; **~ con** (*fam*) to
concern, have to do with; **rezo** *nm*
prayer

rezongar [reθon'gar] *vi* to grumble

rezumar [reθu'mar] *vt* to ooze

ría ['ria] *nf* estuary

riada [ri'aða] *nf* flood

ribera [ri'ßera] *nf* (*de río*) bank; (: *área*)
riverside

ribete [ri'ßete] *nm* (*de vestido*) border;
(*fig*) addition; **~ar** *vt* to edge, border

ricino [ri'θino] *nm*: **aceite de ~** castor oil

rico, a ['riko, a] *adj* rich; (*adinerado*)
wealthy, rich; (*lujoso*) luxurious;
(*comida*) delicious; (*niño*) lovely, cute
♦ *nm/f* rich person

rictus ['riktus] *nm* (*mueca*) sneer, grin

ridiculez [riðiku'leθ] *nf* absurdity

ridiculizar [riðikuli'θar] *vt* to ridicule

ridículo, a [ri'ðikulo, a] *adj* ridiculous;
hacer el ~ to make a fool of o.s.; **poner
a uno en ~** to make a fool of sb

riego ['rjeɣo] *nm* (*aspersión*) watering;
(*irrigación*) irrigation

riel [rjel] *nm* rail

rienda ['rjenda] *nf* rein; **dar ~ suelta a** to
give free rein to

riesgo ['rjesvo] *nm* risk; **correr el ~ de**
to run the risk of

rifa ['rifa] *nf* (*lotería*) raffle; **rifar** *vt* to
raffle

rifle ['rifle] *nm* rifle

rigidez [rixi'ðeθ] *nf* rigidity, stiffness;
(*fig*) strictness; **rígido, a** *adj* rigid, stiff;
strict, inflexible

rigor [ri'ɣor] *nm* strictness, rigour;
(*inclemencia*) harshness; **de ~** de rigueur,
essential; **riguroso, a** *adj* rigorous;
harsh; (*severo*) severe

rimar [ri'mar] *vi* to rhyme

rimbombante [rimbom'bante] *adj* (*fig*) pompous

rímel ['rimel] *nm* mascara

rímmel ['rimel] *nm* = **rímel**

rincón [rin'kon] *nm* corner (*inside*)

rinoceronte [rinoθe'ronte] *nm* rhinoceros

riña ['riɲa] *nf* (*disputa*) argument; (*pelea*) brawl

riñón [ri'ɲon] *nm* kidney; **tener riñones** to have guts

río *etc* ['rio] *vb ver* **reír** ♦ *nm* river; (*fig*) torrent, stream; ~ **abajo/arriba** downstream/upstream; ~ **de la Plata** River Plate

rioja [ri'oxa] *nm* (*vino*) rioja (wine)

rioplatense [riopla'tense] *adj* of o from the River Plate region

riqueza [ri'keθa] *nf* wealth, riches *pl*; (*cualidad*) richness

risa ['risa] *nf* laughter; (*una* ~) laugh; **¡qué ~!** what a laugh!

risco ['risko] *nm* crag, cliff

risible [ri'siβle] *adj* ludicrous, laughable

risotada [riso'taða] *nf* guffaw, loud laugh

ristra ['ristra] *nf* string

risueño, a [ri'sweɲo, a] *adj* (*sonriente*) smiling; (*contento*) cheerful

ritmo ['ritmo] *nm* rhythm; **a ~ lento** slowly; **trabajar a ~ lento** to go slow

rito ['rito] *nm* rite

ritual [ri'twal] *adj, nm* ritual

rival [ri'βal] *adj, nm/f* rival; ~**idad** *nf* rivalry; ~**izar** *vi*: ~**izar con** to rival, vie with

rizado, a [ri'θaðo, a] *adj* curly ♦ *nm* curls *pl*

rizar [ri'θar] *vt* to curl; ~**se** *vr* (*pelo*) to curl; (*agua*) to ripple; **rizo** *nm* curl; ripple

RNE *nf abr* = **Radio Nacional de España**

robar [ro'βar] *vt* to rob; (*objeto*) to steal; (*casa etc*) to break into; (*NAIPES*) to draw

roble ['roβle] *nm* oak; ~**dal** *nm* = **robledo**; ~**do** *nm* oakwood

robo ['roβo] *nm* robbery, theft

robot [ro'βot] *nm* robot; ~ **(de cocina)** food processor

robustecer [roβuste'θer] *vt* to strengthen

robusto, a [ro'βusto, a] *adj* robust, strong

roca ['roka] *nf* rock

roce ['roθe] *nm* (*caricia*) brush; (*TEC*) friction; (*en la piel*) graze; **tener ~ con** to be in close contact with

rociar [ro'θjar] *vt* to spray

rocín [ro'θin] *nm* nag, hack

rocío [ro'θio] *nm* dew

rocoso, a [ro'koso, a] *adj* rocky

rodado, a [ro'ðaðo, a] *adj* (*con ruedas*) wheeled

rodaja [ro'ðaxa] *nf* (*raja*) slice

rodaje [ro'ðaxe] *nm* (*CINE*) shooting, filming; (*AUTO*): **en ~** running in

rodar [ro'ðar] *vt* (*vehículo*) to wheel (along); (*escalera*) to roll down; (*viajar por*) to travel (over) ♦ *vi* to roll; (*coche*) to go, run; (*CINE*) to shoot, film

rodear [roðe'ar] *vt* to surround ♦ *vi* to go round; ~**se** *vr*: ~**se de amigos** to surround o.s. with friends

rodeo [ro'ðeo] *nm* (*ruta indirecta*) detour; (*evasión*) evasion; (*AM*) rodeo; **hablar sin ~s** to come to the point, speak plainly

rodilla [ro'ðiʎa] *nf* knee; **de ~s** kneeling; **ponerse de ~s** to kneel (down)

rodillo [ro'ðiʎo] *nm* roller; (*CULIN*) rolling-pin

roedor, a [roe'ðor, a] *adj* gnawing ♦ *nm* rodent

roer [ro'er] *vt* (*masticar*) to gnaw; (*corroer, fig*) to corrode

rogar [ro'ɣar] *vt, vi* (*pedir*) to ask for; (*suplicar*) to beg, plead; **se ruega no fumar** please do not smoke

rojizo, a [ro'xiθo, a] *adj* reddish

rojo, a ['roxo, a] *adj, nm* red; **al ~ vivo** red-hot

rol [rol] *nm* list, roll; (*AM: papel*) role

rollizo, a [ro'ʎiθo, a] *adj* (*objeto*) cylindrical; (*persona*) plump

rollo ['roʎo] *nm* roll; (*de cuerda*) coil; (*madera*) log; (*fam*) bore; **¡qué ~!** what a carry-on!

ROM [rom] *nf abr* (= *memoria de sólo lectura*) ROM

Roma ['roma] *n* Rome

romance [ro'manθe] *nm* (*idioma*

castellano) Romance language; (*LITE-RATURA*) ballad; **hablar en** ~ to speak plainly

romanticismo [romanti'θismo] *nm* romanticism

romántico, a [ro'mantiko, a] *adj* romantic

rombo ['rombo] *nm* (*GEOM*) rhombus

romería [rome'ria] *nf* (*REL*) pilgrimage; (*excursión*) trip, outing

romero, a [ro'mero, a] *nm/f* pilgrim ♦ *nm* rosemary

romo, a ['romo, a] *adj* blunt; (*fig*) dull

rompecabezas [rompeka'βeθas] *nm inv* riddle, puzzle; (*juego*) jigsaw (puzzle)

rompeolas [rompe'olas] *nm inv* breakwater

romper [rom'per] *vt* to break; (*hacer pedazos*) to smash; (*papel, tela etc*) to tear, rip ♦ *vi* (*olas*) to break; (*sol, diente*) to break through; ~ **un contrato** to break a contract; ~ **a** (*empezar a*) to start (suddenly) to; ~ **a llorar** to burst into tears; ~ **con uno** to fall out with sb

rompimiento [rompi'mjento] *nm* (*acto*) breaking; (*fig*) break; (*quiebra*) crack

ron [ron] *nm* rum

roncar [ron'kar] *vi* to snore

ronco, a ['ronko, a] *adj* (*afónico*) hoarse; (*áspero*) raucous

ronda ['ronda] *nf* (*gen*) round; (*patrulla*) patrol; **rondar** *vt* to patrol ♦ *vi* to patrol; (*fig*) to prowl round

ronquido [ron'kiðo] *nm* snore, snoring

ronronear [ronrone'ar] *vi* to purr; **ronroneo** *nm* purr

roña ['roɲa] *nf* (*VETERINARIA*) mange; (*mugre*) dirt, grime; (*óxido*) rust

roñoso, a [ro'ɲoso, a] *adj* (*mugriento*) filthy; (*tacaño*) mean

ropa ['ropa] *nf* clothes *pl*, clothing; ~ **blanca** linen; ~ **de cama** bed linen; ~ **interior** underwear; ~ **para lavar** washing; ~**je** *nm* gown, robes *pl*

ropero [ro'pero] *nm* linen cupboard; (*guardarropa*) wardrobe

rosa ['rosa] *adj* pink ♦ *nf* rose; (*ANAT*) red birthmark; ~ **de los vientos** the compass

rosado, a [ro'saðo, a] *adj* pink ♦ *nm* rosé

rosal [ro'sal] *nm* rosebush

rosario [ro'sarjo] *nm* (*REL*) rosary; **rezar el** ~ to say the rosary

rosca ['roska] *nf* (*de tornillo*) thread; (*de humo*) coil, spiral; (*pan, postre*) ring-shaped roll/pastry

rosetón [rose'ton] *nm* rosette; (*ARQ*) rose window

rosquilla [ros'kiʎa] *nf* doughnut-shaped fritter

rostro ['rostro] *nm* (*cara*) face

rotación [rota'θjon] *nf* rotation; ~ **de cultivos** crop rotation

rotativo, a [rota'tiβo, a] *adj* rotary

roto, a ['roto, a] *pp de* **romper** ♦ *adj* broken

rótula ['rotula] *nf* kneecap; (*TEC*) ball-and-socket joint

rotulador [rotula'ðor] *nm* felt-tip pen

rotular [rotu'lar] *vt* (*carta, documento*) to head, entitle; (*objeto*) to label; **rótulo** *nm* heading, title; label; (*letrero*) sign

rotundamente [rotunda'mente] *adv* (*negar*) flatly; (*responder, afirmar*) emphatically; **rotundo, a** *adj* round; (*enfático*) emphatic

rotura [ro'tura] *nf* (*rompimiento*) breaking; (*MED*) fracture

roturar [rotu'rar] *vt* to plough

rozadura [roθa'ðura] *nf* abrasion, graze

rozar [ro'θar] *vt* (*frotar*) to rub; (*arañar*) to scratch; (*tocar ligeramente*) to shave, touch lightly; ~**se** *vr* to rub (together); ~**se con** (*fam*) to rub shoulders with

rte. *abr* (= *remite, remitente*) sender

RTVE *nf abr* = **Radiotelevisión Española**

rubí [ru'βi] *nm* ruby; (*de reloj*) jewel

rubio, a ['ruβjo, a] *adj* fair-haired, blond(e) ♦ *nm/f* blond/blonde; **tabaco** ~ Virginia tobacco

rubor [ru'βor] *nm* (*sonrojo*) blush; (*timidez*) bashfulness; ~**izarse** *vr* to blush

rúbrica ['ruβrika] *nf* (*título*) title, heading; (*de la firma*) flourish; **rubricar** *vt* (*firmar*) to sign with a flourish; (*concluir*) to sign and seal

rudeza [ru'ðeθa] *nf* (*tosquedad*)

coarseness; (*sencillez*) simplicity

rudimentario, a [ruðimen'tarjo, a] *adj* (*conocimientos, noción*) rudimentary; **rudimento** *nm* rudiment

rudo, a ['ruðo, a] *adj* (*sin pulir*) unpolished; (*grosero*) coarse; (*violento*) violent; (*sencillo*) simple

rueda ['rweða] *nf* wheel; (*círculo*) ring, circle; (*rodaja*) slice, round; ~ **delantera/trasera/de repuesto** front/back/spare wheel; ~ **de prensa** press conference

ruedo ['rweðo] *nm* (*contorno*) edge, border; (*de vestido*) hem; (*círculo*) circle; (*TAUR*) arena, bullring

ruego *etc* ['rwexo] *vb ver* **rogar** ♦ *nm* request

rufián [ru'fjan] *nm* scoundrel

rugby ['ruɣβi] *nm* rugby

rugido [ru'xiðo] *nm* roar

rugir [ru'xir] *vi* to roar

rugoso, a [ru'xoso, a] *adj* (*arrugado*) wrinkled; (*áspero*) rough; (*desigual*) ridged

ruido ['rwiðo] *nm* noise; (*sonido*) sound; (*alboroto*) racket, row; (*escándalo*) commotion, rumpus; **~so, a** *adj* noisy, loud; (*fig*) sensational

ruin [rwin] *adj* contemptible, mean

ruina ['rwina] *nf* ruin; (*colapso*) collapse; (*de persona*) ruin, downfall

ruindad [rwin'dað] *nf* lowness, meanness; (*acto*) low *o* mean act

ruinoso, a [rwi'noso, a] *adj* ruinous; (*destartalado*) dilapidated, tumbledown; (*COM*) disastrous

ruiseñor [rwise'ɲor] *nm* nightingale

ruleta [ru'leta] *nf* roulette

rulo ['rulo] *nm* (*para el pelo*) curler

Rumania [ru'manja] *nf* Rumania

rumba ['rumba] *nf* rumba

rumbo ['rumbo] *nm* (*ruta*) route, direction; (*ángulo de dirección*) course, bearing; (*fig*) course of events: **ir con ~ a** to be heading for

rumboso, a [rum'boso, a] *adj* (*generoso*) generous

rumiante [ru'mjante] *nm* ruminant

rumiar [ru'mjar] *vt* to chew; (*fig*) to chew

over ♦ *vi* to chew the cud

rumor [ru'mor] *nm* (*ruido sordo*) low sound; (*murmuración*) murmur, buzz

rumorearse *vr*: **se rumorea que** it is rumoured that

runrún [run'run] *nm* (*voces*) murmur, sound of voices; (*fig*) rumour

rupestre [ru'pestre] *adj* rock *cpd*

ruptura [rup'tura] *nf* rupture

rural [ru'ral] *adj* rural

Rusia ['rusja] *nf* Russia; **ruso, a** *adj, nm/f* Russian

rústica ['rustika] *nf*: **libro en ~** paperback (book); *ver tb* **rústico**

rústico, a ['rustiko, a] *adj* rustic; (*ordinario*) coarse, uncouth ♦ *nm/f* yokel

ruta ['ruta] *nf* route

rutina [ru'tina] *nf* routine; **~rio, a** *adj* routine

S s

S *abr* (= *santo, a*) St; (= *sur*) S

s. *abr* (= *siglo*) C.; (= *siguiente*) foll

S.A. *abr* (= *Sociedad Anónima*) Ltd. (*BRIT*), Inc. (*US*)

sábado ['saßaðo] *nm* Saturday

sábana ['saßana] *nf* sheet

sabandija [saßan'dixa] *nf* bug, insect

sabañón [saßa'ɲon] *nm* chilblain

saber [sa'ßer] *vt* to know; (*llegar a conocer*) to find out, learn; (*tener capacidad de*) to know how to ♦ *vi*: ~ **a** to taste of, taste like ♦ *nm* knowledge, learning; **a ~** namely; **¿sabes conducir/nadar?** can you drive/swim?; **¿sabes francés?** do you speak French?; ~ **de memoria** to know by heart; **hacer ~ algo a uno** to inform sb of sth, let sb know sth

sabiduría [saßiðu'ria] *nf* (*conocimientos*) wisdom; (*instrucción*) learning

sabiendas [sa'ßjendas]: **a ~** *adv* knowingly

sabio, a ['saßjo,a] *adj* (*docto*) learned; (*prudente*) wise, sensible

sabor [sa'ßor] *nm* taste, flavour; **~ear** *vt* to taste, savour; (*fig*) to relish

sabotaje [saßo'taxe] *nm* sabotage

saboteador, a [saβotea'ðor, a] *nm/f* saboteur

sabotear [saβote'ar] *vt* to sabotage

sabré *etc vb ver* **saber**

sabroso, a [sa'βroso, a] *adj* tasty; (*fig*: *fam*) racy, salty

sacacorchos [saka'kortʃos] *nm inv* corkscrew

sacapuntas [saka'puntas] *nm inv* pencil sharpener

sacar [sa'kar] *vt* to take out; (*fig: extraer*) to get (out); (*quitar*) to remove, get out; (*hacer salir*) to bring out; (*conclusión*) to draw; (*novela etc*) to publish, bring out; (*ropa*) to take off; (*obra*) to make; (*premio*) to receive; (*entradas*) to get; (*TENIS*) to serve; ~ **adelante** (*niño*) to bring up; (*negocio*) to carry on, go on with; ~ **a uno a bailar** to get sb up to dance; ~ **una foto** to take a photo; ~ **la lengua** to stick out one's tongue; ~ **buenas/malas notas** to get good/bad marks

sacarina [saka'rina] *nf* saccharin(e)

sacerdote [saθer'ðote] *nm* priest

saciar [sa'θjar] *vt* (*hambre, sed*) to satisfy; **~se** *vr* (*de comida*) to get full up; **comer hasta ~se** to eat one's fill

saco ['sako] *nm* bag; (*grande*) sack; (*su contenido*) bagful; (*AM*) jacket; ~ **de dormir** sleeping bag

sacramento [sakra'mento] *nm* sacrament

sacrificar [sakrifi'kar] *vt* to sacrifice; **sacrificio** *nm* sacrifice

sacrilegio [sakri'lexjo] *nm* sacrilege; **sacrílego, a** *adj* sacrilegious

sacristía [sakris'tia] *nf* sacristy

sacro, a ['sakro, a] *adj* sacred

sacudida [saku'ðiða] *nf* (*agitación*) shake, shaking; (*sacudimiento*) jolt, bump; ~ **eléctrica** electric shock

sacudir [saku'ðir] *vt* to shake; (*golpear*) to hit

sádico, a ['saðiko, a] *adj* sadistic ♦ *nm/f* sadist; **sadismo** *nm* sadism

saeta [sa'eta] *nf* (*flecha*) arrow

sagacidad [saɣaθi'ðað] *nf* shrewdness, cleverness; **sagaz** *adj* shrewd, clever

sagitario [saxi'tarjo] *nm* Sagittarius

sagrado, a [sa'ɣraðo, a] *adj* sacred, holy

Sáhara ['saara] *nm*: **el ~** the Sahara (desert)

sal [sal] *vb ver* **salir** ♦ *nf* salt

sala ['sala] *nf* (*cuarto grande*) large room; (~ **de estar**) living room; (*TEATRO*) house, auditorium; (*de hospital*) ward; ~ **de apelación** court; ~ **de espera** waiting room; ~ **de estar** living room; ~ **de fiestas** dance hall

salado, a [sa'laðo, a] *adj* salty; (*fig*) witty, amusing; **agua salada** salt water

salar [sa'lar] *vt* to salt, add salt to

salarial [sala'rjal] *adj* (*aumento, revisión*) wage *cpd*, salary *cpd*

salario [sa'larjo] *nm* wage, pay

salchicha [sal'tʃitʃa] *nf* (pork) sausage; **salchichón** *nm* (salami-type) sausage

saldar [sal'dar] *vt* to pay; (*vender*) to sell off; (*fig*) to settle, resolve; **saldo** *nm* (*pago*) settlement; (*de una cuenta*) balance; (*lo restante*) remnant(s) (*pl*), remainder; **saldos** *nmpl* (*en tienda*) sale

saldré *etc vb ver* **salir**

salero [sa'lero] *nm* salt cellar

salgo *etc vb ver* **salir**

salida [sa'liða] *nf* (*puerta etc*) exit, way out; (*acto*) leaving, going out; (*de tren, AVIAT*) departure; (*TEC*) output, production; (*fig*) way out; (*COM*) opening; (*GEO, válvula*) outlet; (*de gas*) leak; **calle sin ~** cul-de-sac; ~ **de incendios** fire escape

saliente [sa'ljente] *adj* (*ARQ*) projecting; (*sol*) rising; (*fig*) outstanding

---

PALABRA CLAVE

---

salir [sa'lir] *vi* **1** (*partir: tb:* ~ **de**) to leave; **Juan ha salido** Juan is out; **salió de la cocina** he came out of the kitchen

2 (*aparecer*) to appear; (*disco, libro*) to come out; **anoche salió en la tele** she appeared *o* was on TV last night; **salió en todos los periódicos** it was in all the papers

3 (*resultar*): **la muchacha nos salió muy trabajadora** the girl turned out to be a very hard worker; **la comida se ha salido exquisita** the food was delicious; **sale muy caro** it's very expensive

4: ~**le a uno algo: la entrevista que hice me salió bien/mal** the interview I did went o turned out well/badly
5: ~ **adelante: no sé como haré para ~ adelante** I don't know how I'll get by ♦ ~**se** vr (*líquido*) to spill; (*animal*) to escape

saliva [sa'liβa] nf saliva
salmo ['salmo] nm psalm
salmón [sal'mon] nm salmon
salmuera [sal'mwera] nf pickle, brine
salón [sa'lon] nm (*de casa*) living room, lounge; (*muebles*) lounge suite; ~ **de belleza** beauty parlour; ~ **de baile** dance hall
salpicadero [salpika'ðero] nm (AUTO) dashboard
salpicar [salpi'kar] vt (*rociar*) to sprinkle, spatter; (*esparcir*) to scatter
salsa ['salsa] nf sauce; (*con carne asada*) gravy; (*fig*) spice
saltamontes [salta'montes] nm inv grasshopper
saltar [sal'tar] vt to jump (over), leap (over); (*dejar de lado*) to skip, miss out ♦ vi to jump, leap; (*pelota*) to bounce; (*al aire*) to fly up; (*quebrarse*) to break; (*al agua*) to dive; (*fig*) to explode, blow up
salto ['salto] nm jump, leap; (*al agua*) dive; ~ **de agua** waterfall; ~ **de altura** high jump
saltón, ona [sal'ton, ona] adj (*ojos*) bulging, popping; (*dientes*) protruding
salud [sa'luð] nf health; ¡**(a su) ~!** cheers!, good health!; ~**able** adj (*de buena ~*) healthy; (*provechoso*) good, beneficial
saludar [salu'ðar] vt to greet; (MIL) to salute; **saludo** nm greeting; "**saludos**" (*en carta*) "best wishes", "regards"
salva ['salβa] nf: ~ **de aplausos** ovation
salvación [salβa'θjon] nf salvation; (*rescate*) rescue
salvado [sal'βaðo] nm bran
salvaguardar [salβaɣwar'ðar] vt to safeguard
salvajada [salβa'xaða] nf (*una ~*) atrocity
salvaje [sal'βaxe] adj wild; (*tribu*) savage;

salvajismo [salβa'mento] nm savagery
salvamento [salβa'mento] nm rescue
salvar [sal'βar] vt (*rescatar*) to save, rescue; (*resolver*) to overcome, resolve; (*cubrir distancias*) to cover, travel; (*hacer excepción*) to except, exclude; (*un barco*) to salvage
salvavidas [salβa'βiðas] adj inv: **bote/chaleco/cinturón** ~ lifeboat/life jacket/life belt
salvo, a ['salβo, a] adj safe ♦ adv except (for), save; **a** ~ out of danger; ~ **que** unless; ~**conducto** nm safe-conduct
san [san] adj saint; **S~ Juan** St John
sanar [sa'nar] vt (*herida*) to heal; (*persona*) to cure ♦ vi (*persona*) to get well, recover; (*herida*) to heal
sanatorio [sana'torjo] nm sanatorium
sanción [san'θjon] nf sanction; **sancionar** vt to sanction
sandalia [san'dalja] nf sandal
sandez [san'deθ] nf foolishness
sandía [san'dia] nf watermelon
sandwich ['sandwitʃ] (pl ~**s**, ~**es**) nm sandwich
saneamiento [sanea'mjento] nm sanitation
sanear [sane'ar] vt (*terreno*) to drain
sangrar [san'grar] vt, vi to bleed; **sangre** nf blood
sangría [san'gria] nf sangria, *sweetened drink of red wine with fruit*
sangriento, a [san'grjento, a] adj bloody
sanguijuela [sangi'xwela] nf (ZOOL, *fig*) leech
sanguinario, a [sangi'narjo, a] adj bloodthirsty
sanguíneo, a [san'gineo, a] adj blood cpd
sanidad [sani'ðað] nf sanitation; (*calidad de sano*) health, healthiness; ~ **pública** public health
sanitario, a [sani'tarjo, a] adj sanitary; (*de la salud*) health; ~**s** nmpl toilets (BRIT), washroom (US)
sano, a ['sano, a] adj healthy; (*sin daños*) sound; (*comida*) wholesome; (*entero*) whole, intact; ~ **y salvo** safe and sound
Santiago [san'tjaɣo] nm: ~ **(de Chile)** Santiago

santiamén [santja'men] *nm*: **en un ~** in no time at all

santidad [santi'ðað] *nf* holiness, sanctity

santiguarse [santi'ɣwarse] *vr* to make the sign of the cross

santo, a ['santo, a] *adj* holy; (*fig*) wonderful, miraculous ♦ *nm/f* saint ♦ *nm* saint's day; **~ y seña** password

santuario [san'twarjo] *nm* sanctuary, shrine

saña ['saɲa] *nf* rage, fury

sapo ['sapo] *nm* toad

saque ['sake] *nm* (*TENIS*) service, serve; (*FÚTBOL*) throw-in; **~ de esquina** corner (kick)

saquear [sake'ar] *vt* (*MIL*) to sack; (*robar*) to loot, plunder; (*fig*) to ransack; **saqueo** *nm* sacking; looting, plundering; ransacking

sarampión [saram'pjon] *nm* measles *sg*

sarcasmo [sar'kasmo] *nm* sarcasm; **sarcástico, a** *adj* sarcastic

sardina [sar'ðina] *nf* sardine

sargento [sar'xento] *nm* sergeant

sarmiento [sar'mjento] *nm* (*BOT*) vine shoot

sarna ['sarna] *nf* itch; (*MED*) scabies

sarpullido [sarpu'ʎiðo] *nm* (*MED*) rash

sarro ['sarro] *nm* (*en dientes*) tartar, plaque

sartén [sar'ten] *nf* frying pan

sastre ['sastre] *nm* tailor; **~ría** *nf* (*arte*) tailoring; (*tienda*) tailor's (shop)

Satanás [sata'nas] *nm* Satan

satélite [sa'telite] *nm* satellite

sátira ['satira] *nf* satire

satisfacción [satisfak'θjon] *nf* satisfaction

satisfacer [satisfa'θer] *vt* to satisfy; (*gastos*) to meet; (*pérdida*) to make good; **~se** *vr* to satisfy o.s., be satisfied; (*vengarse*) to take revenge; **satisfecho, a** *adj* satisfied; (*contento*) content(ed), happy; (*tb: satisfecho de sí mismo*) self-satisfied, smug

saturar [satu'rar] *vt* to saturate; **~se** *vr* (*mercado, aeropuerto*) to reach saturation point

sauce ['sauθe] *nm* willow; **~ llorón** weeping willow

sauna ['sauna] *nf* sauna

savia ['saβja] *nf* sap

saxofón [sakso'fon] *nm* saxophone

sazonar [saθo'nar] *vt* to ripen; (*CULIN*) to flavour, season

SE *abr* (= *sudeste*) SE

| PALABRA CLAVE |
---

se [se] *pron* **1** (*reflexivo: sg: m*) himself; (: *f*) herself; (: *pl*) themselves; (: *cosa*) itself; (: *de Vd*) yourself; (: *de Vds*) yourselves; **~ está preparando** she's preparing herself; *para usos léxicos del pron ver el vb en cuestión, p.ej.* **arrepentirse**

2 (*con complemento indirecto*) to him; to her; to them; to it; to you; **a usted ~ lo dije ayer** I told you yesterday; **~ compró un sombrero** he bought himself a hat; **~ rompió la pierna** he broke his leg

3 (*uso recíproco*) each other, one another; **~ miraron (el uno al otro)** they looked at each other *o* one another

4 (*en oraciones pasivas*): **se han vendido muchos libros** a lot of books have been sold

5 (*impers*): **~ dice que** people say that, it is said that; **allí ~ come muy bien** the food there is very good, you can eat very well there

sé *vb ver* **saber**; **ser**

sea *etc vb ver* **ser**

sebo ['seβo] *nm* fat, grease

secador [seka'ðor] *nm*: **~ de pelo** hairdryer

secadora [seka'ðora] *nf* (*ELEC*) tumble dryer

secar [se'kar] *vt* to dry; **~se** *vr* to dry (off); (*río, planta*) to dry up

sección [sek'θjon] *nf* section

seco, a ['seko, a] *adj* dry; (*carácter*) cold; (*respuesta*) sharp, curt; **habrá pan a secas** there will be just bread; **decir algo a secas** to say sth curtly; **parar en ~** to stop dead

secretaría [sekreta'ria] *nf* secretariat

secretario, a [sekre'tarjo, a] *nm/f* secretary

secreto, a [se'kreto, a] *adj* secret; (*persona*) secretive ♦ *nm* secret; (*calidad*) secrecy

secta ['sekta] *nf* sect; **~rio, a** *adj* sectarian

sector [sek'tor] *nm* sector

secuela [se'kwela] *nf* consequence

secuencia [se'kwenθja] *nf* sequence

secuestrar [sekwes'trar] *vt* to kidnap; (*bienes*) to seize, confiscate; **secuestro** *nm* kidnapping; seizure, confiscation

secular [seku'lar] *adj* secular

secundar [sekun'dar] *vt* to second, support

secundario, a [sekun'darjo, a] *adj* secondary

sed [seð] *nf* thirst; **tener ~** to be thirsty

seda ['seða] *nf* silk

sedal [se'ðal] *nm* fishing line

sedante [se'ðante] *nm* sedative

sede ['seðe] *nf* (*de gobierno*) seat; (*de compañía*) headquarters *pl*; **Santa S~** Holy See

sedentario, a [seðen'tarjo, a] *adj* sedentary

sediento, a [se'ðjento, a] *adj* thirsty

sedimento [seði'mento] *nm* sediment

sedoso, a [se'ðoso, a] *adj* silky, silken

seducción [seðuk'θjon] *nf* seduction

seducir [seðu'θir] *vt* to seduce; (*sobornar*) to bribe; (*cautivar*) to charm, fascinate; (*atraer*) to attract; **seductor, a** *adj* seductive; charming, fascinating; attractive; (*engañoso*) deceptive, misleading ♦ *nm/f* seducer

segar [se'ɣar] *vt* (*mies*) to reap, cut; (*hierba*) to mow, cut

seglar [se'ɣlar] *adj* secular, lay

segregación [seɣreɣa'θjon] *nf* segregation. **~ racial** racial segregation

segregar [seɣre'ɣar] *vt* to segregate, separate

seguida [se'ɣiða] *nf*: **en ~** at once, right away

seguido, a [se'ɣiðo, a] *adj* (*continuo*) continuous, unbroken; (*recto*) straight ♦ *adv* (*directo*) straight (on); (*después*) after; (*AM: a menudo*) often; **~s** consecutive, successive; **5 días ~s** 5 days

running, 5 days in a row

seguimiento [seɣi'mjento] *nm* chase, pursuit; (*continuación*) continuation

seguir [se'ɣir] *vt* to follow; (*venir después*) to follow on, come after; (*proseguir*) to continue; (*perseguir*) to chase, pursue ♦ *vi* (*gen*) to follow; (*continuar*) to continue, carry o go on; **~se** *vr* to follow; **sigo sin comprender** I still don't understand; **sigue lloviendo** it's still raining

según [se'ɣun] *prep* according to ♦ *adv*: **¿irás? — ~** are you going? — it all depends ♦ *conj* as; **~ caminamos** while we walk

segundo, a [se'ɣundo, a] *adj* second ♦ *nm* second ♦ *nf* second meaning; **de segunda mano** second-hand; **segunda (clase)** second class; **segunda enseñanza** secondary education; **segunda (marcha)** (*AUT*) second (gear)

seguramente [seɣura'mente] *adv* surely; (*con certeza*) for sure, with certainty

seguridad [seɣuri'ðað] *nf* safety; (*del estado, de casa etc*) security; (*certidumbre*) certainty; (*confianza*) confidence; (*estabilidad*) stability; **~ social** social security

seguro, a [se'ɣuro, a] *adj* (*cierto*) sure, certain; (*fiel*) trustworthy; (*libre del peligro*) safe; (*bien defendido, firme*) secure ♦ *adv* for sure, certainly ♦ *nm* (*COM*) insurance; **~ contra terceros/a todo riesgo** third party/comprehensive insurance; **~s sociales** social security *sg*

seis [seis] *num* six

seísmo [se'ismo] *nm* tremor, earthquake

selección [selek'θjon] *nf* selection; **seleccionar** *vt* to pick, choose, select

selectividad [selektiβi'ðað] (*ESP*) *nf* university entrance examination

selecto, a [se'lekto, a] *adj* select, choice; (*escogido*) selected

sellar [se'ʎar] *vt* (*documento oficial*) to seal; (*pasaporte, visado*) to stamp

sello ['seʎo] *nm* stamp; (*precinto*) seal

selva ['selβa] *nf* (*bosque*) forest, woods *pl*; (*jungla*) jungle

semáforo [se'maforo] *nm* (*AUTO*) traffic

lights pl; (FERRO) signal
semana [se'mana] nf week; **entre ~**
during the week; **S~ Santa** Holy Week;
semanal adj weekly
semblante [sem'blante] nm face; (fig)
look
sembrar [sem'brar] vt to sow; (objetos) to
sprinkle, scatter about; (noticias etc) to
spread
semejante [seme'xante] adj (parecido)
similar ♦ nm fellow man, fellow
creature; **~s** alike, similar; **nunca hizo
cosa ~** he never did any such thing;
semejanza nf similarity, resemblance
semejar [seme'xar] vi to seem like,
resemble; **~se** vr to look alike, be
similar
semen ['semen] nm semen; **~tal** nm stud
semestral [semes'tral] adj half-yearly, bi-
annual
semicírculo [semi'θirkulo] nm semicircle
semidesnatado, a [semiðesna'taðo, a]
adj semi-skimmed
semifinal [semifi'nal] nf semifinal
semilla [se'miʎa] nf seed
seminario [semi'narjo] nm (REL)
seminary; (ESCOL) seminar
sémola ['semola] nf semolina
sempiterno, a [sempi'terno, a] adj
everlasting
Sena ['sena] nm: **el ~** the (river) Seine
senado [se'naðo] nm senate; **senador, a**
nm/f senator
sencillez [senθi'ʎeθ] nf simplicity; (de
persona) naturalness; **sencillo, a** adj
simple; natural, unaffected
senda ['senda] nf path, track
sendero [sen'dero] nm path, track
sendos, as ['sendos, as] adj pl: **les dio ~
golpes** he hit both of them
senil [se'nil] adj senile
seno ['seno] nm (ANAT) bosom, bust; (fig)
bosom; **~s** breasts
sensación [sensa'θjon] nf sensation; (sentido) sense; (sentimiento) feeling;
sensacional adj sensational
sensato, a [sen'sato, a] adj sensible
sensible [sen'sible] adj sensitive;
(apreciable) perceptible, appreciable;

(pérdida) considerable; **~ro, a** adj
sentimental
sensitivo, a [sensi'tiβo, a] adj sense cpd
sensorial [senso'rjal] adj sensory
sensual [sen'swal] adj sensual
sentada [sen'taða] nf sitting; (protesta)
sit-in
sentado, a [sen'taðo, a] adj (establecido)
settled; (carácter) sensible; **estar ~** to sit,
be sitting (down); **dar por ~** to take for
granted, assume
sentar [sen'tar] vt to sit, seat; (fig) to
establish ♦ vi (vestido) to suit; (alimento):
~ bien/mal a to agree/disagree with;
~se vr (persona) to sit, sit down; (el
tiempo) to settle (down); (los depósitos) to
settle
sentencia [sen'tenθja] nf (máxima)
maxim, saying; (JUR) sentence;
sentenciar vt to sentence
sentido, a [sen'tiðo, a] adj (pérdida)
regrettable; (carácter) sensitive ♦ nm
sense; (sentimiento) feeling; (significado)
sense, meaning; (dirección) direction; **mi
más ~ pésame** my deepest sympathy; **~
del humor** sense of humour; **~ único**
one-way (street); **tener ~** to make sense
sentimental [sentimen'tal] adj
sentimental; **vida ~** love life
sentimiento [senti'mjento] nm (emoción)
feeling, emotion; (sentido) sense; (pesar)
regret, sorrow
sentir [sen'tir] vt to feel; (percibir) to
perceive, sense; (lamentar) to regret, be
sorry for ♦ vi (tener la sensación) to feel;
(lamentarse) to feel sorry ♦ nm opinion,
judgement; **~se bien/mal** to feel well/ill;
lo siento I'm sorry
seña ['sena] nf sign; (MIL) password; **~s**
nfpl (dirección) address sg; **~s personales** personal description sg
señal [se'nal] nf sign; (síntoma) symptom;
(FERRO, TELEC) signal; (marca) mark; (COM)
deposit; **en ~ de** as a token of, as a sign
of; **~ar** vt to mark; (indicar) to point out,
indicate; (fijar) to fix, settle
señor [se'nor] nm (hombre) man;
(caballero) gentleman; (dueño) owner,
master; (trato: antes de nombre propio)

Mr; (: *hablando directamente*) sir; **muy ~ mío** Dear Sir; **el ~ alcalde/presidente** the mayor/president

señora [se'ɲora] *nf* (*dama*) lady; (*trato: antes de nombre propio*) Mrs; (: *hablando directamente*) madam; (*esposa*) wife; **Nuestra S~** Our Lady

señorita [seɲo'rita] *nf* (*con nombre y/o apellido*) Miss; (*mujer joven*) young lady

señorito [seɲo'rito] *nm* young gentleman; (*pey*) rich kid

señuelo [se'ɲwelo] *nm* decoy

sepa *etc vb ver* **saber**

separación [separa'θjon] *nf* separation; (*división*) division; (*distancia*) gap

separar [sepa'rar] *vt* to separate; (*dividir*) to divide; **~se** *vr* (*parte*) to come away; (*partes*) to come apart; (*persona*) to leave, go away; (*matrimonio*) to separate; **separatismo** *nm* separatism

sepia ['sepja] *nf* cuttlefish

septiembre [sep'tjembre] *nm* September

séptimo, a ['septimo, a] *adj, nm* seventh

sepulcral [sepul'kral] *adj* (*fig: silencio, atmósfera*) deadly; **sepulcro** *nm* tomb, grave

sepultar [sepul'tar] *vt* to bury; **sepultura** *nf* (*acto*) burial; (*tumba*) grave, tomb

sequedad [seke'ðað] *nf* dryness; (*fig*) brusqueness, curtness

sequía [se'kia] *nf* drought

séquito ['sekito] *nm* (*de rey etc*) retinue; (*POL*) followers *pl*

PALABRA CLAVE

---

ser [ser] *vi* **1** (*descripción*) to be; **es médica/muy alta** she's a doctor/very tall; **la familia es de Cuzco** his (*o her etc*) family is from Cuzco; **soy Ana** (*TELEC*) Ana speaking *o* here

2 (*propiedad*): **es de Joaquín** it's Joaquín's, it belongs to Joaquín

3 (*horas, fechas, números*): **es la una** it's one o'clock; **son las seis y media** it's half-past six; **es el 1 de junio** it's the first of June; **somos/son seis** there are six of us/them

4 (*en oraciones pasivas*): **ha sido descubierto ya** it's already been

discovered

5: **es de esperar que ...** it is to be hoped *o I etc* hope that ...

6 (*locuciones con sub*): **o sea** that is to say; **sea él sea su hermana** either him or his sister

7: **a no ~ por él ...** but for him ...

8: **a no ~ que: a no ~ que tenga uno ya** unless he's got one already

♦ *nm* being; **~ humano** human being

---

serenarse [sere'narse] *vr* to calm down

sereno, a [se'reno, a] *adj* (*persona*) calm, unruffled; (*el tiempo*) fine, settled; (*ambiente*) calm, peaceful ♦ *nm* night watchman

serial [ser'jal] *nm* serial

serie ['serje] *nf* series; (*cadena*) sequence, succession; **fuera de ~** out of order; (*fig*) special, out of the ordinary; **fabricación en ~** mass production

seriedad [serje'ðað] *nf* seriousness; (*formalidad*) reliability; (*de crisis*) gravity, seriousness; **serio, a** *adj* serious; (*formalidad*) reliable, dependable; grave, serious; **en serio** *adv* seriously

sermón [ser'mon] *nm* (*REL*) sermon

serpentear [serpente'ar] *vi* to wriggle; (*camino, río*) to wind, snake

serpentina [serpen'tina] *nf* streamer

serpiente [ser'pjente] *nf* snake; **~ boa** boa constrictor; **~ de cascabel** rattlesnake

serranía [serra'nia] *nf* mountainous area

serrar [se'rrar] *vt* = **aserrar**

serrín [se'rrin] *nm* = **aserrín**

serrucho [se'rrutʃo] *nm* saw

servicio [ser'βiθjo] *nm* service; **~s** *nmpl* toilet(s); **~ incluido** service charge included; **~ militar** military service

servidumbre [serβi'ðumbre] *nf* (*sujeción*) servitude; (*criados*) servants *pl*, staff

servil [ser'βil] *adj* servile

servilleta [serβi'ʎeta] *nf* serviette, napkin

servir [ser'βir] *vt* to serve ♦ *vi* to serve; (*tener utilidad*) to be of use, be useful; **~se** *vr* to serve *o* help o.s.; **~se de algo** to make use of sth, use sth; **sírvase pasar** please come in

sesenta [se'senta] *num* sixty

sesgo ['sesɣo] *nm* slant; (*fig*) slant, twist

sesión [se'sjon] *nf* (*POL*) session, sitting; (*CINE*) showing

seso ['seso] *nm* brain; **sesudo**, a *adj* sensible, wise

seta ['seta] *nf* mushroom; ~ **venenosa** toadstool

setecientos, as [sete'θjentos, as] *adj, num* seven hundred

setenta [se'tenta] *num* seventy

seudónimo [seu'ðonimo] *nm* pseudonym

severidad [seβeri'ðað] *nf* severity; **severo**, a *adj* severe

Sevilla [se'βiʎa] *n* Seville; **sevillano**, a *adj* of *o* from Seville ♦ *nm/f* native *o* inhabitant of Seville

sexo ['sekso] *nm* sex

sexto, a ['seksto, a] *adj, nm* sixth

sexual [sek'swal] *adj* sexual; **vida** ~ sex life

si [si] *conj* if; **me pregunto** ~ ... I wonder if *o* whether ...

sí [si] *adv* yes ♦ *nm* consent ♦ *pron* (*uso impersonal*) oneself; (*sg: m*) himself; (*: f*) herself; (*: de cosa*) itself; (*de usted*) yourself; (*pl*) themselves; (*de ustedes*) yourselves; (*recíproco*) each other; **él no quiere pero yo** ~ he doesn't want to but I do; **ella** ~ **vendrá** she will certainly come, she is sure to come; **claro que** ~ of course; **creo que** ~ I think so

siamés, esa [sja'mes, esa] *adj, nm/f* Siamese

SIDA ['siða] *nm abr* (= *Síndrome de Inmunodeficiencia Adquirida*) AIDS

siderúrgico, a [siðe'rurxico, a] *adj* iron and steel *cpd*

sidra ['siðra] *nf* cider

siembra ['sjembra] *nf* sowing

siempre ['sjempre] *adv* always; (*todo el tiempo*) all the time; ~ **que** (*cada vez*) whenever; (*dado que*) provided that; **como** ~ as usual; **para** ~ for ever

sien [sjen] *nf* temple

siento *etc vb ver* **sentar; sentir**

sierra ['sjerra] *nf* (*TEC*) saw; (*cadena de montañas*) mountain range

siervo, a ['sjerβo, a] *nm/f* slave

siesta ['sjesta] *nf* siesta, nap; **echar la** ~ to have an afternoon nap *o* a siesta

siete ['sjete] *num* seven

sífilis ['sifilis] *nf* syphilis

sifón [si'fon] *nm* syphon; **whisky con** ~ whisky and soda

sigilo [si'xilo] *nm* secrecy, discretion; (*al moverse*) stealth

sigla ['siɣla] *nf* abbreviation; acronym

siglo ['siɣlo] *nm* century; (*fig*) age

significación [siɣnifika'θjon] *nf* significance

significado [siɣnifi'kaðo] *nm* significance; (*de palabra etc*) meaning

significar [siɣnifi'kar] *vt* to mean, signify; (*notificar*) to make known, express; **significativo**, a *adj* significant

signo ['siɣno] *nm* sign; ~ **de admiración** *o* **exclamación** exclamation mark; ~ **de interrogación** question mark

sigo *etc vb ver* **seguir**

siguiente [si'ɣjente] *adj* next, following

siguió *etc vb ver* **seguir**

sílaba ['silaβa] *nf* syllable

silbar [sil'βar] *vt, vi* to whistle; **silbato** *nm* whistle; **silbido** *nm* whistle, whistling

silenciador [silenθja'ðor] *nm* silencer

silenciar [silen'θjar] *vt* (*persona*) to silence; (*escándalo*) to hush up; **silencio** *nm* silence, quiet; **silencioso**, a *adj* silent, quiet

silicio [si'liθjo] *nm* silicon

silla ['siʎa] *nf* (*asiento*) chair; (*tb*: ~ **de montar**) saddle; ~ **de ruedas** wheelchair

sillón [si'ʎon] *nm* armchair, easy chair

silueta [si'lweta] *nf* silhouette; (*de edificio*) outline; (*figura*) figure

silvestre [sil'βestre] *adj* (*BOT*) wild; (*fig*) rustic, rural

simbólico, a [sim'boliko, a] *adj* symbolic(al)

simbolizar [simboli'θar] *vt* to symbolize

símbolo ['simbolo] *nm* symbol

simetría [sime'tria] *nf* symmetry

simiente [si'mjente] *nf* seed

similar [simi'lar] *adj* similar

simio ['simjo] *nm* ape

simpatía [simpa'tia] *nf* liking; (*afecto*) affection; (*amabilidad*) kindness;

(*solidaridad*) mutual support, solidarity; simpático, a *adj* nice, pleasant; kind

simpatizante [simpati'θante] *nm/f* sympathizer

simpatizar [simpati'θar] *vi*: ~ **con** to get on well with

simple ['simple] *adj* simple; (*elemental*) simple, easy; (*mero*) mere; (*puro*) pure, sheer ♦ *nm/f* simpleton; ~**za** *nf* simpleness; (*necedad*) silly thing; **simplificar** *vt* to simplify

simposio [sim'posjo] *nm* symposium

simular [simu'lar] *vt* to simulate

simultáneo, a [simul'taneo, a] *adj* simultaneous

sin [sin] *prep* without; **la ropa está ~ lavar** the clothes are unwashed; ~ **que** without; ~ **embargo** however, still

sinagoga [sina'ɣoɣa] *nf* synagogue

sinceridad [sinθeri'ðað] *nf* sincerity; **sincero, a** *adj* sincere

sincronizar [sinkroni'θar] *vt* to synchronize

sindical [sindi'kal] *adj* union *cpd*, trade-union *cpd*; ~**ista** *adj*, *nm/f* trade unionist

sindicato [sindi'kato] *nm* (*de trabajadores*) trade(s) union; (*de negociantes*) syndicate

síndrome ['sindrome] *nm* (*MED*) syndrome; ~ **de abstinencia** (*MED*) withdrawal symptoms

sinfín [sin'fin] *nm*: **un ~ de** a great many, no end of

sinfonía [sinfo'nia] *nf* symphony

singular [singu'lar] *adj* singular; (*fig*) outstanding, exceptional; (*pey*) peculiar, odd; ~**idad** *nf* singularity, peculiarity; ~**izarse** *vr* to distinguish o.s., stand out

siniestro, a [si'njestro, a] *adj* left; (*fig*) sinister ♦ *nm* (*accidente*) accident

sinnúmero [sin'numero] *nm* = **sinfín**

sino ['sino] *nm* fate, destiny ♦ *conj* (*pero*) but; (*salvo*) except, save

sinónimo, a [si'nonimo, a] *adj* synonymous ♦ *nm* synonym

síntesis ['sintesis] *nf* synthesis; **sintético, a** *adj* synthetic

sintetizar [sinteti'θar] *vt* to synthesize

sintió *vb ver* **sentir**

síntoma ['sintoma] *nm* symptom

sintonía [sinto'nia] *nf* (*RADIO, MUS*): *de programa*) tuning; **sintonizar** *vt* (*RADIO*: *emisora*) to tune (in)

sinvergüenza [simber'ɣwenθa] *nm/f* rogue, scoundrel; **¡es un ~!** he's got a nerve!

sionismo [sjo'nismo] *nm* Zionism

siquiera [si'kjera] *conj* even if, even though ♦ *adv* at least; **ni ~** not even

sirena [si'rena] *nf* siren

Siria ['sirja] *nf* Syria

sirviente, a [sir'ßjente, a] *nm/f* servant

sirvo *etc vb ver* **servir**

sisear [sise'ar] *vt, vi* to hiss

sistema [sis'tema] *nm* system; (*método*) method; **sistemático, a** *adj* systematic

sitiar [si'tjar] *vt* to besiege, lay siege to

sitio ['sitjo] *nm* (*lugar*) place; (*espacio*) room, space; (*MIL*) siege

situación [sitwa'θjon] *nf* situation, position; (*estatus*) position, standing

situado, a [situ'aðo] *adj* situated, placed

situar [si'twar] *vt* to place, put; (*edificio*) to locate, situate

slip [slip] *nm* pants *pl*, briefs *pl*

smoking ['smokin, es'mokin] (*pl* ~**s**) *nm* dinner jacket (*BRIT*), tuxedo (*US*)

snob [es'nob] = **esnob**

SO *abr* (= *suroeste*) SW

sobaco [so'ßako] *nm* armpit

sobar [so'ßar] *vt* (*ropa*) to rumple; (*libro*) to dirty (with one's fingers); (*comida*) to play around with

soberanía [soßera'nia] *nf* sovereignty; **soberano, a** *adj* sovereign; (*fig*) supreme ♦ *nm/f* sovereign

soberbia [so'ßerßja] *nf* pride; haughtiness, arrogance; magnificence

soberbio, a [so'ßerßjo, a] *adj* (*orgulloso*) proud; (*altivo*) haughty, arrogant; (*fig*) magnificent, superb

sobornar [soßor'nar] *vt* to bribe; **soborno** *nm* bribe

sobra ['soßra] *nf* excess, surplus; ~**s** *nfpl* left-overs, scraps; **de ~** surplus, extra; **tengo de ~** I've more than enough; ~**do, a** *adj* (*más que suficiente*) more than enough; (*superfluo*) excessive ♦ *adv* too, exceedingly; **sobrante** *adj* remaining, extra ♦ *nm* surplus, remainder

sobrar [so'βrar] *vt* to exceed, surpass ♦ *vi* (*tener de más*) to be more than enough; (*quedar*) to remain, be left (over)

sobrasada [soβra'saða] *nf* pork sausage spread

sobre ['soβre] *prep* (*gen*) on; (*encima*) on (top of); (*por encima de, arriba de*) over, above; (*más que*) more than; (*además*) in addition to, besides; (*alrededor de*) about ♦ *nm* envelope; ~ **todo** above all

sobrecama [soβre'kama] *nf* bedspread

sobrecargar [soβrekar'γar] *vt* (*camión*) to overload; (*COM*) to surcharge

sobredosis [soβre'ðosis] *nf inv* overdose

sobreentender [soβre(e)nten'der] *vt* (*adivinar*) to deduce, infer; **~se** *vr*: **se sobreentiende que ...** it is implied that ...

sobrehumano, a [soβreu'mano, a] *adj* superhuman

sobrellevar [soβreλe'βar] *vt* (*fig*) to bear, endure

sobremesa [soβre'mesa] *nf*: **durante la ~** after dinner; **ordenador de ~** desktop computer

sobrenatural [soβrenatu'ral] *adj* supernatural

sobrenombre [soβre'nombre] *nm* nickname

sobrepasar [soβrepa'sar] *vt* to exceed, surpass

sobreponer [soβrepo'ner] *vt* (*poner encima*) to put on top; (*añadir*) to add; **~se** *vr*: **~se a** to overcome

sobresaliente [soβresa'ljente] *adj* projecting; (*fig*) outstanding, excellent

sobresalir [soβresa'lir] *vi* to project, jut out; (*fig*) to stand out, excel

sobresaltar [soβresal'tar] *vt* (*asustar*) to scare, frighten; (*sobrecoger*) to startle; **sobresalto** *nm* (*movimiento*) start; (*susto*) scare; (*turbación*) sudden shock

sobretodo [soβre'toðo] *nm* overcoat

sobrevenir [soβreβe'nir] *vi* (*ocurrir*) to happen (unexpectedly); (*resultar*) to follow, ensue

sobreviviente [soβreβi'βjente] *adj* surviving ♦ *nm/f* survivor

sobrevivir [soβreβi'βir] *vi* to survive

sobrevolar [soβreβo'lar] *vt* to fly over

sobriedad [soβrje'ðað] *nf* sobriety, soberness; (*moderación*) moderation, restraint

sobrino, a [so'βrino, a] *nm/f* nephew/niece

sobrio, a ['soβrjo, a] *adj* (*moderado*) moderate, restrained

socarrón, ona [soka'rron, ona] *adj* (*sarcástico*) sarcastic, ironic(al)

socavar [soka'βar] *vt* (*tb fig*) to undermine

socavón [soka'βon] *nm* (*hoyo*) hole

sociable [so'θjaβle] *adj* (*persona*) sociable, friendly; (*animal*) social

social [so'θjal] *adj* social; (*COM*) company *cpd*

socialdemócrata [soθjalde'mokrata] *nm/f* social democrat

socialista [soθja'lista] *adj, nm/f* socialist

socializar [soθjali'θar] *vt* to socialize

sociedad [soθje'ðað] *nf* society; (*COM*) company; ~ **anónima** limited company; ~ **de consumo** consumer society

socio, a ['soθjo, a] *nm/f* (*miembro*) member; (*COM*) partner

sociología [soθjolo'xia] *nf* sociology; **sociólogo, a** *nm/f* sociologist

socorrer [soko'rrer] *vt* to help; **socorrista** *nm/f* first aider; (*en piscina, playa*) lifeguard; **socorro** *nm* (*ayuda*) help, aid; (*MIL*) relief; **¡socorro!** help!

soda ['soða] *nf* (*sosa*) soda; (*bebida*) soda (water)

sofá [so'fa] (*pl* ~**s**) *nm* sofa, settee; ~**-cama** *nm* studio couch; sofa bed

sofisticación [sofistika'θjon] *nf* sophistication

sofocar [sofo'kar] *vt* to suffocate; (*apagar*) to smother, put out; **~se** *vr* to suffocate; (*fig*) to blush, feel embarrassed; **sofoco** *nm* suffocation; embarrassment

sofreír [sofre'ir] *vt* (*CULIN*) to fry lightly

soga ['soγa] *nf* rope

sois *vb ver* **ser**

soja ['soxa] *nf* soya

sojuzgar [soxuθ'γar] *vt* to subdue, rule despotically

sol [sol] _nm_ sun; (_luz_) sunshine, sunlight; **hace ~** it is sunny

solamente [sola'mente] _adv_ only, just

solapa [so'lapa] _nf_ (_de chaqueta_) lapel; (_de libro_) jacket

solapado, a [sola'paðo, a] _adj_ (_intenciones_) underhand; (_gestos, movimiento_) sly

solar [so'lar] _adj_ solar, sun _cpd_

solaz [so'laθ] _nm_ recreation, relaxation; **~ar** _vt_ (_divertir_) to amuse

soldada [sol'daða] _nf_ pay

soldado [sol'daðo] _nm_ soldier; **~ raso** private

soldador [solda'ðor] _nm_ soldering iron; (_persona_) welder

soldar [sol'dar] _vt_ to solder, weld; (_unir_) to join, unite

soleado, a [sole'aðo, a] _adj_ sunny

soledad [sole'ðað] _nf_ solitude; (_estado infeliz_) loneliness

solemne [so'lemne] _adj_ solemn; **solemnidad** _nf_ solemnity

soler [so'ler] _vi_ to be in the habit of, be accustomed to; **suele salir a las ocho** she usually goes out at 8 o'clock

solfeo [sol'feo] _nm_ solfa

solicitar [soliθi'tar] _vt_ (_permiso_) to ask for, seek; (_puesto_) to apply for; (_votos_) to canvass for; (_atención_) to attract; (_persona_) to pursue, chase after

solícito, a [so'liθito, a] _adj_ (_diligente_) diligent; (_cuidadoso_) careful; **solicitud** _nf_ (_calidad_) great care; (_petición_) request; (_a un puesto_) application

solidaridad [soliðari'ðað] _nf_ solidarity; **solidario, a** _adj_ (_participación_) joint, common; (_compromiso_) mutually binding

solidez [soli'ðeθ] _nf_ solidity; **sólido, a** _adj_ solid

soliloquio [soli'lokjo] _nm_ soliloquy

solista [so'lista] _nm/f_ soloist

solitario, a [soli'tarjo, a] _adj_ (_persona_) lonely, solitary; (_lugar_) lonely, desolate ♦ _nm/f_ (_recluso_) recluse; (_en la sociedad_) loner ♦ _nm_ solitaire

sollozar [soʎo'θar] _vi_ to sob; **sollozo** _nm_ sob

solo, a ['solo, a] _adj_ (_único_) single, sole;

(_sin compañía_) alone; (_solitario_) lonely; **hay una sola dificultad** there is just one difficulty; **a solas** alone, by oneself

sólo ['solo] _adv_ only, just

solomillo [solo'miʎo] _nm_ sirloin

soltar [sol'tar] _vt_ (_dejar ir_) to let go of; (_desprender_) to unfasten, loosen; (_librar_) to release, set free; (_risa etc_) to let out

soltero, a [sol'tero, a] _adj_ single, unmarried ♦ _nm/f_ bachelor/single woman; **solterón, ona** _nm/f_ old bachelor/spinster

soltura [sol'tura] _nf_ looseness, slackness; (_de los miembros_) agility, ease of movement; (_en el hablar_) fluency, ease

soluble [so'luβle] _adj_ (_QUÍMICA_) soluble; (_problema_) solvable; **~ en agua** soluble in water

solución [solu'θjon] _nf_ solution; **solucionar** _vt_ (_problema_) to solve; (_asunto_) to settle, resolve

solventar [solβen'tar] _vt_ (_pagar_) to settle, pay; (_resolver_) to resolve; **solvente** _adj_ (_ECON: empresa, persona_) solvent

sombra ['sombra] _nf_ shadow; (_como protección_) shade; **~s** _nfpl_ (_oscuridad_) darkness _sg_, shadows; **tener buena/ mala ~** to be lucky/unlucky

sombrero [som'brero] _nm_ hat

sombrilla [som'briʎa] _nf_ parasol, sunshade

sombrío, a [som'brio, a] _adj_ (_oscuro_) dark; (_fig_) sombre, sad; (_persona_) gloomy

somero, a [so'mero, a] _adj_ superficial

someter [some'ter] _vt_ (_país_) to conquer; (_persona_) to subject to one's will; (_informe_) to present, submit; **~se** _vr_ to give in, yield, submit; **~ a** to subject to

somier [so'mjer] (_pl_ **somiers**) _n_ spring mattress

somnífero [som'nifero] _nm_ sleeping pill

somnolencia [somno'lenθja] _nf_ sleepiness, drowsiness

somos [somos] _vb ver_ **ser**

son [son] _vb ver_ **ser** ♦ _nm_ sound; **en ~ de broma** as a joke

sonajero [sona'xero] _nm_ (baby's) rattle

sonambulismo [sonambu'lismo] _nm_ sleepwalking; **sonámbulo, a** _nm/f_ sleepwalker

sonar [so'nar] *vt* to ring ♦ *vi* to sound; (*hacer ruido*) to make a noise; (*pronunciarse*) to be sounded, be pronounced; (*ser conocido*) to sound familiar; (*campana*) to ring; (*reloj*) to strike, chime; **~se** *vr*: **~se (las narices)** to blow one's nose; **me suena ese nombre** that name rings a bell

sonda ['sonda] *nf* (*NAUT*) sounding; (*TEC*) bore, drill; (*MED*) probe

sondear [sonde'ar] *vt* to sound; to bore (into), drill; to probe, sound; (*fig*) to sound out; **sondeo** *nm* sounding, boring, drilling; (*fig*) poll, enquiry

sónico, a ['soniko, a] *adj* sonic, sound *cpd*

sonido [so'niðo] *nm* sound

sonoro, a [so'noro, a] *adj* sonorous; (*resonante*) loud, resonant

sonreír [sonre'ir] *vi* to smile; **~se** *vr* to smile; **sonriente** *adj* smiling; **sonrisa** *nf* smile

sonrojarse [sonro'xarse] *vr* to blush, go red; **sonrojo** *nm* blush

sonsacar [son'sakar] *vt* to coax

soñador, a [sona'ðor, a] *nm/f* dreamer

soñar [so'nar] *vt, vi* to dream; **~ con** to dream about *o* of

soñoliento, a [sono'ljento, a] *adj* sleepy, drowsy

sopa ['sopa] *nf* soup

sopesar [sope'sar] *vt* to consider, weigh up

soplar [so'plar] *vt* (*polvo*) to blow away, blow off; (*inflar*) to blow up; (*vela*) to blow out ♦ *vi* to blow; **soplo** *nm* blow, puff; (*de viento*) puff, gust

soplón, ona [so'plon, ona] (*fam*), *nm/f* (*niño*) telltale; (*de policía*) grass (*fam*)

sopor [so'por] *nm* drowsiness

soporífero [sopo'rifero] *nm* sleeping pill

soportable [sopor'taßle] *adj* bearable

soportar [sopor'tar] *vt* to bear, carry; (*fig*) to bear, put up with; **soporte** *nm* support; (*fig*) pillar, support

soprano [so'prano] *nf* soprano

sorber [sor'ßer] *vt* (*chupar*) to sip; (*inhalar*) to inhale; (*tragar*) to swallow

(up); (*absorber*) to soak up, absorb

sorbete [sor'ßete] *nm* iced fruit drink

sorbo ['sorßo] *nm* (*trago: grande*) gulp, swallow; (: *pequeño*) sip

sordera [sor'ðera] *nf* deafness

sórdido, a ['sorðiðo, a] *adj* dirty, squalid

sordo, a ['sorðo, a] *adj* (*persona*) deaf ♦ *nm/f* deaf person; **~mudo, a** *adj* deaf and dumb

sorna ['sorna] *nf* sarcastic tone

soroche [so'rotʃe] (*AM*) *nm* mountain sickness

sorprendente [sorpren'dente] *adj* surprising

sorprender [sorpren'der] *vt* to surprise; **sorpresa** *nf* surprise

sortear [sorte'ar] *vt* to draw lots for; (*rifar*) to raffle; (*dificultad*) to avoid; **sorteo** *nm* (*en lotería*) draw; (*rifa*) raffle

sortija [sor'tixa] *nf* ring; (*rizo*) ringlet, curl

sosegado, a [sose'ɣaðo, a] *adj* quiet, calm

sosegar [sose'ɣar] *vt* to quieten, calm; (*el ánimo*) to reassure ♦ *vi* to rest; **sosiego** *nm* quiet(ness), calm(ness)

soslayo [sos'lajo]: **de ~** *adv* obliquely, sideways

soso, a ['soso, a] *adj* (*CULIN*) tasteless; (*fig*) dull, uninteresting

sospecha [sos'petʃa] *nf* suspicion; **sospechar** *vt* to suspect; **sospechoso, a** *adj* suspicious; (*testimonio, opinión*) suspect ♦ *nm/f* suspect

sostén [sos'ten] *nm* (*apoyo*) support; (*sujetador*) bra; (*alimentación*) sustenance, food

sostener [soste'ner] *vt* to support; (*mantener*) to keep up, maintain; (*alimentar*) to sustain, keep going; **~se** *vr* to support o.s.; (*seguir*) to continue, remain; **sostenido, a** *adj* continuous, sustained; (*prolongado*) prolonged

sotana [so'tana] *nf* (*REL*) cassock

sótano ['sotano] *nm* basement

soviético, a [so'ßjetiko, a] *adj* Soviet; **los ~s** the Soviets

soy *vb ver* **ser**

Sr. *abr* (≐ *Señor*) Mr

Sra. *abr* (= *Señora*) Mrs

S.R.C. *abr* (= *se ruega contestación*) R.S.V.P.

Sres. *abr* (= *Señores*) Messrs

Srta. *abr* (= *Señorita*) Miss

Sta. *abr* (= *Santa*) St

status ['status, e'status] *nm inv* status

Sto. *abr* (= *Santo*) St

su [su] *pron* (*de él*) his; (*de ella*) her; (*de una cosa*) its; (*de ellos, ellas*) their; (*de usted, ustedes*) your

suave ['swaße] *adj* gentle; (*superficie*) smooth; (*trabajo*) easy; (*música, voz*) soft, sweet; **suavidad** *nf* gentleness; smoothness; softness, sweetness; **suavizar** *vt* to soften; (*quitar la aspereza*) to smooth (out)

subalimentado, a [sußalimen'taðo, a] *adj* undernourished

subasta [su'ßasta] *nf* auction; **subastar** *vt* to auction (off)

subcampeón, ona [sußkampe'on, ona] *nm/f* runner-up

subconsciente [sußkon'sθjente] *adj, nm* subconscious

subdesarrollado, a [sußðesarro'ʎaðo, a] *adj* underdeveloped

subdesarrollo [sußðesa'rroʎo] *nm* underdevelopment

subdirector, a [sußðirek'tor, a] *nm/f* assistant director

súbdito, a ['sußðito, a] *nm/f* subject

subestimar [sußesti'mar] *vt* to underestimate, underrate

subida [su'ßiða] *nf* (*de montaña etc*) ascent, climb; (*de precio*) rise, increase; (*pendiente*) slope, hill

subir [su'ßir] *vt* (*objeto*) to raise, lift up; (*cuesta, calle*) to go up; (*colina, montaña*) to climb; (*precio*) to raise, put up ♦ *vi* to go up, come up; (*a un coche*) to get in; (*a un autobús, tren o avión*) to get on, board; (*precio*) to rise, go up; (*río, marea*) to rise; **~se** *vr* to get up, climb

súbito, a ['sußito, a] *adj* (*repentino*) sudden; (*imprevisto*) unexpected

subjetivo, a [sußxe'tißo, a] *adj* subjective

sublevación [sußleßa'θjon] *nf* revolt, rising

sublevar [sußle'ßar] *vt* to rouse to revolt; **~se** *vr* to revolt, rise

sublime [su'ßlime] *adj* sublime

submarino, a [sußma'rino, a] *adj* underwater ♦ *nm* submarine

subnormal [sußnor'mal] *adj* subnormal ♦ *nm/f* subnormal person

subordinado, a [sußorði'naðo, a] *adj, nm/f* subordinate

subrayar [sußra'jar] *vt* to underline

subsanar [sußsa'nar] *vt* (*reparar*) to make good; (*perdonar*) to excuse; (*sobreponerse a*) to overcome

subscribir [sußskri'ßir] *vt* = **suscribir**

subsidio [suß'siðjo] *nm* (*ayuda*) aid, financial help; (*subvención*) subsidy, grant; (*de enfermedad, paro etc*) benefit, allowance

subsistencia [sußsis'tenθja] *nf* subsistence

subsistir [sußsis'tir] *vi* to subsist; (*vivir*) to live; (*sobrevivir*) to survive, endure

subterráneo, a [sußte'rraneo, a] *adj* underground, subterranean ♦ *nm* underpass, underground passage

subtítulo [suß'titulo] *nm* (*CINE*) subtitle

suburbano, a [sußur'ßano, a] *adj* suburban

suburbio [su'ßurßjo] *nm* (*barrio*) slum quarter; (*afueras*) suburbs *pl*

subvención [sußßen'θjon] *nf* (*ECON*) subsidy, grant; **subvencionar** *vt* to subsidize

subversión [sußßer'sjon] *nf* subversion; **subversivo, a** *adj* subversive

subyugar [sußju'var] *vt* (*país*) to subjugate, subdue; (*enemigo*) to overpower; (*voluntad*) to dominate

succión [suk'θjon] *nf* suction

sucedáneo, a [suθe'ðaneo, a] *adj* substitute ♦ *nm* substitute (food)

suceder [suθe'ðer] *vt, vi* to happen; (*seguir*) to succeed, follow; **lo que sucede es que ...** the fact is that ...; **sucesión** *nf* succession; (*serie*) sequence, series

sucesivamente [suθesißa'mente] *adv*: **y así ~** and so on

sucesivo, a [suθe'sißo, a] *adj* successive,

following; **en lo ~** in future, from now on

suceso [su'θeso] *nm* (*hecho*) event, happening; (*incidente*) incident

suciedad [suθje'ðað] *nf* (*estado*) dirtiness; (*mugre*) dirt, filth

sucinto, a [su'θinto, a] *adj* (*conciso*) succinct, concise

sucio, a [su'θjo, a] *adj* dirty

suculento, a [suku'lento, a] *adj* succulent

sucumbir [sukum'bir] *vi* to succumb

sucursal [sukur'sal] *nf* branch (office)

Sudáfrica [suð'afrika] *nf* South Africa

Sudamérica [suða'merika] *nf* South America; **sudamericano, a** *adj, nm/f* South American

sudar [su'ðar] *vt, vi* to sweat

sudeste [su'ðeste] *nm* south-east

sudoeste [suðo'este] *nm* south-west

sudor [su'ðor] *nm* sweat; **~oso, a** *adj* sweaty, sweating

Suecia ['sweθja] *nf* Sweden; **sueco, a** *adj* Swedish ♦ *nm/f* Swede

suegro, a ['sweɣro, a] *nm/f* father-/mother-in-law

suela ['swela] *nf* sole

sueldo ['sweldo] *nm* pay, wage(s) (*pl*)

suele *etc vb ver* **soler**

suelo ['swelo] *nm* (*tierra*) ground; (*de casa*) floor

suelto, a ['swelto, a] *adj* loose; (*libre*) free; (*separado*) detached; (*ágil*) quick, agile; (*corriente*) fluent, flowing ♦ *nm* (loose) change, small change

sueño *etc* ['sweɲo] *vb ver* **soñar** ♦ *nm* sleep; (*somnolencia*) sleepiness, drowsiness; (*lo soñado, fig*) dream; **tener ~** to be sleepy

suero ['swero] *nm* (*MED*) serum; (*de leche*) whey

suerte ['swerte] *nf* (*fortuna*) luck; (*azar*) chance; (*destino*) fate, destiny; (*condición*) lot; (*género*) sort, kind; **tener ~** to be lucky; **de otra ~** otherwise, if not; **de ~ que** so that, in such a way that

suéter ['sweter] *nm* sweater

suficiente [sufi'θjente] *adj* enough, sufficient ♦ *nm* (*ESCOL*) pass

sufragio [su'fraxjo] *nm* (*voto*) vote;

(*derecho de voto*) suffrage

sufrido, a [su'friðo, a] *adj* (*persona*) tough; (*paciente*) long-suffering, patient

sufrimiento [sufri'mjento] *nm* (*dolor*) suffering

sufrir [su'frir] *vt* (*padecer*) to suffer; (*soportar*) to bear, put up with; (*apoyar*) to hold up, support ♦ *vi* to suffer

sugerencia [suxe'renθja] *nf* suggestion

sugerir [suxe'rir] *vt* to suggest; (*sutilmente*) to hint

sugestión [suxes'tjon] *nf* suggestion; (*sutil*) hint; **sugestionar** *vt* to influence

sugestivo, a [suxes'tiβo, a] *adj* stimulating; (*fascinante*) fascinating

suicida [sui'θiða] *adj* suicidal ♦ *nm/f* suicidal person; (*muerto*) suicide, person who has committed suicide; **suicidarse** *vr* to commit suicide, kill o.s.; **suicidio** *nm* suicide

Suiza ['swiθa] *nf* Switzerland; **suizo, a** *adj, nm/f* Swiss

sujeción [suxe'θjon] *nf* subjection

sujetador [suxeta'ðor] *nm* fastener, clip; (*sostén*) bra

sujetar [suxe'tar] *vt* (*fijar*) to fasten; (*detener*) to hold down; (*fig*) to subject, subjugate; **~se** *vr* to subject o.s.; **sujeto, a** *adj* fastened, secure ♦ *nm* subject; (*individuo*) individual; **sujeto a** subject to

suma ['suma] *nf* (*cantidad*) total, sum; (*de dinero*) sum; (*acto*) adding (up), addition; **en ~** in short

sumamente [suma'mente] *adv* extremely, exceedingly

sumar [su'mar] *vt* to add (up); (*reunir*) to collect, gather ♦ *vi* to add up

sumario, a [su'marjo, a] *adj* brief, concise ♦ *nm* summary

sumergir [sumer'xir] *vt* to submerge; (*hundir*) to sink; (*bañar*) to immerse, dip

suministrar [sumini'strar] *vt* to supply, provide; **suministro** *nm* supply; (*acto*) supplying, providing

sumir [su'mir] *vt* to sink, submerge; (*fig*) to plunge

sumisión [sumi'sjon] *nf* (*acto*) submission; (*calidad*) submissiveness,

docility; **sumiso, a** *adj* submissive,
docile
sumo, a ['sumo, a] *adj* great, extreme;
(*mayor*) highest, supreme
suntuoso, a [sun'twoso, a] *adj* sumptuous, magnificent
supe *etc vb ver* **saber**
supeditar [supeði'tar] *vt*: ~ **algo a algo** to
subordinate sth to sth
super... [super] *prefijo* super..., over...;
~**bueno** *adj* great, fantastic
súper ['super] *nf* (*gasolina*) three-star
(petrol)
superar [supe'rar] *vt* (*sobreponerse a*) to
overcome; (*rebasar*) to surpass, do better
than; (*pasar*) to go beyond; ~**se** *vr* to
excel o.s.
superávit [supe'raßit] *nm inv* surplus
superficial [superfi'θjal] *adj* superficial;
(*medida*) surface *cpd*, of the surface
superficie [super'fiθje] *nf* surface; (*área*)
area
superfluo, a [su'perflwo, a] *adj*
superfluous
superior [supe'rjor] *adj* (*piso, clase*)
upper; (*temperatura, número, nivel*)
higher; (*mejor: calidad, producto*)
superior, better ♦ *nm/f* superior; ~**idad**
nf superiority
supermercado [supermer'kaðo] *nm*
supermarket
superponer [superpo'ner] *vt* to
superimpose
supersónico, a [super'soniko, a] *adj*
supersonic
superstición [supersti'θjon] *nf*
superstition; **supersticioso, a** *adj*
superstitious
supervisar [superßi'sar] *vt* to supervise
supervivencia [superßi'ßenθja] *nf*
survival
superviviente [superßi'ßjente] *adj*
surviving
supiera *etc vb ver* **saber**
suplantar [suplan'tar] *vt* (*persona*) to
supplant; (*documento etc*) to falsify
suplemento [suple'mento] *nm*
supplement
suplente [su'plente] *adj, nm/f* substitute

supletorio, a [suple'torjo, a] *adj*
supplementary ♦ *nm* supplement; **mesa
supletoria** spare table
súplica ['suplika] *nf* request; (*JUR*) petition
suplicar [supli'kar] *vt* (*cosa*) to beg (for),
plead for; (*persona*) to beg, plead with
suplicio [su'pliθjo] *nm* torture
suplir [su'plir] *vt* (*compensar*) to make
good, make up for; (*reemplazar*) to
replace, substitute ♦ *vi*: ~ **a** to take the
place of, substitute for
supo *etc vb ver* **saber**
suponer [supo'ner] *vt* to suppose ♦ *vi* to
have authority; **suposición** *nf*
supposition
supremacía [suprema'θia] *nf* supremacy
supremo, a [su'premo, a] *adj* supreme
supresión [supre'sjon] *nf* suppression; (*de
derecho*) abolition; (*de dificultad*)
removal; (*de palabra etc*) deletion; (*de
restricción*) cancellation, lifting
suprimir [supri'mir] *vt* to suppress; (*derecho, costumbre*) to abolish; (*dificultad*)
to remove; (*palabra etc*) to delete;
(*restricción*) to cancel, lift
supuesto, a [su'pwesto, a] *pp de* **suponer**
♦ *adj* (*hipotético*) supposed; (*falso*) false
♦ *nm* assumption, hypothesis; ~ **que**
since; **por** ~ of course
sur [sur] *nm* south
surcar [sur'kar] *vt* to plough; (*superficie*)
to cut, score; **surco** *nm* (*en metal, disco*)
groove; (*AGR*) furrow
surgir [sur'xir] *vi* to arise, emerge;
(*dificultad*) to come up, crop up
surtido, a [sur'tiðo, a] *adj* mixed,
assorted ♦ *nm* (*selección*) selection,
assortment; (*abastecimiento*) supply,
stock
surtir [sur'tir] *vt* to supply, provide ♦ *vi* to
spout, spurt
susceptible [susθep'tißle] *adj* susceptible;
(*sensible*) sensitive; ~ **de** capable of
suscitar [susθi'tar] *vt* to cause, provoke;
(*interés, sospechas*) to arouse
suscribir [suskri'ßir] *vt* (*firmar*) to sign;
(*respaldar*) to subscribe to, endorse; ~**se**
vr to subscribe; **suscripción** *nf* subscription

susodicho, a [suso'ðitʃo, a] *adj* above-mentioned

suspender [suspen'der] *vt* (*objeto*) to hang (up), suspend; (*trabajo*) to stop, suspend; (*ESCOL*) to fail; **suspensión** *nf* suspension; (*fig*) stoppage, suspension

suspenso, a [sus'penso, a] *adj* hanging, suspended; (*ESCOL*) failed ♦ *nm*: **quedar o estar en ~** to be pending

suspicacia [suspi'kaθja] *nf* suspicion, mistrust; **suspicaz** *adj* suspicious, distrustful

suspirar [suspi'rar] *vi* to sigh; **suspiro** *nm* sigh

sustancia [sus'tanθja] *nf* substance

sustentar [susten'tar] *vt* (*alimentar*) to sustain, nourish; (*objeto*) to hold up, support; (*idea, teoría*) to maintain, uphold; (*fig*) to sustain, keep going; **sustento** *nm* support; (*alimento*) sustenance, food

sustituir [sustitu'ir] *vt* to substitute, replace; **sustituto, a** *nm/f* substitute, replacement

susto ['susto] *nm* fright, scare

sustraer [sustra'er] *vt* to remove, take away; (*MAT*) to subtract

susurrar [susu'rrar] *vi* to whisper; **susurro** *nm* whisper

sutil [su'til] *adj* (*aroma, diferencia*) subtle; (*tenue*) thin; (*inteligencia, persona*) sharp; **~eza** *nf* subtlety; thinness

suyo, a ['sujo, a] (*con artículo o después del verbo* **ser**) *adj* (*de él*) his; (*de ella*) hers; (*de ellos, ellas*) theirs; (*de Ud, Uds*) yours; **un amigo ~** a friend of his (*o* hers *o* theirs *o* yours)

T t

tabacalera [taβaka'lera] *nf*: **T~** Spanish state tobacco monopoly

tabaco [ta'βako] *nm* tobacco; (*fam*) cigarettes *pl*

taberna [ta'βerna] *nf* bar, pub (*BRIT*); **tabernero, a** *nm/f* (*encargado*) publican; (*camarero*) barman/maid

tabique [ta'βike] *nm* partition (wall)

tabla ['taβla] *nf* (*de madera*) plank; (*estante*) shelf; (*de vestido*) pleat; (*ARTE*) panel; **~s** *nfpl*: **estar o quedar en ~s** to draw; **~do** *nm* (*plataforma*) platform; (*TEATRO*) stage

tablao [ta'βlao] *nm* (*tb*: **~ flamenco**) flamenco show

tablero [ta'βlero] *nm* (*de madera*) plank, board; (*de ajedrez, damas*) board; (*AUTO*) dashboard; **~ de anuncios** notice (*BRIT*) *o* bulletin (*US*) board

tableta [ta'βleta] *nf* (*MED*) tablet; (*de chocolate*) bar

tablón [ta'βlon] *nm* (*de suelo*) plank; (*de techo*) beam; **~ de anuncios** notice board (*BRIT*), bulletin board (*US*)

tabú [ta'βu] *nm* taboo

tabular [taβu'lar] *vt* to tabulate

taburete [taβu'rete] *nm* stool

tacaño, a [ta'kaɲo, a] *adj* (*avaro*) mean

tacha ['tatʃa] *nf* flaw; (*TEC*) stud; **tachar** *vt* (*borrar*) to cross out; **tachar de** to accuse of

tácito, a ['taθito, a] *adj* tacit

taciturno, a [taθi'turno, a] *adj* (*callado*) silent; (*malhumorado*) sullen

taco ['tako] *nm* (*BILLAR*) cue; (*libro de billetes*) book; (*AM: de zapato*) heel; (*tarugo*) peg; (*palabrota*) swear word

tacón [ta'kon] *nm* heel; **de ~ alto** high-heeled; **taconeo** *nm* (heel) stamping

táctica ['taktika] *nf* tactics *pl*

táctico, a ['taktiko, a] *adj* tactical

tacto ['takto] *nm* touch; (*fig*) tact

tafetán [tafe'tan] *nm* taffeta

tafilete [tafi'lete] *nm* morocco leather

tahona [ta'ona] *nf* (*panadería*) bakery

taimado, a [tai'maðo, a] *adj* (*astuto*) sly

taita ['taita] (*fam*) *nm* dad, daddy

tajada [ta'xaða] *nf* slice

tajante [ta'xante] *adj* sharp

tajo ['taxo] *nm* (*corte*) cut; (*GEO*) cleft

tal [tal] *adj* such; **~ vez** perhaps ♦ *pron* (*persona*) someone, such a one; (*cosa*) something, such a thing; **~ como** such as; **~ para cual** tit for tat; (*dos iguales*) two of a kind ♦ *adv*: **~ como** (*igual*) just as; **~ cual** (*como es*) just as it is; **¿qué ~?** how are things?; **¿qué ~ te gusta?** how do you like it? ♦ *conj:* **con ~ de que** provided that

taladrar [tala'ðrar] *vt* to drill; **taladro** *nm* drill; *(hoyo)* drill hole

talante [ta'lante] *nm (humor)* mood; *(voluntad)* will, willingness

talar [ta'lar] *vt* to fell, cut down; *(devastar)* to devastate

talco ['talko] *nm (polvos)* talcum powder

talego [ta'leɣo] *nm* sack

talento [ta'lento] *nm* talent; *(capacidad)* ability

TALGO ['talɣo] *(ESP) nm abr* (= *tren articulado ligero Goicoechea-Oriol*) ≈ HST *(BRIT)*

talismán [talis'man] *nm* talisman

talla ['taʎa] *nf (estatura, fig, MED)* height, stature; *(palo)* measuring rod; *(ARTE)* carving; *(medida)* size

tallado, a [ta'ʎaðo, a] *adj* carved ♦ *nm* carving

tallar [ta'ʎar] *vt (madera)* to carve; *(metal etc)* to engrave; *(medir)* to measure

tallarines [taʎa'rines] *nmpl* noodles

talle ['taʎe] *nm (ANAT)* waist; *(fig)* appearance

taller [ta'ʎer] *nm (TEC)* workshop; *(de artista)* studio

tallo ['taʎo] *nm (de planta)* stem; *(de hierba)* blade; *(brote)* shoot

talón [ta'lon] *nm (ANAT)* heel; *(COM)* counterfoil; *(cheque)* cheque *(BRIT)*, check *(US)*

talonario [talo'narjo] *nm (de cheques)* chequebook *(BRIT)*, checkbook *(US)*; *(de billetes)* book of tickets; *(de recibos)* receipt book

tamaño, a [ta'maɲo, a] *adj (tan grande)* such a big; *(tan pequeño)* such a small ♦ *nm* size; **de ~ natural** full-size

tamarindo [tama'rindo] *nm* tamarind

tambalearse [tambale'arse] *vr (persona)* to stagger; *(vehículo)* to sway

también [tam'bjen] *adv (igualmente)* also, too, as well; *(además)* besides

tambor [tam'bor] *nm* drum; *(ANAT)* eardrum; **~ del freno** brake drum

tamiz [ta'miθ] *nm* sieve; **~ar** *vt* to sieve

tampoco [tam'poko] *adv* nor, neither; **yo**

~ lo compré I didn't buy it either

tampón [tam'pon] *nm* tampon

tan [tan] *adv* so; **~ es así que ...** so much so that ....

tanda ['tanda] *nf (gen)* series; *(turno)* shift

tangente [tan'xente] *nf* tangent

Tánger ['tanxer] *n* Tangier(s)

tangible [tan'xiβle] *adj* tangible

tanque ['tanke] *nm (cisterna, MIL)* tank; *(AUTO)* tanker

tantear [tante'ar] *vt (calcular)* to reckon (up); *(medir)* to take the measure of; *(probar)* to test, try out; *(tomar la medida: persona)* to take the measurements of; *(situación)* to weigh up; *(persona: opinión)* to sound out ♦ *vi (DEPORTE)* to score; **tanteo** *nm (cálculo)* (rough) calculation; *(prueba)* test, trial; *(DEPORTE)* scoring

tanto, a ['tanto, a] *adj (cantidad)* so much, as much; **~s** so many, as many; **20 y ~s** 20-odd ♦ *adv (cantidad)* so much, as much; *(tiempo)* so long, as long ♦ *conj:* **en ~ que** while; **hasta ~ (que)** until such time as ♦ *nm (suma)* certain amount; *(proporción)* so much; *(punto)* point; *(gol)* goal; **un ~ perezoso** somewhat lazy ♦ *pron:* **cada uno paga ~** each one pays so much; **~ tú como yo** both you and I; **~ como eso** it's not as bad as that; **~ más ... cuanto que** it's all the more ...' because; **~ mejor/peor** so much the better/the worse; **~ si viene como si va** whether he comes or whether he goes; **~ es así que** so much so that; **por o por lo ~** therefore; **me he vuelto ronco de o con ~ hablar** I have become hoarse with much talking; **a ~s de agosto** on such and such a day in August

tapa ['tapa] *nf (de caja, olla)* lid; *(de botella)* top; *(de libro)* cover; *(comida)* snack

tapadera [tapa'ðera] *nf* lid, cover

tapar [ta'par] *vt (cubrir)* to cover; *(envolver)* to wrap o cover up; *(la vista)* to obstruct; *(persona, falta)* to conceal; *(AM)* to fill; **~se** *vr* to wrap o.s. up

taparrabo [tapa'rraβo] *nm* loincloth

tapete [ta'pete] *nm* table cover

tapia ['tapja] *nf* (garden) wall; **tapiar** *vt* to wall in

tapicería [tapiθe'ria] *nf* tapestry; (*para muebles*) upholstery; (*tienda*) upholsterer's (shop)

tapiz [ta'piθ] *nm* (*alfombra*) carpet; (*tela tejida*) tapestry; **~ar** *vt* (*muebles*) to upholster

tapón [ta'pon] *nm* (*corcho*) stopper; (*TEC*) plug; **~ de rosca** screw-top

taquigrafía [takiɣra'fia] *nf* shorthand; **taquígrafo, a** *nm/f* shorthand writer, stenographer

taquilla [ta'kiʎa] *nf* (*donde se compra*) booking office; (*suma recogida*) takings *pl*; **taquillero, a** *adj*: **función taquillera** box office success ♦ *nm/f* ticket clerk

tara ['tara] *nf* (*defecto*) defect; (*COM*) tare

tarántula [ta'rantula] *nf* tarantula

tararear [tarare'ar] *vi* to hum

tardanza [tar'ðanθa] *nf* (*demora*) delay

tardar [tar'ðar] *vi* (*tomar tiempo*) to take a long time; (*llegar tarde*) to be late; (*demorar*) to delay; **¿tarda mucho el tren?** does the train take (very) long?; **a más ~** at the latest; **no tardes en venir** come soon

tarde ['tarðe] *adv* late ♦ *nf* (*de día*) afternoon; (*al anochecer*) evening; **de ~ en ~** from time to time; **¡buenas ~s!** good afternoon!; **a o por la ~** in the afternoon; in the evening

tardío, a [tar'ðio, a] *adj* (*retrasado*) late; (*lento*) slow (to arrive)

tarea [ta'rea] *nf* task; (*faena*) chore; (*ESCOL*) homework

tarifa [ta'rifa] *nf* (*lista de precios*) price list; (*precio*) tariff

tarima [ta'rima] *nf* (*plataforma*) platform

tarjeta [tar'xeta] *nf* card; **~ postal/de crédito/de Navidad** postcard/credit card/Christmas card

tarro ['tarro] *nm* jar, pot

tarta ['tarta] *nf* (*pastel*) cake; (*torta*) tart

tartamudear [tartamuðe'ar] *vi* to stammer; **tartamudo, a** *adj* stammering ♦ *nm/f* stammerer

tártaro, a ['tartaro, a] *adj*: **salsa tártara** tartar(e) sauce

tasa ['tasa] *nf* (*precio*) (fixed) price, rate; (*valoración*) valuation; (*medida, norma*) measure, standard; **~ de cambio/interés** exchange/interest rate; **~s universitarias** university fees; **~ción** *nf* valuation; **~dor, a** *nm/f* valuer

tasar [ta'sar] *vt* (*arreglar el precio*) to fix a price for; (*valorar*) to value, assess

tasca ['taska] (*fam*) *nf* pub

tatarabuelo, a [tatara'ßwelo, a] *nm/f* great-great-grandfather/mother

tatuaje [ta'twaxe] *nm* (*dibujo*) tattoo; (*acto*) tattooing

tatuar [ta'twar] *vt* to tattoo

taurino, a [tau'rino, a] *adj* bullfighting *cpd*

Tauro ['tauro] *nm* Taurus

tauromaquia [tauro'makja] *nf* tauromachy, (art of) bullfighting

taxi ['taksi] *nm* taxi

taxista [tak'sista] *nm/f* taxi driver

taza ['taθa] *nf* cup; (*de retrete*) bowl; **~ para café** coffee cup; **tazón** *nm* (*taza grande*) mug, large cup; (*de fuente*) basin

te [te] *pron* (*complemento de objeto*) you; (*complemento indirecto*) (to) you; (*reflexivo*) (to) yourself; **¿~ duele mucho el brazo?** does your arm hurt a lot?; **~ equivocas** you're wrong; **¡cálma~!** calm down!

té [te] *nm* tea

tea ['tea] *nf* torch

teatral [tea'tral] *adj* theatre *cpd*; (*fig*) theatrical

teatro [te'atro] *nm* theatre; (*LITERATURA*) plays *pl*, drama

tebeo [te'ßeo] *nm* comic

techo ['tetʃo] *nm* (*externo*) roof; (*interno*) ceiling; **~ corredizo** sunroof

tecla ['tekla] *nf* key; **~do** *nm* keyboard; **teclear** *vi* (*MUS*) to strum; (*con los dedos*) to tap ♦ *vt* (*INFORM*) to key in

técnica ['teknika] *nf* technique; (*arte, oficio*) craft; *ver tb* **técnico**

técnico, a ['tekniko, a] *adj* technical ♦ *nm/f* technician; (*experto*) expert

tecnócrata [tek'nokrata] *nm/f* technocrat

tecnología [teknolo'xia] *nf* technology;

tecnológico, a *adj* technological
tedio ['teðjo] *nm* boredom, tedium; **~so, a** *adj* boring, tedious
teja ['texa] *nf* (*azulejo*) tile; (*BOT*) lime (tree); **~do** *nm* (tiled) roof
tejemaneje [texema'nexe] *nm* (*lío*) fuss; (*intriga*) intrigue
tejer [te'xer] *vt* to weave; (*hacer punto*) to knit; (*fig*) to fabricate; **tejido** *nm* (*tela*) material, fabric; (*telaraña*) web; (*ANAT*) tissue
tel [tel] *abr* (= *teléfono*) tel
tela ['tela] *nf* (*tejido*) material; (*telaraña*) web; (*en líquido*) skin; **telar** *nm* (*máquina*) loom; **telares** *nmpl* (*fábrica*) textile mill *sg*
telaraña [tela'raɲa] *nf* cobweb
tele ['tele] (*fam*) *nf* telly (*BRIT*), tube (*US*)
tele... ['tele] *pref* tele...; **~comunicación** *nf* telecommunication; **~control** *nm* remote control; **~diario** *nm* television news; **~difusión** *nf* (*television*) broadcast; **~dirigido, a** *adj* remote-controlled
teléf *abr* (= *teléfono*) tel
teleférico [tele'feriko] *nm* (*tren*) cable railway; (*de esquí*) ski-lift
telefonear [telefone'ar] *vi* to telephone
telefónico, a [tele'foniko, a] *adj* telephone *cpd*
telefonillo [telefo'niʎo] *nm* (*de puerta*) intercom
telefonista [telefo'nista] *nm/f* telephonist
teléfono [te'lefono] *nm* (tele)phone; **estar hablando al ~** to be on the phone; **llamar a uno por ~** to ring sb (up) o phone sb (up); **~ móvil** car phone; **~ portátil** mobile phone
telegrafía [teleɣra'fia] *nf* telegraphy
telégrafo [te'leɣrafo] *nm* telegraph
telegrama [tele'ɣrama] *nm* telegram
tele: ~impresor *nm* teleprinter (*BRIT*), teletype (*US*); **~objetivo** *nm* telephoto lens; **~patía** *nf* telepathy; **~pático, a** *adj* telepathic; **~scópico, a** *adj* telescopic; **~scopio** *nm* telescope; **~silla** *nm* chairlift; **~spectador, a** *nm/f* viewer; **~squí** *nm* ski-lift; **~tarjeta** *nf* phonecard; **~tipo** *nm* teletype

televidente [teleßi'ðente] *nm/f* viewer
televisar [teleßi'sar] *vt* to televise
televisión [teleßi'sjon] *nf* television; **~ en colores** colour television
televisor [teleßi'sor] *nm* television set
télex ['teleks] *nm inv* telex
telón [te'lon] *nm* curtain; **~ de acero** (*POL*) iron curtain; **~ de fondo** backcloth, background
tema ['tema] *nm* (*asunto*) subject, topic; (*MUS*) theme ♦ *nf* (*obsesión*) obsession; **temática** *nf* (*social, histórica, artística*) range of topics; **temático, a** *adj* thematic
temblar [tem'blar] *vi* to shake, tremble; (*de frío*) to shiver; **temblón, ona** *adj* shaking; **temblor** *nm* trembling; (*de tierra*) earthquake; **tembloroso, a** *adj* trembling
temer [te'mer] *vt* to fear ♦ *vi* to be afraid; **temo que llegue tarde** I am afraid he may be late
temerario, a [teme'rarjo, a] *adj* (*descuidado*) reckless; (*irreflexivo*) hasty; **temeridad** *nf* (*imprudencia*) rashness; (*audacia*) boldness
temeroso, a [teme'roso, a] *adj* (*miedoso*) fearful; (*que inspira temor*) frightful
temible [te'mißle] *adj* fearsome
temor [te'mor] *nm* (*miedo*) fear; (*duda*) suspicion
témpano ['tempano] *nm*: **~ de hielo** ice-floe
temperamento [tempera'mento] *nm* temperament
temperatura [tempera'tura] *nf* temperature
tempestad [tempes'tað] *nf* storm; **tempestuoso, a** *adj* stormy
templado, a [tem'plaðo, a] *adj* (*moderado*) moderate; (: *en el comer*) frugal; (: *en el beber*) abstemious; (*agua*) lukewarm; (*clima*) mild; (*MUS*) well-tuned; **templanza** *nf* moderation; abstemiousness; mildness
templar [tem'plar] *vt* (*moderar*) to moderate; (*furia*) to restrain; (*calor*) to reduce; (*afinar*) to tune (up); (*acero*) to temper; (*tuerca*) to tighten up; temple

nm (ajuste) tempering; *(afinación)* tuning; *(clima)* temperature; *(pintura)* tempera

templo ['templo] *nm (iglesia)* church; *(pagano etc)* temple

temporada [tempo'raða] *nf* time, period; *(estación)* season

temporal [tempo'ral] *adj (no permanente)* temporary; *(REL)* temporal ♦ *nm* storm

tempranero, a [tempra'nero, a] *adj (BOT)* early; *(persona)* early-rising

temprano [tem'prano, a] *adv* early; *(demasiado pronto)* too soon, too early

ten *vb ver* **tener**

tenaces [te'naθes] *adj pl ver* **tenaz**

tenacidad [tenaθi'ðað] *nf* tenacity; *(dureza)* toughness; *(terquedad)* stubbornness

tenacillas [tena'θiʎas] *nfpl* tongs; *(para el pelo)* curling tongs *(BRIT)* o iron *sg (US)*; *(MED)* forceps

tenaz [te'naθ] *adj (material)* tough; *(persona)* tenacious; *(creencia, resistencia)* stubborn

tenaza(s) [te'naθa(s)] *nf(pl) (MED)* forceps; *(TEC)* pliers; *(ZOOL)* pincers

tendedero [tende'ðero] *nm (para ropa)* drying place; *(cuerda)* clothes line

tendencia [ten'denθja] *nf* tendency; *(proceso)* trend; **tener ~ a** to tend to, have a tendency to; **tendencioso, a** *adj* tendentious

tender [ten'der] *vt (extender)* to spread out; *(colgar)* to hang out; *(vía férrea, cable)* to lay; *(estirar)* to stretch ♦ *vi*: **~ a** to tend to, have a tendency towards; **~se** *vr* to lie down; **~ la cama/la mesa** *(AM)* to make the bed/lay *(BRIT)* o set *(US)* the table

tenderete [tende'rete] *nm (puesto)* stall; *(exposición)* display of goods

tendero, a [ten'dero, a] *nm/f* shopkeeper

tendido, a [ten'diðo, a] *adj (acostado)* lying down, flat; *(colgado)* hanging ♦ *nm (TAUR)* front rows of seats; **a galope ~** flat out

tendón [ten'don] *nm* tendon

tendré *etc vb ver* **tener**

tenebroso, a [tene'βroso, a] *adj (oscuro)* dark; *(fig)* gloomy; *(complot)* sinister

tenedor [tene'ðor] *nm (CULIN)* fork; *(poseedor)* holder; **~ de libros** bookkeeper

teneduría [teneðu'ria] *nf* keeping; **~ de libros** book-keeping

tenencia [te'nenθja] *nf (de casa)* tenancy; *(de oficio)* tenure; *(de propiedad)* possession

---

PALABRA CLAVE

---

tener [te'ner] *vt* **1** *(poseer, gen)* to have; *(en la mano)* to hold; **¿tienes un boli?** have you got a pen?; **va a ~ un niño** she's going to have a baby; **¡ten (o tenga)!, ¡aquí tienes (o tiene)!** here you are!

2 *(edad, medidas)* to be; **tiene 7 años** she's 7 (years old); **tiene 15 cm de largo** it's 15 cm long; *ver* **calor; hambre** *etc*

3 *(considerar)*: **lo tengo por brillante** I consider him to be brilliant; **~ en mucho a uno** to think very highly of sb

4 *(+ pp: = pretérito)*: **tengo terminada ya la mitad del trabajo** I've done half the work already

5: **~ que hacer algo** to have to do sth; **tengo que acabar este trabajo hoy** I have to finish this job today

6: **¿qué tienes, estás enfermo?** what's the matter with you, are you ill?

♦ **~se** *vr* **1**: **~se en pie** to stand up

2: **~se por** to think o.s.; **se tiene por muy listo** he thinks himself very clever

---

tengo *etc vb ver* **tener**

tenia ['tenja] *nf* tapeworm

teniente [te'njente] *nm (rango)* lieutenant; *(ayudante)* deputy

tenis ['tenis] *nm* tennis; **~ de mesa** table tennis; **~ta** *nm/f* tennis player

tenor [te'nor] *nm (sentido)* meaning; *(MUS)* tenor; **a ~ de** on the lines of

tensar [ten'sar] *vt* to tauten; *(arco)* to draw

tensión [ten'sjon] *nf* tension; *(TEC)* stress; *(MED)*: **~ arterial** blood pressure; **tener la ~ alta** to have high blood pressure

tenso, a ['tenso, a] *adj* tense

tentación [tenta'θjon] *nf* temptation

tentáculo [ten'takulo] *nm* tentacle

tentador, a [tenta'ðor, a] *adj* tempting ♦ *nm/f* tempter/temptress

tentar [ten'tar] *vt* (*tocar*) to touch, feel; (*seducir*) to tempt; (*atraer*) to attract; **tentativa** *nf* attempt; **tentativa de asesinato** attempted murder

tentempié [tentem'pje] (*fam*) *nm* snack

tenue ['tenwe] *adj* (*delgado*) thin, slender; (*neblina*) light; (*lazo, vínculo*) slight

teñir [te'ɲir] *vt* to dye; (*fig*) to tinge; **~se** *vr* to dye; **~se el pelo** to dye one's hair

teología [teolo'xia] *nf* theology

teorema [teo'rema] *nm* theorem

teoría [teo'ria] *nf* theory; **en ~** in theory; **teóricamente** *adv* theoretically; **teórico, a** *adj* theoretic(al) ♦ *nm/f* theoretician, theorist; **teorizar** *vi* to theorize

terapéutico, a [tera'peutiko, a] *adj* therapeutic

terapia [te'rapja] *nf* therapy

tercer [ter'θer] *adj ver* **tercero**

tercermundista [terθermun'dista] *adj* Third World *cpd*

tercero, a [ter'θero, a] *adj* (*delante de nmsg:* **tercer**) third ♦ *nm* (*JUR*) third party

terceto [ter'θeto] *nm* trio

terciado, a [ter'θjaðo, a] *adj* slanting

terciar [ter'θjar] *vt* (*llevar*) to wear (across the shoulder) ♦ *vi* (*participar*) to take part; (*hacer de árbitro*) to mediate; **~se** *vr* to come up; **~io, a** *adj* tertiary

tercio ['terθjo] *nm* third

terciopelo [terθjo'pelo] *nm* velvet

terco, a ['terko, a] *adj* obstinate

tergal [ter'ɣal] ® *nm* type of polyester

tergiversar [terxißer'sar] *vt* to distort

termal [ter'mal] *adj* thermal

termas ['termas] *nfpl* hot springs

térmico, a ['termiko, a] *adj* thermal

terminación [termina'θjon] *nf* (*final*) end; (*conclusión*) conclusion, ending

terminal [termi'nal] *adj, nm, nf* terminal

terminante [termi'nante] *adj* (*final*) final, definitive; (*tajante*) categorical; **~mente** *adv:* **~mente prohibido** strictly forbidden

terminar [termi'nar] *vt* (*completar*) to complete, finish; (*concluir*) to end ♦ *vi* (*llegar a su fin*) to end; (*parar*) to stop; (*acabar*) to finish; **~se** *vr* to come to an end; **~ por hacer algo** to end up (by) doing sth

término ['termino] *nm* end, conclusion; (*parada*) terminus; (*límite*) boundary; **~ medio** average; (*fig*) middle way; **en último ~** (*a fin de cuentas*) in the last analysis; (*como último recurso*) as a last resort; **en ~s de** in terms of

terminología [terminolo'xia] *nf* terminology

termodinámico, a [termoði'namiko, a] *adj* thermodynamic

termómetro [ter'mometro] *nm* thermometer

termonuclear [termonukle'ar] *adj* thermonuclear

termo(s) ['termo(s)] ® *nm* Thermos ® (flask)

termostato [termo'stato] *nm* thermostat

ternero, a [ter'nero, a] *nm/f* (*animal*) calf ♦ *nf* (*carne*) veal

ternura [ter'nura] *nf* (*trato*) tenderness; (*palabra*) endearment; (*cariño*) fondness

terquedad [terke'ðað] *nf* obstinacy; (*dureza*) harshness

terrado [te'rraðo] *nm* terrace

terraplén [terra'plen] *nm* (*AGR*) terrace; (*cuesta*) slope

terrateniente [terrate'njente] *nm/f* landowner

terraza [te'rraθa] *nf* (*balcón*) balcony; (*techo*) (flat) roof; (*AGR*) terrace

terremoto [terre'moto] *nm* earthquake

terrenal [terre'nal] *adj* earthly

terreno [te'rreno] *nm* (*tierra*) land; (*parcela*) plot; (*suelo*) soil; (*fig*) field; **un ~** a piece of land

terrestre [te'rrestre] *adj* terrestrial; (*ruta*) land *cpd*

terrible [te'rrißle] *adj* terrible, awful

territorio [terri'torjo] *nm* territory

terrón [te'rron] *nm* (*de azúcar*) lump; (*de tierra*) clod, lump

terror [te'rror] *nm* terror; **~ífico, a** *adj* terrifying; **~ista** *adj, nm/f* terrorist

terruño [te'rruɲo] *nm* (*parcela*) plot; (*fig*) native soil

terso, a ['terso, a] *adj* (*liso*) smooth; (*pulido*) polished; **tersura** *nf* smoothness

tertulia [ter'tulja] *nf* (*reunión informal*) social gathering; (*grupo*) group, circle

tesis ['tesis] *nf inv* thesis

tesón [te'son] *nm* (*firmeza*) firmness; (*tenacidad*) tenacity

tesorero, a [teso'rero, a] *nm/f* treasurer

tesoro [te'soro] *nm* treasure; (*COM, POL*) treasury

testaferro [testa'ferro] *nm* figurehead

testamentaría [testamenta'ria] *nf* execution of a will

testamentario, a [testamen'tarjo, a] *adj* testamentary ♦ *nm/f* executor/executrix

testamento [testa'mento] *nm* will

testar [tes'tar] *vi* to make a will

testarudo, a [testa'ruðo, a] *adj* stubborn

testículo [tes'tikulo] *nm* testicle

testificar [testifi'kar] *vt* to testify; (*fig*) to attest ♦ *vi* to give evidence

testigo [tes'tiɣo] *nm/f* witness; ~ **de cargo/descargo** witness for the prosecution/defence; ~ **ocular** eye witness

testimoniar [testimo'njar] *vt* to testify to; (*fig*) to show; **testimonio** *nm* testimony

teta ['teta] *nf* (*de biberón*) teat; (*ANAT: pezón*) nipple; (: *fam*) breast

tétanos ['tetanos] *nm* tetanus

tetera [te'tera] *nf* teapot

tétrico, a ['tetriko, a] *adj* gloomy, dismal

textil [teks'til] *adj* textile

texto ['teksto] *nm* text; **textual** *adj* textual

textura [teks'tura] *nf* (*de tejido*) texture

tez [teθ] *nf* (*cutis*) complexion; (*color*) colouring

ti [ti] *pron* you; (*reflexivo*) yourself

tía ['tia] *nf* (*pariente*) aunt; (*fam*) chick, bird

tibieza [ti'βjeθa] *nf* (*temperatura*) tepidness; (*fig*) coolness; **tibio, a** *adj* lukewarm

tiburón [tiβu'ron] *nm* shark

tic [tik] *nm* (*ruido*) click; (*de reloj*) tick; (*MED*): ~ **nervioso** nervous tic

tictac [tik'tak] *nm* (*de reloj*) tick tock

tiempo ['tjempo] *nm* time; (*época, período*) age, period; (*METEOROLOGÍA*) weather; (*LING*) tense; (*DEPORTE*) half; **a** ~ in time; **a un** *o* **al mismo** ~ at the same time; **al poco** ~ very soon (after); **se quedó poco** ~ he didn't stay very long; **hace poco** ~ not long ago; **mucho** ~ a long time; **de** ~ **en** ~ from time to time; **hace buen/mal** ~ the weather is fine/bad; **estar a** ~ to be in time; **hace** ~ some time ago; **hacer** ~ to while away the time; **motor de 2** ~**s** two-stroke engine; **primer** ~ first half

tienda ['tjenda] *nf* shop, store; ~ **(de campaña)** tent

tienes *etc vb ver* **tener**

tienta *etc* ['tjenta] *vb ver* **tentar** ♦ *nf*: **andar a** ~**s** to grope one's way along

tiento ['tjento] *vb ver* **tentar** ♦ *nm* (*tacto*) touch; (*precaución*) wariness

tierno, a ['tjerno, a] *adj* (*blando*) tender; (*fresco*) fresh; (*amable*) sweet

tierra ['tjerra] *nf* earth; (*suelo*) soil; (*mundo*) earth, world; (*país*) country, land; ~ **adentro** inland

tieso, a ['tjeso, a] *adj* (*rígido*) rigid; (*duro*) stiff; (*fam: orgulloso*) conceited

tiesto ['tjesto] *nm* flowerpot

tifoidea [tifoi'ðea] *nf* typhoid

tifón [ti'fon] *nm* typhoon

tifus ['tifus] *nm* typhus

tigre ['tiɣre] *nm* tiger

tijera [ti'xera] *nf* scissors *pl*; (*ZOOL*) claw; ~**s** *nfpl* scissors; (*para plantas*) shears

tijereta [tixe'reta] *nf* earwig

tijeretear [tixerete'ar] *vt* to snip

tildar [til'dar] *vt*: ~ **de** to brand as

tilde ['tilde] *nf* (*TIP*) tilde

tilín [ti'lin] *nm* tinkle

tilo ['tilo] *nm* lime tree

timar [ti'mar] *vt* (*robar*) to steal; (*estafar*) to swindle

timbal [tim'bal] *nm* small drum

timbrar [tim'brar] *vt* to stamp

timbre ['timbre] *nm* (*sello*) stamp; (*campanilla*) bell; (*tono*) timbre; (*COM*) stamp duty

timidez [timi'ðeθ] *nf* shyness; **tímido, a**

adj shy

timo ['timo] *nm* swindle

timón [ti'mon] *nm* helm, rudder; **timonel** *nm* helmsman

tímpano ['timpano] *nm* (*ANAT*) eardrum; (*MUS*) small drum

tina ['tina] *nf* tub; (*baño*) bath(tub); **tinaja** *nf* large jar

tinglado [tiŋ'glaðo] *nm* (*cobertizo*) shed; (*fig: truco*) trick; (*intriga*) intrigue

tinieblas [ti'njeβlas] *nfpl* darkness *sg*; (*sombras*) shadows

tino ['tino] *nm* (*habilidad*) skill; (*juicio*) insight

tinta ['tinta] *nf* ink; (*TEC*) dye; (*ARTE*) colour

tinte ['tinte] *nm* (*acto*) dyeing

tintero [tin'tero] *nm* inkwell

tintinear [tintine'ar] *vt* to tinkle

tinto, a ['tinto, a] *adj* (*teñido*) dyed ♦ *nm* red wine

tintorería [tintore'ria] *nf* dry cleaner's

tintura [tin'tura] *nf* (*acto*) dyeing; (*QUÍMICA*) dye; (*farmacéutico*) tincture

tío ['tio] *nm* (*pariente*) uncle; (*fam: individuo*) bloke (*BRIT*), guy

tiovivo [tio'βiβo] *nm* merry-go-round

típico, a ['tipiko, a] *adj* typical

tipo ['tipo] *nm* (*clase*) type, kind; (*norma*) norm; (*patrón*) pattern; (*hombre*) fellow; (*ANAT: de hombre*) build; (: *de mujer*) figure; (*IMPRENTA*) type; ~ **bancario/de descuento/de interés/de cambio** bank/discount/interest/exchange rate

tipografía [tipoɣra'fia] *nf* (*tipo*) printing *cpd*; (*lugar*) printing press; **tipográfico, a** *adj* printing *cpd*

tíquet ['tiket] (*pl* ~**s**) *nm* ticket; (*en tienda*) cash slip

tiquismiquis [tikis'mikis] *nm inv* fussy person ♦ *nmpl* (*querellas*) squabbling *sg*; (*escrúpulos*) silly scruples

tira ['tira] *nf* strip; (*fig*) abundance; ~ **y afloja** give and take

tirabuzón [tiraβu'θon] *nm* (*rizo*) curl

tirachinas [tira'tʃinas] *nm inv* catapult

tirada [ti'raða] *nf* (*acto*) cast, throw; (*distancia*) distance; (*serie*) series; (*TIP*) printing, edition; **de una** ~ at one go

tiradero [tira'ðero] *nm* rubbish dump

tirado, a [ti'raðo, a] *adj* (*barato*) dirt-cheap; (*fam: fácil*) very easy

tirador [tira'ðor] *nm* (*mango*) handle

tiranía [tira'nia] *nf* tyranny; **tirano, a** *adj* tyrannical ♦ *nm/f* tyrant

tirante [ti'rante] *adj* (*cuerda etc*) tight, taut; (*relaciones*) strained ♦ *nm* (*ARQ*) brace; (*TEC*) stay; (*correa*) shoulder strap; ~**s** *nmpl* (*de pantalón*) braces (*BRIT*), suspenders (*US*); **tirantez** *nf* tightness; (*fig*) tension

tirar [ti'rar] *vt* to throw; (*dejar caer*) to drop; (*volcar*) to upset; (*derribar*) to knock down *o* over; (*jalar*) to pull; (*desechar*) to throw out *o* away; (*disipar*) to squander; (*imprimir*) to print; (*dar: golpe*) to deal ♦ *vi* (*disparar*) to shoot; (*jalar*) to pull; (*fig*) to draw; (*fam: andar*) to go; (*tender a, buscar realizar*) to tend to; (*DEPORTE*) to shoot; ~**se** *vr* to throw o.s.; (*fig*) to cheapen o.s.; ~ **abajo** to bring down, destroy; **tira más a su padre** he takes more after his father; **ir tirando** to manage; **a todo** ~ at the most

tirita [ti'rita] *nf* (sticking) plaster (*BRIT*), bandaid (*US*)

tiritar [tiri'tar] *vi* to shiver

tiro ['tiro] *nm* (*lanzamiento*) throw; (*disparo*) shot; (*disparar*) shooting; (*DEPORTE*) shot; (*GOLF, TENIS*) drive; (*alcance*) range; (*golpe*) blow; (*engaño*) hoax; ~ **al blanco** target practice; **caballo de** ~ cart-horse; **andar de** ~**s largos** to be all dressed up; **al** ~ (*AM*) at once

tirón [ti'ron] *nm* (*sacudida*) pull, tug; **de un** ~ in one go, all at once

tiroteo [tiro'teo] *nm* exchange of shots, shooting

tísico, a ['tisiko, a] *adj* consumptive

tisis ['tisis] *nf inv* consumption, tuberculosis

títere ['titere] *nm* puppet

titiritero, a [titiri'tero, a] *nm/f* puppeteer

titubeante [tituβe'ante] *adj* (*inestable*) shaky, tottering; (*farfullante*) stammering; (*dudoso*) hesitant

titubear [tituβe'ar] *vi* to stagger; to stammer; (*fig*) to hesitate; **titubeo**

staggering; stammering; hesitation
titulado, a [titu'laðo, a] *adj* (*libro*)
entitled; (*persona*) titled
titular [titu'lar] *adj* titular ♦ *nm/f*
occupant ♦ *nm* headline ♦ *vt* to title; ~**se**
vr to be entitled; **título** *nm* title; (*de
diario*) headline; (*certificado*) professional
qualification; (*universitario*) (university)
degree; (*fig*) right; **a título de** in the
capacity of
tiza ['tiθa] *nf* chalk
tiznar [tiθ'nar] *vt* to blacken; (*fig*) to
tarnish
tizo ['tiθo] *nm* brand
tizón [ti'θon] *nm* brand; (*fig*) stain
toalla [to'aʎa] *nf* towel
tobillo [to'βiʎo] *nm* ankle
tobogán [toβo'ɣan] *nm* toboggan;
(*montaña rusa*) roller-coaster;
(*resbaladilla*) chute, slide
toca ['toka] *nf* headdress
tocadiscos [toka'ðiskos] *nm inv* record
player
tocado, a [to'kaðo, a] *adj* (*fam*) touched
♦ *nm* headdress
tocador [toka'ðor] *nm* (*mueble*) dressing
table; (*cuarto*) boudoir; (*fam*) ladies'
toilet (*BRIT*) o room (*US*)
tocante [to'kante]: ~ **a** *prep* with regard
to
tocar [to'kar] *vt* to touch; (*MUS*) to play;
(*topar con*) to run into, strike; (*referirse
a*) to allude to; (*padecer*) to suffer ♦ *vi* (*a
la puerta*) to knock (on *o* at the door);
(*ser de turno*) to fall to, be the turn of;
(*ser hora*) to be due; (*barco, avión*) to
call at; (*atañer*) to concern; ~**se** *vr*
(*cubrirse la cabeza*) to cover one's head;
(*tener contacto*) to touch (each other);
por lo que a mí me toca as far as I am
concerned
tocayo, a [to'kajo, a] *nm/f* namesake
tocino [to'θino] *nm* bacon
todavía [toða'βia] *adv* (*aun*) even; (*aún*)
still, yet; ~ **más** yet more; ~ **no** not yet

todo, a ['toðo, a] *adj* 1 (*con artículo sg*)
all; **toda la carne** all the meat; **toda la**
noche all night, the whole night; ~ **el
libro** the whole book; **toda una botella**
a whole bottle; ~ **lo contrario** quite the
opposite; **está toda sucia** she's all dirty;
por ~ el país throughout the whole
country
2 (*con artículo pl*) all; every; ~**s los
libros** all the books; **todas las noches**
every night; ~**s los que quieran salir**
all those who want to leave
♦ *pron* 1 everything, all; ~**s** everyone,
everybody; **lo sabemos** ~ we know
everything; ~**s querían más tiempo**
everybody *o* everyone wanted more
time; **nos marchamos** ~**s** all of us left
2: **con** ~: **con** ~ **él me sigue gustando**
even so I still like him
♦ *adv* all; **vaya** ~ **seguido** keep straight
on *o* ahead
♦ *nm*: **como un** ~ as a whole; **del** ~: **no
me agrada del** ~ I don't entirely like it

todopoderoso, a [toðopoðe'roso, a] *adj*
all powerful; (*REL*) almighty
toga ['toɣa] *nf* toga; (*ESCOL*) gown
Tokio ['tokjo] *n* Tokyo
toldo ['toldo] *nm* (*para el sol*) sunshade
(*BRIT*), parasol; (*tienda*) marquee
tolerancia [tole'ranθja] *nf* tolerance;
tolerante *adj* (*sociedad*) liberal; (*persona*)
open-minded
tolerar [tole'rar] *vt* to tolerate; (*resistir*) to
endure
toma ['toma] *nf* (*acto*) taking; (*MED*) dose;
~ **(de corriente)** socket
tomar [to'mar] *vt* to take; (*aspecto*) to
take on; (*beber*) to drink ♦ *vi* to take;
(*AM*) to drink; ~**se** *vr* to take; ~**se por**
to consider o.s. to be; ~ **a bien/a mal** to
take well/badly; ~ **en serio** to take seriously; ~ **el pelo a alguien** to pull sb's
leg; ~**la con uno** to pick a quarrel with
sb
tomate [to'mate] *nm* tomato
tomavistas [toma'βistas] *nm inv* movie
camera
tomillo [to'miʎo] *nm* thyme
tomo ['tomo] *nm* (*libro*) volume
ton [ton] *abr* = **tonelada** ♦ *nm*: **sin** ~ **ni**

son without rhyme or reason
tonada [to'naða] *nf* tune
tonalidad [tonali'ðað] *nf* tone
tonel [to'nel] *nm* barrel
tonelada [tone'laða] *nf* ton; **tonelaje** *nm* tonnage
tónica ['tonika] *nf* (*MUS*) tonic; (*fig*) keynote
tónico, a ['toniko, a] *adj* tonic ♦ *nm* (*MED*) tonic
tonificar [tonifi'kar] *vt* to tone up
tono ['tono] *nm* tone; **fuera de ~** inappropriate; **darse ~** to put on airs
tontería [tonte'ria] *nf* (*estupidez*) foolishness; (*cosa*) stupid thing; (*acto*) foolish act; **~s** *nfpl* (*disparates*) rubbish *sg*, nonsense *sg*
tonto, a ['tonto, a] *adj* stupid, silly ♦ *nm/f* fool; (*payaso*) clown
topar [to'par] *vt* (*tropezar*) to bump into; (*encontrar*) to find, come across; (*ZOOL*) to butt ♦ *vi*: ~ **contra** *o* **en** to run into; ~ **con** to run up against
tope ['tope] *adj* maximum ♦ *nm* (*fin*) end; (*límite*) limit; (*FERRO*) buffer; (*AUTO*) bumper; **al ~** end to end
tópico, a ['topiko, a] *adj* topical ♦ *nm* platitude
topo ['topo] *nm* (*ZOOL*) mole; (*fig*) blunderer
topografía [topoɣra'fia] *nf* topography; **topógrafo, a** *nm/f* topographer
toque *etc* ['toke] *vb ver* **tocar** ♦ *nm* touch; (*MUS*) beat; (*de campana*) peal; (*fig*) crux; **dar un ~ a** to test; ~ **de queda** curfew; **~tear** *vt* to handle
toqué *vb ver* **tocar**
toquilla [to'kiʎa] *nf* (*pañuelo*) headscarf; (*chal*) shawl
tórax ['toraks] *nm* thorax
torbellino [torbe'ʎino] *nm* whirlwind; (*fig*) whirl
torcedura [torθe'ðura] *nf* twist; (*MED*) sprain
torcer [tor'θer] *vt* to twist; (*la esquina*) to turn; (*MED*) to sprain ♦ *vi* (*desviar*) to turn off; **~se** *vr* (*ladearse*) to bend; (*desviarse*) to go astray; (*fracasar*) to go wrong; **torcido, a** *adj* twisted; (*fig*)

crooked ♦ *nm* curl
tordo, a ['torðo, a] *adj* dappled ♦ *nm* thrush
torear [tore'ar] *vt* (*fig: evadir*) to avoid; (*jugar con*) to tease ♦ *vi* to fight bulls; **toreo** *nm* bullfighting; **torero, a** *nm/f* bullfighter
tormenta [tor'menta] *nf* storm; (*fig: confusión*) turmoil
tormento [tor'mento] *nm* torture; (*fig*) anguish
tornar [tor'nar] *vt* (*devolver*) to return, give back; (*transformar*) to transform ♦ *vi* to go back; **~se** *vr* (*ponerse*) to become
tornasolado, a [tornaso'laðo, a] *adj* (*brillante*) iridescent; (*reluciente*) shimmering
torneo [tor'neo] *nm* tournament
tornillo [tor'niʎo] *nm* screw
torniquete [torni'kete] *nm* (*puerta*) turnstile; (*MED*) tourniquet
torno ['torno] *nm* (*TEC*) winch; (*tambor*) drum; **en ~ (a)** round, about
toro ['toro] *nm* bull; (*fam*) he-man; **los ~s** bullfighting
toronja [to'ronxa] *nf* grapefruit
torpe ['torpe] *adj* (*poco hábil*) clumsy, awkward; (*necio*) dim; (*lento*) slow
torpedo [tor'peðo] *nm* torpedo
torpeza [tor'peθa] *nf* (*falta de agilidad*) clumsiness; (*lentitud*) slowness; (*error*) mistake
torre ['torre] *nf* tower; (*de petróleo*) derrick
torrefacto, a [torre'fakto, a] *adj* roasted
torrente [to'rrente] *nm* torrent
tórrido, a ['torriðo, a] *adj* torrid
torrija [to'rrixa] *nf* French toast
torsión [tor'sjon] *nf* twisting
torso ['torso] *nm* torso
torta ['torta] *nf* cake; (*fam*) slap
tortícolis [tor'tikolis] *nm inv* stiff neck
tortilla [tor'tiʎa] *nf* omelette; (*AM*) maize pancake; ~ **francesa/española** plain/potato omelette
tórtola ['tortola] *nf* turtledove
tortuga [tor'tuɣa] *nf* tortoise
tortuoso, a [tor'twoso, a] *adj* winding

tortura [tor'tura] *nf* torture; **torturar** *vt* to torture

tos [tos] *nf* cough; ~ **ferina** whooping cough

tosco, a ['tosko, a] *adj* coarse

toser [to'ser] *vi* to cough

tostada [tos'taða] *nf* piece of toast; **tostado, a** *adj* toasted; (*por el sol*) dark brown; (*piel*) tanned

tostador [tosta'ðor] *nm* toaster

tostar [tos'tar] *vt* to toast; (*café*) to roast; (*persona*) to tan; ~**se** *vr* to get brown

total [to'tal] *adj* total ♦ *adv* in short; (*al fin y al cabo*) when all is said and done ♦ *nm* total; ~ **que** to cut (*BRIT*) o make (*US*) a long story short

totalidad [totali'ðað] *nf* whole

totalitario, a [totali'tarjo, a] *adj* totalitarian

tóxico, a ['toksiko, a] *adj* toxic ♦ *nm* poison; **toxicómano, a** *nm/f* drug addict

toxina [to'ksina] *nf* toxin

tozudo, a [to'θuðo, a] *adj* obstinate

traba ['traβa] *nf* bond, tie; (*cadena*) shackle

trabajador, a [traβaxa'ðor, a] *adj* hard-working ♦ *nm/f* worker

trabajar [traβa'xar] *vt* to work; (*AGR*) to till; (*empeñarse en*) to work at; (*empujar: persona*) to push; (*convencer*) to persuade ♦ *vi* to work; (*esforzarse*) to strive; **trabajo** *nm* work; (*tarea*) task; (*POL*) labour; (*fig*) effort; **tomarse el trabajo de** to take the trouble to; **trabajo por turno/a destajo** shift work/piecework; **trabajoso, a** *adj* hard

trabalenguas [traβa'lengwas] *nm inv* tongue twister

trabar [tra'βar] *vt* (*juntar*) to join, unite; (*atar*) to tie down, fetter; (*agarrar*) to seize; (*amistad*) to strike up; ~**se** *vr* to become entangled; **trabársele a uno la lengua** to be tongue-tied

tracción [trak'θjon] *nf* traction; ~ **delantera/trasera** front-wheel/rear-wheel drive

tractor [trak'tor] *nm* tractor

tradición [traði'θjon] *nf* tradition; **tradicional** *adj* traditional

traducción [traðuk'θjon] *nf* translation

traducir [traðu'θir] *vt* to translate; **traductor, a** *nm/f* translator

traer [tra'er] *vt* to bring; (*llevar*) to carry; (*ropa*) to wear; (*incluir*) to carry; (*fig*) to cause; ~**se** *vr*: ~**se algo** to be up to sth

traficar [trafi'kar] *vi* to trade

tráfico ['trafiko] *nm* (*COM*) trade; (*AUTO*) traffic

tragaluz [traɣa'luθ] *nm* skylight

tragaperras [traɣa'perras] *nm o f inv* slot machine

tragar [tra'ɣar] *vt* to swallow; (*devorar*) to devour, bolt down; ~**se** *vr* to swallow

tragedia [tra'xeðja] *nf* tragedy; **trágico, a** *adj* tragic

trago ['traɣo] *nm* (*líquido*) drink; (*bocado*) gulp; (*fam: de bebida*) swig; (*desgracia*) blow

traición [trai'θjon] *nf* treachery; (*JUR*) treason; (*una ~*) act of treachery; **traicionar** *vt* to betray

traicionero, a [traiθjo'nero, a] *adj* treacherous

traidor, a [trai'ðor, a] *adj* treacherous ♦ *nm/f* traitor

traigo *etc vb ver* **traer**

traje ['traxe] *vb ver* **traer** ♦ *nm* (*de hombre*) suit; (*de mujer*) dress; (*vestido típico*) costume; ~ **de baño** swimsuit; ~ **de luces** bullfighter's costume

trajera *etc vb ver* **traer**

trajín [tra'xin] *nm* haulage; (*fam: movimiento*) bustle; **trajinar** *vt* (*llevar*) to carry, transport ♦ *vi* (*moverse*) to bustle about; (*viajar*) to travel around

trama ['trama] *nf* (*intriga*) plot; (*de tejido*) weft (*BRIT*), woof (*US*); **tramar** *vt* to plot; (*TEC*) to weave

tramitar [trami'tar] *vt* (*asunto*) to transact; (*negociar*) to negotiate; (*manejar*) to handle

trámite ['tramite] *nm* (*paso*) step; (*JUR*) transaction; ~**s** *nmpl* (*burocracia*) procedure *sg*; (*JUR*) proceedings

tramo ['tramo] *nm* (*de tierra*) plot; (*de escalera*) flight; (*de vía*) section

tramoya [tra'moja] *nf* (*TEATRO*) piece of stage machinery; (*fig*) scheme;

tramoyista *nm/f* scene shifter; (*fig*) trickster

trampa ['trampa] *nf* trap; (*en el suelo*) trapdoor; (*engaño*) trick; (*fam*) fiddle; **trampear** *vt, vi* to cheat

trampolín [trampo'lin] *nm* trampoline; (*de piscina etc*) diving board

tramposo, a [tram'poso, a] *adj* crooked, cheating ♦ *nm/f* crook, cheat

tranca ['tranka] *nf* (*palo*) stick; (*de puerta, ventana*) bar; **trancar** *vt* to bar

trance ['tranθe] *nm* (*momento difícil*) difficult moment *o* juncture; (*estado hipnotizado*) trance

tranco ['tranko] *nm* stride

tranquilidad [trankili'ðað] *nf* (*calma*) calmness, stillness; (*paz*) peacefulness

tranquilizar [trankili'θar] *vt* (*calmar*) to calm (down); (*asegurar*) to reassure; **~se** *vr* to calm down; **tranquilo, a** *adj* (*calmado*) calm; (*apacible*) peaceful; (*mar*) calm; (*mente*) untroubled

transacción [transak'θjon] *nf* transaction

transbordador [transβorða'ðor] *nm* ferry

transbordar [transβor'ðar] *vt* to transfer; **transbordo** *nm* transfer; **hacer transbordo** to change (trains *etc*)

transcurrir [transku'rrir] *vi* (*tiempo*) to pass; (*hecho*) to turn out

transcurso [trans'kurso] *nm*: **~ del tiempo** lapse (of time)

transeúnte [transe'unte] *adj* transient ♦ *nm/f* passer-by

transferencia [transfe'renθja] *nf* transference; (*COM*) transfer

transferir [transfe'rir] *vt* to transfer

transformador [transforma'ðor] *nm* (*ELEC*) transformer

transformar [transfor'mar] *vt* to transform; (*convertir*) to convert

tránsfuga ['transfuγa] *nm/f* (*MIL*) deserter; (*POL*) turncoat

transfusión [transfu'sjon] *nf* transfusion

transición [transi'θjon] *nf* transition

transigir [transi'xir] *vi* to compromise, make concessions

transistor [transis'tor] *nm* transistor

transitar [transi'tar] *vi* to go (from place to place); **tránsito** *nm* transit; (*AUTO*)

traffic; **transitorio, a** *adj* transitory

transmisión [transmi'sjon] *nf* (*TEC*) transmission; (*transferencia*) transfer; **~ en directo/exterior** live/outside broadcast

transmitir [transmi'tir] *vt* to transmit; (*RADIO, TV*) to broadcast

transparencia [transpa'renθja] *nf* transparency; (*claridad*) clearness, clarity; (*foto*) slide

transparentar [transparen'tar] *vt* to reveal ♦ *vi* to be transparent; **transparente** *adj* transparent; (*claro*) clear; (*ligero*) diáphanous

transpirar [transpi'rar] *vi* to perspire; (*fig*) to transpire

transportar [transpor'tar] *vt* to transport; (*llevar*) to carry; **transporte** *nm* transport; (*COM*) haulage

transversal [transβer'sal] *adj* transverse, cross

tranvía [tram'bia] *nm* tram

trapecio [tra'peθjo] *nm* trapeze; **trapecista** *nm/f* trapeze artist

trapero, a [tra'pero, a] *nm/f* ragman

trapicheo [trapi'tʃeo] (*fam*) *nm* scheme, fiddle

trapo ['trapo] *nm* (*tela*) rag; (*de cocina*) cloth; **poner un ~ a** (*o* **por**) to dust

tráquea ['trakea] *nf* windpipe

traqueteo [trake'teo] *nm* (*golpeteo*) rattling

tras [tras] *prep* (*detrás*) behind; (*después*) after

trasatlántico [trasat'lantiko] *nm* (*barco*) (cabin) cruiser

trascendencia [trasθen'denθja] *nf* (*importancia*) importance; (*FILOSOFÍA*) transcendence

trascendental [trasθenden'tal] *adj* important; (*FILOSOFÍA*) transcendental

trascender [trasθen'der] *vi* (*noticias*) to come out; (*suceso*) to have a wide effect

trasero, a [tra'sero, a] *adj* back, rear ♦ *nm* (*ANAT*) bottom

trasfondo [tras'fondo] *nm* background

trasgredir [trasγre'ðir] *vt* to contravene

trashumante [trasu'mante] *adj* (*animales*) migrating

trasladar [traslaˈðar] *vt* to move; (*persona*) to transfer; (*postergar*) to postpone; (*copiar*) to copy; **~se** *vr* (*mudarse*) to move; **traslado** *nm* move; (*mudanza*) move, removal

traslucir [trasluˈθir] *vt* to show; **~se** *vr* to be translucent; (*fig*) to be revealed

trasluz [trasˈluθ] *nm* reflected light; **al ~** against the light

trasnochador, a [trasnotʃaˈðor, a] *nm/f* night owl

trasnochar [trasnoˈtʃar] *vi* (*acostarse tarde*) to stay up late; (*no dormir*) to have a sleepless night

traspapelar [traspapeˈlar] *vt* (*document, carta*) to mislay, misplace

traspasar [traspaˈsar] *vt* (*suj: bala etc*) to pierce, go through; (*propiedad*) to sell, transfer; (*calle*) to cross over; (*límites*) to go beyond; (*ley*) to break; **traspaso** *nm* (*venta*) transfer, sale

traspié [trasˈpje] *nm* (*tropezón*) trip; (*fig*) blunder

trasplantar [trasplanˈtar] *vt* to transplant

traste [ˈtraste] *nm* (*MUS*) fret; **dar al ~ con algo** to ruin sth

trastero [trasˈtero] *nm* storage room

trastienda [trasˈtjenda] *nf* back of shop

trasto [ˈtrasto] *nm* (*pey*) (*cosa*) piece of junk; (*persona*) dead loss

trastornado, a [trastorˈnaðo, a] *adj* (*loco*) mad, crazy

trastornar [trastorˈnar] *vt* to overturn, upset; (*fig: ideas*) to confuse; (: *nervios*) to shatter; (: *persona*) to drive crazy; **~se** *vr* (*volverse loco*) to go mad *o* crazy; **trastorno** *nm* (*acto*) overturning; (*confusión*) confusion

tratable [traˈtaβle] *adj* friendly

tratado [traˈtaðo] *nm* (*POL*) treaty; (*COM*) agreement

tratamiento [trataˈmjento] *nm* treatment; **~ de textos** (*INFORM*) word processing *cpd*

tratar [traˈtar] *vt* (*ocuparse de*) to treat; (*manejar, TEC*) to handle; (*MED*) to treat; (*dirigirse a: persona*) to address ♦ *vi:* **~ de** (*hablar sobre*) to deal with, be about; (*intentar*) to try to; **~se** *vr* to treat each

other; **~ con** (*COM*) to trade in; (*negociar*) to negotiate with; (*tener contactos*) to have dealings with; **¿de qué se trata?** what's it about?; **trato** *nm* dealings *pl*; (*relaciones*) relationship; (*comportamiento*) manner; (*COM*) agreement; (*título*) (form of) address

trauma [ˈtrauma] *nm* trauma

través [traˈβes] *nm* (*fig*) reverse; **al ~** across, crossways; **a ~ de** across; (*sobre*) over; (*por*) through

travesaño [traβeˈsaɲo] *nm* (*ARQ*) crossbeam; (*DEPORTE*) crossbar

travesía [traβeˈsia] *nf* (*calle*) cross-street; (*NAUT*) crossing

travesura [traβeˈsura] *nf* (*broma*) prank; (*ingenio*) wit

traviesa [traˈβjesa] *nf* (*ARQ*) crossbeam

travieso, a [traˈβjeso, a] *adj* (*niño*) naughty

trayecto [traˈjekto] *nm* (*ruta*) road, way; (*viaje*) journey; (*tramo*) stretch; (*curso*) course; **~ria** *nf* trajectory; (*fig*) path

traza [ˈtraθa] *nf* (*aspecto*) looks *pl*; (*señal*) sign; **~do, a** *adj:* **bien ~do** shapely, well-formed ♦ *nm* (*ARQ*) plan, design; (*fig*) outline

trazar [traˈθar] *vt* (*ARQ*) to plan; (*ARTE*) to sketch; (*fig*) to trace; (*plan*) to follow; **trazo** *nm* (*línea*) line; (*bosquejo*) sketch

trébol [ˈtreβol] *nm* (*BOT*) clover

trece [ˈtreθe] *num* thirteen

trecho [ˈtretʃo] *nm* (*distancia*) distance; (*de tiempo*) while; (*fam*) piece; **de ~ en ~** at intervals

tregua [ˈtreɣwa] *nf* (*MIL*) truce; (*fig*) lull

treinta [ˈtreinta] *num* thirty

tremendo, a [treˈmendo, a] *adj* (*terrible*) terrible; (*imponente: cosa*) imposing; (*fam: fabuloso*) tremendous

trémulo, a [ˈtremulo, a] *adj* quivering

tren [tren] *nm* train; **~ de aterrizaje** undercarriage

trenca [ˈtrenka] *nf* duffel coat

trenza [ˈtrenθa] *nf* (*de pelo*) plait (*BRIT*), braid (*US*); **trenzar** *vt* (*pelo*) to plait, braid; **trenzarse** *vr* (*AM*) to become involved

trepadora [trepaˈðora] *nf* (*BOT*) climber

trepar [tre'par] *vt, vi* to climb

trepidante [trepi'ðante] *adj* (*acción*) fast; (*ritmo*) hectic

trepidar [trepi'ðar] *vi* to shake, vibrate

tres [tres] *num* three

tresillo [tre'siʎo] *nm* three-piece suite; (*MUS*) triplet

treta ['treta] *nf* (*COM etc*) gimmick; (*fig*) trick

triángulo ['trjangulo] *nm* triangle

tribu ['trißu] *nf* tribe

tribuna [tri'ßuna] *nf* (*plataforma*) platform; (*DEPORTE*) (grand)stand; (*fig*) public speaking

tribunal [trißu'nal] *nm* (*JUR*) court; (*comisión, fig*) tribunal

tributar [trißu'tar] *vt* (*gen*) to pay; **tributo** *nm* (*COM*) tax

tricotar [triko'tar] *vi* to knit

trigal [tri'yal] *nm* wheat field

trigo ['triɣo] *nm* wheat

trigueño, a [tri'ɣeɲo, a] *adj* (*pelo*) corn-coloured; (*piel*) olive-skinned

trillado, a [tri'ʎaðo, a] *adj* threshed; (*fig*) trite, hackneyed; **trilladora** *nf* threshing machine

trillar [tri'ʎar] *vt* (*AGR*) to thresh

trimestral [trimes'tral] *adj* quarterly; (*ESCOL*) termly

trimestre [tri'mestre] *nm* (*ESCOL*) term

trinar [tri'nar] *vi* (*pájaros*) to sing; (*rabiar*) to fume, be angry

trincar [trin'kar] *vt* (*atar*) to tie up; (*inmovilizar*) to pinion

trinchar [trin'tʃar] *vt* to carve

trinchera [trin'tʃera] *nf* (*fosa*) trench

trineo [tri'neo] *nm* sledge

trinidad [trini'ðað] *nf* trio; (*REL*): **la T~** the Trinity

trino ['trino] *nm* trill

tripa ['tripa] *nf* (*ANAT*) intestine; (*fam: tb:* **~s**) insides *pl*

triple ['triple] *adj* triple

triplicado, a [tripli'kaðo, a] *adj*: **por ~** in triplicate

tripulación [tripula'θjon] *nf* crew

tripulante [tripu'lante] *nm/f* crewman/woman

tripular [tripu'lar] *vt* (*barco*) to man;

(*AUTO*) to drive

triquiñuela [triki'ɲwela] *nf* trick

tris [tris] *nm inv* crack; **en un ~** in an instant

triste ['triste] *adj* (*afligido*) sad; (*sombrío*) melancholy, gloomy; (*lamentable*) sorry, miserable; **~za** *nf* (*aflicción*) sadness; (*melancolía*) melancholy

triturar [tritu'rar] *vt* (*moler*) to grind; (*mascar*) to chew

triunfar [trjun'far] *vi* (*tener éxito*) to triumph; (*ganar*) to win; **triunfo** *nm* triumph

trivial [tri'ßjal] *adj* trivial; **~izar** *vt* to minimize, play down

triza ['triθa] *nf*: **hacer ~s** to smash to bits; (*papel*) to tear to shreds

trocar [tro'kar] *vt* to exchange

trocear [troθe'ar] *vt* (*carne, manzana*) to cut up, cut into pieces

trocha ['trotʃa] *nf* short cut

troche ['trotʃe]: **a ~ y moche** *adv* helter-skelter, pell-mell

trofeo [tro'feo] *nm* (*premio*) trophy; (*éxito*) success

tromba ['tromba] *nf* whirlwind

trombón [trom'bon] *nm* trombone

trombosis [trom'bosis] *nf inv* thrombosis

trompa ['trompa] *nf* horn; (*trompo*) humming top; (*hocico*) snout; (*fam*): **cogerse una ~** to get tight

trompazo [trom'paθo] *nm* bump, bang

trompeta [trom'peta] *nf* trumpet; (*clarín*) bugle

trompicón [trompi'kon]: **a ~es** *adv* in fits and starts

trompo ['trompo] *nm* spinning top

trompón [trom'pon] *nm* bump

tronar [tro'nar] *vt* (*AM*) to shoot ♦ *vi* to thunder; (*fig*) to rage

tronchar [tron'tʃar] *vt* (*árbol*) to chop down; (*fig: vida*) to cut short; (*: esperanza*) to shatter; (*persona*) to tire out; **~se** *vr* to fall down

tronco ['tronko] *nm* (*de árbol, ANAT*) trunk

tronera [tro'nera] *nf* (*MIL*) loophole; (*ARQ*) small window

trono ['trono] *nm* throne

tropa ['tropa] *nf* (*MIL*) troop; (*soldados*)

soldiers *pl*

tropel [tro'pel] *nm* (*muchedumbre*) crowd

tropezar [trope'θar] *vi* to trip, stumble;
(*fig*) to slip up; ~ **con** to run into; (*topar con*) to bump into; **tropezón** *nm* trip;
(*fig*) blunder

tropical [tropi'kal] *adj* tropical

trópico ['tropiko] *nm* tropic

tropiezo [tro'pjeθo] *vb ver* **tropezar** ♦ *nm*
(*error*) slip, blunder; (*desgracia*) misfortune; (*obstáculo*) snag

trotamundos [trota'mundos] *nm inv*
globetrotter

trotar [tro'tar] *vi* to trot; **trote** *nm* trot;
(*fam*) travelling; **de mucho trote** hardwearing

trozo ['troθo] *nm* bit, piece

trucha ['trutʃa] *nf* trout

truco ['truko] *nm* (*habilidad*) knack;
(*engaño*) trick

trueno ['trweno] *nm* thunder; (*estampido*)
bang

trueque *etc* ['trweke] *vb ver* **trocar** ♦ *nm*
exchange; (*COM*) barter

trufa ['trufa] *nf* (*BOT*) truffle

truhán, ana [tru'an, ana] *nm/f* rogue

truncar [trun'kar] *vt* (*cortar*) to truncate;
(*fig: la vida etc*) to cut short; (*: el desarrollo*) to stunt

tu [tu] *adj* your

tú [tu] *pron* you

tubérculo [tu'βerkulo] *nm* (*BOT*) tuber

tuberculosis [tuβerku'losis] *nf inv*
tuberculosis

tubería [tuβe'ria] *nf* pipes *pl*; (*conducto*)
pipeline

tubo ['tuβo] *nm* tube, pipe; ~ **de ensayo**
test tube; ~ **de escape** exhaust (pipe)

tuerca ['twerka] *nf* nut

tuerto, a ['twerto, a] *adj* blind in one eye
♦ *nm/f* one-eyed person

tuerza *etc vb ver* **torcer**

tuétano ['twetano] *nm* marrow; (*BOT*) pith

tufo ['tufo] *nm* vapour; (*fig: pey*) stench

tugurio [tu'yurjo] *nm* slum

tul [tul] *nm* tulle

tulipán [tuli'pan] *nm* tulip

tullido, a [tu'ʎiðo, a] *adj* crippled

tumba ['tumba] *nf* (*sepultura*) tomb

tumbar [tum'bar] *vt* to knock down; ~**se**
vr (*echarse*) to lie down; (*extenderse*) to
stretch out

tumbo ['tumbo] *nm* (*caída*) fall; (*de vehículo*) jolt

tumbona [tum'bona] *nf* (*butaca*) easy
chair; (*de playa*) deckchair (*BRIT*), beach
chair (*US*)

tumor [tu'mor] *nm* tumour

tumulto [tu'multo] *nm* turmoil

tuna ['tuna] *nf* (*BOT*) prickly pear; (*MUS*)
student music group; *ver tb* **tuno**

tunante [tu'nante] *nm/f* rascal

tunda ['tunda] *nf* (*golpeo*) beating

túnel ['tunel] *nm* tunnel

Túnez ['tuneθ] *nm* Tunisia; (*ciudad*)
Tunis

tuno, a ['tuno, a] *nm/f* (*fam*) rogue ♦ *nm*
member of student music group

tuntún [tun'tun]: **al** ~ *adv* thoughtlessly

tupido, a [tu'piðo, a] *adj* (*denso*) dense;
(*tela*) close-woven; (*fig*) dim

turba ['turβa] *nf* crowd

turbación [turβa'θjon] *nf* (*molestia*)
disturbance; (*preocupación*) worry;
turbado, a *adj* (*molesto*) disturbed; (*preocupado*) worried

turbante [tur'βante] *nm* turban

turbar [tur'βar] *vt* (*molestar*) to disturb;
(*incomodar*) to upset; ~**se** *vr* to be
disturbed

turbina [tur'βina] *nf* turbine

turbio, a ['turβjo, a] *adj* cloudy; (*tema etc*)
confused ♦ *adv* indistinctly

turbulencia [turβu'lenθja] *nf* turbulence;
(*fig*) restlessness; **turbulento, a** *adj*
turbulent; (*fig: intranquilo*) restless;
(*: ruidoso*) noisy

turco, a ['turko, a] *adj* Turkish ♦ *nm/f*
Turk

turismo [tu'rismo] *nm* tourism; (*coche*)
saloon car; **turista** *nm/f* tourist;
turístico, a *adj* tourist *cpd*

turnar [tur'nar] *vi* to take (it in) turns;
~**se** *vr* to take (it in) turns; **turno** *nm*
(*INDUSTRIA*) shift; (*oportunidad, orden de prioridad*) opportunity; (*juegos etc*) turn

turquesa [tur'kesa] *nf* turquoise

Turquía [tur'kia] *nf* Turkey

turrón [tu'rron] *nm* (*dulce*) nougat

tutear [tute'ar] *vt* to address as familiar "tú"; **~se** *vr* to be on familiar terms

tutela [tu'tela] *nf* (*legal*) guardianship; (*instrucción*) guidance; **tutelar** *adj* tutelary ♦ *vt* to protect

tutor, a [tu'tor, a] *nm/f* (*legal*) guardian; (*ESCOL*) tutor

tuve *etc vb ver* **tener**

tuviera *etc vb ver* **tener**

tuyo, a ['tujo, a] *adj* yours, of yours ♦ *pron* yours; **un amigo ~** a friend of yours; **los ~s** (*fam*) your relations, your family

TV ['te'ße] *nf abr* (= *televisión*) TV

TVE *nf abr* = **Televisión Española**

U u

u [u] *conj* or

ubicar [ußi'kar] *vt* to place, situate; (: *fig*) to install in a post; (*AM: encontrar*) to find; **~se** *vr* to lie, be located

ubre ['ußre] *nf* udder

Ud(s) *abr* = **usted(es)**

UE *nf abr* (= *Unión Europea*) EU

ufanarse [ufa'narse] *vr* to boast; **~ de** to pride o.s. on; **ufano, a** *adj* (*arrogante*) arrogant; (*presumido*) conceited

UGT *nf abr* = **Unión General de Trabajadores**

ujier [u'xjer] *nm* usher; (*portero*) doorkeeper

úlcera ['ulθera] *nf* ulcer

ulcerar [ulθe'rar] *vt* to make sore; **~se** *vr* to ulcerate

ulterior [ulte'rjor] *adj* (*más allá*) farther, further; (*subsecuente, siguiente*) subsequent

últimamente ['ultimamente] *adv* (*recientemente*) lately, recently

ultimar [ulti'mar] *vt* to finish; (*finalizar*) to finalize; (*AM: rematar*) to finish off

ultimátum [ulti'matum] (*pl* **~s**) ultimatum

último, a ['ultimo, a] *adj* last; (*más reciente*) latest, most recent; (*más bajo*) bottom; (*más alto*) top; (*fig*) final, extreme; **en las últimas** on one's last

legs; **por ~** finally

ultra ['ultra] *adj* ultra ♦ *nm/f* extreme right-winger

ultrajar [ultra'xar] *vt* (*escandalizar*) to outrage; (*insultar*) to insult, abuse; **ultraje** *nm* outrage; insult

ultramar [ultra'mar] *nm*: **de o en ~** abroad, overseas

ultramarinos [ultrama'rinos] *nmpl* groceries; **tienda de ~** grocer's (shop)

ultranza [ul'tranθa]: **a ~** *adv* (*a todo trance*) at all costs; (*completo*) outright

ultrasónico, a [ultra'soniko, a] *adj* ultrasonic

ultratumba [ultra'tumba] *nf*: **la vida de ~** the next life

ulular [ulu'lar] *vi* to howl; (*búho*) to hoot

umbral [um'bral] *nm* (*gen*) threshold

umbrío, a [um'brio, a] *adj* shady

un, una [un, 'una] *art indef* a; (*antes de vocal*) an; **una mujer/naranja** a woman/an orange

♦ *adj*: **unos** (*o* **unas**): **hay unos regalos para ti** there are some presents for you; **hay unas cervezas en la nevera** there are some beers in the fridge

unánime [u'nanime] *adj* unanimous; **unanimidad** *nf* unanimity

undécimo, a [un'deθimo, a] *adj* eleventh

ungir [un'xir] *vt* to rub with ointment; (*REL*) to anoint

ungüento [un'gwento] *nm* ointment; (*fig*) salve, balm

únicamente ['unikamente] *adv* solely, only

único, a ['uniko, a] *adj* only, sole; (*sin par*) unique

unidad [uni'ðað] *nf* unity; (*COM, TEC etc*) unit

unido, a [u'niðo, a] *adj* joined, linked; (*fig*) united

unificar [unifi'kar] *vt* to unite, unify

uniformar [unifor'mar] *vt* to make uniform, level up; (*persona*) to put into uniform

uniforme [uni'forme] *adj* uniform, equal;

(*superficie*) even ♦ *nm* uniform;
uniformidad *nf* uniformity; (*llaneza*)
levelness, evenness
unilateral [unilate'ral] *adj* unilateral
unión [u'njon] *nf* union; (*acto*) uniting,
joining; (*calidad*) unity; (*TEC*) joint; (*fig*)
closeness, togetherness; **la U~ Europea**
the European Union; **la U~ Soviética**
the Soviet Union
unir [u'nir] *vt* (*juntar*) to join, unite;
(*atar*) to tie, fasten; (*combinar*) to
combine; **~se** *vr* to join together, unite;
(*empresas*) to merge
unísono [u'nisono] *nm*: **al ~** in unison
universal [unißer'sal] *adj* universal;
(*mundial*) world *cpd*
universidad [unißersi'ðað] *nf* university
universitario, a [unißersi'tarjo, a] *adj*
university *cpd* ♦ *nm/f* (*profesor*) lecturer;
(*estudiante*) (university) student;
(*graduado*) graduate
universo [uni'ßerso] *nm* universe

---

uno, a ['uno, a] *adj* one; **es todo ~** it's all
one and the same; **~s pocos** a few; **~s
cien** about a hundred
♦ *pron* **1** one; **quiero ~ solo** I only want
one; **~ de ellos** one of them
2 (*alguien*) somebody, someone; **conozco
a ~ que se te parece** I know somebody
o someone who looks like you; **~ mismo**
oneself; **~s querían quedarse** some
(people) wanted to stay
3: (**los**) **~s ... (los) otros ...** some ...
others ...; **each other, one another; una y
otra son muy agradables** they're both
very nice
♦ *nf* one; **es la una** it's one o'clock
♦ *nm* (number) one

---

untar [un'tar] *vt* to rub; (*engrasar*) to
grease, oil; (*fig*) to bribe
uña ['uɲa] *nf* (*ANAT*) nail; (*garra*) claw;
(*casco*) hoof; (*arrancaclavos*) claw
uranio [u'ranjo] *nm* uranium
urbanidad [urßani'ðað] *nf* courtesy,
politeness
urbanismo [urßa'nismo] *nm* town

planning
urbanización [urßaniθa'θjon] *nf* (*barrio,
colonia*) housing estate
urbanizar [urßani'θar] *vt* (*zona*) to
develop, urbanize
urbano, a [ur'ßano, a] *adj* (*de ciudad*)
urban; (*cortés*) courteous, polite
urbe ['urße] *nf* large city
urdimbre [ur'ðimbre] *nf* (*de tejido*) warp;
(*intriga*) intrigue
urdir [ur'ðir] *vt* to warp; (*fig*) to plot,
contrive
urgencia [ur'xenθja] *nf* urgency; (*prisa*)
haste, rush; (*emergencia*) emergency;
servicios de ~ emergency services;
urgente *adj* urgent
urgir [ur'xir] *vi* to be urgent; **me urge** I'm
in a hurry for it
urinario, a [uri'narjo, a] *adj* urinary ♦ *nm*
urinal
urna ['urna] *nf* urn; (*POL*) ballot box
urraca [u'rraka] *nf* magpie
URSS *nf*: **la ~** the USSR
Uruguay [uru'ɣwai] *nm*: **el ~** Uruguay;
uruguayo, a *adj, nm/f* Uruguayan
usado, a [u'saðo, a] *adj* used; (*ropa etc*)
worn
usanza [u'sanθa] *nf* custom, usage
usar [u'sar] *vt* to use; (*ropa*) to wear;
(*tener costumbre*) to be in the habit of;
~se *vr* to be used; **uso** *nm* use; wear;
(*costumbre*) usage, custom; (*moda*)
fashion; **al uso** in keeping with custom;
al uso de in the style of
usted [us'teð] *pron* (*sg*) you *sg*; (*pl*): **~es**
you *pl*
usual [u'swal] *adj* usual
usuario, a [usu'arjo, a] *nm/f* user
usufructo [usu'frukto] *nm* use
usura [u'sura] *nf* usury; **usurero, a** *nm/f*
usurer
usurpar [usur'par] *vt* to usurp
utensilio [uten'siljo] *nm* tool; (*CULIN*)
utensil
útero ['utero] *nm* uterus, womb
útil ['util] *adj* useful ♦ *nm* tool; **utilidad**
nf usefulness; (*COM*) profit; **utilizar** *vt* to
use, utilize
utopía [uto'pia] *nf* Utopia; **utópico, a** *adj*

Utopian
uva ['uβa] *nf* grape

V v

v *abr* (= *voltio*) v
va *vb ver* **ir**
vaca ['baka] *nf* (*animal*) cow; **carne de ~** beef
vacaciones [baka'θjones] *nfpl* holidays
vacante [ba'kante] *adj* vacant, empty ♦ *nf* vacancy
vaciar [ba'θjar] *vt* to empty out; (*ahuecar*) to hollow out; (*moldear*) to cast ♦ *vi* (*río*): ~ **(en)** to flow (into); **~se** *vr* to empty
vacilación [baθila'θjon] *nf* hesitation
vacilante [baθi'lante] *adj* unsteady; (*habla*) faltering; (*fig*) hesitant
vacilar [baθi'lar] *vi* to be unsteady; (*al hablar*) to falter; (*fig*) to hesitate, waver; (*memoria*) to fail
vacío, a [ba'θio, a] *adj* empty; (*puesto*) vacant; (*desocupado*) idle; (*vano*) vain ♦ *nm* emptiness; (*FÍSICA*) vacuum; (*un ~*) (empty) space
vacuna [ba'kuna] *nf* vaccine; **vacunar** *vt* to vaccinate
vacuno, a [ba'kuno, a] *adj* cow *cpd*; **ganado ~** cattle
vacuo, a ['bakwo, a] *adj* empty
vadear [baðe'ar] *vt* (*río*) to ford; **vado** *nm* ford
vagabundo, a [baɣa'βundo, a] *adj* wandering; (*pey*) vagrant ♦ *nm* tramp
vagamente [baɣa'mente] *adv* vaguely
vagancia [ba'xanθja] *nf* (*pereza*) idleness, laziness
vagar [ba'ɣar] *vi* to wander; (*no hacer nada*) to idle
vagina [ba'xina] *nf* vagina
vago, a ['baɣo, a] *adj* vague; (*perezoso*) lazy; (*ambulante*) wandering ♦ *nm/f* (*vagabundo*) tramp; (*flojo*) lazybones *sg*, idler
vagón [ba'ɣon] *nm* (*FERRO: de pasajeros*) carriage; (: *de mercancías*) wagon
vaguedad [baɣe'ðað] *nf* vagueness

vaho ['bao] *nm* (*vapor*) vapour, steam; (*respiración*) breath
vaina ['baina] *nf* sheath
vainilla [bai'niʎa] *nf* vanilla
vainita [bai'nita] (*AM*) *nf* green o French bean
vais *vb ver* **ir**
vaivén [bai'βen] *nm* to-and-fro movement; (*de tránsito*) coming and going; **vaivenes** *nmpl* (*fig*) ups and downs
vajilla [ba'xiʎa] *nf* crockery, dishes *pl*; **lavar la ~** to do the washing-up (*BRIT*), wash the dishes (*US*)
valdré *etc vb ver* **valer**
vale ['bale] *nm* voucher; (*recibo*) receipt; (*pagaré*) IOU
valedero, a [bale'ðero, a] *adj* valid
valenciano, a [balen'θjano, a] *adj* Valencian
valentía [balen'tia] *nf* courage, bravery; (*acción*) heroic deed
valer [ba'ler] *vt* to be worth; (*MAT*) to equal; (*costar*) to cost ♦ *vi* (*ser útil*) to be useful; (*ser válido*) to be valid; **~se** *vr* to defend o.s.; **~se de** to make use of, take advantage of; ~ **la pena** to be worthwhile; **¿vale?** (*ESP*) OK?
valeroso, a [bale'roso, a] *adj* brave, valiant
valgo *etc vb ver* **valer**
valía [ba'lia] *nf* worth, value
validar [bali'ðar] *vt* to validate; **validez** *nf* validity; **válido, a** *adj* valid
valiente [ba'ljente] *adj* brave, valiant ♦ *nm* hero
valioso, a [ba'ljoso, a] *adj* valuable; (*rico*) wealthy
valla ['baʎa] *nf* fence; (*DEPORTE*) hurdle; (*fig*) barrier; ~ **publicitaria** hoarding; **vallar** *vt* to fence in
valle ['baʎe] *nm* valley
valor [ba'lor] *nm* value, worth; (*precio*) price; (*valentía*) valour, courage; (*importancia*) importance; **~es** *nmpl* (*COM*) securities; **~ar** *vt* to value
vals [bals] *nm inv* waltz
válvula ['balβula] *nf* valve
vamos *vb ver* **ir**
vampiro, resa [bam'piro, 'resa] *nm/f*

vampire
van *vb ver* **ir**
vanagloriarse [banaɣloˈrjarse] *vr* to boast
vandalismo [bandaˈlismo] *nm* vandalism;
  vándalo, a *nm/f* vandal
vanguardia [banˈgwardja] *nf* vanguard;
  (*ARTE etc*) avant-garde
vanidad [baniˈðað] *nf* vanity; **vanidoso,**
  a *adj* vain, conceited
vano, a [ˈbano, a] *adj* (*irreal*) unreal,
  vain; (*inútil*) useless; (*persona*) vain,
  conceited; (*frívolo*) frivolous
vapor [baˈpor] *nm* vapour; (*vaho*) steam;
  al ~ (*CULIN*) steamed; **~izador** *nm*
  atomizer; **~izar** *vt* to vaporize; **~oso, a**
  adj vaporous
vapulear [bapuleˈar] *vt* to beat, thrash
vaquero, a [baˈkero, a] *adj* cattle *cpd*
  ♦ *nm* cowboy; **~s** *nmpl* (*pantalones*) jeans
vaquilla [baˈkiʎa] *nf* (*ZOOL*) heifer
vara [ˈbara] *nf* stick; (*TEC*) rod; **~ mágica**
  magic wand
variable [baˈrjaβle] *adj, nf* variable
variación [barjaˈθjon] *nf* variation
variar [barˈjar] *vt* to vary; (*modificar*) to
  modify; (*cambiar de posición*) to switch
  around ♦ *vi* to vary
varices [baˈriθes] *nfpl* varicose veins
variedad [barjeˈðað] *nf* variety
varilla [baˈriʎa] *nf* stick; (*BOT*) twig; (*TEC*)
  rod; (*de rueda*) spoke
vario, a [ˈbarjo, a] *adj* varied; **~s** various,
  several
varita [baˈrita] *nf:* **~ mágica** magic wand
varón [baˈron] *nm* male, man; **varonil** *adj*
  manly, virile
Varsovia [barˈsoβja] *n* Warsaw
vas *vb ver* **ir**
vasco, a [ˈbasko, a] *adj, nm/f* Basque
vascongado, a [baskonˈgaðo, a] *adj*
  Basque; **las Vascongadas** the Basque
  Country
vascuence [basˈkwenθe] *adj* =
  vascongado
vaselina [baseˈlina] *nf* Vaseline ®
vasija [baˈsixa] *nf* container, vessel
vaso [ˈbaso] *nm* glass, tumbler; (*ANAT*)
  vessel
vástago [ˈbastaɣo] *nm* (*BOT*) shoot; (*TEC*)

rod; (*fig*) offspring
vasto, a [ˈbasto, a] *adj* vast, huge
Vaticano [batiˈkano] *nm:* **el ~** the Vatican
vaticinio [batiˈθinjo] *nm* prophecy
vatio [ˈbatjo] *nm* (*ELEC*) watt
vaya *etc vb ver* **ir**
Vd(s) *abr* = **usted(es)**
ve *vb ver* **ir; ver**
vecindad [beθinˈdað] *nf* neighbourhood;
  (*habitantes*) residents *pl*
vecindario [beθinˈdarjo] *nm*
  neighbourhood; residents *pl*
vecino, a [beˈθino, a] *adj* neighbouring
  ♦ *nm/f* neighbour; (*residente*) resident
veda [ˈbeða] *nf* prohibition
vedado [beˈðaðo] *nm* preserve
vedar [beˈðar] *vt* (*prohibir*) to ban,
  prohibit; (*impedir*) to stop, prevent
vegetación [bexetaˈθjon] *nf* vegetation
vegetal [bexeˈtal] *adj, nm* vegetable
vegetariano, a [bexetaˈrjano, a] *adj, nm/f*
  vegetarian
vehemencia [be(e)menˈθja] *nf*
  (*insistencia*) vehemence; (*pasión*) passion;
  (*fervor*) fervour; (*violencia*) violence;
  vehemente *adj* vehement; passionate;
  fervent
vehículo [beˈikulo] *nm* vehicle; (*MED*)
  carrier
veía *etc vb ver* **ver**
veinte [ˈbeinte] *num* twenty
vejación [bexaˈθjon] *nf* vexation;
  (*humillación*) humiliation
vejar [beˈxar] *vt* (*irritar*) to annoy, vex;
  (*humillar*) to humiliate
vejez [beˈxeθ] *nf* old age
vejiga [beˈxiɣa] *nf* (*ANAT*) bladder
vela [ˈbela] *nf* (*de cera*) candle; (*NAUT*) sail;
  (*insomnio*) sleeplessness; (*vigilia*) vigil;
  (*MIL*) sentry duty; **estar a dos ~s** (*fam*)
  to be skint
velado, a [beˈlaðo, a] *adj* veiled; (*sonido*)
  muffled; (*FOTO*) blurred ♦ *nf* soirée
velar [beˈlar] *vt* (*vigilar*) to keep watch
  over ♦ *vi* to stay awake; **~ por** to watch
  over, look after
velatorio [belaˈtorjo] *nm* (*funeral*) wake
veleidad [beleiˈðað] *nf* (*ligereza*)
  fickleness; (*capricho*) whim

velero [be'lero] *nm* (*NAUT*) sailing ship; (*AVIAT*) glider

veleta [be'leta] *nf* weather vane

veliz [be'lis] (*AM*) *nm* suitcase

vello ['beʎo] *nm* down, fuzz

velo ['belo] *nm* veil

velocidad [beloθi'ðað] *nf* speed; (*TEC*, *AUTO*) gear

velocímetro [belo'θimetro] *nm* speedometer

veloz [be'loθ] *adj* fast

ven *vb ver* **venir**

vena ['bena] *nf* vein

venado [be'naðo] *nm* deer

vencedor, a [benθe'ðor, a] *adj* victorious ♦ *nm/f* victor, winner

vencer [ben'θer] *vt* (*dominar*) to defeat, beat; (*derrotar*) to vanquish; (*superar*, *controlar*) to overcome, master ♦ *vi* (*triunfar*) to win (through), triumph; (*plazo*) to expire; **vencido, a** *adj* (*derrotado*) defeated, beaten; (*COM*) due ♦ *adv*: **pagar vencido** to pay in arrears; **vencimiento** *nm* (*COM*) maturity

venda ['benda] *nf* bandage; **vendaje** *nm* bandage, dressing; **vendar** *vt* to bandage; **vendar los ojos** to blindfold

vendaval [benda'ßal] *nm* (*viento*) gale

vendedor, a [bende'ðor, a] *nm/f* seller

vender [ben'der] *vt* to sell; ~ **al contado/al por mayor/al por menor** to sell for cash/wholesale/retail

vendimia [ben'dimja] *nf* grape harvest

vendré *etc vb ver* **venir**

veneno [be'neno] *nm* poison; (*de serpiente*) venom; ~**so, a** *adj* poisonous; venomous

venerable [bene'raßle] *adj* venerable; **venerar** *vt* (*respetar*) to revere; (*adorar*) to worship

venéreo, a [be'nereo, a] *adj*: **enfermedad venérea** venereal disease

venezolano, a [beneθo'lano, a] *adj* Venezuelan

Venezuela [bene'θwela] *nf* Venezuela

venganza [ben'ganθa] *nf* vengeance, revenge; **vengar** *vt* to avenge; **vengarse** *vr* to take revenge; **vengativo, a** *adj* (*persona*) vindictive

vengo *etc vb ver* **venir**

venia ['benja] *nf* (*perdón*) pardon; (*permiso*) consent

venial [be'njal] *adj* venial

venida [be'niða] *nf* (*llegada*) arrival; (*regreso*) return

venidero, a [beni'ðero, a] *adj* coming, future

venir [be'nir] *vi* to come; (*llegar*) to arrive; (*ocurrir*) to happen; (*fig*): ~ **de** to stem from; ~ **bien/mal** to be suitable/ unsuitable; **el año que viene** next year; ~**se abajo** to collapse

venta ['benta] *nf* (*COM*) sale; ~ **a plazos** hire purchase; ~ **al contado/al por mayor/al por menor** *o* **al detalle** cash sale/wholesale/retail; ~ **con derecho a retorno** sale or return; **"en** ~**"** "for sale"

ventaja [ben'taxa] *nf* advantage; **ventajoso, a** *adj* advantageous

ventana [ben'tana] *nf* window; **ventanilla** *nf* (*de taquilla*) window (*of booking office etc*)

ventilación [bentila'θjon] *nf* ventilation; (*corriente*) draught; **ventilar** *vt* to ventilate; (*para secar*) to put out to dry; (*fig*) to air, discuss

ventisca [ben'tiska] *nf* blizzard; (*nieve amontonada*) snowdrift

ventrílocuo, a [ben'trilokwo, a] *nm/f* ventriloquist

ventura [ben'tura] *nf* (*felicidad*) happiness; (*buena suerte*) luck; (*destino*) fortune; **a la (buena)** ~ at random; **venturoso, a** *adj* happy; (*afortunado*) lucky, fortunate

veo *etc vb ver* **ver**

ver [ber] *vt* to see; (*mirar*) to look at, watch; (*entender*) to understand; (*investigar*) to look into; ♦ *vi* to see; to understand ♦ *nm* looks *pl*, appearance; ~**se** *vr* (*encontrarse*) to meet; (*dejarse* ~) to be seen; (*hallarse: en un apuro*) to find o.s., be **a** ~ let's see; **dejarse** ~ to become apparent; **no tener nada que** ~ **con** to have nothing to do with; **a mi modo de** ~ as I see it

vera ['bera] *nf* edge, verge; (*de río*) bank

veracidad [beraθi'ðað] *nf* truthfulness

veranear [berane'ar] *vi* to spend the summer; **veraneo** *nm* summer holiday; **veraniego, a** *adj* summer *cpd*

verano [be'rano] *nm* summer

veras ['beras] *nfpl* truth *sg*; **de** ~ really, truly

veraz [be'raθ] *adj* truthful

verbal [ber'βal] *adj* verbal

verbena [ber'βena] *nf* (*fiesta*) fair; (*baile*) open-air dance

verbo ['berβo] *nm* verb; **~so, a** *adj* verbose

verdad [ber'ðað] *nf* truth; (*fiabilidad*) reliability; **de** ~ real, proper; **a decir** ~ to tell the truth; **~ero, a** (*veraz*) true, truthful; (*fiable*) reliable; (*fig*) real

verde ['berðe] *adj* green; (*chiste*) blue, dirty ♦ *nm* green; **viejo** ~ dirty old man; **~ar** *vi* to turn green; **verdor** *nm* (*lo ~*) greenness; (*BOT*) verdure

verdugo [ber'ðuɣo] *nm* executioner

verdulero, a [berðu'lero, a] *nm/f* greengrocer

verduras [ber'ðuras] *nfpl* (*CULIN*) greens

vereda [be'reða] *nf* (*AM*) path; (*AM*) pavement (*BRIT*), sidewalk (*US*)

veredicto [bere'ðikto] *nm* verdict

vergonzoso, a [berɣon'θoso, a] *adj* shameful; (*tímido*) timid, bashful

vergüenza [ber'ɣwenθa] *nf* shame, sense of shame; (*timidez*) bashfulness; (*pudor*) modesty; **me da** ~ I'm ashamed

verídico, a [be'riðiko, a] *adj* true, truthful

verificar [berifi'kar] *vt* to check; (*corroborar*) to verify; (*llevar a cabo*) to carry out; **~se** *vr* to occur, happen

verja ['berxa] *nf* (*cancela*) iron gate; (*valla*) iron railings *pl*; (*de ventana*) grille

vermut [ber'mut] (*pl* ~s) *nm* vermouth

verosímil [bero'simil] *adj* likely, probable; (*relato*) credible

verruga [be'ruɣa] *nf* wart

versado, a [ber'saðo, a] *adj*: ~ **en** versed in

versátil [ber'satil] *adj* versatile

versión [ber'sjon] *nf* version

verso ['berso] *nm* verse; **un** ~ a line of poetry

vértebra ['berteβra] *nf* vertebra

verter [ber'ter] *vt* (*líquido: adrede*) to empty, pour (out); (: *sin querer*) to spill; (*basura*) to dump ♦ *vi* to flow

vertical [berti'kal] *adj* vertical

vértice ['bertiθe] *nm* vertex, apex

vertidos [ber'tiðos] *nmpl* waste *sg*

vertiente [ber'tjente] *nf* slope; (*fig*) aspect

vertiginoso, a [bertixi'noso, a] *adj* giddy, dizzy

vértigo ['bertiɣo] *nm* vertigo; (*mareo*) dizziness

vesícula [be'sikula] *nf* blister

vespertino, a [besper'tino, a] *adj* evening *cpd*

vespino [bes'pino] ® *nm o nf* moped

vestíbulo [bes'tiβulo] *nm* hall; (*de teatro*) foyer

vestido [bes'tiðo] *pp de* **vestir**; ~ **de azul/marinero** dressed in blue/as a sailor ♦ *nm* (*ropa*) clothes *pl*, clothing; (*de mujer*) dress, frock

vestigio [bes'tixjo] *nm* (*huella*) trace; **~s** *nmpl* (*restos*) remains

vestimenta [besti'menta] *nf* clothing

vestir [bes'tir] *vt* (*poner: ropa*) to put on; (*llevar: ropa*) to wear; (*proveer de ropa a*) to clothe; (*suj: sastre*) to make clothes for ♦ *vi* to dress; (*verse bien*) to look good; **~se** *vr* to get dressed, dress o.s.

vestuario [bes'twarjo] *nm* clothes *pl*, wardrobe; (*TEATRO: cuarto*) dressing room; (*DEPORTE*) changing room

veta ['beta] *nf* (*vena*) vein, seam; (*en carne*) streak; (*de madera*) grain

vetar [be'tar] *vt* to veto

veterano, a [bete'rano, a] *adj, nm* veteran

veterinaria [beteri'narja] *nf* veterinary science; *ver tb* **veterinario**

veterinario, a [beteri'narjo, a] *nm/f* vet(erinary surgeon)

veto ['beto] *nm* veto

vetusto, a [be'tusto, a] *adj* ancient

vez [beθ] *nf* time; (*turno*) turn; **a la** ~ **que** at the same time as; **a su** ~ in its turn; **otra** ~ again; **una** ~ once; **de una** ~ in one go; **de una** ~ **para siempre**

once and for all; **en ~ de** instead of; **a o algunas veces** sometimes; **una y otra ~** repeatedly; **de ~ en cuando** from time to time; **7 veces 9** 7 times 9; **hacer las veces de** to stand in for; **tal ~** perhaps

vía ['bia] _nf_ track, route; (_FERRO_) line; (_fig_) way; (_ANAT_) passage, tube ♦ _prep_ via, by way of; **por ~ judicial** by legal means; **por ~ oficial** through official channels; **en ~s de** in the process of; **~ aérea** airway; **V~ Láctea** Milky Way; **~ pública** public road o thoroughfare

viable ['bjaßle] _adj_ (_solución, plan, alternativa_) feasible

viaducto [bja'ðukto] _nm_ viaduct

viajante [bja'xante] _nm_ commercial traveller

viajar [bja'xar] _vi_ to travel; **viaje** _nm_ journey; (_gira_) tour; (_NAUT_) voyage; **estar de viaje** to be on a trip; **viaje de ida y vuelta** round trip; **viaje de novios** honeymoon; **viajero, a** _adj_ travelling; (_ZOOL_) migratory ♦ _nm/f_ (_quien viaja_) traveller; (_pasajero_) passenger

vial [bjal] _adj_ road _cpd_, traffic _cpd_

víbora ['bißora] _nf_ viper; (_AM_) poisonous snake

vibración [bißra'θjon] _nf_ vibration

vibrar [bi'ßrar] _vt, vi_ to vibrate

vicario [bi'karjo] _nm_ curate

vicepresidente [biθepresi'ðente] _nm/f_ vice-president

viceversa [biθe'ßersa] _adv_ vice versa

viciado, a [bi'θjaðo, a] _adj_ (_corrompido_) corrupt; (_contaminado_) foul, contaminated; **viciar** _vt_ (_pervertir_) to pervert; (_JUR_) to nullify; (_estropear_) to spoil; **viciarse** _vr_ to become corrupted

vicio ['biθjo] _nm_ vice; (_mala costumbre_) bad habit; **~so, a** _adj_ (_muy malo_) vicious; (_corrompido_) depraved ♦ _nm/f_ depraved person

vicisitud [biθisi'tuð] _nf_ vicissitude

víctima ['biktima] _nf_ victim

victoria [bik'torja] _nf_ victory; **victorioso, a** _adj_ victorious

vicuña [bi'kuɲa] _nf_ vicuna

vid [bið] _nf_ vine

vida ['biða] _nf_ (_gen_) life; (_duración_) lifetime; **de por ~** for life; **en la/mi ~** never; **estar con ~** to be still alive; **ganarse la ~** to earn one's living

vídeo ['bideo] _nm_ video ♦ _adj inv_: **película ~** video film; **~cámara** _nf_ camcorder; **~club** _nm_ video club; **~juego** _nm_ video game

vidriero, a [bi'ðrjero, a] _nm/f_ glazier ♦ _nf_ (_ventana_) stained-glass window; (_AM: de tienda_) shop window; (_puerta_) glass door

vidrio ['biðrjo] _nm_ glass

vieira ['bjeira] _nf_ scallop

viejo, a ['bjexo, a] _adj_ old ♦ _nm/f_ old man/woman; **hacerse ~** to get old

Viena ['bjena] _n_ Vienna

vienes _etc vb ver_ **venir**

vienés, esa [bje'nes, esa] _adj_ Viennese

viento ['bjento] _nm_ wind; **hacer ~** to be windy

vientre ['bjentre] _nm_ belly; (_matriz_) womb

viernes ['bjernes] _nm inv_ Friday; **V~ Santo** Good Friday

Vietnam [bjet'nam] _nm_: **el ~** Vietnam; **vietnamita** _adj_ Vietnamese

viga ['biɣa] _nf_ beam, rafter; (_de metal_) girder

vigencia [bi'xenθja] _nf_ validity; **estar en ~** to be in force; **vigente** _adj_ valid, in force; (_imperante_) prevailing

vigésimo, a [bi'xesimo, a] _adj_ twentieth

vigía [bi'xia] _nm_ look-out ♦ _nf_ (_atalaya_) watchtower; (_acción_) watching

vigilancia [bixi'lanθja] _nf_: **tener a uno bajo ~** to keep watch on sb

vigilar [bixi'lar] _vt_ to watch over ♦ _vi_ (_gen_) to be vigilant; (_hacer guardia_) to keep watch; **~ por** to take care of

vigilia [vi'xilja] _nf_ wakefulness, being awake; (_REL_) fast

vigor [bi'ɣor] _nm_ vigour, vitality; **en ~** in force; **entrar/poner en ~** to come/put into effect; **~oso, a** _adj_ vigorous

VIH _nm abr_ (= _virus de la inmuno-deficiencia humana_) HIV; **~ positivo/negativo** HIV-positive/-negative

vil [bil] _adj_ vile, low; **~eza** _nf_ vileness; (_acto_) base deed

vilipendiar [bilipen'djar] _vt_ to vilify, revile

villa ['biʎa] *nf (casa)* villa; *(pueblo)* small town; *(municipalidad)* municipality; ~ **miseria** *(AM)* shantytown

villancico [biʎan'θiko] *nm* (Christmas) carol

villorrio [bi'ʎorrjo] *(AM) nm* shantytown

vilo ['bilo]: **en** ~ *adv* in the air, suspended; *(fig)* on tenterhooks, in suspense

vinagre [bi'naɣre] *nm* vinegar

vinagreta [bina'ɣreta] *nf* vinaigrette, French dressing

vinatero, a [bina'tero, a] *adj* wine *cpd* ♦ *nm* wine merchant

vinculación [binkula'θjon] *nf (lazo)* link, bond; *(acción)* linking

vincular [binku'lar] *vt* to link, bind; **vínculo** *nm* link, bond

vine *etc vb ver* **venir**

vinicultura [binikul'tura] *nf* wine growing

viniera *etc vb ver* **venir**

vino ['bino] *vb ver* **venir** ♦ *nm* wine; ~ **blanco/tinto** white/red wine

viña ['biɲa] *nf* vineyard; **viñedo** *nm* vineyard

viola ['bjola] *nf* viola

violación [bjola'θjon] *nf* violation; *(estupro)*: ~ **(sexual)** rape

violar [bjo'lar] *vt* to violate; *(cometer estupro)* to rape

violencia [bjo'lenθja] *nf (fuerza)* violence, force; *(embarazo)* embarrassment; *(acto injusto)* unjust act; **violentar** *vt* to force; *(casa)* to break into; *(agredir)* to assault; *(violar)* to violate; **violento, a** *adj* violent; *(furioso)* furious; *(situación)* embarrassing; *(acto)* forced, unnatural

violeta [bjo'leta] *nf* violet

violín [bjo'lin] *nm* violin

violón [bjo'lon] *nm* double bass

viraje [bi'raxe] *nm* turn; *(de vehículo)* swerve; *(de carretera)* bend; *(fig)* change of direction; **virar** *vi* to change direction

virgen ['birxen] *adj, nf* virgin

Virgo ['birɣo] *nm* Virgo

viril [bi'ril] *adj* virile; ~**idad** *nf* virility

virtud [bir'tuð] *nf* virtue; **en** ~ **de** by virtue of; **virtuoso, a** *adj* virtuous ♦ *nm/f* virtuoso

viruela [bi'rwela] *nf* smallpox; ~**s** *nfpl (granos)* pockmarks

virulento, a [biru'lento, a] *adj* virulent

virus ['birus] *nm inv* virus

visa ['bisa] *(AM) nf* = **visado**

visado [bi'saðo] *nm* visa

víscera ['bisθera] *nf (ANAT, ZOOL)* gut, bowel; ~**s** *nfpl* entrails

visceral [bisθe'ral] *adj (odio)* intense; **reacción** ~ gut reaction

viscoso, a [bis'koso, a] *adj* viscous

visera [bi'sera] *nf* visor

visibilidad [bisiβili'ðað] *nf* visibility; **visible** *adj* visible; *(fig)* obvious

visillos [bi'siʎos] *nmpl* lace curtains

visión [bi'sjon] *nf (ANAT)* vision, (eye)sight; *(fantasía)* vision, fantasy

visita [bi'sita] *nf* call, visit; *(persona)* visitor; **hacer una** ~ to pay a visit

visitar [bisi'tar] *vt* to visit, call on

vislumbrar [bislum'brar] *vt* to glimpse, catch a glimpse of; **vislumbre** *nf* glimpse; *(centelleo)* gleam; *(idea vaga)* glimmer

viso ['biso] *nm (del metal)* glint, gleam; *(de tela)* sheen; *(aspecto)* appearance

visón [bi'son] *nm* mink

visor [bi'sor] *nm (FOTO)* viewfinder

víspera ['bispera] *nf*: **la** ~ **de ...** the day before ...

vista ['bista] *nf* sight, vision; *(capacidad de ver)* (eye)sight; *(mirada)* look(s) *(pl)* ♦ *nm* customs officer; **a primera** ~ at first glance; **hacer la** ~ **gorda** to turn a blind eye; **volver la** ~ to look back; **está a la** ~ **que** it's obvious that; **en** ~ **de** in view of; **en** ~ **de que** in view of the fact that; **¡hasta la** ~**!** so long!, see you!; **con** ~**s a** with a view to; ~**zo** *nm* glance; **dar** *o* **echar un** ~**zo a** to glance at

visto, a ['bisto, a] *pp de* **ver** ♦ *vb ver* **vestir** ♦ *adj* seen; *(considerado)* considered ♦ *nm*: ~ **bueno** approval; "~ **bueno**" "approved"; **por lo** ~ apparently; **está** ~ **que** it's clear that; **está bien/mal** ~ it's acceptable/unacceptable; ~ **que** since, considering that

vistoso, a [bis'toso, a] *adj* colourful

visual [bi'swal] *adj* visual

vital [bi'tal] *adj* life *cpd*, living *cpd*; (*fig*) vital; (*persona*) lively, vivacious; **~icio, a** *adj* for life; **~idad** *nf* (*de persona, negocio*) energy; (*de ciudad*) liveliness

vitamina [bita'mina] *nf* vitamin

viticultor, a [bitikul'tor, a] *nm/f* wine grower; **viticultura** *nf* wine growing

vitorear [bitore'ar] *vt* to cheer, acclaim

vítores ['bitores] *nmpl* cheers

vitrina [bi'trina] *nf* show case; (*AM*) shop window

vituperio [bitu'perjo] *nm* (*condena*) condemnation; (*censura*) censure; (*insulto*) insult

viudez [bju'ðeθ] *nf* widowhood

viudo, a ['bjuðo, a] *nm/f* widower/widow

viva ['bißa] *excl* hurrah!: **¡~ el rey!** long live the king!

vivacidad [bißaθi'ðað] *nf* (*vigor*) vigour; (*vida*) liveliness

vivaracho, a [bißa'ratʃo, a] *adj* jaunty, lively; (*ojos*) bright, twinkling

vivaz [bi'ßaθ] *adj* lively

víveres ['bißeres] *nmpl* provisions

vivero [bi'ßero] *nm* (*para plantas*) nursery; (*para peces*) fish farm; (*fig*) hotbed

viveza [bi'ßeθa] *nf* liveliness; (*agudeza: mental*) sharpness

vivienda [bi'ßjenda] *nf* housing; (*una ~*) house; (*piso*) flat (*BRIT*), apartment (*US*)

viviente [bi'ßjente] *adj* living

vivir [bi'ßir] *vt, vi* to live ♦ *nm* life, living

vivo, a ['bißo, a] *adj* living, alive; (*fig: descripción*) vivid; (*persona: astuto*) smart, clever; **en ~** (*transmisión etc*) live

vocablo [bo'kaßlo] *nm* (*palabra*) word; (*término*) term

vocabulario [bokaßu'larjo] *nm* vocabulary

vocación [boka'θjon] *nf* vocation; **vocacional** (*AM*) *nf* ≈ technical college

vocal [bo'kal] *adj* vocal ♦ *nf* vowel; **~izar** *vt* to vocalize

vocear [boθe'ar] *vt* (*para vender*) to cry; (*aclamar*) to acclaim; (*fig*) to proclaim ♦ *vi* to yell; **vocerío** *nm* shouting

vocero [bo'θero] *nm/f* spokesman/woman

voces ['boθes] *pl de* **voz**

vociferar [boθife'rar] *vt* to shout ♦ *vi* to

yell

vodka ['boðka] *nm o f* vodka

vol *abr* = **volumen**

volador, a [bola'ðor, a] *adj* flying

volandas [bo'landas]: **en ~** *adv* in the air; (*fig*) swiftly

volante [bo'lante] *adj* flying ♦ *nm* (*de coche*) steering wheel; (*de reloj*) balance

volar [bo'lar] *vt* (*edificio*) to blow up ♦ *vi* to fly

volátil [bo'latil] *adj* volatile

volcán [bol'kan] *nm* volcano; **~ico, a** *adj* volcanic

volcar [bol'kar] *vt* to upset, overturn; (*tumbar, derribar*) to knock over; (*vaciar*) to empty out ♦ *vi* to overturn; **~se** *vr* to tip over

voleíbol [bolei'ßol] *nm* volleyball

volqué *etc vb ver* **volcar**

voltaje [bol'taxe] *nm* voltage

voltear [bolte'ar] *vt* to turn over; (*volcar*) to turn upside down

voltereta [bolte'reta] *nf* somersault

voltio ['boltjo] *nm* volt

voluble [bo'lußle] *adj* fickle

volumen [bo'lumen] (*pl* **volúmenes**) *nm* volume; **voluminoso, a** *adj* voluminous; (*enorme*) massive

voluntad [bolun'tað] *nf* will; (*resolución*) willpower; (*deseo*) desire, wish

voluntario, a [bolun'tarjo, a] *adj* voluntary ♦ *nm/f* volunteer

voluntarioso, a [bolunta'rjoso, a] *adj* headstrong

voluptuoso, a [bolup'twoso, a] *adj* voluptuous

volver [bol'ßer] *vt* (*gen*) to turn; (*dar vuelta a*) to turn (over); (*voltear*) to turn round, turn upside down; (*poner al revés*) to turn inside out; (*devolver*) to return ♦ *vi* to return, go back, come back; **~se** *vr* to turn round; **~ la espalda** to turn one's back; **~ triste** *etc* **a uno** to make sb sad *etc*; **~ a hacer** to do again; **~ en sí** to come to; **~se insoportable/ muy caro** to get *o* become unbearable/ very expensive; **~se loco** to go mad

vomitar [bomi'tar] *vt, vi* to vomit; **vómito** *nm* (*acto*) vomiting; (*resultado*) vomit

voraz [boˈraθ] *adj* voracious
vos [bos] (*AM*) *pron* you
vosotros, as [boˈsotros, as] *pron* you;
(*reflexivo*): **entre/para** ~ among/for
yourselves
votación [botaˈθjon] *nf* (*acto*) voting;
(*voto*) vote
votar [boˈtar] *vi* to vote; **voto** *nm* vote;
(*promesa*) vow; **votos** (good) wishes
voy *vb ver* **ir**
voz [boθ] *nf* voice; (*grito*) shout; (*chisme*)
rumour; (*LING*) word; **dar voces** to shout,
yell; **a media** ~ in a low voice; **a** ~ **en
cuello** o **en grito** at the top of one's
voice; **de viva** ~ verbally; **en** ~ **alta**
aloud; ~ **de mando** command
vuelco [ˈbwelko] *vb ver* **volcar** ♦ *nm*
spill, overturning
vuelo [ˈbwelo] *vb ver* **volar** ♦ *nm* flight;
(*encaje*) lace, frill; **coger al** ~ to catch in
flight; ~ **charter/regular** charter/sched-
uled flight; ~ **libre** (*DEPORTE*) hang-
gliding
vuelque *etc vb ver* **volcar**
vuelta [ˈbwelta] *nf* (*gen*) turn; (*curva*)
bend, curve; (*regreso*) return; (*revolución*)
revolution; (*circuito*) lap; (*de papel, tela*)
reverse; (*cambio*) change; **a la** ~ on one's
return; ~ **de correo** by return of post;
dar ~**s** (*suj: cabeza*) to spin; **dar** ~**s a
una idea** to turn over an idea (in one's
head); **estar de** ~ to be back; **dar una** ~
to go for a walk; (*en coche*) to go for a
drive; ~ **ciclista** (*DEPORTE*) (cycle) tour
vuelto *pp de* **volver**
vuelvo *etc vb ver* **volver**
vuestro, a [ˈbwestro, a] *adj* your; **un
amigo** ~ a friend of yours ♦ *pron*: **el** ~/
la vuestra, los ~**s/las vuestras** yours
vulgar [bulˈɣar] *adj* (*ordinario*) vulgar;
(*común*) common; ~**idad** *nf* commonness;
(*acto*) vulgarity; (*expresión*) coarse
expression; ~**idades** *nfpl* (*banalidades*)
banalities; ~**izar** *vt* to popularize
vulgo [ˈbulɣo] *nm* common people
vulnerable [bulneˈraβle] *adj* vulnerable
vulnerar [bulneˈrar] *vt* (*ley, acuerdo*) to
violate, breach; (*derechos, intimidad*) to
violate; (*reputación*) to damage

W w

Walkman [wakˈman] ® *nm* Walkman ®
wáter [ˈbater] *nm* toilet
whisky [ˈwiski] *nm* whisky, whiskey

X x

xenofobia [ksenoˈfoβja] *nf* xenophobia
xilófono [ksiˈlofono] *nm* xylophone

Y y

y [i] *conj* and
ya [ja] *adv* (*gen*) already; (*ahora*) now; (*en
seguida*) at once; (*pronto*) soon ♦ *excl* all
right! ♦ *conj* (*ahora que*) now that; ~ **lo
sé** I know; ~ **que** since
yacer [jaˈθer] *vi* to lie
yacimiento [jaθiˈmjento] *nm* deposit
yanqui [ˈjanki] *adj, nm/f* Yankee
yate [ˈjate] *nm* yacht
yazco *etc vb ver* **yacer**
yedra [ˈjeðra] *nf* ivy
yegua [ˈjeɣwa] *nf* mare
yema [ˈjema] *nf* (*del huevo*) yoke; (*BOT*)
leaf bud; (*fig*) best part; ~ **del dedo**
fingertip
yergo *etc vb ver* **erguir**
yermo, a [ˈjermo, a] *adj* (*despoblado*)
uninhabited; (*estéril, fig*) barren ♦ *nm*
wasteland
yerno [ˈjerno] *nm* son-in-law
yerro *etc vb ver* **errar**
yerto, a [ˈjerto, a] *adj* stiff
yeso [ˈjeso] *nm* (*GEO*) gypsum; (*ARQ*)
plaster
yo [ˈjo] *pron* I; **soy** ~ it's me, it is I
yodo [ˈjoðo] *nm* iodine
yoga [ˈjoɣa] *nm* yoga
yogur(t) [joˈɣur(t)] *nm* yoghurt
yugo [ˈjuɣo] *nm* yoke
Yugoslavia [juɣosˈlaβja] *nf* Yugoslavia
yugular [juɣuˈlar] *adj* jugular
yunque [ˈjunke] *nm* anvil

yunta ['junta] *nf* yoke; **yuntero** *nm* ploughman

yute ['jute] *nm* jute

yuxtaponer [jukstapo'ner] *vt* to juxtapose; **yuxtaposición** *nf* juxtaposition

Z z

zafar [θa'far] *vt* (*soltar*) to untie; (*superficie*) to clear; **~se** *vr* (*escaparse*) to escape; (*TEC*) to slip off

zafio, a ['θafjo, a] *adj* coarse

zafiro [θa'firo] *nm* sapphire

zaga ['θaɣa] *nf*: **a la ~** behind, in the rear

zaguán [θa'ɣwan] *nm* hallway

zaherir [θae'rir] *vt* (*criticar*) to criticize

zaino, a ['θaino, a] *adj* (*color de caballo*) chestnut

zalamería [θalame'ria] *nf* flattery; **zalamero, a** *adj* flattering; (*relamido*) suave

zamarra [θa'marra] *nf* (*piel*) sheepskin; (*chaqueta*) sheepskin jacket

zambullirse [θambu'ʎirse] *vr* to dive; (*ocultarse*) to hide o.s.

zampar [θam'par] *vt* to gobble down ♦ *vi* to gobble (up)

zanahoria [θana'orja] *nf* carrot

zancada [θan'kaða] *nf* stride

zancadilla [θanka'ðiʎa] *nf* trip; (*fig*) stratagem

zanco ['θanko] *nm* stilt

zancudo, a [θan'kuðo, a] *adj* long-legged ♦ *nm* (*AM*) mosquito

zángano ['θangano] *nm* drone

zanja ['θanxa] *nf* ditch; **zanjar** *vt* (*superar*) to surmount; (*resolver*) to resolve

zapata [θa'pata] *nf* half-boot; (*MECÁNICA*) shoe

zapatear [θapate'ar] *vi* to tap with one's feet

zapatería [θapate'ria] *nf* (*oficio*) shoemaking; (*tienda*) shoe shop; (*fábrica*) shoe factory; **zapatero, a** *nm/f* shoemaker

zapatilla [θapa'tiʎa] *nf* slipper; **~ de deporte** training shoe

zapato [θa'pato] *nm* shoe

zapping ['θapin] *nm* channel-hopping; **hacer ~** to flick through the channels

zar [θar] *nm* tsar, czar

zarandear [θaranðe'ar] (*fam*) *vt* to shake vigorously

zarpa ['θarpa] *nf* (*garra*) claw

zarpar [θar'par] *vi* to weigh anchor

zarza ['θarθa] *nf* (*BOT*) bramble; **zarzal** *nm* (*matorral*) bramble patch

zarzamora [θarθa'mora] *nf* blackberry

zarzuela [θar'θwela] *nf* Spanish light opera

zigzag [θiɣ'θaɣ] *nm* zigzag; **zigzaguear** *vi* to zigzag

zinc [θink] *nm* zinc

zócalo ['θokalo] *nm* (*ARQ*) plinth, base

zodíaco [θo'ðiako] *nm* (*ASTRO*) zodiac

zona ['θona] *nf* zone; **~ fronteriza** border area

zoo ['θoo] *nm* zoo

zoología [θoolo'xia] *nf* zoology; **zoológico, a** *adj* zoological ♦ *nm* (*tb: parque ~*) zoo; **zoólogo, a** *nm/f* zoologist

zoom [θum] *nm* zoom lens

zopilote [θopi'lote] (*AM*) *nm* buzzard

zoquete [θo'kete] *nm* (*madera*) block; (*fam*) blockhead

zorro, a ['θorro, a] *adj* crafty ♦ *nm/f* fox/vixen

zozobra [θo'θoβra] *nf* (*fig*) anxiety; **zozobrar** *vi* (*hundirse*) to capsize; (*fig*) to fail

zueco ['θweko] *nm* clog

zumbar [θum'bar] *vt* (*golpear*) to hit ♦ *vi* to buzz; **zumbido** *nm* buzzing

zumo ['θumo] *nm* juice

zurcir [θur'θir] *vt* (*coser*) to darn

zurdo, a ['θurðo, a] *adj* (*mano*) left; (*persona*) left-handed

zurrar [θu'rrar] (*fam*) *vt* to wallop

zurrón [θu'rron] *nm* pouch

USING YOUR COLLINS POCKET DICTIONARY

Supplement
Roy Simon
reproduced by kind permission of
Tayside Region Education Department

USING YOUR COLLINS POCKET DICTIONARY

Introduction

We are delighted that you have decided to invest in this Collins Pocket Dictionary! Whether you intend to use it in school, at home, on holiday or at work, we are sure that you will find it very useful.

The purpose of this supplement is to help you become aware of the wealth of vocabulary and grammatical information your dictionary contains, to explain how this information is presented and also to point out some of the traps one can fall into when using a Spanish-English English-Spanish dictionary.

In the pages which follow you will find explanations and wordgames (not too difficult!) designed to give you practice in exploring the dictionary's contents and in retrieving information for a variety of purposes. Answers are provided at the end. If you spend a little time on these pages you should be able to use your dictionary more efficiently and effectively. Have fun!

Contents

Part One   HOW INFORMATION IS PRESENTED
                IN YOUR DICTIONARY

Part Two   THE DICTIONARY AND GRAMMAR

Part Three   MORE ABOUT MEANING

Part Four   HAVE FUN WITH YOUR DICTIONARY

                ANSWERS

HOW INFORMATION IS PRESENTED IN YOUR DICTIONARY

A great deal of information is packed into your Collins Pocket Dictionary using colour, various typefaces, sizes of type, symbols, abbreviations and brackets. The purpose of this section is to acquaint you with the conventions used in presenting information.

Headwords

A headword is the word you look up in a dictionary. Headwords are listed in alphabetical order throughout the dictionary. They are printed in colour so that they stand out clearly from all the other words on the dictionary page.

Note that at the top of each page two headwords appear. These tell you which is the first and last word dealt with on the page in question. They are there to help you scan through the dictionary more quickly.

The Spanish alphabet consists of 27 letters: the same 26 letters as the English alphabet, in the same order, plus 'ñ', which comes after letter 'n'. You will need to remember that words containing this letter will be listed slightly differently from what you would expect according to English alphabetical order: thus 'caña' does not come immediately after 'cana', but follows the last word beginning with 'can-' in the list, namely 'canuto'.

Where two Spanish words are distinguished only by an accent, the accented form follows the unaccented, e.g. 'de', 'dé'.

A dictionary entry

An entry is made up of a headword and all the information about that headword. Entries will be short or long depending on how frequently a word is used in either English or Spanish and how many meanings it has. Inevitably, the fuller the dictionary entry the more care is needed in sifting through it to find the information you require.

Meanings

The translations of a headword are given in ordinary type. Where there is more than one meaning or usage, a semi-colon separates one from the other.

completo, a [kom'pleto, a] *adj* complete; (*perfecto*) perfect; (*lleno*) full ♦ *nm* full complement

complicado, a [kompli'kaðo, a] *adj* complicated; **estar ~ en** to be mixed up in

complicar [kompli'kar] *vt* to complicate

cómplice ['kompliθe] *nm/f* accomplice

porcelana [porθe'lana] *nf* porcelain; (*china*) china

porcentaje [porθen'taxe] *nm* percentage

porción [por'θjon] *nf* (*parte*) portion,

hall; (*portada*) porch, doorway; (*puerta de entrada*) main door; (*DEPORTE*) goal

portamaletas [portama'letas] *nm inv* (*AUTO: maletero*) boot; (: *baca*) roof rack

nevar [ne'ßar] *vi* to snow

cuenta *etc* ['kwenta] *vb ver* **contar** ♦ *nf* (*cálculo*) count, counting; (*en café, restaurante*) bill (*BRIT*), check (*US*); (*COM*) account; (*de collar*) bead; (*fig*) account; **a fin de ~s** in the end; **caer en la ~** to catch on; **darse ~ de** to realize; **tener en ~** to bear in mind; **echar ~s** to take stock; **~ corriente/de ahorros** current/savings account; **~ atrás** countdown; **~kilómetros** *nm inv* ≈ milometer; (*de velocidad*) speedometer

titubear [tituße'ar] *vi* to stagger; to stammer; (*fig*) to hesitate; **titubeo** *nm* staggering; stammering; hesitation

3

In addition, you will often find other words appearing in *italics* in brackets before the translations. These either give some notion of the contexts in which the headword might appear (as with 'lane' opposite – 'lane in the country', 'lane in a race', etc.) or else they provide synonyms (as with 'hit' opposite – 'hit', 'reach', etc.).

Phonetic spellings

The phonetic spelling of each headword – i.e. its pronunciation – is given in square brackets immediately after it. The phonetic transcription of Spanish and English vowels and consonants is given on pages vi to ix at the front of your dictionary.

Additional information about headwords

Information about the usage or form of certain headwords is given in brackets between the phonetics and the translation of translations. Have a look at the entries for 'COU', 'cuenca', 'mast', 'R.S.V.P.' and 'burócrata' opposite.

This information is usually given in abbreviated form. A helpful list of abbreviations is given on pages iv and v at the front of your dictionary.

You should be particularly careful with colloquial words or phrases. Words labelled (*fam*) would not normally be used in formal speech, while those labelled (*fam!*) would be considered offensive.

Careful consideration of such style labels will help indicate the degree of formality and appropriateness of a word and could help you avoid many an embarrassing situation when using Spanish!

Expressions in which the headword appears

An entry will often feature certain common expressions in which the head-word appears. These expressions are in **bold** type, but in black as opposed to colour. A swung dash (~) is used instead of repeating a headword in an entry. 'Tono' and 'mano' opposite illustrate this point.

Related words

In the Pocket Dictionary words related to certain headwords are sometimes given at the end of an entry, as with 'ambición' and 'accept' opposite. These are easily picked out as they are also in colour. To help you find these words, they are placed in alphabetical order after the headword to which they belong: cf. 'accept, general' opposite.

lane [leɪn] n (in country) camino; (AUT) carril m; (in race) calle f

embrollar [embro'ʎar] vt (el asunto) to confuse, complicate; (persona) to involve, embroil; ~se vr (confundirse) to get into a muddle o mess

COU [kou] (ESP) nm abr (= Curso de Orientación Universitaria) 1 year course leading to final school-leaving certificate and university entrance examinations

cuenca ['kwenka] nf (ANAT) eye socket; (GEO) bowl, deep valley

menudo, a [me'nuðo, a] adj (pequeño) small, tiny; (sin importancia) petty, insignificant; ¡~ **negocio!** (fam) some deal!; **a ~** often, frequently

tono ['tono] nm tone; **fuera de ~** inappropriate; **darse ~** to put on airs

ambición [ambi'θjon] nf ambition; **ambicionar** vt to aspire to; **ambicioso, a** adj ambitious

accept [ək'sɛpt] vt aceptar; (responsibility, blame) admitir; ~**able** adj aceptable; ~**ance** n aceptación

hit [hɪt] (pt, pp **hit**) vt (strike) golpear, pegar; (reach: target) alcanzar; (collide with: car) chocar contra; (fig: affect) afectar ♦ n golpe m; (success) éxito; **to ~ it off with sb** llevarse bien con uno; ~-**and-run driver** n conductor(a) que atropella y huye

repoblación [repoβla'θjon] nf repopulation; (de río) restocking; ~ **forestal** reafforestation

mast [mɑːst] n (NAUT) mástil m; (RADIO etc) torre f

R.S.V.P. abbr (= répondez s'il vous plaît) SRC

burócrata [bu'rokrata] nm/f civil servant; (pey) bureaucrat

bocazas [bo'kaθas] (fam) nm inv bigmouth

cabrón [ka'βron] nm cuckold; (fam!) bastard (!)

mano ['mano] nf hand; (ZOOL) foot, paw; (de pintura) coat; (serie) lot, series; **a ~** by hand; **a ~ derecha/izquierda** on the right(-hand side)/left(-hand side); **de primera ~** (at) first hand; **de segunda ~** (at) second hand; **robo a ~ armada** armed robbery; ~ **de obra** labour, manpower; **estrechar la ~ a uno** to shake sb's hand

general [xene'ral] adj general ♦ nm general; **por lo** o **en ~** in general; G~**itat** nf Catalan parliament; ~**izar** vt to generalize; ~**izarse** vr to become generalized, spread; ~**mente** adv generally

5

'Key' words

Your Collins Pocket Dictionary gives special status to certain Spanish and English words which can be looked on as 'key' words in each language. These are words which have many different usages. 'Poder', 'menos' and 'se' opposite are typical examples in Spanish. You are likely to become familiar with them in your day-to-day language studies.

There will be occasions, however, when you want to check on a particular usage. Your dictionary can be very helpful here. Note how with 'poder', for example, different parts of speech and different usages are clearly indicated by a combination of lozenges - ♦ - and numbers. In addition, further guides to usage are given in the language of the user who needs them. These are bracketed and in italics.

poder [poˈðer] *vi* **1** (*capacidad*) can, be able to; **no puedo hacerlo** I can't do it, I'm unable to do it
2 (*permiso*) can, may, be allowed to; **¿se puede?** may I (*o* we)?; **puedes irte ahora** you may go now; **no se puede fumar en este hospital** smoking is not allowed in this hospital
3 (*posibilidad*) may, might, could; **puede llegar mañana** he may *o* might arrive tomorrow; **pudiste haberte hecho daño** you might *o* could have hurt yourself; **¡podías habérmelo dicho antes!** you might have told me before!
4: **puede ser: puede ser** perhaps; **puede ser que lo sepa Tomás** Tomás may *o* might know
5: **¡no puedo más!** I've had enough!; **no pude menos que dejarlo** I couldn't help but leave it; **es tonto a más no** ~ he's as stupid as they come
6: ~ **con: no puedo con este crío** this kid's too much for me
♦ *nm* power; ~ **adquisitivo** purchasing power; **detentar** *o* **ocupar** *o* **estar en el** ~ to be in power

se [se] *pron* **1** (*reflexivo*: *sg*: *m*) himself; (: *f*) herself; (: *pl*) themselves; (: *cosa*) itself; (: *de Vd*) yourself; (: *de Vds*) yourselves; ~ **está preparando** she's preparing herself; *para usos léxicos del pron ver el vb en cuestión, p.ej.* **arrepentirse**
2 (*con complemento indirecto*) to him; to her; to them; to it; to you; **a usted** ~ **lo dije ayer** I told you yesterday; ~ **compró un sombrero** he bought himself a hat; ~ **rompió la pierna** he broke his leg
3 (*uso recíproco*) each other, one another; ~ **miraron (el uno al otro)** they looked at each other *o* one another
4 (*en oraciones pasivas*): **se han vendido muchos libros** a lot of books have been sold
5 (*impers*): ~ **dice que** people say that, it is said that; **allí** ~ **come muy bien** the food there is very good, you can eat very well there

menos [menos] *adj* **1**: ~ **(que, de)** (*compar*: *cantidad*) less (than); (: *número*) fewer (than); **con** ~ **entusiasmo** with less enthusiasm; ~ **gente** fewer people; *ver tb* **cada**
2 (*superl*): **es el que** ~ **culpa tiene** he is the least to blame
♦ *adv* **1** (*compar*): ~ **(que, de)** less (than); **me gusta** ~ **que el otro** I like it less than the other one
2 (*superl*): **es el** ~ **listo (de su clase)** he's the least bright in his class; **de todas ellas es la que** ~ **me agrada** out of all of them she's the one I like least; **(por) lo** ~ at (the very) least
3 (*locuciones*): **no quiero verle y** ~ **visitarle** I don't want to see him let alone visit him; **tenemos 7 de** ~ we're seven short
♦ *prep* except; (*cifras*) minus; **todos** ~ **él** everyone except (for) him; **5** ~ **2** 5 minus 2
♦ *conj*: **a** ~ **que: a** ~ **que venga mañana** unless he comes tomorrow

WORDGAME 1

HEADWORDS

Study the following sentences. In each sentence a wrong word spelt very similarly to the correct word has deliberately been put in and the sentence doesn't make sense. This word is shaded each time. Write out each sentence again, putting in the <u>correct</u> word which you will find in your dictionary near the wrong word.

Example: Aparcar aquí no es delirio.

['Delirio' (= delirium) is the wrong word and should be replaced by 'delito' (= offence)]

1.   El mecánico se negó a arrebatarme el coche.

2.   El baúl estaba cubierto de pólvora.

3.   Es muy caro reventar las fotos en esa tienda.

4.   Les gusta mucho dar pasillos a caballo.

5.   Para ayunar a su madre pone la mesa todos los días.

6.   La ballesta es el animal más grande del mundo.

7.   Mientras esquiábamos nos cayó una nevera tremenda.

8.   No me gustó el último capitolio del libro.

9.   Tuvimos un pinchito y hubo que parar el coche.

10.   Hay que cerrar la puerta con candidato.

WORDGAME 2
DICTIONARY ENTRIES

Complete the crossword below by looking up the English words in the list and finding the correct Spanish translations. There is a slight catch, however! All the English words can be translated several ways into Spanish, but only one translation will fit correctly into each part of the crossword. So look carefully through the entries in the English-Spanish section of your dictionary.

1. HORN

2. THROW

3. REMEMBER

4. PERFORMANCE

5. SPEECH

6. WHOLE

7. AMUSE

8. OLD

9. BELL

10. MATERIAL

11. ENDING

12. PART

WORDGAME 3
FINDING MEANINGS

In this list there are eight pairs of words that have some sort of connection with each other. For example, **'curso'** (= 'course') and **'estudiante'** (= 'student') are linked. Find the other pairs by looking up the words in your dictionary.

1. bata
2. nido
3. cuero
4. zapatillas
5. campanario
6. estudiante
7. libro
8. bolso
9. pasarela
10. aleta
11. curso
12. estante
13. urraca
14. barco
15. veleta
16. tiburón

WORDGAME 4

SYNONYMS

Complete the crossword by supplying SYNONYMS of the words below. You will sometimes find the synonym you are looking for in italics and bracketed at the entries for the words listed below. Sometimes you will have to turn to the English-Spanish section for help.

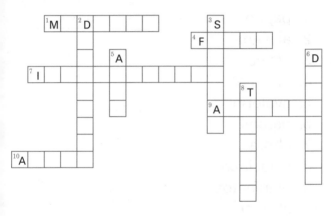

1. maneras
2. desilusión
3. exceder
4. incendio
5. cariño

6. vencer
7. inacabable
8. éxito
9. complacer
10. aeroplano

WORDGAME 5

SPELLING

You will often use your dictionary to check spellings. The person who has compiled this list of ten Spanish words has made <u>three</u> spelling mistakes. Find the three words which have been misspelt and write them out correctly.

1. pájaro
2. acienda
3. oleaje
4. gigante
5. avalorios
6. peregil
7. ahora
8. velocidad
9. quinientos
10. abridor

WORDGAME 6

ANTONYMS

Complete the crossword by supplying ANTONYMS (i.e. opposites) in Spanish of the words below. Use your dictionary to help.

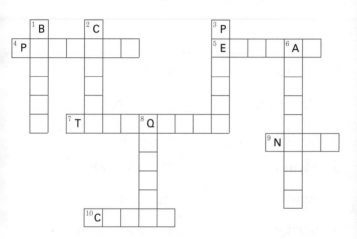

1. feo
2. abrir
3. ligero
4. riqueza
5. salir
6. engordar
7. inquieto
8. poner
9. todo
10. oscuro

WORDGAME 7
PHONETIC SPELLINGS

The phonetic transcriptions of twenty Spanish words are given below. If you study pages vi to ix at the front of your dictionary you should be able to work out what the words are.

1. 'aɣwa

2. θju'ðað

3. alreðe'ðor

4. mu'tʃatʃo

5. 'bjento

6. 'niɲo

7. bol' βer

8. 'kaʎe

9. θiɣ'θaɣ

10. 'xenjo

11. 'gwarða

12. 'tʃoke

13. em'bjar

14. ka'βaʎo

15. aβo'ɣaðo

16. korre'xir

17. ko'mjenθo

18. 'eʎos

19. xer'sei

20. i'ɣwal

WORDGAME 8

EXPRESSIONS IN WHICH THE HEADWORD APPEARS

If you look up the headword 'mismo' in the Spanish-English section of your dictionary you will find that the word can have many meanings. Study the entry carefully and translate the following sentences into English.

1. Ahora mismo se lo llevo.

2. A mí me da lo mismo.

3. Lo mismo que tú estudias francés yo estudio español.

4. En ese mismo momento llegó la policía.

5. Acudió el mismo Presidente.

6. Todos los domingos se ponía el mismo traje.

7. Lo hice yo mismo.

8. Era un hipócrita, y por lo mismo despreciado por todos.

9. Tenemos que empezar hoy mismo.

10. Lo vi aquí mismo.

WORDGAME 9

RELATED WORDS

Fill in the blanks in the pairs of sentences below. The missing words are related to the headwords on the left. Choose the correct 'relative' each time. You will find it in your dictionary near the headword provided.

HEADWORD	RELATED WORDS
estudiante	1. Realiza sus _____ en la Universidad. 2. Hay que _____ bien el texto.
pertenecer	3. Estos son los terrenos _____ al Ayuntamiento. 4. Recogió todas sus _____ y se fue.
empleo	5. Es _____ de banco. 6. Voy a _____ todos los medios a mi alcance.
atractivo	7. Esa perspectiva no me _____ nada. 8. Aquella mujer ejercía una gran _____ sobre él.
terminante	9. Al _____ de la reunión todos se fueron a tomar café. 10. No le dejaron _____ lo que estaba diciendo.
falsedad	11. Lo que estás diciendo es completamente _____. 12. Se dedicaban a _____ billetes de banco.

WORDGAME 10
'KEY' WORDS

Study carefully the entry **'hacer'** in your dictionary and find translations for the following:

1. it's cold

2. I made them come

3. to study Economics

4. this will make it more difficult

5. to do the cooking

6. they became friends

7. I've been going for a month

8. to turn a deaf ear

9. if it's alright with you

10. to get hold of something

THE DICTIONARY AND GRAMMAR

While it is true that a dictionary can never be a substitute for a detailed grammar reference book, it nevertheless provides a great deal of grammatical information. If you know how to extract this information you will be able to use Spanish more accurately both in speech and in writing.

The Collins Pocket Dictionary presents grammatical information as follows.

Parts of speech

Parts of speech are given in italics immediately after the phonetic spellings of headwords. Abbreviated forms are used. Abbreviations can be checked on pages iv and v.

Changes in parts of speech within an entry – for example, from adjective to adverb to noun, or from noun to intransitive verb to transitive verb – are indicated by means of lozenges - ♦ - as with the Spanish 'derecho' and the English 'act' opposite.

Genders of Spanish nouns

The gender of each noun in the Spanish-English section of the dictionary is indicated in the following way:

> *nm* = nombre masculino
> *nf* = nombre femenino

You will occasionally see *nm/f* beside an entry. This indicates that a noun – 'habitante', for example – can be either masculine or feminine.

Feminine forms of nouns are shown, as with 'ministro' opposite: the feminine ending is substituted for the masculine, so that 'ministro' becomes 'ministra' in the feminine.

In the English-Spanish section of the dictionary, genders are not shown for masculine nouns ending in '-o' or feminine nouns ending in '-a'. Otherwise, the gender immediately follows the translation. If a noun can be either masculine or feminine, this is shown by '*m/f*' if the form of the noun does not change, or by the feminine ending if it does change, as with 'graduate' and 'governor' opposite. Note that when an ending is added on to a word rather than substituted for another ending it appears in brackets.

It is most important that you know the correct gender of a Spanish noun, since it is going to determine the form of both adjectives and past participles. If you are in any doubt as to the gender of a noun, it is always best to check it in your dictionary

estría [es'tria] *nf* groove

tenue ['tenwe] *adj* (*delgado*) thin, slender; (*neblina*) light; (*lazo, vínculo*) slight

criterio [kri'terjo] *nm* criterion; (*juicio*) judgement

manguera [man'gera] *nf* (*de riego*) hose; (*tubo*) pipe

habitante [aßi'tante] *nm/f* inhabitant

ministro, a [mi'nistro, a] *nm/f* minister

derecho, a [de'retʃo, a] *adj* right, right-hand ♦ *nm* (*privilegio*) right; (*lado*) right(-hand) side; (*leyes*) law ♦ *adv* straight, directly; ~**s** *nmpl* (*de aduana*) duty *sg*; (*de autor*) royalties; **tener ~ a** to have a right to

act [ækt] *n* acto, acción *f*; (*of play*) acto; (*in music hall etc*) número; (*LAW*) decreto, ley *f* ♦ *vi* (*behave*) comportarse; (*have effect: drug, chemical*) hacer efecto; (*THEATRE*) actuar; (*pretend*) fingir; (*take action*) obrar ♦ *vt* (*part*) hacer el papel de; **in the ~ of: to catch sb in the ~ of** ... pillar a uno en el momento en que ...; **to ~ as** actuar *or* hacer de; ~**ing** *adj* suplente ♦ *n* (*activity*) actuación *f*; (*profession*) profesión *f* de actor

governor ['gʌvənə*] *n* gobernador(a) *m/f*; (*of school etc*) miembro del consejo; (*of jail*) director(a) *m/f*
graduate [*n* 'grædjuɪt, *vb* 'grædjueɪt] *n* (*US: of high school*) graduado/a; (*of university*) licenciado/a ♦ *vi* graduarse; licenciarse; **graduation** [-'eɪʃən] *n* (*ceremony*) entrega del título

19

Adjectives

Adjectives are given in both their masculine and feminine forms, where these are different. The usual rule is to drop the 'o' of the masculine form and add an 'a' to make an adjective feminine, as with 'negro' opposite.

Some adjectives have identical masculine and feminine forms. Where this occurs, there is no 'a' beside the basic masculine form.

Adverbs

The normal 'rule' for forming adverbs in Spanish is to add '-mente' to the feminine form of the adjective. Thus:

seguro > segura > seguramente

The '-mente' ending is often the equivalent of the English '-ly':

seguramente – surely
lentamente – slowly

In your dictionary Spanish adverbs are not generally given, since the English translation can usually be derived from the relevant translation of the adjective headword. Usually the translation can be formed by adding '-ly' to the relevant adjective translation: e.g.

fiel – faithful
fielmente – faithfully

In cases where the basic translation for the adverb cannot be derived from those for the adjective, the adverb is likely to be listed as a headword in alphabetical order. This means it may not be immediately adjacent to the adjective headword: see 'actual' and 'actualmente' opposite.

Information about verbs

A major problem facing language learners is that the form of a verb will change according to the subject and/or the tense being used. A typical Spanish verb can take many different forms – too many to list in a dictionary entry.

negro, a ['neɣro, a] *adj* black; (*suerte*) awful ♦ *nm* black ♦ *nm/f* Negro/Negress, Black

valiente [ba'ljente] *adj* brave, valiant ♦ *nm* hero

seguramente [seɣura'mente] *adv* surely; (*con certeza*) for sure, with certainty

actual [ak'twal] *adj* present(-day), current; *nf* present; ~**idades** *nfpl* (*noticias*) news *sg*; **en la ~idad** at present; (*hoy día*) nowadays

actualizar [aktwali'θar] *vt* to update, modernize

actualmente [aktwal'mente] *adv* at present; (*hoy día*) nowadays

Yet, although verbs are listed in your dictionary in their infinitive forms only, this does not mean that the dictionary is of limited value when it comes to handling the verb system of the Spanish language. On the contrary, it contains much valuable information.

First of all, your dictionary will help you with the meanings of unfamiliar verbs. If you came across the word 'decidió' in a text and looked it up in your dictionary you wouldn't find it. What you must do is assume that it is part of a verb and look for the infinitive form. Thus you will deduce that 'decidió' is a form of the verb 'decidir'. You now have the basic meaning of the word you are concerned with — something to do with the English verb 'decide' — and this should be enough to help you understand the text you are reading.

It is usually an easy task to make the connection between the form of a verb and the infinitive. For example, 'decidieran', 'decidirá', 'decidimos' and 'decidido' are all recognisable as parts of the infinitive 'decidir'. However, sometimes it is less obvious — for example, 'pueda', 'podrán' and 'pude' are all parts of 'poder'. The only real solution to this problem is to learn the various forms of the main Spanish regular and irregular verbs.

And this is the second source of help offered by your dictionary as far as verbs are concerned. The verb tables on page x of the Collins Pocket Dictionary provide a summary of some of the main forms of the main tenses of regular and irregular verbs. Consider the verb 'poder' below where the following information is given:

1 pudiendo	— Present Participle
2 puede	— Imperative
3 puedo, puedes, puede, pueden	— Present Tense forms
4 pude, pudiste, pudo, pudimos, pudisteis, pudieron	— Preterite forms
5 podré *etc*	— 1st Person Singular of the Future Tense
6 pueda, puedas, pueda, puedan	— Present Subjunctive forms
7 pudiera *etc*	— 1st Person Singular of the Imperfect Subjunctive

The regular '-ar', '-er', and '-ir' verbs — 'hablar', 'comer' and 'vivir' — are presented in greater detail. The main tenses and the different endings are given in full. This information can be transferred and applied to all verbs in the list. In addition, the main parts of the most common irregular verbs are listed in the body of the dictionary.

HABLAR

1 hablando
2 habla, hablad
3 hablo, hablas, habla, hablamos, habláis, hablan
4 hablé, hablaste, habló, hablamos, hablasteis, hablaron
5 hablaré, hablarás, hablará, hablaremos, hablaréis, hablarán
6 hable, hables, hable, hablemos, habléis, hablen
7 hablara, hablaras, hablara, habláramos, hablarais, hablaran
8 hablado
9 hablaba, hablabas, hablaba, hablábamos, hablabais, hablaban

In order to make maximum use of the information contained in these pages, a good working knowledge of the various rules affecting Spanish verbs is required. You will acquire this in the course of your Spanish studies and your Collins dictionary will serve as a useful reminder. If you happen to forget how to form the second person singular form of the Future Tense of 'poder' (i.e. how to translate 'you will be able to'), there will be no need to panic — your dictionary contains the information!

WORDGAME 11

PARTS OF SPEECH

In each sentence below a word has been shaded. Put a tick in the appropriate box to indicate the <u>part of speech</u> each time.

SENTENCE	Noun	Adj	Adv	Verb
1. Es estudiante de derecho.				
2. No hables tan alto.				
3. No tiene mucho dinero en su haber.				
4. Es un escrito muy largo.				
5. Vaya todo seguido.				
6. Es un dicho muy frecuente.				
7. Llegamos a casa muy tarde.				
8. Le gusta mucho andar por el campo.				
9. Lo hacemos por tu bien.				
10. A mi parecer es una buena película.				

WORDGAME 12

MEANING CHANGING WITH GENDER

Some Spanish nouns change meaning according to their gender, i.e. according to whether they are masculine or feminine. Look at the pairs of sentences below and fill in the blanks with either **'un'**, **'una'**, **'el'** or **'la'**. Use your dictionary to help.

1. No podía comprender _____ cólera de su padre.

    _____ cólera hace estragos en las regiones tropicales.

2. Perdí _____ pendiente en su casa.

    El coche no podía subir por _____ pendiente.

3. Los niños jugaban con _____ cometa.

    Dicen que en abril caerá _____ cometa.

4. Vimos _____ policía dentro de su coche.

    _____ policía ha descubierto una red de traficantes de droga.

5. Hay que cambiar _____ orden de los números.

    En cuanto recibió _____ orden su puso en camino.

6. ¿Ha llegado _____ parte de la policía?

    _____ parte de atrás de la casa es muy sombría.

7. Pasó dos días en _____ coma profundo.

    Tienes que poner _____ coma ahí.

8. Los soldados están todavía en _____ frente.

    El pelo le cubría _____ frente.

WORDGAME 13

ADVERBS

Translate the following Spanish adverbs into English (generally by adding **-ly** to the adjective).

1. recientemente

2. lamentablemente

3. constantemente

4. mensualmente

5. pesadamente

6. inconscientemente

7. inmediatamente

8. ampliamente

9. tenazmente

10. brillantemente

WORDGAME 14

VERB TENSES

Use your dictionary to help you fill in the blanks in the table below. (Remember the important pages at the front of your dictionary.)

INFINITIVE	PRESENT SUBJUNCTIVE	PRETERITE	FUTURE
tener		yo	
hacer			yo
poder			yo
decir		yo	
agradecer	yo		
saber			yo
reír	yo		
querer		yo	
caber	yo		
ir	yo		
salir			yo
ser		yo	

27

WORDGAME 15

IRREGULAR VERBS

Use your dictionary to find the <u>first person</u> present indicative of these verbs.

INFINITIVE	PRESENT INDICATIVE
conocer	
saber	
estar	
ofrecer	
poder	
ser	
poner	
divertir	
traer	
decir	
preferir	
negar	
dar	
instruir	

WORDGAME 16
IDENTIFYING INFINITIVES

In the sentences below you will see various Spanish verbs shaded. Use your dictionary to help you find the **infinitive** form of each verb.

1. Cuando era pequeño dormía en la misma habitación que mi hermano.

2. Mis amigos vienen conmigo.

3. No cupieron todos los libros en el estante.

4. ¿Es que no veías lo que pasaba?

5. El sábado saldremos todos juntos.

6. Ya hemos visto la casa.

7. ¿Quieres que lo ponga aquí?

8. Le dije que viniera a las ocho.

9. Nos han escrito tres cartas ya.

10. No sabían qué hacer.

11. Tuvimos que salir temprano.

12. En cuanto supe lo de su padre la llamé por teléfono.

13. ¿Por qué no trajiste el dinero?

14. Prefiero quedarme en casa.

15. Quiero que conozcas a mi padre.

MORE ABOUT MEANING

In this section we will consider some of the problems associated with using a bilingual dictionary.

Overdependence on your dictionary

That the dictionary is an invaluable tool for the language learner is beyond dispute. Nevertheless, it is possible to become overdependent on your dictionary, turning to it in an almost automatic fashion every time you come up against a new word or phrase in a Spanish text. Tackling an unfamiliar text in this way will turn reading in Spanish into an extremely tedious activity. It is possible to argue that if you stop to look up every new word you may actually be *hindering* your ability to read in Spanish — you are so concerned with the individual words that you pay no attention to the text as a whole and to the context which gives them meaning. It is therefore important to develop appropriate reading skills — using clues such as titles, headlines, illustrations, etc, understanding relations within a sentence, etc to predict or infer what a text is about.

A detailed study of the development of reading skills is not within the scope of this supplement; we are concerned with knowing how to use a dictionary, which is only one of several important skills involved in reading. Nevertheless, it may be instructive to look at one example. You see the following text in a Spanish newspaper and are interested in working out what it is about.

Contextual clues here include the heading in large type, which indicates that this is some sort of announcement, and the names. The verb 'recibir' is very much like the English 'receive' and you will also know 'form' words such as 'una', 'y' and so forth from your general studies in Spanish, as well as essential vocabulary such as 'niña', 'hijos', 'nombre'. Given that this

> ## Natalicios
> La señora de García Rodríguez (don Alfonso), de soltera Laura Montes de la Torre, ha dado a luz una niña, cuarta de sus hijos, que recibirá el nombre de Beatriz y tendrá como padrinos a doña Mercedes Sánchez Serrano y don Felipe Gómez Morales.

extract appeared in a newspaper, you will probably have worked out by now that this is an announcement placed in the 'Personal Column.'

So you have used contextual and word-formation clues to get you to the point where you have understood that this notice has been placed in the personal column because something has happened to señora de García Rodríguez and that somebody is going to be given the name of 'Beatriz'. And you have reached this point *without* opening your dictionary once. Common sense and your knowledge of newspaper contents in this country will suggest that this must be an announcement of someone's birth or death. Thus 'dar a luz' ('to give birth') and 'padrinos' ('godparents') become the only words that you need to look up in order to confirm that this is indeed a birth announcement.

When learning Spanish we are helped considerably by the fact that many Spanish and English words look and sound alike and have exactly the same meaning. Such words are called 'COGNATES'. Many words which look similar in Spanish and English come from a common Latin root. Other words are the same or nearly the same in both languages because the Spanish language has borrowed a word from English or vice versa. The dictionary will often not be necessary where cognates are concerned — provided you know the English word that the Spanish word resembles!

Words with more than one meaning

The need to examine with care *all* the information contained in a dictionary entry must be stressed. This is particularly important with the many Spanish words which have more than one meaning. For example, the Spanish 'destino' can mean 'destiny' as well as 'destination'. How you translated the word would depend on the context in which you found it.

Similarly, if you were trying to translate a phrase such as 'sigo sin saber', you would have to look through the whole entry for 'seguir' to get the right translation. If you restricted your search to the first line of the entry and saw that the first meaning given is 'to follow', you might be tempted to assume that the phrase meant 'I follow without knowing'. But if you examined the entry closely you would see that 'seguir sin . . .' means 'to still do . . . or 'to still be . . .'. So 'sigo sin saber' means 'I still don't know'.

The same need for care applies when you are using the English-Spanish section of your dictionary to translate a word from English into Spanish. Watch out in particular for the lozenges indicating changes in parts of speech.

The noun 'sink' is 'fregadero', while the verb is 'hundir'. If you don't watch what you are doing, you could end up with ridiculous non-Spanish e.g. 'Dejó los platos en el hundir'!

Phrasal verbs

Another potential source of difficulty is English phrasal verbs. These consist of a common verb ('make', 'get', etc.) plus an adverb and/or a preposition to give English expressions such as 'to make out', 'to get on', etc. Entries for such verbs tend to be fairly full, so close examination of the contents is required. Note how these verbs appear in colour within the entry.

sink [sɪŋk] (*pt* **sank**, *pp* **sunk**) *n* fregadero ♦ *vt* (*ship*) hundir, echar a pique; (*foundations*) excavar ♦ *vi* (*gen*) hundirse; **to ~ sth into** hundir algo en; **~ in** *vi* (*fig*) penetrar, calar.

make [meɪk] (*pt, pp* **made**) *vt* hacer; (*manufacture*) fabricar; (*mistake*) cometer; (*speech*) pronunciar; (*cause to be*): **to ~ sb sad** poner triste a alguien; (*force*): **to ~ sb do sth** obligar a alguien a hacer algo; (*earn*) ganar; (*equal*): **2 and 2 ~ 4** 2 y 2 son 4 ♦ *n* marca; **to ~ the bed** hacer la cama; **to ~ a fool of sb** poner a alguien en ridículo; **to ~ a profit/loss** obtener ganancias/ sufrir pérdidas; **to ~ it** (*arrive*) llegar; (*achieve sth*) tener éxito; **what time do you ~ it?** ¿qué hora tienes?; **to ~ do with** contentarse con; **~ for** *vt fus* (*place*) dirigirse a; **~ out** *vt* (*decipher*) descifrar; (*understand*) entender; (*see*) distinguir; (*cheque*) extender; **~ up** *vt* (*invent*) inventar; (*prepare*) hacer; (*constitute*) constituir ♦ *vi* reconciliarse; (*with cosmetics*) maquillarse; **~ up for** *vt fus* compensar;

Falsos amigos

We noted above that many Spanish and English words have similar forms *and* meanings. There are, however, many Spanish words which *look* like English words but have a completely *different* meaning. For example, 'la carpeta' means 'the folder'; 'sensible' means 'sensitive'. This can easily lead to serious mistranslations.

Sometimes the meaning of the Spanish word is quite close to the English. For example, 'la moneda' means 'coin' rather than 'money'; 'simpático' means 'nice' rather than 'sympethatic'. But some Spanish words which look similar to English words have two meanings, one the same as the English, the other completely different! 'El plato' can mean 'course' (in a meal) as well as 'plate'; ' la cámara' can mean 'camera', but also 'chamber'.

Such words are often referred to as FALSOS AMIGOS ('false friends'). You will have to look at the context in which they appear to arrive at the correct meaning. If they seem to fit in with the sense of the passage as a whole, you will probably not need to look them up. If they don't make sense, however, you may well be dealing with 'falsos amigos'.

WORDS IN CONTEXT

Study the sentences below. Translations of the shaded words are given at the bottom. Match the number of the sentence and the letter of the translation correctly each time.

1. Tendremos que atarlo con una cuerda.
2. La cuerda del reloj se ha roto.
3. Iremos al cine para entretener a los niños.
4. No me entretengas, que llegaré tarde.
5. Le dieron una patada en la espinilla.
6. Tenía una espinilla enorme en la nariz.
7. Siempre le da mucho sueño después de comer.
8. Anoche me desperté sobresaltada por un mal sueño.
9. El niño tocaba todo lo que veía.
10. Su padre tocaba muy bien la guitarra.
11. Tuvo un acceso de tos.
12. Todas las vías de acceso estaban cerradas.
13. Me gustaría estudiar la carrera de Derecho.
14. Todos querían participar en la carrera.
15. He quebrado el plato sin darme cuenta.
16. No sabían que esa empresa había quebrado.

a.	touched	i.	rope
b.	shin(bone)	j.	hold up
c.	entertain	k.	entry
d.	spring	l.	race
e.	fit	m.	gone bankrupt
f.	course	n.	played
g.	sleepiness	o.	dream
h.	blackhead	p.	broken

WORDGAME 18

WORDS WITH MORE THAN ONE MEANING

Look at the advertisements below. The words which are shaded can have more than one meaning. Use your dictionary to help you work out the correct translation in the context.

1

El Pescador
RESTAURANTE

Mariscos de viveros propios
Teléfono 406 12 80 – MADRID 6

P FÁCIL
APARCAMIENTO

2

Restaurante
LOS CEREZOS

ALTA COCINA REGIONAL
Para amantes de lo tradicional

RESERVAS: 574 34 11/12

3

INTERLANGUE
ANUNCIA CURSO MASTER DE
INGLÉS JURÍDICO PARA
PROFESIONALES DEL DERECHO
Inicio: 20 de octubre

4

¡¡¡BUTACAS PIEL A MEDIDA!!!

APROVECHE GRANDES REBAJAS EN OCTUBRE

¡En fábrica, más calidad y menor precio!

Horario continuado de 9,30 a 20,30 –
incluso sábados

34

GRANDES ALMACENES "EL CONDOR"
IMPORTANTES REBAJAS DE FIN DE TEMPORADA

5

6

Guía   **TELEVISION**

JUEVES, 19

19.00. – Partido adelantado de la
JORNADA DE LIGA de PRIMERA DIVISION:
Atlético de Madrid – Barcelona (TV-2)

7

Bar-restaurante **"La Ballena"**

platos combinados desde 300 ptas.

helados, postres nuestra especialidad

8

ULTIMAS VIVIENDAS
de 2 y 3 dormitorios con
plaza de garaje opcional
Lunes a Viernes mañanas de 11 a 13,30.
Tardes de 16,30 a 19,30.

9

Calle de
ISABEL LA CATOLICA
N.ºs 50 – 56

**PISOS EXTERIORES
DE 80 m^2**

FINANCIACION A 11 AÑOS
13 Y 13,5% CON LA CAJA DE BARCELONA

WORDGAME 19
FALSE FRIENDS

Look at the advertisements below. The words which are shaded resemble English words but have different meanings here. Find a correct translation for each word in the context.

1

LA MAYOR COLECCION DE
ALFOMBRAS
PERSAS Y
ORIENTALES
¡¡¡VENTA DE LIQUIDACION
POR CAMBIO DE DOMICILIO!!!

2

Teatro Nacional:
"El Alcalde de Zalamea"
Localidades en venta a partir de mañana

3

PRODUCTOS BENGOLEA
¡NO RECURRA A
LA COMPETENCIA!
Visite nuestro local en Castellana 500

4

OFERTA ESPECIAL
cubiertos de acero inoxidable de
primerísima calidad en planta baja

5

6

7

8

9

HAVE FUN WITH YOUR DICTIONARY

Here are some word games for you to try. You will find your dictionary helpful as you attempt the activities.

WORDGAME 20

In the boxes below the letters of eight Spanish words have been replaced by numbers. A number represents the same letter each time (though an accent may be required sometimes).

Try to crack the code and find eight words. If you need help, use your dictionary.

Here is a clue: all the words you are looking for have something to do with TRANSPORT.

1. | C¹ | A² | M³ | 4 | 5 | 6 |

2. | 2 | 7 | 8 | 5 | 9 | 7 | 10 |

3. | 1 | 5 | 1 | 11 | 12 |

4. | 9 | 4 | 1 | 4 | 1 | 13 | 12 | 8 | 2 |

5. | 8 | 14 | 12 | 6 |

6. | 11 | 12 | 13 | 4 | 1 | 5 | 15 | 8 | 12 | 14 | 5 |

7. | 2 | 3 | 9 | 7 | 13 | 2 | 6 | 1 | 4 | 2 |

8. | 3 | 5 | 8 | 5 |

WORDGAME 21

If you 'behead' certain Spanish words, i.e. take away their first letter, you are left with another Spanish word. For example, if you behead **'aplomo'** (= 'self-assurance'), you get **'plomo'** (= 'lead'), and **'bala'** (= 'bullet') gives **'ala'** (= 'wing').

The following words have their heads chopped off, i.e. the first letter has been removed. Use your dictionary to help you form a new Spanish word by adding one letter to the start of each word below. You will find that some of them can have more than one answer. Write down the new Spanish word and its meaning.

1. bajo (= low)
2. oler (= to smell)
3. año (= year)
4. ora (= gold)
5. reparar (= to repair)
6. ama (= owner)
7. rendido (= worn-out)
8. cuerdo (= sane)
9. ave (= bird)
10. batir (= to beat)
11. resto (= rest)
12. precio (= price)
13. cera (= wax)
14. hora (= hour)
15. pinar (= pine forest)

WORDGAME 22

PALABRAS CRUZADAS

Complete this crossword by looking up the words listed below in the English-Spanish section of your dictionary. Remember to read through the entry carefully to find the word that will fit.

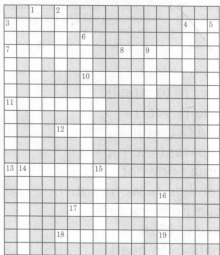

DOWN

1. to identify
2. to go out
3. regrettable
4. to love
5. streamlined
6. heating
9. expensive
14. to oblige
15. tricks
16. now

ACROSS

3. to bark
4. wing
7. lie
8. above
10. to work out
11. to lighten

12. to need
13. usual
17. cornet
18. to stink
19. radius

WORDGAME 23

There are twelve Spanish words hidden in the grid below. Each word is made up of five letters but has been split into two parts.

Find the Spanish words. Each group of letters can only be used once.

Use your dictionary to help you.

bla	lir	bu	ma	que	go
gor	co	ver	vi	asi	jor
cal	me	ha	jo	lar	so
jo	jía	lo	vol	sa	eno

WORDGAME 24

Here is a list of Spanish words for things you will find in the kitchen. Unfortunately, they have all been jumbled up. Try to work out what each word is and put the word in the boxes on the right. You will see that there are seven shaded boxes below. With the seven letters in the shaded boxes make up <u>another</u> Spanish word for an object you can find in the kitchen.

1 azta   ¿Quieres una ____ de café?

2 eanevr   ¡Mete la mantequilla en la ____ !

3 asme   ¡La comida está en la ____!

4 zoac   Su madre está calentando la leche en el ____

5 roegcanldo ¡No saques el helado del ____ todavía!

6 uclclohi ¿Dónde has puesto el ____ del queso?

7 rgoif   ¿Puedes cerrar ya el ____ del agua caliente?

The word you are looking for is:

42

WORDGAME 25
PALABRAS CRUZADAS

Take the four letters given each time and put them in the four empty boxes in the centre of each grid. Arrange them in such a way that you form four six-letter words. Use your dictionary to check the words.

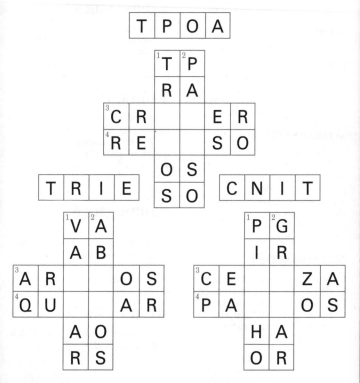

ANSWERS

WORDGAME 1

1	arreglarme	6	ballena
2	polvo	7	nevada
3	revelar	8	capítulo
4	paseos	9	pinchazo
5	ayudar	10	candado

WORDGAME 2

1	cuerno	7	entretener
2	echar	8	antiguo
3	recordar	9	timbre
4	actuación	10	tela
5	habla	11	terminación
6	entero	12	parte

WORDGAME 3

bata + zapatillas
nido + urraca
cuero + bolso
campanario + veleta
estudiante + curso
libro + estante
pasarela + barco
aleta + tiburón

WORDGAME 4

1	modales	6	derrotar
2	decepción	7	interminable
3	superar	8	triunfo
4	fuego	9	agradar
5	amor	10	avión

WORDGAME 5

2	hacienda
5	abalorios
6	perejil

WORDGAME 6

1	bonito	6	adelgazar
2	cerrar	7	tranquilo
3	pesado	8	quitar
4	pobreza	9	nada
5	entrar	10	claro

WORDGAME 7

agua, ciudad, alrededor,
muchacho, viento, niño,
volver, calle, zigzag,
genio, guarda, choque,
enviar, caballo, abogado,
corregir, comienzo, ellos,
jersé, igual

WORDGAME 9

1	estudios	7	atrae
2	estudiar	8	atracción
3	pertenecientes	9	término
4	pertenencias	10	terminar
5	empleado	11	falso
6	emplear	12	falsificar

WORDGAME 11

1 n	2 adv	3 n	4 n	5 adv
6 n	7 adv	8 v	9 n	10 n

44

WORDGAME 12

1 la; El	5 el; la
2 el; la	6 el; La
3 una; un	7 un; una
4 un; La	8 el; la

WORDGAME 14

tuve	ría
haré	quise
podré	quepa
dije	vaya
agradezca	saldré
sabré	fui

WORDGAME 15

conozco	divierto
sé	traigo
estoy	digo
ofrezco	prefiero
puedo	niego
soy	doy
pongo	instruyo

WORDGAME 16

1 dormir	9 escribir
2 venir	10 saber
3 caber	11 tener
4 ver	12 saber
5 salir	13 traer
6 ver	14 preferir
7 poner	15 conocer
8 venir	

WORDGAME 17

1 i	5 b	9 a	13 f
2 d	6 h	10 n	14 l
3 c	7 g	11 e	15 p
4 j	8 o	12 k	16 m

WORDGAME 18

1 fish farm
2 cuisine
3 law
4 leather
5 significant
6 league
7 set main course
8 space
9 savings bank

WORDGAME 19

1 clearance sale;
  home (Here: address)
2 tickets
3 competition
4 cutlery
5 retirement
6 small hotel; rooms
7 guest house
8 premises
9 address

WORDGAME 20

1 camión		5 tren
2 autobús		6 helicóptero
3 coche		7 ambulancia
4 bicicleta		8 moto

45

WORDGAME 21

1 abajo	7 prendido
2 doler; moler; soler	8 acuerdo
	9 nave
3 baño; paño; daño; caño	10 abatir
	11 presto
4 coro; foro; loro; moro; poro	12 aprecio
	13 acera
	14 ahora
5 preparar	15 opinar
6 cama; dama; fama; gama; mama; rama	

WORDGAME 22

ACROSS:
3 ladrar
4 ala
7 mentira
8 encima
10 elaborar
11 aligerar
12 necesitar
13 corriente
17 cucurucho
18 apestar
19 radio

DOWN:
1 identificar
2 salir
3 lamentable
4 amar
5 aerodinámico
6 calefacción
9 caro
14 obligar
15 trucos
16 ahora

WORDGAME 23

enojo	cojo
queso	calma
salir	asilo
volver	largo
vigor	mejor
bujía	habla

WORDGAME 24

1 taza	5 congelador
2 nevera	6 cuchilo
3 mesa	7 grifo
4 cazo	

Missing word – ARMARIO

WORDGAME 25

1)	1 trapos	2 patoso	
	3 cráter	4 reposo	
2)	1 variar	2 abetos	
	3 arreos	4 quitar	
3)	1 pincho	2 gritar	
	3 ceniza	4 pactos	

ENGLISH-SPANISH
INGLÉS-ESPAÑOL

A a

A [eɪ] *n* (*MUS*) la *m*

a [ə] *indef art* (*before vowel or silent h: an*) **1** un(a); ~ **book** un libro; **an apple** una manzana; **she's** ~ **doctor** (ella) es médica
2 (*instead of the number "one"*) un(a); ~ **year ago** hace un año; ~ **hundred/ thousand** *etc* **pounds** cien/mil *etc* libras
3 (*in expressing ratios, prices etc*): **3** ~ **day/week** 3 al día/a la semana; **10 km an hour** 10 km por hora; **£5** ~ **person** £5 por persona; **30p** ~ **kilo** 30p el kilo

A.A. *n abbr* (= *Automobile Association: BRIT*) ≈ RACE *m* (*SP*); (= *Alcoholics Anonymous*) Alcohólicos Anónimos
A.A.A. (*US*) *n abbr* (= *American Automobile Association*) ≈ RACE *m* (*SP*)
aback [ə'bæk] *adv*: **to be taken** ~ quedar desconcertado
abandon [ə'bændən] *vt* abandonar; (*give up*) renunciar a ♦ *n* abandono; (*wild behaviour*): **with** ~ sin reparos
abate [ə'beɪt] *vi* (*storm*) amainar; (*anger*) aplacarse; (*terror*) disminuir
abattoir ['æbətwɑ:*] (*BRIT*) *n* matadero
abbey ['æbɪ] *n* abadía
abbot ['æbət] *n* abad *m*
abbreviation [ə'bri:vɪ'eɪʃən] *n* (*short form*) abreviatura
abdicate ['æbdɪkeɪt] *vt* renunciar a ♦ *vi* abdicar; **abdication** [-'keɪʃən] *n* renuncia; (*of monarch*) abdicación *f*
abdomen ['æbdəmən] *n* abdomen *m*
abduct [æb'dʌkt] *vt* raptar, secuestrar
abet [ə'bet] *vt see* **aid**
abeyance [ə'beɪəns] *n*: **in** ~ (*law*) en desuso; (*matter*) en suspenso
abhor [əb'hɔ:*] *vt* aborrecer, abominar (de)

abide [ə'baɪd] *vt*: **I can't** ~ **it/him** no lo/ le puedo ver; ~ **by** *vt fus* atenerse a
ability [ə'bɪlɪtɪ] *n* habilidad *f*, capacidad *f*; (*talent*) talento
abject ['æbdʒekt] *adj* (*poverty*) miserable; (*apology*) rastrero
ablaze [ə'bleɪz] *adj* en llamas, ardiendo
able ['eɪbl] *adj* capaz; (*skilled*) hábil; **to be** ~ **to do sth** poder hacer algo; ~- **bodied** *adj* sano; **ably** *adv* hábilmente
abnormal [æb'nɔ:məl] *adj* anormal
aboard [ə'bɔ:d] *adv* a bordo ♦ *prep* a bordo de
abode [ə'bəud] *n*: **of no fixed** ~ sin domicilio fijo
abolish [ə'bɔlɪʃ] *vt* suprimir, abolir; **abolition** [æbə'lɪʃən] *n* supresión *f*, abolición *f*
aborigine [æbə'rɪdʒɪnɪ] *n* aborigen *m/f*
abort [ə'bɔ:t] *vt, vi* abortar; ~**ion** [ə'bɔ:ʃən] *n* aborto; **to have an** ~**ion** abortar, hacerse abortar; ~**ive** *adj* malogrado
abound [ə'baund] *vi*: **to** ~ (**in** *or* **with**) abundar (de *or* en)

about [ə'baut] *adv* **1** (*approximately*) más o menos, aproximadamente; ~ **a hundred/thousand** *etc* unos(unas) cien/mil *etc*; **it takes** ~ **10 hours** se tarda unas *or* más o menos 10 horas; **at** ~ **2 o'clock** sobre las dos; **I've just** ~ **finished** casi he terminado
2 (*referring to place*) por todas partes; **to leave things lying** ~ dejar las cosas (tiradas) por ahí; **to run** ~ correr por todas partes; **to walk** ~ pasearse, ir y venir
3: **to be** ~ **to do sth** estar a punto de

hacer algo
♦ *prep* **1** (*relating to*) de, sobre, acerca de; **a book ~ London** un libro sobre *or* acerca de Londres; **what is it ~?** ¿de qué se trata?, ¿qué pasa?; **we talked ~ it** hablamos de eso *or* ello; **what** *or* **how ~ doing this?** ¿qué tal si hacemos esto? **2** (*referring to place*) por; **to walk ~ the town** caminar por la ciudad

above [ə'bʌv] *adv* encima, por encima, arriba ♦ *prep* encima de; (*greater than: in number*) más de; (: *in rank*) superior a; **mentioned ~** susodicho; **~ all** sobre todo; **~ board** *adj* legítimo
abrasive [ə'breɪzɪv] *adj* abrasivo; (*manner*) brusco
abreast [ə'brest] *adv* de frente; **to keep ~ of** (*fig*) mantenerse al corriente de
abridge [ə'brɪdʒ] *vt* abreviar
abroad [ə'brɔːd] *adv* (*to be*) en el extranjero; (*to go*) al extranjero
abrupt [ə'brʌpt] *adj* (*sudden*) brusco; (*curt*) áspero
abruptly [ə'brʌptlɪ] *adv* (*leave*) repentinamente; (*speak*) bruscamente
abscess ['æbsɪs] *n* absceso
abscond [əb'skɔnd] *vi* (*thief*): **to ~ with** fugarse con; (*prisoner*): **to ~ (from)** escaparse (de)
absence ['æbsəns] *n* ausencia
absent ['æbsənt] *adj* ausente; **~ee** [-'tiː] *n* ausente *m/f*; **~-minded** *adj* distraído
absolute ['æbsəluːt] *adj* absoluto; **~ly** [-'luːtlɪ] *adv* (*totally*) totalmente; (*certainly!*) ¡por supuesto (que sí)!
absolve [əb'zɔlv] *vt*: **to ~ sb (from)** absolver a alguien (de)
absorb [əb'zɔːb] *vt* absorber; **to be ~ed in a book** estar absorto en un libro; **~ent cotton** (*US*) *n* algodón *m* hidrófilo; **~ing** *adj* absorbente
absorption [əb'zɔːpʃən] *n* absorción *f*
abstain [əb'steɪn] *vi*: **to ~ (from)** abstenerse (de)
abstinence ['æbstɪnəns] *n* abstinencia
abstract ['æbstrækt] *adj* abstracto
absurd [əb'sɔːd] *adj* absurdo
abundance [ə'bʌndəns] *n* abundancia

abuse [*n* ə'bjuːs, *vb* ə'bjuːz] *n* (*insults*) insultos *mpl*, injurias *fpl*; (*ill-treatment*) malos tratos *mpl*; (*misuse*) abuso ♦ *vt* insultar; maltratar; abusar de; **abusive** *adj* ofensivo
abysmal [ə'bɪzməl] *adj* pésimo; (*failure*) garrafal; (*ignorance*) supino
abyss [ə'bɪs] *n* abismo
AC *abbr* (= *alternating current*) corriente *f* alterna
academic [ækə'demɪk] *adj* académico, universitario; (*pej: issue*) puramente teórico ♦ *n* estudioso/a; profesor(a) *m/f* universitario/a
academy [ə'kædəmɪ] *n* (*learned body*) academia; (*school*) instituto, colegio; **~ of music** conservatorio
accelerate [æk'seləreɪt] *vt, vi* acelerar; **accelerator** (*BRIT*) *n* acelerador *m*
accent ['æksənt] *n* acento; (*fig*) énfasis *m*
accept [ək'sept] *vt* aceptar; (*responsibility, blame*) admitir; **~able** *adj* aceptable; **~ance** *n* aceptación *f*
access ['ækses] *n* acceso; **to have ~ to** tener libre acceso a; **~ible** [-'sesəbl] *adj* (*place, person*) accesible; (*knowledge etc*) asequible
accessory [æk'sesərɪ] *n* accesorio; (*LAW*): **~ to** cómplice de
accident ['æksɪdənt] *n* accidente *m*; (*chance event*) casualidad *f*; **by ~** (*unintentionally*) sin querer; (*by chance*) por casualidad; **~al** [-'dentl] *adj* accidental, fortuito; **~ally** [-'dentəlɪ] *adv* sin querer; por casualidad; **~-prone** *adj* propenso a los accidentes
acclaim [ə'kleɪm] *vt* aclamar, aplaudir ♦ *n* aclamación *f*, aplausos *mpl*
acclimate [ə'klaɪmət] (*US*) *vt* = **acclimatize**
acclimatize [ə'klaɪmətaɪz] (*BRIT*) *vt*: **to become ~d** aclimatarse
accolade ['ækəleɪd] *n* premio
accommodate [ə'kɔmədeɪt] *vt* (*subj: person*) alojar, hospedar; (: *car, hotel etc*) tener cabida para; (*oblige, help*) complacer; **accommodating** *adj* servicial, complaciente
accommodation [əkɔmə'deɪʃən] *n* (*US*

accommodations *npl*) alojamiento
accompaniment [ə'kʌmpənɪmənt] *n*
(*MUS*) acompañamiento
accompany [ə'kʌmpənɪ] *vt* acompañar
accomplice [ə'kʌmplɪs] *n* cómplice *m/f*
accomplish [ə'kʌmplɪʃ] *vt* (*finish*)
concluir; (*achieve*) lograr; **~ed** *adj*
experto, hábil; **~ment** *n* (*skill: gen pl*)
talento; (*completion*) realización *f*
accord [ə'kɔːd] *n* acuerdo ♦ *vt* conceder;
of his own ~ espontáneamente; **~ance**
n: **in ~ance with** de acuerdo con; **~ing**:
~ing to *prep* según; (*in accordance with*)
conforme a; **~ingly** *adv* (*appropriately*)
de acuerdo con esto; (*as a result*) en
consecuencia
accordion [ə'kɔːdɪən] *n* acordeón *m*
accost [ə'kɔst] *vt* abordar, dirigirse a
account [ə'kaunt] *n* (*COMM*) cuenta;
(*report*) informe *m*; **~s** *npl* (*COMM*)
cuentas *fpl*; **of no ~** de ninguna
importancia; **on ~** a cuenta; **on no ~**
bajo ningún concepto; **on ~ of** a causa
de, por motivo de; **to take into ~, take**
~ of tener en cuenta; **~ for** *vt fus*
(*explain*) explicar; (*represent*)
representar; **~able** *adj*: **~able (to)**
responsable (ante)
accountancy [ə'kauntənsɪ] *n* contabilidad
f
accountant [ə'kauntənt] *n* contable *m/f*,
contador(a) *m/f*
account number *n* (*at bank etc*)
número de cuenta
accredited [ə'krɛdɪtɪd] *adj* (*agent etc*)
autorizado
accrued interest [ə'kruː:d-] *n* interés *m*
acumulado
accumulate [ə'kjuːmjuleɪt] *vt* acumular
♦ *vi* acumularse
accuracy ['ækjurəsɪ] *n* (*of total*) exactitud
f; (*of description etc*) precisión *f*
accurate ['ækjurɪt] *adj* (*total*) exacto;
(*description*) preciso; (*person*) cuidadoso;
(*device*) de precisión; **~ly** *adv* con
precisión
accusation [ækjuːˈzeɪʃən] *n* acusación *f*
accuse [ə'kjuːz] *vt*: **to ~ sb (of sth)**
acusar a uno (de algo); **~d** *n* (*LAW*)

acusado/a
accustom [ə'kʌstəm] *vt* acostumbrar;
~ed *adj*: **~ed to** acostumbrado a
ace [eɪs] *n* as *m*
ache [eɪk] *n* dolor *m* ♦ *vi* doler; **my head**
~s me duele la cabeza
achieve [ə'tʃiːv] *vt* (*aim, result*) alcanzar;
(*success*) lograr, conseguir; **~ment** *n*
(*completion*) realización *f*; (*success*) éxito
acid ['æsɪd] *adj* ácido; (*taste*) agrio ♦ *n*
(*CHEM, inf: LSD*) ácido; **~ rain** *n* lluvia
ácida
acknowledge [ək'nɔlɪdʒ] *vt* (*letter: also*:
~ receipt of) acusar recibo de; (*fact,*
situation, person) reconocer; **~ment** *n*
acuse *m* de recibo
acne ['æknɪ] *n* acné *m*
acorn ['eɪkɔːn] *n* bellota
acoustic [ə'kuːstɪk] *adj* acústico; **~s** *n,*
npl acústica *sg*
acquaint [ə'kweɪnt] *vt*: **to ~ sb with sth**
(*inform*) poner a uno al corriente de
algo; **to be ~ed with** conocer; **~ance** *n*
(*person*) conocido/a; (*with person,*
subject) conocimiento
acquiesce [ækwɪ'ɛs] *vi*: **to ~ (to)**
consentir (en)
acquire [ə'kwaɪə*] *vt* adquirir;
acquisition [ækwɪ'zɪʃən] *n* adquisición *f*
acquit [ə'kwɪt] *vt* absolver, exculpar; **to ~**
o.s. well salir con éxito
acre ['eɪkə*] *n* acre *m*
acrid ['ækrɪd] *adj* acre
acrimonious [ækrɪ'məunɪəs] *adj* (*remark*)
mordaz; (*argument*) reñido
acrobat ['ækrəbæt] *n* acróbata *m/f*
acronym ['ækrənɪm] *n* siglas *fpl*
across [ə'krɔs] *prep* (*on the other side of*)
al otro lado de, del otro lado de;
(*crosswise*) a través de ♦ *adv* de un lado
a otro, de una parte a otra; a través, al
través; (*measurement*): **the road is 10m**
~ la carretera tiene 10m de ancho; **to**
run/swim ~ atravesar corriendo/
nadando; **~** de enfrente de
acrylic [ə'krɪlɪk] *adj* acrílico ♦ *n* acrílica
act [ækt] *n* acto, acción *f*; (*of play*) acto;
(*in music hall etc*) número; (*LAW*) decreto,
ley *f* ♦ *vi* (*behave*) comportarse; (*have*

effect: drug, chemical) hacer efecto; (*THEATRE*) actuar; (*pretend*) fingir; (*take action*) obrar ♦ *vt* (*part*) hacer el papel de; **in the ~ of: to catch sb in the ~ of ...** pillar a uno en el momento en que ...; **to ~ as** actuar *or* hacer de; **~ing** *adj* suplente ♦ *n* (*activity*) actuación *f*; (*profession*) profesión *f* de actor

action ['ækʃən] *n* acción *f*, acto; (*MIL*) acción *f*, batalla; (*LAW*) proceso, demanda; **out of ~** (*person*) fuera de combate; (*thing*) estropeado; **to take ~** tomar medidas; **~ replay** *n* (*TV*) repetición *f*

activate ['æktɪveɪt] *vt* activar

active ['æktɪv] *adj* activo, enérgico; (*volcano*) en actividad; (*fig: participate*) activamente; (*discourage, dislike*) enérgicamente; **activist** *n* activista *m/f*; **activity** [-'tɪvɪtɪ] *n* actividad *f*

actor ['æktə*] *n* actor *m*

actress ['æktrɪs] *n* actriz *f*

actual ['æktjuəl] *adj* verdadero, real; (*emphatic use*) propiamente dicho; **~ly** *adv* realmente, en realidad; (*even*) incluso

acumen ['ækjumən] *n* perspicacia

acute [ə'kju:t] *adj* agudo

ad [æd] *n abbr* = **advertisement**

A.D. *adv abbr* (= *anno Domini*) A.C

adamant ['ædəmənt] *adj* firme, inflexible

adapt [ə'dæpt] *vt* adaptar ♦ *vi*: **to ~ (to)** adaptarse (a), ajustarse (a); **~able** *adj* adaptable; **~er, ~or** *n* (*ELEC*) adaptador *m*

add [æd] *vt* añadir, agregar; (*figures: also:* **~ up**) sumar ♦ *vi*: **to ~ to** (*increase*) aumentar, acrecentar; **it doesn't ~ up** (*fig*) no tiene sentido

adder ['ædə*] *n* víbora

addict ['ædɪkt] *n* adicto/a; (*enthusiast*) entusiasta *m/f*; **~ed** [ə'dɪktɪd] *adj*: **to be ~ed to** ser adicto a; (*football etc*) ser fanático de; **~ion** [ə'dɪkʃən] *n* (*to drugs etc*) adicción *f*; **~ive** [ə'dɪktɪv] *adj* que causa adicción

addition [ə'dɪʃən] *n* (*adding up*) adición *f*; (*thing added*) añadidura, añadido; **in ~** además, por añadidura; **in ~ to** además de; **~al** *adj* adicional

additive ['ædɪtɪv] *n* aditivo

address [ə'drɛs] *n* dirección *f*, señas *fpl*; (*speech*) discurso ♦ *vt* (*letter*) dirigir; (*speak to*) dirigirse a, dirigir la palabra a; (*problem*) tratar

adept ['ædɛpt] *adj*: **~ at** experto *or* hábil en

adequate ['ædɪkwɪt] *adj* (*satisfactory*) adecuado; (*enough*) suficiente

adhere [əd'hɪə*] *vi*: **to ~ to** (*stick to*) pegarse a; (*fig: abide by*) observar; (: *belief etc*) ser partidario de

adhesive [əd'hi:zɪv] *n* adhesivo; **~ tape** *n* (*BRIT*) cinta adhesiva; (*US: MED*) esparadrapo

ad hoc [æd'hɔk] *adj* ad hoc

adjacent [ə'dʒeɪsənt] *adj*: **~ to** contiguo a, inmediato a

adjective ['ædʒɛktɪv] *n* adjetivo

adjoining [ə'dʒɔɪnɪŋ] *adj* contiguo, vecino

adjourn [ə'dʒə:n] *vt* aplazar ♦ *vi* suspenderse

adjudicate [ə'dʒu:dɪkeɪt] *vi* sentenciar

adjust [ə'dʒʌst] *vt* (*change*) modificar; (*clothing*) arreglar; (*machine*) ajustar ♦ *vi*: **to ~ (to)** adaptarse (a); **~able** *adj* ajustable; **~ment** *n* adaptación *f*; (*to machine, prices*) ajuste *m*

ad-lib [æd'lɪb] *vt, vi* improvisar; **ad lib** *adv* de forma improvisada

administer [əd'mɪnɪstə*] *vt* administrar; **administration** [-'treɪʃən] *n* (*management*) administración *f*; (*government*) gobierno; **administrative** [-trətɪv] *adj* administrativo

admiral ['ædmərəl] *n* almirante *m*; **A~ty** (*BRIT*) *n* Ministerio de Marina, Almirantazgo

admiration [ædmə'reɪʃən] *n* admiración *f*

admire [əd'maɪə*] *vt* admirar; **~r** *n* (*fan*) admirador(a) *m/f*

admission [əd'mɪʃən] *n* (*to university, club*) ingreso; (*entry fee*) entrada; (*confession*) confesión *f*

admit [əd'mɪt] *vt* (*confess*) confesar; (*permit to enter*) dejar entrar, dar entrada a; (*to club, organization*) admitir; (*accept: defeat*) reconocer; **to be ~ted to hospital** ingresar en el hospital;

~ **to** *vt fus* confesarse culpable de;
~**tance** *n* entrada; ~**tedly** *adv* es cierto
or verdad que
admonish [əd'mɔnɪʃ] *vt* amonestar
ad nauseam [æd'nɔːsɪæm] *adv* hasta el
cansancio
ado [ə'duː] *n*: **without (any) more ~** sin
más (ni más)
adolescent [ædəu'lɛsnt] *adj, n*
adolescente *m/f*
adopt [ə'dɔpt] *vt* adoptar; ~**ed** *adj* adoptivo; ~**ive** *adj* adoptivo; ~**ion** [ə'dɔpʃən] *n*
adopción *f*
adore [ə'dɔː*] *vt* adorar
Adriatic [eɪdrɪ'ætɪk] *n*: **the ~ (Sea)** el
(Mar) Adriático
adrift [ə'drɪft] *adv* a la deriva
adult ['ædʌlt] *n* adulto/a ♦ *adj* (*grown-up*)
adulto; (*for adults*) para adultos
adultery [ə'dʌltərɪ] *n* adulterio
advance [əd'vɑːns] *n* (*progress*) adelanto,
progreso; (*money*) anticipo, préstamo;
(*MIL*) avance *m* ♦ *adj*: ~ **booking** venta
anticipada; ~ **notice**, ~ **warning** previo
aviso ♦ *vt* (*money*) anticipar; (*theory*,
idea) proponer (para la discusión) ♦ *vi*
avanzar, adelantarse; **to make ~s (to sb)**
hacer proposiciones (a alguien); **in ~** por
adelantado; ~**d** *adj* avanzado; (*SCOL:
studies*) adelantado; ~**ment** *n* progreso;
(*in job*) ascenso
advantage [əd'vɑːntɪdʒ] *n* (*also TENNIS*)
ventaja; **to take ~ of** (*person*) aprovecharse de; (*opportunity*) aprovechar;
~**ous** [ædvən'teɪdʒəs] *adj*: ~**ous (to)** ventajoso (para)
Advent ['ædvənt] *n* (*REL*) Adviento
adventure [əd'vɛntʃə*] *n* aventura;
adventurous [-tʃərəs] *adj* atrevido;
aventurero
adverb ['ædvəːb] *n* adverbio
adverse ['ædvəːs] *adj* adverso, contrario
adversity [əd'vəːsɪtɪ] *n* infortunio
advert ['ædvəːt] (*BRIT*) *n abbr* = **advertisement**
advertise ['ædvətaɪz] *vi* (*in newspaper
etc*) anunciar, hacer publicidad; **to ~ for**
(*staff, accommodation etc*) buscar por
medio de anuncios ♦ *vt* anunciar; ~**ment**

[əd'vəːtɪsmənt] *n* (*COMM*) anuncio; ~**r** *n*
anunciante *m/f*; **advertising** *n* publicidad *f*, anuncios *mpl*; (*industry*) industria
publicitaria
advice [əd'vaɪs] *n* consejo, consejos *mpl*;
(*notification*) aviso; **a piece of ~** un
consejo; **to take legal ~** consultar con
un abogado
advisable [əd'vaɪzəbl] *adj* aconsejable,
conveniente
advise [əd'vaɪz] *vt* aconsejar; (*inform*): **to
~ sb of sth** informar a uno de algo; **to ~
sb against sth/doing sth** desaconsejar
algo a uno/aconsejar a uno que no haga
algo; ~**dly** [əd'vaɪzɪdlɪ] *adv* (*deliberately*)
deliberadamente; ~**r** *n* = **adviser**;
advisor *n* consejero/a; (*consultant*)
asesor(a) *m/f*; **advisory** *adj* consultivo
advocate ['ædvəkeɪt] *vt* abogar por ♦ *n*
[-kɪt] (*lawyer*) abogado/a; (*supporter*): ~
of defensor(a) *m/f* de
Aegean [iː'dʒiːən] *n*: **the ~ (Sea)** el (Mar)
Egeo
aerial ['ɛərɪəl] *n* antena ♦ *adj* aéreo
aerobics [ɛə'rəubɪks] *n* aerobic *m*
aeroplane ['ɛərəpleɪn] (*BRIT*) *n* avión *m*
aerosol ['ɛərəsɔl] *n* aerosol *m*
aesthetic [iːs'θɛtɪk] *adj* estético
afar [ə'fɑː*] *adv*: **from ~** desde lejos
affair [ə'fɛə*] *n* asunto; (*also: love ~*)
aventura (amorosa)
affect [ə'fɛkt] *vt* (*influence*) afectar,
influir en; (*afflict, concern*) afectar;
(*move*) conmover; ~**ed** *adj* afectado
affection [ə'fɛkʃən] *n* afecto, cariño; ~**ate**
adj afectuoso, cariñoso
affiliated [əfɪlɪ'eɪtɪd] *adj* afiliado
affinity [ə'fɪnɪtɪ] *n* (*bond, rapport*): **to
feel an ~ with** sentirse identificado con;
(*resemblance*) afinidad *f*
afflict [ə'flɪkt] *vt* afligir
affluence ['æfluəns] *n* opulencia, riqueza
affluent ['æfluənt] *adj* (*wealthy*)
acomodado; **the ~ society** la sociedad
opulenta
afford [ə'fɔːd] *vt* (*provide*) proporcionar;
can we ~ (to buy) it? ¿tenemos bastante
dinero para comprarlo?
Afghanistan [æf'gænɪstæn] *n* Afganistán

m

afield [ə'fiːld] *adv*: **far** ~ muy lejos

afloat [ə'fləʊt] *adv* (*floating*) a flote

afoot [ə'fʊt] *adv*: **there is something** ~ algo se está tramando

afraid [ə'freɪd] *adj*: **to be** ~ **of** (*person*) tener miedo a; (*thing*) tener miedo de; **to be** ~ **to** tener miedo de, temer; **I am** ~ **that** me temo que; **I am** ~ **not/so** lo siento, pero no/es así

afresh [ə'freʃ] *adv* de nuevo, otra vez

Africa ['æfrɪkə] *n* África; ~**n** *adj*, *n* africano/a *m/f*

aft [ɑːft] *adv* (*to be*) en popa; (*to go*) a popa

after ['ɑːftə*] *prep* (*time*) después de; (*place*, *order*) detrás de, tras ♦ *adv* después ♦ *conj* después (de) que; **what/ who are you** ~? ¿qué/a quién busca usted?; ~ **having done/he left** después de haber hecho/después de que se marchó; **to name sb** ~ **sb** llamar a uno por uno; **it's twenty** ~ **eight** (*US*) son las ocho y veinte; **to ask** ~ **sb** preguntar por alguien; ~ **all** después de todo, al fin y al cabo; ~ **you!** ¡pase usted!; ~**effects** *npl* consecuencias *fpl*, efectos *mpl*; ~**math** *n* consecuencias *fpl*, resultados *mpl*; ~**noon** *n* tarde *f*; ~**s** (*inf*) *n* (*dessert*) postre *m*; ~**-sales service** (*BRIT*) *n* servicio de asistencia pos-venta; ~**-shave** (**lotion**) *n* aftershave *m*; ~**thought** *n* ocurrencia (tardía); ~**wards** (*US* ~**ward**) *adv* después, más tarde

again [ə'gɛn] *adv* otra vez, de nuevo; **to do sth** ~ volver a hacer algo; ~ **and** ~ una y otra vez

against [ə'gɛnst] *prep* (*in opposition to*) en contra de; (*leaning on*, *touching*) contra, junto a

age [eɪdʒ] *n* edad *f*; (*period*) época ♦ *vi* envejecer(se) ♦ *vt* envejecer; **she is 20 years of** ~ tiene 20 años; **to come of** ~ llegar a la mayoría de edad; **it's been ~s since I saw you** hace siglos que no te veo; ~**d 10** de 10 años de edad; **the** ~**d** ['eɪdʒɪd] *npl* los ancianos; ~ **group** *n*: **to be in the same** ~ **group** tener la misma edad; ~ **limit** *n* edad *f* mínima (*or*

máxima)

agency ['eɪdʒənsɪ] *n* agencia

agenda [ə'dʒɛndə] *n* orden *m* del día

agent ['eɪdʒənt] *n* agente *m/f*; (*COMM: holding concession*) representante *m/f*, delegado/a; (*CHEM*, *fig*) agente *m*

aggravate ['ægrəveɪt] *vt* (*situation*) agravar; (*person*) irritar

aggregate ['ægrɪgeɪt] *n* conjunto

aggressive [ə'grɛsɪv] *adj* (*belligerent*) agresivo; (*assertive*) enérgico

aggrieved [ə'griːvd] *adj* ofendido, agraviado

aghast [ə'gɑːst] *adj* horrorizado

agile ['ædʒaɪl] *adj* ágil

agitate ['ædʒɪteɪt] *vt* (*trouble*) inquietar ♦ *vi*: **to** ~ **for/against** hacer campaña pro *or* en favor de/en contra de; **agitator** *n* agitador(a) *m/f*

AGM *n abbr* (= *annual general meeting*) asamblea anual

ago [ə'gəʊ] *adv*: **2 days** ~ hace 2 días; **not long** ~ hace poco; **how long** ~? ¿hace cuánto tiempo?

agog [ə'gɒg] *adj* (*eager*) ansioso; (*excited*) emocionado

agonizing ['ægənaɪzɪŋ] *adj* (*pain*) atroz; (*decision*, *wait*) angustioso

agony ['ægənɪ] *n* (*pain*) dolor *m* agudo; (*distress*) angustia; **to be in** ~ retorcerse de dolor

agree [ə'griː] *vt* (*price*, *date*) acordar, quedar en ♦ *vi* (*have same opinion*): **to** ~ (**with/that**) estar de acuerdo (con/ que); (*correspond*) coincidir, concordar; (*consent*) acceder; **to** ~ **with** (*subj: person*) estar de acuerdo con, ponerse de acuerdo con; (: *food*) sentar bien a; (*LING*) concordar con; **to** ~ **to sth/to do sth** consentir en algo/aceptar hacer algo; **to** ~ **that** (*admit*) estar de acuerdo en que; ~**able** *adj* (*sensation*) agradable; (*person*) simpático; (*willing*) de acuerdo, conforme; ~**d** *adj* (*time*, *place*) convenido; ~**ment** *n* acuerdo; (*contract*) contrato; **in** ~**ment** de acuerdo, conforme

agricultural [ægrɪ'kʌltʃərəl] *adj* agrícola

agriculture ['ægrɪkʌltʃə*] *n* agricultura

aground [ə'graʊnd] *adv*: **to run** ~ (*NAUT*)

encallar, embarrancar

ahead [ə'hed] *adv* (*in front*) delante; (*into the future*): **she had no time to think ~** no tenía tiempo de hacer planes para el futuro; **~ of** delante de; (*in advance of*) antes de; **~ of time** antes de la hora; **go right** *or* **straight ~** (*direction*) siga adelante; (*permission*) hazlo (*or* hágalo)

aid [eɪd] *n* ayuda, auxilio; (*device*) aparato ♦ *vt* ayudar, auxiliar; **in ~ of** a beneficio de; **to ~ and abet** (*LAW*) ser cómplice de

aide [eɪd] *n* (*person, also:* MIL) ayudante *m/f*

AIDS [eɪdz] *n abbr* (= *acquired immune deficiency syndrome*) SIDA *m*

ailing [ˈeɪlɪŋ] *adj* (*person*) enfermizo; (*economy*) debilitado

ailment [ˈeɪlmənt] *n* enfermedad *f*, achaque *m*

aim [eɪm] *vt* (*gun, camera*) apuntar; (*missile, remark*) dirigir; (*blow*) asestar ♦ *vi* (*also: take ~*) apuntar ♦ *n* (*in shooting: skill*) puntería; (*objective*) propósito, meta; **to ~ at** (*with weapon*) apuntar a; (*objective*) aspirar a, pretender; **to ~ to do** tener la intención de hacer; **~less** *adj* sin propósito, sin objeto

ain't [eɪnt] (*inf*) = **am not; aren't; isn't**

air [ɛə*] *n* aire *m*; (*appearance*) aspecto ♦ *vt* (*room*) ventilar; (*clothes, ideas*) airear ♦ *cpd* aéreo; **to throw sth into the ~** (*ball etc*) lanzar algo al aire; **by ~** (*travel*) en avión; **to be on the ~** (*RADIO, TV*) estar en antena; **~ bed** *n* (*BRIT*) colchón *m* neumático; **~borne** *adj* (*in the air*) en el aire; **~-conditioned** *adj* climatizado; **~ conditioning** *n* aire acondicionado; **~craft** *n inv* avión *m*; **~craft carrier** *n* porta(a)viones *m inv*; **~field** *n* campo de aviación; **~ force** *n* fuerzas *fpl* aéreas, aviación *f*; **~ freshener** *n* ambientador *m*; **~gun** *n* escopeta de aire comprimido; **~ hostess** (*BRIT*) *n* azafata; **~ letter** (*BRIT*) *n* carta aérea; **~lift** *n* puente *m* aéreo; **~line** *n* línea aérea; **~liner** *n* avión *m* de pasajeros; **~mail** *n*: **by ~mail** por avión; **~plane** (*US*) *n* avión *m*; **~port** *n* aeropuerto; **~ raid** *n* ataque *m* aéreo;

~sick *adj*: **to be ~sick** marearse (en avión); **~space** *n* espacio aéreo; **~ terminal** *n* terminal *f*; **~tight** *adj* hermético; **~-traffic controller** *n* controlador(a) *m/f* aéreo/a; **~y** *adj* (*room*) bien ventilado; (*fig: manner*) desenfadado

aisle [aɪl] *n* (*of church*) nave *f*; (*of theatre, supermarket*) pasillo

ajar [ə'dʒɑ:*] *adj* entreabierto

akin [ə'kɪn] *adj*: **~ to** parecido a

alacrity [ə'lækrɪtɪ] *n* presteza

alarm [ə'lɑ:m] *n* (*in shop, bank*) alarma; (*anxiety*) inquietud *f* ♦ *vt* asustar, inquietar; **~ call** *n* (*in hotel etc*) alarma; **~ clock** *n* despertador *m*

alas [ə'læs] *adv* desgraciadamente

albeit [ɔ:l'bi:ɪt] *conj* aunque

album [ˈælbəm] *n* álbum *m*; (*L.P.*) elepé *m*

alcohol [ˈælkəhɔl] *n* alcohol *m*; **~ic** [-'hɔlɪk] *adj*, *n* alcohólico/a *m/f*

alcove [ˈælkəuv] *n* nicho, hueco

ale [eɪl] *n* cerveza

alert [ə'lɔ:t] *adj* (*attentive*) atento; (*to danger, opportunity*) alerta ♦ *n* alerta *m*, alarma ♦ *vt* poner sobre aviso; **to be on the ~** (*also* MIL) estar alerta *or* sobre aviso

algebra [ˈældʒɪbrə] *n* álgebra

Algeria [æl'dʒɪərɪə] *n* Argelia

alias [ˈeɪlɪəs] *adv* alias, conocido por ♦ *n* (*of criminal*) apodo; (*of writer*) seudónimo

alibi [ˈælɪbaɪ] *n* coartada

alien [ˈeɪlɪən] *n* (*foreigner*) extranjero/a; (*extraterrestrial*) extraterrestre *m/f* ♦ *adj*: **~ to** ajeno a; **~ate** *vt* enajenar, alejar

alight [ə'laɪt] *adj* ardiendo; (*eyes*) brillante ♦ *vi* (*person*) apearse, bajar; (*bird*) posarse

align [ə'laɪn] *vt* alinear

alike [ə'laɪk] *adj* semejantes, iguales ♦ *adv* igualmente, del mismo modo; **to look ~** parecerse

alimony [ˈælɪmənɪ] *n* manutención *f*

alive [ə'laɪv] *adj* vivo; (*lively*) alegre

KEYWORD

all [ɔːl] *adj (sg)* todo/a; *(pl)* todos/as; ~ **day** todo el día; ~ **night** toda la noche; ~ **men** todos los hombres; ~ **five came** vinieron los cinco; ~ **the books** todos los libros; ~ **his life** toda su vida
♦ *pron* 1 todo; **I ate it** ~, **I ate ~ of it** me lo comí todo; ~ **of us went** fuimos todos; ~ **the boys went** fueron todos los chicos; **is that ~?** ¿eso es todo?, ¿algo más?; *(in shop)* ¿algo más?, ¿alguna cosa más?
2 *(in phrases):* **above ~** sobre todo; por encima de todo; **after ~** después de todo; **at ~: not at ~** *(in answer to question)* en absoluto; *(in answer to thanks)* ¡de nada!, ¡no hay de qué!; **I'm not at ~ tired** no estoy nada cansado/a; **anything at ~ will do** cualquier cosa viene bien; ~ **in** ~ a fin de cuentas
♦ *adv:* ~ **alone** completamente solo/a; **it's not as hard as ~ that** no es tan difícil como lo pintas; ~ **the more/the better** tanto más/mejor; ~ **but** casi; **the score is 2** ~ están empatados a 2

allay [əˈleɪ] *vt (fears)* aquietar
all clear *n (after attack etc)* fin *m* de la alerta; *(fig)* luz *f* verde
allegation [ælɪˈgeɪʃən] *n* alegato
allege [əˈlɛdʒ] *vt* pretender; **~dly** [əˈlɛdʒɪdlɪ] *adv* supuestamente, según se afirma
allegiance [əˈliːdʒəns] *n* lealtad *f*
allergy [ˈælədʒɪ] *n* alergia
alleviate [əˈliːvɪeɪt] *vt* aliviar
alley [ˈælɪ] *n* callejuela
alliance [əˈlaɪəns] *n* alianza
allied [ˈælaɪd] *adj* aliado
alligator [ˈælɪgeɪtə*] *n (ZOOL)* caimán *m*
all-in *(BRIT) adj, adv (charge)* todo incluido; ~ **wrestling** *n* lucha libre
all-night *adj (café, shop)* abierto toda la noche; *(party)* que dura toda la noche
allocate [ˈæləkeɪt] *vt (money etc)* asignar
allot [əˈlɔt] *vt* asignar; **~ment** *n* ración *f*; *(garden)* parcela
all-out *adj (effort etc)* supremo; **all out**

adv con todas las fuerzas
allow [əˈlaʊ] *vt* permitir, dejar; *(a claim)* admitir; *(sum, time etc)* dar, conceder; *(concede):* **to ~ that** reconocer que; **to ~ sb to do** permitir a alguien hacer; **he is ~ed to ...** se le permite ...; ~ **for** *vt fus* tener en cuenta; **~ance** *n* subvención *f*; *(welfare payment)* subsidio, pensión *f*; *(pocket money)* dinero de bolsillo; *(tax ~)* desgravación *f*; **to make ~ances for** *(person)* disculpar a; *(thing)* tener en cuenta
alloy [ˈælɔɪ] *n* mezcla
all: ~ **right** *adv* bien; *(as answer)* ¡conforme!, ¡está bien!; **~-rounder** *n:* **he's a good ~-rounder** se le da bien todo; ~-**time** *adj (record)* de todos los tiempos
allude [əˈluːd] *vi:* **to ~ to** aludir a
alluring [əˈljʊərɪŋ] *adj* atractivo, tentador(a)
allusion [əˈluːʒən] *n* referencia, alusión *f*
ally [ˈælaɪ] *n* aliado/a ♦ *vt:* **to ~ o.s. with** aliarse con
almighty [ɔːlˈmaɪtɪ] *adj* todopoderoso; *(row etc)* imponente
almond [ˈɑːmənd] *n* almendra
almost [ˈɔːlməʊst] *adv* casi
alms [ɑːmz] *npl* limosna
aloft [əˈlɔft] *adv* arriba
alone [əˈləʊn] *adj, adv* solo; **to leave sb ~** dejar a uno en paz; **to leave sth ~** no tocar algo, dejar algo sin tocar; **let ~ ...** y mucho menos ...
along [əˈlɔŋ] *prep* a lo largo de, por
♦ *adv:* **is he coming ~ with us?** ¿viene con nosotros?; **he was limping ~** iba cojeando; ~ **with** junto con; **all ~** *(all the time)* desde el principio; **~side** *prep* al lado de ♦ *adv* al lado
aloof [əˈluːf] *adj* reservado ♦ *adv:* **to stand ~** mantenerse apartado
aloud [əˈlaʊd] *adv* en voz alta
alphabet [ˈælfəbɛt] *n* alfabeto
Alps [ælps] *npl:* **the ~** los Alpes
already [ɔːlˈrɛdɪ] *adv* ya
alright [ˈɔːlˈraɪt] *(BRIT) adv* = **all right**
Alsatian [ælˈseɪʃən] *n (dog)* pastor *m* alemán
also [ˈɔːlsəʊ] *adv* también, además

altar ['ɔltə*] *n* altar *m*

alter ['ɔltə*] *vt* cambiar, modificar ♦ *vi* cambiar

alteration [ɔltə'reɪʃən] *n* cambio; (*to clothes*) arreglo; (*to building*) arreglos *mpl*

alternate [*adj* ɔl'tɜːnɪt, *vb* 'ɔltəneɪt] *adj* (*actions etc*) alternativo; (*events*) alterno; (*US*) = **alternative** ♦ *vi*: **to ~ (with)** alternar (con); **on ~ days** un día sí y otro no; **alternating current** [-neɪtɪŋ] *n* corriente *f* alterna

alternative [ɔl'tɜːnətɪv] *adj* alternativo ♦ *n* alternativa; **~ medicine** medicina alternativa; **~ly** *adv*: **~ly one could ...** por otra parte se podría ...

although [ɔːl'ðəʊ] *conj* aunque

altitude ['æltɪtjuːd] *n* altura

alto ['æltəu] *n* (*female*) contralto *f*; (*male*) alto

altogether [ɔːltə'gɛðə*] *adv* completamente, del todo; (*on the whole*) en total, en conjunto

aluminium [æljʊ'mɪnɪəm] (*BRIT*) *n* aluminio

aluminum [ə'luːmɪnəm] (*US*) *n* = **aluminium**

always ['ɔːlweɪz] *adv* siempre

Alzheimer's (disease) ['æltshaɪməz-] *n* enfermedad *f* de Alzheimer

am [æm] *vb see* **be**

a.m. *adv abbr* (= *ante meridiem*) de la mañana

amalgamate [ə'mælgəmeɪt] *vi* amalgamarse ♦ *vt* amalgamar, unir

amass [ə'mæs] *vt* amontonar, acumular

amateur ['æmətə*] *n* aficionado/a, amateur *m/f*; **~ish** *adj* inexperto, superficial

amaze [ə'meɪz] *vt* asombrar, pasmar; **to be ~d (at)** quedar pasmado (de); **~ment** *n* asombro, sorpresa; **amazing** *adj* extraordinario; (*fantastic*) increíble

Amazon ['æməzən] *n* (*GEO*) Amazonas *m*

ambassador [æm'bæsədə*] *n* embajador(a) *m/f*

amber ['æmbə*] *n* ámbar `m; **at ~** (*BRIT*: *AUT*) en el amarillo

ambiguity [æmbɪ'gjuɪtɪ] *n* ambigüedad *f*

ambiguous [æm'bɪgjuəs] *adj* ambiguo

ambition [æm'bɪʃən] *n* ambición *f*; **ambitious** [-ʃəs] *adj* ambicioso

amble ['æmbl] *vi* (*gen*: **~ along**) deambular, andar sin prisa

ambulance ['æmbjʊləns] *n* ambulancia

ambush ['æmbʊʃ] *n* emboscada ♦ *vt* tender una emboscada a

amenable [ə'miːnəbl] *adj*: **to be ~ to** dejarse influir por

amend [ə'mɛnd] *vt* enmendar; **to make ~s** dar cumplida satisfacción; **~ment** *n* enmienda

amenities [ə'miːnɪtɪz] *npl* comodidades *fpl*

America [ə'mɛrɪkə] *n* (*USA*) Estados *mpl* Unidos; **~n** *adj*, *n* norteamericano/a *m/f*; estadounidense *m/f*

amiable ['eɪmɪəbl] *adj* amable, simpático

amicable ['æmɪkəbl] *adj* amistoso, amigable

amid(st) [ə'mɪd(st)] *prep* entre, en medio de

amiss [ə'mɪs] *adv*: **to take sth ~** tomar algo a mal; **there's something ~** pasa algo

ammonia [ə'məunɪə] *n* amoníaco

ammunition [æmjʊ'nɪʃən] *n* municiones *fpl*

amnesty ['æmnɪstɪ] *n* amnistía

amok [ə'mɔk] *adv*: **to run ~** enloquecerse, desbocarse

among(st) [ə'mʌŋ(st)] *prep* entre, en medio de

amorous ['æmərəs] *adj* amoroso

amount [ə'maunt] *n* (*gen*) cantidad *f*; (*of bill etc*) suma, importe *m* ♦ *vi*: **to ~ to** sumar; (*be same as*) equivaler a, significar

amp(ère) ['æmp(ɛə*)] *n* amperio

amphibious [æm'fɪbɪəs] *adj* anfibio

amphitheatre ['æmfɪθɪətə*] (*US* **amphitheater**) *n* anfiteatro

ample ['æmpl] *adj* (*large*) grande; (*abundant*) abundante; (*enough*) bastante, suficiente

amplifier ['æmplɪfaɪə*] *n* amplificador *m*

amputate ['æmpjuteɪt] *vt* amputar

amuse [ə'mjuːz] *vt* divertir; (*distract*)

distraer, entretener; **~ment** *n* diversión *f*; (*pastime*) pasatiempo; (*laughter*) risa; **~ment arcade** *n* salón *m* de juegos

an [æn] *indef art see* **a**

anaemia [əˈniːmɪə] *n* (*US* **anemia**) anemia; **anaemic** [-mɪk] (*US* **anemic**) *adj* anémico; (*fig*) soso, insípido

anaesthetic [ænɪsˈθetɪk] *n* (*US* **anesthetic**) anestesia; **anaesthetist** [æˈniːsθɪtɪst] (*US* **anesthetist**) *n* anestesista *m/f*

analog(ue) [ˈænəlɔɡ] *adj* (*computer, watch*) analógico

analogy [əˈnælədʒɪ] *n* analogía

analyse [ˈænəlaɪz] (*US* **analyze**) *vt* analizar; **analyses** [əˈnæləsiːz] *npl of* **analysis**; **analysis** [əˈnæləsɪs] (*pl* **analyses**) *n* análisis *m inv*; **analyst** [-lɪst] *n* (*political ~, psycho~*) analista *m/f*; **analytic(al)** [-lɪtɪk(ə)l] *adj* analítico

anarchist [ˈænəkɪst] *n* anarquista *m/f*

anarchy [ˈænəkɪ] *n* anarquía

anatomy [əˈnætəmɪ] *n* anatomía

ancestor [ˈænsɪstə*] *n* antepasado

anchor [ˈæŋkə*] *n* ancla, áncora ♦ *vi* (*also: to drop ~*) anclar ♦ *vt* anclar; **to weigh ~** levar anclas

anchovy [ˈæntʃəvɪ] *n* anchoa

ancient [ˈeɪnʃənt] *adj* antiguo

ancillary [ænˈsɪlərɪ] *adj* auxiliar

and [ænd] *conj* y; (*before i-, hi-+consonant*) e; **men ~ women** hombres y mujeres; **father ~ son** padre e hijo; **trees ~ grass** árboles y hierba; **~ so on** etcétera, y así sucesivamente; **try ~ come** procura venir; **he talked ~ talked** habló sin parar; **better ~ better** cada vez mejor

Andes [ˈændiːz] *npl*: **the ~** los Andes

anemia *etc* [əˈniːmɪə] (*US*) = **anaemia** *etc*

anesthetic *etc* [ænɪsˈθetɪk] (*US*) = **anaesthetic** *etc*

anew [əˈnjuː] *adv* de nuevo, otra vez

angel [ˈeɪndʒəl] *n* ángel *m*

anger [ˈæŋɡə*] *n* cólera

angina [ænˈdʒaɪnə] *n* angina (del pecho)

angle [ˈæŋɡl] *n* ángulo; **from their ~** desde su punto de vista

angler [ˈæŋɡlə*] *n* pescador(a) *m/f* (de

caña)

Anglican [ˈæŋɡlɪkən] *adj, n* anglicano/a *m/f*

angling [ˈæŋɡlɪŋ] *n* pesca con caña

Anglo... [æŋɡləu] *prefix* anglo...

angrily [ˈæŋɡrɪlɪ] *adv* coléricamente, airadamente

angry [ˈæŋɡrɪ] *adj* enfadado, airado; (*wound*) inflamado; **to be ~ with sb/at sth** estar enfadado con alguien/por algo; **to get ~** enfadarse, enojarse

anguish [ˈæŋɡwɪʃ] *n* (*physical*) tormentos *mpl*; (*mental*) angustia

angular [ˈæŋɡjulə*] *adj* (*shape*) angular; (*features*) anguloso

animal [ˈænɪməl] *n* animal *m*; (*pej: person*) bestia ♦ *adj* animal

animate [ˈænɪmɪt] *adj* vivo; **~d** [-meɪtɪd] *adj* animado

animosity [ænɪˈmɔsɪtɪ] *n* animosidad *f*, rencor *m*

aniseed [ˈænɪsiːd] *n* anís *m*

ankle [ˈæŋkl] *n* tobillo *m*; **~ sock** *n* calcetín *m* corto

annex [*n* ˈænɛks, *vb* æˈnɛks] *n* (*also: BRIT: annexe*) (*building*) edificio anexo ♦ *vt* (*territory*) anexionar

annihilate [əˈnaɪəleɪt] *vt* aniquilar

anniversary [ænɪˈvɜːsərɪ] *n* aniversario

announce [əˈnauns] *vt* anunciar; **~ment** *n* anuncio; (*official*) declaración *f*; **~r** *n* (*RADIO*) locutor(a) *m/f*; (*TV*) presentador(a) *m/f*

annoy [əˈnɔɪ] *vt* molestar, fastidiar; **don't get ~ed!** ¡no se enfade!; **~ance** *n* enojo; **~ing** *adj* molesto, fastidioso; (*person*) pesado

annual [ˈænjuəl] *adj* anual ♦ *n* (*BOT*) anual *m*; (*book*) anuario; **~ly** *adv* anualmente, cada año

annul [əˈnʌl] *vt* anular

annum [ˈænəm] *n see* **per**

anomaly [əˈnɔməlɪ] *n* anomalía

anonymous [əˈnɔnɪməs] *adj* anónimo

anorak [ˈænəræk] *n* anorak *m*

another [əˈnʌðə*] *adj* (*one more, a different one*) otro ♦ *pron* otro; *see* **one**

answer [ˈɑːnsə*] *n* contestación *f*, respuesta; (*to problem*) solución *f* ♦ *vi*

contestar, responder ♦ *vt (reply to)*
contestar a, responder a; *(problem)*
resolver; *(prayer)* escuchar; **in ~ to your
letter** contestando *or* en contestación a
su carta; **to ~ the phone** contestar *or*
coger el teléfono; **to ~ the bell *or* the
door** acudir a la puerta; ~ **back** *vi*
replicar, ser respondón/ona; ~ **for** *vt fus*
responder de *or* por; ~ **to** *vt fus*
(description) corresponder a; ~**able** *adj*:
~**able to sb for sth** responsable ante
uno de algo; ~**ing machine** *n*
contestador *m* automático
ant [ænt] *n* hormiga
antagonism [æn'tægənɪzm] *n*
antagonismo, hostilidad *f*
antagonize [æn'tægənaɪz] *vt* provocar la
enemistad de
Antarctic [ænt'ɑ:ktɪk] *n*: **the ~** el
Antártico
antelope ['æntɪləup] *n* antílope *m*
antenatal ['æntɪ'neɪtl] *adj* antenatal,
prenatal; ~ **clinic** *n* clínica prenatal
antenna [æn'tɛnə] *(pl* ~**e)** *n* antena
anthem ['ænθəm] *n*: **national ~** himno
nacional
anthology [æn'θɔlədʒɪ] *n* antología
anthropology [ænθrə'pɔlədʒɪ] *n*
antropología
anti... [æntɪ] *prefix* anti...; ~**-aircraft**
[-'ɛəkrɑːft] *adj* antiaéreo; ~**biotic** [-baɪ'ɔtɪk]
n antibiótico; ~**body** ['æntɪbɒdɪ] *n*
anticuerpo
anticipate [æn'tɪsɪpeɪt] *vt* prever; *(expect)*
esperar, contar con; *(look forward to)*
esperar con ilusión; *(do first)* anticiparse
a, adelantarse a; **anticipation** [-'peɪʃən] *n*
(expectation) previsión *f*; *(eagerness)*
ilusión *f*, expectación *f*
anticlimax [æntɪ'klaɪmæks] *n* decepción *f*
anticlockwise [æntɪ'klɔkwaɪz] *(BRIT)* adv
en dirección contraria a la de las agujas
del reloj
antics ['æntɪks] *npl* gracias *fpl*
anticyclone [æntɪ'saɪkləun] *n* anticiclón
m
antidote ['æntɪdəut] *n* antídoto
antifreeze ['æntɪfriːz] *n* anticongelante *m*
antihistamine [æntɪ'hɪstəmiːn] *n*

antihistamínico
antipathy [æn'tɪpəθɪ] *n (between people)*
antipatía; *(to person, thing)* aversión *f*
antiquated ['æntɪkweɪtɪd] *adj* anticuado
antique [æn'tiːk] *n* antigüedad *f* ♦ *adj*
antiguo; ~ **dealer** *n* anticuario/a; ~ **shop**
n tienda de antigüedades
antiquity [æn'tɪkwɪtɪ] *n* antigüedad *f*
anti-Semitism [æntɪ'sɛmɪtɪzm] *n*
antisemitismo
antiseptic [æntɪ'sɛptɪk] *adj, n* antiséptico
antlers ['æntləz] *npl* cuernas *fpl*,
cornamenta *sg*
anus ['eɪnəs] *n* ano
anvil ['ænvɪl] *n* yunque *m*
anxiety [æŋ'zaɪətɪ] *n* inquietud *f*; *(MED)*
ansiedad *f*; ~ **to do** deseo de hacer
anxious ['æŋkʃəs] *adj* inquieto,
preocupado; *(worrying)* preocupante;
(keen): **to be ~ to do** tener muchas
ganas de hacer

KEYWORD

any ['ɛnɪ] *adj* **1** *(in questions etc)* algún/
alguna; **have you ~ butter/children?**
¿tienes mantequilla/hijos?; **if there are
~ tickets left** si quedan billetes, si
queda algún billete
2 *(with negative)*: **I haven't ~ money/
books** no tengo dinero/libros
3 *(no matter which)* cualquier; ~ **excuse
will do** valdrá *or* servirá cualquier
excusa; **choose ~ book you like** escoge
el libro que quieras; ~ **teacher you ask
will tell you** cualquier profesor al que
preguntes te lo dirá
4 *(in phrases)*: **in ~ case** de todas
formas, en cualquier caso; ~ **day now**
cualquier día (de estos); **at ~ moment**
en cualquier momento, de un momento a
otro; **at ~ rate** en todo caso; ~ **time**:
come (at) ~ time venga cuando quieras;
he might come (at) ~ time podría
llegar de un momento a otro
♦ *pron* **1** *(in questions etc)*: **have you got
~?** ¿tienes alguno(s)/a(s)?; **can ~ of you
sing?** ¿sabéis/saben cantar alguno de
vosotros/ustedes?
2 *(with negative)*: **I haven't ~ (of them)**

no tengo ninguno
3 (*no matter which one(s)*): **take ~ of
those books (you like)** toma cualquier
libro que quieras de ésos
♦ *adv* **1** (*in questions etc*): **do you want
~ more soup/sandwiches?** ¿quieres
más sopa/bocadillos?; **are you feeling ~
better?** ¿te sientes algo mejor?
2 (*with negative*): **I can't hear him ~
more** no le oigo; **don't wait ~ longer**
no esperes más

anybody ['ɛnɪbɔdɪ] *pron* cualquiera; (*in
interrogative sentences*) alguien; (*in
negative sentences*): **I don't see ~** no veo
a nadie; **if ~ should phone ...** si llama
alguien ...
anyhow ['ɛnɪhau] *adv* (*at any rate*) de
todos modos, de todas formas; (*haphazard*): **do it ~ you like** hazlo como
quieras; **she leaves things just ~** deja
las cosas como quiera *or* de cualquier
modo; **I shall go ~** de todos modos iré
anyone ['ɛnɪwʌn] *pron* = **anybody**
anything ['ɛnɪθɪŋ] *pron* (*in questions etc*)
algo, alguna cosa; (*with negative*) nada;
can you see ~? ¿ves algo?; **if ~ happens
to me ...** si algo me ocurre ...; (*no matter what*): **you can say ~ you like** puedes
decir lo que quieras; **~ will do** vale todo
or cualquier cosa; **he'll eat ~** come de
todo *or* lo que sea
anyway ['ɛnɪweɪ] *adv* (*at any rate*) de
todos modos, de todas formas; **I shall go
~** iré de todos modos; (*besides*): **~, I
couldn't come even if I wanted to**
además, no podría venir aunque
quisiera; **why are you phoning, ~?**
¿entonces, por qué llamas?, ¿por qué
llamas, pues?
anywhere ['ɛnɪwɛə*] *adv* (*in questions
etc*): **can you see him ~?** ¿le ves por
algún lado?; **are you going ~?** ¿vas a
algún sitio?; (*with negative*): **I can't see
him ~** no le veo por ninguna parte; **~ in
the world** (*no matter where*) en
cualquier parte (del mundo); **put the
books down ~** deja los libros donde
quieras

apart [ə'pɑːt] *adv* (*aside*) aparte;
(*situation*): **~ (from)** separado (de);
(*movement*): **to pull ~** separar; **10 miles
~** separados por 10 millas; **to take ~**
desmontar; **~ from** *prep* aparte de
apartheid [ə'pɑːteɪt] *n* apartheid *m*
apartment [ə'pɑːtmənt] *n* (*US*) piso (*SP*),
departamento (*AM*), apartamento; (*room*)
cuarto; **~ building** (*US*) *n* edificio de
apartamentos
apathetic [æpə'θetɪk] *adj* apático,
indiferente
apathy ['æpəθɪ] *n* apatía, indiferencia
ape [eɪp] *n* mono ♦ *vt* imitar, remedar
aperitif [ə'perɪtɪf] *n* aperitivo
aperture ['æpətʃjuə*] *n* rendija,
resquicio; (*PHOT*) abertura
apex ['eɪpeks] *n* ápice *m*; (*fig*) cumbre *f*
apiece [ə'piːs] *adv* cada uno
aplomb [ə'plɔm] *n* aplomo
apologetic [əpɔlə'dʒetɪk] *adj* de disculpa;
(*person*) arrepentido
apologize [ə'pɔlədʒaɪz] *vi*: **to ~ (for sth
to sb)** disculparse (con alguien de algo)
apology [ə'pɔlədʒɪ] *n* disculpa, excusa
apostrophe [ə'pɔstrəfɪ] *n* apóstrofo *m*
appal [ə'pɔːl] *vt* horrorizar, espantar;
~ling *adj* espantoso; (*awful*) pésimo
apparatus [æpə'reɪtəs] *n* (*equipment*)
equipo; (*organization*) aparato; (*in
gymnasium*) aparatos *mpl*
apparel [ə'pærl] (*US*) *n* ropa
apparent [ə'pærənt] *adj* aparente;
(*obvious*) evidente; **~ly** *adv* por lo visto,
al parecer
appeal [ə'piːl] *vi* (*LAW*) apelar ♦ *n* (*LAW*)
apelación *f*; (*request*) llamamiento; (*plea*)
petición *f*; (*charm*) atractivo; **to ~ for**
reclamar; **to ~ to** (*be attractive to*)
atraer; **it doesn't ~ to me** no me atrae,
no me llama la atención; **~ing** *adj*
(*attractive*) atractivo
appear [ə'pɪə*] *vi* aparecer, presentarse;
(*LAW*) comparecer; (*publication*) salir (a
luz), publicarse; (*seem*) parecer; **to ~ on
TV/in "Hamlet"** salir por la tele/hacer
un papel en "Hamlet"; **it would ~ that**
parecería que; **~ance** *n* aparición *f*;
(*look*) apariencia, aspecto

appease [ə'pi:z] *vt* (*pacify*) apaciguar; (*satisfy*) satisfacer

appendices [ə'pɛndɪsi:z] *npl of* **appendix**

appendicitis [əpɛndɪ'saɪtɪs] *n* apendicitis *f*

appendix [ə'pɛndɪks] (*pl* **appendices**) *n* apéndice *m*

appetite ['æpɪtaɪt] *n* apetito; (*fig*) deseo, anhelo

appetizer ['æpɪtaɪzə*] *n* (*drink*) aperitivo; (*food*) tapas *fpl* (*SP*)

appetizing ['æpɪtaɪzɪŋ] *adj* apetitoso

applaud [ə'plɔ:d] *vt, vi* aplaudir

applause [ə'plɔ:z] *n* aplausos *mpl*

apple ['æpl] *n* manzana; ~ **tree** *n* manzano

appliance [ə'plaɪəns] *n* aparato

applicable [ə'plɪkəbl] *adj* (*relevant*): **to be ~ (to)** referirse a

applicant ['æplɪkənt] *n* candidato/a; solicitante *m/f*

application [æplɪ'keɪʃən] *n* aplicación *f*; (*for a job etc*) solicitud *f*, petición *f*; ~ **form** *n* solicitud *f*

applied [ə'plaɪd] *adj* aplicado

apply [ə'plaɪ] *vt* (*paint etc*) poner; (*law etc: put into practice*) poner en vigor ♦ *vi*: **to ~ to** (*ask*) dirigirse a; (*be applicable*) ser aplicable a; **to ~ for** (*permit, grant, job*) solicitar; **to ~ o.s. to** aplicarse a, dedicarse a

appoint [ə'pɔɪnt] *vt* (*to post*) nombrar; ~**ed** *adj*: **at the ~ed time** a la hora señalada; ~**ment** *n* (*with client*) cita; (*act*) nombramiento; (*post*) puesto; (*at hairdresser etc*): **to have an ~ment** tener hora; **to make an ~ment (with sb)** citarse (con uno)

appraisal [ə'preɪzl] *n* valoración *f*

appreciable [ə'pri:ʃəbl] *adj* sensible

appreciate [ə'pri:ʃɪeɪt] *vt* apreciar, tener en mucho; (*be grateful for*) agradecer; (*be aware of*) comprender ♦ *vi* (*COMM*) aumentar(se) en valor; **appreciation** [-'eɪʃən] *n* apreciación *f*; (*gratitude*) reconocimiento, agradecimiento; (*COMM*) aumento en valor

appreciative [ə'pri:ʃɪətɪv] *adj* apreciativo; (*comment*) agradecido

apprehend [æprɪ'hɛnd] *vt* detener

apprehension [æprɪ'hɛnʃən] *n* (*fear*) aprensión *f*; **apprehensive** [-'hɛnsɪv] *adj* aprensivo

apprentice [ə'prɛntɪs] *n* aprendiz/a *m/f*; ~**ship** *n* aprendizaje *m*

approach [ə'prəʊtʃ] *vi* acercarse ♦ *vt* acercarse a; (*ask, apply to*) dirigirse a; (*situation, problem*) abordar ♦ *n* acercamiento; (*access*) acceso; (*to problem, situation*): ~ **(to)** actitud *f* (ante); ~**able** *adj* (*person*) abordable; (*place*) accesible

appropriate [*adj* ə'prəʊprɪɪt, *vb* ə'prəʊprɪeɪt] *adj* apropiado, conveniente ♦ *vt* (*take*) apropiarse de

approval [ə'pru:vəl] *n* aprobación *f*, visto bueno; (*permission*) consentimiento; **on** ~ (*COMM*) a prueba

approve [ə'pru:v] *vt* aprobar; ~ **of** *vt fus* (*thing*) aprobar; (*person*): **they don't ~ of her** (ella) no les parece bien

approximate [ə'prɒksɪmɪt] *adj* aproximado; ~**ly** *adv* aproximadamente, más o menos

apricot ['eɪprɪkɒt] *n* albaricoque *m* (*SP*), damasco (*AM*)

April ['eɪprəl] *n* abril *m*; ~ **Fools' Day** *n* el primero de abril; ≈ día *m* de los Inocentes (*28 December*)

apron ['eɪprən] *n* delantal *m*

apt [æpt] *adj* (*likely*): ~ **to do** propenso a hacer

aquarium [ə'kwɛərɪəm] *n* acuario

Aquarius [ə'kwɛərɪəs] *n* Acuario

aqueduct ['ækwɪdʌkt] *n* acueducto

Arab ['ærəb] *adj, n* árabe *m/f*

Arabian [ə'reɪbɪən] *adj* árabe

Arabic ['ærəbɪk] *adj* árabe; (*numerals*) arábigo ♦ *n* árabe *m*

arable ['ærəbl] *adj* cultivable

Aragon ['ærəgən] *n* Aragón *m*

arbitrary ['ɑ:bɪtrərɪ] *adj* arbitrario

arbitration [ɑ:bɪ'treɪʃən] *n* arbitraje *m*

arcade [ɑ:'keɪd] *n* (*round a square*) soportales *mpl*; (*shopping mall*) galería comercial

arch [ɑ:tʃ] *n* arco; (*of foot*) arco del pie ♦ *vt* arquear

archaeologist [ɑːkɪˈɔlədʒɪst] (*US* **archeologist**) *n* arqueólogo/a

archaeology [ɑːkɪˈɔlədʒɪ] (*US* **archeology**) *n* arqueología

archaic [ɑːˈkeɪɪk] *adj* arcaico

archbishop [ɑːtʃˈbɪʃəp] *n* arzobispo

archenemy *n* enemigo jurado

archeology *etc* [ɑːkɪˈɔlədʒɪ] (*US*) = **archaeology** *etc*

archery [ˈɑːtʃərɪ] *n* tiro al arco

archipelago [ɑːkɪˈpelɪgəu] *n* archipiélago

architect [ˈɑːkɪtekt] *n* arquitecto/a; **~ural** [-ˈtektʃərəl] *adj* arquitectónico; **~ure** *n* arquitectura

archives [ˈɑːkaɪvz] *npl* archivo

Arctic [ˈɑːktɪk] *adj* ártico ♦ *n*: **the ~** el Ártico

ardent [ˈɑːdənt] *adj* ardiente, apasionado

arduous [ˈɑːdjuəs] *adj* (*task*) arduo; (*journey*) agotador(a)

are [ɑː*] *vb see* **be**

area [ˈɛərɪə] *n* área, región *f*; (*part of place*) zona; (*MATH etc*) área, superficie *f*; (*in room: e.g. dining ~*) parte *f*; (*of knowledge, experience*) campo

arena [əˈriːnə] *n* estadio; (*of circus*) pista

aren't [ɑːnt] = **are not**

Argentina [ɑːdʒənˈtiːnə] *n* Argentina; **Argentinian** [-ˈtɪnɪən] *adj, n* argentino/a *m/f*

arguably [ˈɑːgjuəblɪ] *adv* posiblemente

argue [ˈɑːgjuː] *vi* (*quarrel*) discutir, pelearse; (*reason*) razonar, argumentar; **to ~ that** sostener que

argument [ˈɑːgjumənt] *n* discusión *f*, pelea; (*reasons*) argumento; **~ative** [-ˈmentətɪv] *adj* discutidor(a)

Aries [ˈɛərɪz] *n* Aries *m*

arise [əˈraɪz] (*pt* **arose**, *pp* **arisen**) *vi* surgir, presentarse

arisen [əˈrɪzn] *pp of* **arise**

aristocrat [ˈærɪstəkræt] *n* aristócrata *m/f*

arithmetic [əˈrɪθmətɪk] *n* aritmética

ark [ɑːk] *n*: **Noah's A~** el Arca *f* de Noé

arm [ɑːm] *n* brazo ♦ *vt* armar; **~s** *npl* armas *fpl*; **~ in ~** cogidos del brazo

armaments [ˈɑːməmənts] *npl* armamento

armchair [ˈɑːmtʃɛə*] *n* sillón *m*, butaca

armed [ɑːmd] *adj* armado; **~ robbery** *n* robo a mano armada

armour [ˈɑːmə*] (*US* **armor**) *n* armadura; (*MIL: tanks*) blindaje *m*; **~ed car** *n* coche *m* (*SP*) *or* carro (*AM*) blindado

armpit [ˈɑːmpɪt] *n* sobaco, axila

armrest [ˈɑːmrest] *n* apoyabrazos *m inv*

army [ˈɑːmɪ] *n* ejército; (*fig*) multitud *f*

aroma [əˈrəumə] *n* aroma *m*, fragancia; **~therapy** *n* aromaterapia

arose [əˈrəuz] *pt of* **arise**

around [əˈraund] *adv* alrededor; (*in the area*): **there is no one else ~** no hay nadie más por aquí ♦ *prep* alrededor de

arouse [əˈrauz] *vt* despertar; (*anger*) provocar

arrange [əˈreɪndʒ] *vt* arreglar, ordenar; (*organize*) organizar; **to ~ to do sth** quedar en hacer algo; **~ment** *n* arreglo; (*agreement*) acuerdo; **~ments** *npl* (*preparations*) preparativos *mpl*

array [əˈreɪ] *n*: **~ of** (*things*) serie *f* de; (*people*) conjunto de

arrears [əˈrɪəz] *npl* atrasos *mpl*; **to be in ~ with one's rent** estar retrasado en el pago del alquiler

arrest [əˈrest] *vt* detener; (*sb's attention*) llamar ♦ *n* detención *f*; **under ~** detenido

arrival [əˈraɪvəl] *n* llegada; **new ~** recién llegado/a; (*baby*) recién nacido

arrive [əˈraɪv] *vi* llegar; (*baby*) nacer

arrogant [ˈærəgənt] *adj* arrogante

arrow [ˈærəu] *n* flecha

arse [ɑːs] (*BRIT: inf!*) *n* culo, trasero

arsenal [ˈɑːsɪnl] *n* arsenal *m*

arson [ˈɑːsn] *n* incendio premeditado

art [ɑːt] *n* arte *m*; (*skill*) destreza; **A~s** *npl* (*SCOL*) Letras *fpl*

artery [ˈɑːtərɪ] *n* arteria

artful [ˈɑːtful] *adj* astuto

art gallery *n* pinacoteca; (*saleroom*) galería de arte

arthritis [ɑːˈθraɪtɪs] *n* artritis *f*

artichoke [ˈɑːtɪtʃəuk] *n* alcachofa; **Jerusalem ~** aguaturma

article [ˈɑːtɪkl] *n* artículo; (*BRIT: LAW: training*): **~s** *npl* contrato de aprendizaje; **~ of clothing** prenda de vestir

articulate [*adj* ɑːˈtɪkjulɪt, *vb* ɑːˈtɪkjuleɪt] *adj*

claro, bien expresado ♦ *vt* expresar; **~d
lorry** (*BRIT*) *n* trailer *m*
artificial [ɑːtɪˈfɪʃəl] *adj* artificial; (*affected*) afectado
artillery [ɑːˈtɪlərɪ] *n* artillería
artisan [ˈɑːtɪzæn] *n* artesano
artist [ˈɑːtɪst] *n* artista *m/f*, (*MUS*)
intérprete *m/f*; **~ic** [ɑːˈtɪstɪk] *adj* artístico;
~ry *n* arte *m*, habilidad *f* (artística)
art school *n* escuela de bellas artes

KEYWORD
---

as [æz] *conj* **1** (*referring to time*) cuando,
mientras; a medida que; **~ the years
went by** con el paso de los años; **he
came in ~ I was leaving** entró cuando
me marchaba; **~ from tomorrow** desde
or a partir de mañana
2 (*in comparisons*): **~ big ~** tan grande
como; **twice ~ big ~** el doble de grande
que; **~ much money/many books ~**
tanto dinero/tantos libros como; **~ soon
~** en cuanto
3 (*since, because*) como, ya que; **he left
early ~ he had to be home by 10** se
fue temprano como tenía que estar en
casa a las 10
4 (*referring to manner, way*): **do ~ you
wish** haz lo que quieras; **~ she said**
como dijo; **he gave it to me ~ a
present** me lo dio de regalo
5 (*in the capacity of*): **he works ~ a
barman** trabaja de barman; **~ chairman
of the company, he ...** como presidente
de la compañía, ...
6 (*concerning*): **~ for** *or* **to that** por *or*
en lo que respecta a eso
7: **~ if** *or* **though** como si; **he looked ~
if he was ill** parecía como si estuviera
enfermo, tenía aspecto de enfermo; *see
also* **long**; **such**; **well**

a.s.a.p. *abbr* (= *as soon as possible*)
cuanto antes
asbestos [æzˈbɛstəs] *n* asbesto, amianto
ascend [əˈsɛnd] *vt* subir; (*throne*)
ascender *or* subir a; **~ancy** *n*
ascendiente *m*, dominio
ascent [əˈsɛnt] *n* subida; (*slope*) cuesta,

pendiente *f*
ascertain [æsəˈteɪn] *vt* averiguar
ascribe [əˈskraɪb] *vt*: **to ~ sth to** atribuir
algo a
ash [æʃ] *n* ceniza; (*tree*) fresno
ashamed [əˈʃeɪmd] *adj* avergonzado,
apenado (*AM*); **to be ~ of** avergonzarse de
ashen [ˈæʃn] *adj* pálido
ashore [əˈʃɔː*] *adv* en tierra; (*swim etc*)
a tierra
ashtray [ˈæʃtreɪ] *n* cenicero
Ash Wednesday *n* miércoles *m* de
Ceniza
Asia [ˈeɪʃə] *n* Asia; **~n** *adj*, *n* asiático/a
m/f
aside [əˈsaɪd] *adv* a un lado ♦ *n* aparte *m*
ask [ɑːsk] *vt* (*question*) preguntar; (*invite*)
invitar; **to ~ sb sth/to do sth** preguntar
algo a alguien/pedir a alguien que haga
algo; **to ~ sb about sth** preguntar algo a
alguien; **to ~ (sb) a question** hacer una
pregunta (a alguien); **to ~ sb out to
dinner** invitar a cenar a uno; **~ after** *vt
fus* preguntar por; **~ for** *vt fus* pedir;
(*trouble*) buscar
askance [əˈskɑːns] *adv*: **to look ~ at sb/
sth** mirar con recelo a uno/mirar algo
con recelo
askew [əˈskjuː] *adv* torcido, ladeado
asking price *n* precio inicial
asleep [əˈsliːp] *adj* dormido; **to fall ~**
dormirse, quedarse dormido
asparagus [əsˈpærəgəs] *n* (*plant*)
espárrago; (*food*) espárragos *mpl*
aspect [ˈæspɛkt] *n* aspecto, apariencia;
(*direction in which a building etc faces*)
orientación *f*
aspersions [əsˈpəːʃənz] *npl*: **to cast ~ on**
difamar a, calumniar a
asphyxiation [æsfɪksɪˈeɪʃən] *n* asfixia
aspirations [æspəˈreɪʃənz] *npl* ambición *f*
aspire [əsˈpaɪə*] *vi*: **to ~ to** aspirar a,
ambicionar
aspirin [ˈæsprɪn] *n* aspirina
ass [æs] *n* asno, burro; (*inf: idiot*) imbécil
m/f, (*US: inf!*) culo, trasero
assailant [əˈseɪlənt] *n* asaltador(a) *m/f*,
agresor(a) *m/f*
assassin [əˈsæsɪn] *n* asesino/a; **~ate** *vt*

asesinar; ~ation [-'neɪʃən] n asesinato

assault [ə'sɔːlt] n asalto; (LAW) agresión f
♦ vt asaltar, atacar; (sexually) violar

assemble [ə'sɛmbl] vt reunir, juntar;
(TECH) montar ♦ vi reunirse, juntarse

assembly [ə'sɛmblɪ] n reunión f,
asamblea; (parliament) parlamento; (construction) montaje m; ~ line n cadena de
montaje

assent [ə'sɛnt] n asentimiento,
aprobación f

assert [ə'sɔːt] vt afirmar; (authority)
hacer valer; ~ion [-ʃən] n afirmación f

assess [ə'sɛs] vt valorar, calcular; (tax,
damages) fijar; (for tax) gravar; ~ment n
valoración f; (for tax) gravamen m; ~or
n asesor(a) m/f

asset ['æsɛt] n ventaja; ~s npl (COMM)
activo; (property, funds) fondos mpl

assign [ə'saɪn] vt: to ~ (to) (date) fijar
(para); (task) asignar (a); (resources)
destinar (a); ~ment n tarea

assist [ə'sɪst] vt ayudar; ~ance n ayuda,
auxilio; ~ant n ayudante m/f; (BRIT: also:
shop ~ant) dependiente/a m/f

associate [adj, n ə'səʊʃɪɪt, vb ə'səʊʃɪeɪt] adj
asociado ♦ n (at work) colega m/f ♦ vt
asociar; (ideas) relacionar ♦ vi: to ~
with sb tratar con alguien

association [əsəʊsɪ'eɪʃən] n asociación f

assorted [ə'sɔːtɪd] adj surtido, variado

assortment [ə'sɔːtmənt] n (of shapes, colours) surtido; (of books) colección f; (of
people) mezcla

assume [ə'sjuːm] vt suponer; (responsibilities) asumir; (attitude) adoptar,
tomar; ~d name n nombre m falso

assumption [ə'sʌmpʃən] n suposición f,
presunción f; (of power etc) toma f

assurance [ə'ʃʊərəns] n garantía,
promesa; (confidence) confianza, aplomo;
(insurance) seguro

assure [ə'ʃʊə*] vt asegurar

asthma ['æsmə] n asma

astonish [ə'stɒnɪʃ] vt asombrar, pasmar;
~ment n asombro, sorpresa

astound [ə'staʊnd] vt asombrar, pasmar

astray [ə'streɪ] adv: to go ~ extraviarse;
to lead ~ (morally) llevar por mal

camino

astride [ə'straɪd] prep a caballo or
horcajadas sobre

astrology [æs'trɒlədʒɪ] n astrología

astronaut ['æstrənɔːt] n astronauta m/f

astronomy [æs'trɒnəmɪ] n astronomía

astute [əs'tjuːt] adj astuto

asylum [ə'saɪləm] n (refuge) asilo;
(mental hospital) manicomio

┌─────────────┐
│ KEYWORD │
└─────────────┘

at [æt] prep 1 (referring to position) en;
(direction) a; ~ **the top** en lo alto; ~
home/school en casa/la escuela; **to
look** ~ **sth/sb** mirar algo/a uno
2 (referring to time): ~ **4 o'clock** a las 4;
~ **night** por la noche; ~ **Christmas** en
Navidad; ~ **times** a veces
3 (referring to rates, speed etc): ~ **£1 a
kilo** a una libra el kilo; **two** ~ **a time** de
dos en dos; ~ **50 km/h** a 50 km/h
4 (referring to manner): ~ **a stroke** de
un golpe; ~ **peace** en paz
5 (referring to activity): **to be** ~ **work**
estar trabajando; (in the office etc) estar
en el trabajo; **to play** ~ **cowboys** jugar a
los vaqueros; **to be good** ~ **sth** ser
bueno en algo
6 (referring to cause): **shocked/
surprised/annoyed** ~ **sth** asombrado/
sorprendido/fastidiado por algo; **I went**
~ **his suggestion** fui a instancias suyas

ate [eɪt] pt of **eat**

atheist ['eɪθɪɪst] n ateo/a

Athens ['æθɪnz] n Atenas

athlete ['æθliːt] n atleta m/f

athletic [æθ'lɛtɪk] adj atlético; ~s n
atletismo

Atlantic [ət'læntɪk] adj atlántico ♦ n: the
~ (Ocean) el (Océano) Atlántico

atlas ['ætləs] n atlas m

atmosphere ['ætməsfɪə*] n atmósfera; (of
place) ambiente m

atom ['ætəm] n átomo; ~ic [ə'tɒmɪk] adj
atómico; ~(ic) bomb n bomba atómica;
~izer ['ætəmaɪzə*] n atomizador m

atone [ə'təʊn] vi: to ~ for expiar

atrocious [ə'trəʊʃəs] adj atroz

attach [ə'tætʃ] *vt* (*fasten*) atar; (*join*) unir, sujetar; (*document, letter*) adjuntar; (*importance etc*) dar, conceder; **to be ~ed to sb/sth** (*to like*) tener cariño a alguien/algo

attaché [ə'tæʃeɪ] *n* agregado/a; **~ case** *n* maletín *m*

attachment [ə'tætʃmənt] *n* (*tool*) accesorio; (*love*): **~ (to)** apego (a)

attack [ə'tæk] *vt* (*MIL*) atacar; (*subj: criminal*) agredir, asaltar; (*criticize*) criticar; (*task*) emprender ♦ *n* ataque *m*, asalto; (*on sb's life*) atentado; (*fig: criticism*) crítica; (*of illness*) ataque *m*; **heart ~** infarto (de miocardio); **~er** *n* agresor(a) *m/f*, asaltante *m/f*

attain [ə'teɪn] *vt* (*also*: **~ to**) alcanzar; (*achieve*) lograr, conseguir; **~ments** *npl* logros *mpl*

attempt [ə'tempt] *n* tentativa, intento; (*attack*) atentado ♦ *vt* intentar; **~ed** *adj*: **~ed burglary/murder/suicide** tentativa *or* intento de robo/asesinato/suicidio

attend [ə'tend] *vt* asistir a; (*patient*) atender; **~ to** *vt fus* ocuparse de; (*customer, patient*) atender a; **~ance** *n* asistencia, presencia; (*people present*) concurrencia; **~ant** *n* ayudante *m/f*; (*in garage etc*) encargado/a ♦ *adj* (*dangers*) concomitante

attention [ə'tenʃən] *n* atención *f*; (*care*) atenciones *fpl* ♦ *excl* (*MIL*) ¡firme(s)!; **for the ~ of ...** (*ADMIN*) atención ...

attentive [ə'tentɪv] *adj* atento

attest [ə'test] *vi*: **to ~ to** demostrar; (*LAW: confirm*) dar fe de

attic ['ætɪk] *n* desván *m*

attitude ['ætɪtjuːd] *n* actitud *f*; (*disposition*) disposición *f*

attorney [ə'tɜːnɪ] *n* (*lawyer*) abogado/a; **A~ General** (*BRIT*) ≈ Presidente *m* del Consejo del Poder Judicial (*SP*); (*US*) ≈ ministro de justicia

attract [ə'trækt] *vt* atraer; (*sb's attention*) llamar; **~ion** [ə'trækʃən] *n* encanto; (*gen pl: amusements*) diversiones *fpl*; (*PHYSICS*) atracción *f*; (*fig: towards sb, sth*) atractivo; **~ive** *adj* guapo; (*interesting*) atrayente

attribute [*n* 'ætrɪbjuːt, *vb* ə'trɪbjuːt] *n* atributo ♦ *vt*: **to ~ sth to** atribuir algo a

attrition [ə'trɪʃən] *n*: **war of ~** guerra de agotamiento

aubergine ['əʊbəʒiːn] (*BRIT*) *n* berenjena; (*colour*) morado

auburn ['ɔːbən] *adj* color castaño rojizo

auction ['ɔːkʃən] *n* (*also: sale by ~*) subasta ♦ *vt* subastar; **~eer** [-'nɪə*] *n* subastador(a) *m/f*

audacity [ɔː'dæsɪtɪ] *n* audacia, atrevimiento; (*pej*) descaro

audible ['ɔːdɪbl] *adj* audible, que se puede oír

audience ['ɔːdɪəns] *n* público; (*RADIO*) radioescuchas *mpl*; (*TV*) telespectadores *mpl*; (*interview*) audiencia

audio-typist ['ɔːdɪəʊ'taɪpɪst] *n* mecanógrafo/a de dictáfono

audio-visual ['ɔːdɪəʊ'vɪzjuəl] *adj* audiovisual; **~ aid** *n* ayuda audiovisual

audit ['ɔːdɪt] *vt* revisar, intervenir

audition [ɔː'dɪʃən] *n* audición *f*

auditor ['ɔːdɪtə*] *n* interventor(a) *m/f*, censor(a) *m/f* de cuentas

augment [ɔːg'ment] *vt* aumentar

augur ['ɔːgə*] *vi*: **it ~s well** es un buen augurio

August ['ɔːgəst] *n* agosto

aunt [ɑːnt] *n* tía; **~ie** *n diminutive of* **aunt**; **~y** *n diminutive of* **aunt**

au pair ['əʊ'peə*] *n* (*also*: **~ girl**) (chica) au pair *f*

auspices ['ɔːspɪsɪz] *npl*: **under the ~ of** bajo los auspicios de

auspicious [ɔːs'pɪʃəs] *adj* propicio, de buen augurio

austerity [ɔ'sterɪtɪ] *n* austeridad *f*

Australia [ɔs'treɪlɪə] *n* Australia; **~n** *adj*, *n* australiano/a *m/f*

Austria ['ɔstrɪə] *n* Austria; **~n** *adj*, *n* austríaco/a *m/f*

authentic [ɔː'θentɪk] *adj* auténtico

author ['ɔːθə*] *n* autor(a) *m/f*

authoritarian [ɔːθɒrɪ'tɛərɪən] *adj* autoritario

authoritative [ɔː'θɒrɪtətɪv] *adj* autorizado; (*manner*) autoritario

authority [ɔː'θɒrɪtɪ] *n* autoridad *f*;
(*official permission*) autorización *f*; **the
authorities** *npl* las autoridades
authorize ['ɔːθəraɪz] *vt* autorizar
auto ['ɔːtəu] (*US*) *n* coche *m* (*SP*), carro
m (*AM*), automóvil *m*
autobiography [ɔːtəbaɪ'ɒgrəfɪ] *n*
autobiografía
autograph ['ɔːtəɡrɑːf] *n* autógrafo ♦ *vt*
(*photo etc*) dedicar; (*programme*) firmar
automated ['ɔːtəmeɪtɪd] *adj*
automatizado
automatic [ɔːtə'mætɪk] *adj* automático
♦ *n* (*gun*) pistola automática; (*car*) coche
m automático; **~ally** *adv* automáticamen-
te
automation [ɔːtə'meɪʃən] *n* reconversión
f
automaton [ɔː'tɒmətən] (*pl* **automata**) *n*
autómata *m/f*
automobile ['ɔːtəməbiːl] (*US*) *n* coche *m*
(*SP*), carro (*AM*), automóvil *m*
autonomy [ɔː'tɒnəmɪ] *n* autonomía
autopsy ['ɔːtɒpsɪ] *n* autopsia
autumn ['ɔːtəm] *n* otoño
auxiliary [ɔːg'zɪlɪərɪ] *adj, n* auxiliar *m/f*
avail [ə'veɪl] *vt*: **to ~ o.s. of** aprove-
char(se) de ♦ *n*: **to no ~** en vano, sin resultado
available [ə'veɪləbl] *adj* disponible;
(*unoccupied*) libre; (*person: unattached*)
soltero y sin compromiso
avalanche ['ævəlɑːnʃ] *n* alud *m*,
avalancha
avant-garde ['ævãŋ'gɑːd] *adj* de
vanguardia
Ave. *abbr* = **avenue**
avenge [ə'vɛndʒ] *vt* vengar
avenue ['ævənjuː] *n* avenida; (*fig*) camino
average ['ævərɪdʒ] *n* promedio, término
medio ♦ *adj* medio, de término medio;
(*ordinary*) regular, corriente ♦ *vt* sacar
un promedio de; **on ~** por regla general;
~ out *vi*: **to ~ out at** salir en un
promedio de
averse [ə'vɜːs] *adj*: **to be ~ to** sth/doing
sentir aversión *or* antipatía por algo/por
hacer
avert [ə'vɜːt] *vt* prevenir; (*blow*) desviar;

(*one's eyes*) apartar
aviary ['eɪvɪərɪ] *n* pajarera, avería
avid ['ævɪd] *adj* ávido, ansioso
avocado [ævə'kɑːdəu] *n* (*also: BRIT: ~
pear*) aguacate *m* (*SP*), palta (*AM*)
avoid [ə'vɔɪd] *vt* evitar, eludir
await [ə'weɪt] *vt* esperar, aguardar
awake [ə'weɪk] (*pt* **awoke**, *pp* **awoken**
or **awaked**) *adj* despierto ♦ *vt* despertar
♦ *vi* despertarse; **to be ~** estar despierto;
~ning *n* el despertar
award [ə'wɔːd] *n* premio; (*LAW: damages*)
indemnización *f* ♦ *vt* otorgar, conceder;
(*LAW: damages*) adjudicar
aware [ə'wɛə*] *adj*: **~ (of)** consciente
(de); (*realize*) darse
cuenta de/de que; (*learn*) enterarse de/
de que; **~ness** *n* conciencia; (*knowledge*)
conocimiento
awash [ə'wɒʃ] *adj*: **~ with** (*also fig*)
inundado de
away [ə'weɪ] *adv* fuera; (*movement*): **she
went ~** se marchó; (*far ~*) lejos; **two
kilometres ~** a dos kilómetros de
distancia; **two hours ~ by car** a dos
horas en coche; **the holiday was two
weeks ~** faltaban dos semanas para las
vacaciones; **he's ~ for a week** estará
ausente una semana; **to take ~ (from)**
quitar (a); (*subtract*) substraer (de); **to
work/pedal ~** seguir trabajando/
pedaleando; **to fade ~** (*colour*) desvanecerse; (*sound*) apagarse; **~ game** *n*
(*SPORT*) partido de fuera
awe [ɔː] *n* admiración *f* respetuosa; **~-
inspiring** *adj* imponente; **~some** *adj*
imponente
awful ['ɔːfəl] *adj* horroroso; (*quantity*):
an ~ lot (of) cantidad (de); **~ly** *adv*
(*very*) terriblemente
awhile [ə'waɪl] *adv* (durante) un rato,
algún tiempo
awkward ['ɔːkwəd] *adj* desmañado,
torpe; (*shape*) incómodo; (*embarrassing*)
delicado, difícil
awning ['ɔːnɪŋ] *n* (*of tent, caravan, shop*)
toldo
awoke [ə'wəuk] *pt of* **awake**
awoken [ə'wəukən] *pp of* **awake**

awry [əˈraɪ] *adv*: **to be ~** estar descolocado *or* mal puesto; **to go ~** salir mal, fracasar

axe [æks] (*US* **ax**) *n* hacha ♦ *vt* (*project*) cortar; (*jobs*) reducir

axes [ˈæksiːz] *npl of* **axis**

axis [ˈæksɪs] (*pl* **axes**) *n* eje *m*

axle [ˈæksl] *n* eje *m*, árbol *m*

ay(e) [aɪ] *excl* sí

B b

B [biː] *n* (*MUS*) si *m*

B.A. *abbr* = **Bachelor of Arts**

babble [ˈbæbl] *vi* barbotear; (*brook*) murmurar

baby [ˈbeɪbɪ] *n* bebé *m/f*; (*US: inf: darling*) mi amor; **~ carriage** (*US*) *n* cochecito; **~-sit** *vi* hacer de canguro; **~-sitter** *n* canguro/a

bachelor [ˈbætʃələ*] *n* soltero; **B~ of Arts/Science** licenciado/a en Filosofía y Letras/Ciencias

back [bæk] *n* (*of person*) espalda; (*of animal*) lomo; (*of hand*) dorso; (*as opposed to front*) parte *f* de atrás; (*of chair*) respaldo; (*of page*) reverso; (*of book*) final *m*; (*FOOTBALL*) defensa *m*; (*of crowd*): **the ones at the ~** los del fondo ♦ *vt* (*candidate: also*: **~ up**) respaldar, apoyar; (*horse: at races*) apostar a; (*car*) dar marcha atrás a *or* con ♦ *vi* (*car etc*) ir (*or* salir *or* entrar) marcha atrás ♦ *adj* (*payment, rent*) atrasado; (*seats, wheels*) de atrás ♦ *adv* (*not forward*) (hacia) atrás; (*returned*): **he's ~** está de vuelta, ha vuelto; **he ran ~** volvió corriendo; (*restitution*): **throw the ball ~** devuelve la pelota; **can I have it ~?** ¿me lo devuelve?; (*again*): **he called ~** llamó de nuevo; **~ down** *vi* echarse atrás; **~ out** *vi* (*of promise*) volverse atrás; **~ up** *vt* (*person*) apoyar, respaldar; (*theory*) defender; (*COMPUT*) hacer una copia preventiva *or* de reserva; **~bencher** (*BRIT*) *n* miembro del parlamento sin cargo relevante; **~bone** *n* columna vertebral; **~-cloth** *n* telón *m* de fondo; **~date** *vt*

(*pay rise*) dar efecto retroactivo a; (*letter*) poner fecha atrasada a; **~drop** *n* = **~-cloth**; **~fire** *vi* (*AUT*) petardear; (*plans*) fallar, salir mal; **~ground** *n* fondo; (*of events*) antecedentes *mpl*; (*basic knowledge*) bases *fpl*; (*experience*) conocimientos *mpl*, educación *f*; **family ~ground** origen *m*, antecedentes *mpl*; **~hand** *n* (*TENNIS: also*: **~hand stroke**) revés *m*; **~hander** (*BRIT*) *n* (*bribe*) soborno; **~ing** *n* (*fig*) apoyo, respaldo; **~lash** *n* reacción *f*; **~log** *n*: **~log of work** trabajo atrasado; **~ number** *n* (*of magazine etc*) número atrasado; **~pack** *n* mochila; **~ pay** *n* pago atrasado; **~side** (*inf*) *n* trasero, culo; (*also*: **~-up file**) copia de reserva; **~ward** *adj* (*person, country*) atrasado; **~wards** *adv* hacia atrás; (*read a list*) al revés; (*fall*) de espaldas; **~water** *n* (*fig*) lugar *m* atrasado *or* apartado; **~yard** *n* traspatio

bacon [ˈbeɪkən] *n* tocino, beicon *m*

bad [bæd] *adj* malo; (*mistake, accident*) grave; (*food*) podrido, pasado; **his ~ leg** su pierna lisiada; **to go ~** (*food*) pasarse

bade [bæd, beɪd] *pt of* **bid**

badge [bædʒ] *n* insignia; (*policeman's*) chapa, placa

badger [ˈbædʒə*] *n* tejón *m*

badly [ˈbædlɪ] *adv* mal; **to reflect ~ on sb** influir negativamente en la reputación de uno; **~ wounded** gravemente herido; **he needs it ~** le hace gran falta; **to be ~ off (for money)** andar mal de dinero

badminton [ˈbædmɪntən] *n* bádminton *m*

bad-tempered *adj* de mal genio *or* carácter; (*temporarily*) de mal humor

baffle [ˈbæfl] *vt* desconcertar, confundir

bag [bæg] *n* bolsa; (*handbag*) bolso; (*satchel*) mochila; (*case*) maleta; **~s of** (*inf*) un montón de; **~gage** *n* equipaje *m*; **~gy** *adj* amplio; **~pipes** *npl* gaita

Bahamas [bəˈhɑːməz] *npl*: **the ~** las Islas Bahamas

bail [beɪl] *n* fianza ♦ *vt* (*prisoner: gen*:

grant ~ *to*) poner en libertad bajo fianza; (*boat*: *also*: ~ *out*) achicar; **on** ~ (*prisoner*) bajo fianza; **to** ~ **sb out** obtener la libertad de uno bajo fianza; *see also* **bale**

bailiff ['beɪlɪf] *n* alguacil *m*

bait [beɪt] *n* cebo ♦ *vt* poner cebo en; (*tease*) tomar el pelo a

bake [beɪk] *vt* cocer (al horno) ♦ *vi* cocerse; ~**d beans** *npl* judías *fpl* en salsa de tomate; ~**r** *n* panadero; ~**ry** *n* panadería; (*for cakes*) pastelería; **baking** *n* (*act*) amasar *m*; (*batch*) hornada; **baking powder** *n* levadura (en polvo)

balance ['bæləns] *n* equilibrio; (*COMM*: *sum*) balance *m*; (*remainder*) resto; (*scales*) balanza ♦ *vt* equilibrar; (*budget*) nivelar; (*account*) saldar; (*make equal*) equilibrar; ~ **of trade/payments** balanza de comercio/pagos; ~**d** *adj* (*personality, diet*) equilibrado; (*report*) objetivo; ~ **sheet** *n* balance *m*

balcony ['bælkənɪ] *n* (*open*) balcón *m*; (*closed*) galería; (*in theatre*) anfiteatro

bald [bɔːld] *adj* calvo; (*tyre*) liso

bale [beɪl] *n* (*AGR*) paca, fardo; (*of papers etc*) fajo; ~ **out** *vi* lanzarse en paracaídas

Balearics [bælɪˈærɪks] *npl*: **the** ~ las Baleares

ball [bɔːl] *n* pelota; (*football*) balón *m*; (*of wool, string*) ovillo; (*dance*) baile *m*; **to play** ~ (*fig*) cooperar

ballast ['bæləst] *n* lastre *m*

ball bearings *npl* cojinetes *mpl* de bolas

ballerina [bæləˈriːnə] *n* bailarina

ballet ['bæleɪ] *n* ballet *m*; ~ **dancer** *n* bailarín/ina *m/f*

ballistics [bəˈlɪstɪks] *n* balística

balloon [bəˈluːn] *n* globo

ballot ['bælət] *n* votación *f*; ~ **paper** *n* papeleta (para votar)

ball-point (pen) ['bɔːlpɔɪnt-] *n* bolígrafo

ballroom ['bɔːlrum] *n* salón *m* de baile

balm [bɑːm] *n* bálsamo

Baltic ['bɔːltɪk] *n*: **the** ~ **(Sea)** el (Mar) Báltico

balustrade ['bæləstreɪd] *n* barandilla

ban [bæn] *n* prohibición *f*, proscripción *f*

♦ *vt* prohibir, proscribir

banal [bəˈnɑːl] *adj* banal, vulgar

banana [bəˈnɑːnə] *n* plátano (*SP*), banana (*AM*)

band [bænd] *n* grupo; (*strip*) faja, tira; (*stripe*) lista; (*MUS*: *jazz*) orquesta; (: *rock*) grupo; (: *MIL*) banda; ~ **together** *vi* juntarse, asociarse

bandage ['bændɪdʒ] *n* venda, vendaje *m* ♦ *vt* vendar

Bandaid ['bændeɪd] ® (*US*) *n* tirita

bandit ['bændɪt] *n* bandido

bandwagon ['bændwægən] *n*: **to jump on the** ~ subirse al carro

bandy ['bændɪ] *vt* (*jokes, insults*) cambiar

bandy-legged ['bændɪ'legd] *adj* estevado

bang [bæŋ] *n* (*of gun, exhaust*) estallido, detonación *f*; (*of door*) portazo; (*blow*) golpe *m* ♦ *vt* (*door*) cerrar de golpe; (*one's head*) golpear ♦ *vi* estallar; (*door*) cerrar de golpe

Bangladesh [bɑːŋgləˈdɛʃ] *n* Bangladesh *m*

bangs [bæŋz] (*US*) *npl* flequillo

banish ['bænɪʃ] *vt* desterrar

banister(s) ['bænɪstə(z)] *n(pl)* barandilla, pasamanos *m inv*

bank [bæŋk] *n* (*COMM*) banco; (*of river, lake*) ribera, orilla; (*of earth*) terraplén *m* ♦ *vi* (*AVIAT*) ladearse; ~ **on** *vt fus* contar con; ~ **account** *n* cuenta de banco; ~ **card** *n* tarjeta bancaria; ~**er** *n* banquero; ~**er's card** (*BRIT*) *n* = ~ **card**; **B**~ **holiday** (*BRIT*) *n* día *m* festivo; ~**ing** *n* banca; ~**note** *n* billete *m* de banco; ~ **rate** *n* tipo de interés bancario

bankrupt ['bæŋkrʌpt] *adj* quebrado, insolvente; **to go** ~ hacer bancarrota; **to be** ~ estar en quiebra; ~**cy** *n* quiebra

bank statement *n* balance *m* or detalle *m* de cuenta

banner ['bænə*] *n* pancarta

banns [bænz] *npl* amonestaciones *fpl*

banquet ['bæŋkwɪt] *n* banquete *m*

baptism ['bæptɪzəm] *n* bautismo; (*act*) bautizo

baptize [bæpˈtaɪz] *vt* bautizar

bar [bɑː*] *n* (*pub*) bar *m*; (*counter*) mostrador *m*; (*rod*) barra; (*of window*, *cage*) reja; (*of soap*) pastilla; (*of chocolate*) tableta; (*fig: hindrance*) obstáculo; (*prohibition*) proscripción *f*; (*MUS*) barra ♦ *vt* (*road*) obstruir; (*person*) excluir; (*activity*) prohibir; **behind ~s** entre rejas; **the B~** (*LAW*) la abogacía; **~ none** sin excepción

barbaric [baːˈbærɪk] *adj* bárbaro

barbecue [ˈbaːbɪkjuː] *n* barbacoa

barbed wire [ˈbaːbd-] *n* alambre *m* de púas

barber [ˈbaːbə*] *n* peluquero, barbero

bar code *n* código de barras

bare [beə*] *adj* desnudo; (*trees*) sin hojas; (*necessities etc*) básico ♦ *vt* desnudar; (*teeth*) enseñar; **~back** *adv* a pelo, sin silla; **~faced** *adj* descarado; **~foot** *adj*, *adv* descalzo; **~ly** *adv* apenas

bargain [ˈbaːgɪn] *n* pacto, negocio; (*good buy*) ganga ♦ *vi* negociar; (*haggle*) regatear; **into the ~** además, por añadidura; **~ for** *vt fus*: **he got more than he ~ed for** le resultó peor de lo que esperaba

barge [baːdʒ] *n* barcaza; **~ in** *vi* irrumpir; (*interrupt: conversation*) interrumpir

bark [baːk] *n* (*of tree*) corteza; (*of dog*) ladrido ♦ *vi* ladrar

barley [ˈbaːlɪ] *n* cebada; **~ sugar** *n* azúcar *m* cande

barmaid [ˈbaːmeɪd] *n* camarera

barman [ˈbaːmən] *n* camarero, barman *m*

barn [baːn] *n* granero

barometer [bəˈrɒmɪtə*] *n* barómetro

baron [ˈbærən] *n* barón *m*; (*press ~ etc*) magnate *m*; **~ess** *n* baronesa

barracks [ˈbærəks] *npl* cuartel *m*

barrage [ˈbæraːʒ] *n* (*MIL*) descarga, bombardeo; (*dam*) presa; (*of criticism*) lluvia, aluvión *m*

barrel [ˈbærəl] *n* barril *m*; (*of gun*) cañón *m*

barren [ˈbærən] *adj* estéril

barricade [bærɪˈkeɪd] *n* barricada ♦ *vt* cerrar con barricadas; **to ~ o.s. (in)** hacerse fuerte (en)

barrier [ˈbærɪə*] *n* barrera

barring [ˈbaːrɪŋ] *prep* excepto, salvo

barrister [ˈbærɪstə*] (*BRIT*) *n* abogado/a

barrow [ˈbærəu] *n* (*cart*) carretilla (de mano)

bartender [ˈbaːtendə*] (*US*) *n* camarero, barman *m*

barter [ˈbaːtə*] *vt*: **to ~ sth for sth** trocar algo por algo

base [beɪs] *n* base *f* ♦ *vt*: **to ~ sth on** basar *or* fundar algo en ♦ *adj* bajo, infame

baseball [ˈbeɪsbɔːl] *n* béisbol *m*

basement [ˈbeɪsmənt] *n* sótano

bases[1] [ˈbeɪsiːz] *npl of* **basis**

bases[2] [ˈbeɪsɪz] *npl of* **base**

bash [bæʃ] (*inf*) *vt* golpear

bashful [ˈbæʃful] *adj* tímido, vergonzoso

basic [ˈbeɪsɪk] *adj* básico; **~ally** *adv* fundamentalmente, en el fondo; (*simply*) sencillamente; **~s** *npl*: **the ~s** los fundamentos

basil [ˈbæzl] *n* albahaca

basin [ˈbeɪsn] *n* cuenco, tazón *m*; (*GEO*) cuenca; (*also: wash~*) lavabo

basis [ˈbeɪsɪs] (*pl* **bases**) *n* base *f*; **on a part-time/trial ~** a tiempo parcial/a prueba

bask [baːsk] *vi*: **to ~ in the sun** tomar el sol

basket [ˈbaːskɪt] *n* cesta, cesto; canasta; **~ball** *n* baloncesto

Basque [bæsk] *adj*, *n* vasco/a *m/f*; **~ Country** *n* Euskadi *m*, País *m* Vasco

bass [beɪs] *n* (*MUS: instrument*) bajo; (*double ~*) contrabajo; (*singer*) bajo

bassoon [bəˈsuːn] *n* fagot *m*

bastard [ˈbaːstəd] *n* bastardo; (*inf!*) hijo de puta (*!*)

bastion [ˈbæstɪən] *n* baluarte *m*

bat [bæt] *n* (*ZOOL*) murciélago; (*for ball games*) palo; (*BRIT: for table tennis*) pala ♦ *vt*: **he didn't ~ an eyelid** ni pestañeó

batch [bætʃ] *n* (*of bread*) hornada; (*of letters etc*) lote *m*

bated [ˈbeɪtɪd] *adj*: **with ~ breath** sin respirar

bath [baːθ, *pl* baːðz] *n* (*action*) baño; (*~tub*) baño (*SP*), bañera (*SP*), tina (*AM*) ♦ *vt* bañar; **to have a ~** bañarse, tomar un baño; *see also* **baths**

bathe [beɪð] *vi* bañarse ♦ *vt* (*wound*) lavar; **~r** *n* bañista *m/f*

bathing ['beɪðɪŋ] *n* el bañarse; **~ cap** *n* gorro de baño; **~ costume** (*US* **~ suit**) *n* traje *m* de baño

bath: **~robe** *n* (*man's*) batín *m*; (*woman's*) bata; **~room** *n* (cuarto de) baño; **~s** [bɑːðz] *npl* (*also: swimming* **~s**) piscina; **~ towel** *n* toalla de baño

baton ['bætən] *n* (*MUS*) batuta; (*ATHLETICS*) testigo; (*weapon*) porra

batter ['bætə*] *vt* maltratar; (*subj: rain etc*) azotar ♦ *n* masa (para rebozar); **~ed** *adj* (*hat, pan*) estropeado

battery ['bætərɪ] *n* (*AUT*) batería; (*of torch*) pila

battle ['bætl] *n* batalla; (*fig*) lucha ♦ *vi* luchar; **~ship** *n* acorazado

bawdy ['bɔːdɪ] *adj* (*joke*) verde

bawl [bɔːl] *vi* chillar, gritar; (*child*) berrear

bay [beɪ] *n* (*GEO*) bahía; **B~ of Biscay** ≈ mar Cantábrico; **to hold sb at ~** mantener a alguien a raya; **~ leaf** *n* hoja de laurel

bay window *n* ventana salediza

bazaar [bə'zɑː*] *n* bazar *m*; (*fete*) venta con fines benéficos

B. & B. *n abbr* (= *bed and breakfast*) cama y desayuno

BBC *n abbr* (= *British Broadcasting Corporation*) cadena de radio y televisión estatal británica

B.C. *adv abbr* (= *before Christ*) a. de C

KEYWORD
---

be [biː] (*pt* **was, were**, *pp* **been**) *aux vb* **1** (*with present participle: forming continuous tenses*): **what are you doing?** ¿qué estás haciendo?, ¿qué haces?; **they're coming tomorrow** vienen mañana; **I've been waiting for you for hours** llevo horas esperándote

2 (*with pp: forming passives*) ser (*but often replaced by active or reflexive constructions*); **to ~ murdered** ser asesinado; **the box had been opened** habían abierto la caja; **the thief was nowhere to ~ seen** no se veía al ladrón

por ninguna parte

3 (*in tag questions*): **it was fun, wasn't it?** fue divertido, ¿no? *or* ¿verdad?; **he's good-looking, isn't he?** es guapo, ¿no te parece?; **she's back again, is she?** entonces, ¿ha vuelto?

4 (*+ to + infin*): **the house is to ~ sold** (*necessity*) hay que vender la casa; (*future*) van a vender la casa; **he's not to open it** no tiene que abrirlo

♦ *vb + complement* **1** (*with n or num complement, but see also* **3, 4, 5** *and impers vb below*) ser (*subj: he's a doctor* es médico; **2 and 2 are 4** 2 y 2 son 4

2 (*with adj complement: expressing permanent or inherent quality*) ser; (: *expressing state seen as temporary or reversible*) estar; **I'm English** soy inglés/esa; **she's tall/pretty** es alta/bonita; **he's young** es joven; **~ careful/good/quiet** ten cuidado/pórtate bien/cállate; **I'm tired** estoy cansado/a; **it's dirty** está sucio/a

3 (*of health*) estar; **how are you?** ¿cómo estás?; **he's very ill** está muy enfermo; **I'm better now** ya estoy mejor

4 (*of age*) tener; **how old are you?** ¿cuántos años tienes?; **I'm sixteen (years old)** tengo dieciséis años

5 (*cost*) costar; ser; **how much was the meal?** ¿cuánto fue *or* costó la comida?; **that'll ~ £5.75, please** son £5.75, por favor; **this shirt is £17** esta camisa cuesta £17

♦ *vi* **1** (*exist, occur etc*) existir, haber; **the best singer that ever was** el mejor cantante que existió jamás; **is there a God?** ¿hay un Dios?, ¿existe Dios?; **~ that as it may** sea como sea; **so ~ it** así sea

2 (*referring to place*) estar; **I won't ~ here tomorrow** no estaré aquí mañana

3 (*referring to movement*): **where have you been?** ¿dónde has estado?

♦ *impers vb* **1** (*referring to time*): **it's 5 o'clock** son las 5; **it's the 28th of April** estamos a 28 de abril

2 (*referring to distance*): **it's 10 km to the village** el pueblo está a 10 km

3 (*referring to the weather*): **it's too hot/cold** hace demasiado calor/frío; **it's windy today** hace viento hoy
4 (*emphatic*): **it's me** soy yo; **it was Maria who paid the bill** fue María la que pagó la cuenta

beach [biːtʃ] *n* playa ♦ *vt* varar
beacon ['biːkən] *n* (*lighthouse*) faro; (*marker*) guía
bead [biːd] *n* cuenta; (*of sweat etc*) gota
beak [biːk] *n* pico
beaker ['biːkə*] *n* vaso de plástico
beam [biːm] *n* (*ARCH*) viga, travesaño; (*of light*) rayo, haz *m* de luz ♦ *vi* brillar; (*smile*) sonreír
bean [biːn] *n* judía; **runner/broad ~** habichuela/haba; **coffee ~** grano de café; **~sprouts** *npl* brotes *mpl* de soja
bear [bɛə*] (*pt* **bore**, *pp* **borne**) *n* oso ♦ *vt* (*weight etc*) llevar; (*cost*) pagar; (*responsibility*) tener; (*endure*) soportar, aguantar; (*children*) parir, tener; (*fruit*) dar ♦ *vi*: **to ~ right/left** torcer a la derecha/izquierda; **~ out** *vt* (*suspicions*) corroborar, confirmar; (*person*) dar la razón a; **~ up** *vi* (*remain cheerful*) mantenerse animado
beard [bɪəd] *n* barba; **~ed** *adj* con barba, barbudo
bearer ['bɛərə*] *n* portador(a) *m/f*
bearing ['bɛərɪŋ] *n* porte *m*, comportamiento; (*connection*) relación *f*; **~s** *npl* (*also*: **ball ~s**) cojinetes *mpl* a bolas; **to take a ~** tomar marcaciones; **to find one's ~s** orientarse
beast [biːst] *n* bestia; (*inf*) bruto, salvaje *m*; **~ly** (*inf*) *adj* horrible
beat [biːt] (*pt* **beat**, *pp* **beaten**) *n* (*of heart*) latido; (*MUS*) ritmo, compás *m*; (*of policeman*) ronda ♦ *vt* pegar, golpear; (*eggs*) batir; (*defeat: opponent*) vencer, derrotar; (: *record*) sobrepasar ♦ *vi* (*heart*) latir; (*drum*) redoblar; (*rain, wind*) azotar; **off the ~en track** aislado; **to ~ it** (*inf*) largarse; **~ off** *vt* rechazar; **~ up** *vt* (*attack*) dar una paliza a; **~ing** *n* paliza
beautiful ['bjuːtɪful] *adj* precioso,

hermoso, bello; **~ly** *adv* maravillosamente
beauty ['bjuːtɪ] *n* belleza; **~ salon** *n* salón *m* de belleza; **~ spot** *n* (*TOURISM*) lugar *m* pintoresco
beaver ['biːvə*] *n* castor *m*
became [bɪ'keɪm] *pt of* **become**
because [bɪ'kɒz] *conj* porque; **~ of** debido a, a causa de
beck [bɛk] *n*: **to be at the ~ and call of** estar a disposición de
beckon ['bɛkən] *vt* (*also*: **~ to**) llamar con señas
become [bɪ'kʌm] (*irreg: like* **come**) *vt* (*suit*) favorecer, sentar bien a ♦ *vi* (+ *n*) hacerse, llegar a ser; (+ *adj*) ponerse, volverse; **to ~ fat** engordar
becoming [bɪ'kʌmɪŋ] *adj* (*behaviour*) decoroso; (*clothes*) favorecedor(a)
bed [bɛd] *n* cama; (*of flowers*) macizo; (*of coal, clay*) capa; (*of river*) lecho; (*of sea*) fondo; **to go to ~** acostarse; **~ and breakfast** *n* (*place*) pensión *f*; (*terms*) cama y desayuno; **~clothes** *npl* ropa de cama; **~ding** *n* ropa de cama
bedlam ['bɛdləm] *n* desbarajuste *m*
bedraggled [bɪ'dræɡld] *adj* (*untidy: person*) desastrado; (*clothes, hair*) desordenado
bed: **~ridden** *adj* postrado (en cama); **~room** *n* dormitorio; **~side** *n*: **at the ~side of** a la cabecera de; **~sit(ter)** (*BRIT*) *n* estudio (*SP*), suite *m* (*AM*); **~spread** *n* cubrecama *m*, colcha; **~time** *n* hora de acostarse
bee [biː] *n* abeja
beech [biːtʃ] *n* haya
beef [biːf] *n* carne *f* de vaca; **roast ~** rosbif *m*; **~burger** *n* hamburguesa; **B~eater** *n* alabardero de la Torre de Londres
beehive ['biːhaɪv] *n* colmena
beeline ['biːlaɪn] *n*: **to make a ~ for** ir derecho a
been [biːn] *pp of* **be**
beer [bɪə*] *n* cerveza
beet [biːt] *n* (*US*) (*also*: **red ~**) remolacha
beetle ['biːtl] *n* escarabajo
beetroot ['biːtruːt] (*BRIT*) *n* remolacha

before [bɪ'fɔː*] *prep* (*of time*) antes de; (*of space*) delante de ♦ *conj* antes (de) que ♦ *adv* antes, anteriormente; delante, adelante; ~ **going** antes de marcharse; ~ **she goes** antes de que se vaya; **the week** ~ la semana anterior; **I've never seen it** ~ no lo he visto nunca; **~hand** *adv* de antemano, con anticipación

beg [bɛg] *vi* pedir limosna ♦ *vt* pedir, rogar; (*entreat*) suplicar; **to** ~ **sb to do sth** rogar a uno que haga algo; *see also* **pardon**

began [bɪ'gæn] *pt of* **begin**

beggar ['bɛgə*] *n* mendigo/a

begin [bɪ'gɪn] (*pt* **began**, *pp* **begun**) *vt, vi* empezar, comenzar; **to** ~ **doing** *or* **to do sth** empezar a hacer algo; **~ner** *n* principiante *m/f*; **~ning** *n* principio, comienzo

begun [bɪ'gʌn] *pp of* **begin**

behalf [bɪ'hɑːf] *n*: **on** ~ **of** en nombre de, por; (*for benefit of*) en beneficio de; **on my/his** ~ por mí/él

behave [bɪ'heɪv] *vi* (*person*) portarse, comportarse; (*well: also:* ~ *o.s.*) portarse bien; **behaviour** (*US* **behavior**) *n* comportamiento, conducta

behead [bɪ'hɛd] *vt* decapitar

beheld [bɪ'hɛld] *pt, pp of* **behold**

behind [bɪ'haɪnd] *prep* detrás de; (*supporting*): **to be** ~ **sb** apoyar a alguien; (*lower in rank etc*) estar por detrás de ♦ *adv* detrás, por detrás, atrás ♦ *n* trasero; **to be** ~ (**schedule**) ir retrasado; ~ **the scenes** (*fig*) entre bastidores

behold [bɪ'həuld] (*irreg: like* **hold**) *vt* contemplar

beige [beɪʒ] *adj* color beige

being ['biːɪŋ] *n* ser *m*; (*existence*): **in** ~ existente; **to come into** ~ aparecer

belated [bɪ'leɪtɪd] *adj* atrasado, tardío

belch [bɛltʃ] *vi* eructar ♦ *vt* (*gen:* ~ *out: smoke etc*) arrojar

belfry ['bɛlfrɪ] *n* campanario

Belgian ['bɛldʒən] *adj, n* belga *m/f*

Belgium ['bɛldʒəm] *n* Bélgica

belie [bɪ'laɪ] *vt* desmentir, contradecir

belief [bɪ'liːf] *n* opinión *f*; (*faith*) fe *f*

believe [bɪ'liːv] *vt, vi* creer; **to** ~ **in** creer en; **~r** *n* partidario/a; (*REL*) creyente *m/f*, fiel *m/f*

belittle [bɪ'lɪtl] *vt* quitar importancia a

bell [bɛl] *n* campana; (*small*) campanilla; (*on door*) timbre *m*

belligerent [bɪ'lɪdʒərənt] *adj* agresivo

bellow ['bɛləu] *vi* bramar; (*person*) rugir; ~**s** *npl* fuelle *m*

belly ['bɛlɪ] *n* barriga, panza

belong [bɪ'lɔŋ] *vi*: **to** ~ **to** pertenecer a; (*club etc*) ser socio de; **this book** ~**s here** este libro va aquí; ~**ings** *npl* pertenencias *fpl*

beloved [bɪ'lʌvɪd] *adj* querido/a

below [bɪ'ləu] *prep* bajo, debajo de; (*less than*) inferior a ♦ *adv* abajo, (por) debajo; *see* ~ véase más abajo

belt [bɛlt] *n* cinturón *m*; (*TECH*) correa, cinta ♦ *vt* (*thrash*) pegar con correa; ~**way** (*US*) *n* (*AUT*) carretera de circunvalación

bemused [bɪ'mjuːzd] *adj* aturdido

bench [bɛntʃ] *n* banco; (*BRIT: POL*): **the Government/Opposition** ~**es** (los asientos de) los miembros del Gobierno/ de la Oposición; **the B**~ (*LAW: judges*) magistratura

bend [bɛnd] (*pt, pp* **bent**) *vt* doblar ♦ *vi* inclinarse ♦ *n* (*BRIT: in road, river*) curva; (*in pipe*) codo; ~ **down** *vi* inclinarse, doblarse; ~ **over** *vi* inclinarse

beneath [bɪ'niːθ] *prep* bajo, debajo de; (*unworthy of*) indigno de ♦ *adv* abajo, (por) debajo

benefactor ['bɛnɪfæktə*] *n* bienhechor *m*

beneficial [bɛnɪ'fɪʃl] *adj* beneficioso

benefit ['bɛnɪfɪt] *n* beneficio; (*allowance of money*) subsidio ♦ *vt* beneficiar ♦ *vi*: **he'll** ~ **from it** le sacará provecho

benevolent [bɪ'nɛvələnt] *adj* (*person*) benévolo

benign [bɪ'naɪn] *adj* benigno; (*smile*) afable

bent [bɛnt] *pt, pp of* **bend** ♦ *n* inclinación *f* ♦ *adj*: **to be** ~ **on** estar empeñado en

bequest [bɪ'kwɛst] *n* legado

bereaved [bɪ'riːvd] *npl*: **the** ~ los íntimos de una persona afligidos por su muerte

beret ['bɛreɪ] *n* boina

Berlin [bəː'lɪn] *n* Berlín

berm [bɜːm] *n* (*US*) *n* (*AUT*) arcén *m*

Bermuda [bəː'mjuːdə] *n* las Bermudas

berry ['bɛrɪ] *n* baya

berserk [bə'səːk] *adj*: **to go** ~ perder los estribos

berth [bɜːθ] *n* (*bed*) litera; (*cabin*) camarote *m*; (*for ship*) amarradero ♦ *vi* atracar, amarrar

beseech [bɪ'siːtʃ] (*pt, pp* **besought**) *vt* suplicar

beset [bɪ'sɛt] (*pt, pp* **beset**) *vt* (*person*) acosar

beside [bɪ'saɪd] *prep* junto a, al lado de; **to be** ~ **o.s. with anger** estar fuera de sí; **that's** ~ **the point** eso no tiene nada que ver

besides [bɪ'saɪdz] *adv* además ♦ *prep* además de

besiege [bɪ'siːdʒ] *vt* sitiar; (*fig*) asediar

besought [bɪ'sɔːt] *pt, pp of* **beseech**

best [bɛst] *adj* (el/la) mejor ♦ *adv* (lo) mejor; **the** ~ **part of** (*quantity*) la mayor parte de; **at** ~ en el mejor de los casos; **to make the** ~ **of sth** sacar el mejor partido de algo; **to do one's** ~ hacer todo lo posible; **to the** ~ **of my knowledge** que yo sepa; **to the** ~ **of my ability** como mejor puedo; ~ **man** padrino de boda

bestow [bɪ'stəu] *vt* (*title*) otorgar

bestseller ['bɛst'sɛlə*] *n* éxito de librería, bestseller *m*

bet [bɛt] (*pt, pp* **bet** *or* **betted**) *n* apuesta ♦ *vt*: **to** ~ **money on** apostar dinero por; **to** ~ **sb sth** apostar algo a uno ♦ *vi* apostar

betray [bɪ'treɪ] *vt* traicionar; (*trust*) faltar a; ~**al** *n* traición *f*

better ['bɛtə*] *adj, adv* mejor ♦ *vt* superar ♦ *n*: **to get the** ~ **of sb** quedar por encima de alguien; **you had** ~ **do it** más vale que lo hagas; **he thought** ~ **of it** cambió de parecer; **to get** ~ (*MED*) mejorar(se); ~ **off** *adj* mejor; (*wealthier*) más acomodado

betting ['bɛtɪŋ] *n* juego, el apostar; ~ **shop** (*BRIT*) *n* agencia de apuestas

between [bɪ'twiːn] *prep* entre ♦ *adv* (*time*) mientras tanto; (*place*) en medio

beverage ['bɛvərɪdʒ] *n* bebida

beware [bɪ'wɛə*] *vi*: **to** ~ (**of**) tener cuidado (con); "~ **of the dog**" "perro peligroso"

bewildered [bɪ'wɪldəd] *adj* aturdido, perplejo

bewitching [bɪ'wɪtʃɪŋ] *adj* hechicero, encantador(a)

beyond [bɪ'jɔnd] *prep* más allá de; (*past: understanding*) fuera de; (*after: date*) después de, más allá de; (*above*) superior a ♦ *adv* (*in space*) más allá; (*in time*) posteriormente; ~ **doubt** fuera de toda duda; ~ **repair** irreparable

bias ['baɪəs] *n* (*prejudice*) prejuicio, pasión *f*; (*preference*) predisposición *f*; ~(**s**)**ed** *adj* parcial

bib [bɪb] *n* babero

Bible ['baɪbl] *n* Biblia

bicarbonate of soda [baɪ'kɑːbənɪt-] *n* bicarbonato sódico

bicker ['bɪkə*] *vi* pelearse

bicycle ['baɪsɪkl] *n* bicicleta

bid [bɪd] (*pt* **bade** *or* **bid**, *pp* **bidden** *or* **bid**) *n* oferta, postura; (*in tender*) licitación *f*; (*attempt*) tentativa, conato ♦ *vi* hacer una oferta ♦ *vt* (*offer*) ofrecer; **to** ~ **sb good day** dar a uno los buenos días; ~**der** *n*: **the highest** ~**der** el mejor postor; ~**ding** *n* (*at auction*) ofertas *fpl*

bide [baɪd] *vt*: **to** ~ **one's time** esperar el momento adecuado

bifocals [baɪ'fəuklz] *npl* gafas *fpl* (*SP*) or anteojos *mpl* (*AM*) bifocales

big [bɪg] *adj* grande; (*brother, sister*) mayor

bigheaded ['bɪg'hɛdɪd] *adj* engreído

bigot ['bɪgət] *n* fanático/a, intolerante *m/f*; ~**ed** *adj* fanático, intolerante; ~**ry** *n* fanatismo, intolerancia

big top *n* (*at circus*) carpa

bike [baɪk] *n* bici *f*

bikini [bɪ'kiːnɪ] *n* bikini *m*

bile [baɪl] *n* bilis *f*

bilingual [baɪ'lɪŋgwəl] *adj* bilingüe

bill [bɪl] *n* cuenta; (*invoice*) factura; (*POL*) proyecto de ley; (*US*: *banknote*) billete *m*;

(*of bird*) pico; (*of show*) programa *m*; **"post no ~s"** "prohibido fijar carteles"; **to fit** *or* **fill the ~** (*fig*) cumplir con los requisitos; **~board** (*US*) *n* cartelera

billet ['bɪlɪt] *n* alojamiento

billfold ['bɪlfəʊld] (*US*) *n* cartera

billiards ['bɪljədz] *n* billar *m*

billion ['bɪljən] *n* (*BRIT*) billón *m* (*millón de millones*); (*US*) mil millones *mpl*

bimbo ['bɪmbəʊ] (*inf*) *n* tía buena sin seso

bin [bɪn] *n* (*for rubbish*) cubo (*SP*) *or* bote *m* (*AM*) de la basura; (*container*) recipiente *m*

bind [baɪnd] (*pt, pp* **bound**) *vt* atar; (*book*) encuadernar; (*oblige*) obligar ♦ *n* (*inf: nuisance*) lata; **~ing** *adj* (*contract*) obligatorio

binge [bɪndʒ] (*inf*) *n*: **to go on a ~** ir de juerga

bingo ['bɪŋgəʊ] *n* bingo *m*

binoculars [bɪ'nɔkjuləz] *npl* prismáticos *mpl*

bio... [baɪə] *prefix*: **~chemistry** *n* bioquímica; **~graphy** [baɪ'ɔgrəfɪ] *n* biografía; **~logical** [baɪ'lɔdʒɪl] *adj* biológico; **~logy** [baɪ'ɔlədʒɪ] *n* biología

birch [bəːtʃ] *n* (*tree*) abedul *m*

bird [bəːd] *n* ave *f*, pájaro; (*BRIT: inf: girl*) chica; **~'s eye view** *n* (*aerial view*) vista de pájaro; (*overview*) visión *f* de conjunto; **~ watcher** *n* ornitólogo/a

Biro ['baɪrəʊ] ® *n* bolígrafo

birth [bəːθ] *n* nacimiento; **to give ~ to** parir, dar a luz; **~ certificate** *n* partida de nacimiento; **~ control** *n* (*policy*) control *m* de natalidad; (*methods*) métodos *mpl* anticonceptivos; **~day** *n* cumpleaños *m inv* ♦ *cpd* (*cake, card etc*) de cumpleaños; **~place** *n* lugar *m* de nacimiento; **~ rate** *n* (tasa de) natalidad *f*

biscuit ['bɪskɪt] (*BRIT*) *n* galleta, bizcocho (*AM*)

bisect [baɪ'sɛkt] *vt* bisecar

bishop ['bɪʃəp] *n* obispo; (*CHESS*) alfil *m*

bit [bɪt] *pt of* **bite** ♦ *n* trozo, pedazo, pedacito; (*COMPUT*) bit *m*, bitio; (*for horse*) freno, bocado; **a ~ of** un poco de;

a ~ mad un poco loco; **~ by ~** poco a poco

bitch [bɪtʃ] *n* perra; (*inf!: woman*) zorra (*!*)

bite [baɪt] (*pt* **bit**, *pp* **bitten**) *vt, vi* morder; (*insect etc*) picar ♦ *n* (*insect ~*) picadura; (*mouthful*) bocado; **to ~ one's nails** comerse las uñas; **let's have a ~ (to eat)** (*inf*) vamos a comer algo

bitter ['bɪtə*] *adj* amargo; (*wind*) cortante, penetrante; (*battle*) encarnizado ♦ *n* (*BRIT: beer*) cerveza típica británica a base de lúpulos; **~ness** *n* lo amargo, amargura; (*anger*) rencor *m*

bizarre [bɪ'zɑː*] *adj* raro, extraño

blab [blæb] (*inf*) *vi* soplar

black [blæk] *adj* negro; (*tea, coffee*) solo ♦ *n* color *m* negro; (*person*): **B~** negro/a ♦ *vt* (*BRIT: INDUSTRY*) boicotear; **to give sb a ~ eye** ponerle a uno el ojo morado; **~ and blue** (*bruised*) amoratado; **to be in the ~** (*bank account*) estar en números negros; **~berry** *n* zarzamora; **~bird** *n* mirlo; **~board** *n* pizarra; **~ coffee** *n* café *m* solo; **~currant** *n* grosella negra; **~en** *vt* (*fig*) desacreditar; **~ ice** *n* hielo invisible en la carretera; **~leg** (*BRIT*) *n* esquirol *m*, rompehuelgas *m inv*; **~list** *n* lista negra; **~mail** *n* chantaje *m* ♦ *vt* chantajear; **~ market** *n* mercado negro; **~out** *n* (*MIL*) oscurecimiento; (*power cut*) apagón *m*; (*TV, RADIO*) interrupción *f* de programas; (*fainting*) desvanecimiento; **B~ Sea** *n*: **the B~ Sea** el Mar Negro; **~ sheep** *n* (*fig*) oveja negra; **~smith** *n* herrero; **~ spot** *n* (*AUT*) lugar *m* peligroso; (*for unemployment etc*) punto negro

bladder ['blædə*] *n* vejiga

blade [bleɪd] *n* hoja; (*of propeller*) paleta; **a ~ of grass** una brizna de hierba

blame [bleɪm] *n* culpa ♦ *vt*: **to ~ sb for sth** echar a uno la culpa de algo; **to be to ~** tener la culpa de; **~less** *adj* inocente

bland [blænd] *adj* (*music, taste*) soso

blank [blæŋk] *adj* en blanco; (*look*) sin expresión ♦ *n* (*of memory*): **my mind is a ~** no puedo recordar nada; (*on form*) blanco, espacio en blanco; (*cartridge*) cartucho sin bala *or* de fogueo; ~ cheque *n* cheque *m* en blanco

blanket ['blæŋkɪt] *n* manta (*SP*), cobija (*AM*); (*of snow*) capa; (*of fog*) manto

blare [blɛə*] *vi* sonar estrepitosamente

blasé ['blɑːzeɪ] *adj* hastiado

blasphemy ['blæsfɪmɪ] *n* blasfemia

blast [blɑːst] *n* (*of wind*) ráfaga, soplo; (*of explosive*) explosión *f* ♦ *vt* (*blow up*) volar; ~-off *n* (*SPACE*) lanzamiento

blatant ['bleɪtənt] *adj* descarado

blaze [bleɪz] *n* (*fire*) fuego; (*fig: of colour*) despliegue *m*; (: *of glory*) esplendor *m* ♦ *vi* arder en llamas; (*fig*) brillar ♦ *vt*: to ~ a trail (*fig*) abrir un camino; in a ~ of publicity con gran publicidad

blazer ['bleɪzə*] *n* chaqueta de uniforme de colegial o de socio de club

bleach [bliːtʃ] *n* (*also: household* ~) lejía ♦ *vt* blanquear; ~ed *adj* (*hair*) teñido (de rubio); ~ers (*US*) *npl* (*SPORT*) gradas *fpl* al sol

bleak [bliːk] *adj* (*countryside*) desierto; (*prospect*) poco prometedor(a); (*weather*) crudo; (*smile*) triste

bleary-eyed ['blɪərɪˌaɪd] *adj*: to be ~ tener ojos de cansado

bleat [bliːt] *vi* balar

bleed [bliːd] (*pt, pp* **bled**) *vt, vi* sangrar; my nose is ~ing me está sangrando la nariz

bleeper ['bliːpə*] *n* busca *m*

blemish ['blemɪʃ] *n* marca, mancha; (*on reputation*) tacha

blend [blend] *n* mezcla ♦ *vt* mezclar; (*colours etc*) combinar, mezclar ♦ *vi* (*colours etc: also*: ~ in) combinarse, mezclarse

bless [bles] (*pt, pp* **blessed** *or* **blest**) *vt* bendecir; ~ you! (*after sneeze*) ¡Jesús!; ~ing *n* (*approval*) aprobación *f*; (*godsend*) don *m* del cielo, bendición *f*; (*advantage*) beneficio, ventaja

blew [bluː] *pt of* **blow**

blight [blaɪt] *vt* (*hopes etc*) frustrar, arruinar

blimey ['blaɪmɪ] (*BRIT: inf*) *excl* ¡caray!

blind [blaɪnd] *adj* ciego; (*fig*): ~ (to) ciego (a) ♦ *n* (*for window*) persiana ♦ *vt* cegar;

(*dazzle*) deslumbrar; (*deceive*): to ~ sb to ... cegar a uno a ...; the ~ *npl* los ciegos; ~ alley *n* callejón *m* sin salida; ~ corner (*BRIT*) *n* esquina escondida; ~fold *n* venda ♦ *adv* con los ojos vendados ♦ *vt* vendar los ojos a; ~ly *adv* a ciegas, ciegamente; ~ness *n* ceguera; ~ spot *n* (*AUT*) ángulo ciego

blink [blɪŋk] *vi* parpadear, pestañear; (*light*) oscilar; ~ers *npl* anteojeras *fpl*

bliss [blɪs] *n* felicidad *f*

blister ['blɪstə*] *n* ampolla ♦ *vi* (*paint*) ampollarse

blithely ['blaɪðlɪ] *adv* alegremente

blitz [blɪts] *n* (*MIL*) bombardeo aéreo

blizzard ['blɪzəd] *n* ventisca

bloated ['bləʊtɪd] *adj* hinchado; (*person: full*) ahíto

blob [blɒb] *n* (*drop*) gota; (*indistinct object*) bulto

bloc [blɒk] *n* (*POL*) bloque *m*

block [blɒk] *n* bloque *m*; (*in pipes*) obstáculo; (*of buildings*) manzana (*SP*), cuadra (*AM*) ♦ *vt* obstruir, cerrar; (*progress*) estorbar; ~ of flats (*BRIT*) bloque *m* de pisos; **mental** ~ bloqueo mental; ~ade [-'keɪd] *n* bloqueo ♦ *vt* bloquear; ~age *n* estorbo, obstrucción *f*; ~buster *n* (*book*) bestseller *m*; (*film*) éxito de público; ~ letters *npl* letras *fpl* de molde

bloke [bləʊk] (*BRIT: inf*) *n* tipo, tío

blond(e) [blɒnd] *adj, n* rubio/a *m/f*

blood [blʌd] *n* sangre *f*; ~ donor *n* donante *m/f* de sangre; ~ group *n* grupo sanguíneo; ~hound *n* sabueso; ~ poisoning *n* envenenamiento de la sangre; ~ pressure *n* presión *f* sanguínea; ~shed *n* derramamiento de sangre; ~shot *adj* inyectado en sangre; ~stream *n* corriente *f* sanguínea; ~ test *n* análisis *m inv* de sangre; ~thirsty *adj* sanguinario; ~ vessel *n* vaso sanguíneo; ~y *adj* sangriento; (*nose etc*) lleno de sangre; (*BRIT: inf!*): **this** ~... este condenado *o* puñetero ... (!) ♦ *adv*: ~y **strong/good** (*BRIT: inf!*) terriblemente fuerte/bueno; ~y-minded (*BRIT: inf*) *adj* puñetero (!)

bloom [bluːm] *n* flor *f* ♦ *vi* florecer

blossom ['blɔsəm] *n* flor *f* ♦ *vi* (*also fig*) florecer

blot [blɔt] *n* borrón *m*; (*fig*) mancha ♦ *vt* (*stain*) manchar; ~ **out** *vt* (*view*) tapar

blotchy ['blɔtʃɪ] *adj* (*complexion*) lleno de manchas

blotting paper ['blɔtɪŋ-] *n* papel *m* secante

blouse [blauz] *n* blusa

blow [bləu] (*pt* **blew**, *pp* **blown**) *n* golpe *m*; (*with sword*) espadazo ♦ *vi* soplar; (*dust, sand etc*) volar; (*fuse*) fundirse ♦ *vt* (*subj: wind*) llevarse; (*fuse*) quemar; (*instrument*) tocar; **to ~ one's nose** sonarse; ~ **away** *vi* llevarse, arrancar; ~ **down** *vt* derribar; ~ **off** *vt* arrebatar; ~ **out** *vi* apagarse; ~ **over** *vi* amainar; ~ **up** *vi* estallar ♦ *vt* volar; (*tyre*) inflar; (*PHOT*) ampliar; ~-**dry** *n* moldeado (con secador); ~**lamp** (*BRIT*) *n* soplete *m*, lámpara de soldar; ~-**out** *n* (*of tyre*) pinchazo; ~**torch** *n* = ~**lamp**

blue [bluː] *adj* azul; (*depressed*) deprimido; ~ **film/joke** película/chiste *m* verde; **out of the** ~ (*fig*) de repente; ~**bell** *n* campanilla, campánula azul; ~**bottle** *n* moscarda, mosca azul; ~**print** *n* (*fig*) anteproyecto

bluff [blʌf] *vi* tirarse un farol, farolear ♦ *n* farol *m*; **to call sb's** ~ coger a uno la palabra

blunder ['blʌndə*] *n* patinazo, metedura de pata ♦ *vi* cometer un error, meter la pata

blunt [blʌnt] *adj* (*pencil*) despuntado; (*knife*) desafilado, romo; (*person*) franco, directo

blur [bləː*] *n* (*shape*): **to become a** ~ hacerse borroso ♦ *vt* (*vision*) enturbiar; (*distinction*) borrar

blurb [bləːb] *n* comentario de sobrecubierta

blurt out [bləːt-] *vt* descolgarse con, dejar escapar

blush [blʌʃ] *vi* ruborizarse, ponerse colorado ♦ *n* rubor *m*

blustering ['blʌstərɪŋ] *adj* (*person*) fanfarrón/ona

blustery ['blʌstərɪ] *adj* (*weather*) tempestuoso, tormentoso

boar [bɔː*] *n* verraco, cerdo

board [bɔːd] *n* (*card~*) cartón *m*; (*wooden*) tabla, tablero; (*on wall*) tablón *m*; (*for chess etc*) tablero; (*committee*) junta, consejo; (*in firm*) mesa *or* junta directiva; (*NAUT, AVIAT*): **on** ~ a bordo ♦ *vt* (*ship*) embarcarse en; (*train*) subir a; **full** ~ (*BRIT*) pensión completa; **half** ~ (*BRIT*) media pensión; **to go by the** ~ (*fig*) ser abandonado *or* olvidado; ~ **up** *vt* (*door*) tapiar; ~ **and lodging** *n* casa y comida; ~**er** *n* (*SCOL*) interno/a; ~**ing card** (*BRIT*) *n* tarjeta de embarque; ~**ing house** *n* casa de huéspedes; ~**ing pass** (*US*) *n* = ~**ing card**; ~**ing school** *n* internado; ~ **room** *n* sala de juntas

boast [bəust] *vi*: **to ~ (about *or* of)** alardear (de)

boat [bəut] *n* barco, buque *m*; (*small*) barca, bote *m*; ~**er** *n* (*hat*) canotié *m*

bob [bɔb] *vi* (*also*: ~ **up and down**) menearse, balancearse; ~ **up** *vi* (re)aparecer de repente

bobby ['bɔbɪ] (*BRIT: inf*) *n* poli *m*

bobsleigh ['bɔbsleɪ] *n* bob *m*

bode [bəud] *vi*: **to ~ well/ill (for)** ser prometedor/poco prometedor (para)

bodily ['bɔdɪlɪ] *adj* corporal ♦ *adv* (*move: person*) en peso

body ['bɔdɪ] *n* cuerpo; (*corpse*) cadáver *m*; (*of car*) caja, carrocería; (*fig: group*) grupo; (: *organization*) organismo; ~-**building** *n* culturismo; ~**guard** *n* guardaespaldas *m inv*; ~**work** *n* carrocería

bog [bɔg] *n* pantano, ciénaga ♦ *vt*: **to get** ~**ged down** (*fig*) empantanarse, atascarse

boggle ['bɔgl] *vi*: **the mind** ~**s!** ¡no puedo creerlo!

bogus ['bəugəs] *adj* falso, fraudulento

boil [bɔɪl] *vt* (*water*) hervir; (*eggs*) pasar por agua, cocer ♦ *vi* hervir; (*fig: with anger*) estar furioso; (: *with heat*) asfixiarse ♦ *n* (*MED*) furúnculo, divieso; **to come to the** ~, **to come to a** ~ (*US*) comenzar a hervir; **to ~ down to** (*fig*) reducirse a; ~ **over** *vi* salirse, rebosar; (*anger etc*) llegar al colmo; ~ed egg *n* huevo cocido (*SP*) or pasado (*AM*); ~ed potatoes *npl* patatas *fpl* (*SP*) or papas *fpl* (*AM*) hervidas; ~er *n* caldera; ~er suit (*BRIT*) *n* mono; ~ing point *n* punto de ebullición

boisterous ['bɔɪstərəs] *adj* (*noisy*) bullicioso; (*excitable*) exuberante; (*crowd*) tumultuoso

bold [bəuld] *adj* valiente, audaz; (*pej*) descarado; (*colour*) llamativo

Bolivia [bə'lɪvɪə] *n* Bolivia; ~n *adj, n* boliviano/a *m/f*

bollard ['bɔləd] (*BRIT*) *n* (*AUT*) poste *m*

bolster ['bəulstə*] *vt*: ~ **up** reforzar

bolt [bəult] *n* (*lock*) cerrojo; (*with nut*) perno, tornillo ♦ *adv*: ~ **upright** rígido, erguido ♦ *vt* (*door*) echar el cerrojo a; (*also*: ~ *together*) sujetar con tornillos; (*food*) engullir ♦ *vi* fugarse; (*horse*) desbocarse

bomb [bɔm] *n* bomba ♦ *vt* bombardear; ~ard [-'bɑːd] *vt* bombardear; (*fig*): **to ~ard with questions** acribillar a preguntas; ~ardment [-'bɑːdmənt] *n* bombardeo

bombastic [bɔm'bæstɪk] *adj* rimbombante; (*person*) farolero

bomb: ~ **disposal** *n* desmontaje *m* de explosivos; ~er *n* (*AVIAT*) bombardero; ~shell *n* (*fig*) bomba

bona fide ['bəunə'faɪdɪ] *adj* genuino, auténtico

bond [bɔnd] *n* (*promise*) fianza; (*FINANCE*) bono; (*link*) vínculo, lazo; (*COMM*): **in ~** en depósito bajo fianza

bondage ['bɔndɪdʒ] *n* esclavitud *f*

bone [bəun] *n* hueso; (*of fish*) espina ♦ *vt* deshuesar; quitar las espinas a; ~ **idle** *adj* gandul; ~ **marrow** *n* médula

bonfire ['bɔnfaɪə*] *n* hoguera, fogata

bonnet ['bɔnɪt] *n* gorra; (*BRIT: of car*) capó *m*

bonus ['bəunəs] *n* (*payment*) paga extraordinaria, plus *m*; (*fig*) bendición *f*

bony ['bəunɪ] *adj* (*arm, face*) huesudo; (*MED: tissue*) óseo; (*meat*) lleno de huesos; (*fish*) lleno de espinas

boo [buː] *excl* ¡uh! ♦ *vt* abuchear, rechiflar

booby trap ['buːbɪ-] *n* trampa explosiva

book [buk] *n* libro; (*of tickets*) taco; (*of stamps etc*) librito ♦ *vt* (*ticket*) sacar; (*seat, room*) reservar; ~s *npl* (*COMM*) cuentas *fpl*, contabilidad *f*; ~case *n* librería, estante *m* para libros; ~ing office *n* (*BRIT: RAIL*) despacho de billetes (*SP*) or boletos (*AM*); (*THEATRE*) taquilla (*SP*), boletería (*AM*); ~-keeping *n* contabilidad *f*; ~let *n* folleto; ~maker *n* corredor *m* de apuestas; ~seller *n* librero; ~shop, ~ store *n* librería

boom [buːm] *n* (*noise*) trueno, estampido; (*in prices etc*) alza rápida; (*ECON, in population*) boom *m* ♦ *vi* (*cannon*) hacer gran estruendo, retumbar; (*ECON*) estar en alza

boon [buːn] *n* favor *m*, beneficio

boost [buːst] *n* estímulo, empuje *m* ♦ *vt* estimular, empujar; ~er *n* (*MED*) reinyección *f*

boot [buːt] *n* bota; (*BRIT: of car*) maleta, maletero ♦ *vt* (*COMPUT*) arrancar; **to ~** (*in addition*) además, por añadidura

booth [buːð] *n* (*at fair*) barraca; (*telephone ~, voting ~*) cabina

booty ['buːtɪ] *n* botín *m*

booze [buːz] (*inf*) *n* bebida

border ['bɔːdə*] *n* borde *m*, margen *m*; (*of a country*) frontera; (*for flowers*) arriate *m* ♦ *vt* (*road*) bordear; (*another country: also*: ~ **on**) lindar con; **B~s** *n*: **the B~s** región fronteriza entre Escocia y Inglaterra; ~ **on** *vt fus* (*insanity etc*) rayar en; ~line *n*: **on the ~line** en el límite; ~line case *n* caso dudoso

bore [bɔː*] *pt of* **bear** ♦ *vt* (*hole*) hacer un agujero en; (*well*) perforar; (*person*) aburrir ♦ *n* (*person*) pelmazo, pesado; (*of gun*) calibre *m*; **to be ~d** estar aburrido; ~dom *n* aburrimiento

boring ['bɔːrɪŋ] *adj* aburrido

born [bɔːn] *adj*: **to be ~** nacer; **I was ~ in 1960** nací en 1960

borne [bɔːn] *pp of* **bear**

borough ['bʌrə] *n* municipio

borrow ['bɔrəu] *vt*: **to ~ sth (from sb)**

tomar algo prestado (a alguien)

bosom ['buzəm] *n* pecho; ~ **friend** amigo íntimo

boss [bɔs] *n* jefe *m* ♦ *vt* (*also*: ~ *about or around*) mangonear; ~**y** *adj* mandón/ona

bosun ['bəusn] *n* contramaestre *m*

botany ['bɔtəni] *n* botánica

botch [bɔtʃ] *vt* (*also*: ~ *up*) arruinar, estropear

both [bəuθ] *adj, pron* ambos/as, los/las dos; ~ **of us went, we** ~ **went** fuimos los dos, ambos fuimos ♦ *adv*: ~ **A and B** tanto A como B

bother ['bɔðə*] *vt* (*worry*) preocupar; (*disturb*) molestar, fastidiar ♦ *vi* (*also*: ~ *o.s.*) molestarse ♦ *n* (*trouble*) dificultad *f*; (*nuisance*) molestia, lata; **to** ~ **doing** tomarse la molestia de hacer

bottle ['bɔtl] *n* botella; (*small*) frasco; (*baby's*) biberón *m* ♦ *vt* embotellar; ~ **up** *vt* suprimir; ~ **bank** *n* contenedor *m* de vidrio; ~**neck** *n* (*AUT*) embotellamiento; (*in supply*) obstáculo; ~-**opener** *n* abrebotellas *m inv*

bottom ['bɔtəm] *n* (*of box, sea*) fondo; (*buttocks*) trasero, culo; (*of page*) pie *m*; (*of list*) final *m*; (*of class*) último/a ♦ *adj* (*lowest*) más bajo; (*last*) último; ~**less** *adj* sin fondo, inacabable

bough [bau] *n* rama

bought [bɔːt] *pt, pp of* **buy**

boulder ['bəuldə*] *n* canto rodado

bounce [bauns] *vi* (*ball*) (re)botar; (*cheque*) ser rechazado ♦ *vt* hacer (re)botar ♦ *n* (*rebound*) (re)bote *m*; ~**r** (*inf*) *n* gorila *m* (*que echa a los alborotadores de un bar, club etc*)

bound [baund] *pt, pp of* **bind** ♦ *n* (*leap*) salto; (*gen pl: limit*) límite *m* ♦ *vi* (*leap*) saltar ♦ *vt* (*border*) rodear ♦ *adj*: ~ **by** rodeado de; **to be** ~ **to do sth** (*obliged*) tener el deber de hacer algo; **he's** ~ **to come** es seguro que vendrá; **out of** ~**s** prohibido el paso; ~ **for** con destino a

boundary ['baundri] *n* límite *m*

boundless ['baundlis] *adj* ilimitado

bouquet ['bukei] *n* (*of flowers*) ramo

bourgeois ['buəʒwɑ:] *adj* burgués/esa *m/f*

bout [baut] *n* (*of malaria etc*) ataque *m*; (*of activity*) período; (*BOXING etc*) combate *m*, encuentro

bow[1] [bəu] *n* (*knot*) lazo; (*weapon, MUS*) arco

bow[2] [bau] *n* (*of the head*) reverencia; (*NAUT: also*: ~*s*) proa ♦ *vi* inclinarse, hacer una reverencia; (*yield*): **to** ~ **to** *or* **before** ceder ante, someterse a

bowels [bauəlz] *npl* intestinos *mpl*, vientre *m*; (*fig*) entrañas *fpl*

bowl [bəul] *n* tazón *m*, cuenco; (*ball*) bola ♦ *vi* (*CRICKET*) arrojar la pelota

bow-legged ['bəu'legid] *adj* estevado

bowler ['bəulə*] *n* (*CRICKET*) lanzador *m* (*de la pelota*); (*BRIT: also*: ~ *hat*) hongo, bombín *m*

bowling ['bəuliŋ] *n* (*game*) bochas *fpl*, bolos *mpl*; ~ **alley** *n* bolera; ~ **green** *n* pista para bochas

bowls [bəulz] *n* juego de las bochas, bolos *mpl*

bow tie ['bəu-] *n* corbata de lazo, pajarita

box [bɔks] *n* (*also: cardboard* ~) caja, cajón *m*; (*THEATRE*) palco ♦ *vt* encajonar ♦ *vi* (*SPORT*) boxear; ~**er** *n* (*person*) boxeador *m*; ~**ing** *n* (*SPORT*) boxeo; **B**~**ing Day** (*BRIT*) *n* día en que se dan los aguinaldos, 26 de diciembre; ~**ing gloves** *npl* guantes *mpl* de boxeo; ~**ing ring** *n* ring *m*, cuadrilátero; ~ **office** *n* taquilla (*SP*), boletería (*AM*); ~**room** *n* trastero

boy [bɔi] *n* (*young*) niño; (*older*) muchacho, chico; (*son*) hijo

boycott ['bɔikɔt] *n* boicot *m* ♦ *vt* boicotear

boyfriend ['bɔifrend] *n* novio

boyish ['bɔiiʃ] *adj* juvenil; (*girl*) con aspecto de muchacho

B.R. *n abbr* (= *British Rail*) ≈ RENFE *f* (*SP*)

bra [brɑ:] *n* sostén *m*, sujetador *m*

brace [breis] *n* (*BRIT: also*: ~*s: on teeth*) corrector *m*, aparato; (*tool*) berbiquí *m* ♦ *vt* (*knees, shoulders*) tensionar; ~**s** *npl* (*BRIT*) tirantes *mpl*; **to** ~ **o.s.** (*fig*) prepararse

bracelet ['breislit] *n* pulsera, brazalete *m*

bracing ['breɪsɪŋ] *adj* vigorizante, tónico
bracket ['brækɪt] *n* (TECH) soporte *m*,
puntal *m*; (*group*) clase *f*, categoría;
(*also*: brace ~) soporte *m*, abrazadera;
(*also*: round ~) paréntesis *m inv*; (*also*:
square ~) corchete *m* ♦ *vt* (*word etc*)
poner entre paréntesis
brag [bræg] *vi* jactarse
braid [breɪd] *n* (*trimming*) galón *m*; (*of
hair*) trenza
brain [breɪn] *n* cerebro; ~s *npl* sesos *mpl*;
she's got ~s es muy lista; ~child *n*
invento; ~wash *vt* lavar el cerebro;
~wave *n* idea luminosa; ~y *adj* muy
inteligente
braise [breɪz] *vt* cocer a fuego lento
brake [breɪk] *n* (*on vehicle*) freno ♦ *vi*
frenar; ~ fluid *n* líquido de frenos; ~
light *n* luz *f* de frenado
bran [bræn] *n* salvado
branch [brɑːntʃ] *n* rama; (COMM) sucursal
f; ~ out *vi* (*fig*) extenderse
brand [brænd] *n* marca; (*fig: type*) tipo
♦ *vt* (*cattle*) marcar con hierro candente
brandish ['brændɪʃ] *vt* blandir
brand-new ['brænd'njuː] *adj* flamante,
completamente nuevo
brandy ['brændɪ] *n* coñac *m*
brash [bræʃ] *adj* (*forward*) descarado
brass [brɑːs] *n* latón *m*; the ~ (MUS) los
cobres; ~ band *n* banda de metal
brassière ['bræsɪə*] *n* sostén *m*,
sujetador *m*
brat [bræt] (*pej*) *n* mocoso/a
bravado [brə'vɑːdəu] *n* fanfarronería
brave [breɪv] *adj* valiente, valeroso ♦ *vt*
(*face up to*) desafiar; ~ry *n* valor *m*,
valentía
brawl [brɔːl] *n* pelea, reyerta
brawny ['brɔːnɪ] *adj* fornido, musculoso
bray [breɪ] *vi* rebuznar
brazen ['breɪzn] *adj* descarado, cínico
♦ *vt*: to ~ it out echarle cara
brazier ['breɪzɪə*] *n* brasero
Brazil [brə'zɪl] *n* (el) Brasil; ~ian *adj, n*
brasileño/a *m/f*
breach [briːtʃ] *vt* abrir brecha en ♦ *n*
(*gap*) brecha; (*breaking*): ~ of contract
infracción *f* de contrato; ~ of the peace

perturbación *f* del órden público
bread [bred] *n* pan *m*; ~ and butter *n*
pan con mantequilla; (*fig*) pan (de cada
día); ~bin (US = **box**) *n* panera; ~crumbs
npl migajas *fpl*; (CULIN) pan rallado; ~line
n: on the ~line en la miseria
breadth [bretθ] *n* anchura; (*fig*) amplitud
f
breadwinner ['bredwɪnə*] *n* sustento *m*
de la familia
break [breɪk] (*pt* broke, *pp* broken) *vt*
romper; (*promise*) faltar a; (*law*) violar,
infringir; (*record*) batir ♦ *vi* romperse,
quebrarse; (*storm*) estallar; (*weather*)
cambiar; (*dawn*) despuntar; (*news etc*)
darse a conocer ♦ *n* (*gap*) abertura;
(*fracture*) fractura; (*time*) intervalo; (: *at
school*) (período de) recreo; (*chance*)
oportunidad *f*; to ~ the news to sb
comunicar la noticia a uno; ~ down *vt*
(*figures, data*) analizar, descomponer
♦ *vi* (*machine*) estropearse; (AUT)
averiarse; (*person*) romper a llorar;
(*talks*) fracasar; ~ even *vi* cubrir los
gastos; ~ free or loose *vi* escaparse; ~ in
vt (*horse etc*) domar ♦ *vi* (*burglar*) forzar
una entrada; (*interrupt*) interrumpir; ~
into *vt fus* (*house*) forzar; ~ off *vi*
(*speaker*) pararse, detenerse; (*branch*)
partir; ~ open *vt* (*door etc*) abrir por la
fuerza, forzar; ~ out *vi* estallar;
(*prisoner*) escaparse; to ~ out in spots
salirle a uno granos; ~ up *vi* (*ship*)
hacerse pedazos; (*crowd, meeting*)
disolverse; (*marriage*) deshacerse; (SCOL)
terminar (el curso) ♦ *vt* (*rocks etc*)
partir; (*journey*) partir; (*fight etc*)
acabar con; ~age *n* rotura; ~down
n (AUT) avería; (*in commu-*
nications) interrupción *f*; (MED: *also*:
nervous ~down) colapso, crisis *f*
nerviosa; (*of marriage, talks*) fracaso; (*of
statistics*) análisis *m inv*; ~down van
(BRIT) *n* (camión *m*) grúa; ~er *n* (ola)
rompiente *f*
breakfast ['brekfəst] *n* desayuno
break: ~-in *n* robo con allanamiento de
morada; ~ing and entering *n* (LAW)
violación *f* de domicilio, allanamiento de

morada; ~**through** n (*also fig*) avance m; ~**water** m rompeolas m inv

breast [brɛst] n (*of woman*) pecho, seno; (*chest*) pecho; (*of bird*) pechuga; ~-**feed** (*irreg: like* **feed**) vt, vi amamantar, criar a los pechos; ~-**stroke** n braza (de pecho)

breath [brɛθ] n aliento, respiración f; **to take a deep ~** respirar hondo; **out of ~** sin aliento, sofocado

Breathalyser ['brɛθəlaɪzə*] ® (*BRIT*) n alcoholímetro m

breathe [briːð] vt, vi respirar; ~ **in** vt, vi aspirar; ~ **out** vt, vi espirar; ~**r** n respiro; **breathing** n respiración f

breath-: ~**less** adj sin aliento, jadeante; ~**taking** adj imponente, pasmoso

breed [briːd] (*pt, pp* **bred**) vt criar ♦ vi reproducirse, procrear ♦ n (*ZOOL*) raza, casta; (*type*) tipo; ~**ing** n (*of person*) educación f

breeze [briːz] n brisa

breezy ['briːzɪ] adj de mucho viento, ventoso; (*person*) despreocupado

brevity ['brɛvɪtɪ] n brevedad f

brew [bruː] vt (*tea*) hacer; (*beer*) elaborar ♦ vi (*fig: trouble*) prepararse; (*storm*) amenazar; ~**ery** n fábrica de cerveza, cervecería

bribe [braɪb] n soborno ♦ vt sobornar, cohechar; ~**ry** n soborno, cohecho

bric-a-brac ['brɪkəbræk] n inv baratijas fpl

brick [brɪk] n ladrillo; ~**layer** n albañil m

bridal ['braɪdl] adj nupcial

bride [braɪd] n novia; ~**groom** n novio; ~**smaid** n dama de honor

bridge [brɪdʒ] n puente m; (*NAUT*) puente m de mando; (*of nose*) caballete m; (*CARDS*) bridge m ♦ vt (*fig*): **to ~ a gap** llenar un vacío

bridle ['braɪdl] n brida, freno; ~ **path** n camino de herradura

brief [briːf] adj breve, corto ♦ n (*LAW*) escrito; (*task*) cometido, encargo ♦ vt informar; ~**s** npl (*for men*) calzoncillos mpl; (*for women*) bragas fpl; ~**case** n cartera (*SP*), portafolio (*AM*); ~**ing** n (*PRESS*) informe m; ~**ly** adv (*glance*) fugazmente; (*say*) en pocas palabras

brigadier [brɪgə'dɪə*] n general m de brigada

bright [braɪt] adj brillante; (*room*) luminoso; (*day*) de sol; (*person: clever*) listo, inteligente; (: *lively*) alegre; (*colour*) vivo; (*future*) prometedor(a); ~**en** (*also*: ~**en up**) vt (*room*) hacer más alegre; (*event*) alegrar ♦ vi (*weather*) despejarse; (*person*) animarse, alegrarse; (*prospects*) mejorar

brilliance ['brɪljəns] n brillo, brillantez f; (*of talent etc*) brillantez

brilliant ['brɪljənt] adj brillante; (*inf*) fenomenal

brim [brɪm] n borde m; (*of hat*) ala

brine [braɪn] n (*CULIN*) salmuera

bring [brɪŋ] (*pt, pp* **brought**) vt (*thing, person: with you*) traer; (: *to sb*) llevar, conducir; (*trouble, satisfaction*) causar; ~ **about** vt ocasionar, producir; ~ **back** vt volver a traer; (*return*) devolver; ~ **down** vt (*government, plane*) derribar; (*price*) rebajar; ~ **forward** vt adelantar; ~ **off** vt (*task, plan*) lograr, conseguir; ~ **out** vt sacar; (*book etc*) publicar; (*meaning*) subrayar; ~ **round** vt (*unconscious person*) hacer volver en sí; ~ **up** vt subir; (*person*) educar, criar; (*question*) sacar a colación; (*food: vomit*) devolver, vomitar

brink [brɪŋk] n borde m

brisk [brɪsk] adj (*abrupt: tone*) brusco; (*person*) enérgico, vigoroso; (*pace*) rápido; (*trade*) activo

bristle ['brɪsl] n cerda ♦ vi: **to ~ in anger** temblar de rabia

Britain ['brɪtən] n (*also: Great ~*) Gran Bretaña

British ['brɪtɪʃ] adj británico ♦ npl: **the ~** los británicos; ~ **Isles** npl: **the ~ Isles** las Islas Británicas; ~ **Rail** n ≈ RENFE f (*SP*)

Briton ['brɪtən] n británico/a

brittle ['brɪtl] adj quebradizo, frágil

broach [brəʊtʃ] vt (*subject*) abordar

broad [brɔːd] adj ancho; (*range*) amplio; (*smile*) abierto; (*general: outlines etc*) general; (*accent*) cerrado; **in ~ daylight** en pleno día; ~**cast** (*irreg: like* **cast**) n

emisión *f* ♦ *vt* (*RADIO*) emitir; (*TV*)
transmitir ♦ *vi* emitir; transmitir; ~**en** *vt*
ampliar ♦ *vi* ensancharse; **to ~en one's
mind** hacer más tolerante a uno; ~**ly**
adv en general; ~-**minded** *adj* tolerante,
liberal

broccoli ['brɔkəlɪ] *n* brécol *m*

brochure ['brəʊʃjʊə*] *n* folleto

broil [brɔɪl] *vt* (*CULIN*) asar a la parrilla

broke [brəʊk] *pt of* **break** ♦ *adj* (*inf*)
pelado, sin blanca

broken ['brəʊkən] *pp of* **break** ♦ *adj* roto;
(*machine*: *also*: ~ *down*) averiado; ~ **leg**
pierna rota; **in ~ English** en un inglés
imperfecto; ~-**hearted** *adj* con el corazón
partido

broker ['brəʊkə*] *n* agente *m/f*, bolsista
m/f; (*insurance* ~) agente de seguros

brolly ['brɔlɪ] (*BRIT*: *inf*) *n* paraguas *m inv*

bronchitis [brɔŋ'kaɪtɪs] *n* bronquitis *f*

bronze [brɔnz] *n* bronce *m*

brooch [brəʊtʃ] *n* prendedor *m*, broche *m*

brood [bruːd] *n* camada, cría ♦ *vi*
(*person*) dejarse obsesionar

broom [brum] *n* escoba; (*BOT*) retama;
~**stick** *n* palo de escoba

Bros. *abbr* (= *Brothers*) Hnos

broth [brɔθ] *n* caldo

brothel ['brɔθl] *n* burdel *m*

brother ['brʌðə*] *n* hermano; ~-**in-law** *n*
cuñado

brought [brɔːt] *pt, pp of* **bring**

brow [braʊ] *n* (*forehead*) frente *m*; (*eye~*)
ceja; (*of hill*) cumbre *f*

brown [braʊn] *adj* (*colour*) marrón; (*hair*)
castaño; (*tanned*) moreno, bronceado ♦ *n*
(*colour*) color *m* marrón *or* pardo ♦ *vt*
(*CULIN*) dorar; ~ **bread** *n* pan integral

brownie ['braʊnɪ] *n* niña exploradora;
(*US*: *cake*) pastel de chocolate con nueces

brown paper *n* papel *m* de estraza

brown sugar *n* azúcar *m* terciado

browse [braʊz] *vi* (*through book*) hojear;
(*in shop*) mirar

bruise [bruːz] *n* cardenal *m* (*SP*), moretón
m (*AM*) ♦ *vt* magullar

brunch [brʌnʃ] *n* desayuno-almuerzo

brunette [bruː'net] *n* morena

brunt [brʌnt] *n*: **to bear the ~ of** llevar

el peso de

brush [brʌʃ] *n* cepillo; (*for painting,
shaving etc*) brocha; (*artist's*) pincel *m*;
(*with people etc*) roce *m* ♦ *vt* (*sweep*)
barrer; (*groom*) cepillar; (*also*: ~ *against*)
rozar al pasar; ~ **aside** *vt* rechazar, no
hacer caso a; ~ **up** *vt* (*knowledge*)
repasar, refrescar; ~**wood** *n* (*sticks*) leña

brusque [bruːsk] *adj* brusco, áspero

Brussels ['brʌslz] *n* Bruselas; ~ **sprout** *n*
col *f* de Bruselas

brute [bruːt] *n* bruto; (*person*) bestia
♦ *adj*: **by ~ force** a fuerza bruta

B.Sc. *abbr* (= *Bachelor of Science*)
licenciado en Ciencias

BSE *n abbr* (= *bovine spongiform
encephalopathy*) encefalopatía
espongiforme bovina

bubble ['bʌbl] *n* burbuja ♦ *vi* burbujear,
borbotar; ~ **bath** *n* espuma para el baño;
~ **gum** *n* chicle *m* de globo

buck [bʌk] *n* (*rabbit*) conejo macho;
(*deer*) gamo; (*US*: *inf*) dólar *m* ♦ *vi*
corcovear; **to pass the ~ (to sb)** echar (a
uno) el muerto; ~ **up** *vi* (*cheer up*)
animarse, cobrar ánimo

bucket ['bʌkɪt] *n* cubo, balde *m*

buckle ['bʌkl] *n* hebilla ♦ *vt* abrochar
con hebilla ♦ *vi* combarse

bud [bʌd] *n* (*of plant*) brote *m*, yema; (*of
flower*) capullo ♦ *vi* brotar, echar brotes

Buddhism ['bʊdɪzm] *n* Budismo

budding ['bʌdɪŋ] *adj* en ciernes, en
embrión

buddy ['bʌdɪ] (*US*) *n* compañero,
compinche *m*

budge [bʌdʒ] *vt* mover; (*fig*) hacer ceder
♦ *vi* moverse, ceder

budgerigar ['bʌdʒərɪgaː*] *n* periquito

budget ['bʌdʒɪt] *n* presupuesto ♦ *vi*: **to ~
for sth** presupuestar algo

budgie ['bʌdʒɪ] *n* = **budgerigar**

buff [bʌf] *adj* (*colour*) color de ante ♦ *n*
(*inf*: *enthusiast*) entusiasta *m/f*

buffalo ['bʌfələʊ] (*pl* ~ *or* ~**es**) *n* (*BRIT*)
búfalo; (*US*: *bison*) bisonte *m*

buffer ['bʌfə*] *n* (*COMPUT*) memoria
intermedia; (*RAIL*) tope *m*

buffet[1] ['bʊfeɪ] *n* (*BRIT*: *in station*) bar *m*,

cafetería; (*food*) buffet *m*; ~ **car** (*BRIT*) *n* (*RAIL*) coche-comedor *m*

buffet² ['bʌfɪt] *vt* golpear

bug [bʌg] *n* (*esp US*: *insect*) bicho, sabandija; (*COMPUT*) error *m*; (*germ*) microbio, bacilo; (*spy device*) micrófono oculto ♦ *vt* (*inf*: *annoy*) fastidiar; (*room*) poner micrófono oculto en

buggy ['bʌgɪ] *n* cochecito de niño

bugle ['bjuːgl] *n* corneta, clarín *m*

build [bɪld] (*pt*, *pp* **built**) *n* (*of person*) tipo ♦ *vt* construir, edificar; ~ **up** *vt* (*morale*, *forces*, *production*) acrecentar; (*stocks*) acumular; **~er** *n* (*contractor*) contratista *m/f*; **~ing** *n* construcción *f*; (*structure*) edificio; **~ing society** (*BRIT*) *n* sociedad *f* inmobiliaria, cooperativa de construcciones

built [bɪlt] *pt*, *pp of* **build** ♦ *adj*: **~-in** (*wardrobe etc*) empotrado; **~-up area** *n* zona urbanizada

bulb [bʌlb] *n* (*BOT*) bulbo; (*ELEC*) bombilla (*SP*), foco (*AM*)

Bulgaria [bʌl'gɛərɪə] *n* Bulgaria; **~n** *adj*, *n* búlgaro/a *m/f*

bulge [bʌldʒ] *n* bulto, protuberancia ♦ *vi* bombearse, pandearse; (*pocket etc*): **to ~ (with)** rebosar (de)

bulk [bʌlk] *n* masa, mole *f*; **in ~** (*COMM*) a granel; **the ~ of** la mayor parte de; **~y** *adj* voluminoso, abultado

bull [bul] *n* toro; (*male elephant*, *whale*) macho; **~dog** *n* dogo

bulldozer ['buldəuzə*] *n* bulldozer *m*

bullet ['bulɪt] *n* bala

bulletin ['bulɪtɪn] *n* anuncio, parte *m*; (*journal*) boletín *m*

bulletproof ['bulɪtpruːf] *adj* a prueba de balas

bullfight ['bulfaɪt] *n* corrida de toros; **~er** *n* torero; **~ing** *n* los toros, el toreo

bullion ['buljən] *n* oro (*or* plata) en barras

bullock ['bulək] *n* novillo

bullring ['bulrɪŋ] *n* plaza de toros

bull's-eye *n* centro del blanco

bully ['bulɪ] *n* valentón *m*, matón *m* ♦ *vt* intimidar, tiranizar

bum [bʌm] *n* (*inf*: *backside*) culo; (*esp US*:

tramp) vagabundo

bumblebee ['bʌmblbiː] *n* abejorro

bump [bʌmp] *n* (*blow*) tope *m*, choque *m*; (*jolt*) sacudida; (*on road etc*) bache *m*; (*on head etc*) chichón *m* ♦ *vt* (*strike*) chocar contra; **~ into** *vt fus* chocar contra, tropezar con; (*person*) topar con; **~er** *n* (*AUT*) parachoques *m inv* ♦ *adj*: **~er crop/harvest** cosecha abundante; **~er cars** *npl* coches *mpl* de choque

bumptious ['bʌmpʃəs] *adj* engreído, presuntuoso

bumpy ['bʌmpɪ] *adj* (*road*) lleno de baches

bun [bʌn] *n* (*BRIT*: *cake*) pastel *m*; (*US*: *bread*) bollo; (*of hair*) moño

bunch [bʌntʃ] *n* (*of flowers*) ramo; (*of keys*) manojo; (*of bananas*) piña; (*of people*) grupo; (*pej*) pandilla; **~es** *npl* (*in hair*) coletas *fpl*

bundle ['bʌndl] *n* bulto, fardo; (*of sticks*) haz *m*; (*of papers*) legajo ♦ *vt* (*also*: ~ **up**) atar, envolver; **to ~ sth/sb into** meter algo/a alguien precipitadamente en

bungalow ['bʌŋgələu] *n* bungalow *m*, chalé *m*

bungle ['bʌŋgl] *vt* hacer mal

bunion ['bʌnjən] *n* juanete *m*

bunk [bʌŋk] *n* litera; **~ beds** *npl* literas *fpl*

bunker ['bʌŋkə*] *n* (*coal store*) carbonera; (*MIL*) refugio; (*GOLF*) bunker *m*

bunny ['bʌnɪ] *n* (*also*: ~ *rabbit*) conejito

bunting ['bʌntɪŋ] *n* banderitas *fpl*

buoy [bɔɪ] *n* boya; ~ **up** *vt* (*fig*) animar; **~ant** *adj* (*ship*) capaz de flotar; (*economy*) boyante; (*person*) optimista

burden ['bəːdn] *n* carga ♦ *vt* cargar

bureau [bjuə'rəu] (*pl* **bureaux**) *n* (*BRIT*: *writing desk*) escritorio, buró *m*; (*US*: *chest of drawers*) cómoda; (*office*) oficina, agencia

bureaucracy [bjuə'rɔkrəsɪ] *n* burocracia

bureaux [bjuə'rəuz] *npl of* **bureau**

burglar ['bəːglə*] *n* ladrón/ona *m/f*; ~ **alarm** *n* alarma *f* antirrobo; **~y** *n* robo con allanamiento, robo de una casa

burial ['berɪəl] *n* entierro

burly ['bəːlɪ] *adj* fornido, membrudo

Burma ['bɜːmə] *n* Birmania
burn [bɜːn] (*pt, pp* **burned** *or* **burnt**) *vt*
quemar; (*house*) incendiar ♦ *vi*
quemarse, arder; incendiarse; (*sting*)
escocer ♦ *n* quemadura; ~ **down** *vt*
incendiar; **~er** *n* (*on cooker etc*)
quemador *m*; **~ing** *adj* (*building etc*) en
llamas; (*hot: sand etc*) abrasador(a);
(*ambition*) ardiente; **~t** [bɜːnt] *pt, pp* of
burn
burrow ['bʌrəu] *n* madriguera ♦ *vi* hacer
una madriguera; (*rummage*) hurgar
bursary ['bɜːsərɪ] (*BRIT*) *n* beca
burst [bɜːst] (*pt, pp* **burst**) *vt* reventar;
(*subj: river: banks etc*) romper ♦ *vi*
reventarse; (*tyre*) pincharse ♦ *n* (*of
gunfire*) ráfaga; (*also: ~ pipe*) reventón
m; **a ~ of energy/speed/enthusiasm**
una explosión de energía/un ímpetu de
velocidad/un arranque de entusiasmo;
to ~ into flames estallar en llamas; **to ~
into tears** deshacerse en lágrimas; **to ~
out laughing** soltar la carcajada; **to ~
open** abrirse de golpe; **to be ~ing with**
(*subj: container*) estar lleno a rebosar de;
(*person*) reventar por *or* de; **~ into** *vt fus*
(*room etc*) irrumpir en
bury ['bɛrɪ] *vt* enterrar; (*body*) enterrar,
sepultar
bus [bʌs] *n* autobús *m*
bush [buʃ] *n* arbusto; (*scrub land*) monte
m; **to beat about the ~** andar(se) con
rodeos; **~y** *adj* (*thick*) espeso, poblado
busily ['bɪzɪlɪ] *adv* afanosamente
business ['bɪznɪs] *n* (*matter*) asunto;
(*trading*) comercio, negocios *mpl*; (*firm*)
empresa, casa; (*occupation*) oficio; **to be
away on ~** estar en viaje de negocios;
it's my ~ to ... me toca *or* corresponde
...; **it's none of my ~** yo no tengo nada
que ver; **he means ~** habla en serio;
~like *adj* eficiente; **~man** *n* hombre *m* de
negocios; **~ trip** *n* viaje *m* de negocios;
~woman *n* mujer *f* de negocios
busker ['bʌskə*] (*BRIT*) *n* músico/a
ambulante
bus-stop ['bʌsstɔp] *n* parada de autobús
bust [bʌst] *n* (*ANAT*) pecho; (*sculpture*)
busto ♦ *adj* (*inf: broken*) roto,

estropeado; **to go ~** quebrar
bustle ['bʌsl] *n* bullicio, movimiento ♦ *vi*
menearse, apresurarse; **bustling** *adj*
(*town*) animado, bullicioso
busy ['bɪzɪ] *adj* ocupado, atareado; (*shop,
street*) concurrido, animado; (*TEL: line*)
comunicando ♦ *vt*: **to ~ o.s. with**
ocuparse en; **~body** *n* entrometido/a; **~
signal** (*US*) *n* (*TEL*) señal *f* de
comunicando

KEYWORD

but [bʌt] *conj* **1** pero; **he's not very
bright, ~ he's hard-working** no es muy
inteligente, pero es trabajador
2 (*in direct contradiction*): **he's not
English ~ French** no es inglés sino
francés; **he didn't sing ~ he shouted** no
cantó sino que gritó
3 (*showing disagreement, surprise etc*): **~
that's far too expensive!** ¡pero eso es
carísimo!; **~ it does work!** ¡(pero) sí que
funciona!
♦ *prep* (*apart from, except*) menos, salvo;
we've had nothing ~ trouble no hemos
tenido más que problemas; **no-one ~
him can do it** nadie más que él puede
hacerlo; **who ~ a lunatic would do
such a thing?** ¡sólo un loco haría una
cosa así!; **~ for you/your help** si no
fuera por ti/tu ayuda; **anything ~ that**
cualquier cosa menos eso
♦ *adv* (*just, only*): **she's ~ a child** no es
más que una niña; **had I ~ known** si lo
hubiera sabido; **I can ~ try** al menos lo
puedo intentar; **it's all ~ finished** está
casi acabado

butcher ['butʃə*] *n* carnicero ♦ *vt* hacer
una carnicería con; (*cattle etc*) matar; **~'s
(shop)** *n* carnicería
butler ['bʌtlə*] *n* mayordomo
butt [bʌt] *n* (*barrel*) tonel *m*; (*of gun*)
culata; (*of cigarette*) colilla; (*BRIT: fig:
target*) blanco ♦ *vt* dar cabezadas contra,
top(et)ar; **~ in** *vi* (*interrupt*) interrumpir
butter ['bʌtə*] *n* mantequilla ♦ *vt* untar
con mantequilla; **~cup** *n* botón *m* de oro
butterfly ['bʌtəflaɪ] *n* mariposa;

(SWIMMING: *also:* ~ *stroke*) braza de mariposa

buttocks ['bʌtəks] *npl* nalgas *fpl*

button ['bʌtn] *n* botón *m*; (US) placa, chapa ♦ *vt* (*also:* ~ *up*) abotonar, abrochar ♦ *vi* abrocharse

buttress ['bʌtrɪs] *n* contrafuerte *m*

buxom ['bʌksəm] *adj* exuberante

buy [baɪ] (*pt, pp* **bought**) *vt* comprar ♦ *n* compra; **to** ~ **sb sth/sth from sb** comprarle algo a alguien; **to** ~ **sb a drink** invitar a alguien a tomar algo; ~**er** *n* comprador(a) *m/f*

buzz [bʌz] *n* zumbido; (*inf*: *phone call*) llamada (por teléfono) ♦ *vi* zumbar; ~**er** *n* timbre *m*; ~ **word** *n* palabra que está de moda

---
KEYWORD
---

by [baɪ] *prep* **1** (*referring to cause, agent*) por; de; **killed** ~ **lightning** muerto por un relámpago; **a painting** ~ **Picasso** un cuadro de Picasso

2 (*referring to method, manner, means*): ~ **bus/car/train** en autobús/coche/tren; **to pay** ~ **cheque** pagar con un cheque; ~ **moonlight/candlelight** a la luz de la luna/una vela; ~ **saving hard, he** ... ahorrando, ...

3 (*via, through*) por; **we came** ~ **Dover** vinimos por Dover

4 (*close to, past*): **the house** ~ **the river** la casa junto al río; **she rushed** ~ **me** pasó a mi lado como una exhalación; **I go** ~ **the post office every day** paso por delante de Correos todos los días

5 (*time: not later than*) para; (: *during*): ~ **daylight** de día; ~ **4 o'clock** para las cuatro; ~ **this time tomorrow** mañana a estas horas; ~ **the time I got here it was too late** cuando llegué ya era demasiado tarde

6 (*amount*): ~ **the metre/kilo** por metro/kilo; **paid** ~ **the hour** pagado por hora

7 (MATH, *measure*): **to divide/multiply** ~ **3** dividir/multiplicar por 3; **a room 3 metres** ~ **4** una habitación de 3 metros por 4; **it's broader** ~ **a metre** es un metro más ancho

8 (*according to*) según, de acuerdo con; **it's 3 o'clock** ~ **my watch** según mi reloj, son las tres; **it's all right** ~ **me** por mí, está bien

9: (**all**) ~ **oneself** *etc* todo solo; **he did it (all)** ~ **himself** lo hizo él solo; **he was standing (all)** ~ **himself in a corner** estaba de pie solo en un rincón

10: ~ **the way** a propósito, por cierto; **this wasn't my idea,** ~ **the way** pues, no fue idea mía

♦ *adv* **1** *see* **go; pass** *etc*

2: ~ **and** ~ finalmente; **they'll come back** ~ **and** ~ acabarán volviendo; ~ **and large** en líneas generales, en general

bye(-bye) ['baɪ('baɪ)] *excl* adiós, hasta luego

by(e)-law *n* ordenanza municipal

by-election (BRIT) *n* elección *f* parcial

bygone ['baɪgɔn] *adj* pasado, del pasado ♦ *n*: **let** ~**s be** ~**s** lo pasado, pasado está

bypass ['baɪpɑːs] *n* carretera de circunvalación; (MED) (operación *f* de) by-pass *m* ♦ *vt* evitar

by-product *n* subproducto, derivado; (*of situation*) consecuencia

bystander ['baɪstændə*] *n* espectador(a) *m/f*

byte [baɪt] *n* (COMPUT) byte *m*, octeto

byword ['baɪwɔːd] *n*: **to be a** ~ **for** ser conocidísimo por

by-your-leave *n*: **without so much as a** ~ sin decir nada, sin dar ningún tipo de explicación

C c

C [siː] *n* (MUS) do *m*

C.A. *abbr* = **chartered accountant**

cab [kæb] *n* taxi *m*; (*of truck*) cabina

cabbage ['kæbɪdʒ] *n* col *f*, berza

cabin ['kæbɪn] *n* cabaña; (*on ship*) camarote *m*; (*on plane*) cabina; ~ **cruiser** *n* yate *m* de motor

cabinet ['kæbɪnɪt] *n* (POL) consejo de

ministros; (*furniture*) armario; (*also*: *display* ~) vitrina

cable ['keɪbl] *n* cable *m* ♦ *vt* cablegrafiar; ~**-car** *n* teleférico; ~ **television** *n* televisión *f* por cable

cache [kæʃ] *n* (*of weapons, drugs etc*) alijo

cackle ['kækl] *vi* lanzar risotadas; (*hen*) cacarear

cacti ['kæktaɪ] *npl of* **cactus**

cactus ['kæktəs] (*pl* **cacti**) *n* cacto

cadge [kædʒ] (*inf*) *vt* gorronear

Caesarean [si:'zɛərɪən] *adj*: ~ (**section**) cesárea

café ['kæfeɪ] *n* café *m*

cafeteria [kæfɪ'tɪərɪə] *n* cafetería

cage [keɪdʒ] *n* jaula

cagey ['keɪdʒɪ] (*inf*) *adj* cauteloso, reservado

cagoule [kə'gu:l] *n* chubasquero

cajole [kə'dʒəul] *vt* engatusar

cake [keɪk] *n* (CULIN: *large*) tarta; (: *small*) pastel *m*; (*of soap*) pastilla; ~**d** *adj*: ~**d with** cubierto de

calculate ['kælkjuleɪt] *vt* calcular; **calculating** *adj* (*scheming*) calculador(a); **calculation** [-'leɪʃən] *n* cálculo, cómputo; **calculator** *n* calculadora

calendar ['kæləndə*] *n* calendario; ~ **month/year** *n* mes *m*/año civil

calf [kɑ:f] (*pl* **calves**) *n* (*of cow*) ternero, becerro; (*of other animals*) cría; (*also*: ~*skin*) piel *f* de becerro; (ANAT) pantorrilla

calibre ['kælɪbə*] (US **caliber**) *n* calibre *m*

call [kɔ:l] *vt* llamar; (*meeting*) convocar ♦ *vi* (*shout*) llamar; (TEL) llamar (por teléfono), telefonear (*esp* AM); (*visit: also*: ~ **in**, ~ **round**) hacer una visita ♦ *n* llamada; (*of bird*) canto; **to be** ~**ed** llamarse; **on** ~ (*nurse, doctor etc*) de guardia; ~ **back** *vi* (*return*) volver; (TEL) volver a llamar; ~ **for** *vt fus* (*demand*) pedir, exigir; (*fetch*) venir por (SP), pasar por (AM); ~ **off** *vt* (*cancel: meeting, race*) cancelar; (: *deal*) anular; (: *strike*) desconvocar; ~ **on** *vt fus* (*visit*) visitar; (*turn to*) acudir a; ~ **out** *vi* gritar, dar voces; ~ **up** *vt* (MIL) llamar al servicio

militar; (TEL) llamar; ~**box** (BRIT) *n* cabina telefónica; ~**er** *n* visita; (TEL) usuario/a; ~ **girl** *n* prostituta; ~**-in** (US) *n* (*programa m*) coloquio (por teléfono); ~**ing** *n* vocación *f*; (*occupation*) profesión *f*; ~**ing card** (US) *n* tarjeta comercial *or* de visita

callous ['kæləs] *adj* insensible, cruel

calm [kɑ:m] *adj* tranquilo; (*sea*) liso, en calma ♦ *n* calma, tranquilidad *f* ♦ *vt* calmar, tranquilizar; ~ **down** *vi* calmarse, tranquilizarse ♦ *vt* calmar, tranquilizar

Calor gas ['kælə*-] ® *n* butano

calorie ['kælərɪ] *n* caloría

calves [kɑ:vz] *npl of* **calf**

camber ['kæmbə*] *n* (*of road*) combadura, comba

Cambodia [kæm'bəudjə] *n* Camboya

camcorder ['kæmkɔ:də*] *n* videocámara

came [keɪm] *pt of* **come**

camel ['kæməl] *n* camello

cameo ['kæmɪəu] *n* camafeo

camera ['kæmərə] *n* máquina fotográfica; (CINEMA, TV) cámara; **in** ~ (LAW) a puerta cerrada; ~**man** *n* cámara *m*

camouflage ['kæməflɑ:ʒ] *n* camuflaje *m* ♦ *vt* camuflar

camp [kæmp] *n* campamento, camping *m*; (MIL) campamento; (*for prisoners*) campo; (*fig: faction*) bando ♦ *vi* acampar ♦ *adj* afectado, afeminado

campaign [kæm'peɪn] *n* (MIL, POL *etc*) campaña ♦ *vi* hacer campaña

camp: ~**bed** (BRIT) *n* cama de campaña; ~**er** *n* campista *m/f*; (*vehicle*) caravana; ~**ing** *n* camping *m*; **to go** ~**ing** hacer camping; ~**site** *n* camping *m*

campus ['kæmpəs] *n* ciudad *f* universitaria

can[1] [kæn] *n* (*of oil, water*) bidón *m*; (*tin*) lata, bote *m* ♦ *vt* enlatar

⎯⎯⎯⎯ KEYWORD ⎯⎯⎯⎯

can[2] [kæn] (*negative* **cannot, can't**; *conditional and pt* **could**) *aux vb* **1** (*be able to*) poder; **you ~ do it if you try** puedes hacerlo si lo intentas; **I ~'t see you** no te veo

2 *(know how to)* saber; **I ~ swim/play tennis/drive** sé nadar/jugar al tenis/conducir; **~ you speak French?** ¿hablas *or* sabes hablar francés?
3 *(may)* poder; **~ I use your phone?** ¿me dejas *or* puedo usar tu teléfono?
4 *(expressing disbelief, puzzlement etc)*: **it ~'t be true!** ¡no puede ser (verdad)!; **what CAN he want?** ¿qué querrá?
5 *(expressing possibility, suggestion etc)*: **he could be in the library** podría estar en la biblioteca; **she could have been delayed** pudo haberse retrasado

Canada [ˈkænədə] *n* (el) Canadá; **Canadian** [kəˈneɪdɪən] *adj, n* canadiense *m/f*
canal [kəˈnæl] *n* canal *m*
canary [kəˈnɛərɪ] *n* canario; **the C~ Islands** *npl* las (Islas) Canarias
cancel [ˈkænsəl] *vt* cancelar; *(train)* suprimir; *(cross out)* tachar, borrar; **~lation** [-ˈleɪʃən] *n* cancelación *f*; supresión *f*
cancer [ˈkænsə*] *n* cáncer *m*; **C~** *(ASTROLOGY)* Cáncer *m*
candid [ˈkændɪd] *adj* franco, abierto
candidate [ˈkændɪdeɪt] *n* candidato/a
candle [ˈkændl] *n* vela; *(in church)* cirio; **~light** *n*: **by ~light** a la luz de una vela; **~stick** *n (single)* candelero; *(low)* palmatoria; *(bigger, ornate)* candelabro
candour [ˈkændə*] *(US* **candor**) *n* franqueza
candy [ˈkændɪ] *n* azúcar *m* cande; *(US)* caramelo; **~-floss** *(BRIT)* algodón *m* (azucarado)
cane [keɪn] *n (BOT)* caña; *(stick)* vara, palmeta; *(for furniture)* mimbre *f* ♦ *(BRIT) vt (SCOL)* castigar (con vara)
canister [ˈkænɪstə*] *n* bote *m*, lata; *(of gas)* bombona
cannabis [ˈkænəbɪs] *n* marijuana
canned [kænd] *adj* en lata, de lata
cannibal [ˈkænɪbəl] *n* caníbal *m/f*
cannon [ˈkænən] *(pl ~ or ~s) n* cañón *m*
cannot [ˈkænɔt] = **can not**
canoe [kəˈnuː] *n* canoa; *(SPORT)* piragua
canon [ˈkænən] *n (clergyman)* canónigo;

(standard) canon *m*
can opener *n* abrelatas *m inv*
canopy [ˈkænəpɪ] *n* dosel *m*; toldo
can't [kænt] = **can not**
cantankerous [kænˈtæŋkərəs] *adj* quisquillero
canteen [kænˈtiːn] *n (eating place)* cantina; *(BRIT: of cutlery)* juego
canter [ˈkæntə*] *vi* ir a medio galope
canvas [ˈkænvəs] *n (material)* lona; *(painting)* lienzo; *(NAUT)* velas *fpl*
canvass [ˈkænvəs] *vi (POL)*: **to ~ for** solicitar votos por ♦ *vt (COMM)* sondear
canyon [ˈkænjən] *n* cañón *m*
cap [kæp] *n (hat)* gorra; *(of pen)* capuchón *m*; *(of bottle)* tapa, tapón *m*; *(contraceptive)* diafragma *m*; *(for toy gun)* cápsula ♦ *vt (outdo)* superar; *(limit)* recortar
capability [keɪpəˈbɪlɪtɪ] *n* capacidad *f*
capable [ˈkeɪpəbl] *adj* capaz
capacity [kəˈpæsɪtɪ] *n* capacidad *f*; *(position)* calidad *f*
cape [keɪp] *n* capa; *(GEO)* cabo
caper [ˈkeɪpə*] *n (CULIN: gen: ~s)* alcaparra; *(prank)* broma
capital [ˈkæpɪtl] *n (also: ~ city)* capital *f*; *(money)* capital *m*; *(also: ~ letter)* mayúscula; **~ gains tax** *n* impuesto sobre las ganancias de capital; **~ism** *n* capitalismo; **~ist** *adj, n* capitalista *m/f*; **~ize** on *vt fus* aprovechar; **~ punishment** *n* pena de muerte
capitulate [kəˈpɪtjuleɪt] *vi* capitular, rendirse
Capricorn [ˈkæprɪkɔːn] *n (ASTROLOGY)* Capricornio
capsize [kæpˈsaɪz] *vt* volcar, hacer zozobrar ♦ *vi* volcarse, zozobrar
capsule [ˈkæpsjuːl] *n* cápsula
captain [ˈkæptɪn] *n* capitán *m*
caption [ˈkæpʃən] *n (heading)* título; *(to picture)* leyenda
captive [ˈkæptɪv] *adj, n* cautivo/a *m/f*
capture [ˈkæptʃə*] *vt* prender, apresar; *(animal, COMPUT)* capturar; *(place)* tomar; *(attention)* captar, llamar ♦ *n* apresamiento; captura; toma; *(data ~)* formulación *f* de datos

car [kɑː*] *n* coche *m*, carro (*AM*),
automóvil *m*; (*US: RAIL*) vagón *m*

carafe [kə'ræf] *n* jarra

carat ['kærət] *n* quilate *m*

caravan ['kærəvæn] *n* (*BRIT*) caravana,
ruló *f*; (*in desert*) caravana; ~ **site** (*BRIT*)
n camping *m* para caravanas

carbohydrate [kɑːbəu'haidreit] *n* hidrato
de carbono; (*food*) fécula

carbon ['kɑːbən] *n* carbono; ~ **paper** *n*
papel *m* carbón

carburettor [kɑːbju'retə*] (*US*
carburetor) *n* carburador *m*

carcass ['kɑːkəs] *n* cadáver *m* (de
animal)

card [kɑːd] *n* (*material*) cartulina; (*index
~ etc*) ficha; (*playing ~*) carta, naipe *m*;
(*visiting ~, greetings ~ etc*) tarjeta;
~**board** *n* cartón *m*

cardigan ['kɑːdɪgən] *n* rebeca

cardinal ['kɑːdɪnl] *adj* cardinal;
(*importance, principal*) esencial ♦ *n*
cardenal *m*

card index *n* fichero

care [kɛə*] *n* cuidado; (*worry*) inquietud
f; (*charge*) cargo, custodia ♦ *vi*: **to ~
about** (*person, animal*) tener cariño a;
(*thing, idea*) preocuparse por; ~ **of** en
casa de, al cuidado de; **in sb's ~** a cargo
de uno; **to take ~ to** cuidarse de, tener
cuidado de; **to take ~ of** cuidar de;
(*problem etc*) ocuparse de; **I don't ~** no
me importa; **I couldn't ~ less** eso me
trae sin cuidado; ~ **for** *vt fus* cuidar a;
(*like*) querer

career [kə'rɪə*] *n* profesión *f*; (*in work,
school*) carrera ♦ *vi* (*also:* ~ **along**) correr
a toda velocidad; ~ **woman** *n* mujer *f*
dedicada a su profesión

carefree ['kɛəfriː] *adj* despreocupado

careful ['kɛəful] *adj* cuidadoso; (*cautious*)
cauteloso; **(be) ~!** ¡tenga cuidado!; ~**ly**
adv con cuidado, cuidadosamente; con
cautela

careless ['kɛəlɪs] *adj* descuidado;
(*heedless*) poco atento; ~**ness** *n* descuido;
falta de atención

carer ['kɛərə*] *n* enfermero/a *m/f*
(*official*); (*unpaid*) *persona que cuida a*

un pariente o vecino

caress [kə'rɛs] *n* caricia ♦ *vt* acariciar

caretaker ['kɛəteikə*] *n* portero/a,
conserje *m/f*

car-ferry *n* transbordador *m* para
coches

cargo ['kɑːgəu] (*pl* ~**es**) *n* cargamento,
carga

car hire *n* alquiler *m* de automóviles

Caribbean [kærɪ'biːən] *n*: **the ~ (Sea)** el
(Mar) Caribe

caring ['kɛərɪŋ] *adj* humanitario; (*behaviour*) afectuoso

carnation [kɑː'neiʃən] *n* clavel *m*

carnival ['kɑːnɪvəl] *n* carnaval *m*; (*US:
funfair*) parque *m* de atracciones

carol ['kærəl] *n*: **(Christmas) ~** villancico

carp [kɑːp] *n* (*fish*) carpa; ~ **at** *vt fus*
quejarse de

car park (*BRIT*) *n* aparcamiento, parking
m

carpenter ['kɑːpɪntə*] *n* carpintero/a.

carpet ['kɑːpɪt] *n* alfombra; (*fitted*)
moqueta ♦ *vt* alfombrar; ~ **bombing** *n*
bombardeo de arrasamiento; ~ **slippers**
npl zapatillas *fpl*; ~ **sweeper** *n* aparato
para barrer alfombras

car phone *n* teléfono movil

carriage ['kærɪdʒ] *n* (*BRIT: RAIL*) vagón *m*;
(*horse-drawn*) coche *m*; (*of goods*)
transporte *m*; (: *cost*) porte *m*, flete *m*;
~**way** (*BRIT*) *n* (*part of road*) calzada

carrier ['kærɪə*] *n* (*transport company*)
transportista, empresa de transportes;
(*MED*) portador *m*; ~ **bag** (*BRIT*) *n* bolsa de
papel *or* plástico

carrot ['kærət] *n* zanahoria

carry ['kæri] *vt* (*subj: person*) llevar;
(*transport*) transportar; (*involve:
responsibilities etc*) entrañar, implicar;
(*MED*) ser portador de ♦ *vi* (*sound*) oírse;
to get carried away (*fig*) entusiasmarse;
~ **on** *vi* (*continue*) seguir (adelante),
continuar ♦ *vt* proseguir, continuar; ~
out *vt* (*orders*) cumplir; (*investigation*)
llevar a cabo, realizar; ~ **cot** (*BRIT*) *n*
cuna portátil; ~~**on** (*inf*) *n* (*fuss*) lío

cart [kɑːt] *n* carro, carreta ♦ *vt* (*inf:
transport*) acarrear

carton ['kɑːtən] *n* (*box*) caja (de cartón); (*of milk etc*) bote *m*; (*of yogurt*) tarrina

cartoon [kɑːˈtuːn] *n* (*PRESS*) caricatura; (*comic strip*) tira cómica; (*film*) dibujos *mpl* animados

cartridge ['kɑːtrɪdʒ] *n* cartucho; (*of pen*) recambio; (*of record player*) cápsula

carve [kɑːv] *vt* (*meat*) trinchar; (*wood, stone*) cincelar, esculpir; (*initials etc*) grabar; ~ **up** *vt* dividir, repartir; **carving** *n* (*object*) escultura; (*design*) talla; (*art*) tallado; **carving knife** *n* trinchante *m*

car wash *n* lavado de coches

case [keɪs] *n* (*container*) caja; (*MED*) caso; (*for jewels etc*) estuche *m*; (*LAW*) causa, proceso; (*BRIT: also: suit~*) maleta; **in ~ of** en caso de; **in any ~** en todo caso; **just in ~** por si acaso

cash [kæʃ] *n* dinero en efectivo, dinero contante ♦ *vt* cobrar, hacer efectivo; **to pay (in) ~** pagar al contado; ~ **on delivery** cóbrese al entregar; ~**book** *n* libro de caja; ~ **card** *n* tarjeta *f* dinero; ~**desk** (*BRIT*) *n* caja; ~ **dispenser** *n* cajero automático

cashew [kæˈʃuː] *n* (*also:* ~ *nut*) anacardo

cash flow *n* flujo de fondos, cash-flow *m*

cashier [kæˈʃɪə*] *n* cajero/a

cashmere ['kæʃmɪə*] *n* cachemira

cash register *n* caja

casing ['keɪsɪŋ] *n* revestimiento

casino [kəˈsiːnəu] *n* casino

casket ['kɑːskɪt] *n* cofre *m*, estuche *m*; (*US: coffin*) ataúd *m*

casserole ['kæsərəul] *n* (*food, pot*) cazuela

cassette [kæˈsɛt] *n* cassette *f*; ~ **player/ recorder** *n* tocacassettes *m inv*, cassette *m*

cast [kɑːst] (*pt, pp* **cast**) *vt* (*throw*) echar, arrojar, lanzar; (*glance, eyes*) dirigir; (*THEATRE*): **to ~ sb as Othello** dar a uno el papel de Otelo ♦ *vi* (*FISHING*) lanzar ♦ *n* (*THEATRE*) reparto; (*also: plaster ~*) vaciado; **to ~ one's vote** votar; **to ~ doubt on** suscitar dudas acerca de; ~ **off** *vi* (*NAUT*) desamarrar; (*KNITTING*) cerrar (los puntos); ~ **on** *vi* (*KNITTING*) poner los puntos

castanets [kæstəˈnɛts] *npl* castañuelas *fpl*

castaway ['kɑːstəwəɪ] *n* náufrago/a

caste [kɑːst] *n* casta

caster sugar ['kɑːstə*-] (*BRIT*) *n* azúcar *m* extrafino

Castile [kæsˈtiːl] *n* Castilla; **Castilian** *adj, n* castellano/a *m/f*

casting vote ['kɑːstɪŋ-] (*BRIT*) *n* voto decisivo

cast iron *n* hierro fundido

castle ['kɑːsl] *n* castillo; (*CHESS*) torre *f*

castor ['kɑːstə*] *n* (*wheel*) ruedecilla; ~ **oil** *n* aceite *m* de ricino

casual ['kæʒjul] *adj* fortuito; (*irregular: work etc*) eventual, temporero; (*unconcerned*) despreocupado; (*clothes*) de sport; ~**ly** *adv* de manera despreocupada; (*dress*) de sport

casualty ['kæʒjultɪ] *n* víctima, herido; (*dead*) muerto; (*MED: department*) urgencias *fpl*

cat [kæt] *n* gato; (*big ~*) felino

Catalan ['kætəlæn] *adj, n* catalán/ana *m/f*

catalogue ['kætəlɔg] (*US* **catalog**) *n* catálogo ♦ *vt* catalogar

Catalonia [kætəˈləunɪə] *n* Cataluña

catalyst ['kætəlɪst] *n* catalizador *m*

catalytic convertor [kætəˈlɪtɪk kənˈvɜːtə*] *n* catalizador *m*

catapult ['kætəpʌlt] *n* tirachinas *m inv*

catarrh [kəˈtɑː*] *n* catarro

catastrophe [kəˈtæstrəfɪ] *n* catástrofe *f*

catch [kætʃ] (*pt, pp* **caught**) *vt* coger (*SP*), agarrar (*AM*); (*arrest*) detener; (*grasp*) asir; (*breath*) contener; (*surprise: person*) sorprender; (*attract: attention*) captar; (*hear*) oír; (*MED*) contagiarse de, coger; (*also:* ~ *up*) alcanzar ♦ *vi* (*fire*) encenderse; (*in branches etc*) enredarse ♦ *n* (*fish etc*) pesca; (*act of catching*) cogida; (*hidden problem*) dificultad *f*; (*game*) pilla-pilla; (*of lock*) pestillo, cerradura; **to ~ fire** encenderse; **to ~ sight of** divisar; ~ **on** *vi* (*understand*) caer en la cuenta; (*grow popular*) hacerse popular; ~ **up** *vi* (*fig*) ponerse al día

catching ['kætʃɪŋ] *adj* (*MED*) contagioso

catchment area ['kætʃmənt-] (*BRIT*) *n*

zona de captación

catchphrase ['kætʃfreɪz] *n* lema *m*, eslogan *m*

catchy ['kætʃɪ] *adj* (*tune*) pegadizo

category ['kætɪɡərɪ] *n* categoría, clase *f*

cater ['keɪtə*] *vi*: **to ~ for** (*BRIT*) abastecer a; (*needs*) atender a; (*COMM: parties etc*) proveer comida a; **~er** *n* abastecedor(a) *m/f*, proveedor(a) *m/f*; **~ing** *n* (*trade*) hostelería

caterpillar ['kætəpɪlə*] *n* oruga, gusano; **~ track** *n* rodado de oruga

cathedral [kə'θiːdrəl] *n* catedral *f*

catholic ['kæθəlɪk] *adj* (*tastes etc*) amplio; **C~** *adj*, *n* (*REL*) católico/a *m/f*

cat's-eye (*BRIT*) *n* (*AUT*) catafoto

cattle ['kætl] *npl* ganado

catty ['kætɪ] *adj* malicioso, rencoroso

caucus ['kɔːkəs] *n* (*POL*) camarilla política; (: *US: to elect candidates*) comité *m* electoral

caught [kɔːt] *pt, pp of* **catch**

cauliflower ['kɔlɪflauə*] *n* coliflor *f*

cause [kɔːz] *n* causa, motivo, razón *f*; (*principle: also: POL*) causa ♦ *vt* causar

caustic ['kɔːstɪk] *adj* cáustico; (*fig*) mordaz

caution ['kɔːʃən] *n* cautela, prudencia; (*warning*) advertencia, amonestación *f* ♦ *vt* amonestar

cautious ['kɔːʃəs] *adj* cauteloso, prudente, precavido; **~ly** *adv* con cautela

cavalier [kævə'lɪə*] *adj* arrogante, desdeñoso

cavalry ['kævəlrɪ] *n* caballería

cave [keɪv] *n* cueva, caverna; **~ in** *vi* (*roof etc*) derrumbarse, hundirse; **~man** *n* cavernícola *m*, troglodita *m*

cavity ['kævɪtɪ] *n* hueco, cavidad *f*; (*in tooth*) caries *f inv*

cavort [kə'vɔːt] *vi* dar brincos

CB *n abbr* (= *Citizens' Band* (*Radio*)) banda ciudadana

CBI *n abbr* (= *Confederation of British Industry*) ≈ C.E.O.E. *f* (*SP*)

cc *abbr* = **cubic centimetres**; = **carbon copy**

CD *n abbr* (= *compact disc*) DC *m*; (*player*) (reproductor *m* de) disco

compacto; **~-ROM** [siːdiː'rɔm] *n abbr* CD-ROM *m*

cease [siːs] *vt, vi* cesar; **~fire** *n* alto *m* el fuego; **~less** *adj* incesante

cedar ['siːdə*] *n* cedro

ceiling ['siːlɪŋ] *n* techo; (*fig*) límite *m*

celebrate ['selɪbreɪt] *vt* celebrar ♦ *vi* divertirse; **~d** *adj* célebre; **celebration** [-'breɪʃən] *n* fiesta, celebración *f*

celery ['selərɪ] *n* apio

celibacy ['selɪbəsɪ] *n* celibato

cell [sel] *n* celda; (*BIOL*) célula; (*ELEC*) elemento

cellar ['selə*] *n* sótano; (*for wine*) bodega

'cello ['tʃeləu] *n* violoncelo

cellophane ['seləfeɪn] *n* celofán *m*

cellphone ['selfəun] *n* teléfono celular

Celt [kelt, selt] *adj*, *n* celta *m/f*; **~ic** *adj* celta

cement [sə'ment] *n* cemento; **~ mixer** *n* hormigonera

cemetery ['semɪtrɪ] *n* cementerio

censor ['sensə*] *n* censor *m* ♦ *vt* (*cut*) censurar; **~ship** *n* censura

censure ['senʃə*] *vt* censurar

census ['sensəs] *n* censo

cent [sent] *n* (*US*) (*coin*) centavo, céntimo; *see also* **per**

centenary [sen'tiːnərɪ] *n* centenario

center ['sentə*] (*US*) = **centre**

centi... [sentɪ] *prefix*: **~grade** *adj* centígrado; **~litre** (*US* **~liter**) *n* centilitro; **~metre** (*US* **~meter**) *n* centímetro

centipede ['sentɪpiːd] *n* ciempiés *m inv*

central ['sentrəl] *adj* central; (*of house etc*) céntrico; **C~ America** *n* Centroamérica; **~ heating** *n* calefacción *f* central; **~ize** *vt* centralizar

centre ['sentə*] (*US* **center**) *n* centro; (*fig*) núcleo ♦ *vt* centrar; **~-forward** *n* (*SPORT*) delantero centro; **~-half** *n* (*SPORT*) medio centro

century ['sentjurɪ] *n* siglo; **20th ~** siglo veinte

ceramic [sɪ'ræmɪk] *adj* cerámico; **~s** *n* cerámica

cereal ['siːrɪəl] *n* cereal *m*

cerebral ['serɪbrəl] *adj* cerebral; intelectual

ceremony ['sɛrɪmənɪ] *n* ceremonia; **to stand on** ~ hacer ceremonias, estar de cumplido

certain ['sə:tən] *adj* seguro; (*person*): **a ~ Mr Smith** un tal Sr Smith; (*particular, some*) cierto; **for** ~ a ciencia cierta; **~ly** *adv* (*undoubtedly*) ciertamente; (*of course*) desde luego, por supuesto; **~ty** *n* certeza, certidumbre *f*, seguridad *f*; (*inevitability*) certeza

certificate [sə'tɪfɪkɪt] *n* certificado

certified ['sə:tɪfaɪd]: ~ **mail** (*US*) *n* correo certificado; ~ **public accountant** (*US*) *n* contable *m/f* diplomado/a

certify ['sə:tɪfaɪ] *vt* certificar; (*award diploma to*) conceder un diploma a; (*declare insane*) declarar loco

cervical ['sə:vɪkl] *adj* cervical

cervix ['sə:vɪks] *n* cuello del útero

cf. *abbr* (= *compare*) cfr

CFC *n abbr* (= *chlorofluorocarbon*) CFC *m*

ch. *abbr* (= *chapter*) cap

chafe [tʃeɪf] *vt* (*rub*) rozar

chagrin ['ʃægrɪn] *n* (*annoyance*) disgusto; (*disappointment*) decepción *f*

chain [tʃeɪn] *n* cadena; (*of mountains*) cordillera; (*of events*) sucesión *f* ♦ *vt* (*also*: ~ *up*) encadenar; ~ **reaction** *n* reacción *f* en cadena; **~-smoke** *vi* fumar un cigarrillo tras otro; ~ **store** *n* tienda de una cadena, ≈ gran almacén

chair [tʃeə*] *n* silla; (*armchair*) sillón *m*, butaca; (*of university*) cátedra; (*of meeting etc*) presidencia ♦ *vt* (*meeting*) presidir; **~lift** *n* telesilla; **~man** *n* presidente *m*

chalet ['ʃæleɪ] *n* chalet *m*

chalk [tʃɔ:k] *n* (*GEO*) creta; (*for writing*) tiza (*SP*), gis *m* (*AM*)

challenge ['tʃælɪndʒ] *n* desafío, reto ♦ *vt* desafiar, retar; (*statement, right*) poner en duda; **to ~ sb to do sth** retar a uno a que haga algo; **challenging** *adj* exigente; (*tone*) de desafío

chamber ['tʃeɪmbə*] *n* cámara, sala; (*POL*) cámara; (*BRIT: LAW: gen pl*) despacho; ~ **of commerce** cámara de comercio; **~maid** *n* camarera; ~ **music** *n*

música de cámara

chamois ['ʃæmwɑ:] *n* gamuza

champagne [ʃæm'peɪn] *n* champaña *m*, champán *m*

champion ['tʃæmpɪən] *n* campeón/ona *m/f*; (*of cause*) defensor(a) *m/f*; **~ship** *n* campeonato

chance [tʃɑ:ns] *n* (*opportunity*) ocasión *f*, oportunidad *f*; (*likelihood*) posibilidad *f*; (*risk*) riesgo ♦ *vt* arriesgar, probar ♦ *adj* fortuito, casual; **to ~ it** arriesgarse, intentarlo; **to take a ~** arriesgarse; **by ~** por casualidad

chancellor ['tʃɑ:nsələ*] *n* canciller *m*; **C~ of the Exchequer** (*BRIT*) *n* Ministro de Hacienda

chandelier [ʃændə'lɪə*] *n* araña (de luces)

change [tʃeɪndʒ] *vt* cambiar; (*replace*) cambiar, reemplazar; (*gear, clothes, job*) cambiar de; (*transform*) transformar ♦ *vi* cambiar(se); (*trains*) hacer transbordo; (*traffic lights*) cambiar de color; (*be transformed*): **to ~ into** transformarse en ♦ *n* cambio; (*alteration*) modificación *f*, transformación *f*; (*of clothes*) muda; (*coins*) suelto, sencillo; (*money returned*) vuelta; **to ~ gear** (*AUT*) cambiar de marcha; **to ~ one's mind** cambiar de opinión *or* idea; **for a ~** para variar; **~able** *adj* (*weather*) cambiable; ~ **machine** *n* máquina de cambio; **~over** *n* (*to new system*) cambio

changing ['tʃeɪndʒɪŋ] *adj* cambiante; ~ **room** (*BRIT*) *n* vestuario

channel ['tʃænl] *n* (*TV*) canal *m*; (*of river*) cauce *m*; (*groove*) conducto; (*fig: medium*) medio ♦ *vt* (*river etc*) encauzar; **the (English) C~** el Canal (de la Mancha); **the C~ Islands** las Islas Normandas; **the C~ Tunnel** el túnel del Canal de la Mancha, el Eurotúnel

chant [tʃɑ:nt] *n* (*of crowd*) gritos *mpl*; (*REL*) canto ♦ *vt* (*slogan, word*) repetir a gritos

chaos ['keɪɒs] *n* caos *m*

chap [tʃæp] (*BRIT: inf*) *n* (*man*) tío, tipo

chapel ['tʃæpəl] *n* capilla

chaperone ['ʃæpərəun] *n* carabina

chaplain ['tʃæplɪn] n capellán m
chapped [tʃæpt] adj agrietado
chapter ['tʃæptə*] n capítulo
char [tʃɑː*] vt (burn) carbonizar, chamuscar ♦ n (BRIT) = **charlady**
character ['kærɪktə*] n carácter m, naturaleza, índole f; (moral strength, personality) carácter; (in novel, film) personaje m; ~**istic** [-'rɪstɪk] adj característico ♦ n característica; ~**ize** vt caracterizar
charcoal ['tʃɑːkəʊl] n carbón m vegetal; (ART) carboncillo
charge [tʃɑːdʒ] n (LAW) cargo, acusación f; (cost) precio, coste m; (responsibility) cargo ♦ vt (LAW): **to ~ (with)** acusar (de); (battery) cargar; (price) pedir; (customer) cobrar ♦ vi precipitarse; (MIL) cargar, atacar; ~s npl: **to reverse the ~s** (BRIT: TEL) revertir el cobro; **to take ~ of** hacerse cargo de, encargarse de; **to be in ~ of** estar encargado de; (business) mandar; **how much do you ~?** ¿cuánto cobra usted?; **to ~ an expense (up) to sb's account** cargar algo a cuenta de alguien; ~ **card** n tarjeta de cuenta
charitable ['tʃærɪtəbl] adj benéfico
charity ['tʃærɪtɪ] n caridad f; (organization) sociedad f benéfica; (money, gifts) limosnas fpl
charlady ['tʃɑːleɪdɪ] (BRIT) n mujer f de la limpieza
charlatan ['ʃɑːlətən] n farsante m/f
charm [tʃɑːm] n encanto, atractivo; (talisman) hechizo; (on bracelet) dije m ♦ vt encantar; ~**ing** adj encantador(a)
chart [tʃɑːt] n (diagram) cuadro; (graph) gráfica; (map) carta de navegación ♦ vt (course) trazar; (progress) seguir; ~s npl (Top 40): **the ~s** ≈ los 40 principales (SP)
charter ['tʃɑːtə*] vt (plane) alquilar; (ship) fletar ♦ n (document) carta; (of university, company) estatutos mpl; ~**ed accountant** (BRIT) n contable m/f diplomado/a; ~ **flight** n vuelo chárter
charwoman ['tʃɑːwʊmən] n = **charlady**
chase [tʃeɪs] vt (pursue) perseguir; (also: ~ away) ahuyentar ♦ n persecución f
chasm ['kæzəm] n sima

chassis ['ʃæsɪ] n chasis m
chat [tʃæt] vi (also: have a ~) charlar ♦ n charla; ~ **show** (BRIT) n programa m de entrevistas
chatter ['tʃætə*] vi (person) charlar; (teeth) castañetear ♦ n (of birds) parloteo; (of people) charla, cháchara; ~**box** (inf) n parlanchín/ina m/f
chatty ['tʃætɪ] adj (style) informal; (person) hablador(a)
chauffeur ['ʃəʊfə*] n chófer m
chauvinist ['ʃəʊvɪnɪst] n (male ~) machista m; (nationalist) chovinista m/f
cheap [tʃiːp] adj barato; (joke) de mal gusto; (poor quality) de mala calidad ♦ adv barato; ~**er** adj más barato; ~**ly** adv barato, a bajo precio
cheat [tʃiːt] vi hacer trampa ♦ vt: **to ~ sb (out of sth)** estafar (algo) a uno ♦ n (person) tramposo/a
check [tʃɛk] vt (examine) controlar; (facts) comprobar; (halt) parar, detener; (restrain) refrenar, restringir ♦ n (inspection) control m, inspección f; (curb) freno; (US: bill) nota, cuenta; (US) = **cheque**; (pattern: gen pl) cuadro ♦ adj (also: ~**ed**: pattern, cloth) a cuadros; ~ **in** vi (at hotel) firmar el registro; (at airport) facturar el equipaje ♦ vt (luggage) facturar; ~ **out** vi (of hotel) marcharse; ~ **up** vi: **to ~ up on sth** comprobar algo; **to ~ up on sb** investigar a alguien; ~**ered** (US) adj = **check**; **chequered**; ~**ers** (US) n juego de damas; ~**-in** (desk) n mostrador m de facturación; ~**ing account** (US) n cuenta corriente; ~**mate** n jaque m mate; ~**out** n caja; ~**point** n (punto de) control m; ~**room** (US) n consigna; ~**up** n (MED) reconocimiento general
cheek [tʃiːk] n mejilla; (impudence) descaro; **what a ~!** ¡qué cara!; ~**bone** n pómulo; ~**y** adj fresco, descarado
cheep [tʃiːp] vi piar
cheer [tʃɪə*] vt vitorear, aplaudir; (gladden) alegrar, animar ♦ vi dar vivas ♦ n viva m; ~s npl aplausos mpl; ~s! ¡salud!; ~ **up** vi animarse ♦ vt alegrar, animar; ~**ful** adj alegre

cheerio [tʃɪərɪˈəʊ] (BRIT) excl ¡hasta luego!

cheese [tʃiːz] n queso; ~board n tabla de quesos

cheetah [ˈtʃiːtə] n leopardo cazador

chef [ʃef] n jefe/a m/f de cocina

chemical [ˈkemɪkəl] adj químico ♦ n producto químico

chemist [ˈkemɪst] n (BRIT: pharmacist) farmacéutico/a; (scientist) químico/a; ~ry n química; ~'s (shop) (BRIT) n farmacia

cheque [tʃek] (US check) n cheque m; ~book n talonario de cheques (SP), chequera (AM); ~ card n tarjeta de cheque

chequered [ˈtʃekəd] (US checkered) adj (fig) accidentado

cherish [ˈtʃerɪʃ] vt (love) querer, apreciar; (protect) cuidar; (hope etc) abrigar

cherry [ˈtʃerɪ] n cereza; (also: ~ tree) cerezo

chess [tʃes] n ajedrez m; ~board n tablero de ajedrez

chest [tʃest] n (ANAT) pecho; (box) cofre m, cajón m; ~ of drawers n cómoda

chestnut [ˈtʃesnʌt] n castaña; ~ (tree) n castaño

chew [tʃuː] vt mascar, masticar; ~ing gum n chicle m

chic [ʃiːk] adj elegante

chick [tʃɪk] n pollito, polluelo; (inf: girl) chica

chicken [ˈtʃɪkɪn] n gallina, pollo; (food) pollo; (inf: coward) gallina m/f; ~ out (inf) vi rajarse; ~pox n varicela

chicory [ˈtʃɪkərɪ] n (for coffee) achicoria; (salad) escarola

chief [tʃiːf] n jefe/a m/f ♦ adj principal; ~ executive n director(a) m/f general; ~ly adv principalmente

chiffon [ˈʃɪfɒn] n gasa

chilblain [ˈtʃɪlbleɪn] n sabañón m

child [tʃaɪld] (pl **children**) n niño/a; (offspring) hijo/a; ~birth n parto; ~hood n niñez f, infancia; ~ish adj pueril, aniñado; ~like adj de niño; ~minder (BRIT) n madre f de día; ~ren [ˈtʃɪldrən] npl of **child**

Chile [ˈtʃɪlɪ] n Chile m; ~an adj, n chileno/a m/f

chill [tʃɪl] n frío; (MED) resfriado ♦ vt enfriar; (CULIN) congelar

chil(l)i [ˈtʃɪlɪ] (BRIT) n chile m (SP), ají m (AM)

chilly [ˈtʃɪlɪ] adj frío

chime [tʃaɪm] n repique m; (of clock) campanada ♦ vi repicar; sonar

chimney [ˈtʃɪmnɪ] n chimenea; ~ sweep n deshollinador m

chimpanzee [tʃɪmpænˈziː] n chimpancé m

chin [tʃɪn] n mentón m, barbilla

china [ˈtʃaɪnə] n porcelana; (crockery) loza

China [ˈtʃaɪnə] n China; **Chinese** [tʃaɪˈniːz] adj chino/a; (LING) chino

chink [tʃɪŋk] n (opening) grieta, hendedura; (noise) tintineo

chip [tʃɪp] n (gen pl: CULIN: BRIT) patata (SP) or papa (AM) frita; (: US: also: potato ~) patata or papa frita; (of wood) astilla; (of glass, stone) lasca; (at poker) ficha; (COMPUT) chip m ♦ vt (cup, plate) desconchar; ~ in (inf) vi interrumpir; (contribute) compartir los gastos

chiropodist [kɪˈrɒpədɪst] (BRIT) n pedicuro/a, callista m/f

chirp [tʃɜːp] vi (bird) gorjear, piar

chisel [ˈtʃɪzl] n (for wood) escoplo; (for stone) cincel m

chit [tʃɪt] n nota

chitchat [ˈtʃɪtʃæt] n chismes mpl, habladurías fpl

chivalry [ˈʃɪvəlrɪ] n caballerosidad f

chives [tʃaɪvz] npl cebollinos mpl

chlorine [ˈklɔːriːn] n cloro

chock-a-block [ˈtʃɒkəˈblɒk] adj atestado

chockfull [ˈtʃɒkˈful] adj atestado

chocolate [ˈtʃɒklɪt] n chocolate m; (sweet) bombón m

choice [tʃɔɪs] n elección f, selección f; (option) opción f; (preference) preferencia ♦ adj escogido

choir [ˈkwaɪəʳ] n coro; ~boy n niño de coro

choke [tʃəʊk] vi ahogarse; (on food) atragantarse ♦ vt estrangular, ahogar; (block): **to be ~d with** estar atascado de ♦ n (AUT) estárter m

cholesterol [kəˈlɛstərɒl] n colesterol m

choose [tʃuːz] (*pt* **chose**, *pp* **chosen**) *vt*
escoger, elegir; (*team*) seleccionar; **to ~
to do sth** optar por hacer algo

choosy ['tʃuːzɪ] *adj* delicado

chop [tʃɔp] *vt* (*wood*) cortar, tajar; (*CULIN:
also: ~ up*) picar ♦ *n* (*CULIN*) chuleta; **~s**
npl (*jaws*) boca, labios *mpl*

chopper ['tʃɔpə*] *n* (*helicopter*)
helicóptero

choppy ['tʃɔpɪ] *adj* (*sea*) picado, agitado

chopsticks ['tʃɔpstɪks] *npl* palillos *mpl*

chord [kɔːd] *n* (*MUS*) acorde *m*

chore [tʃɔː*] *n* faena, tarea; (*routine task*)
trabajo rutinario

chortle ['tʃɔːtl] *vi* reír entre dientes

chorus ['kɔːrəs] *n* coro; (*repeated part of
song*) estribillo

chose [tʃəuz] *pt of* **choose**

chosen [tʃəuzn] *pp of* **choose**

Christ [kraɪst] *n* Cristo

christen ['krɪsn] *vt* bautizar

Christian ['krɪstɪən] *adj, n* cristiano/a
m/f; **~ity** [-'ænɪtɪ] *n* cristianismo; **~
name** *n* nombre *m* de pila

Christmas ['krɪsməs] *n* Navidad *f*; **Merry
~!** ¡Felices Pascuas!; **~ card** *n* crismas *m
inv*, tarjeta de Navidad; **~ Day** *n* día *m*
de Navidad; **~ Eve** *n* Nochebuena; **~ tree**
n árbol *m* de Navidad

chrome [krəum] *n* cromo

chronic ['krɔnɪk] *adj* crónico

chronological [krɔnə'lɔdʒɪkəl] *adj*
cronológico

chubby ['tʃʌbɪ] *adj* regordete

chuck [tʃʌk] (*inf*) *vt* lanzar, arrojar; (*BRIT:
also: ~ up*) abandonar; **~ out** (*person*)
echar (fuera); (*rubbish etc*) tirar

chuckle ['tʃʌkl] *vi* reírse entre dientes

chug [tʃʌg] *vi* resoplar; (*car, boat: also: ~
along*) avanzar traqueteando

chum [tʃʌm] *n* compañero/a

chunk [tʃʌŋk] *n* pedazo, trozo

church [tʃəːtʃ] *n* iglesia; **~yard** *n*
cementerio

churlish ['tʃəːlɪʃ] *adj* grosero

churn [tʃəːn] *n* (*for butter*) mantequera;
(*for milk*) lechera; **~ out** *vt* producir en
serie

chute [ʃuːt] *n* (*also: rubbish ~*) vertedero;

(*for coal etc*) rampa de caída

chutney ['tʃʌtnɪ] *n* condimento a base de
frutas de la India

CIA (*US*) *n abbr* (= *Central Intelligence
Agency*) CIA *f*

CID (*BRIT*) *n abbr* (= *Criminal
Investigation Department*) ≈ B.I.C. *f* (*SP*)

cider ['saɪdə*] *n* sidra

cigar [sɪ'gɑː*] *n* puro

cigarette [sɪgə'ret] *n* cigarrillo (*SP*),
cigarro (*AM*); pitillo; **~ case** *n* pitillera; **~
end** *n* colilla

Cinderella [sɪndə'relə] *n* Cenicienta

cinders ['sɪndəz] *npl* cenizas *fpl*

cine-camera ['sɪnɪ-] (*BRIT*) *n* cámara
cinematográfica

cinema ['sɪnəmə] *n* cine *m*

cinnamon ['sɪnəmən] *n* canela

circle ['səːkl] *n* círculo; (*in theatre*)
anfiteatro ♦ *vi* dar vueltas ♦ *vt*
(*surround*) rodear, cercar; (*move round*)
dar la vuelta a

circuit ['səːkɪt] *n* circuito; (*tour*) gira;
(*track*) pista; (*lap*) vuelta; **~ous**
[səː'kjuɪtəs] *adj* indirecto

circular ['səːkjulə*] *adj* circular ♦ *n*
circular *f*

circulate ['səːkjuleɪt] *vi* circular; (*person:
at party etc*) hablar con los invitados
♦ *vt* poner en circulación; **circulation**
[-'leɪʃən] *n* circulación *f*; (*of newspaper*)
tirada

circumcise ['səːkəmsaɪz] *vt* circuncidar

circumspect ['səːkəmspekt] *adj* prudente

circumstances ['səːkəmstənsɪz] *npl*
circunstancias *fpl*; (*financial condition*)
situación *f* económica

circumvent ['səːkəmvent] *vt* burlar

circus ['səːkəs] *n* circo

CIS *n abbr* (= *Commonwealth of
Independent States*) CEI *f*

cistern ['sɪstən] *n* tanque *m*, depósito; (*in
toilet*) cisterna

citizen ['sɪtɪzn] *n* (*POL*) ciudadano/a; (*of
city*) vecino/a, habitante *m/f*; **~ship** *n*
ciudadanía

citrus fruits ['sɪtrəs-] *npl* agrios *mpl*

city ['sɪtɪ] *n* ciudad *f*; **the C~** centro
financiero de Londres

civic ['sɪvɪk] *adj* cívico: (*authorities*) municipal; ~ **centre** (*BRIT*) *n* centro público

civil ['sɪvɪl] *adj* civil; (*polite*) atento, cortés; ~ **engineer** *n* ingeniero de caminos (, canales y puertos); ~**ian** [sɪ'vɪliən] *adj* civil (*no militar*) ♦ *n* civil *m/f*, paisano/a

civilization [sɪvɪlaɪ'zeɪʃən] *n* civilización *f*

civilized ['sɪvɪlaɪzd] *adj* civilizado

civil: ~ **law** *n* derecho civil; ~ **servant** *n* funcionario/a del Estado; **C~ Service** *n* administración *f* pública; ~ **war** *n* guerra civil

clad [klæd] *adj:* ~ **(in)** vestido (de)

claim [kleɪm] *vt* exigir, reclamar; (*rights etc*) reivindicar; (*assert*) pretender ♦ *vi* (*for insurance*) reclamar ♦ *n* reclamación *f*; pretensión *f*; ~**ant** *n* demandante *m/f*

clairvoyant [kleə'vɔɪənt] *n* clarividente *m/f*

clam [klæm] *n* almeja

clamber ['klæmbə*] *vi* trepar

clammy ['klæmɪ] *adj* frío y húmedo

clamour ['klæmə*] (*US* **clamor**) *vi:* **to ~ for** clamar por, pedir a voces

clamp [klæmp] *n* abrazadera, grapa ♦ *vt* (*2 things together*) cerrar fuertemente; (*one thing on another*) afianzar (con abrazadera); ~ **down on** *vt fus* (*subj: government, police*) reforzar la lucha contra

clang [klæŋ] *vi* sonar, hacer estruendo

clap [klæp] *vi* aplaudir; ~**ping** *n* aplausos *mpl*

claret ['klærət] *n* clarete *m*

clarify ['klærɪfaɪ] *vt* aclarar

clarinet [klærɪ'net] *n* clarinete *m*

clash [klæʃ] *n* enfrentamiento; choque *m*; desacuerdo; estruendo ♦ *vi* (*fight*) enfrentarse; (*beliefs*) chocar; (*disagree*) estar en desacuerdo; (*colours*) desentonar; (*two events*) coincidir

clasp [klɑːsp] *n* (*hold*) apretón *m*; (*of necklace, bag*) cierre *m* ♦ *vt* apretar; abrazar

class [klɑːs] *n* clase *f* ♦ *vt* clasificar

classic ['klæsɪk] *adj, n* clásico; ~**al** *adj* clásico

classified ['klæsɪfaɪd] *adj* (*information*) reservado; ~ **advertisement** *n* anuncio por palabras

classify ['klæsɪfaɪ] *vt* clasificar

classmate ['klɑːsmeɪt] *n* compañero/a de clase

classroom ['klɑːsrum] *n* aula

clatter ['klætə*] *n* estrépito ♦ *vi* hacer ruido o estrépito

clause [klɔːz] *n* cláusula; (*LING*) oración *f*

claw [klɔː] *n* (*of cat*) uña; (*of bird of prey*) garra; (*of lobster*) pinza; ~ **at** *vt fus* arañar

clay [kleɪ] *n* arcilla

clean [kliːn] *adj* limpio; (*record, reputation*) intachable; (*joke*) decente ♦ *vt* limpiar; (*hands etc*) lavar; ~ **out** *vt* limpiar; ~ **up** *vt* limpiar, asear; ~**-cut** *adj* (*person*) bien parecido; ~**er** *n* (*person*) asistenta; (*substance*) producto para la limpieza; ~**er's** *n* tintorería; ~**ing** *n* limpieza; **cleanliness** ['klenlɪnɪs] *n* limpieza

cleanse [klenz] *vt* limpiar; ~**r** *n* (*for face*) crema limpiadora

clean-shaven *adj* sin barba, afeitado

cleansing department (*BRIT*) *n* departamento de limpieza

clear [klɪə*] *adj* claro; (*road, way*) libre; (*conscience*) limpio, tranquilo; (*skin*) terso; (*sky*) despejado ♦ *vt* (*space*) despejar, limpiar; (*LAW: suspect*) absolver; (*obstacle*) salvar, saltar por encima de; (*cheque*) aceptar ♦ *vi* (*fog etc*) despejarse ♦ *adv:* ~ **of** a distancia de; **to ~ the table** recoger *o* levantar la mesa; ~ **up** *vt* limpiar; (*mystery*) aclarar, resolver; ~**ance** *n* (*removal*) despeje *m*; (*permission*) acreditación *f*; ~**-cut** *adj* bien definido, nítido; ~**ing** *n* (*in wood*) claro; ~**ing bank** (*BRIT*) *n* cámara de compensación; ~**ly** *adv* claramente; (*evidently*) sin duda; ~**way** (*BRIT*) *n* carretera donde no se puede parar

cleaver ['kliːvə*] *n* cuchilla (de carnicero)

clef [klef] *n* (*MUS*) clave *f*

cleft [kleft] *n* (*in rock*) grieta, hendedura

clench [klentʃ] *vt* apretar, cerrar

clergy ['klɜːdʒɪ] *n* clero; ~**man** *n* clérigo

clerical ['klerɪkəl] *adj* de oficina; (*REL*) clerical

clerk [klɑːk, (*US*) klɜːrk] *n* (*BRIT*) oficinista *m/f*; (*US*) dependiente/a *m/f*, vendedor(a) *m/f*

clever ['klevə*] *adj* (*intelligent*) inteligente, listo; (*skilful*) hábil; (*device, arrangement*) ingenioso

click [klɪk] *vt* (*tongue*) chasquear; (*heels*) taconear

client ['klaɪənt] *n* cliente *m/f*

cliff [klɪf] *n* acantilado

climate ['klaɪmɪt] *n* clima *m*

climax ['klaɪmæks] *n* (*of battle, career*) apogeo; (*of film, book*) punto culminante; (*sexual*) orgasmo

climb [klaɪm] *vi* subir; (*plant*) trepar; (*move with effort*): **to ~ over a wall/into a car** trepar a una tapia/subir a un coche ♦ *vt* (*stairs*) subir; (*tree*) trepar a; (*mountain*) escalar ♦ *n* subida; **~-down** *n* vuelta atrás; **~er** *n* alpinista *m/f* (*SP*), andinista *m/f* (*AM*); **~ing** *n* alpinismo (*SP*), andinismo (*AM*)

clinch [klɪntʃ] *vt* (*deal*) cerrar; (*argument*) remachar

cling [klɪŋ] (*pt, pp* **clung**) *vi*: **to ~ to** agarrarse a; (*clothes*) pegarse a

clinic ['klɪnɪk] *n* clínica; **~al** *adj* clínico; (*fig*) frío

clink [klɪŋk] *vi* tintinar

clip [klɪp] *n* (*for hair*) horquilla; (*also: paper* ~) sujetapapeles *m inv*, clip *m*; (*TV, CINEMA*) fragmento ♦ *vt* (*cut*) cortar; (*also: ~ together*) unir; **~pers** *npl* (*for gardening*) tijeras *fpl*; **~ping** *n* (*newspaper*) recorte *m*

clique [kliːk] *n* camarilla

cloak [kləʊk] *n* capa, manto ♦ *vt* (*fig*) encubrir, disimular; **~room** *n* guardarropa; (*BRIT: WC*) lavabo (*SP*), aseos *mpl* (*SP*), baño (*AM*)

clock [klɒk] *n* reloj *m*; **~ in** *or* **on** *vi* fichar, picar; **~ off** *or* **out** *vi* fichar *or* picar la salida; **~wise** *adv* en el sentido de las agujas del reloj; **~work** *n* aparato de relojería ♦ *adj* (*toy*) de cuerda

clog [klɒg] *n* zueco, chanclo ♦ *vt* atascar ♦ *vi* (*also: ~ up*) atascarse

cloister ['klɔɪstə*] *n* claustro

close¹ [kləʊs] *adj* (*near*): **~ (to)** cerca (de); (*friend*) íntimo; (*connection*) estrecho; (*examination*) detallado, minucioso; (*weather*) bochornoso; **to have a ~ shave** (*fig*) escaparse por un pelo ♦ *adv* cerca; **~ by**, **~ at hand** muy cerca; **~ to** *prep* cerca de

close² [kləʊz] *vt* (*shut*) cerrar; (*end*) concluir, terminar ♦ *vi* (*shop etc*) cerrarse; (*end*) concluirse, terminarse ♦ *n* (*end*) fin *m*, final *m*, conclusión *f*; **~ down** *vi* cerrarse definitivamente; **~d** *adj* (*shop etc*) cerrado; **~d shop** *n* taller *m* gremial

close-knit [kləʊs'nɪt] *adj* (*fig*) muy unido

closely ['kləʊslɪ] *adv* (*study*) con detalle; (*watch*) de cerca; (*resemble*) estrechamente

closet ['klɒzɪt] *n* armario

close-up ['kləʊsʌp] *n* primer plano

closure ['kləʊʒə*] *n* cierre *m*

clot [klɒt] *n* (*gen: blood* ~) coágulo; (*inf: idiot*) imbécil *m/f* ♦ *vi* (*blood*) coagularse

cloth [klɒθ] *n* (*material*) tela, paño; (*rag*) trapo

clothe [kləʊð] *vt* vestir; **~s** *npl* ropa; **~s brush** *n* cepillo (para la ropa); **~s line** *n* cuerda (para tender la ropa); **~s peg** (*US* **~s pin**) *n* pinza

clothing ['kləʊðɪŋ] *n* = **clothes**

cloud [klaud] *n* nube *f*; **~burst** *n* aguacero; **~y** *adj* nublado, nubloso; (*liquid*) turbio

clout [klaut] *vt* dar un tortazo a

clove [kləʊv] *n* clavo; **~ of garlic** diente *m* de ajo

clover ['kləʊvə*] *n* trébol *m*

clown [klaun] *n* payaso ♦ *vi* (*also: ~ about*, **~ around**) hacer el payaso

cloying ['klɔɪɪŋ] *adj* empalagoso

club [klʌb] *n* (*society*) club *m*; (*weapon*) porra, cachiporra; (*also: golf ~*) palo ♦ *vt* aporrear ♦ *vi*: **to ~ together** (*for gift*) comprar entre todos; **~s** *npl* (*CARDS*) tréboles *mpl*; **~ car** (*US*) *n* (*RAIL*) coche *m* salón; **~ class** *n* (*AVIAT*) clase *f* preferente; **~house** *n* local social, sobre todo en *clubs deportivos*

cluck [klʌk] *vi* cloquear
clue [kluː] *n* pista; (*in crosswords*) indicación *f*; **I haven't a ~** no tengo ni idea
clump [klʌmp] *n* (*of trees*) grupo
clumsy ['klʌmzɪ] *adj* (*person*) torpe, desmañado; (*tool*) difícil de manejar; (*movement*) desgarbado
clung [klʌŋ] *pt, pp* of **cling**
cluster ['klʌstə*] *n* grupo ♦ *vi* agruparse, apiñarse
clutch [klʌtʃ] *n* (*AUT*) embrague *m*; (*grasp*): **~es** garras *fpl* ♦ *vt* asir; agarrar
clutter ['klʌtə*] *vt* atestar
cm *abbr* (= *centimetre*) cm
CND *n abbr* (= *Campaign for Nuclear Disarmament*) plataforma pro desarme nuclear
Co. *abbr* = **county; company**
c/o *abbr* (= *care of*) c/a, a/c
coach [kəutʃ] *n* autocar *m* (*SP*), coche *m* de línea; (*horse-drawn*) coche *m*; (*of train*) vagón *m*, coche *m*; (*SPORT*) entrenador(a) *m/f*, instructor(a) *m/f*; (*tutor*) profesor(a) *m/f* particular ♦ *vt* (*SPORT*) entrenar; (*student*) preparar, enseñar; **~ trip** *n* excursión *f* en autocar
coal [kəul] *n* carbón *m*; **~ face** *n* frente *m* de carbón; **~field** *n* yacimiento de carbón
coalition [kəuə'lɪʃən] *n* coalición *f*
coal: ~man *n* carbonero; **~ merchant** *n* = **~man**; **~mine** ['kəulmaɪn] *n* mina de carbón
coarse [kɔːs] *adj* basto, burdo; (*vulgar*) grosero, ordinario
coast [kəust] *n* costa, litoral *m* ♦ *vi* (*AUT*) ir en punto muerto; **~al** *adj* costero, costanero; **~guard** *n* guardacostas *m inv*; **~line** *n* litoral *m*
coat [kəut] *n* abrigo; (*of animal*) pelaje *m*, lana; (*of paint*) mano *f*, capa ♦ *vt* cubrir, revestir; **~ of arms** *n* escudo de armas; **~ hanger** *n* percha (*SP*), gancho (*AM*); **~ing** *n* capa, baño
coax [kəuks] *vt* engatusar
cob [kɔb] *n see* **corn**
cobbler ['kɔblə] *n* zapatero (remendón)
cobbles ['kɔblz] *npl*, **cobblestones**

['kɔblstəunz] *npl* adoquines *mpl*
cobweb ['kɔbwɛb] *n* telaraña
cock [kɔk] *n* (*rooster*) gallo; (*male bird*) macho ♦ *vt* (*gun*) amartillar; **~erel** *n* gallito; **~eyed** *adj* (*idea*) disparatado
cockle ['kɔkl] *n* berberecho
cockney ['kɔknɪ] *n* habitante de ciertos barrios de Londres
cockpit ['kɔkpɪt] *n* cabina
cockroach ['kɔkrəutʃ] *n* cucaracha
cocktail ['kɔkteɪl] *n* coctel *m*, cóctel *m*; **~ cabinet** *n* mueble-bar *m*; **~ party** *n* coctel *m*, cóctel *m*
cocoa ['kəukəu] *n* cacao; (*drink*) chocolate *m*
coconut ['kəukənʌt] *n* coco
cocoon [kə'kuːn] *n* (*ZOOL*) capullo
cod [kɔd] *n* bacalao
C.O.D. *abbr* (= *cash on delivery*) C.A.E
code [kəud] *n* código; (*cipher*) clave *f*; (*dialling ~*) prefijo; (*post ~*) código postal
cod-liver oil ['kɔdlɪvər–] *n* aceite *m* de hígado de bacalao
coercion [kəu'əːʃən] *n* coacción *f*
coffee ['kɔfɪ] *n* café *m*; **~ bar** (*BRIT*) *n* cafetería; **~ bean** *n* grano de café; **~ break** *n* descanso (para tomar café); **~pot** *n* cafetera; **~ table** *n* mesita (para servir el café)
coffin ['kɔfɪn] *n* ataúd *m*
cog [kɔg] *n* (*wheel*) rueda dentada; (*tooth*) diente *m*
cogent ['kəudʒənt] *adj* convincente
cognac ['kɔnjæk] *n* coñac *m*
coil [kɔɪl] *n* rollo; (*ELEC*) bobina, carrete *m*; (*contraceptive*) espiral *f* ♦ *vt* enrollar
coin [kɔɪn] *n* moneda ♦ *vt* (*word*) inventar, idear; **~age** *n* moneda; **~-box** (*BRIT*) *n* cabina telefónica
coincide [kəuɪn'saɪd] *vi* coincidir; (*agree*) estar de acuerdo; **coincidence** [kəu'ɪnsɪdəns] *n* casualidad *f*
coke [kəuk] *n* (*coal*) coque *m*
Coke [kəuk] ® *n* Coca Cola ®
colander ['kɔləndə*] *n* colador *m*, escurridor *m*
cold [kəuld] *adj* frío ♦ *n* frío; (*MED*) resfriado; **it's ~** hace frío; **to be ~** (*person*) tener frío; **to catch ~** enfriarse;

to catch a ~ resfriarse, acatarrarse; **in ~ blood** a sangre fría; ~**-shoulder** *vt* dar *or* volver la espalda a; ~ **sore** *n* herpes *mpl or fpl*

coleslaw ['kəulslɔ:] *n* especie de ensalada de col

colic ['kɒlɪk] *n* cólico

collapse [kə'læps] *vi* hundirse, derrumbarse; (*MED*) sufrir un colapso ♦ *n* hundimiento, derrumbamiento; (*MED*) colapso; **collapsible** *adj* plegable

collar ['kɒlə*] *n* (*of coat, shirt*) cuello; (*of dog etc*) collar; ~**bone** *n* clavícula

collateral [kɒ'lætərəl] *n* garantía colateral

colleague ['kɒli:g] *n* colega *m/f*

collect [kə'lɛkt] *vt* (*litter, mail etc*) recoger; (*as a hobby*) coleccionar; (*BRIT: call and pick up*) recoger; (*debts, subscriptions etc*) recaudar ♦ *vi* reunirse; (*dust*) acumularse; **to call ~** (*US: TEL*) llamar a cobro revertido; ~**ion** [kə'lɛkʃən] *n* colección *f*; (*of mail, for charity*) recogida

collector [kə'lɛktə*] *n* coleccionista *m/f*

college ['kɒlɪdʒ] *n* colegio mayor; (*of agriculture, technology*) escuela universitaria

collide [kə'laɪd] *vi* chocar

collie ['kɒlɪ] *n* perro pastor escocés, collie *m*

colliery ['kɒlɪərɪ] (*BRIT*) *n* mina de carbón

collision [kə'lɪʒən] *n* choque *m*

colloquial [kə'ləukwɪəl] *adj* familiar, coloquial

collusion [kə'lu:ʒən] *n* confabulación *f*, connivencia

Colombia [kə'lɒmbɪə] *n* Colombia; ~**n** *adj, n* colombiano/a

colon ['kəulən] *n* (*sign*) dos puntos; (*MED*) colon *m*

colonel ['kə:nl] *n* coronel *m*

colonial [kə'ləunɪəl] *adj* colonial

colony ['kɒlənɪ] *n* colonia

colour ['kʌlə*] (*US* **color**) *n* color *m* ♦ *vt* color(e)ar; (*dye*) teñir; (*fig: account*) adornar; (: *judgement*) distorsionar ♦ *vi* (*blush*) sonrojarse; ~**s** *npl* (*of party, club*) colores *mpl*; **in ~** en color; ~ **in** *vt* colorear; ~ **bar** *n* segregación *f* racial;

~**-blind** *adj* daltónico; ~**ed** *adj* de color; (*photo*) en color; ~ **film** *n* película en color; ~**ful** *adj* lleno de color; (*story*) fantástico; (*person*) excéntrico; ~**ing** *n* (*complexion*) tez *f*; (*in food*) colorante *m*; ~ **scheme** *n* combinación *f* de colores; ~ **television** *n* televisión *f* en color

colt [kəult] *n* potro

column ['kɒləm] *n* columna; ~**ist** ['kɒləmnɪst] *n* columnista *m/f*

coma ['kəumə] *n* coma *m*

comb [kəum] *n* peine *m*; (*ornamental*) peineta ♦ *vt* (*hair*) peinar; (*area*) registrar a fondo

combat ['kɒmbæt] *n* combate *m* ♦ *vt* combatir

combination [kɒmbɪ'neɪʃən] *n* combinación *f*

combine [*vb* kəm'baɪn, *n* 'kɒmbaɪn] *vt* combinar; (*qualities*) reunir ♦ *vi* combinarse ♦ *n* (*ECON*) cartel *m*; ~ (**harvester**) *n* cosechadora

---

KEYWORD

come [kʌm] (*pt* **came**, *pp* **come**) *vi* **1** (*movement towards*) venir; **to ~ running** venir corriendo

2 (*arrive*) llegar; **he's ~ here to work** ha venido aquí para trabajar; **to ~ home** volver a casa

3 (*reach*): **to ~ to** llegar a; **the bill came to £40** la cuenta ascendía a cuarenta libras

4 (*occur*): **an idea came to me** se me ocurrió una idea

5 (*be, become*): **to ~ loose/undone** *etc* aflojarse/desabrocharse, desatarse *etc*; **I've ~ to like him** por fin ha llegado a gustarme

come about *vi* suceder, ocurrir

come across *vt fus* (*person*) topar con; (*thing*) dar con

come away *vi* (*leave*) marcharse; (*become detached*) desprenderse

come back *vi* (*return*) volver

come by *vt fus* (*acquire*) conseguir

come down *vi* (*price*) bajar; (*tree, building*) ser derribado

come forward *vi* presentarse

come from *vt fus* (*place, source*) ser de
come in *vi* (*visitor*) entrar; (*train, report*) llegar; (*fashion*) ponerse de moda; (*on deal etc*) entrar
come in for *vt fus* (*criticism etc*) recibir
come into *vt fus* (*money*) heredar; (*be involved*) tener que ver con; **to ~ into fashion** ponerse de moda
come off *vi* (*button*) soltarse, desprenderse; (*attempt*) salir bien
come on *vi* (*pupil*) progresar; (*work, project*) desarrollarse; (*lights*) encenderse; (*electricity*) volver; **~ on!** ¡vamos!
come out *vi* (*fact*) salir a la luz; (*book, sun*) salir; (*stain*) quitarse
come round *vi* (*after faint, operation*) volver en sí
come to *vi* (*wake*) volver en sí
come up *vi* (*sun*) salir; (*problem*) surgir; (*event*) aproximarse; (*in conversation*) mencionarse
come up against *vt fus* (*resistance etc*) tropezar con
come up with *vt fus* (*idea*) sugerir; (*money*) conseguir
come upon *vt fus* (*find*) dar con

comeback ['kʌmbæk] *n*: **to make a ~** (*THEATRE*) volver a las tablas
comedian [kə'miːdɪən] *n* cómico; **comedienne** [-'ɛn] *n* cómica
comedy ['kɒmɪdɪ] *n* comedia; (*humour*) comicidad *f*
comet ['kɒmɪt] *n* cometa *m*
comeuppance [kʌm'ʌpəns] *n*: **to get one's ~** llevar su merecido
comfort ['kʌmfət] *n* bienestar *m*; (*relief*) alivio ♦ *vt* consolar; **~s** *npl* (*of home etc*) comodidades *fpl*; **~able** *adj* cómodo; (*financially*) acomodado; (*easy*) fácil; **~ably** *adv* (*sit*) cómodamente; (*live*) holgadamente; **~ station** (*US*) *n* servicios *mpl*
comic ['kɒmɪk] *adj* (*also: ~al*) cómico ♦ *n* (*comedian*) cómico; (*BRIT: for children*) tebeo; (*BRIT: for adults*) comic *m*; **~ strip** *n* tira cómica
coming ['kʌmɪŋ] *n* venida, llegada ♦ *adj* que viene; **~(s) and going(s)** *n(pl)* ir y

venir *m*, ajetreo
comma ['kɒmə] *n* coma
command [kə'mɑːnd] *n* orden *f*, mandato; (*MIL: authority*) mando; (*mastery*) dominio ♦ *vt* (*troops*) mandar; (*give orders to*): **to ~ sb to do** mandar *or* ordenar a uno hacer; **~eer** [kɒmən'dɪə*] *vt* requisar; **~er** *n* (*MIL*) comandante *m/f*, jefe/a *m/f*; **~ment** *n* (*REL*) mandamiento
commemorate [kə'mɛməreɪt] *vt* conmemorar
commence [kə'mɛns] *vt*, *vi* comenzar, empezar
commend [kə'mɛnd] *vt* elogiar, alabar; (*recommend*) recomendar
commensurate [kə'mɛnʃərɪt] *adj*: **~ with** en proporción a, que corresponde a
comment ['kɒmɛnt] *n* comentario ♦ *vi*: **to ~ on** hacer comentarios sobre; **"no ~"** (*written*) "sin comentarios"; (*spoken*) "no tengo nada que decir"; **~ary** ['kɒməntərɪ] *n* comentario; **~ator** ['kɒmənteɪtə*] *n* comentarista *m/f*
commerce ['kɒmɔːs] *n* comercio
commercial [kə'mɔːʃəl] *adj* comercial ♦ *n* (*TV, RADIO*) anuncio
commiserate [kə'mɪzəreɪt] *vi*: **to ~ with** compadecerse de, condolerse de
commission [kə'mɪʃən] *n* (*committee, fee*) comisión *f* ♦ *vt* (*work of art*) encargar; **out of ~** fuera de servicio; **~aire** [kəmɪʃə'nɛə*] (*BRIT*) *n* portero; **~er** *n* (*POLICE*) comisario de policía
commit [kə'mɪt] *vt* (*act*) cometer; (*resources*) dedicar; (*to sb's care*) entregar; **to ~ o.s. (to do)** comprometerse (a hacer); **to ~ suicide** suicidarse; **~ment** *n* compromiso; (*to ideology etc*) entrega
committee [kə'mɪtɪ] *n* comité *m*
commodity [kə'mɒdɪtɪ] *n* mercancía
common ['kɒmən] *adj* común; (*pej*) ordinario ♦ *n* campo común; **the C~s** *npl* (*BRIT*) (la Cámara de) los Comunes *mpl*; **in ~** en común; **~er** *n* plebeyo; **~ law** *n* ley *f* consuetudinaria; **~ly** *adv* comúnmente; **C~ Market** *n* Mercado Común; **~place** *adj* de lo más común; **~room** *n* sala común; **~ sense** *n* sentido

común; the C~wealth *n* la Commonwealth
commotion [kə'məuʃən] *n* tumulto,
confusión *f*
commune [*n* 'kɔmjuːn, *vb* kə'mjuːn] *n*
(*group*) comuna ♦ *vi*: to ~ with
comulgar *or* conversar con
communicate [kə'mjuːnɪkeɪt] *vt*
comunicar ♦ *vi*: to ~ to (with) comunicarse
(con); (*in writing*) estar en contacto (con)
communication [kəmjuːnɪ'keɪʃən] *n*
comunicación *f*; ~ cord (BRIT) *n* timbre *m*
de alarma
communion [kə'mjuːnɪən] *n* (*also: Holy*
C~) comunión *f*
communiqué [kə'mjuːnɪkeɪ] *n* comunicado, parte *f*
communism ['kɔmjunɪzəm] *n*
comunismo; communist *adj, n*
comunista *m/f*
community [kə'mjuːnɪtɪ] *n* comunidad *f*;
(*large group*) colectividad *f*; ~ centre *n*
centro social; ~ chest (US) *n* arca
comunitaria, fondo común; ~ home
(BRIT) *n* correccional *m*
commutation ticket [kɔmjuː'teɪʃən-] (US)
n billete *m* de abono
commute [kə'mjuːt] *vi* viajar a diario de
la casa al trabajo ♦ *vt* conmutar; ~r *n*
persona (que viaja ... *see vi*)
compact [*adj* kəm'pækt, *n* 'kɔmpækt] *adj*
compacto ♦ *n* (*also: powder* ~) polvera; ~
disc *n* compact disc *m*; ~ disc player *n*
reproductor *m* de disco compacto,
compact disc *m*
companion [kəm'pænɪən] *n* compañero/
a; ~ship *n* compañerismo
company ['kʌmpənɪ] *n* compañía; (COMM)
sociedad *f*, compañía; to keep sb ~
acompañar a uno; ~ secretary (BRIT) *n*
secretario/a de compañía
comparative [kəm'pærətɪv] *adj* relativo;
(*study*) comparativo; ~ly *adv* (*relatively*)
relativamente
compare [kəm'pɛə*] *vt*: to ~ sth/sb
with/to comparar algo/a uno con ♦ *vi*:
to ~ (with) compararse (con);
comparison [-'pærɪsn] *n* comparación *f*
compartment [kəm'pɑːtmənt] *n* (*also:*

RAIL) compartim(i)ento
compass ['kʌmpəs] *n* brújula; ~es *npl*
(MATH) compás *m*
compassion [kəm'pæʃən] *n* compasión *f*;
~ate *adj* compasivo
compatible [kəm'pætɪbl] *adj* compatible
compel [kəm'pɛl] *vt* obligar; ~ling *adj*
(*fig: argument*) convincente
compensate ['kɔmpənseɪt] *vt* compensar
♦ *vi*: to ~ for compensar; compensation
[-'seɪʃən] *n* (*for loss*) indemnización *f*
compère ['kɔmpɛə*] *n* presentador *m*
compete [kəm'piːt] *vi* (*take part*) tomar
parte, concurrir; (*vie with*): to ~ with
competir con, hacer competencia a
competence ['kɔmpɪtəns] *n* capacidad *f*,
aptitud *f*
competent ['kɔmpɪtənt] *adj* competente,
capaz
competition [kɔmpɪ'tɪʃən] *n* (*contest*)
concurso; (*rivalry*) competencia
competitive [kəm'pɛtɪtɪv] *adj* (ECON,
SPORT) competitivo
competitor [kəm'pɛtɪtə*] *n* (*rival*)
competidor(a) *m/f*; (*participant*)
concursante *m/f*
compile [kəm'paɪl] *vt* compilar
complacency [kəm'pleɪsnsɪ] *n*
autosatisfacción *f*
complacent [kəm'pleɪsənt] *adj*
autocomplaciente
complain [kəm'pleɪn] *vi* quejarse; (COMM)
reclamar; ~t *n* queja; reclamación *f*;
(MED) enfermedad *f*
complement [*n* 'kɔmplɪmənt, *vb*
'kɔmplɪmɛnt] *n* complemento; (*esp of ship's
crew*) dotación *f* ♦ *vt* (*enhance*) comple-
mentar; ~ary [kɔmplɪ'mɛntərɪ] *adj*
complementario
complete [kəm'pliːt] *adj* (*full*) completo;
(*finished*) acabado ♦ *vt* (*fulfil*) completar;
(*finish*) acabar; (*a form*) llenar; ~ly *adv*
completamente; completion [-'pliːʃən] *n*
terminación *f*; (*of contract*) realización *f*
complex ['kɔmplɛks] *adj, n* complejo
complexion [kəm'plɛkʃən] *n* (*of face*) tez
f, cutis *m*
compliance [kəm'plaɪəns] *n* (*submission*)
sumisión *f*; (*agreement*) conformidad *f*;

in ~ with de acuerdo con

complicate ['kɔmplɪkeɪt] *vt* complicar; ~d *adj* complicado; **complication** [-'keɪʃən] *n* complicación *f*

complicity [kəm'plɪsɪtɪ] *n* complicidad *f*

compliment ['kɔmplɪmənt] *n* (*formal*) cumplido ♦ *vt* felicitar; ~s *npl* (*regards*) saludos *mpl*; **to pay sb a ~** hacer cumplidos a uno; ~**ary** [-'mentərɪ] *adj* lisonjero; (*free*) de favor

comply [kəm'plaɪ] *vi*: **to ~ with** cumplir con

component [kəm'pəʊnənt] *adj* componente ♦ *n* (*TECH*) pieza

compose [kəm'pəʊz] *vt*: **to be ~d of** componerse de; (*music etc*) componer; **to ~ o.s.** tranquilizarse; ~**d** *adj* sosegado; ~**r** *n* (*MUS*) compositor(a) *m/f*; **composition** [kɔmpə'zɪʃən] *n* composición *f*

compost ['kɔmpɔst] *n* abono (vegetal)

composure [kəm'pəʊʒə*] *n* serenidad *f*, calma

compound ['kɔmpaʊnd] *n* (*CHEM*) compuesto; (*LING*) palabra compuesta; (*enclosure*) recinto ♦ *adj* compuesto; (*fracture*) complicado

comprehend [kɔmprɪ'hend] *vt* comprender; **comprehension** [-'henʃən] *n* comprensión *f*

comprehensive [kɔmprɪ'hensɪv] *adj* exhaustivo; (*INSURANCE*) contra todo riesgo; ~ (**school**) *n* centro estatal de enseñanza secundaria; ≈ Instituto Nacional de Bachillerato (*SP*)

compress [*vb* kəm'pres, *n* 'kɔmpres] *vt* comprimir; (*information*) condensar ♦ *n* (*MED*) compresa

comprise [kəm'praɪz] *vt* (*also*: **be ~d of**) comprender, constar de; (*constitute*) constituir

compromise ['kɔmprəmaɪz] *n* (*agreement*) arreglo ♦ *vt* comprometer ♦ *vi* transigir

compulsion [kəm'pʌlʃən] *n* compulsión *f*; (*force*) obligación *f*

compulsive [kəm'pʌlsɪv] *adj* compulsivo; (*viewing, reading*) obligado

compulsory [kəm'pʌlsərɪ] *adj* obligatorio

computer [kəm'pjuːtə*] *n* ordenador *m*, computador *m*, computadora *f*; ~ **game** *n*

juego para ordenador; ~**ize** *vt* (*data*) computerizar; (*system*) informatizar; ~ **programmer** *n* programador(a) *m/f*; ~ **programming** *n* programación *f*; ~ **science** *n* informática; **computing** [kəm'pjuːtɪŋ] *n* (*activity, science*) informática

comrade ['kɔmrɪd] *n* (*POL, MIL*) camarada; (*friend*) compañero/a; ~**ship** *n* camaradería, compañerismo

con [kɔn] *vt* (*deceive*) engañar; (*cheat*) estafar ♦ *n* estafa

conceal [kən'siːl] *vt* ocultar

conceit [kən'siːt] *n* presunción *f*; ~**ed** *adj* presumido

conceivable [kən'siːvəbl] *adj* concebible

conceive [kən'siːv] *vt*, *vi* concebir

concentrate ['kɔnsəntreɪt] *vi* concentrarse ♦ *vt* concentrar

concentration [kɔnsən'treɪʃən] *n* concentración *f*

concept ['kɔnsept] *n* concepto

conception [kən'sepʃən] *n* (*idea*) concepto, idea; (*BIOL*) concepción *f*

concern [kən'sɜːn] *n* (*matter*) asunto; (*COMM*) empresa; (*anxiety*) preocupación *f* ♦ *vt* (*worry*) preocupar; (*involve*) afectar; (*relate to*) tener que ver con; **to be ~ed (about)** interesarse (por), preocuparse (por); ~**ing** *prep* sobre, acerca de

concert ['kɔnsət] *n* concierto; ~**ed** [kən'sɜːtəd] *adj* (*efforts etc*) concertado; ~ **hall** *n* sala de conciertos

concertina [kɔnsə'tiːnə] *n* concertina

concerto [kən'tʃɜːtəʊ] *n* concierto

concession [kən'seʃən] *n* concesión *f*; **tax ~** privilegio fiscal

concise [kən'saɪs] *adj* conciso

conclude [kən'kluːd] *vt* concluir; (*treaty etc*) firmar; (*agreement*) llegar a; (*decide*) llegar a la conclusión de; **conclusion** [-'kluːʒən] *n* conclusión *f*; firma; **conclusive** [-'kluːsɪv] *adj* decisivo, concluyente

concoct [kən'kɔkt] *vt* confeccionar; (*plot*) tramar; ~**ion** [-'kɔkʃən] *n* mezcla

concourse ['kɔŋkɔːs] *n* vestíbulo

concrete ['kɔnkriːt] *n* hormigón *m* ♦ *adj* de hormigón; (*fig*) concreto

concur [kən'kɜː*] *vi* estar de acuerdo,

asentir

concurrently [kən'kʌrntlɪ] *adv* al mismo
tiempo

concussion [kən'kʌʃən] *n* conmoción *f*
cerebral

condemn [kən'dɛm] *vt* condenar; (*building*) declarar en ruina; **~ation**
[kɒndɛm'neɪʃən] *n* condena

condense [kən'dɛns] *vi* condensarse ♦ *vt*
condensar, abreviar; **~d milk** *n* leche *f*
condensada

condescending [kɒndɪ'sɛndɪŋ] *adj*
condescendiente

condition [kən'dɪʃən] *n* condición *f*,
estado; (*requirement*) condición *f* ♦ *vt*
condicionar; **on ~ that** a condición (de)
que; **~al** *adj* condicional; **~er** *n* suavizante

condolences [kən'dəʊlənsɪz] *npl* pésame
m

condom ['kɒndəm] *n* condón *m*

condone [kən'dəʊn] *vt* condonar

conducive [kən'djuːsɪv] *adj*: **~ to**
conducente a

conduct [*n* 'kɒndʌkt, *vb* kən'dʌkt] *n*
conducta, comportamiento ♦ *vt* (*lead*)
conducir; (*manage*) llevar a cabo, dirigir;
(*MUS*) dirigir; **to ~ o.s.** comportarse; **~ed
tour** (*BRIT*) *n* visita acompañada; **~or** *n*
(*of orchestra*) director *m*; (*US: on train*)
revisor(a) *m/f*; (*on bus*) cobrador *m*;
(*ELEC*) conductor *m*; **~ress** *n* (*on bus*)
cobradora

cone [kəʊn] *n* cono; (*pine* ~) piña; (*on
road*) pivote *m*; (*for ice-cream*) cucurucho

confectioner [kən'fɛkʃənə*] *n* repostero/
a; **~'s** (*shop*) *n* confitería; **~y** *n* dulces
mpl

confer [kən'fɜː*] *vt*: **to ~ sth on** otorgar
algo a ♦ *vi* conferenciar

conference ['kɒnfərns] *n* (*meeting*)
reunión *f*; (*convention*) congreso

confess [kən'fɛs] *vt* confesar ♦ *vi*
admitir; **~ion** [-'fɛʃən] *n* confesión *f*

confetti [kən'fɛtɪ] *n* confeti *m*

confide [kən'faɪd] *vi*: **to ~ in** confiar en

confidence ['kɒnfɪdns] *n* (*also: self* ~)
confianza; (*secret*) confidencia; **in ~**
(*speak, write*) en confianza; **~ trick** *n*

timo; **confident** *adj* seguro de sí mismo;
(*certain*) seguro; **confidential**
[kɒnfɪ'dɛnʃəl] *adj* confidencial

confine [kən'faɪn] *vt* (*limit*) limitar; (*shut
up*) encerrar; **~d** *adj* (*space*) reducido;
~ment *n* (*prison*) prisión *f*; **~s** ['kɒnfaɪnz]
npl confines *mpl*

confirm [kən'fɜːm] *vt* confirmar; **~ation**
[kɒnfə'meɪʃən] *n* confirmación *f*; **~ed** *adj*
empedernido

confiscate ['kɒnfɪskeɪt] *vt* confiscar

conflict [*n* 'kɒnflɪkt, *vb* kən'flɪkt] *n* conflicto
♦ *vi* (*opinions*) chocar; **~ing** *adj*
contradictorio

conform [kən'fɔːm] *vi* conformarse; **to ~**
to ajustarse a

confound [kən'faʊnd] *vt* confundir

confront [kən'frʌnt] *vt* (*problems*) hacer
frente a; (*enemy, danger*) enfrentarse
con; **~ation** [kɒnfrən'teɪʃən] *n*
enfrentamiento

confuse [kən'fjuːz] *vt* (*perplex*) aturdir,
desconcertar; (*mix up*) confundir;
(*complicate*) complicar; **~d** *adj* confuso;
(*person*) perplejo; **confusing** *adj* confuso;
confusion [-'fjuːʒən] *n* confusión *f*

congeal [kən'dʒiːl] *vi* (*blood*) coagularse;
(*sauce etc*) cuajarse

congenial [kən'dʒiːnɪəl] *adj* agradable

congenital [kən'dʒɛnɪtl] *adj* congénito

congested [kən'dʒɛstɪd] *adj*
congestionado

congestion [kən'dʒɛstʃən] *n* congestión *f*

conglomerate [kən'glɒmərət] *n* (*COMM,
GEO*) conglomerado

congratulate [kən'grætjuleɪt] *vt*: **to ~ sb
(on)** felicitar a uno (por); **congratulations** [-'leɪʃənz] *npl* felicitaciones *fpl*; **~!**
¡enhorabuena!

congregate ['kɒngrɪgeɪt] *vi* congregarse;
congregation [-'geɪʃən] *n* (*of a church*)
feligreses *mpl*

congress ['kɒngrɛs] *n* congreso; (*US*): **C~**
Congreso; **~man** (*US*) *n* miembro del
Congreso

conifer ['kɒnɪfə*] *n* conífera

conjecture [kən'dʒɛktʃə*] *n* conjetura

conjugal ['kɒndʒugl] *adj* conyugal

conjugate ['kɒndʒugeɪt] *vt* conjugar

conjunctivitis [kəndʒʌŋktɪˈvaɪtɪs] *n*
conjuntivitis *f*

conjure [ˈkʌndʒə*] *vi* hacer juegos de
manos; ~ **up** *vt* (*ghost, spirit*) hacer
aparecer; (*memories*) evocar; ~**r** *n*
ilusionista *m/f*

conk out [kɔŋk-] (*inf*) *vi* averiarse

con man [ˈkɔn-] *n* estafador *m*

connect [kəˈnekt] *vt* juntar, unir; (*ELEC*)
conectar; (*TEL: subscriber*) poner;
(: *caller*) poner al habla; (*fig*) relacionar,
asociar ♦ *vi*: **to ~ with** (*train*) enlazar
con; **to be ~ed with** (*associated*) estar
relacionado con; ~**ion** [-ʃən] *n* juntura,
unión *f*; (*ELEC*) conexión *f*; (*RAIL*) enlace
m; (*TEL*) conexión *f*; (*fig*) relación *f*

connive [kəˈnaɪv] *vi*: **to ~ at** hacer la
vista gorda a

connoisseur [kɔnɪˈsə*] *n* experto/a,
entendido/a

conquer [ˈkɔŋkə*] *vt* (*territory*) conquistar; (*enemy, feelings*) vencer; ~**or** *n*
conquistador *m*

conquest [ˈkɔŋkwest] *n* conquista

cons [kɔnz] *npl see* **convenience; pro**

conscience [ˈkɔnʃəns] *n* conciencia

conscientious [kɔnʃɪˈenʃəs] *adj*
concienzudo; (*objection*) de conciencia

conscious [ˈkɔnʃəs] *adj* (*deliberate*)
deliberado; (*awake, aware*) consciente;
~**ness** *n* conciencia; (*MED*) conocimiento

conscript [ˈkɔnskrɪpt] *n* recluta *m*; ~**ion**
[kənˈskrɪpʃən] *n* servicio militar (obligatorio)

consecrate [ˈkɔnsɪkreɪt] *vt* consagrar

consensus [kənˈsensəs] *n* consenso

consent [kənˈsent] *n* consentimiento ♦ *vi*:
to ~ (to) consentir (en)

consequence [ˈkɔnsɪkwəns] *n*
consecuencia; (*significance*) importancia

consequently [ˈkɔnsɪkwəntlɪ] *adv* por
consiguiente

conservation [kɔnsəˈveɪʃən] *n*
conservación *f*

conservative [kənˈsəːvətɪv] *adj* conser-
vador(a); (*estimate etc*) cauteloso; **C~**
(*BRIT*) *adj, n* (*POL*) conservador(a) *m/f*

conservatory [kənˈsəːvətrɪ] *n*
invernadero; (*MUS*) conservatorio

conserve [kənˈsəːv] *vt* conservar ♦ *n*
conserva

consider [kənˈsɪdə*] *vt* considerar; (*take
into account*) tener en cuenta; (*study*)
estudiar, examinar; **to ~ doing sth**
pensar en (la posibilidad de) hacer algo;
~**able** *adj* considerable; ~**ably** *adv*
notablemente

considerate [kənˈsɪdərɪt] *adj* considerado; **consideration** [-ˈreɪʃən] *n* consideración *f*; (*factor*) factor *m*; **to give sth
further consideration** estudiar algo
más a fondo

considering [kənˈsɪdərɪŋ] *prep* teniendo
en cuenta

consign [kənˈsaɪn] *vt*: **to ~ to** (*sth unwanted*) relegar a; (*person*) destinar a; ~**ment**
n envío

consist [kənˈsɪst] *vi*: **to ~ of** consistir en

consistency [kənˈsɪstənsɪ] *n* (*of argument
etc*) coherencia; consecuencia; (*thickness*)
consistencia

consistent [kənˈsɪstənt] *adj* (*person*)
consecuente; (*argument etc*) coherente

consolation [kɔnsəˈleɪʃən] *n* consuelo

console[1] [kənˈsəul] *vt* consolar

console[2] [ˈkɔnsəul] *n* consola

consonant [ˈkɔnsənənt] *n* consonante *f*

consortium [kənˈsɔːtɪəm] *n* consorcio

conspicuous [kənˈspɪkjuəs] *adj* (*visible*)
visible

conspiracy [kənˈspɪrəsɪ] *n* conjura,
complot *m*

conspire [kənˈspaɪə*] *vi* conspirar; (*events
etc*) unirse

constable [ˈkʌnstəbl] (*BRIT*) *n* policía *m/f*;
chief ~ ≈ jefe *m* de policía

constabulary [kənˈstæbjulərɪ] *n* ≈ policía

constant [ˈkɔnstənt] *adj* constante; ~**ly**
adv constantemente

constipated [ˈkɔnstɪpeɪtɪd] *adj* estreñido;
constipation [kɔnstɪˈpeɪʃən] *n*
estreñimiento

constituency [kənˈstɪtjuənsɪ] *n* (*POL: area*)
distrito electoral; (: *electors*) electorado;
constituent [-ənt] *n* (*POL*) elector(a) *m/f*;
(*part*) componente *m*

constitute [ˈkɔnstɪtjuːt] *vt* constituir;
(*make up: whole*) componer

constitution [kɒnstɪˈtjuːʃən] *n*
constitución *f*; ~**al** *adj* constitucional

constraint [kənˈstreɪnt] *n* obligación *f*;
(*limit*) restricción *f*

construct [kənˈstrʌkt] *vt* construir; ~**ion**
[-ʃən] *n* construcción *f*; ~**ive** *adj*
constructivo

construe [kənˈstruː] *vt* interpretar

consul [ˈkɒnsl] *n* cónsul *m/f*; ~**ate**
[ˈkɒnsjulɪt] *n* consulado

consult [kənˈsʌlt] *vt* consultar; ~**ant** *n*
(*BRIT: MED*) especialista *m/f*; (*other
specialist*) asesor(a) *m/f*; ~**ation**
[kɒnsəlˈteɪʃən] *n* consulta; ~**ing room**
(*BRIT*) *n* consultorio

consume [kənˈsjuːm] *vt* (*eat*) comerse;
(*drink*) beberse; (*fire etc, COMM*)
consumir; ~**r** *n* consumidor(a) *m/f*; ~**r
goods** *npl* bienes *mpl* de consumo;
~**rism** *n* consumismo

consummate [ˈkɒnsʌmeɪt] *vt* consumar

consumption [kənˈsʌmpʃən] *n* consumo

cont. *abbr* (= *continued*) sigue

contact [ˈkɒntækt] *n* contacto; (*person*)
contacto; (: *pej*) enchufe *m* ♦ *vt* ponerse
en contacto con; ~ **lenses** *npl* lentes *fpl*
de contacto

contagious [kənˈteɪdʒəs] *adj* contagioso

contain [kənˈteɪn] *vt* contener; **to ~ o.s.**
contenerse; ~**er** *n* recipiente *m*; (*for
shipping etc*) contenedor *m*

contaminate [kənˈtæmɪneɪt] *vt*
contaminar

cont'd *abbr* (= *continued*) sigue

contemplate [ˈkɒntəmpleɪt] *vt*
contemplar; (*reflect upon*) considerar

contemporary [kənˈtɛmpərərɪ] *adj, n*
contemporáneo/a *m/f*

contempt [kənˈtɛmpt] *n* desprecio; ~ **of
court** (*LAW*) desacato (a los tribunales);
~**ible** *adj* despreciable; ~**uous** *adj*
desdeñoso

contend [kənˈtɛnd] *vt* (*argue*) afirmar
♦ *vi*: **to ~ with/for** luchar contra/por;
~**er** *n* (*SPORT*) contendiente *m/f*

content [*adj, vb* kənˈtɛnt, *n* ˈkɒntɛnt] *adj*
(*happy*) contento; (*satisfied*) satisfecho
♦ *vt* contentar; satisfacer ♦ *n* contenido;
~**s** *npl* contenido; (**table of**) ~**s** índice *m*

de materias; ~**ed** *adj* contento; satisfecho

contention [kənˈtɛnʃən] *n* (*assertion*)
aseveración *f*; (*disagreement*) discusión *f*

contentment [kənˈtɛntmənt] *n* contento

contest [*n* ˈkɒntɛst, *vb* kənˈtɛst] *n* lucha;
(*competition*) concurso ♦ *vt* (*dispute*)
impugnar; (*POL*) presentarse como
candidato/a en; ~**ant** [kənˈtɛstənt] *n* concursante *m/f*; (*in fight*) contendiente *m/f*

context [ˈkɒntɛkst] *n* contexto

continent [ˈkɒntɪnənt] *n* continente *m*;
the C~ (*BRIT*) el continente europeo; ~**al**
[-ˈnɛntl] *adj* continental; ~**al quilt** (*BRIT*) *n*
edredón *m*

contingency [kənˈtɪndʒənsɪ] *n*
contingencia

continual [kənˈtɪnjuəl] *adj* continuo; ~**ly**
adv constantemente

continuation [kəntɪnjuˈeɪʃən] *n*
prolongación *f*; (*after interruption*)
reanudación *f*

continue [kənˈtɪnjuː] *vi, vt* seguir,
continuar

continuous [kənˈtɪnjuəs] *adj* continuo; ~
stationery *n* papel *m* continuo

contort [kənˈtɔːt] *vt* retorcer; ~**ion**
[-ˈtɔːʃən] *n* (*movement*) contorsión *f*

contour [ˈkɒntuə*] *n* contorno; (*also: ~
line*) curva de nivel

contraband [ˈkɒntrəbænd] *n* contrabando

contraception [kɒntrəˈsɛpʃən] *n*
contracepción *f*

contraceptive [kɒntrəˈsɛptɪv] *adj, n*
anticonceptivo

contract [*n* ˈkɒntrækt, *vb* kənˈtrækt] *n*
contrato ♦ *vi* (*COMM*): **to ~ to do sth**
comprometerse por contrato a hacer
algo; (*become smaller*) contraerse,
encogerse ♦ *vt* contraer; ~**ion**
[kənˈtrækʃən] *n* contracción *f*; ~**or** *n*
contratista *m/f*

contradict [kɒntrəˈdɪkt] *vt* contradecir;
~**ion** [-ʃən] *n* contradicción *f*; ~**ory** *adj*
contradictorio

contraption [kənˈtræpʃən] (*pej*) *n*
artilugio *m*

contrary[1] [ˈkɒntrərɪ] *adj* contrario ♦ *n* lo
contrario; **on the ~** al contrario; **unless
you hear to the ~** a no ser que le digan

lo contrario

contrary² [kən'trɛərɪ] *adj* (*perverse*) terco

contrast [n 'kɒntrɑːst, vt kən'trɑːst] *n* contraste *m* ♦ *vt* comparar; **in ~ to** en contraste con; **~ing** *adj* (*opinions*) opuesto; (*colours*) que hace contraste

contravene [kɒntrə'viːn] *vt* infringir

contribute [kən'trɪbjuːt] *vi* contribuir ♦ *vt*: **to ~ £10/an article to** contribuir con 10 libras/un artículo a; **to ~ to** (*charity*) donar a; (*newspaper*) escribir para; (*discussion*) intervenir en; **contribution** [kɒntrɪ'bjuːʃən] *n* (*donation*) donativo; (*BRIT: for social security*) cotización *f*; (*to debate*) intervención *f*; (*to journal*) colaboración *f*; **contributor** *n* contribuyente *m/f*; (*to newspaper*) colaborador(a) *m/f*

contrive [kən'traɪv] *vt* (*invent*) idear ♦ *vi*: **to ~ to do** lograr hacer

control [kən'trəʊl] *vt* controlar; (*process etc*) dirigir; (*machinery*) manejar; (*temper*) dominar; (*disease*) contener ♦ *n* control *m*; **~s** *npl* (*of vehicle*) instrumentos *mpl* de mando; (*of radio*) controles *mpl*; (*governmental*) medidas *fpl* de control; **under ~** bajo control; **to be in ~ of** tener el mando de; **the car went out of ~** se perdió el control del coche; **~ panel** *n* tablero de instrumentos; **~ room** *n* sala de mando; **~ tower** *n* (*AVIAT*) torre *f* de control

controversial [kɒntrə'vəːʃl] *adj* polémico

controversy ['kɒntrəvəːsɪ] *n* polémica

conurbation [kɒnəː'beɪʃən] *n* urbanización *f*

convalesce [kɒnvə'lɛs] *vi* convalecer

convector [kən'vɛktə*] *n* calentador *m* de aire

convene [kən'viːn] *vt* convocar ♦ *vi* reunirse

convenience [kən'viːnɪəns] *n* (*easiness*) comodidad *f*; (*suitability*) idoneidad *f*; (*advantage*) ventaja; **at your ~** cuando le sea conveniente; **all modern ~s, all mod cons** (*BRIT*) todo confort

convenient [kən'viːnɪənt] *adj* (*useful*) útil; (*place, time*) conveniente

convent ['kɒnvənt] *n* convento

convention [kən'vɛnʃən] *n* convención *f*; (*meeting*) asamblea; (*agreement*) convenio; **~al** *adj* convencional

converge [kən'vəːdʒ] *vi* convergir; (*people*): **to ~ on** dirigirse todos a

conversant [kən'vəːsnt] *adj*: **to be ~ with** estar al tanto de

conversation [kɒnvə'seɪʃən] *n* conversación *f*; **~al** *adj* familiar; **~al skill** facilidad *f* de palabra

converse [n 'kɒnvəːs, vb kən'vəːs] *n* inversa ♦ *vi* conversar; **~ly** [-'vəːslɪ] *adv* a la inversa

conversion [kən'vəːʃən] *n* conversión *f*

convert [vb kən'vəːt, n 'kɒnvəːt] *vt* (*REL, COMM*) convertir; (*alter*): **to ~ sth into/to** transformar algo en/convertir algo a ♦ *n* converso/a; **~ible** *adj* convertible ♦ *n* descapotable *m*

convey [kən'veɪ] *vt* llevar; (*thanks*) comunicar; (*idea*) expresar; **~or belt** *n* cinta transportadora

convict [vb kən'vɪkt, n 'kɒnvɪkt] *vt* (*find guilty*) declarar culpable a ♦ *n* presidiario/a; **~ion** [-ʃən] *n* condena; (*belief, certainty*) convicción *f*

convince [kən'vɪns] *vt* convencer; **~d** *adj*: **~d of/that** convencido de/de que; **convincing** *adj* convincente

convoluted ['kɒnvəluːtɪd] *adj* (*argument etc*) enrevesado

convoy ['kɒnvɔɪ] *n* convoy *m*

convulse [kən'vʌls] *vt*: **to be ~d with laughter** desternillarse de risa; **convulsion** [-'vʌlʃən] *n* convulsión *f*

coo [kuː] *vi* arrullar

cook [kʊk] *vt* (*stew etc*) guisar; (*meal*) preparar ♦ *vi* cocer; (*person*) cocinar ♦ *n* cocinero/a; **~ book** *n* libro de cocina; **~er** *n* cocina; **~ery** *n* cocina; **~ery book** (*BRIT*) *n* = **~ book**; **~ie** (*US*) *n* galleta; **~ing** *n* cocina

cool [kuːl] *adj* fresco; (*not afraid*) tranquilo; (*unfriendly*) frío ♦ *vt* enfriar ♦ *vi* enfriarse; **~ness** *n* frescura; tranquilidad *f*; (*indifference*) falta de entusiasmo

coop [kuːp] *n* gallinero ♦ *vt*: **to ~ up** (*fig*) encerrar

cooperate [kəʊˈɒpəreɪt] *vi* cooperar, colaborar; **cooperation** [-ˈreɪʃən] *n* cooperación *f*, colaboración *f*; **cooperative** [-rətɪv] *adj* (*business*) cooperativo; (*person*) servicial ♦ *n* cooperativa

coordinate [*vb* kəʊˈɔːdɪneɪt, *n* kəʊˈɔːdɪnət] *vt* coordinar ♦ *n* (*MATH*) coordenada; **~s** *npl* (*clothes*) coordinados *mpl*; **coordination** [-ˈneɪʃən] *n* coordinación *f*

co-ownership [kəʊˈəʊnəʃɪp] *n* copropiedad *f*

cop [kɒp] (*inf*) *n* poli *m* (*SP*), tira *m* (*AM*)

cope [kəʊp] *vi*: **to ~ with** (*problem*) hacer frente a

copious [ˈkəʊpɪəs] *adj* copioso, abundante

copper [ˈkɒpə*] *n* (*metal*) cobre *m*; (*BRIT*: *inf*) poli *m*; **~s** *npl* (*money*) calderilla (*SP*), centavos *mpl* (*AM*)

coppice [ˈkɒpɪs] *n* bosquecillo

copulate [ˈkɒpjʊleɪt] *vi* copularse

copy [ˈkɒpɪ] *n* copia; (*of book etc*) ejemplar *m* ♦ *vt* copiar; **~right** *n* derechos *mpl* de autor

coral [ˈkɒrəl] *n* coral *m*; **~ reef** *n* arrecife *m* (de coral)

cord [kɔːd] *n* cuerda; (*ELEC*) cable *m*; (*fabric*) pana

cordial [ˈkɔːdɪəl] *adj* cordial ♦ *n* cordial *m*

cordon [ˈkɔːdn] *n* cordón *m*; **~ off** *vt* acordonar

corduroy [ˈkɔːdərɔɪ] *n* pana

core [kɔː*] *n* centro, núcleo; (*of fruit*) corazón *m*; (*of problem*) meollo ♦ *vt* quitar el corazón de

coriander [kɒrɪˈændə*] *n* culantro

cork [kɔːk] *n* corcho; (*tree*) alcornoque *m*; **~screw** *n* sacacorchos *m inv*

corn [kɔːn] *n* (*BRIT*: *cereal crop*) trigo; (*US*: *maize*) maíz *m*; (*on foot*) callo; **~ on the cob** (*CULIN*) maíz en la mazorca (*SP*), choclo (*AM*)

corned beef [ˈkɔːnd-] *n* carne *f* acecinada (en lata)

corner [ˈkɔːnə*] *n* (*outside*) esquina; (*inside*) rincón *m*; (*in road*) curva; (*FOOTBALL*) córner *m*; (*BOXING*) esquina ♦ *vt* (*trap*) arrinconar; (*COMM*) acaparar ♦ *vi* (*in car*) tomar las curvas; **~stone** *n* (*also fig*) piedra angular

cornet [ˈkɔːnɪt] *n* (*MUS*) corneta; (*BRIT*: *of ice-cream*) cucurucho

cornflakes [ˈkɔːnfleɪks] *npl* copos *mpl* de maíz, cornflakes *mpl*

cornflour [ˈkɔːnflaʊə*] (*BRIT*), **cornstarch** [ˈkɔːnstɑːtʃ] (*US*) *n* harina de maíz

Cornwall [ˈkɔːnwəl] *n* Cornualles *m*

corny [ˈkɔːnɪ] (*inf*) *adj* gastado

coronary [ˈkɒrənərɪ] *n* (*also*: ~ *thrombosis*) infarto

coronation [kɒrəˈneɪʃən] *n* coronación *f*

coroner [ˈkɒrənə*] *n* juez *m* (de instrucción)

corporal [ˈkɔːpərl] *n* cabo ♦ *adj*: **~ punishment** castigo corporal

corporate [ˈkɔːpərɪt] *adj* (*action, ownership*) colectivo; (*finance, image*) corporativo

corporation [kɔːpəˈreɪʃən] *n* (*of town*) ayuntamiento; (*COMM*) corporación *f*

corps [kɔː*, *pl* kɔːz] *n inv* cuerpo; **diplomatic ~** cuerpo diplomático; **press ~** gabinete *m* de prensa

corpse [kɔːps] *n* cadáver *m*

corral [kɒˈrɑːl] *n* corral *m*

correct [kəˈrɛkt] *adj* justo, exacto; (*proper*) correcto ♦ *vt* corregir; (*exam*) corregir, calificar; **~ion** [-ʃən] *n* (*act*) corrección *f*; (*instance*) rectificación *f*

correspond [kɒrɪsˈpɒnd] *vi* (*write*): **to ~ (with)** escribirse (con); (*be equivalent to*): **to ~ (to)** corresponder (a); (*be in accordance*): **to ~ (with)** corresponder (con); **~ence** *n* correspondencia; **~ence course** *n* curso por correspondencia; **~ent** *n* corresponsal *m/f*

corridor [ˈkɒrɪdɔː*] *n* pasillo

corroborate [kəˈrɒbəreɪt] *vt* corroborar

corrode [kəˈrəʊd] *vt* corroer ♦ *vi* corroerse; **corrosion** [-ˈrəʊʒən] *n* corrosión *f*

corrugated [ˈkɒrəgeɪtɪd] *adj* ondulado; **~ iron** *n* chapa ondulada

corrupt [kəˈrʌpt] *adj* (*person*) corrupto; (*COMPUT*) corrompido ♦ *vt* corromper; (*COMPUT*) degradar; **~ion** [-ʃən] *n* corrupción *f*

corset ['kɔːsɪt] *n* faja

Corsica ['kɔːsɪkə] *n* Córcega

cosmetic [kɔz'metɪk] *adj, n* cosmético

cosmonaut ['kɔzmənɔːt] *n* cosmonauta *m/f*

cosmopolitan [kɔzmə'pɔlɪtn] *adj* cosmopolita

cosset ['kɔsɪt] *vt* mimar

cost [kɔst] (*pt, pp* cost) *n* (*price*) precio; ~s *npl* (*COMM*) costes *mpl*; (*LAW*) costas *fpl* ♦ *vi* costar, valer ♦ *vt* preparar el presupuesto de; **how much does it ~?** ¿cuánto cuesta?; **to ~ sb time/effort** costarle a uno tiempo/esfuerzo; **it ~ him his life** le costó la vida; **at all ~s** cueste lo que cueste

co-star ['kəʊstɑː*] *n* coprotagonista *m/f*

Costa Rica ['kɔstə'riːkə] *n* Costa Rica; ~n *adj, n* costarriqueño/a *m/f*

cost-effective [kɔst'fektɪv] *adj* rentable

costly ['kɔstlɪ] *adj* costoso

cost-of-living [kɔstəv'lɪvɪŋ] *adj*: ~ **allowance** plus *m* de carestía de vida; ~ **index** índice *m* del costo de vida

cost price (*BRIT*) *n* precio de coste

costume ['kɔstjuːm] *n* traje *m*; (*BRIT: also: swimming ~*) traje de baño; ~ **jewellery** *n* bisutería

cosy ['kəʊzɪ] (*US* cozy) *adj* (*person*) cómodo; (*room*) acogedor(a)

cot [kɔt] *n* (*BRIT: child's*) cuna; (*US: campbed*) cama de campaña

cottage ['kɔtɪdʒ] *n* casita de campo; (*rustic*) barraca; ~ **cheese** *n* requesón *m*

cotton ['kɔtn] *n* algodón *m*; (*thread*) hilo; ~ **on to** (*inf*) *vt fus* caer en la cuenta de; ~ **candy** (*US*) *n* algodón *m* (azucarado); ~ **wool** (*BRIT*) *n* algodón *m* (hidrófilo)

couch [kautʃ] *n* sofá *m*; (*doctor's etc*) diván *m*

couchette [kuː'ʃet] *n* litera

cough [kɔf] *vi* toser ♦ *n* tos *f*; ~ **drop** *n* pastilla para la tos

could [kud] *pt of* can²; ~n't = could not

council ['kaunsl] *n* consejo; **city** *or* **town** ~ consejo municipal; ~ **estate** (*BRIT*) *n* urbanización *f* de viviendas municipales de alquiler; ~ **house** (*BRIT*) *n* vivienda

municipal de alquiler; ~**lor** *n* concejal(a) *m/f*

counsel ['kaunsl] *n* (*advice*) consejo; (*lawyer*) abogado/a ♦ *vt* aconsejar; ~**lor** *n* consejero/a; ~**or** (*US*) *n* abogado/a

count [kaunt] *vt* contar; (*include*) incluir ♦ *vi* contar ♦ *n* cuenta; (*of votes*) escrutinio; (*level*) nivel *m*; (*nobleman*) conde *m*; ~ **on** *vt fus* contar con; ~**down** *n* cuenta atrás

countenance ['kauntɪnəns] *n* semblante *m*, rostro ♦ *vt* (*tolerate*) aprobar, tolerar

counter ['kauntə*] *n* (*in shop*) mostrador *m*; (*in games*) ficha ♦ *vt* contrarrestar ♦ *adv*: **to run ~ to** ser contrario a, ir en contra de; ~**act** *vt* contrarrestar

counterfeit ['kauntəfɪt] *n* falsificación *f*, simulación *f* ♦ *vt* falsificar ♦ *adj* falso, falsificado

counterfoil ['kauntəfɔɪl] *n* talón *m*

countermand ['kauntəmɑːnd] *vt* revocar, cancelar

counterpart ['kauntəpɑːt] *n* homólogo/a

counter-productive [kauntəprə'dʌktɪv] *adj* contraproducente

countersign ['kauntəsaɪn] *vt* refrendar

countess ['kauntɪs] *n* condesa

countless ['kauntlɪs] *adj* innumerable

country ['kʌntrɪ] *n* país *m*; (*native land*) patria; (*as opposed to town*) campo; (*region*) región *f*, tierra; ~ **dancing** (*BRIT*) *n* baile *m* regional; ~ **house** *n* casa de campo; ~**man** *n* (*compatriot*) compatriota *m*; (*rural*) campesino, paisano; ~**side** *n* campo

county ['kauntɪ] *n* condado

coup [kuː] (*pl* ~s) *n* (*also*: ~ *d'état*) golpe *m* (de estado); (*achievement*) éxito

coupé ['kuːpeɪ] *n* cupé *m*

couple ['kʌpl] *n* (*of things*) par *m*; (*of people*) pareja; (*married ~*) matrimonio; **a ~ of** un par de

coupon ['kuːpɔn] *n* cupón *m*; (*voucher*) valé *m*

courage ['kʌrɪdʒ] *n* valor *m*, valentía; ~**ous** [kə'reɪdʒəs] *adj* valiente

courgette [kuə'ʒet] (*BRIT*) *n* calabacín *m* (*SP*), calabacita (*AM*)

courier ['kurɪə*] *n* mensajero/a; (*for*

tourists) guía *m/f* (de turismo)
course [kɔːs] *n* (*direction*) dirección *f*; (*of river*, SCOL) curso; (*process*) transcurso; (MED): ~ **of treatment** tratamiento; (*of ship*) rumbo; (*part of meal*) plato; (GOLF) campo; *of* ~ desde luego, naturalmente; **of** ~! ¡claro!
court [kɔːt] *n* (*royal*) corte *f*; (LAW) tribunal *m*, juzgado; (TENNIS *etc*) pista, cancha ♦ *vt* (*woman*) cortejar a; **to take to** ~ demandar
courteous ['kɔːtɪəs] *adj* cortés
courtesan [kɔːtɪ'zæn] *n* cortesana
courtesy ['kɔːtəsɪ] *n* cortesía; **(by)** ~ **of** por cortesía de
court-house ['kɔːthaus] (US) *n* palacio de justicia
courtier ['kɔːtɪə*] *n* cortesano
court-martial (*pl* **courts-martial**) *n* consejo de guerra
courtroom ['kɔːtrum] *n* sala de justicia
courtyard ['kɔːtjɑːd] *n* patio
cousin ['kʌzn] *n* primo/a; **first** ~ primo/a carnal, primo/a hermano/a
cove [kəuv] *n* cala, ensenada
covenant ['kʌvənənt] *n* pacto
cover ['kʌvə*] *vt* cubrir; (*feelings, mistake*) ocultar; (*with lid*) tapar; (*book etc*) forrar; (*distance*) recorrer; (*include*) abarcar; (*protect: also*: INSURANCE) cubrir; (PRESS) investigar; (*discuss*) tratar ♦ *n* cubierta; (*lid*) tapa; (*for chair etc*) funda; (*envelope*) sobre *m*; (*for book*) forro; (*of magazine*) portada; (*shelter*) abrigo; (INSURANCE) cobertura; (*of spy*) cobertura; ~**s** *npl* (*on bed*) sábanas; mantas; **to take** ~ (*shelter*) protegerse, resguardarse; **under** ~ (*indoors*) bajo techo; **under** ~ **of darkness** al amparo de la oscuridad; **under separate** ~ (COMM) por separado; ~ **up** *vi*: **to** ~ **up for sb** encubrir a uno; ~**age** *n* (TV, PRESS) cobertura; ~**alls** (US) *npl* mono; ~ **charge** *n* precio del cubierto; ~**ing** *n* capa; ~**ing letter** (US ~ **letter**) *n* carta de explicación; ~ **note** *n* (INSURANCE) póliza provisional
covert ['kʌvət] *adj* secreto, encubierto
cover-up *n* encubrimiento
covet ['kʌvɪt] *vt* codiciar

cow [kau] *n* vaca; (*inf!*: *woman*) bruja ♦ *vt* intimidar
coward ['kauəd] *n* cobarde *m/f*; ~**ice** [-ɪs] *n* cobardía; ~**ly** *adj* cobarde
cowboy ['kaubɔɪ] *n* vaquero
cower ['kauə*] *vi* encogerse (de miedo)
coy [kɔɪ] *adj* tímido
cozy ['kəuzɪ] (US) *adj* = **cosy**
CPA (US) *n abbr* = **certified public accountant**
crab [kræb] *n* cangrejo; ~ **apple** *n* manzana silvestre
crack [kræk] *n* grieta; (*noise*) crujido; (*drug*) crack *m* ♦ *vt* agrietar, romper; (*nut*) cascar; (*solve: problem*) resolver; (: *code*) descifrar; (*whip etc*) chasquear; (*knuckles*) crujir; (*joke*) contar ♦ *adj* (*expert*) de primera; ~ **down on** *vt fus* adoptar fuertes medidas contra; ~ **up** *vi* (MED) sufrir una crisis nerviosa; ~**er** *n* (*biscuit*) cráquer *m*; (*Christmas* ~**er**) petardo sorpresa
crackle ['krækl] *vi* crepitar
cradle ['kreɪdl] *n* cuna
craft [krɑːft] *n* (*skill*) arte *m*; (*trade*) oficio; (*cunning*) astucia; (*boat*: *pl inv*) barco; (*plane*: *pl inv*) avión *m*
craftsman ['krɑːftsmən] *n* artesano; ~**ship** *n* (*quality*) destreza
crafty ['krɑːftɪ] *adj* astuto
crag [kræg] *n* peñasco
cram [kræm] *vt* (*fill*): **to** ~ **sth with** llenar algo a (reventar) de; (*put*): **to** ~ **sth into** meter algo a la fuerza en ♦ *vi* (*for exams*) empollar
cramp [kræmp] *n* (MED) calambre *m*; ~**ed** *adj* apretado, estrecho
cranberry ['krænbərɪ] *n* arándano agrio
crane [kreɪn] *n* (TECH) grúa; (*bird*) grulla
crank [kræŋk] *n* manivela; (*person*) chiflado; ~**shaft** *n* cigüeñal *m*
cranny ['krænɪ] *n see* **nook**
crash [kræʃ] *n* (*noise*) estrépito; (*of cars etc*) choque *m*; (*of plane*) accidente *m* de aviación; (COMM) quiebra ♦ *vt* (*car, plane*) estrellar ♦ *vi* (*car, plane*) estrellarse; (*two cars*) chocar; (COMM) quebrar; ~ **course** *n* curso acelerado; ~ **helmet** *n* casco (protector); ~ **landing** *n* aterrizaje

m forzado

crass [kræs] *adj* grosero, maleducado

crate [kreɪt] *n* cajón *m* de embalaje; (*for bottles*) caja

crater ['kreɪtə*] *n* cráter *m*

cravat(e) [krə'væt] *n* pañuelo

crave [kreɪv] *vt*, *vi*: **to ~ (for)** ansiar, anhelar

crawl [krɔːl] *vi* (*drag o.s.*) arrastrarse; (*child*) andar a gatas, gatear; (*vehicle*) avanzar (lentamente) ♦ *n* (SWIMMING) crol *m*

crayfish ['kreɪfɪʃ] *n inv* (*freshwater*) cangrejo de río; (*saltwater*) cigala

crayon ['kreɪən] *n* lápiz *m* de color

craze [kreɪz] *n* (*fashion*) moda

crazy ['kreɪzɪ] *adj* (*person*) loco; (*idea*) disparatado; (*inf*: *keen*): **~ about sb/sth** loco por uno/algo; **~ paving** (BRIT) *n* pavimento de baldosas irregulares

creak [kriːk] *vi* (*floorboard*) crujir; (*hinge etc*) chirriar, rechinar

cream [kriːm] *n* (*of milk*) nata, crema; (*lotion*) crema; (*fig*) flor *f* y nata ♦ *adj* (*colour*) color crema; **~ cake** *n* pastel *m* de nata; **~ cheese** *n* queso blanco; **~y** *adj* cremoso; (*colour*) color crema

crease [kriːs] *n* (*fold*) pliegue *m*; (*in trousers*) raya; (*wrinkle*) arruga ♦ *vt* (*wrinkle*) arrugar ♦ *vi* (*wrinkle up*) arrugarse

create [kriː'eɪt] *vt* crear; **creation** [-ʃən] *n* creación *f*; **creative** *adj* creativo; **creator** *n* creador(a) *m/f*

creature ['kriːtʃə*] *n* (*animal*) animal *m*, bicho; (*person*) criatura

crèche [krɛʃ] *n* guardería (infantil)

credence ['kriːdəns] *n*: **to lend** *or* **give ~ to** creer en, dar crédito a

credentials [krɪ'denʃlz] *npl* (*references*) referencias *fpl*; (*identity papers*) documentos *mpl* de identidad

credible ['kredɪbl] *adj* creíble; (*trustworthy*) digno de confianza

credit ['kredɪt] *n* crédito; (*merit*) honor *m*, mérito ♦ *vt* (COMM) abonar; (*believe*: *also*: **give ~ to**) creer, prestar fe a ♦ *adj* crediticio; **~s** *npl* (CINEMA) fichas *fpl* técnicas; **to be in ~** (*person*) tener saldo

a favor; **to ~ sb with** (*fig*) reconocer a uno el mérito de; **~ card** *n* tarjeta de crédito; **~or** *n* acreedor(a) *m/f*

creed [kriːd] *n* credo

creek [kriːk] *n* cala, ensenada; (US) riachuelo

creep [kriːp] (*pt*, *pp* **crept**) *vi* arrastrarse; **~er** *n* enredadera; **~y** *adj* (*frightening*) horripilante

cremate [krɪ'meɪt] *vt* incinerar

crematorium [krɛmə'tɔːriəm] (*pl* **crematoria**) *n* crematorio

crêpe [kreɪp] *n* (*fabric*) crespón *m*; (*also*: **~ rubber**) crepé *m*; **~ bandage** (BRIT) *n* venda de crepé

crept [krɛpt] *pt*, *pp of* **creep**

crescent ['krɛsnt] *n* media luna; (*street*) calle *f* (*en forma de semicírculo*)

cress [krɛs] *n* berro

crest [krɛst] *n* (*of bird*) cresta; (*of hill*) cima, cumbre *f*; (*of coat of arms*) blasón *m*; **~fallen** *adj* alicaído

crevice ['krɛvɪs] *n* grieta, hendedura

crew [kruː] *n* (*of ship etc*) tripulación *f*; (TV, CINEMA) equipo; **~-cut** *n* corte *m* al rape; **~-neck** *n* cuello a la caja

crib [krɪb] *n* cuna ♦ *vt* (*inf*) plagiar

crick [krɪk] *n* (*in neck*) tortícolis *f*

cricket ['krɪkɪt] *n* (*insect*) grillo; (*game*) críquet *m*

crime [kraɪm] *n* (*no pl*: *illegal activities*) crimen *m*; (*illegal action*) delito; **criminal** ['krɪmɪnl] *n* criminal *m/f*, delincuente *m/f* ♦ *adj* criminal; (*illegal*) delictivo; (*law*) penal

crimson ['krɪmzn] *adj* carmesí

cringe [krɪndʒ] *vi* agacharse, encogerse

crinkle ['krɪŋkl] *vt* arrugar

cripple ['krɪpl] *n* lisiado/a, cojo/a ♦ *vt* lisiar, mutilar

crises ['kraɪsiːz] *npl of* **crisis**

crisis ['kraɪsɪs] (*pl* **crises**) *n* crisis *f inv*

crisp [krɪsp] *adj* fresco; (*vegetables etc*) crujiente; (*manner*) seco; **~s** (BRIT) *npl* patatas *fpl* (SP) *or* papas *fpl* (AM) fritas

criss-cross ['krɪskrɔs] *adj* entrelazado

criterion [kraɪ'tɪəriən] (*pl* **criteria**) *n* criterio

critic ['krɪtɪk] *n* crítico/a; **~al** *adj* crítico;

(*illness*) grave; ~ally *adv* (*speak etc*) en tono crítico; (*ill*) gravemente; ~ism ['krɪtɪsɪzm] *n* crítica; ~ize ['krɪtɪsaɪz] *vt* criticar

croak [krəuk] *vi* (*frog*) croar; (*raven*) graznar; (*person*) gruñir

Croatia [krəu'eɪʃə] *n* Croacia

crochet ['krəuʃeɪ] *n* ganchillo

crockery ['krɔkərɪ] *n* loza, vajilla

crocodile ['krɔkədaɪl] *n* cocodrilo

crocus ['krəukəs] *n* croco, crocus *m*

croft [krɔft] *n* granja pequeña

crony ['krəunɪ] (*inf: pej*) *n* compinche *m/f*

crook [kruk] *n* ladrón/ona *m/f*; (*of shepherd*) cayado; ~ed ['krukɪd] *adj* torcido; (*dishonest*) nada honrado

crop [krɔp] *n* (*produce*) cultivo; (*amount produced*) cosecha; (*riding* ~) látigo de montar ♦ *vt* cortar, recortar; ~ up *vi* surgir, presentarse

croquette [krə'ket] *n* croqueta

cross [krɔs] *n* cruz *f*; (*hybrid*) cruce *m* ♦ *vt* (*street etc*) cruzar, atravesar ♦ *adj* de mal humor, enojado; ~ out *vt* tachar; ~ over *vi* cruzar; ~bar *n* travesaño; ~country (*race*) *n* carrera a campo traviesa, cross *m*; ~-examine *vt* interrogar; ~-eyed *adj* bizco; ~fire *n* fuego cruzado; ~ing *n* (*sea passage*) travesía; (*also: pedestrian* ~ing) paso para peatones; ~ing guard (*US*) *n* persona encargada de ayudar a los niños a cruzar la calle; ~ purposes *npl*: **to be at ~ purposes** no comprenderse uno a otro; ~-reference *n* referencia, llamada; ~roads *n* cruce *m*, encrucijada; ~ section *n* corte *m* transversal; (*of population*) muestra (representativa); ~walk (*US*) *n* paso de peatones; ~wind *n* viento de costado; ~word *n* crucigrama *m*

crotch [krɔtʃ] *n* (*ANAT, of garment*) entrepierna

crotchet ['krɔtʃɪt] *n* (*MUS*) negra

crotchety ['krɔtʃɪtɪ] *adj* antipático

crouch [krautʃ] *vi* agacharse, acurrucarse

crow [krəu] *n* (*bird*) cuervo; (*of cock*) canto, cacareo ♦ *vi* (*cock*) cantar

crowbar ['krəubɑː*] *n* palanca

crowd [kraud] *n* muchedumbre *f*, multitud *f* ♦ *vt* (*fill*) llenar ♦ *vi* (*gather*): **to ~ round** reunirse en torno a; (*cram*): **to ~ in** entrar en tropel; ~ed *adj* (*full*) atestado; (*densely populated*) superpoblado

crown [kraun] *n* corona; (*of head*) coronilla; (*for tooth*) funda; (*of hill*) cumbre *f* ♦ *vt* coronar; (*fig*) completar, rematar; ~ **jewels** *npl* joyas *fpl* reales; ~ **prince** *n* príncipe *m* heredero

crow's feet *npl* patas *fpl* de gallo

crucial ['kruːʃl] *adj* decisivo

crucifix ['kruːsɪfɪks] *n* crucifijo; ~ion [-'fɪkʃən] *n* crucifixión *f*

crude [kruːd] *adj* (*materials*) bruto; (*fig: basic*) tosco; (: *vulgar*) ordinario; ~ (*oil*) *n* (petróleo) crudo

cruel ['kruəl] *adj* cruel; ~ty *n* crueldad *f*

cruise [kruːz] *n* crucero ♦ *vi* (*ship*) hacer un crucero; (*car*) ir a velocidad de crucero; ~r *n* (*motorboat*) yate *m* de motor; (*warship*) crucero

crumb [krʌm] *n* miga, migaja

crumble ['krʌmbl] *vt* desmenuzar ♦ *vi* (*building, also fig*) desmoronarse; **crumbly** *adj* que se desmigaja fácilmente

crumpet ['krʌmpɪt] *n* ≈ bollo para tostar

crumple ['krʌmpl] *vt* (*paper*) estrujar; (*material*) arrugar

crunch [krʌntʃ] *vt* (*with teeth*) mascar; (*underfoot*) hacer crujir ♦ *n* (*fig*) hora o momento de la verdad; ~y *adj* crujiente

crusade [kruː'seɪd] *n* cruzada

crush [krʌʃ] *n* (*crowd*) aglomeración *f*; (*infatuation*): **to have a ~ on sb** estar loco por uno; (*drink*): **lemon ~** limonada ♦ *vt* aplastar; (*paper*) estrujar; (*cloth*) arrugar; (*fruit*) exprimir; (*opposition*) aplastar; (*hopes*) destruir

crust [krʌst] *n* corteza; (*of snow, ice*) costra

crutch [krʌtʃ] *n* muleta

crux [krʌks] *n*: **the ~ of** lo esencial de, el quid de

cry [kraɪ] *vi* llorar; (*shout: also:* ~ **out**) gritar ♦ *n* (*shriek*) chillido; (*shout*) grito; ~ **off** *vi* echarse atrás

cryptic ['krɪptɪk] *adj* enigmático, secreto

crystal ['krɪstl] n cristal m; **~-clear** adj claro como el agua

cub [kʌb] n cachorro; (also: ~ **scout**) niño explorador

Cuba ['kju:bə] n Cuba; **~n** adj, n cubano/a m/f

cubbyhole ['kʌbɪhəul] n cuchitril m

cube [kju:b] n cubo ♦ vt (MATH) cubicar; **cubic** adj cúbico

cubicle ['kju:bɪkl] n (at pool) caseta; (for bed) cubículo

cuckoo ['kuku:] n cuco; ~ **clock** n reloj m de cucú

cucumber ['kju:kʌmbə*] n pepino

cuddle ['kʌdl] vt abrazar ♦ vi abrazarse

cue [kju:] n (snooker ~) taco; (THEATRE etc) señal f

cuff [kʌf] n (of sleeve) puño; (US: of trousers) vuelta; (blow) bofetada; **off the ~** adv de improviso; **~links** npl gemelos mpl

cuisine [kwɪ'zi:n] n cocina

cul-de-sac ['kʌldəsæk] n callejón m sin salida

cull [kʌl] vt (idea) sacar ♦ n (of animals) matanza selectiva

culminate ['kʌlmɪneɪt] vi: **to ~ in** terminar en; **culmination** [-'neɪʃən] n culminación f, colmo

culottes [ku:'lɔts] npl falda pantalón f

culprit ['kʌlprɪt] n culpable m/f

cult [kʌlt] n culto

cultivate ['kʌltɪveɪt] vt (also fig) cultivar; **~d** adj culto; **cultivation** [-'veɪʃən] n cultivo

cultural ['kʌltʃərəl] adj cultural

culture ['kʌltʃə*] n (also fig) cultura; (BIO) cultivo; **~d** adj culto

cumbersome ['kʌmbəsəm] adj de mucho bulto, voluminoso; (process) enrevesado

cunning ['kʌnɪŋ] n astucia ♦ adj astuto

cup [kʌp] n taza; (as prize) copa

cupboard ['kʌbəd] n armario; (kitchen) alacena

cup-tie ['kʌptaɪ] (BRIT) n partido de copa

curate ['kjuərɪt] n cura m

curator [kjuə'reɪtə*] n director(a) m/f

curb [kə:b] vt refrenar; (person) reprimir ♦ n freno; (US) bordillo

curdle ['kə:dl] vi cuajarse

cure [kjuə*] vt curar ♦ n cura, curación f; (fig: solution) remedio

curfew ['kə:fju:] n toque m de queda

curio ['kjuərɪəu] n curiosidad f

curiosity [kjuərɪ'ɔsɪtɪ] n curiosidad f

curious ['kjuərɪəs] adj curioso; (person: interested): **to be ~** sentir curiosidad

curl [kə:l] n rizo ♦ vt (hair) rizar ♦ vi rizarse; **~ up** vi (person) hacerse un ovillo; **~er** n rulo; **~y** adj rizado

currant ['kʌrnt] n pasa (de Corinto); (black~, red~) grosella

currency ['kʌrnsɪ] n moneda; **to gain ~** (fig) difundirse

current ['kʌrnt] n corriente f ♦ adj (accepted) corriente; (present) actual; ~ **account** (BRIT) n cuenta corriente; ~ **affairs** npl noticias fpl de actualidad; **~ly** adv actualmente

curriculum [kə'rɪkjuləm] (pl ~s or **curricula**) n plan m de estudios; ~ **vitae** n currículum m

curry ['kʌrɪ] n curry m ♦ vt: **to ~ favour with** buscar favores con; ~ **powder** n curry m en polvo

curse [kə:s] vi soltar tacos ♦ vt maldecir ♦ n maldición f; (swearword) palabrota, taco

cursor ['kə:sə*] n (COMPUT) cursor m

cursory ['kə:sərɪ] adj rápido, superficial

curt [kə:t] adj corto, seco

curtail [kə:'teɪl] vt (visit etc) acortar; (freedom) restringir; (expenses etc) reducir

curtain ['kə:tn] n cortina; (THEATRE) telón m

curts(e)y ['kə:tsɪ] vi hacer una reverencia

curve [kə:v] n curva ♦ vi (road) hacer una curva; (line etc) curvarse

cushion ['kuʃən] n cojín m; (of air) colchón m ♦ vt (shock) amortiguar

custard ['kʌstəd] n natillas fpl

custody ['kʌstədɪ] n custodia; **to take into ~** detener

custom ['kʌstəm] n costumbre f; (COMM) clientela; **~ary** adj acostumbrado

customer ['kʌstəmə*] n cliente m/f

customized ['kʌstəmaɪzd] *adj* (*car etc*) hecho a encargo

custom-made *adj* hecho a la medida

customs ['kʌstəmz] *npl* aduana; ~ **duty** *n* derechos *mpl* de aduana; ~ **officer** *n* aduanero/a

cut [kʌt] (*pt, pp* **cut**) *vt* cortar; (*price*) rebajar; (*text, programme*) acortar; (*reduce*) reducir ♦ *vi* cortar ♦ *n* (*of garment*) corte *m*; (*in skin*) cortadura; (*in salary etc*) rebaja; (*in spending*) reducción *f*, recorte *m*; (*slice of meat*) tajada; **to ~ a tooth** echar un diente; ~ **down** *vt* (*tree*) derribar; (*reduce*) reducir; ~ **off** *vt* cortar; (*person, place*) aislar; (*TEL*) desconectar; ~ **out** *vt* (*shape*) recortar; (*stop: activity etc*) dejar; (*remove*) quitar; ~ **up** *vt* cortar (en pedazos); ~**back** *n* reducción *f*

cute [kjuːt] *adj* mono

cuticle ['kjuːtɪkl] *n* cutícula

cutlery ['kʌtlərɪ] *n* cubiertos *mpl*

cutlet ['kʌtlɪt] *n* chuleta; (*nut etc* ~) *plato vegetariano hecho con nueces y verdura en forma de chuleta*

cut: ~**out** *n* (*switch*) dispositivo de seguridad, disyuntor *m*; (*cardboard* ~) recortable *m*; ~-**price** (*US* ~-**rate**) *adj* a precio reducido; ~**throat** *n* asesino/a ♦ *adj* feroz

cutting ['kʌtɪŋ] *adj* (*remark*) mordaz ♦ *n* (*BRIT: from newspaper*) recorte *m*; (*from plant*) esqueje *m*

CV *n abbr* = **curriculum vitae**

cwt *abbr* = **hundredweight(s)**

cyanide ['saɪənaɪd] *n* cianuro

cycle ['saɪkl] *n* ciclo; (*bicycle*) bicicleta ♦ *vi* ir en bicicleta; **cycling** *n* ciclismo; **cyclist** *n* ciclista *m/f*

cyclone ['saɪkləun] *n* ciclón *m*

cygnet ['sɪgnɪt] *n* pollo de cisne

cylinder ['sɪlɪndə*] *n* cilindro; (*of gas*) bombona; ~-**head gasket** *n* junta de culata

cymbals ['sɪmblz] *npl* platillos *mpl*

cynic ['sɪnɪk] *n* cínico/a; ~**al** *adj* cínico; ~**ism** ['sɪnɪsɪzəm] *n* cinismo

cypress ['saɪprɪs] *n* ciprés *m*

Cyprus ['saɪprəs] *n* Chipre *f*

cyst [sɪst] *n* quiste *m*; ~**itis** [-'taɪtɪs] *n* cistitis *f*

czar [zɑː*] *n* zar *m*

Czech [tʃɛk] *adj, n* checo/a *m/f*

Czechoslovakia [tʃɛkəslə'vækɪə] *n* Checoslovaquia; ~**n** *adj, n* checo/a *m/f*

D d

D [diː] *n* (*MUS*) re *m*

dab [dæb] *vt* (*eyes, wound*) tocar (ligeramente); (*paint, cream*) poner un poco de

dabble ['dæbl] *vi*: **to ~ in** ser algo aficionado a

dad [dæd] *n* = **daddy**

daddy ['dædɪ] *n* papá *m*

daffodil ['dæfədɪl] *n* narciso

daft [dɑːft] *adj* tonto

dagger ['dægə*] *n* puñal *m*, daga

daily ['deɪlɪ] *adj* diario, cotidiano ♦ *adv* todos los días, cada día

dainty ['deɪntɪ] *adj* delicado

dairy ['dɛərɪ] *n* (*shop*) lechería; (*on farm*) vaquería; ~ **farm** *n* granja; ~ **products** *npl* productos *mpl* lácteos; ~ **store** (*US*) *n* lechería

dais ['deɪɪs] *n* estrado

daisy ['deɪzɪ] *n* margarita; ~ **wheel** *n* margarita

dale [deɪl] *n* valle *m*

dam [dæm] *n* presa ♦ *vt* construir una presa sobre, represar

damage ['dæmɪdʒ] *n* lesión *f*; daño; (*dents etc*) desperfectos *mpl*; (*fig*) perjuicio ♦ *vt* dañar, perjudicar; (*spoil, break*) estropear; ~**s** *npl* (*LAW*) daños *mpl* y perjuicios

damn [dæm] *vt* condenar; (*curse*) maldecir ♦ *n* (*inf*): **I don't give a ~** me importa un pito ♦ *adj* (*inf: also: ~ed*) maldito; ~ (**it!**) ¡maldito sea!; ~**ing** *adj* (*evidence*) irrecusable

damp [dæmp] *adj* húmedo, mojado ♦ *n* humedad *f* ♦ *vt* (*also: ~en: cloth, rag*) mojar; (*: enthusiasm*) enfriar

damson ['dæmzən] *n* ciruela damascena

dance [dɑːns] *n* baile *m* ♦ *vi* bailar; ~

hall *n* salón *m* de baile; **~r** *n* bailador(a) *m/f*; *(professional)* bailarín/ina *m/f*; **dancing** *n* baile *m*

dandelion ['dændɪlaɪən] *n* diente *m* de león

dandruff ['dændrəf] *n* caspa

Dane [deɪn] *n* danés/esa *m/f*

danger ['deɪndʒə*] *n* peligro; *(risk)* riesgo; **~!** *(on sign)* ¡peligro de muerte!; **to be in ~ of** correr riesgo de; **~ous** *adj* peligroso; **~ously** *adv* peligrosamente

dangle ['dæŋgl] *vt* colgar ♦ *vi* pender, colgar

Danish ['deɪnɪʃ] *adj* danés/esa ♦ *n* *(LING)* danés *m*

dapper ['dæpə*] *adj* pulcro, apuesto

dare [dɛə*] *vt*: **to ~ sb to do** desafiar a uno a hacer ♦ *vi*: **to ~ (to) do sth** atreverse a hacer algo; **I ~ say** *(I suppose)* puede ser (que); **~devil** *n* temerario/a, atrevido/a; **daring** *adj* atrevido, osado ♦ *n* atrevimiento, osadía

dark [dɑːk] *adj* oscuro; *(hair, complexion)* moreno ♦ *n*: **in the ~** a oscuras; **to be in the ~ about** *(fig)* no saber nada de; **after ~** después del anochecer; **~en** *vt* *(colour)* hacer más oscuro ♦ *vi* oscurecer-se; **~ glasses** *npl* gafas *fpl* negras *(SP)*, anteojos *mpl* negros *(AM)*; **~ness** *n* oscuridad *f*; **~room** *n* cuarto oscuro

darling ['dɑːlɪŋ] *adj, n* querido/a *m/f*

darn [dɑːn] *vt* zurcir

dart [dɑːt] *n* dardo; *(in sewing)* sisa ♦ *vi* precipitarse; **~ away/along** *vi* salir/marchar disparado; **~board** *n* diana; **~s** *n* dardos *mpl*

dash [dæʃ] *n* *(small quantity: of liquid)* gota, chorrito; *(: of solid)* pizca; *(sign)* raya ♦ *vt* *(throw)* tirar; *(hopes)* defraudar ♦ *vi* precipitarse, ir de prisa; **~ away** *or* **off** *vi* marcharse apresuradamente

dashboard ['dæʃbɔːd] *n* *(AUT)* salpicadero

dashing ['dæʃɪŋ] *adj* gallardo

data ['deɪtə] *npl* datos *mpl*; **~base** *n* base *f* de datos; **~ processing** *n* proceso de datos

date [deɪt] *n* *(day)* fecha; *(with friend)* cita; *(fruit)* dátil *m* ♦ *vt* fechar; *(person)* salir con; **~ of birth** fecha de nacimien-

to; **to ~** *adv* hasta la fecha; **~d** *adj* anticuado; **~ rape** *n* violación ocurrida *durante una cita con un conocido*

daub [dɔːb] *vt* embadurnar

daughter ['dɔːtə*] *n* hija; **~-in-law** *n* nuera, hija política

daunting ['dɔːntɪŋ] *adj* desalentador(a)

dawdle ['dɔːdl] *vi* *(go slowly)* andar muy despacio

dawn [dɔːn] *n* alba, amanecer *m*; *(fig)* nacimiento ♦ *vi* *(day)* amanecer; *(fig)*: **it ~ed on him that ...** cayó en la cuenta de que ...

day [deɪ] *n* día *m*; *(working ~)* jornada; *(hey~)* tiempos *mpl*, días *mpl*; **the ~ before/after** el día anterior/siguiente; **the ~ after tomorrow** pasado mañana; **the ~ before yesterday** anteayer; **the following ~** el día siguiente; **by ~** de día; **~break** *n* amanecer *m*; **~dream** *vi* soñar despierto; **~light** *n* luz *f* (del día); **~ return** *(BRIT)* *n* billete *m* de ida y vuelta (en un día); **~time** *n* día *m*; **~-to-~** *adj* cotidiano

daze [deɪz] *vt* *(stun)* aturdir ♦ *n*: **in a ~** aturdido

dazzle ['dæzl] *vt* deslumbrar

DC *abbr* (= *direct current*) corriente *f* continua

dead [dɛd] *adj* muerto; *(limb)* dormido; *(telephone)* cortado; *(battery)* agotado ♦ *adv* *(completely)* totalmente; *(exactly)* exactamente; **to shoot sb ~** matar a uno a tiros; **~ tired** muerto (de cansancio); **to stop ~** parar en seco; **the ~** *npl* los muertos; **to be a ~ loss** *(inf: person)* ser un inútil; **~en** *vt* *(blow, sound)* amortiguar; *(pain etc)* aliviar; **~ end** *n* callejón *m* sin salida; **~ heat** *n* *(SPORT)* empate *m*; **~line** *n* fecha (*or* hora) tope; **~lock** *n*: **to reach ~lock** llegar a un punto muerto; **~ly** *adj* mortal, fatal; **~pan** *adj* sin expresión; **the D~ Sea** *n* el Mar Muerto

deaf [dɛf] *adj* sordo; **~en** *vt* ensordecer; **~ness** *n* sordera

deal [diːl] *(pt, pp* **dealt**) *n* *(agreement)* pacto, convenio; *(business ~)* trato ♦ *vt* dar; *(card)* repartir; **a great ~ (of)** bastante, mucho; **~ in** *vt fus* tratar en, comerciar en; ~ **with** vt fus (*people*) tratar con; (*problem*) ocuparse de; (*subject*) tratar de; ~**ings** npl (COMM) transacciones fpl; (*relations*) relaciones fpl

dealt [dɛlt] pt, pp of **deal**

dean [diːn] n (REL) deán m; (SCOL: BRIT) decano; (: US) decano; rector m

dear [dɪə*] adj querido; (*expensive*) caro ♦ n: **my** ~ mi querido/a ♦ excl: ~ **me!** ¡Dios mío!; **D~ Sir/Madam** (*in letter*) Muy Señor Mío, Estimado Señor/ Estimada Señora; **D~ Mr/Mrs X** Estimado/a Señor(a) X; ~**ly** adv (*love*) mucho; (*pay*) caro

death [dɛθ] n muerte f; ~ **certificate** n partida de defunción; ~**ly** adj (*white*) como un muerto; (*silence*) sepulcral; ~ **penalty** n pena de muerte; ~ **rate** n mortalidad f; ~ **toll** n número de víctimas

debacle [deɪˈbɑːkl] n desastre m

debar [dɪˈbɑː*] vt: **to** ~ **sb from doing** prohibir a uno hacer

debase [dɪˈbeɪs] vt degradar

debatable [dɪˈbeɪtəbl] adj discutible

debate [dɪˈbeɪt] n debate m ♦ vt discutir

debauchery [dɪˈbɔːtʃərɪ] n libertinaje m

debilitating [dɪˈbɪlɪteɪtɪŋ] adj debilitante

debit [ˈdɛbɪt] n debe m ♦ vt: **to** ~ **a sum to sb** or **to sb's account** cargar una suma en cuenta a alguien

debris [ˈdɛbriː] n escombros mpl

debt [dɛt] n deuda; **to be in** ~ tener deudas; ~**or** n deudor(a) m/f

debunk [diːˈbʌŋk] vt desprestigiar, desacreditar

début [ˈdeɪbjuː] n presentación f

decade [ˈdɛkeɪd] n decenio, década

decadence [ˈdɛkədəns] n decadencia

decaffeinated [dɪˈkæfɪneɪtɪd] adj descafeinado

decanter [dɪˈkæntə*] n garrafa

decay [dɪˈkeɪ] n (*of building*) desmoronamiento; (*of tooth*) caries f inv ♦ vi (*rot*) pudrirse

deceased [dɪˈsiːst] n: **the** ~ el/la difunto/a

deceit [dɪˈsiːt] n engaño; ~**ful** adj engañoso; **deceive** [dɪˈsiːv] vt engañar

December [dɪˈsɛmbə*] n diciembre m

decent [ˈdiːsənt] adj (*proper*) decente; (*person: kind*) amable, bueno

deception [dɪˈsɛpʃən] n engaño

deceptive [dɪˈsɛptɪv] adj engañoso

decibel [ˈdɛsɪbɛl] n decibel(io) m

decide [dɪˈsaɪd] vt (*person*) decidir; (*question, argument*) resolver ♦ vi decidir; **to** ~ **to do/that** decidir hacer/ que; **to** ~ **on sth** decidirse por algo; ~**d** adj (*resolute*) decidido; (*clear, definite*) indudable; ~**dly** [-dɪdlɪ] adv decididamente; (*emphatically*) con resolución

deciduous [dɪˈsɪdjuəs] adj de hoja caduca

decimal [ˈdɛsɪməl] adj decimal ♦ n decimal m; ~ **point** n coma decimal

decimate [ˈdɛsɪmeɪt] vt diezmar

decipher [dɪˈsaɪfə*] vt descifrar

decision [dɪˈsɪʒən] n decisión f

decisive [dɪˈsaɪsɪv] adj decisivo; (*person*) decidido

deck [dɛk] n (NAUT) cubierta; (*of bus*) piso; (*record*) platina; (*of cards*) baraja; ~**chair** n tumbona

declaration [dɛkləˈreɪʃən] n declaración f

declare [dɪˈklɛə*] vt declarar

decline [dɪˈklaɪn] n disminución f, descenso ♦ vt rehusar ♦ vi (*person, business*) decaer; (*strength*) disminuir

decode [diːˈkəud] vt descifrar

decoder [diːˈkəudə*] n (TV) decodificador m

decompose [diːkəmˈpəuz] vi descomponerse

décor [ˈdeɪkɔː*] n decoración f; (THEATRE) decorado

decorate [ˈdɛkəreɪt] vt (*adorn*): **to** ~ **(with)** adornar (de), decorar (de); (*paint*) pintar; (*paper*) empapelar; **decoration** [-ˈreɪʃən] n adorno; (*act*) decoración f; (*medal*) condecoración f; **decorative** [ˈdɛkərətɪv] adj decorativo; **decorator** n (*workman*) pintor m (decorador)

decorum [dɪˈkɔːrəm] n decoro

decoy [ˈdiːkɔɪ] n señuelo

decrease [n ˈdiːkriːs, vb dɪˈkriːs] n: ~ **(in)** disminución f (de) ♦ vt disminuir, reducir ♦ *vi* reducirse

decree [dɪ'kriː] *n* decreto; ~ **nisi** *n* sentencia provisional de divorcio

dedicate ['dɛdɪkeɪt] *vt* dedicar; **dedication** [-'keɪʃən] *n* (*devotion*) dedicación *f*; (*in book*) dedicatoria

deduce [dɪ'djuːs] *vt* deducir

deduct [dɪ'dʌkt] *vt* restar; descontar; ~**ion** [dɪ'dʌkʃən] *n* (*amount deducted*) descuento; (*conclusion*) deducción *f*, conclusión *f*

deed [diːd] *n* hecho, acto; (*feat*) hazaña; (*LAW*) escritura

deem [diːm] *vt* juzgar

deep [diːp] *adj* profundo; (*expressing measurements*) de profundidad; (*voice*) bajo; (*breath*) profundo; (*colour*) intenso ♦ *adv*: **the spectators stood 20 ~** los espectadores se formaron de 20 en fondo; **to be 4 metres ~** tener 4 metros de profundidad; ~**en** *vt* ahondar, profundizar ♦ *vi* aumentar, crecer; ~-**freeze** *n* congelador *m*; ~-**fry** *vt* freír en aceite abundante; ~**ly** *adv* (*breathe*) a pleno pulmón; (*interested, moved, grateful*) profundamente, hondamente; ~-**sea diving** *n* buceo de altura; ~-**seated** *adj* (*beliefs*) (profundamente) arraigado

deer [dɪə*] *n inv* ciervo

deface [dɪ'feɪs] *vt* (*wall, surface*) estropear, pintarrajear

default [dɪ'fɔːlt] *n*: **by ~** (*win*) por incomparecencia ♦ *adj* (*COMPUT*) por defecto

defeat [dɪ'fiːt] *n* derrota ♦ *vt* derrotar, vencer; ~**ist** *adj, n* derrotista *m/f*

defect [*n* 'diːfɛkt, *vb* dɪ'fɛkt] *n* defecto ♦ *vi*: **to ~ to the enemy** pasarse al enemigo; ~**ive** [dɪ'fɛktɪv] *adj* defectuoso

defence [dɪ'fɛns] (*US* **defense**) *n* defensa; ~**less** *adj* indefenso

defend [dɪ'fɛnd] *vt* defender; ~**ant** *n* acusado/a; (*in civil case*) demandado/a; ~**er** *n* defensor(a) *m/f*; (*SPORT*) defensa *m/f*

defense [dɪ'fɛns] (*US*) *n* = **defence**

defensive [dɪ'fɛnsɪv] *adj* defensivo ♦ *n*: **on the ~** a la defensiva

defer [dɪ'fəː*] *vt* aplazar; ~**ence** ['dɛfərəns] *n* deferencia, respeto

defiance [dɪ'faɪəns] *n* desafío; **in ~ of** en contra de; **defiant** [dɪ'faɪənt] *adj* (*challenging*) desafiante, retador(a)

deficiency [dɪ'fɪʃənsɪ] *n* (*lack*) falta; (*defect*) defecto; **deficient** [dɪ'fɪʃənt] *adj* deficiente

deficit ['dɛfɪsɪt] *n* déficit *m*

defile [dɪ'faɪl] *vt* manchar

define [dɪ'faɪn] *vt* (*word etc*) definir; (*limits etc*) determinar

definite ['dɛfɪnɪt] *adj* (*fixed*) determinado; (*obvious*) claro; (*certain*) indudable; **he was ~ about it** no dejó lugar a dudas (sobre ello); ~**ly** *adv* desde luego, por supuesto

definition [dɛfɪ'nɪʃən] *n* definición *f*; (*clearness*) nitidez *f*

deflate [diː'fleɪt] *vt* desinflar

deflect [dɪ'flɛkt] *vt* desviar

defraud [dɪ'frɔːd] *vt*: **to ~ sb of sth** estafar algo a uno

defrost [diː'frɒst] *vt* descongelar; ~**er** (*US*) *n* (*demister*) eliminador *m* de vaho

deft [dɛft] *adj* diestro, hábil

defunct [dɪ'fʌŋkt] *adj* difunto; (*organization etc*) ya que no existe

defuse [diː'fjuːz] *vt* desactivar; (*situation*) calmar

defy [dɪ'faɪ] *vt* (*resist*) oponerse a; (*challenge*) desafiar; (*fig*): **it defies description** resulta imposible describirlo

degenerate [*vb* dɪ'dʒɛnəreɪt, *adj* dɪ'dʒɛnərɪt] *vi* degenerar ♦ *adj* degenerado

degree [dɪ'griː] *n* grado; (*SCOL*) título; **to have a ~ in maths** tener una licenciatura en matemáticas; **by ~s** (*gradually*) poco a poco, por etapas; **to some ~** hasta cierto punto

dehydrated [diːhaɪ'dreɪtɪd] *adj* deshidratado; (*milk*) en polvo

de-ice [diː'aɪs] *vt* deshelar

deign [deɪn] *vi*: **to ~ to do** dignarse hacer

deity ['diːɪtɪ] *n* deidad *f*, divinidad *f*

dejected [dɪ'dʒɛktɪd] *adj* abatido, desanimado

delay [dɪ'leɪ] *vt* demorar, aplazar; (*person*) entretener; (*train*) retrasar ♦ *vi* tardar ♦ *n* demora, retraso; **to be ~ed** retrasarse; **without** ~ en seguida, sin tardar

delectable [dɪ'lɛktəbl] *adj* (*person*) encantador(a); (*food*) delicioso

delegate [*n* 'dɛlɪgɪt, *vb* 'dɛlɪgeɪt] *n* delegado/a ♦ *vt* (*person*) delegar en; (*task*) delegar

delete [dɪ'liːt] *vt* suprimir, tachar

deliberate [*adj* dɪ'lɪbərɪt, *vb* dɪ'lɪbəreɪt] *adj* (*intentional*) intencionado; (*slow*) pausado, lento ♦ *vi* deliberar; ~**ly** *adv* (*on purpose*) a propósito

delicacy ['dɛlɪkəsɪ] *n* delicadeza; (*choice food*) manjar *m*

delicate ['dɛlɪkɪt] *adj* delicado; (*fragile*) frágil

delicatessen [dɛlɪkə'tɛsn] *n* ultramarinos *mpl* finos

delicious [dɪ'lɪʃəs] *adj* delicioso

delight [dɪ'laɪt] *n* (*feeling*) placer *m*, deleite *m*; (*person, experience etc*) encanto, delicia ♦ *vt* encantar, deleitar; **to take ~ in** deleitarse en; ~**ed** *adj:* ~**ed** (**at** *or* **with/to do**) encantado (con/de hacer); ~**ful** *adj* encantador(a), delicioso

delinquent [dɪ'lɪŋkwənt] *adj, n* delincuente *m/f*

delirious [dɪ'lɪrɪəs] *adj:* **to be** ~ delirar, desvariar; **to be** ~ **with** estar loco de

deliver [dɪ'lɪvə*] *vt* (*distribute*) repartir; (*hand over*) entregar; (*message*) comunicar; (*speech*) pronunciar; (*MED*) asistir al parto de; ~**y** *n* reparto; entrega; (*of speaker*) modo de expresarse; (*MED*) parto, alumbramiento; **to take ~y of** recibir

delude [dɪ'luːd] *vt* engañar

deluge ['dɛljuːdʒ] *n* diluvio

delusion [dɪ'luːʒən] *n* ilusión *f*, engaño

de luxe [də'lʌks] *adj* de lujo

delve [dɛlv] *vi:* **to** ~ **into** (*subject*) ahondar en; (*cupboard etc*) hurgar en

demand [dɪ'mɑːnd] *vt* (*gen*) exigir; (*rights*) reclamar ♦ *n* exigencia; (*claim*) reclamación *f*; (*ECON*) demanda; **to be in** ~ ser muy solicitado; **on** ~ a solicitud;

~**ing** *adj* (*boss*) exigente; (*work*) absorbente

demean [dɪ'miːn] *vt:* **to** ~ **o.s.** rebajarse

demeanour [dɪ'miːnə*] (*US* **demeanor**) *n* porte *m*, conducta

demented [dɪ'mɛntɪd] *adj* demente

demise [dɪ'maɪz] *n* (*death*) fallecimiento

demister [diː'mɪstə*] *n* (*AUT*) eliminador *m* de vaho

demo ['dɛməu] (*inf*) *n abbr* (= *demonstration*) manifestación *f*

democracy [dɪ'mɔkrəsɪ] *n* democracia; **democrat** ['dɛməkræt] *n* demócrata *m/f*; **democratic** [dɛmə'krætɪk] *adj* democrático; (*US*) demócrata

demolish [dɪ'mɔlɪʃ] *vt* derribar, demoler; (*fig: argument*) destruir; **demolition** [dɛmə'lɪʃən] *n* derribo, demolición *f*, destrucción *f*

demon ['diːmən] *n* (*evil spirit*) demonio

demonstrate ['dɛmənstreɪt] *vt* demostrar; (*skill, appliance*) mostrar ♦ *vi* manifestarse; **demonstration** [-'streɪʃən] *n* (*POL*) manifestación *f*; (*proof, exhibition*) demostración *f*; **demonstrator** *n* (*POL*) manifestante *m/f*; (*COMM*) demostrador(a) *m/f*; vendedor(a) *m/f*

demoralize [dɪ'mɔrəlaɪz] *vt* desmoralizar

demote [dɪ'məut] *vt* degradar

demure [dɪ'mjuə*] *adj* recatado

den [dɛn] *n* (*of animal*) guarida; (*room*) habitación *f*

denatured alcohol [diː'neɪtʃəd-] (*US*) *n* alcohol *m* desnaturalizado

denial [dɪ'naɪəl] *n* (*refusal*) negativa; (*of report etc*) negación *f*

denim ['dɛnɪm] *n* tela vaquera; ~**s** *npl* vaqueros *mpl*

Denmark ['dɛnmɑːk] *n* Dinamarca

denomination [dɪnɔmɪ'neɪʃən] *n* valor *m*; (*REL*) confesión *f*

denote [dɪ'nəut] *vt* indicar, significar

denounce [dɪ'nauns] *vt* denunciar

dense [dɛns] *adj* (*crowd*) denso; (*thick*) espeso; (*: foliage etc*) tupido; (*inf: stupid*) torpe; ~**ly** *adv:* ~**ly populated** con una alta densidad de población

density ['dɛnsɪtɪ] *n* densidad *f*; **single/double-~ disk** *n* (*COMPUT*) disco de densidad sencilla/doble densidad

dent [dɛnt] *n* abolladura ♦ *vt* (*also: make a ~ in*) abollar

dental ['dɛntl] *adj* dental; ~ **surgeon** *n* odontólogo/a

dentist ['dɛntɪst] *n* dentista *m/f*; ~**ry** *n* odontología

dentures ['dɛntʃəz] *npl* dentadura (postiza)

denunciation [dɪnʌnsɪ'eɪʃən] *n* denuncia, denunciación *f*

deny [dɪ'naɪ] *vt* negar; (*charge*) rechazar

deodorant [diː'əudərənt] *n* desodorante *m*

depart [dɪ'pɑːt] *vi* irse, marcharse; (*train*) salir; **to ~ from** (*fig: differ from*) apartarse de

department [dɪ'pɑːtmənt] *n* (COMM) sección *f*; (SCOL) departamento; (POL) ministerio; ~ **store** *n* gran almacén *m*

departure [dɪ'pɑːtʃə*] *n* partida, ida; (*of train*) salida; (*of employee*) marcha; **a new** ~ un nuevo rumbo; ~ **lounge** *n* (*at airport*) sala de embarque

depend [dɪ'pɛnd] *vi*: **to ~ on** depender de; (*rely on*) contar con; **it ~s** depende, según; ~**ing on the result** según el resultado; ~**able** *adj* (*person*) formal, serio; (*watch*) exacto; (*car*) seguro; ~**ant** *n* dependiente *m/f*; ~**ence** *n* dependencia; ~**ent** *adj*: **to be ~ent on** depender de ♦ *n* = **dependant**

depict [dɪ'pɪkt] *vt* (*in picture*) pintar; (*describe*) representar

depleted [dɪ'pliːtɪd] *adj* reducido

deplorable [dɪ'plɔːrəbl] *adj* deplorable

deploy [dɪ'plɔɪ] *vt* desplegar

depopulation [diːpɔpju'leɪʃən] *n* despoblación *f*

deport [dɪ'pɔːt] *vt* deportar

deportment [dɪ'pɔːtmənt] *n* comportamiento; (*way of walking*) porte *m*

depose [dɪ'pəuz] *vt* deponer

deposit [dɪ'pɔzɪt] *n* depósito; (CHEM) sedimento; (*of ore, oil*) yacimiento ♦ *vt* (*gen*) depositar; ~ **account** *n* (BRIT) cuenta de ahorros

depot ['dɛpəu] *n* (*storehouse*) depósito; (*for vehicles*) parque *m*; (US) estación *f*

depreciate [dɪ'priːʃɪeɪt] *vi* depreciarse, perder valor; **depreciation** [-'eɪʃən] *n* depreciación *f*

depress [dɪ'prɛs] *vt* deprimir; (*wages etc*) hacer bajar; (*press down*) apretar; ~**ed** *adj* deprimido; ~**ing** *adj* deprimente; ~**ion** [dɪ'prɛʃən] *n* depresión *f*

deprivation [dɛprɪ'veɪʃən] *n* privación *f*

deprive [dɪ'praɪv] *vt*: **to ~ sb of** privar a uno de; ~**d** *adj* necesitado

depth [dɛpθ] *n* profundidad *f*; (*of cupboard*) fondo; **to be in the ~s of despair** sentir la mayor desesperación; **to be out of one's ~** (*in water*) no hacer pie; (*fig*) sentirse totalmente perdido

deputation [dɛpju'teɪʃən] *n* delegación *f*

deputize ['dɛpjutaɪz] *vi*: **to ~ for sb** suplir a uno

deputy ['dɛpjutɪ] *adj*: ~ **head** subdirector(a) *m/f* ♦ *n* sustituto/a, suplente *m/f*; (US: POL) diputado/a; (US: *also*: ~ *sheriff*) agente *m* (del sheriff)

derail [dɪ'reɪl] *vt*: **to be ~ed** descarrilarse; ~**ment** *n* descarrilamiento

deranged [dɪ'reɪndʒd] *adj* trastornado

derby ['dɑːbɪ] (US) *n* (*hat*) hongo

derelict ['dɛrɪlɪkt] *adj* abandonado

derisory [dɪ'raɪzərɪ] *adj* (*sum*) irrisorio

derivative [dɪ'rɪvətɪv] *n* derivado

derive [dɪ'raɪv] *vt* (*benefit etc*) obtener ♦ *vi*: **to ~ from** derivarse de

derogatory [dɪ'rɔgətərɪ] *adj* despectivo

descend [dɪ'sɛnd] *vt, vi* descender, bajar; **to ~ from** descender de; **to ~ to** rebajarse a; ~**ant** *n* descendiente *m/f*

descent [dɪ'sɛnt] *n* descenso; (*origin*) descendencia

describe [dɪs'kraɪb] *vt* describir; **description** [-'krɪpʃən] *n* descripción *f*; (*sort*) clase *f*, género

desecrate ['dɛsɪkreɪt] *vt* profanar

desert [*n* 'dezət, *vb* dɪ'zəːt] *n* desierto ♦ *vt* abandonar ♦ *vi* (MIL) desertar; ~**er** [dɪ'zəːtə*] *n* desertor(a) *m/f*; ~**ion** [dɪ'zəːʃən] *n* deserción *f*; (LAW) abandono; ~ **island** *n* isla desierta; ~**s** [dɪ'zəːts] *npl*: **to get one's just ~s** llevar su merecido

deserve [dɪ'zəːv] *vt* merecer, ser digno de; **deserving** *adj* (*person*) digno; (*action*,

cause) meritorio

design [dɪ'zaɪn] n (*sketch*) bosquejo; (*layout, shape*) diseño; (*pattern*) dibujo; (*intention*) intención f ♦ vt diseñar

designate [vb 'dezɪgneɪt, adj 'dezɪgnɪt] vt (*appoint*) nombrar; (*destine*) designar ♦ adj designado

designer [dɪ'zaɪnə*] n diseñador(a) m/f; (*fashion ~*) modisto/a, diseñador(a) m/f de moda

desirable [dɪ'zaɪərəbl] adj (*proper*) deseable; (*attractive*) atractivo

desire [dɪ'zaɪə*] n deseo ♦ vt desear

desk [desk] n (*in office*) escritorio; (*for pupil*) pupitre m; (*in hotel, at airport*) recepción f; (*BRIT: in shop, restaurant*) caja

desolate ['desəlɪt] adj (*place*) desierto; (*person*) afligido; **desolation** [-'leɪʃən] n (*of place*) desolación f; (*of person*) aflicción f

despair [dɪs'pɛə*] n desesperación f ♦ vi: **to ~ of** perder la esperanza de

despatch [dɪs'pætʃ] n, vt = **dispatch**

desperate ['despərɪt] adj desesperado; (*fugitive*) peligroso; **to be ~ for sth/to do** necesitar urgentemente algo/hacer; **~ly** adv desesperadamente; (*very*) terriblemente, gravemente

desperation [despə'reɪʃən] n desesperación f; **in (sheer) ~** (absolutamente) desesperado

despicable [dɪs'pɪkəbl] adj vil, despreciable

despise [dɪs'paɪz] vt despreciar

despite [dɪs'paɪt] prep a pesar de, pese a

despondent [dɪs'pɔndənt] adj deprimido, abatido

dessert [dɪ'zɜːt] n postre m; **~spoon** n cuchara (de postre)

destination [destɪ'neɪʃən] n destino

destiny ['destɪnɪ] n destino

destitute ['destɪtjuːt] adj desamparado, indigente

destroy [dɪs'trɔɪ] vt destruir; (*animal*) sacrificar; **~er** n (*NAUT*) destructor m

destruction [dɪs'trʌkʃən] n destrucción f; **destructive** [dɪs'trʌktɪv] adj destructivo, destructor(a)

detach [dɪ'tætʃ] vt separar; (*unstick*) despegar; **~able** adj de quita y pon; **~ed** adj (*attitude*) objetivo, imparcial; **~ed house** n ≈ chalé m, ≈ chalet m; **~ment** n (*aloofness*) frialdad f; (*MIL*) destacamento

detail ['diːteɪl] n detalle m; (*no pl: in picture etc*) detalles mpl; (*trifle*) pequeñez f ♦ vt detallar; (*MIL*) destacar; **in ~** detalladamente; **~ed** adj detallado

detain [dɪ'teɪn] vt retener; (*in captivity*) detener

detect [dɪ'tekt] vt descubrir; (*MED, POLICE*) identificar; (*MIL, RADAR, TECH*) detectar; **~ion** [dɪ'tekʃən] n descubrimiento; identificación f; **~ive** n detective m/f; **~ive story** n novela policíaca; **~or** n detector m

détente [deɪ'tɑːnt] n distensión f

detention [dɪ'tenʃən] n detención f, arresto; (*SCOL*) castigo

deter [dɪ'tɜː*] vt (*dissuade*) disuadir

detergent [dɪ'tɜːdʒənt] n detergente m

deteriorate [dɪ'tɪərɪəreɪt] vi deteriorarse; **deterioration** [-'reɪʃən] n deterioro

determination [dɪtɜːmɪ'neɪʃən] n resolución f; (*establishment*) establecimiento

determine [dɪ'tɜːmɪn] vt determinar; **~d** adj (*person*) resuelto, decidido; **~d to do** resuelto a hacer

deterrent [dɪ'terənt] n (*MIL*) fuerza de disuasión

detest [dɪ'test] vt aborrecer

detonate ['detəneɪt] vi estallar ♦ vt hacer detonar

detour ['diːtuə*] n (*gen, US: AUT*) desviación f

detract [dɪ'trækt] vt: **to ~ from** quitar mérito a, desvirtuar

detriment ['detrɪmənt] n: **to the ~ of** en perjuicio de; **~al** [detrɪ'mentl] adj: **~al (to)** perjudicial (a)

devaluation [dɪvæljʊ'eɪʃən] n devaluación f

devalue [diː'væljuː] vt (*currency*) devaluar; (*fig*) quitar mérito a

devastate ['devəsteɪt] vt devastar; (*fig*): **to be ~d by** quedar destrozado por;

devastating *adj* devastador(a); (*fig*) arrollador(a)

develop [dɪ'vɛləp] *vt* desarrollar; (*PHOT*) revelar; (*disease*) coger; (*habit*) adquirir; (*fault*) empezar a tener ♦ *vi* desarrollarse; (*advance*) progresar; (*facts, symptoms*) aparecer; **~ing country** *n* país *m* en (vías de) desarrollo; **~er** *n* promotor *m*; **~ment** *n* desarrollo; (*advance*) progreso; (*of affair, case*) desenvolvimiento; (*of land*) urbanización *f*

deviate [ˈdiːvɪeɪt] *vi*: **to ~ (from)** desviarse (de); **deviation** [-ˈeɪʃən] *n* desviación *f*

device [dɪ'vaɪs] *n* (*apparatus*) aparato, mecanismo

devil [ˈdɛvl] *n* diablo, demonio; **~ish** *adj* diabólico

devious [ˈdiːvɪəs] *adj* taimado

devise [dɪ'vaɪz] *vt* idear, inventar

devoid [dɪ'vɔɪd] *adj*: **~ of** desprovisto de

devolution [diːvə'luːʃən] *n* (*POL*) descentralización *f*

devote [dɪ'vəut] *vt*: **to ~ sth to** dedicar algo a; **~d** *adj* (*loyal*) leal, fiel; **to be ~d to sb** querer con devoción a alguien; **the book is ~d to politics** el libro trata de la política; **~e** [dɛvəu'tiː] *n* entusiasta *m/f*; (*REL*) devoto/a

devotion [dɪ'vəuʃən] *n* dedicación *f*; (*REL*) devoción *f*

devour [dɪ'vauə*] *vt* devorar

devout [dɪ'vaut] *adj* devoto

dew [djuː] *n* rocío

dexterity [dɛks'tɛrɪtɪ] *n* destreza

diabetes [daɪə'biːtiːz] *n* diabetes *f*; **diabetic** [-'bɛtɪk] *adj, n* diabético/a *m/f*

diabolical [daɪə'bɔlɪkəl] (*inf*) *adj* (*weather, behaviour*) pésimo

diagnose [daɪəg'nəuz] *vt* diagnosticar; **diagnoses** [-'nəusiːz] *npl of* **diagnosis**; **diagnosis** [-'nəusɪs] (*pl* **-ses**) *n* diagnóstico

diagonal [daɪ'ægənl] *adj, n* diagonal *f*

diagram [ˈdaɪəgræm] *n* diagrama *m*, esquema *m*

dial [ˈdaɪəl] *n* esfera, cuadrante *m*, cara (*AM*); (*on radio etc*) selector *m*; (*of phone*) disco ♦ *vt* (*number*) marcar

dialling [ˈdaɪəlɪŋ]: **~ code** (*US* **dial code**) *n* prefijo; **~ tone** (*US* **dial tone**) *n* (*BRIT*) señal *f or* tono de marcar

dialogue [ˈdaɪəlɔg] (*US* **dialog**) *n* diálogo

diameter [daɪˈæmɪtə*] *n* diámetro

diamond [ˈdaɪəmənd] *n* diamante *m*; (*shape*) rombo; **~s** *npl* (*CARDS*) diamantes *mpl*

diaper [ˈdaɪəpə*] (*US*) *n* pañal *m*

diaphragm [ˈdaɪəfræm] *n* diafragma *m*

diarrhoea [daɪə'riːə] (*US* **diarrhea**) *n* diarrea

diary [ˈdaɪərɪ] *n* (*daily account*) diario; (*book*) agenda

dice [daɪs] *n inv* dados *mpl* ♦ *vt* (*CULIN*) cortar en cuadritos

dichotomy [daɪ'kɔtəmɪ] *n* dicotomía

Dictaphone [ˈdɪktəfəun] ® *n* dictáfono ®

dictate [dɪk'teɪt] *vt* dictar; (*conditions*) imponer; **dictation** [-'teɪʃən] *n* dictado; (*giving of orders*) órdenes *fpl*

dictator [dɪk'teɪtə*] *n* dictador *m*; **~ship** *n* dictadura

dictionary [ˈdɪkʃənrɪ] *n* diccionario

did [dɪd] *pt of* **do**

didn't [ˈdɪdənt] = **did not**

die [daɪ] *vi* morir; (*fig: fade*) desvanecerse, desaparecer; **to be dying for sth/to do sth** morirse por algo/de ganas de hacer algo; **~ away** *vi* (*sound, light*) perderse; **~ down** *vi* apagarse; (*wind*) amainar; **~ out** *vi* desaparecer

diehard [ˈdaɪhɑːd] *n* reaccionario/a

diesel [ˈdiːzəl] *n* vehículo con motor Diesel; **~ engine** *n* motor *m* Diesel; **~ (oil)** *n* gasoil *m*

diet [ˈdaɪət] *n* dieta; (*restricted food*) régimen *m* ♦ *vi* (*also:* **be on a ~**) estar a dieta, hacer régimen

differ [ˈdɪfə*] *vi*: **to ~ (from)** (*be different*) ser distinto (a), diferenciarse (de); (*disagree*) discrepar (de); **~ence** *n* diferencia; (*disagreement*) desacuerdo; **~ent** *adj* diferente, distinto; **~entiate** [-ˈrɛnʃɪeɪt] *vi*: **to ~entiate (between)** distinguir (entre); **~ently** *adv* de otro modo, en forma distinta

difficult [ˈdɪfɪkəlt] *adj* difícil; **~y** *n* dificultad *f*

diffident ['dɪfɪdənt] *adj* tímido

diffuse [*adj* dɪ'fju:s, *vb* dɪ'fju:z] *adj* difuso ♦ *vt* difundir

dig [dɪg] (*pt, pp* dug) *vt* (*hole, ground*) cavar ♦ *n* (*prod*) empujón *m*; (*archaeological*) excavación *f*; (*remark*) indirecta; **to ~ one's nails into** clavar las uñas en; **~ into** *vt fus* (*savings*) consumir; **~ out** *vt* (*hole*) excavar; (*fig*) sacar; **~ up** *vt* (*information*) desenterrar; (*plant*) desarraigar

digest [*vb* daɪ'dʒɛst, *n* 'daɪdʒɛst] *vt* (*food*) digerir; (*facts*) asimilar ♦ *n* resumen *m*; **~ion** [dɪ'dʒɛstʃən] *n* digestión *f*

digit ['dɪdʒɪt] *n* (*number*) dígito; (*finger*) dedo; **~al** *adj* digital

dignified ['dɪgnɪfaɪd] *adj* grave, solemne

dignity ['dɪgnɪtɪ] *n* dignidad *f*

digress [daɪ'grɛs] *vi*: **to ~ from** apartarse de

digs [dɪgz] (*BRIT: inf*) *npl* pensión *f*, alojamiento

dilapidated [dɪ'læpɪdeɪtɪd] *adj* desmoronado, ruinoso

dilemma [daɪ'lɛmə] *n* dilema *m*

diligent ['dɪlɪdʒənt] *adj* diligente

dilute [daɪ'lu:t] *vt* diluir

dim [dɪm] *adj* (*light*) débil; (*outline*) indistinto; (*room*) oscuro; (*inf: stupid*) lerdo ♦ *vt* (*light*) bajar

dime [daɪm] (*US*) *n* moneda de diez centavos

dimension [dɪ'mɛnʃən] *n* dimensión *f*

diminish [dɪ'mɪnɪʃ] *vt, vi* disminuir

diminutive [dɪ'mɪnjutɪv] *adj* diminuto ♦ *n* (*LING*) diminutivo

dimmers ['dɪməz] (*US*) *npl* (*AUT: dipped headlights*) luces *fpl* cortas; (: *parking lights*) luces *fpl* de posición

dimple ['dɪmpl] *n* hoyuelo

din [dɪn] *n* estruendo, estrépito

dine [daɪn] *vi* cenar; **~r** *n* (*person*) comensal *m/f*; (*US*) restaurante *m* económico

dinghy ['dɪŋgɪ] *n* bote *m*; (*also: rubber ~*) lancha (neumática)

dingy ['dɪndʒɪ] *adj* (*room*) sombrío; (*colour*) sucio

dining car ['daɪnɪŋ-] (*BRIT*) *n* (*RAIL*) coche-

comedor *m*

dining room *n* comedor *m*

dinner ['dɪnə*] *n* (*evening meal*) cena; (*lunch*) comida; (*public*) cena, banquete *m*; **~ jacket** *n* smoking *m*; **~ party** *n* cena; **~ time** *n* (*evening*) hora de cenar; (*midday*) hora de comer

dinosaur ['daɪnəsɔ:*] *n* dinosaurio

dint [dɪnt] *n*: **by ~ of** a fuerza de

diocese ['daɪəsɪs] *n* diócesis *f inv*

dip [dɪp] *n* (*slope*) pendiente *m*; (*in sea*) baño; (*CULIN*) salsa ♦ *vt* (*in water*) mojar; (*ladle etc*) meter; (*BRIT: AUT*): **to ~ one's lights** poner luces de cruce ♦ *vi* (*road etc*) descender, bajar

diphthong ['dɪfθɔŋ] *n* diptongo

diploma [dɪ'pləumə] *n* diploma *m*

diplomacy [dɪ'pləuməsɪ] *n* diplomacia

diplomat ['dɪpləmæt] *n* diplomático/a; **~ic** [dɪplə'mætɪk] *adj* diplomático

diprod ['dɪprɔd] (*US*) *n* = **dipstick**

dipstick ['dɪpstɪk] (*BRIT*) *n* (*AUT*) varilla de nivel (del aceite)

dipswitch ['dɪpswɪtʃ] (*BRIT*) *n* (*AUT*) interruptor *m*

dire [daɪə*] *adj* calamitoso

direct [daɪ'rɛkt] *adj* directo; (*challenge*) claro; (*person*) franco ♦ *vt* dirigir; (*order*): **to ~ sb to do sth** mandar a uno hacer algo ♦ *adv* derecho; **can you ~ me to...?** ¿puede indicarme dónde está...?; **~ debit** (*BRIT*) *n* domiciliación *f* bancaria de recibos

direction [dɪ'rɛkʃən] *n* dirección *f*; **sense of ~** sentido de la dirección; **~s** *npl* (*instructions*) instrucciones *fpl*; **~s for use** modo de empleo

directly [dɪ'rɛktlɪ] *adv* (*in straight line*) directamente; (*at once*) en seguida

director [dɪ'rɛktə*] *n* director(a) *m/f*

directory [dɪ'rɛktərɪ] *n* (*TEL*) guía (telefónica); (*COMPUT*) directorio

dirt [də:t] *n* suciedad *f*; (*earth*) tierra; **~-cheap** *adj* baratísimo; **~y** *adj* sucio; (*joke*) verde (*SP*), colorado (*AM*) ♦ *vt* ensuciar; (*stain*) manchar; **~y trick** *n* juego sucio

disability [dɪsə'bɪlɪtɪ] *n* incapacidad *f*

disabled [dɪs'eɪbld] *adj*: **to be physically**

~ ser minusválido/a; **to be mentally ~** ser deficiente mental

disadvantage [dɪsəd'vɑːntɪdʒ] *n* desventaja, inconveniente *m*

disaffection [dɪsə'fekʃən] *n* descontento

disagree [dɪsə'griː] *vi* (*differ*) discrepar; **to ~ (with)** no estar de acuerdo (con); **~able** *adj* desagradable; (*person*) antipático; **~ment** *n* desacuerdo

disallow [dɪsə'lau] *vt* (*goal*) anular; (*claim*) rechazar

disappear [dɪsə'pɪə*] *vi* desaparecer; **~ance** *n* desaparición *f*

disappoint [dɪsə'pɔɪnt] *vt* decepcionar, defraudar; **~ed** *adj* decepcionado; **~ing** *adj* decepcionante; **~ment** *n* decepción *f*

disapproval [dɪsə'pruːvəl] *n* desaprobación *f*

disapprove [dɪsə'pruːv] *vi*: **to ~ of** ver mal

disarm [dɪs'ɑːm] *vt* desarmar; **~ament** *n* desarme *m*; **~ing** *adj* (*smile etc*) que desarma

disarray [dɪsə'reɪ] *n*: **in ~** (*army, organization*) desorganizado; (*hair, clothes*) desarreglado

disaster [dɪ'zɑːstə*] *n* desastre *m*

disband [dɪs'bænd] *vt* disolver ♦ *vi* desbandarse

disbelief [dɪsbə'liːf] *n* incredulidad *f*

disc [dɪsk] *n* disco; (*COMPUT*) = **disk**

discard [dɪs'kɑːd] *vt* (*old things*) tirar; (*fig*) descartar

discern [dɪ'sɜːn] *vt* percibir, discernir; (*understand*) comprender; **~ing** *adj* perspicaz

discharge [*vb* dɪs'tʃɑːdʒ, *n* 'dɪstʃɑːdʒ] *vt* (*task, duty*) cumplir; (*waste*) verter; (*patient*) dar de alta; (*employee*) despedir; (*soldier*) licenciar; (*defendant*) poner en libertad ♦ *n* (*ELEC*) descarga; (*MED*) supuración *f*; (*dismissal*) despedida; (*of duty*) desempeño; (*of debt*) pago, descargo

disciple [dɪ'saɪpl] *n* discípulo

discipline ['dɪsɪplɪn] *n* disciplina ♦ *vt* disciplinar; (*punish*) castigar

disc jockey *n* pinchadiscos *m/f inv*

disclaim [dɪs'kleɪm] *vt* negar

disclose [dɪs'kləuz] *vt* revelar; **disclosure** [-'kləuʒə*] *n* revelación *f*

disco ['dɪskəu] *n abbr* = **discothèque**

discoloured [dɪs'kʌləd] (*US* **discolored**) *adj* descolorido

discomfort [dɪs'kʌmfət] *n* incomodidad *f*; (*unease*) inquietud *f*; (*physical*) malestar *m*

disconcert [dɪskən'sɜːt] *vt* desconcertar

disconnect [dɪskə'nekt] *vt* separar; (*ELEC etc*) desconectar

discontent [dɪskən'tent] *n* descontento; **~ed** *adj* descontento

discontinue [dɪskən'tɪnjuː] *vt* interrumpir; (*payments*) suspender; **"~d"** (*COMM*) "ya no se fabrica"

discord ['dɪskɔːd] *n* discordia; (*MUS*) disonancia; **~ant** [dɪs'kɔːdənt] *adj* discorde

discothèque ['dɪskəutek] *n* discoteca

discount [*n* 'dɪskaunt, *vb* dɪs'kaunt] *n* descuento ♦ *vt* descontar

discourage [dɪs'kʌrɪdʒ] *vt* desalentar; (*advise against*): **to ~ sb from doing** disuadir a uno de hacer; **discouraging** *adj* desalentador(a)

discover [dɪs'kʌvə*] *vt* descubrir; (*error*) darse cuenta de; **~y** *n* descubrimiento

discredit [dɪs'kredɪt] *vt* desacreditar

discreet [dɪ'skriːt] *adj* (*tactful*) discreto; (*careful*) circunspecto, prudente

discrepancy [dɪ'skrepənsɪ] *n* diferencia

discretion [dɪ'skreʃən] *n* (*tact*) discreción *f*; **at the ~ of** a criterio de

discriminate [dɪ'skrɪmɪneɪt] *vi*: **to ~ between** distinguir entre; **to ~ against** discriminar contra; **discriminating** *adj* entendido; **discrimination** [-'neɪʃən] *n* (*discernment*) perspicacia; (*bias*) discriminación *f*

discuss [dɪ'skʌs] *vt* discutir; (*a theme*) tratar; **~ion** *n* discusión *f*

disdain [dɪs'deɪn] *n* desdén *m*

disease [dɪ'ziːz] *n* enfermedad *f*

disembark [dɪsɪm'bɑːk] *vt, vi* desembarcar

disenchanted [dɪsɪn'tʃɑːntɪd] *adj*: **~ (with)** desilusionado (con)

disengage [dɪsɪn'geɪdʒ] *vt*: **to ~ the clutch** (*AUT*) desembragar

disentangle [dɪsɪn'tæŋgl] *vt* soltar; (*wire,*

thread) desenredar

disfigure [dɪs'fɪgə*] *vt* (*person*) desfigurar; (*object*) afear

disgrace [dɪs'greɪs] *n* ignominia; (*shame*) vergüenza, escándalo ♦ *vt* deshonrar; ~**ful** *adj* vergonzoso

disgruntled [dɪs'grʌntld] *adj* disgustado, descontento

disguise [dɪs'gaɪz] *n* disfraz *m* ♦ *vt* disfrazar; **in** ~ disfrazado

disgust [dɪs'gʌst] *n* repugnancia ♦ *vt* repugnar, dar asco a; ~**ing** *adj* repugnante, asqueroso; (*behaviour etc*) vergonzoso

dish [dɪʃ] *n* (*gen*) plato; **to do** *or* **wash the** ~**es** fregar los platos; ~ **up** *vt* servir; ~ **out** *vt* repartir; ~**cloth** *n* estropajo

dishearten [dɪs'hɑːtn] *vt* desalentar

dishevelled [dɪ'ʃevəld] *adj* (*hair*) despeinado; (*appearance*) desarreglado

dishonest [dɪs'ɒnɪst] *adj* (*person*) poco honrado, tramposo; (*means*) fraudulento; ~**y** *n* falta de honradez

dishonour [dɪs'ɒnə*] (*US* **dishonor**) *n* deshonra; ~**able** *adj* deshonroso

dishtowel ['dɪʃtauəl] (*US*) *n* estropajo

dishwasher ['dɪʃwɒʃə*] *n* lavaplatos *m inv*

disillusion [dɪsɪ'luːʒən] *vt* desilusionar

disincentive [dɪsɪn'sentɪv] *n* desincentivo

disinfect [dɪsɪn'fekt] *vt* desinfectar; ~**ant** *n* desinfectante *m*

disintegrate [dɪs'ɪntɪgreɪt] *vi* disgregarse, desintegrarse

disinterested [dɪs'ɪntrəstɪd] *adj* desinteresado

disjointed [dɪs'dʒɔɪntɪd] *adj* inconexo

disk [dɪsk] *n* (*esp US*) = **disc**; (*COMPUT*) disco, disquete *m*; **single-/double-sided** ~ disco de una cara/dos caras; ~ **drive** *n* disc drive *m*; ~**ette** *n* = **disk**

dislike [dɪs'laɪk] *n* antipatía, aversión *f* ♦ *vt* tener antipatía a

dislocate ['dɪsləkeɪt] *vt* dislocar

dislodge [dɪs'lɒdʒ] *vt* sacar

disloyal [dɪs'lɔɪəl] *adj* desleal

dismal ['dɪzml] *adj* (*gloomy*) deprimente, triste; (*very bad*) malísimo, fatal

dismantle [dɪs'mæntl] *vt* desmontar, desarmar

dismay [dɪs'meɪ] *n* consternación *f* ♦ *vt* consternar

dismiss [dɪs'mɪs] *vt* (*worker*) despedir; (*pupils*) dejar marchar; (*soldiers*) dar permiso para irse; (*idea, LAW*) rechazar; (*possibility*) descartar; ~**al** *n* despido

dismount [dɪs'maunt] *vi* apearse

disobedience [dɪsə'biːdɪəns] *n* desobediencia

disobedient [dɪsə'biːdɪənt] *adj* desobediente

disobey [dɪsə'beɪ] *vt* desobedecer

disorder [dɪs'ɔːdə*] *n* desorden *m*; (*rioting*) disturbios *mpl*; (*MED*) trastorno; ~**ly** *adj* desordenado; (*meeting*) alborotado; (*conduct*) escandaloso

disorientated [dɪs'ɔːrɪenteɪtəd] *adj* desorientado

disown [dɪs'əun] *vt* (*action*) renegar de; (*person*) negar cualquier tipo de relación con

disparaging [dɪs'pærɪdʒɪŋ] *adj* despreciativo

disparate ['dɪspərɪt] *adj* dispar

disparity [dɪs'pærɪtɪ] *n* disparidad *f*

dispassionate [dɪs'pæʃənɪt] *adj* (*unbiased*) imparcial

dispatch [dɪs'pætʃ] *vt* enviar ♦ *n* (*sending*) envío; (*PRESS*) informe *m*; (*MIL*) parte *m*

dispel [dɪs'pel] *vt* disipar

dispense [dɪs'pens] *vt* (*medicines*) preparar; ~ **with** *vt fus* prescindir de; ~**r** *n* (*container*) distribuidor *m* automático; **dispensing chemist** (*BRIT*) *n* farmacia

disperse [dɪs'pəːs] *vt* dispersar ♦ *vi* dispersarse

dispirited [dɪ'spɪrɪtɪd] *adj* desanimado, desalentado

displace [dɪs'pleɪs] *vt* desplazar, reemplazar; ~**d person** *n* (*POL*) desplazado/a

display [dɪs'pleɪ] *n* (*in shop window*) escaparate *m*; (*exhibition*) exposición *f*; (*COMPUT*) visualización *f*; (*of feeling*) manifestación *f* ♦ *vt* exponer; manifestar; (*ostentatiously*) lucir

displease [dɪs'pliːz] *vt* (*offend*) ofender;

(*annoy*) fastidiar; ~d *adj*: ~d with disgustado con; **displeasure** [-'plɛʒə*] *n* disgusto

disposable [dɪs'pəuzəbl] *adj* desechable; (*income*) disponible; ~ nappy *n* pañal *m* desechable

disposal [dɪs'pəuzl] *n* (*of rubbish*) destrucción *f*; at one's ~ a su disposición

dispose [dɪs'pəuz] *vi*: to ~ of (*unwanted goods*) deshacerse de; (*problem etc*) resolver; ~d *adj*: ~d to do dispuesto a hacer; to be well-~d towards sb estar bien dispuesto hacia uno; **disposition** [-'zɪʃən] *n* (*nature*) temperamento; (*inclination*) propensión *f*

disproportionate [dɪsprə'pɔːʃənət] *adj* desproporcionado

disprove [dɪs'pruːv] *vt* refutar

dispute [dɪs'pjuːt] *n* disputa; (*also: industrial* ~) conflicto (laboral) ♦ *vt* (*argue*) disputar, discutir; (*question*) cuestionar

disqualify [dɪs'kwɔlɪfaɪ] *vt* (*SPORT*) desclasificar; to ~ sb for sth/from doing sth incapacitar a alguien para algo/hacer algo

disquiet [dɪs'kwaɪət] *n* preocupación *f*, inquietud *f*

disregard [dɪsrɪ'gɑːd] *vt* (*ignore*) no hacer caso de

disrepair [dɪsrɪ'pɛə*] *n*: to fall into ~ (*building*) desmoronarse

disreputable [dɪs'rɛpjutəbl] *adj* (*person*) de mala fama; (*behaviour*) vergonzoso

disrespectful [dɪsrɪ'spɛktful] *adj* irrespetuoso

disrupt [dɪs'rʌpt] *vt* (*plans*) desbaratar, trastornar; (*conversation*) interrumpir; ~ion [-'rʌpʃən] *n* (*disturbance*) trastorno; (*interruption*) interrupción *f*

dissatisfaction [dɪssætɪs'fækʃən] *n* disgusto, descontento

dissect [dɪ'sɛkt] *vt* disecar

dissent [dɪ'sɛnt] *n* disensión *f*

dissertation [dɪsə'teɪʃən] *n* tesina

disservice [dɪs'səːvɪs] *n*: to do sb a ~ perjudicar a alguien

dissident ['dɪsɪdənt] *adj, n* disidente *m/f*

dissimilar [dɪ'sɪmɪlə*] *adj* distinto

dissipate ['dɪsɪpeɪt] *vt* disipar; (*waste*) desperdiciar

dissociate [dɪ'səuʃɪeɪt] *vt* disociar

dissolute ['dɪsəluːt] *adj* disoluto

dissolution [dɪsə'luːʃən] *n* disolución *f*

dissolve [dɪ'zɔlv] *vt* disolver ♦ *vi* disolverse; to ~ in(to) tears deshacerse en lágrimas

dissuade [dɪ'sweɪd] *vt*: to ~ sb (from) disuadir a uno (de)

distance ['dɪstəns] *n* distancia; in the ~ a lo lejos

distant ['dɪstənt] *adj* lejano; (*manner*) reservado, frío

distaste [dɪs'teɪst] *n* repugnancia; ~ful *adj* repugnante, desagradable

distended [dɪ'stɛndɪd] *adj* (*stomach*) hinchado

distil [dɪs'tɪl] (*US* **distill**) *vt* destilar; ~lery *n* destilería

distinct [dɪs'tɪŋkt] *adj* (*different*) distinto; (*clear*) claro; (*unmistakeable*) inequívoco; as ~ from a diferencia de; ~ion [dɪs'tɪŋkʃən] *n* distinción *f*; (*honour*) honor *m*; (*in exam*) sobresaliente *m*; ~ive *adj* distintivo

distinguish [dɪs'tɪŋgwɪʃ] *vt* distinguir; to ~ o.s. destacarse; ~ed *adj* (*eminent*) distinguido; ~ing *adj* (*feature*) distintivo

distort [dɪs'tɔːt] *vt* distorsionar; (*shape, image*) deformar; ~ion [dɪs'tɔːʃən] *n* distorsión *f*; deformación *f*

distract [dɪs'trækt] *vt* distraer; ~ed *adj* distraído; ~ion [dɪs'trækʃən] *n* distracción *f*; (*confusion*) aturdimiento

distraught [dɪs'trɔːt] *adj* loco de inquietud

distress [dɪs'trɛs] *n* (*anguish*) angustia, aflicción *f* ♦ *vt* afligir; ~ing *adj* angustioso; doloroso; ~ signal *n* señal *f* de socorro

distribute [dɪs'trɪbjuːt] *vt* distribuir; (*share out*) repartir; **distribution** [-'bjuːʃən] *n* distribución *f*, reparto; **distributor** *n* (*AUT*) distribuidor *m*; (*COMM*) distribuidora

district ['dɪstrɪkt] *n* (*of country*) zona, región *f*; (*of town*) barrio; (*ADMIN*) distrito; ~ **attorney** (*US*) *n* fiscal *m/f*; ~ **nurse** (*BRIT*) *n* enfermera que atiende a pacientes a domicilio

distrust [dɪsˈtrʌst] *n* desconfianza ♦ *vt* desconfiar de

disturb [dɪsˈtəːb] *vt* (*person: bother, interrupt*) molestar; (: *upset*) perturbar, inquietar; (*disorganize*) alterar; ~**ance** *n* (*upheaval*) perturbación *f*; (*political etc: gen pl*) disturbio; (*of mind*) trastorno; ~**ed** *adj* (*worried, upset*) preocupado, angustiado; **emotionally** ~**ed** trastornado; (*childhood*) inseguro; ~**ing** *adj* inquietante, perturbador(a)

disuse [dɪsˈjuːs] *n*: **to fall into** ~ caer en desuso

disused [dɪsˈjuːzd] *adj* abandonado

ditch [dɪtʃ] *n* zanja; (*irrigation* ~) acequia ♦ *vt* (*inf: partner*) deshacerse de; (: *plan, car etc*) abandonar

dither [ˈdɪðəʳ] (*pej*) *vi* vacilar

ditto [ˈdɪtəu] *adv* ídem, lo mismo

divan [dɪˈvæn] *n* (*also*: ~ **bed**) cama turca

dive [daɪv] *n* (*from board*) salto; (*underwater*) buceo; (*of submarine*) sumersión *f* ♦ *vi* (*swimmer: into water*) saltar; (: *under water*) zambullirse, bucear; (*fish, submarine*) sumergirse; (*bird*) lanzarse en picado; **to** ~ **into** (*bag etc*) meter la mano en; (*place*) meterse de prisa en; ~**r** *n* (*underwater*) buzo

diverge [daɪˈvəːdʒ] *vi* divergir

diverse [daɪˈvəːs] *adj* diversos/as, varios/as

diversion [daɪˈvəːʃən] *n* (*BRIT: AUT*) desviación *f*; (*distraction, MIL*) diversión *f*; (*of funds*) distracción *f*

divert [daɪˈvəːt] *vt* (*turn aside*) desviar

divide [dɪˈvaɪd] *vt* dividir; (*separate*) separar ♦ *vi* dividirse; (*road*) bifurcarse; ~**d highway** (*US*) *n* carretera de doble calzada

dividend [ˈdɪvɪdɛnd] *n* dividendo; (*fig*): **to pay** ~**s** proporcionar beneficios

divine [dɪˈvaɪn] *adj* (*also fig*) divino

diving [ˈdaɪvɪŋ] *n* (*SPORT*) salto; (*underwater*) buceo; ~ **board** *n* trampolín *m*

divinity [dɪˈvɪnɪtɪ] *n* divinidad *f*; (*SCOL*) teología

division [dɪˈvɪʒən] *n* división *f*; (*sharing out*) reparto; (*disagreement*) diferencias *fpl*; (*COMM*) sección *f*

divorce [dɪˈvɔːs] *n* divorcio ♦ *vt* divorciarse de; ~**d** *adj* divorciado; ~**e** [-ˈsiː] *n* divorciado/a

divulge [daɪˈvʌldʒ] *vt* divulgar, revelar

D.I.Y. (*BRIT*) *adj, n abbr* = **do-it-yourself**

dizzy [ˈdɪzɪ] *adj* (*spell*) de mareo; **to feel** ~ marearse

DJ *n abbr* = **disc jockey**

KEYWORD
---

do [duː] (*pt* **did**, *pp* **done**) *n* (*inf: party etc*): **we're having a little** ~ **on Saturday** damos una fiestecita el sábado; **it was rather a grand** ~ fue un acontecimiento a lo grande
♦ *aux vb* **1** (*in negative constructions: not translated*) **I don't understand** no lo entiendo
2 (*to form questions: not translated*) **didn't you know?** ¿no lo sabías?; **what** ~ **you think?** ¿qué opinas?
3 (*for emphasis, in polite expressions*): **people** ~ **make mistakes sometimes** sí que se cometen errores a veces; **she does seem rather late** a mí también me parece que se ha retrasado; ~ **sit down/help yourself** siéntate/sírvete por favor; ~ **take care!** ¡ten cuidado(, te pido)!
4 (*used to avoid repeating vb*): **she sings better than I** ~ canta mejor que yo; ~ **you agree?** — **yes, I** ~/**no, I don't** ¿estás de acuerdo? — sí (lo estoy)/no (lo estoy); **she lives in Glasgow** — **so** ~ **I** vive en Glasgow — yo también; **he didn't like it and neither did we** no le gustó y a nosotros tampoco; **who made this mess?** — **I did** ¿quién hizo esta chapuza? — yo; **he asked me to help him and I did** me pidió que le ayudara y lo hice
5 (*in question tags*): **you like him, don't you?** te gusta, ¿verdad? *or* ¿no?; **I don't know him,** ~ **I?** creo que no le conozco
♦ *vt* **1** (*gen, carry out, perform etc*): **what**

are you ~ing tonight? ¿qué haces esta noche?; **what can I ~ for you?** ¿en qué puedo servirle?; **to ~ the washing-up/cooking** fregar los platos/cocinar; **to ~ one's teeth/hair/nails** lavarse los dientes/arreglarse el pelo/arreglarse las uñas

2 (*AUT etc*): **the car was ~ing 100** el coche iba a 100; **we've done 200 km already** ya hemos hecho 200 km; **he can ~ 100 in that car** puede dar los 100 en ese coche

♦ *vi* 1 (*act, behave*) hacer; **~ as I ~** haz como yo

2 (*get on, fare*): **he's ~ing well/badly at school** va bien/mal en la escuela; **the firm is ~ing well** la empresa anda *or* va bien; **how ~ you ~?** mucho gusto; (*less formal*) ¿qué tal?

3 (*suit*): **will it ~?** ¿sirve?, ¿está *or* va bien?

4 (*be sufficient*) bastar; **will £10 ~?** ¿será bastante con £10?; **that'll ~** así está bien; **that'll ~!** (*in annoyance*) ¡ya está bien!, ¡basta ya!; **to make ~ (with)** arreglárselas (con)

do away with *vt fus* (*kill, disease*) eliminar; (*abolish: law etc*) abolir; (*withdraw*) retirar

do up *vt* (*laces*) atar; (*zip, dress, shirt*) abrochar; (*renovate: room, house*) renovar

do with *vt fus* (*need*): **I could ~ with a drink/some help** no me vendría mal un trago/un poco de ayuda; (*be connected*) tener que ver con; **what has it got to ~ with you?** ¿qué tiene que ver contigo?

do without *vi* pasar sin; **if you're late for tea then you'll ~ without** si llegas tarde para la merienda pasarás sin él

♦ *vt fus* pasar sin; **I can ~ without a car** puedo pasar sin coche

dock [dɔk] *n* (*NAUT*) muelle *m*; (*LAW*) banquillo (de los acusados); **~s** *npl* (*NAUT*) muelles *mpl*, puerto *sg* ♦ *vi* (*enter ~*) atracar (la) muelle; (*SPACE*) acoplarse; **~er** *n* trabajador *m* portuario, estibador *m*; **~yard** *n* astillero

doctor [ˈdɔktə*] *n* médico/a; (*Ph.D. etc*) doctor(a) *m/f* ♦ *vt* (*drink etc*) adulterar; **D~ of Philosophy** *n* Doctor en Filosofía y Letras

doctrine [ˈdɔktrɪn] *n* doctrina

document [ˈdɔkjumənt] *n* documento; **~ary** [-ˈmentərɪ] *adj* documental ♦ *n* documental *m*

dodge [dɔdʒ] *n* (*fig*) truco ♦ *vt* evadir; (*blow*) esquivar

dodgems [ˈdɔdʒəmz] (*BRIT*) *npl* coches *mpl* de choque

doe [dəu] *n* (*deer*) cierva, gama; (*rabbit*) coneja

does [dʌz] *vb see* **do**; **~n't = ~ not**

dog [dɔg] *n* perro ♦ *vt* seguir los pasos de; (*subj: bad luck*) perseguir; **~ collar** *n* collar *m* de perro; (*of clergyman*) alzacuellos *m inv*; **~-eared** *adj* sobado

dogged [ˈdɔgɪd] *adj* tenaz, obstinado

dogsbody [ˈdɔgzbɔdɪ] (*BRIT: inf*) *n* burro de carga

doings [ˈduɪŋz] *npl* (*activities*) actividades *fpl*

do-it-yourself *n* bricolaje *m*

doldrums [ˈdɔldrəmz] *npl*: **to be in the ~** (*person*) estar abatido; (*business*) estar estancado

dole [dəul] (*BRIT*) *n* (*payment*) subsidio de paro; **on the ~** parado; **~ out** *vt* repartir

doleful [ˈdəulful] *adj* triste, lúgubre

doll [dɔl] *n* muñeca; (*US: inf: woman*) muñeca, gachí *f*; **~ed-up** (*inf*) *adj* arreglado

dollar [ˈdɔlə*] *n* dólar *m*

dolphin [ˈdɔlfɪn] *n* delfín *m*

domain [dəˈmeɪn] *n* (*fig*) campo, competencia; (*land*) dominios *mpl*

dome [dəum] *n* (*ARCH*) cúpula

domestic [dəˈmestɪk] *adj* (*animal, duty*) doméstico; (*flight, policy*) nacional; **~ated** *adj* domesticado; (*home-loving*) casero, hogareño

dominant [ˈdɔmɪnənt] *adj* dominante

dominate [ˈdɔmɪneɪt] *vt* dominar

domineering [dɔmɪˈnɪərɪŋ] *adj* dominante

dominion [dəˈmɪnɪən] *n* dominio

domino [ˈdɔmɪnəu] (*pl* ~**es**) *n* ficha de

dominó; ~es n (game) dominó

don [dɔn] (BRIT) n profesor(a) m/f universitario/a

donate [də'neɪt] vt donar; donation [də'neɪʃən] n donativo

done [dʌn] pp of do

donkey ['dɔŋkɪ] n burro

donor ['dəunə*] n donante m/f

don't [dəunt] = do not

doodle ['duːdl] vi hacer dibujitos or garabatos

doom [duːm] n (fate) suerte f ♦ vt: to be ~ed to failure estar condenado al fracaso; ~sday n día m del juicio final

door [dɔː*] n puerta f; ~bell n timbre m; ~ handle n tirador m; (of car) manija; ~man n (in hotel) portero; ~mat n felpudo, estera; ~step n peldaño; ~-to-~ adj de puerta en puerta; ~way n entrada, puerta

dope [dəup] n (inf: illegal drug) droga; (: person) imbécil m/f ♦ vt (horse etc) drogar

dopey ['dəupɪ] (inf) adj (groggy) atontado; (stupid) imbécil

dormant ['dɔːmənt] adj inactivo

dormice ['dɔːmaɪs] npl of dormouse

dormitory ['dɔːmɪtrɪ] n (BRIT) dormitorio; (US) colegio mayor

dormouse ['dɔːmaus] (pl -mice) n lirón m

DOS n abbr (= disk operating system) DOS m

dosage ['dəusɪdʒ] n dosis f inv

dose [dəus] n dósis f inv

doss house ['dɔss-] (BRIT) n pensión f de mala muerte

dossier ['dɔsɪeɪ] n expediente m, dosier m

dot [dɔt] n punto ♦ vi: ~ted with salpicado de, con; on the ~ en punto

dote [dəut]: to ~ on vt fus adorar, idolatrar

dot-matrix printer n impresora matricial (or de matriz) de puntos

double ['dʌbl] adj doble ♦ adv (twice): to cost ~ costar el doble ♦ n doble m ♦ vt doblar ♦ vi doblarse; on the ~, at the ~ (BRIT) corriendo; ~ bass n contrabajo; ~

bed n cama de matrimonio; ~ bend (BRIT) n doble curva; ~-breasted adj cruzado; ~cross vt (trick) engañar; (betray) traicionar; ~decker n autobús m de dos pisos; ~ glazing (BRIT) n doble acristalamiento; ~ room n habitación f doble; ~s n (TENNIS) juego de dobles; doubly adv doblemente

doubt [daut] n duda ♦ vt dudar; (suspect) dudar de; to ~ that dudar que; ~ful adj dudoso; (person): to be ~ful about sth tener dudas sobre algo; ~less adv sin duda

dough [dəu] n masa, pasta; ~nut n ≈ rosquilla

douse [daus] vt (drench) mojar; (extinguish) apagar

dove [dʌv] n paloma

dovetail ['dʌvteɪl] vi (fig) encajar

dowdy ['daudɪ] adj (person) mal vestido; (clothes) pasado de moda

down [daun] n (feathers) plumón m, flojel m ♦ adv (~wards) abajo, hacia abajo; (on the ground) por or en tierra ♦ prep abajo ♦ vt (inf: drink) beberse; ~ with X! ¡abajo X!; ~-and-out n vagabundo/a; ~-at-heel adj venido a menos; (appearance) desaliñado; ~cast adj abatido; ~fall n caída, ruina; ~hearted adj desanimado; ~hill adv: to go ~hill (also fig) ir cuesta abajo; ~ payment n entrada, pago al contado; ~pour n aguacero; ~right adj (nonsense, lie) manifiesto; (refusal) terminante

Down's syndrome ['daunz-] n síndrome m de Down

down [daun]: ~stairs adv (below) (en la casa de) abajo; (~wards) escaleras abajo; ~stream adv aguas or río abajo; ~-to-earth adj práctico; ~town adv en el centro de la ciudad; ~ under adv en Australia (or Nueva Zelanda); ~ward [-wəd] adj, adv hacia abajo; ~wards [-wədz] adv hacia abajo

dowry ['daurɪ] n dote f

doz. abbr = dozen

doze [dəuz] vi dormitar; ~ off vi quedarse medio dormido

dozen ['dʌzn] n docena; a ~ books una

docena de libros; **~s of** cantidad de

Dr. *abbr* = **doctor; drive**

drab [dræb] *adj* gris, monótono

draft [drɑːft] *n* (*first copy*) borrador *m*; (*POL: of bill*) anteproyecto; (*US: call-up*) quinta ♦ *vt* (*plan*) preparar; (*write roughly*) hacer un borrador de; *see also* **draught**

draftsman ['drɑːftsmən] (*US*) *n* = **draughtsman**

drag [dræg] *vt* arrastrar; (*river*) dragar, rastrear ♦ *vi* (*time*) pasar despacio; (*play, film etc*) hacerse pesado ♦ *n* (*inf*) lata *m*; (*women's clothing*): **in ~** vestido de travesti; **~ on** *vi* ser interminable

dragon ['drægən] *n* dragón *m*

dragonfly ['drægənflaɪ] *n* libélula

drain [dreɪn] *n* desaguadero; (*in street*) sumidero; (*source of loss*): **to be a ~ on** consumir, agotar ♦ *vt* (*land, marshes*) desaguar; (*reservoir*) desecar; (*vegetables*) escurrir ♦ *vi* escurrirse; **~age** *n* (*act*) desagüe *m*; (*MED, AGR*) drenaje *m*; (*sewage*) alcantarillado; **~board** ['dreɪnbɔːd] (*US*) *n* = **~ing board**; **~ing board** *n* escurridera, escurridor *m*; **~pipe** *n* tubo de desagüe

drama ['drɑːmə] *n* (*art*) teatro; (*play*) drama *m*; (*excitement*) emoción *f*; **~tic** [drə'mætɪk] *adj* dramático; (*sudden, marked*) espectacular; **~tist** ['dræmətɪst] *n* dramaturgo/a; **~tize** ['dræmətaɪz] *vt* (*events*) dramatizar; (*adapt: for TV, cinema*) adaptar a la televisión/al cine

drank [dræŋk] *pt of* **drink**

drape [dreɪp] *vt* (*cloth*) colocar; (*flag*) colgar; **~s** (*US*) *npl* cortinas *fpl*

drastic ['dræstɪk] *adj* (*measure*) severo; (*change*) radical, drástico

draught [drɑːft] (*US* **draft**) *n* (*of air*) corriente *f* de aire; (*NAUT*) calado; **on ~** (*beer*) de barril; **~board** (*BRIT*) *n* tablero de damas; **~s** (*BRIT*) *n* (*game*) juego de damas

draughtsman ['drɑːftsmən] (*US* **draftsman**) *n* delineante *m*

draw [drɔː] (*pt* **drew**, *pp* **drawn**) *vt* (*picture*) dibujar; (*cart*) tirar de; (*curtain*) correr; (*take out*) sacar; (*attract*) atraer;

(*money*) retirar; (*wages*) cobrar ♦ *vi* (*SPORT*) empatar ♦ *n* (*SPORT*) empate *m*; (*lottery*) sorteo; **~ near** *vi* acercarse; **~ out** *vi* (*lengthen*) alargarse ♦ *vt* sacar; **~ up** *vi* (*stop*) pararse ♦ *vt* (*chair*) acercar; (*document*) redactar; **~back** *n* inconveniente *m*, desventaja; **~bridge** *n* puente *m* levadizo

drawer [drɔː*] *n* cajón *m*

drawing ['drɔːɪŋ] *n* dibujo; **~ board** *n* tablero (de dibujante); **~ pin** (*BRIT*) *n* chincheta; **~ room** *n* salón *m*

drawl [drɔːl] *n* habla lenta y cansina

drawn [drɔːn] *pp of* **draw**

dread [dred] *n* pavor *m*, terror *m* ♦ *vt* temer, tener miedo *or* pavor a; **~ful** *adj* horroroso

dream [driːm] (*pt, pp* **dreamed** *or* **dreamt**) *n* sueño ♦ *vt, vi* soñar; **~er** *n* soñador(a) *m/f*; **dreamt** [dremt] *pt, pp of* **dream**; **~y** *adj* (*distracted*) soñador(a), distraído; (*music*) suave

dreary ['drɪərɪ] *adj* monótono

dredge [dredʒ] *vt* dragar

dregs [dregz] *npl* posos *mpl*; (*of humanity*) hez *f*

drench [drentʃ] *vt* empapar

dress [dres] *n* vestido; (*clothing*) ropa ♦ *vt* vestir; (*wound*) vendar ♦ *vi* vestirse; **to get ~ed** vestirse; **~ up** *vi* vestirse de etiqueta; (*in fancy dress*) disfrazarse; **~ circle** (*BRIT*) *n* principal *m*; **~er** *n* (*furniture*) aparador *m*; (*: US*) cómoda (con espejo); **~ing** *n* (*MED*) vendaje *m*; (*CULIN*) aliño; **~ing gown** (*BRIT*) *n* bata; **~ing room** *n* (*THEATRE*) camarín *m*; (*SPORT*) vestuario; **~ing table** *n* tocador *m*; **~maker** *n* modista, costurera; **~ rehearsal** *n* ensayo general

drew [druː] *pt of* **draw**

dribble ['drɪbl] *vi* (*baby*) babear ♦ *vt* (*ball*) regatear

dried [draɪd] *adj* (*fruit*) seco; (*milk*) en polvo

drier ['draɪə*] *n* = **dryer**

drift [drɪft] *n* (*of current etc*) flujo; (*of snow*) ventisquero; (*meaning*) significado ♦ *vi* (*boat*) ir a la deriva; (*sand, snow*) amontonarse; **~wood** *n* madera de deriva

drill [drɪl] *n* (~ *bit*) broca; (*tool for DIY etc*) taladro; (*of dentist*) fresa; (*for mining etc*) perforadora, barrena; (*MIL*) instrucción *f* ♦ *vt* perforar, taladrar; (*troops*) enseñar la instrucción a ♦ *vi* (*for oil*) perforar

drink [drɪŋk] (*pt* **drank**, *pp* **drunk**) *n* bebida; (*sip*) trago ♦ *vt, vi* beber; **to have a ~** tomar algo; tomar una copa *or* un trago; **a ~ of water** un trago de agua; **~er** *n* bebedor(a) *m/f*; **~ing water** *n* agua potable

drip [drɪp] *n* (*act*) goteo; (*one ~*) gota; (*MED*) gota a gota *m* ♦ *vi* gotear; **~-dry** *adj* (*shirt*) inarrugable; **~ping** *n* (*animal fat*) pringue *m*

drive [draɪv] (*pt* **drove**, *pp* **driven**) *n* (*journey*) viaje *m* (en coche); (*also*: ~*way*) entrada; (*energy*) energía, vigor *m*; (*COMPUT*: *also*: *disk* ~) drive *m* ♦ *vt* (*car*) conducir (*SP*), manejar (*AM*); (*nail*) clavar; (*push*) empujar; (*TECH*: *motor*) impulsar ♦ *vi* (*AUT*: *at controls*) conducir; (: *travel*) pasearse en coche; **left-/right-hand ~** conducción *f* a la izquierda/derecha; **to ~ sb mad** volverle loco a uno

drivel ['drɪvl] (*inf*) *n* tonterías *fpl*

driven ['drɪvn] *pp of* **drive**

driver ['draɪvə*] *n* conductor(a) *m/f* (*SP*), chofer *m* (*AM*); (*of taxi, bus*) chofer; **~'s license** (*US*) *n* carnet *m* de conducir

driveway ['draɪvweɪ] *n* entrada

driving ['draɪvɪŋ] *n* el conducir (*SP*), el manejar (*AM*); **~ instructor** *n* instructor(a) *m/f* de conducción *or* manejo; **~ lesson** *n* clase *f* de conducción *or* manejo; **~ licence** (*BRIT*) *n* permiso de conducir; **~ school** *n* autoescuela; **~ test** *n* examen *m* de conducción *or* manejo

drizzle ['drɪzl] *n* llovizna

drone [drəun] *n* (*noise*) zumbido; (*bee*) zángano

drool [druːl] *vi* babear

droop [druːp] *vi* (*flower*) marchitarse; (*shoulders*) encorvarse; (*head*) inclinarse

drop [drɔp] *n* (*of water*) gota; (*lessening*) baja; (*fall*) caída ♦ *vt* dejar caer; (*voice,*

eyes, price) bajar; (*passenger*) dejar; (*omit*) omitir ♦ *vi* (*object*) caer; (*wind*) amainar; **~s** *npl* (*MED*) gotas *fpl*; **~ off** *vi* (*sleep*) dormirse ♦ *vt* (*passenger*) dejar; **~ out** *vi* (*withdraw*) retirarse; **~-out** *n* marginado/a; (*SCOL*) estudiante *que abandona los estudios*; **~per** *n* cuentagotas *m inv*; **~pings** *npl* excremento

drought [draut] *n* sequía

drove [drəuv] *pt of* **drive**

drown [draun] *vt* ahogar ♦ *vi* ahogarse

drowsy ['drauzɪ] *adj* soñoliento; **to be ~** tener sueño

drudgery ['drʌdʒərɪ] *n* trabajo monótono

drug [drʌg] *n* medicamento; (*narcotic*) droga ♦ *vt* drogar; **to be on ~s** drogarse; **~ addict** *n* drogadicto/a; **~gist** (*US*) *n* farmacéutico; **~store** (*US*) *n* farmacia

drum [drʌm] *n* tambor *m*; (*for oil, petrol*) bidón *m*; **~s** *npl* batería; **~mer** *n* tambor *m*

drunk [drʌŋk] *pp of* **drink** ♦ *adj* borracho ♦ *n* (*also*: ~*ard*) borracho/a; **~en** *adj* borracho; (*laughter, party*) de borrachos

dry [draɪ] *adj* seco; (*day*) sin lluvia; (*climate*) árido, seco ♦ *vt* secar; (*tears*) enjugarse ♦ *vi* secarse; **~ up** *vi* (*river*) secarse; **~-cleaner's** *n* tintorería; **~-cleaning** *n* lavado en seco; **~er** *n* (*for hair*) secador *m*; (*US*: *for clothes*) secadora; **~ness** *n* sequedad *f*; **~ rot** *n* putrefacción *f* fungoide

DSS *n abbr* = **Department of Social Security**

dual ['djuəl] *adj* doble; **~ carriageway** (*BRIT*) *n* carretera de doble calzada; **~ nationality** *n* doble nacionalidad *f*; **~-purpose** *adj* de doble uso

dubbed [dʌbd] *adj* (*CINEMA*) doblado

dubious ['djuːbɪəs] *adj* indeciso; (*reputation, company*) sospechoso

duchess ['dʌtʃɪs] *n* duquesa

duck [dʌk] *n* pato ♦ *vi* agacharse; **~ling** *n* patito

duct [dʌkt] *n* conducto, canal *m*

dud [dʌd] *n* (*object, tool*) engaño, engañifa ♦ *adj*: **~ cheque** (*BRIT*) cheque *m* sin fondos

due [dju:] *adj* (*owed*): **he is ~ £10** se le deben **♦** £10 libras; (*expected: event*): **the meeting is ~ on Wednesday** la reunión tendrá lugar el miércoles; (*: arrival*) **the train is ~ at 8am** el tren tiene su llegada para las 8; (*proper*) debido **♦** *n*: **to give sb his** (*or* **her**) **~** ser justo con alguien **♦** *adv*: **~ north** derecho al norte; **~s** *npl* (*for club, union*) cuota; (*in harbour*) derechos *mpl*; **in ~ course** a su debido tiempo; **~ to** debido a; **to be ~ to** deberse a

duet [dju:'ɛt] *n* dúo

duffel ['dʌfəl] *adj*: **~ bag** *n* bolsa de lona; **~ coat** *n* trenca, abrigo de tres cuartos

dug [dʌg] *pt, pp of* **dig**

duke [dju:k] *n* duque *m*

dull [dʌl] *adj* (*light*) débil; (*stupid*) torpe; (*boring*) pesado; (*sound, pain*) sordo; (*weather, day*) gris **♦** *vt* (*pain, grief*) aliviar; (*mind, senses*) entorpecer

duly ['dju:lɪ] *adv* debidamente; (*on time*) a su debido tiempo

dumb [dʌm] *adj* mudo; (*pej: stupid*) estúpido; **~founded** [dʌm'faundɪd] *adj* pasmado

dummy ['dʌmɪ] *n* (*tailor's*) maniquí *m*; (*mock-up*) maqueta; (*BRIT: for baby*) chupete *m* **♦** *adj* falso, postizo

dump [dʌmp] *n* (*also: rubbish ~*) basurero, vertedero; (*inf: place*) cuchitril *m* **♦** *vt* (*put down*) dejar; (*get rid of*) deshacerse de; (*COMPUT: data*) transferir

dumpling ['dʌmplɪŋ] *n bola de masa hervida*

dumpy ['dʌmpɪ] *adj* regordete/a

dunce [dʌns] *n* zopenco

dung [dʌŋ] *n* estiércol *m*

dungarees [dʌŋgə'ri:z] *npl* mono

dungeon ['dʌndʒən] *n* calabozo

duo ['dju:əu] *n* (*gen, MUS*) dúo

dupe [dju:p] *n* (*victim*) víctima **♦** *vt* engañar

duplex ['dju:plɛks] *n* dúplex *m*

duplicate [*n* 'dju:plɪkət, *vb* 'dju:plɪkeɪt] *n* duplicado **♦** *vt* duplicar; (*photocopy*) fotocopiar; (*repeat*) repetir; **in ~** por duplicado

durable ['djuərəbl] *adj* duradero

duration [djuə'reɪʃən] *n* duración *f*

duress [djuə'rɛs] *n*: **under ~** por compulsión

during ['djuərɪŋ] *prep* durante

dusk [dʌsk] *n* crepúsculo, anochecer *m*

dust [dʌst] *n* polvo **♦** *vt* quitar el polvo a, desempolvar; (*cake etc*): **to ~ with** espolvorear de; **~bin** (*BRIT*) *n* cubo de la basura (*SP*), balde *m* (*AM*); **~er** *n* paño, trapo; **~man** (*BRIT*) *n* basurero; **~y** *adj* polvoriento

Dutch [dʌtʃ] *adj* holandés/esa **♦** *n* (*LING*) holandés *m*; **the ~** *npl* los holandeses; **to go ~** (*inf*) pagar cada uno lo suyo; **~man/woman** *n* holandés/esa *m/f*

dutiful ['dju:tɪful] *adj* obediente, sumiso

duty ['dju:tɪ] *n* deber *m*; (*tax*) derechos *mpl* de aduana; **on ~** de servicio; (*at night etc*) de guardia; **off ~** libre (de servicio); **~-free** *adj* libre de impuestos

duvet ['du:veɪ] (*BRIT*) *n* edredón *m*

dwarf [dwɔ:f] (*pl* **dwarves**) *n* enano/a **♦** *vt* empequeñecer; **dwarves** [dwɔ:vz] *npl of* **dwarf**

dwell [dwɛl] (*pt, pp* **dwelt**) *vi* morar; **~ on** *vt fus* explayarse en; **~ing** *n* vivienda

dwindle ['dwɪndl] *vi* menguar, disminuir

dye [daɪ] *n* tinte *m* **♦** *vt* teñir

dying ['daɪɪŋ] *adj* moribundo, agonizante

dyke [daɪk] (*BRIT*) *n* dique *m*

dynamic [daɪ'næmɪk] *adj* dinámico

dynamite ['daɪnəmaɪt] *n* dinamita

dynamo ['daɪnəməu] *n* dinamo *f*

dynasty ['dɪnəstɪ] *n* dinastía

E e

E [i:] *n* (*MUS*) mi *m*

each [i:tʃ] *adj* cada *inv* **♦** *pron* cada uno; **~ other** el uno al otro; **they hate ~ other** se odian (entre ellos *or* mutuamente); **they have 2 books ~** tienen 2 libros por persona

eager ['i:gə*] *adj* (*keen*) entusiasmado; **to be ~ to do sth** tener muchas ganas de hacer algo, impacientarse por hacer algo; **to be ~ for** tener muchas ganas de

eagle ['iːgl] *n* águila
ear [ɪə*] *n* oreja; oído; (*of corn*) espiga;
~**ache** *n* dolor *m* de oídos; ~**drum** *n*
tímpano
earl [əːl] *n* conde *m*
earlier ['əːlɪə*] *adj* anterior ♦ *adv* antes
early ['əːlɪ] *adv* temprano; (*before time*)
con tiempo, con anticipación ♦ *adj*
temprano; (*settlers etc*) primitivo; (*death,
departure*) prematuro; (*reply*) pronto; **to
have an ~ night** acostarse temprano; **in
the ~ *or* ~ in the spring/19th century**
a principios de primavera/del siglo
diecinueve; ~ **retirement** *n* jubilación *f*
anticipada
earmark ['ɪəmɑːk] *vt*: **to ~ (for)** reservar
(para), destinar (a)
earn [əːn] *vt* (*salary*) percibir; (*interest*)
devengar; (*praise*) merecerse
earnest ['əːnɪst] *adj* (*wish*) fervoroso;
(*person*) serio, formal; **in ~** en serio
earnings ['əːnɪŋz] *npl* (*personal*) sueldo,
ingresos *mpl*; (*company*) ganancias *fpl*
ear: ~**phones** *npl* auriculares *mpl*; ~**ring**
n pendiente *m*, arete *m*; ~**shot** *n*: **within
~shot** al alcance del oído
earth [əːθ] *n* tierra; (*BRIT: ELEC*) cable *m*
de toma de tierra ♦ *vt* (*BRIT: ELEC*)
conectar a tierra; ~**enware** *n* loza (de
barro); ~**quake** *n* terremoto; ~**y** *adj* (*fig:
vulgar*) grosero
ease [iːz] *n* facilidad *f*; (*comfort*) comodidad *f* ♦ *vt* (*lessen: problem*) mitigar;
(: *pain*) aliviar; (: *tension*) reducir; **to ~
sth in/out** meter/sacar algo con
cuidado; **at ~!** (*MIL*) ¡descansen!; ~ **off *or*
up** *vi* (*wind, rain*) amainar; (*slow down*)
aflojar la marcha
easel ['iːzl] *n* caballete *m*
easily ['iːzɪlɪ] *adv* fácilmente
east [iːst] *n* este *m* ♦ *adj* del este,
oriental; (*wind*) este ♦ *adv* al este, hacia
el este; **the E~** el Oriente; (*POL*) los países del Este
Easter ['iːstə*] *n* Pascua (de
Resurrección); ~ **egg** *n* huevo de Pascua
easterly ['iːstəlɪ] *adj* (*to the east*) al este;
(*from the east*) del este
eastern ['iːstən] *adj* del este, oriental;

(*oriental*) oriental; (*communist*) del este
East Germany *n* Alemania Oriental
eastward(s) ['iːstwəd(z)] *adv* hacia el
este
easy ['iːzɪ] *adj* fácil; (*simple*) sencillo;
(*comfortable*) holgado, cómodo; (*relaxed*)
tranquilo ♦ *adv*: **to take it *or* things ~**
(*not worry*) tomarlo con calma; (*rest*)
descansar; ~ **chair** *n* sillón *m*; ~-**going**
adj acomodadizo
eat [iːt] (*pt* **ate**, *pp* **eaten**) *vt* comer; ~
away at *vt fus* corroer; mermar; ~ **into**
vt fus corroer; (*savings*) mermar
eau de Cologne [əudəkə'ləun] *n* (agua
de) Colonia
eaves [iːvz] *npl* alero
eavesdrop ['iːvzdrɒp] *vi*: **to ~ (on)**
escuchar a escondidas
ebb [ɛb] *n* reflujo ♦ *vi* bajar; (*fig: also*: ~
away) decaer
ebony ['ɛbənɪ] *n* ébano
EC *n abbr* (= *European Community*) CE *f*
eccentric [ɪk'sɛntrɪk] *adj, n* excéntrico/a
m/f
echo ['ɛkəu] (*pl* ~**es**) *n* eco *m* ♦ *vt* (*sound*)
repetir ♦ *vi* resonar, hacer eco
éclair [ɪ'kleə*] *n* pastelillo relleno de
crema y con chocolate por encima
eclipse [ɪ'klɪps] *n* eclipse *m*
ecology [ɪ'kɒlədʒɪ] *n* ecología
economic [iːkə'nɒmɪk] *adj* económico;
(*business etc*) rentable; ~**al** *adj* económico; ~**s** *n* (*SCOL*) economía ♦ *npl* (*of project
etc*) rentabilidad *f*
economize [ɪ'kɒnəmaɪz] *vi* economizar,
ahorrar
economy [ɪ'kɒnəmɪ] *n* economía; ~ **class**
n (*AVIAT*) clase *f* económica; ~ **size** *n*
tamaño económico
ecstasy ['ɛkstəsɪ] *n* éxtasis *m inv*;
ecstatic [-'tætɪk] *adj* extático
ECU ['eɪkjuː] *n* (= *European Currency
Unit*) ECU *m*
Ecuador ['ɛkwədɔːr] *n* Ecuador *m*; ~**ian**
adj, n ecuatoriano/a *m/f*
eczema ['ɛksɪmə] *n* eczema *m*
edge [ɛdʒ] *n* (*of knife etc*) filo; (*of object*)
borde *m*; (*of lake etc*) orilla ♦ *vt* (*SEWING*)
ribetear; **on ~** (*fig*) = **edgy**; **to ~ away**

from alejarse poco a poco de; **~ways** *adv*: **he couldn't get a word in ~ways** no pudo meter ni baza

edgy ['ɛdʒɪ] *adj* nervioso, inquieto

edible ['ɛdɪbl] *adj* comestible

Edinburgh ['ɛdɪnbərə] *n* Edimburgo

edit ['ɛdɪt] *vt* (*be editor of*) dirigir; (*text, report*) corregir, preparar; **~ion** [ɪ'dɪʃən] *n* edición *f*; **~or** *n* (*of newspaper*) director(a) *m/f*; (*of column*): **foreign/political ~or** encargado de la sección de extranjero/política; (*of book*) redactor(a) *m/f*; **~orial** [-'tɔːrɪəl] *adj* editorial ♦ *n* editorial *m*

educate ['ɛdjukeɪt] *vt* (*gen*) educar; (*instruct*) instruir

education [ɛdju'keɪʃən] *n* educación *f*; (*schooling*) enseñanza; (*SCOL*) pedagogía; **~al** *adj* (*policy etc*) educacional; (*experience*) docente; (*toy*) educativo

EEC *n abbr* (= *European Economic Community*) CEE *f*

eel [iːl] *n* anguila

eerie ['ɪərɪ] *adj* misterioso

effect [ɪ'fɛkt] *n* efecto ♦ *vt* efectuar, llevar a cabo; **to take ~** (*law*) entrar en vigor *or* vigencia; (*drug*) surtir efecto; **in ~** en realidad; **~ive** *adj* eficaz; (*actual*) verdadero; **~ively** *adv* eficazmente; (*in reality*) efectivamente; **~iveness** *n* eficacia

effeminate [ɪ'fɛmɪnɪt] *adj* afeminado

efficiency [ɪ'fɪʃənsɪ] *n* eficiencia; rendimiento

efficient [ɪ'fɪʃənt] *adj* eficiente; (*machine*) de buen rendimiento

effort ['ɛfət] *n* esfuerzo; **~less** *adj* sin ningún esfuerzo; (*style*) natural

effrontery [ɪ'frʌntərɪ] *n* descaro

effusive [ɪ'fjuːsɪv] *adj* efusivo

e.g. *adv abbr* (= *exempli gratia*) p. ej.

egg [ɛg] *n* huevo; **hard-boiled/soft-boiled ~** huevo duro/pasado por agua; **~ on** *vt* incitar; **~cup** *n* huevera; **~ plant** (*esp US*) *n* berenjena; **~shell** *n* cáscara de huevo

ego ['iːgəu] *n* ego; **~tism** *n* egoísmo; **~tist** *n* egoísta *m/f*

Egypt ['iːdʒɪpt] *n* Egipto; **~ian** [ɪ'dʒɪpʃən] *adj*, *n* egipcio/a *m/f*

eiderdown ['aɪdədaun] *n* edredón *m*

eight [eɪt] *num* ocho; **~een** *num* diez y ocho, dieciocho; **~h** [eɪtθ] *num* octavo; **~y** *num* ochenta

Eire ['ɛərə] *n* Eire *m*

either ['aɪðə*] *adj* cualquiera de los dos; (*both, each*) cada ♦ *pron*: **~ (of them)** cualquiera (de los dos) ♦ *adv* tampoco; **on ~ side** en ambos lados; **I don't like ~ no me gusta ninguno/a de los/las dos; **no, I don't ~** no, yo tampoco ♦ *conj*: **~ yes or no** o sí o no

eject [ɪ'dʒɛkt] *vt* echar, expulsar; (*tenant*) desahuciar; **~or seat** *n* asiento proyectable

eke [iːk]: **to ~ out** *vt* hacer que alcance

elaborate [*adj* ɪ'læbərɪt, *vb* ɪ'læbəreɪt] *adj* (*complex*) complejo ♦ *vt* (*expand*) ampliar; (*refine*) refinar ♦ *vi* explicar con más detalles

elapse [ɪ'læps] *vi* transcurrir

elastic [ɪ'læstɪk] *n* elástico ♦ *adj* elástico; (*fig*) flexible; **~ band** (*BRIT*) *n* gomita

elated [ɪ'leɪtɪd] *adj*: **to be ~** regocijarse

elbow ['ɛlbəu] *n* codo

elder ['ɛldə*] *adj* mayor ♦ *n* (*tree*) saúco; (*person*) mayor; **~ly** *adj* de edad, mayor ♦ *npl*: **the ~ly** los mayores

eldest ['ɛldɪst] *adj*, *n* el/la mayor

elect [ɪ'lɛkt] *vt* elegir ♦ *adj*: **the president ~** el presidente electo; **to ~ to do** optar por hacer; **~ion** [ɪ'lɛkʃən] *n* elección *f*; **~ioneering** [ɪlɛkʃə'nɪərɪŋ] *n* campaña electoral; **~or** *n* elector(a) *m/f*; **~oral** *adj* electoral; **~orate** *n* electorado

electric [ɪ'lɛktrɪk] *adj* eléctrico; **~al** *adj* eléctrico; **~ blanket** *n* manta eléctrica; **~ fire** *n* estufa eléctrica

electrician [ɪlɛk'trɪʃən] *n* electricista *m/f*

electricity [ɪlɛk'trɪsɪtɪ] *n* electricidad *f*

electrify [ɪ'lɛktrɪfaɪ] *vt* (*RAIL*) electrificar; (*fig: audience*) electrizar

electron [ɪ'lɛktrɔn] *n* electrón *m*

electronic [ɪlɛk'trɔnɪk] *adj* electrónico; **~ mail** *n* correo electrónico; **~s** *n* electrónica

elegant ['ɛlɪgənt] *adj* elegante

element ['ɛlɪmənt] *n* elemento; (*of kettle*

etc) resistencia; **~ary** [-'mentərɪ] *adj*
elemental; (*primitive*) rudimentario;
(*school*) primario
elephant ['ɛlɪfənt] *n* elefante *m*
elevation [ɛlɪ'veɪʃən] *n* elevación *f*;
(*height*) altura
elevator ['ɛlɪveɪtə*] *n* (*US*) ascensor *m*;
(*in warehouse etc*) montacargas *m inv*
eleven [ɪ'lɛvn] *num* once; **~ses** (*BRIT*) *npl*
café *m* de las once; **~th** *num* undécimo
elf [ɛlf] (*pl* **elves**) *n* duende *m*
elicit [ɪ'lɪsɪt] *vt*: **to ~ (from)** sacar (de)
eligible ['ɛlɪdʒəbl] *adj*: **an ~ young
man/woman** un buen partido; **to be ~
for sth** llenar los requisitos para algo
eliminate [ɪ'lɪmɪneɪt] *vt* (*eradicate*)
suprimir; (*opponent*) eliminar
elm [ɛlm] *n* olmo *m*
elongated ['iːlɒŋgeɪtɪd] *adj* alargado
elope [ɪ'ləʊp] *vi* fugarse (para casarse);
~ment *n* fuga
eloquent ['ɛləkwənt] *adj* elocuente
else [ɛls] *adv*: **something ~** otra cosa;
somewhere ~ en otra parte;
everywhere ~ en todas partes menos
aquí; **where ~?** ¿dónde más?, ¿en qué
otra parte?; **there was little ~ to do**
apenas quedaba otra cosa que hacer;
nobody ~ spoke no habló nadie más;
~where *adv* (*be*) en otra parte; (*go*) a
otra parte
elucidate [ɪ'luːsɪdeɪt] *vt* aclarar
elude [ɪ'luːd] *vt* (*subj: idea etc*) escaparse
a; (*capture*) esquivar
elusive [ɪ'luːsɪv] *adj* esquivo; (*quality*)
difícil de encontrar
emaciated [ɪ'meɪsɪeɪtɪd] *adj* demacrado
emanate ['ɛməneɪt] *vi*: **to ~ from** (*idea*)
surgir de; (*light, sound*) proceder de
emancipate [ɪ'mænsɪpeɪt] *vt* emancipar
embankment [ɪm'bæŋkmənt] *n* terraplén
m
embargo [ɪm'bɑːgəʊ] (*pl* **~es**) *n*
prohibición *f*, embargo
embark [ɪm'bɑːk] *vi* embarcarse ♦ *vt*
embarcar; **to ~ on** (*journey*) emprender;
(*course of action*) lanzarse a; **~ation**
[ɛmbɑː'keɪʃən] *n* (*people*) embarco; (*goods*)
embarque *m*

embarrass [ɪm'bærəs] *vt* avergonzar;
(*government etc*) dejar en mal lugar; **~ed**
adj (*laugh, silence*) embarazoso; **~ing** *adj*
(*situation*) violento; (*question*) embarazoso; **~ment** *n* (*shame*) vergüenza;
(*problem*): **to be an ~ment for sb** poner
en un aprieto a uno
embassy ['ɛmbəsɪ] *n* embajada
embedded [ɪm'bɛdɪd] *adj* (*object*)
empotrado; (*thorn etc*) clavado
embellish [ɪm'bɛlɪʃ] *vt* embellecer;
(*story*) adornar
embers ['ɛmbəz] *npl* rescoldo, ascua
embezzle [ɪm'bɛzl] *vt* desfalcar,
malversar
embitter [ɪm'bɪtə*] *vt* (*fig: sour*) amargar
embody [ɪm'bɒdɪ] *vt* (*spirit*) encarnar;
(*include*) incorporar
embossed [ɪm'bɒst] *adj* realzado
embrace [ɪm'breɪs] *vt* abrazar, dar un
abrazo a; (*include*) abarcar ♦ *vi*
abrazarse ♦ *n* abrazo
embroider [ɪm'brɔɪdə*] *vt* bordar; **~y** *n*
bordado
embryo ['ɛmbrɪəʊ] *n* embrión *m*
emerald ['ɛmərəld] *n* esmeralda
emerge [ɪ'mɜːdʒ] *vi* salir; (*arise*) surgir
emergency [ɪ'mɜːdʒənsɪ] *n* crisis *f inv*;
in an ~ en caso de urgencia; **state of ~**
estado de emergencia; **~ cord** (*US*) *n*
timbre *m* de alarma; **~ exit** *n* salida de
emergencia; **~ landing** *n* aterrizaje *m*
forzoso; **~ services** *npl* (*fire, police,
ambulance*) servicios *mpl* de urgencia *or*
emergencia
emergent [ɪ'mɜːdʒənt] *adj* (*nation*) recién
independizado; (*group*) recién aparecido
emery board ['ɛmərɪ-] *n* lima de uñas
emigrate ['ɛmɪgreɪt] *vi* emigrar
emissions [ɪ'mɪʃənz] *npl* emisión *f*
emit [ɪ'mɪt] *vt* emitir; (*smoke*) arrojar;
(*smell*) despedir; (*sound*) producir
emotion [ɪ'məʊʃən] *n* emoción *f*; **~al** *adj*
(*needs*) emocional; (*person*) sentimental;
(*scene*) conmovedor(a), emocionante;
(*speech*) emocionado
emperor ['ɛmpərə*] *n* emperador *m*
emphases ['ɛmfəsiːz] *npl of* **emphasis**
emphasis ['ɛmfəsɪs] (*pl* **-ses**) *n* énfasis *m*

inv

emphasize ['ɛmfəsaɪz] *vt* (*word, point*) subrayar, recalcar; (*feature*) hacer resaltar

emphatic [ɛm'fætɪk] *adj* (*reply*) categórico; (*person*) insistente; ~**ally** *adv* con énfasis; (*certainly*) sin ningún género de dudas

empire ['ɛmpaɪə*] *n* (*also fig*) imperio

employ [ɪm'plɔɪ] *vt* emplear; ~**ee** [-'iː] *n* empleado/a; ~**er** *n* patrón/ona *m/f*; empresario; ~**ment** *n* (*work*) trabajo; ~**ment agency** *n* agencia de colocaciones

empower [ɪm'paʊə*] *vt*: **to ~ sb to do sth** autorizar a uno para hacer algo

empress ['ɛmprɪs] *n* emperatriz *f*

emptiness ['ɛmptɪnɪs] *n* vacío; (*of life etc*) vaciedad *f*

empty ['ɛmptɪ] *adj* vacío; (*place*) desierto; (*house*) desocupado; (*threat*) vano ♦ *vt* vaciar; (*place*) dejar vacío ♦ *vi* vaciarse; (*house etc*) quedar desocupado; ~**-handed** *adj* con las manos vacías

emulate ['ɛmjʊleɪt] *vt* emular

emulsion [ɪ'mʌlʃən] *n* emulsión *f*; (*also:* ~ *paint*) pintura emulsión

enable [ɪ'neɪbl] *vt*: **to ~ sb to do sth** permitir a uno hacer algo

enact [ɪn'ækt] *vt* (*law*) promulgar; (*play*) representar; (*role*) hacer

enamel [ɪ'næməl] *n* esmalte *m*; (*also:* ~ *paint*) pintura esmaltada

enamoured [ɪ'næməd] *adj*: **to be ~ of** (*person*) estar enamorado de; (*activity etc*) tener gran afición a; (*idea*) aferrarse a

encased [ɪn'keɪst] *adj*: ~ **in** (*covered*) revestido de

enchant [ɪn'tʃɑːnt] *vt* encantar; ~**ing** *adj* encantador(a)

encircle [ɪn'sɜːkl] *vt* rodear

encl. *abbr* (= *enclosed*) adj

enclose [ɪn'kləuz] *vt* (*land*) cercar; (*letter etc*) adjuntar; **please find ~d** le mandamos adjunto

enclosure [ɪn'kləuʒə*] *n* cercado, recinto

encompass [ɪn'kʌmpəs] *vt* abarcar

encore [ɔŋ'kɔː*] *excl* ¡otra!, ¡bis! ♦ *n* bis

m

encounter [ɪn'kauntə*] *n* encuentro ♦ *vt* encontrar, encontrarse con; (*difficulty*) tropezar con

encourage [ɪn'kʌrɪdʒ] *vt* alentar, animar; (*activity*) fomentar; (*growth*) estimular; ~**ment** *n* estímulo; (*of industry*) fomento

encroach [ɪn'krəutʃ] *vi*: **to ~ (up)on** invadir; (*rights*) usurpar; (*time*) adueñarse de

encumber [ɪn'kʌmbə*] *vt*: **to be ~ed with** (*baggage etc, debts*) estar cargado de

encyclop(a)edia [ɛnsaɪkləu'piːdɪə] *n* enciclopedia

end [ɛnd] *n* (*gen, also aim*) fin *m*; (*of table*) extremo; (*of street*) final *m*; (*SPORT*) lado ♦ *vt* terminar, acabar; (*also: bring to an ~, put an ~ to*) acabar con ♦ *vi* terminar, acabar; **in the ~** al fin; **on ~** (*object*) de punta, de cabeza; **to stand on ~** (*hair*) erizarse; **for hours on ~** hora tras hora; ~ **up** *vi*: **to ~ up in** terminar en; (*place*) ir a parar en

endanger [ɪn'deɪndʒə*] *vt* poner en peligro

endearing [ɪn'dɪərɪŋ] *adj* simpático, atractivo

endeavour [ɪn'dɛvə*] (*US* **endeavor**) *n* esfuerzo; (*attempt*) tentativa ♦ *vi*: **to ~ to do** esforzarse por hacer; (*try*) procurar hacer

ending ['ɛndɪŋ] *n* (*of book*) desenlace *m*; (*LING*) terminación *f*

endive ['ɛndaɪv] *n* (*chicory*) endibia; (*curly*) escarola

endless ['ɛndlɪs] *adj* interminable, inacabable

endorse [ɪn'dɔːs] *vt* (*cheque*) endosar; (*approve*) aprobar; ~**ment** *n* (*on driving licence*) nota de inhabilitación

endow [ɪn'dau] *vt* (*provide with money*): **to ~ (with)** dotar (de); **to be ~ed with** (*fig*) estar dotado de

endurance [ɪn'djuərəns] *n* resistencia

endure [ɪn'djuə*] *vt* (*bear*) aguantar, soportar ♦ *vi* (*last*) durar

enemy ['ɛnəmɪ] *adj, n* enemigo/a *m/f*

energetic [ɛnə'dʒɛtɪk] *adj* enérgico

energy ['ɛnədʒɪ] *n* energía
enforce [ɪn'fɔːs] *vt* (*LAW*) hacer cumplir
engage [ɪn'geɪdʒ] *vt* (*attention*) llamar; (*interest*) ocupar; (*in conversation*) abordar; (*worker*) contratar; (*AUT*): **to ~ the clutch** embragar ♦ *vi* (*TECH*) engranar; **to ~ in** dedicarse a, ocuparse en; **~d** *adj* (*BRIT: busy, in use*) ocupado; (*betrothed*) prometido; **to get ~d** prometerse; **~d tone** (*BRIT*) *n* (*TEL*) señal *f* de comunicando; **~ment** *n* (*appointment*) compromiso, cita; (*booking*) contratación *f*; (*to marry*) compromiso; (*period*) noviazgo; **~ment ring** *n* anillo de prometida
engaging [ɪn'geɪdʒɪŋ] *adj* atractivo
engender [ɪn'dʒɛndə*] *vt* engendrar
engine ['ɛndʒɪn] *n* (*AUT*) motor *m*; (*RAIL*) locomotora; **~ driver** *n* maquinista *m/f*
engineer [ɛndʒɪ'nɪə*] *n* ingeniero; (*BRIT: for repairs*) mecánico; (*on ship, US: RAIL*) maquinista *m*; **~ing** *n* ingeniería
England ['ɪŋglənd] *n* Inglaterra
English ['ɪŋglɪʃ] *adj* inglés/esa ♦ *n* (*LING*) inglés *m*; **the ~** *npl* los ingleses *mpl*; **the ~ Channel** *n* (el Canal de) la Mancha; **~man/woman** *n* inglés/esa *m/f*
engraving [ɪn'greɪvɪŋ] *n* grabado
engrossed [ɪn'grəust] *adj*: **~ in** absorto en
engulf [ɪn'gʌlf] *vt* (*subj: water*) sumergir, hundir; (*: fire*) prender; (*: fear*) apoderarse de
enhance [ɪn'hɑːns] *vt* (*gen*) aumentar; (*beauty*) realzar
enjoy [ɪn'dʒɔɪ] *vt* (*health, fortune*) disfrutar de, gozar de; (*like*) gustarle a uno; **to ~ o.s.** divertirse; **~able** *adj* agradable; (*amusing*) divertido; **~ment** *n* (*joy*) placer *m*; (*activity*) diversión *f*
enlarge [ɪn'lɑːdʒ] *vt* aumentar; (*broaden*) extender; (*PHOT*) ampliar ♦ *vi*: **to ~ on** (*subject*) tratar con más detalles; **~ment** *n* (*PHOT*) ampliación *f*
enlighten [ɪn'laɪtn] *vt* (*inform*) informar; **~ed** *adj* comprensivo; **the E~ment** *n* (*HISTORY*) ≈ la Ilustración, ≈ el Siglo de las Luces
enlist [ɪn'lɪst] *vt* alistar; (*support*) conseguir ♦ *vi* alistarse
enmity ['ɛnmɪtɪ] *n* enemistad *f*
enormous [ɪ'nɔːməs] *adj* enorme
enough [ɪ'nʌf] *adj*: **~ time/books** bastante tiempo/bastantes libros ♦ *pron* bastante(s) ♦ *adv*: **big ~** bastante grande; **he has not worked ~** no ha trabajado bastante; **have you got ~?** ¿tiene usted bastante(s)?; **~ to eat** (lo) suficiente *or* (lo) bastante para comer; **~!** ¡basta ya!; **that's ~, thanks** con eso basta, gracias; **I've had ~ of him** estoy harto de él; **... which, funnily** *or* **oddly ~ ...** ... lo que, por extraño que parezca ...
enquire [ɪn'kwaɪə*] *vt, vi* = **inquire**
enrage [ɪn'reɪdʒ] *vt* enfurecer
enrich [ɪn'rɪtʃ] *vt* enriquecer
enrol [ɪn'rəul] *vt* (*members*) inscribir; (*SCOL*) matricular ♦ *vi* inscribirse; matricularse; **~ment** *n* inscripción *f*; matriculación *f*
en route [ɔn'ruːt] *adv* durante el viaje
ensue [ɪn'sjuː] *vi* seguirse; (*result*) resultar
ensure [ɪn'ʃuə*] *vt* asegurar
entail [ɪn'teɪl] *vt* suponer
entangled [ɪn'tæŋgld] *adj*: **to become ~ (in)** quedarse enredado (en) *or* enmarañado (en)
enter ['ɛntə*] *vt* (*room*) entrar en; (*club*) hacerse socio de; (*army*) alistarse en; (*sb for a competition*) inscribir; (*write down*) anotar, apuntar; (*COMPUT*) meter ♦ *vi* entrar; **~ for** *vt fus* presentarse para; **~ into** *vt fus* (*discussion etc*) entablar; (*agreement*) llegar a, firmar
enterprise ['ɛntəpraɪz] *n* empresa; (*spirit*) iniciativa; **free ~** la libre empresa; **private ~** la iniciativa privada; **enterprising** *adj* emprendedor(a)
entertain [ɛntə'teɪn] *vt* (*amuse*) divertir; (*invite: guest*) invitar (a casa); (*idea*) abrigar; **~er** *n* artista *m/f*; **~ing** *adj* divertido, entretenido; **~ment** *n* (*amusement*) diversión *f*; (*show*) espectáculo
enthralled [ɪn'θrɔːld] *adj* encantado
enthusiasm [ɪn'θuːzɪæzəm] *n* entusiasmo
enthusiast [ɪn'θuːzɪæst] *n* entusiasta *m/f*;

~ic [-'æstɪk] *adj* entusiasta; **to be ~ic about** entusiasmarse por
entice [ɪn'taɪs] *vt* tentar
entire [ɪn'taɪə*] *adj* entero; **~ly** *adv* totalmente; **~ty** [ɪn'taɪərətɪ] *n*: **in its ~ty** en su totalidad
entitle [ɪn'taɪtl] *vt*: **to ~ sb to sth** dar a uno derecho a algo; **~d** *adj* (*book*) titulado; **to be ~d to do** tener derecho a hacer
entourage [ɔntu'rɑːʒ] *n* séquito
entrails ['ɛntreɪlz] *npl* entrañas *fpl*
entrance [*n* 'ɛntrəns, *vb* ɪn'trɑːns] *n* entrada ♦ *vt* encantar, hechizar; **to gain ~ to** (*university etc*) ingresar en; **~ examination** *n* examen *m* de ingreso; **~ fee** *n* cuota; **~ ramp** (*US*) *n* (*AUT*) rampa de acceso
entrant ['ɛntrənt] *n* (*in race, competition*) participante *m/f*; (*in examination*) candidato/a
entreat [ɛn'triːt] *vt* rogar, suplicar
entrenched [ɛn'trɛntʃd] *adj* inamovible
entrepreneur [ɔntrəprə'nəː] *n* empresario
entrust [ɪn'trʌst] *vt*: **to ~ sth to sb** confiar algo a uno
entry ['ɛntrɪ] *n* entrada; (*in competition*) participación *f*; (*in register*) apunte *m*; (*in account*) partida; (*in reference book*) artículo; **"no ~"** "prohibido el paso"; (*AUT*) "dirección prohibida"; **~ form** *n* hoja de inscripción; **~ phone** *n* portero automático
enunciate [ɪ'nʌnsɪeɪt] *vt* pronunciar; (*principle etc*) enunciar
envelop [ɪn'vɛləp] *vt* envolver
envelope ['ɛnvələup] *n* sobre *m*
envious ['ɛnvɪəs] *adj* envidioso; (*look*) de envidia
environment [ɪn'vaɪərnmənt] *n* (*surroundings*) entorno; (*natural world*): **the ~** el medio ambiente; **~al** [-'mɛntl] *adj* ambiental; medioambiental; **~-friendly** *adj* no perjudicial para el medio ambiente
envisage [ɪn'vɪzɪdʒ] *vt* prever
envoy ['ɛnvɔɪ] *n* enviado
envy ['ɛnvɪ] *n* envidia ♦ *vt* tener envidia a; **to ~ sb sth** envidiar algo a uno

epic ['ɛpɪk] *n* épica ♦ *adj* épico
epidemic [ɛpɪ'dɛmɪk] *n* epidemia
epilepsy ['ɛpɪlɛpsɪ] *n* epilepsia
episode ['ɛpɪsəud] *n* episodio
epitomize [ɪ'pɪtəmaɪz] *vt* epitomar, resumir
equable ['ɛkwəbl] *adj* (*climate*) templado; (*character*) tranquilo, afable
equal ['iːkwl] *adj* igual; (*treatment*) equitativo ♦ *n* igual *m/f* ♦ *vt* ser igual a; (*fig*) igualar; **to be ~ to** (*task*) estar a la altura de; **~ity** [iː'kwɔlɪtɪ] *n* igualdad *f*; **~ize** *vi* (*SPORT*) empatar; **~ly** *adv* igualmente; (*share etc*) a partes iguales
equate [ɪ'kweɪt] *vt*: **to ~ sth with** equiparar algo con; **equation** [ɪ'kweɪʒən] *n* (*MATH*) ecuación *f*
equator [ɪ'kweɪtə*] *n* ecuador *m*
equilibrium [iːkwɪ'lɪbrɪəm] *n* equilibrio
equip [ɪ'kwɪp] *vt* equipar; (*person*) proveer; **to be well ~ped** estar bien equipado; **~ment** *n* equipo; (*tools*) avíos *mpl*
equitable ['ɛkwɪtəbl] *adj* equitativo
equities ['ɛkwɪtɪz] (*BRIT*) *npl* (*COMM*) derechos *mpl* sobre or en el activo
equivalent [ɪ'kwɪvələnt] *adj*: **~ (to)** equivalente (a) ♦ *n* equivalente *m*
equivocal [ɪ'kwɪvəkl] *adj* (*ambiguous*) ambiguo; (*open to suspicion*) equívoco
era ['ɪərə] *n* era, época
eradicate [ɪ'rædɪkeɪt] *vt* erradicar
erase [ɪ'reɪz] *vt* borrar; **~r** *n* goma de borrar
erect [ɪ'rɛkt] *adj* erguido ♦ *vt* erigir, levantar; (*assemble*) montar; **~ion** [-ʃən] *n* construcción *f*; (*assembly*) montaje *m*; (*PHYSIOL*) erección *f*
ERM *n abbr* (= *Exchange Rate Mechanism*) tipo de cambio europeo
ermine ['əːmɪn] *n* armiño
erode [ɪ'rəud] *vt* (*GEO*) erosionar; (*metal*) corroer, desgastar; (*fig*) desgastar
erotic [ɪ'rɔtɪk] *adj* erótico
err [əː*] *vi* (*formal*) equivocarse
errand ['ɛrnd] *n* recado (*SP*), mandado (*AM*)
erratic [ɪ'rætɪk] *adj* desigual, poco uniforme

erroneous [ɪˈrəʊnɪəs] *adj* erróneo
error [ˈɛrə*] *n* error *m*, equivocación *f*
erupt [ɪˈrʌpt] *vi* entrar en erupción; *(fig)* estallar; ~**ion** [ɪˈrʌpʃən] *n* erupción *f*; *(of war)* estallido
escalate [ˈɛskəleɪt] *vi* extenderse, intensificarse
escalator [ˈɛskəleɪtə*] *n* escalera móvil
escapade [ɛskəˈpeɪd] *n* travesura
escape [ɪˈskeɪp] *n* fuga ♦ *vi* escaparse; *(flee)* huir, evadirse; *(leak)* fugarse ♦ *vt (responsibility etc)* evitar, eludir; *(consequences)* escapar a; *(elude)*: **his name ~s me** no me sale su nombre; **to ~ from** *(place)* escaparse de; *(person)* escaparse a
escort [*n* ˈɛskɔːt, *vb* ɪˈskɔːt] *n* acompañante *m/f*; *(MIL)* escolta ♦ *vt* acompañar
Eskimo [ˈɛskɪməʊ] *n* esquimal *m/f*
especially [ɪˈspɛʃlɪ] *adv (above all)* sobre todo; *(particularly)* en particular, especialmente
espionage [ˈɛspɪənɑːʒ] *n* espionaje *m*
esplanade [ɛspləˈneɪd] *n (by sea)* paseo marítimo
espouse [ɪˈspaʊz] *vt* adherirse a
Esquire [ɪˈskwaɪə] *(abbr* **Esq.)** *n*: **J. Brown, ~** Sr. D. J. Brown
essay [ˈɛseɪ] *n (LITERATURE)* ensayo; *(SCOL: short)* redacción *f*; *(: long)* trabajo
essence [ˈɛsns] *n* esencia
essential [ɪˈsɛnʃl] *adj (necessary)* imprescindible; *(basic)* esencial; ~**s** *npl* lo imprescindible, lo esencial; ~**ly** *adv* esencialmente
establish [ɪˈstæblɪʃ] *vt* establecer; *(prove)* demostrar; *(relations)* entablar; *(reputation)* ganarse; ~**ed** *adj (business)* conocido; *(practice)* arraigado; ~**ment** *n* establecimiento; **the E~ment** la clase dirigente
estate [ɪˈsteɪt] *n (land)* finca, hacienda; *(inheritance)* herencia; *(BRIT: also: housing ~)* urbanización *f*; ~ **agent** *(BRIT) n* agente *m/f* inmobiliario/a; ~ **car** *(BRIT) n* furgoneta
esteem [ɪˈstiːm] *n*: **to hold sb in high ~** estimar en mucho a uno

esthetic [ɪsˈθɛtɪk] *(US) adj* = **aesthetic**
estimate [*n* ˈɛstɪmət, *vb* ˈɛstɪmeɪt] *n* estimación *f*, apreciación *f*; *(assessment)* tasa, cálculo; *(COMM)* presupuesto ♦ *vt* estimar, tasar; calcular; **estimation** [-ˈmeɪʃən] *n* opinión *f*, juicio; cálculo
estranged [ɪˈstreɪndʒd] *adj* separado
estuary [ˈɛstjʊərɪ] *n* estuario, ría
etc *abbr (= et cetera)* etc
etching [ˈɛtʃɪŋ] *n* aguafuerte *m or f*
eternal [ɪˈtɜːnl] *adj* eterno
eternity [ɪˈtɜːnɪtɪ] *n* eternidad *f*
ethical [ˈɛθɪkl] *adj* ético; **ethics** [ˈɛθɪks] *n* ética ♦ *npl* moralidad *f*
Ethiopia [iːθɪˈəʊpɪə] *n* Etiopía
ethnic [ˈɛθnɪk] *adj* étnico
ethos [ˈiːθɒs] *n* genio, carácter *m*
etiquette [ˈɛtɪkɛt] *n* etiqueta
Eurocheque [ˈjʊərəʊtʃɛk] *n* Eurocheque *m*
Europe [ˈjʊərəp] *n* Europa; ~**an** [-ˈpiːən] *adj*, *n* europeo/a *m/f*
evacuate [ɪˈvækjueɪt] *vt (people)* evacuar; *(place)* desocupar; **evacuation** [-ˈeɪʃən] *n* evacuación *f*
evade [ɪˈveɪd] *vt* evadir, eludir
evaluate [ɪˈvæljueɪt] *vt* evaluar
evaporate [ɪˈvæpəreɪt] *vi* evaporarse; *(fig)* desvanecerse; ~**d milk** *n* leche *f* evaporada
evasion [ɪˈveɪʒən] *n* evasión *f*
eve [iːv] *n*: **on the ~ of** en vísperas de
even [ˈiːvn] *adj (level)* llano; *(smooth)* liso; *(speed, temperature)* uniforme; *(number)* par ♦ *adv* hasta, incluso; *(introducing a comparison)* aún, todavía; ~ **if**, ~ **though** aunque + *sub*; ~ **more** aun más; ~ **so** aun así; **not** ~ ni siquiera; ~ **he was there** hasta él estuvo allí; ~ **on Sundays** incluso los domingos; **to get ~ with sb** ajustar cuentas con uno; ~ **out** *vi* nivelarse
evening [ˈiːvnɪŋ] *n* tarde *f*; *(late)* noche *f*; **in the ~** por la tarde; ~ **class** *n* clase *f* nocturna; ~ **dress** *n (no pl: formal clothes)* traje *m* de etiqueta; *(woman's)* traje *m* de noche
event [ɪˈvɛnt] *n* suceso, acontecimiento; *(SPORT)* prueba; **in the ~ of** en caso de;

~ful *adj* (*life*) activo; (*day*) ajetreado

eventual [ɪ'vɛntʃuəl] *adj* final; **~ity** [-'ælɪtɪ] *n* eventualidad *f*; **~ly** *adv* (*finally*) finalmente; (*in time*) con el tiempo

ever ['ɛvə*] *adv* (*at any time*) nunca, jamás; (*at all times*) siempre; (*in question*): **why ~ not?** ¿y por qué no?; **the best ~** lo nunca visto; **have you ~ seen it?** ¿lo ha visto usted alguna vez?; **better than ~** mejor que nunca; **~ since** *adv* desde entonces ♦ *conj* después de que; **~green** *n* árbol *m* de hoja perenne; **~lasting** *adj* eterno, perpetuo

---

KEYWORD

every ['ɛvrɪ] *adj* **1** (*each*) cada; **~ one of them** (*persons*) todos ellos/as; (*objects*) cada uno de ellos/as; **~ shop in the town was closed** todas las tiendas de la ciudad estaban cerradas

2 (*all possible*) todo/a; **I gave you ~ assistance** te di toda la ayuda posible; **I have ~ confidence in him** tiene toda mi confianza; **we wish you ~ success** te deseamos toda suerte de éxitos

3 (*showing recurrence*) todo/a; **~ day/ week** todos los días/todas las semanas; **~ other car had been broken into** habían forzado uno de cada dos coches; **she visits me ~ other/third day** me visita cada dos/tres días; **~ now and then** de vez en cuando

---

everybody ['ɛvrɪbɔdɪ] *pron* = **everyone**

everyday ['ɛvrɪdeɪ] *adj* (*daily*) cotidiano, de todos los días; (*usual*) acostumbrado

everyone ['ɛvrɪwʌn] *pron* todos/as, todo el mundo

everything ['ɛvrɪθɪŋ] *pron* todo; **this shop sells ~** esta tienda vende de todo

everywhere ['ɛvrɪwɛə*] *adv*: **I've been looking for you ~** te he estado buscando por todas partes; **~ you go you meet ...** en todas partes encuentras ...

evict [ɪ'vɪkt] *vt* desahuciar; **~ion** [ɪ'vɪkʃən] *n* desahucio

evidence ['ɛvɪdəns] *n* (*proof*) prueba; (*of witness*) testimonio; (*sign*) indicios *mpl*; **to give ~** prestar declaración, dar

testimonio

evident ['ɛvɪdənt] *adj* evidente, manifiesto; **~ly** *adv* por lo visto

evil ['iːvl] *adj* malo; (*influence*) funesto ♦ *n* mal *m*

evocative [ɪ'vɔkətɪv] *adj* sugestivo, evocador(a)

evoke [ɪ'vəuk] *vt* evocar

evolution [iːvə'luːʃən] *n* evolución *f*

evolve [ɪ'vɔlv] *vt* desarrollar ♦ *vi* evolucionar, desarrollarse

ewe [juː] *n* oveja

ex- [ɛks] *prefix* ex

exact [ɪg'zækt] *adj* exacto; (*person*) meticuloso ♦ *vt*: **to ~ sth (from)** exigir algo (de); **~ing** *adj* exigente; (*conditions*) arduo; **~ly** *adv* exactamente; (*indicating agreement*) exacto

exaggerate [ɪg'zædʒəreɪt] *vt, vi* exagerar; **exaggeration** [-'reɪʃən] *n* exageración *f*

exalted [ɪg'zɔːltɪd] *adj* eminente

exam [ɪg'zæm] *n abbr* (*SCOL*) = **examination**

examination [ɪgzæmɪ'neɪʃən] *n* examen *m*; (*MED*) reconocimiento

examine [ɪg'zæmɪn] *vt* examinar; (*inspect*) inspeccionar, escudriñar; (*MED*) reconocer; **~r** *n* examinador(a) *m/f*

example [ɪg'zɑːmpl] *n* ejemplo; **for ~** por ejemplo

exasperate [ɪg'zɑːspəreɪt] *vt* exasperar, irritar; **exasperation** [-ʃən] *n* exasperación *f*, irritación *f*

excavate ['ɛkskəveɪt] *vt* excavar

exceed [ɪk'siːd] *vt* (*amount*) exceder; (*number*) pasar de; (*speed limit*) sobrepasar; (*powers*) excederse en; (*hopes*) superar; **~ingly** *adv* sumamente, sobremanera

excel [ɪk'sɛl] *vi*: **to ~ (at/in)** sobresalir (en)

excellent ['ɛksələnt] *adj* excelente

except [ɪk'sɛpt] *prep* (*also*: **~ for**, **~ing**) excepto, salvo ♦ *vt* exceptuar, excluir; **~ if/when** excepto si/cuando; **~ that** salvo que; **~ion** [ɪk'sɛpʃən] *n* excepción *f*; **to take ~ion to** ofenderse por; **~ional** [ɪk'sɛpʃənl] *adj* excepcional

excerpt ['ɛksɔːpt] *n* extracto

excess [ɪkˈsɛs] n exceso; **~es** npl (*of cruelty etc*) atrocidades fpl; **~ baggage** n exceso de equipaje; **~ fare** n suplemento; **~ive** adj excesivo

exchange [ɪksˈtʃeɪndʒ] n intercambio; (*conversation*) diálogo; (*also: telephone ~*) central f (telefónica) ♦ vt: **to ~ (for)** cambiar (por); **~ rate** n tipo de cambio

exchequer [ɪksˈtʃɛkə*] (*BRIT*) n: **the ~** la Hacienda del Fisco

excise [ˈɛksaɪz] n impuestos mpl sobre el alcohol y el tabaco

excite [ɪkˈsaɪt] vt (*stimulate*) estimular; (*arouse*) excitar; **~d** adj: **to get ~d** emocionarse; **~ment** n (*agitation*) excitación f; (*exhilaration*) emoción f; **exciting** adj emocionante

exclaim [ɪkˈskleɪm] vi exclamar; **exclamation** [ɛksklǝˈmeɪʃǝn] n exclamación f; **exclamation mark** n punto de admiración

exclude [ɪkˈskluːd] vt excluir; exceptuar

exclusive [ɪkˈskluːsɪv] adj exclusivo; (*club, district*) selecto; **~ of tax** excluyendo impuestos; **~ly** adv únicamente

excommunicate [ɛkskǝˈmjuːnɪkeɪt] vt excomulgar

excruciating [ɪkˈskruːʃɪeɪtɪŋ] adj (*pain*) agudísimo, atroz; (*noise, embarrassment*) horrible

excursion [ɪkˈskǝːʃǝn] n (*tourist ~*) excursión f

excuse [n ɪkˈskjuːs, vb ɪkˈskjuːz] n disculpa, excusa; (*pretext*) pretexto ♦ vt (*justify*) justificar; (*forgive*) disculpar, perdonar; **to ~ sb from doing sth** dispensar a uno de hacer algo; **~ me!** (*attracting attention*) ¡por favor!; (*apologizing*) ¡perdón!; **if you will ~ me** con su permiso

ex-directory [ˈɛksdɪˈrɛktǝrɪ] (*BRIT*) adj que no consta en la guía

execute [ˈɛksɪkjuːt] vt (*plan*) realizar; (*order*) cumplir; (*person*) ajusticiar, ejecutar; **execution** [-ˈkjuːʃǝn] n realización f; cumplimiento; ejecución f; **executioner** [-ˈkjuːʃǝnǝ*] n verdugo

executive [ɪgˈzɛkjutɪv] n (*person, committee*) ejecutivo; (*POL: committee*) poder m ejecutivo ♦ adj ejecutivo

executor [ɪgˈzɛkjutǝ*] n albacea m, testamentario

exemplify [ɪgˈzɛmplɪfaɪ] vt ejemplificar; (*illustrate*) ilustrar

exempt [ɪgˈzɛmpt] adj: **~ from** exento de ♦ vt: **to ~ sb from** eximir a uno de; **~ion** [-ʃǝn] n exención f

exercise [ˈɛksǝsaɪz] n ejercicio ♦ vt (*patience*) usar de; (*right*) valerse de; (*dog*) llevar de paseo; (*mind*) preocupar ♦ vi (*also: to take ~*) hacer ejercicio(s); **~ bike** n ciclostátic ® m, bicicleta estática; **~ book** n cuaderno

exert [ɪgˈzǝːt] vt ejercer; **to ~ o.s.** esforzarse; **~ion** [-ʃǝn] n esfuerzo

exhale [eksˈheɪl] vt despedir ♦ vi exhalar

exhaust [ɪgˈzɔːst] n (*AUT: also: ~ pipe*) escape m; (: *fumes*) gases mpl de escape ♦ vt agotar; **~ed** adj agotado; **~ion** [ɪgˈzɔːstʃǝn] n agotamiento; **nervous ~ion** postración f nerviosa; **~ive** adj exhaustivo

exhibit [ɪgˈzɪbɪt] n (*ART*) obra expuesta; (*LAW*) objeto expuesto ♦ vt (*show: emotions*) manifestar; (: *courage, skill*) demostrar; (*paintings*) exponer; **~ion** [ɛksɪˈbɪʃǝn] n exposición f; (*of talent etc*) demostración f

exhilarating [ɪgˈzɪlǝreɪtɪŋ] adj estimulante, tónico

exile [ˈɛksaɪl] n exilio; (*person*) exiliado/a ♦ vt desterrar, exiliar

exist [ɪgˈzɪst] vi existir; (*live*) vivir; **~ence** n existencia; **~ing** adj existente, actual

exit [ˈɛksɪt] n salida ♦ vi (*THEATRE*) hacer mutis; (*COMPUT*) salir (al sistema); **~ poll** n encuesta a la salida de los colegios electorales; **~ ramp** (*US*) n (*AUT*) vía de acceso

exodus [ˈɛksǝdǝs] n éxodo

exonerate [ɪgˈzɔnǝreɪt] vt: **to ~ from** exculpar de

exotic [ɪgˈzɔtɪk] adj exótico

expand [ɪkˈspænd] vt ampliar; (*number*) aumentar ♦ vi (*population*) aumentar; (*trade etc*) expandirse; (*gas, metal*) dilatarse

expanse [ɪk'spæns] *n* extensión *f*
expansion [ɪk'spænʃən] *n* (*of population*) aumento; (*of trade*) expansión *f*
expect [ɪk'spɛkt] *vt* esperar; (*require*) contar con; (*suppose*) suponer ♦ *vi*: **to be ~ing** (*pregnant woman*) estar embarazada; **~ancy** *n* (*anticipation*) esperanza; **life ~ancy** esperanza de vida; **~ant mother** *n* futura madre *f*; **~ation** [ɛkspɛk'teɪʃən] *n* (*hope*) esperanza; (*belief*) expectativa
expedient [ɪk'spiːdɪənt] *adj* conveniente, oportuno ♦ *n* recurso, expediente *m*
expedition [ɛkspə'dɪʃən] *n* expedición *f*
expel [ɪk'spɛl] *vt* arrojar; (*from place*) expulsar
expend [ɪk'spɛnd] *vt* (*money*) gastar; (*time, energy*) consumir; **~able** *adj* prescindible; **~iture** *n* gastos *mpl*, desembolso; consumo
expense [ɪk'spɛns] *n* gasto, gastos *mpl*; (*high cost*) costa; **~s** *npl* (*COMM*) gastos *mpl*; **at the ~ of** a costa de; **~ account** *n* cuenta de gastos
expensive [ɪk'spɛnsɪv] *adj* caro, costoso
experience [ɪk'spɪərɪəns] *n* experiencia ♦ *vt* experimentar; (*suffer*) sufrir; **~d** *adj* experimentado
experiment [ɪk'spɛrɪmənt] *n* experimento ♦ *vi* hacer experimentos; **~al** [-'mɛntl] *adj* experimental
expert ['ɛkspəːt] *adj* experto, perito ♦ *n* experto/a, perito/a; (*specialist*) especialista *m/f*; **~ise** [-'tiːz] *n* pericia
expire [ɪk'spaɪə*] *vi* caducar, vencer; **expiry** *n* vencimiento
explain [ɪk'spleɪn] *vt* explicar; **explanation** [ɛksplə'neɪʃən] *n* explicación *f*; **explanatory** [ɪk'splænətrɪ] *adj* explicativo; aclaratorio
explicit [ɪk'splɪsɪt] *adj* explícito
explode [ɪk'spləud] *vi* estallar, explotar; (*population*) crecer rápidamente; (*with anger*) reventar
exploit [*n* 'ɛksplɔɪt, *vb* ɪk'splɔɪt] *n* hazaña ♦ *vt* explotar; **~ation** [-'teɪʃən] *n* explotación *f*
exploratory [ɪk'splɔrətrɪ] *adj* de exploración; (*fig: talks*) exploratorio,

preliminar
explore [ɪk'splɔː*] *vt* explorar; (*fig*) examinar; investigar; **~r** *n* explorador(a) *m/f*
explosion [ɪk'spləuʒən] *n* (*also fig*) explosión *f*; **explosive** [ɪks'pləusɪv] *adj*, *n* explosivo
exponent [ɪk'spəunənt] *n* (*of theory etc*) partidario/a; (*of skill etc*) exponente *m/f*
export [*vb* ɛk'spɔːt, *n* 'ɛkspɔːt] *vt* exportar ♦ *n* (*process*) exportación *f*; (*product*) producto de exportación ♦ *cpd* de exportación; **~er** *n* exportador *m*
expose [ɪk'spəuz] *vt* exponer; (*unmask*) desenmascarar; **~d** *adj* expuesto
exposure [ɪk'spəuʒə*] *n* exposición *f*; (*publicity*) publicidad *f*; (*PHOT: speed*) velocidad *f* de obturación; (: *shot*) fotografía; **to die from ~** (*MED*) morir de frío; **~ meter** *n* fotómetro
expound [ɪk'spaund] *vt* exponer
express [ɪk'sprɛs] *adj* (*definite*) expreso, explícito; (*BRIT: letter etc*) urgente ♦ *n* (*train*) rápido ♦ *vt* expresar; **~ion** [ɪk'sprɛʃən] *n* expresión *f*; (*of actor etc*) sentimiento; **~ly** *adv* expresamente; **~way** (*US*) *n* (*urban motorway*) autopista
exquisite [ɛk'skwɪzɪt] *adj* exquisito
extend [ɪk'stɛnd] *vt* (*visit, street*) prolongar; (*building*) ampliar; (*invitation*) ofrecer ♦ *vi* (*land*) extenderse; (*period of time*) prolongarse
extension [ɪk'stɛnʃən] *n* extensión *f*; (*building*) ampliación *f*; (*of time*) prolongación *f*; (*TEL: in private house*) línea derivada; (: *in office*) extensión *f*
extensive [ɪk'stɛnsɪv] *adj* extenso; (*damage*) importante; (*knowledge*) amplio; **~ly** *adv*: **he's travelled ~ly** ha viajado por muchos países
extent [ɪk'stɛnt] *n* (*breadth*) extensión *f*; (*scope*) alcance *m*; **to some ~** hasta cierto punto; **to the ~ of...** hasta el punto de...; **to such an ~ that...** hasta tal punto que...; **to what ~?** ¿hasta qué punto?
extenuating [ɪk'stɛnjueɪtɪŋ] *adj*: **~ circumstances** circunstancias *fpl* atenuantes

exterior [ɛk'stɪərɪə*] *adj* exterior, externo
♦ *n* exterior *m*
exterminate [ɪk'stə:mɪneɪt] *vt* exterminar
external [ɛk'stə:nl] *adj* externo
extinct [ɪk'stɪŋkt] *adj* (*volcano*)
extinguido; (*race*) extinto
extinguish [ɪk'stɪŋgwɪʃ] *vt* extinguir,
apagar; ~**er** *n* extintor *m*
extort [ɪk'stɔ:t] *vt* obtener por fuerza;
~**ion** [ɪk'stɔ:ʃən] *n* extorsión *f*; ~**ionate**
[ɪk'stɔ:ʃnət] *adj* excesivo, exorbitante
extra ['ɛkstrə] *adj* adicional ♦ *adv* (*in addition*) de más ♦ *n* (*luxury, addition*)
extra *m*; (*CINEMA, THEATRE*) extra *m/f*,
comparsa *m/f*
extra... ['ɛkstrə] *prefix* extra...
extract [*vb* ɪk'strækt, *n* 'ɛkstrækt] *vt* sacar;
(*tooth*) extraer; (*money, promise*) obtener
♦ *n* extracto
extracurricular [ɛkstrəkə'rɪkjulə*] *adj*
extraescolar, extra-académico
extradite ['ɛkstrədaɪt] *vt* extraditar
extramarital [ɛkstrə'mærɪtl] *adj*
extramatrimonial
extramural [ɛkstrə'mjuərl] *adj*
extraescolar
extraordinary [ɪk'strɔ:dnrɪ] *adj*
extraordinario; (*odd*) raro
extravagance [ɪk'strævəgəns] *n* derroche
m, despilfarro; (*thing bought*)
extravagancia
extravagant [ɪk'strævəgənt] *adj* (*lavish: person*) pródigo; (: *gift*) (demasiado) caro;
(*wasteful*) despilfarrador(a)
extreme [ɪk'stri:m] *adj* extremo,
extremado ♦ *n* extremo; ~**ly** *adv*
sumamente, extremadamente
extremity [ɪk'strɛmətɪ] *n* extremidad *f*,
punta; (*of situation*) extremo
extricate ['ɛkstrɪkeɪt] *vt*: **to ~ sth/sb**
from librar algo/a uno de
extrovert ['ɛkstrəvə:t] *n* extrovertido/a
exuberant [ɪg'zju:bərnt] *adj* (*person*)
eufórico; (*imagination*) exuberante
exude [ɪg'zju:d] *vt* (*confidence*) rebosar;
(*liquid, smell*) rezumar
eye [aɪ] *n* ojo ♦ *vt* mirar de soslayo,
ojear; **to keep an ~ on** vigilar; ~**ball** *n*
globo del ojo; ~**bath** *n* ojera; ~**brow** *n*

ceja; ~**brow pencil** *n* lápiz *m* de cejas;
~**drops** *npl* gotas *fpl* para los ojos,
colino; ~**lash** *n* pestaña; ~**lid** *n* párpado;
~**liner** *n* lápiz *m* de ojos; ~-**opener** *n*
revelación *f*, gran sorpresa; ~**shadow** *n*
sombreador *m* de ojos; ~**sight** *n* vista;
~**sore** *n* monstruosidad *f*; ~ **witness** *n*
testigo *m/f* presencial

F f

F [ɛf] *n* (*MUS*) fa *m*
F. *abbr* = **Fahrenheit**
fable ['feɪbl] *n* fábula
fabric ['fæbrɪk] *n* tejido, tela
fabrication [fæbrɪ'keɪʃən] *n* (*lie*)
invención *f*; (*making*) fabricación *f*
fabulous ['fæbjuləs] *adj* fabuloso
façade [fə'sɑ:d] *n* fachada
face [feɪs] *n* (*ANAT*) cara, rostro; (*of clock*)
esfera (*SP*), cara (*AM*); (*of mountain*) cara,
ladera; (*of building*) fachada ♦ *vt*
(*direction*) estar de cara a; (*situation*)
hacer frente a; (*facts*) aceptar; ~ **down**
(*person, card*) boca abajo; **to lose ~**
desprestigiarse; **to make** *or* **pull a ~**
hacer muecas; **in the ~ of** (*difficulties etc*) ante; **on the ~ of it** a primera vista;
~ **to ~** cara a cara; ~ **up to** *vt fus* hacer
frente a, arrostrar; ~ **cloth** (*BRIT*) *n*
manopla; ~ **cream** *n* crema (de belleza);
~ **lift** *n* estirado facial; (*of building*)
renovación *f*; ~ **powder** *n* polvos *mpl*;
~-**saving** *adj* para salvar las apariencias
facetious [fə'si:ʃəs] *adj* gracioso
face value *n* (*of stamp*) valor *m*
nominal; **to take sth at** ~ (*fig*) tomar
algo en sentido literal
facile ['fæsaɪl] *adj* superficial
facilities [fə'sɪlɪtɪz] *npl* (*buildings*)
instalaciones *fpl*; (*equipment*) servicios
mpl; **credit** ~ facilidades *fpl* de crédito
facing ['feɪsɪŋ] *prep* frente a
facsimile [fæk'sɪmɪlɪ] *n* (*replica*)
facsímil(e) *m*; (*machine*) telefax *m*; (*fax*)
fax *m*
fact [fækt] *n* hecho; **in** ~ en realidad
factor ['fæktə*] *n* factor *m*

factory ['fæktərɪ] *n* fábrica
factual ['fæktjʊəl] *adj* basado en los hechos
faculty ['fækəltɪ] *n* facultad *f*; (*US: teaching staff*) personal *m* docente
fad [fæd] *n* novedad *f*, moda
fade [feɪd] *vi* desteñirse; (*sound, smile*) desvanecerse; (*light*) apagarse; (*flower*) marchitarse; (*hope, memory*) perderse
fag [fæg] (*BRIT: inf*) *n* (*cigarette*) pitillo (*SP*), cigarro
fail [feɪl] *vt* (*candidate*) suspender; (*exam*) no aprobar (*SP*), reprobar (*AM*); (*subj: memory etc*) fallar a ♦ *vi* suspender; (*be unsuccessful*) fracasar; (*strength, brakes*) fallar; (*light*) acabarse; **to ~ to do sth** (*neglect*) dejar de hacer algo; (*be unable*) no poder hacer algo; **without ~** sin falta; **~ing** *n* falta, defecto ♦ *prep* a falta de; **~ure** ['feɪljə*] *n* fracaso; (*person*) fracasado/a; (*mechanical etc*) fallo
faint [feɪnt] *adj* débil; (*recollection*) vago; (*mark*) apenas visible ♦ *n* desmayo ♦ *vi* desmayarse; **to feel ~** estar mareado, marearse
fair [fɛə*] *adj* justo; (*hair, person*) rubio; (*weather*) bueno; (*good enough*) regular; (*considerable*) bastante ♦ *adv* (*play*) limpio ♦ *n* feria; (*BRIT: funfair*) parque *m* de atracciones; **~ly** *adv* (*justly*) con justicia; (*quite*) bastante; **~ness** *n* justicia, imparcialidad *f*; **~ play** *n* juego limpio
fairy ['fɛərɪ] *n* hada; **~ tale** *n* cuento de hadas
faith [feɪθ] *n* fe *f*; (*trust*) confianza; (*sect*) religión *f*; **~ful** *adj* (*loyal: troops etc*) leal; (*spouse*) fiel; (*account*) exacto; **~fully** *adv* fielmente; **yours ~fully** (*BRIT: in letters*) le saluda atentamente
fake [feɪk] *n* (*painting etc*) falsificación *f*; (*person*) impostor(a) *m/f* ♦ *adj* falso ♦ *vt* fingir; (*painting etc*) falsificar
falcon ['fɔːlkən] *n* halcón *m*
fall [fɔːl] (*pt* **fell**, *pp* **fallen**) *n* caída; (*in price etc*) descenso; (*US*) otoño ♦ *vi* caer(se); (*price*) bajar, descender; **~s** *npl* (*water~*) cascada, salto de agua; **to ~ flat** (*on one's face*) caerse (boca abajo); (*plan*)

fracasar; (*joke, story*) no hacer gracia; **~ back** *vi* retroceder; **~ back on** *vt fus* (*remedy etc*) recurrir a; **~ behind** *vi* quedarse atrás; **~ down** *vi* (*person*) caerse; (*building, hopes*) derrumbarse; **~ for** *vt fus* (*trick*) dejarse engañar por; (*person*) enamorarse de; **~ in** *vi* (*roof*) hundirse; (*MIL*) alinearse; **~ off** *vi* caerse; (*diminish*) disminuir; **~ out** *vi* (*friends etc*) reñir; (*hair, teeth*) caerse; **~ through** *vi* (*plan, project*) fracasar
fallacy ['fæləsɪ] *n* error *m*
fallen ['fɔːlən] *pp of* **fall**
fallout ['fɔːlaut] *n* lluvia radioactiva; **~ shelter** *n* refugio antiatómico
fallow ['fæləu] *adj* en barbecho
false [fɔːls] *adj* falso; **under ~ pretences** con engaños; **~ alarm** *n* falsa alarma; **~ teeth** (*BRIT*) *npl* dentadura postiza
falter ['fɔːltə*] *vi* vacilar; (*engine*) fallar
fame [feɪm] *n* fama
familiar [fə'mɪlɪə*] *adj* conocido, familiar; (*tone*) de confianza; **to be ~ with** (*subject*) conocer (bien)
family ['fæmɪlɪ] *n* familia; **~ business** *n* negocio familiar; **~ doctor** *n* médico/a de cabecera
famine ['fæmɪn] *n* hambre *f*, hambruna
famished ['fæmɪʃt] *adj* hambriento
famous ['feɪməs] *adj* famoso, célebre; **~ly** *adv* (*get on*) estupendamente
fan [fæn] *n* abanico; (*ELEC*) ventilador *m*; (*of pop star*) fan *m/f*; (*SPORT*) hincha *m/f* ♦ *vt* abanicar; (*fire, quarrel*) atizar; **~ out** *vi* desparramarse
fanatic [fə'nætɪk] *n* fanático/a
fan belt *n* correa del ventilador
fanciful ['fænsɪful] *adj* (*design, name*) fantástico
fancy ['fænsɪ] *n* (*whim*) capricho, antojo; (*imagination*) imaginación *f* ♦ *adj* (*luxury*) lujoso, de lujo ♦ *vt* (*feel like, want*) tener ganas de; (*imagine*) imaginarse; (*think*) creer; **to take a ~ to sb** tomar cariño a uno; **he fancies her** (*inf*) le gusta (ella) mucho; **~ dress** *n* disfraz *m*; **~-dress ball** *n* baile *m* de disfraces
fanfare ['fænfɛə*] *n* fanfarria (de

trompeta)

fang [fæŋ] n colmillo

fantastic [fæn'tæstɪk] adj (*enormous*) enorme; (*strange, wonderful*) fantástico

fantasy ['fæntəzɪ] n (*dream*) sueño; (*unreality*) fantasía

far [fɑː*] adj (*distant*) lejano ♦ adv lejos; (*much, greatly*) mucho; ~ **away**, ~ **off** (a lo) lejos; ~ **better** mucho mejor; ~ **from** lejos de; **by** ~ con mucho; **go as ~ as the farm** vaya hasta la granja; **as ~ as I know** que yo sepa; **how ~?** ¿hasta dónde?; (*fig*) ¿hasta qué punto?; ~**away** adj remoto; (*look*) distraído

farce [fɑːs] n farsa; **farcical** adj absurdo

fare [fɛə*] n (*on trains, buses*) precio (del billete); (*in taxi: cost*) tarifa; (*food*) comida; **half** ~ medio pasaje m; **full** ~ pasaje completo

Far East n: **the** ~ el Extremo Oriente

farewell [fɛə'wɛl] excl, n adiós m

farm [fɑːm] n granja (*SP*), finca (*AM*), estancia (*AM*) ♦ vt cultivar; ~**er** n granjero (*SP*), estanciero (*AM*); ~**hand** n peón m; ~**house** n granja, casa de hacienda (*AM*); ~**ing** n agricultura; (*of crops*) cultivo; (*of animals*) cría; ~**land** n tierra de cultivo; ~ **worker** n = ~**hand**; ~**yard** n corral m

far-reaching [fɑː'riːtʃɪŋ] adj (*reform, effect*) de gran alcance

fart [fɑːt] (*inf!*) vi tirarse un pedo (*!*)

farther ['fɑːðə*] adv más lejos, más allá ♦ adj más lejano

farthest ['fɑːðɪst] superlative of **far**

fascinate ['fæsɪneɪt] vt fascinar; **fascination** [-'neɪʃən] n fascinación f

fascism ['fæʃɪzəm] n fascismo

fashion ['fæʃən] n moda; (~ *industry*) industria de la moda; (*manner*) manera ♦ vt formar; **in** ~ a la moda; **out of** ~ pasado de moda; ~**able** adj de moda; ~ **show** n desfile m de modelos

fast [fɑːst] adj rápido; (*dye, colour*) resistente; (*clock*): **to be** ~ estar adelantado ♦ adv rápidamente, de prisa; (*stuck, held*) firmemente ♦ n ayuno ♦ vi ayunar; ~ **asleep** profundamente dormido

fasten ['fɑːsn] vt atar, sujetar; (*coat, belt*) abrochar ♦ vi atarse; abrocharse; ~**er** n cierre m; (*of door etc*) cerrojo; ~**ing** n = ~**er**

fast food n comida rápida, platos mpl preparados

fastidious [fæs'tɪdɪəs] adj (*fussy*) quisquilloso

fat [fæt] adj gordo; (*book*) grueso; (*profit*) grande, pingüe ♦ n grasa; (*on person*) carnes fpl; (*lard*) manteca

fatal ['feɪtl] adj (*mistake*) fatal; (*injury*) mortal; ~**istic** [-'lɪstɪk] adj fatalista; ~**ity** [fə'tælɪtɪ] n (*road death etc*) víctima; ~**ly** adv fatalmente; mortalmente

fate [feɪt] n destino; (*of person*) suerte f; ~**ful** adj fatídico

father ['fɑːðə*] n padre m; ~-**in-law** n suegro; ~**ly** adj paternal

fathom ['fæðəm] n braza ♦ vt (*mystery*) desentrañar; (*understand*) lograr comprender

fatigue [fə'tiːg] n fatiga, cansancio

fatten ['fætn] vt, vi engordar

fatty ['fætɪ] adj (*food*) graso ♦ n (*inf*) gordito/a, gordinflón/ona m/f

fatuous ['fætjʊəs] adj fatuo, necio

faucet ['fɔːsɪt] (*US*) n grifo (*SP*), llave f (*AM*)

fault [fɔːlt] n (*blame*) culpa; (*defect: in person, machine*) defecto; (*GEO*) falla ♦ vt criticar; **it's my** ~ es culpa mía; **to find** ~ **with** criticar, poner peros a; **at** ~ culpable; ~**y** adj defectuoso

fauna ['fɔːnə] n fauna

faux pas n ['fəʊ'pɑː] n plancha

favour ['feɪvə*] (*US* **favor**) n favor m; (*approval*) aprobación f ♦ vt (*proposition*) estar a favor de, aprobar; (*assist*) ser propicio a; **to do sb a** ~ hacer un favor a uno; **to find** ~ **with sb** caer en gracia a uno; **in** ~ **of** a favor de; ~**able** adj favorable; ~**ite** [-rɪt] adj, n favorito, preferido

fawn [fɔːn] n cervato ♦ adj (*also*: ~-*coloured*) color de cervato, leonado ♦ vi: **to** ~ **(up)on** adular

fax [fæks] n (*document*) fax m; (*machine*) telefax m ♦ vt mandar por telefax

FBI (US) n abbr (= Federal Bureau of Investigation) ≈ BIC f (SP)

fear [fɪə*] n miedo, temor m ♦ vt tener miedo de, temer; **for ~ of** por si; **~ful** adj temeroso, miedoso; (awful) terrible; **~less** adj audaz

feasible ['fiːzəbl] adj factible

feast [fiːst] n banquete m; (REL: also: ~ day) fiesta ♦ vi festejar

feat [fiːt] n hazaña

feather ['fɛðə*] n pluma

feature ['fiːtʃə*] n característica; (article) artículo de fondo ♦ vt (subj: film) presentar ♦ vi: **to ~ in** tener un papel destacado en; **~s** npl (of face) facciones fpl; **~ film** n largometraje m

February ['fɛbruəri] n febrero

fed [fɛd] pt, pp of **feed**

federal ['fɛdərəl] adj federal

fed up [fɛd'ʌp] adj: **to be ~ (with)** estar harto (de)

fee [fiː] n pago; (professional) derechos mpl, honorarios mpl; (of club) cuota; **school ~s** matrícula

feeble ['fiːbl] adj débil; (joke) flojo

feed [fiːd] (pt, pp fed) n comida; (of animal) pienso; (on printer) dispositivo de alimentación ♦ vt alimentar; (BRIT: baby: breast~) dar el pecho a; (animal) dar de comer a; (data, information): **to ~ into** meter en; **~ on** vt fus alimentarse de; **~back** n reacción f, feedback m; **~ing bottle** (BRIT) n biberón m

feel [fiːl] (pt, pp felt) n (sensation) sensación f; (sense of touch) tacto; (impression): **to have the ~ of** parecerse a ♦ vt tocar; (pain etc) sentir; (think, believe) creer; **to ~ hungry/cold** tener hambre/frío; **to ~ lonely/better** sentirse solo/mejor; **I don't ~ well** no me siento bien; **it ~s soft** es suave al tacto; **to ~ like** (want) tener ganas de; **~ about** or **around** vi tantear; **~er** n (of insect) antena; **to put out ~ers** or a **~er** (fig) sondear; **~ing** n (physical) sensación f; (foreboding) presentimiento; (emotion) sentimiento

feet [fiːt] npl of **foot**

feign [feɪn] vt fingir

fell [fɛl] pt of **fall** ♦ vt (tree) talar

fellow ['fɛləu] n tipo, tío (SP); (comrade) compañero; (of learned society) socio/a ♦ cpd: **~ citizen** n conciudadano/a; **~ countryman** n compatriota m; **~ men** npl semejantes mpl; **~ship** n compañerismo; (grant) beca

felony ['fɛləni] n crimen m

felt [fɛlt] pt, pp of **feel** ♦ n fieltro; **~-tip pen** n rotulador m

female ['fiːmeɪl] n (pej: woman) mujer f, tía; (ZOOL) hembra ♦ adj femenino; hembra

feminine ['fɛminin] adj femenino

feminist ['fɛminist] n feminista

fence [fɛns] n valla, cerca ♦ vt (also: ~ in) cercar ♦ vi (SPORT) hacer esgrima; **fencing** n esgrima

fend [fɛnd] vi: **to ~ for o.s.** valerse por sí mismo; **~ off** vt (attack) rechazar; (questions) evadir

fender ['fɛndə*] n guardafuego; (US: AUT) parachoques m inv

ferment [vb fə'mɛnt, n 'fɜːmɛnt] vi fermentar ♦ n (fig) agitación f

fern [fɜːn] n helecho

ferocious [fə'rəuʃəs] adj feroz; **ferocity** [-'rɔsiti] n ferocidad f

ferret ['fɛrit] n hurón m; **~ out** vt desentrañar

ferry ['fɛri] n (small) barca (de pasaje), balsa; (large: also: ~boat) transbordador m (SP), embarcadero (AM) ♦ vt transportar

fertile ['fɜːtaɪl] adj fértil; (BIOL) fecundo; **fertility** [fə'tɪlɪti] n fertilidad f; fecundidad f; **fertilize** ['fɜːtɪlaɪz] vt (BIOL) fecundar; (AGR) abonar; **fertilizer** n abono

fervent ['fɜːvənt] adj ferviente, entusiasta

fervour ['fɜːvə*] n fervor m, ardor m

fester ['fɛstə*] vi ulcerarse

festival ['fɛstɪvəl] n (REL) fiesta; (ART. MUS) festival m

festive ['fɛstɪv] adj festivo; **the ~ season** (BRIT: Christmas) las Navidades

festivities [fɛs'tɪvɪtɪz] npl fiestas fpl

festoon [fɛs'tuːn] vt: **to ~ with** engalanar de

fetch [fɛtʃ] vt ir a buscar; (sell for)

venderse por

fetching ['fɛtʃɪŋ] *adj* atractivo

fête [feɪt] *n* fiesta

fetish ['fɛtɪʃ] *n* obsesión *f*

fetus ['fiːtəs] (*US*) *n* = **foetus**

feud [fjuːd] *n* (*hostility*) enemistad *f*; (*quarrel*) disputa

fever ['fiːvə*] *n* fiebre *f*; ~**ish** *adj* febril

few [fjuː] *adj* (*not many*) pocos ♦ *pron* pocos; algunos; **a** ~ *adj* unos pocos, algunos, ~**er** *adj* menos; ~**est** *adj* los/las menos

fiancé [fɪ'ɑ̃ːŋseɪ] *n* novio, prometido; ~**e** *n* novia, prometida

fiasco [fɪ'æskəu] *n* desastre *m*

fib [fɪb] *n* mentirilla

fibre ['faɪbə*] (*US* **fiber**) *n* fibra; ~-**glass** *n* fibra de vidrio

fickle ['fɪkl] *adj* inconstante

fiction ['fɪkʃən] *n* ficción *f*; ~**al** *adj* novelesco; **fictitious** [fɪk'tɪʃəs] *adj* ficticio

fiddle ['fɪdl] *n* (*MUS*) violín *m*; (*cheating*) trampa ♦ *vt* (*BRIT: accounts*) falsificar; ~ **with** *vt fus* juguetear con

fidget ['fɪdʒɪt] *vi* enredar; **stop** ~**ing!** ¡estáte quieto!

field [fiːld] *n* campo; (*fig*) campo, esfera; (*SPORT*) campo, cancha (*AM*); ~ **marshal** *n* mariscal *m*; ~**work** *n* trabajo de campo

fiend [fiːnd] *n* demonio; ~**ish** *adj* diabólico

fierce [fɪəs] *adj* feroz; (*wind, heat*) fuerte; (*fighting, enemy*) encarnizado

fiery ['faɪərɪ] *adj* (*burning*) ardiente; (*temperament*) apasionado

fifteen [fɪf'tiːn] *num* quince

fifth [fɪfθ] *num* quinto

fifty ['fɪftɪ] *num* cincuenta; ~-~ *adj* (*deal, split*) a medias ♦ *adv* a medias, mitad por mitad

fig [fɪg] *n* higo

fight [faɪt] (*pt, pp* **fought**) *n* (*gen*) pelea; (*MIL*) combate *m*; (*struggle*) lucha ♦ *vt* luchar contra; (*cancer, alcoholism*) combatir; (*election*) intentar ganar; (*emotion*) resistir ♦ *vi* pelear, luchar; ~**er** *n* combatiente *m/f*; (*plane*) caza *m*; ~**ing** *n* combate *m*, pelea

figment ['fɪgmənt] *n*: **a** ~ **of the**

imagination una quimera

figurative ['fɪgjurətɪv] *adj* (*meaning*) figurado; (*style*) figurativo

figure ['fɪgə*] *n* (*DRAWING, GEOM*) figura, dibujo; (*number, cipher*) cifra; (*body, outline*) tipo; (*personality*) figura ♦ *vt* (*esp US*) imaginar ♦ *vi* (*appear*) figurar; ~ **out** *vt* (*work out*) resolver; ~**head** *n* (*NAUT*) mascarón *m* de proa; (*pej: leader*) figura decorativa; ~ **of speech** *n* figura retórica

filch [fɪltʃ] *vt* hurtar, robar

file [faɪl] *n* (*tool*) lima; (*dossier*) expediente *m*; (*folder*) carpeta; (*COMPUT*) fichero; (*row*) fila ♦ *vt* limar; (*LAW: claim*) presentar; (*store*) archivar; ~ **in/out** *vi* entrar/salir en fila; **filing cabinet** *n* fichero, archivador *m*

fill [fɪl] *vt* (*space*): **to** ~ (**with**) llenar (de); (*vacancy, need*) cubrir ♦ *n*: **to eat one's** ~ llenarse; ~ **in** *vt* rellenar; ~ **up** *vt* llenar (hasta el borde) ♦ *vi* (*AUT*) poner gasolina

fillet ['fɪlɪt] *n* filete *m*; ~ **steak** *n* filete *m* de ternera

filling ['fɪlɪŋ] *n* (*CULIN*) relleno; (*for tooth*) empaste *m*; ~ **station** *n* estación *f* de servicio

film [fɪlm] *n* película ♦ *vt* (*scene*) filmar ♦ *vi* rodar (una película); ~ **star** *n* astro, estrella de cine; ~**strip** *n* tira de película

filter ['fɪltə*] *n* filtro ♦ *vt* filtrar; ~ **lane** (*BRIT*) *n* carril *m* de selección; ~-**tipped** *adj* con filtro

filth [fɪlθ] *n* suciedad *f*; ~**y** *adj* sucio; (*language*) obsceno

fin [fɪn] *n* (*gen*) aleta

final ['faɪnl] *adj* (*last*) final, último; (*definitive*) definitivo, terminante ♦ *n* (*BRIT: SPORT*) final *f*; ~**s** *npl* (*SCOL*) examen *m* final; (*US: SPORT*) final *f*

finale [fɪ'nɑːlɪ] *n* final *m*

final: ~**ist** *n* (*SPORT*) finalista *m/f*; ~**ize** *vt* concluir, completar; ~**ly** *adv* (*lastly*) por último, finalmente; (*eventually*) por fin

finance [faɪ'næns] *n* (*money*) fondos *mpl*; ~**s** *npl* finanzas *fpl*; (*personal* ~**s**) situación *f* económica ♦ *vt* financiar; **financial** [-'nænʃəl] *adj* financiero;

financier *n* financiero/a
find [faind] (*pt, pp* found) *vt* encontrar, hallar; (*come upon*) descubrir ♦ *n* hallazgo; descubrimiento; to ~ sb guilty (*LAW*) declarar culpable a uno; ~ out *vt* averiguar; (*truth, secret*) descubrir; to ~ out about (*subject*) informarse sobre; (*by chance*) enterarse de; ~ings *npl* (*LAW*) veredicto, fallo; (*of report*) recomendaciones *fpl*
fine [fain] *adj* excelente; (*thin*) fino ♦ *adv* (*well*) bien ♦ *n* (*LAW*) multa ♦ *vt* (*LAW*) multar; to be ~ (*person*) estar bien; (*weather*) hacer buen tiempo; ~ arts *npl* bellas artes *fpl*
finery ['fainəri] *n* adornos *mpl*
finesse [fɪ'nɛs] *n* sutileza
finger ['fɪŋgə*] *n* dedo ♦ *vt* (*touch*) manosear; little/index ~ (dedo) meñique *m*/índice *m*; ~nail *n* uña; ~print *n* huella dactilar; ~tip *n* yema del dedo
finicky ['fɪnɪkɪ] *adj* delicado
finish ['fɪnɪʃ] *n* (*end*) fin *m*; (*SPORT*) meta; (*polish etc*) acabado ♦ *vt, vi* terminar; to ~ doing sth acabar de hacer algo; to ~ third llegar el tercero; ~ off *vt* acabar, terminar; (*kill*) acabar con; ~ up *vt* acabar, terminar ♦ *vi* ir a parar, terminar; ~ing line *n* línea de llegada *or* meta; ~ing school *n* academia para señoritas
finite ['fainait] *adj* finito; (*verb*) conjugado
Finland ['fɪnlənd] *n* Finlandia
Finn [fɪn] *n* finlandés/esa *m/f*; ~ish *adj* finlandés/esa ♦ *n* (*LING*) finlandés *m*
fir [fə:*] *n* abeto
fire ['faɪə*] *n* fuego; (*in hearth*) lumbre *f*; (*accidental*) incendio; (*heater*) estufa ♦ *vt* (*gun*) disparar; (*interest*) despertar; (*inf: dismiss*) despedir ♦ *vi* (*shoot*) disparar; on ~ ardiendo, en llamas; ~ alarm *n* alarma de incendios; ~arm *n* arma de fuego; ~ brigade (*US* ~ department) *n* (cuerpo de) bomberos *mpl*; ~ engine *n* coche *m* de bomberos; ~ escape *n* escalera de incendios; ~ extinguisher *n* extintor *m* (de incendios); ~guard *n* rejilla de protección; ~man *n* bombero; ~place *n* chimenea; ~side *n*: by the

~side al lado de la chimenea; ~ station *n* parque *m* de bomberos; ~wood *n* leña; ~works *npl* fuegos *mpl* artificiales
firing squad ['faɪrɪŋ-] *n* pelotón *m* de ejecución
firm [fə:m] *adj* firme; (*look, voice*) resuelto ♦ *n* firma, empresa; ~ly *adv* firmemente; resueltamente
first [fə:st] *adj* primero ♦ *adv* (*before others*) primero; (*when listing reasons etc*) en primer lugar, primeramente ♦ *n* (*person: in race*) primero/a; (*AUT*) primera; (*BRIT: SCOL*) título de licenciado con calificación de sobresaliente; at ~ al principio; ~ of all ante todo; ~ aid *n* primera ayuda, primeros auxilios *mpl*; ~-aid kit *n* botiquín *m*; ~-class *adj* (*excellent*) de primera (categoría); (*ticket etc*) de primera clase; ~-hand *adj* de primera mano; F~ Lady (*esp US*) *n* primera dama; ~ly *adv* en primer lugar; ~ name *n* nombre *m* (de pila); ~-rate *adj* estupendo
fish [fɪʃ] *n inv* pez *m*; (*food*) pescado ♦ *vt, vi* pescar; to go ~ing ir de pesca; ~erman *n* pescador *m*; ~ farm *n* criadero de peces; ~ fingers (*BRIT*) *npl* croquetas *fpl* de pescado; ~ing boat *n* barca de pesca; ~ing line *n* sedal *m*; ~ing rod *n* caña (de pescar) ~monger's (shop) (*BRIT*) *n* pescadería; ~ sticks (*US*) *npl* = ~ fingers; (*US*) *npl* = ~ fingers; ~y (*inf*) *adj* sospechoso
fist [fɪst] *n* puño
fit [fɪt] *adj* (*healthy*) en (buena) forma; (*proper*) adecuado, apropiado ♦ *vt* (*subj: clothes*) estar *or* sentar bien a; (*instal*) poner; (*equip*) proveer, dotar; (*facts*) cuadrar *or* corresponder con ♦ *vi* (*clothes*) sentar bien; (*in space, gap*) caber; (*facts*) coincidir ♦ *n* (*MED*) ataque *m*; ~ to (*ready*) a punto de; ~ for apropiado para; a ~ of anger/pride un arranque de cólera/orgullo; this dress is a good ~ este vestido me sienta bien; by ~s and starts a rachas; ~ in *vi* (*fig: person*) llevarse bien (con todos); ~ful *adj* espasmódico, intermitente; ~ment *n* módulo adosable; ~ness *n* (*MED*) salud *f*; ~ted carpet *n* moqueta; ~ted kitchen *n*

cocina amueblada; ~ter *n* ajustador *m*;
~ting *adj* apropiado ♦ *n* (*of dress*)
prueba; (*of piece of equipment*)
instalación *f*; ~ting room *n* probador *m*;
~tings *npl* instalaciones *fpl*

five [faɪv] *num* cinco; ~ (*inf*) *n* (*BRIT*)
billete *m* de cinco libras; (*US*) billete *m*
de cinco dólares

fix [fɪks] *vt* (*secure*) fijar, asegurar; (*mend*)
arreglar; (*prepare*) preparar ♦ *n*: **to be
in a ~** estar en un aprieto; **~ up** *vt*
(*meeting*) arreglar; **to ~ sb up with sth**
proveer a uno de algo; ~**ation** [fɪk'seɪʃən]
n obsesión *f*; ~**ed** [fɪkst] *adj* (*prices etc*)
fijo; ~**ture** ['fɪkstʃə*] *n* (*SPORT*) encuentro;
~**tures** *npl* (*cupboards etc*) instalaciones
fpl fijas

fizzle out ['fɪzl-] *vi* apagarse

fizzy ['fɪzɪ] *adj* (*drink*) gaseoso

fjord [fjɔːd] *n* fiordo

flabbergasted ['flæbəgɑːstɪd] *adj*
pasmado, alucinado

flabby ['flæbɪ] *adj* gordo

flag [flæg] *n* bandera; (*stone*) losa ♦ *vi*
decaer; **to ~ sb down** hacer señas a uno
para que se pare; ~**pole** *n* asta de
bandera; ~**ship** *n* buque *m* insignia; (*fig*)
bandera

flair [flɛə*] *n* aptitud *f* especial

flak [flæk] *n* (*MIL*) fuego antiaéreo; (*inf*:
criticism) lluvia de críticas

flake [fleɪk] *n* (*of rust, paint*) escama; (*of
snow, soap powder*) copo ♦ *vi* (*also*: ~ *off*)
desconcharse

flamboyant [flæm'bɔɪənt] *adj* (*dress*)
vistoso; (*person*) extravagante

flame [fleɪm] *n* llama

flamingo [flə'mɪŋgəu] *n* flamenco

flammable ['flæməbl] *adj* inflamable

flan [flæn] (*BRIT*) *n* tarta

flank [flæŋk] *n* (*of animal*) ijar *m*; (*of
army*) flanco ♦ *vt* flanquear

flannel ['flænl] *n* (*BRIT*: *also*: *face* ~)
manopla; (*fabric*) franela; ~**s** *npl*
(*trousers*) pantalones *mpl* de franela

flap [flæp] *n* (*of pocket, envelope*) solapa
♦ *vt* (*wings, arms*) agitar ♦ *vi* (*sail, flag*)
ondear

flare [flɛə*] *n* llamarada; (*MIL*) bengala;

(*in skirt etc*) vuelo; ~ **up** *vi* encenderse;
(*fig*: *person*) encolerizarse; (: *revolt*)
estallar

flash [flæʃ] *n* relámpago; (*also*: *news* ~)
noticias *fpl* de última hora; (*PHOT*) flash
m ♦ *vt* (*light, headlights*) lanzar un
destello con; (*news, message*) transmitir;
(*smile*) lanzar ♦ *vi* brillar; (*hazard light
etc*) lanzar destellos; **in a ~** en un
instante; **he ~ed by** *or* **past** pasó como
un rayo; ~**back** *n* (*CINEMA*) flashback *m*;
~**bulb** *n* bombilla fusible; ~ **cube** *n* cubo
de flash; ~**light** *n* linterna

flashy ['flæʃɪ] (*pej*) *adj* ostentoso

flask [flɑːsk] *n* frasco; (*also*: *vacuum* ~)
termo

flat [flæt] *adj* llano; (*smooth*) liso; (*tyre*)
desinflado; (*battery*) descargado; (*beer*)
muerto; (*refusal etc*) rotundo; (*MUS*)
desafinado; (*rate*) fijo ♦ *n* (*BRIT*:
apartment) piso (*SP*), departamento (*AM*),
apartamento; (*AUT*) pinchazo; (*MUS*) bemol
m; **to work ~ out** trabajar a toda
mecha; ~**ly** *adv* terminantemente, de
plano; ~**-screen** *adj* de pantalla plana;
~**ten** *vt* (*also*: ~*ten out*) allanar; (*smooth
out*) alisar; (*building, plants*) arrasar

flatter ['flætə*] *vt* adular, halagar; ~**ing**
adj halagüeño; (*dress*) que favorece; ~**y** *n*
adulación *f*

flaunt [flɔːnt] *vt* ostentar, lucir

flavour ['fleɪvə*] (*US* **flavor**) *n* sabor *m*,
gusto ♦ *vt* sazonar, condimentar; **strawberry ~ed** con sabor a fresa; ~**ing** *n* (*in
product*) aromatizante *m*

flaw [flɔː] *n* defecto; ~**less** *adj* impecable

flax [flæks] *n* lino; ~**en** *adj* rubio

flea [fliː] *n* pulga

fleck [flɛk] *n* (*mark*) mota

flee [fliː] (*pt, pp* **fled**) *vt* huir de ♦ *vi*
huir, fugarse

fleece [fliːs] *n* vellón *m*; (*wool*) lana ♦ *vt*
(*inf*) desplumar

fleet [fliːt] *n* flota; (*of lorries etc*) escuadra

fleeting ['fliːtɪŋ] *adj* fugaz

Flemish ['flɛmɪʃ] *adj* flamenco

flesh [flɛʃ] *n* carne *f*; (*skin*) piel *f*; (*of
fruit*) pulpa; ~ **wound** *n* herida
superficial

flew [flu:] *pt of* **fly**

flex [fleks] *n* cordón *m* ♦ *vt* (*muscles*) tensar; **~ibility** [-ɪˈbɪlɪtɪ] *n* flexibilidad *f*; **~ible** *adj* flexible

flick [flɪk] *n* capirotazo; chasquido ♦ *vt* (*with hand*) dar un capirotazo a; (*whip etc*) chasquear; (*switch*) accionar; **~ through** *vt fus* hojear

flicker [ˈflɪkə*] *vi* (*light*) parpadear; (*flame*) vacilar

flier [ˈflaɪə*] *n* aviador(a) *m/f*

flight [flaɪt] *n* vuelo; (*escape*) huida, fuga; (*also:* **~ of steps**) tramo (de escaleras); **~ attendant** (*US*) *n* camarero/azafata; **~ deck** *n* (*AVIAT*) cabina de mandos; (*NAUT*) cubierta de aterrizaje

flimsy [ˈflɪmzɪ] *adj* (*thin*) muy ligero; (*building*) endeble; (*excuse*) flojo

flinch [flɪntʃ] *vi* encogerse; **to ~ from** retroceder ante

fling [flɪŋ] (*pt, pp* **flung**) *vt* arrojar

flint [flɪnt] *n* pedernal *m*; (*in lighter*) piedra

flip [flɪp] *vt* dar la vuelta a; (*switch: turn on*) encender; (*: turn off*) apagar; (*coin*) echar a cara o cruz

flippant [ˈflɪpənt] *adj* poco serio

flipper [ˈflɪpə*] *n* aleta

flirt [flɜːt] *vi* coquetear, flirtear ♦ *n* coqueta

flit [flɪt] *vi* revolotear

float [fləʊt] *n* flotador *m*; (*in procession*) carroza; (*money*) reserva ♦ *vi* flotar; (*swimmer*) hacer la plancha

flock [flɒk] *n* (*of sheep*) rebaño; (*of birds*) bandada ♦ *vi*: **to ~ to** acudir en tropel a

flog [flɒg] *vt* azotar

flood [flʌd] *n* inundación *f*; (*of letters, imports etc*) avalancha ♦ *vt* inundar ♦ *vi* (*place*) inundarse; (*people*): **to ~ into** inundar; **~ing** *n* inundaciones *fpl*; **~light** *n* foco

floor [flɔː*] *n* suelo; (*storey*) piso; (*of sea*) fondo ♦ *vt* (*subj: question*) dejar sin respuesta; (*: blow*) derribar; **ground ~, first ~** (*US*) planta baja; **first ~, second ~** (*US*) primer piso; **~board** *n* tabla; **~ show** *n* cabaret *m*

flop [flɒp] *n* fracaso ♦ *vi* (*fail*) fracasar;

(*fall*) derrumbarse

floppy [ˈflɒpɪ] *adj* flojo ♦ *n* (*COMPUT: also:* **~ disk**) floppy *m*

flora [ˈflɔːrə] *n* flora

floral [ˈflɔːrl] *adj* (*pattern*) floreado

florid [ˈflɒrɪd] *adj* florido; (*complexion*) rubicundo

florist [ˈflɒrɪst] *n* florista *m/f*; **~'s** (*shop*) *n* florería

flounce [flaʊns] *n* volante *m*; **~ out** *vi* salir enfadado

flounder [ˈflaʊndə*] *vi* (*swimmer*) patalear; (*fig: economy*) estar en dificultades ♦ *n* (*ZOOL*) platija

flour [ˈflaʊə*] *n* harina

flourish [ˈflʌrɪʃ] *vi* florecer ♦ *n* ademán *m*, movimiento (ostentoso); **~ing** *adj* floreciente

flout [flaʊt] *vt* burlarse de

flow [fləʊ] *n* (*movement*) flujo; (*of traffic*) circulación *f*; (*tide*) corriente *f* ♦ *vi* (*river, blood*) fluir; (*traffic*) circular; **~ chart** *n* organigrama *m*

flower [ˈflaʊə*] *n* flor *f* ♦ *vi* florecer; **~ bed** *n* macizo; **~pot** *n* tiesto; **~y** *adj* (*fragrance*) floral; (*pattern*) floreado; (*speech*) florido

flown [fləʊn] *pp of* **fly**

flu [flu:] *n*: **to have ~** tener la gripe

fluctuate [ˈflʌktjueɪt] *vi* fluctuar

fluent [ˈfluːənt] *adj* (*linguist*) que habla perfectamente; (*speech*) elocuente; **he speaks ~ French, he's ~ in French** domina el francés; **~ly** *adv* con fluidez

fluff [flʌf] *n* pelusa; **~y** *adj* de pelo suave

fluid [ˈfluːɪd] *adj* (*movement*) fluido, líquido; (*situation*) inestable ♦ *n* fluido, líquido

fluke [fluːk] (*inf*) *n* chiripa

flung [flʌŋ] *pt, pp of* **fling**

fluoride [ˈfluəraɪd] *n* fluoruro

flurry [ˈflʌrɪ] *n* (*of snow*) temporal *m*; **~ of activity** frenesí *m* de actividad

flush [flʌʃ] *n* rubor *m*; (*fig: of youth etc*) resplandor *m* ♦ *vt* limpiar con agua ♦ *vi* ruborizarse ♦ *adj*: **~ with** a ras de; **to ~ the toilet** hacer funcionar la cisterna; **~ out** *vt* (*game, birds*) levantar; **~ed** *adj* ruborizado

flustered ['flʌstəd] *adj* aturdido
flute [fluːt] *n* flauta
flutter ['flʌtə*] *n* (*of wings*) revoloteo, aleteo; **a ~ of panic/excitement** una oleada de pánico/excitación ♦ *vi* revolotear
flux [flʌks] *n*: **to be in a state of ~** estar continuamente cambiando
fly [flaɪ] (*pt* **flew**, *pp* **flown**) *n* mosca; (*on trousers: also:* **flies**) bragueta ♦ *vt* (*plane*) pilot(e)ar; (*cargo*) transportar (en avión); (*distances*) recorrer (en avión) ♦ *vi* volar; (*passengers*) ir en avión; (*escape*) evadirse; (*flag*) ondear; **~ away** *or* **off** *vi* emprender el vuelo; **~ing** *n* (*activity*) (el) volar; (*action*) vuelo ♦ *adj*: **~ing visit** visita relámpago; **with ~ing colours** con lucimiento; **~ing saucer** *n* platillo volante; **~ing start** *n*: **to get off to a ~ing start** empezar con buen pie; **~over** (*BRIT*) *n* paso a desnivel *or* superior; **~sheet** *n* (*for tent*) doble techo
foal [fəul] *n* potro
foam [fəum] *n* espuma ♦ *vi* hacer espuma; **~ rubber** *n* goma espuma
fob [fɔb] *vt*: **to ~ sb off with sth** despachar a uno con algo
focal point ['fəukl-] *n* (*fig*) centro de atención
focus ['fəukəs] (*pl* **~es**) *n* foco; (*centre*) centro ♦ *vt* (*field glasses etc*) enfocar ♦ *vi*: **to ~ (on)** enfocar a; (*issue etc*) centrarse en; **in/out of ~** enfocado/desenfocado·
fodder ['fɔdə*] *n* pienso
foetus ['fiːtəs] (*US* **fetus**) *n* feto
fog [fɔg] *n* niebla; **~gy** *adj*: **it's ~gy** hay niebla, está brumoso; **~ lamp** (*US* **~ light**) *n* (*AUT*) faro de niebla
foil [fɔɪl] *vt* frustrar ♦ *n* hoja; (*kitchen ~*) papel *m* (de) aluminio; (*complement*) complemento; (*FENCING*) florete *m*
fold [fəuld] *n* (*bend, crease*) pliegue *m*; (*AGR*) redil *m* ♦ *vt* doblar; (*arms*) cruzar; **~ up** *vi* plegarse, doblarse; (*business*) quebrar ♦ *vt* (*map etc*) plegar; **~er** *n* (*for papers*) carpeta; **~ing** *adj* (*chair, bed*) plegable
foliage ['fəulɪɪdʒ] *n* follaje *m*

folk [fəuk] *npl* gente *f* ♦ *adj* popular, folklórico; **~s** *npl* (*family*) familia *sg*, parientes *mpl*; **~lore** ['fəuklɔː*] *n* folklore *m*; **~ song** *n* canción *f* popular *or* folklórica
follow ['fɔləu] *vt* seguir ♦ *vi* seguir; (*result*) resultar; **to ~ suit** hacer lo mismo; **~ up** *vt* (*letter, offer*) responder a; (*case*) investigar; **~er** *n* (*of person, belief*) partidario/a; **~ing** *adj* siguiente ♦ *n* afición *f*, partidarios *mpl*
folly ['fɔlɪ] *n* locura
fond [fɔnd] *adj* (*memory, smile etc*) cariñoso; (*hopes*) ilusorio; **to be ~ of** tener cariño a; (*pastime, food*) ser aficionado a
fondle ['fɔndl] *vt* acariciar
font [fɔnt] *n* pila bautismal; (*TYP*) fundición *f*
food [fuːd] *n* comida; **~ mixer** *n* batidora; **~ poisoning** *n* intoxicación *f* alimenticia; **~ processor** *n* robot *m* de cocina; **~stuffs** *npl* comestibles *mpl*
fool [fuːl] *n* tonto/a; (*CULIN*) puré *m* de frutas con nata ♦ *vt* engañar ♦ *vi* (*gen: ~ around*) bromear; **~hardy** *adj* temerario; **~ish** *adj* tonto; (*careless*) imprudente; **~proof** *adj* (*plan etc*) infalible
foot [fut] (*pl* **feet**) *n* pie *m*; (*measure*) pie *m* (= 304 mm); (*of animal*) pata ♦ *vt* (*bill*) pagar; **on ~** a pie; **~age** *n* (*CINEMA*) imágenes *fpl*; **~ball** *n* balón *m*; (*game: BRIT*) fútbol *m*; (: *US*) fútbol *m* americano; **~ball player** *n* (*BRIT: also:* **~baller**) futbolista *m*; (*US*) jugador *m* de fútbol americano; **~brake** *n* freno de pie; **~bridge** *n* puente *m* para peatones; **~hills** *npl* estribaciones *fpl*; **~hold** *n* pie *m* firme; **~ing** *n* (*fig*) posición *f*; **to lose one's ~ing** perder el pie; **~lights** *npl* candilejas *fpl*; **~man** *n* lacayo; **~note** *n* nota (al pie de la página); **~path** *n* sendero; **~print** *n* huella, pisada; **~step** *n* paso; **~wear** *n* calzado

KEYWORD

for [fɔː] *prep* **1** (*indicating destination, intention*) para; **the train ~ London** el tren con destino a *or* de Londres; **he left**

~ **Rome** marchó para Roma; **he went ~ the paper** fue por el periódico; **is this ~ me?** ¿es esto para mí?; **it's time ~ lunch** es la hora de comer

2 (*indicating purpose*) para; **what('s it) ~?** ¿para qué (es)?; **to pray ~ peace** rezar por la paz

3 (*on behalf of, representing*): **the MP ~ Hove** el diputado por Hove; **he works ~ the government/a local firm** trabaja para el gobierno/en una empresa local; **I'll ask him ~ you** se lo pediré por ti; **G ~ George** G de Gerona

4 (*because of*) por esta razón; **~ fear of being criticized** por temor a ser criticado

5 (*with regard to*) para; **it's cold ~ July** hace frío para julio; **he has a gift ~ languages** tiene don de lenguas

6 (*in exchange for*) por; **I sold it ~ £5** lo vendí por £5; **to pay 50 pence ~ a ticket** pagar 50 peniques por un billete

7 (*in favour of*): **are you ~ or against us?** ¿estás con nosotros o contra nosotros?; **I'm all ~ it** estoy totalmente a favor; **vote ~ X** vote (a) X

8 (*referring to distance*): **there are roadworks ~ 5 km** hay obras en 5 km; **we walked ~ miles** caminamos kilómetros y kilómetros

9 (*referring to time*): **he was away ~ 2 years** estuvo fuera (durante) dos años; **it hasn't rained ~ 3 weeks** no ha llovido durante *or* en 3 semanas; **I have known her ~ years** la conozco desde hace años; **can you do it ~ tomorrow?** ¿lo podrás hacer para mañana?

10 (*with infinitive clauses*): **it is not ~ me to decide** la decisión no es cosa mía; **it would be best ~ you to leave** sería mejor que te fueras; **there is still time ~ you to do it** todavía te queda tiempo para hacerlo; **~ this to be possible ...** para que esto sea posible ...

11 (*in spite of*) a pesar de; **~ all his complaints** a pesar de sus quejas
♦ *conj* (*since, as: rather formal*) puesto que

forage ['fɒrɪdʒ] *vi* (*animal*) forrajear; (*person*): **to ~ for** hurgar en busca de

foray ['fɒreɪ] *n* incursión *f*

forbad(e) [fə'bæd] *pt of* **forbid**

forbid [fə'bɪd] (*pt* **forbad(e)**, *pp* **forbidden**) *vt* prohibir; **to ~ sb to do sth** prohibir a uno hacer algo; **~ding** *adj* amenazador(a)

force [fɔːs] *n* fuerza ♦ *vt* forzar; (*push*) meter a la fuerza; **to ~ o.s. to do** hacer un esfuerzo por hacer; **the F~s** *npl* (*BRIT*) las Fuerzas Armadas; **in ~** en vigor; **~d** [fɔːst] *adj* forzado; **~-feed** *vt* alimentar a la fuerza; **~ful** *adj* enérgico

forcibly ['fɔːsəblɪ] *adv* a la fuerza; (*speak*) enérgicamente

ford [fɔːd] *n* vado

fore [fɔː*] *n*: **to come to the ~** empezar a destacar

forearm ['fɔːrɑːm] *n* antebrazo

foreboding [fɔː'bəudɪŋ] *n* presentimiento

forecast ['fɔːkɑːst] *n* pronóstico ♦ *vt* (*irreg: like cast*) pronosticar

forecourt ['fɔːkɔːt] *n* patio

forefathers ['fɔːfɑːðəz] *npl* antepasados *mpl*

forefinger ['fɔːfɪŋgə*] *n* (dedo) índice *m*

forefront ['fɔːfrʌnt] *n*: **in the ~ of** en la vanguardia de

forego *vt* = **forgo**

foregone ['fɔːgɒn] *pp of* **forego** ♦ *adj*: **it's a ~ conclusion** es una conclusión evidente

foreground ['fɔːgraund] *n* primer plano

forehead ['fɒrɪd] *n* frente *f*

foreign ['fɒrɪn] *adj* extranjero; (*trade*) exterior; (*object*) extraño; **~er** *n* extranjero/a; **~ exchange** *n* divisas *fpl*; **F~ Office** (*BRIT*) *n* Ministerio de Asuntos Exteriores; **F~ Secretary** (*BRIT*) *n* Ministro de Asuntos Exteriores

foreleg ['fɔːleg] *n* pata delantera

foreman ['fɔːmən] *n* capataz *m*; (*in construction*) maestro de obras

foremost ['fɔːməust] *adj* principal ♦ *adv*: **first and ~** ante todo

forensic [fə'rɛnsɪk] *adj* forense

forerunner ['fɔːrʌnə*] *n* precursor(a) *m/f*

foresaw [fɔː'sɔː] *pt of* **foresee**

foresee [fɔː'siː] (*pt* **foresaw**, *pp* **foreseen**) *vt* prever; ~**able** *adj* previsible

foreshadow [fɔː'ʃædəu] *vt* prefigurar, anunciar

foresight ['fɔːsaɪt] *n* previsión *f*

forest ['fɒrɪst] *n* bosque *m*

forestall [fɔː'stɔːl] *vt* prevenir

forestry ['fɒrɪstrɪ] *n* silvicultura

foretaste ['fɔːteɪst] *n* muestra

foretell [fɔː'tɛl] (*pt, pp* **foretold**) *vt* predecir, pronosticar

foretold [fɔː'təuld] *pt, pp of* **foretell**

forever [fə'rɛvə*] *adv* para siempre; (*endlessly*) constantemente

forewent [fɔː'wɛnt] *pt of* **forego**

foreword ['fɔːwɜːd] *n* prefacio

forfeit ['fɔːfɪt] *vt* perder

forgave [fə'geɪv] *pt of* **forgive**

forge [fɔːdʒ] *n* herrería ♦ *vt* (*signature, money*) falsificar; (*metal*) forjar; ~ **ahead** *vi* avanzar mucho; ~**ry** *n* falsificación *f*

forget [fə'gɛt] (*pt* **forgot**, *pp* **forgotten**) *vt* olvidar ♦ *vi* olvidarse; ~**ful** *adj* despistado; ~**-me-not** *n* nomeolvides *f* *inv*

forgive [fə'gɪv] (*pt* **forgave**, *pp* **forgiven**) *vt* perdonar; **to** ~ **sb for sth** perdonar algo a uno; ~**ness** *n* perdón *m*

forgo [fɔː'gəu] (*pt* **forwent**, *pp* **forgone**) *vt* (*give up*) renunciar a; (*go without*) privarse de

forgot [fə'gɒt] *pt of* **forget**

forgotten [fə'gɒtn] *pp of* **forget**

fork [fɔːk] *n* (*for eating*) tenedor *m*; (*for gardening*) horca; (*of roads*) bifurcación *f* ♦ *vi* (*road*) bifurcarse; ~ **out** (*inf*) *vt* (*pay*) desembolsar; ~**-lift truck** *n* máquina elevadora

forlorn [fə'lɔːn] *adj* (*person*) triste, melancólico; (*place*) abandonado; (*attempt, hope*) desesperado

form [fɔːm] *n* forma; (*BRIT: SCOL*) clase *f*; (*document*) formulario ♦ *vt* formar; (*idea*) concebir; (*habit*) adquirir; **in top** ~ en plena forma; **to** ~ **a queue** hacer cola

formal ['fɔːməl] *adj* (*offer, receipt*) por escrito; (*person etc*) correcto; (*occasion, dinner*) de etiqueta; (*dress*) correcto; (*garden*) (de estilo) clásico; ~**ity** [-'mælɪtɪ]

n (*procedure*) trámite *m*; corrección *f*; etiqueta; ~**ly** *adv* oficialmente

format ['fɔːmæt] *n* formato ♦ *vt* (*COMPUT*) formatear

formative ['fɔːmətɪv] *adj* (*years*) de formación; (*influence*) formativo

former ['fɔːmə*] *adj* anterior; (*earlier*) antiguo; (*ex*) ex; **the** ~ **... the latter ...** aquél ... éste ...; ~**ly** *adv* antes

formula ['fɔːmjulə] *n* fórmula

forsake [fə'seɪk] (*pt* **forsook**, *pp* **for-saken**) *vt* (*gen*) abandonar; (*plan*) renunciar a

forsaken [fə'seɪkən] *pp of* **forsake**

fort [fɔːt] *n* fuerte *m*

forte ['fɔːtɪ] *n* fuerte *m*

forth [fɔːθ] *adv*: **back and** ~ de acá para allá; **and so** ~ y así sucesivamente; ~**coming** *adj* próximo, venidero; (*help, information*) disponible; (*character*) comunicativo; ~**right** *adj* franco; ~**with** *adv* en el acto

fortify ['fɔːtɪfaɪ] *vt* (*city*) fortificar; (*person*) fortalecer

fortitude ['fɔːtɪtjuːd] *n* fortaleza

fortnight ['fɔːtnaɪt] (*BRIT*) *n* quince días *mpl*; quincena; ~**ly** *adj* de cada quince días, quincenal ♦ *adv* cada quince días, quincenalmente

fortress ['fɔːtrɪs] *n* fortaleza

fortunate ['fɔːtʃənɪt] *adj* afortunado; **it is** ~ **that ...** (es una) suerte que ...; ~**ly** *adv* afortunadamente

fortune ['fɔːtʃən] *n* suerte *f*; (*wealth*) fortuna; ~**-teller** *n* adivino/a

forty ['fɔːtɪ] *num* cuarenta

forum ['fɔːrəm] *n* foro

forward ['fɔːwəd] *adj* (*movement, position*) avanzado; (*front*) delantero; (*in time*) adelantado; (*not shy*) atrevido ♦ *n* (*SPORT*) delantero ♦ *vt* (*letter*) remitir; (*career*) promocionar; **to move** ~ avanzar; ~**(s)** *adv* (hacia) adelante

fossil ['fɒsl] *n* fósil *m*

foster ['fɒstə*] *vt* (*child*) acoger en una familia; fomentar; ~ **child** *n* hijo/a adoptivo/a

fought [fɔːt] *pt, pp of* **fight**

foul [faul] *adj* sucio, puerco; (*weather,*

smell etc) asqueroso; (*language*) grosero; (*temper*) malísimo ♦ *n* (*SPORT*) falta ♦ *vt* (*dirty*) ensuciar; ~ **play** *n* (*LAW*) muerte *f* violenta

found [faund] *pt, pp of* **find** ♦ *vt* fundar; **~ation** [-'deɪʃən] *n* (*act*) fundación *f*; (*basis*) base *f*; (*also*: **~ation cream**) crema base; **~ations** *npl* (*of building*) cimientos *mpl*

founder ['faundə*] *n* fundador(a) *m/f* ♦ *vi* hundirse

foundry ['faundrɪ] *n* fundición *f*

fountain ['fauntɪn] *n* fuente *f*; ~ **pen** *n* pluma (estilográfica) (*SP*), pluma-fuente *f* (*AM*)

four [fɔ:*] *num* cuatro; **on all ~s** a gatas; **~-poster (bed)** *n* cama de dosel; **~some** ['fɔ:səm] *n* grupo de cuatro personas; **~teen** *num* catorce; **~th** *num* cuarto

fowl [faul] *n* ave *f* (de corral)

fox [fɔks] *n* zorro ♦ *vt* confundir

foyer ['fɔɪeɪ] *n* vestíbulo

fraction ['frækʃən] *n* fracción *f*

fracture ['fræktʃə*] *n* fractura

fragile ['frædʒaɪl] *adj* frágil

fragment ['frægmənt] *n* fragmento

fragrant ['freɪgrənt] *adj* fragante, oloroso

frail [freɪl] *adj* frágil; (*person*) débil

frame [freɪm] *n* (*TECH*) armazón *m*; (*of person*) cuerpo; (*of picture, door etc*) marco; (*of spectacles: also*: **~s**) montura ♦ *vt* enmarcar; ~ **of mind** *n* estado de ánimo; **~work** *n* marco

France [frɑ:ns] *n* Francia

franchise ['fræntʃaɪz] *n* (*POL*) derecho de votar, sufragio; (*COMM*) licencia, concesión *f*

frank [fræŋk] *adj* franco ♦ *vt* (*letter*) franquear; **~ly** *adv* francamente; **~ness** *n* franqueza

frantic ['fræntɪk] *adj* (*distraught*) desesperado; (*hectic*) frenético

fraternity [frə'tə:nɪtɪ] *n* (*feeling*) fraternidad *f*; (*group of people*) círculos *mpl*

fraud [frɔ:d] *n* fraude *m*; (*person*) impostor(a) *m/f*

fraught [frɔ:t] *adj*: ~ **with** lleno de

fray [freɪ] *n* combate *m*, lucha ♦ *vi*

deshilacharse; **tempers were ~ed** el ambiente se ponía tenso

freak [fri:k] *n* (*person*) fenómeno; (*event*) suceso anormal

freckle ['frekl] *n* peca

free [fri:] *adj* libre; (*gratis*) gratuito ♦ *vt* (*prisoner etc*) poner en libertad; (*jammed object*) soltar; ~ (**of charge**), **for** ~ gratis; **~dom** ['fri:dəm] *n* libertad *f*; **~-for-all** *n* riña general; ~ **gift** *n* prima; **~hold** *n* propiedad *f* vitalicia; ~ **kick** *n* tiro libre; **~lance** *adj* independiente ♦ *adv* por cuenta propia; **~ly** *adv* libremente; (*liberally*) generosamente; **F~mason** *n* francmasón *m*; **F~post** *n* porte *m* pagado; **~-range** *adj* (*hen, eggs*) de granja; ~ **trade** *n* libre comercio; **~way** (*US*) *n* autopista; ~ **will** *n* libre albedrío; **of one's own** ~ **will** por su propia voluntad

freeze [fri:z] (*pt* **froze**, *pp* **frozen**) *vi* (*weather*) helar; (*liquid, pipe, person*) helarse, congelarse ♦ *vt* helar; (*food, prices, salaries*) congelar ♦ *n* helada; (*on arms, wages*) congelación *f*; **~-dried** *adj* liofilizado; **~r** *n* congelador *m* (*SP*), congeladora (*AM*)

freezing ['fri:zɪŋ] *adj* helado; **3 degrees below** ~ tres grados bajo cero; ~ **point** *n* punto de congelación

freight [freɪt] *n* (*goods*) carga; (*money charged*) flete *m*; ~ **train** (*US*) *n* tren *m* de mercancías

French [frentʃ] *adj* francés/esa ♦ *n* (*LING*) francés *m*; **the** ~ *npl* los franceses; ~ **bean** *n* judía verde; ~ **fried potatoes** *npl* patatas *fpl* (*SP*) or papas *fpl* (*AM*) fritas; ~ **fries** (*US*) *npl* = ~ **fried potatoes**; **~man/woman** *n* francés/esa *m/f*; ~ **window** *n* puerta de cristal

frenzy ['frenzɪ] *n* frenesí *m*

frequent [*adj* 'fri:kwənt, *vb* frɪ'kwent] *adj* frecuente ♦ *vt* frecuentar; **~ly** [-əntlɪ] *adv* frecuentemente, a menudo

fresh [freʃ] *adj* fresco; (*bread*) tierno; (*new*) nuevo; **~en** *vi* (*wind, air*) soplar más recio; **~en up** *vi* (*person*) arreglarse, lavarse; **~er** (*BRIT: inf*) *n* (*SCOL*) estudiante *m/f* de primer año; **~ly** *adv* (*made,*

painted etc) recién; ~man (*US*) n = ~er;
~ness n frescura; ~water adj (*fish*) de
agua dulce

fret [frɛt] vi inquietarse

friar ['fraɪə*] n fraile m; (*before name*)
fray m

friction ['frɪkʃən] n fricción f

Friday ['fraɪdɪ] n viernes m inv

fridge [frɪdʒ] (*BRIT*) n nevera (*SP*),
refrigeradora (*AM*)

fried [fraɪd] adj frito

friend [frɛnd] n amigo/a; ~ly adj
simpático; (*government*) amigo; (*place*)
acogedor(a); (*match*) amistoso; ~ fire
fuego amigo, disparos mpl del propio
bando; ~ship n amistad f

frieze [friːz] n friso

frigate ['frɪɡɪt] n fragata

fright [fraɪt] n (*terror*) terror m; (*scare*)
susto; to take ~ asustarse; ~en vt
asustar; ~ened adj asustado; ~ening adj
espantoso; ~ful adj espantoso, horrible

frigid ['frɪdʒɪd] adj (*MED*) frígido, frío

frill [frɪl] n volante m

fringe [frɪndʒ] n (*BRIT*: of hair*) flequillo;
(*on lampshade etc*) flecos mpl; (*of forest
etc*) borde m, margen m; ~ benefits npl
beneficios mpl marginales

frisk [frɪsk] vt cachear, registrar

frisky ['frɪskɪ] adj juguetón/ona

fritter ['frɪtə*] n buñuelo; ~ away vt
desperdiciar

frivolous ['frɪvələs] adj frívolo

frizzy ['frɪzɪ] adj rizado

fro [frəʊ] see to

frock [frɔk] n vestido

frog [frɔɡ] n rana; ~man n hombre-rana
m

frolic ['frɔlɪk] vi juguetear

KEYWORD

from [frɔm] prep 1 (*indicating starting
place*) de, desde; where do you come ~?
¿de dónde eres?; ~ London to Glasgow
de Londres a Glasgow; to escape ~ sth/
sb escapar de algo/alguien
2 (*indicating origin etc*) de; a letter/
telephone call ~ my sister una carta/
llamada de mi hermana; tell him ~ me

that ... dígale de mi parte que ...
3 (*indicating time*): ~ one o'clock to or
until or till two de(sde) la una a or
hasta las dos; ~ January (on) a partir
de enero
4 (*indicating distance*) de; the hotel is 1
km ~ the beach el hotel está a 1 km de
la playa
5 (*indicating price, number etc*) de;
prices range ~ £10 to £50 los precios
van desde £10 a or hasta £50; the
interest rate was increased ~ 9% to
10% el tipo de interés fue incrementado
de un 9% a un 10%
6 (*indicating difference*) de; he can't tell
red ~ green no sabe distinguir el rojo
del verde; to be different ~ sb/sth ser
diferente a algo/alguien
7 (*because of, on the basis of*): ~ what he
says por lo que dice; weak ~ hunger
debilitado por el hambre

front [frʌnt] n (*foremost part*) parte f
delantera; (*of house*) fachada; (*of dress*)
delantero; (*promenade*: also: sea ~) paseo
marítimo; (*MIL, POL, METEOROLOGY*) frente
m; (*fig: appearances*) apariencias fpl
♦ adj (*wheel, leg*) delantero; (*row, line*)
primero; in ~ (of) delante (de); ~age
['frʌntɪdʒ] n (*of building*) fachada; ~ door
n puerta principal; ~ier ['frʌntɪə*] n
frontera; ~ page n primera plana; ~
room n (*BRIT*) salón m, sala; ~-wheel
drive n tracción f delantera

frost [frɔst] n helada; (*also: hoar~*)
escarcha; ~bite n congelación f; ~ed adj
(*glass*) deslustrado; ~y adj (*weather*) de
helada; (*welcome etc*) glacial

froth [frɔθ] n espuma

frown [fraʊn] vi fruncir el ceño

froze [frəʊz] pt of freeze

frozen ['frəʊzn] pp of freeze

fruit [fruːt] n inv fruta; fruto; (*fig*) fruto;
resultados mpl; ~erer n frutero/a;
~erer's (*shop*) n frutería; ~ful adj
provechoso; ~ion [fruːˈɪʃən] n: to come to
~ion realizarse; ~ juice n zumo (*SP*) or
jugo (*AM*) de fruta; ~ machine (*BRIT*) n
máquina f tragaperras; ~ salad n

macedonia (*SP*) *or* ensalada (*AM*) de frutas

frustrate [frʌs'treɪt] *vt* frustrar; **~d** *adj* frustrado

fry [fraɪ] (*pt, pp* **fried**) *vt* freír; **small ~** gente *f* menuda; **~ing pan** *n* sartén *f*

ft. *abbr* = **foot**; **feet**

fuddy-duddy ['fʌdɪdʌdɪ] (*pej*) *n* carroza *m/f*

fudge [fʌdʒ] *n* (*CULIN*) caramelo blando

fuel [fjuəl] *n* (*for heating*) combustible *m*; (*coal*) carbón *m*; (*wood*) leña; (*for engine*) carburante *m*; **~ oil** *n* fuel oil *m*; **~ tank** *n* depósito (de combustible)

fugitive ['fjuːdʒɪtɪv] *n* fugitivo/a

fulfil [ful'fɪl] *vt* (*function*) cumplir con; (*condition*) satisfacer; (*wish, desire*) realizar; **~ment** *n* satisfacción *f*; (*of promise, desire*) realización *f*

full [ful] *adj* lleno; (*fig*) pleno; (*complete*) completo; (*maximum*) máximo; (*information*) detallado; (*price*) íntegro; (*skirt*) amplio ♦ *adv*: **to know ~ well that** saber perfectamente que; **I'm ~ (up)** no puedo más; **~ employment** pleno empleo; **a ~ two hours** dos horas completas; **at ~ speed** a máxima velocidad; **in ~** (*reproduce, quote*) íntegramente; **~-length** *adj* (*novel etc*) entero; (*coat*) largo; (*portrait*) de cuerpo entero; **~ moon** *n* luna llena; **~-scale** *adj* (*attack, war*) en gran escala; (*model*) de tamaño natural; **~ stop** *n* punto; **~-time** *adj* (*work*) de tiempo completo ♦ *adv*: **to work ~-time** trabajar a tiempo completo; **~y** *adv* completamente; (*at least*) por lo menos; **~y-fledged** *adj* (*teacher, barrister*) diplomado

fulsome ['fulsəm] (*pej*) *adj* (*praise, gratitude*) excesivo, exagerado

fumble ['fʌmbl] *vi*: **to ~ with** manejar torpemente

fume [fjuːm] *vi* (*rage*) estar furioso; **~s** *npl* humo, gases *mpl*

fun [fʌn] *n* (*amusement*) diversión *f*; **to have ~** divertirse; **for ~** en broma; **to make ~ of** burlarse de

function ['fʌŋkʃən] *n* función *f* ♦ *vi* funcionar; **~al** *adj* (*operational*) en buen estado; (*practical*) funcional

fund [fʌnd] *n* fondo; (*reserve*) reserva; **~s** *npl* (*money*) fondos *mpl*

fundamental [fʌndə'mɛntl] *adj* fundamental

funeral ['fjuːnərəl] *n* (*burial*) entierro; (*ceremony*) funerales *mpl*; **~ parlour** (*BRIT*) *n* funeraria; **~ service** *n* misa de difuntos, funeral *m*

funfair ['fʌnfɛə*] (*BRIT*) *n* parque *m* de atracciones

fungi ['fʌŋgaɪ] *npl of* **fungus**

fungus ['fʌŋgəs] (*pl* **fungi**) *n* hongo; (*mould*) moho

funnel ['fʌnl] *n* embudo; (*of ship*) chimenea

funny ['fʌnɪ] *adj* gracioso, divertido; (*strange*) curioso, raro

fur [fəː*] *n* piel *f*; (*BRIT: in kettle etc*) sarro; **~ coat** *n* abrigo de pieles

furious ['fjuərɪəs] *adj* furioso; (*effort*) violento

furlong ['fəːlɒŋ] *n* octava parte de una milla, = 201.17 m

furlough ['fəːləu] *n* (*MIL*) permiso

furnace ['fəːnɪs] *n* horno

furnish ['fəːnɪʃ] *vt* amueblar; (*supply*) suministrar; (*information*) facilitar; **~ings** *npl* muebles *mpl*

furniture ['fəːnɪtʃə*] *n* muebles *mpl*; **piece of ~** mueble *m*

furrow ['fʌrəu] *n* surco

furry ['fəːrɪ] *adj* peludo

further ['fəːðə*] *adj* (*new*) nuevo, adicional ♦ *adv* más lejos; (*more*) más; (*moreover*) además ♦ *vt* promover, adelantar; **~ education** *n* educación *f* superior; **~more** [fəːðə'mɔː*] *adv* además

furthest ['fəːðɪst] *superlative of* **far**

fury ['fjuərɪ] *n* furia

fuse [fjuːz] (*US* **fuze**) *n* fusible *m*; (*for bomb etc*) mecha ♦ *vt* (*metal*) fundir; (*fig*) fusionar ♦ *vi* fundirse; fusionarse; (*BRIT: ELEC*): **to ~ the lights** fundir los plomos; **~ box** *n* caja de fusibles

fuss [fʌs] *n* (*excitement*) conmoción *f*; (*trouble*) alboroto; **to make a ~** armar un lío *or* jaleo; **to make a ~ of sb** mimar a uno; **~y** *adj* (*person*) exigente; (*too ornate*) recargado

futile ['fjuːtaɪl] *adj* vano
future ['fjuːtʃə*] *adj* futuro; (*coming*) venidero ♦ *n* futuro; (*prospects*) porvenir; **in ~** de ahora en adelante
fuze [fjuːz] (*US*) = **fuse**
fuzzy ['fʌzɪ] *adj* (*PHOT*) borroso; (*hair*) muy rizado

G g

G [dʒiː] *n* (*MUS*) sol *m*
g. *abbr* (= *gram(s)*) gr
G7 *abbr* (= *Group of Seven*) el grupo de los 7
gabble ['gæbl] *vi* hablar atropelladamente
gable ['geɪbl] *n* aguilón *m*
gadget ['gædʒɪt] *n* aparato
Gaelic ['geɪlɪk] *adj, n* (*LING*) gaélico
gaffe [gæf] *n* plancha
gag [gæg] *n* (*on mouth*) mordaza; (*joke*) chiste *m* ♦ *vt* amordazar
gaiety ['geɪtɪ] *n* alegría
gaily ['geɪlɪ] *adv* alegremente
gain [geɪn] *n*: **~ (in)** aumento (de); (*profit*) ganancia ♦ *vt* ganar ♦ *vi* (*watch*) adelantarse; **to ~ from/by sth** sacar provecho de algo; **to ~ on sb** ganar terreno a uno; **to ~ 3 lbs (in weight)** engordar 3 libras
gait [geɪt] *n* (*modo de*) andar *m*
gal. *abbr* = **gallon**
gala ['gɑːlə] *n* fiesta
gale [geɪl] *n* (*wind*) vendaval *m*
gallant ['gælənt] *adj* valiente; (*towards ladies*) atento; **~ry** *n* valentía; galantería
gall bladder ['gɔːl-] *n* vesícula biliar
gallery ['gælərɪ] *n* (*also: art ~: public*) pinacoteca; (: *private*) galería de arte; (*for spectators*) tribuna
galley ['gælɪ] *n* (*ship's kitchen*) cocina
gallon ['gælən] *n* galón *m* (*BRIT* = *4,546 litros, US = 3,785 litros*)
gallop ['gæləp] *n* galope *m* ♦ *vi* galopar
gallows ['gæləʊz] *n* horca
gallstone ['gɔːlstəʊn] *n* cálculo biliario
galore [gə'lɔː*] *adv* en cantidad, en abundancia

galvanize ['gælvənaɪz] *vt*: **to ~ sb into action** animar a uno para que haga algo
gambit ['gæmbɪt] *n* (*fig*): **(opening) ~** estrategia (inicial)
gamble ['gæmbl] *n* (*risk*) riesgo ♦ *vt* jugar, apostar ♦ *vi* (*take a risk*) jugárselas; (*bet*) apostar; **to ~ on** apostar a; (*success etc*) contar con; **~r** *n* jugador(a) *m/f*; **gambling** *n* juego
game [geɪm] *n* juego; (*match*) partido; (*of cards*) partida; (*HUNTING*) caza ♦ *adj* (*willing*): **to be ~ for anything** atreverse a todo; **big ~** caza mayor; **~keeper** *n* guardabosques *m inv*
gammon ['gæmən] *n* (*bacon*) tocino ahumado; (*ham*) jamón ahumado
gamut ['gæmət] *n* gama
gang [gæŋ] *n* (*of criminals*) pandilla; (*of friends etc*) grupo; (*of workmen*) brigada; **~ up** *vi*: **to ~ up on sb** aliarse contra uno
gangster ['gæŋstə*] *n* gángster *m*
gangway ['gæŋweɪ] *n* (*on ship*) pasarela; (*BRIT: in theatre, bus etc*) pasillo
gaol [dʒeɪl] (*BRIT*) *n, vt* = **jail**
gap [gæp] *n* vacío, hueco (*AM*); (*in trees, traffic*) claro; (*in time*) intervalo; (*difference*): **~ (between)** diferencia (entre)
gape [geɪp] *vi* mirar boquiabierto; (*shirt etc*) abrirse (completamente); **gaping** *adj* (completamente) abierto
garage ['gærɑːʒ] *n* garaje *m*; (*for repairs*) taller *m*
garbage ['gɑːbɪdʒ] (*US*) *n* basura; (*inf: nonsense*) tonterías *fpl*; **~ can** *n* cubo (*SP*) *or* bote *m* (*AM*) de la basura
garbled ['gɑːbld] *adj* (*distorted*) falsificado, amañado
garden ['gɑːdn] *n* jardín *m*; **~s** *npl* (*park*) parque *m*; **~er** *n* jardinero/a; **~ing** *n* jardinería
gargle ['gɑːgl] *vi* hacer gárgaras, gargarear (*AM*)
garish ['gɛərɪʃ] *adj* chillón/ona
garland ['gɑːlənd] *n* guirnalda
garlic ['gɑːlɪk] *n* ajo
garment ['gɑːmənt] *n* prenda (de vestir)
garnish ['gɑːnɪʃ] *vt* (*CULIN*) aderezar

garrison ['gærɪsn] *n* guarnición *f*

garrulous ['gærjuləs] *adj* charlatán/ana

garter ['gɑːtə*] *n* (*for sock*) liga; (*US*) liguero

gas [gæs] *n* gas *m*; (*fuel*) combustible *m*; (*US: gasoline*) gasolina ♦ *vt* asfixiar con gas; ~ **cooker** (*BRIT*) *n* cocina de gas; ~ **cylinder** *n* bombona de gas; ~ **fire** *n* estufa de gas

gash [gæʃ] *n* raja; (*wound*) cuchillada ♦ *vt* rajar; acuchillar

gasket ['gæskɪt] *n* (*AUT*) junta de culata

gas mask *n* careta antigás

gas meter *n* contador *m* de gas

gasoline ['gæsəliːn] (*US*) *n* gasolina

gasp [gɑːsp] *n* boqueada; (*of shock etc*) grito sofocado ♦ *vi* (*pant*) jadear; ~ **out** *vt* (*say*) decir con voz entrecortada

gas station (*US*) *n* gasolinera

gastric ['gæstrɪk] *adj* gástrico

gate [geɪt] *n* puerta; (*iron* ~) verja; ~**crash** (*BRIT*) *vt* colarse en; ~**way** *n* (*also fig*) puerta

gather ['gæðə*] *vt* (*flowers, fruit*) coger (*SP*), recoger; (*assemble*) reunir; (*pick up*) recoger; (*SEWING*) fruncir; (*understand*) entender ♦ *vi* (*assemble*) reunirse; **to ~ speed** ganar velocidad; ~**ing** *n* reunión *f*, asamblea

gauche [gəuʃ] *adj* torpe

gaudy ['gɔːdɪ] *adj* chillón/ona

gauge [geɪdʒ] *n* (*instrument*) indicador *m* ♦ *vt* medir; (*fig*) juzgar

gaunt [gɔːnt] *adj* (*haggard*) demacrado; (*stark*) desolado

gauntlet ['gɔːntlɪt] *n* guante *m*; (*fig*): **to run the ~ of** exponerse a; **to throw down the ~** arrojar el guante

gauze [gɔːz] *n* gasa

gave [geɪv] *pt of* **give**

gay [geɪ] *adj* (*homosexual*) gay; (*joyful*) alegre; (*colour*) vivo

gaze [geɪz] *n* mirada fija ♦ *vi*: **to ~ at sth** mirar algo fijamente

gazelle [gə'zɛl] *n* gacela

gazetteer [gæzə'tɪə*] *n* diccionario geográfico

gazumping [gə'zʌmpɪŋ] (*BRIT*) *n* la subida del precio de una casa una vez que ya ha sido apalabrado

GB *abbr* = **Great Britain**

GCE *n abbr* (*BRIT*) = *General Certificate of Education*

GCSE (*BRIT*) *n abbr* (= *General Certificate of Secondary Education*) *examen de reválida que se hace a los 16 años*

gear [gɪə*] *n* equipo, herramientas *fpl*; (*TECH*) engranaje *m*; (*AUT*) velocidad *f*, marcha ♦ *vt* (*fig: adapt*): **to ~ sth to** adaptar or ajustar algo a; **top** *or* **high** (*US*)/**low** ~ cuarta/primera velocidad; **in** ~ en marcha; ~ **box** *n* caja de cambios; ~ **lever** *n* palanca de cambio; ~ **shift** (*US*) *n* = ~ **lever**

geese [giːs] *npl of* **goose**

gel [dʒɛl] *n* gel *m*

gem [dʒɛm] *n* piedra preciosa

Gemini ['dʒɛmɪnaɪ] *n* Géminis *m*, Gemelos *mpl*

gender ['dʒɛndə*] *n* género

gene [dʒiːn] *n* gen(e) *m*

general ['dʒɛnərl] *n* general *m* ♦ *adj* general; **in ~** en general; ~ **delivery** (*US*) *n* lista de correos; ~ **election** *n* elecciones *fpl* generales; ~**ization** [-aɪ'zeɪʃən] *n* generalización *f*; ~**ly** *adv* generalmente, en general; ~ **practitioner** *n* médico general

generate ['dʒɛnəreɪt] *vt* (*ELEC*) generar; (*jobs, profits*) producir

generation [dʒɛnə'reɪʃən] *n* generación *f*

generator ['dʒɛnəreɪtə*] *n* generador *m*

generosity [dʒɛnə'rɔsɪtɪ] *n* generosidad *f*

generous ['dʒɛnərəs] *adj* generoso

genetic [dʒɪ'nɛtɪk] *adj*: ~ **engineering** ingeniería genética; ~ **fingerprinting** identificación *f* genética

Geneva [dʒɪ'niːvə] *n* Ginebra

genial ['dʒiːnɪəl] *adj* afable, simpático

genitals ['dʒɛnɪtlz] *npl* (órganos *mpl*) genitales *mpl*

genius ['dʒiːnɪəs] *n* genio

genteel [dʒɛn'tiːl] *adj* fino, elegante

gentle ['dʒɛntl] *adj* apacible, dulce; (*animal*) manso; (*breeze, curve etc*) suave

gentleman ['dʒɛntlmən] *n* señor *m*; (*well-bred man*) caballero

gentleness ['dʒɛntlnɪs] *n* apacibilidad *f*, dulzura; mansedumbre *f*; suavidad *f*

gently ['dʒɛntlɪ] *adv* dulcemente; suavemente

gentry ['dʒɛntrɪ] *n* alta burguesía

gents [dʒɛnts] *n* aseos *mpl* (de caballeros)

genuine ['dʒɛnjuɪn] *adj* auténtico; (*person*) sincero

geography [dʒɪ'ɔgrəfɪ] *n* geografía

geology [dʒɪ'ɔlədʒɪ] *n* geología

geometric(al) [dʒɪə'mɛtrɪk(l)] *adj* geométrico

geranium [dʒɪ'reɪnjəm] *n* geranio

geriatric [dʒɛrɪ'ætrɪk] *adj, n* geriátrico/a *m/f*

germ [dʒɜːm] *n* (*microbe*) microbio, bacteria; (*seed, fig*) germen *m*

German ['dʒɜːmən] *adj* alemán/ana ♦ *n* alemán/ana *m/f*; (*LING*) alemán *m*; ~ **measles** *n* rubéola

Germany ['dʒɜːmənɪ] *n* Alemania

gesture ['dʒɛstjə*] *n* gesto; (*symbol*) muestra

KEYWORD

get [gɛt] (*pt, pp* **got**, *pp* **gotten** (*US*)) *vi* **1** (*become, be*) ponerse, volverse; **to ~ old/ tired** envejecer/cansarse; **to ~ drunk** emborracharse; **to ~ dirty** ensuciarse; **~ married** casarse; **when do I ~ paid?** ¿cuándo me pagan *or* se me paga?; **it's ~ting late** se está haciendo tarde

2 (*go*): **to ~ to/from** llegar a/de; **to ~ home** llegar a casa

3 (*begin*) empezar a; **to ~ to know sb** (llegar a) conocer a uno; **I'm ~ting to like him** me está empezando a gustar; **let's ~ going** *or* **started** ¡vamos (a empezar)!

4 (*modal aux vb*): **you've got to do it** tienes que hacerlo

♦ *vt* **1**: **to ~ sth done** (*finish*) terminar algo; (*have done*) mandar hacer algo; **to ~ one's hair cut** cortarse el pelo; **to ~ the car going** *or* **to go** arrancar el coche; **to ~ sb to do sth** conseguir *or* hacer que alguien haga algo; **to ~ sth/sb ready** preparar algo/a alguien

2 (*obtain: money, permission, results*)

conseguir; (*find: job, flat*) encontrar; (*fetch: person, doctor*) buscar; (*object*) ir a buscar, traer; **to ~ sth for sb** conseguir algo para alguien; **~ me Mr Jones, please** (*TEL*) póngame *or* comuníqueme (*AM*) con el Sr. Jones, por favor; **can I ~ you a drink?** ¿quieres algo de beber?

3 (*receive: present, letter*) recibir; (*acquire: reputation*) alcanzar; (*: prize*) ganar; **what did you ~ for your birthday?** ¿qué te regalaron por tu cumpleaños?; **how much did you ~ for the painting?** ¿cuánto sacaste por el cuadro?

4 (*catch*) coger (*SP*), agarrar (*AM*); (*hit: target etc*) dar en; **to ~ sb by the arm/ throat** coger *or* agarrar a uno por el brazo/cuello; **~ him!** ¡cógelo! (*SP*), ¡atrápalo! (*AM*); **the bullet got him in the leg** la bala le dio en la pierna

5 (*take, move*) llevar; **to ~ sth to sb** hacer llegar algo a alguien; **do you think we'll ~ it through the door?** ¿crees que lo podremos meter por la puerta?

6 (*catch, take: plane, bus etc*) coger (*SP*), tomar (*AM*); **where do I ~ the train for Birmingham?** ¿dónde se coge *or* se toma el tren para Birmingham?

7 (*understand*) entender; (*hear*) oír; **I've got it!** ¡ya lo tengo!, ¡eureka!; **I don't ~ your meaning** no te entiendo; **I'm sorry, I didn't ~ your name** lo siento, no cogí tu nombre

8 (*have, possess*): **to have got** tener

get about *vi* salir mucho; (*news*) divulgarse

get along *vi* (*agree*) llevarse bien; (*depart*) marcharse; (*manage*) = **get by**

get at *vt fus* (*attack*) atacar; (*reach*) alcanzar

get away *vi* marcharse; (*escape*) escaparse

get away with *vt fus* hacer impunemente

get back *vi* (*return*) volver ♦ *vt* recobrar

get by *vi* (*pass*) (lograr) pasar; (*manage*) arreglárselas

get down *vi* bajarse ♦ *vt fus* bajar ♦ *vt*

bajar; (*depress*) deprimir

get down to *vt fus* (*work*) ponerse a

get in *vi* entrar; (*train*) llegar; (*arrive home*) volver a casa, regresar

get into *vt fus* entrar en; (*vehicle*) subir a; **to ~ into a rage** enfadarse

get off *vi* (*from train etc*) bajar; (*depart: person, car*) marcharse ♦ *vt* (*remove*) quitar ♦ *vt fus* (*train, bus*) bajar de

get on *vi* (*at exam etc*): **how are you ~ting on?** ¿cómo te va?; (*agree*): **to ~ on (with)** llevarse bien (con) ♦ *vt fus* subir a

get out *vi* salir; (*of vehicle*) bajar ♦ *vt* sacar

get out of *vt fus* salir de; (*duty etc*) escaparse de

get over *vt fus* (*illness*) recobrarse de

get round *vt fus* rodear; (*fig: person*) engatusar a

get through *vi* (TEL) (lograr) comunicarse

get through to *vt fus* (TEL) comunicar con

get together *vi* reunirse ♦ *vt* reunir, juntar

get up *vi* (*rise*) levantarse ♦ *vt fus* subir

get up to *vt fus* (*reach*) llegar a; (*prank*) hacer

geyser ['giːzə*] *n* (*water heater*) calentador *m* de agua; (GEO) géiser *m*

ghastly ['gɑːstlɪ] *adj* horrible

gherkin ['gɜːkɪn] *n* pepinillo

ghetto blaster ['gɛtəʊblɑːstə*] *n* cassette *m* portátil de gran tamaño

ghost [gəʊst] *n* fantasma *m*

giant ['dʒaɪənt] *n* gigante *m/f* ♦ *adj* gigantesco, gigante

gibberish ['dʒɪbərɪʃ] *n* galimatías *m*

gibe [dʒaɪb] *n* = **jibe**

giblets ['dʒɪblɪts] *npl* menudillos *mpl*

Gibraltar [dʒɪ'brɔːltə*] *n* Gibraltar *m*

giddy ['gɪdɪ] *adj* mareado

gift [gɪft] *n* regalo; (*ability*) talento; **~ed** *adj* dotado; **~ token** *or* **voucher** *n* vale *m* canjeable por un regalo

gigantic [dʒaɪ'gæntɪk] *adj* gigantesco

giggle ['gɪgl] *vi* reírse tontamente

gill [dʒɪl] *n* (*measure*) = *0.25 pints* (BRIT = *0.148l*, US = *0.118l*)

gills [gɪlz] *npl* (*of fish*) branquias *fpl*, agallas *fpl*

gilt [gɪlt] *adj, n* dorado; **~-edged** *adj* (COMM) de máxima garantía

gimmick ['gɪmɪk] *n* truco

gin [dʒɪn] *n* ginebra

ginger ['dʒɪndʒə*] *n* jengibre *m*; **~ ale** = **~ beer**; **~ beer** (BRIT) *n* gaseosa de jengibre; **~bread** *n* pan *m* (*or* galleta) de jengibre

gingerly ['dʒɪndʒəlɪ] *adv* con cautela

gipsy ['dʒɪpsɪ] *n* = **gypsy**

giraffe [dʒɪ'rɑːf] *n* jirafa

girder ['gɜːdə*] *n* viga

girdle ['gɜːdl] *n* (*corset*) faja

girl [gɜːl] *n* (*small*) niña; (*young woman*) chica, joven *f*, muchacha; (*daughter*) hija; **an English ~** una (chica) inglesa; **~friend** *n* (*of girl*) amiga; (*of boy*) novia; **~ish** *adj* de niña

giro ['dʒaɪrəʊ] *n* (BRIT: *bank* ~) giro bancario; (*post office* ~) giro postal; (*state benefit*) cheque quincenal del subsidio de desempleo

girth [gɜːθ] *n* circunferencia; (*of saddle*) cincha

gist [dʒɪst] *n* lo esencial

give [gɪv] (*pt* **gave**, *pp* **given**) *vt* dar; (*deliver*) entregar; (*as gift*) regalar ♦ *vi* (*break*) romperse; (*stretch: fabric*) dar de sí; **to ~ sb sth, ~ sth to sb** dar algo a uno; **~ away** *vt* (*give free*) regalar; (*betray*) traicionar; (*disclose*) revelar; **~ back** *vt* devolver; **~ in** *vi* ceder ♦ *vt* entregar; **~ off** *vt* despedir; **~ out** *vt* distribuir; **~ up** *vi* rendirse, darse por vencido ♦ *vt* renunciar a; **to ~ up smoking** dejar de fumar; **to ~ o.s. up** entregarse; **~ way** *vi* ceder; (BRIT: AUT) ceder el paso

glacier ['glæsɪə*] *n* glaciar *m*

glad [glæd] *adj* contento

gladly ['glædlɪ] *adv* con mucho gusto

glamorous ['glæmərəs] *adj* encantador(a), atractivo; **glamour** ['glæmə*] *n* encanto, atractivo

glance [glɑːns] *n* ojeada, mirada ♦ *vi*: **to**

~ **at** echar una ojeada a; ~ **off** *vt* rebotar en; *glancing adj (blow)* oblicuo

gland [glænd] *n* glándula

glare [gleə*] *n (of anger)* mirada feroz; *(of light)* deslumbramiento, brillo; **to be in the ~ of publicity** ser el foco de la atención pública ♦ *vi* deslumbrar; **to ~ at** mirar con odio a; **glaring** *adj (mistake)* manifiesto

glass [glɑːs] *n* vidrio, cristal *m*; *(for drinking)* vaso; *(: with stem)* copa; ~**es** *npl (spectacles)* gafas *fpl*; ~**house** *n* invernadero; ~**ware** *n* cristalería; ~**y** *adj (eyes)* vidrioso

glaze [gleɪz] *vt (window)* poner cristales a; *(pottery)* vidriar ♦ *n* vidriado; **glazier** ['gleɪzɪə*] *n* vidriero/a

gleam [gliːm] *vi* centellear

glean [gliːn] *vt (information)* recoger

glee [gliː] *n* alegría, regocijo

glen [glɛn] *n* cañada

glib [glɪb] *adj* de mucha labia; *(promise, response)* poco sincero

glide [glaɪd] *vi* deslizarse; *(AVIAT, birds)* planear; ~**r** *n (AVIAT)* planeador *m*; **gliding** *n (AVIAT)* vuelo sin motor

glimmer ['glɪmə*] *n* luz *f* tenue; *(of interest)* muestra; *(of hope)* rayo

glimpse [glɪmps] *n* vislumbre *m* ♦ *vt* vislumbrar, entrever

glint [glɪnt] *vi* centellear

glisten ['glɪsn] *vi* relucir, brillar

glitter ['glɪtə*] *vi* relucir, brillar

gloat [gləʊt] *vi*: **to ~ over** recrearse en

global ['gləʊbl] *adj* mundial; ~ **warming** (re)calentamiento global *or* de la tierra

globe [gləʊb] *n* globo; *(model)* globo terráqueo

gloom [gluːm] *n* tinieblas *fpl*, oscuridad *f*; *(sadness)* tristeza, melancolía; ~**y** *adj (dark)* oscuro; *(sad)* triste; *(pessimistic)* pesimista

glorious ['glɔːrɪəs] *adj* glorioso; *(weather etc)* magnífico

glory ['glɔːrɪ] *n* gloria

gloss [glɒs] *n (shine)* brillo; *(paint)* pintura de aceite; ~ **over** *vt fus* disimular

glossary ['glɒsərɪ] *n* glosario

glossy ['glɒsɪ] *adj* lustroso; *(magazine)* de lujo

glove [glʌv] *n* guante *m*; ~ **compartment** *n (AUT)* guantera

glow [gləʊ] *vi* brillar

glower ['glaʊə*] *vi*: **to ~ at** mirar con ceño

glue [gluː] *n* goma (de pegar), cemento ♦ *vt* pegar

glum [glʌm] *adj (person, tone)* melancólico

glut [glʌt] *n* superabundancia

glutton ['glʌtn] *n* glotón/ona *m/f*; **a ~ for work** un(a) trabajador(a) incansable

gnarled [nɑːld] *adj* nudoso

gnat [næt] *n* mosquito

gnaw [nɔː] *vt* roer

gnome [nəʊm] *n* gnomo

go [gəʊ] *(pt* went, *pp* gone; *pl* ~s) *vi* ir; *(travel)* viajar; *(depart)* irse, marcharse; *(work)* funcionar, marchar; *(be sold)* venderse; *(time)* pasar; *(fit, suit)*: **to ~ with** hacer juego con; *(become)* ponerse; *(break etc)* estropearse, romperse ♦ *n*: **to have a ~ (at)** probar suerte (con); **to be on the ~** no parar; **whose ~ is it?** ¿a quién le toca?; **he's going to do it** va a hacerlo; **to ~ for a walk** ir de paseo; **to ~ dancing** ir a bailar; **how did it ~?** ¿qué tal salió *or* resultó?, ¿cómo ha ido?; **to ~ round the back** pasar por detrás; ~ **about** *vi (rumour)* propagarse ♦ *vt fus*: **how do I ~ about this?** ¿cómo me las arreglo para hacer esto?; ~ **ahead** *vi* seguir adelante; ~ **along** *vi* ir ♦ *vt fus* bordear; **to ~ along with** *(agree)* estar de acuerdo con; ~ **away** *vi* irse, marcharse; ~ **back** *vi* volver; ~ **back on** *vt fus (promise)* faltar a; ~ **by** *vi (time)* pasar ♦ *vt fus* guiarse por; ~ **down** *vi* bajar; *(ship)* hundirse; *(sun)* ponerse ♦ *vt fus* bajar; ~ **for** *vt fus (fetch)* ir por; *(like)* gustar; *(attack)* atacar; ~ **in** *vi* entrar; ~ **in for** *vt fus (competition)* presentarse a; ~ **into** *vt fus* entrar en; *(investigate)* investigar; *(embark on)* dedicarse a; ~ **off** *vi* irse, marcharse; *(food)* pasarse; *(explode)* estallar; *(event)* realizarse ♦ *vt fus* dejar de gustar; **I'm going off him/**

the idea ya no me gusta tanto él/la idea; ~ **on** *vi* (*continue*) seguir, continuar; (*happen*) pasar, ocurrir; **to ~ on doing sth** seguir haciendo algo; ~ **out** *vi* salir; (*fire, light*) apagarse; ~ **over** *vi* (*ship*) zozobrar ♦ *vt fus* (*check*) revisar; ~ **through** *vt fus* (*town etc*) atravesar; ~ **up** *vi, vt fus* subir; ~ **without** *vt fus* pasarse sin

goad [gəud] *vt* aguijonear

go-ahead *adj* (*person*) dinámico; (*firm*) innovador(a) ♦ *n* luz *f* verde

goal [gəul] *n* meta; (*score*) gol *m*; ~**keeper** *n* portero; ~-**post** *n* poste *m* (de la portería)

goat [gəut] *n* cabra

gobble ['gɔbl] *vt* (*also:* ~ **down**, ~ **up**) tragarse, engullir

go-between *n* intermediario/a

god [gɔd] *n* dios *m*; G~ *n* Dios *m*; ~**child** *n* ahijado/a; ~**daughter** *n* ahijada; ~**dess** *n* diosa; ~**father** *n* padrino; ~-**forsaken** *adj* dejado de la mano de Dios; ~**mother** *n* madrina; ~**send** *n* don *m* del cielo; ~**son** *n* ahijado

goggles ['gɔglz] *npl* gafas *fpl*

going ['gəuiŋ] *n* (*conditions*) estado del terreno ♦ *adj*: **the ~ rate** la tarifa corriente *or* en vigor

gold [gəuld] *n* oro ♦ *adj* de oro; ~**en** *adj* (*made of ~*) de oro; (*~ in colour*) dorado; ~**fish** *n* pez *m* de colores; ~**mine** *n* (*also fig*) mina de oro; ~-**plated** *adj* chapado en oro; ~**smith** *n* orfebre *m/f*

golf [gɔlf] *n* golf *m*; ~ **ball** *n* (*for game*) pelota de golf; (*on typewriter*) esfera; ~ **club** *n* club *m* de golf; (*stick*) palo (de golf); ~ **course** *n* campo de golf; ~**er** *n* golfista *m/f*

gone [gɔn] *pp* of **go**

good [gud] *adj* bueno; (*pleasant*) agradable; (*kind*) bueno, amable; (*well-behaved*) educado ♦ *n* bien *m*, provecho; ~**s** *npl* (COMM) mercancías *fpl*; ~! ¡qué bien!; **to be ~ at** tener aptitud para; **to be ~ for** servir para; **it's ~ for you** te hace bien; **would you be ~ enough to ...?** ¿podría hacerme el favor de ...?, ¿sería tan amable de ...?; **a ~ deal (of)**

mucho; **a ~ many** muchos; **to make ~** reparar; **it's no ~ complaining** no vale la pena (de) quejarse; **for ~** para siempre, definitivamente; ~ **morning/afternoon** ¡buenos días/buenas tardes!; ~ **evening!** ¡buenas noches!; ~ **night!** ¡buenas noches!; ~**bye!** ¡adiós!; **to say** ~**bye** despedirse; G~ **Friday** *n* Viernes *m* Santo; ~-**looking** *adj* guapo; ~-**natured** *adj* amable, simpático; ~**ness** *n* (*of person*) bondad *f*; **for ~ness sake!** ¡por Dios!; ~**ness gracious!** ¡Dios mío!; ~**s train** (BRIT) *n* tren *m* de mercancías; ~**will** *n* buena voluntad *f*

goose [guːs] (*pl* **geese**) *n* ganso, oca

gooseberry ['guzbəri] *n* grosella espinosa; **to play ~** hacer de carabina

gooseflesh ['guːsfleʃ] *n* = **goose pimples**

goose pimples *npl* carne *f* de gallina

gore [gɔː*] *vt* cornear ♦ *n* sangre *f*

gorge [gɔːdʒ] *n* barranco ♦ *vr*: **to ~ o.s. (on)** atracarse (de)

gorgeous ['gɔːdʒəs] *adj* (*thing*) precioso; (*weather*) espléndido; (*person*) guapísimo

gorilla [gə'rilə] *n* gorila *m*

gorse [gɔːs] *n* tojo

gory ['gɔːri] *adj* sangriento

go-slow (BRIT) *n* huelga de manos caídas

gospel ['gɔspl] *n* evangelio

gossip ['gɔsip] *n* (*scandal*) cotilleo, chismes *mpl*; (*chat*) charla; (*scandalmonger*) cotilla *m/f*, chismoso/a ♦ *vi* cotillear

got [gɔt] *pt, pp* of **get**; ~**ten** (US) *pp* of **get**

gout [gaut] *n* gota

govern ['gʌvən] *vt* gobernar; (*influence*) dominar

governess ['gʌvənis] *n* institutriz *f*

government ['gʌvnmənt] *n* gobierno

governor ['gʌvənə*] *n* gobernador(a) *m/f*; (*of school etc*) miembro del consejo; (*of jail*) director(a) *m/f*

gown [gaun] *n* traje *m*; (*of teacher*, BRIT: *of judge*) toga

G.P. *n abbr* = **general practitioner**

grab [græb] *vt* coger (SP) *or* agarrar (AM), arrebatar ♦ *vi*: **to ~ at** intentar agarrar

grace [greis] *n* gracia ♦ *vt* honrar;

(*adorn*) adornar; **5 days'** ~ un plazo de 5 días; ~**ful** *adj* grácil, ágil; (*style, shape*) elegante, gracioso; **gracious** ['greɪʃəs] *adj* amable

grade [greɪd] *n* (*quality*) clase *f*, calidad *f*; (*in hierarchy*) grado; (*SCOL: mark*) nota; (*US: school class*) curso ♦ *vt* clasificar; ~ **crossing** (*US*) *n* paso a nivel; ~ **school** (*US*) *n* escuela primaria

gradient ['greɪdɪənt] *n* pendiente *f*

gradual ['grædjuəl] *adj* paulatino; ~**ly** *adv* paulatinamente

graduate [*n* 'grædjuɪt, *vb* 'grædjueɪt] *n* (*US: of high school*) graduado/a; (*of university*) licenciado/a ♦ *vi* graduarse; licenciarse; **graduation** [-'eɪʃən] *n* (*ceremony*) entrega del título

graffiti [grə'fiːtiː] *n* pintadas *fpl*

graft [grɑːft] *n* (*AGR, MED*) injerto; (*BRIT: inf*) trabajo duro; (*bribery*) corrupción *f* ♦ *vt* injertar

grain [greɪn] *n* (*single particle*) grano; (*corn*) granos *mpl*, cereales *mpl*; (*of wood*) fibra

gram [græm] *n* gramo

grammar ['græmə*] *n* gramática; ~ **school** (*BRIT*) *n* ≈ instituto de segunda enseñanza, liceo (*SP*)

grammatical [grə'mætɪkl] *adj* gramatical

gramme [græm] *n* = **gram**

gramophone ['græməfəun] (*BRIT*) *n* tocadiscos *m inv*

grand [grænd] *adj* magnífico, imponente; (*wonderful*) estupendo; (*gesture etc*) grandioso; ~**children** *npl* nietos *mpl*; ~**dad** (*inf*) *n* yayo, abuelito; ~**daughter** *n* nieta; ~**eur** ['grændjə*] *n* magnificencia, lo grandioso; ~**father** *n* abuelo; ~**ma** (*inf*) *n* yaya, abuelita; ~**mother** *n* abuela; ~**pa** (*inf*) *n* = ~**dad**; ~**parents** *npl* abuelos *mpl*; ~ **piano** *n* piano de cola; ~**son** *n* nieto; ~**stand** (*SPORT*) *n* tribuna

granite ['grænɪt] *n* granito

granny ['grænɪ] (*inf*) *n* abuelita, yaya

grant [grɑːnt] *vt* (*concede*) conceder; (*admit*) reconocer ♦ *n* (*SCOL*) beca; (*ADMIN*) subvención *f*; **to take sth/sb for ~ed** dar algo por sentado/no hacer ningún caso a uno

granulated sugar ['grænjuːleɪtɪd-] (*BRIT*) *n* azúcar *m* blanquilla

granule ['grænjuːl] *n* grano, gránulo

grape [greɪp] *n* uva

grapefruit ['greɪpfruːt] *n* pomelo (*SP*), toronja (*AM*)

graph [grɑːf] *n* gráfica; ~**ic** *adj* gráfico; ~**ics** *n* artes *fpl* gráficas ♦ *npl* (*drawings*) dibujos *mpl*

grapple ['græpl] *vi*: **to ~ with sth/sb** agarrar a algo/uno

grasp [grɑːsp] *vt* agarrar, asir; (*understand*) comprender ♦ *n* (*grip*) asimiento; (*understanding*) comprensión *f*; ~**ing** *adj* (*mean*) avaro

grass [grɑːs] *n* hierba; (*lawn*) césped *m*; ~**hopper** *n* saltamontes *m inv*; ~-**roots** *adj* (*fig*) popular

grate [greɪt] *n* parrilla de chimenea ♦ *vi*: **to ~ (on)** chirriar (sobre) ♦ *vt* (*CULIN*) rallar

grateful ['greɪtful] *adj* agradecido

grater ['greɪtə*] *n* rallador *m*

gratifying ['grætɪfaɪɪŋ] *adj* grato

grating ['greɪtɪŋ] *n* (*iron bars*) reja ♦ *adj* (*noise*) áspero

gratitude ['grætɪtjuːd] *n* agradecimiento

gratuity [grə'tjuːɪtɪ] *n* gratificación *f*

grave [greɪv] *n* tumba ♦ *adj* serio, grave

gravel ['grævl] *n* grava

gravestone ['greɪvstəun] *n* lápida

graveyard ['greɪvjɑːd] *n* cementerio

gravity ['grævɪtɪ] *n* gravedad *f*

gravy ['greɪvɪ] *n* salsa de carne

gray [greɪ] *adj* = **grey**

graze [greɪz] *vi* pacer ♦ *vt* (*touch lightly*) rozar; (*scrape*) raspar ♦ *n* (*MED*) abrasión *f*

grease [griːs] *n* (*fat*) grasa; (*lubricant*) lubricante *m* ♦ *vt* engrasar; lubrificar; ~**proof paper** (*BRIT*) *n* papel *m* apergaminado; **greasy** *adj* grasiento

great [greɪt] *adj* grande; (*inf*) magnífico, estupendo; **G~ Britain** *n* Gran Bretaña; ~-**grandfather** *n* bisabuelo; ~-**grandmother** *n* bisabuela; ~**ly** *adv* muy; (*with verb*) mucho; ~**ness** *n* grandeza

Greece [griːs] *n* Grecia

greed [griːd] *n* (*also*: ~**iness**) codicia,

avaricia; (*for food*) gula; (*for power etc*) avidez *f*; ~**y** *adj* avaro; (*for food*) glotón/ona

Greek [gri:k] *adj* griego ♦ *n* griego/a; (*LING*) griego

green [gri:n] *adj* (*also POL*) verde; (*inexperienced*) novato ♦ *n* verde *m*; (*stretch of grass*) césped *m*; (*GOLF*) green *m*; ~**s** *npl* (*vegetables*) verduras *fpl*; **belt** *n* zona verde; ~ **card** *n* (*AUT*) carta verde; (*US: work permit*) permiso de trabajo para los extranjeros en EE. UU.; ~**ery** *n* verdura; ~**grocer** (*BRIT*) *n* verdulero/a; ~**house** *n* invernadero; ~**house effect** *n* efecto invernadero; ~**house gas** *n* gases *mpl* de invernadero; ~**ish** *adj* verdoso

Greenland ['gri:nlənd] *n* Groenlandia

greet [gri:t] *vt* (*welcome*) dar la bienvenida a; (*receive: news*) recibir; ~**ing** *n* (*welcome*) bienvenida; ~**ing(s) card** *n* tarjeta de felicitación

grenade [grə'neɪd] *n* granada

grew [gru:] *pt of* **grow**

grey [greɪ] *adj* gris; (*weather*) sombrío; ~**-haired** *adj* canoso; ~**hound** *n* galgo

grid [grɪd] *n* reja; (*ELEC*) red *f*; ~**lock** *n* (*traffic jam*) retención *f*

grief [gri:f] *n* dolor *m*, pena

grievance ['gri:vəns] *n* motivo de queja, agravio

grieve [gri:v] *vi* afligirse, acongojarse ♦ *vt* dar pena a; **to ~ for** llorar por

grievous ['gri:vəs] *adj*: ~ **bodily harm** (*LAW*) daños *mpl* corporales graves

grill [grɪl] *n* (*on cooker*) parrilla; (*also: mixed ~*) parrillada ♦ *vt* (*BRIT*) asar a la parrilla; (*inf: question*) interrogar

grille [grɪl] *n* reja; (*AUT*) rejilla

grim [grɪm] *adj* (*place*) sombrío; (*situation*) triste; (*person*) ceñudo

grimace [grɪ'meɪs] *n* mueca ♦ *vi* hacer muecas

grime [graɪm] *n* mugre *f*, suciedad *f*

grin [grɪn] *n* sonrisa abierta ♦ *vi* sonreír abiertamente

grind [graɪnd] (*pt, pp* **ground**) *vt* (*coffee, pepper etc*) moler; (*US: meat*) picar; (*make sharp*) afilar ♦ *n* (*work*) rutina

grip [grɪp] *n* (*hold*) asimiento; (*control*) control *m*, dominio; (*of tyre etc*): **to have a good/bad ~** agarrarse bien/mal; (*handle*) asidero; (*holdall*) maletín *m* ♦ *vt* agarrar; (*viewer, reader*) fascinar; **to get to ~s with** enfrentarse con; ~**ping** *adj* absorbente

grisly ['grɪzlɪ] *adj* horripilante, horrible

gristle ['grɪsl] *n* ternilla

grit [grɪt] *n* gravilla; (*courage*) valor *m* ♦ *vt* (*road*) poner gravilla en; **to ~ one's teeth** apretar los dientes

groan [grəun] *n* gemido; quejido ♦ *vi* gemir; quejarse

grocer ['grəusə*] *n* tendero (de ultramarinos (*SP*)); ~**ies** *npl* comestibles *mpl*; ~'**s (shop)** *n* tienda de ultramarinos *or* de abarrotes (*AM*)

groggy ['grɔgɪ] *adj* atontado

groin [grɔɪn] *n* ingle *f*

groom [gru:m] *n* mozo/a de cuadra; (*also: bride~*) novio ♦ *vt* (*horse*) almohazar; (*fig*): **to ~ sb for** preparar a uno para; **well-~ed** de buena presencia

groove [gru:v] *n* ranura, surco

grope [grəup]: **to ~ for** *vt fus* buscar a tientas

gross [grəus] *adj* (*neglect, injustice*) grave; (*vulgar: behaviour*) grosero; (: *appearance*) de mal gusto; (*COMM*) bruto; ~**ly** *adv* (*greatly*) enormemente

grotesque [grə'tɛsk] *adj* grotesco

grotto ['grɔtəu] *n* gruta

grotty ['grɔtɪ] (*inf*) *adj* horrible

ground [graund] *pt, pp of* **grind** ♦ *n* suelo, tierra; (*SPORT*) campo, terreno; (*reason: gen pl*) causa, razón *f*; (*US: also: ~ wire*) tierra ♦ *vt* (*plane*) mantener en tierra; (*US: ELEC*) conectar con tierra; ~**s** *npl* (*of coffee etc*) poso; (*gardens etc*) jardines *mpl*, parque *m*; **on the ~** en el suelo; **to the ~** al suelo; **to gain/lose ~** ganar/perder terreno; ~ **cloth** (*US*) *n* = ~**sheet**; ~**ing** *n* (*in education*) conocimientos *mpl* básicos; ~**less** *adj* infundado; ~**sheet** (*BRIT*) *n* tela impermeable; suelo; ~ **staff** *n* personal *m* de tierra; ~**swell** *n* (*of opinion*) marejada; ~**work** *n* preparación *f*

group [gru:p] *n* grupo; (*musical*) conjunto ♦ *vt* (*also:* ~ *together*) agrupar ♦ *vi* (*also:* ~ *together*) agruparse

grouse [graus] *n inv* (*bird*) urogallo ♦ *vi* (*complain*) quejarse

grove [grəuv] *n* arboleda

grovel ['grɔvl] *vi* (*fig*): **to ~ before** humillarse ante

grow [grəu] (*pt* **grew**, *pp* **grown**) *vi* crecer; (*increase*) aumentar; (*expand*) desarrollarse; (*become*) volverse; **to ~ rich/weak** enriquecerse/debilitarse ♦ *vt* cultivar; (*hair, beard*) dejar crecer; ~ **up** *vi* crecer, hacerse hombre/mujer; ~**er** *n* cultivador(a) *m/f*, productor(a) *m/f*; ~**ing** *adj* creciente

growl [graul] *vi* gruñir

grown [grəun] *pp of* **grow**; ~**-up** *n* adulto, mayor *m/f*

growth [grəuθ] *n* crecimiento, desarrollo; (*what has grown*) brote *m*; (*MED*) tumor *m*

grub [grʌb] *n* larva, gusano; (*inf: food*) comida

grubby ['grʌbɪ] *adj* sucio, mugriento

grudge [grʌdʒ] *n* (motivo de) rencor *m* ♦ *vt*: **to ~ sb sth** dar algo a uno de mala gana; **to bear sb a ~** guardar rencor a uno

gruelling ['gruəlɪŋ] *adj* penoso, duro

gruesome ['gru:səm] *adj* horrible

gruff [grʌf] *adj* (*voice*) ronco; (*manner*) brusco

grumble ['grʌmbl] *vi* refunfuñar, quejarse

grumpy ['grʌmpɪ] *adj* gruñón/ona

grunt [grʌnt] *vi* gruñir

G-string ['dʒi:strɪŋ] *n* taparrabo

guarantee [gærən'ti:] *n* garantía ♦ *vt* garantizar

guard [gɑ:d] *n* (*squad*) guardia; (*one man*) guardia *m*; (*BRIT: RAIL*) jefe *m* de tren; (*on machine*) dispositivo de seguridad; (*also: fire~*) rejilla de protección ♦ *vt* guardar; (*prisoner*) vigilar; **to be on one's ~** estar alerta; ~ **against** *vt fus* (*prevent*) protegerse de; ~**ed** *adj* (*fig*) cauteloso; ~**ian** *n* guardián/ana *m/f*; (*of minor*) tutor(a)

m/f; ~**'s van** *n* (*BRIT: RAIL*) furgón *m*

Guatemala [gwæti'mɑ:lə] *n* Guatemala; ~**n** *adj*, *n* guatemalteco/a *m/f*

guerrilla [gə'rɪlə] *n* guerrillero/a

guess [gɛs] *vi* adivinar; (*US*) suponer ♦ *vt* adivinar; suponer ♦ *n* suposición *f*, conjetura; **to take** *or* **have a ~** tratar de adivinar; ~**work** *n* conjeturas *fpl*

guest [gɛst] *n* invitado/a; (*in hotel*) huésped(a) *m/f*; ~**-house** *n* casa de huéspedes, pensión *f*; ~ **room** *n* cuarto de huéspedes

guffaw [gʌ'fɔ:] *vi* reírse a carcajadas

guidance ['gaɪdəns] *n* (*advice*) consejos *mpl*

guide [gaɪd] *n* (*person*) guía *m/f*; (*book, fig*) guía ♦ *vt* (*round museum etc*) guiar; (*lead*) conducir; (*direct*) orientar; (*girl*) ~ *n* exploradora; ~**book** *n* guía; ~ **dog** *n* perro *m* guía; ~**lines** *npl* (*advice*) directrices *fpl*

guild [gɪld] *n* gremio

guile [gaɪl] *n* astucia

guillotine ['gɪlətiːn] *n* guillotina

guilt [gɪlt] *n* culpabilidad *f*; ~**y** *adj* culpable

guinea ['gɪnɪ] (*BRIT*) *n* (*old*) guinea (= 21 chelines)

guinea pig *n* cobaya; (*fig*) conejillo de Indias

guise [gaɪz] *n*: **in** *or* **under the ~ of** bajo apariencia de

guitar [gɪ'tɑ:*] *n* guitarra

gulf [gʌlf] *n* golfo; (*abyss*) abismo

gull [gʌl] *n* gaviota

gullet ['gʌlɪt] *n* esófago

gullible ['gʌlɪbl] *adj* crédulo

gully ['gʌlɪ] *n* barranco

gulp [gʌlp] *vi* tragar saliva ♦ *vt* (*also:* ~ *down*) tragarse

gum [gʌm] *n* (*ANAT*) encía; (*glue*) goma, cemento; (*sweet*) caramelo de goma; (*also: chewing-~*) chicle *m* ♦ *vt* pegar con goma; ~**boots** (*BRIT*) *npl* botas *fpl* de goma

gumption ['gʌmpʃən] *n* sentido común

gun [gʌn] *n* (*small*) pistola, revólver *m*; (*shotgun*) escopeta; (*rifle*) fusil *m*; (*cannon*) cañón *m*; ~**boat** *n* cañonero;

~fire *n* disparos *mpl*; ~man *n* pistolero; ~point *n*: **at ~point** a mano armada; ~powder *n* pólvora; ~shot *n* escopetazo

gurgle ['gɔːgl] *vi* (*baby*) gorgotear; (*water*) borbotear

gush [gʌʃ] *vi* salir a raudales; (*person*) deshacerse en efusiones

gust [gʌst] *n* (*of wind*) ráfaga

gusto ['gʌstəʊ] *n* entusiasmo

gut [gʌt] *n* intestino; ~**s** *npl* (ANAT) tripas *fpl*; (*courage*) valor *m*

gutter ['gʌtə*] *n* (*of roof*) canalón *m*; (*in street*) cuneta

guy [gaɪ] *n* (*also*: ~*rope*) cuerda; (*inf*: *man*) tío (SP), tipo; (*figure*) monigote *m*

guzzle ['gʌzl] *vi* tragar ♦ *vt* engullir

gym [dʒɪm] *n* (*also*: *gymnasium*) gimnasio; (*also*: *gymnastics*) gimnasia; ~**nast** *n* gimnasta *m/f*; ~ **shoes** *npl* zapatillas *fpl* (de deporte); ~ **slip** (BRIT) *n* túnica de colegiala

gynaecologist [gaɪnɪˈkɔlədʒɪst] (US **gynecologist**) *n* ginecólogo/a

gypsy ['dʒɪpsɪ] *n* gitano/a

gyrate [dʒaɪˈreɪt] *vi* girar

H h

haberdashery [hæbəˈdæʃərɪ] (BRIT) *n* mercería

habit ['hæbɪt] *n* hábito, costumbre *f*; (*drug* ~) adicción *f*; (*costume*) hábito

habitual [həˈbɪtjuəl] *adj* acostumbrado, habitual; (*drinker, liar*) empedernido

hack [hæk] *vt* (*cut*) cortar; (*slice*) tajar ♦ *n* (*pej*: *writer*) escritor(a) *m/f* a sueldo; ~**er** *n* (COMPUT) pirata *m/f* informático/a

hackneyed ['hæknɪd] *adj* trillado

had [hæd] *pt, pp of* **have**

haddock ['hædək] (*pl* ~ *or* ~**s**) *n* especie *de merluza*

hadn't ['hædnt] = **had not**

haemorrhage ['hemərɪdʒ] (US **hemorrhage**) *n* hemorragia

haemorrhoids ['hemərɔɪdz] (US **hemorrhoids**) *npl* hemorroides *fpl*

haggard ['hægəd] *adj* ojeroso

haggle ['hægl] *vi* regatear

Hague [heɪg] *n*: **The ~** La Haya

hail [heɪl] *n* granizo; (*fig*) lluvia ♦ *vt* saludar; (*taxi*) llamar a; (*acclaim*) aclamar ♦ *vi* granizar; ~**stone** *n* (piedra de) granizo

hair [heə*] *n* pelo, cabellos *mpl*; (*one* ~) pelo, cabello; (*on legs etc*) vello; **to do one's ~** arreglarse el pelo; **to have grey ~** tener canas *fpl*; ~**brush** *n* cepillo (para el pelo); ~**cut** *n* corte *m* (de pelo); ~**do** *n* peinado; ~**dresser** *n* peluquero/a; ~**dresser's** *n* peluquería; ~**-dryer** *n* secador *m* de pelo; ~**grip** *n* horquilla; ~**net** *n* redecilla; ~**piece** *n* postizo; ~**pin** *n* horquilla; ~**pin bend** (US ~**pin curve**) *n* curva de horquilla; ~**raising** *adj* espeluznante; ~ **removing cream** *n* crema depilatoria; ~ **spray** *n* laca; ~**style** *n* peinado; ~**y** *adj* peludo; velludo; (*inf*: *frightening*) espeluznante

hake [heɪk] (*pl inv or* ~**s**) *n* merluza

half [hɑːf] (*pl* **halves**) *n* mitad *f*; (*of beer*) ≈ caña (SP), media pinta; (RAIL, BUS) billete *m* de niño ♦ *adj* medio ♦ *adv* medio, a medias; **two and a ~** dos y media; ~ **a dozen** media docena; ~ **a pound** media libra; **to cut sth in ~** cortar algo por la mitad; ~**-caste** *n* mestizo/a; ~**-hearted** *adj* indiferente, poco entusiasta; ~**-hour** *n* media hora; ~**-mast** *n*: **at ~-mast** (*flag*) a media asta; ~**-price** *adj, adv* a mitad de precio; ~ **term** (BRIT) *n* (SCOL) vacaciones de *mediados del trimestre*; ~**-time** *n* descanso; ~**way** *adv* a medio camino; (*in period of time*) a mitad de

hall [hɔːl] *n* (*for concerts*) sala; (*entrance way*) hall *m*; vestíbulo; ~ **of residence** (BRIT) *n* residencia

hallmark ['hɔːlmɑːk] *n* sello

hallo [hə'ləʊ] *excl* = **hello**

Hallowe'en [hæləʊˈiːn] *n* víspera de Todos los Santos

hallucination [həluːsɪˈneɪʃən] *n* alucinación *f*

hallway ['hɔːlweɪ] *n* vestíbulo

halo ['heɪləʊ] *n* (*of saint*) halo, aureola

halt [hɔːlt] *n* (*stop*) alto, parada ♦ *vt* parar; interrumpir ♦ *vi* pararse

halve [hɑːv] vt partir por la mitad
halves [hɑːvz] npl of **half**
ham [hæm] n jamón m (cocido)
hamburger ['hæmbɜːgə*] n hamburguesa
hamlet ['hæmlɪt] n aldea
hammer ['hæmə*] n martillo ♦ vt (nail) clavar; (force): **to ~ an idea into sb/a message across** meter una idea en la cabeza a uno/machacar una idea ♦ vi dar golpes
hammock ['hæmək] n hamaca
hamper ['hæmpə*] vt estorbar ♦ n cesto
hand [hænd] n mano f; (of clock) aguja; (writing) letra; (worker) obrero ♦ vt dar, pasar; **to give** or **lend sb a ~** echar una mano a uno, ayudar a uno; **at ~** a mano; **in ~** (time) libre; (job etc) entre manos; **on ~** (person, services) a mano, al alcance; **to hand** (information etc) a mano; **on the one ~ ..., on the other ~ ...** por una parte ... por otra (parte) ...; **~ in** vt entregar; **~ out** vt distribuir; **~ over** vt (deliver) entregar; **~bag** n bolso (SP), cartera (AM); **~book** n manual m; **~brake** n freno de mano; **~cuffs** npl esposas fpl; **~ful** n puñado
handicap ['hændɪkæp] n minusvalía; (disadvantage) desventaja; (SPORT) handicap m ♦ vt estorbar; **mentally/physically ~ped** deficiente m/f (mental)/minusválido/a (físico/a)
handicraft ['hændɪkrɑːft] n artesanía; (object) objeto de artesanía
handiwork ['hændɪwɜːk] n obra
handkerchief ['hæŋkətʃɪf] n pañuelo
handle ['hændl] n (of door etc) tirador m; (of cup etc) asa; (of knife etc) mango; (for winding) manivela ♦ vt (touch) tocar; (deal with) encargarse de; (treat: people) manejar; **"~ with care"** "(manéjese) con cuidado"; **to fly off the ~** perder los estribos; **~bar(s)** n(pl) manillar m
hand: **~-luggage** n equipaje m de mano; **~made** ['hændmeɪd] adj hecho a mano; **~out** ['hændaʊt] n (money etc) limosna; (leaflet) folleto; **~rail** ['hændreɪl] n pasamanos m inv; **~shake** ['hændʃeɪk] n apretón m de manos
handsome ['hænsəm] adj guapo;

(building) bello; (fig: profit) considerable
handwriting ['hændraɪtɪŋ] n letra
handy ['hændɪ] adj (close at hand) a la mano; (tool etc) práctico; (skilful) hábil, diestro; **~man** n manitas m inv
hang [hæŋ] (pt, pp **hung**) vt colgar; (criminal: pt, pp **hanged**) ahorcar ♦ vi (painting, coat etc) colgar; (hair, drapery) caer; **to get the ~ of sth** (inf) lograr dominar algo; **~ about** or **around** vi haraganear; **~ on** vi (wait) esperar; **~ up** vi (TEL) colgar ♦ vt colgar
hanger ['hæŋə*] n percha; **~-on** n parásito
hang-gliding ['-glaɪdɪŋ] n vuelo libre
hangover ['hæŋəʊvə*] n (after drinking) resaca
hang-up n complejo
hanker ['hæŋkə*] vi: **to ~ after** añorar
hankie ['hæŋkɪ], **hanky** ['hæŋkɪ] n abbr = **handkerchief**
haphazard [hæp'hæzəd] adj fortuito
happen ['hæpən] vi suceder, ocurrir; (chance): **he ~ed to hear/see** dió la casualidad de que oyó/vió; **as it ~s** da la casualidad de que; **~ing** n suceso, acontecimiento
happily ['hæpɪlɪ] adv (luckily) afortunadamente; (cheerfully) alegremente
happiness ['hæpɪnɪs] n felicidad f; (cheerfulness) alegría
happy ['hæpɪ] adj feliz; (cheerful) alegre; **to be ~ (with)** estar contento (con); **to be ~ to do** estar encantado de hacer; **~ birthday!** ¡feliz cumpleaños!; **~-go-lucky** adj despreocupado
harass ['hærəs] vt acosar, hostigar; **~ment** n persecución f
harbour ['hɑːbə*] (US **harbor**) n puerto ♦ vt (fugitive) dar abrigo a; (hope etc) abrigar
hard [hɑːd] adj duro; (difficult) difícil; (work) arduo; (person) severo; (fact) innegable ♦ adv (work) mucho, duro; (think) profundamente; **to look ~ at** clavar los ojos en; **to try ~** esforzarse; **no ~ feelings!** ¡sin rencor(es)!; **to be ~ of hearing** ser duro de oído; **to be ~ done by** ser tratado injustamente; **~back**

n libro en cartoné; ~ **cash** *n* dinero contante; ~ **disk** *n* (*COMPUT*) disco duro *or* rígido; ~**en** *vt* endurecer; (*fig*) curtir ♦ *vi* endurecerse; curtirse; ~**-headed** *adj* realista; ~ **labour** *n* trabajos *mpl* forzados

hardly ['hɑ:dlɪ] *adv* apenas; ~ **ever** casi nunca

hardship ['hɑ:dʃɪp] *n* privación *f*

hard-up (*inf*) *adj* sin un duro (*SP*), sin plata (*AM*)

hardware ['hɑ:dwɛə*] *n* ferretería; (*COMPUT*) hardware *m*; (*MIL*) armamento; ~ **shop** *n* ferretería

hard-wearing *adj* resistente, duradero

hard-working *adj* trabajador(a)

hardy ['hɑ:dɪ] *adj* fuerte; (*plant*) resistente

hare [hɛə*] *n* liebre *f*; ~**-brained** *adj* descabellado

harem [hɑː'riːm] *n* harén *m*

harm [hɑːm] *n* daño, mal *m* ♦ *vt* (*person*) hacer daño a; (*health*, *interests*) perjudicar; (*thing*) dañar; **out of ~'s way** a salvo; ~**ful** *adj* dañino; ~**less** *adj* (*person*) inofensivo; (*joke etc*) inocente

harmony ['hɑːmənɪ] *n* armonía

harness ['hɑːnɪs] *n* arreos *mpl*; (*for child*) arnés *m*; (*safety* ~) arneses *mpl* ♦ *vt* (*horse*) enjaezar; (*resources*) aprovechar

harp [hɑːp] *n* arpa ♦ *vi*: **to ~ on (about)** machacar (con)

harpoon [hɑː'puːn] *n* arpón *m*

harrowing ['hærəʊɪŋ] *adj* angustioso

harsh [hɑːʃ] *adj* (*cruel*) duro, cruel; (*severe*) severo; (*sound*) áspero; (*light*) deslumbrador(a)

harvest ['hɑːvɪst] *n* (~ *time*) siega; (*of cereals etc*) cosecha; (*of grapes*) vendimia ♦ *vt* cosechar

has [hæz] *vb see* **have**

hash [hæʃ] *n* (*CULIN*) picadillo; (*fig: mess*) lío

hashish ['hæʃɪʃ] *n* hachís *m*

hasn't ['hæznt] = **has not**

hassle ['hæsl] (*inf*) *n* lata

haste [heɪst] *n* prisa; ~**n** ['heɪsn] *vt* acelerar ♦ *vi* darse prisa; **hastily** *adv* de prisa; precipitadamente; **hasty** *adj*

apresurado; (*rash*) precipitado

hat [hæt] *n* sombrero

hatch [hætʃ] *n* (*NAUT: also:* ~*way*) escotilla; (*also: service* ~) ventanilla ♦ *vi* (*bird*) salir del cascarón ♦ *vt* incubar; (*plot*) tramar; **5 eggs have ~ed** han salido 5 pollos

hatchback ['hætʃbæk] *n* (*AUT*) tres *or* cinco puertas *m*

hatchet ['hætʃɪt] *n* hacha

hate [heɪt] *vt* odiar, aborrecer ♦ *n* odio; ~**ful** *adj* odioso; **hatred** ['heɪtrɪd] *n* odio

haughty ['hɔːtɪ] *adj* altanero

haul [hɔːl] *vt* tirar ♦ *n* (*of fish*) redada; (*of stolen goods etc*) botín *m*; ~**age** (*BRIT*) *n* transporte *m*; (*costs*) gastos *mpl* de transporte; ~**ier** (*US* ~**er**) *n* transportista *m/f*

haunch [hɔːntʃ] *n* anca; (*of meat*) pierna

haunt [hɔːnt] *vt* (*subj: ghost*) aparecerse en; (*obsess*) obsesionar ♦ *n* guarida

| KEYWORD |

have [hæv] (*pt, pp* **had**) *aux vb* **1** (*gen*) haber; **to ~ arrived/eaten** haber llegado/comido; **having finished** *or* **when I had finished, he left** cuando hubo acabado, se fue

2 (*in tag questions*): **you've done it, ~n't you?** lo has hecho, ¿verdad? *or* ¿no?

3 (*in short answers and questions*): **I ~n't** no; **so I ~** pues, es verdad; **we ~n't paid — yes we ~!** no hemos pagado — ¡sí que hemos pagado!; **I've been there before, ~ you?** he estado allí antes, ¿y tú?

♦ *modal aux vb* (*be obliged*): **to ~ (got) to do sth** tener que hacer algo; **you ~n't to tell her** no hay que *or* no debes decirselo

♦ *vt* **1** (*possess*): **he has (got) blue eyes/dark hair** tiene los ojos azules/el pelo negro

2 (*referring to meals etc*): **to ~ breakfast/lunch/dinner** desayunar/comer/cenar; **to ~ a drink/a cigarette** tomar algo/fumar un cigarrillo

3 (*receive*) recibir; (*obtain*) obtener; **may I ~ your address?** ¿puedes darme tu dirección?; **you can ~ it for £5** te lo

puedes quedar por £5; **I must ~ it by tomorrow** lo necesito para mañana; **to ~ a baby** tener un niño *or* bebé
4 (*maintain, allow*): **I won't ~ it/this nonsense!** ¡no lo permitiré!/¡no permitiré estas tonterías!; **we can't ~ that** no podemos permitir eso
5: to ~ sth done hacer *or* mandar hacer algo; **to ~ one's hair cut** cortarse el pelo; **to ~ sb do sth** hacer que alguien haga algo
6 (*experience, suffer*): **to ~ a cold/flu** tener un resfriado/la gripe; **she had her bag stolen/her arm broken** le robaron el bolso/se rompió un brazo; **to ~ an operation** operarse
7 (+ *noun*): **to ~ a swim/walk/bath/rest** nadar/dar un paseo/darse un baño/descansar; **let's ~ a look** vamos a ver; **to ~ a meeting/party** celebrar una reunión/una fiesta; **let me ~ a try** déjame intentarlo
have out *vt*: **to ~ it out with sb** (*settle a problem etc*) dejar las cosas en claro con alguien

haven ['heɪvn] *n* puerto; (*fig*) refugio
haven't ['hævnt] = **have not**
haversack ['hævəsæk] *n* mochila
havoc ['hævək] *n* estragos *mpl*
hawk [hɔːk] *n* halcón *m*
hay [heɪ] *n* heno; **~ fever** *n* fiebre *f* del heno; **~stack** *n* almiar *m*
haywire ['heɪwaɪə*] (*inf*) *adj*: **to go ~** (*plan*) embrollarse
hazard ['hæzəd] *n* peligro ♦ *vt* aventurar; **~ous** *adj* peligroso; **~ warning lights** *npl* (*AUT*) señales *fpl* de emergencia
haze [heɪz] *n* neblina
hazelnut ['heɪzlnʌt] *n* avellana
hazy ['heɪzɪ] *adj* brumoso; (*idea*) vago
he [hiː] *pron* él; **~ who ...** él que ..., quien ...
head [hɛd] *n* cabeza; (*leader*) jefe/a *m/f*; (*of school*) director(a) *m/f* ♦ *vt* (*list*) encabezar; (*group*) capitanear; (*company*) dirigir; **~s (or tails)** cara (o cruz); **~ first** de cabeza; **~ over heels** (*in love*) perdidamente; **to ~ the ball** cabecear (la

pelota); **~ for** *vt fus* dirigirse a; (*disaster*) ir camino de; **~ache** *n* dolor *m* de cabeza; **~dress** *n* tocado; **~ing** *n* título; **~lamp** (*BRIT*) *n* = **~light**; **~land** *n* promontorio; **~light** *n* faro; **~line** *n* titular *m*; **~long** *adv* (*fall*) de cabeza; (*rush*) precipitadamente; **~master/mistress** *n* director(a) *m/f* (de escuela); **~ office** *n* oficina central, central *f*; **~-on** *adj* (*collision*) de frente; **~phones** *npl* auriculares *mpl*; **~quarters** *npl* sede *f* central; (*MIL*) cuartel *m* general; **~-rest** *n* reposa-cabezas *m inv*; **~room** *n* (*in car*) altura interior; (*under bridge*) (límite *m* de) altura; **~scarf** *n* pañuelo; **~strong** *adj* testarudo; **~ waiter** *n* maître *m*; **~way** *n*: **to make ~way** (*fig*) hacer progresos; **~wind** *n* viento contrario; **~y** *adj* (*experience, period*) apasionante; (*wine*) cabezón; (*atmosphere*) embriagador(a)
heal [hiːl] *vt* curar ♦ *vi* cicatrizarse
health [hɛlθ] *n* salud *f*; **~ food** *n* alimentos *mpl* orgánicos; **the H~ Service** (*BRIT*) *n* el servicio de salud pública; ≈ el Insalud (*SP*); **~y** *adj* sano, saludable
heap [hiːp] *n* montón *m* ♦ *vt*: **to ~ (up)** amontonar; **to ~ sth with** llenar algo hasta arriba de; **~s of** un montón de
hear [hɪə*] (*pt, pp* **heard**) *vt* (*also LAW*) oír; (*news*) saber ♦ *vi* oír; **to ~ about** oír hablar de; **to ~ from sb** tener noticias de uno; **heard** [hɜːd] *pt, pp of* **hear**; **~ing** *n* (*sense*) oído; (*LAW*) vista; **~ing aid** *n* audífono; **~say** *n* rumores *mpl*, hablillas *fpl*
hearse [hɜːs] *n* coche *m* fúnebre
heart [hɑːt] *n* corazón *m*; (*fig*) valor *m*; (*of lettuce*) cogollo; **~s** *npl* (*CARDS*) corazones *mpl*; **to lose/take ~** descorazonarse/cobrar ánimo; **at ~** en el fondo; **by ~** (*learn, know*) de memoria; **~ attack** *n* infarto (de miocardio); **~beat** *n* latido (del corazón); **~breaking** *adj* desgarrador(a); **~broken** *adj*: **she was ~broken about it** esto le partió el corazón; **~burn** *n* acedía; **~ failure** *n* fallo cardíaco; **~felt** *adj* (*deeply felt*) más

sentido
hearth [hɑːθ] *n* (*fireplace*) chimenea
heartless [ˈhɑːtlɪs] *adj* cruel
hearty [ˈhɑːtɪ] *adj* (*person*) campechano; (*laugh*) sano; (*dislike*, *support*) absoluto
heat [hiːt] *n* calor *m*; (*SPORT*: *also*: *qualifying* ~) prueba eliminatoria ♦ *vt* calentar; ~ **up** *vi* calentarse ♦ *vt* calentar; ~**ed** *adj* caliente; (*fig*) acalorado; ~**er** *n* estufa; (*in car*) calefacción *f*
heath [hiːθ] (*BRIT*) *n* brezal *m*
heather [ˈhɛðə*] *n* brezo
heating [ˈhiːtɪŋ] *n* calefacción *f*
heat-seeking [ˈhiːtsiːkɪŋ] *adj* guiado por infrarrojos, termoguiado
heatstroke [ˈhiːtstrəʊk] *n* insolación *f*
heatwave [ˈhiːtweɪv] *n* ola de calor
heave [hiːv] *vt* (*pull*) tirar; (*push*) empujar con esfuerzo; (*lift*) levantar (con esfuerzo) ♦ *vi* (*chest*) palpitar; (*retch*) tener náuseas ♦ *n* tirón *m*; empujón *m*; **to ~ a sigh** suspirar
heaven [ˈhɛvn] *n* cielo; (*fig*) una maravilla; ~**ly** *adj* celestial; (*fig*) maravilloso
heavily [ˈhɛvɪlɪ] *adv* pesadamente; (*drink*, *smoke*) con exceso; (*sleep*, *sigh*) profundamente; (*depend*) mucho
heavy [ˈhɛvɪ] *adj* pesado; (*work*, *blow*) duro; (*sea*, *rain*, *meal*) fuerte; (*drinker*, *smoker*) grande; (*responsibility*) grave; (*schedule*) ocupado; (*weather*) bochornoso; ~ **goods vehicle** *n* vehículo pesado; ~**weight** *n* (*SPORT*) peso pesado
Hebrew [ˈhiːbruː] *adj*, *n* (*LING*) hebreo
heckle [ˈhɛkl] *vt* interrumpir
hectic [ˈhɛktɪk] *adj* agitado
he'd [hiːd] = **he would**; **he had**
hedge [hɛdʒ] *n* seto ♦ *vi* contestar con evasivas; **to ~ one's bets** (*fig*) cubrirse
hedgehog [ˈhɛdʒhɔg] *n* erizo
heed [hiːd] *vt* (*also*: **take ~ of**) (*pay attention to*) hacer caso de; ~**less** *adj*: **to be ~less (of)** no hacer caso (de)
heel [hiːl] *n* talón *m*; (*of shoe*) tacón *m* ♦ *vt* (*shoe*) poner tacón a
hefty [ˈhɛftɪ] *adj* (*person*) fornido; (*parcel*, *profit*) gordo

heifer [ˈhɛfə*] *n* novilla, ternera
height [haɪt] *n* (*of person*) estatura; (*of building*) altura; (*high ground*) cerro; (*altitude*) altitud *f*; (*fig*: *of season*): **at the ~ of summer** en los días más calurosos del verano; (: *of power etc*) cúspide *f*; (: *of stupidity etc*) colmo; ~**en** *vt* elevar; (*fig*) aumentar
heir [ɛə*] *n* heredero; ~**ess** *n* heredera; ~**loom** *n* reliquia de familia
held [hɛld] *pt*, *pp of* **hold**
helicopter [ˈhɛlɪkɔptə*] *n* helicóptero
helium [ˈhiːlɪəm] *n* helio
hell [hɛl] *n* infierno; ~! (*inf*) ¡demonios!
he'll [hiːl] = **he will**; **he shall**
hello [hɑˈləʊ] *excl* ¡hola!; (*to attract attention*) ¡oiga!; (*surprise*) ¡caramba!
helm [hɛlm] *n* (*NAUT*) timón *m*
helmet [ˈhɛlmɪt] *n* casco
help [hɛlp] *n* ayuda; (*cleaner etc*) criada, asistenta ♦ *vt* ayudar; ~! ¡socorro!; ~ **yourself** sírvete; **he can't ~ it** no es culpa suya; ~**er** *n* ayudante *m/f*; ~**ful** *adj* útil; (*person*) servicial; (*advice*) útil; ~**ing** *n* ración *f*; ~**less** *adj* (*incapable*) incapaz; (*defenceless*) indefenso
hem [hɛm] *n* dobladillo ♦ *vt* poner *or* coser el dobladillo; ~ **in** *vt* cercar
hemorrhage [ˈhɛmərɪdʒ] (*US*) *n* = **haemorrhage**
hemorrhoids [ˈhɛmərɔɪdz] (*US*) *npl* = **haemorrhoids**
hen [hɛn] *n* gallina; (*female bird*) hembra
hence [hɛns] *adv* (*therefore*) por lo tanto; **2 years** ~ de aquí a 2 años; ~**forth** *adv* de hoy en adelante
henchman [ˈhɛntʃmən] (*pej*) *n* secuaz *m*
hepatitis [hɛpəˈtaɪtɪs] *n* hepatitis *f*
her [hɜː*] *pron* (*direct*) la; (*indirect*) le; (*stressed*, *after prep*) ella ♦ *adj* su; *see also* **me**, **my**
herald [ˈhɛrəld] *n* heraldo ♦ *vt* anunciar; ~**ry** *n* heráldica
herb [hɜːb] *n* hierba
herd [hɜːd] *n* rebaño
here [hɪə*] *adv* aquí; (*at this point*) en este punto; ~! (*present*) ¡presente!; ~ **is/ are** aquí está/están; ~ **she is** aquí está; ~**after** *adv* en el futuro; ~**by** *adv* (*in*

letter) por la presente

heredity [hɪˈrɛdɪtɪ] *n* herencia

heritage [ˈhɛrɪtɪdʒ] *n* patrimonio

hermit [ˈhəːmɪt] *n* ermitaño/a

hernia [ˈhəːnɪə] *n* hernia

hero [ˈhɪərəʊ] (*pl* ~es) *n* héroe *m*; (*in book, film*) protagonista *m*; ~ic [hɪˈrəʊɪk] *adj* heroico

heroin [ˈhɛrəʊɪn] *n* heroína

heroine [ˈhɛrəʊɪn] *n* heroína; (*in book, film*) protagonista

heron [ˈhɛrən] *n* garza

herring [ˈhɛrɪŋ] *n* arenque *m*

hers [həːz] *pron* (el) suyo/(la) suya *etc*; *see also* **mine**[2]

herself [həːˈsɛlf] *pron* (*reflexive*) se; (*emphatic*) ella misma; (*after prep*) sí (misma); *see also* **oneself**

he's [hiːz] = **he is**; **he has**

hesitant [ˈhɛzɪtənt] *adj* vacilante

hesitate [ˈhɛzɪteɪt] *vi* vacilar; (*in speech*) titubear; (*be unwilling*) resistirse a; **hesitation** [-ˈteɪʃən] *n* indecisión *f*; titubeo; dudas *fpl*

heterosexual [hɛtərəʊˈsɛksjuəl] *adj* heterosexual

hew [hjuː] *vt* (*stone, wood*) labrar

heyday [ˈheɪdeɪ] *n*: **the ~ of** el apogeo de

HGV *n abbr* = **heavy goods vehicle**

hi [haɪ] *excl* ¡hola!; (*to attract attention*) ¡oiga!

hiatus [haɪˈeɪtəs] *n* vacío

hibernate [ˈhaɪbəneɪt] *vi* invernar

hiccough [ˈhɪkʌp] = **hiccup**

hiccup [ˈhɪkʌp] *vi* hipar; ~s *npl* hipo

hide [haɪd] (*pt* **hid**, *pp* **hidden**) *n* (*skin*) piel *f* ♦ *vt* esconder, ocultar ♦ *vi*: **to ~ (from sb)** esconderse *or* ocultarse (de uno); ~-**and-seek** *n* escondite *m*; ~**away** *n* escondrijo

hideous [ˈhɪdɪəs] *adj* horrible

hiding [ˈhaɪdɪŋ] *n* (*beating*) paliza; **to be in ~** (*concealed*) estar escondido

hierarchy [ˈhaɪərɑːkɪ] *n* jerarquía

hi-fi [ˈhaɪfaɪ] *n* estéreo, hifi *m* ♦ *adj* de alta fidelidad

high [haɪ] *adj* alto; (*speed, number*) grande; (*price*) elevado; (*wind*) fuerte; (*voice*) agudo ♦ *adv* alto, a gran altura; **it**

is 20 m ~ tiene 20 m de altura; ~ **in the air** en las alturas; ~**brow** *adj* intelectual; ~**chair** *n* silla alta; ~**er education** *n* educación *f or* enseñanza superior; ~-**handed** *adj* despótico; ~-**heeled** *adj* de tacón alto; ~ **jump** *n* (*SPORT*) salto de altura; **the H~lands** *npl* las tierras altas de Escocia; ~**light** *n* (*fig: of event*) punto culminante; (*in hair*) reflejo ♦ *vt* subrayar; ~**ly** *adv* (*paid*) muy bien; (*critical, confidential*) sumamente; (*a lot*): **to speak/think ~ly of** hablar muy bien de/tener en mucho a; ~**ly strung** *adj* hipertenso; ~**ness** *n* altura; **Her** *or* **His H~ness** Su Alteza; ~-**pitched** *adj* agudo; ~-**rise block** *n* torre *f* de pisos; ~ **school** *n* ≈ Instituto Nacional de Bachillerato (*SP*); ~ **season** (*BRIT*) *n* temporada alta; ~ **street** (*BRIT*) *n* calle *f* mayor; ~**way** *n* carretera; (*US*) carretera nacional; autopista; **H~way Code** (*BRIT*) *n* código de la circulación

hijack [ˈhaɪdʒæk] *vt* secuestrar; ~**er** *n* secuestrador(a) *m/f*

hike [haɪk] *vi* (*go walking*) ir de excursión (a pie) ♦ *n* caminata; ~**r** *n* excursionista *m/f*

hilarious [hɪˈlɛərɪəs] *adj* divertidísimo

hill [hɪl] *n* colina; (*high*) montaña; (*slope*) cuesta; ~**side** *n* ladera; ~**y** *adj* montañoso

hilt [hɪlt] *n* (*of sword*) empuñadura; **to the ~** (*fig: support*) incondicionalmente

him [hɪm] *pron* (*direct*) le, lo; (*indirect*) le; (*stressed, after prep*) él; *see also* **me**; ~**self** *pron* (*reflexive*) se; (*emphatic*) él mismo; (*after prep*) sí (mismo); *see also* **oneself**

hind [haɪnd] *adj* posterior

hinder [ˈhɪndə*] *vt* estorbar, impedir; **hindrance** [ˈhɪndrəns] *n* estorbo

hindsight [ˈhaɪndsaɪt] *n*: **with ~** en retrospectiva

Hindu [ˈhɪnduː] *n* hindú *m/f*

hinge [hɪndʒ] *n* bisagra, gozne *m* ♦ *vi* (*fig*): **to ~ on** depender de

hint [hɪnt] *n* indirecta; (*advice*) consejo; (*sign*) dejo ♦ *vt*: **to ~ that** insinuar que ♦ *vi*: **to ~ at** hacer alusión a

hip [hɪp] *n* cadera

hippopotamus [hɪpə'pɒtəməs] (*pl* ~es *or* -mi) *n* hipopótamo

hire ['haɪə*] *vt* (*BRIT: car, equipment*) alquilar; (*worker*) contratar ♦ *n* alquiler *m*; **for ~** se alquila; (*taxi*) libre; ~ **purchase** (*BRIT*) *n* compra a plazos

his [hɪz] *pron* (el) suyo/(la) suya *etc* ♦ *adj* su; *see also* **mine²**; **my**

Hispanic [hɪs'pænɪk] *adj* hispánico

hiss [hɪs] *vi* silbar

historian [hɪ'stɔːrɪən] *n* historiador(a) *m/f*

historic(al) [hɪ'stɔrɪk(l)] *adj* histórico

history ['hɪstərɪ] *n* historia

hit [hɪt] (*pt, pp* **hit**) *vt* (*strike*) golpear, pegar; (*reach: target*) alcanzar; (*collide with: car*) chocar contra; (*fig: affect*) afectar ♦ *n* golpe *m*; (*success*) éxito; **to ~ it off with sb** llevarse bien con uno; ~-**and-run driver** *n* conductor(a) que atropella y huye

hitch [hɪtʃ] *vt* (*fasten*) atar, amarrar; (*also: ~ up*) remangar ♦ *n* (*difficulty*) dificultad *f*; **to ~ a lift** hacer autostop

hitch-hike *vi* hacer autostop; ~**r** *n* autostopista *m/f*

hi-tech [haɪ'tɛk] *adj* de alta tecnología

hitherto ['hɪðə'tuː] *adv* hasta ahora

HIV *n abbr* (= *human immunodeficiency virus*) VIH *m*; ~-**negative/positive** *adj* VIH negativo/positivo

hive [haɪv] *n* colmena; ~ **off** (*inf*) *vt* (*privatize*) privatizar

HMS *abbr* = **His (Her) Majesty's Ship**

hoard [hɔːd] *n* (*treasure*) tesoro; (*stockpile*) provisión *f* ♦ *vt* acumular; (*goods in short supply*) acaparar; ~**ing** *n* (*for posters*) cartelera

hoarse [hɔːs] *adj* ronco

hoax [həʊks] *n* trampa

hob [hɒb] *n* quemador *m*

hobble ['hɒbl] *vi* cojear

hobby ['hɒbɪ] *n* pasatiempo, afición *f*; ~-**horse** *n* (*fig*) caballo de batalla

hobo ['həʊbəʊ] (*US*) *n* vagabundo

hockey ['hɒkɪ] *n* hockey *m*

hog [hɒg] *n* cerdo, puerco ♦ *vt* (*fig*) acaparar; **to go the whole** ~ poner toda la carne en el asador

hoist [hɔɪst] *n* (*crane*) grúa ♦ *vt* levantar, alzar; (*flag, sail*) izar

hold [həʊld] (*pt, pp* **held**) *vt* sostener; (*contain*) contener; (*have: power, qualification*) tener; (*keep back*) retener; (*believe*) sostener; (*consider*) considerar; (*keep in position*): **to ~ one's head up** mantener la cabeza alta; (*meeting*) celebrar ♦ *vi* (*withstand pressure*) resistir; (*be valid*) valer ♦ *n* (*grasp*) asimiento; (*fig*) dominio; ~ **the line!** (*TEL*) ¡no cuelgue!; **to ~ one's own** (*fig*) defenderse; **to catch** *or* **get** (**a**) ~ **of** agarrarse *or* asirse de; ~ **back** *vt* retener; (*secret*) ocultar; ~ **down** *vt* (*person*) sujetar; (*job*) mantener; ~ **off** *vt* (*enemy*) rechazar; ~ **on** *vi* agarrarse bien; (*wait*) esperar; ~ **on!** (*TEL*) ¡(espere) un momento!; ~ **on to** *vt fus* agarrarse a; (*keep*) guardar; ~ **out** *vt* ofrecer ♦ *vi* (*resist*) resistir; ~ **up** *vt* (*raise*) levantar; (*support*) apoyar; (*delay*) retrasar; (*rob*) asaltar; ~**all** (*BRIT*) *n* bolsa; ~**er** *n* (*container*) receptáculo; (*of ticket, record*) poseedor(a) *m/f*; (*of office, title etc*) titular *m/f*; ~**ing** *n* (*share*) interés *m*; (*farmland*) parcela; ~**up** *n* (*robbery*) atraco; (*delay*) retraso; (*BRIT: in traffic*) embotellamiento

hole [həʊl] *n* agujero ♦ *vt* agujerear

holiday ['hɒlədɪ] *n* vacaciones *fpl*; (*public* ~) (día *m* de) fiesta, día *m* feriado; **on** ~ de vacaciones; ~ **camp** *n* (*BRIT: also: ~ centre*) centro de vacaciones; ~-**maker** (*BRIT*) *n* turista *m/f*; ~ **resort** *n* centro turístico

holiness ['həʊlɪnɪs] *n* santidad *f*

Holland ['hɒlənd] *n* Holanda

hollow ['hɒləʊ] *adj* hueco; (*claim*) vacío; (*eyes*) hundido; (*sound*) sordo ♦ *n* hueco; (*in ground*) hoyo ♦ *vt*: **to ~ out** excavar

holly ['hɒlɪ] *n* acebo

holocaust ['hɒləkɔːst] *n* holocausto

holy ['həʊlɪ] *adj* santo, sagrado; (*water*) bendito

homage ['hɒmɪdʒ] *n* homenaje *m*

home [həʊm] *n* casa; (*country*) patria; (*institution*) asilo ♦ *cpd* (*domestic*) casero, de casa; (*ECON, POL*) nacional ♦ *adv* (*direction*) a casa; (*right in: nail etc*) a fondo; **at ~** en casa; (*in country*) en el país; (*fig*) como pez en el agua; **to go/come ~** ir/volver a casa; **make yourself at ~** ¡estás en tu casa!; **~ address** n domicilio; **~land** n tierra natal; **~less** adj sin hogar, sin casa; **~ly** adj (*simple*) sencillo; **~-made** adj casero; **H~ Office** (*BRIT*) n Ministerio del Interior; **~ rule** n autonomía; **H~ Secretary** (*BRIT*) n Ministro del Interior; **~sick** adj: **to be ~sick** tener morriña, sentir nostalgia; **~ town** n ciudad f natal; **~ward** ['həumwəd] adj (*journey*) hacia casa; **~work** n deberes mpl

homicide ['hɔmɪsaɪd] (*US*) n homicidio
homosexual [hɔməu'sɛksjuəl] adj, n homosexual m/f
Honduran [hɔn'djuərən] adj, n hondureño/a m/f
Honduras [hɔn'djuərəs] n Honduras f
honest ['ɔnɪst] adj honrado; (*sincere*) franco, sincero; **~ly** adv honradamente; francamente; **~y** n honradez f
honey ['hʌnɪ] n miel f; **~comb** n panal m; **~moon** n luna de miel; **~suckle** n madreselva
honk [hɔŋk] vi (*AUT*) tocar el pito, pitar
honorary ['ɔnərərɪ] adj (*member, president*) de honor; (*title*) honorífico; **~ degree** n doctorado honoris causa
honour ['ɔnə*] (*US* **honor**) vt honrar; (*commitment, promise*) cumplir con ♦ n honor m, honra f; **~able** adj honorable; **~s degree** n (*SCOL*) título de licenciado con calificación alta
hood [hud] n capucha; (*BRIT: AUT*) capota; (*US: AUT*) capó m; (*of cooker*) campana de humos
hoodwink ['hudwɪŋk] (*BRIT*) vt timar
hoof [hu:f] (*pl* **hooves**) n pezuña
hook [huk] n gancho; (*on dress*) corchete m, broche m; (*for fishing*) anzuelo ♦ vt enganchar; (*fish*) pescar
hooligan ['hu:lɪgən] n gamberro
hoop [hu:p] n aro
hooray [hu:'reɪ] excl = **hurray**
hoot [hu:t] (*BRIT*) vi (*AUT*) tocar el pito, pitar; (*siren*) sonar la sirena; (*owl*) ulular; **~er** (*BRIT*) n (*AUT*) pito, claxon m;

(*NAUT*) sirena
Hoover ['hu:və*] ® (*BRIT*) n aspiradora ♦ vt: **h~** pasar la aspiradora por
hooves [hu:vz] npl of **hoof**
hop [hɔp] vi saltar, brincar; (*on one foot*) saltar con un pie
hope [həup] vt, vi esperar ♦ n esperanza; **I ~ so/not** espero que sí/no; **~ful** adj (*person*) optimista; (*situation*) prometedor(a); **~fully** adv con esperanza; (*one hopes*): **~fully he will recover** esperamos que se recupere; **~less** adj desesperado; (*person*): **to be ~less** ser un desastre
hops [hɔps] npl lúpulo
horde [hɔ:d] n (*fig*) multitud f
horizon [hə'raɪzn] n horizonte m; **~tal** [hɔrɪ'zɔntl] adj horizontal
hormone ['hɔ:məun] n hormona
horn [hɔ:n] n cuerno; (*MUS: also: French ~*) trompa; (*AUT*) pito, claxon m
hornet ['hɔ:nɪt] n avispón m
horny ['hɔ:nɪ] (*inf*) adj cachondo
horoscope ['hɔrəskəup] n horóscopo
horrible ['hɔrɪbl] adj horrible
horrid ['hɔrɪd] adj horrible, horroroso
horrify ['hɔrɪfaɪ] vt horrorizar
horror ['hɔrə*] n horror m; **~ film** n película de horror
hors d'œuvre [ɔ:'də:vrə] n entremeses mpl
horse [hɔ:s] n caballo; **~back** n: **on ~back** a caballo; **~ chestnut** n (*tree*) castaño de Indias; (*nut*) castaña de Indias; **~man/woman** n jinete/a m/f; **~power** n caballo (de fuerza); **~-racing** n carreras fpl de caballos; **~radish** n rábano picante; **~shoe** n herradura
hose [həuz] n (*also: ~pipe*) manguera
hosiery ['həuzɪərɪ] n (*in shop*) (sección f de) medias fpl
hospitable [hɔs'pɪtəbl] adj hospitalario
hospital ['hɔspɪtl] n hospital m
hospitality [hɔspɪ'tælɪtɪ] n hospitalidad f
host [həust] n anfitrión m; (*TV, RADIO*) presentador m; (*REL*) hostia; (*large number*): **a ~ of** multitud de
hostage ['hɔstɪdʒ] n rehén m
hostel ['hɔstl] n hostal m; **(youth) ~**

albergue *m* juvenil

hostess ['həʊstɪs] *n* anfitriona; (*BRIT*: *air* ~) azafata; (*TV*, *RADIO*) presentadora

hostile ['hɔstaɪl] *adj* hostil

hot [hɔt] *adj* caliente; (*weather*) caluroso, de calor; (*as opposed to warm*) muy caliente; (*spicy*) picante; (*fig*) ardiente, acalorado; **to be** ~ (*person*) tener calor; (*object*) estar caliente; (*weather*) hacer calor; ~**bed** *n* (*fig*) semillero; ~ **dog** *n* perro caliente

hotel [həʊ'tɛl] *n* hotel *m*; ~**ier** *n* hotelero; (*manager*) director *m*

hot: ~**headed** *adj* exaltado; ~**house** *n* invernadero; ~ **line** *n* (*POL*) teléfono rojo; ~**ly** *adv* con pasión, apasionadamente; ~**plate** *n* (*on cooker*) placa calentadora; ~**water bottle** *n* bolsa de agua caliente

hound [haʊnd] *vt* acosar ♦ *n* perro (de caza)

hour ['aʊə*] *n* hora; ~**ly** *adj* (de) cada hora

house [*n* haus, *pl* 'haʊzɪz, *vb* hauz] *n* (*gen*, *firm*) casa; (*POL*) cámara; (*THEATRE*) sala ♦ *vt* (*person*) alojar; (*collection*) albergar; **on the** ~ (*fig*) la casa invita; ~ **arrest** *n* arresto domiciliario; ~**boat** *n* casa flotante; ~**bound** *adj* confinado en casa; ~**breaking** *n* allanamiento de morada; ~**coat** *n* bata; ~**hold** *n* familia; (*home*) casa; ~**keeper** *n* ama de llaves; ~**keeping** (*work*) trabajos *mpl* domésticos; ~**keeping** (*money*) *n* dinero para gastos domésticos; ~**warming party** *n* fiesta de estreno de una casa; ~**wife** *n* ama de casa; ~**work** *n* faenas *fpl* (de la casa)

housing ['haʊzɪŋ] *n* (*act*) alojamiento; (*houses*) viviendas *fpl*; ~ **development** *n* urbanización *f*; ~ **estate** (*BRIT*) *n* = ~ **development**

hovel ['hɔvl] *n* casucha

hover ['hɔvə*] *vi* flotar (en el aire); ~**craft** *n* aerodeslizador *m*

how [haʊ] *adv* (*in what way*) cómo; ~ **are you?** ¿cómo estás?; ~ **much milk/many people?** ¿cuánta leche/gente?; ~ **much does it cost?** ¿cuánto cuesta?; ~ **long have you been here?** ¿cuánto hace que estás aquí?; ~ **old are you?** ¿cuántos

años tienes?; ~ **tall is he?** ¿cómo es de alto?; ~ **is school?** ¿cómo (te) va (en) la escuela?; ~ **was the film?** ¿qué tal la película?; ~ **lovely/awful!** ¡qué bonito/horror!

howl [haʊl] *n* aullido ♦ *vi* aullar; (*person*) dar alaridos; (*wind*) ulular

H.P. *n abbr* = **hire purchase**

h.p. *abbr* = **horse power**

HQ *n abbr* = **headquarters**

hub [hʌb] *n* (*of wheel*) cubo; (*fig*) centro

hubbub ['hʌbʌb] *n* barahúnda

hubcap ['hʌbkæp] *n* tapacubos *m inv*

huddle ['hʌdl] *vi*: **to** ~ **together** acurrucarse

hue [hju:] *n* color *m*, matiz *m*; ~ **and cry** *n* clamor *m*

huff [hʌf] *n*: **in a** ~ enojado

hug [hʌg] *vt* abrazar; (*thing*) apretar con los brazos

huge [hju:dʒ] *adj* enorme

hulk [hʌlk] *n* (*ship*) barco viejo; (*person*, *building etc*) mole *f*

hull [hʌl] *n* (*of ship*) casco

hullo [hə'ləʊ] *excl* = **hello**

hum [hʌm] *vt* tararear, canturrear ♦ *vi* tararear, canturrear; (*insect*) zumbar

human ['hju:mən] *adj*, *n* humano

humane [hju:'meɪn] *adj* humano, humanitario

humanitarian [hju:mænɪ'tɛərɪən] *adj* humanitario

humanity [hju:'mænɪtɪ] *n* humanidad *f*

humble ['hʌmbl] *adj* humilde ♦ *vt* humillar

humbug ['hʌmbʌg] *n* tonterías *fpl*; (*BRIT*: *sweet*) caramelo de menta

humdrum ['hʌmdrʌm] *adj* (*boring*) monótono, aburrido

humid ['hju:mɪd] *adj* húmedo

humiliate [hju:'mɪlɪeɪt] *vt* humillar

humor ['hju:mə*] (*US*) *n* = **humour**

humorous ['hju:mərəs] *adj* gracioso, divertido

humour ['hju:mə*] (*US* **humor**) *n* humorismo, sentido del humor; (*mood*) humor *m* ♦ *vt* (*person*) complacer

hump [hʌmp] *n* (*in ground*) montículo; (*camel's*) giba; ~**backed** *adj*: ~**backed**

bridge puente *m* (*de fuerte pendiente*)
hunch [hʌntʃ] *n* (*premonition*) presentimiento; **~back** *n* joroba *m/f*; **~ed** *adj* jorobado
hundred ['hʌndrəd] *num* ciento; (*before n*) cien; **~s of** centenares de; **~weight** *n* (*BRIT*) = 50.8 kg; 112 lb; (*US*) = 45.3 kg; 100 lb
hung [hʌŋ] *pt, pp of* **hang**
Hungarian [hʌŋˈgeəriən] *adj, n* húngaro/a *m/f*
Hungary ['hʌŋgəri] *n* Hungría
hunger ['hʌŋgəʳ] *n* hambre *f* ♦ *vi*: **to ~ for** (*fig*) tener hambre de, anhelar; **~ strike** *n* huelga de hambre
hungry ['hʌŋgri] *adj*: **~ (for)** hambriento (de); **to be ~** tener hambre
hunk [hʌŋk] *n* (*of bread etc*) trozo, pedazo
hunt [hʌnt] *vt* (*seek*) buscar; (*SPORT*) cazar ♦ *vi* (*search*): **to ~ (for)** buscar; (*SPORT*) cazar ♦ *n* búsqueda; caza, cacería; **~er** *n* cazador(a) *m/f*; **~ing** *n* caza
hurdle ['hə:dl] *n* (*SPORT*) valla; (*fig*) obstáculo
hurl [hə:l] *vt* lanzar, arrojar
hurrah [huˈrɑ:] *excl* = **hurray**
hurray [huˈrei] *excl* ¡viva!
hurricane ['hʌrikən] *n* huracán *m*
hurried ['hʌrid] *adj* (*rushed*) hecho de prisa; **~ly** *adv* con prisa, apresuradamente
hurry ['hʌri] *n* prisa ♦ *vi* (*also*: **~ up**) apresurarse, darse prisa ♦ *vt* (*also*: **~ up**: *person*) dar prisa a; (: *work*) apresurar, hacer de prisa; **to be in a ~** tener prisa
hurt [hə:t] (*pt, pp* **hurt**) *vt* hacer daño a ♦ *vi* doler ♦ *adj* lastimado; **~ful** *adj* (*remark etc*) hiriente
hurtle ['hə:tl] *vi*: **to ~ past** pasar como un rayo; **to ~ down** ir a toda velocidad
husband ['hʌzbənd] *n* marido
hush [hʌʃ] *n* silencio ♦ *vt* hacer callar; **~!** ¡chitón!, ¡cállate!; **~ up** *vt* encubrir
husk [hʌsk] *n* (*of wheat*) cáscara
husky ['hʌski] *adj* ronco ♦ *n* perro esquimal
hustle ['hʌsl] *vt* (*hurry*) dar prisa a ♦ *n*: **~ and bustle** ajetreo
hut [hʌt] *n* cabaña; (*shed*) cobertizo

hutch [hʌtʃ] *n* conejera
hyacinth ['haiəsinθ] *n* jacinto
hydrant ['haidrənt] *n* (*also*: *fire* **~**) boca de incendios
hydraulic [haiˈdrɔ:lik] *adj* hidráulico
hydroelectric [haidrəuˈlektrik] *adj* hidroeléctrico
hydrofoil ['haidrəfɔil] *n* aerodeslizador *m*
hydrogen ['haidrədʒən] *n* hidrógeno
hygiene ['haidʒi:n] *n* higiene *f*; **hygienic** [-'dʒi:nik] *adj* higiénico
hymn [him] *n* himno
hype [haip] (*inf*) *n* bombardeo publicitario
hypermarket ['haipəmɑ:kit] *n* hipermercado
hyphen ['haifn] *n* guión *m*
hypnotize ['hipnətaiz] *vt* hipnotizar
hypochondriac [haipəuˈkɔndriæk] *n* hipocondríaco/a
hypocrisy [hiˈpɔkrisi] *n* hipocresía; **hypocrite** ['hipəkrit] *n* hipócrita *m/f*; **hypocritical** [hipəˈkritikl] *adj* hipócrita
hypothesis [haiˈpɔθisis] (*pl* **hypotheses**) *n* hipótesis *f inv*
hysteria [hiˈstiəriə] *n* histeria; **hysterical** [-'sterikl] *adj* histérico; (*funny*) para morirse de risa; **hysterics** [-'steriks] *npl* histeria; **to be in hysterics** (*fig*) morirse de risa

I i

I [ai] *pron* yo
ice [ais] *n* hielo; (~ *cream*) helado ♦ *vt* (*cake*) alcorzar ♦ *vi* (*also*: **~ over**, **~ up**) helarse; **~berg** *n* iceberg *m*; **~box** *n* (*BRIT*) congelador *m*; (*US*) nevera (*SP*), refrigeradora (*AM*); **~ cream** *n* helado; **~ cube** *n* cubito de hielo; **~d** *adj* (*cake*) escarchado; (*drink*) helado; **~ hockey** *n* hockey *m* sobre hielo
Iceland ['aislənd] *n* Islandia
ice: **~ lolly** (*BRIT*) *n* polo; **~ rink** *n* pista de hielo; **~ skating** *n* patinaje *m* sobre hielo
icicle ['aisikl] *n* carámbano
icing ['aisiŋ] *n* (*CULIN*) alcorza; **~ sugar**

(*BRIT*) *n* azúcar *m* glas(eado)
icy ['aɪsɪ] *adj* helado
I'd [aɪd] = **I would; I had**
idea [aɪ'dɪə] *n* idea
ideal [aɪ'dɪəl] *n* ideal *m* ♦ *adj* ideal; **~ist** *n* idealista *m/f*
identical [aɪ'dɛntɪkəl] *adj* idéntico
identification [aɪdɛntɪfɪ'keɪʃən] *n* identificación *f*; **(means of)** ~ documentos *mpl* personales
identify [aɪ'dɛntɪfaɪ] *vt* identificar
Identikit [aɪ'dɛntɪkɪt] ® *n*: ~ **(picture)** retrato-robot *m*
identity [aɪ'dɛntɪtɪ] *n* identidad *f*; ~ **card** *n* carnet *m* de identidad
ideology [aɪdɪ'ɒlədʒɪ] *n* ideología
idiom ['ɪdɪəm] *n* modismo; **(style of speaking)** lenguaje *m*; **~atic** [-'mætɪk] *adj* idiomático
idiosyncrasy [ɪdɪəu'sɪŋkrəsɪ] *n* idiosincrasia
idiot ['ɪdɪət] *n* idiota *m/f*; **~ic** [-'ɒtɪk] *adj* tonto
idle ['aɪdl] *adj* **(inactive)** ocioso; **(lazy)** holgazán/ana; **(unemployed)** parado, desocupado; **(machinery etc)** parado; **(talk etc)** frívolo ♦ *vi* **(machine)** marchar en vacío; ~ **away** *vt*: **to ~ away the time** malgastar el tiempo
idol ['aɪdl] *n* ídolo; **~ize** *vt* idolatrar
idyllic [ɪ'dɪlɪk] *adj* idílico
i.e. *abbr* (= *that is*) esto es
if [ɪf] *conj* si; ~ **necessary** si fuera necesario, si hiciese falta; ~ **I were you** yo en tu lugar; ~ **so/not** de ser así/si no; ~ **only I could!** ¡ojalá pudiera!; *see also* **as; even**
igloo ['ɪglu:] *n* iglú *m*
ignite [ɪg'naɪt] *vt* **(set fire to)** encender ♦ *vi* encenderse
ignition [ɪg'nɪʃən] *n* **(AUT: process)** ignición *f*; **(: mechanism)** encendido; **to switch on/off the** ~ arrancar/apagar el motor; ~ **key** *n* **(AUT)** llave *f* de contacto
ignorance ['ɪgnərəns] *n* ignorancia
ignorant ['ɪgnərənt] *adj* ignorante; **to be** ~ **of** ignorar
ignore [ɪg'nɔ:*] *vt* **(person, advice)** no hacer caso de; **(fact)** pasar por alto

ill [ɪl] *adj* enfermo, malo ♦ *n* mal *m* ♦ *adv* mal; **to be taken** ~ ponerse enfermo; **~-advised** *adj* **(decision)** imprudente; **~-at-ease** *adj* incómodo
I'll [aɪl] = **I will; I shall**
illegal [ɪ'li:gl] *adj* ilegal
illegible [ɪ'lɛdʒɪbl] *adj* ilegible
illegitimate [ɪlɪ'dʒɪtɪmət] *adj* ilegítimo
ill-fated *adj* malogrado
ill feeling *n* rencor *m*
illicit [ɪ'lɪsɪt] *adj* ilícito
illiterate [ɪ'lɪtərət] *adj* analfabeto
ill-mannered *adj* mal educado
illness ['ɪlnɪs] *n* enfermedad *f*
ill-treat *vt* maltratar
illuminate [ɪ'lu:mɪneɪt] *vt* **(room, street)** iluminar, alumbrar; **illumination** [-'neɪʃən] *n* alumbrado; **illuminations** *npl* **(decorative lights)** iluminaciones *fpl*, luces *fpl*
illusion [ɪ'lu:ʒən] *n* ilusión *f*; **(trick)** truco
illustrate ['ɪləstreɪt] *vt* ilustrar
illustration [ɪlə'streɪʃən] *n* **(act of illustrating)** ilustración *f*; **(example)** ejemplo, ilustración *f*; **(in book)** lámina
illustrious [ɪ'lʌstrɪəs] *adj* ilustre
ill will *n* rencor *m*
I'm [aɪm] = **I am**
image ['ɪmɪdʒ] *n* imagen *f*; **~ry** [-ərɪ] *n* imágenes *fpl*
imaginary [ɪ'mædʒɪnərɪ] *adj* imaginario
imagination [ɪmædʒɪ'neɪʃən] *n* imaginación *f*; **(inventiveness)** inventiva
imaginative [ɪ'mædʒɪnətɪv] *adj* imaginativo
imagine [ɪ'mædʒɪn] *vt* imaginarse
imbalance [ɪm'bæləns] *n* desequilibrio
imbecile ['ɪmbəsi:l] *n* imbécil *m/f*
imitate ['ɪmɪteɪt] *vt* imitar; **imitation** [-'teɪʃən] *n* imitación *f*; **(copy)** copia
immaculate [ɪ'mækjulət] *adj* inmaculado
immaterial [ɪmə'tɪərɪəl] *adj* **(unimportant)** sin importancia
immature [ɪmə'tjuə*] *adj* **(person)** inmaduro
immediate [ɪ'mi:dɪət] *adj* inmediato; **(pressing)** urgente, apremiante; **(nearest: family)** próximo; **(: neighbourhood)** inmediato; **~ly** *adv* **(at once)** en seguida;

(*directly*) inmediatamente; ~**ly next to** muy junto a

immense [ɪ'mɛns] *adj* inmenso, enorme; (*importance*) enorme

immerse [ɪ'məːs] *vt* (*submerge*) sumergir; **to be ~d in** (*fig*) estar absorto en

immersion heater [ɪ'məːʃən-] (*BRIT*) *n* calentador *m* de inmersión

immigrant ['ɪmɪgrənt] *n* inmigrante *m/f*; **immigration** [ɪmɪ'greɪʃən] *n* inmigración *f*

imminent ['ɪmɪnənt] *adj* inminente

immobile [ɪ'məubaɪl] *adj* inmóvil

immoral [ɪ'mɔrl] *adj* inmoral

immortal [ɪ'mɔːtl] *adj* inmortal

immune [ɪ'mjuːn] *adj*: ~ **(to)** inmune (a); **immunity** *n* (*MED, of diplomat*) inmunidad *f*

immunize ['ɪmjunaɪz] *vt* inmunizar

imp [ɪmp] *n* diablillo; (*child*) pícaro

impact ['ɪmpækt] *n* impacto

impair [ɪm'pɛə*] *vt* perjudicar

impale [ɪm'peɪl] *vt* empalar

impart [ɪm'pɑːt] *vt* comunicar; (*flavour*) proporcionar

impartial [ɪm'pɑːʃl] *adj* imparcial

impassable [ɪm'pɑːsəbl] *adj* (*barrier*) infranqueable; (*river, road*) intransitable

impasse [æm'pɑːs] *n* punto muerto

impassive [ɪm'pæsɪv] *adj* impasible

impatience [ɪm'peɪʃəns] *n* impaciencia

impatient [ɪm'peɪʃənt] *adj* impaciente; **to get** *or* **grow** ~ impacientarse

impeccable [ɪm'pɛkəbl] *adj* impecable

impede [ɪm'piːd] *vt* estorbar

impediment [ɪm'pɛdɪmənt] *n* obstáculo, estorbo; (*also:* speech ~) defecto (del habla)

impending [ɪm'pɛndɪŋ] *adj* inminente

impenetrable [ɪm'pɛnɪtrəbl] *adj* impenetrable; (*fig*) insondable

imperative [ɪm'pɛrətɪv] *adj* (*tone*) imperioso; (*need*) imprescindible ♦ *n* (*LING*) imperativo

imperfect [ɪm'pəːfɪkt] *adj* (*goods etc*) defectuoso ♦ *n* (*LING: also:* ~ tense) imperfecto; ~**ion** [-'fɛkʃən] *n* (*blemish*) desperfecto; (*fault*) defecto

imperial [ɪm'pɪərɪəl] *adj* imperial; ~**ism** *n* imperialismo

impersonal [ɪm'pəːsənl] *adj* impersonal

impersonate [ɪm'pəːsəneɪt] *vt* hacerse pasar por; (*THEATRE*) imitar

impertinent [ɪm'pəːtɪnənt] *adj* impertinente, insolente

impervious [ɪm'pəːvɪəs] *adj* impermeable; (*fig*): ~ **to** insensible a

impetuous [ɪm'pɛtjuəs] *adj* impetuoso

impetus ['ɪmpətəs] *n* ímpetu *m*; (*fig*) impulso

impinge [ɪm'pɪndʒ]: **to ~ on** *vt fus* (*affect*) afectar a

implacable [ɪm'plækəbl] *adj* implacable

implement [*n* 'ɪmplɪmənt, *vb* 'ɪmplɪmɛnt] *n* herramienta; (*for cooking*) utensilio ♦ *vt* (*regulation*) hacer efectivo; (*plan*) realizar

implicate ['ɪmplɪkeɪt] *vt* (*in crime etc*) involucrar; **implication** [-'keɪʃən] *n* consecuencia; (*involvement*) implicación *f*

implicit [ɪm'plɪsɪt] *adj* implícito; (*belief, trust*) absoluto

implore [ɪm'plɔː*] *vt* (*person*) suplicar

imply [ɪm'plaɪ] *vt* (*involve*) suponer; (*hint*) dar a entender que

impolite [ɪmpə'laɪt] *adj* mal educado

import [*vb* ɪm'pɔːt, *n* 'ɪmpɔːt] *vt* importar ♦ *n* (*COMM*) importación *f*; (: *article*) producto importado; (*meaning*) significado, sentido

importance [ɪm'pɔːtəns] *n* importancia

important [ɪm'pɔːtənt] *adj* importante; **it's not** ~ no importa, no tiene importancia

importer [ɪm'pɔːtə*] *n* importador(a) *m/f*

impose [ɪm'pəuz] *vt* imponer ♦ *vi*: **to ~ on sb** abusar de uno; **imposing** *adj* imponente, impresionante

imposition [ɪmpə'zɪʃən] *n* (*of tax etc*) imposición *f*; **to be an** ~ **on** (*person*) molestar a

impossible [ɪm'pɔsɪbl] *adj* imposible; (*person*) insoportable

impostor [ɪm'pɔstə*] *n* impostor(a) *m/f*

impotent ['ɪmpətənt] *adj* impotente

impound [ɪm'paund] *vt* embargar

impoverished [ɪm'pɔvərɪʃt] *adj* necesitado

impracticable [ɪm'præktɪkəbl] *adj* no

factible, irrealizable

impractical [ɪmˈpræktɪkl] *adj (person, plan)* poco práctico

imprecise [ɪmprɪˈsaɪs] *adj* impreciso

impregnable [ɪmˈprɛgnəbl] *adj (castle)* inexpugnable

impregnate [ˈɪmprɛgneɪt] *vt (saturate)* impregnar

impress [ɪmˈprɛs] *vt* impresionar; *(mark)* estampar; **to ~ sth on sb** hacer entender algo a uno

impression [ɪmˈprɛʃən] *n* impresión *f*; *(imitation)* imitación *f*; **to be under the ~ that** tener la impresión de que; **~able** *adj* impresionable; **~ist** *n* impresionista *m/f*

impressive [ɪmˈprɛsɪv] *adj* impresionante

imprint [ˈɪmprɪnt] *n (outline)* huella; *(PUBLISHING)* pie *m* de imprenta

imprison [ɪmˈprɪzn] *vt* encarcelar; **~ment** *n* encarcelamiento; *(term of ~ment)* cárcel *f*

improbable [ɪmˈprɔbəbl] *adj* improbable, inverosímil

impromptu [ɪmˈprɔmptjuː] *adj* improvisado

improper [ɪmˈprɔpə*] *adj (unsuitable: conduct etc)* incorrecto; *(: activities)* deshonesto

improve [ɪmˈpruːv] *vt* mejorar; *(foreign language)* perfeccionar ♦ *vi* mejorarse; **~ment** *n* mejoramiento; perfección *f*; progreso

improvise [ˈɪmprəvaɪz] *vt, vi* improvisar

impudent [ˈɪmpjudnt] *adj* descarado, insolente

impulse [ˈɪmpʌls] *n* impulso; **to act on ~** obrar sin reflexión; **impulsive** [-ˈpʌlsɪv] *adj* irreflexivo

impunity [ɪmˈpjuːnɪtɪ] *n*: **with ~** impunemente

impure [ɪmˈpjuə*] *adj (adulterated)* adulterado; *(morally)* impuro; **impurity** *n* impureza

---

KEYWORD

in [ɪn] *prep* **1** *(indicating place, position, with place names)* en; **~ the house/ garden** en (la) casa/el jardín; **~ here/**
there aquí/ahí *or* allí dentro; **~ London/England** en Londres/Inglaterra

2 *(indicating time)* en; **~ spring** en (la) primavera; **~ the afternoon** por la tarde; **at 4 o'clock ~ the afternoon** a las 4 de la tarde; **I did it ~ 3 hours/ days** lo hice en 3 horas/días; **I'll see you ~ 2 weeks** *or* **~ 2 weeks' time** te veré dentro de 2 semanas

3 *(indicating manner etc)* en; **~ a loud/ soft voice** en voz alta/baja; **~ pencil/ ink** a lápiz/bolígrafo; **the boy ~ the blue shirt** el chico de la camisa azul

4 *(indicating circumstances)*: **~ the sun/ shade/rain** al sol/a la sombra/bajo la lluvia; **a change ~ policy** un cambio de política

5 *(indicating mood, state)*: **~ tears** en lágrimas, llorando; **~ anger/despair** enfadado/desesperado; **to live ~ luxury** vivir lujosamente

6 *(with ratios, numbers)*: **1 ~ 10 households, 1 household ~ 10** una de cada 10 familias; **20 pence ~ the pound** 20 peniques por libra; **they lined up ~ twos** se alinearon de dos en dos

7 *(referring to people, works)* en; entre; **the disease is common ~ children** la enfermedad es común entre los niños; **~ (the works of) Dickens** en (las obras de) Dickens

8 *(indicating profession etc)*: **to be ~ teaching** estar en la enseñanza

9 *(after superlative)* de; **the best pupil ~ the class** el/la mejor alumno/a de la clase

10 *(with present participle)*: **~ saying this** al decir esto

♦ *adv*: **to be ~** *(person: at home)* estar en casa; *(work)* estar; *(train, ship, plane)* haber llegado; *(in fashion)* estar de moda; **she'll be ~ later today** llegará más tarde hoy; **to ask sb ~** hacer pasar a uno; **to run/limp** *etc* **~** entrar corriendo/cojeando *etc*

♦ *n*: **the ~s and outs** *(of proposal, situation etc)* los detalles

in. *abbr* = **inch**

inability [ɪnəˈbɪlɪtɪ] *n*: ~ **(to do)** incapacidad *f* (de hacer)

inaccessible [ɪnəkˈsɛsɪbl] *adj* (*also fig*) inaccesible

inaccurate [ɪnˈækjurət] *adj* inexacto, incorrecto

inactivity [ɪnækˈtɪvɪtɪ] *n* inactividad *f*

inadequate [ɪnˈædɪkwət] *adj* (*income, reply etc*) insuficiente; (*person*) incapaz

inadvertently [ɪnədˈvəːtntlɪ] *adv* por descuido

inadvisable [ɪnədˈvaɪzəbl] *adj* poco aconsejable

inane [ɪˈneɪn] *adj* necio, fatuo

inanimate [ɪnˈænɪmət] *adj* inanimado

inappropriate [ɪnəˈprəuprɪət] *adj* inadecuado; (*improper*) poco oportuno

inarticulate [ɪnɑːˈtɪkjulət] *adj* (*person*) incapaz de expresarse; (*speech*) mal pronunciado

inasmuch as [ɪnəzˈmʌtʃ-] *conj* puesto que, ya que

inaudible [ɪnˈɔːdɪbl] *adj* inaudible

inaugurate [ɪˈnɔːgjureɪt] *vt* inaugurar; **inauguration** [-ˈreɪʃən] *n* ceremonia de apertura

inborn [ɪnˈbɔːn] *adj* (*quality*) innato

inbred [ɪnˈbred] *adj* innato; (*family*) engendrado por endogamia

Inc. *abbr* (*US*: = *incorporated*) S.A.

incapable [ɪnˈkeɪpəbl] *adj* incapaz

incapacitate [ɪnkəˈpæsɪteɪt] *vt*: **to ~ sb** incapacitar a uno

incarcerate [ɪnˈkɑːsəreɪt] *vt* encarcelar

incarnation [ɪnkɑːˈneɪʃən] *n* encarnación *f*

incendiary [ɪnˈsɛndɪərɪ] *adj* incendiario

incense [*n* ˈɪnsɛns, *vb* ɪnˈsɛns] *n* incienso ♦ *vt* (*anger*) indignar, encolerizar

incentive [ɪnˈsɛntɪv] *n* incentivo, estímulo

incessant [ɪnˈsɛsnt] *adj* incesante, continuo; ~**ly** *adv* constantemente

incest [ˈɪnsɛst] *n* incesto

inch [ɪntʃ] *n* pulgada; **to be within an ~ of** estar a dos dedos de; **he didn't give an ~** no dio concesión alguna; ~ **forward** *vi* avanzar palmo a palmo

incidence [ˈɪnsɪdns] *n* (*of crime, disease*) incidencia

incident [ˈɪnsɪdnt] *n* incidente *m*

incidental [ɪnsɪˈdɛntl] *adj* accesorio; ~ **to** relacionado con; ~**ly** [-ˈdɛntəlɪ] *adv* (*by the way*) a propósito

incinerator [ɪnˈsɪnəreɪtə*] *n* incinerador *m*

incisive [ɪnˈsaɪsɪv] *adj* (*remark etc*) incisivo

incite [ɪnˈsaɪt] *vt* provocar

inclination [ɪnklɪˈneɪʃən] *n* (*tendency*) tendencia, inclinación *f*; (*desire*) deseo; (*disposition*) propensión *f*

incline [*n* ˈɪnklaɪn, *vb* ɪnˈklaɪn] *n* pendiente *m*, cuesta ♦ *vt* (*head*) poner de lado ♦ *vi* inclinarse; **to be ~d to** (*tend*) ser propenso a

include [ɪnˈkluːd] *vt* (*incorporate*) incluir; (*in letter*) adjuntar; **including** *prep* incluso, inclusive

inclusion [ɪnˈkluːʒən] *n* inclusión *f*

inclusive [ɪnˈkluːsɪv] *adj* inclusivo; ~ **of tax** incluidos los impuestos

incognito [ɪnkɔgˈniːtəu] *adv* de incógnito

incoherent [ɪnkəuˈhɪərənt] *adj* incoherente

income [ˈɪŋkʌm] *n* (*earned*) ingresos *mpl*; (*from property etc*) renta; (*from investment etc*) rédito; ~ **tax** *n* impuesto sobre la renta

incoming [ˈɪnkʌmɪŋ] *adj* (*flight, government etc*) entrante

incomparable [ɪnˈkɔmpərəbl] *adj* incomparable, sin par

incompatible [ɪnkəmˈpætɪbl] *adj* incompatible

incompetent [ɪnˈkɔmpɪtənt] *adj* incompetente

incomplete [ɪnkəmˈpliːt] *adj* (*partial: achievement etc*) incompleto; (*unfinished: painting etc*) inacabado

incomprehensible [ɪnkɔmprɪˈhɛnsɪbl] *adj* incomprensible

inconceivable [ɪnkənˈsiːvəbl] *adj* inconcebible

incongruous [ɪnˈkɔŋgruəs] *adj* (*strange*) discordante; (*inappropriate*) incongruente

inconsiderate [ɪnkənˈsɪdərət] *adj*

desconsiderado
inconsistent [ɪnkən'sɪstənt] *adj* inconsecuente; (*contradictory*) incongruente; ~ **with** (que) no concuerda con
inconspicuous [ɪnkən'spɪkjuəs] *adj* (*colour, building etc*) discreto; (*person*) que llama poco la atención
inconvenience [ɪnkən'viːnjəns] *n* inconvenientes *mpl*; (*trouble*) molestia, incomodidad *f* ♦ *vt* incomodar
inconvenient [ɪnkən'viːnjənt] *adj* incómodo, poco práctico; (*time, place, visitor*) inoportuno
incorporate [ɪn'kɔːpəreɪt] *vt* incorporar; (*contain*) comprender; (*add*) agregar; ~**d** *adj*: ~**d company** (*US*) ≈ sociedad *f* anónima
incorrect [ɪnkə'rɛkt] *adj* incorrecto
incorrigible [ɪn'kɔrɪdʒəbl] *adj* incorregible
incorruptible [ɪnkə'rʌptɪbl] *adj* insobornable
increase [*n* 'ɪnkriːs, *vb* ɪn'kriːs] *n* aumento ♦ *vi* aumentar; (*grow*) crecer; (*price*) subir ♦ *vt* aumentar; (*price*) subir; **increasing** *adj* creciente; **increasingly** *adv* cada vez más, más y más
incredible [ɪn'krɛdɪbl] *adj* increíble
incredulous [ɪn'krɛdjuləs] *adj* incrédulo
incriminate [ɪn'krɪmɪneɪt] *vt* incriminar
incubator ['ɪnkjubeɪtə*] *n* incubadora
incumbent [ɪn'kʌmbənt] *n* titular *m/f* ♦ *adj*: **it is** ~ **on him to ...** le incumbe ...
incur [ɪn'kə:*] *vt* (*expenditure*) incurrir; (*loss*) sufrir; (*anger, disapproval*) provocar
incurable [ɪn'kjuərəbl] *adj* incurable
indebted [ɪn'dɛtɪd] *adj*: **to be** ~ **to sb** estar agradecido a uno
indecent [ɪn'diːsnt] *adj* indecente; ~ **assault** (*BRIT*) atentado contra el pudor; ~ **exposure** *n* exhibicionismo
indecisive [ɪndɪ'saɪsɪv] *adj* indeciso
indeed [ɪn'diːd] *adv* efectivamente, en realidad; (*in fact*) en efecto; (*furthermore*) es más; **yes** ~! ¡claro que sí!
indefinitely [ɪn'dɛfɪnɪtlɪ] *adv* (*wait*) indefinidamente
indelible [ɪn'dɛlɪbl] *adj* imborrable

indemnity [ɪn'dɛmnɪtɪ] *n* (*insurance*) indemnidad *f*; (*compensation*) indemnización *f*
independence [ɪndɪ'pɛndns] *n* independencia
independent [ɪndɪ'pɛndənt] *adj* independiente
indestructible [ɪndɪs'trʌktəbl] *adj* indestructible
index ['ɪndɛks] (*pl* ~**es**) *n* (*in book*) índice *m*; (: *in library etc*) catálogo; (*pl* **indices**: *ratio, sign*) exponente *m*; ~ **card** *n* ficha; ~**ed** (*US*) *adj* = ~-**linked**; ~ **finger** *n* índice *m*; ~-**linked** (*BRIT*) *adj* vinculado al índice del coste de la vida
India ['ɪndɪə] *n* la India; ~**n** *adj, n* indio/a *m/f*; **Red** ~**n** piel roja *m/f*; ~**n Ocean** *n*: **the** ~**n Ocean** el Océano Índico
indicate ['ɪndɪkeɪt] *vt* indicar; **indication** [-'keɪʃən] *n* indicio, señal *f*; **indicative** [ɪn'dɪkətɪv] *adj*: **to be indicative of** indicar ♦ *n* (*LING*) indicativo; **indicator** *n* indicador *m*; (*AUT*) intermitente *m*
indices ['ɪndɪsiːz] *npl of* **index**
indictment [ɪn'daɪtmənt] *n* acusación *f*
indifference [ɪn'dɪfrəns] *n* indiferencia
indifferent [ɪn'dɪfrənt] *adj* indiferente; (*mediocre*) regular
indigenous [ɪn'dɪdʒɪnəs] *adj* indígena
indigestion [ɪndɪ'dʒestʃən] *n* indigestión *f*
indignant [ɪn'dɪgnənt] *adj*: **to be** ~ **at sth/with sb** indignarse por algo/con uno
indigo ['ɪndɪgəu] *adj* de color añil ♦ *n* añil *m*
indirect [ɪndɪ'rɛkt] *adj* indirecto; ~**ly** *adv* indirectamente
indiscreet [ɪndɪ'skriːt] *adj* indiscreto, imprudente
indiscriminate [ɪndɪ'skrɪmɪnət] *adj* indiscriminado
indispensable [ɪndɪ'spɛnsəbl] *adj* indispensable, imprescindible
indisposed [ɪndɪ'spəuzd] *adj* (*unwell*) indispuesto
indisputable [ɪndɪ'spjuːtəbl] *adj* incontestable.
indistinct [ɪndɪ'stɪŋkt] *adj* (*noise, memory etc*) confuso

individual [ˌɪndɪ'vɪdjuəl] *n* individuo ♦ *adj* individual; (*personal*) personal; (*particular*) particular; ~**ist** *n* individualista *m/f*; ~**ly** *adv* (*singly*) individualmente

indoctrinate [ɪn'dɔktrɪneɪt] *vt* adoctrinar

indolent ['ɪndələnt] *adj* indolente, perezoso

indoor ['ɪndɔː*] *adj* (*swimming pool*) cubierto; (*plant*) de interior; (*sport*) bajo cubierta; ~**s** [ɪn'dɔːz] *adv* dentro

induce [ɪn'djuːs] *vt* inducir, persuadir; (*bring about*) producir; (*birth*) provocar; ~**ment** *n* (*incentive*) incentivo; (*pej: bribe*) soborno

indulge [ɪn'dʌldʒ] *vt* (*whim*) satisfacer; (*person*) complacer; (*child*) mimar ♦ *vi*: **to ~ in** darse el gusto de; ~**nce** *n* vicio; (*leniency*) indulgencia; ~**nt** *adj* indulgente

industrial [ɪn'dʌstrɪəl] *adj* industrial; ~ **action** *n* huelga; ~ **estate** (*BRIT*) *n* polígono (*SP*) or zona (*AM*) industrial; ~**ist** *n* industrial *m/f*; ~**ize** *vt* industrializar; ~ **park** (*US*) *n* = ~ **estate**

industrious [ɪn'dʌstrɪəs] *adj* trabajador(a); (*student*) aplicado

industry ['ɪndəstrɪ] *n* industria; (*diligence*) aplicación *f*

inebriated [ɪ'niːbrɪeɪtɪd] *adj* borracho

inedible [ɪn'edɪbl] *adj* incomible; (*poisonous*) no comestible

ineffective [ɪnɪ'fektɪv] *adj* ineficaz, inútil

ineffectual [ɪnɪ'fektjuəl] *adj* = **ineffective**

inefficiency [ɪnɪ'fɪʃənsɪ] *n* ineficacia

inefficient [ɪnɪ'fɪʃənt] *adj* ineficaz, ineficiente

inept [ɪ'nept] *adj* incompetente

inequality [ɪnɪ'kwɔlɪtɪ] *n* desigualdad *f*

inert [ɪ'nɜːt] *adj* inerte, inactivo; (*immobile*) inmóvil; ~**ia** [ɪ'nɜːʃə] *n* inercia; (*laziness*) pereza

inescapable [ɪnɪ'skeɪpəbl] *adj* ineludible

inevitable [ɪn'evɪtəbl] *adj* inevitable; **inevitably** *adv* inevitablemente

inexcusable [ɪnɪks'kjuːzəbl] *adj* imperdonable

inexhaustible [ɪnɪg'zɔːstɪbl] *adj* inagotable

inexpensive [ɪnɪk'spensɪv] *adj* económico

inexperience [ɪnɪk'spɪərɪəns] *n* falta de experiencia; ~**d** *adj* inexperto

inextricably [ɪnɪks'trɪkəblɪ] *adv* indisolublemente

infallible [ɪn'fælɪbl] *adj* infalible

infamous ['ɪnfəməs] *adj* infame

infancy ['ɪnfənsɪ] *n* infancia

infant ['ɪnfənt] *n* niño/a; (*baby*) niño pequeño, bebé *m*; ~**ile** *adj* infantil; (*pej*) aniñado; ~ **school** (*BRIT*) *n* parvulario

infantry ['ɪnfəntrɪ] *n* infantería

infatuated [ɪn'fætjueɪtɪd] *adj*: ~ **with** (*in love*) loco por

infatuation [ɪnfætʃu'eɪʃən] *n* enamoramiento, pasión *f*

infect [ɪn'fekt] *vt* (*wound*) infectar; (*food*) contaminar; (*person, animal*) contagiar; ~**ion** [ɪn'fekʃən] *n* infección *f*; (*fig*) contagio; ~**ious** [ɪn'fekʃəs] *adj* (*also fig*) contagioso

infer [ɪn'fɜː*] *vt* deducir, inferir; ~**ence** ['ɪnfərəns] *n* deducción *f*, inferencia

inferior [ɪn'fɪərɪə*] *adj, n* inferior *m/f*; ~**ity** [-rɪ'ɔrɪtɪ] *n* inferioridad *f*; ~**ity complex** *n* complejo de inferioridad

inferno [ɪn'fɜːnəu] *n* (*fire*) hoguera

infertile [ɪn'fɜːtaɪl] *adj* estéril; (*person*) infecundo; **infertility** [-'tɪlɪtɪ] *n* esterilidad *f*; infecundidad *f*

infested [ɪn'festɪd] *adj*: ~ **with** plagado de

in-fighting *n* (*fig*) lucha(s) *f(pl)* interna(s)

infiltrate ['ɪnfɪltreɪt] *vt* infiltrar en

infinite ['ɪnfɪnɪt] *adj* infinito

infinitive [ɪn'fɪnɪtɪv] *n* infinitivo

infinity [ɪn'fɪnɪtɪ] *n* infinito; (*an ~*) infinidad *f*

infirm [ɪn'fɜːm] *adj* enfermo, débil; ~**ary** *n* hospital *m*; ~**ity** *n* debilidad *f*; (*illness*) enfermedad *f*, achaque *m*

inflamed [ɪn'fleɪmd] *adj*: **to become ~** inflamarse

inflammable [ɪn'flæməbl] *adj* inflamable

inflammation [ɪnflə'meɪʃən] *n* inflamación *f*

inflatable [ɪn'fleɪtəbl] *adj* (*ball, boat*) inflable

inflate [ɪnˈfleɪt] *vt* (*tyre, price etc*) inflar; (*fig*) hinchar; **inflation** [ɪnˈfleɪʃən] *n* (*ECON*) inflación *f*

inflexible [ɪnˈfleksəbl] *adj* (*rule*) rígido; (*person*) inflexible

inflict [ɪnˈflɪkt] *vt*: **to ~ sth on sb** infligir algo en uno

influence [ˈɪnfluəns] *n* influencia ♦ *vt* influir en, influenciar; **under the ~ of alcohol** en estado de embriaguez; **influential** [-ˈenfl] *adj* influyente

influenza [ɪnfluˈenzə] *n* gripe *f*

influx [ˈɪnflʌks] *n* afluencia

inform [ɪnˈfɔːm] *vt*: **to ~ sb of sth** informar a uno sobre *or* de algo ♦ *vi*: **to ~ on sb** delatar a uno

informal [ɪnˈfɔːməl] *adj* (*manner, tone*) familiar; (*dress, interview, occasion*) informal; (*visit, meeting*) extraoficial; **~ity** [-ˈmælɪtɪ] *n* informalidad *f*, sencillez *f*

informant [ɪnˈfɔːmənt] *n* informante *m/f*

information [ɪnfəˈmeɪʃən] *n* información *f*; (*knowledge*) conocimientos *mpl*; **a piece of ~** un dato; **~ office** *n* información *f*

informative [ɪnˈfɔːmətɪv] *adj* informativo

informer [ɪnˈfɔːmə*] *n* (*also: police ~*) soplón/ona *m/f*

infra-red [ɪnfrəˈred] *adj* infrarrojo

infrastructure [ˈɪnfrəstrʌktʃə*] *n* (*of system etc*) infraestructura

infringe [ɪnˈfrɪndʒ] *vt* infringir, violar ♦ *vi*: **to ~ on** abusar de; **~ment** *n* infracción *f*; (*of rights*) usurpación *f*

infuriating [ɪnˈfjuərɪeɪtɪŋ] *adj* (*habit, noise*) enloquecedor/a

ingenious [ɪnˈdʒiːnjəs] *adj* ingenioso; **ingenuity** [-dʒɪˈnjuːɪtɪ] *n* ingeniosidad *f*

ingenuous [ɪnˈdʒenjuəs] *adj* ingenuo

ingot [ˈɪŋgət] *n* lingote *m*, barra

ingrained [ɪnˈgreɪnd] *adj* arraigado

ingratiate [ɪnˈgreɪʃɪeɪt] *vt*: **to ~ o.s. with** congraciarse con

ingredient [ɪnˈgriːdɪənt] *n* ingrediente *m*

inhabit [ɪnˈhæbɪt] *vt* vivir en; **~ant** *n* habitante *m/f*

inhale [ɪnˈheɪl] *vt* inhalar ♦ *vi* (*breathe in*) aspirar; (*in smoking*) tragar

inherent [ɪnˈhɪərənt] *adj*: **~ in** *or* **to** inherente a

inherit [ɪnˈherɪt] *vt* heredar; **~ance** *n* herencia; (*fig*) patrimonio

inhibit [ɪnˈhɪbɪt] *vt* inhibir, impedir; **~ed** *adj* (*PSYCH*) cohibido; **~ion** [-ˈbɪʃən] *n* cohibición *f*

inhospitable [ɪnhɔsˈpɪtəbl] *adj* (*person*) inhospitalario; (*place*) inhóspito

inhuman [ɪnˈhjuːmən] *adj* inhumano

iniquity [ɪˈnɪkwɪtɪ] *n* iniquidad *f*; (*injustice*) injusticia

initial [ɪˈnɪʃl] *adj* primero ♦ *n* inicial *f* ♦ *vt* firmar con las iniciales; **~s** *npl* (*as signature*) iniciales *fpl*; (*abbreviation*) siglas *fpl*; **~ly** *adv* al principio

initiate [ɪˈnɪʃɪeɪt] *vt* iniciar; **to ~ proceedings against sb** (*LAW*) entablar proceso contra uno; **initiation** [-ˈeɪʃən] *n* (*into secret etc*) iniciación *f*; (*beginning*) comienzo

initiative [ɪˈnɪʃɪətɪv] *n* iniciativa

inject [ɪnˈdʒekt] *vt* inyectar; **to ~ sb with sth** inyectar algo a uno; **~ion** [ɪnˈdʒekʃən] *n* inyección *f*

injunction [ɪnˈdʒʌŋkʃən] *n* interdicto

injure [ˈɪndʒə*] *vt* (*hurt*) herir, lastimar; (*fig: reputation etc*) perjudicar; **~d** *adj* (*person, arm*) herido, lastimado; **injury** *n* herida, lesión *f*; (*wrong*) perjuicio, daño; **injury time** *n* (*SPORT*) (tiempo de) descuento

injustice [ɪnˈdʒʌstɪs] *n* injusticia

ink [ɪŋk] *n* tinta

inkling [ˈɪŋklɪŋ] *n* sospecha; (*idea*) idea

inlaid [ˈɪnleɪd] *adj* (*with wood, gems etc*) incrustado

inland [*adj* ˈɪnlənd, *adv* ɪnˈlænd] *adj* (*waterway, port etc*) interior ♦ *adv* tierra adentro; **I~ Revenue** (*BRIT*) *n* departamento de impuestos; ≈ Hacienda (*SP*)

in-laws *npl* suegros *mpl*

inlet [ˈɪnlet] *n* (*GEO*) ensenada, cala; (*TECH*) admisión *f*, entrada

inmate [ˈɪnmeɪt] *n* (*in prison*) preso/a; presidiario/a; (*in asylum*) internado/a

inn [ɪn] *n* posada, mesón *m*

innate [ɪˈneɪt] *adj* innato

inner [ˈɪnə*] *adj* (*courtyard, calm*) interior; (*feelings*) íntimo; **~ city** *n* barrios deprimidos del centro de una ciudad; ~ **tube** n (*of tyre*) cámara (*SP*), llanta (*AM*)

innings ['ɪnɪŋz] n (*CRICKET*) entrada, turno

innocence ['ɪnəsəns] n inocencia

innocent ['ɪnəsnt] adj inocente

innocuous [ɪ'nɔkjuəs] adj inocuo

innovation [ɪnəu'veɪʃən] n novedad f

innuendo [ɪnju'ɛndəu] (*pl* ~**es**) n indirecta

inoculation [ɪnɔkju'leɪʃən] n inoculación f

inopportune [ɪn'ɔpətjuːn] adj inoportuno

inordinately [ɪ'nɔːdɪnɪtlɪ] adv desmesuradamente

in-patient n paciente m/f interno/a

input ['ɪnput] n entrada; (*of resources*) inversión f; (*COMPUT*) entrada de datos

inquest ['ɪnkwɛst] n (*coroner's*) encuesta judicial

inquire [ɪn'kwaɪə*] vi preguntar ♦ vt: to ~ **whether** preguntar si; **to ~ about** (*person*) preguntar por; (*fact*) informarse de; ~ **into** vt fus investigar, indagar; **inquiry** n pregunta; (*investigation*) investigación f, pesquisa; **inquiry office** (*BRIT*) n oficina de información

inquisitive [ɪn'kwɪzɪtɪv] adj (*curious*) curioso

inroads ['ɪnrəudz] npl: **to make ~ into** mermar

ins abbr = **inches**

insane [ɪn'seɪn] adj loco; (*MED*) demente

insanity [ɪn'sænɪtɪ] n demencia, locura

insatiable [ɪn'seɪʃəbl] adj insaciable

inscription [ɪn'skrɪpʃən] n inscripción f; (*in book*) dedicatoria

inscrutable [ɪn'skruːtəbl] adj inescrutable, insondable

insect ['ɪnsɛkt] n insecto; ~**icide** [ɪn'sɛktɪsaɪd] n insecticida m

insecure [ɪnsɪ'kjuə*] adj inseguro

insemination [ɪnsɛmɪ'neɪʃn] n: **artificial ~** inseminación f artificial

insensitive [ɪn'sɛnsɪtɪv] adj insensible

inseparable [ɪn'sɛprəbl] adj inseparable

insert [vb ɪn'səːt, n 'ɪnsəːt] vt (*into sth*) introducir ♦ n encarte m; ~**ion** [ɪn'səːʃən]

n inserción f

in-service ['ɪnsəːvɪs] adj (*training, course*) a cargo de la empresa

inshore [ɪn'ʃɔː*] adj de bajura ♦ adv (*be*) cerca de la orilla; (*move*) hacia la orilla

inside ['ɪn'saɪd] n interior m ♦ adj interior, interno ♦ adv (*be*) (por) dentro; (*go*) hacia dentro ♦ prep dentro de; (*of time*): ~ **10 minutes** en menos de 10 minutos; ~**s** npl (*inf: stomach*) tripas fpl; ~ **information** n información f confidencial; ~ **lane** n (*AUT: in Britain*) carril m izquierdo; (*AUT: in US, Europe etc*) carril m derecho; ~ **out** (*turn*) al revés; (*know*) a fondo

insider dealing, insider trading n (*STOCK EXCHANGE*) abuso de información privilegiada

insidious [ɪn'sɪdɪəs] adj insidioso

insight ['ɪnsaɪt] n perspicacia

insignia [ɪn'sɪgnɪə] npl insignias fpl

insignificant [ɪnsɪg'nɪfɪknt] adj insignificante

insincere [ɪnsɪn'sɪə*] adj poco sincero

insinuate [ɪn'sɪnjueɪt] vt insinuar

insipid [ɪn'sɪpɪd] adj soso, insulso

insist [ɪn'sɪst] vi insistir; **to ~ on** insistir en; **to ~ that** insistir en que; (*claim*) exigir que; ~**ence** n (*determination*) empeño; ~**ent** adj insistente; (*noise, action*) persistente

insole ['ɪnsəul] n plantilla

insolent ['ɪnsələnt] adj insolente, descarado

insoluble [ɪn'sɔljubl] adj insoluble

insomnia [ɪn'sɔmnɪə] n insomnio

inspect [ɪn'spɛkt] vt inspeccionar, examinar; (*troops*) pasar revista a; ~**ion** [ɪn'spɛkʃən] n inspección f, examen m; (*of troops*) revista; ~**or** n inspector(a) m/f; (*BRIT: on buses, trains*) revisor(a) m/f

inspiration [ɪnspə'reɪʃən] n inspiración f; **inspire** [ɪn'spaɪə*] vt inspirar

instability [ɪnstə'bɪlɪtɪ] n inestabilidad f

install [ɪn'stɔːl] vt instalar; (*official*) nombrar; ~**ation** [ɪnstə'leɪʃən] n instalación f

instalment [ɪn'stɔːlmənt] (*US* **installment**) n plazo; (*of story*) entrega; (*of TV* *serial etc*) capítulo; **in ~s** (*pay*, *receive*) a plazos

instance ['ınstəns] *n* ejemplo, caso; **for ~** por ejemplo; **in the first ~** en primer lugar

instant ['ınstənt] *n* instante *m*, momento ♦ *adj* inmediato; (*coffee etc*) instantáneo; **~ly** *adv* en seguida

instead [ın'stɛd] *adv* en cambio; **~ of** en lugar de, en vez de

instep ['ınstɛp] *n* empeine *m*

instil [ın'stıl] *vt*: **to ~ sth into** inculcar algo a

instinct ['ınstıŋkt] *n* instinto; **~ive** [-'stıŋktıv] *adj* instintivo

institute ['ınstıtjuːt] *n* instituto; (*professional body*) colegio ♦ *vt* (*begin*) iniciar, empezar; (*proceedings*) entablar; (*system*, *rule*) establecer

institution [ınstı'tjuːʃən] *n* institución *f*; (*MED*: *home*) asilo; (: *asylum*) manicomio; (*of system etc*) establecimiento; (*of custom*) iniciación *f*

instruct [ın'strʌkt] *vt*: **to ~ sb in sth** instruir a uno en *or* sobre algo; **to ~ sb to do sth** dar instrucciones a uno de hacer algo; **~ion** [ın'strʌkʃən] *n* (*teaching*) instrucción *f*; **~ions** *npl* (*orders*) órdenes *fpl*; **~ions** (*for use*) modo de empleo; **~ive** *adj* instructivo; **~or** *n* instructor(a) *m/f*

instrument ['ınstrəmənt] *n* instrumento; **~al** [-'mɛntl] *adj* (*MUS*) instrumental; **to be ~al in** ser (el) artífice de; **~ panel** *n* tablero (de instrumentos)

insubordination [ınsəbɔːdı'neıʃən] *n* insubordinación *f*

insufferable [ın'sʌfrəbl] *adj* insoportable

insufficient [ınsə'fıʃənt] *adj* insuficiente

insular ['ınsjulə*] *adj* insular; (*person*) estrecho de miras

insulate ['ınsjuleıt] *vt* aislar; **insulating tape** *n* cinta aislante; **insulation** [-'leıʃən] *n* aislamiento

insulin ['ınsjulın] *n* insulina

insult [*n* 'ınsʌlt, *vb* ın'sʌlt] *n* insulto ♦ *vt* insultar; **~ing** *adj* insultante

insurance [ın'ʃuərəns] *n* seguro; **fire/life ~** seguro contra incendios/sobre la vida;

~ agent *n* agente *m/f* de seguros; **~ policy** *n* póliza (de seguros)

insure [ın'ʃuə*] *vt* asegurar

intact [ın'tækt] *adj* íntegro; (*unharmed*) intacto

intake ['ınteık] *n* (*of food*) ingestión *f*; (*of air*) consumo; (*BRIT*: *SCOL*): **an ~ of 200 a year** 200 matriculados al año

integral ['ıntıgrəl] *adj* (*whole*) íntegro; (*part*) integrante

integrate ['ıntıgreıt] *vt* integrar ♦ *vi* integrarse

integrity [ın'tɛgrıtı] *n* honradez *f*, rectitud *f*

intellect ['ıntəlɛkt] *n* intelecto; **~ual** [-'lɛktjuəl] *adj*, *n* intelectual *m/f*

intelligence [ın'tɛlıdʒəns] *n* inteligencia

intelligent [ın'tɛlıdʒənt] *adj* inteligente; **~sia** [ıntɛlı'dʒɛntsıə] *n* intelectualidad *f*

intelligible [ın'tɛlıdʒıbl] *adj* inteligible, comprensible

intend [ın'tɛnd] *vt* (*gift etc*): **to ~ sth for** destinar algo a; **to ~ to do sth** tener intención de *or* pensar hacer algo; **~ed** *adj* intencionado

intense [ın'tɛns] *adj* intenso; **~ly** *adv* (*extremely*) sumamente

intensify [ın'tɛnsıfaı] *vt* intensificar; (*increase*) aumentar

intensive [ın'tɛnsıv] *adj* intensivo; **~ care unit** *n* unidad *f* de vigilancia intensiva

intent [ın'tɛnt] *n* (*LAW*) premeditación *f* ♦ *adj* (*absorbed*) absorto; (*attentive*) atento; **to all ~s and purposes** prácticamente; **to be ~ on doing sth** estar resuelto a hacer algo

intention [ın'tɛnʃən] *n* intención *f*, propósito; **~al** *adj* deliberado; **~ally** *adv* a propósito

intently [ın'tɛntlı] *adv* atentamente, fijamente

interact [ıntər'ækt] *vi* influirse mutuamente; **~ion** [-'ækʃən] *n* interacción *f*; **~ive** *adj* (*COMPUT*) interactivo

intercede [ıntə'siːd] *vi*: **to ~ (with)** interceder (con)

intercept [ıntə'sɛpt] *vt* interceptar

interchange ['ıntətʃeındʒ] *n* intercambio; (*on motorway*) intersección *f*; **~able** *adj* intercambiable

intercom ['ɪntəkɔm] *n* interfono

intercourse ['ɪntəkɔːs] *n* (*sexual*) relaciones *fpl* sexuales

interest ['ɪntrɪst] *n* (*also* COMM) interés *m* ♦ *vt* interesar; **to be ~ed in** interesarse por; ~**ing** *adj* interesante; ~ **rate** *n* tipo *or* tasa de interés

interface ['ɪntəfeɪs] *n* (COMPUT) junción *f*

interfere [ɪntə'fɪə*] *vi*: **to ~ in** (*quarrel, other people's business*) entrometerse en; **to ~ with** (*hinder*) estorbar; (*damage*) estropear

interference [ɪntə'fɪərəns] *n* intromisión *f*, (RADIO, TV) interferencia

interim ['ɪntərɪm] *n*: **in the ~** en el ínterin ♦ *adj* provisional

interior [ɪn'tɪərɪə*] *n* interior *m* ♦ *adj* interior; ~ **designer** *n* interiorista *m/f*

interjection [ɪntə'dʒekʃən] *n* interposición *f*, (LING) interjección *f*

interlock [ɪntə'lɔk] *vi* entrelazarse

interlude ['ɪntəluːd] *n* intervalo; (THEATRE) intermedio

intermarry [ɪntə'mærɪ] *vi* casarse personas de distintas razas (*or* religiones *etc*)

intermediary [ɪntə'miːdɪərɪ] *n* intermediario/a

intermediate [ɪntə'miːdɪət] *adj* intermedio

interminable [ɪn'tɜːmɪnəbl] *adj* inacabable

intermission [ɪntə'mɪʃən] *n* intermisión *f*, (THEATRE) descanso

intermittent [ɪntə'mɪtnt] *adj* intermitente

intern [*vb* ɪn'tɜːn, *n* 'ɪntɜːn] *vt* internar ♦ *n* (US) interno/a

internal [ɪn'tɜːnl] *adj* (*layout, pipes, security*) interior; (*injury, structure, memo*) internal; ~**ly** *adv*: **"not to be taken ~ly"** "uso externo"; **I~ Revenue Service** (US) *n* departamento de impuestos; ≈ Hacienda (SP)

international [ɪntə'næʃənl] *adj* internacional ♦ *n* (BRIT: *match*) partido internacional

interplay ['ɪntəpleɪ] *n* interacción *f*

interpret [ɪn'tɜːprɪt] *vt* interpretar; (*trans-*

late) traducir; (*understand*) entender ♦ *vi* hacer de intérprete; ~**ation** [-'teɪʃən] *n* interpretación *f*, traducción *f*, entendimiento; ~**er** *n* intérprete *m/f*

interrelated [ɪntərɪ'leɪtɪd] *adj* interrelacionado

interrogate [ɪn'tɛrəugeɪt] *vt* interrogar; **interrogation** [-'geɪʃən] *n* interrogatorio; **interrogative** [ɪntə'rɔgətɪv] *adj* (LING) interrogativo

interrupt [ɪntə'rʌpt] *vt*, *vi* interrumpir; ~**ion** [-'rʌpʃən] *n* interrupción *f*

intersect [ɪntə'sekt] *vi* (*roads*) cruzarse; ~**ion** [-'sekʃən] *n* (*of roads*) cruce *m*

intersperse [ɪntə'spəːs] *vt*: **to ~ with** salpicar de

intertwine [ɪntə'twaɪn] *vt* entrelazarse

interval ['ɪntəvl] *n* intervalo; (BRIT: THEATRE, SPORT) descanso; (: SCOL) recreo; **at ~s** a ratos, de vez en cuando

intervene [ɪntə'viːn] *vi* intervenir; (*event*) interponerse; (*time*) transcurrir; **intervention** [-'vɛnʃən] *n* intervención *f*

interview ['ɪntəvjuː] *n* entrevista ♦ *vt* entrevistarse con; ~**er** *n* entrevistador(a) *m/f*

intestine [ɪn'tɛstɪn] *n* intestino

intimacy ['ɪntɪməsɪ] *n* intimidad *f*

intimate [*adj* 'ɪntɪmət, *vb* 'ɪntɪmeɪt] *adj* íntimo; (*friendship*) estrecho; (*knowledge*) profundo ♦ *vt* dar a entender

intimidate [ɪn'tɪmɪdeɪt] *vt* intimidar, amedrentar

into ['ɪntuː] *prep* en; (*towards*) a; (*inside*) hacia el interior de; ~ **3 pieces/French** en 3 pedazos/al francés

intolerable [ɪn'tɔlərəbl] *adj* intolerable, insoportable

intolerant [ɪn'tɔlərənt] *adj*: ~ **(of)** intolerante (con *or* para)

intonation [ɪntəu'neɪʃən] *n* entonación *f*

intoxicated [ɪn'tɔksɪkeɪtɪd] *adj* embriagado; **intoxication** [ɪntɔksɪ'keɪʃən] *n* embriaguez *f*

intractable [ɪn'træktəbl] *adj* (*person*) intratable; (*problem*) espinoso

intransitive [ɪn'trænsɪtɪv] *adj* intransitivo

intravenous [ɪntrə'viːnəs] *adj* intravenoso

in-tray *n* bandeja de entrada
intricate ['ɪntrɪkət] *adj (design, pattern)* intrincado
intrigue [ɪn'triːg] *n* intriga ♦ *vt* fascinar; **intriguing** *adj* fascinante
intrinsic [ɪn'trɪnsɪk] *adj* intrínseco
introduce [ɪntrə'djuːs] *vt* introducir, meter; *(speaker, TV show etc)* presentar; **to ~ sb (to sb)** presentar uno (a otro); **to ~ sb to** *(pastime, technique)* introducir a uno a; **introduction** [-'dʌkʃən] *n* introducción *f*; *(of person)* presentación *f*; **introductory** [-'dʌktərɪ] *adj* introductorio; *(lesson, offer)* de introducción
introvert ['ɪntrəvəːt] *n* introvertido/a ♦ *adj (also: ~ed)* introvertido
intrude [ɪn'truːd] *vi (person)* entrometerse; **to ~ on** estorbar; **~r** *n* intruso/a; **intrusion** [-ʒən] *n* invasión *f*
intuition [ɪntju:'ɪʃən] *n* intuición *f*
inundate ['ɪnʌndeɪt] *vt*: **to ~ with** inundar de
invade [ɪn'veɪd] *vt* invadir
invalid [*n* 'ɪnvəlɪd, *adj* ɪn'vælɪd] *n (MED)* minusválido/a ♦ *adj (not valid)* inválido, nulo
invaluable [ɪn'væljuəbl] *adj* inestimable
invariable [ɪn'vɛərɪəbl] *adj* invariable
invasion [ɪn'veɪʒən] *n* invasión *f*
invent [ɪn'vɛnt] *vt* inventar; **~ion** [ɪn'vɛnʃən] *n* invento; *(lie)* ficción *f*, mentira; **~ive** *adj* inventivo; **~or** *n* inventor(a) *m/f*
inventory ['ɪnvəntrɪ] *n* inventario
invert [ɪn'vəːt] *vt* invertir
invertebrate [ɪn'vəːtɪbrət] *n* invertebrado
inverted commas *(BRIT)* npl comillas *fpl*
invest [ɪn'vɛst] *vt* invertir ♦ *vi*: **to ~ in** *(company etc)* invertir dinero en; *(fig: sth useful)* comprar
investigate [ɪn'vɛstɪgeɪt] *vt* investigar; **investigation** [-'geɪʃən] *n* investigación *f*, pesquisa; **investigator** *n* investigador(a) *m/f*
investment [ɪn'vɛstmənt] *n* inversión *f*
investor [ɪn'vɛstə*] *n* inversionista *m/f*
inveterate [ɪn'vɛtərət] *adj* empedernido
invidious [ɪn'vɪdɪəs] *adj* odioso

invigilator [ɪn'vɪdʒɪleɪtə*] *n* persona que vigila en un examen
invigorating [ɪn'vɪgəreɪtɪŋ] *adj* vigorizante
invincible [ɪn'vɪnsɪbl] *adj* invencible
invisible [ɪn'vɪzɪbl] *adj* invisible
invitation [ɪnvɪ'teɪʃən] *n* invitación *f*
invite [ɪn'vaɪt] *vt* invitar; *(opinions etc)* solicitar, pedir; **inviting** *adj* atractivo; *(food)* apetitoso
invoice ['ɪnvɔɪs] *n* factura ♦ *vt* facturar
invoke [ɪn'vəuk] *vt (law, principle)* recurrir a
involuntary [ɪn'vɔləntrɪ] *adj* involuntario
involve [ɪn'vɔlv] *vt* suponer, implicar; tener que ver con; *(concern, affect)* corresponder; **to ~ sb (in sth)** comprometer a uno (con algo); **~d** *adj* complicado; **to be ~d in** *(take part)* tomar parte en; *(be engrossed)* estar muy metido en; **~ment** *n* participación *f*; dedicación *f*
inward ['ɪnwəd] *adj (movement)* interior, interno; *(thought, feeling)* íntimo; **~(s)** *adv* hacia dentro
I/O *abbr (COMPUT = input/output)* entrada/salida
iodine ['aɪəudiːn] *n* yodo
ion ['aɪən] *n* ion *m*; **ioniser** ['aɪənaɪzə*] *n* ionizador *m*
iota [aɪ'əutə] *n* jota, ápice *m*
IOU *n abbr (= I owe you)* pagaré *m*
IQ *n abbr (= intelligence quotient)* cociente *m* intelectual
IRA *n abbr (= Irish Republican Army)* IRA *m*
Iran [ɪ'rɑːn] *n* Irán *m*; **~ian** [ɪ'reɪnɪən] *adj*, *n* iraní *m/f*
Iraq [ɪ'rɑːk] *n* Iraq; **~i** *adj*, *n* iraquí *m/f*
irascible [ɪ'ræsɪbl] *adj* irascible
irate [aɪ'reɪt] *adj* enojado, airado
Ireland ['aɪələnd] *n* Irlanda
iris ['aɪrɪs] *(pl ~es)* *n (ANAT)* iris *m*; *(BOT)* lirio
Irish ['aɪrɪʃ] *adj* irlandés/esa ♦ *npl*: **the ~** los irlandeses; **~man/woman** *n* irlandés/esa *m/f*; **~ Sea** *n*: **the ~ Sea** el mar de Irlanda
irksome ['əːksʌm] *adj* fastidioso

iron ['aɪən] *n* hierro; (*for clothes*) plancha ♦ *cpd* de hierro ♦ *vt* (*clothes*) planchar; ~ out *vt* (*fig*) allanar; **I~ Curtain** *n*: **the I~ Curtain** el Telón de Acero

ironic(al) [aɪ'rɔnɪk(l)] *adj* irónico

ironing ['aɪənɪŋ] *n* (*activity*) planchado; (*clothes: ironed*) ropa planchada; (: *to be ironed*) ropa por planchar; ~ **board** *n* tabla de planchar

ironmonger's (shop) ['aɪənmʌŋgəz] (*BRIT*) *n* ferretería, quincallería

irony ['aɪrənɪ] *n* ironía

irrational [ɪ'ræʃənl] *adj* irracional

irreconcilable [ɪrɛkən'saɪləbl] *adj* (*ideas*) incompatible; (*enemies*) irreconciliable

irregular [ɪ'rɛgjulə*] *adj* irregular; (*surface*) desigual; (*action, event*) anómalo; (*behaviour*) poco ortodoxo

irrelevant [ɪ'rɛləvənt] *adj* fuera de lugar, inoportuno

irreplaceable [ɪrɪ'pleɪsəbl] *adj* irremplazable

irrepressible [ɪrɪ'prɛsəbl] *adj* incontenible

irresistible [ɪrɪ'zɪstɪbl] *adj* irresistible

irresolute [ɪ'rɛzəluːt] *adj* indeciso

irrespective [ɪrɪ'spɛktɪv]: ~ **of** *prep* sin tener en cuenta, no importa

irresponsible [ɪrɪ'spɔnsɪbl] *adj* (*act*) irresponsable; (*person*) poco serio

irrigate ['ɪrɪgeɪt] *vt* regar; **irrigation** [-'geɪʃən] *n* riego

irritable ['ɪrɪtəbl] *adj* (*person*) de mal humor

irritate ['ɪrɪteɪt] *vt* fastidiar; (*MED*) picar; **irritating** *adj* fastidioso; **irritation** [-'teɪʃən] *n* fastidio; irritación; picazón *f*, picor *m*

IRS (*US*) *n abbr* = **Internal Revenue Service**

is [ɪz] *vb see* **be**

Islam ['ɪzlɑːm] *n* Islam *m*; ~**ic** [ɪz'læmɪk] *adj* islámico

island ['aɪlənd] *n* isla; ~**er** *n* isleño/a

isle [aɪl] *n* isla

isn't ['ɪznt] = **is not**

isolate ['aɪsəleɪt] *vt* aislar; ~**d** *adj* aislado; **isolation** [-'leɪʃən] *n* aislamiento

Israel ['ɪzreɪl] *n* Israel *m*; ~**i** [ɪz'reɪlɪ] *adj, n* israelí *m/f*

issue ['ɪsjuː] *n* (*problem, subject, most important part*) cuestión *f*; (*outcome*) resultado; (*of banknotes etc*) emisión *f*; (*of newspaper etc*) edición *f*; (*offspring*) sucesión *f*, descendencia ♦ *vt* (*rations, equipment*) distribuir, repartir; (*orders*) dar; (*certificate, passport*) expedir; (*decree*) promulgar; (*magazine*) publicar; (*cheques*) extender; (*banknotes, stamps*) emitir; **at ~** en cuestión; **to take ~ with sb (over)** estar en desacuerdo con uno (sobre); **to make an ~ of sth** hacer una cuestión de algo

Istanbul [ɪstæn'buːl] *n* Estambul *m*

isthmus ['ɪsməs] *n* istmo

KEYWORD

---

it [ɪt] *pron* **1** (*specific: subject: not generally translated*) él/ella; (: *direct object*) lo, la; (: *indirect object*) le; (*after prep*) él/ella; (*abstract concept*) ello; ~**'s on the table** está en la mesa; **I can't find ~** no lo (*or* la) encuentro; **give ~ to me** dámelo (*or* dámela); **I spoke to him about ~** le hablé del asunto; **what did you learn from ~?** ¿qué aprendiste de él (*or* ella)?; **did you go to ~?** (*party, concert etc*) ¿fuiste?

2 (*impersonal*): ~**'s raining** llueve, está lloviendo; ~**'s 6 o'clock/the 10th of August** son las 6/es el 10 de agosto; **how far is ~? — ~'s 10 miles/2 hours on the train** ¿a qué distancia está? — a 10 millas/2 horas en tren; **who is ~? — ~'s me** ¿quién es? — soy yo

---

Italian [ɪ'tæljən] *adj* italiano ♦ *n* italiano/a; (*LING*) italiano

italics [ɪ'tælɪks] *npl* cursiva

Italy ['ɪtəlɪ] *n* Italia

itch [ɪtʃ] *n* picazón *f* ♦ *vi* (*part of body*) picar; **to ~ to do sth** rabiar por hacer algo; ~**y** *adj*: **my hand is ~y** me pica la mano

it'd ['ɪtd] = **it would; it had**

item ['aɪtəm] *n* artículo; (*on agenda*) asunto (a tratar); (*also: news ~*) noticia; ~**ize** *vt* detallar

itinerant [ɪˈtɪnərənt] *adj* ambulante
itinerary [aɪˈtɪnərərɪ] *n* itinerario
it'll [ˈɪtl] = **it will; it shall**
its [ɪts] *adj* su; sus *pl*
it's [ɪts] = **it is; it has**
itself [ɪtˈsɛlf] *pron* (*reflexive*) sí mismo/a; (*emphatic*) él mismo/ella misma
ITV *n abbr* (*BRIT*: = *Independent Television*) cadena de televisión comercial independiente del Estado
I.U.D. *n abbr* (= *intra-uterine device*) DIU *m*
I've [aɪv] = **I have**
ivory [ˈaɪvərɪ] *n* marfil *m*; (*colour*) (color) de marfil; ~ **tower** *n* torre *f* de marfil
ivy [ˈaɪvɪ] *n* (*BOT*) hiedra

J j

jab [dʒæb] *vt*: **to ~ sth into sth** clavar algo en algo ♦ *n* (*inf*) (*MED*) pinchazo
jack [dʒæk] *n* (*AUT*) gato; (*CARDS*) sota; ~ **up** *vt* (*AUT*) levantar con gato
jackal [ˈdʒɔːl] *n* (*ZOOL*) chacal *m*
jacket [ˈdʒækɪt] *n* chaqueta, americana, saco (*AM*); (*of book*) sobrecubierta
jack-knife *vi* colear
jack plug *n* (*ELEC*) enchufe *m* de clavija
jackpot [ˈdʒækpɔt] *n* premio gordo
jaded [ˈdʒeɪdɪd] *adj* (*tired*) cansado; (*fed-up*) hastiado
jagged [ˈdʒægɪd] *adj* dentado
jail [dʒeɪl] *n* cárcel *f* ♦ *vt* encarcelar
jam [dʒæm] *n* mermelada; (*also: traffic ~*) embotellamiento; (*inf: difficulty*) apuro ♦ *vt* (*passage etc*) obstruir; (*mechanism, drawer etc*) atascar; (*RADIO*) interferir ♦ *vi* atascarse, trabarse; **to ~ sth into sth** meter algo a la fuerza en algo
Jamaica [dʒəˈmeɪkə] *n* Jamaica
jangle [ˈdʒæŋgl] *vi* entrechocar (ruidosamente)
janitor [ˈdʒænɪtə*] *n* (*caretaker*) portero, conserje *m*
January [ˈdʒænjuərɪ] *n* enero
Japan [dʒəˈpæn] *n* (el) Japón; **~ese** [dʒæpəˈniːz] *adj* japonés/esa ♦ *n inv* japonés/esa *m/f*; (*LING*) japonés *m*

jar [dʒɑː*] *n* tarro, bote *m* ♦ *vi* (*sound*) chirriar; (*colours*) desentonar
jargon [ˈdʒɑːgən] *n* jerga
jasmine [ˈdʒæzmɪn] *n* jazmín *m*
jaundice [ˈdʒɔːndɪs] *n* ictericia; **~d** *adj* desilusionado, poco entusiasta
jaunt [dʒɔːnt] *n* excursión *f*; **~y** *adj* alegre
javelin [ˈdʒævlɪn] *n* jabalina
jaw [dʒɔː] *n* mandíbula
jay [dʒeɪ] *n* (*ZOOL*) arrendajo
jaywalker [ˈdʒeɪwɔːkə*] *n* peatón/ona *m/f* imprudente
jazz [dʒæz] *n* jazz *m*; ~ **up** *vt* (*liven up*) animar, avivar
jealous [ˈdʒɛləs] *adj* celoso; (*envious*) envidioso; **~y** *n* celos *mpl*; envidia
jeans [dʒiːnz] *npl* vaqueros *mpl*, tejanos *mpl*
jeep [dʒiːp] *n* jeep *m*
jeer [dʒɪə*] *vi*: **to ~ (at)** (*mock*) mofarse (de)
jelly [ˈdʒɛlɪ] *n* (*jam*) jalea; (*dessert etc*) gelatina; **~fish** *n inv* medusa (*SP*), aguaviva (*AM*)
jeopardy [ˈdʒɛpədɪ] *n*: **to be in ~** estar en peligro
jerk [dʒɔːk] *n* (*jolt*) sacudida; (*wrench*) tirón *m*; (*inf*) imbécil *m/f* ♦ *vt* tirar bruscamente de ♦ *vi* (*vehicle*) traquetear
jerkin [ˈdʒɔːkɪn] *n* chaleco
jersey [ˈdʒɔːzɪ] *n* jersey *m*; (*fabric*) (tejido de) punto
jest [dʒɛst] *n* broma
Jesus [ˈdʒiːzəs] *n* Jesús *m*
jet [dʒɛt] *n* (*of gas, liquid*) chorro; (*AVIAT*) avión *m* a reacción; **~-black** *adj* negro como el azabache; ~ **engine** *n* motor *m* a reacción; ~ **lag** *n* desorientación *f* después de un largo vuelo
jettison [ˈdʒɛtɪsn] *vt* desechar
jetty [ˈdʒɛtɪ] *n* muelle *m*, embarcadero
Jew [dʒuː] *n* judío
jewel [ˈdʒuːəl] *n* joya; (*in watch*) rubí *m*; **~er** *n* joyero/a; **~er's (shop)** (*US* **~ry store**) *n* joyería; **~lery** (*US* **~ry**) *n* joyas *fpl*, alhajas *fpl*
Jewess [ˈdʒuːɪs] *n* judía
Jewish [ˈdʒuːɪʃ] *adj* judío

jibe [dʒaɪb] *n* mofa

jiffy ['dʒɪfɪ] (*inf*) *n*: **in a ~** en un santiamén

jig [dʒɪg] *n* giga

jigsaw ['dʒɪgsɔː] *n* (*also*: ~ **puzzle**) rompecabezas *m inv*, puzle *m*

jilt [dʒɪlt] *vt* dejar plantado a

jingle ['dʒɪŋgl] *n* musiquilla ♦ *vi* tintinear

jinx [dʒɪŋks] *n*: **there's a ~ on it** está gafado

jitters ['dʒɪtəz] (*inf*) *npl*: **to get the ~** ponerse nervioso

job [dʒɒb] *n* (*task*) tarea; (*post*) empleo; **it's not my ~** no me incumbe a mí; **it's a good ~ that ...** menos mal que ...; **just the ~!** ¡estupendo!; **~ centre** (*BRIT*) *n* oficina estatal de colocaciones; **~less** *adj* sin trabajo

jockey ['dʒɒkɪ] *n* jockey *m/f* ♦ *vi*: **to ~ for position** maniobrar para conseguir una posición

jocular ['dʒɒkjulə*] *adj* gracioso

jog [dʒɒg] *vt* empujar (ligeramente) ♦ *vi* (*run*) hacer footing; **to ~ sb's memory** refrescar la memoria a uno; **~ along** *vi* (*fig*) ir tirando; **~ging** *n* footing *m*

join [dʒɔɪn] *vt* (*things*) juntar, unir; (*club*) hacerse socio de, afiliarse a; (*POL: party*) afiliarse a; (*queue*) ponerse en; (*meet: people*) reunirse con ♦ *vi* (*roads*) juntarse; (*rivers*) confluir ♦ *n* juntura; **~ in** *vi* tomar parte, participar ♦ *vt fus* tomar parte *or* participar en; **~ up** *vi* reunirse; (*MIL*) alistarse

joiner ['dʒɔɪnə*] (*BRIT*) *n* carpintero/a; **~y** *n* carpintería

joint [dʒɔɪnt] *n* (*TECH*) junta, unión *f*; (*ANAT*) articulación *f*; (*BRIT: CULIN*) pieza de carne (para asar); (*inf: place*) tugurio; (: *of cannabis*) porro ♦ *adj* (*common*) común; (*combined*) combinado; **~ account** (*with bank etc*) cuenta común

joke [dʒəuk] *n* chiste *m*; (*also: practical* ~) broma ♦ *vi* bromear; **to play a ~ on** gastar una broma a; **~r** *n* (*CARDS*) comodín *m*

jolly ['dʒɒlɪ] *adj* (*merry*) alegre; (*enjoyable*) divertido ♦ *adv* (*BRIT: inf*) muy, terriblemente

jolt [dʒəult] *n* (*jerk*) sacudida; (*shock*) susto ♦ *vt* (*physically*) sacudir; (*emotionally*) asustar

jostle ['dʒɒsl] *vt* dar empellones a, codear

jot [dʒɒt] *n*: **not one** ~ ni jota, ni pizca; ~ **down** *vt* apuntar; **~ter** (*BRIT*) *n* bloc *m*

journal ['dʒɜːnl] *n* (*magazine*) revista; (*diary*) periódico, diario; **~ism** *n* periodismo; **~ist** *n* periodista *m/f*, reportero/a

journey ['dʒɜːnɪ] *n* viaje *m*; (*distance covered*) trayecto

jovial ['dʒəuvɪəl] *adj* risueño, jovial

joy [dʒɔɪ] *n* alegría; **~ful** *adj* alegre; **~ous** *adj* alegre; ~ **ride** *n* (*illegal*) paseo en coche robado; **~rider** *n* gamberro que roba un coche para dar una vuelta y luego abandonarlo; ~ **stick** *n* (*AVIAT*) palanca de mando; (*COMPUT*) palanca de control

J.P. *n abbr* = **Justice of the Peace**

Jr *abbr* = **junior**

jubilant ['dʒuːbɪlnt] *adj* jubiloso

jubilee ['dʒuːbɪliː] *n* aniversario

judge [dʒʌdʒ] *n* juez *m/f*; (*fig: expert*) perito ♦ *vt* juzgar; (*consider*) considerar; **judg(e)ment** *n* juicio

judiciary [dʒuː'dɪʃɪərɪ] *n* poder *m* judicial

judicious [dʒuː'dɪʃəs] *adj* juicioso

judo ['dʒuːdəu] *n* judo

jug [dʒʌg] *n* jarra

juggernaut ['dʒʌgənɔːt] (*BRIT*) *n* (*huge truck*) trailer *m*

juggle ['dʒʌgl] *vi* hacer juegos malabares; **~r** *n* malabarista *m/f*

Jugoslav ['juːgəuslɑːv] *etc* = **Yugoslav** *etc*

juice [dʒuːs] *n* zumo, jugo (*esp AM*); **juicy** *adj* jugoso

jukebox ['dʒuːkbɒks] *n* tocadiscos *m inv* tragaperras *m inv*

July [dʒuː'laɪ] *n* julio

jumble ['dʒʌmbl] *n* revoltijo ♦ *vt* (*also:* ~ *up*) revolver; ~ **sale** (*BRIT*) *n* venta de objetos usados con fines benéficos

jumbo (jet) ['dʒʌmbəu-] *n* jumbo

jump [dʒʌmp] *vi* saltar, dar saltos; (*with fear, surprise*) pegar un bote; (*increase*) aumentar ♦ *vt* saltar ♦ *n* salto; aumento; **to ~ the queue** (*BRIT*) colarse

jumper ['dʒʌmpə*] *n* (*BRIT: pullover*) suéter *m*, jersey *m*; (*US: dress*) mandil *m*; **~ cables** (*US*) *npl* = **jump leads**

jump leads (*BRIT*) *npl* cables *mpl* puente de batería

jumpy ['dʒʌmpɪ] (*inf*) *adj* nervioso

Jun. *abbr* = **junior**

junction ['dʒʌŋkʃən] *n* (*BRIT: of roads*) cruce *m*; (*RAIL*) empalme *m*

juncture ['dʒʌŋktʃə*] *n*: **at this ~** en este momento, en esta coyuntura

June [dʒuːn] *n* junio

jungle ['dʒʌŋgl] *n* selva, jungla

junior ['dʒuːnɪə*] *adj* (*in age*) menor, más joven; (*brother/sister etc*): **7 years her ~** siete años menor que ella; (*position*) subalterno ♦ *n* menor *m/f*, joven *m/f*; **~ school** (*BRIT*) *n* escuela primaria

junk [dʒʌŋk] *n* (*cheap goods*) baratijas *fpl*; (*rubbish*) basura; **~ bond** *n* (*COMM*) obligación *f* basura; **~ food** *n* alimentos preparados y envasados de escaso valor nutritivo

junkie ['dʒʌŋkɪ] (*inf*) *n* drogadicto/a, yonqui *m/f*

junk mail *n* propaganda de buzón

junk shop *n* tienda de objetos usados

Junr *abbr* = **junior**

jurisdiction [dʒuərɪs'dɪkʃən] *n* jurisdicción *f*

juror ['dʒuərə*] *n* jurado

jury ['dʒuərɪ] *n* jurado

just [dʒʌst] *adj* justo ♦ *adv* (*exactly*) exactamente; (*only*) sólo, solamente; **he's ~ done it/left** acaba de hacerlo/irse; **~ right** perfecto; **~ two o'clock** las dos en punto; **she's ~ as clever as you** (ella) es tan lista como tú; **~ as well that ...** menos mal que ...; **~ as he was leaving** en el momento en que se marchaba; **~ before/enough** justo antes/lo suficiente; **~ here** aquí mismo; **he ~ missed** ha fallado por poco; **~ listen to this** escucha esto un momento

justice ['dʒʌstɪs] *n* justicia; (*US: judge*) juez *m*; **to do ~ to** (*fig*) hacer justicia a; **J~ of the Peace** *n* juez *m* de paz

justify ['dʒʌstɪfaɪ] *vt* justificar; (*text*) alinear

jut [dʒʌt] *vi* (*also:* **~ out**) sobresalir

juvenile ['dʒuːvənaɪl] *adj* (*court*) de menores; (*humour, mentality*) infantil ♦ *n* menor *m* de edad

juxtapose ['dʒʌkstəpəuz] *vt* yuxtaponer

K k

K *abbr* (= *one thousand*) mil; (= *kilobyte*) kilobyte *m*, kilocteto

kaleidoscope [kə'laɪdəskəup] *n* calidoscopio

kangaroo [kæŋgə'ruː] *n* canguro

karate [kə'rɑːtɪ] *n* karate *m*

kebab [kə'bæb] *n* pincho moruno

keel [kiːl] *n* quilla; **on an even ~** (*fig*) en equilibrio

keen [kiːn] *adj* (*interest, desire*) grande, vivo; (*eye, intelligence*) agudo; (*competition*) reñido; (*edge*) afilado; (*eager*) entusiasta; **to be ~ to do** *or* **doing sth** tener muchas ganas de hacer algo; **to be ~ on sth/sb** interesarse por algo/uno

keep [kiːp] (*pt, pp* **kept**) *vt* (*preserve, store*) guardar; (*hold back*) quedarse con; (*maintain*) mantener; (*detain*) detener; (*shop*) ser propietario de; (*feed: family etc*) mantener; (*promise*) cumplir; (*chickens, bees etc*) criar; (*accounts*) llevar; (*diary*) escribir; (*prevent*): **to ~ sb from doing sth** impedir a uno hacer algo ♦ *vi* (*food*) conservarse; (*remain*) seguir, continuar ♦ *n* (*of castle*) torreón *m*; (*food etc*) comida, subsistencia; (*inf*): **for ~s** para siempre; **to ~ doing sth** seguir haciendo algo; **to ~ sb happy** tener a uno contento; **to ~ a place tidy** mantener un lugar limpio; **to ~ sth to o.s.** guardar algo para sí mismo; **to ~ sth (back) from sb** ocultar algo a uno; **to ~ time** (*clock*) mantener la hora exacta; **~ on** *vi*: **to ~ on doing** seguir or continuar haciendo; **to ~ on (about sth)** no parar de hablar (de algo); **~ out** *vi* (*stay out*) permanecer fuera; **"~ out"**

"prohibida la entrada"; ~ **up** *vt* mantener, conservar ♦ *vi* no retrasarse; **to ~ up with** (*pace*) ir al paso de; (*level*) mantenerse a la altura de; ~**er** *n* guardián/ana *m/f*; ~**-fit** *n* gimnasia (para mantenerse en forma); ~**ing** *n* (*care*) cuidado; **in ~ing with** de acuerdo con; ~**sake** *n* recuerdo

kennel ['kɛnl] *n* perrera; ~**s** *npl* residencia canina

Kenya ['kɛnjə] *n* Kenia

kept [kɛpt] *pt*, *pp of* **keep**

kerb [kəːb] (*BRIT*) *n* bordillo

kernel ['kəːnl] *n* (*nut*) almendra; (*fig*) meollo

ketchup ['kɛtʃəp] *n* salsa de tomate, catsup *m*

kettle ['kɛtl] *n* hervidor *m* de agua; ~**drum** *n* (*MUS*) timbal *m*

key [kiː] *n* llave *f*; (*MUS*) tono; (*of piano, typewriter*) tecla ♦ *adj* (*issue etc*) clave *inv* ♦ *vt* (*also:* ~ *in*) teclear; ~**board** *n* teclado; ~**ed up** *adj* (*person*) nervioso; ~**hole** *n* ojo (de la cerradura); ~**note** *n* (*MUS*) tónica; (*of speech*) punto principal *or* clave; ~**ring** *n* llavero

khaki ['kɑːkɪ] *n* caqui

kick [kɪk] *vt* dar una patada *or* un puntapié a; (*inf: habit*) quitarse de ♦ *vi* (*horse*) dar coces ♦ *n* patada; puntapié *m*; (*of animal*) coz *f*; (*thrill*): **he does it for ~s** lo hace por pura diversión; ~ **off** *vi* (*SPORT*) hacer el saque inicial

kid [kɪd] *n* (*inf: child*) chiquillo/a; (*animal*) cabrito; (*leather*) cabritilla ♦ *vi* (*inf*) bromear

kidnap ['kɪdnæp] *vt* secuestrar; ~**per** *n* secuestrador(a) *m/f*; ~**ping** *n* secuestro

kidney ['kɪdnɪ] *n* riñón *m*

kill [kɪl] *vt* matar; (*murder*) asesinar ♦ *n* matanza; **to ~ time** matar el tiempo; ~**er** *n* asesino/a; ~**ing** *n* (*one*) asesinato; (*several*) matanza; **to make a ~ing** (*fig*) hacer su agosto; ~**joy** (*BRIT*) *n* aguafiestas *m/f inv*

kiln [kɪln] *n* horno

kilo ['kiːləu] *n* kilo; ~**byte** *n* (*COMPUT*) kilobyte *m*, kilooicteto; ~**gram(me)** ['kɪləugræm] *n* kilo, kilogramo; ~**metre**

['kɪləmiːtə*] (*US* ~**meter**) *n* kilómetro; ~**watt** ['kɪləuwɔt] *n* kilovatio

kilt [kɪlt] *n* falda escocesa

kin [kɪn] *n see* **kith**; **next**

kind [kaɪnd] *adj* amable, atento ♦ *n* clase *f*, especie *f*; (*species*) género; **in ~** (*COMM*) en especie; **a ~ of** una especie de; **to be two of a ~** ser tal para cual

kindergarten ['kɪndəgɑːtn] *n* jardín *m* de la infancia

kind-hearted *adj* bondadoso, de buen corazón

kindle ['kɪndl] *vt* encender; (*arouse*) despertar

kindly ['kaɪndlɪ] *adj* bondadoso; cariñoso ♦ *adv* bondadosamente, amablemente; **will you ~ ...** sea usted tan amable de ...

kindness ['kaɪndnɪs] *n* (*quality*) bondad *f*, amabilidad *f*; (*act*) favor *m*

kindred ['kɪndrɪd] *n* familia ♦ *adj*: ~ **spirits** almas *fpl* gemelas

kinetic [kɪ'nɛtɪk] *adj* cinético

king [kɪŋ] *n* rey *m*; ~**dom** *n* reino; ~**fisher** *n* martín *m* pescador; ~**-size** *adj* de tamaño extra

kinky ['kɪŋkɪ] (*pej: person, behaviour*) extraño; (*: sexually*) perverso

kiosk ['kiːɔsk] *n* quiosco; (*BRIT: TEL*) cabina

kipper ['kɪpə*] *n* arenque *m* ahumado

kiss [kɪs] *n* beso ♦ *vt* besar; **to ~ (each other)** besarse; ~ **of life** *n* respiración *f* boca a boca

kit [kɪt] *n* (*equipment*) equipo; (*tools etc*) (caja de) herramientas *fpl*; (*assembly ~*) juego de armar

kitchen ['kɪtʃɪn] *n* cocina; ~ **sink** *n* fregadero

kite [kaɪt] *n* (*toy*) cometa

kith [kɪθ] *n*: ~ **and kin** parientes *mpl* y allegados

kitten ['kɪtn] *n* gatito/a

kitty ['kɪtɪ] *n* (*pool of money*) fondo común

kleptomaniac [klɛptəu'meɪnɪæk] *n* cleptómano/a

km *abbr* (= *kilometre*) km

knack [næk] *n*: **to have the ~ of doing sth** tener el don de hacer algo

knapsack ['næpsæk] *n* mochila
knead [niːd] *vt* amasar
knee [niː] *n* rodilla; **~cap** *n* rótula
kneel [niːl] (*pt, pp* **knelt**) *vi* (*also:* ~
down) arrodillarse
knell [nɛl] *n* toque *m* de difuntos
knelt [nɛlt] *pt, pp of* **kneel**
knew [njuː] *pt of* **know**
knickers ['nɪkəz] (*BRIT*) *npl* bragas *fpl*
knife [naɪf] (*pl* **knives**) *n* cuchillo ♦ *vt*
acuchillar
knight [naɪt] *n* caballero; (*CHESS*) caballo;
~hood (*BRIT*) *n* (*title*): **to receive a**
~hood recibir el título de *Sir*
knit [nɪt] *vt* tejer, tricotar ♦ *vi* hacer
punto, tricotar; (*bones*) soldarse; **to ~**
one's brows fruncir el ceño; **~ting** *n*
labor *f* de punto; **~ting machine** *n*
máquina de tricotar; **~ting needle** *n*
aguja de hacer punto; **~wear** *n* prendas
fpl de punto
knives [naɪvz] *npl of* **knife**
knob [nɔb] *n* (*of door*) tirador *m*; (*of*
stick) puño; (*on radio, TV*) botón *m*
knock [nɔk] *vt* (*strike*) golpear; (*bump*
into) chocar contra; (*inf*) criticar ♦ *vi* (*at*
door etc): **to ~ at/on** llamar a ♦ *n* golpe
m; (*on door*) llamada; **~ down** *vt*
atropellar; **~ off** (*inf*) *vi* (*finish*) salir del
trabajo ♦ *vt* (*from price*) descontar; (*inf:*
steal) birlar; **~ out** *vt* dejar sin sentido;
(*BOXING*) poner fuera de combate, dejar
K.O.; (*in competition*) eliminar; **~ over** *vt*
(*object*) tirar; (*person*) atropellar; **~er** *n*
(*on door*) aldabón *m*; **~out** *n* (*BOXING*)
K.O. *m*, knockout *m* ♦ *cpd* (*competition*
etc) eliminatorio
knot [nɔt] *n* nudo ♦ *vt* anudar; **~ty** *adj*
(*fig*) complicado
know [nəu] (*pt* **knew**, *pp* **known**) *vt*
(*facts*) saber; (*be acquainted with*)
conocer; (*recognize*) reconocer, conocer;
to ~ how to swim saber nadar; **to ~**
about *or* **of sb/sth** saber de uno/algo;
~-all *n* sabelotodo *m/f*; **~-how** *n*
conocimientos *mpl*; **~ing** *adj* (*look*) de
complicidad; **~ingly** *adv* (*purposely*)
adrede; (*smile, look*) con complicidad
knowledge ['nɔlɪdʒ] *n* conocimiento;

(*learning*) saber *m*, conocimientos *mpl*;
~able *adj* entendido
known [nəun] *pp of* **know**
knuckle ['nʌkl] *n* nudillo
K.O. *n abbr* = **knockout**
Koran [kɔ'rɑːn] *n* Corán *m*
Korea [kə'rɪə] *n* Corea
kosher ['kəuʃə*] *adj* autorizado por la
ley judía

L l

L (*BRIT*) *abbr* = **learner driver**
l. *abbr* (= *litre*) l
lab [læb] *n abbr* = **laboratory**
label ['leɪbl] *n* etiqueta ♦ *vt* poner
etiqueta a
labor *etc* ['leɪbə*] (*US*) = **labour**
laboratory [lə'bɔrətərɪ] *n* laboratorio
laborious [lə'bɔːrɪəs] *adj* penoso
labour ['leɪbə*] (*US* **labor**) *n* (*hard work*)
trabajo; (~ *force*) mano *f* de obra; (*MED*):
to be in ~ estar de parto ♦ *vi*: **to ~** (**at**
sth) trabajar (en algo) ♦ *vt*: **to ~ a point**
insistir en un punto; **L~, the L~ party**
(*BRIT*) el partido laborista, los laboristas
mpl; **~ed** *adj* (*breathing*) fatigoso; **~er** *n*
peón *m*; **farm ~er** peón *m*; (*day ~er*)
jornalero
labyrinth ['læbɪrɪnθ] *n* laberinto
lace [leɪs] *n* encaje *m*; (*of shoe etc*) cordón
m ♦ *vt* (*shoes: also:* ~ *up*) atarse (los
zapatos)
lack [læk] *n* (*absence*) falta ♦ *vt* faltarle a
uno, carecer de; **through** *or* **for ~ of** por
falta de; **to be ~ing** faltar, no haber; **to**
be ~ing in sth faltarle a uno algo
lacquer ['lækə*] *n* laca
lad [læd] *n* muchacho, chico
ladder ['lædə*] *n* escalera (de mano);
(*BRIT: in tights*) carrera
laden ['leɪdn] *adj*: ~ (**with**) cargado (de)
ladle ['leɪdl] *n* cucharón *m*
lady ['leɪdɪ] *n* señora; (*dignified, graceful*)
dama; **"ladies and gentlemen ..."**
"señoras y caballeros ..."; **young ~**
señorita; **the ladies' (room)** los
servicios de señoras; **~bird** (*US* **~bug**) *n*

mariquita; **~like** adj fino; **L~ship** n:
your L~ship su Señoría
lag [læg] n retraso ♦ vi (also: ~ **behind**)
retrasarse, quedarse atrás ♦ vt (pipes)
revestir
lager ['lɑ:gə*] n cerveza (rubia)
lagoon [lə'gu:n] n laguna
laid [leɪd] pt, pp of **lay**; ~ **back** (inf) adj
relajado; ~ **up** adj: **to be** ~ **up (with)**
tener que guardar cama (a causa de)
lain [leɪn] pp of **lie**
lair [leə*] n guarida
lake [leɪk] n lago
lamb [læm] n cordero; (meat) (carne f de)
cordero; ~ **chop** n chuleta de cordero;
lambswool n lana de cordero
lame [leɪm] adj cojo; (excuse) poco
convincente
lament [lə'mɛnt] n quejo ♦ vt lamentarse
de
laminated ['læmɪneɪtɪd] adj (metal)
laminado; (wood) contrachapado; (surface) plastificado
lamp [læmp] n lámpara
lampoon [læm'pu:n] vt satirizar
lamp: **~post** (BRIT) n (poste m de) farol
m; **~shade** n pantalla
lance [lɑ:ns] n lanza ♦ vt (MED) abrir con
lanceta
land [lænd] n tierra; (country) país m;
(piece of ~) terreno; (estate) tierras fpl,
finca ♦ vi (from ship) desembarcar;
(AVIAT) aterrizar; (fig: fall) caer, terminar
♦ vt (passengers, goods) desembarcar; **to**
~ **sb with sth** (inf) hacer cargar a uno
con algo; ~ **up** vi: **to** ~ **up in/at** ir a
parar a/en; **~ing** n aterrizaje m; (of
staircase) rellano; **~ing gear** n (AVIAT)
tren m de aterrizaje; **~ing strip** n pista
de aterrizaje; **~lady** n (of rented house,
pub etc) dueña; (of pub etc) patrón m;
~lord n propietario; (of pub etc) patrón
m; **~mark** n lugar m co-
nocido; **to be a ~mark** (fig) marcar un
hito histórico; **~owner** n terrateniente
m/f
landscape ['lænskeɪp] n paisaje m; ~
gardener n arquitecto de jardines
landslide ['lændslaɪd] n (GEO) corrimiento
de tierras; (fig: POL) victoria arrolladora

lane [leɪn] n (in country) camino; (AUT)
carril m; (in race) calle f
language ['læŋgwɪdʒ] n lenguaje m;
(national tongue) idioma m, lengua; **bad**
~ palabrotas fpl; ~ **laboratory** n
laboratorio de idiomas
languish ['læŋgwɪʃ] vi languidecer
lank [læŋk] adj (hair) lacio
lanky ['læŋkɪ] adj larguirucho
lantern ['læntn] n linterna, farol m
lap [læp] n (of track) vuelta; (of body)
regazo; **to sit on sb's** ~ sentarse en las
rodillas de uno ♦ vt (also: ~ up) beber a
lengüetadas ♦ vi (waves) chapotear; ~ **up**
vt (fig) tragarse
lapel [lə'pɛl] n solapa
Lapland ['læplænd] n Laponia
lapse [læps] n fallo; (moral) desliz m; (of
time) intervalo ♦ vi (expire) caducar;
(time) pasar, transcurrir; **to** ~ **into bad**
habits caer en malos hábitos
laptop (computer) ['læptɔp-] n
(ordenador m) portátil m
larceny ['lɑ:sənɪ] n latrocinio
larch [lɑ:tʃ] n alerce m
lard [lɑ:d] n manteca (de cerdo)
larder ['lɑ:də*] n despensa
large [lɑ:dʒ] adj grande; **at** ~ (free) en
libertad; (generally) en general; **~ly** adv
(mostly) en su mayor parte; (introducing
reason) en gran parte; **~-scale** adj (map)
en gran escala; (fig) importante
largesse [lɑ:'ʒɛs] n generosidad f
lark [lɑ:k] n (bird) alondra; (joke) broma;
~ **about** vi bromear, hacer el tonto
laryngitis [lærɪn'dʒaɪtɪs] n laringitis f
larynx ['lærɪŋks] n laringe f
laser ['leɪzə*] n láser m; ~ **printer** n
impresora (por) láser
lash [læʃ] n latigazo; (also: eye~) pestaña
♦ vt azotar; (tie): **to** ~ **to/together** atar
a/atar; ~ **out** vi: **to** ~ **out (at sb)** (hit)
arremeter (contra uno); **to** ~ **out**
against sb lanzar invectivas contra uno
lass [læs] n (BRIT) chica
lasso [læ'su:] n lazo
last [lɑ:st] adj último; (end: of series etc)
final ♦ adv (most recently) la última vez;
(finally) por último ♦ vi durar; (continue)

continuar, seguir; **~ night** anoche; **~ week** la semana pasada; **at ~** por fin; **~ but one** penúltimo; **~-ditch** adj (attempt) último, desesperado; **~ing** adj duradero; **~ly** adv por último, finalmente; **~-minute** adj de última hora

latch [lætʃ] n pestillo

late [leɪt] adj (far on: in time, process etc) al final de; (not on time) tarde, atrasado; (dead) fallecido ♦ adv tarde; (behind time, schedule) con retraso; **of ~** últimamente; **~ at night** a última hora de la noche; **in ~ May** hacia fines de mayo; **the ~ Mr X** el difunto Sr X; **~comer** n recién llegado/a; **~ly** adv últimamente

later ['leɪtə*] adj (date etc) posterior; (version etc) más reciente ♦ adv más tarde, después

lateral ['lætərl] adj lateral

latest ['leɪtɪst] adj último; **at the ~** a más tardar

lathe [leɪð] n torno

lather ['lɑ:ðə*] n espuma (de jabón) ♦ vt enjabonar

Latin ['lætɪn] n latín m ♦ adj latino; **~ America** n América latina; **~-American** adj, n latinoamericano/a

latitude ['lætɪtjuːd] n latitud f; (fig) libertad f

latrine [lə'triːn] n letrina

latter ['lætə*] adj último; (of two) segundo ♦ n: **the ~** el último, éste; **~ly** adv últimamente

lattice ['lætɪs] n enrejado

laudable ['lɔːdəbl] adj loable

laugh [lɑːf] n risa ♦ vi reír(se); **(to do sth) for a ~** (hacer algo) en broma; **~ at** vt fus reírse de; **~ off** vt tomar algo a risa; **~able** adj ridículo; **~ing stock** n: **the ~ing stock of** el hazmerreír de; **~ter** n risa

launch [lɔːntʃ] n lanzamiento; (boat) lancha ♦ vt (ship) botar; (rocket etc) lanzar; (fig) comenzar; **~ into** vt fus lanzarse a; **~(ing) pad** n plataforma de lanzamiento

launder ['lɔːndə*] vt lavar

Launderette [lɔːn'drɛt] (®: BRIT) n

lavandería (automática)

Laundromat ['lɔːndrəmæt] (®: US) n = **launderette**

laundry ['lɔːndrɪ] n (dirty) ropa sucia; (clean) colada; (room) lavadero

laureate ['lɔːrɪət] adj see **poet**

lavatory ['lævətərɪ] n wáter m

lavender ['lævəndə*] n lavanda

lavish ['lævɪʃ] adj (amount) abundante; (person): **~ with** pródigo en ♦ vt: **to ~ sth on sb** colmar a uno de algo

law [lɔː] n ley f; (SCOL) derecho; (a rule) regla; (professions connected with ~) jurisprudencia; **~-abiding** adj respetuoso de la ley; **~ and order** n orden m público; **~ court** n tribunal m (de justicia); **~ful** adj legítimo, lícito; **~less** adj (action) criminal

lawn [lɔːn] n césped m; **~mower** n cortacésped m; **~ tennis** n tenis m sobre hierba

law school (US) n (SCOL) facultad f de derecho

lawsuit ['lɔːsuːt] n pleito

lawyer ['lɔːjə*] n abogado/a; (for sales, wills etc) notario/a

lax [læks] adj laxo

laxative ['læksətɪv] n laxante m

lay [leɪ] (pt, pp laid) pt of **lie** ♦ adj laico; (not expert) lego ♦ vt (place) colocar; (eggs, table) poner; (cable) tender; (carpet) extender; **~ aside** or **by** vt dejar a un lado; **~ down** vt (pen etc) dejar; (rules etc) establecer; **to ~ down the law** (pej) imponer las normas; **~ off** vt (workers) despedir; **~ on** vt (meal, facilities) proveer; **~ out** vt (spread out) disponer, exponer; **~about** (inf) n vago/a; **~-by** n (BRIT: AUT) área de aparcamiento

layer ['leɪə*] n capa

layman ['leɪmən] n lego

layout ['leɪaʊt] n (design) plan m, trazado; (PRESS) composición f

laze [leɪz] vi (also: **~ about**) holgazanear

laziness ['leɪzɪnɪs] n pereza

lazy ['leɪzɪ] adj perezoso, vago; (movement) lento

lb. abbr = **pound** (weight)

lead¹ [liːd] (*pt, pp* **led**) *n* (*front position*) delantera; (*clue*) pista; (*ELEC*) cable *m*; (*for dog*) correa; (*THEATRE*) papel *m* principal ♦ *vt* (*walk etc in front of*) ir a la cabeza de; (*guide*): **to ~ sb somewhere** conducir a uno a algún sitio; (*be leader of*) dirigir; (*start, guide: activity*) protagonizar ♦ *vi* (*road, pipe etc*) conducir a; (*SPORT*) ir primero; **to be in the ~** (*SPORT*) llevar la delantera; (*fig*) ir a la cabeza; **to ~ the way** (*also fig*) llevar la delantera; **~ away** *vt* llevar; **~ back** *vt* (*person, route*) llevar de vuelta; **~ on** *vt* (*tease*) engañar; **~ to** *vt fus* producir, provocar; **~ up to** *vt fus* (*events*) conducir a; (*in conversation*) preparar el terreno para

lead² [lɛd] *n* (*metal*) plomo *m*; (*in pencil*) mina

leader ['liːdə*] *n* jefe/a *m/f*, líder *m*; (*SPORT*) líder *m*; **~ship** *n* dirección *f*; (*position*) mando; (*quality*) iniciativa

leading ['liːdɪŋ] *adj* (*main*) principal; (*first*) primero; (*front*) delantero; **~ lady** *n* (*THEATRE*) primera actriz *f*; **~ light** *n* (*person*) figura principal; **~ man** *n* (*THEATRE*) primer galán *m*

lead singer [liːd-] *n* cantante *m/f*

leaf [liːf] (*pl* **leaves**) *n* hoja ♦ *vi*: **to ~ through** hojear; **to turn over a new ~** reformarse

leaflet ['liːflɪt] *n* folleto

league [liːg] *n* sociedad *f*; (*FOOTBALL*) liga; **to be in ~ with** haberse confabulado con

leak [liːk] *n* (*of liquid, gas*) escape *m*, fuga; (*in pipe*) agujero; (*in roof*) gotera; (*in security*) filtración *f* ♦ *vi* (*shoes, ship*) hacer agua; (*pipe*) tener (un) escape; (*roof*) gotear; (*liquid, gas*) escaparse, fugarse; (*fig*) divulgarse ♦ *vt* (*fig*) filtrar

lean [liːn] (*pt, pp* **leaned** *or* **leant**) *adj* (*thin*) flaco; (*meat*) magro ♦ *vt*: **to ~ sth on sth** apoyar algo en algo ♦ *vi* (*slope*) inclinarse; **to ~ against** apoyarse contra; **to ~ on** apoyarse en; **~ back/forward** *vi* inclinarse hacia atrás/adelante; **~ out** *vi* asomarse; **~ over** *vi* inclinarse; **~ing** *n*: **~ing (towards)** inclinación *f* (hacia);

leant [lɛnt] *pt, pp of* **lean**

leap [liːp] (*pt, pp* **leaped** *or* **leapt**) *n* salto ♦ *vi* saltar; **~frog** *n* pídola; **leapt** [lɛpt] *pt, pp of* **leap**; **~ year** *n* año bisiesto

learn [ləːn] (*pt, pp* **learned** *or* **learnt**) *vt* aprender ♦ *vi* aprender; **to ~ about sth** enterarse de algo; **to ~ to do sth** aprender a hacer algo; **~ed** ['ləːnɪd] *adj* erudito; **~er** *n* (*BRIT: also:* **~er driver**) principiante *m/f*; **~ing** *n* el saber *m*, conocimientos *mpl*; **learnt** [ləːnt] *pt, pp of* **learn**

lease [liːs] *n* arriendo ♦ *vt* arrendar

leash [liːʃ] *n* correa

least [liːst] *adj*: **the ~** (*slightest*) el menor, el más pequeño; (*smallest amount of*) mínimo ♦ *adv* (*+ vb*) menos; (*+ adj*): **the ~ expensive** el/la menos costoso/a; **the ~ possible effort** el menor esfuerzo posible; **at ~** por lo menos, al menos; **you could at ~ have written** por lo menos podías haber escrito; **not in the ~** en absoluto

leather ['lɛðə*] *n* cuero

leave [liːv] (*pt, pp* **left**) *vt* dejar; (*go away from*) abandonar; (*place etc: permanently*) salir de ♦ *vi* irse; (*train etc*) salir ♦ *n* permiso; **to ~ sth to sb** (*money etc*) legar algo a uno; (*responsibility etc*) encargar a uno de algo; **to be left** quedar, sobrar; **there's some milk left over** sobra *or* queda algo de leche; **on ~** de permiso; **~ behind** *vt* (*on purpose*) dejar; (*accidentally*) dejarse; **~ out** *vt* omitir; **~ of absence** *n* permiso de ausentarse

leaves [liːvz] *npl of* **leaf**

Lebanon ['lɛbənən] *n*: **the ~** el Líbano

lecherous ['lɛtʃərəs] (*pej*) *adj* lascivo

lecture ['lɛktʃə*] *n* conferencia; (*SCOL*) clase *f* ♦ *vi* dar una clase ♦ *vt* (*scold*): **to ~ sb on** *or* **about sth** echar una reprimenda a uno por algo; **to give a ~ on** dar una conferencia sobre; **~r** *n* conferenciante *m/f*; (*BRIT: at university*) profesor(a) *m/f*

led [lɛd] *pt, pp of* **lead**

ledge [lɛdʒ] *n* repisa; (*of window*) alféizar *m*; (*of mountain*) saliente *m*

ledger ['lɛdʒə*] *n* libro mayor

leech [liːtʃ] *n* sanguijuela

leek [liːk] *n* puerro

leer [lɪə*] *vi*: **to ~ at sb** mirar de manera lasciva a uno

leeway ['liːweɪ] *n* (*fig*): **to have some ~** tener cierta libertad de acción

left [left] *pt, pp of* **leave** ♦ *adj* izquierdo; (*remaining*): **there are 2 ~** quedan dos ♦ *n* izquierda ♦ *adv* a la izquierda; **on** *or* **to the ~** a la izquierda; **the L~** (*POL*) la izquierda; **~-handed** *adj* zurdo; **the ~-hand side** n la izquierda; **~-luggage (office)** (*BRIT*) *n* consigna; **~-overs** *npl* sobras *fpl*; **~-wing** *adj* (*POL*) de izquierdas, izquierdista

leg [leg] *n* pierna; (*of animal, chair*) pata; (*trouser ~*) pernera; (*CULIN: of lamb*) pierna; (*of chicken*) pata; (*of journey*) etapa

legacy ['legəsɪ] *n* herencia

legal ['liːgl] *adj* (*permitted by law*) lícito; (*of law*) legal; **~ holiday** (*US*) *n* fiesta oficial; **~ize** *vt* legalizar; **~ly** *adv* legalmente; **~ tender** *n* moneda de curso legal

legend ['ledʒənd] *n* (*also fig: person*) leyenda

legislation [ledʒɪs'leɪʃən] *n* legislación *f*

legislature ['ledʒɪsleɪtʃə*] *n* cuerpo legislativo

legitimate [lɪ'dʒɪtɪmət] *adj* legítimo

leg-room *n* espacio para las piernas

leisure ['leʒə*] *n* ocio, tiempo libre; **at ~** con tranquilidad; **~ centre** *n* centro de recreo; **~ly** *adj* sin prisa; lento

lemon ['lemən] *n* limón *m*; **~ade** [-'neɪd] *n* (*fizzy*) gaseosa; **~ tea** *n* té *m* con limón

lend [lend] (*pt, pp* **lent**) *vt*: **to ~ sth to sb** prestar algo a alguien; **~ing library** *n* biblioteca de préstamo

length [leŋθ] *n* (*size*) largo, longitud *f*; (*distance*): **the ~ of** todo lo largo de; (*of swimming pool, cloth*) largo; (*of wood, string*) trozo; (*amount of time*) duración *f*; **at ~** (*at last*) por fin, finalmente; (*lengthily*) largamente; **~en** *vt* alargar ♦ *vi* alargarse; **~ways** *adv* a lo largo; **~y** *adj* largo, extenso

lenient ['liːnɪənt] *adj* indulgente

lens [lenz] *n* (*of spectacles*) lente *f*; (*of camera*) objetivo

lent [lent] *pt, pp of* **lend**

Lent [lent] *n* Cuaresma

lentil ['lentl] *n* lenteja

Leo ['liːəu] *n* Leo

leotard ['liːətɑːd] *n* mallas *fpl*

leprosy ['leprəsɪ] *n* lepra

lesbian ['lezbɪən] *n* lesbiana

less [les] *adj* (*in size, degree etc*) menor; (*in quality*) menos ♦ *pron, adv* menos ♦ *prep*: **~ tax/10% discount** menos impuestos/el 10 por ciento de descuento; **~ than half** menos de la mitad; **~ than ever** menos que nunca; **~ and ~** cada vez menos; **the ~ he works …** cuanto menos trabaja …

lessen ['lesn] *vi* disminuir, reducirse ♦ *vt* disminuir, reducir

lesser ['lesə*] *adj* menor; **to a ~ extent** en menor grado

lesson ['lesn] *n* clase *f*; (*warning*) lección *f*

lest [lest] *conj* para que

let [let] (*pt, pp* **let**) *vt* (*allow*) dejar, permitir; (*BRIT: lease*) alquilar; **to ~ sb do sth** dejar que uno haga algo; **to ~ sb know sth** comunicar algo a uno; **~'s go** ¡vamos!; **~ him come** que venga; **"to ~"** "se alquila"; **~ down** *vt* (*tyre*) desinflar; (*disappoint*) defraudar; **~ go** *vi, vt* soltar; **~ in** *vt* dejar entrar; (*visitor etc*) hacer pasar; **~ off** *vt* (*culprit*) dejar escapar; (*gun*) disparar; (*bomb*) accionar; (*firework*) hacer estallar; **~ on** (*inf*) *vt* divulgar; **~ out** *vt* dejar salir; (*sound*) soltar; **~ up** *vi* amainar, disminuir

lethal ['liːθl] *adj* (*weapon*) mortífero; (*poison, wound*) mortal

lethargic [lə'θɑːdʒɪk] *adj* letárgico

letter ['letə*] *n* (*of alphabet*) letra; (*correspondence*) carta; **~ bomb** *n* cartabomba; **~box** (*BRIT*) *n* buzón *m*; **~ing** *n* letras *fpl*

lettuce ['letɪs] *n* lechuga

let-up *n* disminución *f*

leukaemia [luː'kiːmɪə] (*US* **leukemia**) *n* leucemia

level ['levl] *adj* (*flat*) llano ♦ *adv*: **to**

draw ~ **with** llegar a la altura de ♦ *n*
nivel *m*; (*height*) altura ♦ *vt* nivelar;
allanar; (*destroy: building*) derribar;
(*: forest*) arrasar; **to be** ~ **with** estar a
nivel de; **"A"** ~**s** (*BRIT*) *npl* ≈ exámenes
mpl de bachillerato superior, B.U.P.;
"O" ~**s** (*BRIT*) *npl* ≈ exámenes *mpl* de
octavo de básica; **on the** ~ (*fig: honest*)
serio; ~ **off** *or* **out** *vi* (*prices etc*)
estabilizarse; ~ **crossing** (*BRIT*) *n* paso a
nivel; ~**-headed** *adj* sensato
lever ['liːvə*] *n* (*also fig*) palanca ♦ *vt*: **to**
~ **up** levantar con palanca; ~**age** *n*
(*using bar etc*) apalancamiento; (*fig:
influence*) influencia
levity ['levɪtɪ] *n* frivolidad *f*
levy ['levɪ] *n* impuesto ♦ *vt* exigir,
recaudar
lewd [luːd] *adj* lascivo; (*joke*) obsceno,
colorado (*AM*)
liability [laɪə'bɪlɪtɪ] *n* (*pej: person, thing*)
estorbo, lastre *m*; (*JUR: responsibility*)
responsabilidad *f*; **liabilities** *npl* (*COMM*)
pasivo
liable ['laɪəbl] *adj* (*subject*): ~ **to** sujeto a;
(*responsible*): ~ **for** responsable de;
(*likely*): ~ **to do** propenso a hacer
liaise [lɪ'eɪz] *vi*: **to** ~ **with** enlazar con;
liaison [liː'eɪzɔn] *n* (*coordination*) enlace
m; (*affair*) relaciones *fpl* amorosas
liar ['laɪə*] *n* mentiroso/a
libel ['laɪbl] *n* calumnia ♦ *vt* calumniar
liberal ['lɪbərəl] *adj* liberal; (*offer, amount
etc*) generoso
liberate ['lɪbəreɪt] *vt* (*people: from poverty
etc*) librar; (*prisoner*) libertar; (*country*)
liberar
liberty ['lɪbətɪ] *n* libertad *f*; (*criminal*): **to
be at** ~ estar en libertad; **to be at** ~ **to
do** estar libre para hacer; **to take the** ~
of doing sth tomarse la libertad de
hacer algo
Libra ['liːbrə] *n* Libra
librarian [laɪ'brɛərɪən] *n* bibliotecario/a
library ['laɪbrərɪ] *n* biblioteca
libretto [lɪ'brɛtəu] *n* libreto
Libya ['lɪbɪə] *n* Libia; ~**n** *adj*, *n* libio/a
m/f
lice [laɪs] *npl of* **louse**

licence ['laɪsəns] (*US* **license**) *n* licencia;
(*permit*) permiso; (*also: driving* ~, (*US*)
driver's ~) carnet *m* de conducir (*SP*),
permiso (*AM*)
license ['laɪsəns] *n* (*US*) = **licence** ♦ *vt*
autorizar, dar permiso a; ~**d** *adj* (*for
alcohol*) autorizado para vender bebidas
alcohólicas; (*car*) matriculado; ~ **plate**
(*US*) *n* placa (de matrícula)
lichen ['laɪkən] *n* liquen *m*
lick [lɪk] *vt* lamer; (*inf: defeat*) dar una
paliza a; **to** ~ **one's lips** relamerse
licorice ['lɪkərɪs] (*US*) *n* = **liquorice**
lid [lɪd] *n* (*of box, case*) tapa; (*of pan*)
tapadera
lido ['laɪdəu] *n* (*BRIT*) piscina
lie [laɪ] (*pt* **lay**, *pp* **lain**) *vi* (*rest*) estar
echado, estar acostado; (*of object: be
situated*) estar, encontrarse; (*tell lies: pt,
pp* **lied**) mentir ♦ *n* mentira; **to** ~ **low**
(*fig*) mantenerse a escondidas; ~ **about**
or **around** *vi* (*things*) estar tirado; (*BRIT:
people*) estar tumbado; ~**-down** (*BRIT*) *n*:
to have a ~**-down** echarse (una siesta);
~**-in** (*BRIT*) *n*: **to have a** ~**-in** quedarse en
la cama
lieu [luː]: **in** ~ **of** *prep* en lugar de
lieutenant [lɛf'tɛnənt, (*US*) luː'tɛnənt] *n*
(*MIL*) teniente *m*
life [laɪf] (*pl* **lives**) *n* vida; **to come to** ~
animarse; ~ **assurance** (*BRIT*) *n* seguro
de vida; ~**belt** (*BRIT*) *n* cinturón *m*
salvavidas; ~**boat** *n* lancha de socorro;
~**guard** *n* vigilante *m/f*, socorrista *m/f*;
~ **imprisonment** *n* cadena perpetua; ~
insurance *n* = ~ **assurance**; ~ **jacket** *n*
chaleco salvavidas; ~**less** *adj* sin vida;
(*dull*) soso; ~**like** *adj* (*model etc*) que
parece vivo; (*realistic*) realista; ~**line** *n*
(*fig*) cordón *m* umbilical; ~**long** *adj* de
toda la vida; ~ **preserver** (*US*) *n* cinturón
m/chaleco salvavidas; ~ **sentence** *n*
cadena perpetua; ~**size** *adj* de tamaño
natural; ~ **span** *n* vida; ~**style** *n* estilo
de vida; ~ **support system** *n* (*MED*)
sistema *m* de respiración asistida; ~**time**
n (*of person*) vida; (*of thing*) período de
vida
lift [lɪft] *vt* levantar; (*end: ban, rule*)

levantar, suprimir ♦ *vi* (*fog*) disiparse ♦ *n* (BRIT: *machine*) ascensor *m*; **to give sb a ~** (BRIT) llevar a uno en el coche; **~- off** *n* despegue *m*

light [laɪt] (*pt, pp* **lighted** *or* **lit**) *n* luz *f*; (*lamp*) luz *f*, lámpara; (AUT) faro; (*for cigarette etc*): **have you got a ~?** ¿tienes fuego? ♦ *vt* (*candle, cigarette, fire*) encender (SP), prender (AM); (*room*) alumbrar ♦ *adj* (*colour*) claro; (*not heavy, also fig*) ligero; (*room*) con mucha luz; (*gentle, graceful*) ágil; **~s** *npl* (*traffic ~s*) semáforos *mpl*; **to come to ~** salir a luz; **in the ~ of** (*new evidence etc*) a la luz de; **~ up** *vi* (*smoke*) encender un cigarrillo; (*face*) iluminarse ♦ *vt* (*illuminate*) iluminar, alumbrar; (*set fire to*) encender; **~ bulb** *n* bombilla (SP), foco (AM); **~en** *vt* (*make less heavy*) aligerar; **~er** *n* (*also: cigarette ~er*) encendedor *m*, mechero; **~-headed** *adj* (*dizzy*) mareado; (*excited*) exaltado; **~-hearted** *adj* (*person*) alegre; (*remark etc*) divertido; **~house** *n* faro; **~ing** *n* (*system*) alumbrado; **~ly** *adv* ligeramente; (*not seriously*) con poca seriedad; **to get off ~ly** ser castigado con poca severidad; **~ness** *n* (*in weight*) ligereza

lightning [ˈlaɪtnɪŋ] *n* relámpago, rayo; **~ conductor** (US = **rod**) *n* pararrayos *m inv*

light: ~ pen *n* lápiz *m* óptico; **~weight** *adj* (*suit*) ligero ♦ *n* (BOXING) peso ligero; **~ year** *n* año luz

like [laɪk] *vt* gustarle a uno ♦ *prep* como ♦ *adj* parecido, semejante ♦ *n*: **and the ~** y otros por el estilo; **his ~s and dislikes** sus gustos y aversiones; **I would ~, I'd ~** me gustaría; (*for purchase*) quisiera; **would you ~ a coffee?** ¿te apetece un café?; **I ~ swimming** me gusta nadar; **she ~s apples** le gustan las manzanas; **to be** *or* **look ~ sb/sth** parecerse a alguien/algo; **what does it look/taste/ sound ~?** ¿cómo es/a qué sabe/cómo suena?; **that's just ~ him** es muy de él, es característico de él; **do it ~ this** hazlo así; **it is nothing ~ ...** no tiene parecido alguno con ...; **~able** *adj* simpático, agradable

likelihood [ˈlaɪklɪhud] *n* probabilidad *f*

likely [ˈlaɪklɪ] *adj* probable; **he's ~ to leave** es probable que se vaya; **not ~!** ¡ni hablar!

likeness [ˈlaɪknɪs] *n* semejanza, parecido; **that's a good ~** se parece mucho

likewise [ˈlaɪkwaɪz] *adv* igualmente; **to do ~** hacer lo mismo

liking [ˈlaɪkɪŋ] *n* (*person*) cariño (a); (*thing*) afición (a); **to be to sb's ~** ser del gusto de uno

lilac [ˈlaɪlək] *n* (*tree*) lilo; (*flower*) lila

lily [ˈlɪlɪ] *n* lirio, azucena; **~ of the valley** *n* lirio de los valles

limb [lɪm] *n* miembro

limber [ˈlɪmbə*] **to ~ up** *vi* (SPORT) hacer ejercicios de calentamiento

limbo [ˈlɪmbəu] *n*: **to be in ~** (*fig*) quedar a la expectativa

lime [laɪm] *n* (*tree*) limero; (*fruit*) lima; (GEO) cal *f*

limelight [ˈlaɪmlaɪt] *n*: **to be in the ~** (*fig*) ser el centro de atención

limerick [ˈlɪmərɪk] *n especie de poema humorístico*

limestone [ˈlaɪmstəun] *n* piedra caliza

limit [ˈlɪmɪt] *n* límite *m* ♦ *vt* limitar; **limitation** *n* limitación *f*; (*weak point*) punto flaco; (*restriction*) restricción *f*; **~ed** *adj* limitado; **to be ~ed to** limitarse a; **~ed (liability) company** (BRIT) *n* sociedad *f* anónima

limousine [ˈlɪməziːn] *n* limusina

limp [lɪmp] *n*: **to have a ~** tener cojera ♦ *vi* cojear ♦ *adj* flojo; (*material*) fláccido

limpet [ˈlɪmpɪt] *n* lapa

line [laɪn] *n* línea; (*rope*) cuerda; (*for fishing*) sedal *m*; (*wire*) hilo; (*row, series*) fila, hilera; (*of writing*) renglón *m*, línea; (*of song*) verso; (*on face*) arruga; (RAIL) vía ♦ *vt* (*road etc*) llenar; (SEWING) forrar; **to ~ the streets** llenar las aceras; **in ~ with** alineado con; (*according to*) de acuerdo con; **~ up** *vi* hacer cola ♦ *vt* alinear; (*prepare*) preparar; organizar

linear [ˈlɪnɪə*] *adj* lineal

lined [laɪnd] *adj* (*face*) arrugado; (*paper*) rayado

linen ['lɪnɪn] *n* ropa blanca; (*cloth*) lino

liner ['laɪnə*] *n* vapor *m* de línea, transatlántico; (*for bin*) bolsa (de basura)

linesman ['laɪnzmən] *n* (*SPORT*) juez *m* de línea

line-up *n* (*US*: *queue*) cola; (*SPORT*) alineación *f*

linger ['lɪŋgə*] *vi* retrasarse, tardar en marcharse; (*smell, tradition*) persistir

lingerie ['lænʒəriː] *n* lencería

lingo ['lɪŋgəʊ] (*pl* ~es) (*inf*) *n* jerga

linguist ['lɪŋgwɪst] *n* lingüista *m/f*; ~ic [-'gwɪstɪk] *adj* lingüístico; ~ics *n* lingüística

lining ['laɪnɪŋ] *n* forro; (*ANAT*) (membrana) mucosa

link [lɪŋk] *n* (*of a chain*) eslabón *m*; (*relationship*) relación *f*, vínculo ♦ *vt* vincular, unir; (*associate*): **to ~ with** *or* **to** relacionar con; ~s *npl* (*GOLF*) campo de golf; ~ **up** *vt* acoplar ♦ *vi* unirse

lino ['laɪnəʊ] *n* = **linoleum**

linoleum [lɪ'nəʊlɪəm] *n* linóleo

lion ['laɪən] *n* león *m*; ~ess *n* leona

lip [lɪp] *n* labio

liposuction ['lɪpəʊsʌkʃən] *n* liposucción *f*

lip: ~read *vi* leer los labios; ~ salve *n* crema protectora para labios; ~ service *n*: **to pay ~ service to sth** (*pej*) prometer algo de boquilla; ~stick *n* lápiz *m* de labios, carmín *m*

liqueur [lɪ'kjʊə*] *n* licor *m*

liquid ['lɪkwɪd] *adj, n* líquido; ~ize [-aɪz] *vt* (*CULIN*) licuar; ~izer [-aɪzə*] *n* licuadora

liquor ['lɪkə*] *n* licor *m*, bebidas *fpl* alcohólicas

liquorice ['lɪkərɪs] (*BRIT*) *n* regaliz *m*

liquor store (*US*) *n* bodega, *tienda de vinos y bebidas alcohólicas*

Lisbon ['lɪzbən] *n* Lisboa

lisp [lɪsp] *n* ceceo ♦ *vi* cecear

list [lɪst] *n* lista ♦ *vt* (*mention*) enumerar; (*put on a list*) poner en una lista; ~ed building (*BRIT*) *n monumento declarado de interés histórico-artístico*

listen ['lɪsn] *vi* escuchar, oír; **to ~ to sb/ sth** escuchar a uno/algo; ~er *n* oyente *m/f*; (*RADIO*) radioyente *m/f*

listless ['lɪstlɪs] *adj* apático, indiferente

lit [lɪt] *pt, pp of* **light**

litany ['lɪtənɪ] *n* letanía

liter ['liːtə*] (*US*) *n* = **litre**

literacy ['lɪtərəsɪ] *n* capacidad *f* de leer y escribir

literal ['lɪtərl] *adj* literal

literary ['lɪtərərɪ] *adj* literario

literate ['lɪtərət] *adj* que sabe leer y escribir; (*educated*) culto

literature ['lɪtrɪtʃə*] *n* literatura; (*brochures etc*) folletos *mpl*

lithe [laɪð] *adj* ágil

litigation [lɪtɪ'geɪʃən] *n* litigio

litre ['liːtə*] (*US* **liter**) *n* litro

litter ['lɪtə*] *n* (*rubbish*) basura; (*young animals*) camada, cría; ~ **bin** (*BRIT*) *n* papelera; ~ed *adj*: ~ed with (*scattered*) lleno de

little ['lɪtl] *adj* (*small*) pequeño; (*not much*) poco ♦ *adv* poco; **a ~** un poco (de); ~ **house/bird** casita/pajarito; **a ~ bit** un poquito; ~ **by** ~ poco a poco; ~ **finger** *n* dedo meñique

live [*vi* lɪv, *adj* laɪv] *vi* vivir ♦ *adj* (*animal*) vivo; (*wire*) conectado; (*broadcast*) en directo; (*shell*) cargado; ~ **down** *vt* hacer olvidar; ~ **on** *vt fus* (*food, salary*) vivir de; ~ **together** *vi* vivir juntos; ~ **up to** *vt fus* (*fulfil*) cumplir con

livelihood ['laɪvlɪhʊd] *n* sustento

lively ['laɪvlɪ] *adj* vivo; (*interesting: place, book etc*) animado

liven up ['laɪvn-] *vt* animar ♦ *vi* animarse

liver ['lɪvə*] *n* hígado

lives [laɪvz] *npl of* **life**

livestock ['laɪvstɒk] *n* ganado

livid ['lɪvɪd] *adj* lívido; (*furious*) furioso

living ['lɪvɪŋ] *adj* (*alive*) vivo ♦ *n*: **to earn** *or* **make a ~** ganarse la vida; ~ **conditions** *npl* condiciones *fpl* de vida; ~ **room** *n* sala (de estar); ~ **standards** *npl* nivel *m* de vida; ~ **wage** *n* jornal *m* suficiente para vivir

lizard ['lɪzəd] *n* lagarto; (*small*) lagartija

load [ləʊd] *n* carga; (*weight*) peso ♦ *vt* (*COMPUT*) cargar; (*also*: ~ *up*): **to ~ (with)** cargar (con *or* de); **a ~ of rubbish** (*inf*) tonterías *fpl*; **a ~ of,** **~s of** (*fig*) (gran) cantidad de, montones de; **~ed** *adj* (*vehicle*): **to be ~ed with** estar cargado de; (*question*) intencionado; (*inf*: *rich*) forrado (de dinero)

loaf [ləuf] (*pl* **loaves**) *n* (barra de) pan *m*

loan [ləun] *n* préstamo ♦ *vt* prestar; **on ~** prestado

loath [ləuθ] *adj*: **to be ~ to do sth** estar poco dispuesto a hacer algo

loathe [ləuð] *vt* aborrecer; (*person*) odiar; **loathing** *n* aversión *f*; odio

loaves [ləuvz] *npl of* **loaf**

lobby [ˈlɔbɪ] *n* vestíbulo, sala de espera; (*POL*: *pressure group*) grupo de presión ♦ *vt* presionar

lobe [ləub] *n* lóbulo

lobster [ˈlɔbstə*] *n* langosta

local [ˈləukl] *adj* local ♦ *n* (*pub*) bar *m*; **the ~s** los vecinos, los del lugar; **~ anaesthetic** *n* (*MED*) anestesia local; **~ authority** *n* municipio, ayuntamiento (*SP*); **~ call** *n* (*TEL*) llamada local; **~ government** *n* gobierno municipal; **~ity** [-ˈkælɪtɪ] *n* localidad *f*; **~ly** [-kəlɪ] *adv* en la vecindad; por aquí

locate [ləuˈkeɪt] *vt* (*find*) localizar; (*situate*): **to be ~d in** estar situado en

location [ləuˈkeɪʃən] *n* situación *f*; **on ~** (*CINEMA*) en exteriores

loch [lɔx] *n* lago

lock [lɔk] *n* (*of door, box*) cerradura; (*of canal*) esclusa; (*of hair*) mechón *m* ♦ *vt* (*with key*) cerrar (con llave) ♦ *vi* (*door etc*) cerrarse (con llave); (*wheels*) trabarse; **~ in** *vt* encerrar; **~ out** *vt* (*person*) cerrar la puerta a; **~ up** *vt* (*criminal*) meter en la cárcel; (*mental patient*) encerrar; (*house*) cerrar (con llave) ♦ *vi* echar la llave

locker [ˈlɔkə*] *n* casillero

locket [ˈlɔkɪt] *n* medallón *m*

locksmith [ˈlɔksmɪθ] *n* cerrajero/a

lockup [ˈlɔkʌp] *n* (*jail, cell*) cárcel *f*

locomotive [ləukəˈməutɪv] *n* locomotora

locum [ˈləukəm] *n* (*MED*) (médico/a) interino/a

locust [ˈləukəst] *n* langosta

lodge [lɔdʒ] *n* casita (del guarda) ♦ *vi*

(*person*): **to ~ (with)** alojarse (en casa de); (*bullet, bone*) incrustarse ♦ *vt* (*complaint*) presentar; **~r** *n* huésped(a) *m/f*

lodgings [ˈlɔdʒɪŋz] *npl* alojamiento

loft [lɔft] *n* desván *m*

lofty [ˈlɔftɪ] *adj* (*noble*) sublime; (*haughty*) altanero

log [lɔg] *n* (*of wood*) leño, tronco; (*written account*) diario ♦ *vt* anotar

logbook [ˈlɔgbuk] *n* (*NAUT*) diario de a bordo; (*AVIAT*) libro de vuelo; (*of car*) documentación *f* (del coche (*SP*) *or* carro (*AM*))

loggerheads [ˈlɔgəhedz] *npl*: **to be at ~ (with)** estar en desacuerdo (con)

logic [ˈlɔdʒɪk] *n* lógica; **~al** *adj* lógico

logo [ˈləugəu] *n* logotipo

loin [lɔɪn] *n* (*CULIN*) lomo, solomillo

loiter [ˈlɔɪtə*] *vi* (*linger*) entretenerse

loll [lɔl] *vi* (*also*: **~ about**) repantigarse

lollipop [ˈlɔlɪpɔp] *n* chupa-chups *m inv* ®, pirulí *m*; **~ lady/man** (*BRIT*) *n persona encargada de ayudar a los niños a cruzar la calle*

London [ˈlʌndən] *n* Londres; **~er** *n* londinense *m/f*

lone [ləun] *adj* solitario

loneliness [ˈləunlɪnɪs] *n* soledad *f*, aislamiento

lonely [ˈləunlɪ] *adj* (*situation*) solitario; (*person*) solo; (*place*) aislado

long [lɔŋ] *adj* largo ♦ *adv* mucho tiempo, largamente ♦ *vi*: **to ~ for sth** anhelar algo; **so** *or* **as ~ as** mientras, con tal que; **don't be ~!** ¡no tardes!, ¡vuelve pronto!; **how ~ is the street?** ¿cuánto tiene la calle de largo?; **how ~ is the lesson?** ¿cuánto dura la clase?; **6 metres ~** que mide 6 metros, de 6 metros de largo; **6 months ~** que dura 6 meses, de 6 meses de duración; **all night ~** toda la noche; **he no ~er comes** ya no viene; **~ before** mucho antes; **before ~** (+*future*) dentro de poco; (+*past*) poco tiempo después; **at ~ last** al fin, por fin; **~-distance** *adj* (*race*) de larga distancia; (*call*) interurbano; **~-haired** *adj* de pelo largo; **~hand** *n* escritura sin abreviaturas; **~ing** *n* anhelo, ansia; *(nostalgia)* nostalgia ♦ *adj* anhelante

longitude ['lɒŋgɪtjuːd] *n* longitud *f*

long: **~ jump** *n* salto de longitud; **~-life** *adj (batteries)* de larga duración; *(milk)* uperizado; **~-lost** *adj* desaparecido hace mucho tiempo; **~-playing record** *n* elepé *m*, disco de larga duración; **~-range** *adj (plan)* de gran alcance; *(missile)* de largo alcance; **~-sighted** *(BRIT) adj* présbita; **~-standing** *adj* de mucho tiempo; **~-suffering** *adj* sufrido; **~-term** *adj* a largo plazo; **~ wave** *n* onda larga; **~-winded** *adj* prolijo

loo [luː] *(BRIT: inf) n* wáter *m*

look [luk] *vi* mirar; *(seem)* parecer; *(building etc)*: **to ~ south/on to the sea** dar al sur/al mar ♦ *n (gen)*: **to have a ~** mirar; *(glance)* mirada; *(appearance)* aire *m*, aspecto; **~s** *npl (good ~s)* belleza; **~ (here)!** *(expressing annoyance etc)* ¡oye!; **~!** *(expressing surprise)* ¡mira!; **~ after** *vt fus (care for)* cuidar a; *(deal with)* encargarse de; **~ at** *vt fus* mirar; *(read quickly)* echar un vistazo a; **~ back** *vi* mirar hacia atrás; **~ down on** *vt fus (fig)* despreciar, mirar con desprecio; **~ for** *vt fus* buscar; **~ forward to** *vt fus* esperar con ilusión; *(in letters)*: **we ~ forward to hearing from you** quedamos a la espera de sus gratas noticias; **~ into** *vt* investigar; **~ on** *vi* mirar (como espectador); **~ out** *vi (beware)*: **to ~ out (for)** tener cuidado (de); **~ out for** *vt fus (seek)* buscar; *(await)* esperar; **~ round** *vi* volver la cabeza; **~ through** *vt fus (examine)* examinar; **~ to** *vt fus (rely on)* contar con; **~ up** *vi* mirar hacia arriba; *(improve)* mejorar ♦ *vt (word)* buscar; **~ up to** *vt fus* admirar; **~-out** *n (tower etc)* puesto de observación; *(person)* vigía *m/f*; **to be on the ~-out for sth** estar al acecho de algo

loom [luːm] *vi*: **~ (up)** *(threaten)* surgir, amenazar; *(event: approach)* aproximarse

loony ['luːnɪ] *(inf) n, adj* loco/a *m/f*

loop [luːp] *n* lazo ♦ *vt*: **to ~ sth round sth** pasar algo alrededor de algo; **~hole**

n escapatoria

loose [luːs] *adj* suelto; *(clothes)* ancho; *(morals, discipline)* relajado; **to be on the ~** estar en libertad; **to be at a ~ end** *or* **at ~ ends** *(US)* no saber qué hacer; **~ change** *n* cambio; **~ chippings** *npl (on road)* gravilla suelta; **~ly** *adv* libremente, aproximadamente; **~n** *vt* aflojar

loot [luːt] *n* botín *m* ♦ *vt* saquear

lop off [lɒp-] *vt (branches)* podar

lop-sided *adj* torcido

lord [lɔːd] *n* señor *m*; **L~ Smith** Lord Smith; **the L~** el Señor; **my ~** *(to bishop)* Ilustrísima; *(to noble etc)* Señor; **good L~!** ¡Dios mío!; **the (House of) L~s** *(BRIT)* la Cámara de los Lores; **~ship** *n*: **your L~ship** su Señoría

lore [lɔː*] *n* tradiciones *fpl*

lorry ['lɒrɪ] *(BRIT) n* camión *m*; **~ driver** *n* camionero/a

lose [luːz] *(pt, pp lost) vt* perder ♦ *vi* perder, ser vencido; **to ~ (time)** *(clock)* atrasarse; **~r** *n* perdedor/a *m/f*

loss [lɒs] *n* pérdida; **heavy ~es** *(MIL)* grandes pérdidas; **to be at a ~** no saber qué hacer; **to make a ~** sufrir pérdidas

lost [lɒst] *pt, pp of* **lose** ♦ *adj* perdido; **~ property** *(US ~* **and found)** *n* objetos *mpl* perdidos

lot [lɒt] *n (group: of things)* grupo; *(at auctions)* lote *m*; **the ~** el todo, todos; **a ~** *(large number: of books etc)* muchos; *(a great deal)* mucho, bastante; **a ~ of, ~s of** mucho(s) *(pl)*; **I read a ~** leo bastante; **to draw ~s (for sth)** echar suertes (para decidir algo)

lotion ['ləʊʃən] *n* loción *f*

lottery ['lɒtərɪ] *n* lotería

loud [laud] *adj (voice, sound)* fuerte; *(laugh, shout)* estrepitoso; *(condemnation etc)* enérgico; *(gaudy)* chillón/ona ♦ *adv (speak etc)* fuerte; **out ~** en voz alta; **~hailer** *(BRIT) n* megáfono; **~ly** *adv (noisily)* fuerte; *(aloud)* en voz alta; **~speaker** *n* altavoz *m*

lounge [laundʒ] *n* salón *m*, sala (de estar); *(at airport etc)* sala; *(BRIT: also: ~-bar)* salón-bar *m* ♦ *vi (also: ~ about or around)* reposar, holgazanear; **~ suit**

(*BRIT*) *n* traje *m* de calle
louse [laus] (*pl* **lice**) *n* piojo
lousy ['lauzɪ] (*inf*) *adj* (*bad quality*) malísimo, asqueroso; (*ill*) fatal
lout [laut] *n* gamberro/a
lovable ['lʌvəbl] *adj* (*delightful*) amable, simpático
love [lʌv] *n* (*romantic, sexual*) amor *m*; (*kind, caring*) cariño ♦ *vt* amar, querer; (*thing, activity*) encantarle a uno; **"~ from Anne"** (*on letter*) "un abrazo (de) Anne"; **to ~ to do** encantarle a uno hacer; **to be/fall in ~ with** estar enamorado/enamorarse de; **to make ~** hacer el amor; **for the ~ of** por amor de; **"15 ~"** (*TENNIS*) "15 a cero"; **I ~ paella** me encanta la paella; **~ affair** *n* aventura sentimental; **~ letter** *n* carta de amor; **~ life** *n* vida sentimental
lovely ['lʌvlɪ] *adj* (*delightful*) encantador(a); (*beautiful*) precioso
lover ['lʌvə*] *n* amante *m/f*; (*person in love*) enamorado/a; (*amateur*): **a ~ of** un(a) aficionado/a *or* un(a) amante de
loving ['lʌvɪŋ] *adj* amoroso, cariñoso; (*action*) tierno
low [ləu] *adj, ad* bajo ♦ *n* (*METEOROLOGY*) área de baja presión; **to be ~ on** (*supplies etc*) andar mal de; **to feel ~** sentirse deprimido; **to turn (down) ~** bajar; **~-alcohol** *adj* de bajo contenido en alcohol; **~-cut** *adj* (*dress*) escotado
lower ['ləuə*] *adj* más bajo; (*less important*) menos importante ♦ *vt* bajar; (*reduce*) reducir ♦ *vr*: **to ~ o.s. to** (*fig*) rebajarse a
low: **~-fat** *adj* (*milk, yoghurt*) desnatado; (*diet*) bajo en calorías; **~lands** *npl* (*GEO*) tierras *fpl* bajas; **~ly** *adj* humilde, inferior
loyal ['lɔɪəl] *adj* leal; **~ty** *n* lealtad *f*
lozenge ['lɔzɪndʒ] *n* (*MED*) pastilla
L.P. *n abbr* (= *long-playing record*) elepé *m*
L-plates ['εl-] (*BRIT*) *npl* placas *fpl* de aprendiz de conductor
Ltd *abbr* (= *limited company*) S.A
lubricate ['lu:brɪkeɪt] *vt* lubricar, engrasar
lucid ['lu:sɪd] *adj* lúcido

luck [lʌk] *n* suerte *f*; **bad ~** mala suerte; **good ~!** ¡que tengas suerte!, ¡suerte!; **bad or hard or tough ~!** ¡qué pena!; **~ily** *adv* afortunadamente; **~y** *adj* afortunado; (*at cards etc*) con suerte; (*object*) que trae suerte
ludicrous ['lu:dɪkrəs] *adj* absurdo
lug [lʌg] *vt* (*drag*) arrastrar
luggage ['lʌgɪdʒ] *n* equipaje *m*; **~ rack** *n* (*on car*) baca, portaequipajes *m inv*
lukewarm ['lu:kwɔ:m] *adj* tibio
lull [lʌl] *n* tregua ♦ *vt*: **to ~ sb to sleep** arrullar a uno; **to ~ sb into a false sense of security** dar a alguien una falsa sensación de seguridad
lullaby ['lʌləbaɪ] *n* nana
lumbago [lʌm'beɪgəu] *n* lumbago
lumber ['lʌmbə*] *n* (*junk*) trastos *mpl* viejos; (*wood*) maderos *mpl*; ~ *with vt*: **to be ~ed with** tener que cargar con algo; **~jack** *n* maderero
luminous ['lu:mɪnəs] *adj* luminoso
lump [lʌmp] *n* terrón *m*; (*fragment*) trozo; (*swelling*) bulto ♦ *vt* (*also:* ~ **together**) juntar; **~ sum** *n* suma global; **~y** *adj* (*sauce*) lleno de grumos; (*mattress*) lleno de bultos
lunar ['lu:nə*] *adj* lunar
lunatic ['lu:nətɪk] *adj* loco
lunch [lʌntʃ] *n* almuerzo, comida ♦ *vi* almorzar
luncheon ['lʌntʃən] *n* almuerzo; ~ **meat** *n* tipo de fiambre; ~ **voucher** (*BRIT*) *n* vale *m* de comida
lunch time *n* hora de comer
lung [lʌŋ] *n* pulmón *m*
lunge [lʌndʒ] *vi* (*also:* ~ **forward**) abalanzarse; **to ~ at** arremeter contra
lurch [lə:tʃ] *vi* dar sacudidas ♦ *n* sacudida; **to leave sb in the ~** dejar a uno plantado
lure [luə*] *n* (*attraction*) atracción *f* ♦ *vt* tentar
lurid ['luərɪd] *adj* (*colour*) chillón/ona; (*account*) espeluznante
lurk [lə:k] *vi* (*person, animal*) estar al acecho; (*fig*) acechar
luscious ['lʌʃəs] *adj* (*attractive: person, thing*) precioso; (*food*) delicioso

lush [lʌʃ] *adj* exuberante

lust [lʌst] *n* lujuria; (*greed*) codicia; ~ **after** *or* **for** *vt fus* codiciar

lustre ['lʌstə*] (*US* **luster**) *n* lustre *m*, brillo

lusty ['lʌstɪ] *adj* robusto, fuerte

Luxembourg ['lʌksəmbə:g] *n* Luxemburgo

luxuriant [lʌg'zjuərɪənt] *adj* exuberante

luxurious [lʌg'zjuərɪəs] *adj* lujoso

luxury ['lʌkʃərɪ] *n* lujo ♦ *cpd* de lujo

lying ['laɪɪŋ] *n* mentiras *fpl* ♦ *adj* mentiroso

lyrical ['lɪrɪkl] *adj* lírico

lyrics ['lɪrɪks] *npl* (*of song*) letra

M m

m. *abbr* = **metre; mile; million**

M.A. *abbr* = **Master of Arts**

mac [mæk] (*BRIT*) *n* impermeable *m*

macaroni [mækə'rəunɪ] *n* macarrones *mpl*

machine [mə'ʃi:n] *n* máquina ♦ *vt* (*dress etc*) coser a máquina; (*TECH*) hacer a máquina; ~ **gun** *n* ametralladora; ~ **language** *n* (*COMPUT*) lenguaje *m* máquina; ~**ry** *n* maquinaria; (*fig*) mecanismo

macho ['mætʃəu] *adj* machista

mackerel ['mækrl] *n inv* caballa

mackintosh ['mækɪntɔʃ] (*BRIT*) *n* impermeable *m*

mad [mæd] *adj* loco; (*idea*) disparatado; (*angry*) furioso; (*keen*): **to be ~ about sth** volverle loco a uno algo

madam ['mædəm] *n* señora

madden ['mædn] *vt* volver loco

made [meɪd] *pt, pp of* **make**

Madeira [mə'dɪərə] *n* (*GEO*) Madera; (*wine*) vino de Madera

made-to-measure (*BRIT*) *adj* hecho a la medida

madly ['mædlɪ] *adv* locamente

madman ['mædmən] *n* loco

madness ['mædnɪs] *n* locura

Madrid [mə'drɪd] *n* Madrid

Mafia ['mæfɪə] *n* Mafia

magazine [mægə'zi:n] *n* revista; (*RADIO,* *TV*) programa *m* magazina

maggot ['mægət] *n* gusano

magic ['mædʒɪk] *n* magia ♦ *adj* mágico; ~**ian** [mə'dʒɪʃən] *n* mago/a; (*conjurer*) prestidigitador(a) *m/f*

magistrate ['mædʒɪstreɪt] *n* juez *m/f* (municipal)

magnet ['mægnɪt] *n* imán *m*; ~**ic** [-'netɪk] *adj* magnético; (*personality*) atrayente; ~**ic tape** *n* cinta magnética

magnificent [mæg'nɪfɪsənt] *adj* magnífico

magnify ['mægnɪfaɪ] *vt* (*object*) ampliar; (*sound*) aumentar; ~**ing glass** *n* lupa

magpie ['mægpaɪ] *n* urraca

mahogany [mə'hɔgənɪ] *n* caoba

maid [meɪd] *n* criada; **old ~** (*pej*) solterona

maiden ['meɪdn] *n* doncella ♦ *adj* (*aunt etc*) solterona; (*speech, voyage*) inaugural; ~ **name** *n* nombre *m* de soltera

mail [meɪl] *n* correo; (*letters*) cartas *fpl* ♦ *vt* echar al correo; ~**box** (*US*) *n* buzón *m*; ~**ing list** *n* lista de direcciones; ~**-order** *n* pedido postal

maim [meɪm] *vt* mutilar, lisiar

main [meɪn] *adj* principal, mayor ♦ *n* (*pipe*) cañería maestra; (*US*) red *f* eléctrica; **the ~s** *npl* (*BRIT*: *ELEC*) la red eléctrica; **in the ~** = en general; ~**frame** *n* (*COMPUT*) ordenador *m* central; ~**land** *n* tierra firme; ~**ly** *adv* principalmente; ~ **road** *n* carretera; ~**stay** *n* (*fig*) pilar *m*; ~**stream** *n* corriente *f* principal

maintain [meɪn'teɪn] *vt* mantener; **maintenance** ['meɪntənəns] *n* mantenimiento; (*LAW*) manutención *f*

maize [meɪz] (*BRIT*) *n* maíz *m* (*SP*), choclo (*AM*)

majestic [mə'dʒestɪk] *adj* majestuoso

majesty ['mædʒɪstɪ] *n* majestad *f*; (*title*): **Your M~** Su Majestad

major ['meɪdʒə*] *n* (*MIL*) comandante *m* ♦ *adj* principal; (*MUS*) mayor

Majorca [mə'jɔ:kə] *n* Mallorca

majority [mə'dʒɔrɪtɪ] *n* mayoría

make [meɪk] (*pt, pp* **made**) *vt* hacer; (*manufacture*) fabricar; (*mistake*) cometer; (*speech*) pronunciar; (*cause to be*): **to ~ sb sad** poner triste a alguien;

(*force*): **to ~ sb do sth** obligar a alguien a hacer algo; (*earn*) ganar; (*equal*): **2 and 2 ~ 4** 2 y 2 son 4 ♦ *n* marca; **to ~ the bed** hacer la cama; **to ~ a fool of sb** poner a alguien en ridículo; **to ~ a profit/loss** obtener ganancias/sufrir pérdidas; **to ~ it** (*arrive*) llegar; (*achieve sth*) tener éxito; **what time do you ~ it?** ¿qué hora tienes?; **to ~ do with** contentarse con; **~ for** *vt fus* (*place*) dirigirse a; **~ out** *vt* (*decipher*) descifrar; (*understand*) entender; (*see*) distinguir; (*cheque*) extender; **~ up** *vt* (*invent*) inventar; (*prepare*) hacer; (*constitute*) constituir ♦ *vi* reconciliarse; (*with cosmetics*) maquillarse; **~ up for** *vt fus* compensar; **~-believe** *n* ficción *f*, invención *f*; **~r** *n* fabricante *m/f*; (*of film, programme*) autor(a) *m/f*; **~shift** *adj* improvisado; **~-up** *n* maquillaje *m*; **~-up remover** *n* desmaquillador *m*

making ['meɪkɪŋ] *n* (*fig*): **in the ~** en vías de formación; **to have the ~s of** (*person*) tener madera de

malaise [mæ'leɪz] *n* malestar *m*

Malaysia [mə'leɪzɪə] *n* Malasia, Malaysia

male [meɪl] *n* (*BIOL*) macho ♦ *adj* (*sex, attitude*) masculino; (*child etc*) varón

malfunction [mæl'fʌŋkʃən] *n* mal funcionamiento

malice ['mælɪs] *n* malicia; **malicious** [mə'lɪʃəs] *adj* malicioso; rencoroso

malign [mə'laɪn] *vt* difamar, calumniar

malignant [mə'lɪɡnənt] *adj* (*MED*) maligno

mall [mɔːl] (*US*) *n* (*also: shopping ~*) centro comercial

mallet ['mælɪt] *n* mazo

malnutrition [mælnjuː'trɪʃən] *n* desnutrición *f*

malpractice [mæl'præktɪs] *n* negligencia profesional

malt [mɔːlt] *n* malta; (*whisky*) whisky *m* de malta

Malta ['mɔːltə] *n* Malta; **Maltese** [-'tiːz] *adj, n inv* maltés/esa *m/f*

mammal ['mæml] *n* mamífero

mammoth ['mæməθ] *n* mamut *m* ♦ *adj* gigantesco

man [mæn] (*pl* **men**) *n* hombre *m*;

(*~kind*) el hombre ♦ *vt* (*NAUT*) tripular; (*MIL*) guarnecer; (*operate: machine*) manejar; **an old ~** un viejo; **~ and wife** marido y mujer

manage ['mænɪdʒ] *vi* arreglárselas, ir tirando ♦ *vt* (*be in charge of*) dirigir; (*control: person*) manejar; (*: ship*) gobernar; **~able** *adj* manejable; **~ment** *n* dirección *f*; **~r** *n* director(a) *m/f*; (*of pop star*) mánayer *m/f*; (*SPORT*) entrenador(a) *m/f*; **~ress** *n* directora; entrenadora; **~rial** [-ə'dʒɪərɪəl] *adj* directivo; **managing director** *n* director(a) *m/f* general

mandarin ['mændərɪn] *n* (*also: ~ orange*) mandarina; (*person*) mandarín *m*

mandate ['mændeɪt] *n* mandato

mandatory ['mændətərɪ] *adj* obligatorio

mane [meɪn] *n* (*of horse*) crin *f*; (*of lion*) melena

maneuver [mə'nuːvə*] (*US*) = **manoeuvre**

manfully ['mænfəlɪ] *adv* valientemente

mangle ['mæŋɡl] *vt* mutilar, destrozar

mangy ['meɪndʒɪ] *adj* (*animal*) sarnoso

manhandle ['mænhændl] *vt* maltratar

manhole ['mænhəul] *n* agujero de acceso

manhood ['mænhud] *n* edad *f* viril; (*state*) virilidad *f*

man-hour *n* hora-hombre *f*

manhunt ['mænhʌnt] *n* (*POLICE*) búsqueda y captura

mania ['meɪnɪə] *n* manía; **~c** ['meɪnɪæk] *n* maníaco/a; (*fig*) maniático

manic ['mænɪk] *adj* frenético; **~- depressive** *n* maníaco/a depresivo/a

manicure ['mænɪkjuə*] *n* manicura

manifest ['mænɪfest] *vt* manifestar, mostrar ♦ *adj* manifiesto

manifesto [mænɪ'festəu] *n* manifiesto

manipulate [mə'nɪpjuleɪt] *vt* manipular

mankind [mæn'kaɪnd] *n* humanidad *f*, género humano

manly ['mænlɪ] *adj* varonil

man-made *adj* artificial

manner ['mænə*] *n* manera, modo; (*behaviour*) conducta, manera de ser; (*type*): **all ~ of things** toda clase de cosas; **~s** *npl* (*behaviour*) modales *mpl*; **bad ~s** mala educación; **~ism** *n* peculiaridad *f* de lenguaje (*or* de comportamiento)

manoeuvre [mə'nu:və*] (*US* **maneuver**) *vt, vi* maniobrar ♦ *n* maniobra

manor ['mænə*] *n* (*also*: ~ **house**) casa solariega

manpower ['mænpauə*] *n* mano *f* de obra

mansion ['mænʃən] *n* palacio, casa grande

manslaughter ['mænslɔ:tə*] *n* homicidio no premeditado

mantelpiece ['mæntlpi:s] *n* repisa, chimenea

manual ['mænjuəl] *adj* manual ♦ *n* manual *m*

manufacture [mænju'fæktʃə*] *vt* fabricar ♦ *n* fabricación *f*; **~r** *n* fabricante *m/f*

manure [mə'njuə*] *n* estiércol *m*

manuscript ['mænjuskrɪpt] *n* manuscrito

many ['menɪ] *adj, pron* muchos/as; **a great ~** muchísimos, un buen número de; **~ a time** muchas veces

map [mæp] *n* mapa *m*; **to ~ out** *vt* proyectar

maple ['meɪpl] *n* arce *m* (*SP*), maple *m* (*AM*)

mar [mɑ:*] *vt* estropear

marathon ['mærəθən] *n* maratón *m*

marauder [mə'rɔ:də*] *n* merodeador(a) *m/f*

marble ['mɑ:bl] *n* mármol *m*; (*toy*) canica

March [mɑ:tʃ] *n* marzo

march [mɑ:tʃ] *vi* (*MIL*) marchar; (*demonstrators*) manifestarse ♦ *n* marcha; (*demonstration*) manifestación *f*

mare [meə*] *n* yegua

margarine [mɑ:dʒə'ri:n] *n* margarina

margin ['mɑ:dʒɪn] *n* margen *m*; (*COMM*: *profit* ~) margen *m* de beneficios; **~al** *adj* marginal; **~al seat** *n* (*POL*) escaño electoral difícil de asegurar

marigold ['mærɪɡəuld] *n* caléndula

marijuana [mærɪ'wɑ:nə] *n* marijuana

marina [mə'ri:nə] *n* puerto deportivo

marinate ['mærɪneɪt] *vt* marinar

marine [mə'ri:n] *adj* marino ♦ *n* soldado de marina

marital ['mærɪtl] *adj* matrimonial; ~

status estado civil

marjoram ['mɑ:dʒərəm] *n* mejorana

mark [mɑ:k] *n* marca, señal *f*; (*in snow, mud etc*) huella; (*stain*) mancha; (*BRIT: SCOL*) nota; (*currency*) marco ♦ *vt* marcar; manchar; (*damage: furniture*) rayar; (*indicate: place etc*) señalar; (*BRIT: SCOL*) calificar, corregir; **to ~ time** marcar el paso; (*fig*) marcar(se) un ritmo; **~ed** *adj* (*obvious*) marcado, acusado; **~er** *n* (*sign*) marcador *m*; (*bookmark*) señal *f* (de libro)

market ['mɑ:kɪt] *n* mercado ♦ *vt* (*COMM*) comercializar; **~ garden** (*BRIT*) *n* huerto; **~ing** *n* márketing *m*; **~place** *n* mercado; **~ research** *n* análisis *m inv* de mercados

marksman ['mɑ:ksmən] *n* tirador *m*

marmalade ['mɑ:məleɪd] *n* mermelada de naranja

maroon [mə'ru:n] *vt*: **to be ~ed** quedar aislado; (*fig*) quedar abandonado

marquee [mɑ:'ki:] *n* entoldado

marquess ['mɑ:kwɪs] *n* marqués *m*

marquis ['mɑ:kwɪs] *n* = **marquess**

marriage ['mærɪdʒ] *n* (*relationship, institution*) matrimonio; (*wedding*) boda; (*act*) casamiento; **~ bureau** *n* agencia matrimonial; **~ certificate** *n* partida de casamiento

married ['mærɪd] *adj* casado; (*life, love*) conyugal

marrow ['mærəu] *n* médula; (*vegetable*) calabacín *m*

marry ['mærɪ] *vt* casarse con; (*subj: father, priest etc*) casar ♦ *vi* (*also*: get married) casarse

Mars [mɑ:z] *n* Marte *m*

marsh [mɑ:ʃ] *n* pantano; (*salt* ~) marisma

marshal ['mɑ:ʃl] *n* (*MIL*) mariscal *m*; (*at sports meeting etc*) oficial *m*; (*US: of police, fire department*) jefe/a *m/f* ♦ *vt* (*thoughts etc*) ordenar; (*soldiers*) formar

marshy ['mɑ:ʃɪ] *adj* pantanoso

martial ['mɑ:ʃl] *adj* marcial; **~ law** *n* ley *f* marcial

martyr ['mɑ:tə*] *n* mártir *m/f*; **~dom** *n* martirio

marvel ['mɑ:vl] *n* maravilla, prodigio

♦ *vi*: **to ~ (at)** maravillarse (de); **~lous** (*US* **~ous**) *adj* maravilloso

Marxist ['maːksɪst] *adj, n* marxista *m/f*

marzipan ['maːzɪpæn] *n* mazapán *m*

mascara [mæs'kaːrə] *n* rímel *m*

masculine ['mæskjulɪn] *adj* masculino

mash [mæʃ] *vt* machacar; **~ed potatoes** *npl* puré *m* de patatas (*SP*) *or* papas (*AM*)

mask [maːsk] *n* máscara ♦ *vt* (*cover*): **to ~ one's face** ocultarse la cara; (*hide: feelings*) esconder

masochist ['mæsəkɪst] *n* masoquista *m/f*

mason ['meɪsn] *n* (*also: stone~*) albañil *m*; (*also: free~*) masón *m*; **~ry** *n* (*in building*) mampostería

masquerade [mæskə'reɪd] *vi*: **to ~ as** disfrazarse de, hacerse pasar por

mass [mæs] *n* (*people*) muchedumbre *f*; (*of air, liquid etc*) masa; (*of detail, hair etc*) gran cantidad *f*; (*REL*) misa ♦ *cpd* masivo ♦ *vi* reunirse; concentrarse; **the ~es** *npl* las masas; **~es of** (*inf*) montones de

massacre ['mæsəkə*] *n* masacre *f*

massage ['mæsaːʒ] *n* masaje *m* ♦ *vt* dar masaje en

masseur [mæ'səː*] *n* masajista *m*

masseuse [mæ'səːz] *n* masajista *f*

massive ['mæsɪv] *adj* enorme; (*support, changes*) masivo

mass media *npl* medios *mpl* de comunicación

mass-production *n* fabricación *f* en serie

mast [maːst] *n* (*NAUT*) mástil *m*; (*RADIO etc*) torre *f*

master ['maːstə*] *n* (*of servant*) amo; (*of situation*) dueño, maestro; (*in primary school*) maestro; (*in secondary school*) profesor *m*; (*title for boys*): **M~ X** Señorito X ♦ *vt* dominar; **M~ of Arts/ Science** *n* licenciatura superior en Letras/Ciencias; **~ly** *adj* magistral; **~mind** *n* inteligencia superior ♦ *vt* dirigir, planear; **~piece** *n* obra maestra; **~y** *n* maestría

masturbate ['mæstəbeɪt] *vi* masturbarse

mat [mæt] *n* estera; (*also: door~*) felpudo; (*also: table ~*) salvamanteles *m inv*,

posavasos *m inv* ♦ *adj* = **matt**

match [mætʃ] *n* cerilla, fósforo; (*game*) partido; (*equal*) igual *m/f* ♦ *vt* (*go well with*) hacer juego con; (*equal*) igualar; (*correspond to*) corresponderse con; (*pair: also: ~ up*) casar con ♦ *vi* hacer juego; **to be a good ~** hacer juego; **~box** *n* caja de cerillas; **~ing** *adj* que hace juego

mate [meɪt] *n* (*work~*) colega *m/f*; (*inf: friend*) amigo/a; (*animal*) macho *m/* hembra *f*; (*in merchant navy*) segundo de a bordo ♦ *vi* acoplarse, aparearse ♦ *vt* aparear

material [mə'tɪərɪəl] *n* (*substance*) materia; (*information*) material *m*; (*cloth*) tela, tejido ♦ *adj* material; (*important*) esencial; **~s** *npl* materiales *mpl*; **~istic** [-'lɪstɪk] *adj* materialista; **~ize** *vi* materializarse

maternal [mə'təːnl] *adj* maternal

maternity [mə'təːnɪtɪ] *n* maternidad *f*; **~ dress** *n* vestido premamá

math [mæθ] (*US*) *n* = **mathematics**

mathematical [mæθə'mætɪkl] *adj* matemático

mathematician [mæθəmə'tɪʃən] *n* matemático/a

mathematics [mæθə'mætɪks] *n* matemáticas *fpl*

maths [mæθs] (*BRIT*) *n* = **mathematics**

matinée ['mætɪneɪ] *n* sesión *f* de tarde

matrices ['meɪtrɪsiːz] *npl of* **matrix**

matriculation [mətrɪkju'leɪʃən] *n* (formalización *f* de) matrícula

matrimony ['mætrɪmənɪ] *n* matrimonio

matrix ['meɪtrɪks] (*pl* **matrices**) *n* matriz *f*

matron ['meɪtrən] *n* enfermera *f* jefe; (*in school*) ama de llaves

mat(t) [mæt] *adj* mate

matted ['mætɪd] *adj* enmarañado

matter ['mætə*] *n* cuestión *f*, asunto; (*PHYSICS*) sustancia, materia; (*reading ~*) material *m*; (*MED: pus*) pus *m* ♦ *vi* importar; **~s** *npl* (*affairs*) asuntos *mpl*, temas *mpl*; **it doesn't ~** no importa; **what's the ~?** ¿qué pasa?; **no ~ what** pase lo que pase; **as a ~ of course** por rutina; **as a ~ of fact** de hecho; **~-of-fact**

adj prosaico, práctico

mattress ['mætrɪs] *n* colchón *m*

mature [mə'tjuə*] *adj* maduro ♦ *vi* madurar; **maturity** *n* madurez *f*

maul [mɔ:l] *vt* magullar

mauve [məuv] *adj* de color malva (SP) or guinda (AM)

maverick ['mævərɪk] *n* hombre/mujer *m/f* poco ortodoxo/a

maxim ['mæksɪm] *n* máxima

maximum ['mæksɪməm] (*pl* **maxima**) *adj* máximo ♦ *n* máximo

May [meɪ] *n* mayo

may [meɪ] (*conditional:* **might**) *vi* (*indicating possibility*): **he ~ come** puede que venga; (*be allowed to*): **~ I smoke?** ¿puedo fumar?; (*wishes*): **God bless you!** ¡que Dios le bendiga!; **you ~ as well go** bien puedes irte

maybe ['meɪbi:] *adv* quizá(s)

May Day *n* el primero de Mayo

mayhem ['meɪhəm] *n* caos *m* total

mayonnaise [meɪə'neɪz] *n* mayonesa

mayor [mɛə*] *n* alcalde *m*; **~ess** *n* alcaldesa

maze [meɪz] *n* laberinto

M.D. *abbr* = **Doctor of Medicine**

me [mi:] *pron* (*direct*) me; (*stressed, after pron*) mí; **can you hear ~?** ¿me oyes?; **he heard ME!** me oyó a mí; **it's ~** soy yo; **give them to ~** dámelos/las; **with/ without ~** conmigo/sin mí

meadow ['mɛdəu] *n* prado, pradera

meagre ['mi:gə*] (US **meager**) *adj* escaso, pobre

meal [mi:l] *n* comida; (*flour*) harina; **~time** *n* hora de comer

mean [mi:n] (*pt, pp* **meant**) *adj* (*with money*) tacaño; (*unkind*) mezquino, malo; (*shabby*) humilde; (*average*) medio ♦ *vt* (*signify*) querer decir, significar; (*refer to*) referirse a; (*intend*): **to ~ to do sth** pensar or pretender hacer algo ♦ *n* medio, término medio; **~s** *npl* (*way*) medio, manera; (*money*) recursos *mpl*, medios *mpl*; **by ~s of** mediante, por medio de; **by all ~s!** ¡naturalmente!, ¡claro que sí!; **do you ~ it?** ¿lo dices en serio?; **what do you ~?** ¿qué quiere

decir?; **to be meant for sb/sth** ser para uno/algo

meander [mɪ'ændə*] *vi* (*river*) serpentear

meaning ['mi:nɪŋ] *n* significado, sentido; (*purpose*) sentido, propósito; **~ful** *adj* significativo; **~less** *adj* sin sentido

meanness ['mi:nnɪs] *n* (*with money*) tacañería; (*unkindness*) maldad *f*, mezquindad *f*; (*shabbiness*) humildad *f*

meant [mɛnt] *pt, pp of* **mean**

meantime ['mi:ntaɪm] *adv* (*also: in the ~*) mientras tanto

meanwhile ['mi:nwaɪl] *adv* = **meantime**

measles ['mi:zlz] *n* sarampión *m*

measly ['mi:zlɪ] (*inf*) *adj* miserable

measure ['mɛʒə*] *vt, vi* medir ♦ *n* medida; (*ruler*) regla; **~d** *adj* (*tone, step*) comedido; **~ments** *npl* medidas *fpl*

meat [mi:t] *n* carne *f*; **cold ~** fiambre *m*; **~ball** *n* albóndiga; **~ pie** *n* pastel *m* de carne

Mecca ['mɛkə] *n* La Meca

mechanic [mɪ'kænɪk] *n* mecánico/a; **~s** *n* mecánica ♦ *npl* mecanismo; **~al** *adj* mecánico

mechanism ['mɛkənɪzəm] *n* mecanismo

medal ['mɛdl] *n* medalla; **~lion** [mɪ'dælɪən] *n* medallón *m*; **~list** (US **~ist**) *n* (*SPORT*) medallista *m/f*

meddle ['mɛdl] *vi:* **to ~ in** entrometerse en; **to ~ with sth** manosear algo

media ['mi:dɪə] *npl* medios *mpl* de comunicación ♦ *npl of* **medium**

mediaeval [mɛdɪ'i:vl] *adj* = **medieval**

mediate ['mi:dɪeɪt] *vi* mediar; **mediator** *n* intermediario/a, mediador(a) *m/f*

Medicaid ['mɛdɪkeɪd] (US) *n programa de ayuda médica para los pobres*

medical ['mɛdɪkl] *adj* médico ♦ *n* reconocimiento médico

Medicare ['mɛdɪkeə*] (US) *n programa de ayuda médica para los ancianos*

medication [mɛdɪ'keɪʃən] *n* medicación *f*

medicine ['mɛdsɪn] *n* medicina; (*drug*) medicamento

medieval [mɛdɪ'i:vl] *adj* medieval

mediocre [mi:dɪ'əukə*] *adj* mediocre

meditate ['mɛdɪteɪt] *vi* meditar

Mediterranean [mɛdɪtə'reɪnɪən] *adj*

mediterráneo; **the ~ (Sea)** el (Mar) Mediterráneo

medium ['miːdɪəm] (*pl* **media**) *adj* mediano, regular ♦ *n* (*means*) medio; (*pl* *mediums: person*) médium *m/f*; **~ wave** *n* onda media

medley ['mɛdlɪ] *n* mezcla; (*MUS*) popurrí *m*

meek [miːk] *adj* manso, sumiso

meet [miːt] (*pt, pp* **met**) *vt* encontrar; (*accidentally*) encontrarse con, tropezar con; (*by arrangement*) reunirse con; (*for the first time*) conocer; (*go and fetch*) ir a buscar; (*opponent*) enfrentarse con; (*obligations*) cumplir; (*encounter: problem*) hacer frente a; (*need*) satisfacer ♦ *vi* encontrarse; (*in session*) reunirse; (*join: objects*) unirse; (*for the first time*) conocerse; **~ with** *vt fus* (*difficulty*) tropezar con; **to ~ with success** tener éxito; **~ing** *n* encuentro; (*arranged*) cita, compromiso; (*business ~ing*) reunión *f*; (*POL*) mítin *m*

megabyte ['mɛɡəbaɪt] *n* (*COMPUT*) megabyte *m*, megaocteto

megaphone ['mɛɡəfəun] *n* megáfono

melancholy ['mɛlənkəlɪ] *n* melancolía ♦ *adj* melancólico

mellow ['mɛləu] *adj* (*wine*) añejo; (*sound, colour*) suave ♦ *vi* (*person*) ablandar

melody ['mɛlədɪ] *n* melodía

melon ['mɛlən] *n* melón *m*

melt [mɛlt] *vi* (*metal*) fundirse; (*snow*) derretirse ♦ *vt* fundir; **~down** *n* (*in nuclear reactor*) fusión *f* de un reactor (nuclear); **~ing pot** *n* (*fig*) crisol *m*

member ['mɛmbə*] *n* (*gen, ANAT*) miembro; (*of club*) socio/a; **M~ of Parliament** (*BRIT*) diputado/a; **M~ of the European Parliament** (*BRIT*) eurodiputado/a; **~ship** *n* (*members*) número de miembros; (*state*) filiación *f*; **~ship card** *n* carnet *m* de socio

memento [mə'mɛntəu] *n* recuerdo

memo ['mɛməu] *n* apunte *m*, nota

memoirs ['mɛmwɑːz] *npl* memorias *fpl*

memorandum [mɛmə'rændəm] (*pl* **memoranda**) *n* apunte *m*, nota; (*official note*) acta

memorial [mɪ'mɔːrɪəl] *n* monumento conmemorativo ♦ *adj* conmemorativo

memorize ['mɛməraɪz] *vt* aprender de memoria

memory ['mɛmərɪ] *n* (*also: COMPUT*) memoria; (*instance*) recuerdo; (*of dead person*): **in ~ of** a la memoria de

men [mɛn] *npl of* **man**

menace ['mɛnəs] *n* amenaza ♦ *vt* amenazar; **menacing** *adj* amenazador(a)

mend [mɛnd] *vt* reparar, arreglar; (*darn*) zurcir ♦ *vi* reponerse ♦ *n* arreglo, reparación *f*; zurcido ♦ *n*: **to be on the ~** ir mejorando; **to ~ one's ways** enmendarse; **~ing** *n* reparación *f*; (*clothes*) ropa por remendar

menial ['miːnɪəl] (*often pej*) *adj* bajo

meningitis [mɛnɪn'dʒaɪtɪs] *n* meningitis *f*

menopause ['mɛnəupɔːz] *n* menopausia

menstruation [mɛnstru'eɪʃən] *n* menstruación *f*

mental ['mɛntl] *adj* mental; **~ity** [-'tælɪtɪ] *n* mentalidad *f*

mention ['mɛnʃən] *n* mención *f* ♦ *vt* mencionar; (*speak of*) hablar de; **don't ~ it!** ¡de nada!

menu ['mɛnjuː] *n* (*set ~*) menú *m*; (*printed*) carta; (*COMPUT*) menú *m*

MEP *n abbr* = **Member of the European Parliament**

mercenary ['məːsɪnərɪ] *adj, n* mercenario/a *m/f*

merchandise ['məːtʃəndaɪz] *n* mercancías *fpl*

merchant ['məːtʃənt] *n* comerciante *m/f*; **~ bank** (*BRIT*) *n* banco comercial; **~ navy** (*US ~* **marine**) *n* marina mercante

merciful ['məːsɪful] *adj* compasivo; (*fortunate*) afortunado

merciless ['məːsɪlɪs] *adj* despiadado

mercury ['məːkjurɪ] *n* mercurio

mercy ['məːsɪ] *n* compasión *f*; (*REL*) misericordia; **at the ~ of** a la merced de

mere [mɪə*] *adj* simple, mero; **~ly** *adv* simplemente, sólo

merge [məːdʒ] *vt* (*join*) unir ♦ *vi* unirse; (*COMM*) fusionarse; (*colours etc*) fundirse; **~r** *n* (*COMM*) fusión *f*

meringue [mə'ræŋ] *n* merengue *m*

merit ['mɛrɪt] n mérito ♦ vt merecer
mermaid ['mə:meɪd] n sirena
merry ['mɛrɪ] adj alegre; **M~ Christmas!**
¡Felices Pascuas!; **~-go-round** n tiovivo
mesh [mɛʃ] n malla
mesmerize ['mɛzməraɪz] vt hipnotizar
mess [mɛs] n (muddle: of situation)
confusión f; (: of room) revoltijo; (dirt)
porquería; (MIL) comedor m; **~ about** or
around (inf) vi perder el tiempo; (pass
the time) entretenerse; **~ about** or
around with (inf) vt fus divertirse con;
~ up vt (spoil) estropear; (dirty) ensuciar
message ['mɛsɪdʒ] n recado, mensaje m
messenger ['mɛsɪndʒə*] n mensajero/a
Messrs abbr (on letters: = Messieurs)
Sres
messy ['mɛsɪ] adj (dirty) sucio; (untidy)
desordenado
met [mɛt] pt, pp of **meet**
metabolism [mɛ'tæbəlɪzəm] n metabolismo
metal ['mɛtl] n metal m; **~lic** [-'tælɪk] adj
metálico
metaphor ['mɛtəfə*] n metáfora
mete [mi:t]: **to ~ out** vt (punishment)
imponer
meteor ['mi:tɪə*] n meteoro; **~ite** [-aɪt] n
meteorito
meteorology [mi:tɪə'rɔlədʒɪ] n
meteorología
meter ['mi:tə*] n (instrument) contador
m; (US: unit) = **metre** ♦ vt (US: POST)
franquear
method ['mɛθəd] n método
Methodist ['mɛθədɪst] adj, n metodista
m/f
meths [mɛθs] (BRIT) n = **methylated
spirit**
methylated spirit ['mɛθɪleɪtɪd-] (BRIT) n
alcohol m metilado or desnaturalizado
metre ['mi:tə*] (US **meter**) n metro
metric ['mɛtrɪk] adj métrico
metropolis [mɪ'trɔpəlɪs] n metrópoli f
metropolitan [mɛtrə'pɔlɪtən] adj
metropolitano; **the M~ Police** (BRIT) la
policía londinense
mettle ['mɛtl] n: **to be on one's ~** estar
dispuesto a mostrar todo lo que uno vale

mew [mju:] vi (cat) maullar
mews [mju:z] n: **~ flat** (BRIT) piso
acondicionado en antiguos establos o
cocheras
Mexican ['mɛksɪkən] adj, n mejicano/a
m/f, mexicano/a m/f
Mexico ['mɛksɪkəu] n Méjico (SP), México
(AM); **~ City** n Ciudad f de Méjico or
México
miaow [mi:'au] vi maullar
mice [maɪs] npl of **mouse**
micro... [maɪkrəu] prefix micro...; **~chip** n
microplaqueta; **~(computer)** n
microordenador m; **~phone** n micrófono;
~processor n microprocesador m;
~scope n microscopio; **~wave** n (also:
~wave oven) horno microondas
mid [mɪd] adj: **in ~ May** a mediados de
mayo; **in ~ afternoon** a media tarde; **in
~ air** en el aire; **~day** n mediodía m
middle ['mɪdl] n centro; (half-way point)
medio; (waist) cintura ♦ adj de en
medio; (course, way) intermedio; **in the
~ of the night** en plena noche; **~-aged**
adj de mediana edad; **the M~ Ages** npl
la Edad Media; **~-class** adj de clase
media; **the ~ class(es)** n(pl) la clase
media; **M~ East** n Oriente m Medio;
~man n intermediario; **~ name** n
segundo nombre; **~-of-the-road** adj
moderado; **~weight** n (BOXING) peso
medio; **middling** adj mediano
midge [mɪdʒ] n mosquito
midget ['mɪdʒɪt] n enano/a
Midlands ['mɪdləndz] npl: **the ~** la región
central de Inglaterra
midnight ['mɪdnaɪt] n medianoche f
midriff ['mɪdrɪf] n diafragma m
midst [mɪdst] n: **in the ~ of** (crowd) en
medio de; (situation, action) en mitad de
midsummer [mɪd'sʌmə*] n: **in ~** en
pleno verano
midway [mɪd'weɪ] adj, adv: **~ (between)**
a medio camino (entre); **~ through** a la
mitad de
midweek [mɪd'wi:k] adv entre semana
midwife ['mɪdwaɪf] (pl **midwives**) n
comadrona, partera
midwinter [mɪd'wɪntə*] n: **in ~** en pleno

invierno

might [maɪt] *vb see* **may** ♦ *n* fuerza, poder *m*; **~y** *adj* fuerte, poderoso

migraine ['miːɡreɪn] *n* jaqueca

migrant ['maɪɡrənt] *n adj* (*bird*) migratorio; (*worker*) emigrante

migrate [maɪ'ɡreɪt] *vi* emigrar

mike [maɪk] *n abbr* (= *microphone*) micro

mild [maɪld] *adj* (*person*) apacible; (*climate*) templado; (*slight*) ligero; (*taste*) suave; (*illness*) leve

mildew ['mɪldjuː] *n* moho

mildly ['maɪldlɪ] *adv* ligeramente, suavemente; **to put it ~** para no decir más

mile [maɪl] *n* milla; **~age** *n* número de millas, ≈ kilometraje *m*; **~ometer** *n* ≈ cuentakilómetros *m inv*; **~stone** *n* mojón *m*

milieu ['miːljəː] *n* (medio) ambiente *m*

militant ['mɪlɪtnt] *adj, n* militante *m/f*

military ['mɪlɪtərɪ] *adj* militar

militate ['mɪlɪteɪt] *vi*: **to ~ against** ir en contra de, perjudicar

militia [mɪ'lɪʃə] *n* milicia

milk [mɪlk] *n* leche *f* ♦ *vt* (*cow*) ordeñar; (*fig*) chupar; **~ chocolate** *n* chocolate *m* con leche; **~man** *n* lechero; **~ shake** *n* batido, malteada (*AM*); **~y** *adj* lechoso; **M~y Way** *n* Vía Láctea

mill [mɪl] *n* (*windmill etc*) molino; (*coffee* ~) molinillo; (*factory*) fábrica ♦ *vt* moler ♦ *vi* (*also:* ~ *about*) arremolinarse

millennium [mɪ'lɛnɪəm] (*pl* **~s** *or* **millennia**) *n* milenio, milenario

miller ['mɪlə*] *n* molinero

milli... ['mɪlɪ] *prefix*: **~gram(me)** *n* miligramo; **~metre** (*US* **~meter**) *n* milímetro

millinery ['mɪlɪnrɪ] *n* sombrerería

million ['mɪljən] *n* millón *m*; **a ~ times** un millón de veces; **~aire** [-jə'nɛə*] *n* millonario/a

milometer [maɪ'lɒmɪtə*] (*BRIT*) *n* = **mileometer**

mime [maɪm] *n* mímica; (*actor*) mimo/a ♦ *vt* remedar ♦ *vi* actuar de mimo

mimic ['mɪmɪk] *n* imitador(a) *m/f* ♦ *adj* mímico ♦ *vt* remedar, imitar

min. *abbr* = **minimum; minute(s)**

minaret [mɪnə'rɛt] *n* alminar *m*

mince [mɪns] *vt* picar ♦ *vi* (*in walking*) andar con pasos menudos ♦ *n* (*BRIT: CULIN*) carne *f* picada; **~meat** *n* conserva de fruta picada; (*US: meat*) carne *f* picada; **~ pie** *n* empanadilla rellena de fruta picada; **~r** *n* picadora de carne

mind [maɪnd] *n* mente *f*; (*intellect*) intelecto; (*contrasted with matter*) espíritu *m* ♦ *vt* (*attend to, look after*) ocuparse de, cuidar; (*be careful of*) tener cuidado con; (*object to*): **I don't ~ the noise** no me molesta el ruido; **it is on my ~** me preocupa; **to bear sth in ~** tomar *or* tener algo en cuenta; **to make up one's ~** decidirse; **I don't ~** me es igual; **~ you, ...** te advierto que ...; **never ~!** ¡es igual!, ¡no importa!; (*don't worry*) ¡no te preocupes!; **"~ the step"** "cuidado con el escalón"; **~er** *n* guardaespaldas *m inv*; (*child* ~*er*) = niñera; **~ful** *adj*: **~ful of** consciente de; **~less** *adj* (*crime*) sin motivo; (*work*) de autómata

mine[1] [maɪn] *pron* el mío/la mía etc; **a friend of ~** un(a) amigo/a mío/mía ♦ *adj*: **this book is ~** este libro es mío

mine[2] [maɪn] *n* mina ♦ *vt* (*coal*) extraer; (*bomb: beach etc*) minar; **~field** *n* campo de minas; **miner** *n* minero/a

mineral ['mɪnərəl] *adj* mineral ♦ *n* mineral *m*; **~s** *npl* (*BRIT: soft drinks*) refrescos *mpl*; **~ water** *n* agua mineral

mingle ['mɪŋɡl] *vi*: **to ~ with** mezclarse con

miniature ['mɪnətʃə*] *adj* (en) miniatura ♦ *n* miniatura

minibus ['mɪnɪbʌs] *n* microbús *m*

minim ['mɪnɪm] *n* (*MUS*) blanca

minimal ['mɪnɪml] *adj* mínimo

minimize ['mɪnɪmaɪz] *vt* minimizar; (*play down*) empequeñecer

minimum ['mɪnɪməm] (*pl* **minima**) *n, adj* mínimo

mining ['maɪnɪŋ] *n* explotación *f* minera

miniskirt ['mɪnɪskəːt] *n* minifalda

minister ['mɪnɪstə*] *n* (*BRIT: POL*) ministro/a (*SP*), secretario/a (*AM*); (*REL*) pastor *m* ♦ *vi*: **to ~ to** atender a

ministry ['ministri] *n* (*BRIT: POL*) ministerio (*SP*), secretaria (*AM*); (*REL*) sacerdocio

mink [miŋk] *n* visón *m*

minnow ['minəu] *n* pececillo (*de agua dulce*)

minor ['mainə*] *adj* (*repairs, injuries*) leve; (*poet, planet*) menor; (*MUS*) menor ♦ *n* (*LAW*) menor *m* de edad

Minorca [mi'nɔːkə] *n* Menorca

minority [mai'nɔriti] *n* minoría

mint [mint] *n* (*plant*) menta, hierbabuena; (*sweet*) caramelo de menta ♦ *vt* (*coins*) acuñar; **the (Royal) M~, the (US) M~** la Casa de la Moneda; **in ~ condition** en perfecto estado

minus ['mainəs] *n* (*also*: ~ **sign**) signo de menos ♦ *prep* menos; **12 ~ 6 equals 6** 12 menos 6 son 6; **~ 24°C** menos 24 grados

minute [*n* 'minit, *adj* mai'njuːt] *n* minuto; (*fig*) momento; **~s** *npl* (*of meeting*) actas *fpl* ♦ *adj* diminuto; (*search*) minucioso; **at the last ~** a última hora

miracle ['mirəkl] *n* milagro

mirage ['mirɑːʒ] *n* espejismo

mirror ['mirə*] *n* espejo; (*in car*) retrovisor *m*

mirth [məːθ] *n* alegría

misadventure [misəd'ventʃə*] *n* desgracia

misapprehension [misæpri'henʃən] *n* equivocación *f*

misappropriate [misə'prəuprieit] *vt* malversar

misbehave [misbi'heiv] *vi* portarse mal

miscalculate [mis'kælkjuleit] *vt* calcular mal

miscarriage ['miskæridʒ] *n* (*MED*) aborto; **~ of justice** error *m* judicial

miscellaneous [misi'leiniəs] *adj* varios/as, diversos/as

mischief ['mistʃif] *n* travesuras *fpl*, diabluras *fpl*; (*maliciousness*) malicia; **mischievous** [-ʃivəs] *adj* travieso

misconception [miskən'sepʃən] *n* idea equivocada; equivocación *f*

misconduct [mis'kɔndʌkt] *n* mala conducta; **professional ~** falta profesional

misdemeanour [misdi'miːnə*] (*US* **misdemeanor**) *n* delito, ofensa

miser ['maizə*] *n* avaro/a

miserable ['mizərəbl] *adj* (*unhappy*) triste, desgraciado; (*unpleasant, contemptible*) miserable

miserly ['maizəli] *adj* avariento, tacaño

misery ['mizəri] *n* tristeza; (*wretchedness*) miseria, desdicha

misfire [mis'faiə*] *vi* fallar

misfit ['misfit] *n* inadaptado/a

misfortune [mis'fɔːtʃən] *n* desgracia

misgiving [mis'giviŋ] *n* (*apprehension*) presentimiento; **to have ~s about sth** tener dudas acerca de algo

misguided [mis'gaidid] *adj* equivocado

mishandle [mis'hændl] *vt* (*mismanage*) manejar mal

mishap ['mishæp] *n* desgracia, contratiempo

misinform [misin'fɔːm] *vt* informar mal

misinterpret [misin'təːprit] *vt* interpretar mal

misjudge [mis'dʒʌdʒ] *vt* juzgar mal

mislay [mis'lei] (*irreg*) *vt* extraviar, perder

mislead [mis'liːd] (*irreg*) *vt* llevar a conclusiones erróneas; **~ing** *adj* engañoso

mismanage [mis'mænidʒ] *vt* administrar mal

misnomer [mis'nəumə*] *n* término inapropiado *or* equivocado

misogynist [mi'sɔdʒinist] *n* misógino

misplace [mis'pleis] *vt* extraviar

misprint ['misprint] *n* errata, error *m* de imprenta

Miss [mis] *n* Señorita

miss [mis] *vt* (*train etc*) perder; (*fail to hit: target*) errar; (*regret the absence of*): **I ~ him** (yo) le echo de menos *or* a faltar; (*fail to see*): **you can't ~ it** no tiene pérdida ♦ *vi* fallar ♦ *n* (*shot*) tiro fallido *or* perdido; **~ out** (*BRIT*) *vt* omitir

misshapen [mis'ʃeipən] *adj* deforme

missile ['misail] *n* (*AVIAT*) mísil *m*; (*object thrown*) proyectil *m*

missing ['misiŋ] *adj* (*pupil*) ausente; (*thing*) perdido; (*MIL*): **~ in action**

desaparecido en combate

mission ['mɪʃən] n misión f; (*official representation*) delegación f; ~**ary** n misionero/a

misspent ['mɪs'spɛnt] adj: **his ~ youth** su juventud disipada

mist [mɪst] n (*light*) neblina; (*heavy*) niebla; (*at sea*) bruma ♦ vi (*eyes*: also: ~ *over*, ~ *up*) llenarse de lágrimas; (*BRIT*: *windows*: also: ~ *over*, ~ *up*) empañarse

mistake [mɪs'teɪk] (*vt*: *irreg*) n error m ♦ vt entender mal; **by ~** por equivocación; **to make a ~** equivocarse; **to ~ A for B** confundir A con B; **mistaken** pp of **mistake** ♦ adj equivocado; **to be mistaken** equivocarse, engañarse

mister ['mɪstə*] (*inf*) n señor m; see **Mr**

mistletoe ['mɪsltəu] n muérdago

mistook [mɪs'tuk] pt of **mistake**

mistress ['mɪstrɪs] n (*lover*) amante f; (*of house*) señora (de la casa); (*BRIT*: *in primary school*) maestra; (*in secondary school*) profesora; (*of situation*) dueña

mistrust [mɪs'trʌst] vt desconfiar de

misty ['mɪstɪ] adj (*day*) de niebla; (*glasses etc*) empañado

misunderstand [mɪsʌndə'stænd] (*irreg*) vt, vi entender mal; **~ing** n malentendido

misuse [n mɪs'juːs, vb mɪs'juːz] n mal uso; (*of power*) abuso; (*of funds*) malversación f ♦ vt abusar de; malversar

mitt(en) ['mɪt(n)] n manopla

mix [mɪks] vt mezclar; (*combine*) unir ♦ vi mezclarse; (*people*) llevarse bien ♦ n mezcla; **~ up** vt mezclar; (*confuse*) confundir; **~ed** adj mixto; (*feelings etc*) encontrado; **~-ed-up** adj (*confused*) confuso, revuelto; **~er** n (*for food*) licuadora; (*for drinks*) coctelera; (*person*): **he's a good ~er** tiene don de gentes; **~ture** n mezcla; (*also*: *cough ~ture*) jarabe m; **~-up** n confusión f

mm abbr (= *millimetre*) mm

moan [məun] n gemido ♦ vi gemir; (*inf*: *complain*): **to ~ (about)** quejarse (de)

moat [məut] n foso

mob [mɔb] n multitud f ♦ vt acosar

mobile ['məubaɪl] adj móvil ♦ n móvil m;

~ **home** n caravana; ~ **phone** n teléfono portátil

mock [mɔk] vt (*ridicule*) ridiculizar; (*laugh at*) burlarse de ♦ adj fingido; ~ **exam** *examen preparatorio antes de los exámenes oficiales*; ~**ery** n burla; ~**-up** n maqueta

mod [mɔd] adj see **convenience**

mode [məud] n modo

model ['mɔdl] n modelo; (*fashion ~, artist's ~*) modelo m/f ♦ adj modelo ♦ vt (*with clay etc*) modelar (*copy*): **to ~ o.s. on** tomar como modelo a ♦ vi ser modelo; **to ~ clothes** pasar modelos, ser modelo; ~ **railway** n ferrocarril m de juguete

modem ['məudəm] n modem m

moderate [adj 'mɔdərət, vb 'mɔdəreɪt] adj moderado/a ♦ vi moderarse, calmarse ♦ vt moderar

modern ['mɔdən] adj moderno; ~**ize** vt modernizar

modest ['mɔdɪst] adj modesto; (*small*) módico; ~**y** n modestia

modicum ['mɔdɪkəm] n: **a ~ of** un mínimo de

modify ['mɔdɪfaɪ] vt modificar

mogul ['məugəl] n (*fig*) magnate m

mohair ['məuhɛə*] n mohair m

moist [mɔɪst] adj húmedo; ~**en** ['mɔɪsn] vt humedecer; ~**ure** ['mɔɪstʃə*] n humedad f; ~**urizer** ['mɔɪstʃəraɪzə*] n crema hidratante

molar ['məulə*] n muela

mold [məuld] (*US*) n, vt = **mould**

mole [məul] n (*animal, spy*) topo; (*spot*) lunar m

molecule ['mɔlɪkjuːl] n molécula

molest [məu'lɛst] vt importunar; (*assault sexually*) abusar sexualmente de

mollycoddle ['mɔlɪkɔdl] vt mimar

molt [məult] (*US*) vi = **moult**

molten ['məultən] adj fundido; (*lava*) líquido

mom [mɔm] (*US*) n = **mum**

moment ['məumənt] n momento; **at the ~** de momento, por ahora; ~**ary** adj momentáneo; ~**ous** [-'mɛntəs] adj trascendental, importante

momentum [məʊˈmɛntəm] *n* momento; (*fig*) ímpetu *m*; **to gather** ~ cobrar velocidad; (*fig*) ganar fuerza

mommy [ˈmɒmɪ] (*US*) *n* = **mummy**

Monaco [ˈmɒnəkəʊ] *n* Mónaco

monarch [ˈmɒnək] *n* monarca *m/f*; **~y** *n* monarquía

monastery [ˈmɒnəstərɪ] *n* monasterio

Monday [ˈmʌndɪ] *n* lunes *m inv*

monetary [ˈmʌnɪtərɪ] *adj* monetario

money [ˈmʌnɪ] *n* dinero; (*currency*) moneda; **to make** ~ ganar dinero; ~ **order** *n* giro; **~-spinner** (*inf*) *n*: **to be a ~-spinner** dar mucho dinero

mongrel [ˈmʌŋgrəl] *n* (*dog*) perro mestizo

monitor [ˈmɒnɪtə*] *n* (*SCOL*) monitor *m*; (*also*: *television* ~) receptor *m* de control; (*of computer*) monitor *m* ♦ *vt* controlar

monk [mʌŋk] *n* monje *m*

monkey [ˈmʌŋkɪ] *n* mono; ~ **nut** (*BRIT*) *n* cacahuete *m* (*SP*), maní (*AM*); ~ **wrench** *n* llave *f* inglesa

mono [ˈmɒnəʊ] *adj* (*recording*) mono

monopoly [məˈnɒpəlɪ] *n* monopolio

monotone [ˈmɒnətəʊn] *n* voz *f* (*or* tono) monocorde

monotonous [məˈnɒtənəs] *adj* monótono

monsoon [mɒnˈsuːn] *n* monzón *m*

monster [ˈmɒnstə*] *n* monstruo

monstrosity [mɒnsˈtrɒsɪtɪ] *n* monstruosidad *f*

monstrous [ˈmɒnstrəs] *adj* (*huge*) enorme; (*atrocious, ugly*) monstruoso

month [mʌnθ] *n* mes *m*; **~ly** *adj* mensual ♦ *adv* mensualmente

monument [ˈmɒnjumənt] *n* monumento; **~al** [-ˈmɛntl] *adj* monumental

moo [muː] *vi* mugir

mood [muːd] *n* humor *m*; (*of crowd, group*) clima *m*; **to be in a good/bad** ~ estar de buen/mal humor; **~y** *adj* (*changeable*) de humor variable; (*sullen*) malhumorado

moon [muːn] *n* luna; **~light** *n* luz *f* de la luna; **~lighting** *n* pluriempleo; **~lit** *adj*: **a ~lit night** una noche de luna

Moor [mʊə*] *n* moro/a

moor [mʊə*] *n* páramo ♦ *vt* (*ship*) amarrar ♦ *vi* echar las amarras

Moorish [ˈmʊərɪʃ] *adj* moro; (*architecture*) árabe, morisco

moorland [ˈmʊələnd] *n* páramo, brezal *m*

moose [muːs] *n inv* alce *m*

mop [mɒp] *n* fregona; (*of hair*) greña, melena ♦ *vt* fregar; ~ **up** *vt* limpiar

mope [məʊp] *vi* estar *or* andar deprimido

moped [ˈməʊpɛd] *n* ciclomotor *m*

moral [ˈmɒrl] *adj* moral ♦ *n* moraleja; **~s** *npl* moralidad *f*, moral *f*

morale [mɒˈrɑːl] *n* moral *f*

morality [məˈrælɪtɪ] *n* moralidad *f*

morass [məˈræs] *n* pantano

morbid [ˈmɔːbɪd] *adj* (*interest*) morboso

KEYWORD
---

more [mɔː*] *adj* **1** (*greater in number etc*) más; ~ **people/work than before** más gente/trabajo que antes

2 (*additional*) más; **do you want (some)** ~ **tea?** ¿quieres más té?; **is there any** ~ **wine?** ¿queda vino?; **it'll take a few** ~ **weeks** tardará unas semanas más; **it's 2 kms** ~ **to the house** faltan 2 kms para la casa; ~ **time/letters than we expected** más tiempo del que/más cartas de las que esperábamos

♦ *pron* (*greater amount, additional amount*) más; ~ **than 10** más de 10; **it cost** ~ **than the other one/than we expected** costó más que el otro/más de lo que esperábamos; **is there any** ~**?** ¿hay más?; **many/much** ~ muchos(as)/mucho(a) más

♦ *adv* más; ~ **dangerous/easily (than)** más peligroso/fácilmente (than); ~ **and** ~ **expensive** cada vez más caro; ~ **or less** más o menos; ~ **than ever** más que nunca

moreover [mɔːˈrəʊvə*] *adv* además, por otra parte

morgue [mɔːg] *n* depósito de cadáveres

Mormon [ˈmɔːmən] *n* mormón/ona *m/f*

morning [ˈmɔːnɪŋ] *n* mañana; (*early* ~) madrugada ♦ *cpd* matutino, de la mañana; **in the** ~ por la mañana; **7 o'clock in the** ~ las 7 de la mañana; ~ **sickness** *n* náuseas *fpl* matutinas

Morocco [mə'rɔkəu] *n* Marruecos *m*

moron ['mɔ:rɔn] (*inf*) *n* imbécil *m/f*

morose [mə'rəus] *adj* hosco, malhumorado

morphine ['mɔ:fi:n] *n* morfina

Morse [mɔ:s] *n* (*also:* ~ **code**) (código) Morse

morsel ['mɔ:sl] *n* (*of food*) bocado

mortar ['mɔ:tə*] *n* argamasa; (*implement*) mortero

mortgage ['mɔ:gɪdʒ] *n* hipoteca ♦ *vt* hipotecar; ~ **company** (*US*) *n* ≈ banco hipotecario

mortify ['mɔ:tɪfaɪ] *vt* mortificar, humillar

mortuary ['mɔ:tjuərɪ] *n* depósito de cadáveres

Moscow ['mɔskəu] *n* Moscú

Moslem ['mɔzləm] *adj*, *n* = **Muslim**

mosque [mɔsk] *n* mezquita

mosquito [mɔs'ki:təu] (*pl* ~**es**) *n* mosquito (*SP*), zancudo (*AM*)

moss [mɔs] *n* musgo

most [məust] *adj* la mayor parte de, la mayoría de ♦ *pron* la mayor parte, la mayoría ♦ *adv* el más; (*very*) muy; **the ~** (*also:* +*adj*) el más; ~ **of them** la mayor parte de ellos; **I saw the ~** yo vi el que más; **at the (very) ~** a lo sumo, todo lo más; **to make the ~ of** aprovechar (al máximo); **a ~ interesting book** un libro interesantísimo

mostly ['məustlɪ] *adv* en su mayor parte, principalmente

MOT (*BRIT*) *n abbr* (= *Ministry of Transport*): **the ~** (*test*) *inspección (anual) obligatoria de coches y camiones*

motel [məu'tɛl] *n* motel *m*

moth [mɔθ] *n* mariposa nocturna; (*clothes* ~) polilla; ~**ball** *n* bola de naftalina

mother ['mʌðə*] *n* madre *f* ♦ *adj* materno ♦ *vt* (*care for*) cuidar (como una madre); ~**hood** *n* maternidad *f*; ~**-in-law** *n* suegra; ~**ly** *adj* maternal; ~**-of-pearl** *n* nácar *m*; ~**-to-be** *n* futura madre *f*; ~ **tongue** *n* lengua materna

motif [məu'ti:f] *n* motivo

motion ['məuʃən] *n* movimiento; (*gesture*) ademán *m*, señal *f*; (*at meeting*)

moción *f* ♦ *vt*, *vi*: **to ~ (to) sb to do sth** hacer señas a uno para que haga algo; ~**less** *adj* inmóvil; ~ **picture** *n* película

motivated ['məutɪveɪtɪd] *adj* motivado

motive ['məutɪv] *n* motivo

motley ['mɔtlɪ] *adj* variado

motor ['məutə*] *n* motor *m*; (*BRIT*: *inf*: *vehicle*) coche *m* (*SP*), carro (*AM*), automóvil *m* ♦ *adj* motor (*f*: *motora or motriz*); ~**bike** *n* moto *f*; ~**boat** *n* lancha motora; ~**car** (*BRIT*) *n* coche *m*, carro, automóvil *m*; ~**cycle** *n* motocicleta; ~**cycle racing** *n* motociclismo; ~**cyclist** *n* motociclista *m/f*; ~**ing** (*BRIT*) *n* automovilismo; ~**ist** *n* conductor(a) *m/f*, automovilista *m/f*; ~ **racing** (*BRIT*) *n* carreras *fpl* de coches, automovilismo; ~ **vehicle** *n* automóvil *m*; ~**way** (*BRIT*) *n* autopista

mottled ['mɔtld] *adj* abigarrado, multicolor

motto ['mɔtəu] (*pl* ~**es**) *n* lema *m*; (*watchword*) consigna

mould [məuld] (*US* **mold**) *n* molde *m*; (*mildew*) moho ♦ *vt* moldear; (*fig*) formar; ~**y** *adj* enmohecido

moult [məult] (*US* **molt**) *vi* mudar la piel (*or* las plumas)

mound [maund] *n* montón *m*, montículo

mount [maunt] *n* monte *m* ♦ *vt* montar, subir a; (*jewel*) engarzar; (*picture*) enmarcar; (*exhibition etc*) organizar ♦ *vi* (*increase*) aumentar; ~ **up** *vi* aumentar

mountain ['mauntɪn] *n* montaña ♦ *cpd* de montaña; ~ **bike** *n* bicicleta de montaña; ~**eer** [-'nɪə*] *n* montañero/a (*SP*), andinista *m/f* (*AM*); ~**eering** [-'nɪərɪŋ] *n* montañismo, andinismo; ~**ous** *adj* montañoso; ~ **rescue team** *n* equipo de rescate de montaña; ~**side** *n* ladera de la montaña

mourn [mɔ:n] *vt* llorar, lamentar ♦ *vi*: **to ~ for** llorar la muerte de; ~**er** *n* doliente *m/f*; dolorido/a; ~**ful** *adj* triste, lúgubre; ~**ing** *n* luto; **in** ~**ing** de luto

mouse [maus] (*pl* **mice**) *n* (*ZOOL, COMPUT*) ratón *m*; ~**trap** *n* ratonera

mousse [mu:s] *n* (*CULIN*) crema batida; (*for hair*) espuma (moldeadora)

moustache [məs'tɑːʃ] (*US* **mustache**) *n* bigote *m*

mousy ['maʊsɪ] *adj* (*hair*) pardusco

mouth [maʊθ, *pl* maʊðz] *n* boca; (*of river*) desembocadura; **~ful** *n* bocado; **~ organ** *n* armónica; (*spokesman*) portavoz *m/f*; **~wash** *n* enjuague *m*; **~-watering** *adj* apetitoso

movable ['muːvəbl] *adj* movible

move [muːv] *n* (*movement*) movimiento; (*in game*) jugada; (: *turn to play*) turno; (*change: of house*) mudanza; (: *of job*) cambio de trabajo ♦ *vt* mover; (*emotionally*) conmover; (*POL: resolution etc*) proponer ♦ *vi* moverse; (*traffic*) circular; (*also: ~ house*) trasladarse, mudarse; **to ~ sb to do sth** mover a uno a hacer algo; **to get a ~ on** darse prisa; **~ about** *or* **around** *vi* moverse; (*travel*) viajar; **~ along** *vi* avanzar, adelantarse; **~ away** *vi* alejarse; **~ back** *vi* retroceder; **~ forward** *vi* avanzar; **~ in** *vi* (*to a house*) instalarse; (*police, soldiers*) intervenir; **~ on** *vi* ponerse en camino; **~ out** *vi* (*of house*) mudarse; **~ over** *vi* apartarse, hacer sitio; **~ up** *vi* (*employee*) ser ascendido

moveable ['muːvəbl] *adj* = **movable**

movement ['muːvmənt] *n* movimiento

movie ['muːvɪ] *n* película; **to go to the ~s** ir al cine; **~ camera** *n* cámara cinematográfica

moving ['muːvɪŋ] *adj* (*emotional*) conmovedor(a); (*that moves*) móvil

mow [məʊ] (*pt* **mowed**, *pp* **mowed** *or* **mown**) *vt* (*grass, corn*) cortar, segar; **~ down** *vt* (*shoot*) acribillar; **~er** *n* (*also: lawn~er*) cortacéspedes *m inv*, segadora

MP *n abbr* = **Member of Parliament**

m.p.h. *abbr* = *miles per hour* (*60 m.p.h.* *= 96 k.p.h.*)

Mr ['mɪstə*] (*US* **Mr.**) *n*: **~ Smith** (el) Sr. Smith

Mrs ['mɪsɪz] (*US* **Mrs.**) *n*: **~ Smith** (la) Sra. Smith

Ms [mɪz] (*US* **Ms.**) *n* (= *Miss or Mrs*): **~ Smith** (la) Sr(t)a. Smith

M.Sc. *abbr* = **Master of Science**

much [mʌtʃ] *adj* mucho ♦ *adv* mucho; (*before pp*) muy ♦ *n or pron* mucho; **how ~ is it?** ¿cuánto es?, ¿cuánto cuesta?; **too ~** demasiado; **it's not ~** no es mucho; **as ~ as** tanto como; **however ~ he tries** por mucho que se esfuerce

muck [mʌk] *n* suciedad *f*; **~ about** *or* **around** (*inf*) *vi* perder el tiempo; (*enjoy o.s.*) entretenerse; **~ up** (*inf*) *vt* arruinar, estropear

mud [mʌd] *n* barro, lodo

muddle ['mʌdl] *n* desorden *m*, confusión *f*; (*mix-up*) embrollo, lío ♦ *vt* (*also: ~ up*) embrollar, confundir; **~ through** *vi* salir del paso

muddy ['mʌdɪ] *adj* fangoso, cubierto de lodo

mudguard ['mʌdgɑːd] *n* guardabarros *m inv*

muffin ['mʌfɪn] *n* panecillo dulce

muffle ['mʌfl] *vt* (*sound*) amortiguar; (*against cold*) embozar; **~d** *adj* (*noise etc*) amortiguado, apagado; **~r** (*US*) *n* (*AUT*) silenciador *m*

mug [mʌg] *n* taza grande (*sin platillo*); (*for beer*) jarra; (*inf: face*) jeta; (: *fool*) bobo ♦ *vt* (*assault*) asaltar; **~ging** *n* asalto

muggy ['mʌgɪ] *adj* bochornoso

mule [mjuːl] *n* mula

mull over [mʌl-] *vt* meditar sobre

multi... [mʌltɪ] *prefix* multi...

multi-level [mʌltɪ'levl] (*US*) *adj* = **multistorey**

multiple ['mʌltɪpl] *adj* múltiple ♦ *n* múltiplo; **~ sclerosis** *n* esclerosis *f* múltiple

multiplication [mʌltɪplɪ'keɪʃən] *n* multiplicación *f*

multiply ['mʌltɪplaɪ] *vt* multiplicar ♦ *vi* multiplicarse

multistorey [mʌltɪ'stɔːrɪ] (*BRIT*) *adj* de muchos pisos

multitude ['mʌltɪtjuːd] *n* multitud *f*

mum [mʌm] (*BRIT: inf*) *n* mamá ♦ *adj*: **to keep ~** mantener la boca cerrada

mumble ['mʌmbl] *vt*, *vi* hablar entre dientes, refunfuñar

mummy ['mʌmɪ] *n* (*BRIT: mother*) mamá;

(*embalmed*) momia

mumps [mʌmps] *n* paperas *fpl*

munch [mʌntʃ] *vt, vi* mascar

mundane [mʌn'deɪn] *adj* trivial

municipal [mjuː'nɪsɪpl] *adj* municipal

munitions [mjuː'nɪʃənz] *npl* munición *f*

murder ['mɜːdə*] *n* asesinato; (*in law*) homicidio ♦ *vt* asesinar, matar; **~er/ess** *n* asesino/a; **~ous** *adj* homicida

murky ['mɜːkɪ] *adj* (*water*) turbio; (*street, night*) lóbrego

murmur ['mɜːmə*] *n* murmullo ♦ *vt, vi* murmurar

muscle ['mʌsl] *n* músculo; (*fig: strength*) garra, fuerza; **~ in** *vi* entrometerse; **muscular** ['mʌskjulə*] *adj* muscular; (*person*) musculoso

muse [mjuːz] *vi* meditar ♦ *n* musa

museum [mjuː'zɪəm] *n* museo

mushroom ['mʌʃrum] *n* seta, hongo; (*CULIN*) champiñón *m* ♦ *vi* crecer de la noche a la mañana

music ['mjuːzɪk] *n* música; **~al** *adj* musical; (*sound*) melodioso; (*person*) con talento musical ♦ *n* (*show*) comedia musical; **~al instrument** *n* instrumento musical; **~ hall** *n* teatro de variedades; **~ian** [-'zɪʃən] *n* músico/a

musk [mʌsk] *n* almizcle *m*

Muslim ['mʌzlɪm] *adj, n* musulmán/ana *m/f*

muslin ['mʌzlɪn] *n* muselina

mussel ['mʌsl] *n* mejillón *m*

must [mʌst] *aux vb* (*obligation*): **I ~ do it** debo hacerlo, tengo que hacerlo; (*probability*): **he ~ be there by now** ya debe (de) estar allí ♦ *n*: **it's a ~** es imprescindible

mustache ['mʌstæʃ] (*US*) *n* = **moustache**

mustard ['mʌstəd] *n* mostaza

muster ['mʌstə*] *vt* juntar, reunir

mustn't ['mʌsnt] = **must not**

musty ['mʌstɪ] *adj* mohoso, que huele a humedad

mute [mjuːt] *adj, n* mudo/a *m/f*

muted ['mjuːtɪd] *adj* callado; (*colour*) apagado

mutilate ['mjuːtɪleɪt] *vt* (*person*) mutilar; (*thing*) destrozar

mutiny ['mjuːtɪnɪ] *n* motín *m* ♦ *vi* amotinarse

mutter ['mʌtə*] *vt, vi* murmurar

mutton ['mʌtn] *n* carne *f* de cordero

mutual ['mjuːtʃuəl] *adj* mutuo; (*interest*) común; **~ly** *adv* mutuamente

muzzle ['mʌzl] *n* hocico; (*for dog*) bozal *m*; (*of gun*) boca ♦ *vt* (*dog*) poner un bozal a

my [maɪ] *adj* mi(s); **~ house/brother/ sisters** mi casa/mi hermano/mis hermanas; **I've washed ~ hair/cut ~ finger** me he lavado el pelo/cortado un dedo; **is this ~ pen or yours?** ¿es este bolígrafo mío o tuyo?

myopic [maɪ'ɔpɪk] *adj* miope

myself [maɪ'self] *pron* (*reflexive*) me; (*emphatic*) yo mismo; (*after prep*) mí (mismo); *see also* **oneself**

mysterious [mɪs'tɪərɪəs] *adj* misterioso

mystery ['mɪstərɪ] *n* misterio

mystify ['mɪstɪfaɪ] *vt* (*perplex*) dejar perplejo

mystique [mɪs'tiːk] *n* misterio (profesional *etc*)

myth [mɪθ] *n* mito

N n

n/a *abbr* (= *not applicable*) no interesa

nag [næg] *vt* (*scold*) regañar; **~ging** *adj* (*doubt*) persistente; (*pain*) continuo

nail [neɪl] *n* (*human*) uña; (*metal*) clavo ♦ *vt* clavar; **to ~ sth to sth** clavar algo en algo; **to ~ sb down to doing sth** comprometer a uno a que haga algo; **~brush** *n* cepillo para las uñas; **~file** *n* lima para las uñas; **~ polish** *n* esmalte *m or* laca para las uñas; **~ polish remover** *n* quitaesmalte *m*; **~ scissors** *npl* tijeras *fpl* para las uñas; **~ varnish** (*BRIT*) *n* = **polish**

naïve [naɪ'iːv] *adj* ingenuo

naked ['neɪkɪd] *adj* (*nude*) desnudo; (*flame*) expuesto al aire

name [neɪm] *n* nombre *m*; (*surname*) apellido; (*reputation*) fama, renombre *m* ♦ *vt* (*child*) poner nombre a; (*criminal*) identificar; (*price, date etc*) fijar; **what's your ~?** ¿cómo se llama?; **by ~** de nombre; **in the ~ of** en nombre de; **to give one's ~ and address** dar sus señas; **~less** *adj* (*unknown*) desconocido; (*anonymous*) anónimo, sin nombre; **~ly** *adv* a saber; **~sake** *n* tocayo/a

nanny ['nænɪ] *n* niñera

nap [næp] *n* (*sleep*) sueñecito, siesta; **to be caught ~ping** estar desprevenido

nape [neɪp] *n*: **~ of the neck** nuca, cogote *m*

napkin ['næpkɪn] *n* (*also: table ~*) servilleta

nappy ['næpɪ] (*BRIT*) *n* pañal *m*; **~ rash** *n* prurito

narcotic [nɑːˈkɒtɪk] *adj, n* narcótico

narrow ['nærəʊ] *adj* estrecho, angosto; (*fig: majority etc*) corto; (: *ideas etc*) estrecho ♦ *vi* (*road*) estrecharse; (*diminish*) reducirse; **to have a ~ escape** escaparse por los pelos; **to ~ sth down** reducir algo; **~ly** *adv* (*miss*) por poco; **~-minded** *adj* de miras estrechas

nasty ['nɑːstɪ] *adj* (*remark*) feo; (*person*) antipático; (*revolting: taste, smell*) asqueroso; (*wound, disease etc*) peligroso, grave

nation ['neɪʃən] *n* nación *f*

national ['næʃənl] *adj, n* nacional *m/f*; **~ dress** *n* vestido nacional; **N~ Health Service** (*BRIT*) *n* servicio nacional de salud pública; ≈ Insalud *m* (*SP*); **N~ Insurance** (*BRIT*) *n* seguro social nacional; **~ism** *n* nacionalismo; **~ist** *adj, n* nacionalista *m/f*; **~ity** [-ˈnælɪtɪ] *n* nacionalidad *f*; **~ize** *vt* nacionalizar; **~ly** *adv* (*nationwide*) en escala nacional; (*as a nation*) nacionalmente, como nación

nationwide ['neɪʃənwaɪd] *adj* en escala *or* a nivel nacional

native ['neɪtɪv] *n* (*local inhabitant*) natural *m/f*, nacional *m/f*; (*of tribe etc*) indígena *m/f*, nativo/a ♦ *adj* (*indigenous*) indígena; (*country*) natal; (*innate*) natural, innato; **a ~ of Russia** un(a) natural *m/f* de Rusia; **a ~ speaker of French** un hablante nativo de francés; **N~ American** *adj, n* americano/a

indígena, amerindio/a; **~ language** *n* lengua materna

Nativity [nəˈtɪvɪtɪ] *n*: **the ~** Navidad *f*

NATO ['neɪtəʊ] *n abbr* (= *North Atlantic Treaty Organization*) OTAN *f*

natural ['nætʃrəl] *adj* natural; **to become ~ized** (*person*) naturalizarse; (*plant*) aclimatarse; **~ly** *adv* (*speak etc*) naturalmente; (*of course*) desde luego, por supuesto

nature ['neɪtʃə*] *n* (*also: N~*) naturaleza; (*group, sort*) género, clase *f*; (*character*) carácter *m*, genio; **by ~** por *or* de naturaleza

naught [nɔːt] = **nought**

naughty ['nɔːtɪ] *adj* (*child*) travieso

nausea ['nɔːsɪə] *n* náuseas *fpl*; **~te** [-sieit] *vt* dar náuseas a; (*fig*) dar asco a

nautical ['nɔːtɪkl] *adj* náutico, marítimo; (*mile*) marino

naval ['neɪvl] *adj* naval, de marina; **~ officer** *n* oficial *m/f* de marina

nave [neɪv] *n* nave *f*

navel ['neɪvl] *n* ombligo

navigate ['nævɪɡeɪt] *vt* gobernar ♦ *vi* navegar; (*AUT*) ir de copiloto; **navigation** [-ˈɡeɪʃən] *n* (*action*) navegación *f*; (*science*) náutica; **navigator** *n* navegador(a) *m/f*, navegante *m/f*; (*AUT*) copiloto *m/f*

navvy ['nævɪ] (*BRIT*) *n* peón *m* caminero

navy ['neɪvɪ] *n* marina de guerra; (*ships*) armada, flota; **~(-blue)** *adj* azul marino

Nazi ['nɑːtsɪ] *n* nazi *m/f*

NB *abbr* (= *nota bene*) nótese

near [nɪə*] *adj* (*place, relation*) cercano; (*time*) próximo ♦ *adv* cerca ♦ *prep* (*also: ~ to: space*) cerca de, junto a; (: *time*) cerca de ♦ *vt* acercarse a, aproximarse a; **~by** [nɪəˈbaɪ] *adj* cercano, próximo ♦ *adv* cerca; **~ly** *adv* casi, por poco; **I ~ly fell** por poco me caigo; **~ miss** *n* tiro cercano; **~side** *n* (*AUT: in Britain*) lado izquierdo; (: *in US, Europe etc*) lado derecho; **~-sighted** *adj* miope, corto de vista

neat [niːt] *adj* (*place*) ordenado, bien cuidado; (*person*) pulcro; (*plan*) ingenioso; (*spirits*) solo; **~ly** *adv* (*tidily*) con esmero; (*skilfully*) ingeniosamente

necessarily ['nesɪsrɪlɪ] *adv*
necesariamente

necessary ['nesɪsrɪ] *adj* necesario,
preciso

necessitate [nɪ'sesɪteɪt] *vt* hacer
necesario

necessity [nɪ'sesɪtɪ] *n* necesidad *f*;
necessities *npl* artículos *mpl* de primera
necesidad

neck [nek] *n* (*of person, garment, bottle*)
cuello; (*of animal*) pescuezo ♦ *vi* (*inf*)
besuquearse; **~ and ~** parejos; **~lace**
['neklɪs] *n* collar *m*; **~line** *n* escote *m*; **~tie**
['nektaɪ] *n* corbata

née [neɪ] *adj*: **~ Scott** de soltera Scott

need [niːd] *n* (*lack*) escasez *f*, falta;
(*necessity*) necesidad *f* ♦ *vt* (*require*)
necesitar; **I ~ to do it** tengo que *or* debo
hacerlo; **you don't ~ to go** no hace falta
que (te) vayas

needle ['niːdl] *n* aguja ♦ *vt* (*fig: inf*)
picar, fastidiar

needless ['niːdlɪs] *adj* innecesario; **~ to
say** huelga decir que

needlework ['niːdlwəːk] *n* (*activity*)
costura, labor *f* de aguja

needn't ['niːdnt] = **need not**

needy ['niːdɪ] *adj* necesitado

negative ['negətɪv] *n* (*PHOT*) negativo;
(*LING*) negación *f* ♦ *adj* negativo

neglect [nɪ'glekt] *vt* (*one's duty*) faltar a,
no cumplir con; (*child*) descuidar,
desatender ♦ *n* (*of house, garden etc*)
abandono; (*of child*) desatención *f*; (*of
duty*) incumplimiento

negligee ['neglɪʒeɪ] *n* (*nightgown*) salto
de cama

negligence ['neglɪdʒəns] *n* negligencia,
descuido

negligible ['neglɪdʒɪbl] *adj* insignificante,
despreciable

negotiate [nɪ'gəuʃɪeɪt] *vt* (*treaty, loan*)
negociar; (*obstacle*) franquear; (*bend in
road*) tomar ♦ *vi*: **to ~ (with)** negociar
(con); **negotiation** [-'eɪʃən] *n* negociación
f, gestión *f*

Negress ['niːgrɪs] *n* negra

Negro ['niːgrəu] *adj, n* negro

neigh [neɪ] *vi* relinchar

neighbour ['neɪbə*] (*US* **neighbor**) *n*
vecino/a; **~hood** *n* (*place*) vecindad *f*,
barrio; (*people*) vecindario; **~ing** *adj*
vecino; **~ly** *adj* (*person*) amable;
(*attitude*) de buen vecino

neither ['naɪðə*] *adj* ni ♦ *conj*: **I didn't
move and ~ did John** no me he
movido, ni Juan tampoco ♦ *pron*
ninguno ♦ *adv*: **~ good nor bad** ni
bueno ni malo; **~ is true** ninguno/a de
los/las dos es cierto/a

neon ['niːɔn] *n* neón *m*; **~ light** *n*
lámpara de neón

nephew ['nevjuː] *n* sobrino

nerve [nəːv] *n* (*ANAT*) nervio; (*courage*)
valor *m*; (*impudence*) descaro, frescura; **a
fit of ~s** un ataque de nervios; **~-racking**
adj desquiciante

nervous ['nəːvəs] *adj* (*anxious, ANAT*)
nervioso; (*timid*) tímido, miedoso; **~
breakdown** *n* crisis *f* nerviosa

nest [nest] *n* (*of bird*) nido; (*wasps' ~*)
avispero ♦ *vi* anidar; **~ egg** *n* (*fig*)
ahorros *mpl*

nestle ['nesl] *vi*: **to ~ down** acurrucarse

net [net] *n* (*gen*) red *f*; (*fabric*) tul *m*
♦ *adj* (*COMM*) neto, líquido ♦ *vt* coger (*SP*)
or agarrar (*AM*) con red; (*SPORT*) marcar;
~ball *n* básquet *m*; **~ curtains** *npl*
visillos *mpl*

Netherlands ['neðələndz] *npl*: **the ~** los
Países Bajos

nett [net] *adj* = **net**

netting ['netɪŋ] *n* red *f*, redes *fpl*

nettle ['netl] *n* ortiga

network ['netwəːk] *n* red *f*

neurotic [njuə'rɔtɪk] *adj, n* neurótico/a
m/f

neuter ['njuːtə*] *adj* (*LING*) neutro ♦ *vt*
castrar, capar

neutral ['njuːtrəl] *adj* (*person*) neutral;
(*colour etc, ELEC*) neutro ♦ *n* (*AUT*) punto
muerto; **~ize** *vt* neutralizar

never ['nevə*] *adv* nunca, jamás; **I ~
went** no fui nunca; **~ in my life** jamás
en la vida; *see also* **mind**; **~-ending** *adj*
interminable, sin fin; **~theless** [nevəðə-
'les] *adv* sin embargo, no obstante

new [njuː] *adj* nuevo; (*brand new*) a

estrenar; (*recent*) reciente; **N~ Age** *n* Nueva Era; **~born** *adj* recién nacido; **~comer** ['njuːkʌmə*] *n* recién venido/a *or* llegado/a; **~-fangled** (*pej*) *adj* modernísimo; **~-found** *adj* (*friend*) nuevo; (*enthusiasm*) recién adquirido; **~ly** *adv* nuevamente, recién; **~ly-weds** *npl* recién casados *mpl*

news [njuːz] *n* noticias *fpl*; **a piece of ~** una noticia; **the ~** (*RADIO, TV*) las noticias *fpl*; **~ agency** *n* agencia de noticias; **~agent** (*BRIT*) *n* vendedor(a) *m/f* de periódicos; **~caster** *n* presentador(a) *m/f*, locutor(a) *m/f*; **~ dealer** (*US*) *n* = **~agent**; **~ flash** *n* noticia de última hora; **~letter** *n* hoja informativa, boletín *m*; **~paper** *n* periódico, diario; **~print** *n* papel *m* de periódico; **~reader** *n* = **~caster**; **~reel** *n* noticiario; **~ stand** *n* quiosco *or* puesto de periódicos

newt [njuːt] *n* tritón *m*

New Year *n* Año Nuevo; **~'s Day** *n* Día *m* de Año Nuevo; **~'s Eve** *n* Nochevieja

New York ['njuː'jɔːk] *n* Nueva York

New Zealand [njuː'ziːlənd] *n* Nueva Zelanda; **~er** *n* neozelandés/esa *m/f*

next [nɛkst] *adj* (*house, room*) vecino; (*bus stop, meeting*) próximo; (*following: page etc*) siguiente ♦ *adv* después; **the ~ day** el día siguiente; **~ time** la próxima vez; **~ year** el año próximo *or* que viene; **~ to** junto a, al lado de; **~ to nothing** casi nada; **~ please!** ¡el siguiente! **~ door** *adv* en la casa de al lado ♦ *adj* vecino, de al lado; **~-of-kin** *n* pariente *m* más cercano

NHS *n abbr* = **National Health Service**

nib [nɪb] *n* plumilla

nibble ['nɪbl] *vt* mordisquear, mordiscar

Nicaragua [nɪkə'ræɡjuə] *n* Nicaragua; **~n** *adj, n* nicaragüense *m/f*

nice [naɪs] *adj* (*likeable*) simpático; (*kind*) amable; (*pleasant*) agradable; (*attractive*) bonito, mono, lindo (*AM*); **~ly** *adv* amablemente; bien

nick [nɪk] *n* (*wound*) rasguño; (*cut, indentation*) mella, muesca ♦ *vt* (*inf*) birlar, robar; **in the ~ of time** justo a tiempo

nickel ['nɪkl] *n* níquel *m*; (*US*) *moneda de 5 centavos*

nickname ['nɪkneɪm] *n* apodo, mote *m* ♦ *vt* apodar

nicotine ['nɪkətiːn] *n* nicotina

niece [niːs] *n* sobrina

Nigeria [naɪ'dʒɪərɪə] *n* Nigeria; **~n** *adj, n* nigeriano/a *m/f*

niggling ['nɪɡlɪŋ] *adj* (*trifling*) nimio, insignificante; (*annoying*) molesto

night [naɪt] *n* noche *f*; (*evening*) tarde *f*; **the ~ before last** anteanoche; **at ~, by ~** de noche, por la noche; **~cap** *n* (*drink*) *bebida que se toma antes de acostarse*; **~ club** *n* cabaret *m*; **~dress** (*BRIT*) *n* camisón *m*; **~fall** *n* anochecer *m*; **~gown** *n* = **~dress**; **~ie** ['naɪtɪ] *n* = **~dress**

nightingale ['naɪtɪŋɡeɪl] *n* ruiseñor *m*

nightlife ['naɪtlaɪf] *n* vida nocturna

nightly ['naɪtlɪ] *adj* de todas las noches ♦ *adv* todas las noches, cada noche

nightmare ['naɪtmeə*] *n* pesadilla

night: **~ porter** *n* portero de noche; **~ school** *n* clase(s) *f(pl)* nocturna(s); **~ shift** *n* turno nocturno *or* de noche; **~ time** *n* noche *f*; **~ watchman** *n* vigilante *m* nocturno

nil [nɪl] (*BRIT*) *n* (*SPORT*) cero, nada

Nile [naɪl] *n*: **the ~** el Nilo

nimble ['nɪmbl] *adj* (*agile*) ágil, ligero; (*skilful*) diestro

nine [naɪn] *num* nueve; **~teen** *num* diecinueve, diez y nueve; **~ty** *num* noventa

ninth [naɪnθ] *adj* noveno

nip [nɪp] *vt* (*pinch*) pellizcar; (*bite*) morder

nipple ['nɪpl] *n* (*ANAT*) pezón *m*

nitrogen ['naɪtrədʒən] *n* nitrógeno

KEYWORD

no [nəu] (*pl* **~es**) *adv* (*opposite of "yes"*) no; **are you coming?** — **~ (I'm not)** ¿vienes? — no; **would you like some more?** — **~ thank you** ¿quieres más? — no gracias

♦ *adj* (*not any*): **I have ~ money/time/ books** no tengo dinero/tiempo/libros; **~ other man would have done it** ningún

otro lo hubiera hecho; "**~ entry**"
"prohibido el paso"; "**~ smoking**"
"prohibido fumar"
♦ *n* no *m*

---

nobility [nəu'bɪlɪtɪ] *n* nobleza
noble ['nəubl] *adj* noble
nobody ['nəubədɪ] *pron* nadie
nod [nɔd] *vi* saludar con la cabeza; (*in agreement*) decir que sí con la cabeza; (*doze*) dar cabezadas ♦ *vt*: **to ~ one's head** inclinar la cabeza ♦ *n* inclinación *f* de cabeza; ~ **off** *vi* dar cabezadas
noise [nɔɪz] *n* ruido; (*din*) escándalo, estrépito; **noisy** *adj* ruidoso; (*child*) escandaloso
nominate ['nɔmɪneɪt] *vt* (*propose*) proponer; (*appoint*) nombrar; **nomination** [-'neɪʃən] *n* propuesta; nombramiento; **nominee** [-'niː] *n* candidato/a
non... [nɔn] *prefix* no, des..., in...; ~**alcoholic** *adj* no alcohólico; ~**-aligned** *adj* no alineado
nonchalant ['nɔnʃələnt] *adj* indiferente
non-committal ['nɔnkə'mɪtl] *adj* evasivo
nondescript ['nɔndɪskrɪpt] *adj* soso
none [nʌn] *pron* ninguno/a ♦ *adv* de ninguna manera; ~ **of you** ninguno de vosotros; **I've ~ left** no me queda ninguno/a; **he's ~ the worse for it** no le ha hecho ningún mal
nonentity [nɔ'nentɪtɪ] *n* cero a la izquierda, nulidad *f*
nonetheless [nʌnðə'les] *adv* sin embargo, no obstante
non-existent *adj* inexistente
non-fiction *n* literatura no novelesca
nonplussed [nɔn'plʌst] *adj* perplejo
nonsense ['nɔnsəns] *n* tonterías *fpl*, disparates *fpl*; ~! ¡qué tonterías!
non: ~**-smoker** *n* no fumador/a *m/f*; ~**-stick** *adj* (*pan, surface*) antiadherente; ~**-stop** *adj* continuo; (*RAIL*) directo ♦ *adv* sin parar
noodles ['nuːdlz] *npl* tallarines *mpl*
nook [nuk] *n*: ~**s and crannies** escondrijos *mpl*
noon [nuːn] *n* mediodía *m*

no-one *pron* = **nobody**
noose [nuːs] *n* (*hangman's*) dogal *m*
nor [nɔː*] *conj* = **neither** ♦ *adv see* **neither**
norm [nɔːm] *n* norma
normal ['nɔːml] *adj* normal; ~**ly** *adv* normalmente
north [nɔːθ] *n* norte *m* ♦ *adj* del norte, norteño ♦ *adv* al *or* hacia el norte; **N~ Africa** *n* África del Norte; **N~ America** *n* América del Norte; ~**-east** *n* nor(d)este *m*; ~**erly** ['nɔːðəlɪ] *adj* (*point, direction*) norteño; ~**ern** ['nɔːðən] *adj* norteño, del norte; **N~ern Ireland** *n* Irlanda del Norte; **N~ Pole** *n* Polo Norte; **N~ Sea** *n* Mar *m* del Norte; ~**ward(s)** ['nɔːθwəd(z)] *adv* hacia el norte; ~**-west** *n* nor(d)oeste *m*
Norway ['nɔːweɪ] *n* Noruega; **Norwegian** [-'wiːdʒən] *adj* noruego/a ♦ *n* noruego/a; (*LING*) noruego
nose [nəuz] *n* (*ANAT*) nariz *f*; (*ZOOL*) hocico; (*sense of smell*) olfato ♦ *vi*: **to ~ about** curiosear; ~**bleed** *n* hemorragia nasal; ~**-dive** *n* (*of plane: deliberate*) picado vertical; (: *involuntary*) caída en picado; ~**y** (*inf*) *adj* curioso, fisgón/ona
nostalgia [nɔs'tældʒɪə] *n* nostalgia
nostril ['nɔstrɪl] *n* ventana de la nariz
nosy ['nəuzɪ] (*inf*) *adj* = **nosey**
not [nɔt] *adv* no; ~ **that ...** no es que ...; **it's too late, isn't it?** es demasiado tarde, ¿verdad *or* no?; ~ **yet/now** todavía/ahora no; **why ~?** ¿por qué no?; *see also* **all**; **only**
notably ['nəutəblɪ] *adv* especialmente
notary ['nəutərɪ] *n* notario/a
notch [nɔtʃ] *n* muesca, corte *m*
note [nəut] *n* (*MUS, record, letter*) nota; (*banknote*) billete *m*; (*tone*) tono ♦ *vt* (*observe*) notar, observar; (*write down*) apuntar, anotar; ~**book** *n* libreta, cuaderno; ~**d** ['nəutɪd] *adj* célebre, conocido; ~**pad** *n* bloc *m*; ~**paper** *n* papel *m* para cartas
nothing ['nʌθɪŋ] *n* nada; (*zero*) cero; **he does ~** no hace nada; ~ **new** nada nuevo; ~ **much** no mucho; **for ~** (*free*) gratis, sin pago; (*in vain*) en balde

notice ['nəutɪs] n (*announcement*) anuncio; (*warning*) aviso; (*dismissal*) despido; (*resignation*) dimisión f; (*period of time*) plazo ♦ vt (*observe*) notar, observar; **to bring sth to sb's ~** (*attention*) llamar la atención de uno sobre algo; **to take ~ of** tomar nota de, prestar atención a; **at short ~** con poca anticipación; **until further ~** hasta nuevo aviso; **to hand in one's ~** dimitir; **~able** adj evidente, obvio; **~ board** (BRIT) n tablón m de anuncios

notify ['nəutɪfaɪ] vt: **to ~ sb (of sth)** comunicar (algo) a uno

notion ['nəuʃən] n idea; (*opinion*) opinión f

notorious [nəu'tɔːrɪəs] adj notorio

notwithstanding [nɔtwɪθ'stændɪŋ] adv no obstante, sin embargo ♦ prep a pesar de

nougat ['nuːgɑː] n turrón m

nought [nɔːt] n cero

noun [naun] n nombre m, sustantivo

nourish ['nʌrɪʃ] vt nutrir; (*fig*) alimentar; **~ing** adj nutritivo; **~ment** n alimento, sustento

novel ['nɔvl] n novela ♦ adj (*new*) nuevo, original; (*unexpected*) insólito; **~ist** n novelista m/f; **~ty** n novedad f

November [nəu'vɛmbə*] n noviembre m

novice ['nɔvɪs] n principiante m/f, novato/a; (REL) novicio/a

now [nau] adv (*at the present time*) ahora; (*these days*) actualmente, hoy día ♦ conj: **~ (that)** ya que, ahora que; **right ~** ahora mismo; **by ~** ya; **just ~** ahora mismo; **~ and then, ~ and again** de vez en cuando; **from ~ on** de ahora en adelante; **~adays** ['nauədeɪz] adv hoy (en) día, actualmente

nowhere ['nəuwɛə*] adv (*direction*) a ninguna parte; (*location*) en ninguna parte

nozzle ['nɔzl] n boquilla

nuance ['njuːɑːns] n matiz m

nuclear ['njuːklɪə*] adj nuclear

nuclei ['njuːklɪaɪ] npl of **nucleus**

nucleus ['njuːklɪəs] (pl **nuclei**) n núcleo

nude [njuːd] adj, n desnudo/a m/f; **in the ~** desnudo

nudge [nʌdʒ] vt dar un codazo a

nudist ['njuːdɪst] n nudista m/f

nuisance ['njuːsns] n molestia, fastidio; (*person*) pesado, latoso; **what a ~!** ¡qué lata!

nuke ['njuːk] (*inf*) n bomba atómica ♦ vt atacar con arma nuclear

null [nʌl] adj: **~ and void** nulo y sin efecto

numb [nʌm] adj: **~ with cold/fear** entumecido por el frío/paralizado de miedo

number ['nʌmbə*] n número; (*quantity*) cantidad f ♦ vt (*pages etc*) numerar, poner número a; (*amount to*) sumar, ascender a; **to be ~ed among** figurar entre; **a ~ of** varios, algunos; **they were ten in ~** eran diez; **~ plate** (BRIT) n matrícula, placa

numeral ['njuːmərəl] n número, cifra

numerate ['njuːmərɪt] adj competente en la aritmética

numerous ['njuːmərəs] adj numeroso

nun [nʌn] n monja, religiosa

nurse [nəːs] n enfermero/a; (*also*: **~maid**) niñera ♦ vt (*patient*) cuidar, atender

nursery ['nəːsərɪ] n (*institution*) guardería infantil; (*room*) cuarto de los niños; (*for plants*) criadero, semillero; **~ rhyme** n canción f infantil; **~ school** n parvulario, escuela de párvulos; **~ slope** (BRIT) n (SKI) cuesta para principiantes

nursing ['nəːsɪŋ] n (*profession*) profesión f de enfermera; (*care*) asistencia, cuidado; **~ home** n clínica de reposo; **~ mother** n madre f lactante

nurture ['nəːtʃə*] vt (*child, plant*) alimentar, nutrir

nut [nʌt] n (TECH) tuerca; (BOT) nuez f; **~crackers** npl cascanueces m inv

nutmeg ['nʌtmɛg] n nuez f moscada

nutritious [njuː'trɪʃəs] adj nutritivo, alimenticio

nuts [nʌts] (*inf*) adj loco

nutshell ['nʌtʃɛl] n: **in a ~** en resumidas cuentas

nylon ['naɪlɔn] n nilón m ♦ adj de nilón

O o

oak [əuk] *n* roble *m* ♦ *adj* de roble

O.A.P. (*BRIT*) *n abbr* = **old-age pensioner**

oar [ɔː*] *n* remo

oases [əu'eɪsiːz] *npl of* **oasis**

oasis [əu'eɪsɪs] (*pl* **oases**) *n* oasis *m inv*

oath [əuθ] *n* juramento; (*swear word*) palabrota; **on** (*BRIT*) *or* **under** ~ bajo juramento

oatmeal ['əutmiːl] *n* harina de avena

oats [əuts] *n* avena

obedience [ə'biːdɪəns] *n* obediencia

obedient [ə'biːdɪənt] *adj* obediente

obey [ə'beɪ] *vt* obedecer; (*instructions, regulations*) cumplir

obituary [ə'bɪtjuərɪ] *n* necrología

object [*n* 'ɔbdʒɪkt, *vb* əb'dʒɛkt] *n* objeto; (*purpose*) objeto, propósito; (*LING*) complemento ♦ *vi*: **to ~ to** estar en contra de; (*proposal*) oponerse a; **to ~ that** objetar que; **expense is no** ~ no importa cuánto cuesta; **I ~!** ¡yo protesto!; ~**ion** [əb'dʒɛkʃən] *n* protesta; **I have no** ~**ion to ...** no tengo inconveniente en que ...; ~**ionable** [əb'dʒɛkʃənəbl] *adj* desagradable; (*conduct*) censurable; ~**ive** *adj, n* objetivo

obligation [ɔblɪ'geɪʃən] *n* obligación *f*, (*debt*) deber *m*; **without** ~ sin compromiso

oblige [ə'blaɪdʒ] *vt* (*do a favour for*) complacer, hacer un favor a; **to ~ sb to do sth** forzar *or* obligar a uno a hacer algo; **to be ~d to sb for sth** estarle agradecido a uno por algo; **obliging** *adj* servicial, atento

oblique [ə'bliːk] *adj* oblicuo; (*allusion*) indirecto

obliterate [ə'blɪtəreɪt] *vt* borrar

oblivion [ə'blɪvɪən] *n* olvido; **oblivious** [-ɪəs] *adj*: **oblivious of** inconsciente de

oblong ['ɔblɔŋ] *adj* rectangular ♦ *n* rectángulo

obnoxious [əb'nɔkʃəs] *adj* odioso, detestable; (*smell*) nauseabundo

oboe ['əubəu] *n* oboe *m*

obscene [əb'siːn] *adj* obsceno

obscure [əb'skjuə*] *adj* oscuro ♦ *vt* oscurecer; (*hide*: *sun*) esconder

obsequious [əb'siːkwɪəs] *adj* servil

observance [əb'zə:vns] *n* observancia, cumplimiento

observant [əb'zə:vnt] *adj* observador(a)

observation [ɔbzə'veɪʃən] *n* observación *f*; (*MED*) examen *m*

observe [əb'zə:v] *vt* observar; (*rule*) cumplir; ~**r** *n* observador(a) *m/f*

obsess [əb'sɛs] *vt* obsesionar; ~**ive** *adj* obsesivo; obsesionante

obsolete ['ɔbsəliːt] *adj*: **to be** ~ estar en desuso

obstacle ['ɔbstəkl] *n* obstáculo; (*nuisance*) estorbo; ~ **race** *n* carrera de obstáculos

obstinate ['ɔbstɪnɪt] *adj* terco, porfiado; (*determined*) obstinado

obstruct [əb'strʌkt] *vt* obstruir; (*hinder*) estorbar, obstaculizar; ~**ion** [əb'strʌkʃən] *n* (*action*) obstrucción *f*; (*object*) estorbo, obstáculo

obtain [əb'teɪn] *vt* obtener; (*achieve*) conseguir; ~**able** *adj* asequible

obvious ['ɔbvɪəs] *adj* obvio, evidente; ~**ly** *adv* evidentemente, naturalmente; ~**ly not** por supuesto que no

occasion [ə'keɪʒən] *n* oportunidad *f*, ocasión *f*; (*event*) acontecimiento; ~**al** *adj* poco frecuente, ocasional; ~**ally** *adv* de vez en cuando

occult [ə'kʌlt] *n*: **the** ~ lo sobrenatural, lo oculto

occupant ['ɔkjupənt] *n* (*of house*) inquilino/a; (*of car*) ocupante *m/f*

occupation [ɔkju'peɪʃən] *n* ocupación *f*; (*job*) trabajo; (*pastime*) ocupaciones *fpl*; ~**al hazard** *n* riesgo profesional

occupier ['ɔkjupaɪə*] *n* inquilino/a

occupy ['ɔkjupaɪ] *vt* (*seat, post, time*) ocupar; (*house*) habitar; **to ~ o.s. in doing** pasar el tiempo haciendo

occur [ə'kə:*] *vi* pasar, suceder; **to ~ to sb** ocurrírsele a uno; ~**rence** [ə'kʌrəns] *n* acontecimiento; (*existence*) existencia

ocean ['əuʃən] *n* océano; ~-**going** *adj* de alta mar

ochre ['əukə*] (*US* **ocher**) *n* ocre *m*

o'clock [ə'klɔk] *adv*: **it is 5 ~** son las 5

OCR *n abbr* = **optical character recognition/reader**

octave ['ɔktɪv] *n* octava

October [ɔk'təubə*] *n* octubre *m*

octopus ['ɔktəpəs] *n* pulpo

odd [ɔd] *adj* extraño, raro; (*number*) impar; (*sock, shoe etc*) suelto; **60-~** 60 y pico; **at ~ times** de vez en cuando; **to be the ~ one out** estar de más; **~ity** *n* rareza; (*person*) excéntrico; **~-job man** *n* chico para todo; **~ jobs** *npl* bricolaje *m*; **~ly** *adv* curiosamente, extrañamente; *see also* **enough**; **~ments** *npl* (*COMM*) retales *mpl*; **~s** *npl* (*in betting*) puntos *mpl* de ventaja; **it makes no ~s** da lo mismo; **at ~s** reñidos/as; **~s and ends** minucias *fpl*

ode [əud] *n* oda

odometer [ɔ'dɔmɪtə*] (*US*) *n* cuentakilómetros *m inv*

odour ['əudə*] (*US* **odor**) *n* olor *m*; (*unpleasant*) hedor *m*

of [ɔv, əv] *prep* **1** (*gen*) de; **a friend ~ ours** un amigo nuestro; **a boy ~ 10** un chico de 10 años; **that was kind ~ you** eso fue muy amable por *or* de tu parte
2 (*expressing quantity, amount, dates etc*) de; **a kilo ~ flour** un kilo de harina; **there were 3 ~ them** había tres; **3 ~ us went** tres de nosotros fuimos; **the 5th ~ July** el 5 de julio
3 (*from, out of*) de; **made ~ wood** (hecho) de madera

off [ɔf] *adj, adv* (*engine*) desconectado; (*light*) apagado; (*tap*) cerrado; (*BRIT: food: bad*) pasado, malo; (*: milk*) cortado; (*cancelled*) cancelado ♦ *prep* de; **to be ~** (*to leave*) irse, marcharse; **to be ~ sick** estar enfermo *or* de baja; **a day ~** un día libre *or* sin trabajar; **to have an ~ day** tener un día malo; **he had his coat ~** se había quitado el abrigo; **10% ~** (*COMM*) (con el) 10% de descuento; **5 km ~ (the road)** a 5 km (de la carretera); **~ the coast** frente a la costa; **I'm ~ meat** (*no*

longer eat/like it) paso de la carne; **on the ~ chance** por si acaso; **~ and on** de vez en cuando

offal ['ɔfl] (*BRIT*) *n* (*CULIN*) menudencias *fpl*

off-colour [ɔf'kʌlə*] (*BRIT*) *adj* (*ill*) indispuesto

offence [ə'fɛns] (*US* **offense**) *n* (*crime*) delito; **to take ~ at** ofenderse por

offend [ə'fɛnd] *vt* (*person*) ofender; **~er** *n* delincuente *m/f*

offensive [ə'fɛnsɪv] *adj* ofensivo; (*smell etc*) repugnante ♦ *n* (*MIL*) ofensiva

offer ['ɔfə*] *n* oferta, ofrecimiento *m*; (*proposal*) propuesta ♦ *vt* ofrecer; (*opportunity*) facilitar; **"on ~"** (*COMM*) "en oferta"; **~ing** *n* ofrenda

offhand [ɔf'hænd] *adj* informal ♦ *adv* de improviso

office ['ɔfɪs] *n* (*place*) oficina; (*room*) despacho; (*position*) carga, oficio; **doctor's ~** (*US*) consultorio; **to take ~** entrar en funciones; **~ automation** *n* ofimática, buromática; **~ block** (*US* **~ building**) *n* bloque *m* de oficinas; **~ hours** *npl* horas *fpl* de oficina; (*US: MED*) horas *fpl* de consulta

officer ['ɔfɪsə*] *n* (*MIL etc*) oficial *m/f*; (*also*: **police ~**) agente *m/f* de policía; (*of organization*) director(a) *m/f*

office worker *n* oficinista *m/f*

official [ə'fɪʃl] *adj* oficial, autorizado ♦ *n* funcionario, oficial *m*; **~dom** *n* burocracia

offing ['ɔfɪŋ] *n*: **in the ~** (*fig*) en perspectiva

off: **~-licence** (*BRIT*) *n* (*shop*) bodega, *tienda de vinos y bebidas alcohólicas*; **~-line** *adj, adv* (*COMPUT*) fuera de línea; **~-peak** *adj* (*electricity*) de banda económica; (*ticket*) *billete de precio reducido por viajar fuera de las horas punta*; **~-putting** (*BRIT*) *adj* (*person*) asqueroso; (*remark*) desalentador(a); **~-season** *adj, adv* fuera de temporada

offset ['ɔfsɛt] (*irreg*) *vt* contrarrestar, compensar

offshoot ['ɔfʃuːt] *n* (*fig*) ramificación *f*

offshore [ɔf'ʃɔː*] *adj* (*breeze, island*)

costera; (*fishing*) de bajura

offside ['ɔf'saɪd] *adj* (*SPORT*) fuera de juego; (*AUT: in Britain*) del lado derecho; (: *in US, Europe etc*) del lado izquierdo

offspring ['ɔfsprɪŋ] *n inv* descendencia

off: ~**stage** *adv* entre bastidores; ~**-the-peg** (*US* ~**-the-rack**) *adv* confeccionado; ~**-white** *adj* blanco grisáceo

often ['ɔfn] *adv* a menudo, con frecuencia; **how** ~ **do you go?** ¿cada cuánto vas?

ogle ['əʊgl] *vt* comerse con los ojos a

oh [əʊ] *excl* ¡ah!

oil [ɔɪl] *n* aceite *m*; (*petroleum*) petróleo; (*for heating*) aceite *m* combustible ♦ *vt* engrasar; ~**can** *n* lata de aceite; ~**field** *n* campo petrolífero; ~ **filter** *n* (*AUT*) filtro de aceite; ~ **painting** *n* pintura al óleo; ~ **rig** *n* torre *f* de perforación; ~**skins** *npl* impermeables *mpl* de hule, chubasquero; ~ **tanker** *n* petrolero; (*truck*) camión *m* cisterna; ~ **well** *n* pozo (de petróleo); ~**y** *adj* aceitoso; (*food*) grasiento

ointment ['ɔɪntmənt] *n* ungüento

O.K., okay ['əʊ'keɪ] *excl* O.K., ¡está bien!, ¡vale! (*SP*) ♦ *adj* bien ♦ *vt* dar el visto bueno a

old [əʊld] *adj* viejo; (*former*) antiguo; **how** ~ **are you?** ¿cuántos años tienes?, ¿qué edad tienes?; **he's 10 years** ~ tiene 10 años; ~**er brother** hermano mayor; ~ **age** *n* vejez *f*; ~**-age pensioner** (*BRIT*) *n* jubilado/a; ~**-fashioned** *adj* anticuado, pasado de moda

olive ['ɔlɪv] *n* (*fruit*) aceituna; (*tree*) olivo ♦ *adj* (*also:* ~-**green**) verde oliva; ~ **oil** *n* aceite *m* de oliva

Olympic [əʊ'lɪmpɪk] *adj* olímpico; **the** ~ **Games, the** ~**s** las Olimpiadas

omelet(te) ['ɔmlɪt] *n* tortilla (*SP*), tortilla de huevo (*AM*)

omen ['əʊmən] *n* presagio

ominous ['ɔmɪnəs] *adj* de mal agüero, amenazador(a)

omit [əʊ'mɪt] *vt* omitir

KEYWORD

on [ɔn] *prep* **1** (*indicating position*) en; sobre; ~ **the wall** en la pared; **it's** ~ **the**
table está sobre *or* en la mesa; ~ **the left** a la izquierda

2 (*indicating means, method, condition etc*): ~ **foot** a pie; ~ **the train/plane** (*go*) en tren/avión; (*be*) en el tren/el avión; ~ **the radio/television/telephone** por *or* en la radio/televisión/al teléfono; **to be** ~ **drugs** drogarse; (*MED*) estar a tratamiento; **to be** ~ **holiday/business** estar de vacaciones/en viaje de negocios

3 (*referring to time*): ~ **Friday** el viernes; ~ **Fridays** los viernes; ~ **June 20th** el 20 de junio; ~ **a week** ~ **Friday** del viernes en una semana; ~ **arrival** al llegar; ~ **seeing this** al ver esto

4 (*about, concerning*) sobre, acerca de; **a book** ~ **physics** un libro de *or* sobre física

♦ *adv* **1** (*referring to dress*): **to have one's coat** ~ tener *or* llevar el abrigo puesto; **she put her gloves** ~ se puso los guantes

2 (*referring to covering*): **"screw the lid** ~ **tightly"** "cerrar bien la tapa"

3 (*further, continuously*): **to walk** *etc* ~ seguir caminando *etc*

♦ *adj* **1** (*functioning, in operation*: *machine, radio, TV, light*) encendido/a (*SP*), prendido/a (*AM*); (: *tap*) abierto/a; (: *brakes*) echado/a, puesto/a; **is the meeting still** ~? (*in progress*) ¿todavía continúa la reunión?; (*not cancelled*) ¿va a haber reunión al fin?; **there's a good film** ~ **at the cinema** ponen una buena película en el cine

2: that's not ~! (*inf: not possible*) ¡eso ni hablar!; (: *not acceptable*) ¡eso no se hace!

---
once [wʌns] *adv* una vez; (*formerly*) antiguamente ♦ *conj* una vez que; ~ **he had left/it was done** una vez que se había marchado/se hizo; **at** ~ en seguida, inmediatamente; (*simultaneously*) a la vez; ~ **a week** una vez por semana; ~ **more** otra vez; ~ **and for all** de una vez por todas; ~ **upon a time** érase una vez

oncoming ['ɔnkʌmɪŋ] *adj* (*traffic*) que viene de frente

KEYWORD

one [wʌn] *num* un(o)/una; ~ **hundred and fifty** ciento cincuenta; ~ **by** ~ uno a uno
♦ *adj* 1 (*sole*) único; **the** ~ **book which** el único libro que; **the** ~ **man who** el único que
2 (*same*) mismo/a; **they came in the** ~ **car** vinieron en un solo coche
♦ *pron* 1: **this** ~ éste/ésta; **that** ~ ése/ésa; (*more remote*) aquél/aquélla; **I've already got (a red)** ~ ya tengo uno/a (rojo/a); ~ **by** ~ uno/a por uno/a
2: ~ **another** os (*SP*), se (+ *el uno al otro, unos a otros etc*); **do you two ever see** ~ **another?** ¿vosotros dos os veis alguna vez? (*SP*), ¿se ven ustedes dos alguna vez?; **the boys didn't dare look at** ~ **another** los chicos no se atrevieron a mirarse (el uno al otro); **they all kissed** ~ **another** se besaron unos a otros
3 (*impers*): ~ **never knows** nunca se sabe; **to cut** ~**'s finger** cortarse el dedo; ~ **needs to eat** hay que comer

one: ~**-day excursion** (*US*) *n* billete *m* de ida y vuelta en un día; ~**-man** *adj* (*business*) individual; ~**-man band** *n* hombre-orquesta *m*; ~**-off** (*BRIT: inf*) *n* (*event*) acontecimiento único
oneself [wʌn'sɛlf] *pron* (*reflexive*) se; (*after prep*) sí; (*emphatic*) uno/a mismo/a; **to hurt** ~ hacerse daño; **to keep sth for** ~ guardarse algo; **to talk to** ~ hablar solo
one: ~**-sided** *adj* (*argument*) parcial; ~**-to-**~ *adj* (*relationship*) de dos; ~**-upmanship** *n* arte *m* de aventajar a los demás; ~**-way** *adj* (*street*) de sentido único
ongoing ['ɔngəuɪŋ] *adj* continuo
onion ['ʌnjən] *n* cebolla
on-line *adj, adv* (*COMPUT*) en línea
onlooker ['ɔnlukə*] *n* espectador(a) *m/f*
only ['əunlɪ] *adv* solamente, sólo ♦ *adj* único, solo ♦ *conj* solamente que, pero; **an** ~ **child** un hijo único; **not** ~ ... **but also** ... no sólo ... sino también ...

onset ['ɔnsɛt] *n* comienzo
onshore ['ɔnʃɔː*] *adj* (*wind*) que sopla del mar hacia la tierra
onslaught ['ɔnslɔːt] *n* ataque *m*, embestida
onto ['ɔntu] *prep* = **on to**
onus ['əunəs] *n* responsabilidad *f*
onward(s) ['ɔnwəd(z)] *adv* (*move*) (hacia) adelante; **from that time** ~ desde entonces en adelante
onyx ['ɔnɪks] *n* ónice *m*
ooze [uːz] *vi* rezumar
opaque [əu'peɪk] *adj* opaco
OPEC ['əupɛk] *n abbr* (= *Organization of Petroleum-Exporting Countries*) OPEP *f*
open ['əupn] *adj* abierto; (*car*) descubierto; (*road, view*) despejado; (*meeting*) público; (*admiration*) manifiesto ♦ *vt* abrir ♦ *vi* abrirse; (*book etc: commence*) comenzar; **in the** ~ **(air)** al aire libre; ~ **on to** *vt fus* (*subj: room, door*) dar a; ~ **up** *vt* abrir; (*blocked road*) despejar ♦ *vi* abrirse, empezar; ~**ing** *n* abertura; (*start*) comienzo; (*opportunity*) oportunidad *f*; ~ **learning** *n* enseñanza flexible a tiempo parcial; ~**ly** *adv* abiertamente; ~**-minded** *adj* imparcial; ~**-necked** *adj* (*shirt*) desabrochado; sin corbata; ~**-plan office** *adj*: ~**-plan office** gran oficina sin particiones
opera ['ɔpərə] *n* ópera; ~ **house** *n* teatro de la ópera
operate ['ɔpəreɪt] *vt* (*machine*) hacer funcionar; (*company*) dirigir ♦ *vi* funcionar; **to** ~ **on sb** (*MED*) operar a uno
operatic [ɔpə'rætɪk] *adj* de ópera
operating table ['ɔpəreɪtɪŋ-] *n* mesa de operaciones
operating theatre *n* sala de operaciones
operation [ɔpə'reɪʃən] *n* operación *f*; (*of machine*) funcionamiento; **to be in** ~ estar funcionando *or* en funcionamiento; **to have an** ~ (*MED*) ser operado; ~**al** *adj* operacional, en buen estado
operative ['ɔpərətɪv] *adj* en vigor
operator ['ɔpəreɪtə*] *n* (*of machine*) maquinista *m/f*, operario/a; (*TEL*) operador(a) *m/f*, telefonista *m/f*

opinion [ə'pɪnɪən] *n* opinión *f*; **in my ~** en mi opinión, a mi juicio; **~ated** *adj* testarudo; **~ poll** *n* encuesta, sondeo

opponent [ə'pəunənt] *n* adversario/a, contrincante *m/f*

opportunist [ɔpə'tjuːnɪst] *n* oportunista *m/f*

opportunity [ɔpə'tjuːnɪtɪ] *n* oportunidad *f*; **to take the ~ of doing** aprovechar la ocasión para hacer

oppose [ə'pəuz] *vt* oponerse a; **to be ~d to sth** oponerse a algo; **as ~d to** a diferencia de; **opposing** *adj* opuesto, contrario

opposite ['ɔpəzɪt] *adj* opuesto, contrario a; (*house etc*) de enfrente ♦ *adv* en frente ♦ *prep* en frente de, frente a ♦ *n* lo contrario

opposition [ɔpə'zɪʃən] *n* oposición *f*

oppress [ə'prɛs] *vt* oprimir; **~ion** [ə'prɛʃən] *n* opresión *f*; **~ive** *adj* opresivo; (*weather*) agobiante

opt [ɔpt] *vi*: **to ~ for** optar por; **to ~ to do** optar por hacer; **~ out** *vi*: **to ~ out of** optar por no hacer

optical ['ɔptɪkl] *adj* óptico

optician [ɔp'tɪʃən] *n* óptico *m/f*

optimist ['ɔptɪmɪst] *n* optimista *m/f*; **~ic** [-'mɪstɪk] *adj* optimista

optimum ['ɔptɪməm] *adj* óptimo

option ['ɔpʃən] *n* opción *f*, **~al** *adj* facultativo, discrecional

or [ɔː*] *conj* o; (*before o, ho*) u; (*with negative*): **he hasn't seen ~ heard anything** no ha visto ni oído nada; **~ else** si no

oracle ['ɔrəkl] *n* oráculo

oral ['ɔːrəl] *adj* oral ♦ *n* examen *m* oral

orange ['ɔrɪndʒ] *n* (*fruit*) naranja ♦ *adj* color naranja

orator ['ɔrətə*] *n* orador(a) *m/f*

orbit ['ɔːbɪt] *n* órbita ♦ *vt, vi* orbitar

orchard ['ɔːtʃəd] *n* huerto

orchestra ['ɔːkɪstrə] *n* orquesta; (*US: seating*) platea

orchid ['ɔːkɪd] *n* orquídea

ordain [ɔː'deɪn] *vt* (*REL*) ordenar, decretar

ordeal [ɔː'diːl] *n* experiencia horrorosa

order ['ɔːdə*] *n* orden *m*; (*command*)

orden *f*; (*good* ~) buen estado; (*COMM*) pedido ♦ *vt* (*also: put in* ~) arreglar, poner en orden; (*COMM*) pedir; (*command*) mandar, ordenar; **in ~** en orden; (*of document*) en regla; **in (working) ~** en funcionamiento; **in ~ to do/that** para hacer/que; **on ~** (*COMM*) pedido; **to be out of ~** estar desordenado; (*not working*) no funcionar; **in ~ to ~ sb to do sth** mandar a uno hacer algo; **~ form** *n* hoja de pedido; **~ly** *n* (*MIL*) ordenanza *m*; (*MED*) enfermero/a (auxiliar) ♦ *adj* ordenado

ordinary ['ɔːdnrɪ] *adj* corriente, normal; (*pej*) común y corriente; **out of the ~** fuera de lo común

Ordnance Survey ['ɔːdnəns-] (*BRIT*) *n* *servicio oficial de topografía*

ore [ɔː*] *n* mineral *m*

organ ['ɔːgən] *n* órgano *m*; **~ic** [ɔː'gænɪk] *adj* orgánico; **~ism** *n* organismo

organization [ɔːgənaɪ'zeɪʃən] *n* organización *f*

organize ['ɔːgənaɪz] *vt* organizar; **~r** *n* organizador(a) *m/f*

orgasm ['ɔːgæzəm] *n* orgasmo

orgy ['ɔːdʒɪ] *n* orgía

Orient ['ɔːrɪənt] *n* Oriente *m*; **oriental** [-'ɛntl] *adj* oriental

orientate ['ɔːrɪənteɪt] *vt*: **to ~ o.s.** orientarse

origin ['ɔrɪdʒɪn] *n* origen *m*

original [ə'rɪdʒɪnl] *adj* original; (*first*) primero; (*earlier*) primitivo ♦ *n* original *m*; **~ity** [-'nælɪtɪ] *n* originalidad *f*; **~ly** *adv* al principio

originate [ə'rɪdʒɪneɪt] *vi*: **to ~ from, to ~ in** surgir de, tener su origen en

Orkneys ['ɔːknɪz] *npl*: **the ~** (*also: the Orkney Islands*) las Orcadas

ornament ['ɔːnəmənt] *n* adorno; (*trinket*) chuchería; **~al** [-'mɛntl] *adj* decorativo, de adorno

ornate [ɔː'neɪt] *adj* muy ornado, vistoso

orphan ['ɔːfn] *n* huérfano/a; **~age** *n* orfanato

orthodox ['ɔːθədɔks] *adj* ortodoxo; **~y** *n* ortodoxia

orthopaedic [ɔːθə'piːdɪk] (*US* **orthopedic**)

adj ortopédico

oscillate ['ɒsɪleɪt] *vi* oscilar; (*person*) vacilar

ostensibly [ɔs'tɛnsɪblɪ] *adv* aparentemente

ostentatious [ɔstɛn'teɪʃəs] *adj* ostentoso

osteopath ['ɒstɪəpæθ] *n* osteópata *m/f*

ostracize ['ɒstrəsaɪz] *vt* hacer el vacio a

ostrich ['ɒstrɪtʃ] *n* avestruz *m*

other ['ʌðə*] *adj* otro ♦ *pron*: **the ~ (one)** el/la otro/a ♦ *adv*: **~ than** aparte de; **~s** (**~** *people*) otros; **the ~ day** el otro día; **~wise** *adv* de otra manera ♦ *conj* (*if not*) si no

otter ['ɒtə*] *n* nutria

ouch [autʃ] *excl* ¡ay!

ought [ɔːt] (*pt* **ought**) *aux vb*: **I ~ to do it** debería hacerlo; **this ~ to have been corrected** esto debiera haberse corregido; **he ~ to win** (*probability*) debe *or* debiera ganar

ounce [auns] *n* onza (*28.35g*)

our ['auə*] *adj* nuestro; *see also* **my**; **~s** *pron* (el) nuestro/(la) nuestra *etc*; *see also* **mine²**; **~selves** *pron pl* (*reflexive, after prep*) nosotros; (*emphatic*) nosotros mismos; *see also* **oneself**

oust [aust] *vt* desalojar

out [aut] *adv* fuera, afuera; (*not at home*) fuera (de casa); (*light, fire*) apagado; **~ there** allí (fuera); **he's ~** (*absent*) no está, ha salido; **to be ~ in one's calculations** equivocarse (en sus cálculos); **to run ~** salir corriendo; **~ loud** en alta voz; **~ of** (*outside*) fuera de; (*because of: anger etc*) por; **~ of petrol** sin gasolina; "**~ of order**" "no funciona"

out-and-out *adj* (*liar, thief etc*) redomado, empedernido

outback ['autbæk] *n* interior *m*

outboard ['autbɔːd] *adj*: **~ motor** (*motor m*) fuera borda *m*

outbreak ['autbreɪk] *n* (*of war*) comienzo; (*of disease*) epidemia; (*of violence etc*) ola

outburst ['autbɜːst] *n* explosión *f*, arranque *m*

outcast ['autkɑːst] *n* paria *m/f*

outcome ['autkʌm] *n* resultado

outcrop ['autkrɒp] *n* (*of rock*)

afloramiento

outcry ['autkraɪ] *n* protestas *fpl*

outdated [aut'deɪtɪd] *adj* anticuado, fuera de moda

outdo [aut'duː] (*irreg*) *vt* superar

outdoor [aut'dɔː*] *adj* exterior, de aire libre; (*clothes*) de calle; **~s** *adv* al aire libre

outer ['autə*] *adj* exterior, externo; **~ space** *n* espacio exterior

outfit ['autfɪt] *n* (*clothes*) conjunto

outgoing ['autgəuɪŋ] *adj* (*character*) extrovertido; (*retiring: president etc*) saliente; **~s** *npl* gastos *mpl*

outgrow [aut'grəu] (*irreg*) *vt*: **he has ~n his clothes** su ropa le queda pequeña ya

outhouse ['authaus] *n* dependencia

outing ['autɪŋ] *n* excursión *f*, paseo

outlandish [aut'lændɪʃ] *adj* estrafalario

outlaw ['autlɔː] *n* proscrito ♦ *vt* proscribir

outlay ['autleɪ] *n* inversión *f*

outlet ['autlet] *n* salida; (*of pipe*) desagüe *m*; (*US: ELEC*) toma de corriente; (*also: retail ~*) punto de venta

outline ['autlaɪn] *n* (*shape*) contorno, perfil *m*; (*sketch, plan*) esbozo ♦ *vt* (*plan etc*) esbozar; **in ~** (*fig*) a grandes rasgos

outlive [aut'lɪv] *vt* sobrevivir a

outlook ['autluk] *n* (*fig: prospects*) perspectivas *fpl*; (: *for weather*) pronóstico

outlying ['autlaɪɪŋ] *adj* remoto, aislado

outmoded [aut'məudɪd] *adj* anticuado, pasado de moda

outnumber [aut'nʌmbə*] *vt* superar en número

out-of-date *adj* (*passport*) caducado; (*clothes*) pasado de moda

out-of-the-way *adj* apartado

outpatient ['autpeɪʃənt] *n* paciente *m/f* externo/a

outpost ['autpəust] *n* puesto avanzado

output ['autput] *n* (*volumen m de*) producción *f*, rendimiento; (*COMPUT*) salida

outrage ['autreɪdʒ] *n* escándalo; (*atrocity*) atrocidad *f* ♦ *vt* ultrajar; **~ous** [-'reɪdʒəs] *adj* monstruoso

outright [*adv* aut'raɪt, *adj* 'autraɪt] *adv* (*ask*,

deny) francamente; (*refuse*) rotundamente; (*win*) de manera absoluta; (*be killed*) en el acto ♦ *adj* franco; rotundo

outset ['autsɛt] *n* principio

outside [aut'saɪd] *n* exterior *m* ♦ *adj* exterior, externo ♦ *adv* fuera ♦ *prep* fuera de; (*beyond*) más allá de; **at the ~** (*fig*) a lo sumo; **~ lane** *n* (*AUT: in Britain*) carril *m* de la derecha; (: *in US, Europe etc*) carril *m* de la izquierda; **~ line** *n* (*TEL*) línea (exterior); **~r** *n* (*stranger*) extraño, forastero

outsize ['autsaɪz] *adj* (*clothes*) de talla grande

outskirts ['autskə:ts] *npl* alrededores *mpl*, afueras *fpl*

outspoken [aut'spəukən] *adj* muy franco

outstanding [aut'stændɪŋ] *adj* excepcional, destacado; (*remaining*) pendiente

outstay [aut'steɪ] *vt*: **to ~ one's welcome** quedarse más de la cuenta

outstretched [aut'strɛtʃt] *adj* (*hand*) extendido

outstrip [aut'strɪp] *vt* (*competitors, demand*) dejar atrás, aventajar

out-tray *n* bandeja de salida

outward ['autwəd] *adj* externo; (*journey*) de ida; **~ly** *adv* por fuera

outweigh [aut'weɪ] *vt* pesar más que

outwit [aut'wɪt] *vt* ser más listo que

oval ['əuvl] *adj* ovalado ♦ *n* óvalo

ovary ['əuvərɪ] *n* ovario

oven ['ʌvn] *n* horno; **~proof** *adj* resistente al horno

over ['əuvə*] *adv* encima, por encima ♦ *adj* (*or adv*) (*finished*) terminado; (*surplus*) de sobra ♦ *prep* (por) encima de; (*above*) sobre; (*on the other side of*) al otro lado de; (*more than*) más de; (*during*) durante; **~ here** (por) aquí; **~ there** (por) allí *or* allá; **all ~** (*everywhere*) por todas partes; **~ and ~ (again)** una y otra vez; **~ and above** además de; **to ask sb ~** invitar a uno a una casa; **to bend ~** inclinarse

overall [*adj, n* 'əuvərɔ:l, *adv* əuvər'ɔ:l] *adj* (*length etc*) total; (*study*) de conjunto ♦ *adv* en conjunto ♦ *n* (*BRIT*) guardapol-

vo; **~s** *npl* mono (*SP*), overol *m* (*AM*)

overawe [əuvər'ɔ:] *vt*: **to be ~d (by)** quedar impresionado (con)

overbalance [əuvə'bæləns] *vi* perder el equilibrio

overbearing [əuvə'bɛərɪŋ] *adj* autoritario, imperioso

overboard ['əuvəbɔ:d] *adv* (*NAUT*) por la borda

overbook [əuvə'buk] *vt* sobrereservar

overcast ['əuvəkɑ:st] *adj* encapotado

overcharge [əuvə'tʃɑ:dʒ] *vt*: **to ~ sb** cobrar un precio excesivo a uno

overcoat ['əuvəkəut] *n* abrigo, sobretodo

overcome [əuvə'kʌm] (*irreg*) *vt* vencer; (*difficulty*) superar

overcrowded [əuvə'kraudɪd] *adj* atestado de gente; (*city, country*) superpoblado

overdo [əuvə'du:] (*irreg*) *vt* exagerar; (*overcook*) cocer demasiado; **to ~ it** (*work etc*) pasarse

overdose ['əuvədəus] *n* sobredosis *f inv*

overdraft ['əuvədrɑ:ft] *n* saldo deudor

overdrawn [əuvə'drɔ:n] *adj* (*account*) en descubierto

overdue [əuvə'dju:] *adj* retrasado

overestimate [əuvər'ɛstɪmeɪt] *vt* sobreestimar

overflow [*vb* əuvə'fləu, *n* 'əuvəfləu] *vi* desbordarse ♦ *n* (*also:* **~ pipe**) (cañería de) desagüe *m*

overgrown [əuvə'grəun] *adj* (*garden*) invadido por la vegetación

overhaul [*vb* əuvə'hɔ:l, *n* 'əuvəhɔ:l] *vt* revisar, repasar ♦ *n* revisión *f*

overhead [*adv* əuvə'hɛd, *adj, n* 'əuvəhɛd] *adv* por arriba *or* encima ♦ *adj* (*cable*) aéreo ♦ *n* (*US*) = **~s**; **~s** *npl* (*expenses*) gastos *mpl* generales

overhear [əuvə'hɪə*] (*irreg*) *vt* oír por casualidad

overheat [əuvə'hi:t] *vi* (*engine*) recalentarse

overjoyed [əuvə'dʒɔɪd] *adj* encantado, lleno de alegría

overkill ['əuvəkɪl] *n* excesos *mpl*

overland ['əuvəlænd] *adj, adv* por tierra

overlap [əuvə'læp] *vi* traslaparse

overleaf [əuvə'li:f] *adv* al dorso

overload [əuvə'ləud] *vt* sobrecargar

overlook [əuvə'luk] *vt* (*have view of*) dar a, tener vistas a; (*miss: by mistake*) pasar por alto; (*excuse*) perdonar

overnight [əuvə'naɪt] *adv* durante la noche; (*fig*) de la noche a la mañana ♦ *adj* de noche; **to stay ~** pasar la noche

overpass ['əuvəpɑːs] (*US*) *n* paso superior

overpower [əuvə'pauə*] *vt* dominar; (*fig*) embargar; **~ing** *adj* (*heat*) agobiante; (*smell*) penetrante

overrate [əuvə'reɪt] *vt* sobreestimar

override [əuvə'raɪd] (*irreg*) *vt* no hacer caso de; **overriding** *adj* predominante

overrule [əuvə'ruːl] *vt* (*decision*) anular; (*claim*) denegar

overrun [əuvə'rʌn] (*irreg*) *vt* (*country*) invadir; (*time limit*) rebasar, exceder

overseas [əuvə'siːz] *adv* (*abroad*: *live*) en el extranjero; (: *travel*) al extranjero ♦ *adj* (*trade*) exterior; (*visitor*) extranjero

overshadow [əuvə'ʃædəu] *vt*: **to be ~ed by** estar a la sombra de

overshoot [əuvə'ʃuːt] (*irreg*) *vt* excederse

oversight ['əuvəsaɪt] *n* descuido

oversleep [əuvə'sliːp] (*irreg*) *vi* quedarse dormido

overstate [əuvə'steɪt] *vt* exagerar

overstep [əuvə'step] *vt*: **to ~ the mark** pasarse de la raya

overt [əu'vəːt] *adj* abierto

overtake [əuvə'teɪk] (*irreg*) *vt* sobrepasar; (*BRIT*: *AUT*) adelantar

overthrow [əuvə'θrəu] (*irreg*) *vt* (*government*) derrocar

overtime ['əuvətaɪm] *n* horas *fpl* extraordinarias

overtone ['əuvətəun] *n* (*fig*) tono

overture ['əuvətʃuə*] *n* (*MUS*) obertura; (*fig*) preludio

overturn [əuvə'təːn] *vt* volcar; (*fig: plan*) desbaratar; (: *government*) derrocar ♦ *vi* volcar

overweight [əuvə'weɪt] *adj* demasiado gordo *or* pesado

overwhelm [əuvə'welm] *vt* aplastar; (*subj: emotion*) sobrecoger; **~ing** *adj* (*victory, defeat*) arrollador(a); (*feeling*) irresistible

overwork [əuvə'wəːk] *n* trabajo excesivo ♦ *vi* trabajar demasiado

overwrought [əuvə'rɔːt] *adj* sobreexcitado

owe [əu] *vt*: **to ~ sb sth, to ~ sth to sb** deber algo a uno; **owing to** *prep* debido a, por causa de

owl [aul] *n* búho, lechuza

own [əun] *vt* tener, poseer ♦ *adj* propio; **a room of my ~** una habitación propia; **to get one's ~ back** tomar revancha; **on one's ~** solo, a solas; **~ up** *vi* confesar; **~er** *n* dueño/a; **~ership** *n* posesión *f*

ox [ɔks] (*pl* **~en**) *n* buey *m*; **~tail** *n*: **~tail soup** sopa de rabo de buey

oxygen ['ɔksɪdʒən] *n* oxígeno; **~ mask/ tent** *n* máscara/tienda de oxígeno

oyster ['ɔɪstə*] *n* ostra

oz. *abbr* = **ounce(s)**

ozone hole ['əuzəun-] *n* agujero *m* de/en la capa de ozono

ozone layer ['əuzəun-] *n* capa *f* de ozono

P p

p [piː] *abbr* = **penny; pence**

P.A. *n abbr* = **personal assistant; public address system**

p.a. *abbr* = **per annum**

pa [pɑː] (*inf*) *n* papá *m*

pace [peɪs] *n* paso ♦ *vi*: **to ~ up and down** pasearse de un lado a otro; **to keep ~ with** llevar el mismo paso que; **~maker** *n* (*MED*) regulador *m* cardíaco, marcapasos *m inv*; (*SPORT: also*: **~setter**) liebre *f*

Pacific [pə'sɪfɪk] *n*: **the ~ (Ocean)** el (Océano) Pacífico

pacify ['pæsɪfaɪ] *vt* apaciguar

pack [pæk] *n* (*packet*) paquete *m*; (*of hounds*) jauría; (*of people*) manada, bando; (*of cards*) baraja; (*bundle*) fardo; (*US: of cigarettes*) paquete *m*; (*back ~*) mochila ♦ *vt* (*fill*) llenar; (*in suitcase etc*) meter, poner; (*cram*) llenar, atestar; **to ~ (one's bags)** hacerse la maleta; **to ~ sb off** despachar a uno; **~ it in!** (*inf*) ¡déjalo!

package ['pækɪdʒ] n paquete m; (*bulky*) bulto; (*also:* ~ **deal**) acuerdo global; ~ **holiday** n vacaciones *fpl* organizadas; ~ **tour** n viaje m organizado

packed lunch n almuerzo frío

packet ['pækɪt] n paquete m

packing ['pækɪŋ] n embalaje m; ~ **case** n cajón m de embalaje

pact [pækt] n pacto

pad [pæd] n (*of paper*) bloc m; (*cushion*) cojinete m; (*inf: home*) casa ♦ vt rellenar; ~**ding** n (*material*) relleno

paddle ['pædl] n (*oar*) canalete m; (*US: for table tennis*) paleta ♦ vt impulsar con canalete ♦ vi (*with feet*) chapotear; ~ **steamer** n vapor m de ruedas; **paddling pool** (*BRIT*) n estanque m de juegos

paddock ['pædək] n corral m

paddy field ['pædɪ-] n arrozal m

padlock ['pædlɔk] n candado

paediatrics [piːdɪˈætrɪks] (*US* **pediatrics**) n pediatría

pagan ['peɪgən] adj, n pagano/a m/f

page [peɪdʒ] n (*of book*) página; (*of newspaper*) plana; (*also:* ~ **boy**) paje m ♦ vt (*in hotel etc*) llamar por altavoz a

pageant ['pædʒənt] n (*procession*) desfile m; (*show*) espectáculo; ~**ry** n pompa

pager ['peɪdʒə*] n (*TEL*) busca m

paging device ['peɪdʒɪŋ-] n (*TEL*) busca m

paid [peɪd] pt, pp of **pay** ♦ adj (*work*) remunerado; (*holiday*) pagado; (*official etc*) a sueldo; **to put** ~ **to** (*BRIT*) acabar con

pail [peɪl] n cubo, balde m

pain [peɪn] n dolor m; **to be in** ~ sufrir; **to take** ~**s to do sth** tomarse grandes molestias en hacer algo; ~**ed** adj (*expression*) afligido; ~**ful** adj doloroso; (*difficult*) penoso; (*disagreeable*) desagradable; ~**fully** adv (*fig: very*) terriblemente; ~**killer** n analgésico; ~**less** adj que no causa dolor; ~**staking** ['peɪnzteɪkɪŋ] adj (*person*) concienzudo, esmerado

paint [peɪnt] n pintura ♦ vt pintar; **to** ~ **the door blue** pintar la puerta de azul; ~**brush** n (*artist's*) pincel m; (*decorator's*)

brocha; ~**er** n pintor(a) m/f; ~**ing** n pintura; ~**work** n pintura

pair [peə*] n (*of shoes, gloves etc*) par m; (*of people*) pareja; **a** ~ **of scissors** unas tijeras; **a** ~ **of trousers** unos pantalones, un pantalón

pajamas [pəˈdʒɑːməz] (*US*) npl pijama m

Pakistan [pɑːkɪˈstɑːn] n Paquistán m; ~**i** adj, n paquistaní m/f

pal [pæl] (*inf*) n compinche m/f, compañero/a

palace ['pæləs] n palacio

palatable ['pælɪtəbl] adj sabroso

palate ['pælɪt] n paladar m

palatial [pəˈleɪʃəl] adj suntuoso, espléndido

pale [peɪl] adj (*gen*) pálido; (*colour*) claro ♦ n: **to be beyond the** ~ pasarse de la raya

Palestine ['pælɪstaɪn] n Palestina; **Palestinian** [-ˈtɪnɪən] adj, n palestino/a m/f

palette ['pælɪt] n paleta

pall [pɔːl] n (*of smoke*) capa (de humo) ♦ vi perder el sabor

pallet ['pælɪt] n (*for goods*) pallet m

pallid ['pælɪd] adj pálido

pallor ['pælə*] n palidez f

palm [pɑːm] n (*ANAT*) palma; (*also:* ~ **tree**) palmera, palma ♦ vt: **to** ~ **sth off on sb** (*inf*) encajar algo a uno; **P~ Sunday** n Domingo de Ramos

palpable ['pælpəbl] adj palpable

paltry ['pɔːltrɪ] adj irrisorio

pamper ['pæmpə*] vt mimar

pamphlet ['pæmflət] n folleto

pan [pæn] n (*also: sauce*~) cacerola, cazuela, olla; (*also: frying* ~) sartén f

panache [pəˈnæʃ] n: **with** ~ con estilo

Panama ['pænəmɑː] n Panamá m; **the** ~ **Canal** el Canal de Panamá

pancake ['pænkeɪk] n crepe f

panda ['pændə] n panda m; ~ **car** (*BRIT*) n coche m Z (*SP*)

pandemonium [pændɪˈməʊnɪəm] n jaleo

pander ['pændə*] vi: **to** ~ **to** complacer a

pane [peɪn] n cristal m

panel ['pænl] n (*of wood etc*) panel m; (*RADIO, TV*) panel m de invitados; ~**ling** (*US* ~**ing**) n paneles *mpl*

pang [pæŋ] *n*: **a ~ of regret** (una punzada de) remordimiento; **hunger ~s** dolores *mpl* del hambre

panic ['pænɪk] *n* (terror *m*) pánico ♦ *vi* dejarse llevar por el pánico; **~ky** *adj* (*person*) asustadizo; **~-stricken** *adj* preso de pánico

pansy ['pænzɪ] *n* (*BOT*) pensamiento; (*inf*: *pej*) maricón *m*

pant [pænt] *vi* jadear

panther ['pænθə*] *n* pantera

panties ['pæntɪz] *npl* bragas *fpl*, pantis *mpl*

pantihose ['pæntɪhəuz] (*US*) *n* pantimedias *fpl*

pantomime ['pæntəmaɪm] (*BRIT*) *n* revista musical representada en Navidad, basada en cuentos de hadas

pantry ['pæntrɪ] *n* despensa

pants [pænts] *n* (*BRIT: underwear: woman's*) bragas *fpl*; (: *man's*) calzoncillos *mpl*; (*US: trousers*) pantalones *mpl*

paper ['peɪpə*] *n* papel *m*; (*also: news~*) periódico, diario; (*academic essay*) ensayo; (*exam*) examen *m* ♦ *adj* de papel ♦ *vt* empapelar (*SP*), tapizar (*AM*); **~s** *npl* (*also: identity ~s*) papeles *mpl*, documentos *mpl*; **~back** *n* libro en rústica; **~ bag** *n* bolsa de papel; **~ clip** *n* clip *m*; **~ hankie** *n* pañuelo de papel; **~weight** *n* pisapapeles *m inv*; **~work** *n* trabajo administrativo

papier-mâché ['pæpɪeɪ'mæʃeɪ] *n* cartón *m* piedra

paprika ['pæprɪkə] *n* pimentón *m*

par [pɑː*] *n* par *f*; (*GOLF*) par *m*; **to be on a ~ with** estar a la par con

parable ['pærəbl] *n* parábola

parachute ['pærəʃuːt] *n* paracaídas *m inv*

parade [pə'reɪd] *n* desfile *m* ♦ *vt* (*show off*) hacer alarde de ♦ *vi* desfilar; (*MIL*) pasar revista

paradise ['pærədaɪs] *n* paraíso

paradox ['pærədɒks] *n* paradoja; **~ically** [-'dɒksɪklɪ] *adv* paradójicamente

paraffin ['pærəfɪn] (*BRIT*) *n* (*also: ~ oil*) parafina

paragon ['pærəgən] *n* modelo

paragraph ['pærəgrɑːf] *n* párrafo

parallel ['pærəlɛl] *adj* en paralelo; (*fig*) semejante ♦ *n* (*line*) paralela; (*fig, GEO*) paralelo

paralyse ['pærəlaɪz] *vt* paralizar

paralysis [pə'rælɪsɪs] *n* parálisis *f inv*

paralyze ['pærəlaɪz] (*US*) *vt* = **paralyse**

paramount ['pærəmaunt] *adj*: **of ~ importance** de suma importancia

paranoid ['pærənɔɪd] *adj* (*person, feeling*) paranoico

paraphernalia [pærəfə'neɪlɪə] *n* (*gear*) avíos *mpl*

paraphrase ['pærəfreɪz] *vt* parafrasear

parasite ['pærəsaɪt] *n* parásito/a

parasol ['pærəsɒl] *n* sombrilla, quitasol *m*

paratrooper ['pærətruːpə*] *n* paracaidista *m/f*

parcel ['pɑːsl] *n* paquete *m* ♦ *vt* (*also: ~ up*) empaquetar, embalar

parch [pɑːtʃ] *vt* secar, resecar; **~ed** *adj* (*person*) muerto de sed

parchment ['pɑːtʃmənt] *n* pergamino

pardon ['pɑːdn] *n* (*LAW*) indulto ♦ *vt* perdonar; **~ me!, I beg your ~!** (*I'm sorry!*) ¡perdone usted!; (**I beg your**) **~?**, **~ me?** (*US*) (*what did you say?*) ¿cómo?

parent ['pɛərənt] *n* (*mother*) madre *f*; (*father*) padre *m*; **~s** *npl* padres *mpl*; **~al** [pə'rɛntl] *adj* paternal/maternal

parentheses [pə'rɛnθɪsiːz] *npl* of **parenthesis**

parenthesis [pə'rɛnθɪsɪs] (*pl* **parentheses**) *n* paréntesis *m inv*

Paris ['pærɪs] *n* París

parish ['pærɪʃ] *n* parroquia

Parisian [pə'rɪzɪən] *adj, n* parisiense *m/f*

parity ['pærɪtɪ] *n* paridad *f*, igualdad *f*

park [pɑːk] *n* parque *m* ♦ *vt* aparcar, estacionar ♦ *vi* aparcar, estacionarse

parka ['pɑːkə] *n* anorak *m*

parking ['pɑːkɪŋ] *n* aparcamiento, estacionamiento; **"no ~"** "prohibido estacionarse"; **~ lot** (*US*) *n* parking *m*; **~ meter** *n* parquímetro; **~ ticket** *n* multa de aparcamiento

parlance ['pɑːləns] *n* lenguaje *m*

parliament ['pɑːləmənt] *n* parlamento; (*Spanish*) Cortes *fpl*; **~ary** [-'mɛntərɪ] *adj* parlamentario

parlour ['pɑːlə*] (*US* **parlor**) *n* sala de recibo, salón *m*, living *m* (*AM*)

parochial [pə'rəʊkɪəl] (*pej*) *adj* de miras estrechas

parody ['pærədɪ] *n* parodia

parole [pə'rəʊl] *n*: **on** ~ libre bajo palabra

parquet ['pɑːkeɪ] *n*: ~ **floor(ing)** parquet *m*

parrot ['pærət] *n* loro, papagayo

parry ['pærɪ] *vt* parar

parsimonious [pɑːsɪ'məʊnɪəs] *adj* tacaño

parsley ['pɑːslɪ] *n* perejil *m*

parsnip ['pɑːsnɪp] *n* chirivía

parson ['pɑːsn] *n* cura *m*

part [pɑːt] *n* (*gen*, *MUS*) parte *f*; (*bit*) trozo; (*of machine*) pieza; (*THEATRE etc*) papel *m*; (*of serial*) entrega; (*US*: *in hair*) raya ♦ *adv* = **partly** ♦ *vt* separar ♦ *vi* (*people*) separarse; (*crowd*) apartarse; **to take ~ in** tomar parte *or* participar en; **to take sth in good** ~ tomar algo en buena parte; **to take sb's** ~ defender a uno; **for my** ~ por mi parte; **for the most** ~ en su mayor parte; **to** ~ **one's hair** hacerse la raya; ~ *with vt fus* ceder, entregar; (*money*) pagar; ~ **exchange** (*BRIT*) *n*: **in ~ exchange** como parte del pago

partial ['pɑːʃl] *adj* parcial; **to be ~ to** ser aficionado a

participant [pɑː'tɪsɪpənt] *n* (*in competition*) concursante *m/f*; (*in campaign etc*) participante *m/f*

participate [pɑː'tɪsɪpeɪt] *vi*: **to ~ in** participar en; **participation** [-'peɪʃən] *n* participación *f*

participle ['pɑːtɪsɪpl] *n* participio

particle ['pɑːtɪkl] *n* partícula; (*of dust*) grano

particular [pə'tɪkjʊlə*] *adj* (*special*) particular; (*concrete*) concreto; (*given*) determinado; (*fussy*) quisquilloso; (*demanding*) exigente; ~**s** *npl* (*information*) datos *mpl*; (*details*) pormenores *mpl*; **in** ~ en particular; ~**ly** *adv* (*in particular*) sobre todo; (*difficult, good etc*) especialmente

parting ['pɑːtɪŋ] *n* (*act of*) separación *f*; (*farewell*) despedida; (*BRIT*: *in hair*) raya ♦ *adj* de despedida

partisan [pɑːtɪ'zæn] *adj* partidista ♦ *n* partidario/a

partition [pɑː'tɪʃən] *n* (*POL*) división *f*; (*wall*) tabique *m*

partly ['pɑːtlɪ] *adv* en parte

partner ['pɑːtnə*] *n* (*COMM*) socio/a; (*SPORT, at dance*) pareja; (*spouse*) cónyuge *m/f*; (*lover*) compañero/a; ~**ship** *n* asociación *f*; (*COMM*) sociedad *f*

partridge ['pɑːtrɪdʒ] *n* perdiz *f*

part-time *adj, adv* a tiempo parcial

party ['pɑːtɪ] *n* (*POL*) partido; (*celebration*) fiesta; (*group*) grupo; (*LAW*) parte *f* interesada ♦ *cpd* (*POL*) de partido; ~ **dress** *n* vestido de fiesta; ~ **line** *n* (*TEL*) línea compartida

pass [pɑːs] *vt* (*time, object*) pasar; (*place*) pasar por; (*overtake*) rebasar; (*exam*) aprobar; (*approve*) aprobar ♦ *vi* pasar; (*SCOL*) aprobar, ser aprobado ♦ *n* (*permit*) permiso; (*membership card*) carnet *m*; (*in mountains*) puerto, desfiladero; (*SPORT*) pase *m*; (*SCOL*: *also*: ~ **mark**): **to get a ~ in** aprobar en; **to ~ sth through sth** pasar algo por algo; **to make a ~ at sb** (*inf*) hacer proposiciones a uno; ~ **away** *vi* fallecer; ~ **by** *vi* pasar ♦ *vt* (*ignore*) pasar por alto; ~ **for** *vt fus* pasar por; ~ **on** *vt* transmitir; ~ **out** *vi* desmayarse; ~ **up** *vt* (*opportunity*) renunciar a; ~**able** *adj* (*road*) transitable; (*tolerable*) pasable

passage ['pæsɪdʒ] *n* (*also*: ~*way*) pasillo; (*act of passing*) tránsito; (*fare, in book*) pasaje *m*; (*by boat*) travesía; (*ANAT*) tubo

passbook ['pɑːsbʊk] *n* libreta de banco

passenger ['pæsɪndʒə*] *n* pasajero/a, viajero/a

passer-by [pɑːsə'baɪ] *n* transeúnte *m/f*

passing ['pɑːsɪŋ] *adj* pasajero; **in** ~ de paso; ~ **place** *n* (*AUT*) apartadero

passion ['pæʃən] *n* pasión *f*; ~**ate** *adj* apasionado

passive ['pæsɪv] *adj* (*gen, also LING*) pasivo; ~ **smoker** *n* fumador(a) *m/f* pasivo/a; ~ **smoking** *n* efectos del tabaco *en fumadores pasivos*

Passover ['pɑːsəʊvə*] *n* Pascua (de los judíos)

passport ['pɑːspɔːt] n pasaporte m; ~ **control** n control m de pasaporte

password ['pɑːswɜːd] n contraseña

past [pɑːst] prep (in front of) por delante de; (further than) más allá de; (later than) después de ♦ adj pasado; (president etc) antiguo ♦ n (time) pasado; (of person) antecedentes mpl; **he's ~ forty** tiene más de cuarenta años; **ten/quarter ~ eight** las ocho y diez/cuarto; **for the ~ few/3 days** durante los últimos días/ últimos 3 días; **to run ~ sb** pasar a uno corriendo

pasta ['pæstə] n pasta

paste [peɪst] n pasta; (glue) engrudo ♦ vt pegar

pastel ['pæstl] adj pastel

pasteurized ['pæstəraɪzd] adj pasteurizado

pastille ['pæstl] n pastilla

pastime ['pɑːstaɪm] n pasatiempo

pastry ['peɪstrɪ] n (dough) pasta; (cake) pastel m

pasture ['pɑːstʃə*] n pasto

pasty[1] ['pæstɪ] n empanada

pasty[2] ['peɪstɪ] adj (complexion) pálido

pat [pæt] vt dar una palmadita a; (dog etc) acariciar

patch [pætʃ] n (of material, eye ~) parche m; (mended part) remiendo; (of land) terreno ♦ vt remendar; **(to go through) a bad ~** (pasar por) una mala racha; ~ **up** vt reparar; (quarrel) hacer las paces en; ~**work** n labor m de retazos; ~**y** adj desigual

pâté ['pæteɪ] n paté m

patent ['peɪtnt] n patente f ♦ vt patentar ♦ adj patente, evidente; ~ **leather** n charol m

paternal [pə'tɜːnl] adj paternal; (relation) paterno

path [pɑːθ] n camino, sendero; (trail, track) pista; (of missile) trayectoria

pathetic [pə'θetɪk] adj patético, lastimoso; (very bad) malísimo

pathological [pæθə'lɔdʒɪkəl] adj patológico

pathos ['peɪθɔs] n patetismo

pathway ['pɑːθweɪ] n camino, vereda

patience ['peɪʃns] n paciencia; (BRIT: CARDS) solitario

patient ['peɪʃnt] n paciente m/f ♦ adj paciente, sufrido

patio ['pætɪəu] n patio

patriot ['peɪtrɪət] n patriota m/f; ~**ic** [pætrɪ'ɔtɪk] adj patriótico

patrol [pə'trəul] n patrulla ♦ vt patrullar por; ~ **car** n coche m patrulla; ~**man** (US) n policía m

patron ['peɪtrən] n (in shop) cliente m/f; (of charity) patrocinador(a) m/f; ~ **of the arts** mecenas m; ~**age** ['pætrənɪdʒ] n patrocinio; ~**ize** ['pætrənaɪz] vt (shop) ser cliente de; (artist etc) proteger; (look down on) condescender con; ~ **saint** n santo/a patrón/ona m/f

patter ['pætə*] n golpeteo; (sales talk) labia ♦ vi (rain) tamborilear

pattern ['pætən] n (SEWING) patrón m; (design) dibujo

paunch [pɔːntʃ] n panza, barriga

pauper ['pɔːpə*] n pobre m/f

pause [pɔːz] n pausa ♦ vi hacer una pausa

pave [peɪv] vt pavimentar; **to ~ the way for** preparar el terreno para

pavement ['peɪvmənt] (BRIT) n acera (SP), vereda (AM)

pavilion [pə'vɪlɪən] n (SPORT) caseta

paving ['peɪvɪŋ] n pavimento, enlosado; ~ **stone** n losa

paw [pɔː] n pata

pawn [pɔːn] n (CHESS) peón m; (fig) instrumento ♦ vt empeñar; ~ **broker** n prestamista m/f; ~**shop** n monte m de piedad

pay [peɪ] (pt, pp **paid**) n (wage etc) sueldo, salario ♦ vt pagar ♦ vi (be profitable) rendir; **to ~ attention (to)** prestar atención (a); **to ~ sb a visit** hacer una visita a uno; **to ~ one's respects to sb** presentar sus respetos a uno; ~ **back** vt (money) reembolsar; (person) pagar; ~ **for** vt fus pagar; ~ **in** vt ingresar; ~ **off** vt saldar ♦ vi (scheme, decision) dar resultado; ~ **up** vt pagar (de mala gana); ~**able** adj; ~**able to** pagadero a; ~ **day** n día m de paga; ~**ee**

n portador(a) *m/f*; ~ **envelope** (*US*) *n* =
~ **packet**; ~**ment** *n* pago; **monthly**
~**ment** mensualidad *f*; ~ **packet** (*BRIT*) *n*
sobre *m* (de paga); ~ **phone** *n* teléfono
público; ~**roll** *n* nómina; ~ **slip** *n* recibo
de sueldo; ~ **television** *n* televisión *f* de
pago

PC *n abbr* = **personal computer**; (*BRIT*)
= **police constable**

p.c. *abbr* = **per cent**

pea [piː] *n* guisante *m* (*SP*), chícharo (*AM*),
arveja (*AM*)

peace [piːs] *n* paz *f*; (*calm*) paz *f*,
tranquilidad *f*; ~**ful** *adj* (*gentle*) pacífico;
(*calm*) tranquilo, sosegado

peach [piːtʃ] *n* melocotón *m* (*SP*), durazno
(*AM*)

peacock ['piːkɔk] *n* pavo real

peak [piːk] *n* (*of mountain*) cumbre *f*,
cima; (*of cap*) visera; (*fig*) cumbre *f*; ~
hours *npl*, ~ **period** *n* horas *fpl* punta

peal [piːl] *n* (*of bells*) repique *m*; ~ **of**
laughter carcajada

peanut ['piːnʌt] *n* cacahuete *m* (*SP*), maní
m (*AM*); ~ **butter** manteca de cacahuete
or maní

pear [pɛə*] *n* pera

pearl [pɜːl] *n* perla

peasant ['pɛznt] *n* campesino/a

peat [piːt] *n* turba

pebble ['pɛbl] *n* guijarro

peck [pɛk] *vt* (*also*: ~ **at**) picotear ♦ *vi*
picotazo; (*kiss*) besito; ~**ing order** *n*
orden *m* de jerarquía; ~**ish** (*BRIT: inf*) *adj*:
I feel ~**ish** tengo ganas de picar algo

peculiar [pɪ'kjuːlɪə*] *adj* (*odd*) extraño,
raro; (*typical*) propio, característico; ~ **to**
propio de; ~**ity** [pɪkjuːlɪˈærɪtɪ] *n*
peculiaridad *f*, característica

pedal ['pɛdl] *n* pedal *m* ♦ *vi* pedalear

pedantic [pɪ'dæntɪk] *adj* pedante

peddler ['pɛdlə*] *n*: **drugs** ~ traficante
m/f; camello

pedestrian [pɪ'dɛstrɪən] *n* peatón/ona
m/f ♦ *adj* pedestre; ~ **crossing** (*BRIT*) *n*
paso de peatones

pediatrics [piːdɪ'ætrɪks] (*US*) *n* = **paediat-**
rics

pedigree ['pɛdɪgriː] *n* genealogía; (*of*

animal) raza, pedigrí *m* ♦ *cpd* (*animal*)
de raza, de casta

pee [piː] (*inf*) *vi* mear

peek [piːk] *vi* mirar a hurtadillas

peel [piːl] *n* piel *f*; (*of orange, lemon*)
cáscara; (: *removed*) peladuras *fpl* ♦ *vt*
pelar ♦ *vi* (*paint etc*) desconcharse;
(*wallpaper*) despegarse, desprenderse;
(*skin*) pelar

peep [piːp] *n* (*BRIT: look*) mirada furtiva;
(*sound*) pío ♦ *vi* (*BRIT: look*) mirar
furtivamente; ~ **out** *vi* salir (un poco);
~**hole** *n* mirilla

peer [pɪə*] *vi*: **to** ~ **at** esudriñar ♦ *n*
(*noble*) par *m*; (*equal*) igual *m*; (*contem-*
porary) contemporáneo/a; ~**age** *n*
nobleza

peeved [piːvd] *adj* enojado

peg [pɛg] *n* (*for coat etc*) gancho,
colgadero; (*BRIT: also: clothes* ~) pinza

Pekingese [piːkɪˈniːz] *n* (*dog*) pequinés/
esa *m/f*

pelican ['pɛlɪkən] *n* pelícano; ~ **crossing**
(*BRIT*) *n* (*AUT*) paso de peatones señalizado

pellet ['pɛlɪt] *n* bolita; (*bullet*) perdigón *m*

pelt [pɛlt] *vt*: **to** ~ **sb with sth** arrojarle
algo a uno ♦ *vi* (*rain*) llover a cántaros;
(*inf: run*) correr ♦ *n* pellejo

pen [pɛn] *n* (*fountain* ~) pluma; (*ballpoint*
~) bolígrafo; (*for sheep*) redil *m*

penal ['piːnl] *adj* penal; ~**ize** *vt* castigar

penalty ['pɛnltɪ] *n* (*gen*) pena; (*fine*)
multa; ~ (**kick**) *n* (*FOOTBALL*) penalty *m*;
(*RUGBY*) golpe *m* de castigo

penance ['pɛnəns] *n* penitencia

pence [pɛns] *npl of* **penny**

pencil ['pɛnsl] *n* lápiz *m*, lapicero (*AM*); ~
case *n* estuche *m*; ~ **sharpener** *n*
sacapuntas *m inv*

pendant ['pɛndnt] *n* pendiente *m*

pending ['pɛndɪŋ] *prep* antes de ♦ *adj*
pendiente

pendulum ['pɛndjuləm] *n* péndulo

penetrate ['pɛnɪtreɪt] *vt* penetrar; **pen-**
etrating *adj* penetrante

penfriend ['pɛnfrɛnd] (*BRIT*) *n* amigo/a
por carta

penguin ['pɛŋgwɪn] *n* pingüino

penicillin [pɛnɪ'sɪlɪn] *n* penicilina

peninsula [pə'nɪnsjulə] *n* península
penis ['piːnɪs] *n* pene *m*
penitent ['penɪtnt] *adj* arrepentido
penitentiary [penɪ'tenʃərɪ] (*US*) *n* cárcel *f*, presidio
penknife ['pennaɪf] *n* navaja
pen name *n* seudónimo
penniless ['penɪlɪs] *adj* sin dinero
penny ['penɪ] (*pl* **pennies** *or* (*BRIT*) **pence**) *n* penique *m*; (*US*) centavo
penpal ['penpæl] *n* amigo/a por carta
pension ['penʃən] *n* (*state benefit*) jubilación *f*; ~**er** (*BRIT*) *n* jubilado/a; ~ **fund** *n* caja *or* fondo de pensiones
pensive ['pensɪv] *adj* pensativo; (*withdrawn*) preocupado
pentagon ['pentəgən] *n*: **the P~** (*US*: *POL*) el Pentágono
Pentecost ['pentɪkɔst] *n* Pentecostés *m*
penthouse ['penthaus] *n* ático de lujo
pent-up ['pentʌp] *adj* reprimido
people ['piːpl] *npl* gente *f*; (*citizens*) pueblo, ciudadanos *mpl*; (*POL*): **the** ~ el pueblo ♦ *n* (*nation, race*) pueblo, nación *f*; **several** ~ **came** vinieron varias personas; ~ **say that ...** dice la gente que ...
pep [pep] (*inf*) *n* energía; ~ **up** *vt* animar
pepper ['pepə*] *n* (*spice*) pimienta; (*vegetable*) pimiento ♦ *vt*: **to** ~ **with** (*fig*) salpicar de; ~**mint** *n* (*sweet*) pastilla de menta
peptalk ['peptɔːk] *n*: **to give sb a** ~ darle a uno una inyección de ánimo
per [pəː*] *prep* por; ~ **day/person** per día/persona; ~ **annum** al año; ~ **capita** *adj*, *adv* per cápita
perceive [pə'siːv] *vt* percibir; (*realize*) darse cuenta de
per cent *n* por ciento
percentage [pə'sentɪdʒ] *n* porcentaje *m*
perception [pə'sepʃən] *n* percepción *f*; (*insight*) perspicacia; (*opinion etc*) opinión *f*; **perceptive** [-'septɪv] *adj* perspicaz
perch [pəːtʃ] *n* (*fish*) perca; (*for bird*) percha ♦ *vi*: **to** ~ **(on)** (*bird*) posarse (en); (*person*) encaramarse (en)
percolator ['pəːkəleɪtə*] *n* (*also*: *coffee* ~)

cafetera de filtro
peremptory [pə'remptərɪ] *adj* perentorio; (*person*) autoritario
perennial [pə'renɪəl] *adj* perenne
perfect [*adj, n* 'pəːfɪkt, *vb* pə'fekt] *adj* perfecto ♦ *n* (*also*: ~ **tense**) perfecto ♦ *vt* perfeccionar; ~**ly** ['pəːfɪktlɪ] *adv* perfectamente
perforate ['pəːfəreɪt] *vt* perforar
perform [pə'fɔːm] *vt* (*carry out*) realizar, llevar a cabo; (*THEATRE*) representar; (*piece of music*) interpretar ♦ *vi* (*well, badly*) funcionar; ~**ance** *n* (*of a play*) representación *f*; (*of actor, athlete etc*) actuación *f*; (*of car, engine, company*) rendimiento; (*of economy*) resultados *mpl*; ~**er** *n* (*actor*) actor *m*, actriz *f*
perfume ['pəːfjuːm] *n* perfume *m*
perfunctory [pə'fʌŋktərɪ] *adj* superficial
perhaps [pə'hæps] *adv* quizá(s), tal vez
peril ['perɪl] *n* peligro, riesgo
perimeter [pə'rɪmɪtə*] *n* perímetro
period ['pɪərɪəd] *n* período; (*SCOL*) clase *f*; (*full stop*) punto; (*MED*) regla ♦ *adj* (*costume, furniture*) de época; ~**ic** [-'ɔdɪk(l)] *adj* periódico; ~**ical** [-'ɔdɪkl] *n* periódico; ~**ically** [-'ɔdɪklɪ] *adv* de vez en cuando, cada cierto tiempo
peripheral [pə'rɪfərəl] *adj* periférico ♦ *n* (*COMPUT*) periférico, unidad *f* periférica
perish ['perɪʃ] *vi* perecer; (*decay*) echarse a perder; ~**able** *adj* perecedero
perjury ['pəːdʒərɪ] *n* (*LAW*) perjurio
perk [pəːk] *n* extra *m*; ~ **up** *vi* (*cheer up*) animarse; ~**y** *adj* alegre, despabilado
perm [pəːm] *n* permanente *f*
permanent ['pəːmənənt] *adj* permanente
permeate ['pəːmɪeɪt] *vi* penetrar, trascender ♦ *vt* penetrar, trascender a
permissible [pə'mɪsɪbl] *adj* permisible, lícito
permission [pə'mɪʃən] *n* permiso
permissive [pə'mɪsɪv] *adj* permisivo
permit [*n* 'pəːmɪt, *vt* pə'mɪt] *n* permiso, licencia ♦ *vt* permitir
pernicious [pəː'nɪʃəs] *adj* nocivo; (*MED*) pernicioso
perpetrate ['pəːpɪtreɪt] *vt* cometer
perpetual [pə'petjuəl] *adj* perpetuo

perpetuate [pə'pɛtjueɪt] *vt* perpetuar
perplex [pə'plɛks] *vt* dejar perplejo
persecute [ˈpɜːsɪkjuːt] *vt* perseguir
perseverance [pɜːsɪ'vɪərəns] *n* perseverancia
persevere [pɜːsɪ'vɪə*] *vi* persistir
Persian ['pɜːʃən] *adj, n* persa *m/f*; **the ~ Gulf** el Golfo Pérsico
persist [pə'sɪst] *vi*: **to ~ (in doing sth)** persistir (en hacer algo); **~ence** *n* empeño; **~ent** *adj* persistente; *(determined)* porfiado
person ['pɜːsn] *n* persona; **in ~** en persona; **~al** *adj* personal; individual; *(visit)* en persona; **~al assistant** *n* ayudante *m/f* personal; **~al call** *n (TEL)* llamada persona a persona; **~al column** *n* anuncios *mpl* personales; **~al computer** *n* ordenador *m* personal; **~ality** [-'nælɪtɪ] *n* personalidad *f*; **~ally** *adv* personalmente; *(in person)* en persona; **to take sth ~ally** tomarse algo a mal; **~al organizer** *n* agenda; **~al stereo** *n* Walkman *m* ®; **~ify** [-'sɒnɪfaɪ] *vt* encarnar
personnel [pɜːsə'nɛl] *n* personal *m*
perspective [pə'spɛktɪv] *n* perspectiva
Perspex ['pɜːspɛks] ® *n* plexiglás *m* ®
perspiration [pɜːspɪ'reɪʃən] *n* transpiración *f*
persuade [pə'sweɪd] *vt*: **to ~ sb to do sth** persuadir a uno para que haga algo
pertaining [pə:'teɪnɪŋ]: **~ to** *prep* relacionado con
pertinent ['pɜːtɪnənt] *adj* pertinente, a propósito
Peru [pə'ruː] *n* el Perú
peruse [pə'ruːz] *vt* leer con detención, examinar
Peruvian [pə'ruːvɪən] *adj, n* peruano/a *m/f*
pervade [pə'veɪd] *vt* impregnar, infundirse en
perverse [pə'vɜːs] *adj* perverso; *(wayward)* travieso
pervert [*n* 'pɜːvɜːt, *vb* pə'vɜːt] *n* pervertido/a ♦ *vt* pervertir; *(truth, sb's words)* tergiversar
pessimist ['pɛsɪmɪst] *n* pesimista *m/f*; **~ic** [-'mɪstɪk] *adj* pesimista

pest [pɛst] *n (insect)* insecto nocivo; *(fig)* lata, molestia
pester ['pɛstə*] *vt* molestar, acosar
pesticide ['pɛstɪsaɪd] *n* pesticida *m*
pet [pɛt] *n* animal *m* doméstico ♦ *cpd* favorito ♦ *vt* acariciar ♦ *vi (inf)* besuquearse; **teacher's ~** favorito/a (del profesor); **~ hate** manía
petal ['pɛtl] *n* pétalo
peter ['piːtə*]: **to ~ out** *vi* agotarse, acabarse
petite [pə'tiːt] *adj* chiquita
petition [pə'tɪʃən] *n* petición *f*
petrified ['pɛtrɪfaɪd] *adj* horrorizado
petrol ['pɛtrəl] *(BRIT) n* gasolina; **two/four-star ~** gasolina normal/súper; **~ can** *n* bidón *m* de gasolina
petroleum [pə'trəʊlɪəm] *n* petróleo
petrol: **~ pump** *(BRIT) n (in garage)* surtidor *m* de gasolina; **~ station** *(BRIT) n* gasolinera; **~ tank** *(BRIT) n* depósito (de gasolina)
petticoat ['pɛtɪkəʊt] *n* enaguas *fpl*
petty ['pɛtɪ] *adj (mean)* mezquino; *(unimportant)* insignificante; **~ cash** *n* dinero para gastos menores; **~ officer** *n* contramaestre *m*
petulant ['pɛtjʊlənt] *adj* malhumorado
pew [pjuː] *n* banco
pewter ['pjuːtə*] *n* peltre *m*
phantom ['fæntəm] *n* fantasma *m*
pharmacist ['fɑːməsɪst] *n* farmacéutico/a
pharmacy ['fɑːməsɪ] *n* farmacia
phase [feɪz] *n* fase *f* ♦ *vt*: **to ~ sth in/out** introducir/retirar algo por etapas
Ph.D. *abbr* = **Doctor of Philosophy**
pheasant ['fɛznt] *n* faisán *m*
phenomenon [fə'nɒmɪnən] *(pl* **phenomena)** *n* fenómeno
philanthropist [fɪ'lænθrəpɪst] *n* filántropo/a
Philippines ['fɪlɪpiːnz] *npl*: **the ~** las Filipinas
philosopher [fɪ'lɒsəfə*] *n* filósofo/a
philosophy [fɪ'lɒsəfɪ] *n* filosofía
phlegm [flɛm] *n* flema; **~atic** [flɛg'mætɪk] *adj* flemático
phobia ['fəʊbjə] *n* fobia

phone [fəun] n teléfono ♦ vt telefonear, llamar por teléfono; **to be on the ~** tener teléfono; (*be calling*) estar hablando por teléfono; **~ back** vt, vi volver a llamar; **~ up** vt, vi llamar por teléfono; **~ book** n guía telefónica; **~ booth** n cabina telefónica; **~ box** (BRIT) n = **~ booth**; **~ call** n llamada (telefónica); **~card** n teletarjeta; **~-in** (BRIT) n (RADIO, TV) programa m de participación (telefónica)

phonetics [fə'nɛtiks] n fonética

phoney ['fəuni] adj falso

photo ['fəutəu] n foto f

photo... ['fəutəu] prefix: **~copier** n fotocopiadora; **~copy** n fotocopia ♦ vt fotocopiar

photograph ['fəutəgrɑːf] n fotografía ♦ vt fotografiar; **~er** [fə'tɔgrəfə*] n fotógrafo; **~y** [fə'tɔgrəfi] n fotografía

phrase [freiz] n frase f ♦ vt expresar; **~ book** n libro de frases

physical ['fizikl] adj físico; **~ education** n educación f física; **~ly** adv físicamente

physician [fi'ziʃən] n médico/a

physicist ['fizisist] n físico/a

physics ['fiziks] n física

physiotherapy [fiziəu'θɛrəpi] n fisioterapia

physique [fi'ziːk] n físico

pianist ['piːənist] n pianista m/f

piano [pi'ænəu] n piano

piccolo ['pikələu] n (MUS) flautín m

pick [pik] n (tool: also: **~axe**) pico, piqueta ♦ vt (select) elegir, escoger; (gather) coger (SP), recoger; (remove, take out) sacar, quitar; (lock) abrir con ganzúa; **take your ~** escoja lo que quiera; **the ~ of** lo mejor de; **to ~ one's nose/teeth** hurgarse las narices/ limpiarse los dientes; **to ~ a quarrel with sb** meterse con alguien; **~ at** vt fus: **to ~ at one's food** comer con poco apetito; **~ on** vt fus (person) meterse con; **~ out** vt (choose) escoger; (distinguish) identificar; **~ up** vi (improve: sales) ir mejor; (: patient) reponerse; (: FINANCE) recobrarse ♦ vt recoger; (learn) aprender; (POLICE: arrest) detener;

(person: for sex) ligar; (RADIO) captar; **to ~ up speed** acelerarse; **to ~ o.s. up** levantarse

picket ['pikit] n piquete m ♦ vt piquetear

pickle ['pikl] n (also: **~s**: as condiment) escabeche m; (fig: mess) apuro ♦ vt encurtir

pickpocket ['pikpɔkit] n carterista m/f

pickup ['pikʌp] n (small truck) furgoneta

picnic ['piknik] n merienda ♦ vi ir de merienda

picture ['piktʃə*] n cuadro; (painting) pintura; (photograph) fotografía; (TV) imagen f; (film) película; (fig: description) descripción f; (: situation) situación f ♦ vt (imagine) imaginar; **~s** npl: **the ~s** (BRIT) el cine; **~ book** n libro de dibujos

picturesque [piktʃə'rɛsk] adj pintoresco

pie [pai] n pastel m; (open) tarta; (small: of meat) empanada

piece [piːs] n pedazo, trozo; (of cake) trozo; (item): **a ~ of clothing/ furniture/advice** una prenda (de vestir)/un mueble/un consejo ♦ vt: **to ~ together** juntar; (TECH) armar; **to take to ~s** desmontar; **~meal** adv poco a poco; **~work** n trabajo a destajo

pie chart n gráfico de sectores or tarta

pier [piə*] n muelle m, embarcadero

pierce [piəs] vt perforar

piercing ['piəsiŋ] adj penetrante

piety ['paiəti] n piedad f

pig [pig] n cerdo (SP), puerco (SP), chancho (AM); (pej: unkind person) asqueroso; (: greedy person) glotón/ona m/f

pigeon ['pidʒən] n paloma; (as food) pichón m; **~hole** n casilla

piggy bank ['pigi-] n hucha (en forma de cerdito)

pig: ~headed ['pig'hɛdid] adj terco, testarudo; **~let** ['piglit] n cochinillo; **~skin** n piel f de cerdo; **~sty** ['pigstai] n pocilga; **~tail** n (girl's) trenza; (Chinese, TAUR) coleta

pike [paik] n (fish) lucio

pilchard ['piltʃəd] n sardina

pile [pail] n montón m; (of carpet, cloth) pelo ♦ vt (also: **~ up**) amontonar; (fig) acumular ♦ *vi* (*also:* ~ up) amontonarse; acumularse; ~ into *vt fus* (*car*) meterse en; ~s [pailz] *npl* (*MED*) almorranas *fpl*, hemorroides *mpl*; ~-up *n* (*AUT*) accidente *m* múltiple

pilfering ['pilfəriŋ] *n* ratería

pilgrim ['pilgrim] *n* peregrino/a; ~age [ədʒ] *n* peregrinación *f*, romería

pill [pil] *n* píldora; the ~ la píldora

pillage ['pilidʒ] *vt* pillar, saquear

pillar ['pilə*] *n* pilar *m*; ~ box (*BRIT*) *n* buzón *m*

pillion ['piljən] *n* (*of motorcycle*) asiento trasero

pillory ['piləri] *vt* poner en la picota, criticar con dureza

pillow ['piləʊ] *n* almohada; ~case *n* funda

pilot ['pailət] *n* piloto ♦ *cpd* (*scheme etc*) piloto ♦ *vt* pilotar; ~ light *n* piloto

pimp [pimp] *n* chulo (*SP*), cafiche *m* (*AM*)

pimple ['pimpl] *n* grano

PIN *n abbr* (= *personal identification number*) número personal

pin [pin] *n* alfiler *m* ♦ *vt* prender (con alfiler); ~s and needles hormigueo; to ~ sb down (*fig*) hacer que uno concrete; to ~ sth on sb (*fig*) colgarle a uno el sambenito de algo

pinafore ['pinəfɔ:*] *n* delantal *m*; ~ dress (*BRIT*) *n* mandil *m*

pinball ['pinbɔ:l] *n* mesa americana

pincers ['pinsəz] *npl* pinzas *fpl*, tenazas *fpl*

pinch [pintʃ] *n* (*of salt etc*) pizca ♦ *vt* pellizcar; (*inf: steal*) birlar; at a ~ en caso de apuro

pincushion ['pinkuʃən] *n* acerico

pine [pain] *n* (*also:* ~ tree, wood) pino ♦ *vi:* to ~ for suspirar por; ~ away *vi* morirse de pena

pineapple ['painæpl] *n* piña, ananás *m*

ping [piŋ] *n* (*noise*) sonido agudo; ~-pong ® *n* pingpong *m* ®

pink [piŋk] *adj* rosado, (color de) rosa ♦ *n* (*colour*) rosa, (*BOT*) clavel *m*, clavellina

pinnacle ['pinəkl] *n* cumbre *f*

pinpoint ['pinpɔint] *vt* precisar

pint [paint] *n* pinta (*BRIT* = 568cc; *US* = 473cc); (*BRIT: inf: of beer*) pinta de cerveza, ≈ jarra (*SP*)

pin-up *n* fotografía erótica

pioneer [paiə'niə*] *n* pionero/a

pious ['paiəs] *adj* piadoso, devoto

pip [pip] *n* (*seed*) pepita; the ~s (*BRIT*) la señal

pipe [paip] *n* tubo, caño; (*for smoking*) pipa ♦ *vt* conducir en cañerías; ~s *npl* (*gen*) cañería; (*also: bag~s*) gaita; ~ down (*inf*) *vi* callarse; ~ cleaner *n* limpiapipas *m inv*; ~ dream *n* sueño imposible; ~line *n* (*for oil*) oleoducto; (*for gas*) gasoducto; ~r *n* gaitero/a

piping ['paipiŋ] *adv:* to be ~ hot estar que quema

piquant ['pi:kənt] *adj* picante; (*fig*) agudo

pique [pi:k] *n* pique *m*, resentimiento

pirate ['paiərət] *n* pirata *m/f* ♦ *vt* (*cassette, book*) piratear; ~ radio (*BRIT*) *n* emisora pirata

pirouette [piru'ɛt] *n* pirueta

Pisces ['paisi:z] *n* Piscis *m*

piss [pis] (*inf!*) *vi* mear; ~ed (*inf!*) *adj* (*drunk*) borracho

pistol ['pistl] *n* pistola

piston ['pistən] *n* pistón *m*, émbolo

pit [pit] *n* hoyo; (*also: coal* ~) mina; (*in garage*) foso de inspección; (*also: orchestra* ~) platea ♦ *vt:* to ~ one's wits against sb medir fuerzas con uno; ~s *npl* (*AUT*) box *m*

pitch [pitʃ] *n* (*MUS*) tono; (*BRIT: SPORT*) campo, terreno; (*fig*) punto; (*tar*) brea ♦ *vt* (*throw*) arrojar, lanzar ♦ *vi* (*fall*) caer(se); to ~ a tent montar una tienda (de campaña); ~-black *adj* negro como boca de lobo; ~ed battle *n* batalla campal

piteous ['pitiəs] *adj* lastimoso

pitfall ['pitfɔ:l] *n* riesgo

pith [piθ] *n* (*of orange*) médula

pithy ['piθi] *adj* (*fig*) jugoso

pitiful ['pitiful] *adj* (*touching*) lastimoso, conmovedor(a)

pitiless ['pitilis] *adj* despiadado

pittance ['pitns] *n* miseria

pity ['piti] *n* compasión *f*, piedad *f* ♦ *vt*

compadecer(se de); **what a ~!** ¡qué pena!

pivot ['pɪvət] *n* eje *m*

pizza ['piːtsə] *n* pizza

placard ['plækɑːd] *n* letrero; (*in march etc*) pancarta

placate [plə'keɪt] *vt* apaciguar

place [pleɪs] *n* lugar *m*, sitio; (*seat*) plaza, asiento; (*post*) puesto; (*home*): **at/to his ~** en/a su casa; (*role: in society etc*) papel *m* ♦ *vt* (*object*) poner, colocar; (*identify*) reconocer; **to take ~** tener lugar; **to be ~d** (*in race, exam*) colocarse; **out of ~** (*not suitable*) fuera de lugar; **in the first ~** en primer lugar; **to change ~s with sb** cambiarse de sitio con uno; **~ of birth** lugar *m* de nacimiento

placid ['plæsɪd] *adj* apacible

plagiarism ['pleɪdʒɪərɪzəm] *n* plagio

plague [pleɪg] *n* plaga; (*MED*) peste *f* ♦ *vt* (*fig*) acosar, atormentar

plaice [pleɪs] *n inv* platija

plaid [plæd] *n* (*material*) tartán *m*

plain [pleɪn] *adj* (*unpatterned*) liso; (*clear*) claro, evidente; (*simple*) sencillo; (*not handsome*) poco atractivo ♦ *adv* claramente ♦ *n* llano, llanura; **~ chocolate** *n* chocolate *m* amargo; **~ clothes** *adj* (*police*) vestido de paisano; **~ly** *adv* claramente

plaintiff ['pleɪntɪf] *n* demandante *m/f*

plaintive ['pleɪntɪv] *adj* lastimero

plait [plæt] *n* trenza

plan [plæn] *n* (*drawing*) plano; (*scheme*) plan *m*, proyecto ♦ *vt* proyectar, planificar ♦ *vi* hacer proyectos; **to ~ to do** pensar hacer

plane [pleɪn] *n* (*AVIAT*) avión *m*; (*MATH, fig*) plano; (*also: ~ tree*) plátano; (*tool*) cepillo

planet ['plænɪt] *n* planeta *m*

plank [plæŋk] *n* tabla

planner ['plænə*] *n* planificador(a) *m/f*

planning ['plænɪŋ] *n* planificación *f*; **family ~** planificación familiar; **~ permission** *n* permiso para realizar obras

plant [plɑːnt] *n* planta; (*machinery*) maquinaria; (*factory*) fábrica ♦ *vt* plantar; (*field*) sembrar; (*bomb*) colocar

plaque [plæk] *n* placa

plaster ['plɑːstə*] *n* (*for walls*) yeso; (*also: ~ of Paris*) yeso mate; (*BRIT: also: sticking ~*) tirita (*SP*), esparadrapo, curita (*AM*) ♦ *vt* enyesar; (*cover*): **to ~ with** llenar *or* cubrir de; **~ed** (*inf*) *adj* borracho; **~er** *n* yesero

plastic ['plæstɪk] *n* plástico ♦ *adj* de plástico; **~ bag** *n* bolsa de plástico

plasticine ['plæstɪsiːn] ® (*BRIT*) *n* plastilina ®

plastic surgery *n* cirujía plástica

plate [pleɪt] *n* (*dish*) plato; (*metal, in book*) lámina; (*dental ~*) placa de dentadura postiza

plateau ['plætəʊ] (*pl* **~s** *or* **~x**) *n* meseta, altiplanicie *f*

plateaux ['plætəʊz] *npl of* **plateau**

plate glass *n* vidrio cilindrado

platform ['plætfɔːm] *n* (*RAIL*) andén *m*; (*stage, BRIT: on bus*) plataforma; (*at meeting*) tribuna; (*POL*) programa *m* (*electoral*)

platinum ['plætɪnəm] *adj, n* platino

platitude ['plætɪtjuːd] *n* lugar *m* común, tópico

platoon [plə'tuːn] *n* pelotón *m*

platter ['plætə*] *n* fuente *f*

plausible ['plɔːzɪbl] *adj* verosímil; (*person*) convincente

play [pleɪ] *n* (*THEATRE*) obra, comedia ♦ *vt* (*game*) jugar; (*compete against*) jugar contra; (*instrument*) tocar; (*part: in play etc*) hacer el papel de; (*tape, record*) poner ♦ *vi* jugar; (*band*) tocar; (*tape, record*) sonar; **to ~ safe** ir a lo seguro; **~ down** *vt* quitar importancia a; **~ up** *vi* (*cause trouble to*) dar guerra; **~boy** *n* playboy *m*; **~er** *n* jugador(a) *m/f*; (*THEATRE*) actor/actriz *m/f*; (*MUS*) músico/a; **~ful** *adj* juguetón/ona; **~ground** *n* (*in school*) patio de recreo; (*in park*) parque *m* infantil; **~group** *n* jardín *m* de niños; **~ing card** *n* naipe *m*, carta; **~ing field** *n* campo de deportes; **~mate** *n* compañero/a de juego; **~-off** *n* (*SPORT*) (*partido de*) desempate *m*; **~pen** *n* corral *m*; **~thing** *n* juguete *m*; **~time** *n* (*SCOL*) recreo; **~wright** *n* dramaturgo/a

plc *abbr* (= *public limited company*) ≈

S.A.

plea [pliː] *n* súplica, petición *f*; (*LAW*) alegato, defensa; **~ bargaining** *n* (*LAW*) *acuerdo entre fiscal y defensor para agilizar los trámites judiciales*

plead [pliːd] *vt* (*LAW*): **to ~ sb's case** defender a uno; (*give as excuse*) poner como pretexto ♦ *vi* (*LAW*) declararse; (*beg*): **to ~ with sb** suplicar *or* rogar a uno

pleasant ['plɛznt] *adj* agradable; **~ries** *npl* cortesías *fpl*

please [pliːz] *excl* ¡por favor! ♦ *vt* (*give pleasure to*) dar gusto a, agradar ♦ *vi* (*think fit*): **do as you ~** haz lo que quieras; **~ yourself!** (*inf*) ¡haz lo que quieras!, ¡como quieras!; **~d** *adj* (*happy*) alegre, contento; **~d (with)** satisfecho (de); **~d to meet you** ¡encantado!, ¡tanto gusto!; **pleasing** *adj* agradable, grato

pleasure ['plɛʒə*] *n* placer *m*, gusto; "**it's a ~**" "el gusto es mío"; **~ boat** *n* barco de recreo

pleat [pliːt] *n* pliegue *m*

pledge [plɛdʒ] *n* (*promise*) promesa, voto ♦ *vt* prometer

plentiful ['plɛntɪful] *adj* copioso, abundante

plenty ['plɛntɪ] *n*: **~ of** mucho(s)/a(s)

pliable ['plaɪəbl] *adj* flexible

pliant ['plaɪənt] *adj* = **pliable**

pliers ['plaɪəz] *npl* alicates *mpl*, tenazas *fpl*

plight [plaɪt] *n* situación *f* difícil

plimsolls ['plɪmsəlz] (*BRIT*) *npl* zapatos *mpl* de tenis

plinth [plɪnθ] *n* plinto

plod [plɔd] *vi* caminar con paso pesado; (*fig*) trabajar laboriosamente

plonk [plɔŋk] (*inf*) *n* (*BRIT*: *wine*) vino peleón ♦ *vt*: **to ~ sth down** dejar caer algo

plot [plɔt] *n* (*scheme*) complot *m*, conjura; (*of story, play*) argumento; (*of land*) terreno, lote *m* ♦ *vt* (*mark out*) trazar; (*conspire*) tramar, urdir ♦ *vi* conspirar; **~ter** *n* (*instrument*) trazador *m* de gráficos

plough [plau] (*US* **plow**) *n* arado ♦ *vt*

(*earth*) arar; **to ~ money into** invertir dinero en; **~ through** *vt fus* (*crowd*) abrirse paso por la fuerza por; **~man's lunch** (*BRIT*) *n* almuerzo de pub a base de pan, queso y encurtidos

ploy [plɔɪ] *n* truco, estratagema

pluck [plʌk] *vt* (*fruit*) coger (*SP*), recoger (*AM*); (*musical instrument*) puntear; (*bird*) desplumar; (*eyebrows*) depilar ♦ *n* valor *m*, ánimo; **to ~ up courage** hacer de tripas corazón

plug [plʌg] *n* tapón *m*; (*ELEC*) enchufe *m*, clavija; (*AUT*: *also*: **spark(ing) ~**) bujía ♦ *vt* (*hole*) tapar; (*inf*: *advertise*) dar publicidad a; **~ in** *vt* (*ELEC*) enchufar

plum [plʌm] *n* (*fruit*) ciruela ♦ *cpd*: **~ job** (*inf*) puesto (*de trabajo*) muy codiciado

plumb [plʌm] *vt*: **to ~ the depths of** alcanzar los mayores extremos de

plumber ['plʌmə*] *n* fontanero/a (*SP*), plomero/a (*AM*)

plumbing ['plʌmɪŋ] *n* (*trade*) fontanería, plomería; (*piping*) cañería

plume [pluːm] *n* pluma; (*on helmet etc*) penacho

plummet ['plʌmɪt] *vi*: **to ~ (down)** caer a plomo

plump [plʌmp] *adj* rechoncho, rollizo ♦ *vi*: **to ~ for** (*inf*: *choose*) optar por; **~ up** *vt* mullir

plunder ['plʌndə*] *n* pillaje *m*; (*loot*) botín *m* ♦ *vt* pillar, saquear

plunge [plʌndʒ] *n* zambullida ♦ *vt* sumergir, hundir ♦ *vi* (*fall*) caer; (*dive*) saltar; (*person*) arrojarse; **to take the ~** lanzarse; **~r** *n* (*for drain*) desatascador *m*; **plunging** *adj*: **plunging neckline** escote *m* pronunciado

pluperfect [pluː'pəːfɪkt] *n* pluscuamperfecto

plural ['pluərl] *adj* plural ♦ *n* plural *m*

plus [plʌs] *n* (*also*: **~ sign**) signo más ♦ *prep* más, y, además de; **ten/twenty ~** más de diez/veinte

plush [plʌʃ] *adj* lujoso

plutonium [pluː'təʊnɪəm] *n* plutonio

ply [plaɪ] *vt* (*a trade*) ejercer ♦ *vi* (*ship*) ir y venir ♦ *n* (*of wool, rope*) cabo; **to ~ sb with drink** insistir en ofrecer a uno muchas copas; **~wood** n madera contrachapada

P.M. n abbr = **Prime Minister**

p.m. adv abbr (= post meridiem) de la tarde or noche

pneumatic [njuːˈmætɪk] adj neumático; **~ drill** n martillo neumático

pneumonia [njuːˈməʊnɪə] n pulmonía

poach [pəʊtʃ] vt (cook) escalfar; (steal) cazar (or pescar) en vedado ♦ vi cazar (or pescar) en vedado; **~ed** adj escalfado; **~er** n cazador(a) m/f furtivo/a

P.O. Box n abbr = **Post Office Box**

pocket [ˈpɒkɪt] n bolsillo; (fig: small area) bolsa ♦ vt meter en el bolsillo; (steal) embolsar; **to be out of ~** (BRIT) salir perdiendo; **~book** (US) n cartera; **~ calculator** n calculadora de bolsillo; **~ knife** n navaja; **~ money** n asignación f

pod [pɒd] n vaina

podgy [ˈpɒdʒɪ] adj gordinflón/ona

podiatrist [pəˈdiːətrɪst] (US) n pedicuro/a

poem [ˈpəʊɪm] n poema m

poet [ˈpəʊɪt] n poeta m/f; **~ic** [-ˈɛtɪk] adj poético; **~ laureate** n poeta m laureado; **~ry** n poesía

poignant [ˈpɔɪnjənt] adj conmovedor(a)

point [pɔɪnt] n punto; (tip) punta; (purpose) fin m, propósito; (use) utilidad f; (significant part) lo significativo; (moment) momento; (ELEC) toma (de corriente); (also: decimal ~): **2 ~ 3 (2.3)** dos coma tres (2,3) ♦ vt señalar; (gun etc): **to ~ sth at sb** apuntar algo a uno ♦ vi: **to ~ at** señalar; **~s** npl (AUT) contactos mpl; (RAIL) agujas fpl; **to be on the ~ of doing sth** estar a punto de hacer algo; **to make a ~ of** poner empeño en; **to get/miss the ~** comprender/no comprender; **to come to the ~** ir al meollo; **there's no ~ (in doing)** no tiene sentido (hacer); **~ out** vt señalar; **~ to** vt fus (fig) indicar, señalar; **~-blank** adv (say, refuse) sin más hablar; (also: **at ~-blank range**) a quemarropa; **~ed** adj (shape) puntiagudo, afilado; (remark) intencionado; **~edly** adv intencionadamente; **~er** n (needle) aguja, indicador m; **~less** adj sin sentido; **~ of**

view n punto de vista

poise [pɔɪz] n aplomo, elegancia

poison [ˈpɔɪzn] n veneno ♦ vt envenenar; **~ing** n envenenamiento; **~ous** adj venenoso; (fumes etc) tóxico

poke [pəʊk] vt (jab with finger, stick etc) empujar; (put): **to ~ sth in(to)** introducir algo en; **~ about** vi fisgonear

poker [ˈpəʊkə*] n atizador m; (CARDS) póker m; **~-faced** adj de cara impasible

poky [ˈpəʊkɪ] adj estrecho

Poland [ˈpəʊlənd] n Polonia

polar [ˈpəʊlə*] adj polar; **~ bear** n oso polar

Pole [pəʊl] n polaco/a

pole [pəʊl] n palo; (fixed) poste m; (GEO) polo; **~ bean** (US) n ≈ judía verde; **~ vault** n salto con pértiga

police [pəˈliːs] n policía ♦ vt vigilar; **~ car** n coche-patrulla m; **~man** n policía m, guardia m; **~ state** n estado policial; **~ station** n comisaría; **~woman** n mujer f policía

policy [ˈpɒlɪsɪ] n política; (also: insurance ~) póliza

polio [ˈpəʊlɪəu] n polio f

Polish [ˈpəʊlɪʃ] adj polaco ♦ n (LING) polaco

polish [ˈpɒlɪʃ] n (for shoes) betún m; (for floor) cera (de lustrar); (shine) brillo, lustre m; (fig: refinement) educación f ♦ vt (shoes) limpiar; (make shiny) pulir, sacar brillo a; **~ off** vt (work) terminar; (food) despachar; **~ed** adj (fig: person) elegante

polite [pəˈlaɪt] adj cortés, atento; **~ness** n cortesía

political [pəˈlɪtɪkl] adj político

politician [pɒlɪˈtɪʃən] n político/a

politics [ˈpɒlɪtɪks] n política

poll [pəʊl] n (election) votación f; (also: opinion ~) sondeo, encuesta ♦ vt encuestar; (votes) obtener

pollen [ˈpɒlən] n polen m

polling day [ˈpəʊlɪŋ-] n día m de elecciones

polling station n centro electoral

pollute [pəˈluːt] vt contaminar

pollution [pəˈluːʃən] n polución f,

contaminación *f* del medio ambiente

polo ['pəuləu] *n* (*sport*) polo; **~-necked** *adj* de cuello vuelto; **~ shirt** *n* polo, niqui *m*

polyester [pɒlɪ'estə*] *n* poliéster *m*

polystyrene [pɒlɪ'staɪriːn] *n* poliestireno

polytechnic [pɒlɪ'teknɪk] *n* politécnico

polythene ['pɒlɪθiːn] (*BRIT*) *n* politeno

pomegranate ['pɒmɪgrænɪt] *n* granada

pomp [pɒmp] *n* pompa

pompom ['pɒmpɒm] *n* borla, pompón *m*

pompous ['pɒmpəs] *adj* pomposo

pond [pɒnd] *n* (*natural*) charca; (*artificial*) estanque *m*

ponder ['pɒndə*] *vt* meditar

ponderous ['pɒndərəs] *adj* pesado

pong [pɒŋ] (*BRIT: inf*) *n* hedor *m*

pontoon [pɒn'tuːn] *n* pontón *m*

pony ['pəunɪ] *n* poney *m*, jaca, potro (*AM*); **~tail** *n* cola de caballo; **~ trekking** (*BRIT*) *n* excursión *f* a caballo

poodle ['puːdl] *n* caniche *m*

pool [puːl] *n* (*natural*) charca; (*also: swimming ~*) piscina (*SP*), alberca (*AM*); (*fig: of light etc*) charco; (*SPORT*) chapolín *m* ♦ *vt* juntar; **~s** *npl* (*football ~s*) quinielas *fpl*; **typing ~** servicio de mecanografía

poor [puə*] *adj* pobre; (*bad*) de mala calidad ♦ *npl*: **the ~** los pobres; **~ly** *adj* mal, enfermo ♦ *adv* mal

pop [pɒp] *n* (*sound*) ruido seco; (*MUS*) (música) pop *m*; (*inf: father*) papá *m*; (*drink*) gaseosa ♦ *vt* (*put quickly*) meter (de prisa) ♦ *vi* reventar; (*cork*) saltar; **~ in/out** *vi* entrar/salir un momento; **~ up** *vi* aparecer inesperadamente; **~corn** *n* palomitas *fpl*

pope [pəup] *n* papa *m*

poplar ['pɒplə*] *n* álamo

poplin ['pɒplɪn] *n* popelina

popper ['pɒpə*] (*BRIT*) *n* automático

poppy ['pɒpɪ] *n* amapola

popsicle ['pɒpsɪkl] (*US*) *n* polo

pop star *n* estrella del pop

populace ['pɒpjuləs] *n* pueblo, plebe *f*

popular ['pɒpjulə*] *adj* popular; **~ize** *vt* popularizar; (*disseminate*) vulgarizar

population [pɒpju'leɪʃən] *n* población *f*

porcelain ['pɔːslɪn] *n* porcelana

porch [pɔːtʃ] *n* pórtico, entrada; (*US*) veranda

porcupine ['pɔːkjupaɪn] *n* puerco *m* espín

pore [pɔː*] *n* poro ♦ *vi*: **to ~ over** engolfarse en

pork [pɔːk] *n* carne *f* de cerdo (*SP*) or chancho (*AM*)

pornography [pɔː'nɒgrəfɪ] *n* pornografía

porpoise ['pɔːpəs] *n* marsopa

porridge ['pɒrɪdʒ] *n* gachas *fpl* de avena

port [pɔːt] *n* puerto; (*NAUT: left side*) babor *m*; (*wine*) vino de Oporto; **~ of call** puerto de escala

portable ['pɔːtəbl] *adj* portátil

porter ['pɔːtə*] *n* (*for luggage*) maletero; (*doorkeeper*) portero/a, conserje *m/f*

portfolio [pɔːt'fəuləu] *n* cartera

porthole ['pɔːthəul] *n* portilla

portion ['pɔːʃən] *n* porción *f*; (*of food*) ración *f*

portly ['pɔːtlɪ] *adj* corpulento

portrait ['pɔːtreɪt] *n* retrato

portray [pɔː'treɪ] *vt* retratar; (*subj: actor*) representar; **~al** *n* retrato; representación *f*

Portugal ['pɔːtjugl] *n* Portugal *m*

Portuguese [pɔːtju'giːz] *adj* portugués/esa ♦ *n inv* portugués/esa *m/f*; (*LING*) portugués *m*

pose [pəuz] *n* postura, actitud *f* ♦ *vi* (*pretend*): **to ~ as** hacerse pasar por ♦ *vt* (*question*) plantear; **to ~ for** posar para

posh [pɒʃ] (*inf*) *adj* elegante, de lujo

position [pə'zɪʃən] *n* posición *f*; (*job*) puesto; (*situation*) situación *f* ♦ *vt* colocar

positive ['pɒzɪtɪv] *adj* positivo; (*certain*) seguro; (*definite*) definitivo

possess [pə'zes] *vt* poseer; **~ion** [pə'zeʃən] *n* posesión *f*; **~ions** *npl* (*belongings*) pertenencias *fpl*

possibility [pɒsɪ'bɪlɪtɪ] *n* posibilidad *f*

possible ['pɒsɪbl] *adj* posible; **as big as ~** lo más grande posible; **possibly** *adv* posiblemente; **I cannot possibly come** me es imposible venir

post [pəust] *n* (*BRIT: system*) correos *mpl*; (*BRIT: letters, delivery*) correo; (*job,* *situation*) puesto; (*pole*) poste *m* ♦ *vt* (*BRIT*: *send by post*) echar al correo; (*BRIT*: *appoint*): **to ~ to** enviar a; **~age** *n* porte *m*, franqueo; **~age stamp** *n* sello de correos; **~al** *adj* postal, de correos; **~al order** *n* giro postal; **~box** (*BRIT*) *n* buzón *m*; **~card** *n* tarjeta postal; **~code** (*BRIT*) *n* código postal

postdate [pəust'deɪt] *vt* (*cheque*) poner fecha adelantada a

poster ['pəustə*] *n* cartel *m*

poste restante [pəust'rɛstɔ̃nt] (*BRIT*) *n* lista de correos

postgraduate [pəust'grædjuət] *n* posgraduado/a

posthumous ['pɔstjuməs] *adj* póstumo

postman ['pəustmən] *n* cartero

postmark ['pəustmɑːk] *n* matasellos *m inv*

post-mortem [-'mɔːtəm] *n* autopsia

post office *n* (*building*) (oficina de) correos *m*; (*organization*): **the Post Office** Administración *f* General de Correos; **Post Office Box** *n* apartado postal (*SP*), casilla de correos (*AM*)

postpone [pəs'pəun] *vt* aplazar

postscript ['pəustskrɪpt] *n* posdata

posture ['pɔstʃə*] *n* postura, actitud *f*

postwar [pəust'wɔː*] *adj* de la posguerra

posy ['pəuzɪ] *n* ramillete *m* (de flores)

pot [pɔt] *n* (*for cooking*) olla; (*tea~*) tetera; (*coffee~*) cafetera; (*for flowers*) maceta; (*for jam*) tarro, pote *m*; (*inf*: *marijuana*) chocolate *m* ♦ *vt* (*plant*) poner en tiesto; **to go to ~** (*inf*) irse al traste

potato [pə'teɪtəu] (*pl* ~**es**) *n* patata (*SP*), papa (*AM*); **~ peeler** *n* pelapatatas *m inv*

potent ['pəutnt] *adj* potente, poderoso; (*drink*) fuerte

potential [pə'tɛnʃl] *adj* potencial, posible ♦ *n* potencial *m*; **~ly** *adv* en potencia

pothole ['pɔthəul] *n* (*in road*) bache *m*; (*BRIT*: *underground*) gruta; **potholing** (*BRIT*) *n*: **to go potholing** dedicarse a la espeleología

potluck [pɔt'lʌk] *n*: **to take ~** tomar lo que haya

potted ['pɔtɪd] *adj* (*food*) en conserva;

(*plant*) en tiesto or maceta; (*shortened*) resumido

potter ['pɔtə*] *n* alfarero/a ♦ *vi*: **to ~ around, ~ about** (*BRIT*) hacer trabajitos; **~y** *n* cerámica; (*factory*) alfarería

potty ['pɔtɪ] *adj* (*inf*: *mad*) chiflado ♦ *n* orinal *m* de niño

pouch [pautʃ] *n* (*ZOOL*) bolsa; (*for tobacco*) petaca

poultry ['pəultrɪ] *n* aves *fpl* de corral; (*meat*) pollo

pounce [pauns] *vi*: **to ~ on** precipitarse sobre

pound [paund] *n* libra (*weight = 453g or 16oz; money = 100 pence*) ♦ *vt* (*beat*) golpear; (*crush*) machacar ♦ *vi* (*heart*) latir; **~ sterling** *n* libra esterlina

pour [pɔː*] *vt* echar; (*tea etc*) servir ♦ *vi* correr, fluir; **to ~ sb a drink** servirle a uno una copa; **~ away** *or* **off** *vt* vaciar, verter; **~ in** *vi* (*people*) entrar en tropel; **~ out** *vi* salir en tropel ♦ *vt* (*drink*) echar, servir; (*fig*): **to ~ out one's feelings** desahogarse; **~ing** *adj*: **~ing rain** lluvia torrencial

pout [paut] *vi* hacer pucheros

poverty ['pɔvətɪ] *n* pobreza, miseria; **~-stricken** *adj* necesitado

powder ['paudə*] *n* polvo; (*face ~*) polvos *mpl* ♦ *vt* polvorear; **to ~ one's face** empolvarse la cara; **~ compact** *n* polvera; **~ed milk** *n* leche *f* en polvo; **~ puff** *n* borla; **~ room** *n* aseos *mpl*

power ['pauə*] *n* (*strength*) fuerza; (*nation, TECH*) potencia; (*drive*) empuje *m*; (*ELEC*) fuerza, energía ♦ *vt* impulsar; **to be in ~** (*POL*) estar en el poder; **~ cut** (*BRIT*) *n* apagón *m*; **~ed** *adj*: **~ed by** impulsado por; **~ failure** *n* = **~ cut**; **~ful** *adj* poderoso; (*engine*) potente; (*speech etc*) convincente; **~less** *adj*: **~less (to do)** incapaz (de hacer); **~ point** (*BRIT*) *n* enchufe *m*; **~ station** *n* central *f* eléctrica

p.p. *abbr* (= *per procurationem*): **~ J. Smith** p.p. (por poder de) J. Smith; (= *pages*) págs

PR *n abbr* = **public relations**

practicable ['præktɪkəbl] *adj* factible

practical ['præktɪkl] *adj* práctico; **~ity** [-'kælɪtɪ] *n* factibilidad *f*; **~ joke** *n* broma pesada; **~ly** *adv* (*almost*) casi

practice ['præktɪs] *n* (*habit*) costumbre *f*; (*exercise*) práctica, ejercicio; (*training*) adiestramiento; (*MED: of profession*) práctica, ejercicio; (*MED, LAW: business*) consulta ♦ *vt, vi* (*US*) = **practise**; **in ~** (*in reality*) en la práctica; **out of ~** desentrenado

practise ['præktɪs] (*US* **practice**) *vt* (*carry out*) practicar; (*profession*) ejercer; (*train at*) practicar ♦ *vi* ejercer; (*train*) practicar; **practising** *adj* (*Christian etc*) practicante; (*lawyer*) en ejercicio

practitioner [præk'tɪʃənə*] *n* (*MED*) médico/a

prairie ['prɛərɪ] *n* pampa

praise [preɪz] *n* alabanza(s) *f(pl)*, elogio(s) *m(pl)* ♦ *vt* alabar, elogiar; **~worthy** *adj* loable

pram [præm] (*BRIT*) *n* cochecito de niño

prance [prɑːns] *vi* (*person*) contonearse

prank [præŋk] *n* travesura

prawn [prɔːn] *n* gamba

pray [preɪ] *vi* rezar

prayer [prɛə*] *n* oración *f*, rezo; (*entreaty*) ruego, súplica

preach [priːtʃ] *vi* (*also fig*) predicar; **~er** *n* predicador(a) *m/f*

precaution [prɪ'kɔːʃən] *n* precaución *f*

precede [prɪ'siːd] *vt, vi* preceder

precedent ['prɛsɪdənt] *n* precedente *m*

preceding [prɪ'siːdɪŋ] *adj* anterior

precinct ['priːsɪŋkt] *n* recinto; **~s** *npl* contornos *mpl*; **pedestrian ~** (*BRIT*) zona peatonal; **shopping ~** (*BRIT*) centro comercial

precious ['prɛʃəs] *adj* precioso

precipice ['prɛsɪpɪs] *n* precipicio

precipitate [prɪ'sɪpɪteɪt] *vt* precipitar

precise [prɪ'saɪs] *adj* preciso, exacto; **~ly** *adv* precisamente, exactamente

preclude [prɪ'kluːd] *vt* excluir

precocious [prɪ'kəʊʃəs] *adj* precoz

preconceived [priːkən'siːvd] *adj* preconcebido

precondition [priːkən'dɪʃən] *n* condición *f* previa

predator ['prɛdətə*] *n* animal *m* de rapiña, depredador *m*

predecessor ['priːdɪsɛsə*] *n* antecesor(a) *m/f*

predicament [prɪ'dɪkəmənt] *n* apuro

predict [prɪ'dɪkt] *vt* pronosticar; **~able** *adj* previsible; **~ion** [-'dɪkʃən] *n* predicción *f*

predominantly [prɪ'dɒmɪnəntlɪ] *adv* en su mayoría

predominate [prɪ'dɒmɪneɪt] *vi* predominar

pre-empt [priː'ɛmt] *vt* adelantarse a

preen [priːn] *vt*: **to ~ itself** (*bird*) limpiarse (las plumas); **to ~ o.s.** pavonearse

prefab ['priːfæb] *n* casa prefabricada

preface ['prɛfəs] *n* prefacio

prefect ['priːfɛkt] (*BRIT*) *n* (*in school*) monitor(a) *m/f*

prefer [prɪ'fɜː*] *vt* preferir; **to ~ doing** *or* **to do** preferir hacer; **~able** ['prɛfrəbl] *adj* preferible; **~ably** ['prɛfrəblɪ] *adv* de preferencia; **~ence** ['prɛfrəns] *n* preferencia; (*priority*) prioridad *f*; **~ential** [prɛfə'rɛnʃəl] *adj* preferente

prefix ['priːfɪks] *n* prefijo

pregnancy ['prɛgnənsɪ] *n* (*of woman*) embarazo; (*of animal*) preñez *f*

pregnant ['prɛgnənt] *adj* (*woman*) embarazada; (*animal*) preñada

prehistoric ['priːhɪs'tɒrɪk] *adj* prehistórico

prejudice ['prɛdʒʊdɪs] *n* prejuicio; **~d** *adj* (*person*) predispuesto

preliminary [prɪ'lɪmɪnərɪ] *adj* preliminar

prelude ['prɛljuːd] *n* preludio

premarital ['priː'mærɪtl] *adj* premarital

premature ['prɛmətʃuə*] *adj* prematuro

premier ['prɛmɪə*] *adj* primero, principal ♦ *n* (*POL*) primer(a) ministro/a

première ['prɛmɪɛə*] *n* estreno

premise ['prɛmɪs] *n* premisa; **~s** *npl* (*of business etc*) local *m*; **on the ~s** en el lugar mismo

premium ['priːmɪəm] *n* premio; (*insurance*) prima; **to be at a ~** ser muy solicitado; **~ bond** (*BRIT*) *n* bono del estado que participa en una lotería nacional

premonition [prɛmə'nɪʃən] *n* presentimiento

preoccupied [pri:'ɔkjupaɪd] *adj* ensimismado

prep [prɛp] *n* (*SCOL: study*) deberes *mpl*

prepaid [pri:'peɪd] *adj* porte pagado

preparation [prɛpə'reɪʃən] *n* preparación *f*; ~s *npl* preparativos *mpl*

preparatory [prɪ'pærətərɪ] *adj* preparatorio, preliminar; ~ **school** *n* escuela preparatoria

prepare [prɪ'pɛə*] *vt* preparar, disponer; (*CULIN*) preparar ♦ *vi*: **to ~ for** (*action*) prepararse *or* disponerse para; (*event*) hacer preparativos para; ~**d to** dispuesto a; ~**d for** listo para

preponderance [prɪ'pɔndərns] *n* predominio

preposition [prɛpə'zɪʃən] *n* preposición *f*

preposterous [prɪ'pɔstərəs] *adj* absurdo, ridículo

prep school *n* = **preparatory school**

prerequisite [pri:'rɛkwɪzɪt] *n* requisito

prerogative [prɪ'rɔgətɪv] *n* prerrogativa

Presbyterian [prɛzbɪ'tɪərɪən] *adj, n* presbiteriano/a *m/f*

preschool ['pri:'sku:l] *adj* preescolar

prescribe [prɪ'skraɪb] *vt* (*MED*) recetar

prescription [prɪ'skrɪpʃən] *n* (*MED*) receta

presence ['prɛzns] *n* presencia; **in sb's ~** en presencia de uno; ~ **of mind** aplomo

present [*adj, n* 'prɛznt, *vb* prɪ'zɛnt] *adj* (*in attendance*) presente; (*current*) actual ♦ *n* (*gift*) regalo; (*actuality*): **the ~** la actualidad, el presente ♦ *vt* (*introduce, describe*) presentar; (*expound*) exponer; (*give*) presentar, dar, ofrecer; (*THEATRE*) representar; **to give sb a ~** regalar algo a uno; **at ~** actualmente; ~**able** [prɪ'zɛntəbl] *adj*: **to make o.s. ~able** arreglarse; ~**ation** [-'teɪʃən] *n* presentación *f*; (*of report etc*) exposición *f*; (*formal ceremony*) entrega de un regalo; ~**day** *adj* actual; ~**er** [prɪ'zɛntə*] *n* (*RADIO, TV*) locutor(a) *m/f*; ~**ly** *adv* (*soon*) dentro de poco; (*now*) ahora

preservation [prɛzə'veɪʃən] *n* conservación *f*

preservative [prɪ'zə:vətɪv] *n* conservante *m*

preserve [prɪ'zə:v] *vt* (*keep safe*) preservar, proteger; (*maintain*) mantener; (*food*) conservar ♦ *n* (*for game*) coto, vedado; (*often pl: jam*) conserva, confitura

preside [prɪ'zaɪd] *vi*: **to ~ over** presidir

president ['prɛzɪdənt] *n* presidente *m/f*; ~**ial** [-'dɛnʃl] *adj* presidencial

press [prɛs] *n* (*newspapers*): **the P~** la prensa; (*printer's*) imprenta; (*of button*) pulsación *f* ♦ *vt* empujar; (*button etc*) apretar; (*clothes: iron*) planchar; (*put pressure on: person*) presionar; (*insist*): **to ~ sth on sb** insistir en que uno acepte algo ♦ *vi* (*squeeze*) apretar; (*pressurize*): **to ~ for** presionar por; **we are ~ed for time/money** estamos apurados de tiempo/dinero; ~ **on** *vi* avanzar; (*hurry*) apretar el paso; ~ **agency** *n* agencia de prensa; ~ **conference** *n* rueda de prensa; ~**ing** *adj* apremiante; ~ **stud** (*BRIT*) *n* botón *m* de presión; ~~**up** (*BRIT*) *n* plancha

pressure ['prɛʃə*] *n* presión *f*; **to put ~ on sb** presionar a uno; ~ **cooker** *n* olla a presión; ~ **gauge** *n* manómetro; ~ **group** *n* grupo de presión; **pressurized** *adj* (*container*) a presión

prestige [prɛs'ti:ʒ] *n* prestigio

presumably [prɪ'zju:məblɪ] *adv* es de suponer que, cabe presumir que

presume [prɪ'zju:m] *vt*: **to ~ (that)** presumir (que), suponer (que)

presumption [prɪ'zʌmpʃən] *n* suposición *f*

presumptuous [prɪ'zʌmptjuəs] *adj* presumido

presuppose [pri:sə'pəuz] *vt* presuponer

pretence [prɪ'tɛns] (*US* **pretense**) *n* fingimiento; **under false ~s** con engaños

pretend [prɪ'tɛnd] *vt, vi* (*feign*) fingir

pretense [prɪ'tɛns] (*US*) *n* = **pretence**

pretentious [prɪ'tɛnʃəs] *adj* presumido; (*ostentatious*) ostentoso, aparatoso

pretext ['pri:tɛkst] *n* pretexto

pretty ['prɪtɪ] *adj* bonito (*SP*), lindo (*AM*) ♦ *adv* bastante

prevail [prɪ'veɪl] *vi* (*gain mastery*)

prevalecer; *(be current)* predominar;
~ing *adj (dominant)* predominante
prevalent ['prɛvələnt] *adj (widespread)*
extendido
prevent [prɪ'vɛnt] *vt:* **to ~ sb from doing
sth** impedir a uno hacer algo; **to ~ sth
from happening** evitar que ocurra algo;
~ative *adj* = **preventive**; ~ive *adj*
preventivo
preview ['pri:vju:] *n (of film)* preestreno
previous ['pri:vɪəs] *adj* previo, anterior;
~ly *adv* antes
prewar [pri:'wɔ:*] *adj* de antes de la
guerra
prey [preɪ] *n* presa ♦ *vi:* **to ~ on** *(feed on)*
alimentarse de; **it was ~ing on his
mind** le preocupaba, le obsesionaba
price [praɪs] *n* precio ♦ *vt (goods)* fijar el
precio de; ~**less** *adj* que no tiene precio;
~ **list** *n* tarifa
prick [prɪk] *n (sting)* picadura ♦ *vt*
pinchar; *(hurt)* picar; **to ~ up one's ears**
aguzar el oído
prickle ['prɪkl] *n (sensation)* picor *m*;
(BOT) espina; **prickly** *adj* espinoso; *(fig:
person)* enojadizo; **prickly heat** *n*
sarpullido causado por exceso de calor
pride [praɪd] *n* orgullo; *(pej)* soberbia
♦ *vt:* **to ~ o.s.** on enorgullecerse de
priest [pri:st] *n* sacerdote *m*; ~**ess** *n*
sacerdotisa; ~**hood** *n* sacerdocio
prig [prɪg] *n* gazmoño/a
prim [prɪm] *adj (demure)* remilgado;
(prudish) gazmoño
primarily ['praɪmərɪlɪ] *adv* ante todo
primary ['praɪmərɪ] *adj (first in importance)* principal ♦ *n (US: POL)* (elección *f)*
primaria; ~ **school** *(BRIT)* *n* escuela
primaria
primate [praɪmeɪt] *n (ZOOL)* primate *m*
prime [praɪm] *adj* primero, principal;
(excellent) selecto, de primera clase ♦ *n:*
in the ~ of life en la flor de la vida ♦ *vt*
(wood, fig) preparar; ~ **example** ejemplo
típico; P~ **Minister** *n* primer(a)
ministro/a
primeval [praɪ'mi:vəl] *adj* primitivo
primitive ['prɪmɪtɪv] *adj* primitivo;
(crude) rudimentario

primrose ['prɪmrəuz] *n* primavera,
prímula
Primus (stove) ['praɪməs-] ® *(BRIT)* *n*
hornillo de camping
prince [prɪns] *n* príncipe *m*
princess [prɪn'sɛs] *n* princesa
principal ['prɪnsɪpl] *adj* principal, mayor
♦ *n* director(a) *m/f*; ~**ity** [-'pælɪtɪ] *n*
principado
principle ['prɪnsɪpl] *n* principio; **in ~** en
principio; **on ~** por principio
print [prɪnt] *n (foot~)* huella; *(finger~)*
huella dactilar; *(letters)* letra de molde;
(fabric) estampado; *(ART)* grabado; *(PHOT)*
impresión *f* ♦ *vt* imprimir; *(cloth)*
estampar; *(write in capitals)* escribir en
letras de molde; **out of ~** agotado; ~**ed
matter** *n* impresos *mpl*; ~**er** *n (person)*
impresor(a) *m/f*; *(machine)* impresora;
~**ing** *n (art)* imprenta; *(act)* impresión *f*;
~**out** *n (COMPUT)* impresión *f*
prior ['praɪə*] *adj* anterior, previo; *(more
important)* más importante; ~ **to** antes
de
priority [praɪ'ɔrɪtɪ] *n* prioridad *f*; **to have
~ (over)** tener prioridad (sobre)
prise [praɪz] *vt:* **to ~ open** abrir con
palanca
prison ['prɪzn] *n* cárcel *f*, prisión *f* ♦ *cpd*
carcelario; ~**er** *n (in prison)* preso/a;
(captured person) prisionero; ~**er-of-war**
n prisionero de guerra
pristine ['prɪsti:n] *adj* inmaculado
privacy ['prɪvəsɪ] *n* intimidad *f*
private ['praɪvɪt] *adj (personal)*
particular; *(property, industry, discussion
etc)* privado; *(person)* reservado; *(place)*
tranquilo ♦ *n* soldado raso; **"~"** *(on
envelope)* "confidencial"; *(on door)*
"prohibido el paso"; **in ~** en privado; ~
enterprise *n* empresa privada; ~ **eye** *n*
detective *m/f* privado/a; ~ **property** *n*
propiedad *f* privada; ~ **school** *n* colegio
particular
privet ['prɪvɪt] *n* alheña
privilege ['prɪvɪlɪdʒ] *n* privilegio; *(prerogative)* prerrogativa
privy ['prɪvɪ] *adj:* **to be ~ to** estar
enterado de

prize [praɪz] n premio ♦ adj de primera clase ♦ vt apreciar, estimar; **~-giving** n distribución f de premios; **~winner** n premiado/a

pro [prəu] n (*SPORT*) profesional m/f ♦ prep a favor de; **the ~s and cons** los pros y los contras

probability [prɔbə'bɪlɪtɪ] n probabilidad f; **in all ~** con toda probabilidad

probable ['prɔbəbl] adj probable

probably ['prɔbəblɪ] adv probablemente

probation [prə'beɪʃən] n: **on ~** (*employee*) a prueba; (*LAW*) en libertad condicional

probe [prəub] n (*MED, SPACE*) sonda; (*enquiry*) encuesta, investigación f ♦ vt sondar; (*investigate*) investigar

problem ['prɔbləm] n problema m

procedure [prə'siːdʒə*] n procedimiento; (*bureaucratic*) trámites mpl

proceed [prə'siːd] vi (*do afterwards*): **to ~ to do sth** proceder a hacer algo; (*continue*): **to ~ (with)** continuar or seguir (con); **~ings** npl acto(s) (pl); (*LAW*) proceso; **~s** ['prəusiːdz] npl (*money*) ganancias fpl, ingresos mpl

process ['prəuses] n proceso ♦ vt tratar, elaborar; **~ing** n tratamiento, elaboración f; (*PHOT*) revelado

procession [prə'seʃən] n desfile m; **funeral ~** cortejo fúnebre

pro-choice [prəu'tʃɔɪs] adj en favor del derecho a elegir de la madre

proclaim [prə'kleɪm] vt (*announce*) anunciar; **proclamation** [prɔklə'meɪʃən] n proclamación f; (*written*) proclama

procrastinate [prəu'kræstɪneɪt] vi demorarse

procure [prə'kjuə*] vt conseguir

prod [prɔd] vt empujar ♦ n empujón m

prodigal ['prɔdɪgl] adj pródigo

prodigy ['prɔdɪdʒɪ] n prodigio

produce [n 'prɔdjuːs, vt prə'djuːs] n (*AGR*) productos mpl agrícolas ♦ vt producir; (*play, film, programme*) presentar; **~r** n productor(a) m/f; (*of film, programme*) director(a) m/f; (*of record*) productor(a) m/f

product ['prɔdʌkt] n producto

production [prə'dʌkʃən] n producción f;

(*THEATRE*) presentación f; **~ line** n línea de producción

productive [prə'dʌktɪv] adj productivo; **productivity** [prɔdʌk'tɪvɪtɪ] n productividad f

profane [prə'feɪn] adj profano

profession [prə'feʃən] n profesión f; **~al** adj profesional ♦ n profesional m/f; (*skilled person*) perito

professor [prə'fesə*] n (*BRIT*) catedrático/a; (*US, Canada*) profesor(a) m/f

proficiency [prə'fɪʃənsɪ] n capacidad f, habilidad f

proficient [prə'fɪʃənt] adj experto, hábil

profile ['prəufaɪl] n perfil m

profit ['prɔfɪt] n (*COMM*) ganancia ♦ vi: **to ~ by** or **from** aprovechar or sacar provecho de; **~ability** [-ə'bɪlɪtɪ] n rentabilidad f; **~able** adj (*ECON*) rentable

profound [prə'faund] adj profundo

profusely [prə'fjuːslɪ] adv profusamente

profusion [prə'fjuːʒən] n profusión f, abundancia

programme ['prəugræm] (*US* **program**) n programa m ♦ vt programar; **~r** (*US* **programer**) n programador(a) m/f; **programming** (*US* **programing**) n programación f

progress [n 'prəugres, vi prə'gres] n progreso; (*development*) desarrollo ♦ vi progresar, avanzar; **in ~** en curso; **~ive** [-'gresɪv] adj progresivo; (*person*) progresista

prohibit [prə'hɪbɪt] vt prohibir; **to ~ sb from doing sth** prohibir a uno hacer algo; **~ion** [-'bɪʃn] n prohibición f; (*US*): **P~ion** Ley f Seca

project [n 'prɔdʒekt, vb prə'dʒekt] n proyecto ♦ vt proyectar ♦ vi (*stick out*) salir, sobresalir; **projectile** [prə'dʒektaɪl] n proyectil m; **projection** [prə'dʒekʃən] n proyección f; (*overhang*) saliente m; **projector** [prə'dʒektə*] n proyector m

proletarian [prəulɪ'tɛərɪən] n proletario/a

proletariat [prəulɪ'tɛərɪət] n proletariado

pro-life [prəu'laɪf] adj pro-vida

prologue ['prəulɔg] n prólogo

prolong [prə'lɔŋ] vt prolongar, extender

prom [prɔm] n abbr = **promenade**; (*US:*

ball) baile *m* de gala

promenade [prɔmə'nɑːd] *n* (*by sea*) paseo marítimo; ~ **concert** (*BRIT*) *n* concierto (en que parte del público permanece de pie)

prominence ['prɔmɪnəns] *n* importancia

prominent ['prɔmɪnənt] *adj* (*standing out*) saliente; (*important*) eminente, importante

promiscuous [prə'mɪskjuəs] *adj* (*sexually*) promiscuo

promise ['prɔmɪs] *n* promesa ♦ *vt, vi* prometer; **promising** *adj* prometedor(a)

promote [prə'məut] *vt* (*employee*) ascender; (*product, pop star*) hacer propaganda por; (*ideas*) fomentar; ~**r** *n* (*of event*) promotor(a) *m/f*; (*of cause etc*) impulsor(a) *m/f*; **promotion** [-'məuʃən] *n* (*advertising campaign*) campaña de promoción *f*; (*in rank*) ascenso

prompt [prɔmpt] *adj* rápido ♦ *adv*: **at 6 o'clock** ~ a las seis en punto ♦ *n* (*COMPUT*) aviso ♦ *vt* (*urge*) mover, incitar; (*when talking*) instar; (*THEATRE*) apuntar; **to** ~ **sb to do sth** instar a uno a hacer algo; ~**ly** *adv* rápidamente; (*exactly*) puntualmente

prone [prəun] *adj* (*lying*) postrado; ~ **to** propenso a

prong [prɔŋ] *n* diente *m*, punta

pronoun ['prəunaun] *n* pronombre *m*

pronounce [prə'nauns] *vt* pronunciar; ~**d** *adj* (*marked*) marcado

pronunciation [prənʌnsɪ'eɪʃən] *n* pronunciación *f*

proof [pruːf] *n* prueba ♦ *adj*: ~ **against** a prueba de

prop [prɔp] *n* apoyo *m* ♦ *vt* (*also*: ~ *up*) apoyar; (*lean*): **to** ~ **sth against** apoyar algo contra

propaganda [prɔpə'gændə] *n* propaganda

propagate ['prɔpəgeɪt] *vt* (*idea, information*) difundir

propel [prə'pɛl] *vt* impulsar, propulsar; ~**ler** *n* hélice *f*

propensity [prə'pɛnsɪtɪ] *n* propensión *f*

proper ['prɔpə*] *adj* (*suited, right*) propio; (*exact*) justo; (*seemly*) correcto, decente; (*authentic*) verdadero; (*referring to place*):

the village ~ el pueblo mismo; ~**ly** *adv* (*adequately*) correctamente; (*decently*) decentemente; ~ **noun** *n* nombre *m* propio

property ['prɔpətɪ] *n* propiedad *f*; (*personal*) bienes *mpl* muebles; ~ **owner** *n* dueño/a de propiedades

prophecy ['prɔfɪsɪ] *n* profecía

prophesy ['prɔfɪsaɪ] *vt* (*fig*) predecir

prophet ['prɔfɪt] *n* profeta *m*

proportion [prə'pɔːʃən] *n* proporción *f*; (*share*) parte *f*; ~**al** *adj*: ~**al (to)** en proporción (con); ~**al representation** *n* representación *f* proporcional; ~**ate** *adj*: ~**ate (to)** en proporción (con)

proposal [prə'pəuzl] *n* (*offer of marriage*) oferta de matrimonio; (*plan*) proyecto

propose [prə'pəuz] *vt* proponer ♦ *vi* declararse; **to** ~ **to do** tener intención de hacer

proposition [prɔpə'zɪʃən] *n* propuesta

proprietor [prə'praɪətə*] *n* propietario/a, dueño/a

propriety [prə'praɪətɪ] *n* decoro

pro rata [-'rɑːtə] *adv* a prorrateo

prose [prəuz] *n* prosa

prosecute ['prɔsɪkjuːt] *vt* (*LAW*) procesar; **prosecution** [-'kjuːʃən] *n* proceso, causa; (*accusing side*) acusación *f*; **prosecutor** *n* acusador(a) *m/f*; (*also: public prosecutor*) fiscal *m*

prospect [*n* 'prɔspɛkt, *vb* prə'spɛkt] *n* (*possibility*) posibilidad *f*; (*outlook*) perspectiva ♦ *vi*: **to** ~ **for** buscar; ~**s** *npl* (*for work etc*) perspectivas *fpl*; ~**ing** *n* prospección *f*; ~**ive** [prə'spɛktɪv] *adj* futuro

prospectus [prə'spɛktəs] *n* prospecto

prosper ['prɔspə*] *vi* prosperar; ~**ity** [-'spɛrɪtɪ] *n* prosperidad *f*; ~**ous** *adj* próspero

prostitute ['prɔstɪtjuːt] *n* prostituta; (*male*) hombre que se dedica a la prostitución

prostrate ['prɔstreɪt] *adj* postrado

protagonist [prə'tægənɪst] *n* protagonista *m/f*

protect [prə'tɛkt] *vt* proteger; ~**ion** [-'tɛkʃən] *n* protección *f*; ~**ive** *adj* protector(a)

protégé ['prəʊtɛʒeɪ] *n* protegido/a
protein ['prəʊtiːn] *n* proteína
protest [*n* 'prəʊtɛst, *vb* prə'tɛst] *n* protesta
♦ *vi*: to ~ **about** *or* **at/against** protestar
de/contra ♦ *vt* (*insist*): to ~ **(that)**
insistir en (que)
Protestant ['prɒtɪstənt] *adj*, *n* protestante
m/f
protester [prə'tɛstə*] *n* manifestante *m/f*
protracted [prə'træktɪd] *adj* prolongado
protrude [prə'truːd] *vi* salir, sobresalir
proud [praʊd] *adj* orgulloso; (*pej*)
soberbio, altanero
prove [pruːv] *vt* probar; (*show*) demostrar
♦ *vi*: to ~ **(to be) correct** resultar
correcto; to ~ **o.s.** probar su valía
proverb ['prɒvəːb] *n* refrán *m*
provide [prə'vaɪd] *vt* proporcionar, dar;
to ~ **sb with sth** proveer a uno de algo;
~**d (that)** *conj* con tal de que, a condición de que; ~ **for** *vt fus* (*person*) mantener a; (*problem etc*) tener en cuenta;
providing [prə'vaɪdɪŋ] *conj*: **providing
(that)** a condición de que, con tal de que
province ['prɒvɪns] *n* provincia; (*fig*)
esfera; **provincial** [prə'vɪnʃəl] *adj*
provincial; (*pej*) provinciano
provision [prə'vɪʒən] *n* (*supplying*)
suministro, abastecimiento; (*of contract
etc*) disposición *f*; ~**s** *npl* (*food*)
comestibles *mpl*; ~**al** *adj* provisional
proviso [prə'vaɪzəʊ] *n* condición *f*,
estipulación *f*
provocative [prə'vɒkətɪv] *adj* provocativo
provoke [prə'vəʊk] *vt* (*cause*) provocar,
incitar; (*anger*) enojar
prow [praʊ] *n* proa
prowess ['praʊɪs] *n* destreza
prowl [praʊl] *vi* (*also*: ~ **about**, ~ **around**)
merodear ♦ *n*: **on the** ~ de merodeo; ~**er**
n merodeador(a) *m/f*
proxy ['prɒksɪ] *n*: **by** ~ por poderes
prude [pruːd] *n* remilgado/a
prudent ['pruːdənt] *adj* prudente
prune [pruːn] *n* ciruela pasa ♦ *vt* podar
pry [praɪ] *vi*: to ~ **(into)** entrometerse
(en)
PS *n abbr* (= *postscript*) P.D.
psalm [sɑːm] *n* salmo

pseudo- [sjuːdəʊ] *prefix* seudo-;
pseudonym *n* seudónimo
psyche ['saɪkɪ] *n* psique *f*
psychiatric [saɪkɪ'ætrɪk] *adj* psiquiátrico
psychiatrist [saɪ'kaɪətrɪst] *n* psiquiatra
m/f
psychic ['saɪkɪk] *adj* (*also*: ~**al**) psíquico
psychoanalyse [saɪkəʊ'ænəlaɪz] *vt*
psicoanalizar; **psychoanalysis** [-ə'næləsɪs]
n psicoanálisis *m inv*
psychological [saɪkə'lɒdʒɪkl] *adj*
psicológico
psychologist [saɪ'kɒlədʒɪst] *n* psicólogo/a
psychology [saɪ'kɒlədʒɪ] *n* psicología
PTO *abbr* (= *please turn over*) sigue
pub [pʌb] *n abbr* (= *public house*) pub *m*,
taberna
puberty ['pjuːbətɪ] *n* pubertad *f*
public ['pʌblɪk] *adj* público ♦ *n*: **the** ~ el
público; **in** ~ en público; **to make** ~
hacer público; ~ **address system** *n*
megafonía
publican ['pʌblɪkən] *n* tabernero/a
publication [pʌblɪ'keɪʃən] *n* publicación *f*
public: ~ **company** *n* sociedad *f*
anónima; ~ **convenience** (*BRIT*) *n* aseos
mpl públicos (*SP*), sanitarios *mpl* (*AM*); ~
holiday *n* día de fiesta (*SP*), (día) feriado
(*AM*); ~ **house** (*BRIT*) *n* bar *m*, pub *M*
publicity [pʌb'lɪsɪtɪ] *n* publicidad *f*
publicize ['pʌblɪsaɪz] *vt* publicitar
publicly ['pʌblɪklɪ] *adv* públicamente, en
público
public: ~ **opinion** *n* opinión *f* pública; ~
relations *fpl* relaciones *fpl* públicas; ~
school *n* (*BRIT*) escuela privada; (*US*)
instituto; ~**-spirited** *adj* que tiene
sentido del deber ciudadano; ~ **transport**
n transporte *m* público
publish ['pʌblɪʃ] *vt* publicar; ~**er** *n*
(*person*) editor(a) *m/f*; (*firm*) editorial *f*;
~**ing** *n* (*industry*) industria del libro
puce [pjuːs] *adj* de color pardo rojizo
pucker ['pʌkə*] *vt* (*pleat*) arrugar; (*brow
etc*) fruncir
pudding ['pʊdɪŋ] *n* pudín *m*; (*BRIT*:
dessert) postre *m*; **black** ~ morcilla
puddle ['pʌdl] *n* charco
puff [pʌf] *n* soplo; (*of smoke*, *air*)

bocanada; (*of breathing*) resoplido ♦ *vt*:
to ~ one's pipe chupar la pipa ♦ *vi*
(*pant*) jadear; ~ out *vt* hinchar; ~ed (*inf*)
adj (*out of breath*) sin aliento; ~ pastry
n hojaldre *m*; ~y *adj* hinchado
pull [pul] *n* (*tug*): to give sth a ~ dar un
tirón a algo ♦ *vt* tirar de; (*press: trigger*)
apretar; (*haul*) tirar, arrastrar; (*close:
curtain*) echar ♦ *vi* tirar; to ~ to pieces
hacer pedazos; to not ~ one's punches
no andarse con bromas; to ~ one's
weight hacer su parte; to ~ o.s.
together sobreponerse; to ~ sb's leg
tomar el pelo a uno; ~ apart *vt* (*break*)
romper; ~ down *vt* (*building*) derribar;
~ in *vi* (*car etc*) parar (junto a la acera);
(*train*) llegar a la estación; ~ off *vt* (*deal
etc*) cerrar; ~ out *vi* (*car, train etc*) salir
♦ *vt* sacar, arrancar; ~ over *vi* (*AUT*)
hacerse a un lado; ~ through *vi* (*MED*)
reponerse; ~ up *vi* (*stop*) parar ♦ *vt*
(*raise*) levantar; (*uproot*) arrancar,
desarraigar
pulley ['puli] *n* polea
pullover ['puləuvə*] *n* jersey *m*, suéter *m*
pulp [pʌlp] *n* (*of fruit*) pulpa
pulpit ['pulpit] *n* púlpito
pulsate [pʌl'seit] *vi* pulsar, latir
pulse [pʌls] *n* (*ANAT*) pulso; (*rhythm*)
pulsación *f*; (*BOT*) legumbre *f*
pummel ['pʌml] *vt* aporrear
pump [pʌmp] *n* bomba; (*shoe*) zapatilla
♦ *vt* sacar con una bomba; ~ up *vt* inflar
pumpkin ['pʌmpkin] *n* calabaza
pun [pʌn] *n* juego de palabras
punch [pʌntʃ] *n* (*blow*) golpe *m*,
puñetazo; (*tool*) punzón *m*; (*drink*)
ponche *m* ♦ *vt* (*hit*): to ~ sb/sth dar un
puñetazo *or* golpear a uno/algo; ~line *n*
palabras que rematan un chiste; ~-up
(*BRIT: inf*) *n* riña
punctual ['pʌŋktjuəl] *adj* puntual
punctuation [pʌŋktju'eiʃən] *n* puntuación
f
puncture ['pʌŋktʃə*] (*BRIT*) *n* pinchazo
♦ *vt* pinchar
pundit ['pʌndit] *n* experto/a
pungent ['pʌndʒənt] *adj* acre
punish ['pʌniʃ] *vt* castigar; ~ment *n*

castigo
punk [pʌŋk] *n* (*also*: ~ rocker) punki *m/f*;
(*also*: ~ rock) música punk; (*US: inf*:
hoodlum) rufián *m*
punt [pʌnt] *n* (*boat*) batea
punter ['pʌntə*] (*BRIT*) *n* (*gambler*)
jugador(a) *m/f*; (*inf*) cliente *m/f*
puny ['pjuːni] *adj* débil
pup [pʌp] *n* cachorro
pupil ['pjuːpl] *n* alumno/a; (*of eye*) pupila
puppet ['pʌpit] *n* títere *m*
puppy ['pʌpi] *n* cachorro, perrito
purchase ['pəːtʃis] *n* compra ♦ *vt*
comprar; ~r *n* comprador(a) *m/f*
pure [pjuə*] *adj* puro
purée ['pjuərei] *n* puré *m*
purely ['pjuəli] *adv* puramente
purge [pəːdʒ] *n* (*MED, POL*) purga ♦ *vt*
purgar
purify ['pjuərifai] *vt* purificar, depurar
puritan ['pjuəritən] *n* puritano/a
purity ['pjuəriti] *n* pureza
purple ['pəːpl] *adj* purpúreo; morado
purport [pəː'pɔːt] *vi*: to ~ to be/do dar a
entender que es/hace
purpose ['pəːpəs] *n* propósito; on ~ a
propósito, adrede; ~ful *adj* resuelto,
determinado
purr [pəː*] *vi* ronronear
purse [pəːs] *n* monedero; (*US*) bolsa (*SP*),
cartera (*AM*) ♦ *vt* fruncir
purser ['pəːsə*] *n* (*NAUT*) comisario/a
pursue [pə'sjuː] *vt* seguir; ~r *n*
perseguidor(a) *m/f*
pursuit [pə'sjuːt] *n* (*chase*) caza;
(*occupation*) actividad *f*
push [puʃ] *n* empuje *m*, empujón *m*; (*of
button*) presión *f*; (*drive*) empuje *m* ♦ *vt*
empujar; (*button*) apretar; (*promote*)
promover ♦ *vi* empujar; (*demand*): to ~
for luchar por; ~ aside *vt* apartar con la
mano; ~ off (*inf*) *vi* largarse; ~ on *vi*
seguir adelante; ~ through *vi* (*crowd*)
abrirse paso a empujones ♦ *vt* (*measure*)
despachar; ~ up *vt* (*total, prices*) hacer
subir; ~chair (*BRIT*) *n* sillita de ruedas;
~er *n* (*drug* ~*er*) traficante *m/f* de
drogas; ~over (*inf*) *n*: it's a ~over está
tirado; ~-up (*US*) *n* plancha; ~y (*pej*) *adj*

agresivo

puss [pus] (*inf*) *n* minino

pussy(-cat) ['pusɪ-] (*inf*) *n* = **puss**

put [put] (*pt, pp* put) *vt* (*place*) poner, colocar; (~ *into*) meter; (*say*) expresar; (*a question*) hacer; (*estimate*) estimar; ~ **about** *or* **around** *vt* (*rumour*) diseminar; ~ **across** *vt* (*ideas etc*) comunicar; ~ **away** *vt* (*store*) guardar; ~ **back** *vt* (*replace*) devolver a su lugar; (*postpone*) aplazar; ~ **by** *vt* (*money*) guardar; ~ **down** *vt* (*on ground*) poner en el suelo; (*animal*) sacrificar; (*in writing*) apuntar; (*revolt etc*) sofocar; (*attribute*): **to** ~ **sth down to** atribuir algo a; ~ **forward** *vt* (*ideas*) presentar, proponer; ~ **in** *vt* (*complaint*) presentar; (*time*) dedicar; ~ **off** *vt* (*postpone*) aplazar; (*discourage*) desanimar; ~ **on** *vt* ponerse; (*light etc*) encender; (*play etc*) presentar; (*gain*): **to** ~ **on weight** engordar; (*brake*) echar; (*record, kettle etc*) poner; (*assume*) adoptar; ~ **out** *vt* (*fire, light*) apagar; (*rubbish etc*) sacar; (*cat etc*) echar; (*one's hand*) alargar; (*inf: person*): **to be** ~ **out** alterarse; ~ **through** *vt* (*TEL*) poner; (*plan etc*) hacer aprobar; ~ **up** *vt* (*raise*) levantar, alzar; (*hang*) colgar; (*build*) construir; (*increase*) aumentar; (*accommodate*) alojar; ~ **up with** *vt fus* aguantar

putrid ['pju:trɪd] *adj* podrido

putt [pʌt] *n* putt *m*, golpe *m* corto; ~**ing green** *n* green *m*; minigolf *m*

putty ['pʌtɪ] *n* masilla

put-up ['putʌp] *adj*: ~ **job** (*BRIT*) amaño

puzzle ['pʌzl] *n* rompecabezas *m inv*; (*also: crossword* ~) crucigrama *m*; (*mystery*) misterio ♦ *vt* dejar perplejo, confundir ♦ *vi*: **to** ~ **over sth** devanarse los sesos con algo; **puzzling** *adj* misterioso, extraño

pyjamas [pɪ'dʒɑ:məz] (*BRIT*) *npl* pijama *m*

pylon ['paɪlən] *n* torre *f* de conducción eléctrica

pyramid ['pɪrəmɪd] *n* pirámide *f*

Pyrenees [pɪrə'ni:z] *npl*: **the** ~ los Pirineos

python ['paɪθən] *n* pitón *m*

Q q

quack [kwæk] *n* graznido; (*pej: doctor*) curandero/a

quad [kwɒd] *n abbr* = **quadrangle**; **quadruplet**

quadrangle ['kwɒdræŋgl] *n* patio

quadruple [kwɒ'dru:pl] *vt, vi* cuadruplicar

quadruplets [kwɔ:'dru:plɪts] *npl* cuatrillizos/as

quagmire ['kwægmaɪə*] *n* lodazal *m*, cenagal *m*

quail [kweɪl] *n* codorniz *f* ♦ *vi*: **to** ~ **at** *or* **before** amedrentarse ante

quaint [kweɪnt] *adj* extraño; (*picturesque*) pintoresco

quake [kweɪk] *vi* temblar ♦ *n abbr* = **earthquake**

Quaker ['kweɪkə*] *n* cuáquero/a

qualification [kwɒlɪfɪ'keɪʃən] *n* (*ability*) capacidad *f*; (*often pl: diploma etc*) título; (*reservation*) salvedad *f*

qualified ['kwɒlɪfaɪd] *adj* capacitado; (*professionally*) titulado; (*limited*) limitado

qualify ['kwɒlɪfaɪ] *vt* (*make competent*) capacitar; (*modify*) modificar ♦ *vi* (*in competition*): **to** ~ (**for**) calificarse (para); (*pass examination(s)*): **to** ~ (**as**) calificarse (de), graduarse (en); (*be eligible*): **to** ~ (**for**) reunir los requisitos (para)

quality ['kwɒlɪtɪ] *n* calidad *f*; (*of person*) cualidad *f*

qualm [kwɑ:m] *n* escrúpulo

quandary ['kwɒndrɪ] *n*: **to be in a** ~ tener dudas

quantity ['kwɒntɪtɪ] *n* cantidad *f*; **in** ~ en grandes cantidades; ~ **surveyor** *n* aparejador(a) *m/f*

quarantine ['kwɒrənti:n] *n* cuarentena

quarrel ['kwɒrl] *n* riña, pelea ♦ *vi* reñir, pelearse; ~**some** *adj* pendenciero

quarry ['kwɒrɪ] *n* cantera; (*animal*) presa

quart [kwɔ:t] *n* = litro

quarter ['kwɔ:tə*] *n* cuarto, cuarta parte *f*; (*US: coin*) *moneda de 25 centavos*; (*of year*) trimestre *m*; (*district*) barrio ♦ *vt* dividir en cuartos; (*MIL*: *lodge*) alojar; ~s *npl* (*barracks*) cuartel *m*; (*living* ~s) alojamiento; **a ~ of an hour** un cuarto de hora; ~ **final** *n* cuarto de final; **~ly** *adj* trimestral ♦ *adv* cada 3 meses, trimestralmente

quartet(te) [kwɔːˈtɛt] *n* cuarteto

quartz [kwɔːts] *n* cuarzo

quash [kwɔʃ] *vt* (*verdict*) anular

quasi- [ˈkweɪzaɪ] *prefix* cuasi

quaver [ˈkweɪvə*] (*BRIT*) *n* (*MUS*) corchea ♦ *vi* temblar

quay [kiː] *n* (*also:* ~*side*) muelle *m*

queasy [ˈkwiːzɪ] *adj*: **to feel ~** tener náuseas

queen [kwiːn] *n* reina; (*CARDS etc*) dama; ~ **mother** *n* reina madre

queer [kwɪə*] *adj* raro, extraño ♦ *n* (*inf*: *highly offensive*) maricón *m*

quell [kwɛl] *vt* (*feeling*) calmar; (*rebellion etc*) sofocar

quench [kwɛntʃ] *vt*: **to ~ one's thirst** apagar la sed

querulous [ˈkwɛruləs] *adj* quejumbroso

query [ˈkwɪərɪ] *n* (*question*) pregunta ♦ *vt* dudar de

quest [kwɛst] *n* busca, búsqueda

question [ˈkwɛstʃən] *n* pregunta; (*doubt*) duda; (*matter*) asunto, cuestión *f* ♦ *vt* (*doubt*) dudar de; (*interrogate*) interrogar, hacer preguntas a; **beyond ~** fuera de toda duda; **out of the ~** imposible; ni hablar; **~able** *adj* dudoso; ~ **mark** *n* punto de interrogación; **~naire** [-'nɛə*] *n* cuestionario

queue [kjuː] (*BRIT*) *n* cola ♦ *vi* (*also:* ~ *up*) hacer cola

quibble [ˈkwɪbl] *vi* sutilizar

quick [kwɪk] *adj* rápido, (*agile*) ágil; (*mind*) listo ♦ *n*: **cut to the ~** (*fig*) herido en lo vivo; **be ~!** ¡date prisa!; **~en** *vt* apresurar ♦ *vi* apresurarse, darse prisa; **~ly** *adv* rápidamente, de prisa; **~sand** *n* arenas *fpl* movedizas; **~-witted** *adj* perspicaz

quid [kwɪd] (*BRIT*: *inf*) *n inv* libra

quiet [ˈkwaɪət] *adj* (*voice*, *music etc*) bajo; (*person*, *place*) tranquilo; (*ceremony*) íntimo ♦ *n* silencio; (*calm*) tranquilidad *f*

♦ *vt*, *vi* (*US*) = **~en**; **~en** (*also:* ~*en down*) *vi* calmarse; (*grow silent*) callarse ♦ *vt* calmar; hacer callar; **~ly** *adv* tranquilamente; (*silently*) silenciosamente; **~ness** *n* silencio; tranquilidad *f*

quilt [kwɪlt] *n* edredón *m*

quin [kwɪn] *n abbr* = **quintuplet**

quinine [kwɪˈniːn] *n* quinina

quintet(te) [kwɪnˈtɛt] *n* quinteto

quintuplets [kwɪnˈtjuːplɪts] *npl* quintillizos/as

quip [kwɪp] *n* pulla

quirk [kwɜːk] *n* peculiaridad *f*; (*accident*) capricho

quit [kwɪt] (*pt*, *pp* quit *or* quitted) *vt* dejar, abandonar; (*premises*) desocupar ♦ *vi* (*give up*) renunciar; (*resign*) dimitir

quite [kwaɪt] *adv* (*rather*) bastante; (*entirely*) completamente; **that's not ~ big enough** no acaba de ser lo bastante grande; ~ **a few of them** un buen número de ellos; ~ **(so)!** ¡así es!, ¡exactamente!

quits [kwɪts] *adj*: ~ **(with)** en paz (con); **let's call it ~** dejémoslo en tablas

quiver [ˈkwɪvə*] *vi* estremecerse

quiz [kwɪz] *n* concurso ♦ *vt* interrogar; **~zical** *adj* burlón(ona)

quota [ˈkwəʊtə] *n* cuota

quotation [kwəʊˈteɪʃən] *n* cita; (*estimate*) presupuesto; ~ **marks** *npl* comillas *fpl*

quote [kwəʊt] *n* cita; (*estimate*) presupuesto ♦ *vt* citar; (*price*) cotizar ♦ *vi*: **to ~ from** citar de; **~s** *npl* (*inverted commas*) comillas *fpl*

quotient [ˈkwəʊʃənt] *n* cociente *m*

R r

rabbi [ˈræbaɪ] *n* rabino

rabbit [ˈræbɪt] *n* conejo; ~ **hutch** *n* conejera

rabble [ˈræbl] (*pej*) *n* chusma, populacho

rabies [ˈreɪbiːz] *n* rabia

RAC (*BRIT*) *n abbr* = **Royal Automobile Club**

rac(c)oon [rəˈkuːn] *n* mapache *m*

race [reɪs] *n* carrera; (*species*) raza ♦ *vt*

(*horse*) hacer correr; (*engine*) acelerar ♦ *vi* (*compete*) competir; (*run*) correr; (*pulse*) latir a ritmo acelerado; **~ car** (*US*) *n* = **racing car; ~ car driver** (*US*) *n* = **racing driver; ~course** *n* hipódromo; **~horse** *n* caballo de carreras; **~track** *n* pista; (*for cars*) autódromo

racial ['reɪʃl] *adj* racial

racing ['reɪsɪŋ] *n* carreras *fpl*; **~ car** (*BRIT*) *n* coche *m* de carreras; **~ driver** (*BRIT*) *n* corredor(a) *m/f* de coches

racism ['reɪsɪzəm] *n* racismo; **racist** [-sɪst] *adj*, *n* racista *m/f*

rack [ræk] *n* (*also: luggage ~*) rejilla; (*shelf*) estante *m*; (*also: roof ~*) baca, portaequipajes *m inv*; (*dish ~*) escurre-platos *m inv*; (*clothes ~*) percha ♦ *vt* ator-mentar; **to ~ one's brains** devanarse los sesos

racket ['rækɪt] *n* (*for tennis*) raqueta; (*noise*) ruido, estrépito; (*swindle*) estafa, timo

racquet ['rækɪt] *n* raqueta

racy ['reɪsɪ] *adj* picante, salado

radar ['reɪdɑː*] *n* radar *m*

radiance ['reɪdɪəns] *n* brillantez *f*, resplandor *m*

radiant ['reɪdɪənt] *adj* radiante (de felicidad)

radiate ['reɪdɪeɪt] *vt* (*heat*) radiar; (*emotion*) irradiar ♦ *vi* (*lines*) extenderse

radiation [reɪdɪ'eɪʃən] *n* radiación *f*

radiator ['reɪdɪeɪtə*] *n* radiador *m*

radical ['rædɪkl] *adj* radical

radii ['reɪdɪaɪ] *npl of* **radius**

radio ['reɪdɪəu] *n* radio *f*; **on the ~** por radio

radio... [reɪdɪəu] *prefix:* **~active** *adj* radioactivo; **radiography** [-'ɔgrəfɪ] *n* radiografía; **radiology** [-'ɔlədʒɪ] *n* radiología

radio station *n* emisora

radiotherapy [-'θεrəpɪ] *n* radioterapia

radish ['rædɪʃ] *n* rábano

radius ['reɪdɪəs] (*pl* **radii**) *n* radio

RAF *n abbr* = **Royal Air Force**

raffle ['ræfl] *n* rifa, sorteo

raft [rɑːft] *n* balsa; (*also: life ~*) balsa salvavidas

rafter ['rɑːftə*] *n* viga

rag [ræg] *n* (*piece of cloth*) trapo; (*torn cloth*) harapo; (*pej: newspaper*) periodicucho; (*for charity*) actividades estudiantiles benéficas; **~s** *npl* (*torn clothes*) harapos *mpl*; **~-and-bone man** (*BRIT*) *n* = **~man; ~ doll** *n* muñeca de trapo

rage [reɪdʒ] *n* rabia, furor *m* ♦ *vi* (*person*) rabiar, estar furioso; (*storm*) bramar; **it's all the ~** (*very fashionable*) está muy de moda

ragged ['rægɪd] *adj* (*edge*) desigual, mellado; (*appearance*) andrajoso, harapiento

ragman ['rægmæn] *n* trapero

raid [reɪd] *n* (*MIL*) incursión *f*; (*criminal*) asalto; (*by police*) redada ♦ *vt* invadir, atacar; asaltar

rail [reɪl] *n* (*on stair*) barandilla, pasamanos *m inv*; (*on bridge, balcony*) pretil *m*; (*of ship*) barandilla; (*also: towel ~*) toallero; **~s** *npl* (*RAIL*) vía; **by ~** por ferrocarril; **~ing(s)** *n(pl)* vallado; **~road** (*US*) *n* = **~way; ~way** (*BRIT*) *n* ferrocarril *m*, vía férrea; **~way line** (*BRIT*) *n* línea (de ferrocarril); **~wayman** (*BRIT*) *n* ferroviario; **~way station** (*BRIT*) *n* estación *f* de ferrocarril

rain [reɪn] *n* lluvia ♦ *vi* llover; **in the ~** bajo la lluvia; **it's ~ing** llueve, está lloviendo; **~bow** *n* arco iris; **~coat** *n* impermeable *m*; **~drop** *n* gota de lluvia; **~fall** *n* lluvia; **~forest** *n* selvas *fpl* tropicales; **~y** *adj* lluvioso

raise [reɪz] *n* aumento ♦ *vt* levantar; (*increase*) aumentar; (*improve: morale*) subir; (: *standards*) mejorar; (*doubts*) suscitar; (*a question*) plantear; (*cattle, family*) criar; (*crop*) cultivar; (*army*) reclutar; (*loan*) obtener; **to ~ one's voice** alzar la voz

raisin ['reɪzn] *n* pasa de Corinto

rake [reɪk] *n* (*tool*) rastrillo; (*person*) libertino ♦ *vt* (*garden*) rastrillar; (*with machine gun*) barrer

rally ['rælɪ] *n* (*POL etc*) reunión *f*, mitin *m*; (*AUT*) rallye *m*; (*TENNIS*) peloteo ♦ *vt* reu-nir ♦ *vi* recuperarse; **~ round** *vt fus* (*fig*) dar apoyo a

RAM [ræm] *n abbr* (= *random access memory*) RAM *f*

ram [ræm] *n* carnero; (*also*: *battering* ~) ariete *m* ♦ *vt* (*crash into*) dar contra, chocar con; (*push*: *fist etc*) empujar con fuerza

ramble ['ræmbl] *n* caminata, excursión *f* en el campo ♦ *vi* (*pej*: *also*: ~ *on*) divagar; ~**r** *n* excursionista *m/f*; (*BOT*) trepadora; **rambling** *adj* (*speech*) inconexo; (*house*) laberíntico; (*BOT*) trepador(a)

ramp [ræmp] *n* rampa; **on/off** ~ (*US*: *AUT*) vía de acceso/salida

rampage [ræm'peɪdʒ] *n*: **to be on the** ~ desmandarse ♦ *vi*: **they went rampaging through the town** recorrieron la ciudad armando alboroto

rampant ['ræmpənt] *adj* (*disease etc*): **to be** ~ estar extendiéndose mucho

rampart ['ræmpɑːt] *n* (*fortification*) baluarte *m*

ram raid *vt* atracar (*rompiendo el escaparate con un coche*)

ramshackle ['ræmʃækl] *adj* destartalado

ran [ræn] *pt of* **run**

ranch [rɑːntʃ] *n* hacienda, estancia; ~**er** *n* ganadero

rancid ['rænsɪd] *adj* rancio

rancour ['ræŋkə*] (*US* **rancor**) *n* rencor *m*

random ['rændəm] *adj* fortuito, sin orden; (*COMPUT*, *MATH*) aleatorio ♦ *n*: **at** ~ al azar

randy ['rændɪ] (*BRIT*: *inf*) *adj* cachondo

rang [ræŋ] *pt of* **ring**

range [reɪndʒ] *n* (*of mountains*) cadena de montañas, cordillera; (*of missile*) alcance *m*; (*of voice*) registro; (*series*) serie *f*; (*of products*) surtido; (*MIL*: *also*: *shooting* ~) campo de tiro; (*also*: *kitchen* ~) fogón *m* ♦ *vt* (*place*) colocar; (*arrange*) arreglar ♦ *vi*: **to** ~ **over** (*extend*) extenderse por; **to** ~ **from ... to ...** oscilar entre ... y ...

ranger [reɪndʒə*] *n* guardabosques *m inv*

rank [ræŋk] *n* (*row*) fila; (*MIL*) rango; (*status*) categoría; (*BRIT*: *also*: *taxi* ~) parada de taxis ♦ *vi*: **to** ~ **among** figurar

entre ♦ *adj* fétido, rancio; **the** ~ **and file** (*fig*) la base

rankle ['ræŋkl] *vi* doler

ransack ['rænsæk] *vt* (*search*) registrar; (*plunder*) saquear

ransom ['rænsəm] *n* rescate *m*; **to hold to** ~ (*fig*) hacer chantaje a

rant [rænt] *vi* divagar, desvariar

rap [ræp] *vt* golpear, dar un golpecito en ♦ *n* (*music*) rap *m*

rape [reɪp] *n* violación *f*; (*BOT*) colza ♦ *vt* violar; ~ (**seed**) **oil** *n* aceite *m* de colza

rapid ['ræpɪd] *adj* rápido; ~**ity** [rə'pɪdɪtɪ] *n* rapidez *f*; ~**ly** *adv* rápidamente; ~**s** *npl* (*GEO*) rápidos *mpl*

rapist ['reɪpɪst] *n* violador *m*

rapport [ræ'pɔː*] *n* simpatía

rapture ['ræptʃə*] *n* éxtasis *m*; **rapturous** *adj* extático

rare [rɛə*] *adj* raro, poco común; (*CULIN*: *steak*) poco hecho

rarely ['rɛəlɪ] *adv* pocas veces

raring ['rɛərɪŋ] *adj*: **to be** ~ **to go** (*inf*) tener muchas ganas de empezar

rarity ['rɛərɪtɪ] *n* rareza, escasez *f*

rascal ['rɑːskl] *n* pillo, pícaro

rash [ræʃ] *adj* imprudente, precipitado ♦ *n* (*MED*) sarpullido, erupción *f* (*cutánea*); (*of events*) serie *f*

rasher ['ræʃə*] *n* lonja

raspberry ['rɑːzbərɪ] *n* frambuesa

rasping ['rɑːspɪŋ] *adj*: **a** ~ **noise** un ruido áspero

rat [ræt] *n* rata

rate [reɪt] *n* (*ratio*) razón *f*; (*price*) precio; (: *of hotel etc*) tarifa; (*of interest*) tipo; (*speed*) velocidad *f* ♦ *vt* (*value*) tasar; (*estimate*) estimar; ~**s** *npl* (*BRIT*: *property tax*) impuesto municipal; (*fees*) tarifa; **to** ~ **sth/sb as** considerar algo/a uno como; ~**able value** (*BRIT*) *n* valor *m* impuesto; ~**payer** (*BRIT*) *n* contribuyente *m/f*

rather ['rɑːðə*] *adv*: **it's** ~ **expensive** es algo caro; (*too much*) es demasiado caro; (*to some extent*) más bien; **there's** ~ **a lot** hay bastante; **I would** *or* **I'd** ~ **go** preferiría ir; **or** ~ mejor dicho

ratify ['rætɪfaɪ] *vt* ratificar

rating ['reɪtɪŋ] *n* tasación *f*; (*score*) índice

m; (*BRIT: NAUT: sailor*) marinero; (*of ship*) clase *f*; ~s *npl* (*RADIO, TV*) niveles *mpl* de audiencia

ratio ['reɪʃɪəʊ] *n* razón *f*; **in the ~ of 100 to 1** a razón de 100 a 1

ration ['ræʃən] *n* ración *f* ♦ *vt* racionar; ~s *npl* víveres *mpl*

rational ['ræʃənl] *adj* (*solution, reasoning*) lógico, razonable; (*person*) cuerdo, sensato; ~e [-'nɑːl] *n* razón *f* fundamental; ~ize *vt* justificar

rationing ['ræʃnɪŋ] *n* racionamiento

rat race *n* lucha incesante por la supervivencia

rattle ['rætl] *n* golpeteo; (*of train etc*) traqueteo; (*for baby*) sonaja, sonajero ♦ *vi* castañetear; (*car, bus*): **to ~ along** traquetear ♦ *vt* hacer sonar agitando; ~**snake** *n* serpiente *f* de cascabel

raucous ['rɔːkəs] *adj* estridente, ronco

ravage ['rævɪdʒ] *vt* hacer estragos en, destrozar; ~s *npl* estragos *mpl*

rave [reɪv] *vi* (*in anger*) encolerizarse; (*with enthusiasm*) entusiasmarse; (*MED*) delirar, desvariar

raven ['reɪvən] *n* cuervo

ravenous ['rævənəs] *adj* hambriento

ravine [rə'viːn] *n* barranco

raving ['reɪvɪŋ] *adj*: ~ **lunatic** loco/a de atar

ravishing ['rævɪʃɪŋ] *adj* encantador(a)

raw [rɔː] *adj* crudo; (*not processed*) bruto; (*sore*) vivo; (*inexperienced*) novato, inexperto; ~ **deal** (*inf*) *n* injusticia; ~ **material** *n* materia prima

ray [reɪ] *n* rayo; ~ **of hope** (rayo de) esperanza

rayon ['reɪɔn] *n* rayón *m*

raze [reɪz] *vt* arrasar

razor ['reɪzə*] *n* (*open*) navaja; (*safety ~*) máquina de afeitar; (*electric ~*) máquina (eléctrica) de afeitar; ~ **blade** *n* hoja de afeitar

Rd *abbr* = **road**

re [riː] *prep* con referencia a

reach [riːtʃ] *n* alcance *m*; (*of river etc*) extensión *f* entre dos recodos ♦ *vt* alcanzar, llegar a; (*achieve*) lograr ♦ *vi* extenderse; **within ~** al alcance (de la

mano); **out of ~** fuera del alcance; ~ **out** *vt* (*hand*) tender ♦ *vi*: **to ~ out for sth** alargar *or* tender la mano para tomar algo

react [riː'ækt] *vi* reaccionar; ~**ion** [-'ækʃən] *n* reacción *f*

reactor [riː'æktə*] *n* (*also: nuclear ~*) reactor *m* (nuclear)

read [riːd, *pt, pp* rɛd] (*pt, pp* **read**) *vi* leer ♦ *vt* leer; (*understand*) entender; (*study*) estudiar; ~ **out** *vt* leer en alta voz; ~**able** *adj* (*writing*) legible; (*book*) leíble; ~**er** *n* lector(a) *m/f*; (*book*) libro de lecturas; (*BRIT: at university*) profesor(a) *m/f* adjunto/a; ~**ership** *n* (*of paper etc*) (número de) lectores *mpl*

readily ['rɛdɪlɪ] *adv* (*willingly*) de buena gana; (*easily*) fácilmente; (*quickly*) en seguida

readiness ['rɛdɪnɪs] *n* buena voluntad *f*; (*preparedness*) preparación *f*; **in ~** (*prepared*) listo, preparado

reading ['riːdɪŋ] *n* lectura *f*; (*on instrument*) indicación *f*

readjust [riːə'dʒʌst] *vt* reajustar ♦ *vi* (*adapt*): **to ~ (to)** reajustarse (a)

ready ['rɛdɪ] *adj* listo, preparado; (*willing*) dispuesto; (*available*) disponible ♦ *adv*: ~**-cooked** listo para comer ♦ *n*: **at the ~** (*MIL*) listo para tirar; **to get ~** *vi* prepararse ♦ *vt* preparar; ~**-made** *adj* confeccionado; ~ **money** *n* dinero contante; ~ **reckoner** *n* libro de cálculos hechos; ~**-to-wear** *adj* confeccionado

real [rɪəl] *adj* verdadero, auténtico; **in ~ terms** en términos reales; ~ **estate** *n* bienes *mpl* raíces; ~**istic** [-'lɪstɪk] *adj* realista

reality [riː'ælɪtɪ] *n* realidad *f*

realization [rɪəlaɪ'zeɪʃən] *n* comprensión *f*; (*fulfilment, COMM*) realización *f*

realize ['rɪəlaɪz] *vt* (*understand*) darse cuenta de; (*fulfil, COMM: asset*) realizar

really ['rɪəlɪ] *adv* realmente; (*for emphasis*) verdaderamente; (*actually*): **what ~ happened** lo que pasó en realidad; ~? ¿de veras?; ~! (*annoyance*) ¡vamos!, ¡por favor!

realm [rɛlm] *n* reino; (*fig*) esfera

realtor ['rɪəltɔː*] (*US*) *n* corredor(a) *m/f* de bienes raíces

reap [riːp] *vt* segar; (*fig*) cosechar, recoger

reappear [riːə'pɪə*] *vi* reaparecer

rear [rɪə*] *adj* trasero ♦ *n* parte *f* trasera ♦ *vt* (*cattle, family*) criar ♦ *vi* (*also: ~ up*) (*animal*) encabritarse; **~guard** *n* retaguardia

rearmament [riːˈɑːməmənt] *n* rearme *m*

rearrange [riːəˈreɪndʒ] *vt* ordenar *or* arreglar de nuevo

rear-view: **~ mirror** *n* (*AUT*) (espejo) retrovisor *m*

reason ['riːzn] *n* razón *f* ♦ *vi*: **to ~ with sb** tratar de que uno entre en razón; **it stands to ~ that** es lógico que; **~able** *adj* razonable; (*sensible*) sensato; **~ably** *adv* razonablemente; **~ed** *adj* (*argument*) razonado; **~ing** *n* razonamiento, argumentos *mpl*

reassurance [riːəˈʃuərəns] *n* consuelo

reassure [riːəˈʃuə*] *vt* tranquilizar, alentar; **to ~ sb that** tranquilizar a uno asegurando que; **reassuring** *adj* alentador(a)

rebate ['riːbeɪt] *n* (*on tax etc*) desgravación *f*

rebel [*n* 'rɛbl, *vi* rɪ'bɛl] *n* rebelde *m/f* ♦ *vi* rebelarse, sublevarse; **~lion** [rɪ'bɛljən] *n* rebelión *f*, sublevación *f*; **~lious** [rɪ'bɛljəs] *adj* rebelde; (*child*) revoltoso

rebirth ['riːbəːθ] *n* renacimiento

rebound [*vi* rɪ'baund, *n* 'riːbaund] *vi* (*ball*) rebotar ♦ *n* rebote *m*; **on the ~** (*also fig*) de rebote

rebuff [rɪ'bʌf] *n* desaire *m*, rechazo

rebuild [riː'bɪld] (*irreg*) *vt* reconstruir

rebuke [rɪ'bjuːk] *n* reprimenda ♦ *vt* reprender

rebut [rɪ'bʌt] *vt* rebatir

recall [rɪ'kɔːl] *vt* (*remember*) recordar; (*ambassador etc*) retirar ♦ *n* recuerdo; retirada

recant [rɪ'kænt] *vi* retractarse

recap ['riːkæp] *vt*, *vi* recapitular

recapitulate [riːkə'pɪtjuleɪt] *vt*, *vi* = **recap**

recapture [riː'kæptʃə*] *vt* recobrar

rec'd *abbr* (= *received*) rbdo

recede [rɪ'siːd] *vi* (*memory*) ir borrándose; (*hair*) retroceder; **receding** *adj* (*forehead, chin*) huidizo; **to have a receding hairline** tener entradas

receipt [rɪ'siːt] *n* (*document*) recibo; (*for parcel etc*) recibo; (*act of receiving*) recepción *f*; **~s** *npl* (*COMM*) ingresos *mpl*

receive [rɪ'siːv] *vt* recibir; (*guest*) acoger; (*wound*) sufrir; **~r** *n* (*TEL*) auricular *m*; (*RADIO*) receptor *m*; (*of stolen goods*) perista *m/f*; (*COMM*) administrador *m* jurídico

recent ['riːsnt] *adj* reciente; **~ly** *adv* recientemente; **~ly arrived** recién llegado

receptacle [rɪ'sɛptɪkl] *n* receptáculo

reception [rɪ'sɛpʃən] *n* recepción *f*; (*welcome*) acogida; **~ desk** *n* recepción *f*; **~ist** *n* recepcionista *m/f*

recess [rɪ'sɛs] *n* (*in room*) hueco; (*for bed*) nicho; (*secret place*) escondrijo; (*POL etc: holiday*) clausura; **~ion** [-'sɛʃən] *n* recesión *f*

recharge [riː'tʃɑːdʒ] *vt* (*battery*) recargar

recipe ['rɛsɪpɪ] *n* receta; (*for disaster, success*) fórmula

recipient [rɪ'sɪpɪənt] *n* recibidor(a) *m/f*; (*of letter*) destinatario/a

recital [rɪ'saɪtl] *n* recital *m*

recite [rɪ'saɪt] *vt* (*poem*) recitar

reckless ['rɛkləs] *adj* temerario, imprudente; (*driving, driver*) peligroso; **~ly** *adv* imprudentemente; de modo peligroso

reckon ['rɛkən] *vt* calcular; (*consider*) considerar; (*think*): **I ~ that ...** me parece que ...; **~ on** *vt fus* contar con; **~ing** *n* cálculo

reclaim [rɪ'kleɪm] *vt* (*land, waste*) recuperar; (*land: from sea*) rescatar; (*demand back*) reclamar

reclamation [rɛklə'meɪʃən] *n* (*of land*) acondicionamiento de tierras

recline [rɪ'klaɪn] *vi* reclinarse; **reclining** *adj* (*seat*) reclinable

recluse [rɪ'kluːs] *n* recluso/a

recognition [rɛkəg'nɪʃən] *n* reconocimiento; **transformed beyond** ~ irreconocible

recognizable ['rekəgnaɪzəbl] *adj*: ~ **(by)** reconocible (por)

recognize ['rekəgnaɪz] *vt*: **to** ~ **(by/as)** reconocer (por/como)

recoil [*vi* rɪ'kɔɪl, *n* 'riːkɔɪl] *vi* (*person*): **to** ~ **from doing sth** retraerse de hacer algo ♦ *n* (*of gun*) retroceso

recollect [rekə'lekt] *vt* recordar, acordarse de; **~ion** [-'lekʃən] *n* recuerdo

recommend [rekə'mend] *vt* recomendar

reconcile ['rekənsaɪl] *vt* (*two people*) reconciliar; (*two facts*) compaginar; **to** ~ **o.s. to sth** conformarse a algo

recondition [riːkən'dɪʃən] *vt* (*machine*) reacondicionar

reconnaissance [rɪ'kɔnɪsns] *n* (*MIL*) reconocimiento

reconnoitre [rekə'nɔɪtə*] (*US* **reconnoiter**) *vt, vi* (*MIL*) reconocer

reconsider [riːkən'sɪdə*] *vt* repensar

reconstruct [riːkən'strʌkt] *vt* reconstruir

record [*n* 'rekɔːd, *vt* rɪ'kɔːd] *n* (*MUS*) disco; (*of meeting etc*) acta; (*register*) registro, partida; (*file*) archivo; (*also: criminal* ~) antecedentes *mpl*; (*written*) expediente *m*; (*SPORT, COMPUT*) récord *m* ♦ *vt* registrar; (*MUS: song etc*) grabar; **in** ~ **time** en un tiempo récord; **off the** ~ *adj* no oficial ♦ *adv* confidencialmente; ~ **card** *n* (*in file*) ficha; **~ed delivery** (*BRIT*) *n* (*POST*) entrega con acuse de recibo; **~er** *n* (*MUS*) flauta de pico; ~ **holder** *n* (*SPORT*) actual poseedor(a) *m/f* del récord; **~ing** *n* (*MUS*) grabación *f*; ~ **player** *n* tocadiscos *m inv*

recount [rɪ'kaunt] *vt* contar

re-count [*n* 'riːkaunt, *vb* riː'kaunt] *n* (*POL: of votes*) segundo escrutinio ♦ *vt* volver a contar

recoup [rɪ'kuːp] *vt*: **to** ~ **one's losses** recuperar las pérdidas

recourse [rɪ'kɔːs] *n*: **to have** ~ **to** recurrir a

recover [rɪ'kʌvə*] *vt* recuperar ♦ *vi* (*from illness, shock*) recuperarse; **~y** *n* recuperación *f*

recreation [rekrɪ'eɪʃən] *n* recreo; **~al** *adj*

de recreo; **~al drug** droga recreativa

recruit [rɪ'kruːt] *n* recluta *m/f* ♦ *vt* reclutar; (*staff*) contratar; **~ment** *n* reclutamiento

rectangle ['rektæŋgl] *n* rectángulo; **rectangular** [-'tæŋgjulə*] *adj* rectangular

rectify ['rektɪfaɪ] *vt* rectificar

rector ['rektə*] *n* (*REL*) párroco; **~y** *n* casa del párroco

recuperate [rɪ'kuːpəreɪt] *vi* reponerse, restablecerse

recur [rɪ'kəː*] *vi* repetirse; (*pain, illness*) producirse de nuevo; **~rence** [rɪ'kʌrəns] *n* repetición *f*; **~rent** [rɪ'kʌrənt] *adj* repetido

recycle [riː'saɪkl] *vt* reciclar

red [red] *n* rojo ♦ *adj* rojo; (*hair*) pelirrojo; (*wine*) tinto; **to be in the** ~ (*account*) estar en números rojos; (*business*) tener un saldo negativo; **to give sb the** ~ **carpet treatment** recibir a uno con todos los honores; **R~ Cross** *n* Cruz *f* Roja; **~currant** *n* grosella roja; **~den** *vt* enrojecer ♦ *vi* enrojecerse; **~dish** *adj* rojizo

redeem [rɪ'diːm] *vt* redimir; (*promises*) cumplir; (*sth in pawn*) desempeñar; (*fig, also REL*) rescatar; **~ing** *adj*: **~ing feature** rasgo bueno *or* favorable

redeploy [riːdɪ'plɔɪ] *vt* (*resources*) reorganizar

red: **~-haired** *adj* pelirrojo; **~-handed** *adj*: **to be caught ~-handed** cogerse (*SP*) *or* pillarse (*AM*) con las manos en la masa; **~head** *n* pelirrojo/a; ~ **herring** *n* (*fig*) pista falsa; **~-hot** *adj* candente

redirect [riːdaɪ'rekt] *vt* (*mail*) reexpedir

red light *n*: **to go through a** ~ (*AUT*) pasar la luz roja; **red-light district** *n* barrio chino

redo [riː'duː] (*irreg*) *vt* rehacer

redolent ['redələnt] *adj*: ~ **of** (*smell*) con fragancia a; **to be** ~ **of** (*fig*) recordar

redouble [riː'dʌbl] *vt*: **to** ~ **one's efforts** intensificar los esfuerzos

redress [rɪ'dres] *n* reparación *f* ♦ *vt* reparar

Red Sea *n*: **the** ~ el mar Rojo

redskin ['redskɪn] *n* piel roja *m/f*

red tape *n* (*fig*) trámites *mpl*

reduce [rɪˈdjuːs] *vt* reducir; **to ~ sb to tears** hacer llorar a uno; **to be ~d to begging** no quedarle a uno otro remedio que pedir limosna; **"~ speed now"** (*AUT*) "reduzca la velocidad"; **at a ~d price** (*of goods*) (a precio) rebajado; **reduction** [rɪˈdʌkʃən] *n* reducción *f*; (*of price*) rebaja; (*discount*) descuento; (*smaller-scale copy*) copia reducida

redundancy [rɪˈdʌndənsɪ] *n* (*dismissal*) despido; (*unemployment*) desempleo

redundant [rɪˈdʌndnt] *adj* (*BRIT: worker*) parado, sin trabajo; (*detail, object*) superfluo; **to be made ~** quedar(se) sin trabajo

reed [riːd] *n* (*BOT*) junco, caña; (*MUS*) lengüeta

reef [riːf] *n* (*at sea*) arrecife *m*

reek [riːk] *vi*: **to ~ (of)** apestar (a)

reel [riːl] *n* carrete *m*, bobina; (*of film*) rollo; (*dance*) baile *m* escocés ♦ *vt* (*also: ~ up*) devanar; (*also: ~ in*) sacar ♦ *vi* (*sway*) tambalear(se)

ref [rɛf] (*inf*) *n abbr* = **referee**

refectory [rɪˈfɛktərɪ] *n* comedor *m*

refer [rɪˈfəː*] *vt* (*send: patient*) referir; (*: matter*) remitir ♦ *vi*: **to ~ to** (*allude to*) referirse a, aludir a; (*apply to*) relacionarse con; (*consult*) consultar

referee [rɛfəˈriː] *n* árbitro; (*BRIT: for job application*): **to be a ~ for sb** proporcionar referencias a uno ♦ *vt* (*match*) arbitrar a

reference [ˈrɛfrəns] *n* referencia; (*for job application: letter*) carta de recomendación; **with ~ to** (*COMM: in letter*) me remito a; **~ book** *n* libro de consulta; **~ number** *n* número de referencia

refill [*vt* riːˈfɪl, *n* ˈriːfɪl] *vt* rellenar ♦ *n* repuesto, recambio

refine [rɪˈfaɪn] *vt* refinar; **~d** *adj* (*person*) fino; **~ment** *n* cultura, educación *f*; (*of system*) refinamiento

reflect [rɪˈflɛkt] *vt* reflejar ♦ *vi* (*think*) reflexionar, pensar; **it ~s badly/well on him** le perjudica/le hace honor; **~ion** [-ˈflɛkʃən] *n* (*act*) reflexión *f*; (*image*) reflejo; (*criticism*) crítica; **on ~ion** pensándolo bien; **~or** *n* (*AUT*) captafaros

m inv; (*of light, heat*) reflector *m*

reflex [ˈriːflɛks] *adj, n* reflejo; **~ive** [rɪˈflɛksɪv] *adj* (*LING*) reflexivo

reform [rɪˈfɔːm] *n* reforma ♦ *vt* reformar; **the R~ation** [rɛfəˈmeɪʃən] *n* la Reforma; **~atory** (*US*) *n* reformatorio

refrain [rɪˈfreɪn] *vi*: **to ~ from doing** abstenerse de hacer ♦ *n* estribillo

refresh [rɪˈfrɛʃ] *vt* refrescar; **~er course** (*BRIT*) *n* curso de repaso; **~ing** *adj* refrescante; **~ments** *npl* refrescos *mpl*

refrigerator [rɪˈfrɪdʒəreɪtə*] *n* nevera (*SP*), refrigeradora (*AM*)

refuel [riːˈfjuəl] *vi* repostar (combustible)

refuge [ˈrɛfjuːdʒ] *n* refugio, asilo; **to take ~ in** refugiarse en

refugee [rɛfjuˈdʒiː] *n* refugiado/a

refund [*n* ˈriːfʌnd, *vb* rɪˈfʌnd] *n* reembolso ♦ *vt* devolver, reembolsar

refurbish [riːˈfəːbɪʃ] *vt* restaurar, renovar

refusal [rɪˈfjuːzəl] *n* negativa; **to have first ~ on** tener la primera opción a

refuse [*n* ˈrɛfjuːs, *vb* rɪˈfjuːz] *n* basura ♦ *vt* rechazar; (*invitation*) declinar; (*permission*) denegar ♦ *vi*: **to ~ to do sth** negarse a hacer algo; (*horse*) rehusar; **~ collection** *n* recolección *f* de basuras

regain [rɪˈgeɪn] *vt* recobrar, recuperar

regal [ˈriːgl] *adj* regio, real

regalia [rɪˈgeɪlɪə] *n* insignias *fpl*

regard [rɪˈgɑːd] *n* mirada; (*esteem*) respeto; (*attention*) consideración *f* ♦ *vt* (*consider*) considerar; **to give one's ~s to** saludar de su parte a; **"with kindest ~s"** "con muchos recuerdos"; **~ing, as ~s, with ~ to** con respecto a, en cuanto a; **~less** *adv* a pesar de todo; **~less of** sin reparar en

régime [reɪˈʒiːm] *n* régimen *m*

regiment [ˈrɛdʒɪmənt] *n* regimiento; **~al** [-ˈmɛntl] *adj* militar

region [ˈriːdʒən] *n* región *f*; **in the ~ of** (*fig*) alrededor de; **~al** *adj* regional

register [ˈrɛdʒɪstə*] *n* registro ♦ *vt* registrar; (*birth*) declarar; (*car*) matricular; (*letter*) certificar; (*subj: instrument*) marcar, indicar ♦ *vi* (*at hotel*) registrarse; (*as student*) matricularse; (*make impression*) producir impresión; ~ed *adj* (*letter, parcel*) certificado; ~ed trademark *n* marca registrada

registrar ['rɛdʒɪstrɑː*] *n* secretario/a (del registro civil)

registration [rɛdʒɪs'treɪʃən] *n* (*act*) declaración *f*; (*AUT: also*: ~ *number*) matrícula

registry ['rɛdʒɪstrɪ] *n* registro; ~ office (*BRIT*) *n* registro civil; **to get married in a ~ office** casarse por lo civil

regret [rɪ'grɛt] *n* sentimiento, pesar *m* ♦ *vt* sentir, lamentar; ~fully *adv* con pesar; ~table *adj* lamentable

regular ['rɛgjulə*] *adj* regular; (*soldier*) profesional; (*usual*) habitual; (: *doctor*) de cabecera ♦ *n* (*client etc*) cliente/a *m/f* habitual; ~ity [-'lærɪtɪ] *n* regularidad *f*; ~ly *adv* con regularidad; (*often*) repetidas veces

regulate ['rɛgjuleɪt] *vt* controlar; **regulation** [-'leɪʃən] *n* (*rule*) regla, reglamento

rehearsal [rɪ'həːsəl] *n* ensayo

rehearse [rɪ'həːs] *vt* ensayar

reign [reɪn] *n* reinado; (*fig*) predominio ♦ *vi* reinar; (*fig*) imperar

reimburse [riːɪm'bəːs] *vt* reembolsar

rein [reɪn] *n* (*for horse*) rienda

reindeer ['reɪndɪə*] *n inv* reno

reinforce [riːɪn'fɔːs] *vt* reforzar; ~d concrete *n* hormigón *m* armado; ~ment *n* (*action*) refuerzo; ~ments *npl* (*MIL*) refuerzos *mpl*

reinstate [riːɪn'steɪt] *vt* reintegrar; (*tax, law*) reinstaurar

reiterate [riː'ɪtəreɪt] *vt* reiterar, repetir

reject [*n* 'riːdʒɛkt, *vb* rɪ'dʒɛkt] *n* (*thing*) desecho ♦ *vt* rechazar; (*suggestion*) descartar; (*coin*) expulsar; ~ion [rɪ'dʒɛkʃən] *n* rechazo

rejoice [rɪ'dʒɔɪs] *vi*: **to ~ at** *or* **over** regocijarse *or* alegrarse de

rejuvenate [rɪ'dʒuːvəneɪt] *vt* rejuvenecer

relapse [rɪ'læps] *n* recaída

relate [rɪ'leɪt] *vt* (*tell*) contar, relatar; (*connect*) relacionar ♦ *vi* relacionarse; ~d *adj* afín; (*person*) emparentado; ~d to (*subject*) relacionado con; **relating to**

prep referente a

relation [rɪ'leɪʃən] *n* (*person*) familiar *m/f*, pariente/a *m/f*; (*link*) relación *f*; ~s *npl* (*relatives*) familiares *mpl*; ~ship *n* relación *f*; (*personal*) relaciones *fpl*; (*also: family ~ship*) parentesco

relative ['rɛlətɪv] *n* pariente/a *m/f*, familiar *m/f* ♦ *adj* relativo; ~ly *adv* (*comparatively*) relativamente

relax [rɪ'læks] *vi* descansar; (*unwind*) relajarse ♦ *vt* (*one's grip*) soltar, aflojar; (*control*) relajar; (*mind, person*) descansar; ~ation [riːlæk'seɪʃən] *n* descanso; (*of rule, control*) relajamiento; (*entertainment*) diversión *f*; ~ed *adj* relajado; (*tranquil*) tranquilo; ~ing *adj* relajante

relay ['riːleɪ] *n* (*race*) carrera de relevos ♦ *vt* (*RADIO, TV*) retransmitir

release [rɪ'liːs] *n* (*liberation*) liberación *f*; (*from prison*) puesta en libertad; (*of gas etc*) escape *m*; (*of film etc*) estreno; (*of record*) lanzamiento ♦ *vt* (*prisoner*) poner en libertad; (*gas*) despedir, arrojar; (*from wreckage*) soltar; (*catch, spring etc*) desenganchar; (*film*) estrenar; (*book*) publicar; (*news*) difundir

relegate ['rɛləgeɪt] *vt* relegar; (*BRIT: SPORT*): **to be ~d** bajar a

relent [rɪ'lɛnt] *vi* ablandarse; ~less *adj* implacable

relevant ['rɛləvənt] *adj* (*fact*) pertinente; ~ **to** relacionado con

reliability [rɪlaɪə'bɪlɪtɪ] *n* fiabilidad *f*; seguridad *f*; veracidad *f*

reliable [rɪ'laɪəbl] *adj* (*person, firm*) de confianza, de fiar; (*method, machine*) seguro; (*source*) fidedigno; **reliably** *adv*: **to be reliably informed that ...** saber de fuente fidedigna que ...

reliance [rɪ'laɪəns] *n*: ~ **(on)** dependencia (de)

relic ['rɛlɪk] *n* (*REL*) reliquia; (*of the past*) vestigio

relief [rɪ'liːf] *n* (*from pain, anxiety*) alivio; (*help, supplies*) socorro, ayuda; (*ART, GEO*) relieve *m*

relieve [rɪ'liːv] *vt* (*pain*) aliviar; (*bring help to*) ayudar, socorrer; (*take over* *from*) sustituir; (: *guard*) relevar; **to ~ sb of sth** quitar algo a uno; **to ~ o.s.** hacer sus necesidades

religion [rɪ'lɪdʒən] *n* religión *f*; **religious** *adj* religioso

relinquish [rɪ'lɪŋkwɪʃ] *vt* abandonar; (*plan, habit*) renunciar a

relish ['rɛlɪʃ] *n* (*CULIN*) salsa; (*enjoyment*) entusiasmo ♦ *vt* (*food etc*) saborear; (*enjoy*): **to ~ sth** hacerle mucha ilusión a uno algo

relocate [riːləʊ'keɪt] *vt* cambiar de lugar, mudar ♦ *vi* mudarse

reluctance [rɪ'lʌktəns] *n* renuencia; **reluctant** *adj* renuente; **reluctantly** *adv* de mala gana

rely on [rɪ'laɪ-] *vt fus* depender de; (*trust*) contar con

remain [rɪ'meɪn] *vi* (*survive*) quedar; (*be left*) quedar; (*continue*) quedar(se), permanecer; **~der** *n* resto; **~ing** *adj* que queda(n); (*surviving*) restante(s); **~s** *npl* restos *mpl*

remand [rɪ'mɑːnd] *n*: **on ~** detenido (bajo custodia) ♦ *vt*: **to be ~ed in custody** quedar detenido bajo custodia; **~ home** (*BRIT*) *n* reformatorio

remark [rɪ'mɑːk] *n* comentario ♦ *vt* comentar; **~able** *adj* (*outstanding*) extraordinario

remarry [riː'mærɪ] *vi* volver a casarse

remedial [rɪ'miːdɪəl] *adj* de recuperación

remedy ['rɛmədɪ] *n* remedio ♦ *vt* remediar, curar

remember [rɪ'mɛmbə*] *vt* recordar, acordarse de; (*bear in mind*) tener presente; (*send greetings to*): **~ me to him** dale recuerdos de mi parte; **remembrance** *n* recuerdo

remind [rɪ'maɪnd] *vt*: **to ~ sb to do sth** recordar a uno que haga algo; **to ~ sb of sth** (*of fact*) recordar algo a uno; **she ~s me of her mother** me recuerda a su madre; **~er** *n* notificación *f*; (*memento*) recuerdo

reminisce [rɛmɪ'nɪs] *vi* recordar (viejas historias); **~nt** *adj*: **to be ~nt of sth** recordar algo

remiss [rɪ'mɪs] *adj* descuidado; **it was ~**

of him fue un descuido de su parte

remission [rɪ'mɪʃən] *n* remisión *f*; (*of prison sentence*) disminución *f* de pena; (*REL*) perdón *m*

remit [rɪ'mɪt] *vt* (*send: money*) remitir, enviar; **~tance** *n* remesa, envío

remnant ['rɛmnənt] *n* resto; (*of cloth*) retal *m*; **~s** *npl* (*COMM*) restos *mpl* de serie

remorse [rɪ'mɔːs] *n* remordimientos *mpl*; **~ful** *adj* arrepentido; **~less** *adj* (*fig*) implacable, inexorable

remote [rɪ'məʊt] *adj* (*distant*) lejano; (*person*) distante; **~ control** *n* telecontrol *m*; **~ly** *adv* remotamente; (*slightly*) levemente

remould ['riːməʊld] (*BRIT*) *n* (*tyre*) neumático *or* llanta (*AM*) recauchutado/a

removable [rɪ'muːvəbl] *adj* (*detachable*) separable

removal [rɪ'muːvəl] *n* (*taking away*) el quitar; (*BRIT: from house*) mudanza; (*from office: dismissal*) destitución *f*; (*MED*) extirpación *f*; **~ van** (*BRIT*) *n* camión *m* de mudanzas

remove [rɪ'muːv] *vt* quitar; (*employee*) destituir; (*name: from list*) tachar, borrar; (*doubt*) disipar; (*abuse*) suprimir, acabar con; (*MED*) extirpar; **~rs** (*BRIT*) *npl* (*company*) agencia de mudanzas

Renaissance [rɪ'neɪsɒns] *n*: **the ~** el Renacimiento

render ['rɛndə*] *vt* (*thanks*) dar; (*aid*) proporcionar, prestar; (*make*): **to ~ sth useless** hacer algo inútil; **~ing** *n* (*MUS etc*) interpretación *f*

rendezvous ['rɒndɪvuː] *n* cita

renew [rɪ'njuː] *vt* renovar; (*resume*) reanudar; (*loan etc*) prorrogar; **~able** *adj* renovable; **~al** *n* reanudación *f*; prórroga

renounce [rɪ'naʊns] *vt* renunciar a; (*right, inheritance*) renunciar

renovate ['rɛnəʊveɪt] *vt* renovar

renown [rɪ'naʊn] *n* renombre *m*; **~ed** *adj* renombrado

rent [rɛnt] *n* (*for house*) arriendo, renta ♦ *vt* alquilar; **~al** *n* (*for television, car*) alquiler *m*

renunciation [rɪnʌnsɪ'eɪʃən] *n* renuncia

rep [rɛp] *n abbr* = **representative**;
repertory

repair [rɪ'pɛə*] *n* reparación *f*,
compostura ♦ *vt* reparar, componer;
(*shoes*) remendar; **in good/bad ~** en
buen/mal estado; **~ kit** *n* caja de
herramientas

repatriate [ri:pætrɪ'eɪt] *vt* repatriar

repay [ri:'peɪ] (*irreg*) *vt* (*money*) devolver,
reembolsar; (*person*) pagar; (*debt*)
liquidar; (*sb's efforts*) devolver,
corresponder a; **~ment** *n* reembolso,
devolución *f*; (*sum of money*) recompensa

repeal [rɪ'pi:l] *n* revocación *f* ♦ *vt*
revocar

repeat [rɪ'pi:t] *n* (*RADIO, TV*) reposición *f*
♦ *vt* repetir ♦ *vi* repetirse; **~edly** *adv*
repetidas veces

repel [rɪ'pɛl] *vt* (*drive away*) rechazar;
(*disgust*) repugnar; **~lent** *adj* repugnante
♦ *n*: **insect ~lent** crema (*or* loción *f*)
anti-insectos

repent [rɪ'pɛnt] *vi*: **to ~ (of)** arrepentirse
(de); **~ance** *n* arrepentimiento

repercussions [ri:pə'kʌʃənz] *npl*
consecuencias *fpl*

repertoire ['rɛpətwɑ:*] *n* repertorio

repertory ['rɛpətərɪ] *n* (*also*: ~ *theatre*)
teatro de repertorio

repetition [rɛpɪ'tɪʃən] *n* repetición *f*

repetitive [rɪ'pɛtɪtɪv] *adj* repetitivo

replace [rɪ'pleɪs] *vt* (*put back*) devolver a
su sitio; (*take the place of*) reemplazar,
sustituir; **~ment** *n* (*act*) reposición *f*;
(*thing*) recambio; (*person*) suplente *m/f*

replay ['ri:pleɪ] *n* (*SPORT*) desempate *m*; (*of
tape, film*) repetición *f*

replenish [rɪ'plɛnɪʃ] *vt* rellenar; (*stock
etc*) reponer

replica ['rɛplɪkə] *n* copia, reproducción *f*
(exacta)

reply [rɪ'plaɪ] *n* respuesta, contestación *f*
♦ *vi* contestar, responder; **~ coupon** *n*
cupón-respuesta *m*

report [rɪ'pɔ:t] *n* informe *m*; (*PRESS etc*)
reportaje *m*; (*BRIT: also: school ~*) boletín
m escolar; (*of gun*) estallido ♦ *vt*
informar de; (*PRESS etc*) hacer un
reportaje sobre; (*notify: accident, culprit*)

denunciar ♦ *vi* (*make a report*) presentar
un informe; (*present o.s.*): **to ~ (to sb)**
presentarse (ante uno); **~ card** *n* (*US,
Scottish*) cartilla escolar; **~edly** *adv*
según se dice; **~er** *n* periodista *m/f*

repose [rɪ'pəuz] *n*: **in ~** (*face, mouth*) en
reposo

reprehensible [rɛprɪ'hɛnsɪbl] *adj*
reprensible, censurable

represent [rɛprɪ'zɛnt] *vt* representar;
(*COMM*) ser agente de; (*describe*): **to ~ sth
as** describir algo como; **~ation** [-'teɪʃən] *n*
representación *f*; **~ations** *npl* (*protest*)
quejas *fpl*; **~ative** *n* representante *m/f*;
(*US: POL*) diputado/a *m/f* ♦ *adj*
representativo

repress [rɪ'prɛs] *vt* reprimir; **~ion**
[-'prɛʃən] *n* represión *f*

reprieve [rɪ'pri:v] *n* (*LAW*) indulto; (*fig*)
alivio

reprimand ['rɛprɪmɑ:nd] *n* reprimenda
♦ *vt* reprender

reprint ['ri:prɪnt] *n* reimpresión *f* ♦ *vt*
reimprimir

reprisals [rɪ'praɪzlz] *npl* represalias *fpl*

reproach [rɪ'prəutʃ] *n* reproche *m* ♦ *vt*: **to
~ sb for sth** reprochar algo a uno; **~ful**
adj de reproche, de acusación

reproduce [ri:prə'dju:s] *vt* reproducir ♦ *vi*
reproducirse; **reproduction** [-'dʌkʃən] *n*
reproducción *f*

reproof [rɪ'pru:f] *n* reproche *m*

reprove [rɪ'pru:v] *vt*: **to ~ sb for sth**
reprochar algo a uno

reptile ['rɛptaɪl] *n* reptil *m*

republic [rɪ'pʌblɪk] *n* república *f*; **~an** *adj*,
n republicano/a *m/f*

repudiate [rɪ'pju:dɪeɪt] *vt* rechazar;
(*violence etc*) repudiar

repulse [rɪ'pʌls] *vt* rechazar; **repulsive**
adj repulsivo

reputable ['rɛpjutəbl] *adj* (*make etc*) de
renombre

reputation [rɛpju'teɪʃən] *n* reputación *f*

reputed [rɪ'pju:tɪd] *adj* supuesto; **~ly** *adv*
según dicen *or* se dice

request [rɪ'kwɛst] *n* petición *f*; (*formal*)
solicitud *f* ♦ *vt*: **to ~ sth of** *or* **from sb**
solicitar algo a uno; **~ stop** (*BRIT*) *n*

parada discrecional

require [rɪ'kwaɪə*] *vt* (*need: subj: person*) necesitar, tener necesidad de; (: *thing, situation*) exigir; (*want*) pedir; **to ~ sb to do sth** pedir a uno que haga algo; ~**ment** *n* requisito; (*need*) necesidad *f*

requisite ['rɛkwɪzɪt] *n* requisito ♦ *adj* necesario

requisition [rɛkwɪ'zɪʃən] *n*: ~ **(for)** solicitud *f* (de) ♦ *vt* (*MIL*) requisar

resale ['riːseɪl] *n* reventa

rescind [rɪ'sɪnd] *vt* (*law*) abrogar; (*contract, order etc*) anular

rescue ['rɛskjuː] *n* rescate *m* ♦ *vt* rescatar; ~ **party** *n* expedición *f* de salvamento; ~**r** *n* salvador(a) *m/f*

research [rɪ'sɜːtʃ] *n* investigaciones *fpl* ♦ *vt* investigar; ~**er** *n* investigador(a) *m/f*

resemblance [rɪ'zɛmbləns] *n* parecido

resemble [rɪ'zɛmbl] *vt* parecerse a

resent [rɪ'zɛnt] *vt* tomar a mal; ~**ful** *adj* resentido; ~**ment** *n* resentimiento

reservation [rɛzə'veɪʃən] *n* reserva

reserve [rɪ'zɜːv] *n* reserva; (*SPORT*) suplente *m/f* ♦ *vt* (*seats etc*) reservar; ~**s** *npl* (*MIL*) reserva; **in** ~ de reserva; ~**d** *adj* reservado

reservoir ['rɛzəvwaː*] *n* embalse *m*

reshuffle [riː'ʃʌfl] *n*: **Cabinet** ~ (*POL*) remodelación *f* del gabinete

reside [rɪ'zaɪd] *vi* residir, vivir

residence ['rɛzɪdəns] *n* (*formal: home*) domicilio; (*length of stay*) permanencia; ~ **permit** (*BRIT*) *n* permiso de permanencia

resident ['rɛzɪdənt] *n* (*of area*) vecino/a; (*in hotel*) huésped(a) *m/f* ♦ *adj* (*population*) permanente; (*doctor*) residente; ~**ial** [-'dɛnʃəl] *adj* residencial

residue ['rɛzɪdjuː] *n* resto

resign [rɪ'zaɪn] *vt* renunciar a ♦ *vi* dimitir; **to ~ o.s. to** (*situation*) resignarse a; ~**ation** [rɛzɪg'neɪʃən] *n* dimisión *f*; (*state of mind*) resignación *f*; ~**ed** *adj* resignado

resilient [rɪ'zɪlɪənt] *adj* (*material*) elástico; (*person*) resistente

resin ['rɛzɪn] *n* resina

resist [rɪ'zɪst] *vt* resistir, oponerse a; ~**ance** *n* resistencia

resolute ['rɛzəluːt] *adj* resuelto; (*refusal*) tajante

resolution [rɛzə'luːʃən] *n* (*gen*) resolución *f*

resolve [rɪ'zɔlv] *n* resolución *f* ♦ *vt* resolver ♦ *vi*: **to ~ to do** resolver hacer; ~**d** *adj* resuelto

resort [rɪ'zɔːt] *n* (*town*) centro turístico; (*recourse*) recurso ♦ *vi*: **to ~ to** recurrir a; **in the last** ~ como último recurso

resound [rɪ'zaund] *vi*: **to ~ (with)** resonar (con); ~**ing** *adj* sonoro; (*fig*) clamoroso

resource [rɪ'sɔːs] *n* recurso; ~**s** *npl* recursos *mpl*; ~**ful** *adj* despabilado, ingenioso

respect [rɪs'pɛkt] *n* respeto ♦ *vt* respetar; ~**s** *npl* recuerdos *mpl*, saludos *mpl*; **with** ~ **to** con respecto a; **in this** ~ en cuanto a eso; ~**able** *adj* respetable; (*large: amount*) apreciable; (*passable*) tolerable; ~**ful** *adj* respetuoso

respective [rɪs'pɛktɪv] *adj* respectivo; ~**ly** *adv* respectivamente

respite ['rɛspaɪt] *n* respiro

resplendent [rɪs'plɛndənt] *adj* resplandeciente

respond [rɪs'pɔnd] *vi* responder; (*react*) reaccionar; **response** [-'pɔns] *n* respuesta; reacción *f*

responsibility [rɪspɔnsɪ'bɪlɪtɪ] *n* responsabilidad *f*

responsible [rɪs'pɔnsɪbl] *adj* (*character*) serio, formal; (*job*) de confianza; (*liable*): ~ **(for)** responsable (de)

responsive [rɪs'pɔnsɪv] *adj* sensible

rest [rɛst] *n* descanso, reposo; (*MUS, pause*) pausa, silencio; (*support*) apoyo; (*remainder*) resto ♦ *vi* descansar; (*be supported*): **to ~ on** descansar sobre ♦ *vt* (*lean*): **to ~ sth on/against** apoyar algo en *or* sobre/contra; **the ~ of them** (*people, objects*) los demás; **it ~s with him to ...** depende de él el que ...

restaurant ['rɛstərɔŋ] *n* restaurante *m*; ~ **car** (*BRIT*) *n* (*RAIL*) coche-comedor *m*

restful ['rɛstful] *adj* descansado, tranquilo

rest home *n* residencia para jubilados
restive ['rɛstɪv] *adj* inquieto; (*horse*) rebelón(ona)
restless ['rɛstlɪs] *adj* inquieto
restoration [rɛstə'reɪʃən] *n* restauración *f*; devolución *f*
restore [rɪ'stɔ:*] *vt* (*building*) restaurar; (*sth stolen*) devolver; (*health*) restablecer; (*to power*) volver a poner a
restrain [rɪs'treɪn] *vt* (*feeling*) contener, refrenar; (*person*): **to ~ (from doing)** disuadir (de hacer); **~ed** *adj* reservado; **~t** *n* (*restriction*) restricción *f*; (*moderation*) moderación *f*; (*of manner*) reserva
restrict [rɪs'trɪkt] *vt* restringir, limitar; **~ion** [-kʃən] *n* restricción *f*, limitación *f*; **~ive** *adj* restrictivo
rest room (*US*) *n* aseos *mpl*
result [rɪ'zʌlt] *n* resultado ♦ *vi*: **to ~ in** terminar en, tener por resultado; **as a ~ of** a consecuencia de
resume [rɪ'zju:m] *vt* reanudar ♦ *vi* comenzar de nuevo
résumé ['reɪzju:meɪ] *n* resumen *m*; (*US*) currículum *m*
resumption [rɪ'zʌmpʃən] *n* reanudación *f*
resurgence [rɪ'sɔ:dʒəns] *n* resurgimiento *m*
resurrection [rɛzə'rɛkʃən] *n* resurrección *f*
resuscitate [rɪ'sʌsɪteɪt] *vt* (*MED*) resucitar
retail ['ri:teɪl] *adj*, *adv* al por menor; **~er** *n* detallista *m/f* ~ **price** *n* precio de venta al público
retain [rɪ'teɪn] *vt* (*keep*) retener, conservar; **~er** *n* (*fee*) anticipo
retaliate [rɪ'tælieɪt] *vi*: **to ~ (against)** tomar represalias (contra); **retaliation** [-'eɪʃən] *n* represalias *fpl*
retarded [rɪ'tɑ:dɪd] *adj* retrasado
retch [rɛtʃ] *vi* dársele a uno arcadas
retentive [rɪ'tɛntɪv] *adj* (*memory*) retentivo
reticent ['rɛtɪsnt] *adj* reservado
retire [rɪ'taɪə*] *vi* (*give up work*) jubilarse; (*withdraw*) retirarse; (*go to bed*) acostarse; **~d** *adj* (*person*) jubilado; **~ment** *n* (*giving up work: state*) retiro; (: *act*) jubilación *f*; **retiring** *adj* (*leaving*)

saliente; (*shy*) retraído
retort [rɪ'tɔ:t] *vi* contestar
retrace [ri:'treɪs] *vt*: **to ~ one's steps** volver sobre sus pasos, desandar lo andado
retract [rɪ'trækt] *vt* (*statement*) retirar; (*claws*) retraer; (*undercarriage, aerial*) replegar
retrain [ri:'treɪn] *vt* reciclar; **~ing** *n* readaptación *f* profesional
retread ['ri:trɛd] *n* neumático (*SP*) *or* llanta (*AM*) recauchutado/a
retreat [rɪ'tri:t] *n* (*place*) retiro; (*MIL*) retirada ♦ *vi* retirarse
retribution [rɛtrɪ'bju:ʃən] *n* desquite *m*
retrieval [rɪ'tri:vəl] *n* recuperación *f*
retrieve [rɪ'tri:v] *vt* recobrar; (*situation, honour*) salvar; (*COMPUT*) recuperar; (*error*) reparar; **~r** *n* perro cobrador
retrograde ['rɛtrəgreɪd] *adj* retrógrado
retrospect ['rɛtrəspɛkt] *n*: **in ~** retrospectivamente; **~ive** [-'spɛktɪv] *adj* retrospectivo; (*law*) retroactivo
return [rɪ'tɔ:n] *n* (*going or coming back*) vuelta, regreso; (*of sth stolen etc*) devolución *f*; (*FINANCE: from land, shares*) ganancia, ingresos *mpl* ♦ *cpd* (*journey*) de regreso; (*BRIT: ticket*) de ida y vuelta; (*match*) de vuelta ♦ *vi* (*person etc: come or go back*) volver, regresar; (*symptoms etc*) reaparecer; (*regain*): **to ~ to** recuperar ♦ *vt* devolver; (*favour, love etc*) corresponder a; (*verdict*) pronunciar; (*POL: candidate*) elegir; **~s** *npl* (*COMM*) ingresos *mpl*; **in ~ (for)** a cambio (de); **by ~ of post** a vuelta de correo; **many happy ~s (of the day)!** ¡feliz cumpleaños!
reunion [ri:'ju:nɪən] *n* (*of family*) reunión *f*; (*of two people, school*) reencuentro
reunite [ri:ju:'naɪt] *vt* reunir; (*reconcile*) reconciliar
rev [rɛv] (*AUT*) *n* abbr (= *revolution*) revolución *f* ♦ *vt* (*also*: ~ **up**) acelerar
revamp [ri:'væmp] *vt* (*company etc*) reorganizar
reveal [rɪ'vi:l] *vt* revelar; **~ing** *adj* revelador(a)
reveille [rɪ'vælɪ] *n* (*MIL*) diana

revel ['rɛvl] *vi*: **to ~ in** sth/in doing sth gozar de algo/con hacer algo

revelry ['rɛvlrɪ] *n* jarana, juerga

revenge [rɪ'vɛndʒ] *n* venganza; **to take ~ on** vengarse de

revenue ['rɛvənjuː] *n* ingresos *mpl*, rentas *fpl*

reverberate [rɪ'vəːbəreɪt] *vi* (*sound*) resonar, retumbar; (*fig: shock*) repercutir; **reverberation** [-'reɪʃən] *n* retumbo, eco; repercusión *f*

revere [rɪ'vɪə*] *vt* venerar; **~nce** ['rɛvərəns] *n* reverencia

Reverend ['rɛvərənd] *adj* (*in titles*): **the ~ John Smith** (*Anglican*) el Reverendo John Smith; (*Catholic*) el Padre John Smith; (*Protestant*) el Pastor John Smith

reversal [rɪ'vəːsl] *n* (*of order*) inversión *f*; (*of direction, policy*) cambio; (*of decision*) revocación *f*

reverse [rɪ'vəːs] *n* (*opposite*) contrario, (*back: of cloth*) revés *m*; (: *of coin*) reverso; (: *of paper*) dorso; (AUT: *also*: ~ **gear**) marcha atrás; (*setback*) revés *m* ♦ *adj* (*order*) inverso; (*direction*) contrario; (*process*) opuesto ♦ *vt* (*decision, AUT*) dar marcha atrás a; (*position, function*) invertir ♦ *vi* (BRIT: AUT) dar marcha atrás; **~-charge call** (BRIT) *n* llamada a cobro revertido; **reversing lights** (BRIT) *npl* (AUT) luces *fpl* de retroceso

revert [rɪ'vəːt] *vi*: **to ~ to** volver a

review [rɪ'vjuː] *n* (*magazine, MIL*) revista; (*of book, film*) reseña; (US: *examination*) repaso, examen *m* ♦ *vt* repasar, examinar; (MIL) pasar revista a; (*book, film*) reseñar; **~er** *n* crítico/a

revile [rɪ'vaɪl] *vt* injuriar, vilipendiar

revise [rɪ'vaɪz] *vt* (*manuscript*) corregir; (*opinion*) modificar; (*price, procedure*) revisar ♦ *vi* (*study*) repasar; **revision** [rɪ'vɪʒən] *n* corrección *f*; modificación *f*; (*for exam*) repaso

revitalize [riː'vaɪtəlaɪz] *vt* revivificar

revival [rɪ'vaɪvəl] *n* (*recovery*) reanimación *f*; (*of interest*) renacimiento; (THEATRE) reestreno; (*of faith*) despertar *m*

revive [rɪ'vaɪv] *vt* resucitar; (*custom*) restablecer; (*hope*) despertar; (*play*)

reestrenar ♦ *vi* (*person*) volver en sí; (*business*) reactivarse

revolt [rɪ'vəult] *n* rebelión *f* ♦ *vi* rebelarse, sublevarse ♦ *vt* dar asco a, repugnar; **~ing** *adj* asqueroso, repugnante

revolution [rɛvə'luːʃən] *n* revolución *f*; **~ary** *adj*, *n* revolucionario/a *m/f*; **~ize** *vt* revolucionar

revolve [rɪ'vɔlv] *vi* dar vueltas, girar; (*life, discussion*): **to ~ (a)round** girar en torno a

revolver [rɪ'vɔlvə*] *n* revólver *m*

revolving [rɪ'vɔlvɪŋ] *adj* (*chair, door etc*) giratorio

revue [rɪ'vjuː] *n* (THEATRE) revista

revulsion [rɪ'vʌlʃən] *n* asco, repugnancia

reward [rɪ'wɔːd] *n* premio, recompensa ♦ *vt*: **to ~ (for)** recompensar *or* premiar (por); **~ing** *adj* (*fig*) valioso

rewind [riː'waɪnd] (*irreg*) rebobinar

rewire [riː'waɪə*] *vt* (*house*) renovar la instalación eléctrica de

rewrite [riː'raɪt] (*irreg*) *vt* reescribir

rhapsody ['ræpsədɪ] *n* (MUS) rapsodia

rhetorical [rɪ'tɔrɪkl] *adj* retórico

rheumatism ['ruːmətɪzəm] *n* reumatismo, reúma *m*

Rhine [raɪn] *n*: **the ~** (el) Rin

rhinoceros [raɪ'nɔsərəs] *n* rinoceronte *m*

rhododendron [rəudə'dɛndrn] *n* rododendro

Rhone [rəun] *n*: **the ~** el (río) Ródano

rhubarb ['ruːbɑːb] *n* ruibarbo

rhyme [raɪm] *n* rima; (*verse*) poesía

rhythm ['rɪðm] *n* ritmo

rib [rɪb] *n* (ANAT) costilla ♦ *vt* (*mock*) tomar el pelo a

ribbon ['rɪbən] *n* cinta; **in ~s** (*torn*) hecho trizas

rice [raɪs] *n* arroz *m*; **~ pudding** *n* arroz *m* con leche

rich [rɪtʃ] *adj* rico; (*soil*) fértil; (*food*) pesado; (: *sweet*) empalagoso; (*abundant*): **~ in** (*minerals etc*) rico en; **the ~** *npl* los ricos; **~es** *npl* riqueza; **~ly** *adv* ricamente; (*deserved, earned*) bien

rickets ['rɪkɪts] *n* raquitismo

rickety ['rɪkɪtɪ] *adj* tambaleante

rickshaw ['rɪkʃɔ:] *n* carro de culi
ricochet ['rɪkəʃeɪ] *vi* rebotar
rid [rɪd] (*pt, pp* **rid**) *vt*: **to ~ sb of sth** librar a uno de algo; **to get ~ of** deshacerse *or* desembarazarse de
ridden ['rɪdn] *pp of* **ride**
riddle ['rɪdl] *n* (*puzzle*) acertijo; (*mystery*) enigma *m*, misterio ♦ *vt*: **to be ~d with** ser lleno *or* plagado de
ride [raɪd] (*pt* **rode**, *pp* **ridden**) *n* paseo; (*distance covered*) viaje *m*, recorrido ♦ *vi* (*as sport*) montar; (*go somewhere: on horse, bicycle*) dar un paseo, pasearse; (*travel: on bicycle, motorcycle, bus*) viajar ♦ *vt* (*a horse*) montar a; (*a bicycle, motorcycle*) andar en; (*distance*) recorrer; **to take sb for a ~** (*fig*) engañar a uno; **~r** *n* (*on horse*) jinete/a *m/f*; (*on bicycle*) ciclista *m/f*; (*on motorcycle*) motociclista *m/f*
ridge [rɪdʒ] *n* (*of hill*) cresta; (*of roof*) caballete *m*; (*wrinkle*) arruga
ridicule ['rɪdɪkjuːl] *n* irrisión *f*, burla ♦ *vt* poner en ridículo, burlarse de; **ridiculous** [-'dɪkjuləs] *adj* ridículo
riding ['raɪdɪŋ] *n* equitación *f*; **I like ~** me gusta montar a caballo; **~ school** *n* escuela de equitación
rife [raɪf] *adj*: **to be ~** ser muy común; **to be ~ with** abundar en
riffraff ['rɪfræf] *n* gentuza
rifle ['raɪfl] *n* rifle *m*, fusil *m* ♦ *vt* saquear; **~ through** *vt* (*papers*) registrar; **~ range** *n* campo de tiro; (*at fair*) tiro al blanco
rift [rɪft] *n* (*in clouds*) claro; (*fig: disagreement*) desavenencia
rig [rɪg] *n* (*also: oil ~: at sea*) plataforma petrolera (*election etc*) amañar; **~ out** (*BRIT*) *vt* disfrazar; **~ up** *vt* improvisar; **~ging** *n* (*NAUT*) aparejo
right [raɪt] *adj* (*correct*) correcto, exacto; (*suitable*) indicado, debido; (*proper*) apropiado; (*just*) justo; (*morally good*) bueno; (*not left*) derecho ♦ *n* bueno; (*title, claim*) derecho; (*not left*) derecha ♦ *adv* bien, correctamente; (*not left*) a la derecha; (*exactly*): **~ now** ahora mismo ♦ *vt* enderezar; (*correct*) corregir ♦ *excl*

¡bueno!, ¡está bien!; **to be ~** (*person*) tener razón; (*answer*) ser correcto; **is that the ~ time?** (*of clock*) ¿es esa la hora buena?; **by ~s** en justicia; **on the ~** a la derecha; **to be in the ~** tener razón; **~ away** en seguida; **~ in the middle** exactamente en el centro; **~ angle** *n* ángulo recto; **~eous** ['raɪtʃəs] *adj* justado, honrado; (*anger*) justificado; **~ful** *adj* legítimo; **~-handed** *adj* diestro; **~-hand man** *n* brazo derecho; **~-hand side** *n* derecha; **~ly** *adv* correctamente, debidamente; (*with reason*) con razón; **~ of way** *n* (*on path etc*) derecho de paso; (*AUT*) prioridad *f*; **~-wing** *adj* (*POL*) derechista
rigid ['rɪdʒɪd] *adj* rígido; (*person, ideas*) inflexible
rigmarole ['rɪgmərəʊl] *n* galimatías *m inv*
rigorous ['rɪgərəs] *adj* riguroso
rigour ['rɪgə*] (*US* **rigor**) *n* rigor *m*, severidad *f*
rile [raɪl] *vt* irritar
rim [rɪm] *n* borde *m*; (*of spectacles*) aro; (*of wheel*) llanta
rind [raɪnd] *n* (*of bacon*) corteza; (*of lemon etc*) cáscara; (*of cheese*) costra
ring [rɪŋ] (*pt* **rang**, *pp* **rung**) *n* (*of metal*) aro; (*on finger*) anillo; (*of people*) corro; (*of objects*) círculo; (*gang*) banda; (*for boxing*) cuadrilátero; (*of circus*) pista; (*bull ~*) ruedo, plaza; (*sound of bell*) toque *m* ♦ *vi* (*on telephone*) llamar por teléfono; (*bell*) repicar; (*doorbell, phone*) sonar; (*also: ~ out*) sonar; (*ears*) zumbar ♦ *vt* (*BRIT: TEL*) llamar, telefonear; (*bell etc*) hacer sonar; (*doorbell*) tocar; **to give sb a ~** (*BRIT: TEL*) llamar *or* telefonear a alguien; **~ back** (*BRIT*) *vt, vi* (*TEL*) devolver la llamada; **~ off** (*BRIT*) *vi* (*TEL*) colgar, cortar la comunicación; **~ up** (*BRIT*) *vt* (*TEL*) llamar, telefonear; **~ing** *n* (*of bell*) repique *m*; (*of phone*) el sonar; (*in ears*) zumbido; **~ing tone** *n* (*TEL*) tono de llamada; **~leader** *n* (*of gang*) cabecilla *m*; **~lets** *npl* rizos *mpl*, bucles *mpl*; **~ road** (*BRIT*) *n* carretera periférica *or* de circunvalación
rink [rɪŋk] *n* (*also: ice ~*) pista de hielo

rinse [rɪns] *n* aclarado; (*dye*) tinte *m* ♦ *vt* aclarar; (*mouth*) enjuagar

riot ['raɪət] *n* motín *m*, disturbio ♦ *vi* amotinarse; **to run ~** desmandarse; **~ous** *adj* alborotado; (*party*) bullicioso

rip [rɪp] *n* rasgón *m*, rasgadura ♦ *vt* rasgar, desgarrar ♦ *vi* rasgarse, desgarrarse; **~cord** *n* cabo de desgarre

ripe [raɪp] *adj* maduro; **~n** *vt* madurar; (*cheese*) curar ♦ *vi* madurar

ripple ['rɪpl] *n* onda, rizo; (*sound*) murmullo ♦ *vi* rizarse

rise [raɪz] (*pt* **rose**, *pp* **risen**) *n* (*slope*) cuesta, pendiente *f*; (*hill*) altura; (*BRIT: in wages*) aumento; (*in prices, temperature*) subida; (*fig: to power etc*) ascenso ♦ *vi* subir; (*waters*) crecer; (*sun, moon*) salir; (*person: from bed etc*) levantarse; (*also: ~ up: rebel*) sublevarse; (*in rank*) ascender; **to give ~ to** dar lugar *or* origen a; **to ~ to the occasion** ponerse a la altura de las circunstancias; **risen** ['rɪzn] *pp of* **rise**; **rising** *adj* (*increasing: number*) creciente; (*: prices*) en aumento *or* alza; (*tide*) creciente; (*sun, moon*) naciente

risk [rɪsk] *n* riesgo, peligro ♦ *vt* arriesgar; (*run the ~ of*) exponerse a; **to take** *or* **run the ~ of doing** correr el riesgo de hacer; **at ~** en peligro; **at one's own ~** bajo su propia responsabilidad; **~y** *adj* arriesgado, peligroso

risqué ['riːskeɪ] *adj* verde

rissole ['rɪsəʊl] *n* croqueta

rite [raɪt] *n* rito; **last ~s** exequias *fpl*

ritual ['rɪtjuəl] *adj* ritual ♦ *n* ritual *m*, rito

rival ['raɪvl] *n* rival *m/f*; (*in business*) competidor(a) *m/f* ♦ *adj* rival, opuesto ♦ *vt* competir con; **~ry** *n* competencia

river ['rɪvə*] *n* río ♦ *cpd* (*port*) de río; (*traffic*) fluvial; **up/down ~** río arriba/ abajo; **~bank** *n* orilla (del río); **~bed** *n* lecho, cauce *m*

rivet ['rɪvɪt] *n* roblón *m*, remache *m* ♦ *vt* (*fig*) captar

Riviera [rɪvɪ'ɛərə] *n*: **the (French) ~** la Costa Azul (francesa)

road [rəʊd] *n* camino; (*motorway etc*) carretera; (*in town*) calle *f* ♦ *cpd* (*accident*) de tráfico; **major/minor ~** carretera principal/secundaria; **~block** *n* barricada; **~hog** *n* loco/a del volante; **~ map** *n* mapa *m* de carreteras; **~ safety** *n* seguridad *f* vial; **~side** *n* borde *m* (del camino); **~sign** *n* señal *f* de tráfico; **~ user** *n* usuario/a de la vía pública; **~way** *n* calzada; **~works** *npl* obras *fpl*; **~worthy** *adj* (*car*) en buen estado para circular

roam [rəʊm] *vi* vagar

roar [rɔː*] *n* rugido; (*of vehicle, storm*) estruendo; (*of laughter*) carcajada ♦ *vi* rugir; hacer estruendo; **to ~ with laughter** reírse a carcajadas; **to do a ~ing trade** hacer buen negocio

roast [rəʊst] *n* carne *f* asada, asado ♦ *vt* asar; (*coffee*) tostar; **~ beef** *n* rosbif *m*

rob [rɒb] *vt* robar; **to ~ sb of sth** robar algo a uno; (*fig: deprive*) quitar algo a uno; **~ber** *n* ladrón/ona *m/f*; **~bery** *n* robo

robe [rəʊb] *n* (*for ceremony etc*) toga; (*also: bath ~, US*) albornoz *m*

robin ['rɒbɪn] *n* petirrojo

robot ['rəʊbɒt] *n* robot *m*

robust [rəʊ'bʌst] *adj* robusto, fuerte

rock [rɒk] *n* roca; (*boulder*) peña, peñasco; (*US: small stone*) piedrecita; (*BRIT: sweet*) ≈ pirulí ♦ *vt* (*swing gently: cradle*) balancear, mecer; (*: child*) arrullar; (*shake*) sacudir ♦ *vi* mecerse, balancearse; sacudirse; **on the ~s** (*drink*) con hielo; (*marriage etc*) en ruinas; **~ and roll** *n* rocanrol *m*; **~-bottom** *n* (*fig*) punto más bajo; **~ery** *n* cuadro alpino

rocket ['rɒkɪt] *n* cohete *m*

rocking ['rɒkɪŋ]: **~ chair** *n* mecedora; **~ horse** *n* caballo de balancín

rocky ['rɒkɪ] *adj* rocoso

rod [rɒd] *n* vara, varilla; (*also: fishing ~*) caña

rode [rəʊd] *pt of* **ride**

rodent ['rəʊdnt] *n* roedor *m*

roe [rəʊ] *n* (*species: also: ~ deer*) corzo; (*of fish*): **hard/soft ~** hueva/lecha

rogue [rəʊg] *n* pícaro, pillo

role [rəʊl] *n* papel *m*

roll [rəʊl] *n* rollo; (*of bank notes*) fajo;

(*also*: *bread* ~) panecillo; (*register, list*) lista, nómina; (*sound: of drums etc*) redoble *m* ♦ *vt* hacer rodar; (*also*: ~ *up*: *string*) enrollar; (: *sleeves*) arremangar; (*cigarette*) liar; (*also*: ~ *out*: *pastry*) aplanar; (*flatten: road, lawn*) apisonar ♦ *vi* rodar; (*drum*) redoblar; (*ship*) balancearse; ~ **about or around** *vi* (*person*) revolcarse; (*object*) rodar (por); ~ **by** *vi* (*time*) pasar; ~ **in** *vi* (*mail, cash*) entrar a raudales; ~ **over** *vi* dar una vuelta; ~ **up** *vi* (*inf: arrive*) aparecer ♦ *vt* (*carpet*) arrollar; ~ **call** *n*: **to take a ~ call** pasar lista; ~**er** *n* rodillo; (*wheel*) rueda; (*for road*) apisonadora; (*for hair*) rulo; ~**er coaster** *n* montaña rusa; ~**er skates** *npl* patines *mpl* de rueda

rolling [ˈrəʊlɪŋ] *adj* (*landscape*) ondulado; ~ **pin** *n* rodillo (de cocina); ~ **stock** *n* (*RAIL*) material *m* rodante

ROM [rɔm] *n abbr* (*COMPUT*: = *read only memory*) ROM *f*

Roman [ˈrəʊmən] *adj* romano/a; ~ **Catholic** *adj, n* católico/a *m/f* (romano/a)

romance [rəˈmæns] *n* (*love affair*) amor *m*; (*charm*) lo romántico; (*novel*) novela de amor

Romania [ruːˈmeɪnɪə] *n* = **Rumania**

Roman numeral *n* número romano

romantic [rəˈmæntɪk] *adj* romántico

Rome [rəʊm] *n* Roma

romp [rɔmp] *n* retozo, juego ♦ *vi* (*also*: ~ *about*) jugar, brincar

rompers [ˈrɔmpəz] *npl* pelele *m*

roof [ruːf] (*pl* ~**s**) *n* (*gen*) techo; (*of house*) techo, tejado ♦ *vt* techar, poner techo a; **the ~ of the mouth** el paladar; ~**ing** *n* techumbre *f*; ~ **rack** *n* (*AUT*) baca, portaequipajes *m inv*

rook [ruk] *n* (*bird*) graja; (*CHESS*) torre *f*

room [ruːm] *n* cuarto, habitación *f*, pieza (*esp AM*); (*also*: *bed*~) dormitorio; (*in school etc*) sala; (*space, scope*) sitio, cabida; ~**s** *npl* (*lodging*) alojamiento; "~**s to let**", "~**s for rent**" "se alquilan cuartos"; **single/double** ~ habitación individual/doble *or* para dos personas; ~**ing house** (*US*) *n* pensión *f*; ~**mate** *n*

compañero/a de cuarto; ~ **service** *n* servicio de habitaciones; ~**y** *adj* espacioso; (*garment*) amplio

roost [ruːst] *vi* pasar la noche

rooster [ˈruːstə*] *n* gallo

root [ruːt] *n* raíz *f* ♦ *vi* arraigarse; ~ **about** *vi* (*fig*) buscar y rebuscar; ~ **for** *vt fus* (*support*) apoyar a; ~ **out** *vt* desarraigar

rope [rəʊp] *n* cuerda; (*NAUT*) cable *m* ♦ *vt* (*tie*) atar *or* amarrar con (una) cuerda; (*climbers: also*: ~ *together*) encordarse; (*an area: also*: ~ *off*) acordonar; **to know the ~s** (*fig*) conocer los trucos (del oficio); ~ **in** *vt* (*fig*): **to ~ sb in** persuadir a uno a tomar parte; ~ **ladder** *n* escala de cuerda

rosary [ˈrəʊzərɪ] *n* rosario

rose [rəʊz] *pt of* **rise** ♦ *n* rosa; (*shrub*) rosal *m*; (*on watering can*) roseta

rosé [ˈrəʊzeɪ] *n* vino rosado

rosebud [ˈrəʊzbʌd] *n* capullo de rosa

rosebush [ˈrəʊzbʊʃ] *n* rosal *m*

rosemary [ˈrəʊzmərɪ] *n* romero

rosette [rəʊˈzɛt] *n* escarapela

roster [ˈrɔstə*] *n*: **duty ~** lista de deberes

rostrum [ˈrɔstrəm] *n* tribuna

rosy [ˈrəʊzɪ] *adj* rosado, sonrosado; **a ~ future** un futuro prometedor

rot [rɔt] *n* podredumbre *f*; (*fig: pej*) tonterías *fpl* ♦ *vt* pudrir ♦ *vi* pudrirse

rota [ˈrəʊtə] *n* (sistema *m* de) turnos *mpl*

rotary [ˈrəʊtərɪ] *adj* rotativo

rotate [rəʊˈteɪt] *vt* (*revolve*) hacer girar, dar vueltas a; (*jobs*) alternar ♦ *vi* girar, dar vueltas; **rotating** *adj* rotativo; **rotation** [-ˈteɪʃən] *n* rotación *f*

rote [rəʊt] *n*: **by ~** maquinalmente, de memoria

rotten [ˈrɔtn] *adj* podrido; (*dishonest*) corrompido; (*inf: bad*) pocho; **to feel ~** (*ill*) sentirse fatal

rotund [rəʊˈtʌnd] *adj* regordete

rouble [ˈruːbl] (*US* **ruble**) *n* rublo

rouge [ruːʒ] *n* colorete *m*

rough [rʌf] *adj* (*skin, surface*) áspero; (*terrain*) quebrado; (*road*) desigual; (*voice*) bronco; (*person, manner*) tosco, grosero; (*weather*) borrascoso; (*treatment*)

brutal; (*sea*) picado; (*town, area*)
peligroso; (*cloth*) basto; (*plan*)
preliminar; (*guess*) aproximado ♦ *n*
(*GOLF*): **in the ~** en las hierbas altas; **to
~ it** vivir sin comodidades; **to sleep ~**
(*BRIT*) pasar la noche al raso; **~age** *n*
fibra(s) *f(pl)*; **~-and-ready** *adj*
improvisado; **~ copy** *n* borrador *m*; **~
draft** *n* = **~ copy**; **~en** *vt* (*a surface*)
poner áspero; **~ly** *adv* (*handle*)
torpemente; (*make*) toscamente; (*speak*)
groseramente; (*approximately*)
aproximadamente; **~ness** *n* (*of surface*)
aspereza; (*of person*) rudeza
roulette [ruː'let] *n* ruleta
Roumania [ruː'meɪnɪə] *n* = **Rumania**
round [raund] *adj* redondo ♦ *n* círculo;
(*BRIT*: *of toast*) rebanada; (*of policeman*)
ronda; (*of milkman*) recorrido; (*of doctor*)
visitas *fpl*; (*game: of cards, in competition*) partida; (*of ammunition*) cartucho;
(*BOXING*) asalto; (*of talks*) ronda ♦ *vt* (*corner*) doblar ♦ *prep* alrededor de; (*surrounding*): **~ his neck/the table** en su
cuello/alrededor de la mesa; (*in a
circular movement*): **to move ~ the
room/sail ~ the world** dar una vuelta a
la habitación/circunnavegar el mundo;
(*in various directions*): **to move ~ a
room/house** moverse por toda la
habitación/casa; (*approximately*)
alrededor de ♦ *adv*: **all ~** por todos
lados; **the long way ~** por el camino
menos directo; **all the year ~** durante
todo el año; **it's just ~ the corner** (*fig*)
está a la vuelta de la esquina; **~ the
clock** *adv* las 24 horas; **to go ~ to sb's
(house)** ir a casa de uno; **to go ~ the
back** pasar por atrás; **to go ~ a house**
visitar una casa; **enough to go ~**
bastante (para todos); **a ~ of applause**
una salva de aplausos; **a ~ of drinks/
sandwiches** una ronda de bebidas/
bocadillos; **~ off** *vt* (*speech etc*) acabar,
poner término a; **~ up** *vt* (*cattle*)
acorralar; (*people*) reunir; (*price*)
redondear; **~about** (*BRIT*) *n* (*AUT*) isleta;
(*at fair*) tiovivo ♦ *adj* (*route, means*)
indirecto; **~ers** *n* (*game*) juego similar al

béisbol; **~ly** *adv* (*fig*) rotundamente; **~-
shouldered** *adj* cargado de espaldas; **~
trip** *n* viaje *m* de ida y vuelta; **~up** *n*
rodeo; (*of criminals*) redada; (*of news*)
resumen *m*
rouse [rauz] *vt* (*wake up*) despertar; (*stir
up*) suscitar; **rousing** *adj* (*cheer, welcome*) caluroso
rout [raut] *n* (*MIL*) derrota ♦ *vt* derrotar
route [ruːt] *n* ruta, camino; (*of bus*)
recorrido; (*of shipping*) derrota; **~ map**
(*BRIT*) *n* (*for journey*) mapa *m* de carreteras
routine [ruː'tiːn] *adj* rutinario ♦ *n* rutina;
(*THEATRE*) número
rove [rəuv] *vt* vagar *or* errar por
row[1] [rəu] *n* (*line*) fila, hilera; (*KNITTING*)
pasada ♦ *vi* (*in boat*) remar ♦ *vt*
conducir remando; **4 days in a ~** 4 días
seguidos
row[2] [rau] *n* (*racket*) escándalo; (*dispute*)
bronca, pelea; (*scolding*) regaño ♦ *vi*
pelear(se)
rowboat ['rəubəut] (*US*) *n* bote *m* de
remos
rowdy ['raudɪ] *adj* (*person: noisy*)
ruidoso; (*occasion*) alborotado
rowing ['rəuɪŋ] *n* remo; **~ boat** (*BRIT*) *n*
bote *m* de remos
royal ['rɔɪəl] *adj* real; **R~ Air Force** *n*
Fuerzas *fpl* Aéreas Británicas; **~ty** *n* (*~
persons*) familia real; (*payment to author*)
derechos *mpl* de autor
rpm *abbr* (= *revs per minute*) r.p.m.
R.S.V.P. *abbr* (= *répondez s'il vous
plaît*) SRC
Rt. Hon. *abbr* (*BRIT*: = *Right Honourable*) título honorífico de diputado
rub [rʌb] *vt* frotar; (*scrub*) restregar ♦ *n*:
to give sth a ~ frotar algo; **to ~ sb up**
or **~ sb** (*US*) **the wrong way** entrarle
uno por mal ojo; **~ off** *vi* borrarse; **~ off
on** *vt fus* influir en; **~ out** *vt* borrar
rubber ['rʌbə*] *n* caucho, goma; (*BRIT*:
eraser) goma de borrar; **~ band** *n* goma,
gomita; **~ plant** *n* ficus *m*; **~y** *adj*
elástico; (*meat*) gomoso
rubbish ['rʌbɪʃ] *n* basura; (*waste*)
desperdicios *mpl*; (*fig: pej*) tonterías *fpl*;

(*junk*) pacotilla; ~ **bin** (*BRIT*) n cubo (*SP*) or bote m (*AM*) de la basura; ~ **dump** n vertedero, basurero

rubble ['rʌbl] n escombros mpl

ruble ['ru:bl] (*US*) n = **rouble**

ruby ['ru:bɪ] n rubí m

rucksack ['rʌksæk] n mochila

rudder ['rʌdə*] n timón m

ruddy ['rʌdɪ] adj (*face*) rubicundo; (*inf*: *damned*) condenado

rude [ru:d] adj (*impolite*: *person*) mal educado; (: *word, manners*) grosero; (*crude*) crudo; (*indecent*) indecente; ~**ness** n descortesía

rueful ['ru:ful] adj arrepentido

ruffian ['rʌfɪən] n matón m, criminal m

ruffle ['rʌfl] vt (*hair*) despeinar; (*clothes*) arrugar; **to get ~d** (*fig*: *person*) alterarse

rug [rʌg] n alfombra; (*BRIT*: *blanket*) manta

rugby ['rʌgbɪ] n (*also*: ~ **football**) rugby m

rugged ['rʌgɪd] adj (*landscape*) accidentado; (*features*) robusto

rugger ['rʌgə*] (*BRIT*: *inf*) n rugby m

ruin ['ru:ɪn] n ruina ♦ vt arruinar; (*spoil*) estropear; ~**s** npl ruinas fpl, restos mpl; ~**ous** adj desastroso

rule [ru:l] n (*norm*) norma, costumbre f; (*regulation, ruler*) regla; (*government*) dominio ♦ vt (*country, person*) gobernar ♦ vi gobernar; (*LAW*) fallar; **as a** ~ por regla general; ~ **out** vt excluir; ~**d** adj (*paper*) rayado; ~**r** n (*sovereign*) soberano; (*for measuring*) regla; **ruling** adj (*party*) gobernante; (*class*) dirigente ♦ n (*LAW*) fallo, decisión f

rum [rʌm] n ron m

Rumania [ru:'meɪnɪə] n Rumanía; ~**n** adj rumano/a ♦ n rumano/a m/f; (*LING*) rumano

rumble ['rʌmbl] n (*noise*) ruido sordo ♦ vi retumbar, hacer un ruido sordo; (*stomach, pipe*) sonar

rummage ['rʌmɪdʒ] vi (*search*) hurgar

rumour ['ru:mə*] (*US* **rumor**) n rumor m ♦ vt: **it is ~ed that ...** se rumorea que ...

rump [rʌmp] n (*of animal*) ancas fpl, grupa; ~ **steak** n filete m de lomo

rumpus ['rʌmpəs] n lío, jaleo

run [rʌn] (*pt* **ran**, *pp* **run**) n (*fast pace*): **at a** ~ corriendo; (*SPORT, in tights*) carrera; (*outing*) paseo, excursión f; (*distance travelled*) trayecto; (*series*) serie f; (*THEATRE*) temporada; (*SKI*) pista ♦ vt correr; (*operate: business*) dirigir; (: *competition, course*) organizar; (: *hotel, house*) administrar, llevar; (*COMPUT*) ejecutar; (*pass: hand*) pasar; (*PRESS*: *feature*) publicar ♦ vi correr; (*work*: *machine*) funcionar, marchar; (*bus, train*: *operate*) circular, ir; (: *travel*) ir; (*continue: play*) seguir; (: *contract*) ser válido; (*flow: river*) fluir; (*colours, washing*) desteñirse; (*in election*) ser candidato; **there was a ~ on** (*meat, tickets*) hubo mucha demanda de; **in the long ~** a la larga; **on the ~** en fuga; **I'll ~ you to the station** te llevaré a la estación (en coche); **to ~ a risk** correr un riesgo; **to ~ a bath** llenar la bañera; ~ **about** *or* **around** vi (*children*) correr por todos lados; ~ **across** vt fus (*find*) dar *or* topar con; ~ **away** vi huir; ~ **down** vt (*production*) ir reduciendo; (*factory*) ir restringiendo la producción en; (*subj: car*) atropellar; (*criticize*) criticar; **to be ~ down** (*person: tired*) estar debilitado; ~ **in** (*BRIT*) vt (*car*) rodar; ~ **into** vt fus (*meet: person, trouble*) tropezar con; (*collide with*) chocar con; ~ **off** vt (*water*) dejar correr; (*copies*) sacar ♦ vi huir corriendo; ~ **out** vi (*person*) salir corriendo; (*liquid*) irse; (*lease*) caducar, vencer; (*money etc*) acabarse; ~ **out of** vt fus quedar sin; ~ **over** vt (*AUT*) atropellar ♦ vt fus (*revise*) repasar; ~ **through** vt fus (*instructions*) repasar; ~ **up** vt (*debt*) contraer; **to ~ up against** (*difficulties*) tropezar con; ~**away** adj (*horse*) desbocado; (*truck*) sin frenos; (*child*) escapado de casa

rung [rʌŋ] pp of **ring** ♦ n (*of ladder*) escalón m, peldaño

runner ['rʌnə*] n (*in race: person*) corredor(a) m/f; (: *horse*) caballo; (*on sledge*) patín m; ~ **bean** (*BRIT*) n ≈ judía verde; ~-**up** n subcampeón/ona m/f

running ['rʌnɪŋ] *n* (*sport*) atletismo; (*business*) administración *f* ♦ *adj* (*water*, *costs*) corriente; (*commentary*) continuo; **to be in/out of the ~ for sth** tener/no tener posibilidades de ganar algo; **6 days** ~ 6 días seguidos; ~ **commentary** *n* (*TV*, *RADIO*) comentario en directo; (*on guided tour etc*) comentario detallado; ~ **costs** *npl* gastos *mpl* corrientes

runny ['rʌnɪ] *adj* fluido; (*nose*, *eyes*) gastante

run-of-the-mill *adj* común y corriente

runt [rʌnt] *n* (*also pej*) redrojo, enano

run-up *n*: ~ **to** (*election etc*) período previo a

runway ['rʌnweɪ] *n* (*AVIAT*) pista de aterrizaje

rupee [ruː'piː] *n* rupia

rupture ['rʌptʃə*] *n* (*MED*) hernia

rural ['ruərl] *adj* rural

ruse [ruːz] *n* ardid *m*

rush [rʌʃ] *n* ímpetu *m*; (*hurry*) prisa; (*COMM*) demanda repentina; (*current*) corriente *f* fuerte; (*of feeling*) torrente; (*BOT*) junco ♦ *vt* apresurar; (*work*) hacer de prisa ♦ *vi* correr, precipitarse; ~ **hour** *n* horas *fpl* punta

rusk [rʌsk] *n* bizcocho tostado

Russia ['rʌʃə] *n* Rusia; ~**n** *adj* ruso/a ♦ *n* ruso/a *m/f*; (*LING*) ruso

rust [rʌst] *n* herrumbre *f*, moho ♦ *vi* oxidarse

rustic ['rʌstɪk] *adj* rústico

rustle ['rʌsl] *vi* susurrar ♦ *vt* (*paper*) hacer crujir; (*US*: *cattle*) hurtar, robar

rustproof ['rʌstpruːf] *adj* inoxidable

rusty ['rʌstɪ] *adj* oxidado

rut [rʌt] *n* surco; (*ZOOL*) celo; **to be in a ~** ser esclavo de la rutina

ruthless ['ruːθlɪs] *adj* despiadado

rye [raɪ] *n* centeno; ~ **bread** *n* pan de centeno

S s

Sabbath ['sæbəθ] *n* domingo; (*Jewish*) sábado

sabotage ['sæbətɑːʒ] *n* sabotaje *m* ♦ *vt* sabotear

saccharin(e) ['sækərɪn] *n* sacarina

sachet ['sæʃeɪ] *n* sobrecito

sack [sæk] *n* (*bag*) saco, costal *m* ♦ *vt* (*dismiss*) despedir; (*plunder*) saquear; **to get the ~** ser despedido; ~**ing** *n* despido; (*material*) arpillera

sacred ['seɪkrɪd] *adj* sagrado, santo

sacrifice ['sækrɪfaɪs] *n* sacrificio ♦ *vt* sacrificar

sacrilege ['sækrɪlɪdʒ] *n* sacrilegio

sad [sæd] *adj* (*unhappy*) triste; (*deplorable*) lamentable

saddle ['sædl] *n* silla (de montar); (*of cycle*) sillín *m* ♦ *vt* (*horse*) ensillar; **to be ~d with sth** (*inf*) quedar cargado con algo; ~**bag** *n* alforja

sadistic [sə'dɪstɪk] *adj* sádico

sadly ['sædlɪ] *adv* lamentablemente; **to be ~ lacking in** estar por desgracia carente de

sadness ['sædnɪs] *n* tristeza

s.a.e. *abbr* (= *stamped addressed envelope*) sobre con las propias señas de uno y con sello

safari [sə'fɑːrɪ] *n* safari *m*

safe [seɪf] *adj* (*out of danger*) fuera de peligro; (*not dangerous*, *sure*) seguro; (*unharmed*) ileso ♦ *n* caja de caudales, caja fuerte; ~ **and sound** sano y salvo; (**just**) **to be on the ~ side** para mayor seguridad; ~**-conduct** *n* salvoconducto; ~**-deposit** *n* (*vault*) cámara acorazada; (*box*) caja de seguridad; ~**guard** *n* protección *f*, garantía ♦ *vt* proteger, defender; ~**keeping** *n* custodia; ~**ly** *adv* seguramente, con seguridad; **to arrive ~ly** llegar bien; ~ **sex** *n* sexo seguro *or* sin riesgo

safety ['seɪftɪ] *n* seguridad *f*; ~ **belt** *n* cinturón *m* (de seguridad); ~ **pin** *n* imperdible *m* (*SP*), seguro (*AM*); ~ **valve** *n* válvula de seguridad

saffron ['sæfrən] *n* azafrán *m*

sag [sæg] *vi* aflojarse

sage [seɪdʒ] *n* (*herb*) salvia; (*man*) sabio

Sagittarius [sædʒɪ'tɛərɪəs] *n* Sagitario

Sahara [sə'hɑːrə] *n*: **the ~** (*Desert*) el (desierto del) Sáhara

said [sɛd] *pt, pp of* **say**
sail [seɪl] *n* (*on boat*) vela; (*trip*): **to go for a ~** dar un paseo en barco ♦ *vt* (*boat*) gobernar ♦ *vi* (*travel: ship*) navegar; (*SPORT*) hacer vela; (*begin voyage*) salir; **they ~ed into Copenhagen** arribaron a Copenhague; **~ through** *vt fus* (*exam*) aprobar sin ningún problema; **~boat** (*US*) *n* velero, barco de vela; **~ing** *n* (*SPORT*) vela; **to go ~ing** hacer de vela; **~ing boat** *n* barco de vela; **~ing ship** *n* velero; **~or** *n* marinero, marino
saint [seɪnt] *n* santo; **~ly** *adj* santo
sake [seɪk] *n*: **for the ~ of** por
salad ['sæləd] *n* ensalada; **~ bowl** *n* ensaladera; **~ cream** (*BRIT*) *n* (*especie f* de) mayonesa; **~ dressing** *n* aliño
salary ['sælərɪ] *n* sueldo
sale [seɪl] *n* venta; (*at reduced prices*) liquidación *f*, saldo; (*auction*) subasta; **~s** *npl* (*total amount sold*) ventas *fpl*, facturación *f*; **"for ~"** "se vende"; **on ~** en venta; **on ~ or return** (*goods*) venta por reposición; **~room** *n* sala de subastas; **~s assistant** (*US* **~s clerk**) *n* dependiente/a *m/f*; **salesman/woman** *n* (*in shop*) dependiente/a *m/f*; (*representative*) viajante *m/f*
salient ['seɪlɪənt] *adj* sobresaliente
saliva [sə'laɪvə] *n* saliva
sallow ['sæləʊ] *adj* cetrino
salmon ['sæmən] *n inv* salmón *m*
salon ['sælɒn] *n* (*hairdressing ~*) peluquería; (*beauty ~*) salón *m* de belleza
saloon [sə'luːn] *n* (*US*) bar *m*, taberna; (*BRIT: AUT*) (coche *m* de) turismo; (*ship's lounge*) cámara, salón *m*
salt [sɔːlt] *n* sal *f* ♦ *vt* salar; (*put ~ on*) poner sal en; **~ away** (*inf*) *vt* (*money*) ahorrar; **~ cellar** *n* salero; **~water** *adj* de agua salada; **~y** *adj* salado
salutary ['sæljutərɪ] *adj* saludable
salute [sə'luːt] *n* saludo; (*of guns*) salva ♦ *vt* saludar
salvage ['sælvɪdʒ] *n* (*saving*) salvamento, recuperación *f*; (*things saved*) objetos *mpl* salvados ♦ *vt* salvar
salvation [sæl'veɪʃən] *n* salvación *f*; **S~ Army** *n* Ejército de Salvación

salvo ['sælvəʊ] *n* (*MIL*) salva
same [seɪm] *adj* mismo ♦ *pron*: **the ~** el/la mismo/a, los/las mismos/as; **the ~ book as** el mismo libro que; **at the ~ time** (*at the ~ moment*) al mismo tiempo; (*yet*) sin embargo; **all** *or* **just the ~** sin embargo, aun así; **to do the ~ (as sb)** hacer lo mismo (que uno); **the ~ to you!** ¡igualmente!
sample ['sɑːmpl] *n* muestra ♦ *vt* (*food*) probar; (*wine*) catar
sanatorium [sænə'tɔːrɪəm] (*pl* **sanatoria**) (*BRIT*) *n* sanatorio
sanctimonious [sæŋktɪ'məʊnɪəs] *adj* mojigato
sanction ['sæŋkʃən] *n* aprobación *f* ♦ *vt* sancionar; aprobar; **~s** *npl* (*POL*) sanciones *fpl*
sanctity ['sæŋktɪtɪ] *n* santidad *f*; (*inviolability*) inviolabilidad *f*
sanctuary ['sæŋktjʊərɪ] *n* santuario; (*refuge*) asilo, refugio; (*for wildlife*) reserva
sand [sænd] *n* arena; (*beach*) playa ♦ *vt* (*also: ~ down*) lijar
sandal ['sændl] *n* sandalia
sand: **~box** (*US*) *n* = **~pit**; **~castle** *n* castillo de arena; **~ dune** *n* duna; **~paper** *n* papel *m* de lija; **~pit** *n* (*for children*) cajón *m* de arena; **~stone** *n* piedra arenisca
sandwich ['sændwɪtʃ] *n* bocadillo (*SP*), sandwich *m*, emparedado (*AM*) ♦ *vt* intercalar; **~ed between** apretujado entre; **cheese/ham ~** sandwich de queso/jamón; **~ course** (*BRIT*) *n* curso de medio tiempo
sandy ['sændɪ] *adj* arenoso; (*colour*) rojizo
sane [seɪn] *adj* cuerdo; (*sensible*) sensato
sang [sæŋ] *pt of* **sing**
sanitarium [sænɪ'tɛərɪəm] (*US*) *n* = **sanitarium**
sanitary ['sænɪtərɪ] *adj* sanitario; (*clean*) higiénico; **~ towel** (*US* **~ napkin**) *n* paño higiénico, compresa
sanitation [sænɪ'teɪʃən] *n* (*in house*) servicios *mpl* higiénicos; (*in town*) servicio de desinfección; **~ department** (*US*) *n* departamento de limpieza y

recogida de basuras

sanity ['sænɪtɪ] *n* cordura; (*of judgment*) sensatez *f*

sank [sæŋk] *pt of* **sink**

Santa Claus [sæntə'klɔːz] *n* San Nicolás, Papá Noel

sap [sæp] *n* (*of plants*) savia ♦ *vt* (*strength*) minar, agotar

sapling ['sæplɪŋ] *n* árbol nuevo *or* joven

sapphire ['sæfaɪə*] *n* zafiro

sarcasm ['sɑːkæzm] *n* sarcasmo

sardine [sɑː'diːn] *n* sardina

Sardinia [sɑː'dɪnɪə] *n* Cerdeña

sash [sæʃ] *n* faja

sat [sæt] *pt, pp of* **sit**

Satan ['seɪtn] *n* Satanás *m*

satchel ['sætʃl] *n* (*child's*) cartera (*SP*), mochila (*AM*)

satellite ['sætəlaɪt] *n* satélite *m*; ~ **dish** *n* antena de televisión por satélite; ~ **television** *n* televisión *f* vía satélite

satin ['sætɪn] *n* raso ♦ *adj* de raso

satire ['sætaɪə*] *n* sátira

satisfaction [sætɪs'fækʃən] *n* satisfacción *f*

satisfactory [sætɪs'fæktərɪ] *adj* satisfactorio

satisfy ['sætɪsfaɪ] *vt* satisfacer; (*convince*) convencer; ~**ing** *adj* satisfactorio

saturate ['sætʃəreɪt] *vt*: **to ~ (with)** empapar *or* saturar (de)

Saturday ['sætədɪ] *n* sábado

sauce [sɔːs] *n* salsa; (*sweet*) crema; jarabe *m*; ~**pan** *n* cacerola, olla

saucer ['sɔːsə*] *n* platillo

saucy ['sɔːsɪ] *adj* fresco, descarado

Saudi ['saʊdɪ]: ~ **Arabia** *n* Arabia Saudí *or* Saudita; ~ **(Arabian)** *adj*, *n* saudí *m/f*, saudita *m/f*

sauna ['sɔːnə] *n* sauna

saunter ['sɔːntə*] *vi*: **to ~ in/out** entrar/salir sin prisa

sausage ['sɔsɪdʒ] *n* salchicha; ~ **roll** *n* empanadita de salchicha

sauté ['səʊteɪ] *adj* salteado

savage ['sævɪdʒ] *adj* (*cruel, fierce*) feroz, furioso; (*primitive*) salvaje ♦ *n* salvaje *m/f* ♦ *vt* (*attack*) embestir; ~**ry** *n* salvajismo, salvajería

save [seɪv] *vt* (*rescue*) salvar, rescatar; (*money, time*) ahorrar; (*put by, keep: seat*) guardar; (*COMPUT*) salvar (y guardar); (*avoid: trouble*) evitar; (*SPORT*) parar ♦ *vi* (*also*: ~ **up**) ahorrar ♦ *n* (*SPORT*) parada ♦ *prep* salvo, excepto

saving ['seɪvɪŋ] *n* (*on price etc*) economía ♦ *adj*: **the ~ grace of** el único mérito de; ~**s** *npl* ahorros *mpl*; ~**s account** *n* cuenta de ahorros; ~**s bank** *n* caja de ahorros

saviour ['seɪvjə*] (*US* **savior**) *n* salvador(a) *m/f*

savour ['seɪvə*] (*US* **savor**) *vt* saborear; ~**y** *adj* sabroso; (*dish: not sweet*) salado

saw [sɔː] (*pt* **sawed**, *pp* **sawed** *or* **sawn**) *pt of* **see** ♦ *n* (*tool*) sierra; (*SPORT*) *vt* serrar; ~**dust** *n* (a)serrín *m*; ~**mill** *n* aserradero; ~**n-off shotgun** *n* escopeta de cañones recortados

saxophone ['sæksəfəʊn] *n* saxófono

say [seɪ] (*pt, pp* **said**) *n*: **to have one's ~** expresar su opinión ♦ *vt* decir; **to have a** *or* **some ~ in sth** tener voz *or* tener que ver en algo; **to ~ yes/no** decir que sí/no; **could you ~ that again?** ¿podría repetir eso?; **that is to ~** es decir; **that goes without ~ing** ni que decir tiene; ~**ing** *n* dicho, refrán *m*

scab [skæb] *n* costra; (*pej*) esquirol *m*

scaffold ['skæfəʊld] *n* cadalso; ~**ing** *n* andamio, andamiaje *m*

scald [skɔːld] *n* escaldadura ♦ *vt* escaldar

scale [skeɪl] *n* (*gen, MUS*) escala; (*of fish*) escama; (*of salaries, fees etc*) escalafón *m* ♦ *vt* (*mountain*) escalar; (*tree*) trepar; ~**s** *npl* (*for weighing: small*) balanza; (: *large*) báscula; **on a large ~** en gran escala; ~ **of charges** tarifa, lista de precios; ~ **down** *vt* reducir a escala

scallop ['skɔləp] *n* (*ZOOL*) venera; (*SEWING*) festón *m*

scalp [skælp] *n* cabellera ♦ *vt* escalpar

scalpel ['skælpl] *n* bisturí *m*

scamper ['skæmpə*] *vi*: **to ~ away** *or* **off** irse corriendo

scampi ['skæmpɪ] *npl* gambas *fpl*

scan [skæn] *vt* (*examine*) escudriñar; (*glance at quickly*) dar un vistazo a; (*TV*,

RADAR) explorar, registrar ♦ n (*MED*): **to have a ~** pasar por el escáner

scandal ['skændl] n escándalo; (*gossip*) chismes *mpl*

Scandinavia [skændɪ'neɪvɪə] n Escandinavia; **~n** adj, n escandinavo/a *m/f*

scant [skænt] adj escaso; **~y** adj (*meal*) insuficiente; (*clothes*) ligero

scapegoat ['skeɪpgəut] n cabeza de turco, chivo expiatorio

scar [skɑː] n cicatriz f; (*fig*) señal f ♦ vt dejar señales en

scarce [skɛəs] adj escaso; **to make o.s. ~** (*inf*) esfumarse; **~ly** adv apenas; **scarcity** n escasez f

scare [skɛə*] n susto, sobresalto; (*panic*) pánico ♦ vt asustar, espantar; **to ~ sb stiff** dar a uno un susto de muerte; **bomb ~** amenaza de bomba; **~ off** or **away** vt ahuyentar; **~crow** n espanta-pájaros m inv; **~d** adj: **to be ~d** estar asustado

scarf [skɑːf] (pl **~s** or **scarves**) n (*long*) bufanda; (*square*) pañuelo

scarlet ['skɑːlɪt] adj escarlata; **~ fever** n escarlatina

scarves [skɑːvz] npl of **scarf**

scary ['skɛərɪ] (*inf*) adj espeluznante

scathing ['skeɪðɪŋ] adj mordaz

scatter ['skætə*] vt (*spread*) esparcir, desparramar; (*put to flight*) dispersar ♦ vi dispersarse; **~brained** adj ligero de cascos

scavenger ['skævəndʒə*] n (*person*) basurero/a

scenario [sɪ'nɑːrɪəu] n (*THEATRE*) argumento; (*CINEMA*) guión m; (*fig*) escenario

scene [siːn] n (*THEATRE, fig etc*) escena; (*of crime etc*) escenario; (*view*) panorama m; (*fuss*) escándalo; **~ry** n (*THEATRE*) decorado; (*landscape*) paisaje m; **scenic** adj pintoresco

scent [sɛnt] n perfume m, olor m; (*fig: track*) rastro, pista

sceptic ['skɛptɪk] (*US* **skeptic**) n escéptico/a; **~al** adj escéptico; **~ism** ['skɛptɪsɪzm] n escepticismo

sceptre ['sɛptə*] (*US* **scepter**) n cetro

schedule ['ʃɛdjuːl, (*US*) 'skɛdjuːl] n (*timetable*) horario; (*of events*) programa m; (*list*) lista ♦ vt (*visit*) fijar la hora de; **to arrive on ~** llegar a la hora debida; **to be ahead of/behind ~** estar adelantado/en retraso; **~d flight** n vuelo regular

schematic [skɪ'mætɪk] adj (*diagram etc*) esquemático

scheme [skiːm] n (*plan*) plan m, proyecto; (*plot*) intriga; (*arrangement*) disposición f; (*pension ~ etc*) sistema m ♦ vi (*intrigue*) intrigar; **scheming** adj intrigante ♦ n intrigas *fpl*

schism ['skɪzəm] n cisma m

schizophrenic [skɪtzə'frɛnɪk] adj esquizofrénico

scholar ['skɔlə*] n (*pupil*) alumno/a; (*learned person*) sabio/a, erudito/a; **~ly** adj erudito; **~ship** n erudición f; (*grant*) beca

school [skuːl] n escuela, colegio; (*in university*) facultad f ♦ cpd escolar; **~ age** n edad f escolar; **~book** n libro de texto; **~boy** n alumno; **~children** npl alumnos *mpl*; **~days** npl años *mpl* del colegio; **~girl** n alumna; **~ing** n enseñanza; **~master/mistress** n (*primary*) maestro/a; (*secondary*) profesor(a) *m/f*; **~teacher** n (*primary*) maestro/a; (*secondary*) profesor(a) *m/f*

schooner ['skuːnə*] n (*ship*) goleta

sciatica [saɪ'ætɪkə] n ciática

science ['saɪəns] n ciencia; **~ fiction** n ciencia-ficción f; **scientific** [-'tɪfɪk] adj científico; **scientist** n científico/a

scintillating ['sɪntɪleɪtɪŋ] adj brillante, ingenioso

scissors ['sɪzəz] npl tijeras *fpl*; **a pair of ~** unas tijeras

scoff [skɔf] vt (*BRIT: inf: eat*) engullir ♦ vi: **to ~ (at)** (*mock*) mofarse (de)

scold [skəuld] vt regañar

scone [skɔn] n pastel de pan

scoop [skuːp] n (*for flour etc*) pala; (*PRESS*) exclusiva f; **~ out** vt excavar; **~ up** vt recoger

scooter ['skuːtə*] n moto f; (*toy*) patinete

m

scope [skəup] *n* (*of plan*) ámbito; (*of person*) competencia; (*opportunity*) libertad *f* (de acción)

scorch [skɔːtʃ] *vt* (*clothes*) chamuscar; (*earth, grass*) quemar, secar

score [skɔː*] *n* (*points etc*) puntuación *f*; (*MUS*) partitura; (*twenty*) veintena ♦ *vt* (*goal, point*) ganar; (*mark*) rayar; (*achieve: success*) conseguir ♦ *vi* marcar un tanto; (*FOOTBALL*) marcar (un) gol; (*keep score*) llevar el tanteo; ~s of (*very many*) decenas de; **on that** ~ en lo que se refiere a eso; **to ~ 6 out of 10** obtener una puntuación de 6 sobre 10; ~ **out** *vt* tachar; ~ **over** *vt fus* obtener una victoria sobre; ~**board** *n* marcador *m*

scorn [skɔːn] *n* desprecio ♦ *vt* despreciar; ~**ful** *adj* desdeñoso, despreciativo

Scorpio ['skɔːpɪəu] *n* Escorpión *m*

scorpion ['skɔːpɪən] *n* alacrán *m*

Scot [skɔt] *n* escocés/esa *m/f*

scotch [skɔtʃ] *vt* (*rumour*) desmentir; (*plan*) abandonar; **S~** *n* whisky *m* escocés

scot-free *adv*: **to get off** ~ (*unpunished*) salir impune

Scotland ['skɔtlənd] *n* Escocia

Scots [skɔts] *adj* escocés/esa; ~**man/ woman** *n* escocés/esa *m/f*; **Scottish** ['skɔtɪʃ] *adj* escocés/esa

scoundrel ['skaundrl] *n* canalla *m/f*, sinvergüenza *m/f*

scour ['skauə*] *vt* (*search*) recorrer, registrar

scourge [skɜːdʒ] *n* azote *m*

scout [skaut] *n* (*MIL, also: boy* ~) explorador *m*; **girl** ~ (*US*) niña exploradora; ~ **around** *vi* reconocer el terreno

scowl [skaul] *vi* fruncir el ceño; **to** ~ **at sb** mirar con ceño a uno

scrabble ['skræbl] *vi* (*claw*): **to** ~ (**at**) arañar; (*also: to* ~ *around: search*) revolver todo buscando ♦ *n*: **S~** ® Scrabble *m* ®

scraggy ['skrægɪ] *adj* descarnado

scram [skræm] (*inf*) *vi* largarse

scramble ['skræmbl] *n* (*climb*) subida

through/out abrirse paso/salir con dificultad; **to** ~ **for** pelear por; ~**d eggs** *npl* huevos *mpl* revueltos

scrap [skræp] *n* (*bit*) pedacito; (*fig*) pizca; (*fight*) riña, bronca; (*also:* ~ *iron*) chatarra, hierro viejo ♦ *vt* (*discard*) desechar, descartar ♦ *vi* reñir, armar (una) bronca; ~**s** *npl* (*waste*) sobras *fpl*, desperdicios *mpl*; ~**book** *n* álbum *m* de recortes; ~ **dealer** *n* chatarrero/a

scrape [skreip] *n*: **to get into a** ~ meterse en un lío ♦ *vt* raspar; (*skin etc*) rasguñar; (~ *against*) rozar ♦ *vi*: **to** ~ **through** (*exam*) aprobar por los pelos; ~ **together** *vt* (*money*) arañar, juntar

scrap: ~ **heap** *n* (*fig*): **to be on the** ~ **heap** estar acabado; ~ **merchant** (*BRIT*) *n* chatarrero/a; ~ **paper** *n* pedazos *mpl* de papel; ~**py** *adj* (*work*) imperfecto

scratch [skrætʃ] *n* rasguño; (*from claw*) arañazo ♦ *cpd*: ~ **team** equipo improvisado ♦ *vt* (*paint, car*) rayar; (*with claw, nail*) rasguñar, arañar; (*rub: nose etc*) rascarse ♦ *vi* rascarse; **to start from** ~ partir de cero; **to be up to** ~ cumplir con los requisitos

scrawl [skrɔːl] *n* garabatos *mpl* ♦ *vi* hacer garabatos

scrawny ['skrɔːnɪ] *adj* flaco

scream [skriːm] *n* chillido ♦ *vi* chillar

screech [skriːtʃ] *vi* chirriar

screen [skriːn] *n* (*CINEMA, TV*) pantalla; (*movable barrier*) biombo ♦ *vt* (*conceal*) tapar; (*from the wind etc*) proteger; (*film*) proyectar; (*candidates etc*) investigar a; ~**ing** *n* (*MED*) investigación *f* médica; ~**play** *n* guión *m*

screw [skruː] *n* tornillo ♦ *vt* (*also:* ~ *in*) atornillar; ~ **up** *vt* (*paper etc*) arrugar; **to** ~ **up one's eyes** arrugar el entrecejo; ~**driver** *n* destornillador *m*

scribble ['skrɪbl] *n* garabatos *mpl* ♦ *vt, vi* garabatear

script [skrɪpt] *n* (*CINEMA etc*) guión *m*; (*writing*) escritura, letra

scripture(s) ['skrɪptʃə*(z)] *n(pl)* Sagrada Escritura

scroll [skrəul] *n* rollo

scrounge [skraundʒ] (*inf*) *vt*: **to ~ sth off** *or* **from sb** obtener algo de uno de gorra ♦ *n*: **on the ~** de gorra; **~r** *n* gorrón/ona *m/f*

scrub [skrʌb] *n* (*land*) maleza ♦ *vt* fregar, restregar; (*inf*: *reject*) cancelar, anular

scruff [skrʌf] *n*: **by the ~ of the neck** por el pescuezo

scruffy ['skrʌfɪ] *adj* desaliñado, piojoso

scrum(mage) ['skrʌm(mɪdʒ)] *n* (*RUGBY*) melée *f*

scruple ['skruːpl] *n* (*gen pl*) escrúpulo

scrutinize ['skruːtɪnaɪz] *vt* escudriñar; (*votes*) escrutar; **scrutiny** ['skruːtɪnɪ] *n* escrutinio, examen *m*

scuff [skʌf] *vt* (*shoes, floor*) rayar

scuffle ['skʌfl] *n* refriega

sculptor ['skʌlptə*] *n* escultor(a) *m/f*

sculpture ['skʌlptʃə*] *n* escultura

scum [skʌm] *n* (*on liquid*) espuma; (*pej*: *people*) escoria

scupper ['skʌpə*] (*BRIT*: *inf*) *vt* (*plans*) dar al traste con

scurrilous ['skʌrɪləs] *adj* difamatorio, calumnioso

scurry ['skʌrɪ] *vi* correr; **to ~ off** escabullirse

scuttle ['skʌtl] *n* (*also*: *coal ~*) cubo, carbonera ♦ *vt* (*ship*) barrenar ♦ *vi* (*scamper*): **to ~ away, ~ off** escabullirse

scythe [saɪð] *n* guadaña

SDP (*BRIT*) *n abbr* = **Social Democratic Party**

sea [siː] *n* mar *m* ♦ *cpd* de mar, marítimo; **by ~** (*travel*) en barco; **on the ~** (*boat*) en el mar; (*town*) junto al mar; **to be all at ~** (*fig*) estar despistado; **out to ~, at ~** en alta mar; **~board** *n* litoral *m*; **~food** *n* mariscos *mpl*; **~ front** *n* paseo marítimo; **~-going** *adj* de altura; **~gull** *n* gaviota

seal [siːl] *n* (*animal*) foca; (*stamp*) sello ♦ *vt* (*close*) cerrar; **~ off** *vt* (*area*) acordonar

sea level *n* nivel *m* del mar

sea lion *n* león *m* marino

seam [siːm] *n* costura; (*of metal*) juntura; (*of coal*) veta, filón *m*

seaman ['siːmən] *n* marinero

seamy ['siːmɪ] *adj* sórdido

seance ['seɪɔns] *n* sesión *f* de espiritismo

seaplane ['siːpleɪn] *n* hidroavión *m*

seaport ['siːpɔːt] *n* puerto de mar

search [sɔːtʃ] *n* (*for person, thing*) busca, búsqueda; (*COMPUT*) búsqueda; (*inspection: of sb's home*) registro ♦ *vt* (*look in*) buscar en; (*examine*) examinar; (*person, place*) registrar ♦ *vi*: **to ~ for** buscar; **in ~ of** en busca de; **~ through** *vt fus* registrar; **~ing** *adj* penetrante; **~light** *n* reflector *m*; **~ party** *n* pelotón *m* de salvamento; **~ warrant** *n* mandamiento (judicial)

sea: **~shore** *n* playa, orilla del mar; **~sick** *adj* mareado; **~side** *n* playa, orilla del mar; **~side resort** *n* centro turístico costero

season ['siːzn] *n* (*of year*) estación *f*; (*sporting etc*) temporada; (*of films etc*) ciclo ♦ *vt* (*food*) sazonar; **in/out of ~** en sazón/fuera de temporada; **~al** *adj* estacional; **~ed** *adj* (*fig*) experimentado; **~ing** *n* condimento, aderezo; **~ ticket** *n* abono

seat [siːt] *n* (*in bus, train*) asiento; (*chair*) silla; (*PARLIAMENT*) escaño; (*buttocks*) culo, trasero; (*of trousers*) culera ♦ *vt* sentar; (*have room for*) tener cabida para; **to be ~ed** sentarse; **~ belt** *n* cinturón *m* de seguridad

sea: **~ water** *n* agua del mar; **~weed** *n* alga marina; **~worthy** *adj* en condiciones de navegar

sec. *abbr* = **second(s)**

secluded [sɪ'kluːdɪd] *adj* retirado

seclusion [sɪ'kluːʒən] *n* reclusión *f*

second ['sɛkənd] *adj* segundo ♦ *adv* en segundo lugar ♦ *n* (*AUT*: *also*: *~ gear*) segunda; (*COMM*) artículo con algún desperfecto; (*BRIT*: *SCOL*: *degree*) título de licenciado con calificación de notable ♦ *vt* (*motion*) apoyar; **~ary** *adj* secundario; **~ary school** *n* escuela secundaria; **~-class** *adj* de segunda clase ♦ *adv* (*RAIL*) en segunda; **~hand** *adj* de segunda mano, usado; **~ hand** *n* (*on clock*) segundero; **~ly** *adv* en segundo lugar; **~ment** [sɪ'kɔndmənt] (*BRIT*) *n* traslado temporal; **~-rate** *adj* de segunda categoría; **~ thoughts** *npl*: **to have ~ thoughts** cambiar de opinión; **on ~ thoughts** *or* **thought** (*US*) pensándolo bien

secrecy ['si:krəsɪ] *n* secreto

secret ['si:krɪt] *adj, n* secreto; **in ~** en secreto

secretarial [sɛkrɪ'tɛərɪəl] *adj* de secretario; (*course, staff*) de secretariado

secretariat [sɛkrɪ'tɛərɪət] *n* secretaría

secretary ['sɛkrətərɪ] *n* secretario/a; **S~ of State (for)** (*BRIT: POL*) Ministro (de)

secretive ['si:krətɪv] *adj* reservado, sigiloso

secretly ['si:krɪtlɪ] *adv* en secreto

sect [sɛkt] *n* secta; **~arian** [-'tɛərɪən] *adj* sectario

section ['sɛkʃən] *n* sección *f*; (*part*) parte *f*; (*of document*) artículo; (*of opinion*) sector *m*; (*cross-~*) corte *m* transversal

sector ['sɛktə*] *n* sector *m*

secular ['sɛkjulə*] *adj* secular, seglar

secure [sɪ'kjuə*] *adj* seguro; (*firmly fixed*) firme, fijo ♦ *vt* (*fix*) asegurar, afianzar; (*get*) conseguir

security [sɪ'kjuərɪtɪ] *n* seguridad *f*; (*for loan*) fianza; (: *object*) prenda

sedan [sɪ'dæn] (*US*) *n* (*AUT*) sedán *m*

sedate [sɪ'deɪt] *adj* tranquilo; ♦ *vt* tratar con sedantes

sedation [sɪ'deɪʃən] *n* (*MED*) sedación *f*

sedative ['sɛdɪtɪv] *n* sedante *m*, sedativo

seduce [sɪ'dju:s] *vt* seducir; **seduction** [-'dʌkʃən] *n* seducción *f*; **seductive** [-'dʌktɪv] *adj* seductor(a)

see [si:] (*pt* **saw**, *pp* **seen**) *vt* ver; (*accompany*): **to ~ sb to the door** acompañar a uno a la puerta; (*understand*) ver, comprender ♦ *vi* ver ♦ *n* (*arz*)obispado; **to ~ that** (*ensure*) asegurar que; **~ you soon!** ¡hasta pronto!; **~ about** *vt fus* atender a, encargarse de; **~ off** *vt* despedir; **~ through** *vt fus* (*fig*) calar ♦ *vt* (*plan*) llevar a cabo; **~ to** *vt fus* atender a, encargarse de

seed [si:d] *n* semilla; (*in fruit*) pepita; (*fig: gen pl*) germen *m*; (*TENNIS*)

preseleccionado/a; **to go to ~** (*plant*) granar; (*fig*) descuidarse; **~ling** *n* planta de semillero; **~y** *adj* (*shabby*) desaseado, raído

seeing ['si:ɪŋ] *conj*: **~ (that)** visto que, en vista de que

seek [si:k] (*pt, pp* **sought**) *vt* buscar; (*post*) solicitar

seem [si:m] *vi* parecer; **there ~s to be ...** parece que hay ...; **~ingly** *adv* aparentemente, según parece

seen [si:n] *pp of* **see**

seep [si:p] *vi* filtrarse

seesaw ['si:sɔ:] *n* subibaja

seethe [si:ð] *vi* hervir; **to ~ with anger** estar furioso

see-through *adj* transparente

segment ['sɛgmənt] *n* (*part*) sección *f*; (*of orange*) gajo

segregate ['sɛgrɪgeɪt] *vt* segregar

seismic ['saɪzmɪk] *adj* sísmico

seize [si:z] *vt* (*grasp*) agarrar, asir; (*take possession of*) secuestrar; (: *territory*) apoderarse de; (*opportunity*) aprovecharse de; **~ (up)on** *vt fus* aprovechar; **~ up** *vi* (*TECH*) agarrotarse

seizure ['si:ʒə*] *n* (*MED*) ataque *m*; (*LAW, of power*) incautación *f*

seldom ['sɛldəm] *adv* rara vez

select [sɪ'lɛkt] *adj* selecto, escogido ♦ *vt* escoger, elegir; (*SPORT*) seleccionar; **~ion** [-'lɛkʃən] *n* selección *f*, elección *f*; (*COMM*) surtido

self [sɛlf] (*pl* **selves**) *n* uno mismo; **the ~** el yo ♦ *prefix* auto...; **~-assured** *adj* seguro de sí mismo; **~-catering** (*BRIT*) (*flat etc*) con cocina; **~-centred** (*US* **~-centered**) *adj* egocéntrico; **~-confidence** *n* confianza en sí mismo; **~-conscious** *adj* cohibido; **~-contained** (*BRIT*) *adj* (*flat*) con entrada particular; **~-control** *n* autodominio; **~-defence** (*US* **~-defense**) *n* defensa propia; **~-discipline** *n* autodisciplina; **~-employed** *adj* que trabaja por cuenta propia; **~-evident** *adj* patente; **~-governing** *adj* autónomo; **~-indulgent** *adj* autocomplaciente; **~-interest** *n* egoísmo; **~ish** *adj* egoísta; **~ishness** *n* egoísmo; **~less** *adj* desinteresado; **~-made** *adj*: **~-made man** hombre *m* que se ha hecho a sí mismo; **~-pity** *n* lástima de sí mismo; **~-portrait** *n* autorretrato; **~-possessed** *adj* sereno, dueño de sí mismo; **~-preservation** *n* propia conservación *f*; **~-respect** *n* amor *m* propio; **~-righteous** *adj* santurrón/ona; **~-sacrifice** *n* abnegación *f*; **~-satisfied** *adj* satisfecho de sí mismo; **~-service** *adj* de autoservicio; **~-sufficient** *adj* autosuficiente; **~-taught** *adj* autodidacta

sell [sɛl] (*pt, pp* **sold**) *vt* vender ♦ *vi* venderse; **to ~ at** *or* **for £10** venderse a 10 libras; **~ off** *vt* liquidar; **~ out** *vi*: **to ~ out of tickets/milk** vender todas las entradas/toda la leche; **~-by date** *n* fecha de caducidad; **~er** *n* vendedor(a) *m/f*; **~ing price** *n* precio de venta

Sellotape ['sɛləʊteɪp] ® (*BRIT*) *n* cinta adhesiva, celo (*SP*), scotch *m* (*AM*)

selves [sɛlvz] *npl of* **self**

semaphore ['sɛməfɔː*] *n* semáforo

semblance ['sɛmbləns] *n* apariencia

semen ['siːmən] *n* semen *m*

semester [sɪ'mɛstə*] (*US*) *n* semestre *m*

semi... [sɛmɪ] *prefix* semi..., medio...; **~circle** *n* semicírculo; **~colon** *n* punto y coma; **~conductor** *n* semiconductor *m*; **~detached (house)** *n* (casa) semisepa-rada; **~final** *n* semi-final *m*; **~skimmed milk** *n* leche semidesnatada

seminar ['sɛmɪnɑː*] *n* seminario

seminary ['sɛmɪnərɪ] *n* (*REL*) seminario

semiskilled ['sɛmɪskɪld] *adj* (*work, worker*) semi-cualificado

senate ['sɛnɪt] *n* senado; **senator** *n* senador(a) *m/f*

send [sɛnd] (*pt, pp* **sent**) *vt* mandar, enviar; (*signal*) transmitir; **~ away** *vt* despachar; **~ away for** *vt fus* pedir; **~ back** *vt* devolver; **~ for** *vt fus* mandar traer; **~ off** *vt* (*goods*) despachar; (*BRIT*: *SPORT*: *player*) expulsar; **~ out** *vt* (*invitation*) mandar; (*signal*) emitir; **~ up** *vt* (*person, price*) hacer subir; (*BRIT*: *parody*) parodiar; **~er** *n* remitente *m/f*; **~-off** *n*: **a good ~-off** una buena despedida

senior ['siːnɪə*] *adj* (*older*) mayor, más viejo; (: *on staff*) de más antigüedad; (*of higher rank*) superior; **~ citizen** *n* per-sona de la tercera edad; **~ity** [-'ɔrɪtɪ] *n* antigüedad *f*

sensation [sɛn'seɪʃən] *n* sensación *f*; **~al** *adj* sensacional

sense [sɛns] *n* (*faculty, meaning*) sentido; (*feeling*) sensación *f*; (*good ~*) sentido común, juicio ♦ *vt* sentir, percibir; **it makes ~** tiene sentido; **~less** *adj* estúpido, insensato; (*unconscious*) sin conocimiento; **~ of humour** *n* sentido del humor

sensible ['sɛnsɪbl] *adj* sensato; (*rea-sonable*) razonable, lógico

sensitive ['sɛnsɪtɪv] *adj* sensible; (*touchy*) susceptible

sensual ['sɛnsjʊəl] *adj* sensual

sensuous ['sɛnsjʊəs] *adj* sensual

sent [sɛnt] *pt, pp of* **send**

sentence ['sɛntns] *n* (*LING*) oración *f*; (*LAW*) sentencia, fallo ♦ *vt*: **to ~ sb to death/to 5 years (in prison)** condenar a uno a muerte/a 5 años de cárcel

sentiment ['sɛntɪmənt] *n* sentimiento; (*opinion*) opinión *f*; **~al** [-'mɛntl] *adj* sentimental

sentry ['sɛntrɪ] *n* centinela *m*

separate [*adj* 'sɛprɪt, *vb* 'sɛpəreɪt] *adj* separado; (*distinct*) distinto ♦ *vt* separar; (*part*) dividir ♦ *vi* separarse; **~s** *npl* (*clothes*) coordinados *mpl*; **~ly** *adv* por separado; **separation** [-'reɪʃən] *n* separación *f*

September [sɛp'tɛmbə*] *n* se(p)tiembre *m*

septic ['sɛptɪk] *adj* séptico; **~ tank** *n* fosa séptica

sequel ['siːkwl] *n* consecuencia, resultado; (*of story*) continuación *f*

sequence ['siːkwəns] *n* sucesión *f*, serie *f*; (*CINEMA*) secuencia

sequin ['siːkwɪn] *n* lentejuela

serene [sɪ'riːn] *adj* sereno, tranquilo

sergeant ['sɑːdʒənt] *n* sargento

serial ['sɪərɪəl] *n* (*TV*) telenovela, serie *f* televisiva; (*BOOK*) serie *f*; **~ize** *vt* emitir como serial; **~ killer** *n* asesino/a múltiple; ~ **number** *n* número de serie

series ['sɪəriːs] *n inv* serie *f*

serious ['sɪərɪəs] *adj* serio; (*grave*) grave; ~**ly** *adv* en serio; (*ill, wounded etc*) gravemente; ~**ness** *n* seriedad *f*; gravedad *f*

sermon ['sɜːmən] *n* sermón *m*

serrated [sɪ'reɪtɪd] *adj* serrado, dentellado

serum ['sɪərəm] *n* suero

servant ['sɜːvənt] *n* servidor(a) *m/f*; (*house* ~) criado/a

serve [sɜːv] *vt* servir; (*customer*) atender; (*subj: train*) pasar por; (*apprenticeship*) hacer; (*prison term*) cumplir ♦ *vi* (*at table*) servir; (*TENNIS*) sacar; **to ~ as/for/ to do** servir de/para/para hacer ♦ *n* (*TENNIS*) saque *m*; **it ~s him right** se lo tiene merecido; ~ **out** *vt* (*food*) servir; ~ **up** *vt* = ~ **out**

service ['sɜːvɪs] *n* servicio; (*REL*) misa; (*AUT*) mantenimiento; (*dishes etc*) juego ♦ *vt* (*car etc*) revisar; (: *repair*) reparar; **the S~s** *npl* las fuerzas armadas; **to be of ~ to sb** ser útil a uno; ~**able** *adj* servible, utilizable; ~ **area** *n* (*on motorway*) area de servicio; ~ **charge** (*BRIT*) *n* servicio; ~**man** *n* militar *m*; ~ **station** *n* estación *f* de servicio

serviette [sɜːvɪ'et] (*BRIT*) *n* servilleta

session ['seʃən] *n* sesión *f*; **to be in ~** estar en sesión

set [set] (*pt, pp* **set**) *n* juego; (*RADIO*) aparato; (*TV*) televisor *m*; (*of utensils*) batería; (*of cutlery*) cubierto; (*of books*) colección *f*; (*TENNIS*) set *m*; (*group of people*) grupo; (*CINEMA*) plató *m*; (*THEATRE*) decorado ♦ *adj* (*fixed*) fijo; (*ready*) listo ♦ *vt* (*place*) poner, colocar; (*fix*) fijar; (*adjust*) ajustar, arreglar; (*decide: rules etc*) establecer, decidir ♦ *vi* (*sun*) ponerse; (*jam, jelly*) cuajarse; (*concrete*) fraguar; (*bone*) componerse; **to be ~ on doing sth** estar empeñado en hacer algo; **to ~ to music** poner música a; **to ~ on fire** incendiar, poner fuego a; **to ~ free** poner en libertad; **to ~ sth going** poner algo en marcha; **to ~ sail** zarpar,

hacerse a la vela; ~ **about** *vt fus* ponerse a; ~ **aside** *vt* poner aparte, dejar de lado; (*money, time*) reservar; ~ **back** *vt* (*cost*): **to ~ sb back £5** costar a uno cinco libras; (: *in time*): **to ~ back (by)** retrasar (por); ~ **off** *vi* partir ♦ *vt* (*bomb*) hacer estallar; (*events*) poner en marcha; (*show up well*) hacer resaltar; ~ **out** *vi* partir ♦ *vt* (*arrange*) disponer; (*state*) exponer; **to ~ out to do sth** proponerse hacer algo; ~ **up** *vt* establecer; ~**back** *n* revés *m*, contratiempo; ~ **menu** *n* menú *m*

settee [se'tiː] *n* sofá *m*

setting ['setɪŋ] *n* (*scenery*) marco; (*position*) disposición *f*; (*of sun*) puesta; (*of jewel*) engaste *m*, montadura

settle ['setl] *vt* (*argument*) resolver; (*accounts*) ajustar, liquidar; (*MED: calm*) calmar, sosegar ♦ *vi* (*dust etc*) depositarse; (*weather*) serenarse; (*also:* ~ **down**) instalarse; tranquilizarse; **to ~ for sth** convenir en aceptar algo; **to ~ on sth** decidirse por algo; ~ **in** *vi* instalarse; ~ **up** *vi*: **to ~ up with sb** ajustar cuentas con uno; ~**ment** *n* (*payment*) liquidación *f*; (*agreement*) acuerdo, convenio; (*village etc*) pueblo; ~**r** *n* colono/a, colonizador(a) *m/f*

setup ['setʌp] *n* sistema *m*; (*situation*) situación *f*

seven ['sevn] *num* siete; ~**teen** *num* diez y siete, diecisiete; ~**th** *num* séptimo; ~**ty** *num* setenta

sever ['sevə*] *vt* cortar; (*relations*) romper

several ['sevrl] *adj, pron* varios/as *m/fpl*, algunos/as *m/fpl*; ~ **of us** varios de nosotros

severance ['sevərəns] *n* (*of relations*) ruptura; ~ **pay** *n* indemnización *f* por despido

severe [sɪ'vɪə*] *adj* severo; (*serious*) grave; (*hard*) duro; (*pain*) intenso; **severity** [sɪ'verɪtɪ] *n* severidad *f*; gravedad *f*; intensidad *f*

sew [səʊ] (*pt* **sewed**, *pp* **sewn**) *vt, vi* coser; ~ **up** *vt* coser, zurcir

sewage ['suːɪdʒ] *n* aguas *fpl* residuales

sewer ['suːə*] *n* alcantarilla, cloaca
sewing ['səʊɪŋ] *n* costura; ~ **machine** *n* máquina de coser
sewn [səʊn] *pp of* **sew**
sex [sɛks] *n* sexo; (*lovemaking*): **to have ~** hacer el amor; **~ist** *adj, n* sexista *m/f*; **sexual** ['sɛksjʊəl] *adj* sexual; **sexy** *adj* sexy
shabby ['ʃæbɪ] *adj* (*person*) desharrapado; (*clothes*) raído, gastado; (*behaviour*) ruin *inv*
shack [ʃæk] *n* choza, chabola
shackles ['ʃæklz] *npl* grillos *mpl*, grilletes *mpl*
shade [ʃeɪd] *n* sombra; (*for lamp*) pantalla; (*for eyes*) visera; (*of colour*) matiz *m*, tonalidad *f*; (*small quantity*): **a ~** (**too big/more**) un poquitín (grande/más) ♦ *vt* dar sombra a; (*eyes*) proteger del sol; **in the ~** en la sombra
shadow ['ʃædəʊ] *n* sombra ♦ *vt* (*follow*) seguir y vigilar; **~ cabinet** (*BRIT*) *n* (*POL*) gabinete paralelo formado por el partido de oposición; **~y** *adj* oscuro; (*dim*) indistinto
shady ['ʃeɪdɪ] *adj* sombreado; (*fig: dishonest*) sospechoso; (: *deal*) turbio
shaft [ʃɑːft] *n* (*of arrow, spear*) astil *m*; (*AUT, TECH*) eje *m*, árbol *m*; (*of mine*) pozo; (*of lift*) hueco, caja; (*of light*) rayo
shaggy ['ʃægɪ] *adj* peludo
shake [ʃeɪk] (*pt* **shook**, *pp* **shaken**) *vt* sacudir; (*building*) hacer temblar; (*bottle, cocktail*) agitar ♦ *vi* (*tremble*) temblar; **to ~ one's head** (*in refusal*) negar con la cabeza; (*in dismay*) mover *or* menear la cabeza, incrédulo; **to ~ hands with sb** estrechar la mano a uno; **~ off** *vt* sacudirse; (*fig*) deshacerse de; **~ up** *vt* agitar; (*fig*) reorganizar; **shaky** *adj* (*hand, voice*) trémulo; (*building*) inestable
shall [ʃæl] *aux vb*: **~ I help you?** ¿quieres que te ayude?; **I'll buy three, ~ I?** compro tres, ¿no te parece?
shallow ['ʃæləʊ] *adj* poco profundo; (*fig*) superficial
sham [ʃæm] *n* fraude *m*, engaño ♦ *vt* fingir, simular

shambles ['ʃæmblz] *n* confusión *f*
shame [ʃeɪm] *n* vergüenza ♦ *vt* avergonzar; **it is a ~ that/to do** es una lástima que/hacer; **what a ~!** ¡qué lástima!; **~faced** *adj* avergonzado; **~ful** *adj* vergonzoso; **~less** *adj* desvergonzado
shampoo [ʃæm'puː] *n* champú *m* ♦ *vt* lavar con champú; **~ and set** *n* lavado y marcado
shamrock ['ʃæmrɔk] *n* trébol *m* (*emblema nacional irlandés*)
shandy ['ʃændɪ] *n* mezcla de cerveza con gaseosa
shan't [ʃɑːnt] = **shall not**
shanty town ['ʃæntɪ-] *n* barrio de chabolas
shape [ʃeɪp] *n* forma ♦ *vt* formar, dar forma a; (*sb's ideas*) formar; (*sb's life*) determinar; **to take ~** tomar forma; **~ up** *vi* (*events*) desarrollarse; (*person*) formarse; **~d** *suffix*: **heart-~d** en forma de corazón; **~less** *adj* informe, sin forma definida; **~ly** *adj* (*body etc*) esbelto
share [ʃɛə*] *n* (*part*) parte *f*, porción *f*; (*contribution*) cuota; (*COMM*) acción *f* ♦ *vt* dividir; (*have in common*) compartir; **to ~ out** (**among** *or* **between**) repartir (entre); **~holder** (*BRIT*) *n* accionista *m/f*
shark [ʃɑːk] *n* tiburón *m*
sharp [ʃɑːp] *adj* (*blade, nose*) afilado; (*point*) puntiagudo; (*outline*) definido; (*pain*) intenso; (*MUS*) desafinado; (*contrast*) marcado; (*voice*) agudo; (*person: quick-witted*) astuto; (: *dishonest*) poco escrupuloso ♦ *n* (*MUS*) sostenido ♦ *adv*: **at 2 o'clock ~** a las 2 en punto; **~en** *vt* afilar; (*pencil*) sacar punta a; (*fig*) agudizar; **~ener** *n* (*also*: **pencil ~ener**) sacapuntas *m inv*; **~-eyed** *adj* de vista aguda; **~ly** *adv* (*turn, stop*) bruscamente; (*stand out, contrast*) claramente; (*criticize, retort*) severamente
shatter ['ʃætə*] *vt* hacer añicos *or* pedazos; (*fig: ruin*) destruir, acabar con ♦ *vi* hacerse añicos
shave [ʃeɪv] *vt* afeitar, rasurar ♦ *vi* afeitarse, rasurarse ♦ *n*: **to have a ~** afeitarse; **~r** *n* (*also: electric ~r*) máquina de afeitar (eléctrica)

shaving ['ʃeɪvɪŋ] n (*action*) el afeitarse, rasurado; **~s** npl (*of wood etc*) virutas fpl; **~ brush** n brocha (de afeitar); **~ cream** n crema de afeitar; **~ foam** n espuma de afeitar

shawl [ʃɔːl] n chal m

she [ʃiː] pron ella; **~-cat** n gata

sheaf [ʃiːf] (pl **sheaves**) n (*of corn*) gavilla; (*of papers*) fajo

shear [ʃɪə*] (pt **sheared**, pp **sheared** or **shorn**) vt esquilar, trasquilar; **~ off** vi romperse; **~s** npl (*for hedge*) tijeras fpl de jardín

sheath [ʃiːθ] n vaina; (*contraceptive*) preservativo

sheaves [ʃiːvz] npl of **sheaf**

shed [ʃed] (pt, pp **shed**) n cobertizo ♦ vt (*skin*) mudar; (*tears, blood*) derramar; (*load*) derramar; (*workers*) despedir

she'd [ʃiːd] = **she had; she would**

sheen [ʃiːn] n brillo, lustre m

sheep [ʃiːp] n inv oveja; **~dog** n perro pastor; **~ish** adj tímido, vergonzoso; **~skin** n piel f de carnero

sheer [ʃɪə*] adj (*utter*) puro, completo; (*steep*) escarpado; (*material*) diáfano ♦ adv verticalmente

sheet [ʃiːt] n (*on bed*) sábana; (*of paper*) hoja; (*of glass, metal*) lámina; (*of ice*) capa

sheik(h) [ʃeɪk] n jeque m

shelf [ʃelf] (pl **shelves**) n estante m

shell [ʃel] n (*on beach*) concha; (*of egg, nut etc*) cáscara; (*explosive*) proyectil m, obús m; (*of building*) armazón f ♦ vt (*peas*) desenvainar; (*MIL*) bombardear

she'll [ʃiːl] = **she will; she shall**

shellfish ['ʃelfɪʃ] n inv crustáceo; (*as food*) mariscos mpl

shell suit n chándal m de calle

shelter ['ʃeltə*] n abrigo, refugio ♦ vt (*aid*) amparar, proteger; (*give lodging to*) abrigar ♦ vi abrigarse, refugiarse; **~ed** adj (*life*) protegido; (*spot*) abrigado; **~ed housing** n viviendas vigiladas para ancianos y minusválidos

shelve [ʃelv] vt (*fig*) aplazar; **~s** npl of **shelf**

shepherd ['ʃepəd] n pastor m ♦ vt

(*guide*) guiar, conducir; **~'s pie** (*BRIT*) n pastel de carne y patatas

sherry ['ʃerɪ] n jerez m

she's [ʃiːz] = **she is; she has**

Shetland ['ʃetlənd] n (*also: the* ~s, *the* ~ *Isles*) las Islas de Zetlandia

shield [ʃiːld] n escudo; (*protection*) blindaje m ♦ vt: **to ~ (from)** proteger (de)

shift [ʃɪft] n (*change*) cambio; (*at work*) turno ♦ vt trasladar; (*remove*) quitar ♦ vi moverse; **~less** adj (*person*) perezoso; **~ work** n trabajo a turnos; **~y** adj tramposo; (*eyes*) furtivo

shilling ['ʃɪlɪŋ] (*BRIT*) n chelín m

shilly-shally ['ʃɪlɪʃælɪ] vi titubear, vacilar

shimmer ['ʃɪmə*] n reflejo trémulo

shin [ʃɪn] n espinilla

shine [ʃaɪn] (pt, pp **shone**) n brillo, lustre m ♦ vi brillar, relucir ♦ vt (*shoes*) lustrar, sacar brillo a; **to ~ a torch on sth** dirigir una linterna hacia algo

shingle ['ʃɪŋgl] n (*on beach*) guijarros mpl; **~s** n (*MED*) herpes mpl or fpl

shiny ['ʃaɪnɪ] adj brillante, lustroso

ship [ʃɪp] n buque m, barco ♦ vt (*goods*) embarcar; (*send*) transportar or enviar por vía marítima; **~building** n construcción f de buques; **~ment** n (*goods*) envío; **~per** n exportador(a) m/f; **~ping** n (*act*) embarque m; (*traffic*) buques mpl; **~wreck** n naufragio ♦ vt: **to be ~wrecked** naufragar; **~yard** n astillero

shire ['ʃaɪə*] (*BRIT*) n condado

shirk [ʃəːk] vt (*obligations*) faltar a

shirt [ʃəːt] n camisa; **in (one's) ~ sleeves** en mangas de camisa

shit [ʃɪt] (*inf!*) excl ¡mierda! (*!*)

shiver ['ʃɪvə*] n escalofrío ♦ vi temblar, estremecerse; (*with cold*) tiritar

shoal [ʃəʊl] n (*of fish*) banco; (*fig: also:* ~s) tropel m

shock [ʃɔk] n (*impact*) choque m; (*ELEC*) descarga (eléctrica); (*emotional*) conmoción f; (*start*) sobresalto, susto; (*MED*) postración f nerviosa ♦ vt dar un susto a; (*offend*) escandalizar; **~**

absorber *n* amortiguador *m*; **~ing** *adj* (*awful*) espantoso; (*outrageous*) escandaloso

shod [ʃɔd] *pt, pp of* **shoe**

shoddy [ˈʃɔdɪ] *adj* de pacotilla

shoe [ʃuː] (*pt, pp* **shod**) *n* zapato; (*for horse*) herradura ♦ *vt* (*horse*) herrar; **~brush** *n* cepillo para zapatos; **~lace** *n* cordón *m*; **~ polish** *n* betún *m*; **~shop** *n* zapatería; **~string** *n* (*fig*): **on a ~string** con muy poco dinero

shone [ʃɔn] *pt, pp of* **shine**

shoo [ʃuː] *excl* ¡fuera!

shook [ʃuk] *pt of* **shake**

shoot [ʃuːt] (*pt, pp* **shot**) *n* (*on branch, seedling*) retoño, vástago ♦ *vt* disparar; (*kill*) matar a tiros; (*wound*) pegar un tiro; (*execute*) fusilar; (*film*) rodar, filmar ♦ *vi* (*FOOTBALL*) chutar; **~ down** *vt* (*plane*) derribar; **~ in/out** *vi* entrar corriendo/salir disparado; **~ up** *vi* (*prices*) dispararse; **~ing** *n* (*shots*) tiros *mpl*; (*HUNTING*) caza con escopeta; **~ing star** *n* estrella fugaz

shop [ʃɔp] *n* tienda; (*workshop*) taller *m* ♦ *vi* (*also:* **go ~ping**) ir de compras; **~ assistant** (*BRIT*) *n* dependiente/a *m/f*; **~ floor** (*BRIT*) *n* (*fig*) taller *m*, fábrica; **~keeper** *n* tendero/a; **~lifting** *n* mechería; **~per** *n* comprador(a) *m/f*; **~ping** *n* (*goods*) compras *fpl*; **~ping bag** *n* bolsa (de compras); **~ping centre** (*US* **~ping center**) *n* centro comercial; **~soiled** *adj* usado; **~ steward** (*BRIT*) *n* (*INDUSTRY*) enlace *m* sindical; **~ window** *n* escaparate *m* (*SP*), vidriera (*AM*)

shore [ʃɔː*] *n* orilla ♦ *vt*: **to ~ (up)** reforzar; **on ~** en tierra

shorn [ʃɔːn] *pp of* **shear**

short [ʃɔːt] *adj* corto; (*in time*) breve, de corta duración; (*person*) bajo; (*curt*) brusco, seco; (*insufficient*) insuficiente; **to be ~ of sth** estar falto de algo; **in ~** en pocas palabras; **~ of doing ...** fuera de hacer ...; **it is ~ for** es la forma abreviada de; **to cut ~** (*speech, visit*) interrumpir, terminar inesperadamente; **everything ~ of ...** todo menos ...; **to fall ~ of** no alcanzar; **to run ~ of**

quedarle a uno poco; **to stop ~** parar en seco; **to stop ~ of** detenerse antes de; **~age** *n*: **a ~age of** una falta de; **~bread** *n* especie de mantecada); **~change** *vt* no dar el cambio completo a; **~circuit** *n* cortocircuito; **~coming** *n* defecto, deficiencia; **~(crust) pastry** (*BRIT*) *n* pasta quebradiza; **~cut** *n* atajo; **~en** *vt* acortar; (*visit*) interrumpir; **~fall** *n* déficit *m*; **~hand** (*BRIT*) *n* taquigrafía; **~hand typist** (*BRIT*) *n* taquimecanógrafo/a; **~ list** (*BRIT*) *n* (*for job*) lista de candidatos escogidos; **~lived** *adj* efímero; **~ly** *adv* en breve, dentro de poco; **~sighted** (*BRIT*) *adj* miope; (*fig*) imprudente; **~staffed** *adj*: **to be ~staffed** estar falto de personal; **~ story** *n* cuento; **~tempered** *adj* enojadizo; **~term** *adj* (*effect*) a corto plazo; **~wave** *n* (*RADIO*) onda corta

shot [ʃɔt] *pt, pp of* **shoot** ♦ *n* (*sound*) tiro, disparo; (*try*) tentativa; (*injection*) inyección *f*; (*PHOT*) toma, fotografía; **to be a good/poor ~** (*person*) tener buena/mala puntería; **like a ~** (*without any delay*) como un rayo; **~gun** *n* escopeta

should [ʃud] *aux vb*: **I ~ go now** debo irme ahora; **he ~ be there now** debe de haber llegado (ya); **I ~ go if I were you** yo en tu lugar me iría; **I ~ like to** me gustaría

shoulder [ˈʃəuldə*] *n* hombro ♦ *vt* (*fig*) cargar con; **~ bag** *n* cartera de bandolera; **~ blade** *n* omóplato; **~ strap** *n* tirante *m*

shouldn't [ˈʃudnt] = **should not**

shout [ʃaut] *n* grito ♦ *vt* gritar ♦ *vi* gritar, dar voces; **~ down** *vt* acallar a gritos; **~ing** *n* griterío

shove [ʃʌv] *n* empujón *m* ♦ *vt* empujar; (*inf: put*): **to ~ sth in** meter algo a empellones; **~ off** (*inf*) *vi* largarse

shovel [ˈʃʌvl] *n* pala; (*mechanical*) excavadora ♦ *vt* mover con pala

show [ʃəu] (*pt* **showed**, *pp* **shown**) *n* (*of emotion*) demostración *f*; (*semblance*) apariencia; (*exhibition*) exposición *f*; (*THEATRE*) función *f*, espectáculo; (*TV*) show *m* ♦ *vt* mostrar, enseñar; (*courage etc*) mostrar, manifestar; (*exhibit*) exponer; (*film*) proyectar ♦ *vi* mostrarse; (*appear*) aparecer; **for** ~ para impresionar; **on** ~ (*exhibits etc*) expuesto; ~ **in** *vt* (*person*) hacer pasar; ~ **off** (*pej*) *vi* presumir ♦ *vt* (*display*) lucir; ~ **out** *vt*: **to** ~ **sb out** acompañar a uno a la puerta; ~ **up** *vi* (*stand out*) destacar; (*inf: turn up*) aparecer ♦ *vt* (*unmask*) desenmascarar; ~ **business** *n* mundo del espectáculo; **~down** *n* enfrentamiento (final)

shower ['ʃauə*] *n* (*rain*) chaparrón *m*, chubasco; (*of stones etc*) lluvia; (*for bathing*) ducha (*SP*), regadera (*AM*) ♦ *vi* llover ♦ *vt* (*fig*): **to** ~ **sb with sth** colmar a uno de algo; **to have a** ~ ducharse; **~proof** *adj* impermeable

showing ['ʃəuɪŋ] *n* (*of film*) proyección *f*

show jumping *n* hípica

shown [ʃəun] *pp of* **show**

show: **~-off** (*inf*) *n* (*person*) presumido/a; **~piece** *n* (*of exhibition etc*) objeto cumbre; **~room** *n* sala de muestras

shrank [ʃræŋk] *pt of* **shrink**

shrapnel ['ʃræpnl] *n* metralla

shred [ʃrɛd] *n* (*gen pl*) triza, jirón *m* ♦ *vt* hacer trizas; (*CULIN*) desmenuzar; **~der** *n* (*vegetable ~der*) picadora; (*document ~der*) trituradora (de papel)

shrewd [ʃru:d] *adj* astuto

shriek [ʃri:k] *n* chillido ♦ *vi* chillar

shrill [ʃrɪl] *adj* agudo, estridente

shrimp [ʃrɪmp] *n* camarón *m*

shrine [ʃraɪn] *n* santuario, sepulcro

shrink [ʃrɪŋk] (*pt* **shrank**, *pp* **shrunk**) *vi* encogerse; (*be reduced*) reducirse; (*also:* ~ *away*) retroceder ♦ *vt* encoger ♦ *n* (*inf: pej*) loquero/a; **to** ~ **from (doing) sth** no atreverse a hacer algo; **~age** *n* encogimiento; reducción *f*; **~wrap** *vt* embalar con película de plástico

shrivel ['ʃrɪvl] (*also:* ~ *up*) *vt* (*dry*) secar ♦ *vi* secarse

shroud [ʃraud] *n* sudario ♦ *vt*: **~ed in mystery** envuelto en el misterio

Shrove Tuesday ['ʃrəuv-] *n* martes *m* de carnaval

shrub [ʃrʌb] *n* arbusto; **~bery** *n* arbustos *mpl*

shrug [ʃrʌg] *n* encogimiento de hombros

♦ *vt*, *vi*: **to** ~ (**one's shoulders**) encogerse de hombros; ~ **off** *vt* negar importancia a

shrunk [ʃrʌŋk] *pp of* **shrink**

shudder ['ʃʌdə*] *n* estremecimiento, escalofrío ♦ *vi* estremecerse

shuffle ['ʃʌfl] *vt* (*cards*) barajar ♦ *vi*: **to** ~ (**one's feet**) arrastrar los pies

shun [ʃʌn] *vt* rehuir, esquivar

shunt [ʃʌnt] *vt* (*train*) maniobrar; (*object*) empujar

shut [ʃʌt] (*pt, pp* **shut**) *vt* cerrar ♦ *vi* cerrarse; ~ **down** *vt, vi* cerrar; ~ **off** *vt* (*supply etc*) cortar; ~ **up** *vi* (*inf: keep quiet*) callarse ♦ *vt* (*close*) cerrar; (*silence*) hacer callar; **~ter** *n* contraventana; (*PHOT*) obturador *m*

shuttle ['ʃʌtl] *n* lanzadera; (*also:* ~ *service*) servicio rápido y continuo entre dos puntos: (: *AER*) puente *m* aéreo; **~cock** *n* volante *m*; ~ **diplomacy** *n* viajes *mpl* diplomáticos

shy [ʃaɪ] *adj* tímido; **~ness** *n* timidez *f*

sibling ['sɪblɪŋ] *n* hermano/a

Sicily ['sɪsɪlɪ] *n* Sicilia

sick [sɪk] *adj* (*ill*) enfermo; (*nauseated*) mareado; (*humour*) negro; (*vomiting*): **to be** ~ (*BRIT*) vomitar; **to feel** ~ tener náuseas; **to be** ~ **of** (*fig*) estar harto de; ~ **bay** *n* enfermería; **~en** *vt* dar asco a; **~ening** *adj* (*fig*) asqueroso

sickle ['sɪkl] *n* hoz *f*

sick: ~ **leave** *n* baja por enfermedad; **~ly** *adj* enfermizo; (*smell*) nauseabundo; **~ness** *n* enfermedad *f*, mal *m*; (*vomiting*) náuseas *fpl*; ~ **pay** *n* subsidio de enfermedad

side [saɪd] *n* (*gen*) lado; (*of body*) costado; (*of lake*) orilla; (*of hill*) ladera; (*team*) equipo; ♦ *adj* (*door, entrance*) lateral ♦ *vi*: **to** ~ **with sb** tomar el partido de uno; **by the** ~ **of** al lado de; ~ **by** ~ juntos/as; **from** ~ **to** ~ de un lado para otro; **from all** ~**s** de todos lados; **to take** ~**s (with)** tomar partido (con); **~board** *n* aparador *m*; **~boards** (*BRIT*) *npl* = **~burns;** **~burns** *npl* patillas *fpl*; ~ **drum** *n* tambor *m*; ~ **effect** *n* efecto secundario; **~light** *n* (*AUT*) luz *f* lateral; **~line** *n*

(*SPORT*) línea de banda; (*fig*) empleo suplementario; **~long** *adj* de soslayo; **~saddle** *adv* a mujeriegas, a la inglesa; **~ show** *n* (*stall*) caseta; **~step** *vt* (*fig*) esquivar; **~ street** *n* calle *f* lateral; **~track** *vt* (*fig*) desviar (de su propósito); **~walk** (*US*) *n* acera; **~ways** *adv* de lado

siding ['saɪdɪŋ] *n* (*RAIL*) apartadero, vía muerta

sidle ['saɪdl] *vi*: **to ~ up (to)** acercarse furtivamente (a)

siege [siːdʒ] *n* cerco, sitio

sieve [sɪv] *n* colador *m* ♦ *vt* cribar

sift [sɪft] *vt* cribar; (*fig: information*) escudriñar

sigh [saɪ] *n* suspiro ♦ *vi* suspirar

sight [saɪt] *n* (*faculty*) vista; (*spectacle*) espectáculo; (*on gun*) mira, alza ♦ *vt* divisar; **in ~ a la vista; out of ~** fuera de (la) vista; **on ~** (*shoot*) sin previo aviso; **~seeing** *n* excursionismo, turismo; **to go ~seeing** hacer turismo

sign [saɪn] *n* (*with hand*) señal *f*, seña; (*trace*) huella, rastro; (*notice*) letrero; (*written*) signo ♦ *vt* firmar; (*SPORT*) fichar; **to ~ sth over to sb** firmar el traspaso de algo a uno; **~ on** *vi* (*MIL*) alistarse; (*BRIT: as unemployed*) registrarse como desempleado; (*for course*) inscribirse ♦ *vt* (*MIL*) alistar; (*employee*) contratar; **~ up** *vi* (*MIL*) alistarse; (*for course*) inscribirse ♦ *vt* (*player*) fichar

signal ['sɪgnl] *n* señal *f* ♦ *vi* señalizar ♦ *vt* (*person*) hacer señas a; (*message*) comunicar por señales; **~man** *n* (*RAIL*) guardavía *m*

signature ['sɪgnətʃə*] *n* firma; **~ tune** *n* sintonía de apertura de un programa

signet ring ['sɪgnət-] *n* anillo de sello

significance [sɪg'nɪfɪkəns] *n* (*importance*) trascendencia

significant [sɪg'nɪfɪkənt] *adj* significativo; (*important*) trascendente

signify ['sɪgnɪfaɪ] *vt* significar

sign language *n* lenguaje *m* para sordomudos

signpost ['saɪnpəust] *n* indicador *m*

silence ['saɪlns] *n* silencio ♦ *vt* acallar; (*guns*) reducir al silencio; **~r** *n* (*on gun*,

BRIT: AUT) silenciador *m*

silent ['saɪlnt] *adj* silencioso; (*not speaking*) callado; (*film*) mudo; **to remain ~** guardar silencio; **~ partner** *n* (*COMM*) socio/a comanditario/a

silhouette [sɪluː'ɛt] *n* silueta

silicon chip ['sɪlɪkən-] *n* plaqueta de silicio

silk [sɪlk] *n* seda ♦ *adj* de seda; **~y** *adj* sedoso

silly ['sɪlɪ] *adj* (*person*) tonto; (*idea*) absurdo

silt [sɪlt] *n* sedimento

silver ['sɪlvə*] *n* plata; (*money*) moneda suelta ♦ *adj* de plata; (*colour*) plateado; **~ paper** (*BRIT*) *n* papel *m* de plata; **~-plated** *adj* plateado; **~smith** *n* platero/a; **~ware** *n* plata; **~y** *adj* argentino

similar ['sɪmɪlə*] *adj*: **~ (to)** parecido *or* semejante (a); **~ity** [-'lærɪtɪ] *n* semejanza; **~ly** *adv* del mismo modo

simile ['sɪmɪlɪ] *n* símil *m*

simmer ['sɪmə*] *vi* hervir a fuego lento

simpering ['sɪmpərɪŋ] *adj* (*foolish*) bobo

simple ['sɪmpl] *adj* (*easy*) sencillo; (*foolish*, *COMM: interest*) simple; **simplicity** [-'plɪsɪtɪ] *n* sencillez *f*; **simplify** ['sɪmplɪfaɪ] *vt* simplificar

simply ['sɪmplɪ] *adv* (*live*, *talk*) sencillamente; (*just*, *merely*) sólo

simulate ['sɪmjuːleɪt] *vt* fingir, simular; **~d** *adj* simulado; (*fur*) de imitación

simultaneous [sɪməl'teɪnɪəs] *adj* simultáneo; **~ly** *adv* simultáneamente

sin [sɪn] *n* pecado ♦ *vi* pecar

since [sɪns] *adv* desde entonces, después ♦ *prep* desde ♦ *conj* (*time*) desde que; (*because*) ya que, puesto que; **~ then**, **ever ~** desde entonces

sincere [sɪn'sɪə*] *adj* sincero; **~ly** *adv*: **yours ~ly** (*in letters*) le saluda atentamente; **sincerity** [-'sɛrɪtɪ] *n* sinceridad *f*

sinew ['sɪnjuː] *n* tendón *m*

sinful ['sɪnful] *adj* (*thought*) pecaminoso; (*person*) pecador(a)

sing [sɪŋ] (*pt* **sang**, *pp* **sung**) *vt*, *vi* cantar

Singapore [sɪŋə'pɔː*] *n* Singapur *m*

singe [sɪndʒ] *vt* chamuscar

singer ['sɪŋə*] *n* cantante *m/f*

singing ['sɪŋɪŋ] *n* canto
single ['sɪŋgl] *adj* único, solo; (*unmarried*) soltero; (*not double*) simple, sencillo ♦ *n* (*BRIT: also:* ~ **ticket**) billete *m* sencillo; (*record*) sencillo, single *m*; ~**s** *npl* (*TENNIS*) individual *m*; ~ **bed** cama individual; ~ **out** *vt* (*choose*) escoger; ~**-breasted** *adj* recto; ~ **file** *n:* **in** ~ **file** en fila de uno; ~**-handed** *adv* sin ayuda; ~**-minded** *adj* resuelto, firme; ~ **room** cama cuarto individual
singly ['sɪŋglɪ] *adv* uno por uno
singular ['sɪŋgjulə*] *adj* (*odd*) raro, extraño; (*outstanding*) excepcional; (*LING*) singular ♦ *n* (*LING*) singular *m*
sinister ['sɪnɪstə*] *adj* siniestro
sink [sɪŋk] (*pt* **sank**, *pp* **sunk**) *n* fregadero ♦ *vt* (*ship*) hundir, echar a pique; (*foundations*) excavar ♦ *vi* (*gen*) hundirse; **to** ~ **sth into** hundir algo en; ~ **in** *vi* (*fig*) penetrar, calar
sinner ['sɪnə*] *n* pecador(a) *m/f*
sinus ['saɪnəs] *n* (*ANAT*) seno
sip [sɪp] *n* sorbo ♦ *vt* sorber, beber a sorbitos
siphon ['saɪfən] *n* sifón *m*; ~ **off** *vt* desviar
sir [sə*] *n* señor *m*; **S~ John Smith** Sir John Smith; **yes** ~ sí, señor
siren ['saɪərn] *n* sirena
sirloin ['sə:lɔɪn] *n* (*also:* ~ **steak**) solomillo
sissy ['sɪsɪ] (*inf*) *n* marica *m*
sister ['sɪstə*] *n* hermana; (*BRIT: nurse*) enfermera jefe; ~**-in-law** *n* cuñada
sit [sɪt] (*pt, pp* **sat**) *vi* sentarse; (*be sitting*) estar sentado; (*assembly*) reunirse; (*for painter*) posar ♦ *vt* (*exam*) presentarse a; ~ **down** *vi* sentarse; ~ **in on** *vt fus* asistir a; ~ **up** *vi* incorporarse; (*not go to bed*) velar
sitcom ['sɪtkɔm] *n abbr* (= *situation comedy*) comedia de situación
site [saɪt] *n* sitio; (*also: building* ~) solar *m* ♦ *vt* situar
sit-in *n* (*demonstration*) sentada
sitting ['sɪtɪŋ] *n* (*of assembly etc*) sesión *f*; (*in canteen*) turno; ~ **room** *n* sala de estar

situated ['sɪtjueɪtɪd] *adj* situado
situation [sɪtju'eɪʃən] *n* situación *f*; "~**s vacant**" (*BRIT*) "ofrecen trabajo"
six [sɪks] *num* seis; ~**teen** *num* diez y seis, dieciséis; ~**th** *num* sexto; ~**ty** *num* sesenta
size [saɪz] *n* tamaño *m*; (*extent*) extensión *f*; (*of clothing*) talla; (*of shoes*) número; ~ **up** *vt* formarse una idea de; ~**able** *adj* importante, considerable
sizzle ['sɪzl] *vi* crepitar
skate [skeɪt] *n* patín *m*; (*fish: pl inv*) raya ♦ *vi* patinar; ~**board** *n* monopatín *m*; ~**r** *n* patinador(a) *m/f*; **skating** *n* patinaje *m*; **skating rink** *n* pista de patinaje
skeleton ['skelɪtn] *n* esqueleto; (*outline*) esquema *m*; ~ **staff** *n* personal *m* reducido
skeptic *etc* ['skeptɪk] (*US*) = **sceptic**
sketch [sketʃ] *n* (*drawing*) dibujo; (*outline*) esbozo, bosquejo; (*THEATRE*) sketch *m* ♦ *vt* dibujar; (*plan etc: also:* ~ **out**) esbozar; ~ **book** *n* libro de dibujos; ~**y** *adj* incompleto
skewer ['skju:ə*] *n* broqueta
ski [ski:] *n* esquí *m* ♦ *vi* esquiar; ~ **boot** *n* bota de esquí
skid [skɪd] *n* patinazo ♦ *vi* patinar
ski: ~**er** *n* esquiador(a) *m/f*; ~**ing** *n* esquí *m*; ~ **jump** *n* salto con esquís
skilful ['skɪlful] (*BRIT*) *adj* diestro, experto
ski lift *n* telesilla *m*, telesquí *m*
skill [skɪl] *n* destreza, pericia, técnica; ~**ed** *adj* hábil, diestro; (*worker*) cualificado; ~**full** (*US*) *adj* = **skilful**
skim [skɪm] *vt* (*milk*) desnatar; (*glide over*) rozar, rasar ♦ *vi:* **to** ~ **through** (*book*) hojear; ~**med milk** *n* leche *f* desnatada
skimp [skɪmp] *vt* (*also:* ~ **on:** *work*) chapucear; (*cloth etc*) escatimar; ~**y** *adj* escaso; (*skirt*) muy corto
skin [skɪn] *n* piel *f*; (*complexion*) cutis *m* ♦ *vt* (*fruit etc*) pelar; (*animal*) despellejar; ~ **cancer** *n* cáncer *m* de piel; ~**-deep** *adj* superficial; ~ **diving** *n* buceo; ~**ny** *adj* flaco; ~**tight** *adj* (*dress etc*) muy ajustado
skip [skɪp] *n* brinco, salto; (*BRIT: container*) contenedor *m* ♦ *vi* brincar;

(*with rope*) saltar a la comba ♦ *vt* saltarse

ski pants *npl* pantalones *mpl* de esquí

ski pole *n* bastón *m* de esquiar

skipper ['skɪpə*] *n* (*NAUT, SPORT*) capitán *m*

skipping rope ['skɪpɪŋ-] (*BRIT*) *n* comba

skirmish ['skə:mɪʃ] *n* escaramuza

skirt [skə:t] *n* falda (*SP*), pollera (*AM*) ♦ *vt* (*go round*) ladear; **~ing board** (*BRIT*) *n* rodapié *m*

ski slope *n* pista de esquí

ski suit *n* traje *m* de esquiar

skittle ['skɪtl] *n* bolo; **~s** *n* (*game*) boliche *m*

skive [skaɪv] (*BRIT: inf*) *vi* gandulear

skulk [skʌlk] *vi* esconderse

skull [skʌl] *n* calavera; (*ANAT*) cráneo

skunk [skʌŋk] *n* mofeta

sky [skaɪ] *n* cielo; **~light** *n* tragaluz *m*, claraboya; **~scraper** *n* rascacielos *m inv*

slab [slæb] *n* (*stone*) bloque *m*; (*flat*) losa; (*of cake*) trozo

slack [slæk] *adj* (*loose*) flojo; (*slow*) de poca actividad; (*careless*) descuidado; **~s** *npl* pantalones *mpl*; **~en** (*also:* **~en off**) *vi* aflojarse ♦ *vt* aflojar; (*speed*) disminuir

slag heap ['slæg-] *n* escorial *m*, escombrera

slag off (*BRIT: inf*) *vt* poner como un trapo

slain [sleɪn] *pp of* **slay**

slam [slæm] *vt* (*throw*) arrojar (violentamente); (*criticize*) criticar duramente ♦ *vi* (*door*) cerrarse de golpe; **to ~ the door** dar un portazo

slander ['slɑ:ndə*] *n* calumnia, difamación *f*

slang [slæŋ] *n* argot *m*; (*jargon*) jerga

slant [slɑ:nt] *n* sesgo, inclinación *f*; (*fig*) interpretación *f*; **~ed** *adj* (*fig*) parcial; **~ing** *adj* inclinado; (*eyes*) rasgado

slap [slæp] *n* palmada; (*in face*) bofetada ♦ *vt* dar una palmada *or* bofetada a; (*paint etc*): **to ~ sth on sth** embadurnar algo con algo ♦ *adv* (*directly*) exactamente, directamente; **~dash** *adj* descuidado; **~stick** *n* comedia de golpe y porrazo; **~up** *adj*: **a ~-up meal** (*BRIT*) un

banquetazo, una comilona

slash [slæʃ] *vt* acuchillar; (*fig: prices*) fulminar

slat [slæt] *n* tablilla, listón *m*

slate [sleɪt] *n* pizarra ♦ *vt* (*fig: criticize*) criticar duramente

slaughter ['slɔ:tə*] *n* (*of animals*) matanza; (*of people*) carnicería ♦ *vt* matar; **~house** *n* matadero

Slav [slɑ:v] *adj* eslavo

slave [sleɪv] *n* esclavo/a ♦ *vi* (*also:* **~ away**) sudar tinta; **~ry** *n* esclavitud *f*

slay [sleɪ] (*pt* **slew**, *pp* **slain**) *vt* matar

sleazy ['sli:zɪ] *adj* de mala fama

sledge [slɛdʒ] *n* trineo; **~hammer** *n* mazo

sleek [sli:k] *adj* (*shiny*) lustroso; (*car etc*) elegante

sleep [sli:p] (*pt, pp* **slept**) *n* sueño ♦ *vi* dormir; **to go to ~** quedarse dormido; **~ around** *vi* acostarse con cualquiera; **~ in** *vi* (*oversleep*) quedarse dormido; **~er** *n* (*person*) durmiente *m/f*; (*BRIT: RAIL: on track*) traviesa; (: *train*) coche-cama *m*; **~ing bag** *n* saco de dormir; **~ing car** *n* coche-cama *m*; **~ing partner** (*BRIT*) *n* (*COMM*) socio comanditario; **~ing pill** *n* somnífero; **~less** *adj*: **a ~less night** una noche en blanco; **~walker** *n* sonámbulo/a; **~y** *adj* soñoliento; (*place*) soporífero

sleet [sli:t] *n* aguanieve *f*

sleeve [sli:v] *n* manga; (*TECH*) manguito; (*of record*) portada; **~less** *adj* sin mangas

sleigh [sleɪ] *n* trineo

sleight [slaɪt] *n*: **~ of hand** escamoteo

slender ['slɛndə*] *adj* delgado; (*means*) escaso

slept [slɛpt] *pt, pp of* **sleep**

slew [slu:] *pt of* **slay** ♦ *vi* (*BRIT: veer*) torcerse

slice [slaɪs] *n* (*of meat*) tajada; (*of bread*) rebanada; (*of lemon*) rodaja; (*utensil*) pala ♦ *vt* cortar (en tajos); rebanar

slick [slɪk] *adj* (*skilful*) hábil, diestro; (*clever*) astuto ♦ *n* (*also:* **oil ~**) marea negra

slide [slaɪd] (*pt, pp* **slid**) *n* (*movement*) descenso, desprendimiento; (*in playground*) tobogán *m*; (*PHOT*) diapositiva;

(*BRIT: also: hair* ~) pasador *m* ♦ *vt* correr,
deslizar ♦ *vi* (*slip*) resbalarse; (*glide*)
deslizarse; **sliding** *adj* (*door*) corredizo;
sliding scale *n* escala móvil
slight [slaɪt] *adj* (*slim*) delgado; (*frail*)
delicado; (*pain etc*) leve; (*trivial*)
insignificante; (*small*) pequeño ♦ *n*
desaire *m* ♦ *vt* (*insult*) ofender, desairar;
not in the ~est en absoluto; **~ly** *adv*
ligeramente, un poco
slim [slɪm] *adj* delgado, esbelto; (*fig:
chance*) remoto ♦ *vi* adelgazar
slime [slaɪm] *n* limo, cieno; **slimy** *adj*
cenagoso
slimming ['slɪmɪŋ] *n* adelgazamiento
sling [slɪŋ] (*pt, pp* **slung**) *n* (*MED*)
cabestrillo; (*weapon*) honda ♦ *vt* tirar,
arrojar
slip [slɪp] *n* (*slide*) resbalón *m*; (*mistake*)
descuido; (*underskirt*) combinación *f*; (*of
paper*) papelito ♦ *vt* (*slide*) deslizar ♦ *vi*
deslizarse; (*stumble*) resbalar(se);
(*decline*) decaer; (*move smoothly*): **to ~
into/out of** (*room etc*) introducirse en/
salirse de (*room etc*); **to give sb the ~** eludir a uno;
a ~ of the tongue un lapsus; **to ~ sth
on/off** ponerse/quitarse algo; **~ away** *vi*
escabullirse; **~ in** *vt* meter ♦ *vi* meterse;
~ out *vi* (*go out*) salir (un momento); **~
up** *vi* (*make mistake*) equivocarse; meter
la pata; **~ped disc** *n* vértebra dislocada
slipper ['slɪpə*] *n* zapatilla, pantufla
slippery ['slɪpərɪ] *adj* resbaladizo
slip: ~ road (*BRIT*) *n* carretera de acceso;
~shod *adj* descuidado; **~-up** *n* (*error*)
desliz *m*; **~way** *n* grada, gradas *fpl*
slit [slɪt] (*pt, pp* **slit**) *n* raja; (*cut*) corte *m*
♦ *vt* rajar; cortar
slither ['slɪðə*] *vi* deslizarse
sliver ['slɪvə*] *n* (*of glass, wood*) astilla;
(*of cheese etc*) raja
slob [slɔb] (*inf*) *n* abandonado/a
slog [slɔg] (*BRIT*) *vi* sudar tinta; **it was a
~** costó trabajo (hacerlo)
slogan ['sləugən] *n* eslogan *m*, lema *m*
slop [slɔp] *vi* (*also:* ~ *over*) derramarse,
desbordarse ♦ *vt* derramar, verter
slope [sləup] *n* (*up*) cuesta, pendiente *f*;
(*down*) declive *m*; (*side of mountain*)

falda, vertiente *m* ♦ *vi*: **to ~ down** estar
en declive; **to ~ up** inclinarse; **sloping**
adj en pendiente; en declive; (*writing*)
inclinado
sloppy ['slɔpɪ] *adj* (*work*) descuidado;
(*appearance*) desaliñado
slot [slɔt] *n* ranura ♦ *vt*: **to ~ into**
encajar en
sloth [sləuθ] *n* (*laziness*) pereza
slot machine *n* (*BRIT: vending machine*)
distribuidor *m* automático; (*for
gambling*) tragaperras *m inv*
slouch [slautʃ] *vi* andar *etc* con los
hombros caídos
Slovenia [sləʊˈviːnɪə] *n* Eslovenia
slovenly ['slʌvənlɪ] *adj* desaliñado,
desaseado; (*careless*) descuidado
slow [sləu] *adj* lento; (*not clever*) lerdo;
(*watch*): **to be ~** atrasar ♦ *adv*
lentamente, despacio ♦ *vt, vi* (*also:* ~
down, ~ *up*) retardar; "~" (*road sign*)
"disminuir velocidad"; **~down** (*US*) *n*
huelga de manos caídas; **~ly** *adv*
lentamente, despacio; **~ motion** *n*: **in ~
motion** a cámara lenta
sludge [slʌdʒ] *n* lodo, fango
slue [sluː] (*US*) *vi* = **slew**
slug [slʌg] *n* babosa; (*bullet*) posta; **~gish**
adj lento; (*person*) perezoso
sluice [sluːs] *n* (*gate*) esclusa; (*channel*)
canal *m*
slum [slʌm] *n* casucha
slump [slʌmp] *n* (*economic*) depresión *f*
♦ *vi* hundirse; (*prices*) caer en picado
slung [slʌŋ] *pt, pp of* **sling**
slur [slə:*] *n*: **to cast a ~ on** insultar ♦ *vt*
(*speech*) pronunciar mal
slush [slʌʃ] *n* nieve *f* a medio derretir; **~
fund** *n* caja negra (*fondos para sobornar*)
slut [slʌt] *n* putona
sly [slaɪ] *adj* astuto; (*smile*) taimado
smack [smæk] *n* bofetada ♦ *vt* dar con la
mano a; (*child, on face*) abofetear ♦ *vi*: **to
~ of** saber a, oler a
small [smɔ:l] *adj* pequeño; **~ ads** (*BRIT*)
npl anuncios *mpl* por palabras; **~
change** *n* suelto, cambio; **~ fry** *npl* gente
f del montón; **~holder** (*BRIT*) *n* granjero/
a, parcelero/a; **~ hours** *npl*: **in the ~**

hours a las altas horas (de la noche);
~**pox** *n* viruela; ~ **talk** *n* cháchara
smart [smɑːt] *adj* elegante; (*clever*) listo,
inteligente; (*quick*) rápido, vivo ♦ *vi*
escocer, picar; ~**en up** *vi* arreglarse ♦ *vt*
arreglar
smash [smæʃ] *n* (*also:* ~-*up*) choque *m*;
(*MUS*) exitazo ♦ *vt* (*break*) hacer pedazos;
(*car etc*) estrellar; (*SPORT: record*) batir
♦ *vi* hacerse pedazos; (*against wall etc*)
estrellarse; ~**ing** (*inf*) *adj* estupendo
smattering [ˈsmætərɪŋ] *n*: **a** ~ **of** algo de
smear [smɪə*] *n* mancha; (*MED*) frotis *m*
inv ♦ *vt* untar; ~ **campaign** *n* campaña
de desprestigio
smell [smɛl] (*pt, pp* **smelt** *or* **smelled**) *n*
olor *m*; (*sense*) olfato ♦ *vt, vi* oler; ~**y** *adj*
maloliente
smile [smaɪl] *n* sonrisa ♦ *vi* sonreír
smirk [smɔːk] *n* sonrisa falsa *or* afectada
smith [smɪθ] *n* herrero; ~**y** [ˈsmɪðɪ] *n*
herrería
smock [smɔk] *n* blusa; (*children's*)
mandilón *m*; (*US: overall*) guardapolvo
smog [smɔg] *n* esmog *m*
smoke [sməuk] *n* humo ♦ *vi* fumar;
(*chimney*) echar humo ♦ *vt* (*cigarettes*)
fumar; ~**d** *adj* (*bacon, glass*) ahumado;
~**r** *n* fumador(a) *m/f*; (*RAIL*) coche *m*
fumador; ~ **screen** *n* cortina de humo; ~
shop (*US*) *n* estanco (*SP*), tabaquería (*AM*);
smoking *n*: **"no smoking"** "prohibido
fumar"; **smoky** *adj* (*room*) lleno de
humo; (*taste*) ahumado
smolder [ˈsməuldə*] (*US*) *vi* = **smoulder**
smooth [smuːð] *adj* liso; (*sea*) tranquilo;
(*flavour, movement*) suave; (*sauce*) fino;
(*person: pej*) meloso ♦ *vt* (*also:* ~ *out*)
alisar; (*creases, difficulties*) allanar
smother [ˈsmʌðə*] *vt* sofocar; (*repress*)
contener
smoulder [ˈsməuldə*] (*US* **smolder**) *vi*
arder sin llama
smudge [smʌdʒ] *n* mancha ♦ *vt* manchar
smug [smʌg] *adj* presumido; orondo
smuggle [ˈsmʌgl] *vt* pasar de contrabando; ~**r** *n* contrabandista *m/f*;
smuggling *n* contrabando
smutty [ˈsmʌtɪ] *adj* (*fig*) verde, obsceno

snack [snæk] *n* bocado; ~ **bar** *n* cafetería
snag [snæg] *n* problema *m*
snail [sneɪl] *n* caracol *m*
snake [sneɪk] *n* serpiente *f*
snap [snæp] *n* (*sound*) chasquido;
(*photograph*) foto *f* ♦ *adj* (*decision*)
instantáneo ♦ *vt* (*break*) quebrar;
(*fingers*) castañetear ♦ *vi* quebrarse; (*fig:
speak sharply*) contestar bruscamente; **to**
~ **shut** cerrarse de golpe; ~ **at** *vt fus*
(*subj: dog*) intentar morder; ~ **off** *vi*
partirse; ~ **up** *vt* agarrar; ~ **fastener** (*US*)
n botón *m* de presión; ~**py** (*inf*) *adj*
(*answer*) instantáneo; (*slogan*) conciso;
make it ~**py!** (*hurry up*) ¡date prisa!;
~**shot** *n* foto *f* (instantánea)
snare [snɛə*] *n* trampa
snarl [snɑːl] *vi* gruñir
snatch [snætʃ] *n* (*small piece*) fragmento
♦ *vt* (~ *away*) arrebatar; (*fig*) agarrar; **to**
~ **some sleep** encontrar tiempo para
dormir
sneak [sniːk] (*pt* (*US*) **snuck**) *vi*: **to** ~ **in/
out** entrar/salir a hurtadillas ♦ *n* (*inf*)
soplón/ona *m/f*; **to** ~ **up on sb** aparecér-
sele de improviso a uno; ~**ers** *npl* zapatos *mpl* de lona; ~**y** *adj* furtivo
sneer [snɪə*] *vi* reír con sarcasmo;
(*mock*): **to** ~ **at** burlarse de
sneeze [sniːz] *vi* estornudar
sniff [snɪf] *vi* sollozar ♦ *vt* husmear, oler;
(*drugs*) esnifar
snigger [ˈsnɪgə*] *vi* reírse con disimulo
snip [snɪp] *n* tijeretazo; (*BRIT: inf:
bargain*) ganga ♦ *vt* tijeretear
sniper [ˈsnaɪpə*] *n* francotirador(a) *m/f*
snippet [ˈsnɪpɪt] *n* retazo
snivelling [ˈsnɪvlɪŋ] *adj* llorón/ona
snob [snɔb] *n* (e)snob *m/f*; ~**bery** *n*
(e)snobismo; ~**bish** *adj* (e)snob
snooker [ˈsnuːkə*] *n* especie de billar
snoop [snuːp] *vi*: **to** ~ **about** fisgonear
snooty [ˈsnuːtɪ] *adj* (e)snob
snooze [snuːz] *n* siesta ♦ *vi* echar una
siesta
snore [snɔː*] *n* ronquido ♦ *vi* roncar
snorkel [ˈsnɔːkl] *n* (tubo) respirador *m*
snort [snɔːt] *n* bufido ♦ *vi* bufar
snout [snaut] *n* hocico, morro

snow [snəu] *n* nieve *f* ♦ *vi* nevar; **~ball** *n* bola de nieve ♦ *vi* (*fig*) agrandirse, ampliarse; **~bound** *adj* bloqueado por la nieve; **~drift** *n* ventisquero; **~drop** *n* campanilla; **~fall** *n* nevada; **~flake** *n* copo de nieve; **~man** *n* figura de nieve; **~plough** (*US* **~plow**) *n* quitanieves *m inv*; **~shoe** *n* raqueta (de nieve); **~storm** *n* nevada, nevasca

snub [snʌb] *vt* (*person*) desairar ♦ *n* desaire *m*, repulsa; **~-nosed** *adj* chato

snuff [snʌf] *n* rapé *m*

snug [snʌg] *adj* (*cosy*) cómodo; (*fitted*) ajustado

snuggle [ˈsnʌgl] *vi*: **to ~ up to sb** arrimarse a uno

KEYWORD

so [səu] *adv* **1** (*thus, likewise*) así, de este modo; **if ~** de ser así; **I like swimming — ~ do I** a mí me gusta nadar — a mí también; **I've got work to do — ~ has Paul** tengo trabajo que hacer — Paul también; **it's 5 o'clock — ~ it is!** son las cinco — ¡pues es verdad!; **I hope/think ~** espero/creo que sí; **~ far** hasta ahora; (*in past*) hasta este momento

2 (*in comparisons etc: to such a degree*) tan; **~ quickly (that)** tan rápido (que); **~ big (that)** tan grande (que); **she's not ~ clever as her brother** no es tan lista como su hermano; **we were ~ worried** estábamos preocupadísimos

3: **~ much** *adj, adv* tanto/as; **~ many** tantos/as

4 (*phrases*): **10 or ~** unos 10, 10 o así; **~ long!** (*inf: goodbye*) ¡hasta luego!

♦ *conj* **1** (*expressing purpose*): **~ as to do** para hacer; **~ (that)** para que + *sub*

2 (*expressing result*) así que; **~ you see, I could have gone** así que ya ves, (yo) podría haber ido

---

soak [səuk] *vt* (*drench*) empapar; (*steep in water*) remojar ♦ *vi* remojarse, estar a remojo; **~ in** *vi* penetrar; **~ up** *vt* absorber

soap [səup] *n* jabón *m*; **~flakes** *npl* escamas *fpl* de jabón; **~ opera** *n*

telenovela; **~ powder** *n* jabón *m* en polvo; **~y** *adj* jabonoso

soar [sɔ:*] *vi* (*on wings*) remontarse; (*rocket, prices*) dispararse; (*building etc*) elevarse

sob [sɔb] *n* sollozo ♦ *vi* sollozar

sober [ˈsəubə*] *adj* (*serious*) serio; (*not drunk*) sobrio; (*colour, style*) discreto; **~ up** *vt* quitar la borrachera

so-called *adj* así llamado

soccer [ˈsɔkə*] *n* fútbol *m*

social [ˈsəuʃl] *adj* social ♦ *n* velada, fiesta; **~ club** *n* club *m*; **~ism** *n* socialismo; **~ist** *adj, n* socialista *m/f*; **~ize** *vi*: **to ~ize (with)** alternar (con); **~ly** *adv* socialmente; **~ security** *n* seguridad *f* social; **~ work** *n* asistencia social; **~ worker** *n* asistente/a *m/f* social

society [səˈsaɪətɪ] *n* sociedad *f*; (*club*) asociación *f*; (*also: high ~*) alta sociedad

sociology [səusɪˈɔlədʒɪ] *n* sociología

sock [sɔk] *n* calcetín *m* (*SP*), media (*AM*)

socket [ˈsɔkɪt] *n* cavidad *f*; (*BRIT: ELEC*) enchufe *m*

sod [sɔd] *n* (*of earth*) césped *m*; (*BRIT: inf!*) cabrón/ona *m/f* (!)

soda [ˈsəudə] *n* (*CHEM*) sosa; (*also: ~ water*) soda; (*US: also: ~ pop*) gaseosa

sodden [ˈsɔdn] *adj* empapado

sodium [ˈsəudɪəm] *n* sodio

sofa [ˈsəufə] *n* sofá *m*

soft [sɔft] *adj* (*lenient, not hard*) blando; (*gentle, not bright*) suave; **~ drink** *n* bebida no alcohólica; **~en** [ˈsɔfn] *vt* ablandar; suavizar; (*effect*) amortiguar ♦ *vi* ablandarse; suavizarse; **~ly** *adv* suavemente; (*gently*) delicadamente, con delicadeza; **~ness** *n* blandura; suavidad *f*; **~ spot** *n*: **to have a ~ spot for sb** tener debilidad por uno; **~ware** *n* (*COMPUT*) software *m*

soggy [ˈsɔgɪ] *adj* empapado

soil [sɔɪl] *n* (*earth*) tierra, suelo ♦ *vt* ensuciar; **~ed** *adj* sucio

solace [ˈsɔlɪs] *n* consuelo

solar [ˈsəulə*] *adj*: **~ energy** *n* energía solar; **~ panel** *n* panel *m* solar

sold [səuld] *pt, pp of* **sell**; **~ out** *adj* (*COMM*) agotado

solder ['səuldə*] *vt* soldar ♦ *n* soldadura
soldier ['səuldʒə*] *n* soldado; (*army man*)
militar *m*
sole [səul] *n* (*of foot*) planta; (*of shoe*)
suela; (*fish: pl inv*) lenguado ♦ *adj* único
solemn ['sɔləm] *adj* solemne
sole trader *n* (*COMM*) comerciante *m*
exclusivo
solicit [sə'lɪsɪt] *vt* (*request*) solicitar ♦ *vi*
(*prostitute*) importunar
solicitor [sə'lɪsɪtə*] (*BRIT*) *n* (*for wills etc*)
≈ notario/a; (*in court*) ≈ abogado/a
solid ['sɔlɪd] *adj* sólido; (*gold etc*) macizo
♦ *n* sólido; ~s *npl* (*food*) alimentos *mpl*
sólidos
solidarity [sɔlɪ'dærɪtɪ] *n* solidaridad *f*
solitaire [sɔlɪ'tɛə*] *n* (*game, gem*)
solitario
solitary ['sɔlɪtərɪ] *adj* solitario, solo; ~
confinement *n* incomunicación *f*
solitude ['sɔlɪtjuːd] *n* soledad *f*
solo ['səuləu] *n* solo ♦ *adv* (*fly*) en
solitario; ~**ist** *n* solista *m/f*
soluble ['sɔljuːbl] *adj* soluble
solution [sə'luːʃən] *n* solución *f*
solve [sɔlv] *vt* resolver, solucionar
solvent ['sɔlvənt] *adj* (*COMM*) solvente ♦ *n*
(*CHEM*) solvente *m*
sombre ['sɔmbə*] (*US* **somber**) *adj*
sombrío

some [sʌm] *adj* **1** (*a certain amount or
number of*): ~ tea/water/biscuits té/
agua/(unas) galletas; **there's** ~ **milk in
the fridge** hay leche en el frigo; **there
were** ~ **people outside** había algunas
personas fuera; **I've got** ~ **money, but
not much** tengo algo de dinero, pero no
mucho
2 (*certain: in contrasts*) algunos/as; ~
people say that ... hay quien dice que
...; ~ **films were excellent, but most
were mediocre** hubo películas excelen-
tes, pero la mayoría fueron mediocres
3 (*unspecified*): ~ **woman was asking
for you** una mujer estuvo preguntando
por ti; **he was asking for** ~ **book (or
other)** pedía un libro; ~ **day** algún día;

~ **day next week** un día de la semana
que viene
♦ *pron* **1** (*a certain number*): **I've got** ~
(*books etc*) tengo algunos/as
2 (*a certain amount*) algo; **I've got** ~
(*money, milk*) tengo algo; **could I have** ~
of that cheese? ¿me puede dar un poco
de ese queso?; **I've read** ~ **of the book**
he leído parte del libro
♦ *adv*: ~ **10 people** unas 10 personas,
una decena de personas

somebody ['sʌmbədɪ] *pron* = **someone**
somehow ['sʌmhau] *adv* de alguna
manera; (*for some reason*) por una u otra
razón
someone ['sʌmwʌn] *pron* alguien
someplace ['sʌmpleɪs] (*US*) *adv* =
somewhere
somersault ['sʌməsɔːlt] *n* (*deliberate*)
salto mortal; (*accidental*) vuelco ♦ *vi* dar
un salto mortal; dar vuelcos
something ['sʌmθɪŋ] *pron* algo; **would
you like** ~ **to eat/drink?** ¿te gustaría
cenar/tomar algo?
sometime ['sʌmtaɪm] *adv* (*in future*)
algún día, en algún momento; (*in past*):
~ **last month** durante el mes pasado
sometimes ['sʌmtaɪmz] *adv* a veces
somewhat ['sʌmwɔt] *adv* algo
somewhere ['sʌmwɛə*] *adv* (*be*) en
alguna parte; (*go*) a alguna parte; ~ **else**
(*be*) en otra parte; (*go*) a otra parte
son [sʌn] *n* hijo
song [sɔŋ] *n* canción *f*
son-in-law *n* yerno
sonnet ['sɔnɪt] *n* soneto
sonny ['sʌnɪ] (*inf*) *n* hijo
soon [suːn] *adv* pronto, dentro de poco; ~
afterwards poco después; *see also* **as**;
~**er** *adv* (*time*) antes, más temprano;
(*preference*): **I would** ~**er do that**
preferiría hacer eso; ~**er or later** tarde
o temprano
soot [sut] *n* hollín *m*
soothe [suːð] *vt* tranquilizar; (*pain*)
aliviar
sophisticated [sə'fɪstɪkeɪtɪd] *adj*
sofisticado

sophomore ['sɔfəmɔ:*] (*US*) *n* estudiante *m/f* de segundo año

sopping ['sɔpɪŋ] *adj*: ~ (**wet**) empapado

soppy ['sɔpɪ] (*pej*) *adj* tonto

soprano [sə'prɑ:nəu] *n* soprano *f*

sorcerer ['sɔ:sərə*] *n* hechicero

sore [sɔ:*] *adj* (*painful*) doloroso, que duele ♦ *n* llaga; **~ly** *adv*: **I am ~ly tempted** to estoy muy tentado a

sorrow ['sɔrəu] *n* pena, dolor *m*; **~s** *npl* pesares *mpl*; **~ful** *adj* triste

sorry ['sɔrɪ] *adj* (*regretful*) arrepentido; (*condition, excuse*) lastimoso; **~!** ¡perdón!, ¡perdone!; **~?** ¿cómo?; **to feel ~ for sb** tener lástima a uno; **I feel ~ for him** me da lástima

sort [sɔ:t] *n* clase *f*, género, tipo ♦ *vt* (*also*: ~ **out**: *papers*) clasificar; (: *problems*) arreglar, solucionar; **~ing office** *n* sala de batalla

SOS *n* SOS *m*

so-so *adv* regular, así así

soufflé ['su:fleɪ] *n* suflé *m*

sought [sɔ:t] *pt, pp of* **seek**

soul [səul] *n* alma; **~-destroying** *adj* (*work*) deprimente; **~ful** *adj* lleno de sentimiento

sound [saund] *n* (*noise*) sonido, ruido; (*volume: on TV etc*) volumen *m*; (*GEO*) estrecho ♦ *adj* (*healthy*) sano; (*safe, not damaged*) en buen estado; (*reliable: person*) digno de confianza; (*sensible*) sensato, razonable; (*secure: investment*) seguro ♦ *adv*: ~ **asleep** profundamente dormido ♦ *vt* (*alarm*) sonar ♦ *vi* sonar, resonar; (*fig: seem*) parecer; **to ~ like** sonar a; ~ **out** *vt* sondear; ~ **barrier** *n* barrera del sonido; **~bite** *n* cita jugosa; ~ **effects** *npl* efectos *mpl* sonoros; **~ly** *adv* (*sleep*) profundamente; (*defeated*) completamente; **~proof** *adj* insonorizado; **~track** *n* (*of film*) banda sonora

soup [su:p] *n* (*thick*) sopa; (*thin*) caldo; **in the ~** (*fig*) en apuros; ~ **plate** *n* plato sopero; **~spoon** *n* cuchara sopera

sour ['sauə*] *adj* agrio; (*milk*) cortado; **it's ~ grapes** (*fig*) están verdes

source [sɔ:s] *n* fuente *f*

south [sauθ] *n* sur *m* ♦ *adj* del sur, sureño ♦ *adv* al sur, hacia el sur; **S~ Africa** *n* África del Sur; **S~ African** *adj*, *n* sudafricano/a *m/f*; **S~ America** *n* América del Sur, Sudamérica; **S~ American** *adj*, *n* sudamericano/a *m/f*; **~-east** *n* sudeste *m*; **~erly** ['sʌðəlɪ] *adj* sur; (*from the ~*) del sur; **~ern** ['sʌðən] *adj* del sur, meridional; **S~ Pole** *n* Polo Sur; **~ward(s)** *adv* hacia el sur; **~-west** *n* suroeste *m*

souvenir [su:və'nɪə*] *n* recuerdo

sovereign ['sɔvrɪn] *adj*, *n* soberano/a *m/f*; **~ty** *n* soberanía

soviet ['səuvɪət] *adj* soviético; **the S~ Union** la Unión Soviética

sow¹ [səu] (*pt* **sowed**, *pp* **sown**) *vt* sembrar

sow² [sau] *n* cerda (*SP*), puerca (*SP*), chancha (*AM*)

soy [sɔɪ] (*US*) *n* = **soya**

soya ['sɔɪə] (*BRIT*) *n* soja; ~ **bean** *n* haba de soja; ~ **sauce** *n* salsa de soja

spa [spɑ:] *n* balneario

space [speɪs] *n* espacio; (*room*) sitio ♦ *cpd* espacial ♦ *vt* (*also*: ~ **out**) espaciar; **~craft** *n* nave *f* espacial; **~man/woman** *n* astronauta *m/f*, cosmonauta *m/f*; **~ship** *n* = **~craft**; **spacing** *n* espaciado

spacious ['speɪʃəs] *adj* amplio

spade [speɪd] *n* (*tool*) pala, laya; **~s** *npl* (*CARDS: British*) picas *fpl*; (: *Spanish*) espadas *fpl*

spaghetti [spə'gɛtɪ] *n* espaguetis *mpl*, fideos *mpl*

Spain [speɪn] *n* España

span [spæn] *n* (*of bird, plane*) envergadura; (*of arch*) luz *f*; (*in time*) lapso ♦ *vt* extenderse sobre, cruzar; (*fig*) abarcar

Spaniard ['spænjəd] *n* español(a) *m/f*

spaniel ['spænjəl] *n* perro de aguas

Spanish ['spænɪʃ] *adj* español(a) ♦ *n* (*LING*) español *m*, castellano; **the ~** *npl* los españoles

spank [spæŋk] *vt* zurrar

spanner ['spænə*] (*BRIT*) *n* llave *f* (inglesa)

spar [spɑ:*] *n* palo, verga ♦ *vi* (*BOXING*) entrenarse

spare [spɛə*] *adj* de reserva; (*surplus*)

sobrante, de más ♦ *n* = ~ **part** ♦ *vt* (*do without*) pasarse sin; (*refrain from hurting*) perdonar; **to** ~ (*surplus*) sobrante, de sobra; ~ **part** *n* pieza de repuesto; ~ **time** *n* tiempo libre; ~ **wheel** *n* (AUT) rueda de recambio

sparing ['spɛərɪŋ] *adj*: **to be** ~ **with** ser parco en; **~ly** *adv* con moderación

spark [spɑːk] *n* chispa; (*fig*) chispazo; **~(ing) plug** *n* bujía

sparkle ['spɑːkl] *n* centelleo, destello ♦ *vi* (*shine*) relucir, brillar; **sparkling** *adj* (*eyes, conversation*) brillante; (*wine*) espumoso; (*mineral water*) con gas

sparrow ['spærəu] *n* gorrión *m*

sparse [spɑːs] *adj* esparcido, escaso

spartan ['spɑːtən] *adj* (*fig*) espartano

spasm ['spæzəm] *n* (MED) espasmo

spastic ['spæstɪk] *n* espástico/a

spat [spæt] *pt, pp of* spit

spate [speɪt] *n* (*fig*): **a** ~ **of** un torrente de

spatter ['spætə*] *vt*: **to** ~ **with** salpicar de

spawn [spɔːn] *vi* desovar, frezar ♦ *n* huevas *fpl*

speak [spiːk] (*pt* **spoke**, *pp* **spoken**) *vt* (*language*) hablar; (*truth*) decir ♦ *vi* hablar; (*make a speech*) intervenir; **to** ~ **to sb/of** *or* **about sth** hablar con uno/ de *or* sobre algo; ~ **up!** ¡habla fuerte!; **~er** *n* (*in public*) orador(a) *m/f*; (*also: loud~er*) altavoz *m*; (*for stereo etc*) bafle *m*; (POL): **the S~er** (BRIT) el Presidente de la Cámara de los Comunes; (US) el Presidente del Congreso

spear [spɪə*] *n* lanza ♦ *vt* alancear; **~head** *vt* (*attack etc*) encabezar

spec [spɛk] (*inf*) *n*: **on** ~ como especulación

special ['spɛʃl] *adj* especial; (*edition etc*) extraordinario; (*delivery*) urgente; **~ist** *n* especialista *m/f*, **~ity** [spɛʃɪˈælɪtɪ] (BRIT) *n* especialidad *f*; **~ize** *vi*: **to** ~**ize (in)** especializarse (en); **~ly** *adv* sobre todo, en particular; **~ty** (US) *n* = **~ity**

species ['spiːʃiːz] *n inv* especie *f*

specific [spəˈsɪfɪk] *adj* específico; **~ally** *adv* específicamente

specify ['spɛsɪfaɪ] *vt, vi* especificar, precisar

specimen ['spɛsɪmən] *n* ejemplar *m*; (MED: *of urine*) espécimen *m* (: *of blood*) muestra

speck [spɛk] *n* grano, mota

speckled ['spɛkld] *adj* moteado

specs [spɛks] (*inf*) *npl* gafas *fpl* (SP), anteojos *mpl*

spectacle ['spɛktəkl] *n* espectáculo; **~s** *npl* (BRIT: *glasses*) gafas *fpl* (SP), anteojos *mpl*; **spectacular** [-'tækjulə*] *adj* espectacular; (*success*) impresionante

spectator [spɛkˈteɪtə*] *n* espectador(a) *m/f*

spectre ['spɛktə*] (US **specter**) *n* espectro, fantasma *m*

spectrum ['spɛktrəm] (*pl* **spectra**) *n* espectro

speculate ['spɛkjuleɪt] *vi*: **to** ~ **(on)** especular (en)

speculation [spɛkjuˈleɪʃən] *n* especulación *f*

speech [spiːtʃ] *n* (*faculty*) habla; (*formal talk*) discurso; (*spoken language*) lenguaje *m*; **~less** *adj* mudo, estupefacto; ~ **therapist** *n* especialista que corrige defectos de pronunciación en los niños

speed [spiːd] *n* velocidad *f*; (*haste*) prisa; (*promptness*) rapidez *f*; **at full** *or* **top** ~ a máxima velocidad; ~ **up** *vi* acelerarse ♦ *vt* acelerar; **~boat** *n* lancha motora; **~ily** *adv* rápido, rápidamente; **~ing** *n* (AUT) exceso de velocidad; ~ **limit** *n* límite *m* de velocidad, velocidad *f* máxima; **~ometer** [spɪˈdɔmɪtə*] *n* velocímetro; **~way** *n* (*sport*) pista de carrera; **~y** *adj* (*fast*) veloz, rápido; (*prompt*) pronto

spell [spɛl] (*pt, pp* **spelt** (BRIT) *or* **spelled**) *n* (*also: magic* ~) encanto, hechizo; (*period of time*) rato, período ♦ *vt* deletrear; (*fig*) anunciar, presagiar; **to cast a** ~ **on sb** hechizar a uno; **he can't** ~ pone faltas de ortografía; **~bound** *adj* embelesado, hechizado; **~ing** *n* ortografía

spend [spɛnd] (*pt, pp* **spent**) *vt* (*money*) gastar; (*time*) pasar; (*life*) dedicar; **~thrift** *n* derrochador(a) *m/f*, pródigo/a

sperm [spəːm] *n* esperma

spew [spjuː] *vt* vomitar, arrojar

sphere [sfɪə*] *n* esfera

sphinx [sfɪŋks] *n* esfinge *f*

spice [spaɪs] *n* especia ♦ *vt* condimentar

spick-and-span ['spɪkən'spæn] *adj* aseado, (bien) arreglado

spicy ['spaɪsɪ] *adj* picante

spider ['spaɪdə*] *n* araña

spike [spaɪk] *n* (*point*) punta; (*BOT*) espiga

spill [spɪl] (*pt, pp* **spilt** *or* **spilled**) *vt* derramar, verter ♦ *vi* derramarse; **to ~ over** desbordarse

spin [spɪn] (*pt, pp* **spun**) *n* (*AVIAT*) barrena; (*trip in car*) paseo (en coche); (*on ball*) efecto ♦ *vt* (*wool etc*) hilar; (*ball etc*) hacer girar ♦ *vi* girar, dar vueltas; ~ **out** *vt* alargar, prolongar

spinach ['spɪnɪtʃ] *n* espinaca; (*as food*) espinacas *fpl*

spinal ['spaɪnl] *adj* espinal; ~ **cord** *n* columna vertebral

spindly ['spɪndlɪ] *adj* (*leg*) zanquivano

spin doctor *n* informador(a) parcial al servicio de un partido político etc

spin-dryer (*BRIT*) *n* secador *m* centrifugo

spine [spaɪn] *n* espinazo, columna vertebral; (*thorn*) espina; ~**less** *adj* (*fig*) débil, pusilánime

spinning ['spɪnɪŋ] *n* hilandería; ~ **top** *n* peonza; ~ **wheel** *n* torno de hilar

spin-off *n* derivado, producto secundario

spinster ['spɪnstə*] *n* solterona

spiral ['spaɪərl] *n* espiral *f* ♦ *vi* (*fig: prices*) subir desorbitadamente; ~ **staircase** *n* escalera de caracol

spire ['spaɪə*] *n* aguja, chapitel *m*

spirit ['spɪrɪt] *n* (*soul*) alma *f*; (*ghost*) fantasma *m*; (*attitude, sense*) espíritu *m*; (*courage*) valor *m*, ánimo; ~**s** *npl* (*drink*) licor(es) *m(pl)*; **in good ~s** alegre, de buen ánimo; ~**ed** *adj* enérgico, vigoroso; ~ **level** *n* nivel *m* de aire

spiritual ['spɪrɪtjuəl] *adj* espiritual ♦ *n* espiritual *m*

spit [spɪt] (*pt, pp* **spat**) *n* (*for roasting*) asador *m*, espetón *m*; (*saliva*) saliva ♦ *vi* escupir; (*sound*) chisporrotear; (*rain*) lloviznar

spite [spaɪt] *n* rencor *m*, ojeriza ♦ *vt* causar pena a, mortificar; **in ~ of** a pesar de, pese a; ~**ful** *adj* rencoroso, malévolo

spittle ['spɪtl] *n* saliva, baba

splash [splæʃ] *n* (*sound*) chapoteo; (*of colour*) mancha ♦ *vt* salpicar ♦ *vi* (*also: ~ about*) chapotear

spleen [spliːn] *n* (*ANAT*) bazo

splendid ['splendɪd] *adj* espléndido

splint [splɪnt] *n* tablilla

splinter ['splɪntə*] *n* (*of wood etc*) astilla; (*in finger*) espigón *m* ♦ *vi* astillarse, hacer astillas

split [splɪt] (*pt, pp* **split**) *n* hendedura, raja; (*fig*) división *f*; (*POL*) escisión *f* ♦ *vt* partir, rajar; (*party*) dividir; (*share*) repartir ♦ *vi* dividirse, escindirse; ~ **up** *vi* (*couple*) separarse; (*meeting*) acabarse

splutter ['splʌtə*] *vi* chisporrotear; (*person*) balbucear

spoil [spɔɪl] (*pt, pp* **spoilt** *or* **spoiled**) *vt* (*damage*) dañar; (*mar*) estropear; (*child*) mimar, consentir; ~**s** *npl* despojo, botín *m*; ~**sport** *n* aguafiestas *m inv*

spoke [spəuk] *pt of* **speak** ♦ *n* rayo, radio

spoken ['spəukn] *pp of* **speak**

spokesman ['spəuksmən] *n* portavoz *m*; **spokeswoman** ['spəukswumən] *n* portavoz *f*

sponge [spʌndʒ] *n* esponja; (*also: ~ cake*) bizcocho ♦ *vt* (*wash*) lavar con esponja ♦ *vi*: **to ~ off** *or* **on sb** vivir a costa de uno; ~ **bag** (*BRIT*) *n* esponjera

sponsor ['spɒnsə*] *n* patrocinador(a) *m/f* ♦ *vt* (*applicant, proposal etc*) proponer; ~**ship** *n* patrocinio

spontaneous [spɒn'teɪnɪəs] *adj* espontáneo

spooky ['spuːkɪ] (*inf*) *adj* espeluznante, horripilante

spool [spuːl] *n* carrete *m*

spoon [spuːn] *n* cuchara; ~**-feed** *vt* dar de comer con cuchara a; (*fig*) tratar como un niño a; ~**ful** *n* cucharada

sport [spɔːt] *n* deporte *m*; (*person*): **to be a good ~** ser muy majo ♦ *vt* (*wear*) lucir, ostentar; ~**ing** *adj* deportivo; (*generous*) caballeroso; **to give sb a ~ing chance**

darle a uno una (buena) oportunidad; ~ **jacket** (*US*) n = ~**s jacket**; ~**s car** n coche m deportivo; ~**s jacket** (*BRIT*) n chaqueta deportiva; ~**sman** n deportista m; ~**smanship** n deportividad f; ~**swear** n trajes mpl de deporte *or* sport; ~**swoman** n deportista f; ~**y** adj deportista

spot [spɔt] n sitio, lugar m; (*dot: on pattern*) punto, mancha; (*pimple*) grano; (*RADIO*) cuña publicitaria; (*TV*) espacio publicitario; (*small amount*): **a ~ of** un poquito de ♦ vt (*notice*) notar, observar; **on the ~** allí mismo; ~ **check** n reconocimiento rápido; ~**less** adj perfectamente limpio; ~**light** n foco, reflector m; (*AUT*) faro auxiliar; ~**ted** adj (*pattern*) de puntos; ~**ty** adj (*face*) con granos

spouse [spauz] n cónyuge m/f

spout [spaut] n (*of jug*) pico; (*of pipe*) caño ♦ vi salir en chorro

sprain [spreɪn] n torcedura ♦ vt: **to ~ one's ankle/wrist** torcerse el tobillo/la muñeca

sprang [spræŋ] pt of **spring**

sprawl [sprɔːl] vi tumbarse

spray [spreɪ] n rociada; (*of sea*) espuma; (*container*) atomizador m; (*for paint etc*) pistola rociadora; (*of flowers*) ramita ♦ vt rociar; (*crops*) regar

spread [sprɛd] (pt, pp **spread**) n extensión f; (*for bread etc*) pasta para untar; (*inf: food*) comilona ♦ vt extender; (*butter*) untar; (*wings, sails*) desplegar; (*work, wealth*) repartir; (*scatter*) esparcir ♦ vi (*also: ~ out: stain*) extenderse; (*news*) diseminarse; ~ **out** vi (*move apart*) separarse; ~**-eagled** adj a pata tendida; ~**sheet** n (*COMPUT*) hoja electrónica *or* de cálculo

spree [spriː] n: **to go on a ~** ir de juerga

sprightly [spraɪtlɪ] adj vivo, enérgico

spring [sprɪŋ] (pt **sprang**, pp **sprung**) n (*season*) primavera; (*leap*) salto, brinco; (*coiled metal*) resorte m; (*of water*) fuente f, manantial m ♦ vi saltar, brincar; ~ **up** vi (*thing: appear*) aparecer; (*problem*) surgir; ~**board** n trampolín m; ~-

clean(ing) n limpieza general; ~**time** n primavera

sprinkle [sprɪŋkl] vt (*pour: liquid*) rociar; (*: salt, sugar*) espolvorear; **to ~ water etc on,** ~ **with water etc** rociar *or* salpicar de agua etc; ~r n (*for lawn*) rociadera; (*to put out fire*) aparato de rociadura automática

sprint [sprɪnt] n esprint m ♦ vi esprintar

sprout [spraut] vi brotar, retoñar; (*Brussels*) ~**s** npl coles fpl de Bruselas

spruce [spruːs] n inv (*BOT*) pícea ♦ adj aseado, pulcro

sprung [sprʌŋ] pp of **spring**

spry [spraɪ] adj ágil, activo

spun [spʌn] pt, pp of **spin**

spur [spəː*] n espuela; (*fig*) estímulo, aguijón m ♦ vt (*also: ~ on*) estimular, incitar; **on the ~ of the moment** de improviso

spurious [spjuərɪəs] adj falso

spurn [spəːn] vt desdeñar, rechazar

spurt [spəːt] n chorro; (*of energy*) arrebato ♦ vi chorrear

spy [spaɪ] n espía m/f ♦ vi: **to ~ on** espiar a ♦ vt (*see*) divisar, lograr ver; ~**ing** n espionaje m

sq. abbr = **square**

squabble [skwɔbl] vi reñir, pelear

squad [skwɔd] n (*MIL*) pelotón m; (*POLICE*) brigada; (*SPORT*) equipo

squadron [skwɔdrn] n (*MIL*) escuadrón m; (*AVIAT, NAUT*) escuadra

squalid [skwɔlɪd] adj vil; (*fig: sordid*) sórdido

squall [skwɔːl] n (*storm*) chubasco; (*wind*) ráfaga

squalor [skwɔlə*] n miseria

squander [skwɔndə*] vt (*money*) derrochar, despilfarrar; (*chances*) desperdiciar

square [skwɛə*] n cuadro; (*in town*) plaza; (*inf: person*) carca m/f ♦ adj cuadrado; (*inf: ideas, tastes*) trasnochado ♦ vt (*arrange*) arreglar; (*MATH*) cuadrar; (*reconcile*) compaginar; **all ~** igual(es); **to have a ~ meal** comer caliente; **2 metres ~ 2** metros en cuadro; **2 ~ metres** 2 metros cuadrados; ~**ly** adv de lleno

squash [skwɔʃ] *n* (*BRIT*: *drink*): **lemon/ orange ~** zumo *m* (*SP*) *or* jugo (*AM*) de limón/naranja; (*US*: *BOT*) calabacín *m*; (*SPORT*) squash *m*, frontenis *m* ♦ *vt* aplastar

squat [skwɔt] *adj* achaparrado ♦ *vi* (*also*: *~ down*) agacharse, sentarse en cuclillas; **~ter** *n* persona que ocupa ilegalmente una casa

squawk [skwɔːk] *vi* graznar

squeak [skwiːk] *vi* (*hinge*) chirriar, rechinar; (*mouse*) chillar

squeal [skwiːl] *vi* chillar, dar gritos agudos

squeamish ['skwiːmɪʃ] *adj* delicado, remilgado

squeeze [skwiːz] *n* presión *f*; (*of hand*) apretón *m*; (*COMM*) restricción *f* ♦ *vt* (*hand*, *arm*) apretar; **~ out** *vt* exprimir

squelch [skweltʃ] *vi* chapotear

squid [skwɪd] *n inv* calamar *m*; (*CULIN*) calamares *mpl*

squiggle ['skwɪgl] *n* garabato

squint [skwɪnt] *vi* bizquear, ser bizco ♦ *n* (*MED*) estrabismo

squire ['skwaɪə*] (*BRIT*) *n* terrateniente *m*

squirm [skwəːm] *vi* retorcerse, revolverse

squirrel ['skwɪrəl] *n* ardilla

squirt [skwəːt] *vi* salir a chorros ♦ *vt* chiscar

Sr *abbr* = **senior**

St *abbr* = **saint; street**

stab [stæb] *n* (*with knife*) puñalada; (*of pain*) pinchazo; (*inf*: *try*): **to have a ~ at (doing) sth** intentar (hacer) algo ♦ *vt* apuñalar

stable ['steɪbl] *adj* estable ♦ *n* cuadra, caballeriza

stack [stæk] *n* montón *m*, pila ♦ *vt* amontonar, apilar

stadium ['steɪdɪəm] *n* estadio

staff [stɑːf] *n* (*work force*) personal *m*, plantilla; (*BRIT*: *SCOL*) cuerpo docente ♦ *vt* proveer de personal

stag [stæg] *n* ciervo, venado

stage [steɪdʒ] *n* escena; (*point*) etapa; (*platform*) plataforma; (*profession*): **the ~** el teatro ♦ *vt* (*play*) poner en escena, representar; (*organize*) montar, organi-

zar; **in ~s** por etapas; **~coach** *n* diligencia; **~ manager** *n* director(a) *m/f* de escena

stagger ['stægə*] *vi* tambalearse ♦ *vt* (*amaze*) asombrar; (*hours*, *holidays*) escalonar; **~ing** *adj* asombroso

stagnant ['stægnənt] *adj* estancado

stagnate [stæg'neɪt] *vi* estancarse

stag party *n* despedida de soltero

staid [steɪd] *adj* serio, formal

stain [steɪn] *n* mancha; (*colouring*) tintura ♦ *vt* manchar; (*wood*) teñir; **~ed glass window** *n* vidriera de colores; **~less steel** *n* acero inoxidable; **~ remover** *n* quitamanchas *m inv*

stair [stɛə*] *n* (*step*) peldaño, escalón *m*; **~s** *npl* escaleras *fpl*; **~case** *n* = **~way**; **~way** *n* escalera

stake [steɪk] *n* estaca, poste *m*; (*COMM*) interés *m*; (*BETTING*) apuesta ♦ *vt* (*money*) apostar; (*life*) arriesgar; (*reputation*) poner en juego; (*claim*) presentar una reclamación; **to be at ~** estar en juego

stale [steɪl] *adj* (*bread*) duro; (*food*) pasado; (*smell*) rancio; (*beer*) agrio

stalemate ['steɪlmeɪt] *n* tablas *fpl* (por ahogado); (*fig*) estancamiento

stalk [stɔːk] *n* tallo, caña ♦ *vt* acechar, cazar al acecho; **~ off** *vi* irse airado

stall [stɔːl] *n* (*in market*) puesto; (*in stable*) casilla (de establo) ♦ *vt* (*AUT*) calar; (*fig*) dar largas a ♦ *vi* (*AUT*) calarse; (*fig*) andarse con rodeos; **~s** *npl* (*BRIT*: *in cinema*, *theatre*) butacas *fpl*

stallion ['stælɪən] *n* semental *m*

stalwart ['stɔːlwət] *n* leal

stamina ['stæmɪnə] *n* resistencia

stammer ['stæmə*] *n* tartamudeo ♦ *vi* tartamudear

stamp [stæmp] *n* sello, estampilla (*AM*); (*mark*, *also fig*) marca, huella; (*on document*) timbre *m* ♦ *vi* (*also*: *~ one's foot*) patear ♦ *vt* (*mark*) marcar; (*letter*) poner sellos *or* estampillas en; (*with rubber ~*) sellar; **~ album** *n* álbum *m* para sellos *or* estampillas; **~ collecting** *n* filatelia

stampede [stæm'piːd] *n* estampida

stance [stæns] *n* postura

stand [stænd] (*pt, pp* **stood**) *n* (*position*)
posición *f*, postura; (*for taxis*) parada;
(*hall ~*) perchero; (*music ~*) atril *m*;
(*SPORT*) tribuna; (*at exhibition*) stand *m*
♦ *vi* (*be*) estar, encontrarse; (*be on foot*)
estar de pie; (*rise*) levantarse; (*remain*)
quedar en pie; (*in election*) presentar
candidatura ♦ *vt* (*place*) poner, colocar;
(*withstand*) aguantar, soportar; (*invite to*)
invitar; **to make a ~** (*fig*) mantener una
postura firme; **to ~ for parliament**
(*BRIT*) presentarse (como candidato) a las
elecciones; **~ by** *vi* (*be ready*) estar listo
♦ *vt fus* (*opinion*) aferrarse a; (*person*)
apoyar; **~ down** *vi* (*withdraw*) ceder el
puesto; **~ for** *vt fus* (*signify*) significar;
(*tolerate*) aguantar, permitir; **~ in for** *vt
fus* suplir a; **~ out** *vi* destacarse; **~ up** *vi*
levantarse, ponerse de pie; **~ up for** *vt
fus* defender; **~ up to** *vt fus* hacer frente
a

standard ['stændəd] *n* patrón *m*, norma;
(*level*) nivel *m*; (*flag*) estandarte *m* ♦ *adj*
(*size etc*) normal, corriente; (*text*) básico;
~s *npl* (*morals*) valores *mpl* morales;
~ize *vt* normalizar; **~ lamp** (*BRIT*) *n*
lámpara de pie; **~ of living** *n* nivel *m* de
vida

stand-by ['stændbaɪ] *n* (*reserve*) recurso
seguro; **to be on ~** estar sobre aviso; **~
ticket** *n* (*AVIAT*) (billete *m*) standby *m*

stand-in ['stændɪn] *n* suplente *m/f*

standing ['stændɪŋ] *adj* (*on foot*) de pie,
en pie; (*permanent*) permanente ♦ *n*
reputación *f*; **of many years'** que
lleva muchos años; **~ joke** *n* broma
permanente; **~ order** (*BRIT*) *n* (*at bank*)
orden *f* de pago permanente; **~ room** *n*
sitio para estar de pie

stand: **~-offish** *adj* reservado, poco
afable; **~point** *n* punto de vista; **~still** *n*:
at a ~still (*industry, traffic*) paralizado;
(*car*) parado; **to come to a ~still** quedar
paralizado; pararse

stank [stæŋk] *pt of* **stink**

staple ['steɪpl] *n* (*for papers*) grapa ♦ *adj*
(*food etc*) básico ♦ *vt* grapar; **~r** *n*
grapadora

star [stɑ:*] *n* estrella; (*celebrity*) estrella,

astro ♦ *vt* (*THEATRE, CINEMA*) ser el/la
protagonista de; **the ~s** *npl* (*ASTROLOGY*) el
horóscopo

starboard ['stɑ:bəd] *n* estribor *m*

starch [stɑ:tʃ] *n* almidón *m*

stardom ['stɑ:dəm] *n* estrellato

stare [stɛə*] *n* mirada fija ♦ *vi*: **to ~ at**
mirar fijo

starfish ['stɑ:fɪʃ] *n* estrella de mar

stark [stɑ:k] *adj* (*bleak*) severo, escueto
♦ *adv*: **~ naked** en cueros

starling ['stɑ:lɪŋ] *n* estornino

starry ['stɑ:rɪ] *adj* estrellado; **~-eyed** *adj*
(*innocent*) inocentón/ona, ingenuo

start [stɑ:t] *n* principio, comienzo;
(*departure*) salida; (*sudden movement*)
salto, sobresalto; (*advantage*) ventaja
♦ *vt* empezar, comenzar; (*cause*) causar;
(*found*) fundar; (*engine*) poner en marcha
♦ *vi* comenzar, empezar; (*with fright*)
asustarse, sobresaltarse; (*train etc*) salir;
to ~ doing *or* **to do sth** empezar a
hacer algo; **~ off** *vi* empezar, comenzar;
(*leave*) salir, ponerse en camino; **~ up** *vi*
comenzar; (*car*) ponerse en marcha ♦ *vt*
comenzar; poner en marcha; **~er** *n* (*AUT*)
botón *m* de arranque; (*SPORT: official*)
juez *m/f* de salida; (*BRIT: CULIN*) entrada;
~ing point *n* punto de partida

startle ['stɑ:tl] *vt* asustar, sobrecoger;
startling *adj* alarmante

starvation [stɑ:'veɪʃən] *n* hambre *f*

starve [stɑ:v] *vi* tener mucha hambre; (*to
death*) morir de hambre ♦ *vt* hacer pasar
hambre

state [steɪt] *n* estado ♦ *vt* (*say, declare*)
afirmar; **the S~s** los Estados Unidos; **to
be in a ~** estar agitado; (*of anxiety*) maje-
tuoso, imponente; **~ment** *n* afirmación *f*;
statesman *n* estadista *m*

static ['stætɪk] *n* (*RADIO*) parásitos *mpl*
♦ *adj* estático; **~ electricity** *n* estática

station ['steɪʃən] *n* (*gen*) estación *f*;
(*RADIO*) emisora; (*rank*) posición *f* social
♦ *vt* colocar, situar; (*MIL*) apostar

stationary ['steɪʃnərɪ] *adj* estacionario,
fijo

stationer ['steɪʃənə*] *n* papelero/a; **~'s
(shop)** (*BRIT*) *n* papelería; **~y** [-nərɪ] *n*

papel *m* de escribir, artículos *mpl* de escritorio

station master *n* (RAIL) jefe *m* de estación

station wagon (US) *n* ranchera

statistic [stə'tɪstɪk] *n* estadística; **~al** *adj* estadístico; **~s** *n* (science) estadística

statue ['stætjuː] *n* estatua

status ['steɪtəs] *n* estado; (reputation) estatus *m*; **~ symbol** *n* símbolo de prestigio

statute ['stætjuːt] *n* estatuto, ley *f*; **statutory** *adj* estatutario

staunch [stɔːntʃ] *adj* leal, incondicional

stave [steɪv] *vt*: **to ~ off** (attack) rechazar; (threat) evitar

stay [steɪ] *n* estancia ♦ *vi* quedar(se); (as guest) hospedarse; **to ~ put** seguir en el mismo sitio; **to ~ the night/5 days** pasar la noche/estar 5 días; **~ behind** *vi* quedar atrás; **~ in** *vi* quedarse en casa; **~ on** *vi* quedarse; **~ out** *vi* (of house) no volver a casa; (on strike) permanecer en huelga; **~ up** *vi* (at night) velar, no acostarse; **~ing power** *n* aguante *m*

stead [stɛd] *n*: **in sb's ~** en lugar de uno; **to stand sb in good ~** ser muy útil a uno

steadfast ['stɛdfɑːst] *adj* firme, resuelto

steadily ['stɛdɪlɪ] *adv* constantemente; (firmly) firmemente; (work, walk) sin parar; (gaze) fijamente

steady ['stɛdɪ] *adj* (firm) firme; (regular) regular; (person, character) sensato, juicioso; (boyfriend) formal; (look, voice) tranquilo ♦ *vt* (stabilize) estabilizar; (nerves) calmar

steak [steɪk] *n* (gen) filete *m*; (beef) bistec *m*

steal [stiːl] (pt **stole**, pp **stolen**) *vt* robar ♦ *vi* robar; (move secretly) andar a hurtadillas

stealth [stɛlθ] *n*: **by ~** a escondidas, sigilosamente; **~y** *adj* cauteloso, sigiloso

steam [stiːm] *n* vapor *m*; (mist) vaho, humo ♦ *vt* (CULIN) cocer al vapor ♦ *vi* echar vapor; **~ engine** *n* máquina de vapor; **~er** *n* (buque *m* de) vapor *m*; **~roller** *n* apisonadora; **~ship** *n* = **~er**;

~y *adj* (room) lleno de vapor; (window) empañado; (heat, atmosphere) bochornoso

steel [stiːl] *n* acero ♦ *adj* de acero; **~works** *n* acería

steep [stiːp] *adj* escarpado, abrupto; (stair) empinado; (price) exorbitante, excesivo ♦ *vt* empapar, remojar

steeple ['stiːpl] *n* aguja; **~chase** *n* carrera de obstáculos

steer [stɪə*] *vt* (car) conducir (SP), manejar (AM); (person) dirigir ♦ *vi* conducir, manejar; **~ing** *n* (AUT) dirección *f*; **~ing wheel** *n* volante *m*

stem [stɛm] *n* (of plant) tallo; (of glass) pie *m* ♦ *vt* detener; (blood) restañar; **~ from** *vt fus* ser consecuencia de

stench [stɛntʃ] *n* hedor *m*

stencil ['stɛnsl] *n* (pattern) plantilla ♦ *vt* hacer un cliché de

stenographer [stɛ'nɔɡrəfə*] (US) *n* taquígrafo/a

step [stɛp] *n* paso; (on stair) peldaño, escalón *m* ♦ *vi*: **to ~ forward/back** dar un paso adelante/hacia atrás; **~s** *npl* (BRIT) = **~ladder**; **in/out of ~ (with)** acorde/en disonancia (con); **~ down** *vi* (fig) retirarse; **~ on** *vt fus* pisar; **~ up** *vt* (increase) aumentar; **~brother** *n* hermanastro; **~daughter** *n* hijastra; **~father** *n* padrastro; **~ladder** *n* escalera doble *or* de tijera; **~mother** *n* madrastra; **~ping stone** *n* pasadera; **~sister** *n* hermanastra; **~son** *n* hijastro

stereo ['stɛrɪəu] *n* estéreo ♦ *adj* (also: **~phonic**) estéreo, estereofónico

sterile ['stɛraɪl] *adj* estéril; **sterilize** ['stɛrɪlaɪz] *vt* esterilizar

sterling ['stɜːlɪŋ] *adj* (silver) de ley ♦ *n* (ECON) (libras *fpl*) esterlinas *fpl*; **one pound ~** una libra esterlina

stern [stɜːn] *adj* severo, austero ♦ *n* (NAUT) popa

stethoscope ['stɛθəskəup] *n* estetoscopio

stew [stjuː] *n* cocido (SP), estofado (SP), guisado (AM) ♦ *vt* estofar, guisar; (fruit) cocer

steward ['stjuːəd] *n* camarero; **~ess** *n* (esp on plane) azafata

stick [stɪk] (*pt, pp* **stuck**) *n* palo; (*of dynamite*) barreno; (*as weapon*) porra; (*walking ~*) bastón *m* ♦ *vt* (*glue*) pegar; (*inf: put*) meter; (: *tolerate*) aguantar, soportar; (*thrust*): **to ~ sth into** clavar *or* hincar algo en ♦ *vi* pegarse; (*be unmoveable*) quedarse parado; (*in mind*) quedarse grabado; **~ out** *vi* sobresalir; **~ up** *vi* sobresalir; **~ up for** *vt fus* defender; **~er** *n* (*label*) etiqueta engomada; (*with slogan*) pegatina; **~ing plaster** *n* esparadrapo

stickler ['stɪklə*] *n*: **to be a ~ for** insistir mucho en

stick-up ['stɪkʌp] (*inf*) *n* asalto, atraco

sticky ['stɪkɪ] *adj* pegajoso; (*label*) engomado; (*fig*) difícil

stiff [stɪf] *adj* rígido, tieso; (*hard*) duro; (*manner*) estirado; (*difficult*) difícil; (*person*) inflexible; (*price*) exorbitante ♦ *adv*: **scared/bored ~** muerto de miedo/aburrimiento; **~en** *vi* (*muscles etc*) agarrotarse; **~ neck** *n* tortícolis *m inv*; **~ness** *n* rigidez *f*, tiesura

stifle ['staɪfl] *vt* ahogar, sofocar; **stifling** *adj* (*heat*) sofocante, bochornoso

stigma ['stɪɡmə] *n* (*fig*) estigma *m*

stile [staɪl] *n* portillo, portilla

stiletto [stɪ'letəʊ] (*BRIT*) *n* (*also*: ~ *heel*) tacón *m* de aguja

still [stɪl] *adj* inmóvil, quieto ♦ *adv* todavía; (*even*) aun; (*nonetheless*) sin embargo, aun así; **~born** *adj* nacido muerto; **~ life** *n* naturaleza muerta

stilt [stɪlt] *n* zanco; (*pile*) pilar *m*, soporte *m*

stilted ['stɪltɪd] *adj* afectado

stimulate ['stɪmjuleɪt] *vt* estimular

stimuli ['stɪmjulaɪ] *npl of* **stimulus**

stimulus ['stɪmjuləs] (*pl* **stimuli**) *n* estímulo, incentivo

sting [stɪŋ] (*pt, pp* **stung**) *n* picadura; (*pain*) escozor *m*, picazón *f*; (*organ*) aguijón *m* ♦ *vt, vi* picar

stingy ['stɪndʒɪ] *adj* tacaño

stink [stɪŋk] (*pt* **stank**, *pp* **stunk**) *n* hedor *m*, tufo ♦ *vi* heder, apestar; **~ing** *adj* hediondo, fétido; (*fig: inf*) horrible

stint [stɪnt] *n* tarea, trabajo ♦ *vi*: **to ~ on** escatimar

stir [stə:*] *n* (*fig: agitation*) conmoción *f* ♦ *vt* (*tea etc*) remover; (*fig: emotions*) provocar ♦ *vi* moverse; **~ up** *vt* (*trouble*) fomentar

stirrup ['stɪrəp] *n* estribo

stitch [stɪtʃ] *n* (*SEWING*) puntada; (*KNITTING*) punto; (*MED*) punto (de sutura); (*pain*) punzada ♦ *vt* coser; (*MED*) suturar

stoat [stəʊt] *n* armiño

stock [stɔk] *n* (*COMM: reserves*) existencias *fpl*, stock *m*; (: *selection*) surtido; (*AGR*) ganado, ganadería; (*CULIN*) caldo; (*descent*) raza, estirpe *f*; (*FINANCE*) capital *m* ♦ *adj* (*fig: reply etc*) clásico ♦ *vt* (*have in ~*) tener existencias de; **~s and shares** acciones y valores; **in ~** en existencia *or* almacén; **out of ~** agotado; **to take ~ of** (*fig*) asesorar, examinar; **~ up with** *vt fus* abastecerse de; **~broker** ['stɔkbrəʊkə*] *n* agente *m/f* *or* corredor(a) *m/f* de bolsa; **~ cube** (*BRIT*) *n* pastilla de caldo; **~ exchange** *n* bolsa

stocking ['stɔkɪŋ] *n* media

stock: **~ist** (*BRIT*) *n* distribuidor(a) *m/f*; **~ market** *n* bolsa (de valores); **~ phrase** *n* cliché *m*; **~pile** *n* reserva ♦ *vt* acumular, almacenar; **~taking** (*BRIT*) *n* (*COMM*) inventario

stocky ['stɔkɪ] *adj* (*strong*) robusto; (*short*) achaparrado

stodgy ['stɔdʒɪ] *adj* indigesto, pesado

stoke [stəʊk] *vt* atizar

stole [stəʊl] *pt of* **steal** ♦ *n* estola

stolen ['stəʊln] *pp of* **steal**

stolid ['stɔlɪd] *adj* imperturbable, impasible

stomach ['stʌmək] *n* (*ANAT*) estómago; (*belly*) vientre *m* ♦ *vt* tragar, aguantar; **~ache** *n* dolor *m* de estómago

stone [stəʊn] *n* piedra; (*in fruit*) hueso; = *6.348kg; 14 libras* ♦ *adj* de piedra ♦ *vt* apedrear; (*fruit*) deshuesar; **~-cold** *adj* helado; **~-deaf** *adj* sordo como una tapia; **~work** *n* (*art*) cantería; **stony** *adj* pedregoso; (*fig*) frío

stood [stud] *pt, pp of* **stand**

stool [stu:l] *n* taburete *m*

stoop [stu:p] *vi* (*also*: ~ *down*) doblarse,

agacharse; (*also*: *have a ~*) ser cargado de espaldas

stop [stɔp] *n* parada; (*in punctuation*) punto ♦ *vt* parar, detener; (*break off*) suspender; (*block*: *pay*) suspender; (: *cheque*) invalidar; (*also*: *put a ~ to*) poner término a ♦ *vi* pararse, detenerse; (*end*) acabarse; **to ~ doing sth** dejar de hacer algo; **~ dead** *vi* pararse en seco; **~ off** *vi* interrumpir el viaje; **~ up** *vt* (*hole*) tapar; **~gap** *n* (*person*) interino/a; (*thing*) recurso provisional; **~over** *n* parada; (*AVIAT*) escala

stoppage ['stɔpɪdʒ] *n* (*strike*) paro *m*; (*blockage*) obstrucción *f*

stopper ['stɔpə*] *n* tapón *m*

stop press *n* noticias *fpl* de última hora

stopwatch ['stɔpwɔtʃ] *n* cronómetro *m*

storage ['stɔ:rɪdʒ] *n* almacenaje *m*; **~ heater** *n* acumulador *m*

store [stɔ:*] *n* (*stock*) provisión *f*; (*depot*: *BRIT*: *large shop*) almacén *m*; (*US*) tienda; (*reserve*) reserva, repuesto ♦ *vt* almacenar; **~s** *npl* víveres *mpl*; **in ~** (*fig*): **to be in ~ for sb** esperarle a uno; **~ up** *vt* acumular; **~room** *n* despensa

storey ['stɔ:rɪ] (*US* **story**) *n* piso

stork [stɔ:k] *n* cigüeña

storm [stɔ:m] *n* tormenta; (*fig*: *of applause*) salva; (: *of criticism*) nube *f* ♦ *vi* (*fig*) rabiar ♦ *vt* tomar por asalto; **~y** *adj* tempestuoso

story ['stɔ:rɪ] *n* historia; (*lie*) mentira; (*US*) = **storey**; **~book** *n* libro de cuentos

stout [staut] *adj* (*strong*) sólido; (*fat*) gordo, corpulento; (*resolute*) resuelto ♦ *n* cerveza negra

stove [stəuv] *n* (*for cooking*) cocina; (*for heating*) estufa

stow [stəu] *vt* (*also*: ~ *away*) meter, poner; (*NAUT*) estibar; **~away** *n* polizón/ona *m/f*

straddle ['strædl] *vt* montar a horcajadas; (*fig*) abarcar

straggle ['strægl] *vi* (*houses etc*) extenderse; (*lag behind*) rezagarse; **straggly** *adj* (*hair*) desordenado

straight [streɪt] *adj* recto, derecho;

(*frank*) franco, directo; (*simple*) sencillo ♦ *adv* derecho, directamente; (*drink*) sin mezcla; **to put** *or* **set sth** en claro; **~ away**, **~ off** en seguida; **~en** *vt* (*also*: **~en out**) enderezar, poner derecho; **~-faced** *adj* serio; **~forward** *adj* (*simple*) sencillo; (*honest*) honrado, franco

strain [streɪn] *n* tensión *f*; (*TECH*) presión *f*; (*MED*) torcedura; (*breed*) tipo, variedad *f* ♦ *vt* (*back etc*) torcerse; (*resources*) agotar; (*stretch*) estirar; (*food, tea*) colar; **~s** *npl* (*MUS*) son *m*; **~ed** *adj* (*muscle*) torcido; (*laugh*) forzado; (*relations*) tenso; **~er** *n* colador *m*

strait [streɪt] *n* (*GEO*) estrecho; **to be in dire ~s** pasar grandes apuros; **~-jacket** *n* camisa de fuerza; **~-laced** *adj* mojigato, gazmoño

strand [strænd] *n* (*of thread*) hebra; (*of hair*) trenza; (*of rope*) ramal *m*

stranded ['strændɪd] *adj* (*person*: *without money*) desamparado; (: *without transport*) colgado

strange [streɪndʒ] *adj* (*not known*) desconocido; (*odd*) extraño, raro; **~ly** *adv* de un modo raro; *see also* **enough**; **~r** *n* desconocido/a; (*from another area*) forastero/a

strangle ['stræŋgl] *vt* estrangular; **~hold** *n* (*fig*) dominio completo

strap [stræp] *n* correa; (*of slip, dress*) tirante *m*

strapping ['stræpɪŋ] *adj* robusto, fornido

strategic [strə'ti:dʒɪk] *adj* estratégico

strategy ['strætɪdʒɪ] *n* estrategia

straw [strɔ:] *n* paja; (*drinking ~*) caña, pajita; **that's the last ~!** ¡eso es el colmo!

strawberry ['strɔ:bərɪ] *n* fresa (*SP*), frutilla (*AM*)

stray [streɪ] *adj* (*animal*) extraviado; (*bullet*) perdido; (*scattered*) disperso ♦ *vi* extraviarse, perderse; (*thoughts*) vagar

streak [stri:k] *n* raya; (*in hair*) raya ♦ *vt* rayar ♦ *vi*: **to ~ past** pasar como un rayo

stream [stri:m] *n* riachuelo, arroyo; (*of people, vehicles*) riada, caravana; (*of* *smoke, insults etc*) chorro ♦ *vt* (*SCOL*) dividir en grupos por habilidad ♦ *vi* correr, fluir; **to ~ in/out** (*people*) entrar/salir en tropel

streamer ['striːmə*] *n* serpentina

streamlined ['striːmlaɪnd] *adj* aerodinámico

street [striːt] *n* calle *f*; **~car** (*US*) *n* tranvía *m*; **~ lamp** *n* farol *m*; **~ plan** *n* plano; **~wise** (*inf*) *adj* que tiene mucha calle

strength [strɛŋθ] *n* fuerza; (*of girder, knot etc*) resistencia; (*fig: power*) poder *m*; **~en** *vt* fortalecer, reforzar

strenuous ['strɛnjuəs] *adj* (*energetic, determined*) enérgico

stress [strɛs] *n* presión *f*; (*mental strain*) estrés *m*; (*accent*) acento ♦ *vt* subrayar, recalcar; (*syllable*) acentuar

stretch [strɛtʃ] *n* (*of sand etc*) trecho ♦ *vi* estirarse; (*extend*): **to ~ to** *or* **as far as** extenderse hasta ♦ *vt* extender, estirar; (*make demands of*) exigir el máximo esfuerzo a; **~ out** *vi* tenderse ♦ *vt* (*arm etc*) extender; (*spread*) estirar

stretcher ['strɛtʃə*] *n* camilla

strewn [struːn] *adj*: **~ with** cubierto *or* sembrado de

stricken ['strɪkən] *adj* (*person*) herido; (*city, industry etc*) condenado; **~ with** (*disease*) afectado por

strict [strɪkt] *adj* severo; (*exact*) estricto; **~ly** *adv* severamente; estrictamente

stride [straɪd] *n* (*pt* **strode**, *pp* **stridden**) *n* zancada, tranco ♦ *vi* dar zancadas, andar a trancos

strident ['straɪdnt] *adj* estridente

strife [straɪf] *n* lucha

strike [straɪk] *n* (*pt*, *pp* **struck**) *n* huelga; (*of oil etc*) descubrimiento; (*attack*) ataque *m* ♦ *vt* golpear, pegar; (*oil etc*) descubrir; (*bargain, deal*) cerrar ♦ *vi* declarar la huelga; (*attack*) atacar; (*clock*) dar la hora; **on ~** (*workers*) en huelga; **to ~ a match** encender un fósforo; **~ down** *vt* derribar; **~ up** *vt* entablar; (*friendship*) trabar; **~r** *n* huelguista *m/f*; (*SPORT*) delantero; **striking** *adj* llamativo

string [strɪŋ] (*pt*, *pp* **strung**) *n* (*gen*) cuerda; (*row*) hilera ♦ *vt*: **to ~ together** ensartar; **to ~ out** extenderse; **the ~s** *npl* (*MUS*) los instrumentos de cuerda; **to pull ~s** (*fig*) mover palancas; **~ bean** *n* judía verde, habichuela; **~(ed) instrument** *n* (*MUS*) instrumento de cuerda

stringent ['strɪndʒənt] *adj* riguroso, severo

strip [strɪp] *n* tira; (*of land*) franja; (*of metal*) cinta, lámina ♦ *vt* desnudar; (*paint*) quitar; (*also*: **~ down**: *machine*) desmontar ♦ *vi* desnudarse; **~ cartoon** *n* tira cómica (*SP*), historieta (*AM*)

stripe [straɪp] *n* raya; (*MIL*) galón *m*; **~d** *adj* a rayas, rayado

strip lighting *n* alumbrado fluorescente

stripper ['strɪpə*] *n* artista *m/f* de striptease

strive [straɪv] (*pt* **strove**, *pp* **striven**) *vi*: **to ~ for sth/to do sth** luchar por conseguir/hacer algo; **striven** ['strɪvn] *pp* of **strive**

strode [strəud] *pt of* **stride**

stroke [strəuk] *n* (*blow*) golpe *m*; (*SWIMMING*) brazada; (*MED*) apoplejía; (*of paintbrush*) toque *m* ♦ *vt* acariciar; **at a ~ de un solo golpe**

stroll [strəul] *n* paseo, vuelta ♦ *vi* dar un paseo *or* una vuelta; **~er** (*US*) *n* (*for child*) sillita de ruedas

strong [strɔŋ] *adj* fuerte; **they are 50 ~** son 50; **~hold** *n* fortaleza; (*fig*) baluarte *m*; **~ly** *adv* fuertemente, con fuerza; (*believe*) firmemente; **~room** *n* cámara acorazada

strove [strəuv] *pt of* **strive**

struck [strʌk] *pt*, *pp of* **strike**

structure ['strʌktʃə*] *n* estructura; (*building*) construcción *f*

struggle ['strʌgl] *n* lucha ♦ *vi* luchar

strum [strʌm] *vt* (*guitar*) rasguear

strung [strʌŋ] *pt*, *pp of* **string**

strut [strʌt] *n* puntal *m* ♦ *vi* pavonearse

stub [stʌb] *n* (*of ticket etc*) talón *m*; (*of cigarette*) colilla; **to ~ one's toe on sth** dar con el dedo (del pie) contra algo; **~**

out *vt* apagar
stubble ['stʌbl] *n* rastrojo; (*on chin*) barba (incipiente)
stubborn ['stʌbən] *adj* terco, testarudo
stuck [stʌk] *pt, pp of* **stick** ♦ *adj* (*jammed*) atascado; **~-up** *adj* engreído, presumido
stud [stʌd] *n* (*shirt ~*) corchete *m*; (*of boot*) taco; (*earring*) pendiente *m* (de bolita); (*also*: *~ farm*) caballeriza; (*also*: *~ horse*) caballo semental ♦ *vt* (*fig*): **~ded with** salpicado de
student ['stju:dənt] *n* estudiante *m/f* ♦ *adj* estudiantil; **~ driver** (*US*) *n* aprendiz(a) *m/f*
studio ['stju:dɪəu] *n* estudio; (*artist's*) taller *m*; **~ flat** (*US* **~ apartment**) *n* estudio
studious ['stju:dɪəs] *adj* estudioso; (*studied*) calculado; **~ly** *adv* (*carefully*) con esmero
study ['stʌdɪ] *n* estudio ♦ *vt* estudiar; (*examine*) examinar, investigar ♦ *vi* estudiar
stuff [stʌf] *n* materia; (*substance*) material *m*, sustancia; (*things*) cosas *fpl* ♦ *vt* llenar; (*CULIN*) rellenar; (*animals*) disecar; (*inf: push*) meter; **~ing** *n* relleno; **~y** *adj* (*room*) mal ventilado; (*person*) de miras estrechas
stumble ['stʌmbl] *vi* tropezar, dar un traspié; **to ~ across, ~ on** (*fig*) tropezar con; **stumbling block** *n* tropiezo, obstáculo
stump [stʌmp] *n* (*of tree*) tocón *m*; (*of limb*) muñón *m* ♦ *vt*: **to be ~ed for an answer** no saber qué contestar
stun [stʌn] *vt* dejar sin sentido
stung [stʌŋ] *pt, pp of* **sting**
stunk [stʌŋk] *pp of* **stink**
stunning ['stʌnɪŋ] *adj* (*fig: news*) pasmoso; (: *outfit etc*) sensacional
stunt [stʌnt] *n* (*in film*) escena peligrosa; (*publicity ~*) truco publicitario; **~ed** *adj* enano, achaparrado; **~man** *n* doble *m*
stupefy ['stju:pɪfaɪ] *vt* dejar estupefacto
stupendous [stju:'pɛndəs] *adj* estupendo, asombroso
stupid ['stju:pɪd] *adj* estúpido, tonto; **~ity** [-'pɪdɪtɪ] *n* estupidez *f*
sturdy ['stɜ:dɪ] *adj* robusto, fuerte
stutter ['stʌtə*] *n* tartamudeo ♦ *vi* tartamudear
sty [staɪ] *n* (*for pigs*) pocilga
stye [staɪ] *n* (*MED*) orzuelo
style [staɪl] *n* estilo; **stylish** *adj* elegante, a la moda
stylus ['staɪləs] *adj* aguja
suave [swɑ:v] *adj* cortés
sub... [sʌb] *prefix* sub...; **~conscious** *adj* subconsciente; **~contract** *vt* subcontratar; **~divide** *vt* subdividir
subdue [səb'dju:] *vt* sojuzgar; (*passions*) dominar; **~d** *adj* (*light*) tenue; (*person*) sumiso, manso
subject [*n* 'sʌbdʒɪkt, *vb* səb'dʒɛkt] *n* súbdito; (*SCOL*) asignatura; (*matter*) tema *m*; (*GRAMMAR*) sujeto ♦ *vt*: **to be ~ to** someter a uno a algo; **to be ~ to** (*law*) estar sujeto a; (*subj: person*) ser propenso a; **~ive** [-'dʒɛktɪv] *adj* subjetivo; **~ matter** *n* (*content*) contenido
subjunctive [səb'dʒʌŋktɪv] *adj, n* subjuntivo
sublet [sʌb'lɛt] *vt* subarrendar
sub-machine-gun ['sʌbmə'ʃi:n-] *n* metralleta
submarine [sʌbmə'ri:n] *n* submarino
submerge [səb'mə:dʒ] *vt* sumergir ♦ *vi* sumergirse
submissive [səb'mɪsɪv] *adj* sumiso
submit [səb'mɪt] *vt* someter ♦ *vi*: **to ~ to sth** someterse a algo
subnormal [sʌb'nɔ:məl] *adj* anormal
subordinate [sə'bɔ:dɪnət] *adj, n* subordinado/a *m/f*
subpoena [səb'pi:nə] *n* (*LAW*) citación *f*
subscribe [səb'skraɪb] *vi* suscribir; **to ~ to** (*opinion, fund*) suscribir, aprobar; (*newspaper*) suscribirse a; **~r** *n* (*to periodical*) subscriptor(a) *m/f*; (*to telephone*) abonado/a
subscription [səb'skrɪpʃən] *n* abono; (*to magazine*) subscripción *f*
subsequent ['sʌbsɪkwənt] *adj* subsiguiente, posterior; **~ly** *adv* posteriormente, más tarde
subside [səb'saɪd] *vi* hundirse; (*flood*)

bajar; (*wind*) amainar; ~**nce** [-'saɪdns] *n* hundimiento; (*in road*) socavón *m*

subsidiarity [sʌbsɪdɪ'ærɪtɪ] *n* (*POL*) subsidiariedad *f*

subsidiary [səb'sɪdɪərɪ] *adj* secundario ♦ *n* (*also*: ~ *company*) sucursal *f*, filial *f*

subsidize ['sʌbsɪdaɪz] *vt* subvencionar

subsidy ['sʌbsɪdɪ] *n* subvención *f*

subsistence [səb'sɪstəns] *n* subsistencia; ~ **allowance** *n* salario mínimo

substance ['sʌbstəns] *n* sustancia

substantial [səb'stænʃl] *adj* sustancial, sustancioso; (*fig*) importante

substantiate [səb'stænʃɪeɪt] *vt* comprobar

substitute ['sʌbstɪtjuːt] *n* (*person*) suplente *m/f*; (*thing*) sustituto ♦ *vt*: **to ~ A for B** sustituir A por B, reemplazar B por A

subtitle ['sʌbtaɪtl] *n* subtítulo

subtle ['sʌtl] *adj* sutil; ~**ty** *n* sutileza

subtotal [sʌb'teutl] *n* total *m* parcial

subtract [səb'trækt] *vt* restar, sustraer; ~**ion** [-'trækʃən] *n* resta, sustracción *f*

suburb ['sʌbəːb] *n* barrio residencial; **the ~s** las afueras (de la ciudad); ~**an** [sə'bəːbən] *adj* suburbano; (*train etc*) de cercanías; ~**ia** [sə'bəːbɪə] *n* barrios *mpl* residenciales

subway ['sʌbweɪ] *n* (*BRIT*) paso subterráneo *or* inferior; (*US*) metro

succeed [sək'siːd] *vi* (*person*) tener éxito; (*plan*) salir bien ♦ *vt* suceder a; **to ~ in doing** lograr hacer; ~**ing** *adj* (*following*) sucesivo

success [sək'sɛs] *n* éxito; ~**ful** *adj* exitoso; (*business*) próspero; **to be ~ful (in doing)** lograr (hacer); ~**fully** *adv* con éxito

succession [sək'sɛʃən] *n* sucesión *f*, serie *f*

successive [sək'sɛsɪv] *adj* sucesivo, consecutivo

succinct [sək'sɪŋkt] *adj* sucinto

succumb [sə'kʌm] *vi*: **to ~ to** sucumbir a; (*illness*) ser víctima de

such [sʌtʃ] *adj* tal, semejante; (*of that kind*): **~ a book** tal libro; (*so much*): **~ courage** tanto valor ♦ *adv* tan; **~ a long trip** un viaje tan largo; **~ a lot of**

tanto(s)/a(s); **~ as** (*like*) tal como; **as ~** como tal; **~-and-~** *adj* tal o cual

suck [sʌk] *vt* chupar; (*bottle*) sorber; (*breast*) mamar; ~**er** *n* (*ZOOL*) ventosa; (*inf*) bobo, primo

suction ['sʌkʃən] *n* succión *f*

Sudan [su'dæn] *n* Sudán *m*

sudden ['sʌdn] *adj* (*rapid*) repentino, súbito; (*unexpected*) imprevisto; **all of a ~** de repente; ~**ly** *adv* de repente

suds [sʌdz] *npl* espuma de jabón

sue [suː] *vt* demandar

suede [sweɪd] *n* ante *m* (*SP*), gamuza (*AM*)

suet ['suɪt] *n* sebo

Suez ['suːɪz] *n*: **the ~ Canal** el Canal de Suez

suffer ['sʌfə*] *vt* sufrir, padecer; (*tolerate*) aguantar, soportar ♦ *vi* sufrir; **to ~ from** (*illness etc*) padecer; ~**er** *n* víctima, (*MED*) enfermo/a; ~**ing** *n* sufrimiento

suffice [sə'faɪs] *vi* bastar, ser suficiente

sufficient [sə'fɪʃənt] *adj* suficiente, bastante; ~**ly** *ad* suficientemente, bastante

suffix ['sʌfɪks] *n* sufijo

suffocate ['sʌfəkeɪt] *vi* ahogarse, asfixiarse; **suffocation** [-'keɪʃən] *n* asfixia

suffrage ['sʌfrɪdʒ] *n* sufragio

suffused [sə'fjuːzd] *adj*: **~ with** bañado de

sugar ['ʃugə*] *n* azúcar *m* ♦ *vt* echar azúcar a, azucarar; **~ beet** *n* remolacha; **~ cane** *n* caña de azúcar

suggest [sə'dʒɛst] *vt* sugerir; ~**ion** [-'dʒɛstʃən] *n* sugerencia; ~**ive** (*pej*) *adj* indecente

suicide ['suɪsaɪd] *n* suicidio; (*person*) suicida *m/f*; *see also* **commit**

suit [suːt] *n* (*man's*) traje *m*; (*woman's*) conjunto; (*LAW*) pleito; (*CARDS*) palo ♦ *vt* convenir; (*clothes*) sentar a, ir bien a; (*adapt*): **to ~ sth to** adaptar *or* ajustar algo a; **well ~ed** (*well matched: couple*) hecho el uno para el otro; ~**able** *adj* conveniente; (*apt*) indicado; ~**ably** *adv* convenientemente; (*impressed*) apropiadamente

suitcase ['suːtkeɪs] *n* maleta (*SP*), valija (*AM*)

suite [swi:t] *n* (*of rooms*, *MUS*) suite *f*; (*furniture*): **bedroom/dining room** ~ (juego de) dormitorio/comedor

suitor ['su:tə*] *n* pretendiente *m*

sulfur ['sʌlfə*] (*US*) *n* = **sulphur**

sulk [sʌlk] *vi* estar de mal humor; **~y** *adj* malhumorado

sullen ['sʌlən] *adj* hosco, malhumorado

sulphur ['sʌlfə*] (*US* **sulfur**) *n* azufre *m*

sultana [sʌl'tɑ:nə] *n* (*fruit*) pasa de Esmirna

sultry ['sʌltrɪ] *adj* (*weather*) bochornoso

sum [sʌm] *n* suma; (*total*) total *m*; ~ **up** *vt* resumir ♦ *vi* hacer un resumen

summarize ['sʌməraɪz] *vt* resumir

summary ['sʌmərɪ] *n* resumen *m* ♦ *adj* (*justice*) sumario

summer ['sʌmə*] *n* verano ♦ *cpd* de verano; **in** ~ en verano; ~ **holidays** *npl* vacaciones *fpl* de verano; **~house** *n* (*in garden*) cenador *m*, glorieta; **~time** *n* (*season*) verano; ~ **time** *n* (*by clock*) hora de verano

summit ['sʌmɪt] *n* cima, cumbre *f*; (*also*: ~ *conference*, ~ *meeting*) (conferencia) cumbre *f*

summon ['sʌmən] *vt* (*person*) llamar; (*meeting*) convocar; (*LAW*) citar; ~ **up** *vt* (*courage*) armarse de; **~s** *n* llamamiento, llamada ♦ *vt* (*LAW*) citar

sump [sʌmp] (*BRIT*) *n* (*AUT*) cárter *m*

sumptuous ['sʌmptjuəs] *adj* suntuoso

sun [sʌn] *n* sol *m*

sunbathe ['sʌnbeɪð] *vi* tomar el sol

sunburn ['sʌnbə:n] *n* (*painful*) quemadura; (*tan*) bronceado

Sunday ['sʌndɪ] *n* domingo; ~ **school** *n* catequesis *f* dominical

sundial ['sʌndaɪəl] *n* reloj *m* de sol

sundown ['sʌndaun] *n* anochecer *m*

sundry ['sʌndrɪ] *adj* varios/as, diversos/as; **all and** ~ todos sin excepción; **sundries** *npl* géneros *mpl* diversos

sunflower ['sʌnflauə*] *n* girasol *m*

sung [sʌŋ] *pp of* **sing**

sunglasses ['sʌnɡlɑ:sɪz] *npl* gafas *fpl* (*SP*) *or* anteojos *mpl* de sol

sunk [sʌŋk] *pp of* **sink**

sun: **~light** *n* luz *f* del sol; **~lit** *adj*
iluminado por el sol; **~ny** *adj* soleado; (*day*) de sol; (*fig*) alegre; **~rise** *n* salida del sol; ~ **roof** *n* (*AUT*) techo corredizo; **~set** *n* puesta del sol; **~shade** *n* (*over table*) sombrilla; **~shine** *n* sol *m*; **~stroke** *n* insolación *f*; **~tan** *n* bronceado; **~tan oil** *n* aceite *m* bronceador

super ['su:pə*] (*inf*) *adj* genial

superannuation [su:pərænju'eɪʃən] *n* cuota de jubilación

superb [su:'pə:b] *adj* magnífico, espléndido

supercilious [su:pə'sɪlɪəs] *adj* altanero

superfluous [su'pə:fluəs] *adj* superfluo, de sobra

superhuman [su:pə'hju:mən] *adj* sobrehumano

superimpose ['su:pərɪm'pəuz] *vt* sobreponer

superintendent [su:pərɪn'tendənt] *n* director(a) *m/f*; (*POLICE*) subjefe/a *m/f*

superior [su'pɪərɪə*] *adj* superior; (*smug*) desdeñoso ♦ *n* superior *m*; **~ity** [-'ɔrɪtɪ] *n* superioridad *f*

superlative [su'pə:lətɪv] *n* superlativo

superman ['su:pəmæn] *n* superhombre *m*

supermarket ['su:pəmɑ:kɪt] *n* supermercado

supernatural [su:pə'nætʃərəl] *adj* sobrenatural ♦ *n*: **the** ~ lo sobrenatural

superpower ['su:pəpauə*] *n* (*POL*) superpotencia

supersede [su:pə'si:d] *vt* suplantar

superstar ['su:pəstɑ:*] *n* gran estrella

superstitious [su:pə'stɪʃəs] *adj* supersticioso

supertanker ['su:pətæŋkə*] *n* super-petrolero

supervise ['su:pəvaɪz] *vt* supervisar; **supervision** [-'vɪʒən] *n* supervisión *f*; **supervisor** *n* supervisor(a) *m/f*

supper ['sʌpə*] *n* cena

supplant [sə'plɑ:nt] *vt* suplantar

supple ['sʌpl] *adj* flexible

supplement [*n* 'sʌplɪmənt, *vb* sʌplɪ'ment] *n* suplemento ♦ *vt* suplir; **~ary** [-'mentərɪ] *adj* suplementario; **~ary benefit** (*BRIT*) *n* subsidio suplementario de la seguridad social

supplier [sə'plaɪə*] n (COMM) distribuidor(a) m/f

supply [sə'plaɪ] vt (provide) suministrar; (equip): **to ~ (with)** proveer (de) ♦ n provisión f; (gas, water etc) suministro; **supplies** npl (food) víveres mpl; (MIL) pertrechos mpl; **~ teacher** n profesor(a) m/f suplente

support [sə'pɔːt] n apoyo; (TECH) soporte m ♦ vt apoyar; (financially) mantener; (uphold, TECH) sostener; **~er** n (POL etc) partidario/a; (SPORT) aficionado/a

suppose [sə'pəuz] vt suponer; (imagine) imaginarse; (duty): **to be ~d to do sth** deber hacer algo; **~dly** [sə'pəuzɪdlɪ] adv según cabe suponer; **supposing** conj en caso de que

suppress [sə'prɛs] vt suprimir; (yawn) ahogar

supreme [su'priːm] adj supremo

surcharge ['səːtʃɑːdʒ] n sobretasa, recargo

sure [ʃuə*] adj seguro; (definite, convinced) cierto; **to make ~ of sth/that** asegurarse de algo/asegurar que; **~!** (of course) ¡claro!, ¡por supuesto!; **~ enough** efectivamente; **~-footed** adj ágil y seguro; **~ly** adv (certainly) seguramente

surety ['ʃuərətɪ] n fianza

surf [səːf] n olas fpl

surface ['səːfɪs] n superficie f ♦ vt (road) revestir ♦ vi (also fig) salir a la superficie; **by ~ mail** por vía terrestre

surfboard ['səːfbɔːd] n tabla (de surf)

surfeit ['səːfɪt] n: **a ~ of** un exceso de

surfing ['səːfɪŋ] n surf m

surge [səːdʒ] n oleada, oleaje m ♦ vi (wave) romper; (people) avanzar en tropel

surgeon ['səːdʒən] n cirujano/a

surgery ['səːdʒərɪ] n cirugía; (BRIT: room) consultorio; **~ hours** (BRIT) npl horas fpl de consulta

surgical ['səːdʒɪkl] adj quirúrgico; **~ spirit** (BRIT) n alcohol m de 90°

surly ['səːlɪ] adj hosco, malhumorado

surmount [səː'maunt] vt superar, vencer

surname ['səːneɪm] n apellido

surpass [səː'pɑːs] vt superar, exceder

surplus ['səːpləs] n excedente m; (COMM) superávit m ♦ adj excedente, sobrante

surprise [sə'praɪz] n sorpresa ♦ vt sorprender; **surprising** adj sorprendente; **surprisingly** adv: **it was surprisingly easy** me etc sorprendió lo fácil que fue

surrender [sə'rɛndə*] n rendición f, entrega ♦ vi rendirse, entregarse

surreptitious [sʌrəp'tɪʃəs] adj subrepticio

surrogate ['sʌrəgɪt] n sucedáneo; **~ mother** n madre f portadora

surround [sə'raund] vt rodear, circundar; (MIL etc) cercar; **~ing** adj circundante; **~ings** npl alrededores mpl, cercanías fpl

surveillance [səː'veɪləns] n vigilancia

survey [n 'səːveɪ, vb səː'veɪ] n inspección f, reconocimiento; (inquiry) encuesta ♦ vt examinar, inspeccionar; (look at) mirar, contemplar; **~or** n agrimensor(a) m/f

survival [sə'vaɪvl] n supervivencia

survive [sə'vaɪv] vi sobrevivir; (custom etc) perdurar ♦ vt sobrevivir a; **survivor** n superviviente m/f

susceptible [sə'sɛptəbl] adj: **~ (to)** (disease) susceptible (a); (flattery) sensible (a)

suspect [adj, n 'sʌspɛkt, vb səs'pɛkt] adj, n sospechoso/a m/f ♦ vt (person) sospechar de; (think) sospechar

suspend [səs'pɛnd] vt suspender; **~ed sentence** n (LAW) libertad f condicional; **~er belt** n portaligas m inv; **~ers** npl (BRIT) ligas fpl; (US) tirantes mpl

suspense [səs'pɛns] n incertidumbre f, duda; (in film etc) suspense m; **to keep sb in ~** mantener a uno en suspense

suspension [səs'pɛnʃən] n (gen, AUT) suspensión f; (of driving licence) privación f; **~ bridge** n puente m colgante

suspicion [səs'pɪʃən] n sospecha; (distrust) recelo; **suspicious** [-ʃəs] adj receloso; (causing suspicion) sospechoso

sustain [səs'teɪn] vt sostener, apoyar; (suffer) sufrir, padecer; **~able** adj sostenible; **~ed** adj (effort) sostenido

sustenance ['sʌstɪnəns] n sustento

swab [swɔb] n (MED) algodón m

swagger ['swægə*] *vi* pavonearse

swallow ['swɔləu] *n* (*bird*) golondrina ♦ *vt* tragar; (*fig, pride*) tragarse; ~ **up** *vt* (*savings etc*) consumir

swam [swæm] *pt of* **swim**

swamp [swɔmp] *n* pantano, ciénaga ♦ *vt* (*with water etc*) inundar; (*fig*) abrumar, agobiar; ~**y** *adj* pantanoso

swan [swɔn] *n* cisne *m*

swap [swɔp] *n* canje *m*, intercambio ♦ *vt*: **to ~ (for)** cambiar (por)

swarm [swɔːm] *n* (*of bees*) enjambre *m*; (*fig*) multitud *f* ♦ *vi* (*bees*) formar un enjambre; (*people*) pulular; **to be ~ing with** ser un hervidero de

swarthy ['swɔːði] *adj* moreno

swastika ['swɔstıkə] *n* esvástica

swat [swɔt] *vt* aplastar

sway [sweı] *vi* mecerse, balancearse ♦ *vt* (*influence*) mover, influir en

swear [sweə*] (*pt* swore, *pp* sworn) *vi* (*curse*) maldecir; (*promise*) jurar ♦ *vt* jurar; ~**word** *n* taco, palabrota

sweat [swɛt] *n* sudor *m* ♦ *vi* sudar

sweater ['swɛtə*] *n* suéter *m*

sweatshirt ['swɛtʃəːt] *n* suéter *m*

sweaty ['swɛtı] *adj* sudoroso

Swede [swiːd] *n* sueco/a

swede [swiːd] (*BRIT*) *n* nabo

Sweden ['swiːdn] *n* Suecia; **Swedish** ['swiːdıʃ] *adj* sueco ♦ *n* (*LING*) sueco

sweep [swiːp] (*pt, pp* swept) *n* (*act*) barrido; (*also*: *chimney* ~) deshollinador(a) *m/f* ♦ *vt* barrer; (*with arm*) empujar; (*subj*: *current*) arrastrar ♦ *vi* barrer; (*arm etc*) moverse rápidamente; (*wind*) soplar con violencia; ~ **away** *vt* barrer; ~ **past** *vi* pasar majestuosamente; ~ **up** *vi* barrer; ~**ing** *adj* (*gesture*) dramático; (*generalized*: *statement*) generalizado

sweet [swiːt] *n* (*candy*) dulce *m*, caramelo; (*BRIT*: *pudding*) postre *m* ♦ *adj* dulce; (*fig*: *kind*) dulce, amable; (: *attractive*) mono; ~**corn** *n* maíz *m*; ~**en** *vt* (*add sugar to*) poner azúcar a; (*person*) endulzar; ~**heart** *n* novio/a; ~**ness** *n* dulzura; ~ **pea** *n* guisante *m* de olor

swell [swɛl] (*pt* swelled, *pp* swollen *or*

swelled) *n* (*of sea*) marejada, oleaje *m* ♦ *adj* (*US*: *inf*: *excellent*) estupendo, fenomenal ♦ *vt* hinchar, inflar ♦ *vi* (*also*: ~ *up*) hincharse; (*numbers*) aumentar; (*sound, feeling*) ir aumentando; ~**ing** *n* (*MED*) hinchazón *f*

sweltering ['swɛltərıŋ] *adj* sofocante, de mucho calor

swept [swɛpt] *pt, pp of* **sweep**

swerve [swəːv] *vi* desviarse bruscamente

swift [swıft] *n* (*bird*) vencejo ♦ *adj* rápido, veloz; ~**ly** *adv* rápidamente

swig [swıg] (*inf*) *n* (*drink*) trago

swill [swıl] *vt* (*also*: ~ *out*, ~ *down*) lavar, limpiar con agua

swim [swım] (*pt* swam, *pp* swum) *n*: **to go for a ~** ir a nadar *or* a bañarse ♦ *vi* nadar; (*head, room*) dar vueltas ♦ *vt* nadar; (*the Channel etc*) cruzar a nado; ~**mer** *n* nadador(a) *m/f*; ~**ming** *n* natación *f*; ~**ming cap** *n* gorro de baño; ~**ming costume** (*BRIT*) *n* bañador *m*, traje *m* de baño; ~**ming pool** *n* piscina (*SP*), alberca (*AM*); ~**ming trunks** *n* bañador *m* (de hombre); ~**suit** *n* = ~**ming costume**

swindle ['swındl] *n* estafa ♦ *vt* estafar

swine [swaın] (*inf!*) *n* canalla (*!*)

swing [swıŋ] (*pt, pp* swung) *n* (*in playground*) columpio; (*movement*) balanceo, vaivén *m*; (*change of direction*) viraje *m*; (*rhythm*) ritmo ♦ *vt* balancear; (*also*: ~ *round*) voltear, girar ♦ *vi* balancearse, columpiarse; (*also*: ~ *round*) dar media vuelta; **to be in full** ~ estar en plena marcha; ~ **bridge** *n* puente *m* giratorio; ~ **door** (*US* ~**ing door**) *n* puerta giratoria

swingeing ['swındʒıŋ] (*BRIT*) *adj* (*blow*) abrumador(a); (*cuts*) atroz

swipe [swaıp] *vt* (*hit*) golpear fuerte; (*inf*: *steal*) guindar

swirl [swəːl] *vi* arremolinarse

swish [swıʃ] *vi* chasquear

Swiss [swıs] *adj, n inv* suizo/a *m/f*

switch [swıtʃ] *n* (*for light etc*) interruptor *m*; (*change*) cambio ♦ *vt* (*change*) cambiar de; ~ **off** *vt* apagar; (*engine*) parar; ~ **on** *vt* encender (*SP*), prender

(AM); (*engine, machine*) arrancar; ~board n (TEL) centralita (de teléfonos) (SP), conmutador m (AM)

Switzerland ['switsələnd] n Suiza

swivel ['swivl] vi (*also:* ~ *round*) girar

swollen ['swəulən] pp of **swell**

swoon [swu:n] vi desmayarse

swoop [swu:p] n (*by police etc*) redada
♦ vi (*also:* ~ *down*) calarse

swop [swɔp] = **swap**

sword [sɔ:d] n espada; ~fish n pez m espada

swore [swɔ:*] pt of **swear**

sworn [swɔ:n] pp of **swear** ♦ adj (*statement*) bajo juramento; (*enemy*) implacable

swot [swɔt] (BRIT) vt, vi empollar

swum [swʌm] pp of **swim**

swung [swʌŋ] pt, pp of **swing**

sycamore ['sɪkəmɔ:*] n sicomoro

syllable ['sɪləbl] n sílaba

syllabus ['sɪləbəs] n programa m de estudios

symbol ['sɪmbl] n símbolo

symmetry ['sɪmɪtrɪ] n simetría

sympathetic [sɪmpə'θɛtɪk] adj (*understanding*) comprensivo; (*likeable*) simpático; (*showing support*): ~ **to(wards)** bien dispuesto hacia

sympathize ['sɪmpəθaɪz] vi: **to** ~ **with** (*person*) compadecerse de; (*feelings*) comprender; (*cause*) apoyar; ~**r** n (POL) simpatizante m/f

sympathy ['sɪmpəθɪ] n (*pity*) compasión f; **sympathies** npl (*tendencies*) tendencias fpl; **with our deepest** ~ nuestro más sentido pésame; **in** ~ en solidaridad

symphony ['sɪmfənɪ] n sinfonía

symptom ['sɪmptəm] n síntoma m, indicio

synagogue ['sɪnəgɔg] n sinagoga

syndicate ['sɪndɪkɪt] n (*gen*) sindicato; (*of newspapers*) agencia (de noticias)

syndrome ['sɪndrəum] n síndrome m

synonym ['sɪnənɪm] n sinónimo

synopses [sɪ'nɔpsi:z] npl of **synopsis**

synopsis [sɪ'nɔpsɪs] (pl **synopses**) n sinopsis f inv

syntax ['sɪntæks] n sintaxis f inv

syntheses ['sɪnθəsi:z] npl of **synthesis**

synthesis ['sɪnθəsɪs] (pl **syntheses**) n síntesis f inv

synthetic [sɪn'θɛtɪk] adj sintético

syphilis ['sɪfɪlɪs] n sífilis f

syphon ['saɪfən] = **siphon**

Syria ['sɪrɪə] n Siria; ~**n** adj, n sirio/a

syringe [sɪ'rɪndʒ] n jeringa

syrup ['sɪrəp] n jarabe m; (*also:* golden ~) almíbar m

system ['sɪstəm] n sistema m; (ANAT) organismo; ~**atic** [-'mætɪk] adj sistemático, metódico; ~ **disk** n (COMPUT) disco del sistema; ~**s analyst** n analista m/f de sistemas

T t

ta [tɑ:] (BRIT: inf) excl ¡gracias!

tab [tæb] n lengüeta; (*label*) etiqueta; **to keep ~s on** (fig) vigilar

tabby ['tæbɪ] n (*also:* ~ cat) gato atigrado

table ['teɪbl] n mesa; (*of statistics etc*) cuadro, tabla ♦ vt (BRIT: motion etc) presentar; **to lay** or **set the** ~ poner la mesa; ~**cloth** n mantel m; ~ **of contents** n índice m de materias; ~ **d'hôte** [tɑ:bl'dəut] adj del menú; ~ **lamp** n lámpara de mesa; ~**mat** n (*for plate*) posaplatos m inv; (*for hot dish*) salvamantel m; ~**spoon** n cuchara de servir; (*also:* ~spoonful: as measurement) cucharada

tablet ['tæblɪt] n (MED) pastilla, comprimido; (*of stone*) lápida

table tennis n ping-pong m, tenis m de mesa

table wine n vino de mesa

tabloid ['tæblɔɪd] n periódico popular sensacionalista

tabulate ['tæbjuleɪt] vt disponer en tablas

tack [tæk] n (*nail*) tachuela; (fig) rumbo
♦ vt (*nail*) clavar con tachuelas; (*stitch*) hilvanar ♦ vi virar

tackle ['tækl] n (*fishing* ~) aparejo (de pescar); (*for lifting*) aparejo ♦ vt (*difficulty*) enfrentarse con; (*challenge: person*) hacer frente a; (*grapple with*) agarrar; (*FOOTBALL*) cargar; (*RUGBY*) placar

tacky ['tækɪ] *adj* pegajoso; (*pej*) cutre

tact [tækt] *n* tacto, discreción *f*; **~ful** *adj* discreto, diplomático

tactics ['tæktɪks] *n*, *npl* táctica

tactless ['tæktlɪs] *adj* indiscreto

tadpole ['tædpəul] *n* renacuajo

taffy ['tæfɪ] (*US*) *n* toffee *m*

tag [tæg] *n* (*label*) etiqueta; **~ along** *vi* ir (*or* venir) también

tail [teɪl] *n* cola; (*of shirt, coat*) faldón *m* ♦ *vt* (*follow*) vigilar a; **~s** *npl* (*formal suit*) levita; **~ away** *vi* (*in size, quality etc*) ir disminuyendo; **~ off** *vi* = **~ away**; **~back** (*BRIT*) *n* (*AUT*) cola; **~ end** *n* cola, parte *f* final; **~gate** *n* (*AUT*) puerta trasera

tailor ['teɪlə*] *n* sastre *m*; **~ing** *n* (*cut*) corte *m*; (*craft*) sastrería; **~-made** *adj* (*also fig*) hecho a la medida

tailwind ['teɪlwɪnd] *n* viento de cola

tainted ['teɪntɪd] *adj* (*food*) pasado; (*water, air*) contaminado; (*fig*) manchado

take [teɪk] (*pt* **took**, *pp* **taken**) *vt* tomar; (*grab*) coger (*SP*), agarrar (*AM*); (*gain: prize*) ganar; (*require: effort, courage*) exigir; (*tolerate: pain etc*) aguantar; (*hold: passengers etc*) tener cabida para; (*accompany, bring, carry*) llevar; (*exam*) presentarse a; **to ~ sth from** (*drawer etc*) sacar algo de; (*person*) quitar algo a; **I ~ it that ...** supongo que ...; **~ after** *vt fus* parecerse a; **~ apart** *vt* desmontar; **~ away** *vt* (*remove*) quitar; (*carry off*) llevar; (*MATH*) restar; **~ back** *vt* (*return*) devolver; (*one's words*) retractarse de; **~ down** *vt* (*building*) derribar; (*letter etc*) apuntar; **~ in** *vt* (*deceive*) engañar; (*understand*) entender; (*include*) abarcar; (*lodger*) acoger, recibir; **~ off** *vi* (*AVIAT*) despegar ♦ *vt* (*remove*) quitar; **~ on** *vt* (*work*) aceptar; (*employee*) contratar; (*opponent*) desafiar; **~ out** *vt* sacar; **~ over** *vt* (*business*) tomar posesión de; (*country*) tomar el poder ♦ *vi*: **to ~ over from sb** reemplazar a uno; **~ to** *vt fus* (*person*) coger cariño a, encariñarse con; (*activity*) aficionarse a; **~ up** *vt* (*a dress*) acortar; (*occupy: time, space*) ocupar;

(*engage in: hobby etc*) dedicarse a; (*accept*): **to ~ sb up on** aceptar; **~away** (*BRIT*) *adj* (*food*) para llevar ♦ *n* tienda (*or* restaurante *m*) de comida para llevar; **~off** *n* (*AVIAT*) despegue *m*; **~over** *n* (*COMM*) absorción *f*; **~out** (*US*) *n* = **~away**

takings ['teɪkɪŋz] *npl* (*COMM*) ingresos *mpl*

talc [tælk] *n* (*also*: **~um powder**) (polvos de) talco

tale [teɪl] *n* (*story*) cuento; (*account*) relación *f*; **to tell ~s** (*fig*) chivarse

talent ['tælnt] *n* talento; **~ed** *adj* de talento

talk [tɔːk] *n* charla; (*conversation*) conversación *f*; (*gossip*) habladurías *fpl*, chismes *mpl* ♦ *vi* hablar; **~s** *npl* (*POL etc*) conversaciones *fpl*; **to ~ about** hablar de; **to ~ sb into doing sth** convencer a uno para que haga algo; **to ~ sb out of doing sth** disuadir a uno de que haga algo; **to ~ shop** hablar del trabajo; **~ over** *vt* discutir; **~ative** *adj* hablador(a); **~ show** *n* programa *m* de entrevistas

tall [tɔːl] *adj* alto; (*object*) grande; **to be 6 feet ~** (*person*) ≈ medir 1 metro 80

tally ['tælɪ] *n* cuenta ♦ *vi*: **to ~ (with)** corresponder (con)

talon ['tælən] *n* garra

tambourine [tæmbə'riːn] *n* pandereta

tame [teɪm] *adj* domesticado; (*fig*) mediocre

tamper ['tæmpə*] *vi*: **to ~ with** tocar, andar con

tampon ['tæmpɔn] *n* tampón *m*

tan [tæn] *n* (*also: sun~*) bronceado ♦ *vi* ponerse moreno ♦ *adj* (*colour*) marrón

tang [tæŋ] *n* sabor *m* fuerte

tangent ['tændʒənt] *n* (*MATH*) tangente *f*; **to go off at a ~** (*fig*) salirse por la tangente

tangerine [tændʒə'riːn] *n* mandarina

tangle ['tæŋgl] *n* enredo; **to get in(to) a ~** enredarse

tank [tæŋk] *n* (*water ~*) depósito, tanque *m*; (*for fish*) acuario; (*MIL*) tanque *m*

tanker ['tæŋkə*] *n* (*ship*) buque *m* cisterna; (*truck*) camión *m* cisterna

tanned [tænd] *adj (skin)* moreno
tantalizing ['tæntəlaızıŋ] *adj* tentador(a)
tantamount ['tæntəmaunt] *adj*: ~ **to** equivalente a
tantrum ['tæntrəm] *n* rabieta
tap [tæp] *n (BRIT: on sink etc)* grifo *(SP)*, canilla *(AM)*; *(gas ~)* llave *f*; *(gentle blow)* golpecito ♦ *vt (hit gently)* dar golpecitos en; *(resources)* utilizar, explotar; *(telephone)* intervenir; **on ~** *(fig: resources)* a mano; **~-dancing** *n* claqué *m*
tape [teıp] *n (also: magnetic ~)* cinta magnética; *(cassette)* cassette *f*, cinta; *(sticky ~)* cinta adhesiva; *(for tying)* cinta ♦ *vt (record)* grabar (en cinta); *(stick with ~)* pegar con cinta adhesiva; ~ **deck** *n* grabadora; ~ **measure** *n* cinta métrica, metro
taper ['teıpə*] *n* cirio ♦ *vi* afilarse
tape recorder *n* grabadora
tapestry ['tæpıstrı] *n (object)* tapiz *m*; *(art)* tapicería
tar [ta:] *n* alquitrán *m*, brea
target ['ta:gıt] *n (gen)* blanco
tariff ['tærıf] *n (on goods)* arancel *m*; *(BRIT: in hotels etc)* tarifa
tarmac ['ta:mæk] *n (BRIT: on road)* asfaltado; *(AVIAT)* pista (de aterrizaje)
tarnish ['ta:nıʃ] *vt* deslustrar
tarpaulin [ta:'pɔ:lın] *n* lona impermeabilizada
tarragon ['tærəgən] *n* estragón *m*
tart [ta:t] *n (CULIN)* tarta; *(BRIT: inf: prostitute)* puta ♦ *adj* agrio, ácido; ~ **up** *(BRIT: inf)* vt *(building)* remozar; **to ~ o.s. up** acicalarse
tartan ['ta:tn] *n* tejido escocés *m*
tartar ['ta:tə*] *n (on teeth)* sarro; ~**(e) sauce** *n* salsa tártara
task [ta:sk] *n* tarea; **to take to ~** reprender; ~ **force** *n (MIL, POLICE)* grupo de operaciones
taste [teıst] *n (sense)* gusto; *(flavour)* sabor *m*; *(also: after~)* sabor *m*, dejo; *(sample)*: **have a ~!** ¡prueba un poquito!; *(fig)* muestra, idea ♦ *vt (also fig)* probar ♦ *vi*: **to ~ of** *or* **like** *(fish, garlic etc)* saber a; **you can ~ the garlic (in it)** se nota el sabor a ajo; **in good/bad ~ de**

buen/mal gusto; ~**ful** *adj* de buen gusto; ~**less** *adj (food)* soso; *(remark etc)* de mal gusto; **tasty** *adj* sabroso, rico
tatters ['tætəz] *npl*: **in ~** hecho jirones
tattoo [tə'tu:] *n* tatuaje *m*; *(spectacle)* espectáculo militar ♦ *vt* tatuar
tatty ['tætı] *(BRIT: inf) adj* cochambroso
taught [tɔ:t] *pt, pp of* **teach**
taunt [tɔ:nt] *n* burla ♦ *vt* burlarse de
Taurus ['tɔ:rəs] *n* Tauro
taut [tɔ:t] *adj* tirante, tenso
tax [tæks] *n* impuesto ♦ *vt* gravar (con un impuesto); *(fig: memory)* poner a prueba (: *patience)* agotar; ~**able** *adj (income)* gravable; ~**ation** [-'seıʃən] *n* impuestos *mpl*; ~ **avoidance** *n* evasión *f* de impuestos; ~ **disc** *(BRIT) n (AUT)* pegatina del impuesto de circulación; ~ **evasion** *n* evasión *f* fiscal; ~**-free** *adj* libre de impuestos
taxi ['tæksı] *n* taxi *m* ♦ *vi (AVIAT)* rodar por la pista; ~ **driver** *n* taxista *m/f*; ~ **rank** *(BRIT) n* = ~ **stand**; ~ **stand** *n* parada de taxis
tax: ~ **payer** *n* contribuyente *m/f*; ~ **relief** *n* desgravación *f* fiscal; ~ **return** *n* declaración *f* de ingresos
TB *n abbr* = **tuberculosis**
tea [ti:] *n* té *m*; *(BRIT: meal)* ≈ merienda *(SP)*; cena; **high ~** *(BRIT)* merienda-cena *(SP)*; ~ **bag** *n* bolsita de té; ~ **break** *(BRIT) n* descanso para el té
teach [ti:tʃ] *(pt, pp taught) vt*: **to ~ sb sth, ~ sth to sb** enseñar algo a uno ♦ *vi (be a teacher)* ser profesor(a), enseñar; ~**er** *n (in secondary school)* profesor(a) *m/f*; *(in primary school)* maestro/a, profesor(a) de EGB; ~**ing** *n* enseñanza
tea cosy *n* cubretetera *m*
teacup ['ti:kʌp] *n* taza para el té
teak [ti:k] *n (madera de)* teca
team [ti:m] *n* equipo; *(of horses)* tiro; ~**work** *n* trabajo en equipo
teapot ['ti:pɔt] *n* tetera
tear[1] [tıə*] *n* lágrima; **in ~s** llorando
tear[2] [tɛə*] *(pt tore, pp torn) n* rasgón *m*, desgarrón *m* ♦ *vt* romper, rasgar ♦ *vi* rasgarse; ~ **along** *vi (rush)* precipitarse; ~ **up** *vt (sheet of paper etc)* romper

tearful ['tɪəfəl] *adj* lloroso

tear gas ['tɪə-] *n* gas *m* lacrimógeno

tearoom ['tiːruːm] *n* salón *m* de té

tease [tiːz] *vt* tomar el pelo a

tea: ~ **set** *n* servicio de té; **~spoon** *n* cucharita; (*also*: ~*spoonful*: *as measurement*) cucharadita

teat [tiːt] *n* (*of bottle*) tetina

teatime ['tiːtaɪm] *n* hora del té

tea towel (*BRIT*) *n* paño de cocina

technical ['tɛknɪkl] *adj* técnico; ~ **college** (*BRIT n* ≈ escuela de artes y oficios (*SP*); **~ity** [-'kælɪtɪ] *n* (*point of law*) formalismo; (*detail*) detalle *m* técnico; **~ly** *adv* en teoría; (*regarding technique*) técnicamente

technician [tɛk'nɪʃn] *n* técnico/a

technique [tɛk'niːk] *n* técnica

technology [tɛk'nɔlədʒɪ] *n* tecnología

teddy (bear) ['tɛdɪ-] *n* osito de felpa

tedious ['tiːdɪəs] *adj* pesado, aburrido

teem [tiːm] *vi*: **to ~ with** rebosar de; **it is ~ing (with rain)** llueve a cántaros

teenage ['tiːneɪdʒ] *adj* (*fashions etc*) juvenil; (*children*) quinceañero; **~r** *n* quinceañero/a

teens [tiːnz] *npl*: **to be in one's ~** ser adolescente

tee-shirt ['tiːʃəːt] *n* = **T-shirt**

teeter ['tiːtə*] *vi* balancearse; (*fig*): **to ~ on the edge of ...** estar al borde de ...

teeth [tiːθ] *npl of* **tooth**

teethe [tiːð] *vi* echar los dientes

teething ['tiːðɪŋ]: ~ **ring** *n* mordedor *m*; ~ **troubles** *npl* (*fig*) dificultades *fpl* iniciales

teetotal ['tiː'təutl] *adj* abstemio

telegram ['tɛlɪgræm] *n* telegrama *m*

telegraph ['tɛlɪɡrɑːf] *n* telégrafo; ~ **pole** *n* poste *m* telegráfico

telepathy [tə'lɛpəθɪ] *n* telepatía

telephone ['tɛlɪfəun] *n* teléfono ♦ *vt* llamar por teléfono, telefonear; (*message*) dar por teléfono; **to be on the ~** (*talking*) hablar por teléfono; (*possessing ~*) tener teléfono; ~ **booth** *n* cabina telefónica; ~ **box** (*BRIT*) *n* = ~ **booth**; ~ **call** *n* llamada (telefónica); ~ **directory** *n* guía (telefónica); ~ **number** *n* número de

teléfono; **telephonist** [tə'lɛfənɪst] (*BRIT*) *n* telefonista *m/f*

telescope ['tɛlɪskəup] *n* telescopio

television ['tɛlɪvɪʒən] *n* televisión *f*; **on ~** en la televisión; ~ **set** *n* televisor *m*

telex ['tɛlɛks] *n* télex *m* ♦ *vt* enviar un télex a

tell [tɛl] (*pt, pp* **told**) *vt* decir; (*relate*: *story*) contar; (*distinguish*): **to ~ sth from** distinguir algo de ♦ *vi* (*talk*): **to ~ (of)** contar; (*have effect*) tener efecto; **to ~ sb to do sth** mandar a uno hacer algo; ~ **off** *vt*: **to ~ sb off** regañar a uno; **~er** *n* (*in bank*) cajero/a; **~ing** *adj* (*remark, detail*) revelador(a); **~tale** *adj* (*sign*) indicador(a)

telly ['tɛlɪ] (*BRIT*: *inf*) *n abbr* (= *television*) tele *f*

temp [tɛmp] *n abbr* (*BRIT*: = *temporary*) temporero/a

temper ['tɛmpə*] *n* (*nature*) carácter *m*; (*mood*) humor *m*; (*bad ~*) (mal) genio; (*fit of anger*) acceso de ira ♦ *vt* (*moderate*) moderar; **to be in a ~** estar furioso; **to lose one's ~** enfadarse, enojarse

temperament ['tɛmprəmənt] *n* (*nature*) temperamento

temperate ['tɛmprət] *adj* (*climate etc*) templado

temperature ['tɛmprətʃə*] *n* temperatura; **to have** *or* **run a ~** tener fiebre

temple ['tɛmpl] *n* (*building*) templo; (*ANAT*) sien *f*

tempo ['tɛmpəu] (*pl* **tempos** *or* **tempi**) *n* (*MUS*) tempo, tiempo; (*fig*) ritmo

temporarily ['tɛmpərərɪlɪ] *adv* temporalmente

temporary ['tɛmpərərɪ] *adj* provisional; (*passing*) transitorio; (*worker*) temporero; (*job*) temporal

tempt [tɛmpt] *vt* tentar; **to ~ sb into doing sth** tentar *or* inducir a uno a hacer algo; **~ation** [-'teɪʃən] *n* tentación *f*; **~ing** *adj* tentador(a); (*food*) apetitoso/a

ten [tɛn] *num* diez

tenacity [tə'næsɪtɪ] *n* tenacidad *f*

tenancy ['tɛnənsɪ] *n* arrendamiento, alquiler *m*

tenant ['tɛnənt] *n* inquilino/a

tend [tɛnd] vt cuidar ♦ vi: **to ~ to do sth** tener tendencia a hacer algo

tendency ['tɛndənsɪ] n tendencia

tender ['tɛndə*] adj (person, care) tierno, cariñoso; (meat) tierno; (sore) sensible ♦ n (COMM: offer) oferta; (money): **legal ~** moneda de curso legal ♦ vt ofrecer; **~ness** n ternura; (of meat) blandura

tenement ['tɛnəmənt] n casa de pisos (SP)

tenet ['tɛnət] n principio

tennis ['tɛnɪs] n tenis m; **~ ball** n pelota de tenis; **~ court** n cancha de tenis; **~ player** n tenista m/f; **~ racket** n raqueta de tenis

tenor ['tɛnə*] n (MUS) tenor m

tenpin bowling ['tɛnpɪn-] n (juego de los) bolos

tense [tɛns] adj (person) nervioso; (moment, atmosphere) tenso; (muscle) tenso, en tensión ♦ n (LING) tiempo

tension ['tɛnʃən] n tensión f

tent [tɛnt] n tienda (de campaña) (SP), carpa (AM)

tentative ['tɛntətɪv] adj (person, smile) indeciso; (conclusion, plans) provisional

tenterhooks ['tɛntəhuks] npl: **on ~** sobre ascuas

tenth [tɛnθ] num décimo

tent peg n clavija, estaca

tent pole n mástil m

tenuous ['tɛnjuəs] adj tenue

tenure ['tɛnjuə*] n (of land etc) tenencia; (of office) ejercicio

tepid ['tɛpɪd] adj tibio

term [tɜ:m] n (word) término; (period) período; (SCOL) trimestre m ♦ vt llamar; **~s** npl (conditions, COMM) condiciones fpl; **in the short/long ~** a corto/largo plazo; **to be on good ~s with sb** llevarse bien con uno; **to come to ~s with** (problem) aceptar

terminal ['tɜ:mɪnl] adj (disease) mortal; (patient) terminal ♦ n (ELEC) borne m; (COMPUT) terminal m; (also: air ~) terminal f; (BRIT: also: coach ~) (estación f) terminal f

terminate ['tɜ:mɪneɪt] vt terminar

terminus ['tɜ:mɪnəs] (pl termini) n término, (estación f) terminal f

terrace ['tɛrəs] n terraza; (BRIT: row of houses) hilera de casas adosadas; **the ~s** (BRIT: SPORT) las gradas fpl; **~d** adj (garden) en terrazas; (house) adosado

terrain [tɛ'reɪn] n terreno

terrible ['tɛrɪbl] adj terrible, horrible; (inf) atroz; **terribly** adv terriblemente; (very badly) malísimamente

terrier ['tɛrɪə*] n terrier m

terrific [tə'rɪfɪk] adj (very great) tremendo; (wonderful) fantástico, fenomenal

terrify ['tɛrɪfaɪ] vt aterrorizar

territory ['tɛrɪtərɪ] n (also fig) territorio

terror ['tɛrə*] n terror m; **~ism** n terrorismo; **~ist** n terrorista m/f

terse [tɜ:s] adj brusco, lacónico

test [tɛst] n (gen, CHEM) prueba; (MED) examen m; (SCOL) examen m, test m; (also: driving ~) examen m de conducir ♦ vt probar, poner a prueba; (MED, SCOL) examinar

testament ['tɛstəmənt] n testamento; **the Old/New T~** el Antiguo/Nuevo Testamento

testicle ['tɛstɪkl] n testículo

testify ['tɛstɪfaɪ] vi (LAW) prestar declaración; **to ~ to sth** atestiguar algo

testimony ['tɛstɪmənɪ] n (LAW) testimonio

test: ~ match n (CRICKET, RUGBY) partido internacional; **~ pilot** n piloto/mujer piloto m/f de pruebas; **~ tube** n probeta

tetanus ['tɛtənəs] n tétano

tether ['tɛðə*] vt atar (con una cuerda) ♦ n: **to be at the end of one's ~** no aguantar más

text [tɛkst] n texto; **~book** n libro de texto

textiles ['tɛkstaɪlz] npl textiles mpl; (textile industry) industria textil

texture ['tɛkstʃə*] n textura

Thailand ['taɪlænd] n Tailandia

Thames [tɛmz] n: **the ~** el (río) Támesis

than [ðæn] conj (in comparisons): **more ~ 10/once** más de 10/una vez; **I have more/less ~ you/Paul** tengo más/menos que tú/Paul; **she is older ~ you think** es mayor de lo que piensas

thank [θæŋk] vt dar las gracias a,

agradecer; ~ **you (very much)** muchas gracias; ~ **God!** ¡gracias a Dios!; ~**s** *npl* gracias *fpl* ♦ *excl* (*also:* **many ~s, ~s a lot**) ¡gracias!; ~**s to** *prep* gracias a; ~**ful** *adj:* ~**ful (for)** agradecido (por); ~**less** *adj* ingrato; **T~sgiving (Day)** *n* día *m* de Acción de Gracias

that [ðæt] (*pl* **those**) *adj* (*demonstrative*) ese/a, *pl* esos/as; (*more remote*) aquel/aquella, *pl* aquellos/as; **leave those books on the table** deja esos libros sobre la mesa; ~ **one** ése/ésa; (*more remote*) aquél/aquélla; ~ **one over there** ése/ésa de ahí; aquél/aquélla de allí
♦ *pron* **1** (*demonstrative*) ése/a, *pl* ésos/as; (*neuter*) eso; (*more remote*) aquél/aquélla, *pl* aquéllos/as; (*neuter*) aquello; **what's ~?** ¿qué es eso (*or* aquello)?; **who's ~?** ¿quién es ése/a (*or* aquél/aquélla)?; **is ~ you?** ¿eres tú?; **will you eat all ~?** ¿vas a comer todo eso?; ~**'s my house** ésa es mi casa; ~**'s what he said** eso es lo que dijo; ~ **is (to say)** es decir
2 (*relative: subject, object*) que; (*with preposition*) (el/la) que *etc*, el/la cual *etc*; **the book (~) I read** el libro que leí; **the books ~ are in the library** los libros que están en la biblioteca; **all (~) I have** todo lo que tengo; **the box (~) I put it in** la caja en la que *or* donde lo puse; **the people (~) I spoke to** la gente con la que hablé
3 (*relative: of time*) que; **the day (~) he came** el día (en) que vino
♦ *conj* que; **he thought ~ I was ill** creyó que yo estaba enfermo
♦ *adv* (*demonstrative*): **I can't work ~ much** no puedo trabajar tanto; **I didn't realise it was ~ bad** no creí que fuera tan malo; ~ **high** así de alto

thatched [θætʃt] *adj* (*roof*) de paja; (*cottage*) con tejado de paja
thaw [θɔ:] *n* deshielo ♦ *vi* (*ice*) derretirse; (*food*) descongelarse ♦ *vt* (*food*) descongelar

the [ði:, ðə] *def art* **1** (*gen*) el, *f* la, *pl* los, *fpl* las (*NB* = el *immediately before f n beginning with stressed (h)a; a+el* = al; *de+el* = del); ~ **boy/girl** el chico/la chica; ~ **books/flowers** los libros/las flores; **to ~ postman/from ~ drawer** al cartero/del cajón; **I haven't ~ time/money** no tengo tiempo/dinero
2 (*+ adj to form n*) los; lo; ~ **rich and ~ poor** los ricos y los pobres; **to attempt ~ impossible** intentar lo imposible
3 (*in titles*): **Elizabeth ~ First** Isabel primera; **Peter ~ Great** Pedro el Grande
4 (*in comparisons*): ~ **more he works ~ more he earns** cuanto más trabaja más gana

theatre ['θɪətə*] (*US* **theater**) *n* teatro; (*also: lecture* ~) aula; (*MED: also: operating* ~) quirófano; ~**-goer** *n* aficionado/a al teatro
theatrical [θɪ'ætrɪkl] *adj* teatral
theft [θɛft] *n* robo
their [ðɛə*] *adj* su; ~**s** *pron* (el) suyo/(la) suya *etc*; *see also* **my**; **mine**[2]
them [ðɛm, ðəm] *pron* (*direct*) los/las; (*indirect*) les; (*stressed, after prep*) ellos/ellas; *see also* **me**
theme [θi:m] *n* tema *m*; ~ **park** *n* parque de atracciones (*en torno a un tema central*); ~ **song** *n* tema *m* (musical)
themselves [ðəm'sɛlvz] *pl pron* (*subject*) ellos mismos/ellas mismas; (*complement*) se; (*after prep*) sí (mismos/as); *see also* **oneself**
then [ðɛn] *adv* (*at that time*) entonces; (*next*) después; (*later*) luego, después; (*and also*) además ♦ *conj* (*therefore*) en ese caso, entonces ♦ *adj*: **the ~ president** el entonces presidente; **by ~** para entonces; **from ~ on** desde entonces
theology [θɪ'ɔlədʒɪ] *n* teología
theoretical [θɪə'rɛtɪkl] *adj* teórico
theory ['θɪərɪ] *n* teoría
therapist ['θɛrəpɪst] *n* terapeuta *m/f*
therapy [θɛrəpɪ] *n* terapia

there ['ðεə*] adv **1**: ~ **is**, ~ **are** hay; ~ **is no-one here/no bread left** no hay nadie aquí/no queda pan; ~ **has been an accident** ha habido un accidente **2** (*referring to place*) ahí; (*distant*) allí; **it's** ~ está ahí; **put it in/on/up/down** ~ ponlo ahí dentro/encima/arriba/abajo; **I want that book** ~ quiero ese libro de ahí; ~ **he is!** ¡ahí está! **3**: ~, ~ (*esp to child*) ea, ea

there: ~**abouts** adv por ahí; ~**after** adv después; ~**by** adv así, de ese modo; ~**fore** adv por lo tanto; ~'**s** = **there is**; **there has**

thermal ['θə:ml] adj termal; (*paper*) térmico

thermometer [θə'mɒmɪtə*] n termómetro

Thermos ['θə:məs] ® n (*also*: ~ *flask*) termo

thermostat ['θə:məustæt] n termostato

thesaurus [θɪ'sɔ:rəs] n tesoro

these [ði:z] pl adj estos/as ♦ pl pron éstos/as

theses ['θi:si:z] npl of **thesis**

thesis ['θi:sɪs] (pl **theses**) n tesis f inv

they [ðeɪ] pl pron ellos/ellas; (*stressed*) ellos (mismos)/ellas (mismas); ~ **say that ...** (*it is said that*) se dice que ...; ~'**d** = **they had**; **they would**; ~'**ll** = **they shall**; **they will**; ~'**re** = **they are**; ~'**ve** = **they have**

thick [θɪk] adj (*in consistency*) espeso; (*in size*) grueso; (*stupid*) torpe ♦ n: **in the** ~ **of the battle** en lo más reñido de la batalla; **it's 20 cm** ~ tiene 20 cm de espesor; ~**en** vi espesarse ♦ vt (*sauce etc*) espesar; ~**ness** n espesor m; grueso; ~**set** adj fornido; ~**skinned** adj (*fig*) insensible

thief [θi:f] (pl **thieves**) n ladrón/ona m/f

thieves [θi:vz] npl of **thief**

thigh [θaɪ] n muslo

thimble ['θɪmbl] n dedal m

thin [θɪn] adj (*person, animal*) flaco; (*in size*) delgado; (*in consistency*) poco espeso; (*hair, crowd*) escaso ♦ vt: **to** ~

(**down**) diluir

thing [θɪŋ] n cosa; (*object*) objeto, artículo; (*matter*) asunto; (*mania*): **to have a** ~ **about sb/sth** estar obsesionado con uno/algo; ~**s** npl (*belongings*) efectos mpl (personales); **the best** ~ **would be to ...** lo mejor sería ...; **how are** ~**s?** ¿qué tal?

think [θɪŋk] (pt, pp **thought**) vi pensar ♦ vt pensar, creer; **what did you** ~ **of them?** ¿qué te parecieron?; **to** ~ **about sth/sb** pensar en algo/uno; **I'll** ~ **about it** lo pensaré; **to** ~ **of doing sth** pensar en hacer algo; **I** ~ **so/not** creo que sí/no; **to** ~ **well of sb** tener buen concepto de uno; ~ **over** vt reflexionar sobre, meditar; ~ **up** vt (*plan etc*) idear; ~ **tank** n gabinete m de estrategia

thinly ['θɪnlɪ] adv (*cut*) fino; (*spread*) ligeramente

third [θə:d] adj (*before n*) tercer(a); (*following n*) tercero/a ♦ n tercero/a; (*fraction*) tercio; (*BRIT: SCOL: degree*) título de licenciado con calificación de aprobado; ~**ly** adv en tercer lugar; ~ **party insurance** (*BRIT*) n seguro contra terceros; ~**rate** adj (de calidad) mediocre; **T~ World** n Tercer Mundo

thirst [θə:st] n sed f; ~**y** adj (*person, animal*) sediento; (*work*) que da sed; **to be** ~**y** tener sed

thirteen ['θə:'ti:n] num trece

thirty ['θə:tɪ] num treinta

this [ðɪs] (pl **these**) adj (*demonstrative*) este/a; pl estos/as; (*neuter*) esto; ~ **man/woman** este hombre/esta mujer; **these children/flowers** estos chicos/estas flores; ~ **one (here)** éste/a, esto (de aquí)

♦ pron (*demonstrative*) éste/a; pl éstos/as; (*neuter*) esto; **who is** ~? ¿quién es éste/ésta?; **what is** ~? ¿qué es esto?; ~ **is where I live** aquí vivo; ~ **is what he said** esto es lo que dijo; ~ **is Mr Brown** (*in introductions*) le presento al Sr. Brown; (*photo*) éste es el Sr. Brown; (*on telephone*) habla el Sr. Brown

♦ adv (*demonstrative*): ~ **high/long** etc

así de alto/largo *etc*; ~ **far** hasta aquí

thistle ['θɪsl] *n* cardo

thorn [θɔːn] *n* espina

thorough ['θʌrə] *adj* (*search*) minucioso; (*wash*) a fondo; (*knowledge, research*) profundo; (*person*) meticuloso; ~**bred** *adj* (*horse*) de pura sangre; ~**fare** *n* calle *f*; "**no** ~**fare**" "prohibido el paso"; ~**ly** *adv* (*search*) minuciosamente; (*study*) profundamente; (*wash*) a fondo; (*utterly: bad, wet etc*) completamente, totalmente

those [ðəuz] *pl adj* esos/esas; (*more remote*) aquellos/as

though [ðəu] *conj* aunque ♦ *adv* sin embargo

thought [θɔːt] *pt, pp of* **think** ♦ *n* pensamiento; (*opinion*) opinión *f*; ~**ful** *adj* (*serious*) serio; (*considerate*) atento; ~**less** *adj* desconsiderado

thousand ['θauzənd] *num* mil; **two** ~ dos mil; ~**s of** miles de; ~**th** *num* milésimo

thrash [θræʃ] *vt* azotar; (*defeat*) derrotar; ~ **about** *or* **around** *vi* debatirse; ~ **out** *vt* discutir a fondo

thread [θrɛd] *n* hilo; (*of screw*) rosca ♦ *vt* (*needle*) enhebrar; ~**bare** *adj* raído

threat [θrɛt] *n* amenaza; ~**en** *vi* amenazar ♦ *vt*: **to** ~ **sb with/to do** amenazar a uno con/con hacer

three [θriː] *num* tres; ~-**dimensional** *adj* tridimensional; ~-**piece suit** *n* traje *m* de tres piezas; ~-**piece suite** *n* tresillo; ~-**ply** *adj* (*wool*) de tres cabos

thresh [θrɛʃ] *vt* trillar

threshold ['θrɛʃhəuld] *n* umbral *m*

threw [θruː] *pt of* **throw**

thrifty ['θrɪftɪ] *adj* económico

thrill [θrɪl] *n* (*excitement*) emoción *f*; (*shudder*) estremecimiento ♦ *vt* emocionar; **to be** ~**ed** (*with gift etc*) estar encantado; ~**er** *n* novela (*or obra or película*) de suspense; ~**ing** *adj* emocionante

thrive [θraɪv] (*pt* **thrived** *or* **throve**, *pp* **thrived** *or* **thriven**) *vi* (*grow*) crecer; (*do well*): **to** ~ **on sth** sentarle muy bien a uno algo; **thriven** ['θrɪvn] *pp of* **thrive**; **thriving** *adj* próspero

throat [θrəut] *n* garganta; **to have a sore** ~ tener dolor de garganta

throb [θrɔb] *n* (*of heart*) latido; (*of wound*) punzada; (*of engine*) vibración *f* ♦ *vi* latir; dar punzadas; vibrar

throes [θrəuz] *npl*: **in the** ~ **of** en medio de

throne [θrəun] *n* trono

throng [θrɔŋ] *n* multitud *f*, muchedumbre *f* ♦ *vt* agolparse en

throttle ['θrɔtl] *n* (*AUT*) acelerador *m* ♦ *vt* estrangular

through [θruː] *prep* por, a través de; (*time*) durante; (*by means of*) por medio de, mediante; (*owing to*) gracias a ♦ *adj* (*ticket, train*) directo ♦ *adv* completamente, de parte a parte; de principio a fin; **to put sb** ~ **to sb** (*TEL*) poner *or* pasar a uno con uno; **to be** ~ (*TEL*) tener comunicación; (*have finished*) haber terminado; "**no** ~ **road**" (*BRIT*) "calle sin salida"; ~**out** *prep* (*place*) por todas partes de, por todo; (*time*) durante todo ♦ *adv* por *or* en todas partes

throve [θrəuv] *pt of* **thrive**

throw [θrəu] (*pt* **threw**, *pp* **thrown**) *n* tiro; (*SPORT*) lanzamiento ♦ *vt* tirar, echar; (*SPORT*) lanzar; (*rider*) derribar; (*fig*) desconcertar; **to** ~ **a party** dar una fiesta; ~ **away** *vt* tirar; (*money*) derrochar; ~ **off** *vt* deshacerse de; ~ **out** *vt* tirar; (*person*) echar; expulsar; ~ **up** *vi* vomitar; ~**away** *adj* para tirar, desechable; (*remark*) hecho de paso; ~-**in** *n* (*SPORT*) saque *m*

thru [θruː] (*US*) = **through**

thrush [θrʌʃ] *n* zorzal *m*, tordo

thrust [θrʌst] (*pt, pp* **thrust**) *n* (*TECH*) empuje *m* ♦ *vt* empujar (con fuerza)

thud [θʌd] *n* golpe *m* sordo

thug [θʌg] *n* gamberro *m*

thumb [θʌm] *n* (*ANAT*) pulgar *m*; **to** ~ **a lift** hacer autostop; ~ **through** *vt fus* (*book*) hojear; ~**tack** (*US*) *n* chincheta (*SP*)

thump [θʌmp] *n* golpe *m*; (*sound*) ruido seco *or* sordo ♦ *vt* golpear ♦ *vi* (*heart etc*) palpitar

thunder ['θʌndə*] *n* trueno ♦ *vi* tronar; (*train etc*): **to** ~ **past** pasar como un

trueno; ~**bolt** n rayo; ~**clap** n trueno;
~**storm** n tormenta; ~**y** adj tormentoso
Thursday ['θəːzdɪ] n jueves m inv
thus [ðʌs] adv así, de este modo
thwart [θwɔːt] vt frustrar
thyme [taɪm] n tomillo
thyroid ['θaɪrɔɪd] n (also: ~ **gland**)
tiroides m inv
tic [tɪk] n tic m
tick [tɪk] n (sound: of clock) tictac m;
(mark) palomita; (ZOOL) garrapata; (BRIT:
inf): **in a** ~ en un instante ♦ vi hacer
tictac ♦ vt marcar; ~ **off** vt marcar;
(person) reñir; ~ **over** vi (engine) girar
en marcha lenta; (fig) ir tirando
ticket ['tɪkɪt] n billete m (SP), tíquet m,
boleto (AM); (for cinema etc) entrada (SP),
boleto (AM); (in shop: on goods) etiqueta;
(for raffle) papeleta; (for library) tarjeta;
(parking ~) multa por estacionamiento
ilegal; ~ **collector** n revisor(a) m/f; ~
office n taquilla (SP), boletería
(AM); (RAIL) despacho de billetes (SP) or
boletos (AM)
tickle ['tɪkl] vt hacer cosquillas a ♦ vi
hacer cosquillas; **ticklish** adj (person)
cosquilloso; (problem) delicado
tidal ['taɪdl] adj de marea; ~ **wave** n
maremoto
tidbit ['tɪdbɪt] (US) n = **titbit**
tiddlywinks ['tɪdlɪwɪŋks] n juego infantil
con fichas de plástico
tide [taɪd] n marea; (fig: of events etc)
curso, marcha; ~ **over** vt (help out)
ayudar a salir del apuro
tidy ['taɪdɪ] adj (room etc) ordenado;
(dress, work) limpio; (person) (bien)
arreglado ♦ vt (also: ~ **up**) poner en
orden
tie [taɪ] n (string etc) atadura; (BRIT: also:
neck~) corbata; (fig: link) vínculo, lazo;
(SPORT etc: draw) empate m ♦ vt atar ♦ vi
(SPORT etc) empatar; **to ~ in a bow** atar
con un lazo; **to ~ a knot in sth** hacer
un nudo en algo; ~ **down** vt (fig: person:
restrict) atar; (: to price, date etc) obligar
a; ~ **up** vt (parcel) envolver; (dog, person)
atar; (arrangements) concluir; **to be ~d
up** (busy) estar ocupado

tier [tɪə*] n grada; (of cake) piso
tiger ['taɪgə*] n tigre m
tight [taɪt] adj (rope) tirante; (money)
escaso; (clothes) ajustado; (bend) cerrado;
(shoes, schedule) apretado; (budget)
ajustado; (security) estricto; (inf: drunk)
borracho ♦ adv (squeeze) muy fuerte;
(shut) bien; ~**en** vt (rope) estirar; (screw,
grip) apretar; (security) reforzar ♦ vi
estirarse; apretarse; ~**-fisted** adj tacaño;
~**ly** adv (grasp) muy fuerte; ~**rope** n
cuerda floja; ~**s** (BRIT) npl panti mpl
tile [taɪl] n (on roof) teja; (on floor)
baldosa; (on wall) azulejo; ~**d** adj de
tejas; embaldosado; (wall) alicatado
till [tɪl] n caja (registradora) ♦ vt (land)
cultivar ♦ prep, conj = **until**
tilt [tɪlt] vt inclinar ♦ vi inclinarse
timber ['tɪmbə*] n (material) madera;
(trees) árboles mpl
time [taɪm] n tiempo; (epoch: often pl)
época; (by clock) hora; (moment)
momento; (occasion) vez f; (MUS) compás
m ♦ vt calcular or medir el tiempo de;
(race) cronometrar; (remark, visit etc)
elegir el momento para; **a long** ~ mucho
tiempo; **4 at a** ~ de 4 en 4; **4 a la vez**;
for the ~ **being** de momento, por ahora;
from ~ **to** ~ de vez en cuando; **at** ~**s** a
veces; **in** ~ (soon enough) a tiempo; (after
some time) con el tiempo; (MUS) al
compás; **in a week's** ~ dentro de una
semana; **in no** ~ en un abrir y cerrar de
ojos; **any** ~ cuando sea; **on** ~ a la hora;
5 ~**s 5** 5 por 5; **what** ~ **is it?** ¿qué hora
es?; **to have a good** ~ pasarlo bien,
divertirse; ~ **bomb** n bomba de efecto
retardado; ~**less** adj eterno; ~ **limit** n
plazo; ~**ly** adj oportuno; ~ **off** n tiempo
libre; ~**r** n (in kitchen etc) programador
m horario; ~ **scale** (BRIT) n escala de
tiempo; ~ **share** n apartamento (or casa)
a tiempo compartido; ~ **switch** (BRIT) n
interruptor m (horario); ~**table** n
horario; ~ **zone** n huso horario
timid ['tɪmɪd] adj tímido
timing ['taɪmɪŋ] n (SPORT) cronometraje
m; **the** ~ **of his resignation** el momento
que eligió para dimitir

timpani ['tɪmpənɪ] *npl* tímpanos *mpl*

tin [tɪn] *n* estaño; (*also*: ~ **plate**) hojalata; (*BRIT*: *can*) lata; **~foil** *n* papel *m* de estaño

tinge [tɪndʒ] *n* matiz *m* ♦ *vt*: **~d with** teñido de

tingle ['tɪŋgl] *vi* (*person*): **to ~ (with)** estremecerse (de); (*hands etc*) hormiguear

tinker ['tɪŋkə*]: **~ with** *vt fus* jugar con, tocar

tinned [tɪnd] (*BRIT*) *adj* (*food*) en lata, en conserva

tin opener [-əupnə*] (*BRIT*) *n* abrelatas *m inv*

tinsel ['tɪnsl] *n* (guirnalda de) espumillón *m*

tint [tɪnt] *n* matiz *m*; (*for hair*) tinte *m*; **~ed** *adj* (*hair*) teñido; (*glass, spectacles*) ahumado

tiny ['taɪnɪ] *adj* minúsculo, pequeñito

tip [tɪp] *n* (*end*) punta; (*gratuity*) propina; (*BRIT*: *for rubbish*) vertedero; (*advice*) consejo ♦ *vt* (*waiter*) dar una propina a; (*tilt*) inclinar; (*empty*: *also*: ~ **out**) vaciar, echar; (*overturn*: *also*: ~ **over**) volcar; **~-off** *n* (*hint*) advertencia; **~ped** (*BRIT*) *adj* (*cigarette*) con filtro

Tipp-Ex ['tɪpɛks] ® *n* Tipp-Ex ® *m*

tipsy ['tɪpsɪ] (*inf*) *adj* alegre, mareado

tiptoe ['tɪptəu] *n*: **on ~** de puntillas

tiptop ['tɪp'tɔp] *adj*: **in ~ condition** en perfectas condiciones

tire ['taɪə*] *n* (*US*) = **tyre** ♦ *vt* cansar ♦ *vi* (*gen*) cansarse; (*become bored*) aburrirse; **~d** *adj* cansado; **to be ~d of sth** estar harto de algo; **~less** *adj* incansable; **~some** *adj* aburrido; **tiring** *adj* cansado

tissue ['tɪʃuː] *n* tejido; (*paper handkerchief*) pañuelo de papel, kleenex ® *m*; **~ paper** *n* papel *m* de seda

tit [tɪt] *n* (*bird*) herrerillo común; **to give ~ for tat** dar ojo por ojo

titbit ['tɪtbɪt] (*US* **tidbit**) *n* (*food*) golosina; (*news*) noticia sabrosa

titillate ['tɪtɪleɪt] *vt* estimular, excitar

title ['taɪtl] *n* título; **~ deed** *n* (*LAW*) título de propiedad; **~ role** *n* papel *m* principal

titter ['tɪtə*] *vi* reírse entre dientes

TM *abbr* = **trademark**

KEYWORD

to [tuː, tə] *prep* **1** (*direction*) a; **to go ~ France/London/school/the station** ir a Francia/Londres/al colegio/a la estación; **to go ~ Claude's/the doctor's** ir a casa de Claude/al médico; **the road ~ Edinburgh** la carretera de Edimburgo

2 (*as far as*) hasta, a; **from here ~ London** de aquí a *or* hasta Londres; **to count ~ 10** contar hasta 10; **from 40 ~ 50 people** entre 40 y 50 personas

3 (*with expressions of time*): **a quarter/twenty ~ 5** las 5 menos cuarto/veinte

4 (*for, of*): **the key ~ the front door** la llave de la puerta principal; **she is secretary ~ the director** es la secretaria del director; **a letter ~ his wife** una carta a *or* para su mujer

5 (*expressing indirect object*) a; **to give sth ~ sb** darle algo a alguien; **to talk ~ sb** hablar con alguien; **to be a danger ~ sb** ser un peligro para alguien; **to carry out repairs ~ sth** hacer reparaciones en algo

6 (*in relation to*): **3 goals ~ 2** 3 goles a 2; **30 miles ~ the gallon** ≈ 9,4 litros a los cien (kms)

7 (*purpose, result*): **to come ~ sb's aid** venir en auxilio *or* ayuda de alguien; **to sentence sb ~ death** condenar a uno a muerte; **~ my great surprise** con gran sorpresa mía

♦ *with vb* **1** (*simple infin*): **~ go/eat** ir/comer

2 (*following another vb*): **to want/try/start ~ do** querer/intentar/empezar a hacer; *see also relevant vb*

3 (*with vb omitted*): **I don't want ~** no quiero

4 (*purpose, result*) para; **I did it ~ help you** lo hice para ayudarte; **he came ~ see you** vino a verte

5 (*equivalent to relative clause*): **I have things ~ do** tengo cosas que hacer; **the main thing is ~ try** lo principal es intentarlo

6 (*after adj etc*): **ready ~ go** listo para irse; **too old ~ ...** demasiado viejo

(como) para ...
♦ adv: **pull/push the door ~** tirar de/
empujar la puerta

toad [təud] n sapo; **~stool** n hongo
venenoso

toast [təust] n (CULIN) tostada; (drink,
speech) brindis m ♦ vt (CULIN) tostar;
(drink to) brindar por; **~er** n tostador m

tobacco [tə'bækəu] n tabaco; **~nist** n
estanquero/a (SP), tabaquero/a (AM);
~nist's (shop) (BRIT) n estanco (SP),
tabaquería (AM)

toboggan [tə'bɔgən] n tobogán m

today [tə'deɪ] adv, n (also fig) hoy m

toddler ['tɔdlə*] n niño/a (que empieza a
andar)

to-do n (fuss) lío

toe [təu] n dedo (del pie); (of shoe) punta;
to ~ the line (fig) conformarse; **~nail** n
uña del pie

toffee ['tɔfi] n toffee m; **~ apple** (BRIT) n
manzana acaramelada

together [tə'gɛðə*] adv juntos; (at same
time) al mismo tiempo, a la vez; **~ with**
junto con

toil [tɔɪl] n trabajo duro, labor f ♦ vi
trabajar duramente

toilet ['tɔɪlət] n retrete m; (BRIT: room)
servicios mpl (SP), wáter m (SP), sanitario
(AM) ♦ cpd (soap etc) de aseo; **~ paper** n
papel m higiénico; **~ries** npl artículos
mpl de tocador; **~ roll** n rollo de papel
higiénico; **~ water** n (agua de) colonia

token ['təukən] n (sign) señal f, muestra;
(souvenir) recuerdo; (disc) ficha ♦ adj
(strike, payment etc) simbólico; **book/
record ~** (BRIT) vale m para comprar
libros/discos; **gift ~** (BRIT) vale-regalo

Tokyo ['təukjəu] n Tokio, Tokío

told [təuld] pt, pp of **tell**

tolerable ['tɔlərəbl] adj (bearable)
soportable; (fairly good) pasable

tolerant ['tɔlərnt] adj: **~ of** tolerante con

tolerate ['tɔləreɪt] vt tolerar

toll [təul] n (of casualties) número de
víctimas; (tax, charge) peaje m ♦ vi (bell)
doblar

tomato [tə'mɑːtəu] (pl ~es) n tomate m

tomb [tuːm] n tumba

tomboy ['tɔmbɔɪ] n marimacho

tombstone ['tuːmstəun] n lápida

tomcat ['tɔmkæt] n gato (macho)

tomorrow [tə'mɔrəu] adv, n (also: fig)
mañana; **the day after ~** pasado
mañana; **~ morning** mañana por la
mañana

ton [tʌn] n tonelada (BRIT = 1016 kg; US =
907 kg); (metric ~) tonelada métrica; **~s
of** (inf) montones de

tone [təun] n tono ♦ vi (also: ~ in)
armonizar; **~ down** vt (criticism)
suavizar; (colour) atenuar; **~ up** vt
(muscles) tonificar; **~-deaf** adj con mal
oído

tongs [tɔŋz] npl (for coal) tenazas fpl;
(curling ~) tenacillas fpl

tongue [tʌŋ] n lengua; **~ in cheek**
irónicamente; **~-tied** adj (fig) mudo; **~-
twister** n trabalenguas m inv

tonic ['tɔnɪk] n (MED, also fig) tónico;
(also: ~ water) (agua) tónica

tonight [tə'naɪt] adv, n esta noche; esta
tarde

tonnage ['tʌnɪdʒ] n (NAUT) tonelaje m

tonsil ['tɔnsl] n amígdala; **~litis** [-'laɪtɪs] n
amigdalitis f

too [tuː] adv (excessively) demasiado;
(also) también; **~ much** demasiado; **~
many** demasiados/as

took [tuk] pt of **take**

tool [tuːl] n herramienta; **~ box** n caja de
herramientas

toot [tuːt] n pitido ♦ vi tocar el pito

tooth [tuːθ] (pl teeth) n (ANAT, TECH)
diente m; (molar) muela; **~ache** n dolor
m de muelas; **~brush** n cepillo de
dientes; **~paste** n pasta de dientes; **~pick**
n palillo

top [tɔp] n (of mountain) cumbre f, cima; (of
tree) copa; (of head) coronilla; (of
ladder, page) lo alto; (of table) superficie
f; (of cupboard) parte f de arriba; (lid: of
box) tapa; (: of bottle, jar) tapón m; (of
list etc) cabeza; (toy) peonza; (garment)
blusa; camiseta ♦ adj de arriba; (in
rank) principal, primero; (best) mejor
♦ vt (exceed) exceder; (be first in)

encabezar; **on ~ of** (*above*) sobre, encima de; (*in addition to*) además de; **from ~ to bottom** de pies a cabeza; **~ off** (*US*) *vt* = **~ up**; **~ up** *vt* llenar; **~ floor** *n* último piso; **~ hat** *n* sombrero de copa; **~-heavy** *adj* (*object*) mal equilibrado

topic ['tɔpɪk] *n* tema *m*; **~al** *adj* actual

top: **~less** *adj* (*bather, bikini*) topless *inv*; **~-level** *adj* (*talks*) al más alto nivel; **~most** *adj* más alto

topple ['tɔpl] *vt* derribar ♦ *vi* caerse

top-secret *adj* de alto secreto

topsy-turvy ['tɔpsɪ'tə:vɪ] *adj* al revés ♦ *adv* patas arriba

torch [tɔ:tʃ] *n* antorcha; (*BRIT*: *electric*) linterna

tore [tɔ:*] *pt of* **tear**

torment [*n* 'tɔ:mɛnt, *vt* tɔ:'mɛnt] *n* tormento ♦ *vt* atormentar; (*fig*: *annoy*) fastidiar

torn [tɔ:n] *pp of* **tear**

torrent ['tɔrnt] *n* torrente *m*

torrid ['tɔrɪd] *adj* (*fig*) apasionado

tortoise ['tɔ:təs] *n* tortuga; **~shell** ['tɔ:təʃɛl] *adj* de carey

torture ['tɔ:tʃə*] *n* tortura ♦ *vt* torturar; (*fig*) atormentar

Tory ['tɔ:rɪ] (*BRIT*) *adj*, *n* (*POL*) conservador(a) *m/f*

toss [tɔs] *vt* tirar, echar; (*one's head*) sacudir; **to ~ a coin** echar a cara o cruz; **to ~ up for sth** jugar a cara o cruz algo; **to ~ and turn** (*in bed*) dar vueltas

tot [tɔt] *n* (*BRIT*: *drink*) copita; (*child*) nene/a *m/f*

total ['təutl] *adj* total, entero; (*emphatic*: *failure etc*) completo, total ♦ *n* total *m*, suma ♦ *vt* (*add up*) sumar; (*amount to*) ascender a

totalitarian [təutælɪ'tɛərɪən] *adj* totalitario

totally ['təutəlɪ] *adv* totalmente

totter ['tɔtə*] *vi* tambalearse

touch [tʌtʃ] *n* tacto; (*contact*) contacto ♦ *vt* tocar; (*emotionally*) conmover; **a ~ of** (*fig*) un poquito de; **to get in ~ with sb** ponerse en contacto con uno; **to lose ~** (*friends*) perder contacto; **~ on** *vt fus* (*topic*) aludir (*brevemente*) a; **~ up** *vt*

(*paint*) retocar; **~-and-go** *adj* arriesgado; **~down** *n* aterrizaje *m*; (*on sea*) amerizaje *m*; (*US*: *FOOTBALL*) ensayo; **~ed** *adj* (*moved*) conmovido; **~ing** *adj* (*moving*) conmovedor(a); **~line** *n* (*SPORT*) línea de banda; **~y** *adj* (*person*) quisquilloso

tough [tʌf] *adj* (*material*) resistente; (*meat*) duro; (*problem etc*) difícil; (*policy, stance*) inflexible; (*person*) fuerte; **~en** *vt* endurecer

toupée ['tu:peɪ] *n* peluca

tour ['tuə*] *n* viaje *m*, vuelta; (*also*: *package ~*) viaje *m* todo comprendido; (*of town, museum*) visita; (*by band etc*) gira ♦ *vt* recorrer, visitar

tourism ['tuərɪzm] *n* turismo

tourist ['tuərɪst] *n* turista *m/f* ♦ *cpd* turístico; **~ office** *n* oficina de turismo

tournament ['tuənəmənt] *n* torneo

tousled ['tauzld] *adj* (*hair*) despeinado

tout [taut] *vi*: **to ~ for business** solicitar clientes ♦ *n* (*also*: *ticket ~*) revendedor(a) *m/f*

tow [təu] *vt* remolcar; **"on** *or* **in** (*US*) **~"** (*AUT*) "a remolque"

toward(s) [tə'wɔ:d(z)] *prep* hacia; (*attitude*) respecto a, con; (*purpose*) para

towel ['tauəl] *n* toalla; **~ling** *n* (*fabric*) felpa; **~ rail** (*US* **~ rack**) *n* toallero

tower ['tauə*] *n* torre *f*; **~ block** (*BRIT*) torre *f* (de pisos); **~ing** *adj* muy alto, imponente

town [taun] *n* ciudad *f*; **to go to ~** ir a la ciudad; (*fig*) echar la casa por la ventana; **~ centre** *n* centro de la ciudad; **~ council** *n* ayuntamiento, consejo municipal; **~ hall** *n* ayuntamiento; **~ plan** *n* plano de la ciudad; **~ planning** *n* urbanismo

towrope ['təurəup] *n* cable *m* de remolque

tow truck *n* camión *m* grúa

toy [tɔɪ] *n* juguete *m*; **~ with** *vt fus* jugar con; (*idea*) acariciar; **~shop** *n* juguetería

trace [treɪs] *n* rastro ♦ *vt* (*draw*) trazar, delinear; (*locate*) encontrar; (*follow*) seguir la pista de; **tracing paper** *n* papel *m* de calco

track [træk] *n* (*mark*) huella, pista; (*path*:

gen) camino, senda; (: *of bullet etc*) trayectoria; (RAIL) vía; (SPORT) pista; (*on tape, record*) canción ♦ *vt* seguir la pista de; **to keep ~ of** mantenerse al tanto de, seguir; **~ down** *vt* (*prey*) seguir el rastro de; (*sth lost*) encontrar; **~suit** *n* chandal *m*

tract [trækt] *n* (GEO) región *f*; (*pamphlet*) folleto

traction ['trækʃən] *n* (*power*) tracción *f*; **in ~** (MED) en tracción

tractor ['træktə*] *n* tractor *m*

trade [treɪd] *n* comercio; (*skill, job*) oficio ♦ *vi* negociar, comerciar ♦ *vt* (*exchange*): **to ~ sth (for sth)** cambiar algo (por algo); **~ in** *vt* (*old car etc*) ofrecer como parte del pago; **~ fair** *n* feria comercial; **~mark** *n* marca de fábrica; **~ name** *n* marca registrada; **~r** *n* comerciante *m/f*; **~sman** (*shopkeeper*) tendero; **~ union** *n* sindicato; **~ unionist** *n* sindicalista *m/f*

tradition [trə'dɪʃən] *n* tradición *f*; **~al** *adj* tradicional

traffic ['træfɪk] *n* (*gen*, AUT) tráfico, circulación *f*, tránsito (AM) ♦ *vi*: **to ~ in** (*pej: liquor, drugs*) traficar en; **~ circle** (US) *n* isleta; **~ jam** *n* embotellamiento; **~ lights** *npl* semáforo; **~ warden** *n* guardia *m/f* de tráfico

tragedy ['trædʒədɪ] *n* tragedia

tragic ['trædʒɪk] *adj* trágico

trail [treɪl] *n* (*tracks*) rastro, pista; (*path*) camino, sendero; (*dust, smoke*) estela ♦ *vt* (*drag*) arrastrar; (*follow*) seguir la pista de ♦ *vi* arrastrar; (*in contest etc*) ir perdiendo; **~ behind** *vi* quedar a la zaga; **~er** *n* (AUT) remolque *m*; (*caravan*) caravana; (CINEMA) trailer *m*, avance *m*; **~er truck** (US) *n* trailer *m*

train [treɪn] *n* tren *m*; (*of dress*) cola; (*series*) serie *f* ♦ *vt* (*educate, teach skills to*) formar; (*sportsman*) entrenar; (*dog*) adiestrar; (*point: gun etc*): **to ~ on** apuntar a ♦ *vi* (SPORT) entrenarse; (*learn a skill*): **to ~ as a teacher** *etc* estudiar para profesor *etc*; **one's ~ of thought** el razonamiento de uno; **~ed** *adj* (*worker*)

cualificado; (*animal*) amaestrado; **~ee** [treɪ'niː] *n* aprendiz(a) *m/f*; **~er** *n* (SPORT: *coach*) entrenador(a) *m/f*; (: *shoe*): **~ers** zapatillas *fpl* (de deporte); (*of animals*) domador(a) *m/f*; **~ing** *n* formación *f*; entrenamiento; **to be in ~ing** (SPORT) estar entrenando; **~ing college** *n* (*gen*) colegio de formación profesional; (*for teachers*) escuela de formación del profesorado; **~ing shoes** *npl* zapatillas *fpl* (de deporte)

traipse [treɪps] *vi* andar penosamente

trait [treɪt] *n* rasgo

traitor ['treɪtə*] *n* traidor(a) *m/f*

tram [træm] (BRIT) *n* (*also:* **~car**) tranvía *m*

tramp [træmp] *n* (*person*) vagabundo/a; (*inf: pej: woman*) puta ♦ *vi* andar con pasos pesados

trample ['træmpl] *vt*: **to ~ (underfoot)** pisotear

trampoline ['træmpəliːn] *n* trampolín *m*

tranquil ['træŋkwɪl] *adj* tranquilo; **~lizer** *n* (MED) tranquilizante *m*

transact [træn'zækt] *vt* (*business*) despachar; **~ion** [-'zækʃən] *n* transacción *f*, operación *f*

transcend [træn'send] *vt* rebasar

transcript ['trænskrɪpt] *n* copia

transfer [*n* 'trænsfə:*, *vb* træns'fə:*] *n* (*of employees*) traslado; (*of money, power*) transferencia; (SPORT) traspaso; (*picture, design*) calcomanía ♦ *vt* trasladar; transferir; **to ~ the charges** (BRIT: TEL) llamar a cobro revertido

transform [træns'fɔːm] *vt* transformar

transfusion [træns'fjuːʒən] *n* transfusión *f*

transient ['trænzɪənt] *adj* transitorio

transistor [træn'zɪstə*] *n* (ELEC) transistor *m*; **~ radio** *n* transistor *m*

transit ['trænzɪt] *n*: **in ~** en tránsito

transitional [træn'zɪʃənl] *adj* de transición

transitive ['trænzɪtɪv] *adj* (LING) transitivo

transit lounge *n* sala de tránsito

translate [trænz'leɪt] *vt* traducir; **translation** [-'leɪʃən] *n* traducción *f*; **translator** *n* traductor(a) *m/f*

transmit [trænz'mɪt] *vt* transmitir; **~ter** *n* transmisor *m*

transparency [træns'peərnsɪ] *n* transparencia; (*BRIT: PHOT*) diapositiva

transparent [træns'pærnt] *adj* transparente

transpire [træns'paɪə*] *vi* (*turn out*) resultar; (*happen*) ocurrir, suceder; **it ~d that ...** se supo que ...

transplant ['trænsplɑ:nt] *n* (*MED*) transplante *m*

transport [*n* 'trænspɔ:t, *vt* træns'pɔ:t] *n* transporte *m*; (*car*) coche *m* (*SP*), carro (*AM*), automóvil *m* ♦ *vt* transportar; **~ation** [-'teɪʃən] *n* transporte *m*; **~ café** (*BRIT*) *n* bar-restaurant *m* de carretera

transvestite [trænz'vestaɪt] *n* travestí *m/f*

trap [træp] *n* (*snare, trick*) trampa; (*carriage*) cabriolé *m* ♦ *vt* coger (*SP*) *or* agarrar (*AM*) en una trampa; (*trick*) engañar; (*confine*) atrapar; **~ door** *n* escotilla

trapeze [trə'pi:z] *n* trapecio

trappings ['træpɪŋz] *npl* adornos *mpl*

trash [træʃ] *n* (*rubbish*) basura; (*pej*): **the book/film is ~** el libro/la película no vale nada; (*nonsense*) tonterías *fpl*; **~ can** (*US*) *n* cubo (*SP*) *or* balde *m* (*AM*) de la basura

travel ['trævl] *n* el viajar ♦ *vi* viajar ♦ *vt* (*distance*) recorrer; **~s** *npl* (*journeys*) viajes *mpl*; **~ agent** *n* agente *m/f* de viajes; **~ler** (*US* **~er**) *n* viajero/a; **~ler's cheque** (*US* **~er's check**) *n* cheque *m* de viajero; **~ling** (*US* **~ing**) *n* los viajes, el viajar; **~ sickness** *n* mareo

travesty ['trævəstɪ] *n* parodia

trawler ['trɔ:lə*] *n* pesquero de arrastre

tray [treɪ] *n* bandeja; (*on desk*) cajón *m*

treacherous ['tretʃərəs] *adj* traidor, traicionero; (*dangerous*) peligroso

treacle ['tri:kl] (*BRIT*) *n* melaza

tread [tred] (*pt* **trod**, *pp* **trodden**) *n* (*step*) paso, pisada; (*sound*) ruido de pasos; (*of stair*) escalón *m*; (*of tyre*) banda de rodadura ♦ *vi* pisar; **~ on** *vt fus* pisar

treason ['tri:zn] *n* traición *f*

treasure ['treʒə*] *n* (*also fig*) tesoro ♦ *vt* (*value: object, friendship*) apreciar;

(*: memory*) guardar

treasurer ['treʒərə*] *n* tesorero/a

treasury ['treʒərɪ] *n*: **the T~** el Ministerio de Hacienda

treat [tri:t] *n* (*present*) regalo ♦ *vt* tratar; **to ~ sb to sth** invitar a uno a algo

treatment ['tri:tmənt] *n* tratamiento

treaty ['tri:tɪ] *n* tratado

treble ['trebl] *adj* triple ♦ *vt* triplicar ♦ *vi* triplicarse; **~ clef** *n* (*MUS*) clave *f* de sol

tree [tri:] *n* árbol *m*; **~ trunk** tronco (de árbol)

trek [trek] *n* (*long journey*) viaje *m* largo y difícil; (*tiring walk*) caminata

trellis ['trelɪs] *n* enrejado

tremble ['trembl] *vi* temblar

tremendous [trɪ'mendəs] *adj* tremendo, enorme; (*excellent*) estupendo

tremor ['tremə*] *n* temblor *m*; (*also: earth ~*) temblor *m* de tierra

trench [trentʃ] *n* zanja

trend [trend] *n* (*tendency*) tendencia; (*of events*) curso; (*fashion*) moda; **~y** *adj* de moda

trepidation [trepɪ'deɪʃən] *n* inquietud *f*

trespass ['trespəs] *vi*: **to ~ on** entrar sin permiso en; **"no ~ing"** "prohibido el paso"

trestle ['tresl] *n* caballete *m*

trial ['traɪəl] *n* (*LAW*) juicio, proceso; (*test: of machine etc*) prueba; **~s** *npl* (*hardships*) dificultades *fpl*; **by ~ and error** a fuerza de probar

triangle ['traɪæŋgl] *n* (*MATH, MUS*) triángulo

tribe [traɪb] *n* tribu *f*

tribulations [trɪbju'leɪʃənz] *npl* dificultades *fpl*, sufrimientos

tribunal [traɪ'bju:nl] *n* tribunal *m*

tributary ['trɪbju:tərɪ] *n* (*river*) afluente *m*

tribute ['trɪbju:t] *n* homenaje *m*, tributo; **to pay ~ to** rendir homenaje a

trick [trɪk] *n* (*skill, knack*) tino, truco; (*conjuring ~*) truco; (*joke*) broma; (*CARDS*) baza ♦ *vt* engañar; **to play a ~ on sb** gastar una broma a uno; **that should do the ~** a ver si funciona así; **~ery** *n* engaño

trickle ['trɪkl] *n* (*of water etc*) goteo ♦ *vi* gotear

tricky ['trɪkɪ] *adj* difícil; delicado

tricycle ['traɪsɪkl] *n* triciclo

trifle ['traɪfl] *n* bagatela; (*CULIN*) dulce de bizcocho borracho, gelatina, fruta y natillas ♦ *vt*: **a ~ long** un poquito largo; **trifling** *adj* insignificante

trigger ['trɪgə*] *n* (*of gun*) gatillo; **~ off** *vt* desencadenar

trill [trɪl] *vi* trinar, gorjear

trim [trɪm] *adj* (*house, garden*) en buen estado; (*person, figure*) esbelto ♦ *n* (*haircut etc*) recorte *m*; (*on car*) guarnición *f* ♦ *vt* (*neaten*) arreglar; (*cut*) recortar; (*decorate*) adornar; (*NAUT: a sail*) orientar; **~mings** *npl* (*CULIN*) guarnición *f*

trinket ['trɪŋkɪt] *n* chuchería

trip [trɪp] *n* viaje *m*; (*excursion*) excursión *f*; (*stumble*) traspié *m* ♦ *vi* (*stumble*) tropezar; (*go lightly*) andar a paso ligero; **on a ~** de viaje; **~ up** *vi* tropezar, caerse ♦ *vt* hacer tropezar or caer

tripe [traɪp] *n* (*CULIN*) callos *mpl*; (*pej: rubbish*) tonterías *fpl*

triple ['trɪpl] *adj* triple; **triplets** ['trɪplɪts] *npl* trillizos/as *mpl/fpl*; **triplicate** ['trɪplɪkət] *n*: **in triplicate** por triplicado

trite [traɪt] *adj* trillado

triumph ['traɪʌmf] *n* triunfo ♦ *vi*: **to ~ (over)** vencer; **~ant** [traɪˈʌmfənt] *adj* (*team etc*) vencedor/a; (*wave, return*) triunfal

trivia ['trɪvɪə] *npl* trivialidades *fpl*

trivial ['trɪvɪəl] *adj* insignificante; (*commonplace*) banal

trod [trɒd] *pt of* **tread**

trodden ['trɒdn] *pp of* **tread**

trolley ['trɒlɪ] *n* carrito; (*also*: **~ bus**) trolebús *m*

trombone [trɒm'bəun] *n* trombón *m*

troop [tru:p] *n* grupo, banda; **~s** *npl* (*MIL*) tropas *fpl*; **~ in/out** *vi* entrar/salir en tropel; **~ing the colour** *n* (*ceremony*) presentación *f* de la bandera

trophy ['trəufɪ] *n* trofeo

tropical ['trɒpɪkl] *adj* tropical

trot [trɒt] *n* trote *m* ♦ *vi* trotar; **on the ~** (*BRIT: fig*) seguidos/as

trouble ['trʌbl] *n* problema *m*, dificultad *f*; (*worry*) preocupación *f*; (*bother, effort*) molestia, esfuerzo; (*unrest*) inquietud *f*; (*MED*): **stomach** *etc* **~** problemas *mpl* gástricos *etc* ♦ *vt* (*disturb*) molestar; (*worry*) preocupar, inquietar ♦ *vi*: **to ~ to do sth** molestarse en hacer algo; **~s** *npl* (*POL etc*) conflictos *mpl*; (*personal*) problemas *mpl*; **to be in ~** estar en un apuro; **it's no ~!** ¡no es molestia (ninguna)!; **what's the ~?** (*with broken TV etc*) ¿cuál es el problema?; (*doctor to patient*) ¿qué pasa?; **~d** *adj* (*person*) preocupado; (*country, epoch, life*) agitado; **~maker** *n* agitador(a) *m/f*; (*child*) alborotador *m*; **~shooter** *n* (*in conflict*) conciliador(a) *m/f*; **~some** *adj* molesto

trough [trɒf] *n* (*also: drinking ~*) abrevadero; (*also: feeding ~*) comedero; (*depression*) depresión *f*

troupe [tru:p] *n* grupo

trousers ['trauzəz] *npl* pantalones *mpl*; **short ~** pantalones *mpl* cortos

trousseau ['tru:səu] (*pl* **~x** *or* **~s**) *n* ajuar *m*

trout [traut] *n inv* trucha

trowel ['trauəl] *n* (*of gardener*) palita; (*of builder*) paleta

truant ['truənt] *n*: **to play ~** (*BRIT*) hacer novillos

truce [tru:s] *n* tregua

truck [trʌk] *n* (*lorry*) camión *m*; (*RAIL*) vagón *m*; **~ driver** *n* camionero; **~ farm** (*US*) *n* huerto

trudge [trʌdʒ] *vi* (*also: ~ along*) caminar penosamente

true [tru:] *adj* verdadero; (*accurate*) exacto; (*genuine*) auténtico; (*faithful*) fiel; **to come ~** realizarse

truffle ['trʌfl] *n* trufa

truly ['tru:lɪ] *adv* (*really*) realmente; (*truthfully*) verdaderamente; (*faithfully*): **yours ~** (*in letter*) le saluda atentamente

trump [trʌmp] *n* triunfo; **~ed-up** *adj* inventado

trumpet ['trʌmpɪt] *n* trompeta

truncheon ['trʌntʃən] *n* porra

trundle ['trʌndl] *vt* (*pushchair etc*) empujar; hacer rodar ♦ *vi*: **to ~ along** ir sin prisas

trunk [trʌŋk] *n* (*of tree, person*) tronco; (*of*

elephant) trompa; (*case*) baúl *m*; (*US: AUT*) maletero; **~s** *npl* (*also: swimming ~s*) bañador *m* (de hombre)

truss [trʌs] *n* (*MED*) braguero; **~ (up)** *vt* atar

trust [trʌst] *n* confianza; (*responsibility*) responsabilidad *f*; (*LAW*) fideicomiso ♦ *vt* (*rely on*) tener confianza en; (*hope*) esperar; (*entrust*): **to ~ sth to sb** confiar algo a uno; **to take sth on ~** aceptar algo a ojos cerrados; **~ed** *adj* de confianza; **~ee** [trʌs'tiː] *n* (*LAW*) fideicomisario; (*of school*) administrador *m*; **~ful** *adj* confiado; **~ing** *adj* confiado; **~worthy** *adj* digno de confianza

truth [truːθ, *pl* truːðz] *n* verdad *f*; **~ful** *adj* veraz

try [traɪ] *n* tentativa, intento; (*RUGBY*) ensayo ♦ *vt* (*attempt*) intentar; (*test: also:* **~ out**) probar, someter a prueba; (*LAW*) juzgar, procesar; (*strain: patience*) hacer perder ♦ *vi* probar; **to have a ~** probar suerte; **to ~ to do sth** intentar hacer algo; **~ again!** ¡vuelve a probar!; **~ harder!** ¡esfuérzate más!; **well, I tried** al menos lo intenté; **~ on** *vt* (*clothes*) probarse; **~ing** *adj* (*experience*) cansado; (*person*) pesado

tsar [zɑː*] *n* zar *m*

T-shirt [ˈtiːʃəːt] *n* camiseta

T-square *n* regla en T

tub [tʌb] *n* cubo (*SP*), balde *m* (*AM*); (*bath*) tina, bañera

tubby [ˈtʌbɪ] *adj* regordete

tube [tjuːb] *n* tubo; (*BRIT: underground*) metro; (*for tyre*) cámara de aire

tuberculosis [tjubəːkjuˈləusɪs] *n* tuberculosis *f inv*

tube station (*BRIT*) *n* estación *f* de metro

tubular [ˈtjuːbjuləˈ*] *adj* tubular

TUC (*BRIT*) *n abbr* (= *Trades Union Congress*) federación nacional de sindicatos

tuck [tʌk] *vt* (*put*) poner; **~ away** *vt* (*money*) guardar; (*building*): **to be ~ed away** esconderse, ocultarse; **~ in** *vt* meter dentro; (*child*) arropar ♦ *vi* (*eat*) comer con apetito; **~ up** *vt* (*child*)

arropar; **~ shop** *n* (*SCOL*) tienda; ≈ bar *m* (del colegio) (*SP*)

Tuesday [ˈtjuːzdɪ] *n* martes *m inv*

tuft [tʌft] *n* mechón *m*; (*of grass etc*) manojo

tug [tʌg] *n* (*ship*) remolcador *m* ♦ *vt* tirar de; **~-of-war** *n* lucha de tiro de cuerda; (*fig*) tira y afloja *m*

tuition [tjuːˈɪʃən] *n* (*BRIT*) enseñanza; (: *private ~*) clases *fpl* particulares; (*US: school fees*) matrícula

tulip [ˈtjuːlɪp] *n* tulipán *m*

tumble [ˈtʌmbl] *n* (*fall*) caída ♦ *vi* caer; **to ~ to sth** (*inf*) caer en la cuenta de algo; **~down** *adj* destartalado; **~ dryer** (*BRIT*) *n* secadora

tumbler [ˈtʌmbləˈ*] *n* (*glass*) vaso

tummy [ˈtʌmɪ] (*inf*) *n* barriga, tripa

tumour [ˈtjuːməˈ*] (*US* **tumor**) *n* tumor *m*

tuna [ˈtjuːnə] *n inv* (*also:* **~ fish**) atún *m*

tune [tjuːn] *n* melodía ♦ *vt* (*MUS*) afinar; (*RADIO, TV, AUT*) sintonizar; **to be in/out of ~** (*instrument*) estar afinado/desafinado; (*singer*) cantar afinadamente/desafinar; **to be in/out of ~ with** (*fig*) estar de acuerdo/en desacuerdo con; **~ in** *vi*: **to ~ in (to)** (*RADIO, TV*) sintonizar (con); **~ up** *vi* (*musician*) afinar (su instrumento); **~ful** *adj* melodioso; **~r** *n*: **piano ~r** afinador(a) *m/f* de pianos

tunic [ˈtjuːnɪk] *n* túnica

Tunisia [tjuːˈnɪzɪə] *n* Túnez *m*

tunnel [ˈtʌnl] *n* túnel *m*; (*in mine*) galería ♦ *vi* construir un túnel/una galería

turban [ˈtəːbən] *n* turbante *m*

turbine [ˈtəːbaɪn] *n* turbina

turbulent [ˈtəːbjulənt] *adj* turbulento

tureen [təˈriːn] *n* sopera

turf [təːf] *n* césped *m*; (*clod*) tepe *m* ♦ *vt* cubrir con césped; **~ out** (*inf*) *vt* echar a la calle

turgid [ˈtəːdʒɪd] *adj* (*prose*) pesado

Turk [təːk] *n* turco/a

Turkey [ˈtəːkɪ] *n* Turquía

turkey [ˈtəːkɪ] *n* pavo

Turkish [ˈtəːkɪʃ] *adj, n* turco

turmoil [ˈtəːmɔɪl] *n* desorden *m*, alboroto; **in ~** revuelto

turn [təːn] *n* turno; (*in road*) curva; (*of*

mind, events) rumbo; (*THEATRE*) número; (*MED*) ataque *m* ♦ *vt* girar, volver; (*collar, steak*) dar la vuelta a; (*page*) pasar; (*change*): **to ~ sth into** convertir algo en ♦ vi volver; (*person: look back*) volverse; (*reverse direction*) dar la vuelta; (*milk*) cortarse; (*become*): **to ~ nasty/forty** ponerse feo/cumplir los cuarenta; **a good ~** un favor; **it gave me quite a ~** me dio un susto; **"no left ~"** (*AUT*) "prohibido girar a la izquierda"; **it's your ~** te toca a ti; **in ~** por turnos; **to take ~s (at)** turnarse (en); **~ away** *vi* apartar la vista ♦ *vi* rechazar; **~ back** *vi* volverse atrás ♦ *vt* hacer retroceder; (*clock*) retrasar; **~ down** *vt* (*refuse*) rechazar; (*reduce*) bajar; (*fold*) doblar; **~ in** (*inf: go to bed*) acostarse ♦ *vt* (*fold*) doblar hacia dentro; **~ off** *vi* (*from road*) desviarse ♦ *vt* (*light, radio etc*) apagar; (*tap*) cerrar; (*engine*) parar; **~ on** *vt* (*light, radio etc*) encender (*SP*), prender (*AM*); (*tap*) abrir; (*engine*) poner en marcha; **~ out** *vt* (*light, gas*) apagar; (*produce*) producir ♦ *vi* (*voters*) concurrir; **to ~ out to be ...** resultar ser ...; **~ over** *vi* (*person*) volverse ♦ *vt* (*object*) dar la vuelta a; (*page*) volver; **~ round** *vi* volverse; (*rotate*) girar; **~ up** *vi* (*person*) llegar, presentarse; (*lost object*) aparecer ♦ *vt* (*gen*) subir; **~ing** *n* (*in road*) vuelta; **~ing point** *n* (*fig*) momento decisivo
turnip ['tə:nɪp] *n* nabo
turnout ['tə:naʊt] *n* concurrencia
turnover ['tə:nəʊvə*] *n* (*COMM: amount of money*) volumen *m* de ventas; (: *of goods*) movimiento
turnpike ['tə:npaɪk] (*US*) *n* autopista de peaje
turnstile ['tə:nstaɪl] *n* torniquete *m*
turntable ['tə:nteɪbl] *n* plato
turn-up (*BRIT*) *n* (*on trousers*) vuelta
turpentine ['tə:pəntaɪn] *n* (*also: turps*) trementina
turquoise ['tə:kwɔɪz] *n* (*stone*) turquesa ♦ *adj* color turquesa
turret ['tʌrɪt] *n* torreón *m*
turtle ['tə:tl] *n* galápago; **~neck (sweater)** *n* jersey *m* de cuello vuelto

tusk [tʌsk] *n* colmillo
tussle ['tʌsl] *n* pelea
tutor ['tju:tə*] *n* profesor(a) *m/f*; **~ial** [-'tɔ:rɪəl] *n* (*SCOL*) seminario
tuxedo [tʌk'si:dəu] (*US*) *n* smóking *m*, esmoquin *m*
TV [ti:'vi:] *n abbr* (= *television*) tele *f*
twang [twæŋ] *n* (*of instrument*) punteado; (*of voice*) timbre *m* nasal
tweezers ['twi:zəz] *npl* pinzas *fpl* (de depilar)
twelfth [twɛlfθ] *num* duodécimo
twelve [twɛlv] *num* doce; **at ~ o'clock** (*midday*) a mediodía; (*midnight*) a medianoche
twentieth ['twɛntɪɪθ] *adj* vigésimo
twenty ['twɛntɪ] *num* veinte
twice [twaɪs] *adv* dos veces; **~ as much** dos veces más
twiddle ['twɪdl] *vt* juguetear con ♦ *vi*: **to ~ (with) sth** dar vueltas a algo; **to ~ one's thumbs** (*fig*) estar mano sobre mano
twig [twɪg] *n* ramita ♦ *vi* (*inf*) caer en la cuenta
twilight ['twaɪlaɪt] *n* crepúsculo
twin [twɪn] *adj, n* gemelo/a *m/f* ♦ *vt* hermanar; **~-bedded room** *n* habitación *f* doble
twine [twaɪn] *n* bramante *m* ♦ *vi* (*plant*) enroscarse
twinge [twɪndʒ] *n* (*of pain*) punzada; (*of conscience*) remordimiento
twinkle ['twɪŋkl] *vi* centellear; (*eyes*) brillar
twirl [twə:l] *vt* dar vueltas a ♦ *vi* dar vueltas
twist [twɪst] *n* (*action*) torsión *f*; (*in road, coil*) vuelta; (*in wire, flex*) doblez *f*; (*in story*) giro ♦ *vt* torcer; (*weave*) trenzar; (*roll around*) enrollar; (*fig*) deformar ♦ *vi* serpentear
twit [twɪt] (*inf*) *n* tonto
twitch [twɪtʃ] *n* (*pull*) tirón *m*; (*nervous*) tic *m* ♦ *vi* crisparse
two [tu:] *num* dos; **to put ~ and ~ together** (*fig*) atar cabos; **~-door** *adj* (*AUT*) de dos puertas; **~-faced** *adj* (*pej: person*) falso; **~fold** *adv*: **to increase**

~fold doblarse; ~-piece (suit) n traje m
de dos piezas; ~-piece (swimsuit) n dos
piezas m inv, bikini m; ~some n (people)
pareja; ~-way adj: ~-way traffic
circulación f de dos sentidos

tycoon [taɪˈkuːn] n: (business) ~ magnate
m

type [taɪp] n (category) tipo, género;
(model) tipo; (TYP) tipo, letra ♦ vt (letter
etc) escribir a máquina; ~-cast adj
(actor) encasillado; ~face n letra; ~script
n texto mecanografiado; ~writer n
máquina de escribir; ~written adj
mecanografiado

typhoid [ˈtaɪfɔɪd] n tifoidea

typical [ˈtɪpɪkl] adj típico

typing [ˈtaɪpɪŋ] n mecanografía

typist [ˈtaɪpɪst] n mecanógrafo/a

tyranny [ˈtɪrənɪ] n tiranía

tyrant [ˈtaɪərnt] n tirano/a

tyre [ˈtaɪə*] (US tire) n neumático (SP),
llanta (AM); ~ pressure n presión f de los
neumáticos

tzar [zɑː*] n = tsar

U u

U-bend [ˈjuːbɛnd] n (AUT, in pipe) recodo

udder [ˈʌdə*] n ubre f

UFO [ˈjuːfəu] n abbr = (unidentified
flying object) OVNI m

ugh [əːh] excl ¡uf!

ugly [ˈʌɡlɪ] adj feo; (dangerous) peligroso

UK n abbr = United Kingdom

ulcer [ˈʌlsə*] n úlcera; (mouth ~) llaga

Ulster [ˈʌlstə*] n Ulster m

ulterior [ʌlˈtɪərɪə*] adj: ~ motive
segundas intenciones fpl

ultimate [ˈʌltɪmət] adj último, final;
(greatest) máximo; ~ly adv (in the end)
por último, al final; (fundamentally) a or
en fin de cuentas

umbilical cord [ʌmˈbɪlɪkl-] n cordón m
umbilical

umbrella [ʌmˈbrɛlə] n paraguas m inv;
(for sun) sombrilla

umpire [ˈʌmpaɪə*] n árbitro

umpteen [ʌmpˈtiːn] adj enésimos/as; ~th

adj: for the ~th time por enésima vez

UN n abbr (= United Nations) NN. UU.

unable [ʌnˈeɪbl] adj: to be ~ to do sth
no poder hacer algo

unaccompanied [ʌnəˈkʌmpənɪd] adj no
acompañado; (song) sin acompañamiento

unaccountably [ʌnəˈkauntəblɪ] adv
inexplicablemente

unaccustomed [ʌnəˈkʌstəmd] adj: to be
~ to no estar acostumbrado a

unanimous [juːˈnænɪməs] adj unánime

unarmed [ʌnˈɑːmd] adj (defenceless)
inerme; (without weapon) desarmado

unashamed [ʌnəˈʃeɪmd] adj descarado

unassuming [ʌnəˈsjuːmɪŋ] adj modesto,
sin pretensiones

unattached [ʌnəˈtætʃt] adj (person)
soltero y sin compromiso; (part etc)
suelto

unattended [ʌnəˈtɛndɪd] adj desatendido

unattractive [ʌnəˈtræktɪv] adj poco
atractivo

unauthorized [ʌnˈɔːθəraɪzd] adj no
autorizado

unavoidable [ʌnəˈvɔɪdəbl] adj inevitable

unaware [ʌnəˈwɛə*] adj: to be ~ of
ignorar; ~s adv de improviso

unbalanced [ʌnˈbælənst] adj (report)
poco objetivo; (mentally) trastornado

unbearable [ʌnˈbɛərəbl] adj insoportable

unbeatable [ʌnˈbiːtəbl] adj (team)
invencible; (price) inmejorable; (quality)
insuperable

unbelievable [ʌnbɪˈliːvəbl] adj increíble

unbend [ʌnˈbɛnd] (irreg) vi (relax)
relajarse ♦ vt (wire) enderezar

unbiased [ʌnˈbaɪəst] adj imparcial

unborn [ʌnˈbɔːn] adj que va a nacer

unbroken [ʌnˈbrəukən] adj (seal) intacto;
(series) continuo; (record) no batido;
(spirit) indómito

unbutton [ʌnˈbʌtn] vt desabrochar

uncalled-for [ʌnˈkɔːldfɔː*] adj gratuito,
inmerecido

uncanny [ʌnˈkænɪ] adj extraño

unceremonious [ˈʌnsɛrɪˈməunɪəs] adj
(abrupt, rude) brusco, hosco

uncertain [ʌnˈsɜːtn] adj incierto;
(indecisive) indeciso

unchanged [ʌn'tʃeɪndʒd] *adj* igual, sin cambios

unchecked [ʌn'tʃɛkt] *adv* sin estorbo, sin restricción

uncivilized [ʌn'sɪvɪlaɪzd] *adj* inculto; (*fig: behaviour etc*) bárbaro; (*hour*) inoportuno

uncle ['ʌŋkl] *n* tío

uncomfortable [ʌn'kʌmfətəbl] *adj* incómodo; (*uneasy*) inquieto

uncommon [ʌn'kɔmən] *adj* poco común, raro

uncompromising [ʌn'kɔmprəmaɪzɪŋ] *adj* intransigente

unconcerned [ʌnkən'səːnd] *adj* indiferente, despreocupado

unconditional [ʌnkən'dɪʃənl] *adj* incondicional

unconscious [ʌn'kɔnʃəs] *adj* sin sentido; (*unaware*): **to be ~ of** no darse cuenta de ♦ *n*: **the ~** el inconsciente

uncontrollable [ʌnkən'trəuləbl] *adj* (*child etc*) incontrolable; (*temper*) indomable; (*laughter*) incontenible

unconventional [ʌnkən'vɛnʃənl] *adj* poco convencional

uncouth [ʌn'kuːθ] *adj* grosero, inculto

uncover [ʌn'kʌvə*] *vt* descubrir; (*take lid off*) destapar

undecided [ʌndɪ'saɪdd] *adj* (*character*) indeciso; (*question*) no resuelto

under ['ʌndə*] *prep* debajo de; (*less than*) menos de; (*according to*) según, de acuerdo con; (*sb's leadership*) bajo ♦ *adv* debajo, abajo; ~ **there** allí abajo; ~ **repair** en reparación

under... ['ʌndə*] *prefix* sub; **~-age** *adj* menor de edad; (*drinking etc*) de los menores de edad; **~carriage** (*BRIT*) *n* (*AVIAT*) tren *m* de aterrizaje; **~charge** *vt* cobrar menos de la cuenta; **~clothes** *npl* ropa interior (*SP*) or íntima (*AM*); **~coat** *n* (*paint*) primera mano; **~cover** *adj* clandestino; **~current** *n* (*fig*) corriente *f* oculta; **~cut** *vt irreg* vender más barato que; **~developed** *adj* subdesarrollado; **~dog** *n* desvalido/a; **~done** *adj* (*CULIN*) poco hecho; **~estimate** *vt* subestimar; **~exposed** *adj* (*PHOT*) subexpuesto; **~fed**

adj subalimentado; **~foot** *adv* con los pies; **~go** *vt irreg* sufrir; (*treatment*) recibir; **~graduate** *n* estudiante *m/f*; **~ground** *n* (*BRIT: railway*) metro; (*POL*) movimiento clandestino ♦ *adj* (*car park*) subterráneo ♦ *adv* (*work*) en la clandestinidad; **~growth** *n* maleza; **~hand(ed)** *adj* (*fig*) socarrón; **~lie** *vt irreg* (*fig*) ser la razón fundamental de; **~line** *vt* subrayar; **~ling** ['ʌndəlɪŋ] (*pej*) *n* subalterno/a; **~mine** *vt* socavar, minar; **~neath** [ʌndə'niːθ] *adv* debajo ♦ *prep* debajo de, bajo; **~paid** *adj* mal pagado; **~pants** *npl* calzoncillos *mpl*; **~pass** (*BRIT*) *n* paso subterráneo; **~privileged** *adj* desposeído; **~rate** *vt* menospreciar, subestimar; **~shirt** (*US*) *n* camiseta; **~shorts** (*US*) *npl* calzoncillos *mpl*; **~side** *n* parte *f* inferior; **~skirt** (*BRIT*) *n* enaguas *fpl*

understand [ʌndə'stænd] (*irreg*) *vt, vi* entender, comprender; (*assume*) tener entendido; **~able** *adj* comprensible; **~ing** *adj* comprensivo ♦ *n* comprensión *f*, entendimiento; (*agreement*) acuerdo

understatement ['ʌndəsteɪtmənt] *n* modestia (excesiva); **that's an ~!** ¡eso es decir poco!

understood [ʌndə'stud] *pt, pp of* **understand** ♦ *adj* (*agreed*) acordado; (*implied*): **it is ~ that** se sobreentiende que

understudy ['ʌndəstʌdɪ] *n* suplente *m/f*

undertake [ʌndə'teɪk] (*irreg*) *vt* emprender; **to ~ to do sth** comprometerse a hacer algo

undertaker ['ʌndəteɪkə*] *n* director(a) *m/f* de pompas fúnebres

undertaking ['ʌndəteɪkɪŋ] *n* empresa; (*promise*) promesa

undertone ['ʌndətəun] *n*: **in an ~** en voz baja

underwater [ʌndə'wɔːtə*] *adv* bajo el agua ♦ *adj* submarino

underwear ['ʌndəwɛə*] *n* ropa interior (*SP*) or íntima (*AM*)

underworld ['ʌndəwəːld] *n* (*of crime*) hampa, inframundo

underwriter ['ʌndəraɪtə*] *n* (*INSURANCE*)

asegurador(a) *m/f*

undesirable [ʌndɪˈzaɪrəbl] *adj* (*person*) indeseable; (*thing*) poco aconsejable

undies [ˈʌndɪz] (*inf*) *npl* ropa interior (*SP*) *or* íntima (*AM*)

undo [ʌnˈduː] (*irreg*) *vt* (*laces*) desatar; (*button etc*) desabrochar; (*spoil*) deshacer; ~**ing** *n* ruina, perdición *f*

undoubted [ʌnˈdautɪd] *adj* indudable

undress [ʌnˈdrɛs] *vi* desnudarse

undulating [ˈʌndjuleɪtɪŋ] *adj* ondulante

unduly [ʌnˈdjuːlɪ] *adv* excesivamente, demasiado

unearth [ʌnˈɜːθ] *vt* desenterrar

unearthly [ʌnˈɜːθlɪ] *adj* (*hour*) inverosímil

uneasy [ʌnˈiːzɪ] *adj* intranquilo, preocupado; (*feeling*) desagradable; (*peace*) inseguro

uneducated [ʌnˈɛdjukeɪtɪd] *adj* ignorante, inculto

unemployed [ʌnɪmˈplɔɪd] *adj* parado, sin trabajo ♦ *npl*: **the** ~ los parados

unemployment [ʌnɪmˈplɔɪmənt] *n* paro, desempleo

unending [ʌnˈɛndɪŋ] *adj* interminable

unerring [ʌnˈɜːrɪŋ] *adj* infalible

uneven [ʌnˈiːvn] *adj* desigual; (*road etc*) lleno de baches

unexpected [ʌnɪkˈspɛktɪd] *adj* inesperado; ~**ly** *adv* inesperadamente

unfailing [ʌnˈfeɪlɪŋ] *adj* (*support*) indefectible; (*energy*) inagotable

unfair [ʌnˈfɛə*] *adj*: ~ **(to sb)** injusto (con uno)

unfaithful [ʌnˈfeɪθful] *adj* infiel

unfamiliar [ʌnfəˈmɪlɪə*] *adj* extraño, desconocido; **to be ~ with** desconocer

unfashionable [ʌnˈfæʃnəbl] *adj* pasado *or* fuera de moda

unfasten [ʌnˈfɑːsn] *vt* (*knot*) desatar; (*dress*) desabrochar; (*open*) abrir

unfavourable [ʌnˈfeɪvərəbl] (*US* **unfavorable**) *adj* desfavorable

unfeeling [ʌnˈfiːlɪŋ] *adj* insensible

unfinished [ʌnˈfɪnɪʃt] *adj* inacabado, sin terminar

unfit [ʌnˈfɪt] *adj* bajo de forma; (*incompetent*): ~ **(for)** incapaz (de); ~ **for work**

no apto para trabajar

unfold [ʌnˈfəuld] *vt* desdoblar ♦ *vi* abrirse

unforeseen [ˈʌnfɔːˈsiːn] *adj* imprevisto

unforgettable [ʌnfəˈgɛtəbl] *adj* inolvidable

unfortunate [ʌnˈfɔːtʃnət] *adj* desgraciado; (*event, remark*) inoportuno; ~**ly** *adv* desgraciadamente

unfounded [ʌnˈfaundɪd] *adj* infundado

unfriendly [ʌnˈfrɛndlɪ] *adj* antipático; (*behaviour, remark*) hostil, poco amigable

ungainly [ʌnˈgeɪnlɪ] *adj* desgarbado

ungodly [ʌnˈgɒdlɪ] *adj*: **at an ~ hour** a una hora inverosímil

ungrateful [ʌnˈgreɪtful] *adj* ingrato

unhappiness [ʌnˈhæpɪnɪs] *n* tristeza, desdicha

unhappy [ʌnˈhæpɪ] *adj* (*sad*) triste; (*unfortunate*) desgraciado; (*childhood*) infeliz; ~ **about/with** (*arrangements etc*) poco contento con, descontento de

unharmed [ʌnˈhɑːmd] *adj* ileso

unhealthy [ʌnˈhɛlθɪ] *adj* (*place*) malsano; (*person*) enfermizo; (*fig: interest*) morboso

unheard-of [ʌnˈhɜːdɔv] *adj* inaudito, sin precedente

unhurt [ʌnˈhɜːt] *adj* ileso

unidentified [ʌnaɪˈdɛntɪfaɪd] *adj* no identificado, sin identificar; *see also* **UFO**

uniform [ˈjuːnɪfɔːm] *n* uniforme *m* ♦ *adj* uniforme

unify [ˈjuːnɪfaɪ] *vt* unificar, unir

uninhabited [ʌnɪnˈhæbɪtɪd] *adj* desierto

unintentional [ʌnɪnˈtɛnʃənəl] *adj* involuntario

union [ˈjuːnjən] *n* unión *f*; (*also: trade ~*) sindicato ♦ *cpd* sindical; **U~ Jack** *n* bandera del Reino Unido

unique [juːˈniːk] *adj* único

unison [ˈjuːnɪsn] *n*: **in ~** (*speak, reply, sing*) al unísono

unit [ˈjuːnɪt] *n* unidad *f*; (*section: of furniture etc*) elemento; (*team*) grupo; **kitchen ~** módulo de cocina

unite [juːˈnaɪt] *vt* unir ♦ *vi* unirse; ~**d** *adj* unido; (*effort*) conjunto; **U~d Kingdom** *n* Reino Unido; **U~d Nations (Organization)** *n* Naciones *fpl* Unidas; **U~d States (of America)** *n* Estados *mpl* Unidos

unit trust (*BRIT*) *n* bono fiduciario
unity ['ju:nɪtɪ] *n* unidad *f*
universe ['ju:nɪvɜ:s] *n* universo
university [ju:nɪ'vɜ:sɪtɪ] *n* universidad *f*
unjust [ʌn'dʒʌst] *adj* injusto
unkempt [ʌn'kɛmpt] *adj* (*appearance*) descuidado; (*hair*) despeinado
unkind [ʌn'kaɪnd] *adj* poco amable; (*behaviour, comment*) cruel
unknown [ʌn'nəun] *adj* desconocido
unlawful [ʌn'lɔ:ful] *adj* ilegal, ilícito
unleaded [ʌn'lɛdɪd] *adj* (*petrol, fuel*) sin plombo
unleash [ʌn'li:ʃ] *vt* desatar
unless [ʌn'lɛs] *conj* a menos que; ~ **he comes** a menos que venga; ~ **otherwise stated** salvo indicación contraria
unlike [ʌn'laɪk] *adj* (*not alike*) distinto de *or* a; (*not like*) poco propio de ♦ *prep* a diferencia de
unlikely [ʌn'laɪklɪ] *adj* improbable; (*unexpected*) inverosímil
unlimited [ʌn'lɪmɪtɪd] *adj* ilimitado
unlisted [ʌn'lɪstɪd] (*US*) *adj* (*TEL*) que no consta en la guía
unload [ʌn'ləud] *vt* descargar
unlock [ʌn'lɔk] *vt* abrir (con llave)
unlucky [ʌn'lʌkɪ] *adj* desgraciado; (*object, number*) que da mala suerte; **to be ~** tener mala suerte
unmarried [ʌn'mærɪd] *adj* soltero
unmistakable [ʌnmɪs'teɪkəbl] *adj* inconfundible
unnatural [ʌn'nætʃrəl] *adj* (*gen*) antinatural; (*manner*) afectado; (*habit*) perverso
unnecessary [ʌn'nɛsəsərɪ] *adj* innecesario, inútil
unnoticed [ʌn'nəutɪst] *adj*: **to go** *or* **pass** ~ pasar desapercibido
UNO ['ju:nəu] *n abbr* (= *United Nations Organization*) ONU *f*
unobtainable [ʌnəb'teɪnəbl] *adj* inconseguible; (*TEL*) inexistente
unobtrusive [ʌnəb'tru:sɪv] *adj* discreto
unofficial [ʌnə'fɪʃl] *adj* no oficial; (*news*) sin confirmar
unorthodox [ʌn'ɔ:θədɔks] *adj* poco ortodoxo; (*REL*) heterodoxo

unpack [ʌn'pæk] *vi* deshacer las maletas ♦ *vt* deshacer
unpalatable [ʌn'pælətəbl] *adj* incomible; (*truth*) desagradable
unparalleled [ʌn'pærəlɛld] *adj* (*unequalled*) incomparable
unpleasant [ʌn'plɛznt] *adj* (*disagreeable*) desagradable; (*person, manner*) antipático
unplug [ʌn'plʌg] *vt* desenchufar, desconectar
unpopular [ʌn'pɔpjulə*] *adj* impopular, poco popular
unprecedented [ʌn'prɛsɪdəntɪd] *adj* sin precedentes
unpredictable [ʌnprɪ'dɪktəbl] *adj* imprevisible
unprofessional [ʌnprə'fɛʃənl] *adj* (*attitude, conduct*) poco ético
unqualified [ʌn'kwɔlɪfaɪd] *adj* sin título, no cualificado; (*success*) total
unquestionably [ʌn'kwɛstʃənəblɪ] *adv* indiscutiblemente
unravel [ʌn'rævl] *vt* desenmarañar; (*mystery*) desentrañar
unreal [ʌn'rɪəl] *adj* irreal; (*extraordinary*) increíble
unrealistic [ʌnrɪə'lɪstɪk] *adj* poco realista
unreasonable [ʌn'ri:znəbl] *adj* irrazonable; (*demand*) excesivo
unrelated [ʌnrɪ'leɪtɪd] *adj* sin relación; (*family*) no emparentado
unrelenting [ʌnrɪ'lɛntɪŋ] *adj* inexorable
unreliable [ʌnrɪ'laɪəblɪ] *adj* (*person*) informal; (*machine*) poco fiable
unremitting [ʌnrɪ'mɪtɪŋ] *adj* constante
unreservedly [ʌnrɪ'zɜ:vɪdlɪ] *adv* sin reserva
unrest [ʌn'rɛst] *n* inquietud *f*, malestar *m*; (*POL*) disturbios *mpl*
unroll [ʌn'rəul] *vt* desenrollar
unruly [ʌn'ru:lɪ] *adj* indisciplinado
unsafe [ʌn'seɪf] *adj* peligroso
unsaid [ʌn'sɛd] *adj*: **to leave sth** ~ dejar algo sin decir
unsatisfactory ['ʌnsætɪs'fæktərɪ] *adj* poco satisfactorio
unsavoury [ʌn'seɪvərɪ] (*US* **unsavory**) *adj* (*fig*) repugnante

unscathed [ʌnˈskeɪðd] *adj* ileso
unscrew [ʌnˈskruː] *vt* destornillar
unscrupulous [ʌnˈskruːpjuləs] *adj* sin escrúpulos
unsettled [ʌnˈsɛtld] *adj* inquieto, intranquilo; (*weather*) variable
unshaven [ʌnˈʃeɪvn] *adj* sin afeitar
unsightly [ʌnˈsaɪtlɪ] *adj* feo
unskilled [ʌnˈskɪld] *adj* (*work*) no especializado; (*worker*) no cualificado
unspeakable [ʌnˈspiːkəbl] *adj* indecible; (*awful*) incalificable
unstable [ʌnˈsteɪbl] *adj* inestable
unsteady [ʌnˈstɛdɪ] *adj* inestable
unstuck [ʌnˈstʌk] *adj*: **to come ~** despegarse, (*fig*) fracasar
unsuccessful [ʌnsəkˈsɛsful] *adj* (*attempt*) infructuoso; (*writer, proposal*) sin éxito; **to be ~** (*in attempting sth*) no tener éxito, fracasar; **~ly** *adv* en vano, sin éxito
unsuitable [ʌnˈsuːtəbl] *adj* inapropiado; (*time*) inoportuno
unsure [ʌnˈʃuə*] *adj* inseguro, poco seguro
unsuspecting [ˈʌnsəsˈpɛktɪŋ] *adj* desprevenido
unsympathetic [ʌnsɪmpəˈθɛtɪk] *adj* poco comprensivo; (*unlikeable*) antipático
untapped [ʌnˈtæpt] *adj* (*resources*) sin explotar
unthinkable [ʌnˈθɪŋkəbl] *adj* inconcebible, impensable
untidy [ʌnˈtaɪdɪ] *adj* (*room*) desordenado; (*appearance*) desaliñado
untie [ʌnˈtaɪ] *vt* desatar
until [ənˈtɪl] *prep* hasta ♦ *conj* hasta que; **~ he comes** hasta que venga; **~ now** hasta ahora; **~ then** hasta entonces
untimely [ʌnˈtaɪmlɪ] *adj* inoportuno; (*death*) prematuro
untold [ʌnˈtəuld] *adj* (*story*) nunca contado; (*suffering*) indecible; (*wealth*) incalculable
untoward [ʌntəˈwɔːd] *adj* adverso
unused [ʌnˈjuːzd] *adj* sin usar
unusual [ʌnˈjuːʒuəl] *adj* insólito, poco común; (*exceptional*) inusitado
unveil [ʌnˈveɪl] *vt* (*statue*) descubrir
unwanted [ʌnˈwɒntɪd] *adj* (*clothing*)

viejo; (*pregnancy*) no deseado
unwelcome [ʌnˈwɛlkəm] *adj* inoportuno; (*news*) desagradable
unwell [ʌnˈwɛl] *adj*: **to be/feel ~** estar indispuesto/sentirse mal
unwieldy [ʌnˈwiːldɪ] *adj* difícil de manejar
unwilling [ʌnˈwɪlɪŋ] *adj*: **to be ~ to do sth** estar poco dispuesto a hacer algo; **~ly** *adv* de mala gana
unwind [ʌnˈwaɪnd] (*irg: like* **wind²**) *vt* desenvolver ♦ *vi* (*relax*) relajarse
unwise [ʌnˈwaɪz] *adj* imprudente
unwitting [ʌnˈwɪtɪŋ] *adj* inconsciente
unworkable [ʌnˈwɔːkəbl] *adj* (*plan*) imprácticable
unworthy [ʌnˈwɔːðɪ] *adj* indigno
unwrap [ʌnˈræp] *vt* desenvolver
unwritten [ʌnˈrɪtn] *adj* (*agreement*) tácito; (*rules, law*) no escrito

KEYWORD

up [ʌp] *prep*: **to go/be ~ sth** subir/estar subido en algo; **he went ~ the stairs/ the hill** subió las escaleras/la colina; **we walked/climbed ~ the hill** subimos la colina; **they live further ~ the street** viven más arriba en la calle; **go ~ that road and turn left** sigue por esa calle y gira a la izquierda
♦ *adv* 1 (*upwards, higher*) más arriba; **~ in the mountains** en lo alto (de la montaña); **put it a bit higher ~** ponlo un poco más arriba *or* alto; **~ there** ahí *or* allí arriba; **~ above** en lo alto, por encima, arriba
2: **to be ~** (*out of bed*) estar levantado; (*prices, level*) haber subido
3: **~ to** (*as far as*) hasta; **~ to now** hasta ahora *or* la fecha
4: **to be ~ to** (*depending on*): **it's ~ to you** depende de ti; **he's not ~ to it** (*job, task etc*) no es capaz de hacerlo; **his work is not ~ to the required standard** su trabajo no da la talla; (*inf: be doing*): **what is he ~ to?** ¿que estará tramando?
♦ *n*: **~s and downs** altibajos *mpl*

upbringing ['ʌpbrɪŋɪŋ] *n* educación *f*
update [ʌp'deɪt] *vt* poner al día
upgrade [ʌp'greɪd] *vt* (*house*) modernizar; (*employee*) ascender
upheaval [ʌp'hi:vl] *n* trastornos *mpl*; (*POL*) agitación *f*
uphill [ʌp'hɪl] *adj* cuesta arriba; (*fig: task*) penoso, difícil ♦ *adv*: **to go ~** ir cuesta arriba
uphold [ʌp'həʊld] (*irreg*) *vt* defender
upholstery [ʌp'həʊlstərɪ] *n* tapicería
upkeep ['ʌpki:p] *n* mantenimiento
upon [ə'pɔn] *prep* sobre
upper ['ʌpə*] *adj* superior, de arriba ♦ *n* (*of shoe: also:* ~s) empeine *m*; **~-class** *adj* de clase alta; **~ hand** *n*: **to have the ~ hand** tener la sartén por el mango; **~most** *adj* el más alto; **what was ~most in my mind** lo que me preocupaba más
upright ['ʌpraɪt] *adj* derecho; (*vertical*) vertical; (*fig*) honrado
uprising ['ʌpraɪzɪŋ] *n* sublevación *f*
uproar ['ʌprɔ:*] *n* escándalo
uproot [ʌp'ru:t] *vt* (*also fig*) desarraigar
upset [*n* 'ʌpsɛt, *vb, adj* ʌp'sɛt] *n* (*to plan etc*) revés *m*, contratiempo; (*MED*) trastorno ♦ (*irreg*) *vt* (*glass etc*) volcar; (*plan*) alterar; (*person*) molestar, disgustar ♦ *adj* molesto, disgustado; (*stomach*) revuelto
upshot ['ʌpʃɔt] *n* resultado
upside-down *adv* al revés; **to turn a place ~** (*fig*) revolverlo todo
upstairs [ʌp'stɛəz] *adv* arriba ♦ *adj* (*room*) de arriba ♦ *n* el piso superior
upstart ['ʌpstɑ:t] *n* advenedizo/a
upstream [ʌp'stri:m] *adv* río arriba
uptake ['ʌpteɪk] *n*: **to be quick/slow on the ~** ser muy listo/torpe
uptight [ʌp'taɪt] *adj* tenso, nervioso
up-to-date *adj* al día
upturn ['ʌptə:n] *n* (*in luck*) mejora; (*COMM: in market*) resurgimiento económico
upward ['ʌpwəd] *adj* ascendente; **~(s)** *adv* hacia arriba; (*more than*): **~(s) of** más de
urban ['ə:bən] *adj* urbano

urchin ['ə:tʃɪn] *n* pilluelo, golfillo
urge [ə:dʒ] *n* (*desire*) deseo ♦ *vt*: **to ~ sb to do sth** animar a uno a hacer algo
urgent ['ə:dʒənt] *adj* urgente; (*voice*) perentorio
urinate ['juərɪneɪt] *vi* orinar
urine ['juərɪn] *n* orina, orines *mpl*
urn [ə:n] *n* urna; (*also: tea ~*) cacharro metálico grande para hacer té
Uruguay ['juərəgwaɪ] *n* (el) Uruguay; **~an** [-'gwaɪən] *adj, n* uruguayo/a *m/f*
US *n abbr* (= *United States*) EE. UU.
us [ʌs] *pron* nos; (*after prep*) nosotros/as; *see also* **me**
USA *n abbr* (= *United States of America*) EE. UU
usage ['ju:zɪdʒ] *n* (*LING*) uso
use [*n* ju:s, *vb* ju:z] *n* uso, empleo; (*usefulness*) utilidad *f* ♦ *vt* usar, emplear; **she ~d to do it** (ella) solía *or* acostumbraba hacerlo; **in ~** en uso; **out of ~** en desuso; **to be of ~** servir; **it's no ~** (*pointless*) es inútil; (*not useful*) no sirve; **to be ~d to** estar acostumbrado a, acostumbrar; **~ up** *vt* (*food*) consumir; (*money*) gastar; **~d** *adj* (*car*) usado; **~ful** *adj* útil; **~fulness** *n* utilidad *f*; **~less** *adj* (*unusable*) inservible; (*pointless*) inútil; (*person*) inepto; **~r** *n* usuario/a; **~r-friendly** *adj* (*computer*) amistoso
usher ['ʌʃə*] *n* (*at wedding*) ujier *m*; **~ette** [-'rɛt] *n* (*in cinema*) acomodadora
USSR *n*: **the ~** la URSS
usual ['ju:ʒuəl] *adj* normal, corriente; **as ~** como de costumbre; **~ly** *adv* normalmente
utensil [ju:'tɛnsl] *n* utensilio; **kitchen ~s** batería de cocina
uterus ['ju:tərəs] *n* útero
utility [ju:'tɪlɪtɪ] *n* utilidad *f*; (*public ~*) (empresa de) servicio público; **~ room** *n* ofis *m*
utilize ['ju:tɪlaɪz] *vt* utilizar
utmost ['ʌtməʊst] *adj* mayor ♦ *n*: **to do one's ~** hacer todo lo posible
utter ['ʌtə*] *adj* total, completo ♦ *vt* pronunciar, proferir; **~ance** *n* palabras *fpl*, declaración *f*; **~ly** *adv* completamente, totalmente

U-turn ['juː'təːn] *n* viraje *m* en redondo

V v

v. *abbr* = **verse; versus;** (= *volt*) v; (= *vide*) véase

vacancy ['veɪkənsɪ] *n* (*BRIT: job*) vacante *f*; (*room*) habitación *f* libre

vacant ['veɪkənt] *adj* desocupado, libre; (*expression*) distraído; ~ **lot** (*US*) *n* solar *m*

vacate [və'keɪt] *vt* (*house, room*) desocupar; (*job*) dejar (vacante)

vacation [və'keɪʃən] *n* vacaciones *fpl*

vaccinate ['væksɪneɪt] *vt* vacunar

vaccine ['væksiːn] *n* vacuna

vacuum ['vækjum] *n* vacío; ~ **cleaner** *n* aspiradora; ~-**packed** *adj* empaquetado al vacío

vagina [və'dʒaɪnə] *n* vagina

vagrant ['veɪgrnt] *n* vagabundo/a

vague [veɪg] *adj* vago; (*blurred: memory*) borroso; (*ambiguous*) impreciso; (*person: absent-minded*) distraído; (: *evasive*): **to be** ~ no decir las cosas claramente; ~**ly** *adv* vagamente; distraídamente; con evasivas

vain [veɪn] *adj* (*conceited*) presumido; (*useless*) vano, inútil; **in** ~ en vano

valentine ['væləntaɪn] *n* (*also*: ~ *card*) tarjeta del Día de los Enamorados

valet ['væleɪ] *n* ayuda *m* de cámara

valid ['vælɪd] *adj* válido; (*ticket*) valedero; (*law*) vigente

valley ['vælɪ] *n* valle *m*

valuable ['væljuəbl] *adj* (*jewel*) de valor; (*time*) valioso; ~**s** *npl* objetos *mpl* de valor

valuation [vælju'eɪʃən] *n* tasación *f*, valuación *f*; (*judgement of quality*) valoración *f*

value ['væljuː] *n* valor *m*; (*importance*) importancia ♦ *vt* (*fix price of*) tasar, valorar; (*esteem*) apreciar; ~**s** *npl* (*principles*) principios *mpl*; ~ **added tax** (*BRIT*) *n* impuesto sobre el valor añadido; ~**d** *adj* (*appreciated*) apreciado

valve [vælv] *n* válvula

van [væn] *n* (*AUT*) furgoneta (*SP*), camioneta (*AM*)

vandal ['vændl] *n* vándalo/a; ~**ism** *n* vandalismo; ~**ize** *vt* dañar, destruir

vanilla [və'nɪlə] *n* vainilla

vanish ['vænɪʃ] *vi* desaparecer

vanity ['vænɪtɪ] *n* vanidad *f*

vantage point ['vɑːntɪdʒ-] *n* (*for views*) punto panorámico

vapour ['veɪpə*] (*US* **vapor**) *n* vapor *m*; (*on breath, window*) vaho

variable ['vɛərɪəbl] *adj* variable

variance ['vɛərɪəns] *n*: **to be at** ~ (**with**) estar en desacuerdo (con)

variation [vɛərɪ'eɪʃən] *n* variación *f*

varicose ['værɪkəus] *adj*: ~ **veins** varices *fpl*

varied ['vɛərɪd] *adj* variado

variety [və'raɪətɪ] *n* (*diversity*) diversidad *f*; (*type*) variedad *f*; ~ **show** *n* espectáculo de variedades

various ['vɛərɪəs] *adj* (*several: people*) varios/as; (*reasons*) diversos/as

varnish ['vɑːnɪʃ] *n* barniz *m*; (*nail* ~) esmalte *m* ♦ *vt* barnizar; (*nails*) pintar (con esmalte)

vary ['vɛərɪ] *vt* variar; (*change*) cambiar ♦ *vi* variar

vase [vɑːz] *n* florero

Vaseline ['væsɪliːn] ® *n* vaselina ®

vast [vɑːst] *adj* enorme

VAT [væt] (*BRIT*) *n abbr* (= *value added tax*) IVA *m*

vat [væt] *n* tina, tinaja

Vatican ['vætɪkən] *n*: **the** ~ el Vaticano

vault [vɔːlt] *n* (*of roof*) bóveda; (*tomb*) panteón *m*; (*in bank*) cámara acorazada ♦ *vt* (*also*: ~ *over*) saltar (por encima de)

vaunted ['vɔːntɪd] *adj*: **much** ~ cacareado, alardeado

VCR *n abbr* = **video cassette recorder**

VD *n abbr* = **venereal disease**

VDU *n abbr* (= *visual display unit*) UPV *f*

veal [viːl] *n* ternera

veer [vɪə*] *vi* (*vehicle*) virar; (*wind*) girar

vegeburger ['vedʒɪbəːgə*] *n* hamburguesa vegetal

vegetable ['vedʒtəbl] *n* (*BOT*) vegetal *m*;

(*edible plant*) legumbre *f*, hortaliza ♦ *adj*
vegetal; **~s** *npl* (*cooked*) verduras *fpl*

vegetarian [vɛdʒɪ'tɛərɪən] *adj, n*
vegetariano/a *m/f*

vehement ['viːmənt] *adj* vehemente,
apasionado

vehicle ['viːɪkl] *n* vehículo; (*fig*) medio

veil [veɪl] *n* velo ♦ *vt* velar; **~ed** *adj* (*fig*)
velado

vein [veɪn] *n* vena; (*of ore etc*) veta

velocity [vɪ'lɒsɪtɪ] *n* velocidad *f*

velvet ['vɛlvɪt] *n* terciopelo

vending machine ['vɛndɪŋ-] *n*
distribuidor *m* automático

vendor ['vɛndə*] *n* vendedor(a) *m/f*

veneer [və'nɪə*] *n* chapa, enchapado;
(*fig*) barniz *m*

venereal disease [vɪ'nɪərɪəl-] *n*
enfermedad *f* venérea

Venetian blind [vɪ'niːʃən-] *n* persiana

Venezuela [vɛnɪ'zweɪlə] *n* Venezuela; **~n**
adj, n venezolano/a *m/f*

vengeance ['vɛndʒəns] *n* venganza; **with
a ~** (*fig*) con creces

venison ['vɛnɪsn] *n* carne *f* de venado

venom ['vɛnəm] *n* veneno; (*bitterness*)
odio; **~ous** *adj* venenoso; lleno de odio

vent [vɛnt] *n* (*in jacket*) respiradero; (*in
wall*) rejilla (de ventilación) ♦ *vt* (*fig:
feelings*) desahogar

ventilator ['vɛntɪleɪtə*] *n* ventilador *m*

venture ['vɛntʃə*] *n* empresa ♦ *vt*
(*opinion*) ofrecer ♦ *vi* arriesgarse,
lanzarse; **business ~** empresa comercial

venue ['vɛnjuː] *n* lugar *m*

veranda(h) [və'rændə] *n* terraza

verb [vəːb] *n* verbo; **~al** *adj* verbal

verbatim [vəː'beɪtɪm] *adj, adv* palabra
por palabra

verbose [vəː'bəʊs] *adj* prolijo

verdict ['vəːdɪkt] *n* veredicto, fallo; (*fig*)
opinión *f*, juicio

verge [vəːdʒ] (*BRIT*) *n* borde *m*; **"soft ~s"**
(*AUT*) "arcén *m* no asfaltado"; **to be on
the ~ of doing sth** estar a punto de
hacer algo; **~ on** *vt fus* rayar en

verify ['vɛrɪfaɪ] *vt* comprobar, verificar

veritable ['vɛrɪtəbl] *adj* verdadero,
auténtico

vermin ['vəːmɪn] *npl* (*animals*) alimañas
fpl; (*insects, fig*) parásitos *mpl*

vermouth ['vəːməθ] *n* vermut *m*

vernacular [və'nækjulə*] *n* lengua
vernácula

versatile ['vəːsətaɪl] *adj* (*person*)
polifacético; (*machine, tool etc*) versátil.

verse [vəːs] *n* poesía; (*stanza*) estrofa; (*in
bible*) versículo

versed [vəːst] *adj*: **(well-)~ in** versado en

version ['vəːʃən] *n* versión *f*

versus ['vəːsəs] *prep* contra

vertebra ['vəːtɪbrə] (*pl* **~e**) *n* vértebra

vertical ['vəːtɪkl] *adj* vertical

verve [vəːv] *n* brío

very ['vɛrɪ] *adv* muy ♦ *adj*: **the ~ book
which** el mismo libro que; **the ~ last** el
último de todos; **at the ~ least** al
menos; **~ much** muchísimo

vessel ['vɛsl] *n* (*ship*) barco; (*container*)
vasija; *see* **blood**

vest [vɛst] *n* (*BRIT*) camiseta; (*US:
waistcoat*) chaleco; **~ed interests** *npl*
(*COMM*) intereses *mpl* creados

vestige ['vɛstɪdʒ] *n* vestigio, rastro

vet [vɛt] *vt* (*candidate*) investigar ♦ *n
abbr* (*BRIT*) = **veterinary surgeon**

veteran ['vɛtərn] *n* veterano

veterinary surgeon ['vɛtrɪnərɪ] (*US* **vet-
erinarian**) *n* veterinario/a *m/f*

veto ['viːtəu] (*pl* **~es**) *n* veto ♦ *vt*
prohibir, poner el veto a

vex [vɛks] *vt* fastidiar; **~ed** *adj* (*question*)
controvertido

VHF *abbr* (= *very high frequency*) muy
alta frecuencia

via ['vaɪə] *prep* por, por medio de

vibrant ['vaɪbrənt] *adj* (*lively*) animado;
(*bright*) vivo; (*voice*) vibrante

vibrate [vaɪ'breɪt] *vi* vibrar

vicar ['vɪkə*] *n* párroco (de la Iglesia
Anglicana); **~age** *n* parroquia

vice [vaɪs] *n* (*evil*) vicio; (*TECH*) torno de
banco

vice- [vaɪs] *prefix* vice-; **~-chairman** *n*
vicepresidente *m*

vice squad *n* brigada antivicio

vice versa ['vaɪsɪ'vəːsə] *adv* viceversa

vicinity [vɪ'sɪnɪtɪ] *n*: **in the ~ (of)**

cercano (a)

vicious ['vɪʃəs] *adj* (*attack*) violento; (*words*) cruel; (*horse, dog*) resabido; ~ **circle** *n* círculo vicioso

victim ['vɪktɪm] *n* víctima; ~**ize** *vt* tomar represalias contra

victor ['vɪktə*] *n* vencedor(a) *m/f*

victorious [vɪk'tɔːrɪəs] *adj* (*team*) vencedor(a)

victory ['vɪktərɪ] *n* victoria

video ['vɪdɪəʊ] *cpd* video ♦ *n* (~ *film*) videofilm *m*; (*also:* ~ *cassette*) videocassette *f*; (*also:* ~ *cassette recorder*) magnetoscopio; ~ **game** *n* videojuego; ~ **tape** *n* cinta de vídeo

vie [vaɪ] *vi:* **to** ~ (**with sb for sth**) competir (con uno por algo)

Vienna [vɪ'enə] *n* Viena

Vietnam [vjɛt'næm] *n* Vietnam *m*; ~**ese** [-nə'miːz] *n inv, adj* vietnamita *m/f*

view [vjuː] *n* vista; (*outlook*) perspectiva; (*opinion*) opinión *f*, criterio ♦ *vt* (*look at*) mirar; (*fig*) considerar; **on** ~ (*in museum etc*) expuesto; **in full** ~ (**of**) en plena vista (de); **in** ~ **of the weather/the fact that** en vista del tiempo/del hecho de que; **in my** ~ en mi opinión; ~**er** *n* espectador(a) *m/f*; (*TV*) telespectador(a) *m/f*; ~**finder** *n* visor *m* de imagen; ~**point** *n* (*attitude*) punto de vista; (*place*) mirador *m*

vigour ['vɪgə*] (*US* **vigor**) *n* energía, vigor *m*

vile [vaɪl] *adj* vil, infame; (*smell*) asqueroso; (*temper*) endemoniado

villa ['vɪlə] *n* (*country house*) casa de campo; (*suburban house*) chalet *m*

village ['vɪlɪdʒ] *n* aldea; ~**r** *n* aldeano/a

villain ['vɪlən] *n* (*scoundrel*) malvado/a; (*in novel*) malo; (*BRIT: criminal*) maleante *m/f*

vindicate ['vɪndɪkeɪt] *vt* vindicar, justificar

vindictive [vɪn'dɪktɪv] *adj* vengativo

vine [vaɪn] *n* vid *f*

vinegar ['vɪnɪgə*] *n* vinagre *m*

vineyard ['vɪnjɑːd] *n* viña, viñedo

vintage ['vɪntɪdʒ] *n* (*year*) vendimia, cosecha ♦ *cpd* de época; ~ **wine** *n* vino

añejo

vinyl ['vaɪnl] *n* vinilo

viola [vɪ'əʊlə] *n* (*MUS*) viola

violate ['vaɪəleɪt] *vt* violar

violence ['vaɪələns] *n* violencia

violent ['vaɪələnt] *adj* violento; (*intense*) intenso

violet ['vaɪələt] *adj* violado, violeta ♦ *n* (*plant*) violeta

violin [vaɪə'lɪn] *n* violín *m*; ~**ist** *n* violinista *m/f*

VIP *n abbr* (= *very important person*) VIP *m*

virgin ['vɜːdʒɪn] *n* virgen *f*

Virgo ['vɜːgəʊ] *n* Virgo *m*

virtually ['vɜːtjʊəlɪ] *adv* prácticamente

virtual reality ['vɜːtjʊəl-] *n* (*COMPUT*) mundo *or* realidad *f* virtual

virtue ['vɜːtjuː] *n* virtud *f*; (*advantage*) ventaja; **by** ~ **of** en virtud de

virtuous ['vɜːtjʊəs] *adj* virtuoso

virus ['vaɪərəs] *n* (*also: COMPUT*) virus *m*

visa ['viːzə] *n* visado (*SP*), visa (*AM*)

vis-à-vis [viːzə'viː] *prep* con respecto a

visible ['vɪzəbl] *adj* visible

vision ['vɪʒən] *n* (*sight*) vista; (*foresight, in dream*) visión *f*

visit ['vɪzɪt] *n* visita ♦ *vt* (*person: US: also:* ~ *with*) visitar, hacer una visita a; (*place*) ir a, (ir a) conocer; ~**ing hours** *npl* (*in hospital etc*) horas *fpl* de visita; ~**or** *n* (*in museum*) visitante *m/f*; (*invited to house*) visita; (*tourist*) turista *m/f*

visor ['vaɪzə*] *n* visera

vista ['vɪstə] *n* vista, panorama *m*

visual ['vɪzjʊəl] *adj* visual; ~ **aid** *n* medio visual; ~ **display unit** *n* unidad *f* de presentación visual; ~**ize** *vt* imaginarse

vital ['vaɪtl] *adj* (*essential*) esencial, imprescindible; (*dynamic*) dinámico; (*organ*) vital; ~**ly** *adv*: ~**ly important** de primera importancia; ~ **statistics** *npl* (*fig*) medidas *fpl* vitales

vitamin ['vɪtəmɪn] *n* vitamina

vivacious [vɪ'veɪʃəs] *adj* vivaz, alegre

vivid ['vɪvɪd] *adj* (*account*) gráfico; (*light*) intenso; (*imagination, memory*) vivo; ~**ly** *adv* gráficamente; (*remember*) como si fuera hoy

V-neck ['viːnɛk] n cuello de pico
vocabulary [vəu'kæbjulərɪ] n vocabulario
vocal ['vəukl] adj vocal; (*articulate*) elocuente; ~ **chords** npl cuerdas fpl vocales
vocation [vəu'keɪʃən] n vocación f; **~al** adj profesional
vodka ['vɔdkə] n vodka m
vogue [vəug] n: **in** ~ en boga, de moda
voice [vɔɪs] n voz f ♦ vt expresar
void [vɔɪd] n vacío; (*hole*) hueco ♦ adj (*invalid*) nulo, inválido; (*empty*): ~ **of** carente or desprovisto de
volatile ['vɔlətaɪl] adj (*situation*) inestable; (*person*) voluble; (*liquid*) volátil
volcano [vɔl'keɪnəu] (pl ~**es**) n volcán m
volition [və'lɪʃən] n: **of one's own** ~ de su propia voluntad
volley ['vɔlɪ] n (*of gunfire*) descarga; (*of stones etc*) lluvia; (*fig*) torrente m; (*TENNIS etc*) volea; **~ball** n vol(e)ibol m
volt [vəult] n voltio; **~age** n voltaje m
volume ['vɔljuːm] n (*gen*) volumen m; (*book*) tomo
voluminous [və'luːmɪnəs] adj (*clothes*) amplio; (*notes*) prolijo
voluntary ['vɔləntərɪ] adj voluntario
volunteer [vɔlən'tɪə*] n voluntario/a ♦ vt (*information*) ofrecer ♦ vi ofrecerse (de voluntario); **to** ~ **to do** ofrecerse a hacer
vomit ['vɔmɪt] n vómito ♦ vt, vi vomitar
vote [vəut] n voto; (*votes cast*) votación f; (*right to* ~) derecho de votar; (*franchise*) sufragio ♦ vt (*chairman*) elegir; (*propose*): **to** ~ **that** proponer que ♦ vi votar, ir a votar; ~ **of thanks** voto de gracias; **~r** n votante m/f; **voting** n votación f
vouch [vautʃ] n: **to** ~ **for** vt fus garantizar, responder de
voucher ['vautʃə*] n (*for meal, petrol*) vale m
vow [vau] n voto ♦ vt: **to** ~ **to do/that** jurar hacer/que
vowel ['vauəl] n vocal f
voyage ['vɔɪdʒ] n viaje m
V-sign (*BRIT*) n ≈ corte m de mangas
vulgar ['vʌlgə*] adj (*rude*) ordinario, grosero; (*in bad taste*) de mal gusto; **~ity**

[-'gærɪtɪ] n grosería; mal gusto
vulnerable ['vʌlnərəbl] adj vulnerable
vulture ['vʌltʃə*] n buitre m

W w

wad [wɔd] n bolita; (*of banknotes etc*) fajo
waddle ['wɔdl] vi anadear
wade [weɪd] vi: **to** ~ **through** (*water*) vadear; (*fig: book*) leer con dificultad; **wading pool** (*US*) n piscina para niños
wafer ['weɪfə*] n galleta, barquillo
waffle ['wɔfl] n (*CULIN*) gofre m ♦ vi dar el rollo
waft [wɔft] vt llevar por el aire ♦ vi flotar
wag [wæg] vt menear, agitar ♦ vi moverse, menearse
wage [weɪdʒ] n (*also:* ~s) sueldo, salario ♦ vt: **to** ~ **war** hacer la guerra; ~ **earner** n asalariado/a; ~ **packet** n sobre m de paga
wager ['weɪdʒə*] n apuesta
waggle ['wægl] vt menear, mover
wag(g)on ['wægən] n (*horse-drawn*) carro; (*BRIT: RAIL*) vagón m
wail [weɪl] n gemido ♦ vi gemir
waist [weɪst] n cintura, talle m; **~coat** (*BRIT*) n chaleco; **~line** n talle m
wait [weɪt] n (*interval*) pausa ♦ vi esperar; **to lie in** ~ **for** acechar a; **I can't** ~ **to** (*fig*) estoy deseando; **to** ~ **for** esperar (a); ~ **behind** vi quedarse; ~ **on** vt fus servir a; **~er** n camarero; **~ing** n: **"no ~ing"** (*BRIT: AUT*) "prohibido estacionarse"; **~ing list** n lista de espera; **~ing room** n sala de espera; **~ress** n camarera
waive [weɪv] vt suspender
wake [weɪk] (pt **woke** or **waked**, pp **woken** or **waked**) vt (*also:* ~ **up**) despertar ♦ vi (*also:* ~ **up**) despertarse ♦ n (*for dead person*) vela, velatorio; (*NAUT*) estela; **waken** vt, vi = **wake**
Wales [weɪlz] n País m de Gales; **the Prince of** ~ el príncipe de Gales
walk [wɔːk] n (*stroll*) paseo; (*hike*) excursión f a pie, caminata; (*gait*) paso,

andar *m*; (*in park etc*) paseo, alameda
♦ *vi* andar, caminar; (*for pleasure,
exercise*) pasear ♦ *vt* (*distance*) recorrer a
pie, andar; (*dog*) pasear; **10 minutes' ~
from here** a 10 minutos de aquí
andando; **people from all ~s of life**
gente de todas las esferas; **~ out** *vi*
(*audience*) salir; (*workers*) declararse en
huelga; **~ out on** (*inf*) *vt fus* abandonar;
~er *n* (*person*) paseante *m/f*, caminante
m/f, **~ie-talkie** ['wɔːkɪ'tɔːkɪ] *n* walkie-
talkie *m*; **~ing** *n* el andar; **~ing shoes**
npl zapatos *mpl* para andar; **~ing stick** *n*
bastón *m*; **~out** *n* huelga; **~over** (*inf*) *n*:
it was a ~over fue pan comido; **~way** *n*
paseo
wall [wɔːl] *n* pared *f*; (*exterior*) muro;
(*city ~ etc*) muralla; **~ed** *adj* amurallado;
(*garden*) con tapia
wallet ['wɔlɪt] *n* cartera (*SP*), billetera
(*AM*)
wallflower ['wɔːlflauə*] *n* alhelí *m*; **to be
a ~** (*fig*) comer pavo
wallop ['wɔləp] (*inf*) *vt* zurrar
wallow ['wɔləu] *vi* revolcarse
wallpaper ['wɔːlpeɪpə*] *n* papel *m*
pintado ♦ *vt* empapelar
walnut ['wɔːlnʌt] *n* nuez *f*; (*tree*) nogal *m*
walrus ['wɔːlrəs] (*pl* **~** *or* **~es**) *pl* morsa
waltz [wɔːlts] *n* vals *m* ♦ *vi* bailar el vals
wan [wɔn] *adj* pálido
wand [wɔnd] *n* (*also: magic ~*) varita
(mágica)
wander ['wɔndə*] *vi* (*person*) vagar;
deambular; (*thoughts*) divagar ♦ *vt*
recorrer, vagar por
wane [weɪn] *vi* menguar
wangle ['wæŋgl] (*BRIT: inf*) *vt* agenciarse
want [wɔnt] *vt* querer, desear; (*need*)
necesitar ♦ *n*: **for ~ of** por falta de; **~s**
npl (*needs*) necesidades *fpl*; **to ~ to do**
querer hacer; **to ~ sb to do sth** querer
que uno haga algo; **~ed** *adj* (*criminal*)
buscado; "**~ed**" (*in advertisements*) "se
busca"; **~ing** *adj*: **to be found ~ing** no
estar a la altura de las circunstancias
wanton ['wɔntn] *adj* (*playful*) juguetón/
ona; (*licentious*) lascivo
war [wɔː*] *n* guerra; **to make ~ (on)**

(*also fig*) declarar la guerra (a)
ward [wɔːd] *n* (*in hospital*) sala; (*POL*)
distrito electoral; (*LAW: child: also: ~ of
court*) pupilo/a *m/f*; **~ off** *vt* (*blow*) desviar,
parar; (*attack*) rechazar
warden ['wɔːdn] *n* (*BRIT: of institution*)
director(a) *m/f*; (*of park, game reserve*)
guardián/ana *m/f*; (*BRIT: also: traffic ~*)
guardia *m/f*
warder ['wɔːdə*] (*BRIT*) *n* guardián/ana
m/f, carcelero/a
wardrobe ['wɔːdrəub] *n* armario,
guardarropa, ropero (*esp AM*)
warehouse ['wεəhaus] *n* almacén *m*,
depósito
wares [wεəz] *npl* mercancías *fpl*
warfare ['wɔːfεə*] *n* guerra
warhead ['wɔːhed] *n* cabeza armada
warily ['wεərɪlɪ] *adv* con cautela,
cautelosamente
warlike ['wɔːlaɪk] *adj* guerrero; (*appearance*) belicoso
warm [wɔːm] *adj* caliente; (*thanks*)
efusivo; (*clothes etc*) abrigado; (*welcome,
day*) caluroso; **it's ~** hace calor; **I'm ~**
tengo calor; **~ up** *vi* (*room*) calentarse;
(*person*) entrar en calor; (*athlete*) hacer
ejercicios de calentamiento ♦ *vt* calentar;
~-hearted *adj* afectuoso; **~ly** *adv*
afectuosamente; **~th** *n* calor *m*
warn [wɔːn] *vt* avisar, advertir; **~ing** *n*
aviso, advertencia; **~ing light** *n* luz *f* de
advertencia; **~ing triangle** *n* (*AUT*)
triángulo señalizador
warp [wɔːp] *vi* (*wood*) combarse ♦ *vt*
combar; (*mind*) pervertir
warrant ['wɔrnt] *n* autorización *f*; (*LAW: to
arrest*) orden *f* de detención; (: *to search*)
mandamiento de registro
warranty ['wɔrəntɪ] *n* garantía
warren ['wɔrən] *n* (*of rabbits*)
madriguera; (*fig*) laberinto
warrior ['wɔrɪə*] *n* guerrero/a
Warsaw ['wɔːsɔː] *n* Varsovia
warship ['wɔːʃɪp] *n* buque *m* o barco de
guerra
wart [wɔːt] *n* verruga
wartime ['wɔːtaɪm] *n*: **in ~** en tiempos de
guerra, en la guerra

wary ['wεərɪ] *adj* cauteloso
was [wɔz] *pt of* be
wash [wɔʃ] *vt* lavar ♦ *vi* lavarse; (*sea etc*): **to ~ against/over sth** llegar hasta/cubrir algo ♦ *n* (*clothes etc*) lavado; (*of ship*) estela; **to have a ~** lavarse; **~ away** *vt* (*stain*) quitar lavando; (*subj: river etc*) llevarse; **~ off** *vi* quitarse (al lavar); **~ up** *vi* (*BRIT*) fregar los platos; (*US*) lavarse; **~able** *adj* lavable; **~basin** (*US* **~bowl**) *n* lavabo; **~ cloth** (*US*) *n* manopla; **~er** *n* (*TECH*) arandela; **~ing** *n* (*dirty*) ropa sucia; (*clean*) colada; **~ing machine** *n* lavadora; **~ing powder** (*BRIT*) *n* detergente *m* (en polvo)
Washington ['wɔʃɪŋtən] *n* Washington *m*
wash: ~ing-up (*BRIT*) *n* fregado, platos *mpl* (para fregar); **~ing-up liquid** (*BRIT*) *n* líquido lavavajillas; **~-out** (*inf*) *n* fracaso; **~room** (*US*) *n* servicios *mpl*
wasn't ['wɔznt] = **was not**
wasp [wɔsp] *n* avispa
wastage ['weɪstɪdʒ] *n* desgaste *m*; (*loss*) pérdida
waste [weɪst] *n* derroche *m*, despilfarro; (*of time*) pérdida; (*food*) sobras *fpl*; (*rubbish*) basura, desperdicios *mpl* ♦ *adj* (*material*) de desecho; (*left over*) sobrante; (*land*) baldío, descampado ♦ *vt* malgastar, derrochar; (*time*) perder; (*opportunity*) desperdiciar; **~s** *npl* (*area of land*) tierras *fpl* baldías; **~ away** *vi* consumirse; **~ disposal unit** (*BRIT*) *n* triturador *m* de basura; **~ful** *adj* derrochador(a); (*process*) antieconómico; **~ ground** (*BRIT*) *n* terreno baldío; **~paper basket** *n* papelera; **~ pipe** *n* tubo de desagüe
watch [wɔtʃ] *n* (*also: wrist ~*) reloj *m*; (*MIL: group of guards*) centinela *m*; (*act*) vigilancia; (*NAUT: spell of duty*) guardia ♦ *vt* (*look at*) mirar, observar; (: *match, programme*) ver; (*spy on, guard*) vigilar; (*be careful of*) cuidarse de, tener cuidado de ♦ *vi* ver, mirar; (*keep guard*) montar guardia; **~ out** *vi* cuidarse, tener cuidado; **~dog** *n* perro guardián; (*fig*) persona u organismo encargado de asegurarse de

que las empresas actúan dentro de la legalidad; **~ful** *adj* vigilante, sobre aviso; **~maker** *n* relojero/a; **~man** *n see* **night**; **~ strap** *n* pulsera (de reloj)
water ['wɔ:tə*] *n* agua ♦ *vt* (*plant*) regar ♦ *vi* (*eyes*) llorar; (*mouth*) hacerse la boca agua; **~ down** *vt* (*milk etc*) aguar; (*fig: story*) dulcificar, diluir; **~ closet** *n* wáter *m*; **~colour** *n* acuarela; **~cress** *n* berro; **~fall** *n* cascada, salto de agua; **~ heater** *n* calentador *m* de agua; **~ing can** *n* regadera; **~ lily** *n* nenúfar *m*; **~line** *n* (*NAUT*) línea de flotación; **~logged** *adj* (*ground*) inundado; **~ main** *n* cañería del agua; **~melon** *n* sandía; **~proof** *adj* impermeable; **~shed** *n* (*GEO*) cuenca; (*fig*) momento crítico; **~-skiing** *n* esquí *m* acuático; **~tight** *adj* hermético; **~way** *n* vía fluvial *or* navegable; **~works** *n* central *f* depuradora; **~y** *adj* (*coffee etc*) aguado; (*eyes*) lloroso
watt [wɔt] *n* vatio
wave [weɪv] *n* (*of hand*) señal *f* con la mano; (*on water*) ola; (*RADIO, in hair*) onda; (*fig*) oleada ♦ *vi* saludar con la mano; (*flag etc*) ondear ♦ *vt* (*handkerchief, gun*) agitar; **~length** *n* longitud *f* de onda
waver ['weɪvə*] *vi* (*voice, love etc*) flaquear; (*person*) vacilar
wavy ['weɪvɪ] *adj* ondulado
wax [wæks] *n* cera ♦ *vt* encerar ♦ *vi* (*moon*) crecer; **~ paper** (*US*) *n* papel *m* apergaminado; **~works** *n* museo de cera ♦ *npl* figuras *fpl* de cera
way [weɪ] *n* camino; (*distance*) trayecto, recorrido; (*direction*) dirección *f*, sentido; (*manner*) modo, manera; (*habit*) costumbre *f*; **which ~? — this ~** ¿por dónde?, ¿en qué dirección? — por aquí; **on the ~** (*en route*) en (el) camino; **to be on one's ~** estar en camino; **to be in the ~** bloquear el camino; (*fig*) estorbar; **to go out of one's ~ to do sth** desvivirse por hacer algo; **under ~** en marcha; **to lose one's ~** extraviarse; **in a ~** en cierto modo *or* sentido; **no ~!** (*inf*) ¡de eso nada!; **by the ~ ...** a propósito ...; **"~ in"** (*BRIT*) "entrada"; **"~ out"** (*BRIT*) "salida"; **the ~ back** el

camino de vuelta; **"give ~"** (*BRIT: AUT*) "ceda el paso"

waylay [weɪˈleɪ] (*irreg*) *vt* salir al paso a

wayward [ˈweɪwəd] *adj* díscolo

W.C. *n* (*BRIT*) wáter *m*

we [wiː] *pl pron* nosotros/as

weak [wiːk] *adj* débil, flojo; (*tea etc*) claro; **~en** *vi* debilitarse; (*give way*) ceder ♦ *vt* debilitar; **~ling** *n* debilucho/a; (*morally*) persona de poco carácter; **~ness** *n* debilidad *f*; (*fault*) punto débil; **to have a ~ness for** tener debilidad por

wealth [wɛlθ] *n* riqueza; (*of details*) abundancia; **~y** *adj* rico

wean [wiːn] *vt* destetar

weapon [ˈwɛpən] *n* arma

wear [wɛə*] (*pt* **wore**, *pp* **worn**) *n* (*use*) uso; (*deterioration through use*) desgaste *m*; (*clothing*) **sports/baby~** ropa de deportes/de niños ♦ *vt* (*clothes*) llevar; (*shoes*) calzar; (*damage: through use*) gastar, usar ♦ *vi* (*last*) durar; (*rub through etc*) desgastarse; **evening ~** ropa de etiqueta; **~ away** *vt* gastar ♦ *vi* desgastarse; **~ down** *vt* gastar; (*strength*) agotar; **~ off** *vi* (*pain etc*) pasar, desaparecer; **~ out** *vt* desgastar; (*person, strength*) agotar; **~ and tear** *n* desgaste *m*

weary [ˈwɪərɪ] *adj* cansado; (*dispirited*) abatido ♦ *vi*: **to ~ of** cansarse de

weasel [ˈwiːzl] *n* (*ZOOL*) comadreja

weather [ˈwɛðə*] *n* tiempo ♦ *vt* (*storm, crisis*) hacer frente a; **under the ~** (*fig: ill*) indispuesto, pachucho; **~-beaten** *adj* (*skin*) curtido; (*building*) deteriorado por la intemperie; **~cock** *n* veleta; **~ forecast** *n* boletín *m* meteorológico; **~man** (*inf*) *n* hombre *m* del tiempo; **~ vane** *n* = **~cock**

weave [wiːv] (*pt* **wove**, *pp* **woven**) *vt* (*cloth*) tejer; (*fig*) entretejer; **~r** *n* tejedor(a) *m/f*; **weaving** *n* tejeduría

web [wɛb] *n* (*of spider*) telaraña; (*on duck's foot*) membrana; (*network*) red *f*

wed [wɛd] (*pt, pp* **wedded**) *vt* casar ♦ *vi* casarse

we'd [wiːd] = **we had; we would**

wedding [ˈwɛdɪŋ] *n* boda, casamiento;

silver/golden ~ **(anniversary)** bodas *fpl* de plata/de oro; **~ day** *n* día *m* de la boda; **~ dress** *n* traje *m* de novia; **~ present** *n* regalo de boda; **~ ring** *n* alianza

wedge [wɛdʒ] *n* (*of wood etc*) cuña; (*of cake*) trozo ♦ *vt* acuñar; (*push*) apretar

Wednesday [ˈwɛnzdɪ] *n* miércoles *m inv*

wee [wiː] (*Scottish*) *adj* pequeñito

weed [wiːd] *n* mala hierba, maleza ♦ *vt* escardar, desherbar; **~killer** *n* herbicida *m*; **~y** *adj* (*person*) mequetréfico

week [wiːk] *n* semana; **a ~ today/on Friday** de hoy/del viernes en ocho días; **~day** *n* día *m* laborable; **~end** *n* fin *m* de semana; **~ly** *adv* semanalmente, cada semana ♦ *adj* semanal ♦ *n* semanario

weep [wiːp] (*pt, pp* **wept**) *vi, vt* llorar; **~ing willow** *n* sauce *m* llorón

weigh [weɪ] *vt, vi* pesar; **to ~ anchor** levar anclas; **~ down** *vt* sobrecargar; (*fig: with worry*) agobiar; **~ up** *vt* sopesar

weight [weɪt] *n* peso; (*metal ~*) pesa; **to lose/put on ~** adelgazar/engordar; **~ing** *n* (*allowance*): **(London) ~ing** dietas (*por residir en Londres*); **~lifter** *n* levantador *m* de pesas; **~y** *adj* pesado; (*matters*) de relevancia *or* peso

weir [wɪə*] *n* presa

weird [wɪəd] *adj* raro, extraño

welcome [ˈwɛlkəm] *adj* bienvenido ♦ *n* bienvenida ♦ *vt* dar la bienvenida a; (*be glad of*) alegrarse de; **thank you — you're ~** gracias — de nada

weld [wɛld] *n* soldadura ♦ *vt* soldar

welfare [ˈwɛlfɛə*] *n* bienestar *m*; (*social aid*) asistencia social; **~ state** *n* estado del bienestar; **~ work** *n* asistencia social

well [wɛl] *n* fuente *f*, pozo ♦ *adv* bien ♦ *adj*: **to be ~** estar bien (de salud) ♦ *excl* ¡vaya!, ¡bueno!; **as ~** también; **as ~ as** además de; **~ done!** ¡bien hecho!; **get ~ soon!** ¡que te mejores pronto!; **to do ~** (*business*) ir bien; (*person*) tener éxito; **~ up** *vi* (*tears*) saltar

we'll [wiːl] = **we will; we shall**

well- : **~-behaved** *adj* bueno; **~-being** *n* bienestar *m*; **~-built** *adj* (*person*) fornido;

~-deserved *adj* merecido; **~-dressed** *adj* bien vestido; **~-groomed** *adj* de buena presencia; **~-heeled** (*inf*) *adj* (*wealthy*) rico

wellingtons ['welɪŋtənz] *npl* (*also: wellington boots*) botas *fpl* de goma

well: **~-known** *adj* (*person*) conocido; **~-mannered** *adj* educado; **~-meaning** *adj* bienintencionado; **~-off** *adj* acomodado; **~-read** *adj* leído; **~-to-do** *adj* acomodado; **~-wisher** *n* admirador(a) *m/f*

Welsh [welʃ] *adj* galés/esa ♦ *n* (*LING*) galés *m*; **the ~** *npl* los galeses; **~man** *n* galés *m*; **~ rarebit** *n* pan *m* con queso tostado; **~woman** *n* galesa

went [went] *pt of* **go**

wept [wept] *pt, pp of* **weep**

were [wəː*] *pt of* **be**

we're [wɪə*] = **we are**

weren't [wəːnt] = **were not**

west [west] *n* oeste *m* ♦ *adj* occidental, del oeste ♦ *adv* al *or* hacia el oeste; **the W~** el Oeste, el Occidente; **W~ Country** (*BRIT*) *n*: **the W~ Country** el suroeste de Inglaterra; **~erly** *adj* occidental; (*wind*) del oeste; **~ern** *adj* occidental ♦ *n* (*CINEMA*) película del oeste; **W~ Germany** *n* Alemania Occidental; **W~ Indian** *adj*, *n* antillano/a *m/f*; **W~ Indies** *npl* Antillas *fpl*; **~ward(s)** *adv* hacia el oeste

wet [wet] *adj* (*damp*) húmedo; (*~ through*) mojado; (*rainy*) lluvioso ♦ (*BRIT*) *n* (*POL*) conservador(a) *m/f* moderado/a; **to get ~** mojarse; **"~ paint"** "recién pintado"; **~ blanket** *n*: **to be a ~ blanket** (*fig*) ser un/una aguafiestas; **~suit** *n* traje *m* térmico

we've [wiːv] = **we have**

whack [wæk] *vt* dar un buen golpe a

whale [weɪl] *n* (*ZOOL*) ballena

wharf [wɔːf] *n* muelle *m*; **wharves** [wɔːvz] *npl of* **wharf**

what [wɔt] *adj* **1** (*in direct/indirect questions*) qué; **~ size is he?** ¿qué talla usa?; **~ colour/shape is it?** ¿de qué color/forma es?
2 (*in exclamations*): **~ a mess!** ¡qué

desastre!; **~ a fool I am!** ¡qué tonto soy!
♦ *pron* **1** (*interrogative*) qué; **~ are you doing?** ¿qué haces *or* estás haciendo?; **~ is happening?** ¿qué pasa *or* está pasando?; **~ is it called?** ¿cómo se llama?; **~ about me?** ¿y yo qué?; **~ about doing ...?** ¿qué tal si hacemos ...?
2 (*relative*) lo que; **I saw ~ you did/was on the table** vi lo que hiciste/había en la mesa
♦ *excl* (*disbelieving*) ¡cómo!; **~, no coffee!** ¡que no hay café!

whatever [wɔt'ɛvə*] *adj*: **~ book you choose** cualquier libro que elijas ♦ *pron*: **do ~ is necessary** haga lo que sea necesario; **~ happens** pase lo que pase; **no reason ~** *or* **whatsoever** ninguna razón sea la que sea; **nothing ~** nada en absoluto

whatsoever [wɔtsəu'ɛvə*] *adj see* **whatever**

wheat [wiːt] *n* trigo

wheedle ['wiːdl] *vt*: **to ~ sb into doing sth** engatusar a uno para que haga algo; **to ~ sth out of sb** sonsacar algo a uno

wheel [wiːl] *n* rueda; (*AUT: also: steering ~*) volante *m*; (*NAUT*) timón *m* ♦ *vt* (*pram etc*) empujar ♦ *vi* (*also: ~ round*) dar la vuelta, girar; **~barrow** *n* carretilla; **~chair** *n* silla de ruedas; **~ clamp** *n* (*AUT*) cepo

wheeze [wiːz] *vi* resollar

when [wen] *adv* cuando; **~ did it happen?** ¿cuándo ocurrió?; **I know ~ it happened** sé cuándo ocurrió
♦ *conj* **1** (*at, during, after the time that*) cuando; **be careful ~ you cross the road** ten cuidado al cruzar la calle; **that was ~ I needed you** fue entonces que te necesité
2 (*on, at which*): **on the day ~ I met him** el día en qué lo conocí
3 (*whereas*) cuando

whenever [wen'ɛvə*] *conj* cuando; (*every time that*) cada vez que ♦ *adv* cuando sea

where [wεə*] *adv* dónde ♦ *conj* donde; **this is** ~ aquí es donde; **~abouts** *adv* dónde ♦ *n*: **nobody knows his ~abouts** nadie conoce su paradero; **~as** *conj* visto que, mientras; **~by** *pron* por lo cual; **~upon** *conj* con lo cual, después de lo cual; **~ver** [-'εvə*] *conj* dondequiera que; (*interrogative*) dónde; **~withal** *n* recursos *mpl*

whet [wεt] *vt* estimular

whether ['wεðə*] *conj* si; **I don't know ~ to accept or not** no sé si aceptar o no; **~ you go or not** vayas o no vayas

──────────
| KEYWORD |
──────────

which [wɪtʃ] *adj* **1** (*interrogative: direct, indirect*) qué; **~ picture(s) do you want?** ¿qué cuadro(s) quieres?; **~ one?** ¿cuál?
2: **in ~ case** en cuyo caso; **we got there at 8 pm, by ~ time the cinema was full** llegamos allí a las 8, cuando el cine estaba lleno
♦ *pron* **1** (*interrogative*) cual; **I don't mind** ~ el/la que sea
2 (*relative: replacing noun*) que; (: *replacing clause*) lo que; (: *after preposition*) (el/la) que *etc*, el/la cual *etc*; **the apple ~ you ate/~ is on the table** la manzana que comiste/que está en la mesa; **the chair on ~ you are sitting** la silla en la que estás sentado; **he said he knew, ~ is true/I feared** dijo que lo sabía, lo cual *or* lo que es cierto/me temía

──────────

whichever [wɪtʃ'εvə*] *adj*: **take ~ book you prefer** coja (*SP*) el libro que prefiera; **~ book you take** cualquier libro que coja

whiff [wɪf] *n* vaharada

while [waɪl] *n* rato, momento ♦ *conj* mientras; (*although*) aunque; **for a ~** durante algún tiempo; **~ away** *vt* pasar

whim [wɪm] *n* capricho

whimper ['wɪmpə*] *n* sollozo ♦ *vi* lloriquear

whimsical ['wɪmzɪkl] *adj* (*person*) caprichoso; (*look*) juguetón/ona

whine [waɪn] *n* (*of pain*) gemido; (*of*

engine) zumbido; (*of siren*) aullido ♦ *vi* gemir; zumbar; (*fig: complain*) gimotear

whip [wɪp] *n* látigo; (*POL: person*) *encargado de la disciplina partidaria en el parlamento* ♦ *vt* azotar; (*CULIN*) batir; (*move quickly*): **to ~ sth out/off** sacar/quitar algo de un tirón; **~ped cream** *n* nata *or* crema montada; **~-round** (*BRIT*) *n* colecta

whirl [wə:l] *vt* hacer girar, dar vueltas a ♦ *vi* girar, dar vueltas; (*leaves etc*) arremolinarse; **~pool** *n* remolino; **~wind** *n* torbellino

whirr [wə:*] *vi* zumbar

whisk [wɪsk] *n* (*CULIN*) batidor *m* ♦ *vt* (*CULIN*) batir; **to ~ sb away** *or* **off** llevar volando a uno

whiskers ['wɪskəz] *npl* (*of animal*) bigotes *mpl*; (*of man*) patillas *fpl*

whiskey ['wɪskɪ] (*US, Ireland*) *n* = **whisky**

whisky ['wɪskɪ] *n* whisky *m*

whisper ['wɪspə*] *n* susurro ♦ *vi, vt* susurrar

whist [wɪst] (*BRIT*) *n* juego de naipes

whistle ['wɪsl] *n* (*sound*) silbido; (*object*) silbato ♦ *vi* silbar

white [waɪt] *adj* blanco; (*pale*) pálido ♦ *n* blanco; (*of egg*) clara; **~ coffee** (*BRIT*) *n* café *m* con leche; **~-collar worker** *n* oficinista *m/f*; **~ elephant** *n* (*fig*) maula; **~ lie** *n* mentirilla; **~ness** *n* blancura; **~ noise** *n* sonido blanco; **~ paper** *n* (*POL*) libro rojo; **~wash** *n* (*paint*) jalbegue *m*, cal *f* ♦ *vt* (*also fig*) blanquear

whiting ['waɪtɪŋ] *n inv* (*fish*) pescadilla

Whitsun ['wɪtsn] *n* pentecostés *m*

whittle ['wɪtl] *vt*: **to ~ away**, **~ down** ir reduciendo

whizz [wɪz] *vi*: **to ~ past** *or* **by** pasar a toda velocidad; **~ kid** (*inf*) *n* prodigio

──────────
| KEYWORD |
──────────

who [hu:] *pron* **1** (*interrogative*) quién; **~ is it?**, **~'s there?** ¿quién es?; **~ are you looking for?** ¿a quién buscas?; **I told her** ~ **I was** le dije quién era yo
2 (*relative*) que; **the man/woman ~ spoke to me** el hombre/la mujer que

habló conmigo; **those ~ can swim** los que saben *or* sepan nadar

whodun(n)it [huːˈdʌnɪt] (*inf*) *n* novela policíaca

whoever [huːˈɛvə*] *pron*: ~ **finds it** cualquiera *or* quienquiera que lo encuentre; **ask ~ you like** pregunta a quien quieras; ~ **he marries** no importa con quién se case

whole [həʊl] *adj* (*entire*) todo, entero; (*not broken*) intacto ♦ *n* todo; (*all*): **the ~ of the town** toda la ciudad, la ciudad entera ♦ *n* (*total*) total *m*; (*sum*) conjunto; **on the ~, as a ~** en general; ~ **food(s)** *n(pl)* alimento(s) *m(pl)* integral(es); **~hearted** *adj* sincero, cordial; **~meal** *adj* integral; **~sale** *n* venta al por mayor ♦ *adj* al por mayor; (*fig: destruction*) sistemático; **~saler** *n* mayorista *m/f*; **~some** *adj* sano; **~wheat** *adj* = **~meal**; **wholly** *adv* totalmente, enteramente

whom [huːm] *pron* **1** (*interrogative*): ~ **did you see?** ¿a quién viste?; **to ~ did you give it?** ¿a quién se lo diste?; **tell me from ~ you received it** dígame de quién lo recibió
2 (*relative*) que; **to ~** a quien(es); **of ~** de quien(es), del/de la que *etc*; **the man ~ I saw/to ~ I wrote** el hombre que vi/a quien escribí; **the lady about/with ~ I was talking** la señora de (la) que/con quien *or* (la) que hablaba

whooping cough [ˈhuːpɪŋ-] *n* tos *f* ferina

whore [hɔː*] (*inf: pej*) *n* puta

whose [huːz] *adj* **1** (*possessive: interrogative*): ~ **book is this?**, ~ **is this book?** ¿de quién es este libro?; ~ **pencil have you taken?** ¿de quién es el lápiz que has cogido?; ~ **daughter are you?** ¿de quién eres hija?
2 (*possessive: relative*) cuyo/a, *pl* cuyos/

as; **the man ~ son you rescued** el hombre cuyo hijo rescataste; **those ~ passports I have** aquellas personas cuyos pasaportes tengo; **the woman ~ car was stolen** la mujer a quien le robaron el coche
♦ *pron* de quién; ~ **is this?** ¿de quién es esto?; **I know ~ it is** sé de quién es

why [waɪ] *adv* por qué; ~ **not?** ¿por qué no?; ~ **not do it now?** ¿por qué no lo haces (*or* hacemos *etc*) ahora?
♦ *conj*: **I wonder ~ he said that** me pregunto por qué dijo eso; **that's not ~ I'm here** no es por eso (por lo) que estoy aquí; **the reason ~** la razón por la que
♦ *excl* (*expressing surprise, shock, annoyance*) ¡hombre!, ¡vaya! (*explaining*): ~, **it's you!** ¡hombre, eres tú!; ~, **that's impossible!** ¡pero sí eso es imposible!

wicked [ˈwɪkɪd] *adj* malvado, cruel

wickerwork [ˈwɪkəwɜːk] *n* artículos *mpl* de mimbre ♦ *adj* de mimbre

wicket [ˈwɪkɪt] *n* (CRICKET: *stumps*) palos *mpl*; (: *grass area*) terreno de juego

wide [waɪd] *adj* ancho; (*area, knowledge*) vasto, grande; (*choice*) amplio ♦ *adv*: **to open** ~ abrir de par en par; **to shoot** ~ errar el tiro; **~-angle lens** *n* objetivo de gran angular; **~-awake** *adj* bien despierto; **~ly** *adv* (*travelled*) mucho; (*spaced*) muy; **it is ~ly believed/known that ...** mucha gente piensa/sabe que ...; **~n** *vt* ensanchar; (*experience*) ampliar ♦ *vi* ensancharse; ~ **open** *adj* abierto de par en par; **~spread** *adj* extendido, general

widow [ˈwɪdəʊ] *n* viuda, **~ed** *adj* viudo; **~er** *n* viudo

width [wɪdθ] *n* anchura; (*of cloth*) ancho

wield [wiːld] *vt* (*sword*) blandir; (*power*) ejercer

wife [waɪf] (*pl* **wives**) *n* mujer *f*, esposa

wig [wɪg] *n* peluca

wiggle [ˈwɪgl] *vt* menear

wild [waɪld] *adj* (*animal*) salvaje; (*plant*) silvestre; (*person*) furioso, violento; (*idea*) descabellado; (*rough: sea*) bravo; (: *land*) agreste; (: *weather*) muy revuelto; **~s** *npl* regiones *fpl* salvajes, tierras *fpl* vírgenes; **~erness** ['wɪldənɪs] *n* desierto; **~-goose chase** *n* (*fig*) búsqueda inútil; **~life** *n* fauna; **~ly** *adv* (*behave*) locamente; (*lash out*) a diestro y siniestro; (*guess*) a lo loco; (*happy*) a más no poder

wilful ['wɪlful] (*US* **willful**) *adj* (*action*) deliberado; (*obstinate*) testarudo

──── KEYWORD ────

will [wɪl] *aux vb* **1** (*forming future tense*): **I ~ finish it tomorrow** lo terminaré *or* voy a terminar mañana; **I ~ have finished it by tomorrow** lo habré terminado para mañana; **~ you do it? — yes I ~/no I won't** ¿lo harás? — sí/no

2 (*in conjectures, predictions*): **he ~** *or* **he'll be there by now** ya habrá *or* debe (de) haber llegado; **that ~ be the postman** será *or* debe ser el cartero

3 (*in commands, requests, offers*): **~ you be quiet!** ¿quieres callarte?; **~ you help me?** ¿quieres ayudarme?; **~ you have a cup of tea?** ¿te apetece un té?; **I won't put up with it!** ¡no lo soporto!

♦ *vt* (*pt, pp* **willed**): **to ~ sb to do sth** desear que alguien haga algo; **he ~ed himself to go on** con gran fuerza de voluntad, continuó

♦ *n* voluntad *f*; (*testament*) testamento

─────────────

willful ['wɪlful] (*US*) *adj* = **wilful**

willing ['wɪlɪŋ] *adj* (*with goodwill*) de buena voluntad; (*enthusiastic*) entusiasta; **he's ~ to do it** está dispuesto a hacerlo; **~ly** *adv* con mucho gusto; **~ness** *n* buena voluntad

willow ['wɪləu] *n* sauce *m*

willpower ['wɪlpauə*] *n* fuerza de voluntad

willy-nilly [wɪlɪ'nɪlɪ] *adv* quiérase o no

wilt [wɪlt] *vi* marchitarse

wily ['waɪlɪ] *adj* astuto

win [wɪn] (*pt, pp* **won**) *n* victoria, triunfo

♦ *vt* ganar; (*obtain*) conseguir, lograr

♦ *vi* ganar; **~ over** *vt* convencer a; **~ round** (*BRIT*) *vt* = **~ over**

wince [wɪns] *vi* encogerse

winch [wɪntʃ] *n* torno

wind[1] [wɪnd] *n* viento; (*MED*) gases *mpl*

♦ *vt* (*take breath away from*) dejar sin aliento a

wind[2] [waɪnd] (*pt, pp* **wound**) *vt* enrollar; (*wrap*) envolver; (*clock, toy*) dar cuerda a

♦ *vi* (*road, river*) serpentear; **~ up** *vt* (*clock*) dar cuerda a; (*debate, meeting*) concluir, terminar

windfall ['wɪndfɔːl] *n* golpe *m* de suerte

winding ['waɪndɪŋ] *adj* (*road*) tortuoso; (*staircase*) de caracol

wind instrument [wɪnd-] *n* (*MUS*) instrumento de viento

windmill ['wɪndmɪl] *n* molino de viento

window ['wɪndəu] *n* ventana; (*in car, train*) ventanilla; (*in shop etc*) escaparate *m* (*SP*), vitrina (*AM*); **~ box** *n* jardinera de ventana; **~ cleaner** *n* (*person*) limpiador *m* de cristales; **~ ledge** *n* alféizar *m*, repisa; **~ pane** *n* cristal *m*; **~-shopping** *n*: **to go ~-shopping** ir de escaparates; **~sill** *n* alféizar *m*, repisa

windpipe ['wɪndpaɪp] *n* tráquea

wind power *n* energía eólica

windscreen ['wɪndskriːn] (*US* **windshield**) *n* parabrisas *m inv*; **~ washer** *n* lavaparabrisas *m inv*; **~ wiper** *n* limpiaparabrisas *m inv*

windswept ['wɪndswept] *adj* azotado por el viento

windy ['wɪndɪ] *adj* de mucho viento; **it's ~** hace viento

wine [waɪn] *n* vino; **~ bar** *n* enoteca; **~ cellar** *n* bodega; **~ glass** *n* copa (para vino); **~ list** *n* lista de vinos; **~ merchant** *n* vinatero; **~ waiter** *n* escanciador *m*

wing [wɪŋ] *n* ala; (*AUT*) aleta; **~s** *npl* (*THEATRE*) bastidores *mpl*; **~er** *n* (*SPORT*) extremo

wink [wɪŋk] *n* guiño, pestañeo ♦ *vi* guiñar, pestañear

winner ['wɪnə*] *n* ganador(a) *m/f*

winning ['wɪnɪŋ] *adj* (*team*) ganador(a);

(*goal*) decisivo; (*smile*) encantador(a); **~s** *npl* ganancias *fpl*

winter ['wɪntə*] *n* invierno ♦ *vi* invernar; **wintry** ['wɪntrɪ] *adj* invernal

wipe [waɪp] *n*: **to give sth a ~** pasar un trapo sobre algo ♦ *vt* limpiar; (*tape*) borrar; **~ off** *vt* limpiar con un trapo; (*remove*) quitar; **~ out** *vt* (*debt*) liquidar; (*memory*) borrar; (*destroy*) destruir; **~ up** *vt* limpiar

wire ['waɪə*] *n* alambre *m*; (*ELEC*) cable *m* (eléctrico); (*TEL*) telegrama *m* ♦ *vt* (*house*) poner la instalación eléctrica en; (*also: ~ up*) conectar; (*person: telegram*) telegrafiar

wireless ['waɪəlɪs] (*BRIT*) *n* radio *f*

wiring ['waɪərɪŋ] *n* instalación *f* eléctrica

wiry ['waɪərɪ] *adj* (*person*) enjuto y fuerte; (*hair*) crespo

wisdom ['wɪzdəm] *n* sabiduría, saber *m*; (*good sense*) cordura; **~ tooth** *n* muela del juicio

wise [waɪz] *adj* sabio; (*sensible*) juicioso

...wise [waɪz] *suffix*: **time~** en cuanto a *or* respecto al tiempo

wisecrack ['waɪzkræk] *n* broma

wish [wɪʃ] *n* deseo ♦ *vt* querer; **best ~es** (*on birthday etc*) felicidades *fpl*; **with best ~es** (*in letter*) saludos *mpl*, recuerdos *mpl*; **to ~ sb goodbye** despedirse de uno; **he ~ed me well** me deseó mucha suerte; **to ~ to do/sb to do sth** querer hacer/que alguien haga algo; **to ~ for** desear; **~ful** *adj*: **it's ~ful thinking** eso sería soñar

wishy-washy ['wɪʃɪwɔʃɪ] (*inf*) *adj* (*colour, ideas*) desvaído

wisp [wɪsp] *n* mechón *m*; (*of smoke*) voluta

wistful ['wɪstful] *adj* pensativo

wit [wɪt] *n* ingenio, gracia; (*also: ~s*) inteligencia; (*person*) chistoso/a

witch [wɪtʃ] *n* bruja; **~craft** *n* brujería; **~-hunt** *n* (*fig*) caza de brujas

---
KEYWORD
---

with [wɪð, wɪθ] *prep* **1** (*accompanying, in the company of*) con (*con+mí, ti, sí = conmigo, contigo, consigo*); **I was ~ him**
estaba con él; **we stayed ~ friends** nos hospedamos en casa de unos amigos; **I'm (not) ~ you** (*understand*) (no) te entiendo; **to be ~ it** (*inf: person: up-to-date*) estar al tanto; (: *alert*) ser despabilado
2 (*descriptive, indicating manner etc*) con; de; **a room ~ a view** una habitación con vistas; **the man ~ the grey hat/blue eyes** el hombre del sombrero gris/de los ojos azules; **red ~ anger** rojo de ira; **to shake ~ fear** temblar de miedo; **to fill sth ~ water** llenar algo de agua

withdraw [wɪθ'drɔ:] (*irreg*) *vt* retirar, sacar ♦ *vi* retirarse; **to ~ money (from the bank)** retirar fondos (del banco); **~al** *n* retirada; (*of money*) reintegro; **~al symptoms** *npl* (*MED*) síndrome *m* de abstinencia; **~n** *adj* (*person*) reservado, introvertido

wither ['wɪðə*] *vi* marchitarse

withhold [wɪθ'həuld] (*irreg*) *vt* (*money*) retener; (*decision*) aplazar; (*permission*) negar; (*information*) ocultar

within [wɪð'ɪn] *prep* dentro de ♦ *adv* dentro; **~ reach (of)** al alcance (de); **~ sight (of)** a la vista (de); **~ the week** antes de acabar la semana; **~ a mile (of)** a menos de una milla (de)

without [wɪð'aut] *prep* sin; **to go ~ sth** pasar sin algo

withstand [wɪθ'stænd] (*irreg*) *vt* resistir a

witness ['wɪtnɪs] *n* testigo *m/f* ♦ *vt* (*event*) presenciar; (*document*) atestiguar la veracidad de; **to bear ~ to** (*fig*) ser testimonio de; **~ box** *n* tribuna de los testigos; **~ stand** (*US*) *n* = **~ box**

witty ['wɪtɪ] *adj* ingenioso

wives [waɪvz] *npl of* **wife**

wizard ['wɪzəd] *n* hechicero

wk *abbr* = **week**

wobble ['wɔbl] *vi* temblar; (*chair*) cojear

woe [wəu] *n* desgracia

woke [wəuk] *pt of* **wake**

woken ['wəukən] *pp of* **wake**

wolf [wulf] *n* lobo; **wolves** [wulvz] *npl of* **wolf**

woman ['wumən] (*pl* **women**) *n* mujer *f*; **~ doctor** *n* médica; **women's lib** (*inf*:

pej) *n* liberación *f* de la mujer; ~**ly** *adj* femenino

womb [wuːm] *n* matriz *f*, útero

women ['wɪmɪn] *npl of* **woman**

won [wʌn] *pt, pp of* **win**

wonder ['wʌndə*] *n* maravilla, prodigio; (*feeling*) asombro ♦ *vi*: to ~ **whether/ why** preguntarse si/por qué; **to ~ at** asombrarse de; **to ~ about** pensar sobre *or* en; **it's no ~ (that)** no es de extrañarse (que + *subjun*); ~**ful** *adj* maravilloso; ~**fully** *adv* maravillosamente, estupendamente

won't [wəunt] = **will not**

woo [wuː] *vt* (*woman*) cortejar

wood [wud] *n* (*timber*) madera; (*forest*) bosque *m*; ~ **carving** *n* (*act*) tallado en madera; (*object*) talla en madera; ~**ed** *adj* arbolado; ~**en** *adj* de madera; (*fig*) inexpresivo; ~**pecker** *n* pájaro carpintero; ~**wind** *n* (*MUS*) instrumentos *mpl* de viento de madera; ~**work** *n* carpintería; ~**worm** *n* carcoma

wool [wul] *n* lana; **to pull the ~ over sb's eyes** (*fig*) engañar a uno; ~**en** (*US*) *adj* = ~**len**; ~**len** *adj* de lana; ~**lens** *npl* géneros *mpl* de lana; ~**ly** *adj* lanudo, de lana; (*fig*: *ideas*) confuso; ~**y** (*US*) *adj* = ~**ly**

word [wəːd] *n* palabra; (*news*) noticia; (*promise*) palabra (de honor) ♦ *vt* redactar; **in other ~s** en otras palabras, **to break/keep one's** ~ faltar a la palabra/cumplir la promesa; **to have ~s with sb** reñir con uno; ~**ing** *n* redacción *f*; ~ **processing** *n* proceso de textos; ~ **processor** *n* procesador *m* de textos

wore [wɔː*] *pt of* **wear**

work [wəːk] *n* trabajo; (*job*) empleo, trabajo; (*ART, LITERATURE*) obra ♦ *vi* trabajar; (*mechanism*) funcionar, marchar; (*medicine*) ser eficaz, surtir efecto ♦ *vt* (*shape*) trabajar; (*stone etc*) tallar; (*mine etc*) explotar; (*machine*) manejar, hacer funcionar; ~**s** *n* (*BRIT: factory*) fábrica ♦ *npl* (*of clock, machine*) mecanismo; **to be out of** ~ estar parado, no tener trabajo; **to ~ loose** (*part*) desprenderse; (*knot*) aflojarse; ~ **on** *vt*

fus trabajar en, dedicarse a; (*principle*) basarse en; ~ **out** *vi* (*plans etc*) salir bien, funcionar ♦ *vt* (*problem*) resolver; (*plan*) elaborar; **it ~s out at £100** suma 100 libras; ~ **up** *vt*: **to get ~ed up** excitarse; ~**able** *adj* (*solution*) práctico, factible; ~**aholic** [wəːkə'hɒlɪk] *n* trabajador(a) obsesivo/a *m/f*; ~**er** *n* trabajador(a) *m/f*, obrero/a; ~**force** *n* mano *f* de obra; ~**ing class** *n* clase *f* obrera; ~**ing-class** *adj* obrero; ~**ing order** *n*: **in ~ing order** en funcionamiento; ~**man** *n* obrero; ~**manship** *n* habilidad *f*, trabajo; ~**sheet** *n* hoja de trabajo; ~**shop** *n* taller *m*; ~ **station** *n* puesto *or* estación *f* de trabajo; ~**-to-rule** *n* huelga de celo

world [wəːld] *n* mundo ♦ *cpd* (*champion*) del mundo; (*power, war*) mundial; **to think the ~ of sb** (*fig*) tener un concepto muy alto de uno; ~**ly** *adj* mundano; ~**-wide** *adj* mundial, universal

worm [wəːm] *n* (*also: earth~*) lombriz *f*

worn [wɔːn] *pp of* **wear** ♦ *adj* usado; ~**out** *adj* (*object*) gastado; (*person*) rendido, agotado

worried ['wʌrɪd] *adj* preocupado

worry ['wʌrɪ] *n* preocupación *f* ♦ *vt* preocupar, inquietar ♦ *vi* preocuparse; ~**ing** *adj* inquietante

worse [wəːs] *adj, adv* peor ♦ *n* lo peor; **a change for the ~** un empeoramiento; ~**n** *vt, vi* empeorar; ~ **off** *adj* (*financially*): **to be ~ off** tener menos dinero; (*fig*): **you'll be ~ off this way** de esta forma estarás peor que nunca

worship ['wəːʃɪp] *n* adoración *f* ♦ *vt* adorar; **Your W~** (*BRIT: to mayor*) señor alcalde; (: *to judge*) señor juez

worst [wəːst] *adj, adv* peor ♦ *n* lo peor; **at ~** en lo peor de los casos

worth [wəːθ] *n* valor *m* ♦ *adj*: **to be ~** valer; **it's ~ it** vale *or* merece la pena; **to be ~ one's while (to do)** merecer la pena (hacer); ~**less** *adj* sin valor; (*useless*) inútil; ~**while** *adj* (*activity*) que merece la pena; (*cause*) loable

worthy ['wəːðɪ] *adj* respetable; (*motive*) honesto; ~ **of** digno de

KEYWORD

would [wud] *aux vb* **1** (*conditional tense*): **if you asked him he ~ do it** si se lo pidieras, lo haría; **if you had asked him he ~ have done it** si se lo hubieras pedido, lo habría *or* hubiera hecho
2 (*in offers, invitations, requests*): **~ you like a biscuit?** ¿quieres una galleta?; (*formal*) ¿querría una galleta?; **~ you ask him to come in?** ¿quiere hacerle pasar?; **~ you open the window please?** ¿quiere *or* podría abrir la ventana, por favor?
3 (*in indirect speech*): **I said I ~ do it** dije que lo haría
4 (*emphatic*): **it WOULD have to snow today!** ¡tenía que nevar precisamente hoy!
5 (*insistence*): **she ~n't behave** no quiso comportarse bien
6 (*conjecture*): **it ~ have been midnight** sería medianoche; **it ~ seem so** parece ser que sí
7 (*indicating habit*): **he ~ go there on Mondays** iba allí los lunes

would-be (*pej*) *adj* presunto
wouldn't ['wudnt] = **would not**
wound¹ [wu:nd] *n* herida ♦ *vt* herir
wound² [waund] *pt, pp of* **wind**
wove [wəuv] *pt of* **weave**
woven ['wəuvən] *pp of* **weave**
wrangle ['ræŋgl] *n* riña
wrap [ræp] *n* (*stole*) chal *m*; (*cape*) capa ♦ *vt* (*also: ~ up*) envolver; **~per** *n* (*on chocolate*) papel *m*; (*BRIT: of book*) sobrecubierta; **~ping paper** *n* papel *m* de envolver; (*fancy*) papel *m* de regalo
wrath [rɔθ] *n* cólera
wreak [ri:k] *vt*: **to ~ havoc (on)** hacer estragos (en); **to ~ vengeance (on)** vengarse (de)
wreath [ri:θ, *pl* ri:ðz] *n* (*funeral ~*) corona
wreck [rɛk] *n* (*ship: destruction*) naufragio; (: *remains*) restos *mpl* del barco; (*pej: person*) ruina ♦ *vt* (*car etc*) destrozar; (*chances*) arruinar; **~age** *n* restos *mpl*; (*of building*) escombros *mpl*

wren [rɛn] *n* (*ZOOL*) reyezuelo
wrench [rɛntʃ] *n* (*TECH*) llave *f* inglesa; (*tug*) tirón *m*; (*fig*) dolor *m* ♦ *vt* arrancar; **to ~ sth from sb** arrebatar algo violentamente a uno
wrestle ['rɛsl] *vi*: **to ~ (with sb)** luchar (con *or* contra uno); **~r** *n* luchador(a) *m/f* (de lucha libre); **wrestling** *n* lucha libre
wretched ['rɛtʃɪd] *adj* miserable
wriggle ['rɪgl] *vi* (*also: ~ about*) menearse, retorcerse
wring [rɪŋ] (*pt, pp* **wrung**) *vt* retorcer; (*wet clothes*) escurrir; (*fig*): **to ~ sth out of sb** sacar algo por la fuerza a uno
wrinkle ['rɪŋkl] *n* arruga ♦ *vt* arrugar ♦ *vi* arrugarse
wrist [rɪst] *n* muñeca; **~ watch** *n* reloj *m* de pulsera
writ [rɪt] *n* mandato judicial
write [raɪt] (*pt* **wrote**, *pp* **written**) *vt* escribir; (*cheque*) extender ♦ *vi* escribir; **~ down** *vt* escribir; (*note*) apuntar; **~ off** *vt* (*debt*) borrar (como incobrable); (*fig*) desechar por inútil; **~ out** *vt* escribir; **~ up** *vt* redactar; **~-off** *n* siniestro total; **~r** *n* escritor(a) *m/f*
writhe [raɪð] *vi* retorcerse
writing ['raɪtɪŋ] *n* escritura; (*hand-~*) letra; (*of author*) obras *fpl*; **in ~** por escrito; **~ paper** *n* papel *m* de escribir
written ['rɪtn] *pp of* **write**
wrong [rɔŋ] *adj* (*wicked*) malo; (*unfair*) injusto; (*incorrect*) equivocado, incorrecto; (*not suitable*) inoportuno, inconveniente; (*reverse*) del revés ♦ *adv* equivocadamente ♦ *n* injusticia ♦ *vt* ser injusto con; **you are ~ to do it** haces mal en hacerlo; **you are ~ about that, you've got it ~** en eso estás equivocado; **to be in the ~** no tener razón, tener la culpa; **what's ~?** ¿qué pasa?; **to go ~** (*person*) equivocarse; (*plan*) salir mal; (*machine*) estropearse; **~ful** *adj* injusto; **~ly** *adv* mal, incorrectamente; (*by mistake*) por error
wrote [raut] *pt of* **write**
wrought [rɔ:t] *adj*: **~ iron** hierro forjado
wrung [rʌŋ] *pt, pp of* **wring**

wry [raɪ] *adj* irónico
wt. *abbr* = **weight**

X x

Xmas ['ɛksməs] *n abbr* = **Christmas**
X-ray [ɛks'reɪ] *n* radiografía ♦ *vt*
radiografiar, sacar radiografías de
xylophone ['zaɪləfəun] *n* xilófono

Y y

yacht [jɔt] *n* yate *m*; **~ing** *n* (*sport*)
balandrismo; **~sman/woman** *n*
balandrista *m/f*
Yank [jæŋk] (*pej*) *n* yanqui *m/f*
Yankee ['jæŋkɪ] (*pej*) *n* = **Yank**
yap [jæp] *vi* (*dog*) aullar
yard [jɑːd] *n* patio; (*measure*) yarda;
~stick *n* (*fig*) criterio, norma
yarn [jɑːn] *n* hilo; (*tale*) cuento, historia
yawn [jɔːn] *n* bostezo ♦ *vi* bostezar; **~ing**
adj (*gap*) muy abierto
yd(s). *abbr* = **yard(s)**
yeah [jɛə] (*inf*) *adv* sí
year [jɪə*] *n* año; **to be 8 ~s old** tener 8
años; **an eight-~-old child** un niño de
ocho años (de edad); **~ly** *adj* anual ♦ *adv*
anualmente, cada año
yearn [jəːn] *vi*: **to ~ for sth** añorar algo,
suspirar por algo; **~ing** *n* ansia,
añoranza
yeast [jiːst] *n* levadura
yell [jɛl] *n* grito, alarido ♦ *vi* gritar
yellow ['jɛləu] *adj* amarillo
yelp [jɛlp] *n* aullido ♦ *vi* aullar
yeoman ['jəumən] *n*: **Y~ of the Guard**
alabardero de la Casa Real
yes [jɛs] *adv* sí ♦ *n* sí *m*; **to say/answer
~** decir/contestar que sí
yesterday ['jɛstədɪ] *adv* ayer ♦ *n* ayer *m*;
~ morning/evening ayer por la
mañana/tarde; **all day ~** todo el día de
ayer
yet [jɛt] *adv* ya; (*negative*) todavía ♦ *conj*
sin embargo, a pesar de todo; **it is not
finished ~** todavía no está acabado; **the**

best ~ el/la mejor hasta ahora; **as ~**
hasta ahora, todavía
yew [juː] *n* tejo
yield [jiːld] *n* (*AGR*) cosecha; (*COMM*)
rendimiento ♦ *vt* ceder; (*results*)
producir, dar; (*profit*) rendir ♦ *vi*
rendirse, ceder; (*US: AUT*) ceder el paso
YMCA *n abbr* (= *Young Men's Christian
Association*) Asociación *f* de Jóvenes
Cristianos
yog(h)ourt ['jəugət] *n* yogur *m*
yog(h)urt ['jəugət] *n* = **yog(h)ourt**
yoke [jəuk] *n* yugo
yolk [jəuk] *n* yema (de huevo)
yonder ['jɔndə*] *adv* allá (a lo lejos)

KEYWORD

you [juː] *pron* **1** (*subject: familiar*) tú, *pl*
vosotros/as (*SP*), ustedes (*AM*); (*polite*)
usted, *pl* ustedes; **~ are very kind** eres/
es *etc* muy amable; **~ Spanish enjoy
your food** a vosotros (*or* ustedes) los
españoles os (*or* les) gusta la comida; **~
and I will go** iremos tú y yo
2 (*object: direct: familiar*) te, *pl* os (*SP*),
les (*AM*); (*polite*) le, *pl* les, *f* la, *pl* las; **I
know ~** te/le *etc* conozco
3 (*object: indirect: familiar*) te, *pl* os (*SP*),
les (*AM*); (*polite*) le, *pl* les; **I gave the
letter to ~ yesterday** te/os *etc* di la
carta ayer
4 (*stressed*): **I told ~ to do it** te dije a
ti que lo hicieras, es a ti a quien dije
que lo hicieras; *see also* 3, 5
5 (*after prep: NB: con+ ti = contigo*:
familiar) ti, *pl* vosotros/as (*SP*), ustedes
(*AM*); (: *polite*) usted, *pl* ustedes; **it's for ~**
es para ti/vosotros *etc*
6 (*comparisons: familiar*) tú, *pl* voso-
tros/as (*SP*), ustedes (*AM*); (: *polite*) usted,
pl ustedes; **she's younger than ~** es
más joven que tú/vosotros *etc*
7 (*impersonal: one*): **fresh air does ~
good** el aire puro (te) hace bien; **~
never know** nunca se sabe; **~ can't do
that!** ¡eso no se hace!

you'd [juːd] = **you had**; **you would**
you'll [juːl] = **you will**; **you shall**

young [jʌŋ] *adj* joven ♦ *npl* (*of animal*)
cría; (*people*): **the ~** los jóvenes, la
juventud; **~ster** *n* joven *m/f*
your [jɔː*] *adj* tu; (*pl*) vuestro; (*formal*)
su; *see also* **my**
you're [juə*] = **you are**
yours [jɔːz] *pron* tuyo; (*pl*) vuestro;
(*formal*) suyo; *see also* **faithfully**; **mine**²;
sincerely
yourself [jɔːˈsɛlf] *pron* tú mismo;
(*complement*) te; (*after prep*) tí (mismo);
(*formal*) usted mismo; (: *complement*) se;
(: *after prep*) sí (mismo); **yourselves** *pl*
pron vosotros mismos; (*after prep*)
vosotros (mismos); (*formal*) ustedes
(mismos); (: *complement*) se; (: *after prep*)
sí mismos; *see also* **oneself**
youth [juːθ, *pl* juːðz] *n* juventud *f*; (*young
man*) joven *m*; **~ club** *n* club *m* juvenil;
~ful *adj* juvenil; **~ hostel** *n* albergue *m*
de juventud
you've [juːv] = **you have**
Yugoslav [ˈjuːgəuslɑːv] *adj, n*
yugo(e)slavo/a *m/f*
Yugoslavia [juːgəuˈslɑːvɪə] *n* Yugoslavia
yuppie [ˈjʌpɪ] (*inf*) *adj, n* yupi *m/f*, yupy
m/f
YWCA *n abbr* (= *Young Women's
Christian Association*) Asociación *f* de
Jóvenes Cristianas

Z z ·

zany [ˈzeɪnɪ] *adj* estrafalario
zap [zæp] *vt* (*COMPUT*) borrar
zeal [ziːl] *n* celo, entusiasmo; **~ous**
[ˈzɛləs] *adj* celoso, entusiasta
zebra [ˈziːbrə] *n* cebra; **~ crossing** (*BRIT*)
n paso de peatones
zenith [ˈzɛnɪθ] *n* cénit *m*
zero [ˈzɪərəu] *n* cero
zest [zɛst] *n* ánimo, vivacidad *f*; (*of
orange*) piel *f*
zigzag [ˈzɪgzæg] *n* zigzag *m* ♦ *vi*
zigzaguear, hacer eses
zinc [zɪŋk] *n* cinc *m*, zinc *m*
zip [zip] *n* (*also*: ~ *fastener*, (*US*) ~*per*)
cremallera (*SP*), cierre *m* (*AM*) ♦ *vt* (*also*:
~ *up*) cerrar la cremallera de; **~ code**
(*US*) *n* código postal
zodiac [ˈzəudɪæk] *n* zodíaco
zone [zəun] *n* zona
zoo [zuː] *n* (jardín *m*) zoo *m*
zoology [zuˈɔlədʒɪ] *n* zoología
zoom [zuːm] *vi*: **to ~ past** pasar
zumbando; **~ lens** *n* zoom *m*
zucchini [zuːˈkiːnɪ] (*US*) *n(pl)*
calabacín(ines) *m(pl)*